SECOND EDITION

The SAGE Encyclopedia of
TERRORISM

SECOND EDITION

The SAGE Encyclopedia of TERRORISM

EDITOR
GUS MARTIN
California State University, Dominguez Hills

SAGE | reference

Los Angeles | London | New Delhi
Singapore | Washington DC

Los Angeles | London | New Delhi
Singapore | Washington DC

FOR INFORMATION:

SAGE Publications, Inc.
2455 Teller Road
Thousand Oaks, California 91320
E-mail: order@sagepub.com

SAGE Publications Ltd.
1 Oliver's Yard
55 City Road
London, EC1Y 1SP

SAGE Publications India Pvt. Ltd.
B 1/I 1 Mohan Cooperative Industrial Area
Mathura Road, New Delhi 110 044
India

SAGE Publications Asia-Pacific Pte. Ltd.
33 Pekin Street #02-01
Far East Square
Singapore 048763

SAGE REFERENCE

Publisher: Rolf A. Janke
Assistant to the Publisher: Michele Thompson
Acquisitions Editor: Jim Brace-Thompson
Production Editor: Tracy Buyan
Photo Research: Karen Wiley
Reference Systems Coordinator: Laura Notton
Typesetter: C&M Digitals (P) Ltd.
Proofreader: Christina West
Indexer: Wendy Allex
Cover Designer: Ravi Balasuriya
Marketing Manager: Kristi Ward

MTM PUBLISHING
(Project Development, Editing, and Management, New York City)

Publisher: Valerie Tomaselli
Editor: Hilary J. Poole
Editorial Coordinators: Tim Anderson, Zach Gajewski
Copy Editor: Peter Jaskowiak
Editorial Assistance/Research: Lavanya Narasimhan,
    Abby Rugg, Min Jeong Yoon

Printed in the United States of America.

Library of Congress Cataloging-in-Publication Data

The SAGE encyclopedia of terrorism, second edition / edited by Gus Martin.

p. cm.
Includes bibliographical references and index.

ISBN 978-1-4129-8016-6 (cloth)

1. Terrorism—Encyclopedias. 2. Terrorism—United States–Encyclopedias. I. Martin, Gus.

HV6431.S225 2011
363.32503—dc22   2011009896

11 12 13 14 15 10 9 8 7 6 5 4 3 2 1

Contents

List of Entries

Reader's Guide

Counterterrorism

Airport Security
Bureau of Alcohol, Tobacco, Firearms and
  Explosives
Central Intelligence Agency
Counterterrorism
Criminal Prosecution of Terrorists
Decommissioning in Northern Ireland
Department of Justice, U.S.
Federal Bureau of Investigation
Force Protection Conditions
Foreign Intelligence Surveillance Act
Forensic Science and Terrorism
Grenzschutzgruppe 9
Guantánamo Bay
Homeland Security
Intelligence Gathering
International Relations and Terrorism
Interrogation Techniques
Law and Terrorism
Mossad
National Security Agency
National Security Council
9/11 Commission
Operation Eagle Claw
Patriot Act
Rehabilitation of Terrorists
Rendition, Extraordinary
Rewards for Justice
Sayeret Matkal
Special Air Service Regiment
Special Operations Wing
Torture Debate
United Nations

Culture and Ideology of Terrorism

Anarchism
Christian Identity

Ethnic Cleansing
Fatwa
Gender-Based Terrorism
Homegrown Jihadi Movement
Media and Terrorism
New Terrorism, The
Patriot Movement
Popular Culture, Terrorism in
Posse Comitatus
Religious and Spiritual Perspectives on Terrorism
Stockholm Syndrome
Taliban Code of Conduct
Training of Terrorists
Turner Diaries, The
White Supremacy Movement
Women Terrorists

Economics, Politics, and the Law

Bureau of Alcohol, Tobacco, Firearms and
  Explosives
Central Intelligence Agency
Counterterrorism
Criminal Prosecution of Terrorists
Department of Justice, U.S.
Economics and Terrorism
Federal Bureau of Investigation
Financing Terrorism
Foreign Intelligence Surveillance Act
Homeland Security
Insurance and Terrorism
International Relations and Terrorism
Law and Terrorism
National Security Agency
National Security Council
9/11 Commission
Patriot Act
Rendition, Extraordinary
Torture Debate
United Nations

Individuals

Types and Methods of Terrorism

Homegrown Jihadi Movement
Hostage Taking
Kneecapping
Leaderless Resistance
Lone-Wolf Terrorism
Lynching
Narcoterrorism
Nuclear Terrorism
State Terrorism
State-Sponsored Terrorism
Suicide Terrorism
Weapons of Mass Destruction

Regional Categories

Africa: Eastern, Central, and Southern

al Shabab
Democratic Front for the Liberation of
    Rwanda
East Africa Embassy Bombings
Lord's Resistance Army
People Against Gangsterism and Drugs
Revolutionary United Front

Africa: Northern

al Jihad
al Qaeda in the Islamic Maghreb
Armed Islamic Front
Armed Islamic Group
Gama'a al Islamiyya
Tripoli and Benghazi Bombing

Americas: Central and South America

Farabundo Martí National
    Liberation Front
FARC
Lautaro Youth Movement
Manuel Rodriquez Patriotic Front
Morazanist Patriotic Front
Movement of the Revolutionary Left
National Liberation Army–Bolivia
National Liberation Army–Columbia
People's Revolutionary Army
Popular Liberation Army
Shining Path
Tupac Amaru Revolutionary Movement
Tupac Katari Guerrilla Army
Tupamaros
United Self-Defense Forces of Columbia

Americas: North America

Animal Liberation Front
Anti-Abortion Terrorism
Army of God
Aryan Nations
Aryan Republican Army
Black Panther Party
Branch Davidian Compound Siege
Brooklyn Bridge Shooting
Centennial Park Bombing
Covenant, the Sword and the Arm of the
    Lord, The
Earth First!
Earth Liberation Front
El Rukns
Empire State Building Shooting
Evan Mecham Eco-Terrorist International
    Conspiracy
FALN
Fort Smith, Arkansas, Trial
Fraunces Tavern Bombing
Grand Central Station Bombing
Hanafi Muslim Movement
Homegrown Jihadi Movement
Jewish Terrorist Groups in the United States
Ku Klux Klan
LaGuardia Airport Bombing
Macheteros
May 19 Communist Organization
9/11 Commission
Oklahoma City Bombing
Order, The
Puerto Rican Nationalist Terrorism
September 11 Attacks
Sixteenth Street Baptist Church Bombing
Statue of Liberty Bombing
Subway Suicide Bombing Plot
Symbionese Liberation Army
TWA Flight 355 Hijacking
Wall Street Bombing
Weatherman
White Patriot Party
World Trade Center Bombing, 1993
Y2K Plot
Zetas, Los

Asia: East and Southeast

Abu Sayyaf Group
Alex Boncayao Brigade

About the Editor

C. Augustus "Gus" Martin is Associate Vice President for Faculty Affairs at California State University, Dominguez Hills, where he regularly teaches a course on the subject of terrorism and extremism. He has also served as chair of the Department of Public Administration and Public Policy. He began his academic career as a member of the faculty of the Graduate School of Public and International Affairs, University of Pittsburgh, where he was an Administration of Justice professor. His current research and professional interests are terrorism and extremism, administration of justice, juvenile justice, and fair housing.

He is author of several books on the subject of terrorism, including *Terrorism and Homeland Security* (SAGE, 2011), *Essentials of Terrorism: Concepts and Controversies* (SAGE, 2011), *Understanding Terrorism: Challenges, Perspectives, and Issues* (SAGE, 2010), and *The New Era of Terrorism: Selected Readings* (SAGE, 2004). He has served as a panelist for university and community symposia on the subjects of administration of justice, terrorism, and fair housing. He has also been a consultant to governmental and private agencies.

Prior to joining academia, he served as managing attorney for the Fair Housing Partnership of Greater Pittsburgh, where he was also director of a program created under a federal consent decree to desegregate public and assisted housing. He was also Special Counsel to the Attorney General of the U.S. Virgin Islands on the island of St. Thomas. As Special Counsel he provided personal and confidential service in the central office of the Department of Justice; sat as a hearing officer for disciplinary hearings and departmental grievances; served as chair of the drug policy committee; served as a liaison to the intergovernmental Law Enforcement Coordinating Committee as well as to the Narcotics Strike Force; and provided daily legal and policy advice to the Attorney General. Prior to serving as Special Counsel, he was a "floor" Legislative Assistant to Congressman Charles B. Rangel of New York. As Legislative Assistant, he researched, evaluated, and drafted legislation in the areas of foreign policy, foreign aid, human rights, housing, education, social services and poverty; he also drafted House floor statements, Congressional Record inserts, press releases, and news articles; and he composed speeches, briefing materials, and legislative correspondence.

Contributors

Joseph Almog
The Hebrew University

Tim Anderson
Independent Author/Scholar

Bader Araj
University of Toronto

Randy Blazak
Portland State University

Randy Borum
University of South Florida

Jarret Brachman
*North Dakota State
    University*

Kristian Brown
University of Ulster

Robert J. Brym
University of Toronto

Ikaweba Bunting
*California State University,
    Long Beach*

Brian Burton
*Center for a New Economic
    Security*

David B. Cook
Rice University

Stuart Croft
University of Warwick

Nancy Egan
*John Jay College of Criminal
    Justice, The City University
    of New York*

Steven Emerson
*The Investigative Project on
    Terrorism*

Kathryn Farr
Portland State University

Hall Gardner
American University of Paris

David Glazier
*Loyola Law School,
    Los Angeles*

Rohan Gunaratna
*Nanyang Technological
    University*

Dipak Gupta
*California State University,
    San Diego*

Mohammed Hafez
Naval Postgraduate School

Phil Hirschkorn
CNN

Jennifer Holmes
University of Texas, Dallas

Richard Horowitz
Attorney-at-Law

Brian Jackson
RAND Corporation

Bill Jensen
Independent Author/Scholar

Larry C. Johnson
*Business Exposure Reduction
    Group*

Maria Kiriakova
*John Jay College of Criminal
    Justice, The City University
    of New York*

Harvey Kushner
Long Island University

Najib Lafraie
University of Otago

Laura Lambert
*Independent Author/
    Scholar*

Genevieve Lennon
University of Leeds

Jay Levinson
The Hebrew University

Benjamin Lieberman
Fitchburg State University

Brenda J. Lutz
University of Dundee

James Lutz
*Indiana University–Purdue
    University, Fort Wayne*

Lisa Magloff
Independent Author/Scholar

Samuel M. Makinda
Murdoch University

Jonathan Martin
Stanford University

Richard McHugh
*Independent Author/
    Scholar*

Erwann Michel-Kerjan
University of Pennsylvania

Harvey Morley
*California State University,
    Long Beach*

Les Paldy
*State University of New York
    at Stonybrook*

Marie Palladini
*California State University,
Dominguez Hills*

Erica Pearson
Independent Author/Scholar

Mark Pitcavage
Anti-Defamation League

Noelle Quenivet
*University of the West of
England, Bristol*

Rafael Reuveny
Indiana University

Bruce Riedel
Brookings Institution

Paxton Roberts
University of Arkansas

Ann E. Robertson
Independent Author/Scholar

Michael Ronczkowski
Florida Atlantic University

Kenneth J. Ryan
*California State University,
Fresno*

Tahmina Sadat Hadjer
University of Konstanz

Hamoud Salhi
*California State University,
Dominguez Hills*

Jonathan Schanzer
Middle Eastern Forum

Gerald Schneider
University of Konstanz

Harold Scott
Howard University

Olga B. Semukhina
Marquette University

Ellen Sexton
*John Jay College of Criminal
Justice, The City University
of New York*

Mary Sisson
Independent Author/Scholar

Brent Smith
University of Arkansas

Aglaya Snetkov
University of Birmingham

John Stanton
*National Defense Industrial
Organization*

Kenneth Stern
American Jewish Committee

Colleen Sullivan
Independent Author/Scholar

Joseph Szyliowicz
*Josef Korbel School of
International Studies,
University of Denver*

Rhiannon Talbot-English
University of Newcastle

Anna Lisa Tota
University of Rome III

Mark Ungar
Brooklyn College

Lorenzo Vidino
Harvard University

Clive Walker
University of Leeds

Philip Williams
University of Pittsburgh

Leonard Zeskind
Independent Author/Scholar

Introduction

Welcome to the second edition of *The SAGE Encyclopedia of Terrorism*. The publication of this edition is a significant milestone in the examination of modern terrorism on the tenth anniversary of the September 11, 2001, terrorist assault on the United States. The first edition of the *Encyclopedia of Terrorism* was literally in production when this seminal event occurred, and since that time the subject of terrorism has become indelibly embedded in the political and cultural consciousness of the United States and the global community. For this reason, the second edition offers a uniquely comprehensive and complete presentation of the terrorist environment in the post-9/11 era. The tenth anniversary is particularly significant because its commemoration occurs concurrently with the death of Osama bin Laden, symbolic architect of the modern era of terrorism, who was killed in Pakistan on May 1, 2011.

Since the publication of the first edition, much has changed on the national security scene. Despite the dark promises of Osama bin Laden following the 9/11 attacks, the United States has thus far avoided another significant attack, although many other nations have not been as fortunate. The U.S. wars in Afghanistan and Iraq have significantly changed the national security picture, as have the arrival of the Obama administration and a new balance of power within Congress. Securing the American home front has become an indelible part of domestic culture. A ubiquitous homeland security bureaucracy is now embedded at every level of federal, state, and local government and law enforcement. Significantly, the appearance of the "homegrown jihadi" in the United States has created a hitherto unprecedented threat of links between foreign jihadist movements and domestic extremists, often via the Internet. Thus, the threat of economic chaos and massive loss of life due to terror attacks has not abated. Indeed, some experts have argued that a biological, chemical, or even nuclear attack on a major U.S. city is all but inevitable.

The global community has collectively adapted to a grave new reality: Asymmetrical tactics and mass casualty attacks by determined terrorists pose an unprecedented threat to civil society. In the era of what has become known as "the New Terrorism," violent extremists respond to increasingly expansive counterterrorist policies and countermeasures by launching surprisingly sophisticated and unanticipated attacks. Since the September 11, 2001, assault on the U.S. homeland, terrorists have demonstrated an aptitude for striking in the heart of Western democracies, as evidenced by the March 2004 commuter train attacks in Madrid and the July 2005 bombings in London. Repeated mass casualty attacks such as those in Mumbai, Iraq, Pakistan, and Bali likewise test the ability of governments to sustain internal security. Individual extremists have creatively infiltrated secure facilities and institutions on numerous occasions, often deploying as suicide bombers; this particular phenomenon is a hallmark of the New Terrorism, and it has proven to be an especially potent option.

The second edition of the *Encyclopedia of Terrorism* frankly and comprehensively engages the idiosyncrasies and features of the modern era of political violence. It is replete with new entries exploring the characteristics, challenges, and controversies of a dynamic and evolving post-9/11 era. In particular, the new edition expands the original edition's academic grounding through fresh theoretical entries on such topics as economics and terrorism, international relations and terrorism, and religious and spiritual perspectives. The thorough presentation of such broad topics in this edition provides readers with a solid theoretical foundation on a broad range of subject areas. These foundational entries are interwoven with focused topical entries, which serve as case studies investigating more specialized subjects. Thus, a comprehensive theoretical grounding is established in broad discussions on economics, law, religion, and popular culture. The use of terror by governments—such as, for example, Libya's attacks on its own citizens during the 2011 revolution—is explored in entries on state terror and state-sponsored terror. These and entries on various other topics provide informative background analysis to researchers in the field of political violence.

An important entry on the New Terrorism establishes a conceptual context for the modern environment. Because the asymmetrical nature of the New Terrorism has inspired the deployment of large numbers of armed forces in a series of military suppression campaigns, the second edition also offers a thorough examination of the international war on terrorism in new essays discussing the wars in Afghanistan and Iraq. These essays complement and upgrade entries from the first edition, which present precursor information on the modern terrorist environment.

Asymmetry and mass casualty attacks have become prevalent attributes of terrorism in the modern era. Terrorists have repeatedly assaulted civilian populations, public venues, transportation systems, and other "soft," nonmilitary targets, with the specific intention of maximizing the number of victims. The second edition of *The SAGE Encyclopedia of Terrorism* examines in detail many significant post-9/11 terrorist incidents. These include new entries discussing the Bali nightclub bombing, Chechen incidents, the London Underground bombings, the Madrid bombings, and the Mumbai 2008 attacks. Such incidents are presented as case studies within a longitudinal framework of terrorism extending back to the 9/11 attacks and before.

Domestic security culture and institutions responded to these and other attacks by extensively redesigning bureaucratic networks, laws, and procedures in the post-9/11 environment. Hitherto controversial counterterrorist options were reassessed and implemented to manage political violence in the new era. In consideration of the revamped security culture, major new policies and domestic responses are discussed in the second

edition. Controversial alternatives and debates are explored in entries addressing airport security, interrogation techniques, extraordinary rendition, Guantánamo Bay, the Foreign Intelligence Surveillance Act, and the torture debate. Legalistic options and concerns have become increasingly integral concerns for framing national policy, and they pose important challenges to national institutions. For this reason, new essays assess the criminal prosecution of terrorists, forensics and terrorism, insurance and terrorism, and law and terrorism. Similarly, the central roles of homeland security and intelligence gathering are featured in policy-focused entries. Interestingly, the modern era has witnessed a rapidly growing portrayal of terrorism in popular cultural venues, and an entry on popular culture and terrorism examines the impact of the modern terrorist environment on mainstream culture.

Religious extremism has become a primary, though not exclusive, motivation for political violence internationally. Groups and individuals inspired by al Qaeda have become embedded in many societies, ranging from Western democracies to Muslim countries, as well as Asian and African nations. These groups and individuals are responsible for a large number of successful and attempted terrorist incidents. The second edition of *The SAGE Encyclopedia of Terrorism* incorporates extensive discussions of newly emergent movements and organizations, many of which exhibit ideological and theological similarities as participants in a resurgent Islamist international organization. These al Qaeda–like organizations include al Shabab, al Qaeda in Iraq, al Qaeda in the Islamic Maghreb, Ansar al Islam, the East Turkestan Islamic Movement, and Tehrik-i-Taliban Pakistan. As in previous eras of terrorist violence, individual extremists have stepped forward to become infamously known among fellow believers and counterterrorist authorities. Consequently, interesting new case studies include personal profiles of Abd al Aziz Awda, Anwar al Awlaki, Abu Bakar Bashir, Jaber A. Elbaneh, Adam Yahiye Gadahn, John Walker Lindh, José Padilla, and Abu Musab al Zarqawi. Codes of conduct framing the motivational foundation for members and radical Islamist organizations are discussed in an entry on the Taliban "code of conduct."

The modern terrorist environment continues to exhibit historically intractable motivations for political violence, such as nationalism, ideology, and communal enmity. Non-Islamist movements and organizations continue to apply significant pressure on regional politics, and they are sometimes a determining factor in charting the course of regional and national policies. Several new entries investigate these important cases, including nationalistic Chechen incidents, the ideological terrorism of the Communist Party of Nepal (Maoists), the conflict between ethnic Uighurs and the Chinese government in an article on Xinjiang, and an entry exploring communal terrorism as exemplified by ethnic cleansing. A relatively unique case, the Lord's Resistance Army's cult-like campaign in Central Africa, is also discussed. The second edition of *The SAGE Encyclopedia of Terrorism* addresses important "cutting-edge" subjects that pose increasingly important challenges to policymakers. In this regard, a timely update of the role of transnational organized crime is presented in an entry on the narcoterrorism of Los Zetas in Mexico. Significantly, the underinvestigated and underreported role of women as victims and perpetrators of terrorism are specifically addressed in entries on gender-based terrorism and women terrorists.

Topics originally presented in the first edition are augmented in the second edition by featuring expanded coverage of critical case studies and concepts. Subjects mentioned or alluded to in other articles are explored in greater detail in new entries. For example, several case studies having an impact on the modern environment are examined within historical contexts. Discussions of terrorism in the recent past include new entries on the Afghan Arabs, Black September, Bloody Sunday, death squads, the intifada, kneecapping, and the Tupamaros. These events and cases pose enduring questions for counterterrorist policymakers in the modern era. The first edition's coverage of domestic terrorism in the United States has also been augmented with the inclusion of new entries. Case studies and discussions include the Christian Identity, the murder of William Andrew Long, lynching, the Phineas Priesthood, and Daniel Andreas San Diego.

In keeping with the many new topics, entries previously published in the first edition have been thoroughly updated. The outcome is a resource that is designed as a primary reference source for libraries, researchers, and professionals. The content of the second edition presents information from multidisciplinary perspectives. Readers will find that *The SAGE Encyclopedia of Terrorism* is a resource that analytically investigates the multivariate issues inherent in the field of political violence, while at the same time encouraging critical thinking on the subject. In this way, *The SAGE Encyclopedia of Terrorism* is a comprehensive and reliable contribution to the literature on terrorism.

—*C. Augustus "Gus" Martin*

ABBAS, MUHAMMAD "ABU" (1948–2004)

Muhammad "Abu" Abbas (aka Muhammad Zaidan) was the leader of the Palestine Liberation Front–Abu Abbas Faction (PLF), a Marxist militant group perhaps best known for its hijacking of the *Achille Lauro* cruise ship in 1985. Abbas was a member of the Palestine Liberation Organization (PLO) Executive Committee for many years, remaining loyal to Yasir Arafat, the PLO leader, during the 1980s when many other militant Palestinian leaders split with the PLO. Abbas was captured by U.S. troops during the Iraq invasion in 2003.

Abbas was born in 1948 in Haifa, in what is now Israel. He has often told interviewers that he was just 13 days old when his family fled to a refugee camp in Lebanon. He reportedly joined the PLO's army in 1964, and he fought with the Vietcong against U.S. forces in Vietnam. Abbas joined Ahmed Jibril's Popular Front for the Liberation of Palestine–General Command (PFLP-GC) in the late 1960s. In 1977 he became alienated by the pro-Syrian leanings of the PFLP-GC and left to form the Palestine Liberation Front. As a leader of the PLF, Abbas plotted several unorthodox attacks on Israel. In 1981, PLF members twice attempted to invade Israel by flying over the Lebanese border—once in hang gliders and once a hot air balloon—but both attempts were foiled by the Israeli military.

Abbas was deputy secretary of the PLF when the group split into three factions: pro-Arafat and his Palestine Liberation Organization, pro-Syrian,

and pro-Libyan. Abbas led the pro-PLO faction and remained loyal to Arafat during the 1980s when many others began to defect from the PLO leader's control. Abbas became a member of the PLO executive committee in 1984, and his close association with Arafat and the PLO soon came under international scrutiny.

On October 7, 1985, four PLF members hijacked the *Achille Lauro* off Port Said, Egypt, as it sailed toward Israel. Abbas's men demanded the release of 50 Palestinians held in Israel and threatened to blow up the ship. They held hundreds of passengers hostage for two days. During the ordeal, the hijackers shot and killed Leon Klinghoffer, an elderly Jewish man in a wheelchair, and threw his body overboard. While the ship was in the hands of the hijackers, Abbas negotiated with Egyptian officials and secured safe passage to Tunisia for himself, the hijackers, and another PLF official in return for the hostages' release. An EgyptAir plane carrying the PLF members took off for Tunisia, but U.S. Air Force fighter jets forced the plane to land in Sicily, where Italian forces arrested three of the hijackers. Abbas and other PLF members, however, fled to the former Yugoslavia with the help of Italian authorities, provoking protests by the U.S. government.

Abbas repeatedly claimed that the hijacking was a mistake, and that he had planned for his men to travel undercover on the *Achille Lauro* until it docked at Ashdod, Israel. The PLF subsequently moved its base of operations to Iraq. Abbas never served time in jail, although an Italian court tried him in absentia for his leadership role in the

Achille Lauro hijacking and sentenced him to life in prison. The U.S. Justice Department dropped its international warrant for Abbas's arrest after the Italian conviction, saying that there was not enough evidence to try him in a U.S. court.

Abbas left the PLO in 1991, after a foiled PLF raid on an Israeli beach created a diplomatic crisis between the PLO and Washington. He did support the Oslo accords in 1993, and he publicly supported the peace process in 1996, announcing that the PLF would follow a political path.

In 1998, Israeli officials allowed Abbas to travel through Israel to the Gaza Strip for a Palestinian National Council meeting. At the meeting, he voted to revoke the parts of the PLO's charter that call for Israel's destruction. After the meeting, he established himself and the PLF in Gaza City. Peace talks broke down in 2000, however, and Abbas returned to Baghdad. In November 2001, Israeli forces arrested at least 15 PLF members and accused them of plotting bombing attacks.

In March 2003, U.S.-led forces invaded Iraq to overthrow the government of Saddam Hussein, which the United States argued supported terrorist organizations, including the PLF. Abbas was captured in Baghdad by U.S. troops the following month. He was never brought to trial, however. The United States had earlier agreed not to press charges against Palestinians who had acted against Israel before the peace accords of the 1990s. The Palestinian Authority demanded Abbas's release, but the United States argued that it had the right to hold him. Abbas died of a heart attack on March 8, 2004, while in U.S. custody in Baghdad.

Erica Pearson

See also *Achille Lauro* Hijacking; Palestine Liberation Front–Abu Abbas Faction; Palestine Liberation Organization; Popular Front for the Liberation of Palestine–General Command

Further Readings

"Abu Abbas." *The Daily Telegraph*, March 11, 2004, p. 25.

"Abu Abbas: Maverick Palestinian Guerilla Leader." *The Herald*, March 11, 2004, p. 18.

Bohn, Michael K. *The* Achille Lauro *Hijacking: Lessons in the Politics and Prejudice of Terrorism.* Washington, DC: Brassey's, 2004.

Cockburn, Patrick. "Leader of *Achille Lauro* Hijack Turns to the Ballot-box." *The Independent (London)*, May 27, 1998.

Sennott, Charles M. "*Achille Lauro* Plotter Recast as Proponent of Mideast Peace." *The Boston Globe*, June 26, 1998, p. A1.

Smothers, Ronald. "Hostages and Hijackers: An Ally of Arafat: Palestinian Guerilla: Man of Many Factions." *The New York Times*, October 13, 1985.

U.S. State Department. "Foreign Terrorist Organizations." *Country Reports on Terrorism 2008.* http://www.state.gov/s/ct/rls/crt/2008/122449.htm.

ABDEL RAHMAN, OMAR (1938–)

The blind cleric Sheikh Omar Abdel Rahman is serving a life sentence in the United States for inciting and masterminding the terror ring that carried out the 1993 bombing of the World Trade Center in New York City.

Born in Egypt, Abdel Rahman was the spiritual leader of Gama'a al Islamiyya, which was Egypt's largest terrorist organization in the late 20th century. Gama'a al Islamiyya sought to overthrow the Egyptian government and replace it with an Islamic theocracy. As the organization grew, Abdel Rahman himself became an internationally known symbol of opposition to the Egyptian secular authorities. When Egypt severely cracked down on militant groups, Abdel Rahman fled in 1990 to live in exile in Brooklyn, New York.

According to U.S. officials, Abdel Rahman's U.S. terror cell planned to implement Islamic terrorism by attacking civilians, government officials, and landmarks. In 1990 a gunman shot and killed the Jewish extremist Rabbi Meir Kahane in New York. El Sayyid Nosair, an Egyptian man linked to Abdel Rahman, was arrested and tried for the murder. Nosair was convicted of gun charges related to the murder but acquitted of the actual crime. According to press reports, when federal agents raided Nosair's New Jersey apartment after his arrest, they found many incriminating items, including an Abdel Rahman sermon that urged followers to attack "the edifices of capitalism."

One interpretation of this phrase became immediately clear after the February 1993 bombing of the World Trade Center in New York City. The blast killed six people, injured a thousand more, and caused millions of dollars in damage. At least three of the suspects in the bombing worshipped at Abdel Rahman's mosque in Jersey City, New Jersey. In the trial following the bombing, Abdel Rahman was convicted of preparing what prosecutors called a "war of urban terrorism" in New York City. Under a rarely used Civil War–era seditious conspiracy law, prosecutors proved that the cleric had conspired to "overthrow or put down or destroy by force the Government of the United States." The indictment tied together a three-year series of terrorist incidents, including a purported plan to blow up the George Washington Bridge, the Lincoln and Holland Tunnels, the United Nations building, and other Manhattan landmarks. According to prosecutors, these bombs would have all hit their targets on the same day, just minutes apart. Abdel Rahman was also linked to the Kahane murder and convicted of trying to orchestrate the assassination of Egyptian president Hosni Mubarak. He was jailed for life.

Even in prison, Abdel Rahman has wielded considerable influence and inspired acts of terror, many of which have aimed at securing his release. Early in his prison term, according to the *Los Angeles Times,* he called upon his followers to "avenge" him. In 1997, Gama'a al Islamiyya did just that, making its most infamous attack. At a tourist site near the Valley of the Kings at Luxor, gunmen disguised as police officers opened fire into a crowd. Fifty-eight foreign tourists and four Egyptians were killed. When group members called to take responsibility for the attack, they said that they had only intended to take hostages in an attempt to secure Abdel Rahman's release. Witnesses, however, saw no attempt to take hostages.

After the attack, Abdel Rahman was put in solitary confinement, and his lawyer, Lynne Stewart, was made to agree not to share his views with the media. She violated that agreement in May 2000, telling Reuters that Abdel Rahman no longer thought that Gama'a al Islamiyya should follow a cease-fire. In April 2002 the FBI arrested Stewart and charged her with helping the cleric pass messages along to his followers. Stewart was convicted in February 2005 on five counts, including conspiracy, making false statements, and providing material aid to terrorists. Originally sentenced to serve 28 months in prison, the sentence was raised to 10 years in July 2010 due to perjury issues that arose at the 2005 trial.

Allegedly, there are several links between Abdel Rahman and al Qaeda leader Osama bin Laden. Two of Abdel Rahman's sons were said to be close to bin Laden, moving with him to Sudan in 1993 and fighting with al Qaeda in Afghanistan. According to Associated Press reports, Abdel Rahman's son Mohammed was killed during the December 2001 U.S. bombings of the Tora Bora caves, while his son Ahmed was captured a month earlier by anti-Taliban forces.

Abdel Rahman was transferred from his prison cell in Missouri to a nearby hospital for a blood transfusion in late 2006. He had reportedly urged his followers to seek revenge if he died in U.S. custody, but authorities told *The New York Times* that no credible threats had emerged due to his apparent illness, and he was returned to prison after his condition improved.

Erica Pearson

See also Gama'a al Islamiyya; Kahane, Meir; Nosair, El Sayyid; World Trade Center Bombing (1993)

Further Readings

El-Dakhakhny, Mohamed. "Egypt Terrorists Want Leader Back." *Chicago Sun-Times,* November 19, 1997, p. 3.

Jabbur, Nabil. *The Rumbling Volcano: Islamic Fundamentalism in Egypt.* Pasadena, CA: Mandate Press, 1993.

Johnston, David. "Sheik's Illness Prompts Bulletin." *The New York Times,* December 15, 2006.

McCarthy, Andrew. *Willful Blindness: A Memoir of the Jihad.* New York: Encounter Books, 2008.

Moynihan, Colin. "Radical Lawyer Convicted of Aiding Terrorist is Jailed." *The New York Times,* November 20, 2009, p. A32.

Smolowe, Jill. "Sheik Omar Abdel-Rahman Speaks Out." *Time,* March 15, 1993. http://www.time.com/time/magazine/article/0,9171,977984,00.html.

Usborne, David. "New York's Terrorist Sheikh Jailed for Life." *The Independent* (London), January 18, 1996, p. 11.

ABDULLAH, ABDULLAH AHMED (1963–2010)

Born in Egypt, Abdullah Ahmed Abdullah (aka Abu Mohamed al Masri, Saleh) was an alleged al Qaeda conspirator said to have been a top lieutenant and advisor to Osama bin Laden. He was indicted by the United States for his role in the August 7, 1998 bombings of U.S. embassies in the African countries of Tanzania and Kenya. The FBI listed him as one of its "most wanted terrorists" for his role in those attacks, and also for the assistance he provided to the terrorists who attacked the United States on September 11, 2001.

According to the indictment, Abdullah is a member of al Qaeda's tightest circle and sits on bin Laden's consultative council, or *majlis al shura*. al Qaeda, an Arabic term meaning "the base," is a violent international network bent on driving the United States from Saudi Arabia and other Islamic countries. The group carried out the devastating September 11, 2001, attacks on the World Trade Center in New York City and the Pentagon near Washington, D.C., and Abdullah himself is believed to have given money to the lead bomber, Mohamed Atta, to assist him in carrying out the operation. al Qaeda is known for establishing cells worldwide in areas where attacks are carried out, and it often serves as an umbrella group for other militant organizations.

In the embassy bombings case, the U.S. indictment charged that prior to collaborating on the bombings, Abdullah was involved in other anti-U.S. activities in Africa. He and other members of al Qaeda allegedly provided military assistance and training to tribes opposed to the U.N. and U.S. presence in Somalia during that country's civil unrest in 1993. He later became involved in the al Qaeda operations in Kenya. According to the indictment, Abdullah spied on the Kenyan embassy with co-conspirators three days before the bombings. Having given the order for all al Qaeda members to leave Kenya by August 6, Abdullah fled the country for Karachi, Pakistan. On August 7, a bomb-laden pick-up truck left the Nairobi villa rented by al Qaeda operatives and drove to the U.S. embassy. In a synchronized attack 400 miles away, a truck bomb also approached the U.S. embassy in Dar es Salaam, Tanzania. The bombs

exploded just minutes apart, killing a combined total of 224 people.

According to the indictment, Abdullah had also arranged for a fake passport for one of the accused Kenyan embassy bombers, Mohammed Saddiq Odeh. That document enabled Odeh to travel with other al Qaeda members to Afghanistan to meet with bin Laden. In the fall of 1998, the United States asserted that Osama bin Laden and other al Qaeda operatives were responsible for the embassy bombings. As retaliation, President Clinton ordered air attacks on al Qaeda training grounds in Afghanistan and a pharmaceutical plant in the center of Khartoum, Sudan. Three suspects in the bombing case pleaded guilty and cooperated with the prosecution. Their testimony was used in the 2001 trial that convicted four other men with ties to bin Laden. The four were sentenced to life in prison without parole.

Abdullah was reportedly killed in a U.S. predator drone attack in Pakistan in May 2010. Experts believed that the loss of Abdullah would be a significant blow to al Qaeda due to his close relationship with bin Laden.

Erica Pearson

See also al Qaeda; bin Laden, Osama; East Africa Embassy Bombings

Further Readings

Bergen, Peter. *Holy War, Inc.: Inside the Secret World of Osama bin Laden*. New York: Free Press, 2001.

Bergen, Peter. *The Longest War: Inside the Enduring Conflict between America and al-Qaeda*. New York: Free Press, 2011.

Eggen, Dan, and David A. Vise. "More Indicted in Embassy Attacks; 5 Fugitives Alleged to Be Part of bin Laden Terrorist Group." *Washington Post*, December 21, 2000, p. A15.

Federal Bureau of Investigation. "Most Wanted Terrorists." http://www.fbi.gov/wanted/terrorists/fugitives.htm.

Giustozzi, Antonio, ed. *Decoding the New Taliban: Insights from the Afghan Field*. New York: Columbia University Press, 2009.

Reeve, Simon. *The New Jackals: Ramzi Yousef, Osama bin Laden, and the Future of Terrorism*. Boston: Northeastern University Press, 1999.

Smith, Martin, and Lowell Bergman. "Hunting bin Laden." *Frontline*, PBS, September 13, 2001. http://www.pbs.org/wgbh/pages/frontline/shows/binladen.

ABU NIDAL ORGANIZATION

Also known as Arab Revolutionary Brigade, Black June, Black September, and Fatah Revolutionary Council, the Abu Nidal Organization (ANO), a Palestinian terrorist group, was the best-organized, best-funded, and most active terrorist network of the late 1970s and 1980s.

Sabri al Banna, better known by his nom de guerre, Abu Nidal (meaning "father of struggle"), founded the ANO in 1974. Previously a high-ranking member of Yasir Arafat's Fatah, a part of the Palestine Liberation Organization (PLO), Banna broke with that group in 1974 over what he perceived to be its abandonment of the armed struggle for Palestinian liberation in favor of political settlement. Both Banna and the ANO were influenced by the ideology of the Baath Party, which called for the unification of the Arab peoples into a single state. The ANO saw the elimination of Israel as a necessary precursor to Arab unity and hoped that fighting a common enemy (the Israelis) would help forge such unity. The ANO reviled Arafat and other pro-Western Arab leaders, who, at the time, were willing to support the continued existence of Israel in exchange for an independent Palestine. Accordingly, ANO has targeted moderate Arabs as frequently as it has Israelis.

While working as a recruiter for Fatah, Banna was based in Baghdad, Iraq, a Baath stronghold run by the dictator Saddam Hussein. Following Banna's 1974 defection, Hussein helped him to organize the ANO and provided him with funds in exchange for the use of the ANO's services, primarily against Syrian targets. (The Syrian division of the Baath had been feuding with the Iraqi Baath for years.)

The ANO, as created by Banna, would emerge as one of the most extensive and effective terrorist networks of the 1980s. Front organizations for the ANO were established in almost every Arab nation to attract recruits, who were then sent to training camps in the ANO's host country (at various times Iraq, Syria, and Libya). Once proficient in the necessary terrorist skills—weapons training, explosives, intelligence, and covert operations—members joined a small four- or five-person cell and awaited instructions. The ANO was estimated to have about 500 members at its peak, carrying out operations in more than 20 countries across Europe and the Middle East.

A striking feature of the ANO in its early years was its versatility and ability to adapt its tactics to various situations. ANO attacks took the form of car bombings, kidnappings, hijackings, suicide bombings, and assassinations. The ANO attacked the Syrian embassies in Rome, Italy, and Islamabad, Pakistan, and it assassinated PLO representatives in London, Paris, Kuwait, and Brussels. Its most significant action, however, was a June 1982 assassination attempt on the Israeli ambassador to England, Shlomo Argov, in London. This attack precipitated the Israeli invasion of Lebanon, where the PLO had its headquarters, and was a serious blow to that organization.

In 1983, Hussein expelled Banna and the ANO, in the hope of acquiring Western support for his war with Iran (1980–1988). Banna resettled the ANO in Syria, displaying his willingness to abandon former enmities when it was to his advantage, a trait that has led some observers to characterize the ANO as merely a mercenary organization. The Syrians never fully trusted Banna, however, and less than two years later he moved the organization to Libya. This period, the mid-1980s, was the most active for the ANO. The ANO carried out a campaign against Jordan at this time, assassinating several Jordanian ambassadors. The ANO also attacked the El Al counters at the Rome and Vienna airports on December 27, 1985, killing 17 people and wounding more than 100. On September 6, 1986, the ANO massacred 22 worshippers at a synagogue in Istanbul, Turkey, and on that same day ANO terrorists hijacked Pan Am Flight 73 in Karachi, Pakistan, eventually massacring 22 people when negotiations failed.

The ANO also began to recruit more actively during this period. Banna, renowned for his paranoia, began to worry that his underlings might be plotting to overthrow him. In 1989, two of his top deputies accused him of massacring 150 of his own men in an effort to forestall a coup. This internal dissension was magnified by the efforts of the Jordanian government to counter terrorism: some sources suggest that the Jordanian security forces threatened to kill members of Banna's family if he did not stop his campaign. These threats seriously affected the ANO's ability to carry out attacks.

Following a July 1988 an attack in Athens, Greece, in which nine people were killed, the only major attack attributed to the ANO has been the 1991 assassination of Abu Iyad, a former colleague of Banna and a high-ranking figure within the PLO.

During the 1990s, state support for the ANO—which was the organization's major source of funds—declined rapidly in response to that decade's apparent progress in bringing peace to the Middle East. By the end of the 1990s, Banna had been forced to leave Libya. In 1999, he was reported to be in Cairo, Egypt, receiving medical treatment. He eventually left Cairo and returned to Baghdad, where he was found shot to death on August 16, 2002.

Colleen Sullivan

See also al Asifa; Fatah; Hijacking; Hussein, Saddam; Pan Am Flight 73 Hijacking

Further Readings

Hoffman, Bruce. *Inside Terrorism.* New York: Columbia University Press, 2006.

Melman, Yossi. *The Master Terrorist: The True Story of Abu-Nidal.* New York: Adama Books, 1986.

Nasr, Kameel B. *Arab and Israeli Terrorism: The Causes and Effects of Political Violence, 1936–1993.* Jefferson, NC: McFarland, 1997.

Richardson, Louise. *What Terrorists Want: Understanding the Enemy, Containing the Threat.* New York: Random House: 2006.

Seale, Patrick. *Abu Nidal: A Gun for Hire.* New York: Random House, 1992.

Steinberg, Matti. "The Radical Worldview of the Abu-Nidal Faction." *The Jerusalem Quarterly* 48 (Fall 1988): 88–104.

Abu Sayyaf Group

The Abu Sayyaf Group is a Muslim terrorist organization based on Basilan Island, one of the southern islands in the Philippine archipelago. Since the mid-1990s, the group, whose origins are somewhat obscure, has carried out terrorist attacks in the Philippines, including a series of high-profile kidnappings in 2000 and 2001.

The southern Philippines have had a substantial Muslim population for centuries. Sixteenth-century Spanish colonizers spread Christianity to the northern islands, treating the Muslims as a despised minority, and the area has seen periodic violence ever since. The people of the southern islands are among the poorest in the country. In the early 1970s, the Moro National Liberation Front (MNLF) began a war of secession against the Philippine government. Although the fortunes of the MNLF and its splinter group, the Moro Islamic Liberation Front (MILF), have risen and fallen since that time, violence and lawlessness have been a constant in the southern islands. Defections, desertions, and ideological disputes have resulted in many armed bands roaming the islands.

Abu Sayyaf (meaning "bearer of the sword") began as one such band of former guerrillas, led by Abdurajak Abubakar Janjalani, a charismatic former Islamic scholar who had fought against the Soviets in Afghanistan. The group first came to light about 1994, when it was thought to be a small splinter faction of the MILF. Most observers now consider it to be an entirely independent group, however. Early in its existence, Abu Sayyaf established connections with international Muslim terrorist organizations, including al Qaeda, and group members may have received training and support from these organizations.

Abu Sayyaf professes a desire for an independent Muslim state for the Philippines' Muslim population, to be governed under Shariah law. In practice, however, the group's attacks—and particularly its kidnappings—seem to be motivated more by potential profit than by ideological or military significance, and the Philippine government has long considered them to be mere bandits. In the mid-1990s, Abu Sayyaf's strength was estimated at 500 members. Ransom money received from kidnappings has since increased that number, with some commentators believing the group to have as many as 4,000 members. Its stronghold is Basilan Island, though it operates on other Muslim-populated islands as well.

Starting in the late 1990s, Abu Sayyaf increased its numbers of kidnappings in Basilan and elsewhere. At first it targeted wealthy Filipino businessmen, usually releasing the captives after a ransom had been paid, but sometimes killing its victims regardless. In March 2000 the group gained international attention after raiding a local school and taking 27 hostages, most of them children. On April 23, the army launched a dangerous raid against the Abu Sayyaf compound housing the hostages. Four terrorists were killed, and 15 hostages were freed, 10 of whom were seriously wounded. Most of the terrorists escaped into the jungle, taking 5 hostages with them.

Later that day, a different faction of Abu Sayyaf struck again, this time abducting victims from a resort on the nearby island of Sipidan, which is part of Malaysia. The second group took 23 hostages, including 19 Malaysian and Filipino hotel staff, as well as several foreign tourists. Some of the journalists covering the kidnappings were also abducted. The hostages eventually included French, German, Finnish, Lebanese, U.S., and South African nationals. The international spotlight was now focused on the Philippine government, which felt compelled to act. Concerned for the safety of their citizens, the French, German, and South African governments prevailed upon the Filipinos to negotiate with the second group of hostage takers rather than launch another risky raid. A Libyan diplomat offered to act as a go-between, and negotiations began. After months of negotiations, a ransom of an undisclosed amount was paid to Abu Sayyaf and a dozen of the hostages were released. The kidnappers refused to part with the remainder, and President Joseph Estrada launched a massive military strike against the group in September 2000. The move was risky, but it secured the release of the hostages. In May 2001 another kidnapping was similarly resolved through military action.

Following the terrorist attacks on the United States on September 11, 2001, and taking into consideration Abu Sayyaf's connections to the al Qaeda terrorist network, in January 2002 the United States government acceded to the request of the new Philippine president, Gloria Arroyo, and pledged $100 million in military aid for the elimination of Abu Sayyaf. The United States sent 660 U.S. Army Special Forces troops to act as military advisors and train the Philippine army in counterterrorism tactics. The aid package caused considerable controversy in the Philippines but seems to have the support of the public, especially because U.S. forces have not taken part in actual combat. The United States has also offered significant monetary rewards for information leading to the capture of top Abu Sayyaf members.

The collaboration has resulted in some successes, including the capture or death of several of Abu Sayyaf's leaders, but the organization continues to kidnap Filipino and foreign civilians for ransom and to attack police and other targets. In February 2004, Abu Sayyaf bombed a ferry departing from Manila, causing a fire and killing at least 116 people. The following year, the group set off bombs in three cities, killing more than a dozen people. In both cases, Philippine authorities were able to capture and try many of those responsible. While Abu Sayyaf is considered weaker than it was in its 2000 heyday, the organization has also apparently formed alliances with other radical Muslim groups in the Philippines, and it remains a threat. As of 2010, the leader of Abu Sayyaf was believed to be Isnilon Totoni Hapilon, also known as "The Deputy," who is on the FBI's Most Wanted Terrorists list.

Colleen Sullivan

See also Alex Boncayao Brigade; New People's Army

Further Readings

Aglinoby, John. "Basilan Is Home to Separatist Violence and Kidnappings." *The Guardian,* January 12, 2001.

Aglionsouth, John. "Forgotten Hostages of Island Hell: Philippine Terror Group Is Growing Rich as $1m Ransoms Begin to Be Paid to Free Its Prisoners." *The Observer* August 13, 2000, p. 20.

Banlaoi, Rommel C. *Philippine Security in the Age of Terror.* Boca Raton, FL: CRC Press, 2010.

Bowden, Mark. "Jihadists in Paradise." *The Atlantic,* March 2007.

Crisp, Penny, and Raissa Robles. "A Past Traced in Terror." *The Observer,* May 5, 2000, p. 22.

Hookway, James. "A Dangerous New Alliance." *Far Eastern Economic Review,* May 6, 2004.

"A Hostage Crisis Confronts Estrada." *The Economist,* May 6, 2001.

Martin, Gus. *Essentials of Terrorism: Concepts and Controversies.* 2nd ed. Thousand Oaks, CA: Sage, 2011.

Rabasa, Angel, et al. *Ungoverned Territories: Understanding and Reducing Terrorism Risks.* Santa Monica, CA: RAND Corporation, 2007.

"Tourists Are Seized in Malaysia; Tie to Philippine Clash Claimed." *The New York Times,* April 25, 2000, p. 14.

Weymouth, Lally. "Terrorist Cells All Over." *Newsweek,* February 11, 2002, p. 36.

AÇÃO LIBERTADORA NACIONAL

See Marighella, Carlos

ACHILLE LAURO HIJACKING

On October 7, 1985, four Palestinian militants seized the Italian cruise liner *Achille Lauro* off Port Said, Egypt. The hijackers, under the command of the Palestine Liberation Front (PLF) leader Abu Abbas, held the more than 400 people aboard hostage for two days. The hijackers shot Leon Klinghoffer, an elderly, wheelchair-bound, Jewish passenger from New York, and dumped his body overboard. Klinghoffer's body later washed ashore on a Syrian beach.

Threatening to blow up the ship, the hijackers demanded the release of 50 Palestinian prisoners held in Israel. Egyptian and Palestine Liberation Organization (PLO) officials negotiated with the hijackers, and Abbas, who was not on the liner but claimed responsibility as the leader of the men on board. Abbas had commanded the radical PLF faction for many years and was known for having sent his men on surprise raids into the heart of Israel on hang gliders and balloons. However, at the time of the hijacking, he was also a member of the PLO's executive committee.

Six British women aboard the ship—five members of a dance troupe and the ship's beautician—later spoke to the press. The women explained that one of the hijackers had watched over them amid death threats from the other three, and that the British and American passengers had been separated from other passengers. The ship docked in Cairo, where Abbas negotiated the exchange of the ship and the hostages for free passage to Tunis in North Africa for himself and his men. However, U.S. fighter planes intercepted the plane carrying the five men to Tunis and forced it to land in Sicily. Three of the hijackers were arrested in Italy, but the Italian government refused to turn Abbas and two associates over to the U.S. Marines. Instead, Abbas and his cohorts were assisted in fleeing to the former Yugoslavia.

In 1986 an Italian court tried Abbas in absentia and sentenced him to life in prison. He was never arrested, however. That same year, Abbas discussed the *Achille Lauro* hijacking in a controversial NBC news interview. He denied that his men had killed Klinghoffer, only to later publicly acknowledge that they had. He also maintained that the men did not know that Klinghoffer was American or Jewish. During countless interviews, however, Abbas always maintained that the *Achille Lauro* hijacking had not gone according to plan. He asserted that the goal of the hijackers was to use the *Achille Lauro* to sail to the Israeli port of Ashdod, and to then attack the nearby naval base.

In 1996 Abbas publicly embraced the peace process and Israel allowed him to enter Gaza despite the international warrant for his arrest. The U.S. government abandoned efforts to extradite Abbas and dropped the warrant for his arrest after the statute of limitations expired. In 2003, Abbas was captured by U.S. troops in Baghdad during the overthrow of the Iraqi leader Saddam Hussein, but he died in U.S. custody before he could be extradited or tried.

Marilyn Klinghoffer, who had been forcibly separated from her husband by the hijackers before they murdered him, died of cancer several months after the hijacking. In her obituary, *The Washington Post* reported that, after returning from Italy, Mrs. Klinghoffer told President Reagan that she had spit in the faces of the hijackers as she identified them. "God bless you," Reagan reportedly replied. Although the PLO settled a $1.5 billion court case with the Klinghoffer family in 1997, the group has always asserted that the hijackers were working without their support.

Erica Pearson

See also Abbas, Muhammad "Abu"; Palestine Liberation Front–Abu Abbas Faction; Palestine Liberation Organization

Further Readings

Bohn, Michael K. *The* Achille Lauro *Hijacking: Lessons in the Politics and Prejudice of Terrorism.* Washington, DC: Brassey's, 2004.

Borger, Julian. "Homecoming of a Hijacker; Julian Borger Talks with the *Achille Lauro* Mastermind Abbul Abbas, at His Political Party's New Offices in Gaza." *The Guardian* (London), May 28, 1998, p. 14.

Cowell, Alan. "Hijacker Defends *Achille Lauro* Killing." *The New York Times,* November 14, 1988, p. A3.

"85 *Achille Lauro* Killing 'a Mistake.'" *The New York Times,* April 23, 1996, p. A12.

Fisk, Robert. "Abbas—Symbol of Guerrilla Disunity/ Profile of Instigator of *Achille Lauro* Hijacking Incident." *The Times* (London), October 14, 1985.

Fisk, Robert. "Gunman Saved Britons' Lives/Women Relive Ordeal of *Achille Lauro* Hijacking Incident." *The Times* (London), October 14, 1985.

Phillips, Don. "Marilyn Klinghoffer, Hijacking Survivor, Dies; *Achille Lauro* Victim Pushed Antiterror Fight." *Washington Post,* February 10, 1986, p. A5.

ADEL, SAIF AL (1960 OR 1963–)

Saif al Adel (aka Ibrahim al Madani; Muhamad Ibrahim Makkawi; Seif al Adel), an Egyptian, has been a high-ranking member of al Qaeda and head of Osama bin Laden's personal security force. In addition to providing personal security to bin Laden, Adel also served on al Qaeda's military committee, reporting to the group's military commander Muhammad Atef. He is thought to have trained several of the hijackers responsible for the September 11, 2001, attacks on the World Trade Center and the Pentagon in the United States. In 1998 the U.S. accused Adel of participating in the conspiracy to bomb U.S. embassies in East Africa. The FBI lists him as one of its "most wanted terrorists."

Little is known about Adel's early life. Before joining al Qaeda, he was member of the Egyptian Islamic Jihad. That group, led by the Egyptian doctor Ayman al Zawahiri, merged with al Qaeda in the late 1990s. Zawahiri is now widely considered to be bin Laden's second in command.

According to the 1998 U.S. indictment in the embassy bombings case, Adel sits on al Qaeda's *majlis al shura,* or consultative council. This body discusses and approves all acts of terror carried out by the international al Qaeda network. al Qaeda, an Arabic term meaning "the base," serves as an umbrella group for other terrorist organizations and has declared war against the United States. The indictment also charges Adel with providing military, explosives, and intelligence training to recruits for as long as a decade in al Qaeda camps in Afghanistan, Pakistan, and Sudan. The indictment further charges that, in 1993, Adel and other al Qaeda operatives trained the tribe members who attacked U.N. peacekeeping forces in Somalia. An

attack in Mogadishu, the capital of Somalia, led to the death of 18 U.S. Marines later that year.

Adel remains a fugitive, as do many other al Qaeda members indicted in the embassy case. The U.S. State Department offers a reward of up to $5 million for information leading directly to his apprehension or conviction.

Erica Pearson

See also al Qaeda; bin Laden, Osama; East Africa Embassy Bombings; September 11 Attacks; Zawahiri, Ayman al

Further Readings

Akhahenda, Elijah F. *When Blood and Tears United a Country: The Bombing of the American Embassy in Kenya.* Lanham, MD: University Press of America, 2002.

Bergen, Peter. *The Longest War: Inside the Enduring Conflict between America and al-Qaeda.* New York: Free Press, 2011.

Federal Bureau of Investigation. "Most Wanted Terrorists." http://www.fbi.gov/wanted/terrorists/fugitives.htm.

Hoffman, Bruce. *Inside Terrorism.* New York: Columbia University Press, 2006.

"A Nation Challenged: The Hunted; The 22 Most Wanted Suspects, in a Five-act Drama of Global Terror." *The New York Times,* October 14, 2001, p. 1B.

Reeve, Simon. *The New Jackals: Ramzi Yousef, Osama bin Laden, and the Future of Terrorism.* Boston: Northeastern University Press, 1999.

Smith, Martin, and Lowell Bergman. "Hunting bin Laden." *Frontline,* PBS, September 13, 2001. http://www.pbs.org/wgbh/pages/frontline/shows/binladen.

United States District Court Southern District of New York. *United States v. Osama bin Laden et al.* Indictment S(10) 98 Cr. 1023 (LBS).

Wright, Lawrence. *The Looming Tower: al Qaeda and the Road to 9/11.* New York: Alfred A. Knopf, 2006.

ADEN-ABYAN ISLAMIC ARMY

The Aden-Abyan Islamic Army, most recognized for its involvement in the 2000 bombing of the USS *Cole,* is allegedly affiliated with Osama bin Laden's al Qaeda network. The Yemen-based group has been implicated in several acts of terror since the late 1990s.

Aden-Abyan was formed sometime in 1996 or 1997 as a loose guerrilla network of a few dozen men, with a mix of veterans of the Soviet-Afghan war and Islamists from various countries. In May 1998 the group issued the first of a series of political and religious statements on Yemeni and world affairs. In December 1998, Aden-Abyan kidnapped a party of 16 Western tourists in southern Yemen, 4 of whom later died during a botched rescue by Yemeni security forces. Group leader Abu al Hassan al Mihdar was executed for his role in the kidnappings.

Numerous connections have been drawn between Aden-Abyan and the al Qaeda network. After the 1998 attack on the U.S. embassies in Kenya and Tanzania, Aden-Abyan claimed they were a "heroic operation carried out by heroes of the jihad." Later, following an American raid on Osama bin Laden's camp in Afghanistan, Aden-Abyan announced their support for him and asked Yemeni people to kill Americans and destroy their property. It is also believed that Aden-Abyan ran a training camp in a remote part of southern Yemen; when the government tried to close it, a bin Laden representative attempted to intervene.

In October 2000 two suicide bombers aligned with Aden-Abyan exploded their boat alongside the USS *Cole*, then in port in Aden. Most experts agree that the attack was the combined work of Aden-Abyan and al Qaeda. One day after the *Cole* incident, a bomb was lobbed into the British Embassy, shattering windows at both the embassy and nearby buildings. Four members of Aden-Abyan were later sentenced for the embassy bombing.

Aden-Abyan also claimed responsibility for the October 2002 bombing of a French oil tanker, which killed a crew member. As with the *Cole*, the tanker was attacked by a small boat laden with explosives. The following June, Aden-Abyan operatives attacked a military medical convoy, triggering a substantial military response. That October, the leader of Aden-Abyan, Khalid Abd al Nabi, surrendered to Yemeni authorities.

The Yemeni government claims that Aden-Abyan no longer exists. U.S. terrorism experts, on the other hand, believe it likely that some form of the group still does exist, but as a loose, less organized band of Yemenis and non-Yemenis. In general, though, foreign involvement in jihad activity in Yemen has been decreasing as a result of more stringent security.

Richard McHugh

See also al Qaeda

Further Readings

"Aden Islamic Army Threatens the American and British Ambassadors If They Do Not Leave Yemen." March 12, 1999. *Middle East and Islamic Studies Collection.* http://www.library.cornell.edu/colldev/mideast/feat9en .htm.

Carapico, Sheila. "Yemen and the Aden-Abyan Islamic Army." *Middle East Research and Information Report,* October 18, 2000. http://www.merip.org/ mero/mero101800.html.

Gunaratna, Rohan. *Inside al Qaeda: Global Network of Terror.* New York: Columbia University Press, 2002.

Rabasa, Angel, et al. *Ungoverned Territories: Understanding and Reducing Terrorism Risks.* Santa Monica, CA: RAND Corporation, 2007.

Sciolino, Elaine. "Preliminary Investigation Indicates Oil Tanker Was Attacked." *The New York Times,* October 11, 2002, p. A21.

AFGHAN ARABS

The term *Afghan Arabs* (or *Arab Afghans*) refers to Muslims who volunteered to aid the Afghan jihad against the Soviet occupation of Afghanistan between 1979 and 1989. These volunteers became active in national and regional conflicts upon their return from Afghanistan. Some of these international volunteers functioned as commanders of guerrilla training camps in Pakistan and Afghanistan during the 1990s, giving safe haven to revolutionary Muslims seeking skills in terrorism and warfare. Some participated in insurgencies and civil wars around the world, including Algeria, Egypt, Kashmir, Tajikistan, Bosnia, and Chechnya. The most famous Afghan Arab was Osama bin Laden, the founder of the al Qaeda terrorist network.

In 1979, the Soviet Union invaded Afghanistan in an effort to maintain that nation's beleaguered Communist regime, which was facing an insurgency from multiple Islamist factions. The Afghan insurgents, or mujahideen, called on Pakistan and other governments around the world to help them with military, financial, and humanitarian assistance. Muslim antipathy toward the atheistic ideology of communism and images of suffering Afghanis along the Afghanistan-Pakistan border inspired several thousand Arabs and other Muslims to volunteer as aid and humanitarian workers. Some went a step farther by volunteering to join mujahideen factions in rolling

U.S. Army General David H. Petraeus, center, commander of the International Security Assistance Force, meets with Afghans in the Bala Murghab valley of western Afghanistan on August 2, 2010. (U.S. Air Force photo by Staff Sgt. Bradley Lail/Released)

back the Soviet invasion through combat. In the context of the Cold War, the United States and Muslim governments allied with the United States, such as Pakistan, did not hesitate to give material support to the mujahideen and the foreign Muslim volunteers.

The Afghan Arabs were inspired and organized by Sheikh Abdullah Azzam, one of the fund-raisers and recruiters for the Afghan jihad and the founder of the Services Bureau that hosted Arab volunteers in Peshawar, Pakistan. The Afghan Arabs were a tiny contingent in the anti-Soviet struggle. Estimates of foreign Muslim volunteers vary, but it is likely that no more than 3,000 to 4,000 came at any one time. Most of the volunteers served in Peshawar and other Pakistani cities bordering on Afghanistan. They were humanitarian aid workers, cooks, drivers, doctors, accountants, teachers, engineers, and religious preachers. They built camps, mosques, and makeshift hospitals and schools; they dug and treated water wells; and they attended to the sick and wounded. However, some came with jihad in mind.

The motivations of the volunteers can be divided into five general categories: religious fulfillment, employment opportunities, safe havens, military training, and adventure. Afghan Arabs were mainly men in their twenties recruited from the Persian Gulf and North Africa. Volunteers from the Gulf included guest workers who came from impoverished countries such as Mauritania, Somalia, Sudan, and Yemen. By and large they were seeking jobs and salaries with Gulf-based nongovernmental organizations in Pakistan, not martyrdom in Afghanistan.

The influence of the Afghan Arabs on the rise of global jihadism is significant. The crucible of Afghanistan provided this emergent vanguard with training, socialization, and networking opportunities that they could not dream of in their authoritarian countries. Away from their home governments and free to propagate their radical views, Afghan Arabs developed a culture of jihad and martyrdom, as well as a template for mobilizing Muslims in defense of Islamic causes. Their experiences and skills became manifest in several insurgencies and civil wars during the 1990s, and, tragically, in the terrorist attacks of September 11, 2001.

Mohammed Hafez

See also al Qaeda; bin Laden, Osama; Mujahideen

Further Readings

Bergen, Peter. *The Osama bin Laden I Know: An Oral History of al Qaeda's Leader.* New York: Free Press, 2006.

Coll, Steve. *Ghost Wars.* New York: Penguin, 2005.

Giustozzi, Antonio, ed. *Decoding the New Taliban: Insights from the Afghan Field*. New York: Columbia University Press, 2009.

Kakar, M. Hassan. *Afghanistan: The Soviet Invasion and the Afghan Response, 1979–1982*. Berkeley: University of California Press, 1997.

Margolis, Eric S. *War at the Top of the World: The Struggle for Afghanistan, Kashmir, and Tibet*. New York: Routledge, 2002.

Tanner, Stephen. *Afghanistan: A Military History from Alexander the Great to the War against the Taliban*. Updated edition. New York: Da Capo, 2009.

Wright, Lawrence. *The Looming Tower: al Qaeda and the Road to 9/11*. New York: Knopf, 2006.

AFGHANISTAN WAR

Afghanistan, subject to war and instability since the late 1970s, became the first arena of the "war on terror" after the terrorist attacks of September 11, 2001. Operation Enduring Freedom (OEF) was launched to dislodge the Taliban from power and capture al Qaeda leaders. The Taliban regime was replaced by an Interim Administration led by Hamid Karzai, who continued as president beyond 2010. The International Security Assistance Force (ISAF) was deployed to Kabul as a peacekeeping mission in December 2001, and then expanded around the country in the following years after the North Atlantic Treaty Organization (NATO) assumed its command and control. Provincial Reconstruction Teams (PRTs) were the vehicles through which NATO wanted to carry out its peacekeeping operations. However, the resurgence of the Taliban, who originally seemed like a spent force, compelled NATO to pursue a counterinsurgency strategy. A troop surge by the Barack Obama administration in 2009 increased the number of Western troops in Afghanistan to about 150,000, but whether they would be able to subdue the Taliban and restore peace and stability remained in question as of 2011.

Operation Enduring Freedom

The terrorist network known as al Qaeda was found responsible for the attacks on the World Trade Center and the Pentagon on September 11, 2001. The George W. Bush administration then decided to destroy al Qaeda's safe havens in Afghanistan; capture its leader, Osama bin Laden, "dead or alive"; and punish the Taliban regime for hosting the organization within its borders. Operation Enduring Freedom (OEF), initially termed Operation Infinite Justice, was launched October 7, 2001, with aerial bombardments and cruise missile attacks on Taliban positions. The U.S. forces on the ground consisted of about 350 Army Special Forces and about 100 CIA (Central Intelligence Agency) officers. These forces had begun entering Afghanistan soon after the Bush administration's "War Cabinet" had decided to attack. Their main tasks were to support the anti-Taliban Northern Alliance and to pinpoint the Taliban positions for bombardment. The Northern Alliance, or the "United Front," as they called themselves, was an umbrella organization formed after the Taliban captured Kabul in September 1996. Its main component was the former government, which had relocated to the north and was still the internationally recognized government of Afghanistan. It was joined by some of its former rivals—who were also against the Taliban—in the northern, central, and eastern parts of the country. Some 15,000 troops from the Northern Alliance were the main ground force in the initial stage of OEF.

The first major victory against the Taliban was achieved on November 9, 2001, when the city of Mazar-e-Sharif, the largest city in the north, was captured by the Northern Alliance forces. Kabul, the capital, followed soon after, falling to the Northern Alliance on November 13. The city of Kandahar, the birthplace of the Taliban in the south, was their last stronghold, but they were force to surrender it on December 7. The Battle of Tora Bora followed soon after the fall of Kandahar. It became well known as a near miss in the quest to capture Osama bin Laden. The Tora Bora mountain cave complex is located in eastern Afghanistan, not very far from the border with Pakistan. al Qaeda fighters, including bin Laden, took shelter there after running away from areas conquered by pro-American forces. The Tora Bora battle was carried out by Afghan militias, who were supported by the Special Forces and intelligence officers of the United States and its allies, which also provided aerial bombardment. Either due to negligence or some secret deals, however, bin Laden and other al Qaeda leaders managed to escape the siege.

The United States and its allies were able to remove the Taliban from power without suffering casualties. After OEF was launched, several Special Forces teams from Britain and other U.S. allies also arrived in Afghanistan. Since they were not engaged in direct fighting, they avoided suffering battlefield casualties, though a few Americans were killed in some incidents. Northern Alliance casualties were not very high either. The Taliban, on the other hand, suffered very heavy casualties. In what is known as the Dasht-i-Leili massacre, Taliban prisoners were killed while being transported in metal shipping containers from one northern city to another by the Abdul Rashid Dostum militias, part of the Northern Alliance. Civilian casualties were high as well. Most estimates put the number of civilians killed in the first months of the war at above 1,000.

The Bonn Agreement

After the removal of the Taliban, the Northern Alliance returned to power in Kabul. as well as in northern, central, and western Afghanistan. The southern and eastern parts of the country were dominated by tribal leaders allied with the United States. At the initiative of Lakhdar Brahimi, the Special Representative of the UN Secretary General, a conference was held among the Northern Alliance and three other Afghan groups in Bonn, Germany, from November 25 to December 5, 2001. In addition to the United Nations, the United States, Russia, Germany, and Afghanistan's neighboring countries were other sponsors of the conference. It was not a peace conference, however, because there was no Taliban representation. Its aim was to come up with a government acceptable to the majority of Afghans, as well as to outside players.

The Bonn Conference appointed an Interim Administration and charted a political course that became known as the "Bonn Process." Hamid Karzai, a little-known small player in Afghan politics, was chosen as the chair of the Interim Authority. He was affirmed as the president of the Afghan Transitional Administration in the Emergency *Loya Jirga* (a traditional Afghan grand assembly) in June 2002, and he won the presidential elections in October 2004 and August 2009, though the latter was marred by fraud allegations and controversy. The approval of a new constitution in January 2004 was another step in fulfillment of the Bonn Agreement. The Bonn Process came to an end with parliamentary elections in September 2005. Parliamentary elections were held again in September 2010.

International Security Assistance Force

The Bonn Agreement provided for a UN-mandated security force to "assist in the maintenance of security for Kabul and its surrounding areas," with the possibility of future expansion. The UN Security Council passed a resolution for its establishment on December 20, 2001, and the International Security Assistance Force (ISAF) was deployed shortly thereafter. Before NATO assumed ISAF's command and control in August 2003, European nations were the only ones to contribute troops to the effort in Afghanistan. ISAF was first led by Britain, then by Turkey, and finally jointly by Germany and Holland. The number of ISAF troops eventually reached 4,500, and its mandate remained limited to the Kabul province until the end of 2003.

Despite numerous calls by President Karzai and the UN Special Envoy, the United States initially did not agree with the expansion of the ISAF to other provinces, fearing this would interfere with the U.S. "war on terror." This created a security deficiency in most parts of the country, due to a lack of viable Afghan security forces and the limited focus of OEF. To alleviate the situation, the U.S. military came up with the idea of Provincial Reconstruction Teams (PRTs), which began their deployment in December 2002. A PRT consisted of about 100 to 200 soldiers, engineers, medical staff, and civil affairs officers. The aim was to help the Kabul government expand its authority around the country, promote security, and undertake some construction projects. The program was sharply criticized by humanitarian organizations for legitimizing the local warlords, on whose goodwill the PRT had to rely, and for blurring the line between humanitarian work and military operations. Despite this criticism, NATO decided on PRT as its modus operandi after assuming the command of ISAF.

From Peacekeeping to Counterinsurgency

In an unprecedented move, NATO invoked Article 5 of its charter, which considers an attack against one member state to be an attack against all the member states. This was done as an expression of solidarity with the United States in the wake of the 9/11 terrorist attacks. It received a cold shoulder from the United States, however, because the Bush administration did not want to bind itself to

NATO's cumbersome decision-making process. Among the factors that induced the United States to seek a greater role for NATO in the Afghanistan war in early 2003 were ISAF's difficulty in finding volunteers to lead the force and the U.S. involvement in the unpopular war in Iraq. A UN Security Council resolution in October 2003 then authorized the expansion of the ISAF mission beyond Kabul. The German-led PRT in Kunduz City was transferred to ISAF authority as a pilot project in December 2003, marking the beginning of Stage 1 of NATO expansion to the north, which was completed in October 2004. In Stage 2, completed in September 2005, ISAF expanded to the west. Stage 3, an expansion to the south, involved the transfer of command from the United States to NATO in July 2006 and the replacement of some U.S. PRTs by those run by other NATO member states. Finally. in Stage 4 of the expansion in October 2006, more than half of the U.S. forces in the east, as well as the PRTs run by the United States and its allies there and in central Afghanistan, were put under the command of NATO. The other half of the U.S. troops in the east remained outside NATO and part of OEF.

ISAF expansion to the north and the west did not involve any combat. NATO commanders expected the same in the south and the east, but they soon found they were mistaken. As soon the British and Canadian troops were deployed in Helmand and Kandahar, they had to engage in fierce battles with the Taliban, leading their commanders to ask for more troops from other NATO members. The call fell on deaf ears, however.

The reluctance of many NATO members to contribute more troops to ISAF is a sign of an internal rift from which NATO has suffered at least since the end of the Cold War, according to some scholars. The other sign of the rift is the caveats imposed by some nations on the operations of their troops, including the area where they are deployed, the timing of operations, and the type of operations. For many years, NATO forces in Afghanistan also suffered from the lack of a coherent strategy, problems of coordination, and differences of opinion on how to deal with the Taliban, what to do with the drug problem, and how to achieve a balance between effectively fighting the Taliban and minimizing civilian casualties.

NATO's internal rifts made its job in dealing with a resurgent Taliban much more difficult. Taliban fighters were described by informed observers as fierce, dynamic, highly motivated, well organized, well trained, and very resilient. They used various tactics in their war against NATO and the Karzai government, including the use of IEDs (improvised explosive devices) for roadside bombing, suicide attack, ambush, sniper shooting, assassination, kidnapping and hostage taking, and occasional frontal fighting. They also seemed very skillful in propaganda war and the use of multimedia.

Resurgence of the Taliban

Many observers blame the Bush administration's shift of focus to the war on Iraq for the resurgence of the Taliban in Afghanistan. There is some truth in this, but the situation was much more complicated. The initial decision for a "light footprint," which led to a power vacuum around the country and the emergence of local warlords, was also a contributing factor in the reemergence of the Taliban. The mistreatment of the Taliban by pro-U.S. militias and new Afghan authorities was another factor. Thousands of fighters became prisoners of war and were held under what were often described as appalling circumstances, while those who returned to their villages to resume a normal life were subjected to persecution, forcing many to flee and fill the Taliban ranks. The Taliban leadership sought refuge in Pakistan, finding sanctuaries in the tribal areas along the border and support from the Pakistani intelligence agencies. Many believe that the Pakistani government essentially played a double game: while vigorously hunting al Qaeda, it simultaneously supported the Taliban, not only to retain U.S. interest in the region but also to be able to play a role in future Afghan politics.

The Bonn Agreement also had an impact on the rise of the Taliban. The Interim Administration that had been agreed upon gave the impression that the Pashtuns, the ethnic group to which most Taliban belonged, had been marginalized in the new political setup. Despite being a Pashtun himself, Karzai failed to gain widespread legitimacy among Pashtuns because he was perceived as a U.S. stooge, and because he adopted policies seen as anti-Islamic. He also failed to curb factionalism in his cabinet, particularly among those associated with the former resistance movement and the "technocrats" who previously lived in exile in the West. The appointments were based on nepotism and personal relations more than on competence, creating extensive resentment toward the government. Rampant corruption, mostly due to the flow of large amount of funds without much accountability, made the situation worse. The misuse of the reconstruction assistance by the donor agencies, nongovernmental organizations (NGOs), foreign contractors, domestic contractors, and the Afghan authorities, as well as misguided development policies and the "free market" economy enshrined in the new Afghan constitution, led to unprecedented levels of poverty and inequality, further helping the cause of the Taliban.

Moreover, the Karzai government and its foreign supporters failed to curb poppy cultivation and drug production, which were important sources of finance for the Taliban. Their failure to raise reliable Afghan security forces was also spectacular. Until mid-2006, the United States seemed more interested in having an "auxiliary force" in Afghanistan, rather than having a strong national army and police force. Despite the subsequent enormous efforts in their training, the ability of the Afghan security forces to undertake responsibilities from NATO troops by 2014, as agreed at a NATO summit in Lisbon in November 2010, remained questionable.

Another important factor contributing to the resurgence of the Taliban was the behavior of the American and allied forces. Their lack of sensitivity to Afghans' cultural and religious values was part of the problem. As Thomas Johnson and M. Chris Mason noted in 2007, "the United States is losing the war in Afghanistan one Pashtun village at a time, bursting into schoolyards full of children with guns bristling, kicking in village doors, searching women, speeding down city streets, . . . all of which are anathema to the Afghans." They were also implicated in the mistreatment of prisoners and human rights abuses. Furthermore, large numbers of civilian casualties caused by careless aerial bombardments and "trigger happy" shootings by the Western soldiers and private contractors, whose number has been reported to be equivalent to the number of the troops, created immense bitterness. Finally, the Afghans' historical memory of past

aggressions and strong resentment toward foreign intervention further contributed to general population's hostility toward foreign troops and promoted the insurgency.

President Obama's Troop Surge

The newly elected President Obama, who had campaigned on withdrawal from Iraq and focusing on Afghanistan and Pakistan, faced a request from his commander in Afghanistan for an additional 30,000 troops soon after assuming power. After some deliberation, he approved deployment of 17,000 extra troops. A few weeks later, he announced a "new comprehensive strategy" for Afghanistan and Pakistan, which led to the "Af-Pak" neologism. Linking the problem in Afghanistan to Pakistan was a welcome departure from the Bush administration's policies, which had long remained oblivious to the role of Pakistan. General Stanley McChrystal, who was appointed as the U.S. and NATO top commander in Afghanistan in June 2009, undertook a strategic review of the situation as soon as he assumed command. It was a bleak assessment, with a warning of failure if the strategy did not change and the number of troops did not increase. He advocated a surge of at least 40,000 troops, and it took President Obama more than three months of consultations to approve deployment of 30,000 more soldiers, with the hope of the remaining 10,000 being contributed by the allies.

The troop surge reached its peak under McChrystal's replacement, General David Petraeus, in mid-2010. Most of the new troops were deployed to the south and the east. Their presence did put the Taliban under pressure, but there was no expectation that it would lead to their defeat. The hope was that the military pressure in Afghanistan and the drone attacks on the Taliban and al Qaeda positions on the Pakistani side of the border—attacks that multiplied exponentially under the Obama administration—would force the Taliban into negotiation with the Karzai government. Some preliminary talks had started by 2010, but an agreement seemed far off. In the meantime, the Taliban expanded their operations to the previously peaceful areas in the north and the west. The capital, Kabul, also came under attack from time to time.

The Longest War

The Afghanistan war, described as a litmus test of NATO's future relevance and viability, became the United States' longest war in mid-2010. The war also cost NATO allies several hundred billion dollars up to that point. The financial cost increased steadily over the years, as did the number of allied troops killed. In addition, the war became unpopular in Europe, and even in the United States. Holland ended its mission in Afghanistan in August 2010, and Canada planned to do the same in 2011. President Obama declared July 2011 as the date to start drawdown of U.S. troops, and at the 2010 NATO summit in Portugal it was decided that 2014 would be the year military operations in the country would end. Thus, getting out of Afghanistan will be riddled with multiple complications, as was winning the initial war there.

Najib Lafraie

See also al Qaeda; bin Laden, Osama; Central Intelligence Agency; September 11 Attacks; Taliban; United Nations

Further Readings

Giustozzi, Antonio, ed. *Decoding the New Taliban: Insights from the Afghan Field*. New York: Columbia University Press, 2009.

Giustozzi, Antonio. *Koran, Kalashnikov, and Laptop: The Neo-taliban Insurgency in Afghanistan*. New York: Columbia University Press, 2008.

Giustozzi, Antonio. *The Taliban beyond the Pashtuns*. Afghanistan Papers No. 5 (July 2010). Waterloo, Ontario: Centre for International Governance Innovation. http://www.cigionline.org/publications/2010/7/taliban-beyond-pashtuns.

Johnson, Thomas H. "On the Edge of the Big Muddy: The Taliban Resurgence in Afghanistan." *China and Eurasia Forum Quarterly* 5, no. 2 (2007): 93–129.

Johnson, Thomas H., and M. Chris Mason. "Understanding the Taliban and Insurgency in Afghanistan," *Orbis* 51, no. 1 (2007): 71–89.

Lafraie, Najibullah. "NATO in Afghanistan: Perilous Mission Dire Ramifications." *International Politics* 46, no. 5 (2009): 550–572.

Lafraie, Najibullah. "Resurgence of Taliban Insurgency in Afghanistan: How and Why?" *International Politics* 46, no. 1 (2009): 102–113.

Maley, William. *The Afghanistan War*. 2nd ed. New York: Palgrave Macmillan, 2009.

Rashid, Ahmed. *Descent into Chaos: the United States and the Failure of Nation Building in Pakistan, Afghanistan, and Central Asia*. New York: Viking, 2008.

Rohde, David, and David E. Sanger. "How a 'Good War' in Afghanistan Went Bad." *The New York Times*, August 12, 2007.

Suhrke, Astri. "A Contradictory Mission? NATO from Stabilization to Combat in Afghanistan." *International Peacekeeping* 15, no. 2 (2008): 214–236.

AGRICULTURAL TERRORISM

Possible terrorist attacks on the agricultures of the world's advanced economies receive less attention than the possibility of attacks that kill immediately. Damaged crops and sickened herds will never get as much attention or instill as much fear as an attack on a major population center. Yet the agricultural sector of advanced economies is very vulnerable. Attacks could cause severe food shortages and would certainly result in severe trade and economic disruption. While there is no evidence that the 2001 outbreak of foot-and-mouth disease (FMD) in Great Britain was the result of terrorist activity, the economic and psychological impact of the epidemic raised the specter of terrorist attacks against agricultural economies and raised fears that the food supplies of nations might be vulnerable.

There have been at least a few historical examples of military attacks against crops and animals. Both the former Soviet Union and the United States once conducted research and development on pathogens for use against crops and animals, for example. Few doubt that determined terrorists could obtain small quantities of plant and animal pathogens. What is less certain is whether terrorists could succeed in spreading the pathogens widely enough to infect large crop areas or large numbers of animals. An outbreak of an animal disease such as FMD, or a crop blight such as wheat smut, would elicit an immediate reaction, which would include both treatment and quarantine. Environmental factors, such as the natural resistance of plants to disease and weather conditions at the time of the initial attack, might limit the effectiveness of even a well-planned attack. On the other hand, diseases such as FMD are highly infectious, and even a small attack could demoralize a population and lead to disruptions in complex economies.

Tools of the Agroterrorist

Terrorists have, or could develop, the capability of using biological agents to attack crops and livestock. Such agents include viruses such as the highly contagious foot-and-mouth disease and rinderpest, which kill or weaken cattle, sheep, pigs, and other livestock. Anti-plant agents include fungi such as rice blast and stem rust, which attack rice, wheat, and other important crops. Many of these diseases are endemic in various parts of the world, particularly in countries without well-developed procedures to monitor crop and animal health.

Early detection is necessary to cull infected animals and destroy infected crops to keep diseases from spreading. Many of the diseases that terrorists are most likely to use occur naturally, and a terrorist team could travel to the scene of an outbreak to obtain infectious material from a sick animal or crop. At the attack site, the pathogen could be administered clandestinely, so that any resulting sickness would appear to be the result of natural causes. One expert has indicated how easy this would be: "If I wanted to spread foot-and-mouth disease, I would just get a saliva smear from a sick cow and then rub it on the noses of some healthy cows in the country I wanted to attack."

The development of biological agents explicitly for use against animals and crops has a long history. Germany used anthrax and glanders against pack and food animals during World War I. Germany and Japan conducted active research during World War II to develop anti-crop and anti-animal weapons. They rarely used them, however, probably because they feared retaliation in kind from the United States and its allies, which were engaged in similar research. Some nations may have refrained from using biological agents only because they feared the prospect of having the diseases spread to their own homelands.

The United States ended its biological weapons program in 1969 and has honored its commitment to the 1972 Biological and Toxin Weapons Convention of (BWC). This agreement outlawed offensive bioweapon research and development and required signatories to destroy their stockpiles. In the 1990s, however, citizens of the Soviet Union and Iraq reported that their countries continued to pursue clandestine research programs. Some of those bioweapons may still exist in stockpile sites or laboratories, and in any case the knowledge needed to cultivate these organisms is widespread and relatively easy to acquire.

Defensive biological warfare research, such as vaccine development, is permitted under the terms of the BWC, but an outside observer may find distinguishing between the development of a vaccine and the development of a weapon under the cover of vaccine research difficult or impossible. Scientists involved in defensive agroterror research need supplies of plant and animal pathogens. Terrorists seeking these pathogens might obtain them from nations willing to sponsor terrorist activities, by theft from research laboratories, or by misrepresenting themselves to commercial suppliers of pathogens.

The United States has tightened standards considerably in this area, so that it is no longer possible to merely invent a company name, print a letterhead, and obtain a pathogen from a supplier. Many other countries do not have comparable safeguards, however. A small quantity of almost any pathogen could easily be smuggled into the United States by packaging it as a medicine. In addition, persons with modest training in microbiology can cultivate greater quantities of many pathogens if supplied with a starter culture. Some animal diseases are so infectious that only a small quantity is needed to start an infection that would sweep through herds if not caught very early.

Prevention, Detection, and Mitigation of Outbreaks

Crops can be genetically engineered to make them more resistant to pathogens, and their cultivation schedules can be rotated to reduce the risk of exposing an entire crop to a disease. In addition, growing conditions can be optimized to reduce the spread of infection should a disease outbreak occur. Animals, meanwhile, can be vaccinated against some of the most threatening diseases, and antibiotic use can be minimized to reduce the risk of having livestock vulnerable to attack with strains of antibiotic-resistant bacteria. Factory farms that pack thousands of animals into confined spaces are likely to be very vulnerable, making them potentially attractive to terrorists.

Research laboratories in many parts of the world are working on developing instruments that can detect and identify pathogens quickly, eliminating the need for long delays while waiting for laboratory reports. The swift exchange of information about agricultural diseases by veterinary and crop specialists can be accomplished through computer and other information technologies, and international organizations can cooperate to adopt measures to reduce the chance of a disease crossing oceans. An outbreak of a highly infectious plant or animal disease on one continent is only a commercial airline flight away from anyplace else in the world, so timely detection and notification are essential.

Although an agroterror attack might not cause severe food shortages in highly developed countries with diversified food supplies, a terrorist-instigated outbreak of a virulent agricultural disease in a less-developed region could cause local famine. Refugees could carry the disease beyond borders and across oceans to places where it could disrupt economies, cause food price increases, and create widespread panic if the disease were transmissible to humans.

Les Paldy

See also Anthrax; Biological Terrorism; Counterterrorism

Further Readings

Alibek, Ken, with Stephen Handelman. *Biohazard: The Chilling Story of the Largest Covert Biological Weapons Program in the History of the World.* New York: Random House, 1999

Cameron, Gavin, Jason Pate, and Katherine M. Vogel. "Planting Fear: How Real Is the Threat of Agricultural Terrorism?" *Bulletin of the Atomic Scientists* 57, no. 5 (September/October 2001).

Chalk, Peter. *Hitting America's Soft Underbelly: The Potential Threat of Deliberate Biological Attacks against the U.S. Agricultural and Food Industry.* Santa Monica, CA: RAND Corporation, 2004.

Katona, Peter, John P. Sullivan, and Michael D. Intriligator, eds. *Global Biosecurity: Threats and Responses.* Abingdon, UK: Routledge, 2010.

Moats, Jason B. *Agroterrorism: A Guide for First Responders.* College Station: Texas A&M University Press, 2007.

Monterey Institute of International Studies, James Martin Center for Nonproliferation Studies. http://cns.miis.edu.

Rogers, Paul, Simon Whitby, and Malcolm Dando. "Biological Warfare against Crops." *Scientific American* 280 (June 1999).

AIR INDIA FLIGHT 182 BOMBING

On June 23, 1985, a bomb exploded in a cargo hold of Air India Flight 182, which was flying over the Atlantic Ocean near Ireland at the time of the explosion. A handful of the 329 passengers survived the explosion, only to drown in the ocean. Members of the Babbar Khalsa Society, or Babbar Khalsa International (BKI), a Sikh extremist group, were implicated in this attack.

Sikhs are a religious minority who have lived in northern India since the 1500s. The vast majority of Sikhs live in the Indian state of Punjab, but significant Sikh populations exist in Canada, the United States, and Great Britain. In the mid-1970s, a radical Sikh movement emerged advocating the establishment of an independent Sikh nation. In 1984 the Indian government launched a military attack on the Golden Temple in Amritsar, the Sikhs' holiest shrine, which was then occupied by militant Sikhs. The attack was deeply offensive to Sikhs and led to further violence, with the Air India bombings believed to be carried out in retaliation for the attack on the Golden Temple.

The bombs most likely originated in Vancouver, British Columbia, where an unidentified man booked two different itineraries from Vancouver to New Delhi, India's capital. One travel itinerary went east, from Vancouver to Toronto to London to New Delhi; the second went west, from Vancouver to New Delhi via Tokyo. In both cases, bags were checked through to New Delhi, but whoever checked the bags never boarded the flights.

Early in the morning on June 23, 1985, a bag taken off the Vancouver-to-Tokyo flight exploded at Tokyo's Narita Airport. The explosion killed two baggage handlers and wounded four others. An hour later, Flight 182, traveling from Toronto to London at an altitude of 31,000 feet, disappeared from the radar of flight controllers. An examination of the wreckage revealed that a sudden explosion, most likely a bomb, destroyed the plane.

Talwinder Singh Paramar, a leader of Babbar Khalsa Society living in British Columbia, had been under surveillance for weeks before the bombings because he was thought to pose a security threat following the attack on the Golden Temple. Paramar's behavior during the surveillance indicated that he might have been responsible, and he was arrested. Canadian police had mishandled his surveillance—no one was watching him on the day the bombs were delivered to the Vancouver airport, for example—and key evidence was lost. Charges against Paramar were dropped, and he eventually returned to India, where he was killed by Indian security forces in 1992. An accomplice of Paramar, Inderjet Singh Reyat, a mechanic who apparently built the bombs, was also arrested and released; he was re-arrested, convicted, and sentenced in 1991 to 10 years in prison on manslaughter charges connected to the Narita bombing.

In late 2000, the Canadian government charged two Sikh men from British Columbia in the Flight 182 bombing, the cleric Ajaib Singh Bagri and the businessman Ripudaman Singh Malik. In June 2001, Reyat was also charged in the Flight 182 bombing, mere days before completing his 10-year sentence for manslaughter. Reyat pled guilty to manslaughter and received a 5-year sentence. Bagri and Malik, however, went to trial in 2005 and were acquitted. Reyat—to this day, the only person ever convicted for the bombing—currently faces charges of perjury stemming from his testimony in Bagri and Malik's trial.

Most of those who died in the bombing of Flight 182 were Canadian citizens of Indian descent, including Sikhs; the failure of the Canadian government to apprehend and convict those responsible for their deaths has been seen by many as an insult to the community. The acquittal of Bagri and Malik in 2005 fueled calls for a judicial inquiry into the government's handling of the case. The inquiry, which ended public hearings in 2008, revealed a host of security and communication lapses that enabled the bombing to take place and later prevented successful prosecutions.

Mary Sisson

See also Sikh Terrorism

Further Readings

Blaise, Clark, and Bharati Mukherjee. *The Sorrow and the Terror: The Haunting Legacy of the Air India Tragedy.* Markham, Ontario: Viking, 1987.

Bolan, Kim. *Loss of Faith: How the Air-India Bombers Got Away with Murder.* Toronto, Ontario: McClelland and Stewart, 2006.

Commission of Inquiry into the Investigation of the Bombing of Air India Flight 182. http://www.majorcomm.ca/EN/INDEX.ASP.

Jiwa, Salem, and Donald J. Hauka. *Margin of Terror: A Reporter's 20-Year Odyssey Covering the Tragedies of the Air India Bombing.* Mumbai: Jaico, 2007.

MacQueen, Ken, and John Geddes. "Air India: After 22 Years, Now's the Time for the Truth." *MacLean's,* May 28, 2007.

Martin, Douglas. "As Indians' Ranks Grow in Canada, Old Conflicts Are Also Transplanted." *The New York Times,* June 26, 1985, p. A11.

Nickerson, Colin. "15-year Probe of Jet Bombing Brings 2 Arrests: Canada Detains Sikh Militants." *Boston Globe,* October 29, 2000, p. A3.

Swardson, Anne. "Bomb Victims' Families: No Resolution, No Comfort: Air India Crash Case Still Open 10 Years Later." *Washington Post,* July 26, 1995, p. A18.

AIRPORT SECURITY

Of all the targets available to terrorists, airports have proven to be one of the most important. Although there have been comparatively few attacks on airports and aviation, such attacks have been among the deadliest in terms of human lives and economic impact.

Airports make attractive targets because a successful strike can inflict a large number of casualties and disrupt air travel. Terrorists seeking to attack planes must usually try to smuggle themselves or their explosives, or both, through airport checkpoints. Thus, airport security involves not only ensuring a secure environment at the airport itself, but also implementing effective procedures to prevent terrorists from attacking planes.

Safeguarding airports is extremely difficult because of the volume of flights involved. To handle the thousands of flights, millions of passengers, billions of pieces of baggage, and tons of freight that flow through American airports every year, aviation relies on an extensive infrastructure that is highly dependent on complex telecommunications technologies. The tragedy of the 9/11 attacks vividly demonstrated the inadequacy of the measures that

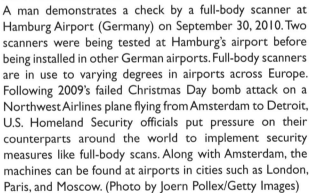

A man demonstrates a check by a full-body scanner at Hamburg Airport (Germany) on September 30, 2010. Two scanners were being tested at Hamburg's airport before being installed in other German airports. Full-body scanners are in use to varying degrees in airports across Europe. Following 2009's failed Christmas Day bomb attack on a Northwest Airlines plane flying from Amsterdam to Detroit, U.S. Homeland Security officials put pressure on their counterparts around the world to implement security measures like full-body scans. Along with Amsterdam, the machines can be found at airports in cities such as London, Paris, and Moscow. (Photo by Joern Pollex/Getty Images)

Images created by a "backscatter" scanner are displayed during a demonstration at the Transportation Security Administration's Systems Integration Facility at Ronald Reagan National Airport on December 30, 2009, in Arlington, Virginia. Backscatter technology uses low-level x-rays to create a two-sided image. The scan can detect hidden metallic and nonmetallic objects such as weapons and explosives without physical contact. The TSA rolled out approximately 150 backscatter scanners in 2010 and has budgeted for 300 additional imaging units. (Photo by Chip Somodevilla/Getty Images)

had been in place at U.S. airports and brought about the implementation of numerous new measures designed to enhance security.

Because aviation is a global activity, airport security also requires international cooperation. U.S. airlines fly to numerous foreign airports and are linked through code sharing and other arrangements with other airlines. At the same time, planes from any different countries bring millions of passengers to the United States. The interconnected nature of air travel raises complex security issues. For example, the bomb that destroyed Pan Am Flight 103 in 1988 was placed onboard a plane in

Malta, transferred to a Pan Am flight in Frankfurt, and subsequently placed on board a B-747 (Flight 103) in London for the trip across the Atlantic. Foreign airports have also been attacked. In December 1985 terrorists struck the El Al and TWA ticket counters in Rome and the El Al counter in Vienna, killing 19 and wounding 140. The International Civil Aviation Organization has attempted to promote essential international cooperation and establish effective international standards, but not all nations are able or willing to comply, and these goals have only been partially achieved.

Before 9/11

Attacks on aviation date back many years. At first, they largely took the form of individual hijackings; the first of which occurred in 1931 at Arequipa Airport in Peru when armed persons tried to commandeer a plane to drop revolutionary leaflets on Lima. At times, hijackers hoped to obtain ransoms, but more frequently they sought to escape from Communist regimes such as that in Cuba. As relations worsened between the United States and Cuba in the early 1960s, hijackings to and from Cuba by Cuban exiles, political refugees, and criminals seeking asylum or ransom intensified. By the late 1960s, however, a new pattern emerged, as terrorists realized that hijacking planes provided great publicity and hostages made great bargaining chips. In 1968, members of the Popular Front for the Liberation of Palestine (PFLP) hijacked an El Al flight in Rome. The frequency of hijackings and bombings increased greatly in the 1980s, especially against American and European airlines. These airlines soon proved to be easier targets than El Al, which had adopted effective measures to screen passengers boarding its planes.

The United States adopted various measures to stem such attacks, including a sky marshal program and passenger screening. The United States also signed various international treaties, including one with Cuba in 1973, but the bombing of Pan Am 103 highlighted the need for additional measures. The President's Commission on Aviation Security and Terrorism was established in 1989, and the Aviation Security Improvement Act was enacted in 1990. Although this legislation mandated various reforms, especially within the Federal Aviation Administration (FAA), they were never implemented adequately owing to administrative mismanagement, a lack of proactive planning, and a fundamental conflict of interest stemming from its basic responsibilities—promoting aviation while also overseeing its safety and security.

The 1996 crash of Flight 800, which crashed into the Atlantic Ocean off of Long Island, New York, prompted the establishment of the White House Commission on Aviation Safety and Security, but the FAA failed to implement many of its recommendations adequately. Airlines and airports continued to implement the FAA's rules as cheaply as possible, showing very limited concern for the security implications.

9/11 and the Policy Response

The successful and devastating 9/11 attack forced a comprehensive reappraisal of the state of airport security and led to a range of dramatic and far-ranging policy initiatives. Within two months, Congress passed the Aviation and Transportation Security Act (ATSA). Designed to eliminate numerous existing weaknesses, it established the Transportation Security Administration (TSA) within the Department of Transportation (DOT). The TSA was one of 22 agencies absorbed by the Department of Homeland Security (DHS) when it was established on November 25, 2002.

To strengthen airport security, the TSA was required to recruit, assess, hire, train, and deploy Security Officers for all the major commercial U.S. airports within 12 months; airport workers and staff were to be subjected to background checks; and access to various areas was restricted. In addition, cockpit doors were strengthened, the number of air marshals increased, and, after considerable debate, pilots were allowed to carry guns.

The most expensive and visible action was the replacement of private company screeners—who tended to be poorly paid, badly trained, and inefficient—with a force of 60,000 federal workers. Although these workers have confiscated millions of potential weapons, questions continue to be raised about the degree to which these costly procedures have truly enhanced security. Many people now cynically characterize screening as "security theater," as a performance designed to help the airlines by making people *feel* safer. The TSA vigorously disputes such assessments and continues to strive to improve screening efficiency through training and the deployment of new technologies. For example, at many airports, magnetometers have been replaced by advanced imaging technology machines (body scanners), though these have been criticized by experts for their inability to see inside body cavities, and by privacy groups for their ability to look through people's clothing. The TSA has responded to these concerns by ensuring that the screeners are far from the subjects and that images cannot be stored or copied.

The failure of the TSA to anticipate predictable threats, in addition to its reactive approach, has been vividly highlighted by several incidents. About three months after 9/11, Richard Reid, a London-born member of al Qaeda, tried to blow up American Airlines Flight 63 en route from Paris to Miami with an explosive compound hidden in his shoes. Though he was unsuccessful, the TSA reacted by mandating that all shoes be screened. In 2006 a plot to use liquid explosives for planes flying from London to North America was detected and the TSA reacted by decreeing that no liquids or gels could be carried on board a plane. Subsequently, after considerable public outcry, the ban was eased. At the time of publication, the "3-1-1 rule" was in place, allowing three-ounce bottles in one quart-size plastic bag per passenger.

To deal with the threat of hidden bombs in baggage, Congress mandated that the TSA screen 100 percent of all checked luggage for explosives by December 31, 2002. The TSA met that deadline with difficulty, and it has now installed over 2,000 Explosive Detection System (EDS) machines, as well as more than 6,000 Explosive Trace Detection (EDT) machines for secondary screening. However, not all of this equipment has been integrated into online baggage systems, a necessary step to optimize baggage screening and enhance worker safety. Moreover, although the TSA was mandated to screen all of the air cargo carried on passenger planes by August 2010, security challenges remained, including how to ensure that the many people involved in the global supply chains have been adequately screened, how to allocate the costs, and how to minimize the economic impacts for manufacturers and their supply chains.

Given the huge volume of passengers and baggage, identifying potential threats is essential. As early as 1994, a computerized system, the Computer Assisted Passenger Prescreening System (CAPPS), was developed but it has also been criticized for privacy concerns and potential discrimination. An advanced version, CAPPS II, was abandoned by the TSA in 2004 for similar reasons. A more limited program, called "Secure Flight," was designed to prescreen passengers and was expected to replace the present system by which the intelligence community provides the airlines with lists of specific individuals who require extra screening or who are not permitted to board a plane. The TSA has also developed the Screening of Passengers by Observation Techniques (SPOT) program. This program, however, has been deployed even in the absence of a scientific consensus that it is possible to detect a potential risk through a person's appearance and behavior.

The problems associated with the existing system (and the continuing inventiveness of al Qaeda) were again vividly illustrated in 2009, when Umar Farouk Abdulmutallab was not placed on the No Fly List, despite being a suspected terrorist. On Christmas Day of that year, he attempted to detonate an explosive device sewn in his underwear on Northwest Airlines Flight 253 from Amsterdam to Detroit. The Senate Select Committee on Intelligence, which studied the case, issued a report on May 18, 2010, identifying 14 specific failures by various intelligence agencies. Subsequent to the report,

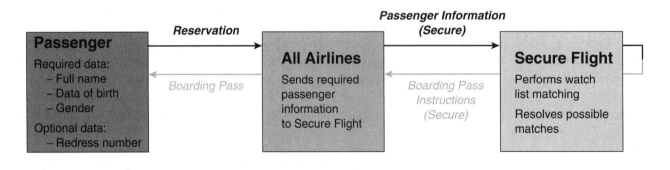

Figure 1   TSA Secure Flight Process.

Source: Adapted from Transportation Security Administration. (n.d.). *Secure Flight Program.* Retrieved 12/21/2010 from http://www.tsa.gov/what_we_do/layers/secureflight/index.shtm.

when specific intelligence information identified people as potential risks, they were to be placed on a third list that would be distributed to the airlines. These additional reforms, however, likewise failed to prevent Faisal Shahzad (the "Times Square bomber"), from boarding an Emirates Airlines plane bound for Dubai in 2010. Though his name had been added to the TSA's No Fly List and the airlines have 24 hours to ascertain whether a passenger is on that list, Emirates had not yet checked the list. Since Shahzad's near-escape from U.S. authorities, airlines have been required to check the No Fly List within two hours. Other obstacles remain, however, including the potential use of false names by terrorists, though the Secure Flight program is expected to prevent such abuses. Clearly, the existing structures and processes by which intelligence is analyzed and integrated by the various agencies and utilized to enhance homeland security continue to need attention.

That airports need to be protected from direct attack was again demonstrated by the June 2007 attack at the Glasgow International Airport, when a car laden with propane attempted to crash into the terminal. While terminal design should clearly incorporate security dimensions, many experts have questioned the degree to which existing facilities have been amended to prevent and minimize the impact of suicide attacks, and even whether the new terminals that have been built across the world in recent years provide adequate security against attacks. Moreover, airport perimeters must also be safeguarded. Here, too, much remains to be done, including vulnerability and consequence assessments. One perimeter threat comes from surface-to-air-missiles known as man-portable air-defense systems (MANPADS), which are readily available to terrorists. Although no plane has yet been downed by such a missile, the existence of this threat has generated a variety of possible solutions, ranging from aircraft hardening to missile protection systems to manned and even unmanned escorts. Nor can one overlook the very large number of general aviation airports. Safeguarding these is a very costly proposition, and though some modest steps have been taken, access to these airports and their planes remains relatively open.

Of course, it is not only the United States that confronts these issues, and airport security policies vary greatly from country to country. At some overseas airports, for example, travelers are not required to remove their shoes. Armed soldiers often patrol terminals, as is the case at Israel's Ben Gurion Airport, which is widely considered the most secure airport in the world. It has not been attacked since 1972, and no departing plane has ever been hijacked or bombed. The greatest difference between European, and especially Israeli, practice and the U.S. approach, however, is probably their risk-based decision making, which assigns people into various categories for differential attention, on the basis of extensive passenger profiling. Because of privacy and discrimination concerns, the United States treats all passengers and their baggage equally, with only a few exceptions, such as the No Fly and Selectee lists. However, the United States has been gradually moving toward the adoption of a trusted passenger program as well. Clearly, despite all the policies and the billions of dollars that have been invested, safeguarding airports remains a work in progress.

Joseph Szyliowicz

See also al Qaeda; Bombings and Bomb Scares; Hijacking; Homeland Security; Intelligence Gathering; LaGuardia Airport Bombing; Pan Am Flight 73 Hijacking; Pan Am Flight 103 Bombing; September 11 Attacks; TWA Flight 355 Hijacking; TWA Flight 840 Hijacking; TWA Flight 847 Hijacking

Further Readings

Duffy, Michael, et al. "The Lessons of Flight 253." *Time*, January 11, 2010, pp. 26–30.

Elias, Bartholomew. *Airport and Aviation Security*. Boca Raton, FL: Auerbach Publications/Taylor & Francis, 2010.

Martin, Gus. *Essentials of Terrorism: Concepts and Controversies*. 2nd ed. Thousand Oaks, CA: Sage, 2011.

Sweet, Kathleen. *Aviation and Airport Security: Terrorism and Safety Concerns*. 2nd ed. Boca Raton, FL: CRC Press, 2008.

Szyliowicz, Joseph S. "Aviation Security: Promise or Reality?" *Studies in Conflict & Terrorism* 27, no. 1 (2004): 47–63.

U.S. Government Accountability Office (GAO). *Aviation Security: A National Strategy and Other Actions Would Strengthen TSA's Efforts to Secure Commercial Airport Perimeters and Access Controls.* GAO-09-399. Washington, DC: GAO, September 30, 2009. http://www.gao.gov/products/GAO-09-399.

U.S. Government Accountability Office (GAO). *Aviation Security: TSA Is Increasing Procurement and Deployment of the Advanced Imaging Technology, but Challenges to This Effort and Other Areas of Aviation Security Remain.* GAO-10-484T. Washington, DC: GAO, March 17, 2010. http://www.gao.gov/products/GAO-10-484T.

AJAJ, AHMAD

See World Trade Center Bombing (1993)

AL AQSA MARTYRS BRIGADES

A coalition of Palestinian West Bank militias that became increasingly violent during 2002, the al Aqsa Martyrs Brigades are known for committing deadly suicide bombing attacks against Israel. Unlike Hamas and other Palestinian groups that use suicide-bombing tactics, the brigades' ideology is reportedly based on Palestinian nationalism rather than Muslim fundamentalism.

The group's name refers to the al Aqsa Mosque, which is located at the top of the Jerusalem holy site known as the Noble Sanctuary by Muslims and as the Temple Mount by Jews. Muslims revere the site as the place where the Prophet Muhammad ascended to heaven, and Jews revere it as the site of the Second Temple, which was destroyed by the Romans in 70 CE. The al Aqsa Martyrs Brigades were formed in the West Bank refugee camp of Balata, near Nablus, shortly after the Israeli prime minister Ariel Sharon and a large police contingent visited the compound where the mosque is located in September 2000. Seven young Palestinians who are said to have grown up together in the Fatah youth movement developed the group.

The brigades have been affiliated with the Palestinian Fatah Party, a connection that appears to have been at its closest while Fatah was under the leadership of Yasir Arafat. The extent of Arafat's involvement with the group has been highly contested, however. He publicly condemned the group's suicide bombings, but press reports have quoted brigade leaders who claimed that Arafat gives their orders.

al Aqsa began with drive-by shootings and suicide bombings, and then started targeting Israeli roadblocks and settlers in the West Bank. At first, the group did not carry out attacks outside of the West Bank. In August 2001, al Aqsa's leader and cofounder, Yasser Badawi, was killed by a car bomb. After his death, the brigades began attacking civilians inside Israel. The attacks escalated, and on January 17, 2002, an al Aqsa member killed 6 people at a bat mitzvah in Hadera, Israel. On March 21, 2002, a suicide bomber killed 3 people and injured more than 20 in West Jerusalem. al Aqsa claimed responsibility for that attack. After the West Jerusalem bombing, the U.S. State Department added al Aqsa to its list of foreign terrorist organizations.

On March 30, 2002, Ayat Akhras, a Palestinian teenager and member of al Aqsa, blew herself up in a suburban Jerusalem supermarket, killing herself and two Israelis. Another 22 people were wounded. The group called the Associated Press to claim responsibility. In a prerecorded video broadcast on Arab television, Akhras, who was 18 at the time of her suicide, said she was sacrificing herself for the al Aqsa Mosque. She is believed to be just the third female Palestinian suicide bomber.

Following Arafat's death in 2004, al Aqsa's relationship with Fatah appears to have loosened, although the group is still considered to be aligned with that political party. In 2005, Fatah announced that the brigades would be dissolved and incorporated into Fatah's security forces. The group remained active, however, threatening to kill senior members of Hamas after the group won elections in 2006 and took over the Gaza Strip.

In 2007, Israel offered amnesty to al Aqsa militants in an effort to strengthen Fatah and undermine Hamas. Under the offer, al Aqsa militants would give up their arms and be incorporated into Fatah's security services. While this has led to a lessening of violence, al Aqsa continues to claim responsibility for a large number of shootings and suicide bombings, sometimes carried out in cooperation with other radical groups, such as Palestinian Islamic Jihad. al Aqsa appears to be a highly decentralized organization, and various al

Aqsa factions seem to act independently of—and to some degree, at cross-purposes with—each other.

Erica Pearson

See also Arafat, Yasir; Fatah; Hamas; Palestine Liberation Organization

Further Readings

BBC. "Profile: al Aqsa Martyrs' Brigade." BBC News, March 5, 2002. http://news.bbc.co.uk/hi/english/world/middle_east/newsid_1760000/1760492.stm.

Davis, Joyce M. *Martyrs: Innocence, Vengeance, and Despair in the Middle East.* New York: Palgrave, 2003.

Gaza, Hala Jaber. "Inside the World of the Palestinian Suicide Bomber." *Sunday Times* (London), March 24, 2002.

Juergensmeyer, Mark. *Terror in the Mind of God: The Global Rise of Religious Violence.* Berkeley: University of California Press, 2000.

McAllester, Matthew. "A Potent, Deadly Militia." *Newsday* (New York), March 10, 2002.

Murphy, Dan. "Israeli Amnesty Offer Divides Militants." *Christian Science Monitor,* July 23, 2007.

Richardson, Louise. *What Terrorists Want: Understanding the Enemy, Containing the Threat.* New York: Random House: 2006.

Sageman, Marc. *Leaderless Jihad: Terror Networks in the Twenty-First Century.* Philadelphia: University of Pennsylvania, 2008.

Stern, Jessica. *Terror in the Name of God: Why Religious Militants Kill.* New York: HarperCollins, 2003.

Williams, Daniel. "A Magnet for Palestinian 'Martyrs': al Aqsa Brigades Lead New Wave of Attacks on Israeli Civilians." *The Washington Post,* March 7, 2002.

AL ASIFA

The Palestinian leader Yasir Arafat gave the name al Asifa, or "the Storm," to the military wing of his al Fatah movement at its founding in 1957. In the early days of Fatah, Arafat signed communiqués and leaflets calling for "armed revolution" with the name al Asifa.

Calling for an armed struggle for Palestine carried out by Palestinians themselves, Fatah launched its first raid into Israel in 1965, claiming responsibility under the name al Asifa. As Fatah emerged further from the underground and gained leadership of the Palestine Liberation Organization, the group gradually stopped making distinctions between Fatah and al Asifa. Some Arafat biographers have claimed that al Asifa was merely the cover name that Fatah used to launch its first operations, and that at its beginning al Fatah had no separate military wing.

al Asifa made international headlines when Sabri al Banna (also known as Abu Nidal) split from Arafat and the al Fatah movement in the early 1970s. Banna condemned Fatah's work for political settlement between Israel and the Palestinians, and is said to have been expelled from the organization for plotting to assassinate Arafat. In what many saw as a move to prove himself to be the legitimate representative of the true Fatah ideology, Banna gave institutions in his organization names identical to those in al Fatah, including calling his military operations wing "al Asifa," and his operatives often claimed responsibility for violent acts under that name.

Erica Pearson

See also Abu Nidal Organization; Banna, Sabri al; Fatah

Further Readings

Aburish, Said K. *Arafat: From Defender to Dictator.* New York: Bloomsbury, 1998.

Burleigh, Michael. *Blood and Rage.* New York and London: HarperPerennial, 2008.

Martin, Gus. *Essentials of Terrorism: Concepts and Controversies.* 2nd ed. Thousand Oaks, CA: Sage, 2011.

Rubin, Barry, and Judith Colp Rubin. *Yasir Arafat: A Political Biography.* New York: Oxford University Press, 2003.

Wallach, Janet, and John Wallach. *Arafat: In the Eyes of the Beholder.* Rev. ed. Secaucus, NJ: Carol Publishing Group, 1997.

Williams, Christian. "Abu Nidal Targets Backers of Mideast Compromise." *The Washington Post,* February 5, 1984.

AL JIHAD

The Egyptian Islamic extremist group al Jihad (aka Egyptian Islamic Jihad; Egyptian al Jihad; Islamic Jihad; Jihad Group; New Jihad) is said to maintain close ties with Osama bin Laden's al Qaeda network. Although exact numbers are unknown, the organization is believed to have several hundred committed members. Active since the 1970s, the militant organization's goal is to overthrow the secular Egyptian government and replace it with an Islamic state. al Jihad developed into a powerful force in the 1980s, specializing in armed attacks against high-level members of the Egyptian government. Unlike the Egyptian extremist group Gama'a al Islamiyya, however, al Jihad has never targeted foreign tourists in Egypt.

In November 1981, group members assassinated Egyptian President Anwar Sadat. During a military parade, they disguised themselves as soldiers, surrounded Sadat, and they shot and killed him in front of Egyptian television cameras. al Jihad also claimed responsibility for the foiled assassination attempts on Interior Minister Hassan al Alfi in August 1993 and Prime Minister Atef Sedky in November 1993. As a consequence of these attacks, Egyptian security forces began to crack down on fundamentalists. Despite international protests, officials held suspects without trial and used torture during interrogation. In response, many al Jihad members fled the country.

According to the U.S. State Department, al Jihad has not carried out an attack inside Egypt since 1993, preferring to work outside that country. In 1995, al Jihad bombed the Egyptian embassy in Islamabad, Pakistan, killing 17 people. Three years later, the group planned an attack against the U.S. embassy in Albania, but the effort was foiled.

During the 1990s, al Jihad divided into two factions: the first, and perhaps less notorious, faction led by Abbud al Zumar, an original Jihad leader currently imprisoned in Egypt; the second faction led by the Egyptian physician Ayman al Zawahiri, who was a close advisor to bin Laden. One of al Jihad's founding members, Zawahiri met bin Laden during the Afghan guerrilla war against the Soviet Union. He is said to have influenced al Qaeda's growing anti-Americanism, and he is suspected of having been instrumental in planning the attacks on the World Trade Center and the Pentagon in 2001.

al Jihad and al Qaeda announced a merger in 1998, saying that they had formed the World Islamic Front for Jihad against Jews and Crusaders.

After Zawahiri merged his faction of al Jihad with al Qaeda, many of his members became known as bin Laden's foot soldiers. Egyptian authorities have accused al Jihad members of providing tactical support to al Qaeda, including forging documents and transferring money. al Jihad operatives have been arrested worldwide, and in 1999, Egyptian courts conducted a large-scale trial of 107 terror suspects, largely al Jihad members.

In mid-2007, as part of its "de-radicalization" program, Egypt released more than 130 jailed members of al Jihad in exchange for their renouncing violence. The year also saw a series of publications by Sayyid Imam al Sharif, better known by the nom de guerre Dr. Fadl, who led al Jihad along with Zawahiri in the 1980s and 1990s. Sharif was arrested in Yemen in 2001 and extradited to Egypt three years later. In his 2007 publications, he denounced terrorist violence as un-Islamic, sparking a lengthy rebuttal from Zawahiri. Sharif's refutation of violence is seen as especially important because his earlier writings provided doctrinal justification for terrorism and were frequently cited by al Qaeda.

Erica Pearson

See also al Qaeda; bin Laden, Osama; Zawahiri, Ayman al

Further Readings

Bergen, Peter. *Holy War, Inc.: Inside the Secret World of Osama bin Laden.* New York: Free Press, 2001.

Knickmeyer, Ellen. "Egyptian Extremist Rewriting Rationale for Armed Struggle: Jailhouse Dissent Seen as Challenge to al Qaeda." *The Washington Post,* July 15, 2007.

"A Nation Challenged: The Hunted; The 22 Most Wanted Suspects, in a Five-Act Drama of Global Terror." *The New York Times,* October 14, 2001.

Sachs, Susan. "An Investigation in Egypt Illustrates al Qaeda's Web." *The New York Times,* November 21, 2001.

U.S. District Court, Southern District of New York. *United States v. Osama bin Laden et al.* Indictment S(10) 98 Cr. 1023 (LBS).

U.S. State Department. "Terrorist Groups." *2008 Country Reports on Terrorism.* http://www.state.gov/s/ct/rls/crt/2008/122449.htm.

Wright, Lawrence. "The Rebellion Within." *The New Yorker,* June 2, 2008.

AL MUHAJIROUN

The extremist Muslim group al Muhajiroun was founded in Jeddah, Saudi Arabia, in 1983 by the radical cleric Sheikh Omar Bakri Muhammad. The group moved to London three years later, when Muhammad was expelled from Saudi Arabia. The small group was largely dismissed by mainstream Muslim religious leaders as a band of "propaganda-seeking extremists," and it was initially written off by British commentators as a bothersome joke, but revelations that several suicide bombers were at one point members of the organization would ultimately result in the British government barring Muhammad from the country.

Muhammad, a Syrian, was known in British tabloid headlines as the "Tottenham Ayatollah." He urged his followers to fight to reestablish "true" Islam, often using harsh anti-Semitic language to call for the wiping out of other religions. Although his application for British citizenship was rejected several times before 2005, he was granted "exceptional leave to remain" because the Syrian government rescinded his passport and was not likely to issue him another one.

al Muhajiroun came under increased scrutiny by Scotland Yard following the September 11, 2001, attacks on the World Trade Center and the Pentagon. Nonetheless, the possibility that the group might be dangerous was largely dismissed. The chairman of the Muslim Parliament of Great Britain called the group "nutters" in London's *Independent* newspaper, advising that a crackdown on the group's activities would exaggerate its importance.

During the U.S.-led air raids on Afghanistan in retaliation for the 9/11 attacks, al Muhajiroun leaders gave public lectures telling young British Muslims that their duty was to travel to Afghanistan and fight on the side of Osama bin Laden and the Taliban. Members of the group later boasted that as many as 600 British Muslims had gone to Afghanistan to fight. They were unable to substantiate these claims, however.

When Britain joined the military strikes against Afghanistan in October 2001, an al Muhajiroun spokesperson in Pakistan told the London-based Arabic newspaper *Asharq al Awsat* that Prime Minister Tony Blair was a "legitimate target" for assassination. Under intense press scrutiny, Muhammad told British journalists that his group engaged in "political and intellectual attacks, not violent ones." He also condemned the attacks on the World Trade Center and the Pentagon. He said, however, that the attacks were not the work of bin Laden and al Qaeda, but were instead carried out by a covert group of "Anglo-Saxon Americans" who wanted to provoke war between the West and Islam.

In November 2001, al Muhajiroun provoked further outcry in Britain by claiming that at least three British Muslims fighting with the Taliban and al Qaeda in Afghanistan had died during the bombing. However, the group was again unable to provide solid facts to back up its claim. Family members of one of the men named by al Muhajiroun said that he was in Afghanistan as an aid worker. A year after the 9/11 attacks, al Muhajiroun hosted a celebratory anniversary event, in which Muhammed praised the al Qaeda operatives responsible as the "magnificent 19."

al Muhajiroun's connection with terrorism began to seem more real in 2003, when two British Muslims conducted a suicide bombing operation in Tel Aviv, Israel, that killed three people. One of the men was an active member of al Muhajiroun. In 2004, British police arrested five men on charges of plotting to bomb targets in London; some of the bombers were members of al Muhajiroun. Later that year, Muhammed announced that he was disbanding the organization so that Muslims would be unified in their struggle against the United States.

On July 7, 2005, four suicide bombers set off explosions in London that killed 52 people and injured hundreds more; the ringleader had formerly been a member of al Muhajiroun. The bombing was followed by a botched bomb attack later that month, and some of the would-be bombers were also former members of al Muhajiroun. Particularly disturbing to many Britons was the fact that several of the bombers were second- or third-generation immigrants who appeared at first glance to be well integrated into British society.

The British government announced that it would ban the organization, and Muhammed left the country in August, traveling to Lebanon. The British government barred him from returning, and in 2006, under a new law that forbade glorifying terrorism, it banned two groups that were believed to be offshoots of al Muhajiroun. In 2009 a former spokesman for Muhammed announced that, because al Muhajiroun had never officially been banned, he would re-form it, resulting in calls in the British press for the group to be banned.

Erica Pearson

See also bin Laden, Osama; London Underground Bombings; Taliban

Further Readings

Carrell, Severin and Jakob Menge. "Attack on Afghanistan: Home-grown Extremists; We Help Britons Join Taliban, Say Militants." *Independent on Sunday* (London), November 4, 2001, p. 5.

Cowell, Alan. "At a Mosque in London, bin Laden Is Hailed as a Hero." *The New York Times*, September 13, 2002, p. A12.

Craig, Olga, and Adam Lusher. "The Making of a Terrorist." *The Sunday Telegraph*, May 6, 2007, p. 16.

Dodd, Vikram. "Attack on Afghanistan: Volunteers: Muslim Leaders Attack Extremists' Claims: Doubts Cast on Story of Britons Killed Fighting for Taliban." *The Guardian* (London), October 31, 2001, p. 5.

Doward, Jamie, and Andrew Wander. "Terror Links: The Network." *The Observer*, May 6, 2007, p. 26.

Lyall, Sarah. "What Drove Two Britons to Bomb a Club in Tel Aviv?" *The New York Times*, May 12, 2003, p. A3.

McGrory, Daniel, and Dominic Kennedy. "Radical Sheikh Revels in Notoriety." *The Times* (London), October 10, 2001.

Raynor, Gordon. "How the Preachers of Hate Turned Suburban Boys into Zealots Bent on Mass Murder." *Daily Mail*, May 1, 2007, p. 6.

AL QAEDA

al Qaeda (Arabic for "the base," aka Islamic Army for the Liberation of the Holy Places; Islamic Salvation Foundation; Osama bin Laden Network; World Islamic Front for Jihad against Jews and Crusaders) is a loosely knit terrorist network that facilitates the activities of like-minded militant Islamic groups in some 55 countries around the globe. al Qaeda is now known to have been behind both attacks on the World Trade Center (1993 and 2001) and the 1998 bombings of two U.S. embassies, among many other incidents.

Organizationally, al Qaeda is governed by a small core of leaders the *majlis al shura,* or consultative council, which makes the final decisions on major policy decisions, including the approval of terrorist operations and the issuing of Islamic decrees, or fatwas. al Qaeda also has a military committee, a business committee, a media committee, and a religious committee. Most al Qaeda operatives never have contact with the top leadership and are dispatched for duty at the last moment, without prior knowledge of the organization's plans. For this reason, intelligence analysts have experienced great difficulty breaking into the network.

The network was established in 1989 by the Saudi militant Osama bin Laden and the Palestinian Muslim Brotherhood figure Abdullah Azzam. al Qaeda was based in Afghanistan from 1989 to 1991, in Sudan from 1991 to 1996, and again in Afghanistan from 1996 to 2001. The group was forced into exile after the United States launched Operation Enduring Freedom into Afghanistan on October 7, 2002.

al Qaeda seeks to overthrow the current world order and replace it with a fundamentalist Islamic order, characterized by a unified Muslim world under the leadership of a Muslim caliph. Accordingly, it has set several goals. First, it seeks to topple what it considers to be the morally bankrupt and heretical regimes of the Middle East. al Qaeda chastises these regimes for not properly implementing Islamic law, or Shariah. The organization's top target is Saudi Arabia, the home of Islam's two holiest sites. bin Laden has lambasted the Saudi regime for allowing U.S. soldiers to be stationed on its soil. Second, al Qaeda sees the United States as the foremost enemy of Islam because of what it perceives to be an oppressive foreign policy. As the world's lone superpower, the United States also represents the largest impediment to an Islamic order. al Qaeda, therefore, seeks to destroy it. Finally, al Qaeda calls for the destruction of the Jewish state of Israel, and replacing it with a Muslim state of Palestine. al Qaeda, however, has never directly attacked a Jewish or Israeli target.

The Beginnings of al Qaeda

The history of al Qaeda is inextricably tied to the life and ideology of bin Laden, the son of a Saudi multimillionaire, whose inheritance was once estimated at $270 million to $300 million. bin Laden left his life of luxury in Saudi Arabia to become a guerrilla fighter in 1979, after the Soviet Union invaded Afghanistan. He contributed millions of dollars to the mujahideen, helping build roads, bunkers, and other vital infrastructure. In tandem with Azzam, bin Laden founded *Maktab al Khidamat* (the Services Office), which recruited thousands of mujahideen from around the globe, financed their travel to Afghanistan, and trained them in guerrilla tactics and terrorist operations.

By one estimate, between 175,000 and 250,000 mujahideen fought yearly in Afghanistan, and only a small percentage of them were native Afghans. Almost half of the fighters hailed from Saudi Arabia, about 3,000 were Algerian, approximately 2,000 were Egyptian, and thousands of others arrived from Sudan, Yemen, and neighboring Pakistan. These fighters would become the core of al Qaeda's fighters.

With the help of American CIA funding and training, the mujahideen defeated the Soviets, who withdrew from Afghanistan on February 15, 1989. The fighting did not end for bin Laden, however. In 1989 he formed al Qaeda to continue the jihad. Through a network of the thousands of jihad fighters that had trained in his Services Office, bin Laden sent militant Muslims home to create terror cells and wage guerrilla warfare to topple what he perceived to be heretical regimes. Other mujahideen were sent to join the jihad struggles in Somalia, the Balkans, and Chechnya.

It has been reported that the first terrorist attack carried out by al Qaeda was the bombing of two hotels in Aden, Yemen, in December 1992. The attack injured several tourists but was likely intended for U.S. troops that were on their way to carry out the humanitarian mission Operation Restore Hope in Somalia. At the time, however, according to various reports, Western intelligence did not link the attack in Yemen to bin Laden's newly formed network.

al Qaeda was also associated with the 1993 attack on the World Trade Center, where 6 people were killed and 1,000 were injured. The attacks were linked to a cell of the Egyptian group Gama'a al Islamiyya, which operated under the aegis of al Qaeda. It was later learned that the convicted bombmaker, Ramzi Yousef, had lived in one of bin Laden's "guest houses" in Peshawar, Pakistan, both before and after the attack.

al Qaeda was next linked to the attacks on American servicemen in Mogadishu, Somalia, in 1993. In this attack, al Qaeda–trained guerrillas thwarted a U.S. attempt to capture a radical Muslim warlord. The guerrillas shot down two American Black Hawk helicopters and forced a third to make a crash-landing. In the end, 18 American soldiers were killed, and 78 were injured. In 1994, additional al Qaeda plots were thwarted, including plans to assassinate the pope and to blow up 11 passenger jets in the air.

All the while, from 1989 through 1991, bin Laden lived again in Saudi Arabia, where he launched a campaign against the House of Saud. He believed that the regime did not rule Saudi Arabia in a way that was consistent with the "proper" interpretation of Islam. After the 1991 Gulf War, he vociferously opposed the presence of America troops on Saudi soil. His speeches were recorded and distributed by the thousands throughout Saudi Arabia. Because of his activism, he was put under surveillance by the Saudi intelligence.

Under pressure from the angered Saudi regime, bin Laden left the country. He, his family, and an estimated 300 to 480 dedicated al Qaeda cadres left for Sudan, a country that had come under the control of Omar al Bashir of the Muslim Brotherhood in 1989. In coordination with Sudan's leading radical ideologue and leader of the National Islamic Front (NIF), Hassan al Turabi, bin Laden established new roots for al Qaeda in Khartoum and its environs. Sudan provided asylum for al Qaeda, land for new training camps, and hundreds of passports so that members could travel under different identities. In return, bin Laden helped finance infrastructure for Sudan's Islamic fundamentalist regime. It is also believed that, through the government of Sudan, al Qaeda established ties with the Government of Iran and the terrorist organization Hezbollah at this time. al Qaeda was growing.

In April 1994, bin Laden's dissatisfaction with the Saudi regime culminated in the creation of the Advice and Reform Committee, which was set up in London to produce literature criticizing the

Saudi regime. While in Sudan, al Qaeda is believed to have participated in two attacks on U.S. military personnel in Saudi Arabia. The first took place in Riyadh on November 1995. Five Americans and two Indians were killed when a large truck bomb exploded just outside of an American-run Saudi National Guard training center. The second was an attack on the Khobar Towers, a U.S. military barracks in Dhahran, in June 1996. Nineteen Americans were killed and 500 were injured when a large truck bomb was detonated just outside the barracks.

al Qaeda was definitively linked to two other attacks in 1995—an assassination attempt on Egyptian president Hosni Mubarak in Addis Ababa, Ethiopia, in June 1995, and a car bombing at Egypt's embassy in Pakistan that killed 15 Pakistanis and Egyptians and injured 80 others.

Jihad Against America

After the attacks against Americans in Saudi Arabia, America levied sanctions against Sudan for harboring bin Laden and al Qaeda. Under intense U.S. pressure, Sudan ousted bin Laden in May 1996. bin Laden and his entourage left for Afghanistan, where a brutal regime of radical Muslims called the Taliban had recently conquered more than half of Afghanistan in a civil war between rival factions.

Soon after his arrival in Afghanistan, bin Laden issued a declaration of war against the United States. On August 23, 1996, he declared a "Jihad on the Americans Occupying the Country of the Two Sacred Places." Two years later, in February 1998, bin Laden also announced the creation of an umbrella organization he called the "Islamic World Front for the Struggle against the Jews and the Crusaders." bin Laden stated, in the form of a fatwa, that Muslims should kill Americans, including civilians, wherever they were to be found.

On May 28, 1998, bin Laden announced the formation of yet another umbrella group: the World Islamic Front for Jihad against Jews and Crusaders. The creation of this front organization finally provided analysts with an idea of the depth and breadth of the al Qaeda network. The front included the Egyptian Islamic Jihad (al Jihad), the Egyptian Armed Group, the Pakistan Scholars Society, the Partisans Movement in Kashmir, the Jihad Movement in Bangladesh, and the Afghan military wing of the Advice and Reform Committee. In his announcement, bin Laden declared war on America and Israel, stating that the United States was vulnerable, that it could be defeated in war, and that civilians were now fair targets in al Qaeda's jihad.

On August 7, 1998, al Qaeda orchestrated the near-simultaneous bombing of the American embassies in Nairobi, Kenya, and Dar es Salaam, Tanzania. The attacks killed 224 people and wounded thousands of others. The embassy in Kenya was attacked, bin Laden noted, because "it was considered to be the biggest intelligence gathering center in the Middle East." The date of the bombings was significant in that it was seven years, to the day, since U.S. troops were dispatched to Saudi Arabia in Operation Desert Shield.

On the heels of these attacks came the biggest breakthrough for U.S. intelligence. It came on August 15, 1998, with the arrest of Mohammed Saddiq Odeh at the Karachi International Airport in Pakistan. Under intense interrogation, Odeh, an al Qaeda operative, divulged detailed information about al Qaeda's international network, his specific activities in the African embassy bombings, and bin Laden's role in the network. Odeh's testimony provided U.S. intelligence with enough information to better monitor al Qaeda.

Having now linked al Qaeda to the two embassy bombings, America opted to retaliate. On August 20, 1998, the United States launched a barrage of cruise missiles at al Qaeda in Afghanistan and Sudan. The targets in Afghanistan included six training camps, while the Sudanese target was a pharmaceutical factory that American intelligence believed was producing the chemical agent, EMPTA (O-ethyl methylphosphonothioic acid), a key ingredient in VX nerve gas. The U.S. missiles killed at least six al Qaeda members in the attacks on Afghanistan.

On September 28, 1998, the Egyptian national Ali Mohamed was arrested in the United States upon suspicions that he was part of al Qaeda. Mohamed had risen to the position of instructor at a sensitive military training site at Fort Bragg, North Carolina. During his time there, he gleaned a great deal of intelligence about the American armed forces, and his story served as an example of how al Qaeda "sleepers," or dormant operatives, could be successful. Despite the fact that he had fought in Afghanistan, and that he regularly returned to the Middle East for al Qaeda activities, Mohamed had managed to infiltrate the higher echelons of the U.S. Army.

Investigating al Qaeda

In June 1999, the FBI added bin Laden to its Most Wanted Terrorists list. In July, President Bill Clinton imposed sanctions on Afghanistan's Taliban regime for harboring bin Laden. Later that year, two members of an al Qaeda commando team were arrested in Turkey after crossing the border from Iran. One suspect admitted his links to bin Laden and warned of an al Qaeda plot to attack a conference on European cooperation and security.

In December 1999, the U.S. government obtained a six-volume terror manual from the Hashemite Kingdom of Jordan. The volume belonged to a group of men arrested in Jordan and was said to be a training manual for al Qaeda operatives. They were apparently consulting it in making plans to participate in an al Qaeda terrorist plot during the forthcoming Millennium festivities. Indeed, a ring of al Qaeda operatives would eventually be arrested in Jordan, the United States, Canada, England, Spain, Germany, Italy, and Syria in connection with this plot. al Qaeda had become truly global.

It was also in 1999 that the Saudi regime uncovered an operation that was funneling approximately $50 million to al Qaeda, given in the form of *zakat*, or alms. Sources also report that al Qaeda received monies funneled from the United Arab Emirates. By early 2000, U.S. officials had revealed that they possessed documents outlining the operational structure of al Qaeda, including weapons purchases, fund-raising, and the falsification of documents. Indeed, U.S. intelligence finally appeared to be gaining ground on al Qaeda. On June 30, 2000, eight alleged al Qaeda members were convicted in a Lebanese military court, with charges ranging from conspiracy to commit terrorism to forgery. In the fall of that year, Jordan convicted several suspects for their role in the Millennium plot. In December, the United States indicted five individuals for their connection to the East African embassy bombings.

Still, al Qaeda attacks continued. In 2000, the Abu Sayyaf Group, an al Qaeda affiliate in the Philippines, kidnapped 58 people from a school, demanding the release of Ramzi Yousef, the al Qaeda operative behind the 1993 World Trade Center bombing. Yousef is currently serving a sentence of life plus 240 years in a U.S. prison. The Abu Sayyaf Group has made tens of millions of dollars in kidnapping operations since its inception in 1991.

On October 12, 2000, an American naval warship, the USS *Cole* was attacked by suicide bombers while the vessel was refueling in the Yemeni port of Aden. Seventeen American sailors were killed and 39 were injured in an attack that caused an estimated quarter-billion dollars in damage. While no group has claimed responsibility for the attack, it is suspected that al Qaeda was behind it. American investigators, including the FBI, are investigating the attack.

al Qaeda carried out its most heinous and successful operation on American soil on September 11, 2001. On that day, a crew of 19 hijackers, with the support of an untold number of "sleepers" in America, hijacked four aircraft. Two of the aircraft were flown into the World Trade Center towers in New York City, bringing them both to the ground. A third airplane was flown into the Pentagon, just outside of Washington, D.C. And a fourth plane, also headed for metropolitan Washington, D.C., was overtaken by passengers and crashed in Western Pennsylvania. In the end, approximately 3,000 Americans were killed, marking the highest number of casualties recorded in America on any one day.

On October 7, 2001, America launched Operation Enduring Freedom as part of its new "war on terror." Within two months, the American military dismantled the totalitarian Taliban regime in Afghanistan. al Qaeda operatives and Taliban fighters alike fled during the fighting, and are thought to have reconstituted elsewhere. Even without a base, however, the organization continues to use modern technology as a means to maintain its far-reaching international network for militant Muslims.

Accordingly, there are hundreds, or perhaps thousands, of al Qaeda members associated with these groups throughout the Muslim world, North America, South America, Europe, and Asia. Indeed, attempts to attack U.S. embassies in France, Italy, Bosnia, Yemen, and Singapore, even after the attacks of September 2001, are evidence of the network's continued global reach. More daunting, however, is the popularity of bin Laden in the Muslim world. He is seen as a modern day Salah al Din (Saladin), promising to liberate the Muslim world from foreign invaders.

Videos of bin Laden released after the attacks of September 11, 2001, threatened continued violence against American targets. Such attacks are credible. Armed with deep pockets, modern technology, and an unwavering hatred of the West, al Qaeda has continued to share resources and reconstitute for the next wave of attacks.

After September 11

In the post–9/11 period, al Qaeda has expanded, both in terms of the number of its small-scale operations and in its influence to areas beyond Afghanistan. After the United States' invasion of Iraq in 2003, several affiliates of al Qaeda emerged, such as al Qaeda in Iraq, a branch of the main organization. Among the notable newer groups was al Qaeda in the Islamic Maghreb (AQIM). Previously known as the Salafist Group for Preaching and Combat, AQIM is an Algerian-based terrorist organization, founded with the original goal of overthrowing the Algerian government and establishing a new state under Islam. They publicly announced their name change and alliance with al Qaeda in 2007. AQIM has taken responsibility for several terrorist acts since then, including the kidnapping of seven foreign nationals, the killing of several hostages, and a series of bombings and attacks in Algeria.

Harakat al Shabab al Mujahideen, more commonly known as al Shabab, began as an insurgent group in the war in Somalia, and it has been responsible for acts such as a suicide bomb attack in a hotel that killed more than 30 people. It confirmed its alignment with al Qaeda in early 2010, releasing a statement asserting that "the jihad of Horn of Africa must be combined with the international jihad led by the al Qaeda network."

al Qaeda in Yemen was formed after 23 suspected members escaped from a Yemeni prison in 2006. They subsequently established the branch,

which then became al Qaeda in the Arabian Peninsula (AQAP), encompassing both Yemen and Saudi Arabia. The group, like its parent organization, opposes the rule of the House of Saud.

With these various offshoots in different counties, al Qaeda's center of operations has shifted from Afghanistan to places such as Pakistan, eastern Africa, and the Arabian Peninsula. With the U.S. invasion of Afghanistan after the 9/11 attacks, al Qaeda sought to move its home base elsewhere, finding the Federally Administered Tribal Area (FATA) of Pakistan—which shares an extensive border with Afghanistan—to be a suitable location. The influence and extent of al Qaeda became apparent in several other terrorist attacks around the world that were perpetrated on behalf of the organization. After several trains in Madrid were bombed in March 2004, recordings of Koranic verses and video messages were found at the site. In addition, two of the bombers in the July 2007 London Underground attacks left behind a videotape that featured an al Qaeda leader, as if to imply the group's involvement. Responsibility for a failed attempt by the Nigerian Umar Farouk Abdulmutallab to bomb an American airline on Christmas Day 2009 was also claimed by al Qaeda.

The al Qaeda ideology, which embraces martyrdom in the name of jihad, has spread globally, influencing other terrorist attacks. al Qaeda even launched its own online magazine in 2010, using the Internet to attract more Westerners. The magazine included articles such as "Make a Bomb in the Kitchen of Your Mom," as well as columns from al Qaeda leaders bin Laden and Ayman al Zawahiri. One particular figure who has utilized media—in particular the web—to spread al Qaeda beliefs is the U.S.–Yemeni dual citizen Anwar al Awlaki. While Awlaki is not suspected of having tactical involvement, he is purported to be a source of far-reaching influence. Faisal Shahzad, the suspect believed to have attempted to detonate a car bomb in Times Square, New York City, on May 1, 2010, is quoted as saying he drew inspiration from the teaching of Awlaki.

Countering al Qaeda

One victory against the ascendancy of al Qaeda was the capture of Khalid Shaikh Mohammed, believed to be the group's chief of operations on March 1, 2003, in Rawalpindi, Pakistan. At the time of his capture, Mohammed was widely thought to be responsible for planning the September 11 attacks, as well as for several other terrorist undertakings, including a foiled plain to blow up 21 U.S. aircraft mid-flight in 1996, the 1998 bombings of the Kenyan and Tanzanian U.S. embassies, the USS *Cole* attack in 2000, and the January 2002 murder of *Wall Street Journal* reporter Daniel Pearl after his kidnapping. And indeed, while detained in Guantánamo Bay, Mohammed confessed he was responsible for the 9/11 attacks "from A to Z," and also for the bombings in a nightclub in Bali, the direct murder of Pearl, planned attacks on Heathrow Airport and Big Ben, and up to 31 other attacks. However, Mohammed's confession generated intense controversy in the world media and protests from human rights' groups when it was revealed that he and his fellow detainees were interrogated using a widely condemned method known as "waterboarding" for a period of as long as six months.

Zawahiri, the head of the Egyptian Islamic Jihad (al Jihad) and a high-ranking al Qaeda official, has helped steer the post-Afghanistan al Qaeda. Other prominent leaders have included Mustafa Abu al Yazid and Abu Musab al Zarqawi, who was deemed "the prince of al Qaeda in Iraq" by bin Laden himself. Zarqawi, however, was killed in June 2007 by a U.S. bomb strike, while Yazid was killed by a drone attack on May 21, 2010. Aside from the group's U.S. targets, these leaders ushered a new era under the seeming minimal presence of bin Laden. They have planned attacks on not only America, but Europe as well, including alleged plans in 2009 to attack Charles de Gaulle Airport in Paris and Heathrow Airport in London. al Qaeda has also continued its campaign of destruction in the Middle East and attempted to destabilize the already-shaky relations between India and Pakistan over the disputed territory of Kashmir, in tandem with the Lashkar-e-Taiba, a Pakistani terrorist organization suspected of being funded by al Qaeda.

While the deaths of its high-ranking leaders—most notably, the killing of bin Laden himself by U.S. Navy SEALs in May 2011—have unquestionably damaged the organization, the speedy growth of al Qaeda and its global influence has ensured that the security, defense, and anti-terrorist measures being developed and implemented will color the state of world affairs well into the twenty-first century.

Jonathan Schanzer

See also Abu Sayyaaf Group; al Qaeda in Iraq; al Qaeda in the Islamic Maghreb; Bali Nightclub Bombing; bin Laden, Osama; East Africa Embassy Bombings; Fatwa; Guantánamo Bay; London Underground Bombings; Madrid Bombings; September 11 Attacks; Taliban; USS *Cole* Bombing; Yousef, Ramzi Ahmed; Zarqawi, Abu Musab al; Zawahiri, Ayman al

Further Readings

Alexander, Yonah, and Michael Swetman. *Usama bin Laden's al Qaeda: Profile of a Terrorist Network.* Ardsley, NY: Transnational Publishers, 2001.

Atwan, Abdel Bari. *The Secret History of al Qaeda.* Berkeley: University of California Press, 2008.

Bergen, Peter. *Holy War, Inc.: Inside the Secret World of Osama bin Laden.* New York: Free Press, 2001.

Bergen, Peter. *The Longest War: Inside the Enduring Conflict between America and al-Qaeda.* New York: Free Press, 2011. Bergen, Peter. *The Osama bin Laden I Know: An Oral History of al Qaeda's Leader.* New York: Free Press, 2006.

Chaliand, Gérard, Arnaud Blin, Edward D. Schneider, Kathryn Pulver, and Jesse Browner. *The History of Terrorism: from Antiquity to al Qaeda.* Berkeley: University of California, 2007.

Ibrahim, Raymond, Ayman Zawahiri, and Osama bin Laden. *The al Qaeda Reader.* New York: Doubleday, 2007.

MacFarquhar, Neil. "Word for Word/Jihad Lit; Beware of Hidden Enemies and Their Wolves and Foxes." *The New York Times,* December 9, 2001.

Rabasa, Angel, et al. *Beyond al Qaeda.* Part 1, *The Global Jihadist Movement.* Santa Monica, CA: RAND Corporation, 2006.

Riedel, Bruce O. *The Search for al Qaeda: Its Leadership, Ideology, and Future.* Washington, DC: Brookings Institution Press, 2008.

Smith, Martin, and Lowell Bergman. "Hunting bin Laden." *Frontline,* PBS, September 13, 2001. http://www.pbs.org/wgbh/pages/frontline/shows/binladen.

Ungoed-Thomas, Jon. "Egypt Used Torture to Crack Network." *Sunday Times* (London), November 25, 2001.

U.S. District Court for the Eastern District of Virginia, Alexandria Division. *United States v. Zacarias Moussaoui.* Indictment, December 11, 2001. http://www.justice.gov/ag/moussaouiindictment.htm.

U.S. District Court for the Southern District of New York. *United States v. Usama bin Laden.* Indictment, November 5, 1998. http://www.fas.org/irp/news/1998/11/98110602_nlt.html.

U.S. District Court for the Southern District of New York. *United States v. Usama bin Laden, et al.* Indictment, April 20, 2001. http://www.uniset.ca/other/cs5/93FSupp2d484.html.

Vidino, Lorenzo. *al Qaeda in Europe: The New Battleground of International Jihad.* Amherst, NY: Prometheus Books, 2006.

Wright, Lawrence. *The Looming Tower: al Qaeda and the Road to 9/11.* New York: Alfred A. Knopf, 2006.

AL QAEDA IN IRAQ

al Qaeda in Iraq (AQI, aka al Qaeda in Mesopotamia; al Qaeda in the Land of the Two Rivers) is an Iraqi Sunni insurgent group led by foreign leaders with anti-Shiite beliefs, extreme tactics, and connections to al Qaeda's transnational terrorist network. It was formed in October 2004 by Abu Musab al Zarqawi, a radical Jordanian Islamist who had operated a guerrilla training camp in Herat, Afghanistan, before the demise of the Taliban regime in 2001. AQI, also referred to as al Qaeda in Mesopotamia and al Qaeda in the Land of the Two Rivers, became notorious for beheadings of hostages and was responsible for the vast majority of mass-casualty suicide bombings in Iraq. It targeted coalition forces, Iraq's government and security services, Shiite militias and civilians, and Sunnis that turned against it.

AQI was created after the United States and its allies invaded Iraq to topple the Baathist regime of Saddam Hussein. Initially, AQI consisted of foreign fighters from neighboring states, but it also attracted volunteers from as far away as North Africa and Europe. Many of these foreign volunteers ended up carrying out suicide attacks on behalf of AQI. By 2006, however, AQI transformed itself into a primarily Iraqi organization with foreign leaders at the helm. It received the political support of al Qaeda's original leaders, Osama bin Laden and Ayman al Zawahiri, but operated independently of their command and control structure.

AQI's immediate objectives are to drive foreign forces out of Iraq, topple the democratic regime in that country, and establish an Islamic state based on Sunni hegemony over the majority Shiite nation. Its ultimate aims are to create a base for radical Sunni jihadists in the Middle East, from which they could topple neighboring secular regimes, and form a pan-Islamic union akin to the caliphates that reigned over the region for many centuries prior to the advent of the modern nation state. AQI uses a variety of tactics to achieve its aims, including beheading its hostages, summarily executing captured Iraqi police and soldiers, detonating improvised explosive devices (IEDs) against coalition forces, and deploying male and female suicide bombers to kill scores of civilians and destroy the institutions of the new Iraqi order.

AQI's extremism stems from its fundamentalist religious ideology and strategic objectives. It harbors an extremist Salafist worldview that depicts Shiites as heretics because of their rejection of Sunni orthodoxy. This ideology has been used to justify mass-casualty bombings against Shiite religious processions, leaders, and shrines. In February 2006, AQI was a major catalyst in a sectarian civil war between Shiites and Sunnis after it destroyed the golden dome of the Askariya Shrine in Samarra, one of Iraq's four major Shiite shrines. The Samarra bombing was not the first catastrophic strike against the symbols of Shiism in Iraq, nor would it be the last. On August 29, 2003, a group known as Tawhid and Jihad (the precursor to AQI) detonated a car bomb outside the Imam Ali Shrine in Najaf, killing the Grand Ayatollah Mohammed Baqir al Hakim, along with several dozen worshippers. Seven months later, on March 2, 2004, insurgents set off several explosions in Baghdad and Karbala during the Shiite Ashura processions, killing 181 people.

In addition to attacks on the symbols of Shiite identity, AQI targets ordinary Shiites in markets and neighborhoods. One of the most devastating attacks was carried out by Raed Mansour al

Banna, a Jordanian suicide bomber deployed by AQI on February 28, 2005, in Hilla, south of Baghdad, killing 125 people. AQI stokes sectarian strife in order to build a base of support among Iraq's Sunni population. It calculates that a sustained campaign of violence against Iraq's Shiite communities will provoke the Shiite-led government and Shiite militias to undertake indiscriminate retaliatory violence against Sunnis. Sectarian polarization hinders Sunni-Shiite reconciliation and enables AQI to position itself as the sole protector of Iraq's Sunnis.

AQI seeks a failed Iraqi state, and it directs its attacks against Iraq's security forces to intimidate and annihilate the security apparatus. To deprive Iraq of stability and reconstruction, AQI uses suicide bombers to attack political, civic, and humanitarian organizations in Iraq, such as United Nations and Red Cross facilities.

In 2010, AQI's leader was an Egyptian by the name of Abu Ayyub al Masri (also known as Abu Hamza al Muhajir), who replaced Zarqawi after he was killed by a U.S. airstrike in June 2006. In October 2006, AQI merged with a coalition of insurgent groups known as the Islamic State of Iraq, allegedly led by an Iraqi named Abu Omar al Baghdadi.

AQI's violence diminished substantially from its peak in 2007 in large part because Iraq's Sunni population, tribes, and insurgents rejected its ideology and tactics. Anti-AQI militias consisting of Sunni tribesmen and former insurgents were deputized by Coalition Forces to drive out AQI from their regions, cities, and neighborhoods. Known as the Awakening Councils or Sons of Iraq, they dealt a serious blow to AQI's organizational capacity, reduced its operational space, and set back its ambition of making Iraq a safe haven for global jihadists.

Mohammed Hafez

See also al Qaeda; Bombings and Bomb Scares; Iraq War; Zarqawi, Abu Musab al

Further Readings

Bergen, Peter I. *The Longest War: Inside the Enduring Conflict between America and al-Qaeda.* New York: Free Press, 2011.
Fishman, Brian. ed. *Bombers, Bank Accounts, and Bleedout: al Qaeda's Road in and out of Iraq.* West Point, NY: Combating Terrorism Center, 2008.
Fishman, Brian. *Dysfunction and Decline: Lessons Learned from Inside al Qa'ida in Iraq.* West Point, NY: Combating Terrorism Center, 2009.
Hafez, Mohammed M. "Martyrdom Mythology in Iraq: How Jihadists Frame Suicide Terrorism in Videos and Biographies." *Terrorism and Political Violence* 19 (2007): 95–115.
Hafez, Mohammed M. *Suicide Bombers in Iraq: The Strategy and Ideology of Martyrdom.* Washington, DC: United States Institute of Peace, 2007.
Hashim, Ahmed S. "Iraq's Chaos: Why the Insurgency Won't Go Away." *Boston Review,* October-November 2004.
Richardson, Louise. *What Terrorists Want: Understanding the Enemy, Containing the Threat.* New York: Random House, 2006.
Sageman, Marc. *Leaderless Jihad: Terror Networks in the Twenty-first Century.* Philadelphia: University of Pennsylvania, 2008.
Shah, Niaz A. *Self-defense in Islamic and International Law.* New York: Palgrave Macmillan, 2008.

AL QAEDA IN THE ISLAMIC MAGHREB

al Qaeda in the Islamic Maghreb (AQIM) was officially created in January 2007, following an announcement made by Ayman al Zawahiri, al Qaeda's second in command. Formerly known as the Salafist Group for Preaching and Combat (GSPC), AQIM aims to establish by violent means a pan-Islamic Shariah state covering the region of the Maghreb (Algeria, Tunisia, Morocco, Western Sahara, Mauritania, and Libya), Niger, and Mali. AQIM has been involved in the kidnapping of foreign citizens and nationals to raise funds for its terrorist operations, as well as attacks on government facilities and banks in the region. It is estimated that AQIM has received a total of $6 million to $10 million in ransoms from kidnapping foreigners and bank robberies.

Many terrorist experts, particularly in Algeria, dispute the transnational regional character of AQIM, arguing that its affiliation with al Qaeda is superficial. To them, AQIM is just GSPC under a different name, and they point out that, since its inception in 1999, GSPC has sought to establish ties with al Qaeda. The French journalist Jason Burke and the Algerian terrorist specialist Anoir Malek have detailed a series of contacts between al Qaeda leader Osama bin Laden and GSPC members. Desperate for financial assistance and weapons, GSPC sought bin Laden's help in exchange for providing al Qaeda with new recruits and training them for terrorist activities in Europe. According to Algerian observers, it took years for al Qaeda to trust GSPC. That trust finally came with Zawahiri's announcement, but the relationship between al Qaeda and AQIM remains weak.

AQIM continues to appear independent from al Qaeda, giving credence to those who believe that GSPC sought the name change to benefit from al Qaeda's notoriety as the leading enemy of the West. It is for this reason that Algerian authorities and media are adamant about not using "AQIM" as an alternate name for "GSPC," and have further claimed that GSPC is but a memory.

This sentiment is true to a degree, for GSPC suffered a serious setback as a result of an aggressive war on terror pursued by the Algerian state. Since the late 1990s, Algerian authorities have engaged in a massive campaign to uproot terrorism, including offering terrorists amnesty under a national reconciliation plan in exchange for giving up violence; launching highly coordinated military operations in areas once deemed impenetrable and under terrorist control; and mobilizing well-known and respected clerics to issue fatwas (edicts) condemning terrorism as un-Islamic. Throughout this anti-terrorism campaign, the state has emphasized testimony by former terrorist leaders—including former GSPC leader Hassan Hattab—condemning terrorism and calling on terrorists to take advantage of the government's national reconciliation policy. As a result, the state has succeeded in bringing normalcy back to the country.

But terrorism is by no means over in the region. AQIM has been active in the kidnapping of Westerners visiting the region, and the group was responsible for killing four French tourists in Mauritania in 2007 and a Briton in Mali in 2009. Several U.S. reports have warned against AQIM's terrorist activities in Algeria. In January 2010, the U.S. State Department identified Algeria as a "country of interest" because of possible support

of terrorists, and the country is on a list of 14 countries whose citizens, and those traveling from or through the 14 countries, are subject to enhanced screening at U.S. airports.

Other indicators show that AQIM has adapted to Algeria's counterterrorism policy in at least two different ways. First, while cornered in Algeria, AQIM has been able to shift its terrorist operations to Mali and Niger, neighboring countries with fewer military capabilities to deter its operations. Similarly, AQIM has infiltrated Western Sahara, benefiting from the contention between the political rivals Algeria and Morocco. This has led European intelligence specialists to warn against a potential takeover of the region's governments or the creation of a volatile environment similar to the one that existed in Algeria during the 1990s.

Second, inside Algeria, AQIM has used psychological warfare against government security forces and the population. Using bombs and threats of suicide bombings to project its power, AQIM has maintained an air of sustainability and endurance. In anticipation of terrorist attacks, authorities routinely place roadblocks on major highways and routes to major cities, causing traffic delays and frustration for commuters. As a result, the country's citizens question the government's claim that the terrorism has ended or that the government is sincere in its attempt to liquidate it.

While it is difficult to measure how much this fear and frustration helps AQIM recruit new members, the psychological warfare appears to have helped AQIM stay alive in the psyche of the Algerian people while undermining those forces seeking to dismantle it. This suggests that AQIM's threat to regional security will most likely persist for at least a few more years.

Hamoud Salhi

See also al Qaeda; Armed Islamic Front; Zawahiri, Ayman al

Further Readings

Badcock, James. "Facing al Qaeda in the Maghreb Threat." *The Daily Star* (Lebanon), February 9, 2010, p. 5.

Bourka, Liess. *Jihadism: Islam and the Challenge of History*. Algiers, Algeria: APIC Dissonances, 2009.

Evans, Martin, and John Phillips. *Algeria: Anger of the Dispossessed*. New Haven, CT: Yale University Press, 2007.

Gerges, Fawaz A. *The Far Enemy: Why Jihad Went Global*. Cambridge, UK: Cambridge University Press, 2009.

Hansen, Andrew, and Lauren Vriens. *al Qaeda in the Islamic Maghreb (AQIM)*. Washington, DC: Council on Foreign Relations, July 21, 2009. http://www.cfr.org/publication/12717.

Malek, Anoir. "The End of al Qaeda in Algeria: Is There a Relationship between Droudkel and Osama bin Laden?" *Ech Chorouk el Youmi* (Algeria), January 24, 2010. (Arabic)

Muslim, Mohammed. "Three Eminent Hijazzi (Saudis) Clerics Call On SGPC Members Not to Be a Tool for Foreign Intelligence." *Ech Chorouk el Youmi* (Algeria), December 23, 2009. (Arabic.) http:www.echoroukonline.com/ara/interviews/45995.html.

AL SHABAB

According to the U.S. State Department, Somalia's Harakat al Shabab al Mujahideen (Arabic for "Movement of the Youth"), known most commonly as simply al Shabab (or al Shabaab), has become one of the most lethal terrorist groups in East Africa.

At the close of the twentieth century, all of the elements were present for radicalism to flourish in Somalia. The collapse of President Siad Barre's government in 1991 left a power vacuum that would be filled by unrestrained violence and a humanitarian tragedy of unparalleled proportions. The country became divided into three separate entities—Somaliland, Puntland, and South Central Somalia—each controlled by tribes and subset clans. These frail entities had no power to impose order or rein in would-be challengers to their authority. Lawlessness ensued, hundreds of millions fled their homes, and tens of thousands have been killed. Somalia's situation was further complicated by the United Nations' establishment of a Transitional Federal Government (TFG) in Mogadishu, Somalia's capital, in 2004, and by an invasion by Ethiopia in 2006. Both of these events lent credence to the charge that Somalia's problems were manufactured outside the country, and by enemies of Islam.

These conditions gave rise to al Shabab. With fighters trained in Afghanistan and Iraq, al Shabab is an offshoot of the Islamic Courts Union (ICU), a group that had been removed from power by the Ethiopia invasion in December 2006. al Shabab's ideological modus operandi is centered on Islamism and nationalism, which resonate in the Somali psyche for a number of reasons, including the UIC's relative success (despite its short-lived experience in power) in establishing order and enticing Somali businesses to invest in Somalia, the widespread presence of Islam in Somalia, and the highly contested presence of foreign troops in the country. al Shabab called for the establishment of a Shariah state (i.e., a state governed by Islam), proclaimed jihad against unbelievers, and urged nationalist resistance against foreign forces, specifically the African Union (AU), the United Nations, Ethiopia, and, more recently, Uganda.

al Shabab has used several tactics to gain recruits, including threatening the family members of those who refuse to join, providing financial help to those in desperate need, and offering refuge for criminals and stipends as salaries for recruits. The group has also had a strong following among some Somalis living in the United States and Europe since 2006.

As a group, al Shabab remains deeply divided, and its terrorist tactics have only exacerbated those fragmentations. It has claimed responsibility for attacks launched against civilians, government officials, and United Africa peacekeeping forces. In July 2010, al Shabab fighters killed 32 people, including 6 politicians, in Mogadishu, and a month later 76 people were killed by al Shabab in a crowded restaurant in Kampala, Uganda. Other terrorist tactics have also been used, including stoning and cutting off people's limbs. These tactics have been vehemently condemned by Somali Sufi Muslims and reformist religious clerics, and they have been rejected by the Somali civilian population at large. Additionally, many of the pretexts used by al Shabab to lure recruits have been taken away. In particular, moderate ICU religious leaders were appointed to top TFG leadership positions, and Ethiopian forces have been withdrawn.

Still, it is difficult to predict whether al Shabab's days are over. Conflicting reports suggest a strong propensity for its survival as a transnational group. Indicators are that it might seek, or might have already established, formal ties with al Qaeda, thereby giving it a raison d'étre and name recognition. In the general scheme of things, however, much of al Shabab's future is tied to Somalia's internal predicament. A drastic improvement of Somalia's internal condition, along with a genuine resolution of its conflict, would go a long way to deflect any pretenses al Shabab uses to justify its terrorism.

Hamoud Salhi

See also al Qaeda

Further Readings

Dagne, Ted. "Somalia: Current Conditions and Prospects for a Long Lasting Peace." Congressional Research Service, February 4, 2010.

Gartenstein-Ross, Daveed. 2009. "The Strategic Challenge of Somalia's Al Shabaab Dimensions of Jihad." *Middle East Quarterly* (Fall 2009): 25–36.

Kaplan, Seth. "Rethinking State-building in a Failed State." *Washington Quarterly* (January 2010): 81–97.

Le Sage, Andre. "Somalia's Endless Transition: Breaking the Deadlock." *Strategic Forum* 257 (June 2010): 1–7.

Shank, Michael. "Understanding Political Islam in Somalia." *Contemporary Islam* 1, no. 1 (2007): 89–103.

Shay, Shaul. *Somalia between Jihad and Restoration.* Piscataway, NJ: Transaction Publishers, 2010.

ALEX BONCAYAO BRIGADE

The Alex Boncayao Brigade (ABB) is a Manila-based Communist hit squad that assassinated dozens of people on the orders of the Communist Party of the Philippines (CPP) during the 1980s and 1990s. The CPP was formed by a group of leftist intellectuals in the mid-1960s, and in 1969 the party created the New People's Army (NPA) and went to war against the Philippine government.

The NPA operated mostly in the countryside surrounding Manila and the outlying islands of the archipelago. Throughout the 1970s, fighting was fierce between the Communists and the government, but the government was never able to completely eliminate the guerrillas. The guerrillas,

however, were unable to consolidate their territorial gains. In the early 1980s, the NPA leadership decided that a strike at the heart of Philippine economic and political power was necessary. An attack on Manila, the capital, was planned.

The NPA, however, lacked the resources for a conventional military assault. Furthermore, the NPA's structure (forces were grouped into brigades of up to 100 men) was unsuited for attacking and fighting in a large city. The leadership had learned valuable lessons from its experiences in assaulting military outposts in the southern Philippines, and they decided that the new force would consist of hit squads of up to four men, who would carry out targeted assassinations of government officials, businessmen, soldiers, and police. Although the number of actual assassins was quite small—some sources estimate as few as 30, even during the peak of the brigade's activity—their support system was vast, with as many as 500 other members providing intelligence, supplies, and safe houses. The new squad would come to be known as the Alex Boncayao Brigade (ABB), after a labor leader turned guerrilla who was killed by security forces in 1983.

The ABB operated independently of its parent organization, launching its first attack in May 1984. It soon acquired a reputation for vicious efficiency. The ABB's hit men were nicknamed "sparrow squads" for their swiftness and skill at fluttering out of the hands of police. Throughout the 1980s, they killed dozens of people a year. The ABB did not limit its targets to Filipinos; the group is believed to have murdered Col. James Row and several other U.S. nationals.

In the early 1990s, the ABB's fortunes declined. The end of the Cold War had thrown the NPA into disarray, and factionalism and power struggles diminished its abilities as a fighting force. In 1994, the ABB's commanding officer, Felimon Lagman, was arrested, and the organization was left without leadership. Unexpectedly, however, the ABB reemerged in December 1995, carrying out a series of attacks on local business executives. The NPA disavowed any connection with these attacks, and in March 1997 the ABB announced that it had allied itself with the Revolutionary Proletariat Army (RPA).

Despite the arrest of ABB leader Nilo de la Cruz later that year, the new alliance began an offensive directed mostly at industrialists and business executives, particularly those in the oil industry. It also added bombings to its tactics. During the late 1990s, however, police arrested several key leaders. In December 2000, the remnant of the RPA-ABB signed a peace pact with the government of President Joseph Estrada. This pact included provisions for disarmament and the release of RPA-ABB prisoners. While the ABB has been accused of assassinating rival leftists, it appears to be largely abiding by the peace pact.

Colleen Sullivan

See also Abu Sayyaf Group; New People's Army

Further Readings

Banlaoi, Rommel C. *Philippine Security in the Age of Terror*. Boca Raton, FL: Auerbach Publications/Taylor & Francis Group, 2010.

"Bosses the Target, Says Filipino Death Squad." *Singapore Business Times*, December 14, 1995, p. 5.

Branigin, William. "Manila Captures Head of Communist Rebels; Underground Chief Ran Urban Hit Squad." *The Washington Post*, May 27, 1994, p. A30.

Dikkenberg, John. "Ambushes Mark Return of Communist Hit Squad." *South China Morning Post*, December 15, 1995, p. 18.

Ghosh, Nirmal. "Capture of Head Honcho a Crushing Blow to Manila Reds." *Singapore Straits Times*, July 14, 1997, p. 20.

Kessler, Richard J. *Rebellion and Repression in the Philippines*. New Haven, CT: Yale University Press, 1989.

Rabasa, Angel. *Ungoverned Territories: Understanding and Reducing Terrorism Risks*. Santa Monica, CA: RAND Corporation, 2007.

ALI, AHMED MOHAMED HAMED (1965–)

Ahmed Mohamed Hamed Ali (aka Abu Fatima; Abu Islam; Abu Islam al Surir; Abu Khadiijah; Ahmad al Masri; Ahmed Ahmed; Ahmed Hamed; Ahmed Hemed; Ahmed Mohamed Abdurehman; Ahmed Mohamed Ali; Ahmed Shieb; Ahmed the Egyptian; Hamed Ali), an Egyptian, has been described as a top lieutenant in Osama bin Laden's al Qaeda network. In 1998 Ali was indicted in the United States for his involvement in the conspiracy to bomb U.S. embassies in East Africa, though he is not accused of playing a direct role in the attacks. He is, however, on the FBI's Most Wanted Terrorists list. *al Qaeda*, from an Arabic word meaning "the base," is an international network of terrorist groups that have committed violent acts against the United States, including the September 11, 2001, attacks on the World Trade Center in New York City and the Pentagon near Washington, D.C.

According to the FBI, Ali may have formal training in agriculture. He fled from Kenya, where he lived, to Pakistan on August 2, 1998, just five days before the August 7 embassy bombings. On that date, the U.S. embassies in Nairobi, Kenya, and Dar es Salaam, Tanzania, were destroyed in synchronized truck bomb attacks that killed 224 people. Shortly thereafter, the U.S. government declared that bin Laden and al Qaeda operatives were responsible.

The 1998 U.S. indictment charges that Ali participated in other anti-U.S. activities in Africa prior to conspiring to bomb the two U.S. embassies. In 1993 he allegedly provided military training and assistance to Somali tribes, preparing them to violently oppose the U.N. and U.S. peacekeeping intervention during Somalia's civil unrest. In 1998 he told al Qaeda members in Kenya that bin Laden had formed a united front with other militant Islamic groups against the United States. Ali remains a fugitive, and the U.S. State Department has offered a reward of up to $5 million for information leading to his arrest or conviction.

Erica Pearson

See also al Qaeda; bin Laden, Osama; East Africa Embassy Bombings

Further Readings

Akhahenda, Elijah F. *When Blood and Tears United a Country: The Bombing of the American Embassy in Kenya*. Lanham, MD: University Press of America/Rowman & Littlefield, 2002.

Bergen, Peter. *Holy War, Inc.: Inside the Secret World of Osama bin Laden*. New York: Free Press, 2001.

Federal Bureau of Investigation. "Most Wanted Terrorists." http://www.fbi.gov/wanted/terrorists/fugitives.htm.

"A Nation Challenged: The Hunted; The 22 Most Wanted Suspects, in a Five-act Drama of Global Terror." *The New York Times*, October 14, 2001, p. 1B.

Reeve, Simon. *The New Jackals: Ramzi Yousef, Osama bin Laden, and the Future of Terrorism.* Boston: Northeastern University Press, 1999.

Smith, Martin, and Lowell Bergman. "Hunting bin Laden." *Frontline*, PBS, September 13, 2001. http://www.pbs.org/wgbh/pages/frontline/shows/binladen.

U.S. District Court for the Southern District of New York. *United States v. Usama bin Laden.* Indictment, November 5, 1998. http://www.fas.org/irp/news/1998/11/98110602_nlt.html.

ANARCHISM

Anarchism is a theory of human governance that rejects any coercive form of central authority and offers a view of the future based on the voluntary cooperation of free individuals and groups forming the backbone of the social order. In such a system, external authority—laws, government, police, church, and so forth—would be eliminated because it would be unnecessary. Crime would also not exist, and should an offense occur, psychological methods of discipline, such as shaming, would suffice.

Anarchists have divergent views on the level of community cooperation, ranging from individualism to mutualism and from syndicalism to communism, and on how these ideals can be achieved. Known tactics of anarchism range between the extremes of terrorism and pacifism. Anarchists have developed various methods of accomplishing social change ever since the French philosopher P. J. Proudhon (1809–1865) first introduced the term in 1840. The mass media and the general public, however, continue to present and perceive anarchists as unruly, and usually angry, individuals hiding a knife, a pistol, or a bomb and awaiting the moment for violent action.

"Propaganda by Deed"

Anarchism was a product of the miserable social, economic, and political conditions of working people in the nineteenth century. Industrial development and significantly greater mobility brought rapid urban growth and the expansion of the gap in wealth and geography between social classes. Where working and living conditions were intolerable and hunger claimed many lives, anarchist ideas found adherents.

Anarchism was the first revolutionary movement in history that not only criticized authority but also agitated for immediate and radical social change. Anarchists, however, are stymied by their very concept of social relations, for organizing is anathema to them. Thus, with a theoretical prohibition against large group action, the Russian anarchist Mikhail Bakunin (1814–1876) made the proposal for "propaganda by deed," the most extreme method of struggle. He thought that individuals or small groups of people should kill those who represented an existing social order, causing such dread and horror that the masses would spontaneously revolt and overthrow the state itself. Similarly, the German radical thinker Karl Heinzen theorized in an 1848 essay called "Der Mord" ("Murder") that all forms of violence (including not only murder but suicide) are both justified and necessary in revolutionary struggles.

Bakunin's ideas found many followers. During the last quarter of the nineteenth century and before the outbreak of World War I, an epidemic of terrorist attacks spread from Europe all over the world. These attacks included an attempted assassination of German emperor Wilhelm I in 1878; an attempt on the life of the German princess in 1883; the attempted assassination of General Martinez Campos in Barcelona, Spain, in 1892; and the assassinations of President Sadi Carnot of France in 1894, of the Empress Elizabeth of Austria-Hungary in 1898, of King Humbert I of Italy in 1900, of President William McKinley of the United States in 1901, and of Prime Minister José Canalejas y Mendez of Spain in 1912.

To fulfill their wish to have the state wither away, some devoted anarchists began to attack institutions and organizations that represented the "false" values of bourgeois society. In 1882 a bomb exploded in a popular music hall in Lyons, France; in 1886 Charles Gallo threw a bottle of vitriol and fired a revolver into the crowd of brokers in the Paris stock exchange; and in 1893 Auguste Vaillant detonated a bomb in the Chamber of Deputies in Paris. Vaillant was sentenced to death and executed, though no one had been killed by his bomb. A year later, Emile Henry, in an act of retaliation for the execution of Vaillant, deposited a bomb in the Café Terminus, where shopkeepers, clerks, and even some workers were drinking and listening to a band. Twenty people were wounded, one of whom later died. The majority of anarchists condemned terrorist actions that would cause damage and death to so many people, but uncompromising individuals such as Henry would explain their position by their total disdain of the lives of the bourgeoisie.

The anarchist movement accepted François-Claudius Königstein (known as Ravachol), a criminal with a long history of theft and murder, as one of its own only after his death. Ravachol, who never claimed to be an anarchist, was captured after police determined that he was responsible for two bomb explosions in Paris in 1892. His trial was conducted in an atmosphere of vengeance. Cesare Lombroso, a famous Italian criminologist, who developed a physiognomy of the "born criminal," declared that Ravachol's physical features exemplified the criminal. The French verb *ravacholiser* (to blow up) is derived from his name.

Based on the many assassinations and bombings in different countries, police postulated an international conspiracy of anarchists. French police, for example, had some agents pretending to be anarchists and run an anarchist newspaper to trap true militants. Prominent anarchists such as Peter Kropotkin (1842–1921) and Errico (or Enrico) Malatesta (1853–1932) were arrested several times in connection with cases they were ignorant of. Kropotkin, like Bakunin, supported violence as justifiable in certain circumstances, especially if it offered the only possibility of social change. Because Kropotkin was a materialist and scientist, he also had a great belief in anarchist "propaganda by word"—the education and inspiration of the public by use of subversive publications.

American Anarchy

At the end of the nineteenth century, most anarchists in the United States were recent immigrants from Europe. John (Johann) Most, a German anarchist, founded the anarchist weekly *Die Freiheit* in 1882 in New York City. Soon other anarchist papers in French, Czech, Yiddish, and Italian joined this German-language newspaper. These publications endorsed the labor movement's fight for the eight-hour working day in the hope of providing an impulse for a revolutionary upheaval. The openness and fervency of these newspapers prompted authorities to assume that anarchists were responsible for many violent disturbances and common crimes.

The most famous incident involving American anarchists occurred in Chicago in 1886 during the Haymarket Riot, when a bomb killed eight policemen. Although the police had no evidence, the state of public terror and fear of conspiracy was so high that eight anarchists were convicted, four of whom were later hanged. Publicity surrounding anarchist and antigovernment activities kept the public and the authorities fearful of radicals, especially if the radicals were foreigners. Two years after the 1901 assassination of President McKinley in Buffalo, New York, by Leon Czolgosz, a young anarchist of Polish origin, Congress passed a law that allowed known anarchists to be barred from entering the United States and the deportation of anarchist aliens already in the country. These laws became more stringent a decade later during the wave of political repression known as the Red Scare, which was directed against those who agitated against capitalism and war and for the rights of working people. As a result of these laws, 247 anarchist aliens had been deported by the year 1917. Emma Goldman (1869–1940), a radical thinker and passionate speaker, and one of the founders of modern feminism in the United States, was deported to Russia.

U.S. anarchist history also includes the 1920 trial and subsequent execution of Nicola Sacco (1891–1927) and Bartolomeo Vanzetti (1888–1927). Active in the antiwar and labor movements, these two Italian immigrants were convicted on controversial murder charges in South Braintree, Massachusetts, in a trial that was more political than criminal.

Violence, Not Inspiration

Individual acts of terror did not inspire the great majority of people, however; most found the violence frightening and shocking. Without coherent organization, anarchism could not develop. Militant anarchism was even rejected by the violent Russian revolutionaries of 1917, and the anarchists were both defeated and persecuted by the Communists. In the twentieth century, many radical thinkers started to realize that they could achieve greater social changes if they joined a political party or trade union. The short success of anarcho-syndicalism in Spain during the civil war of 1936–1939 indicated a new direction that anarchism might take, with workers organizing and taking control of industry and other aspects of the economy.

Since the 1950s, anarchist groups have used terror as end in itself. Such groups have included the Japanese Red Army, the Angry Brigade in England, the Baader-Meinhof Gang in Germany, and the Weatherman in the United States. Such anarchistic elements as the acceptance of violence as a part of culture, and as an opposition method to all conventions and restrictions, also influenced the student movement of the 1960s and 1970s.

In the early twenty-first century, many radical activists, especially those involved in anti-globalization protests, call themselves anarchists. They demonstrate against the expansion of capitalism in the form of transnational corporations at international meetings of the World Bank, the International Monetary Fund, the World Trade Organization, and others of that ilk. The public reputation of the anarchists continues to decline, however, because many such protests culminate in the destruction of property (e.g., the smashing of windows), and sometimes in a violent confrontation with police. Sporadic bomb attacks by self-professed anarchists continue to occur, especially in Europe: in December 2010, a group calling itself the Informal Federation of Anarchy took credit for several mail bomb attacks on embassies in Rome.

Maria Kiriakova

See also Baader-Meinhof Gang; Bakunin, Mikhail; Kropotkin, Peter; Weatherman

Further Readings

Bakunin, Mikhail. *Selected Writings from Mikhail Bakunin: Essays on Anarchism*. St. Petersburg, FL: Red and Black Publishers, 2010.

Epstein, Barbara. "Anarchism and the Anti-globalization Movement." *Monthly Review: An Independent Socialist Magazine* 53, no. 4 (2001): 1–14. http://www.monthlyreview.org/0901epstein.htm.

Guerin, Daniel. *Anarchism: From Theory to Practice*. New York: Monthly Review Press, 1970.

Joll, James. *The Anarchists*. 2nd ed. Cambridge, MA: Harvard University Press, 1980.

Kedward, Roderick. *The Anarchists: The Men Who Shocked an Era*. New York: American Heritage Press, 1971.

Marshall, Peter. *Demanding the Impossible: A History of Anarchism*. Oakland, CA: PM Press, 2010.

Nozick, Robert. *Anarchy, State, and Utopia*. 1974. New York: Basic Books, 2011.

Pennock, Roland J., and John W. Chapman. *Anarchism*. New York: New York University Press, 1978.

Purkis, Jon, and James Bowen, eds. *Twenty-first Century Anarchism: Unorthodox Ideas for a New Millennium*. London: Cassell, 1997.

ANDERSON, TERRY A. (1949–)

The journalist Terry A. Anderson was the longest-held American during the Lebanon hostage crisis, having endured 2,454 days of captivity. One of the first Americans to be abducted in Beirut, and the last to be set free, Anderson's nearly seven years in captivity mark the era of hostage-taking in Lebanon.

Anderson, a former combat correspondent in Vietnam, became the Middle East Bureau Chief for the Associated Press (AP) in 1982, covering the civil war in Lebanon and the Israeli invasion of that country from the Beirut office. By the mid-1980s, Westerners, including several journalists, had been "disappearing" throughout Beirut, seized by anti-Western Shiite Muslim fundamentalist groups. When four Lebanese AP employees were abducted in October 1984, Anderson worked military contacts to secure their release. Colleagues of Anderson believe his fate was sealed when he appeared on Lebanese television, celebrating the return of his coworkers.

Shortly after 8 A.M. on March 16, 1985, Anderson was abducted at gunpoint near the Ain el Mreisse Mosque in West Beirut. The next day, Islamic Jihad (al Jihad) claimed responsibility, stating that Anderson's kidnapping was part of a campaign to rid the Muslim regions of Lebanon of "spies" masquerading as "journalists, industrialists, scientists and men of religion." (Anderson's fellow hostages included American University professors David Jacobsen and Thomas Sutherland, Father Lawrence Martin Jenco, and Rev. Benjamin Weir.) Aside from purging Lebanon of alleged "spies," Islamic Jihad also wanted to use the hostages as bargaining chips for the release of 17 Lebanese and Iraqi prisoners held in Kuwait. These 17 were suspects in the 1983 bombings of the French and American embassies. One of them was the brother-in-law of Imad Mugniyah, a senior Hezbollah official believed to have masterminded Anderson's abduction.

For the next six and a half years, Anderson languished in dank basements and windowless rooms throughout Beirut and southern Lebanon, blindfolded, chained to the floor, and eating meals of stale bread and cheese or cold rice. With the help of his fellow inmates, Anderson endeavored to keep his mind sharp. The captives argued politics, played chess with a set Anderson fashioned from salvaged tinfoil, and, enchained, ran in circles for exercise. For a time, Anderson, Sutherland, Weir, and Jenco read the Bible aloud, praying in what they called the "Church of the Locked Door."

Negotiations for the freedom of the hostages were caught up in the tangled web of international politics that defined the late 1980s, most notably the Iran-Contra Affair. The Reagan administration, publicly committed to "no negotiation" with terrorists, orchestrated an arms-for-hostages deal with Iran, initially to rescue CIA Station Chief William Buckley, who, unbeknownst to them, had died while a captive. Weir, Jenco, and Jacobsen were released under this arrangement. However, by 1987, after the Iran-Contra scandal broke, hope for freedom for Anderson and the remaining hostages dwindled.

In the end, a confluence of world events worked to secure the release of Anderson and the others. Ayatollah Ruhollah Khomeini died, to be replaced by the more pragmatic Hashemi Rafsanjani. Communism fell. Israel's security concerns turned from its borders to its occupied territories. Iraq invaded Kuwait, and the 17 prisoners were freed, leaving the hostage-holders without a clear demand. The United States then easily defeated Iraq during the Gulf War. When Anderson was released, on December 4, 1991, at the age of 44, his captors apologized for what they called a mistake and gave him a half-dozen carnations to give to Madeline Bassil, his soon-to-be wife and the mother of his daughter.

In March 2000, Anderson and his family were awarded $341 million in a lawsuit against the country of Iran, who backed Hezbollah and Islamic Jihad, the groups responsible for his incarceration. Although Anderson has never collected anywhere near the full amount awarded, he used the money he did receive to found the Jenco Foundation, an organization named after his fellow hostage, that seeks to promote leadership in Appalachia.

Laura Lambert

See also al Jihad; Buckley, William; Hezbollah; Hostage Taking; Mugniyah, Imad Fayez; Sutherland, Thomas; Waite, Terry

Further Readings

Anderson, Terry A. *Den of Lions: Memoirs of Seven Years*. New York: Crown, 1993.

Fisk, Robert. *Pity the Nation: Lebanon at War*. London: A. Deutsch, 1990.

Kerr, Ann Zwicker. *Come with Me from Lebanon: An American Family Odyssey*. Syracuse, NY: Syracuse University Press, 1994.

McGovern, Glenn P. *Targeted Violence: A Statistical and Tactical Analysis of Assassinations, Contract Killings, and Kidnappings*. Boca Raton, FL: CRC Press/Taylor & Francis Group, 2010.

Sutherland, Tom, and Jean Sutherland. *At Your Own Risk: An American Chronicle of Crisis and Captivity in the Middle East*. Golden, CO: Fulcrum, 1996.

Van de Ven, and Susan Kerr. *One Family's Response to Terrorism: A Daughter's Memoir*. Syracuse, NY: Syracuse University Press, 2008.

ANIMAL LIBERATION FRONT

The Animal Liberation Front (ALF) is an underground group of animal rights activists made up of small, autonomous cells. ALF cells can be found throughout the world but are located primarily in North America and the United Kingdom. Since its creation in 1976, the ALF has become one of the most active radical animal rights groups, and it is considered a domestic terrorist organization by both the FBI and the Scotland Yard.

The ALF was founded in England by the animal rights activist Ronnie Lee. Frustrated with traditional forms of protest, Lee created the ALF with the intent to end animal exploitation by inflicting economic hardship on the businesses and persons involved in animal industries, usually through the damage and destruction of property. The ALF guidelines, which include "taking precautions against harming any animal, human and nonhuman," instruct members to liberate animals, inflict economic damage, and reveal atrocities against animals. The group uses a range of tactics, including civil disobedience, arson, and burglary. Vandalism is the most common action, with members spray-painting slogans on targeted businesses, such as "McMurder" inside McDonald's restaurants.

By the mid-1980s, the initial 30 ALF members had grown to more than 1,500. ALF cells now operate in over a dozen countries, including France, New Zealand, Poland, Italy, and Slovakia. Because the ALF has no central authority, and because any individual who follows ALF guidelines may be considered part of the organization, determining current ALF membership is difficult. In Great Britain, animal rights activities have consistently been more frequent and more violent than elsewhere. In 1991 alone, activists in Britain engaged in 1,718 actions. British ALF groups have also been more likely to use crude incendiary devices, including mail bombs and car bombs. Since the late 1990s, the use of such devices has been increasingly common among American ALF groups as well.

ALF activities in North America, which began in 1979, include major attacks on universities, federal research centers, medical labs, fur farms, and meatpackers, causing millions of dollars of damage and lost or compromised data, as well as smaller attacks on fast-food restaurants, pet stores, banks, and corporations. Members have also used stolen footage from labs to create publicity materials and films, at times to good effect. In 1986, after seeing an ALF film, *Breaking Barriers,* the renowned primatologist Jane Goodall used her influence to change conditions for primates at the SEMA research center in Maryland.

In 1987, the American ALF committed a multi-million-dollar arson at a University of California, Davis, laboratory; in consequence, the FBI placed ALF on its domestic terrorist list. In the 1990s, Operation Bite Back and Operation Bite Back II, multistate campaigns against the U.S. fur industry, included the freeing of more than 10,000 mink from the Arritola Mink Farm in Mt. Angel, Oregon—the largest liberation of animals to that time.

ALF actions have closed businesses, stopped or altered inhumane research, and hobbled some animal industry economies, but many pro–animal rights groups and individuals consider ALF's actions to be ineffective. "Liberated" animals are often recaptured or killed, and break-ins have led to the installation of stronger security systems and more stringent security controls. Some more moderate animal rights' campaigners have argued that the ALF's reliance on illegal and violent activities, especially following the September 11, 2001, terrorist attacks, could taint the cause of animal rights in the eyes of the public. ALF actions have also led to legislation, including the Animal Enterprise Protection Act (1992), which made causing more than $10,000 in damages at commercial and academic institutions that utilize animals a federal crime.

The first convictions under that act occurred in 2006 in response to an ALF campaign against the Huntingdon Life Sciences, a company that conducts animal tests for pharmaceutical and other companies. An ALF group in Britain began the campaign in 2000, operating publicly under the name Stop Huntingdon Animal Cruelty (SHAC). ALF/SHAC targeted not only Huntingdon but suppliers, banks, and any other companies, both in the United States and Britain, that did business with the firm or somehow enabled its existence. The anti-Huntingdon campaign was not only remarkably broad, but it was quite violent, and harassment in some instances went on for years. Individuals were threatened and beaten, their homes and cars were vandalized, and their addresses and phone numbers were posted on the web.

Six members of ALF/SHAC were convicted in the United States in 2006 and given prison sentences of up to six years. Two years later, seven British ALF/SHAC members, including the campaign's leader, Gregg Avery, were also convicted, receiving sentences of up to 11 years. But despite tougher laws and better enforcement, the decentralized nature of the ALF means that it is likely that extremists will continue to operate under its name in the future.

Laura Lambert

See also Animal Rights Movement; Coronado, Rodney; Ecoterrorism

Further Readings

Best, Steven, and Anthony J. Nocella II, eds. *Terrorists or Freedom Fighters? Reflections on the Liberation of Animals.* New York: Lantern, 2004.

Grimston, Jack. "Animal Terrorist Group Foiled by Captain Nancy, the Police Mole." *Sunday Times,* March 1, 2009, p. 4.

Harden, Blain. "The Fur Flies and Crawls and Bites: Minks Released by Activists Raise a Stink Near Seattle." *The Washington Post,* October 18, 2003, p. A1.

Kinkerbocker, Brad. "A Troubling Rise in Violence for Green Causes." *Christian Science Monitor,* June 6, 2005, p. 3.

Liddick, Donald R. *Eco-terrorism: Radical Environmental and Animal Liberation Movements.* Westport, CT: Praeger, 2006.

Newkirk, Ingrid. *Free the Animals: The Amazing Story of the Animal Liberation Front.* New York: Lantern Books, 2000.

Singer, Peter. *Animal Liberation.* 1975. Reprint, New York: HarperPerennial Modern Classics, 2009.

ANIMAL RIGHTS MOVEMENT

By the 1980s, both the FBI and Scotland Yard viewed radical animal rights organizations, such at the Animal Liberation Front (ALF), as domestic terrorist organizations. Indeed, animal rights activists in the United States make up one-third of what are called "special interest" or "single issue" terrorists, a category that includes anti-abortionists and radical environmentalists.

Today's animal rights movement has its roots in nineteenth-century England, beginning with the Royal Society for the Prevention of Cruelty to Animals (RSPCA). This group, founded in 1824, recognized the legitimate use of animals for research but sought ways to make the conditions for the animals more humane—what is now known as an *animal welfarist* philosophy. By 1875, a faction of the RSPCA had come together against the practice of vivisection—the cutting open or injuring of animals for scientific research—and formed the Society for the Protection of Animals Liable to Vivisection. Shortly thereafter, thanks to the lobbying efforts of such groups, the 1876 Cruelty to Animals Act was passed by Parliament to regulate animal experimentation. America has a similar animal rights history to that of Great Britain: the American Society for the Prevention of Cruelty to Animals (ASPCA) was founded in 1867, and anti-vivisection societies emerged as early as 1883.

The late 1800s saw remarkable advances in medicine based on animal experimentation, including Louis Pasteur's treatments for anthrax and rabies, as well as advances in the study of diabetes. In light of such successes, the animal rights movement in England faded from view for well over half a century. The movement resurfaced in the 1960s in opposition to fox hunting, a cause in which animal rights activists forged bonds with activists engaged in class struggle, as fox hunting has historically been strictly an upper-class sport. This bond also arose in later campaigns against wearing fur.

The Animal Liberation Front

In 1971, an animal rights activist named Ronnie Lee founded a Hunt Saboteur chapter in Luton, England. Convinced that more violent tactics should be used in the struggle for animal rights, Lee created another group, Band of Mercy, a year later. In 1973, Band of Mercy committed two acts of arson at a pharmaceutical plant. The group became increasingly violent until 1975, when Lee was apprehended. Upon his release in 1976, Lee created the Animal Liberation Front (ALF), now one of the most recognized radical animal rights groups in the world.

The founding goal of the ALF was to cause economic damage to people and businesses that exploited animals, with the ultimate objective of wreaking havoc on entire animal-use industries. Lee's cause was greatly assisted by the 1975 release of *Animal Liberation,* a book by the Australian philosopher Peter Singer that has since become a veritable bible of the animal rights movement. Singer wrote that "speciesism" was akin to racism and sexism, thus linking animal rights to the civil and women's rights struggles underway in the United States and abroad, and instilling a previously dormant movement with a sense of purpose and context.

The movement arose in North America at approximately the same time. In 1977, a group called the "Underground Railroad" released two dolphins from a marine lab at the University of Hawaii, in what is often cited as the first animal rights action in the United States. Two years later, the first North American ALF action occurred, in which one cat, two dogs, and two guinea pigs were freed from New York Medical Center. By the early 1980s, ALF cells were active in both Canada and the United States.

In conjunction with the growing underground aspect of the animal rights movement, in 1980, Alex Pacheco and Ingrid Newkirk founded the group People for the Ethical Treatment of Animals (PETA), now the largest and most active animal rights group in the United States. PETA utilizes legal forms of protest, including sit-ins, marches, boycotts, and propaganda campaigns. The group later began acting as the mouthpiece for the ALF, distributing press releases about ALF actions and films of stolen footage revealing conditions inside targeted research facilities.

With aboveground groups such as PETA in the mix, the 1980s were an active time for extremist animal rights activists in North America. In December 1982, the ALF perpetrated the "Christmas Cat Burglary," in which 35 cats were freed from the Howard University Medical School in Washington, D.C. The ALF then raided the Head Injury Lab at the University of Pennsylvania in May 1984. Sixty hours of research videos stolen from the lab became *Unnecessary Fuss,* a film that documented scientists taunting animals after experiments were performed.

In December 1984, the ALF released 115 animals from the City of Hope National Medical Center in California. By November 8, 1985, due to information revealed through ALF propaganda, City of Hope had been fined $11,000 for violations of the Animal Welfare Act. Meanwhile, in Canada, the first-ever primate liberation occurred

in January 1985, when the Canadian ALF rescued a rhesus monkey from labs at the University of Western Ontario.

While authorities were aware of the activities of the American ALF, the federal government did not target the group until April 1987, when activists set fire to the Animal Diagnostics Lab at the University of California, Davis, causing more than $3.5 million in damages. This act elevated the ALF from an underground activist group to a domestic terrorist threat in the eyes of the FBI, who began to closely track the movement's actions the FBI had already heightened investigations of domestic terrorist threats following the 1995 Oklahoma City bombing. Similarly, in England, Scotland Yard created a database of the animal rights movement, called the Animal Rights National Index, to monitor the activities of the British ALF as well as other groups, including the more extreme and violent Animal Rights Militia (ARM).

Contemporary Animal Rights Activities

The 1990s saw renewed action by the ALF, along with the development of other militant animal rights groups that went beyond ALF's tactics of animal liberation and property destruction. England's ARM had established itself in Canada by 1990, perpetrating a food contamination scare against Cold Buster candy bars in 1992, similar to Britain's ARM contamination scare against Mars Bars in 1984. By claiming to have poisoned a certain number of candy bars, ARM forced the targeted food companies to recall their products, causing financial losses upward of $1 million. In both cases, ARM later admitted the poisonings were a hoax.

In 1993 another extreme animal rights group was born, the British-based Justice Department. The Justice Department, now active in both England and North America, gained notoriety by mailing envelopes with razor blades tainted with rat poison or HIV-infected blood to individuals involved in "animal exploitation."

While these more extreme groups employed increasingly violent scare tactics, the Western Wildlife Unit of the ALF began to carry out "Operation Bite Back," one of the most successful campaigns against the fur industry to date. During 1991–1992, the ALF targeted mink farming, considered the backbone of the fur industry, in an attempt to undermine the fur economy in the United States. (Previous attacks on commercial fur stores proved to be highly sensational, but they were largely ineffective.) Based on undercover work conducted by the ALF activist Rodney Coronado, the multistate arson campaign began in June 1991 at the Experimental Fur Farm at Oregon State University in Corvallis. A warning spray-painted on the wall of the facilities read, "This is only the beginning." Over the next 16 months, Operation Bite Back struck at universities and research labs in Washington, Utah, and Michigan, and at fur farms and feed co-ops in the Pacific Northwest. The ALF claimed responsibility for the Michigan State University attack, which caused over $200,000 in damages, in a press release distributed by PETA.

In 1994, Coronado was arrested for his actions at Michigan State University (the first federal arrest of any ALF member). Just as authorities began to believe that ALF activity had died down, the group rebounded in 1995 with Operation Bite Back II, another multistate campaign that focused on animal liberation rather than economic sabotage. As part of the operation, the ALF perpetrated the largest animal liberation ever, releasing 10,000 mink from the Arritola Mink Farm in Mt. Angel, Oregon.

Similar anti-fur actions in Canada during the late 1980s and early 1990s eroded the once-powerful Canadian fur industry. That is not to say, however, that radical animal rights activism has been effective in attaining the goal of ending all human use of animals, or even ending the exploitation of fur-bearing animals. In America, after the slew of attacks in the mid-1980s, research institutions began to install much more elaborate security systems, making them more difficult to penetrate, and Congress passed the Animal Enterprise Protection Act (amended in 2006 by the Animal Enterprise Terrorism Act), which allows the federal government to prosecute any animal rights actions that caused more than $10,000 in damage. In the United States, Canada, England, and Sweden, animal rights activists remain in jail for their activities and are considered "prisoners of war" by their organizations.

The ALF has been fiercely criticized for continuing its actions in the wake of the September 11, 2001, terrorist attacks. Universities, medical school, veterinary clinics, research labs, butcher shops, fish markets, meatpacking plants, chicken and egg producers, dog kennels, mink and fox farms, furriers, and fast-food restaurants remain targets of the organization. The individuals behind these establishments have been targeted as well. From 2000 to 2008, the ALF conducted an extensive campaign of harassment, including beatings, of people associated with the animal testing company Huntingdon Life Sciences. Since 2006, several bomb attacks have been leveled against animal researchers at University of California campuses.

The list of targets has extended to politicians as well. On May 6, 2002, in the Netherlands, Volkert van der Graaf, an animal rights activist and cofounder of a group called Environment Offensive, shot and killed Pim Fortuyn, a right-wing Prime Minister hopeful, allegedly over Fortuyn's plan to lift restrictions on fur-farming if elected. Van der Graaf can be seen as part of a new breed of animal rights activists, who draws strength and community from other like-minded movements, such as environmentalism, feminism, and anti-globalization.

Laura Lambert

See also Animal Liberation Front; Coronado, Rodney; Ecoterrorism; Justice Department

Further Readings

Best, Steven, and Anthony J. Nocella II, eds. *Igniting a Revolution: Voices in Defense of the Earth.* Oakland, CA: AK Press, 2006.

Best, Steven, and Anthony J. Nocella II, eds. *Terrorists or Freedom Fighters? Reflections on the Liberation of Animals.* New York: Lantern, 2004.

Frankel, Glenn. "Animal Rights Group Aims at Enemy's Allies." *The Washington Post,* January 31, 2005, p. A16.

Kinkerbocker, Brad. "New Laws Target Increase in Acts of Ecoterrorism." *Christian Science Monitor,* November 26, 2003, p. 2.

Kistler, John M. *Animal Rights: A Subject Guide, Bibliography, and Internet Companion.* Westport, CT: Greenwood Press, 2000.

Liddick, Donald R. *Eco-terrorism: Radical Environmental and Animal Liberation Movements.* Westport, CT: Praeger, 2006.

Lutherer, Lorenz Otto, and Margaret Sheffield Simon. *Targeted: The Anatomy of an Animal Rights Attack.* Norman: University of Oklahoma Press, 1992.

Newkirk, Ingrid. *Free the Animals: The Amazing Story of the Animal Liberation Front.* New York: Lantern Books, 2000.

Paddock, Richard C., and Maria L. LaGanga. "Officials Decry Attacks on UC Staff." *Los Angeles Times,* August 5, 2008, p. B1.

Rudacille, Deborah. *The Scalpel and the Butterfly: The War between Animal Research and Animal Protection.* New York: Farrar, Straus and Giroux, 2000.

Ryder, Richard D. *Animal Revolution: Changing Attitudes toward Speciesism.* Rev. ed. Oxford and New York: Berg, 2000.

Scarce, Rik. *Eco-warriors: Understanding the Radical Environmental Movement.* Chicago: Noble Press, 1990.

Scully, Matthew. *Dominion: The Power of Man, the Suffering of Animals, and the Call to Mercy.* New York: St. Martin's, 2002.

Singer, Peter. *Animal Liberation.* 1975. Reprint, New York: HarperPerennial Modern Classics, 2009.

ANSAR AL ISLAM

Ansar al Islam (in English, Partisans of Islam) is a Sunni insurgent group of Kurdish origin operating primarily in northern Iraq, especially the governorates of Sulaymaniyah and Ninawa. Ansar al Islam holds to a Salafist worldview, which insists on a puritanical form of Islam and seeks to emulate the practices of the Prophet Muhammad and his companions. It aims to create an Islamic state in Iraq through a violent jihad against the Iraqi government and its institutions. Ansar al Islam has deployed violence against mainstream secular Kurdish groups, including the Kurdistan Democratic Party (KDP) and Patriotic Union of Kurdistan (PUK).

Ansar al Islam was founded in December 2001 by Najmuddin Faraj Ahmad (better known as Mullah Krekar), who as of 2010 was residing in Norway as a refugee. His goal was to challenge the grip of traditional Kurdish leaders over Kurdistan. In 2010 the group's leader was Abu Abdullah al Shafi'i (real name Wirya Salih), a Kurdish Iraqi veteran of jihad in Afghanistan and Chechnya. In addition to targeting its Kurdish adversaries, Ansar al Islam has regularly claimed responsibility for attacks against coalition forces in Iraq, the Iraqi government and its security personnel, Shiite militias, and anyone it accused of cooperating with these groups. Along with al Qaeda in Iraq, Ansar al Islam has regularly deployed suicide bombers and is known to behead its captives.

Prior to its 2003 invasion of Iraq, the United States accused Saddam Hussein, then president of Iraq, of willingly harboring Ansar al Islam and other terrorists, but these charges have largely not been proven. Following the invasion, Ansar al Islam was decimated by a combined U.S. aerial bombardment campaign and a ground attack led by Kurdish militias, known as the Peshmerga, loyal to the KDP and PUK. In September 2003, surviving members of the group reorganized under the name of Ansar al Sunna Army, which later changed its name to Ansar al Sunna Group. Then, on November 28, 2007, Abu Abdullah al Shafi'i announced that his group would return to the name Ansar al Islam. In all likelihood, this "rebranding" was intended to differentiate his men from another group that split from his ranks a few months earlier and adopted the name of Ansar al Sunna. The return to the original title was also intended to highlight Ansar al Islam's history of jihad in Iraq, which predates the invasion of the country and the rise of competing insurgent factions.

Ansar al Islam was the first organization to host foreign jihadists seeking a haven in Iraq, chief among them Abu Musab al Zarqawi, the founder of al Qaeda in Iraq (AQI). While both AQI and Ansar al Islam share a similar worldview, serious tensions between the two groups emerged in 2007 due to charges that AQI had killed some members of Ansar al Islam.

Ansar al Islam has regularly produced online magazines and videos highlighting its ideology and celebrating its insurgent attacks. These online productions feature suicide bombings, killings of Iraqi police and military personnel, attacks against mainstream Kurdish parties and forces, and the execution of Shiites accused on being anti-Sunni militia members.

Mohammed Hafez

See also al Qaeda in Iraq; Bombings and Bomb Scares; Hussein, Saddam; Zarqawi, Abu Musab al

Further Readings

Hafez, Mohammed M. *Suicide Bombers in Iraq: The Strategy and Ideology of Martyrdom.* Washington, DC: United States Institute of Peace, 2007.

While searching for al Qaeda and Ansar al Sunna forces, members of the Multi-Iraqi Transitional Team, 4th Battalion, 2nd Brigade, 5th Division, question the locals during Operation Orange Justice in Buhriz, Iraq, on February 10, 2007. (U.S. Air Force photo by Staff Sgt. Stacy L. Pearsall/Released)

Rabasa, Angel, et al. *Beyond al Qaeda.* Part 1, *The Global Jihadist Movement.* Santa Monica, CA: RAND Corporation, 2006.

Shah, Niaz A. *Self-defense in Islamic and International Law.* New York: Palgrave Macmillan, 2008.

Vidino, Lorenzo. *Al Qaeda in Europe: The New Battleground of International Jihad.* Amherst, NY: Prometheus Books, 2006.

ANTHRAX

Anthrax is caused by the bacterium *Bacillus anthracis,* which is usually seen in herbivores, rarely in humans. If left untreated, infection can be fatal. Anthrax is an attractive biological weapon because of the relative ease with which it can be grown, the lethality of the inhaled form of the disease, and the hardiness of its spores.

Anthrax is the oldest known animal disease, familiar to farmers in ancient Greece right up to the present day. Few countries are completely free of anthrax. The United States has sporadic outbreaks among livestock and wild animals. The disease is controlled in animals by a vaccine developed by Louis Pasteur in 1881. Herbivores take in anthrax spores from the soil as they graze. The spores then germinate into bacteria and multiply within the animal. In the final stages of the disease, bacteria released from the body in blood and other fluids form spores that can remain dormant in the soil for decades. Anthrax spores are very hardy and can withstand drying, heat, and cold.

Anthrax is not contagious, however. Cutaneous, or skin, anthrax is the most common and most treatable form of the disease. Indeed, 95 percent of all human cases are cutaneous, which occurs when spores contaminate a skin abrasion. The incubation period varies from a couple of days to up to six weeks after exposure. After contamination, a lesion quickly appears, and it is covered by a black scab within days. This black scab gives anthrax, which is derived from the Greek word for coal, its name. Most cases of skin anthrax do not become systemic infections.

More serious is gastrointestinal anthrax, which results from eating the meat of infected animals. Inhalation anthrax, the most rare and deadly form, was believed to be almost invariably fatal before 2001. Symptoms in the first stage of inhalation anthrax may resemble those of the flu or a stomach virus. The bacteria multiply first in the lymph nodes, particularly in the mediastinal and peribronchial nodes, creating characteristic images on chest X-rays. In the second stage of the disease, high concentrations of bacteria and toxins are found in the blood. The resulting shock and organ failure cause death.

Natural outbreaks of human anthrax may follow epidemics among livestock. In Zimbabwe, between 1979 and 1985, more than 100,000 cases of human anthrax (mostly cutaneous) were seen during an animal epidemic. Historically, anthrax in the United States was associated with the wool and animal-skin industries. From 1900 to 2000, the United States had 18 cases of inhalation anthrax, the latest occurring in 1978. The death rate was over 85 percent.

Anthrax as a Weapon

Japan, the United States, Britain, the Soviet Union, and Iraq are all known to have developed weapons using anthrax. During and following World War II, the United States developed anthrax weapons, but it became more interested in organisms that would incapacitate rather than kill. Great Britain exploded an anthrax bomb on Gruinard Island off Scotland in 1942. The contaminated island was unusable until cleanup work was completed a half century later. In 1969, President Richard Nixon ordered all offensive biowarfare research to cease, but defensive research continued.

Weapons-grade anthrax is grown as bacteria in wet solutions using fermentation vats. It is stressed to form spores, dried, and then milled into a powder fine enough to be inhaled. The earliest anthrax bombs were not very effective, because the anthrax was in a wet solution, so that most of the bacteria would be killed when the explosive charge detonated. More efficient delivery mechanisms have since been developed that can distribute anthrax spores in an aerosol.

In the spring of 1979, an outbreak of anthrax in Sverdlovsk (Yekaterinburg) in the Soviet Union caused at least 68 deaths. The official explanation attributed the deaths to the consumption of infected meat. More than a decade later, a team of Russian and U.S. scientists investigated and concluded that spores had been accidentally released into the air from a military manufacturing facility, and that the majority of cases in Sverdlovsk occurred in people who were directly downwind of

the facility. Ken Alibek, who defected to the United States after decades of managing the Soviet Biopreparat biological warfare program, confirmed this conclusion. By 1990, the Soviet Union had created the largest and most advanced biological warfare establishment ever known. This enormous program collapsed along with the Soviet Union. From 1985 to 1991, Iraq manufactured anthrax weapons.

Terrorist Attacks

During World War I, the German Secret Service used anthrax to infect horses, sheep, and cattle in Romania, the United States, and Argentina in an effort to prevent the transport of livestock to Russia, Britain, and India. In the 1970s, the Baader-Meinhof Gang threatened to disseminate anthrax in German shopping malls, but it never did. In 1981, a British group called Dark Harvest collected anthrax-contaminated soil from Gruinard Island and left a bag of it near the British military research laboratories at Porton Down, and another at the site of a Conservative Party meeting. The group wanted to force the British government to decontaminate the island. A Japanese terrorist group, Aum Shinrikyo, attempted to disperse anthrax spores in Tokyo on at least eight occasions during the 1990s, but the attacks failed to cause any illness. Evidence uncovered in Afghanistan indicates that the terrorist network al Qaeda attempted to create an anthrax weapon, although apparently it was unsuccessful.

In the fall of 2001, the Centers for Disease Control and Prevention (CDC) reported 22 cases of anthrax in the United States. Eleven cases were inhalation anthrax, five of which were fatal. The epidemic resulted from a terrorist attack that used the U.S. mail as a delivery system. Four envelopes containing anthrax spores were found, all of them postmarked Trenton, New Jersey. Each envelope contained a short note referring to the September 11, 2001, attacks on the World Trade Center. The envelopes were addressed to two U.S. senators, Tom Daschle and Patrick J. Leahy; to NBC in New York City; and to the *New York Post*.

The first case of anthrax attributed to the mailings was that of a 63-year-old photo editor at the *Sun* newspaper in Florida, who died on October 5, a day after the case was made public. One of his colleagues also fell ill but recovered. Six cases involved media workers in New York, but the majority of cases (10, including 3 deaths) involved postal workers. The other four victims were an infant who had visited a media office in New York, a woman in New York, a woman in Connecticut, and a bookkeeper who worked near Hamilton, New Jersey. The last three cases were thought to have resulted from the cross-contamination of mail.

The spores in each envelope were of the same strain of anthrax and were in the form of a very fine powder, minute enough to be inhaled into the deepest parts of the lungs. Each envelope had been tightly sealed, but spores leaked out through pores in the paper. The jets of compressed air that are routinely used to clean mail-sorting machines were powerful enough to resuspend spores on the machines into the air. These resuspended spores are thought to have infected the postal workers.

The anthrax strain used was not resistant to antibiotics, and demand soared for both respirators and ciprofloxacin, the only antibiotic approved by the U.S. Food and Drug Administration at that time for treating anthrax. The 2001 cases demonstrated that early treatment with modern antibiotics such as doxycycline and ciprofloxacin, combined with supportive medical procedures, can successfully treat inhalation anthrax.

No one has been charged in the attacks, but on July 29, 2008, a U.S. Army microbiologist named Bruce Ivins committed suicide after being informed by the FBI that he would likely be indicted. Following Ivins's death, the FBI released evidence that the agency claimed demonstrated that Ivins was solely responsible for the attack. The evidence included Ivins's deteriorating mental health, his access to the strain of anthrax used in the attack, the unexplained late hours he spent in the laboratory before the attack, and the fact that he delayed the investigation by not providing complete samples of the anthrax strains he worked with when investigators were trying to match the strain used in the attack to strains available at various laboratories. Defenders of Ivins have argued that the evidence against him was circumstantial, and that his failure to provide investigators with complete samples of the anthrax he worked with was the result of a misunderstanding, not an effort to conceal his guilt.

Numerous anthrax hoaxes followed the actual cases. In November 2001, at least 250 abortion clinics and gynecological offices received mailed letters containing a harmless white powder, while another 200 or so received powder in Federal Express packages. The mailed letters contained the statement "you have been exposed to anthrax" and were signed by the Army of God. Two years later, Clayton Lee Waagner, an anti-abortion extremist, was convicted for sending the letters, which he did while on the run following a prison escape.

By late 2008, harmless white powder had been sent to the offices of nearly all 50 state governors, as well as about 100 U.S. embassies in other countries. In 2007 and 2008, the FBI handled roughly 1,000 "white powder" incidents, each of which could include multiple mailings. Anthrax hoaxes also occurred prior to the 9/11 attacks.

The 2001 anthrax attacks were deadly, but they were much smaller in scale than had been feared by bioweapons experts. A typical scenario imagined a release of massive amounts of a deadly agent into the air over a city, resulting in hundreds of thousands of deaths and massive panic. A number of cities in the United States have held war games and training exercises simulating biowarfare attacks. The war games have demonstrated that responding to a large-scale attack would be overwhelming, and that such an attack would likely cause the complete collapse of emergency response and public health systems.

Ellen Sexton

See also Army of God; Aum Shinrikyo; Biological Terrorism; Chemical Terrorism; Hussein, Saddam

Further Readings

Alibek, Ken, with Stephen Handelman. *Biohazard.* New York: Random House, 1999.

Coen, Bob, and Eric Nadler. *Dead Silence: Fear and Terror on the Anthrax Trail.* Berkeley, CA: Counterpoint, 2009.

Cole, Leonard. *The Anthrax Letters: A Medical Detective Story.* Washington, DC: Joseph Henry Press, 2003.

Dixon, Terry, Matthew Meselson, Jeanne Guillemin, and Philip C. Hanna. "Anthrax" (review article). *New England Journal of Medicine* 341, no. 11 (1999): 815–826. http://content.nejm.org/cgi/content/full/341/11/815.

Drogin, Bob. "Anthrax Hoaxes, and Costs, Pile Up." *Los Angeles Times,* March 8, 2009, p. A3.

Guillemin, Jeanne. *Anthrax: The Investigation of a Deadly Outbreak.* Berkeley: University of California Press, 1999.

Inglesby, Thomas V., et al. "Anthrax as a Biological Weapon: Medical and Public Health Management." *Journal of the American Medical Association* 281, no. 18 (1999): 1735–1745. http://jama.ama-assn.org/cgi/content/full/281/18/1735.

Jernigan, John A., et al. "Bioterrorism-Related Inhalational Anthrax: The First 10 Cases Reported in the United States." *Emerging Infectious Diseases* 7, no. 6 (November–December 2001): 933–944. http://www.cdc.gov/ncidod/EID/vol7no6/jernigan.htm.

Lipton, Erik, and Kirk Johnson. "The Anthrax Trail: Tracking Bioterror's Tangled Course." *The New York Times,* December 26, 2001, p. A1.

Miller, Judith, Stephen Engelberg, and William Broad. *Germs: Biological Weapons and America's Secret War.* New York: Simon & Schuster, 2001.

Perez, Evan. "FBI Paints Chilling Portrait of Anthrax-Attack Suspect." *The Wall Street Journal,* August 7, 2008, p. A1.

Swarns, Rachel, and Eric Lipton. "From Offering Help in the Anthrax Investigation to Being Named the Suspect." *The New York Times,* August 8, 2008, p. A12.

Thompson, Marilyn W. *The Killer Strain: Anthrax and a Government Exposed.* New York: HarperCollins, 2003.

Warrick, Joby. "Suspect and a Setback in al Qaeda Anthrax Case." *The Washington Post,* October 31, 2006, p. A1.

ANTI-ABORTION TERRORISM

In the years following *Roe v. Wade,* the 1973 case that brought the issue of legalizing abortion before the Supreme Court, anti-abortion terrorism has plagued abortion providers throughout the United States. The FBI considers militant anti-abortionists, like radical animal rights and environmentalist groups, to be "special interest" or "single-issue" terrorists, whose adherents use violence to achieve one end.

Anti-abortion direct action in the United States dates to 1975, when six women in Rockville, Maryland, were arrested for the first clinic sit-in. Although violent incidents were relatively rare in the mid-1970s, the level of violence rose quickly.

In February 1977, an activist entered the Concern Women's Clinic in Cleveland, Ohio, and set fire to its interior after throwing flammable liquid in the receptionist's face. Two years later, Peter Burkin, then 21 years old, stormed into a Hempstead, New York, clinic with a two-foot flaming torch, threatening to "cleanse the soul" of the abortion provider, Dr. Bill Baird. (Baird was then known for his 1972 Supreme Court case that legalized the sale of contraceptives to unmarried couples.)

Early Organizations

By 1980, two of the most significant direct-action anti-abortion groups had been founded. Paul and Judie Brown, of Stafford, Virginia, started the American Life League (ALL) in 1979. A year later, Joseph Scheidler, widely considered to be the father of anti-abortion direct action, created the Pro-Life Action League (PLAL) in Chicago. The Browns and Scheidler were part of the National Right to Life Committee (NRLC), the largest anti-abortion group in the United States. Scheidler had been the executive director of the Illinois chapter of the NRLC from 1973 until he was dismissed in 1978 because of his radical tactics. Similarly, the Browns formed ALL to raise the level of direct action in their protests.

Bolstered by the conservative political climate of the 1980s, ALL and PLAL chapters, and other like-minded groups, sprung up around the country. Clinic violence and anti-abortion picketing were regular features on the news by the early 1980s. In January 1982, the Hope Clinic for Women in Granite City, Illinois, was gutted by fire. Four months later, the anti-abortion activist Don Benny Anderson set fire to two clinics in Florida. That August, Anderson and Matthew and Wayne Moore, who are brothers, kidnapped Dr. Hector Zevallos, of the Hope Clinic for Women, and held him, along with his wife, for eight days. During that time, Zevallos was ordered to make an anti-abortion tape to be sent to President Ronald Reagan in support of anti-*Roe* legislation. The kidnapping was the first of its kind and it was the debut action of the Army of God, a group that, by the end of the 1990s, would become one of the most feared in the country.

While clinic staffs were terrorized by the threat of more kidnappings, anti-abortion activists continued to disrupt clinics in increasingly creative ways.

Activists cut the hoses to abortion equipment in Toledo, Ohio, placed nails in parking lots in Ft. Lauderdale, Florida, called in bomb scares in Tulsa, Oklahoma, and successfully firebombed clinics in Washington, Maryland, and Florida. In 1984, activists twice bombed The Ladies Center, one of two abortion clinics in Pensacola, Florida, as part of a well-coordinated attack that included two private physician's offices. Despite the escalating violence, in December 1984, FBI Director William H. Webster claimed that clinic bombings did not conform to the federal definition of terrorism and were therefore not a federal priority.

The 1985 publication of Joseph Scheidler's direct action manual, *Closed: 99 Ways to Stop Abortion,* and Kevin Sherlock's *The Abortion Buster's Manual* encouraged anti-abortion forces. Sherlock's book focused on ways to identify and harass abortion providers, which had been pinpointed as the weak link in the abortion "industry." Activists were encouraged to search all public records for any evidence of malpractice, criminal history, or abortion-related deaths, which, if found, would be used as propaganda. Scheidler's volume discussed a number of actions that could create a maximum level of disruption at clinics, including aggressive sidewalk counseling techniques and full-scale clinic blockades. Scheidler included instructions for using license plates to identify individuals, both patients and staff, and obtaining personal contact information. Activists would later confront the individuals, "outing" doctors in public places or calling women at their homes.

One of Scheidler's protégés, Randall Terry, a former used-car salesman, began Operation Rescue, an anti-abortion group that was, for a time, the most active and successful in the movement. Founded in Binghamton, New York, in 1986, Operation Rescue focused its efforts on "rescues"—large-scale sit-ins and blockades in which hundreds of activists faced arrest. In 1987, the group engaged in its first major blockade at a clinic in Cherry Hill, New Jersey. The New Jersey "rescue" was followed by protests nearly every weekend thereafter through 1990, when Terry closed the Binghamton office and passed leadership of Operation Rescue to Rev. Keith Tucci. Under Tucci, in 1991, Operation Rescue conducted a seven-week occupation of three clinics in Wichita, Kansas, in which 1,734 people were arrested. Since 1988, Operation Rescue California, headed by Jeff White, had been waging some of the most aggressive rescue campaigns in the country, dubbed "No Place to Hide," in which doctors, nurses, and clinic staff were besieged with harassment.

The *Army of God Manual* advocated an array of tactics, from gluing locks and using foul-smelling butyric acid, sometimes referred to as "liquid rescue," to shut down clinics, to arson and bomb threats. The anti-abortion movement had previously used many of the tactics; however, the manual also contained step-by-step instructions for making plastic bombs, and, in a November 1992 epilogue, advocated the murder of abortion providers. (The *Army of God Manual* has undergone at least three clandestine reprintings.)

Moving on to Murder

On March 10, 1993, Michael Griffin, a 31-year-old chemical plant employee, shot and killed Dr. David Gunn as he entered the Pensacola Women's Medical Services clinic in Florida, while members of the anti-abortion group Rescue America protested outside. Griffin's actions quickly transformed the movement. Five months later, Rachelle "Shelley" Shannon, a prolific anti-abortion activist from Oregon who was linked to arson attacks in Eugene and Portland, Oregon, as well as butyric acid attacks in Reno, Nevada, and Chico, California, shot Dr. George Tiller in both arms as he left his Wichita, Kansas, clinic. (On August 21, 1993, Dr. George Wayne Patterson, owner of Pensacola Women's Medical Services, was shot to death in Mobile, Alabama. Although authorities attribute the murder to a botched robbery, many pro-choice activists believe this was another anti-abortion murder.) In February 1994, the FBI announced that it would begin investigating death threats received by abortion providers and clinic staff in several states, including Florida.

Anti-abortion groups now grappled with the choice of murder as an anti-abortion tactic, and with what that tactic meant for their movement. In April 1994, more than 80 anti-abortion leaders met in Chicago specifically to discuss the new level of violence. Among the attendees was the former Presbyterian minister Paul Hill, an extremely vocal proponent of anti-abortion violence. In July 1993, Hill had drafted a "Defensive Action Statement," in which he called Griffin's actions "justifiable homicide." Hill and those who supported his views split from the majority of anti-abortion leaders to form the American Coalition of Life Activists.

The following six months were among the most violent in the history of the anti-abortion movement. On the morning of July 29, 1994, Hill shot Dr. John Bayard Britton and his bodyguard to death outside the Ladies Center in Pensacola, Florida. That September, Michael Bray, a convicted clinic bomber, published *A Time to Kill,* in which he gave theological rationale for "justifiable homicide" in the anti-abortion battle. Three months later, on December 30, 1994, John Salvi III, a hairdresser, murdered two clinic receptionists outside a clinic in Brookline, Massachusetts. During this same period, anti-abortion forces engaged in significant violence, including bombings and arson, against 52 percent of all clinics in the United States. Similar violence was perpetrated concurrently in Canada, with several abortion doctors shot in their homes by snipers.

Legislative Responses

Many attribute the wave of violence in the 1990s to the change in the U.S. political climate caused by the election of President Bill Clinton in 1992. Clinton had rescinded many of the anti-*Roe* regulations put in place by the preceding Reagan and Bush administrations.

In May 1994, Clinton signed the Freedom of Access to Clinic Entrances (FACE) Act, which, by prohibiting the use or threat of force or physical obstruction that interferes with reproductive health services, created stronger legal protections for clinics. The FACE Act, along with two Supreme Court decisions—*Madsen v. Women's Health Center* and *Scheidler, et al. v. National Organization of Women, et al.,* which, respectively, established "buffer zones" around clinics and allowed anti-abortion groups to be investigated under federal racketeering charges—helped to prevent the spiral of violence the country experienced in 1994 from being repeated. Clinic violence dropped significantly over the next several years, though more moderate anti-abortion activism continued throughout the country.

In January 1997, after the anti-abortion activist Neal Horsley first posted the "Nuremberg Files"

on the Internet, anti-abortion violence experienced another surge. Sponsored by the American Coalition of Life Activists, the Nuremberg Files website listed the names and home addresses of over 200 abortion providers and clinic staff, with three possible statuses for each: still working, wounded, or dead. The information was used to target and terrorize abortion providers in their homes. The stalking of abortion providers, which had been declining steadily since 1994, increased, and within hours of the sniper murder of Dr. Barnett Slepian at his home in Amherst, New York, on October 23, 1998, Horsley put a line through Slepian's name.

Slepian's murder—as well as the first fatal clinic bombing, on January 29, 1998, in Birmingham, Alabama—seemed to mark a change in attitude among anti-abortion terrorists. Unlike Griffin and Hill, who willingly turned themselves over to police, becoming martyrs for the movement, both James Kopp, who was charged with Slepian's murder, and Eric Rudolph, charged with the Birmingham clinic and other Atlanta-area bombings, fled from the law. Kopp was eventually arrested in France in March 2001 and extradited the following year. In 2007, after a trial and numerous appeals, Kopp was sentenced to life in prison plus 10 years for killing Slepian. Rudolph, meanwhile, was captured in North Carolina in 2003 and pled guilty to numerous homicide charges. While both men had loose ties to anti-abortion and fundamentalist religious groups, they were considered to be loners by both sides of the abortion issue. Rudolph also exemplified an apparent convergence of anti-abortion and other right-wing movements, including racist and militia movements.

Following the murder of Slepian, the FBI, under the orders of Attorney General Janet Reno, began investigating anti-abortion groups for conspiracy, even though a grand jury in Alexandria, Virginia, had failed to deliver any indictments in a similar investigation two years earlier. Senior FBI officials expressed misgivings about the investigation, questioning the boundary between legitimate, if unpopular, political causes and criminal activity. Such federal ambivalence about pursuing anti-abortion violence has plagued pro-choice activists since the beginning of the abortion struggle.

By the year 2000, clinic violence had dropped considerably from its peak in 1994. Nonetheless,

Table 1 Incidents of Violence and Disruption Against Abortion Providers in the United States and Canada

VIOLENCE	1977–93	1994	1995	1996	1997	1998	1999	2000	2001	2002	2003	2004	2005	2006	2007	2008	2009*	TOTAL
Murder[1]	1	4	0	0	0	2	0	0	0	0	0	0	0	0	0	0	1	8
Attempted Murder	3	8	1	1	2	1	0	1	0	0	0	0	0	0	0	0	0	17
Bombing[1]	28	1	1	2	6	1	1	0	1	0	0	0	0	0	0	0	0	41
Arson[1]	113	11	14	3	8	4	8	2	2	1	3	2	2	0	2	0	0	175
Attempted Bomb/Arson[1]	61	3	1	4	2	5	1	3	2	0	0	1	6	4	2	1	1	97
Invasion	345	2	4	0	7	5	3	4	2	1	0	0	0	4	7	6	1	391
Vandalism	543	42	31	29	105	46	63	56	58	60	48	49	83	72	59	45	40	1429
Trespassing	0	0	0	0	0	0	193	81	144	163	66	67	633	336	122	148	104	2057
Butyric Acid Attacks	72	8	0	1	0	19	0	0	0	0	0	0	0	0	0	0	0	100
Anthrax Threats	0	0	0	0	0	12	35	30	554	23	0	1	77	0	1	0	2	661
Assault & Battery	88	7	2	1	9	4	2	7	2	1	7	8	8	11	12	6	9	184
Death Threats	166	59	41	13	11	25	13	9	14	3	7	4	10	10	13	2	16	416
Kidnapping	2	0	0	0	0	1	0	0	0	0	0	0	0	1	0	0	0	4
Burglary	31	3	3	6	6	6	4	5	6	1	9	5	11	30	12	7	12	157
Stalking[2]	188	22	61	52	67	13	13	17	10	12	3	15	8	6	19	19	1	526
TOTAL	1641	170	159	112	223	144	336	215	795	265	143	152	761	474	249	237	187	6263
DISRUPTION																		
Hate Mail/Harassing Calls	1452	381	255	605	2829	915	1646	1011	404	230	432	453	515	548	522	396	1699	14293
E-Mail/Internet Harassment	0	0	0	0	0	0	0	0	0	24	70	51	77	25	38	44	16	345
Hoax Device/Susp. Package	0	0	0	0	0	0	0	0	0	41	13	9	16	17	23	24	17	160
Bomb Threats	297	14	41	13	79	31	39	20	31	7	17	13	11	7	6	13	4	643
Picketing	6361	1407	1356	3932	7518	8402	8727	8478	9969	10241	11348	11640	13415	13505	11113	12503	8388	148303
TOTAL	8110	1802	1652	4550	10426	9348	10412	9509	10404	10543	11880	12166	14034	14102	11702	12980	10124	163744
CLINIC BLOCKADES																		
Number of Incidents	609	25	5	7	25	2	3	4	2	0	10	34	4	13	7	8	1	763
Number of Arrests[3]	33444	217	54	65	29	16	5	0	0	0	0	0	0	0	3	1	0	33834

Source: National Abortion Federation. Reprinted by permission.

Notes: All numbers represent incidents reported to or obtained by NAF. Actual incidents are likely much higher. Tabulation of trespassing began in 1999 and tabulation of e-mail harassment and hoax devices began in 2002.

1. Incidents recorded are those classified as such by the appropriate law enforcement agency. Incidents that were ruled inconclusive or accidental are not included.

2. Stalking is defined as the persistent following, threatening, and harassing of an abortion provider, staff member, or patient away from the clinic. Tabulation of stalking incidents began in 1993.

3. The "number of arrests" represents the total number of arrests, not the total number of persons arrested. Many blockaders are arrested multiple times.

* Through December 2009.

every year at least one in five abortion clinics has a serious violent incident, including vandalism, arson, death threats, and assaults. Further, a new trend in anti-abortion terrorism began in 1997—anthrax hoaxes. Mimicking the anthrax-contaminated letters of October 2001, over 550 hoax anthrax letters were sent to abortion clinics and advocacy groups throughout the country, many of them signed "Army of God, Virginia Dare Chapter," or "Virginia Dare Cell." In December 2001, authorities arrested Clayton Lee Waagner, an anti-abortion activist, who confessed to sending the letters.

After years of comparative quiet, Dr. George Tiller was shot and killed while attending church in Wichita, Kansas, on May 31, 2009. Tiller had long been a lightning rod for the anti-abortion movement, as he was one of an ever-dwindling number of doctors willing to perform late-term abortions in a clinic setting. In addition to the attack by Shannon in 1993, pro-life groups had protested Tiller for years. His clinic had been blockaded, vandalized, and even fire-bombed. Tiller's murderer, Scott Roeder, was convicted after a 37-minute deliberation by a jury in January 2010. Several months later, Roeder was sentenced to life in prison (without parole for the first 50 years), the maximum allowable under Kansas law. Some mainstream anti-abortion groups, such as the National Right to Life Committee, condemned the murder, but Randall Terry told reporters that Doctor Tiller had "reaped what he sowed."

Laura Lambert

See also Army of God; Griffin, Michael Frederick; Hill, Paul Jennings; Rudolph, Eric

Further Readings

Baird-Windle, Patricia, and Eleanor J. Bader. *Targets of Hatred: Anti-abortion Terrorism*. New York: Palgrave Macmillan, 2001.

Blanchard, Dallas A. *The Anti-abortion Movement and the Rise of the Religious Right: From Polite to Fiery Protest*. New York: G.K. Hall, 1996.

Joffe, Carole. *Dispatches from the Abortion Wars: The Costs of Fanaticism to Doctors, Patients, and the Rest of Us*. Boston: Beacon Press, 2010.

Kurst-Swanger, Karl. *Worship and Sin: An Exploration of Religion-related Crime in the United States*. New York: Peter Lang, 2008.

Reiter, Jerry. *Live from the Gates of Hell: An Insider's Look at the Antiabortion Underground*. Amherst, NY: Prometheus Books, 2000.

Risen, James, and Judy L. Thomas. *Wrath of Angels: The American Abortion War*. New York: Basic Books, 1998.

Rose, Melody. *Safe, Legal, and Unavailable? Abortion Politics in the United States*. Washington, DC: CQ Press, 2006.

Singular, Steven. *The Wichita Divide: The Murder of Dr. George Tiller, the Battle over Abortion, and the New Civil War*. New York: St. Martin's, 2011.

Solinger, Rickie. *Abortion Wars: A Half Century of Struggle, 1950–2000*. Berkeley: University of California Press, 1998.

Vollers, Maryanne. *Lone Wolf: Eric Rudolph and the Legacy of American Terror*. New York: HarperPerennial, 2008.

Wells, Jon. *Sniper: The True Story of Anti-abortion Killer James Kopp*. Mississauga, Ontario: Wiley, 2008.

APRIL 19

Terrorists have been known to time their attacks to coincide with the anniversary of a particular historical event or the birthday of someone special to them. The date can even be the anniversary of a past terrorist or terrorist-related event. One example is October 16, the annual "Worldwide Day of Action Against McDonald's," which was started in 1984 to coincide with United Nations' World Food Day. On that date, activists target McDonald's restaurants as a protest against animal cruelty, the exploitation of workers, and the global domination of corporations. However, the most infamous of these terror anniversaries by far is April 19.

On April 19, 1993, the 51-day siege at David Koresh's Branch Davidian compound near Waco, Texas, ended, when Koresh and 75 followers, including 21 children, perished in a fire. Known as the Mount Carmel Center, the compound was occupied by members of an apocalyptic religious cult led by Koresh. It was rumored that the compound contained an arsenal of explosives and weapons. After the siege ended in tragedy, April 19 became known as the "Date of Doom" or "Militia Day." The militia movement, made up of armed paramilitary groups, exploded on the scene in the mid-1990s, sparked by a belief that the American public needed protection against a tyrannical federal government controlled by international interests.

The significance of April 19 dates back even further, however. April 19, 1775, is the date of the Battle of Lexington, which ushered in the American Revolution, while April 19, 1943, was the day Nazis turned flame-throwers on apartment buildings and gunned down Jews in the Warsaw Ghetto. Adding to the presumed significance of the date is that Adolph Hitler's birthday is the following day. These events are celebrated anniversaries within extremist camps within the United States. They have come to symbolize the beginning of a pure Aryan society within North America and an attempt to exterminate the Jews, who are viewed as something less than human by neo-Nazis and Aryan extremists of all stripes.

In addition to the events mentioned above, April 19, 1992, was the day that surveillance of the Randy Weaver family atop Ruby Ridge, Idaho, began. Weaver, a white separatist, was wanted by federal marshals for failing to appear in court on a weapons charge. The stakeout ended tragically with the deaths of Weaver's son, Sammy, his wife, Vicki, and a federal officer, William Degan. Further, on April 19, 1995, Richard Wayne Snell, a white supremacist and member of The Covenant, the Sword, and the Arm of the Lord (CSA), a Christian Identity paramilitary group, was executed for the 1983 murder of a Texarkana pawnshop owner.

However, the most famous event to take place on April 19 was the 1995 bombing of the Alfred P. Murrah Federal Building in Oklahoma City, in which 168 individuals lost their lives. Many believe that Timothy McVeigh, who was executed for carrying out the bombing, selected April 19 to take revenge against the U.S. government for its role in the Waco and Ruby Ridge tragedies, as well as the upcoming execution of Snell.

Terrorists commemorate anniversaries with further attacks, primarily as a way of wringing every possible drop of publicity out of their actions. Scheduling an operation on the anniversary of a past one almost certainly guarantees press coverage, even if the new operation is a rather insignificant one. Counterterrorism experts have therefore learned to keep an eye on the calendar when trying to anticipate terrorists' next moves.

Harvey Kushner

See also Branch Davidian Compound Siege; Covenant, the Sword and the Arm of the Lord, The; McVeigh, Timothy James; Oklahoma City Bombing; Snell, Richard Wayne; White Supremacy Movement

Further Readings

Dees, Morris, with James Corcoran. *Gathering Storm: America's Militia Threat.* New York: HarperCollins, 1996.

Hamm, Mark S. *Apocalypse in Oklahoma: Waco and Ruby Ridge Revenged.* Boston: Northeastern University Press, 1997.

Oklahoma Today, comp. *The Official Record of the Oklahoma City Bombing.* Norman: University of Oklahoma Press, 2005.

Southern Poverty Law Center. *False Patriots: The Threat of Antigovernment Extremists.* Montgomery, AL: Southern Poverty Law Center, 1996.

Torpy, Bill. "Heat Still on Domestic Terror Groups: FBI Scrutinizes Homegrown Extremists." *Atlanta Journal Constitution,* April 19, 2003, p. A5.

ARAB REVOLUTIONARY BRIGADE

See Abu Nidal Organization

ARAFAT, YASIR (1929–2004)

During his lengthy tenure as a Palestinian leader, Yasir Arafat (aka Abu Ammar) played many roles, from terrorist to recipient of the Nobel Peace Prize. While serving a chairman of the Palestine Liberation Organization (PLO) and leader of the Palestinian Authority, Arafat remained an iconic figure, as famous for his fiery speeches as for sporting an unshaven chin and a checkered *kaffiyeh,* always shaped into a point to symbolize the map of Palestine.

Although Arafat, whose nom de guerre is Abu Ammar, cooperated with many biographers and gave countless interviews, many details of his life are uncertain. No consensus exists on his date or place of birth, for instance. His birth certificate shows he was born Mohammed Abder Rauf Arafat al Kudwa al Husseini in Cairo on August 24, 1929;

Arafat maintained that he was born in Jerusalem on August 4, 1929, however. The sixth of seven children, he spent his early years in Cairo. His mother died when he was four, and Arafat and his younger brother were sent to live with an uncle in Jerusalem. He later returned to Cairo when his father, a Palestinian wholesale trader, remarried.

Arafat was active in politics from an early age, working as an aide for a relative in the Palestinian national movement. Before he entered his twenties, he was involved in smuggling guns from Egypt to Palestine. During his first years as an engineering student at Cairo University, he worked to organize fellow Palestinian students. In 1948 he left school to fight for Palestine as a volunteer in the first Arab-Israeli war.

After the Arab defeat, Arafat returned to Cairo. He later told biographers that he was so devastated that he considered abandoning the cause. He toyed with the idea of traveling to the United States to finish his studies, and even applied for a visa. Instead, he returned to the university in Cairo and decided to stay in Egypt. He continued to organize, and in 1952 he was elected president of the Union of Palestinian Students, and he created a student magazine called *The Voice of Palestine.*

Arafat later left Egypt for Kuwait, where he worked as a construction and contacting engineer. In 1957 he and his closest colleagues formed an underground movement, which became the first cell of his al Fatah group, which advocated an armed struggle for Palestine carried out by Palestinians themselves, not by other Arab countries and their armies. The group published a magazine, *Our Palestine: The Call to Life,* that called for the eradication of Israel. The publication helped al Fatah draw in new members, and Arafat gained the support of the Syrian government. With this backing, Fatah mounted its first raid into Israel in 1965. The group continued to infiltrate and attack Israel, crossing from Lebanon and Jordan. Arafat is said to have used multiple disguises when traveling, including that of an Egyptian tourist, a Pakistani businessman, and a shepherd.

In June 1967, Israel defeated Egypt, Syria, and Jordan in what has become known as the Six-Day War. Israel then occupied the Sinai Peninsula, the Golan Heights, the Gaza Strip, and the West Bank, forcing many Palestinians to become refugees. Arafat and other top Fatah leaders worked quickly to recruit displaced Palestinians. Fatah increased the number of its raids, attacking Israel from Jordan, Lebanon, and Syria. Arafat and about 300 fighters set up a base in the town of Karameh, on the road between the West Bank and Jordan.

Israeli forces counterattacked Fatah bases and the homes of suspected terrorists. In March 1968, Israeli forces struck Karameh, in what was said to be the biggest single military action since the end of the Six-Day War. Fatah, backed by Jordanian artillery, held off the attack. Although Fatah had suffered many losses, Arafat celebrated the battle as a tactical victory, and many in the Arab world saw it as some remediation of the devastating 1967 defeat. At the same time, Fatah's ranks swelled. Arafat, already wearing his trademark *kaffiyeh,* became a famous symbol of Palestine and Palestinians, appearing on the cover of *Time* in December 1968.

In 1969, Fatah joined and gained control of the Palestine Liberation Organization (PLO), the coordinating body for Palestinian groups, and Arafat was elected chairman of the organization's executive committee. The PLO's primary bases of operation at this time were Palestinian refugee camps in eastern Jordan. The group suffered a major setback in September 1970, after members of the Popular Front for the Liberation of Palestine hijacked four international airliners and forced them to land outside of Amman, Jordan. Once the crisis was resolved, King Hussein of Jordan launched an offensive against the Palestinian forces, which were seen to be undermining the Jordanian government. PLO forces were defeated in the 10 days of fighting now called "Black September." Arafat reportedly fled Amman disguised as an Arab woman, and he and the PLO fighters were expelled from Jordan and settled in Lebanon.

After this setback, the remnants of the PLO staged further terror attacks to bring international attention to the situation of Palestinians. During the 1972 Olympics in Munich, Germany, 11 Israeli team members were killed in an attack perpetrated by an extremist group within al Fatah calling itself "Black September."

In November 1974, dressed in military fatigues and with a holstered gun on his hip, Arafat addressed the United Nations General Assembly in New York. He told the Assembly that he came "bearing an olive branch and a freedom fighter's gun." Diplomats from countries sympathetic to the PLO gave him a friendly reception, and by 1977 more than 100 nations had given the PLO diplomatic recognition.

Arafat and the PLO spent 11 years in Lebanon, which was home to many Palestinian refugees. However, the PLO's presence added to the strife among different groups in Lebanon and helped fuel the Lebanese civil war. The Israeli Defense Minister, Gen. Ariel Sharon, advocated the destruction of the PLO. When Israel invaded Lebanon in 1982, Arafat and many PLO guerrillas evacuated Beirut under international guarantees of safety. Just two weeks after their departure, a militia of Lebanese Christians allied with Israel massacred hundreds of unarmed Palestinian refugees in the city's Sabra and Shatila refugee camps. Many Palestinians have never forgiven Arafat for evacuating and leaving those in the camps unprotected.

In 1983, senior al Fatah officials broke with Arafat. With Syrian backing, they attacked Arafat and his fighters in Tripoli, Lebanon. Arafat and his troops were evacuated and PLO forces were dispersed throughout Tunisia, Yemen, Algeria, Jordan, Iraq, and Syria. Arafat moved PLO headquarters to Tunis, Tunisia. In 1985, members of Force 17, Arafat's personal security squad, killed three Israelis on a hijacked yacht at Larnaca, Cyprus. The PLO claimed that the men were members of Mossad, Israel's secret intelligence service. Israel responded by bombing PLO headquarters; 65 people were killed, but Arafat was unharmed.

In the late 1980s, Arafat began strong and effective negotiations for peace. What motivated Arafat's shift to a political strategy—and, indeed, whether it was a sincere shift on Arafat's part or merely a smokescreen to hide terrorist activities—is a matter of heated debate. Many experts point to Arafat's plane crash in the Libyan desert in October 1992 as an essential turning point. Arafat may also have become more aware of his own vulnerability due to the assassination of some of his comrades: Khalil al Wazir, the head of the PLO terrorist operations against Israel, was killed by Mossad, Israel's intelligence service, in Tunis in 1988, while Salah Khalef, a PLO intelligence officer and key figure in al Fatah, and Hayil Abd al Hamid, the security chief of al Fatah, were both killed in 1991 by the rival Abu Nidal Organization

in a campaign of inter-Palestinian fratricide stemming from Saddam Hussein's invasion of Kuwait. Arafat's own encroaching age may also have been a factor in his shift toward a political solution.

Speaking in Stockholm in 1988, Arafat declared that the PLO accepted the existence of Israel. Under his leadership, the PLO accepted UN Security Council Resolution 242, which had laid out the basis for Middle East peace negotiations two decades before, and agreed that Israel had a right to coexist with Palestine. Later that year, Arafat spoke before a special session of the United Nations General Assembly in Geneva and called on Israel to join peace talks. The following day, President Ronald Reagan of the United States authorized the start of what he called a "substantive dialogue" with the PLO, saying that it had met the U.S. conditions.

As Arafat became an ever more public figure, he increasingly kept his private life hidden. Arafat was seen by the press as a notorious bachelor, famous for saying, "I am married to all the women of Palestine." In fact, Arafat was secretly married in 1990, to Suha al Taweel, a Paris-educated Christian. She converted to Islam but is still not entirely accepted by some extremists inside the Arafat camp. Arafat didn't publicly admit to the marriage until 1992.

As the PLO advocated a more moderate stance and worked to join in diplomatic negotiations, Arafat's leadership came under fire from militant Palestinian groups, including Hamas and Abu Nidal's breakaway Fatah Revolutionary Council, both of which supported a build up of Palestinian military strength.

Arafat would again become persona non grata in the United States when he stridently supported Iraq during the Persian Gulf War. During the war, many Arab countries stopped supporting the PLO financially and began supporting the more extreme group (and Fatah rival) Hamas, instead.

In 1993 Arafat took part in secret meetings with Israeli diplomats in Oslo, Norway. These meetings culminated in the signing of the 1993 PLO-Israel Declaration of Principles. After signing the declaration in Washington on September 13, Arafat and Prime Minister Yitzhak Rabin of Israel shook hands on the White House lawn—an unprecedented and historic moment. In 1994 Arafat was awarded the Nobel Peace Prize, along with Rabin and Israeli foreign minister Shimon Peres. During the same year, Arafat signed the Gaza-Jericho accord and returned to the Gaza Strip after 27 years in exile.

In January 1996 Arafat was elected president of the Palestinian Authority, which governed the West Bank and Gaza Strip. Two years later, during negotiations at the Wye River Plantation in Maryland, he and Israeli Prime Minister Benjamin Netanyahu signed an agreement that guaranteed the return of an additional 13 percent of West Bank land to Palestinian control.

In 2000 Arafat walked away from negotiations with Israeli Prime Minister Ehud Barak at Camp David in the United States. Peace negotiations reached a stalemate in the years that followed. In December 2001, responding to a series of suicide bombings committed by the al Aqsa Martyrs Brigades, which many experts believed to be under Arafat's control, the Israeli military began a siege of Ramallah on the West Bank. Arafat was trapped in the city and then confined to his headquarters. He remained in his compound until May 2, 2002, when he and his staff were released as part of an international agreement that required the convicted murderers of an Israeli minister serve time in a Palestinian jail, supervised by the United States and Britain.

The United States government was often disappointed with Arafat's leadership, but U.S. administrations were usually willing to work with him in pursuit of a political solution—he was, after all, the elected president of the Palestinian Authority. Others accused Arafat of hypocrisy, saying that he claimed to be in favor of peace but consistently failed to discipline those who perpetrated acts of terror. Some experts doubted Arafat's ability to govern the violent elements of his community, while others questioned his desire to do so.

Arafat died in 2004 while receiving medical treatment in a Paris suburb for a mysterious illness. Controversial even in death, rumors swirled that Arafat might have had the flu, AIDS, or even been poisoned by Israel's Mossad. Leaked reports of Arafat's confidential medical records suggested that cirrhosis of the liver might have been the true culprit; observers suggested that the illness's association with alcoholism in the public mind was the true motivation for all the secrecy. (Arafat was not known to have consumed alcohol, and not all cases of cirrhosis are caused by it.)

Mahmoud Abbas succeeded Arafat as the chairman of the PLO, but the years following Arafat's death have been marked by vicious infighting between various Palestinian groups, with Hamas and Fatah struggling violently for domination. So far, no leader has emerged who comes close to possessing Arafat's ability to maintain an equilibrium between the many competing factions.

Erica Pearson

See also al Aqsa Martyrs Brigades; al Asifa; Fatah; Force 17; Munich Olympics Massacre; Palestine Liberation Organization

Further Readings

Abukhalil, Asad. "Arab Israeli Conflict." In *The Middle East,* edited by Robin Surratt. 9th ed. Washington DC: CQ Press, 2000.

Aburish, Said K. *Arafat: From Defender to Dictator.* New York: Bloomsbury, 1998.

Gowers, Andrew. *Behind the Myth: Arafat, the biography.* London: Virgin, 1994.

Hart, Alan. *Arafat: A Political Biography.* London: Sidgwick & Jackson, 1994.

Kiernan, Thomas. *Arafat, The Man and the Myth.* New York: Norton, 1976.

Mishal, Shaul. *The PLO under Arafat: Between Gun and Olive Branch.* New Haven, CT: Yale University Press, 1986.

Rubinstein, Danny. *The Mystery of Arafat.* South Royalton, VT: Steerforth Press, 1995.

Sontag, Deborah. "The Palestinian Conversation." *The New York Times Magazine,* February 3, 2002.

"Talking with the PLO; The P.L.O.: From Birth through Terrorism to Dialogue with the U.S." *The New York Times,* December 16, 1988.

Walker, Tony, and Andrew Bowers. *Arafat: The Biography.* London: Virgin Books, 2003.

Wallach, Janet, and John Wallach. *Arafat: In the Eyes of the Beholder.* Rev. ed. Secaucus, NJ: Carol Publishing Group, 1997.

ARMED FORCES OF NATIONAL LIBERATION

See FALN

ARMED ISLAMIC FRONT

The Armed Islamic Front (aka Algerian Jihad Islamic Front) is the military wing of Algeria's largest opposition party, the Islamic Salvation Front (FIS). In January 1992, the Algerian military cancelled a second round of elections that the banned FIS was likely to win; in response, the Armed Islamic Front began a campaign of terror. Members of the Armed Islamic Front and other Islamic militant groups first carried out bombings and killings targeting government institutions and security forces, but the violence soon spilled over into attacks on civilians, foreigners, journalists, and intellectuals. More than 100,000 people were killed in these attacks.

As civil order in Algeria continued to disintegrate, the Islamic opposition splintered into a confusing array of groups. The Armed Islamic Front is generally considered to be the same group as the Jihad Armed Islamic Front, or Armed Islamic Front for the Jihad. The international press also sometimes refers to the Armed Islamic Front with the Islamic Salvation Front's acronym FIS. The Front, said to be slightly more moderate than the radical and better-known Armed Islamic Group (GIA), gained a reputation for targeting intellectuals and public figures.

Most of the massacres and car bombings in Algeria's bloody conflict have been attributed to GIA, the most extreme Islamic organization. GIA has become known for kidnapping victims and slitting their throats. However, international analysts have raised the possibility of Algerian military infiltration of such groups, and the military may therefore be responsible for many of the deaths.

When a deadly car bomb exploded at the press headquarters in the capital city of Algiers on February 11, 1996, killing 21 people, including two journalists and a chief editor of *Soir d'Algerie*, authorities at first suspected the GIA; however, the Armed Islamic Front was later shown to be the perpetrator.

In March 1997, Algerian security forces killed Armed Islamic Front leader Abdelkadur Seddouki. During the same week, security forces assassinated the prominent GIA member Yihad Riane in his apartment. The international press reported that the killings were part of a government campaign to crack down on militants before local elections. In September 1997, the Armed Islamic Front publicly urged Islamic militants to honor a truce proposed by the government. However, according to press reports, during the very weekend that the Front called for peace, members of the GIA killed at least 30 civilians.

Abdelaziz Bouteflika became president of Algeria in 1999 and offered an amnesty to Algerian militants not directly implicated in rape or murder. In response, thousands of fighters, including many Armed Islamic Front members, laid down their weapons.

Erica Pearson

See also Armed Islamic Group

Further Readings

Bowker, Hilary. "No End in Site to Algerian Conflict; Expert Gives Insight." *CNN Worldview*, September 29, 1997.

Evans, Martin, and John Phillips. *Algeria: Anger of the Dispossessed.* New Haven, CT: Yale University Press, 2007.

Huband, Mark. *Warriors of the Prophet: the Struggle for Islam.* Boulder, CO: Westview Press, 1998.

ARMED ISLAMIC GROUP

The Armed Islamic Group (GIA, aka al Jama'ah al Islamiyah al Musallah; GIA; Groupement Islamique Arme) is an extremist Islamic organization bent on overthrowing Algeria's military-backed regime and creating an Islamic state. The Algerian government has accused Iran and Sudan of supporting the GIA and other Algerian extremist groups.

The GIA began a terror campaign in 1992 after the Algerian army declared a state of emergency and blocked an election that the Islamic Salvation Front (FIS), Algeria's largest opposition party, appeared certain to win. More than 100,000 people were killed in the civil conflict that followed.

The GIA (the French acronym for Groupement Islamique Arme) has carried out scores of attacks against civilians—targeting journalists, foreign residents, and government workers. The GIA wiped out entire villages during its campaign of civilian massacres. The group uses tactics such as assassinations and car bombings and is known for kidnapping victims and slitting their throats. However, international analysts have cautioned that the GIA may have been manipulated and infiltrated by the Algerian military, and that some attacks attributed to the group may not be its responsibility.

In 1993 the GIA announced a campaign against foreigners living in Algeria. Group operatives have since killed more than 100 foreign nationals—both men and women. In December 1994, GIA members hijacked Air France Flight 8969 to Algiers. Two years later, GIA operatives claimed responsibility for a wave of bombings in Paris and Lyon, France, that killed 12 and wounded more than 200. Several GIA members were later convicted in France of the attacks.

During the spring of 1996, seven monks were kidnapped from the Our Lady of the Atlas monastery, located south of Algiers. More than two months later, Moroccan radio broadcast a communiqué said to be from the GIA, stating, "We have cut the throats of the seven monks." Later press reports noted evidence that the Algerian military may have been involved, perhaps in an attempt to sabotage negotiations between the French government and Islamic militants.

When President Abdelaziz Bouteflika came to power in Algeria in 1999, he offered an amnesty to Algerian militants who were not directly implicated in murder. Thousands of fighters surrendered their weapons, but violence continued to wrack the country. GIA leader Antar Zouabri called on GIA members to reject the offer of amnesty. In February 2002, Algerian security forces assaulted a GIA hideout and killed Zouabri. Algerian authorities had declared Zouabri dead many times before, but this report appears to be accurate. Since then, GIA leadership has only stayed in place for a short time before being arrested or killed by Algerian police. For example, one GIA leader, Boulenouar Oukil, was arrested in April 2005 after GIA ambushed and killed 14 civilians at a fake roadblock outside Algiers.

The Salafist Group for Preaching and Combat (GSPC), a splinter faction of GIA thought to be aligned with al Qaeda, largely eclipsed its parent organization. Assessments by the U.S. State Department call the GSPC the most effective remaining armed group inside Algeria. The group rechristened itself as al Qaeda in the Islamic Maghreb, emphasizing its supposed ties with Osama bin Laden's organization. The GIA, meanwhile, seems to have been largely broken up, due to the intense efforts of the Algerian army. As of 2005, the Algerian government reported that there were fewer than 800 terrorists active in the country. Yet another GIA leader, Rachid Abou Tourab, was arrested in 2008.

Erica Pearson

See also al Qaeda; al Qaeda in the Islamic Maghreb; Armed Islamic Front

Further Readings

Evans, Martin, and John Phillips. *Algeria: Anger of the Dispossessed.* New Haven, CT: Yale University Press, 2007.

Gerges, Fawaz A. *The Far Enemy: Why Jihad Went Global.* Cambridge, UK: Cambridge University Press, 2009.

Touati, Abdelmalek. "Algerian Terrorist Reported Slain; Leader of Radical Islamic Group Was Nation's 'Most Wanted.'" *Washington Post,* February 10, 2002.

U.S. State Department. "Armed Islamic Group." In *Country Reports on Terrorism 2004,* 95. Department of State Publication 11248. Washington, DC: Office of the Coordinator for Counterterrorism, 2005. http://www.state.gov/documents/organization/45313.pdf.

Vriens, Lauren. "Armed Islamic Group." Council on Foreign Relations website. http://www.cfr.org/publication/9154/armed_islamic_group_algeria_islamists.html.

ARMED REVOLUTIONARY NUCLEI

See Ordine Nuovo

ARMENIAN SECRET ARMY FOR THE LIBERATION OF ARMENIA

The Armenian Secret Army for the Liberation of Armenia (ASALA) was a terrorist group formed in 1975 to force Turkey to admit its guilt for the Armenian genocide of 1915. In that year, the government of what is now Turkey engaged in a deliberate campaign to expel the Christian Armenian minority from their homes, resulting in an Armenian diaspora that continues to this day.

The current Turkish government insists that this campaign was not a genocide, while Armenians contend that 1.5 million of their compatriots were massacred. ASALA's stated goals were to force the Turkish government to acknowledge the genocide, pay reparations, and support the creation of an Armenian state. The group was founded in 1975 by Hagop Hagopian, a Lebanese-born Armenian who had become involved with Palestinian resistance groups in the early 1970s. Some sources claim that Hagopian was a member of the Popular Front for the Liberation of Palestine (PFLP), and that the PFLP helped fund the Armenian group. Like the PFLP, ASALA was Marxist in ideology.

ASALA started with six or seven members, and at the height of its support, in the early 1980s, it may have had about 100 active members and sympathizers. ASALA's first attack was the bombing of the World Council of Churches office in Beirut, Lebanon, in January 1975; no one was hurt in the attack. The group's next attack, the assassination of Oktay Cirit, the first secretary of the Turkish embassy in Beirut, in 1976, established assassination as a primary tactic. Throughout the late 1970s and early 1980s, ASALA perpetuated a series of attacks on Turkish diplomats around the world— more than 30 diplomats and members of their families were assassinated between 1975 and 1984. (Another Armenian terrorist group, the Justice Commandoes of the Armenian Genocide [JCAG], which later became the Armenian Revolutionary Army [ARA], also carried out assassinations during this period.)

The assassination campaign attracted international attention to the claimed Armenian genocide, and by 1980 ASALA had begun to receive considerable clandestine support from the Armenian community in the United States and Europe. Unlike JCAG/ARA, ASALA also carried out dozens of bombings. Between 1980 and 1982, ASALA initiated several bombing campaigns in Switzerland and France with the aim of freeing comrades imprisoned in those countries; the bombings injured dozens of people, and several terrorists were released from prison in response.

More often, however, ASALA targeted Turkish institutions. Its most devastating attacks were made at the Ankara Esenboga Airport in Ankara, Turkey, on August 7, 1982, and at the Turkish Airlines counter at France's Orly Airport on July 15, 1983. Eighteen people were killed and more than 120 injured in these two attacks.

When Israel invaded Lebanon in June 1982, ASALA was forced to flee its Beirut headquarters. This shakeup exacerbated tensions within the group, and following the Orly attack, the ASALA split in two. One faction, which felt that the group's attacks on civilians were hurting its cause, labeled itself the ASALA Revolutionary Movement (ASALA-RM) and vowed to pursue a more openly political path; the second faction, led by Hagopian, remained committed to terrorist tactics and associated itself with the Abu Nidal Organization. The split weakened both groups considerably, and the number of their attacks declined drastically. In 1988 Hagopian was killed in Athens, Greece. He is believed to have been assassinated by Turkish agents. ASALA's steady decline only worsened after his death, and, despite 1991 and 1994 attacks claimed by the group, most observers believed that by the early twenty-first century the group no longer posed a threat.

Colleen Sullivan

See also Abu Nidal Organization; Popular Front for the Liberation of Palestine

Further Readings

Bal, Idris, ed. *Turkish Foreign Policy in the Post Cold War Era.* Boca Raton, FL: Brown Walker Press, 2004.

Foreman, Adrian. "Turks Deny Killing Armenian Activist: Faction Fighting Blamed for Assassination of Agopian." *The Guardian,* April 30, 1988.

Gunter, Michael M. *"Pursuing the Just Cause of Their People": A Study of Contemporary Armenian Terrorism.* New York: Greenwood Press, 1986.

Melkonian, Markar. *My Brother's Road: An American's Fateful Journey to Armenia.* New York: I.B. Tauris, 2005.

Army for the Liberation of Rwanda

See Democratic Front for the Liberation of Rwanda

ARMY OF GOD

In the early 1980s, a shadowy group calling itself the Army of God emerged in the anti-abortion movement. While the group has often been linked to threatening or violent acts, investigators believe that it does not necessarily represent an organized group but has instead become an umbrella label for some extremists. However, many pro-choice advocates maintain that there is a conspiracy among the more violent factions of the anti-abortion movement, arguing that if the Army of God did not start as an organized group, certainly the vast networking capability spurred by the World Wide Web has given it some cohesion.

The group first surfaced in 1982, when it claimed responsibility for the kidnapping of an Illinois doctor and his wife, and for the firebombing of two Florida abortion clinics. Authorities eventually arrested three men in the case. Don Benny Anderson, the ringleader in the abduction and the founder of the group, told investigators he was acting on orders from God and the Archangel Michael. Although authorities originally believed the group consisted of only these three men, subsequent anti-abortion activity throughout the following decades, including fires and explosions in several abortion clinics, has been attributed to the group. The Army of God has also sent threatening letters to prominent figures such as Supreme Court justice Harry A. Blackmun, the author of the landmark *Roe v. Wade* decision that legalized abortion.

The name "Army of God" became more widely known in 1997, when it was signed on letters claiming credit for the bombings of an abortion clinic and a gay nightclub in Atlanta. Examination of the letters in these cases, however, led investigators to believe that the suspect had a larger agenda than abortion and was more antigovernment and militia-like. These incidents were eventually linked to the highly publicized Olympic Park bombing in 1996 and the bombing of a Birmingham, Alabama clinic in 1998. The suspect named in the case, Eric Robert Rudolph, was found to have links with followers of Christian Identity, a racist, anti-Semitic, anti-abortion, and anti-gay ideology.

Some experts theorize that it is becoming more common for anti-abortion proponents to be taking a militant antigovernment stance. Since the 1994 Freedom of Access to Clinic Entrances Act, which made it illegal to obstruct access to reproductive health clinics, the number of clinic blockades and arrests decreased dramatically, while violent abortion-related crimes increased.

Also in 1994, the *Army of God Manual* surfaced. Similar to one found a year earlier buried in the yard of a woman convicted for the attempted murder of a doctor, the manual outlines methods for causing disruption at what it calls "abortuaries." It offers suggestions on how to use the putrid-smelling butyric acid to disrupt activities, and it encourages violent acts like cutting off the thumbs of doctors and firebombing clinics. The manual became a focus of a federal grand jury investigation into the possibility of a conspiracy. Abortion rights activists testified that many of the methods described in the book have been used to disrupt clinics throughout the country, and many vandals have tagged the letters "AOG" on abortion clinic walls. The grand jury found no evidence, however, of a nationwide conspiracy.

The possibility of a conspiracy became evident again in the autumn of 2001. A spate of letters to reproductive health clinics and professionals threatening anthrax exposure were credited to the Army of God. Clayton Lee Waagner, an escapee from an Illinois jail, was arrested in December of that year and admitted to mailing more than 500 anthrax hoax letters in two waves, in late October and November. The extent of Waagner's fear campaign while a fugitive from justice has made many people, including some authorities, suspect that he was receiving aid while on the run. Some authorities also think he may have had an associate working with him in the anthrax hoax. He did manage to keep in contact with many supporters of the anti-abortion movement by posting messages on the "Army of God" website. Donald Spitz, who maintains the site, claims to not know if anyone aided Waagner, and he expressed disappointment in Waagner's capture.

Likewise, other anti-abortion extremists affiliated with the Army of God have evaded authorities for extended periods of time. Eric Rudolph, who bombed two abortion clinics as well as the 1996 Summer Olympics in Atlanta, hid out from law enforcement in the mountains of North Carolina for five years before he was captured in 2003. Letters were sent to news outlets following Rudolph's clinic bombings claiming that the attacks were the work of the Army of God. While Rudolph was an experienced outdoorsman, the amount of time he was able to survive and evade the police has raised the possibility that he had organized assistance.

Nancy Egan

See also Anthrax; Anti-Abortion Terrorism; Rudolph, Eric

Further Readings

Carman, Diane. "Terror Outrage Lacking in Rudolph Case." *Denver Post*, June 8, 2003, p. B1.

Cole, Leonard A. *The Anthrax Letter: A Bioterrorism Expert Investigates the Attacks That Shocked America.* New York: Skyhorse, 2009.

Cooperman, Alan. "Is Terrorism Tied to Christian Sect? Religion May Have Motivated Bombing Suspect." *The Washington Post*, June 2, 2003, p. A3.

Jacoby, Mary. "Domestic Terrorist: Waagner on the Run." *St. Petersburg Times*, August 5, 2002, p. 1A.

Juergensmeyer, Mark. *Terror in the Mind of God: The Global Rise of Religious Violence.* Berkeley: University of California Press, 2001.

Kifner, John. "The Nation; Finding a Common Foe, Fringe Groups Join Forces." *The New York Times*, December 6, 1998.

Kressel, Neil J. *Bad Faith: The Danger of Religious Extremism.* Amherst, NY: Prometheus Books, 2007.

Martz, Ron, and Kathy Scruggs. "Atlanta Bombings: Looking for Answers; Agents Skeptical of Letter's Claims, Writer's Identity; 'Army of God' Claim Is Doubtful, Could Be a Ruse." *Atlanta Journal and Constitution*, February 27, 1997.

Nifong, Christina. "Anti-abortion Violence Defines 'Army of God'" *Christian Science Monitor*, February 4, 1998.

Schuster, Henry. *Hunting Eric Rudolph: An Insider's Account of the Five-year Search for the Olympic Bomber.* New York: Berkley Books, 2005.

Scruggs, Kathy, and Ron Martz. "Atlanta Bombings: Looking for Answers; 'Army of God' Was Started by Texas Con Man." *Atlanta Journal and Constitution*, February 25, 1997.

Vollers, Maryanne. *Lone Wolf: Eric Rudolph: Murder, Myth, and the Pursuit of an American Outlaw.* New York: HarperCollins, 2006.

ARMY OF MOHAMMED

See Jaish-e-Mohammed

ARMY OF THE RIGHTEOUS

See Lashkar-e-Taiba

AROCENA, EDUARDO (1943–)

Eduardo Arocena was the leader of the anticommunist Cuban terror group Omega 7, which carried out several attacks against Cuban government officials in the late 1970s and early 1980s.

Born in Cuba in 1943, Arocena fled that country in 1965 as a stowaway on a cargo boat to Spain. He later immigrated to the United States, where he worked as a dockworker in Union City, New Jersey. A fervent anticommunist, Arocena soon became involved in the movement to overthrow Fidel Castro, Cuba's Communist dictator. In the early 1970s, Arocena came to feel that the existing anti-Castro groups were doing too little to actively attack the Castro regime. With the support of the larger organizations, he began to recruit a small elite force to carry out assassinations and bombings against those deemed to be pro-Castro.

Founded on September 11, 1974, Arocena's group became known as Omega 7, after the original number of members. The organization seems to have had no more than 20 members at any time. Omega 7 received funds from Cuban businessmen and by conducting surveillance and other activities for a wealthy Cuban marijuana trafficker, though the group did not aid in the actual selling or transport of drugs. The FBI found the group extremely difficult to penetrate—for several years, the FBI thought "Omega 7" was merely a cover name for the larger Cuban Nationalist Movement (CNM), an impression that the CNM actively fostered.

Omega 7 carried out its first attacks on February 1, 1975, bombing the Venezuelan consulate in New York City. Over the next seven years, its targets included Soviet businesses and ships, Latin American embassies, and pro-Castro Cuban exiles and businesses in New York, New Jersey, Washington, D.C., and Florida. In the more than 30 attacks attributed to Omega 7, two people were killed and a few were injured, though property damage was extensive. Its most devastating attacks were against the Cuban Mission to the United Nations. On March 25, 1980, the group attached a radio-controlled bomb to the car of Dr. Raul Roa Kouri, the Cuban ambassador to the United Nations. While he was parking the car, the device was jostled loose from the undercarriage, and Arocena decided not to detonate it. On September 11, 1980, an Omega 7 gunman killed a Cuban attaché, Felix Garcia Rodriguez.

FBI agents investigating the attacks on the consulate approached Arocena, asking for information about the group's activities. Apparently convinced that his comrades were informing on him in an attempt to oust him from the leadership, Arocena submitted to an interview by the FBI, in which he admitted to being "Omar," his nom de guerre as Omega 7's leader, and implicated himself and several colleagues in the murder of Rodriguez and the attempted murder of Doctor Kouri.

After five days, Arocena fled New York for Miami, where he resumed his anti-Castro activities. Found and arrested on July 22, 1983, Arocena was tried in New York for murder and attempted murder; in addition, he was twice tried in Miami for charges relating to the hundreds of pounds of weapons and explosives seized from his Florida apartment. Found guilty in all three of his trials, he is currently serving a life sentence in federal prison.

Colleen Sullivan

See also Omega 7

Further Readings

Didion, Joan. *Miami*. New York: Vintage Books, 1998.

Elfrink, Tim. "Let Terrorist Eduardo Arocena Go: *El Exilio* Wants Him out of Jail." *Miami New Times*, September 25, 2008. http://www.miaminewtimes.com/2008-09-25/news/let-terrorist-eduardo-arocena-go.

Federal Bureau of Investigation. "Cuban Information Archives: Omega 7." http://cuban-exile.com/menu1/!group.html.

Lubasch, Arnold H. "Cuban Exile Group Reportedly Planned to Kill Castro on His '79 U.N. Trip." *The New York Times*, September 22, 1983, p. B1.

Treaster, Joseph B. "Suspected Head of Omega 7 Terrorist Group Seized." *The New York Times*, July 23, 1983, p. 1.

Treaster, Joseph B. "Weapons Seized in Apartment of Omega 7 Suspect." *The New York Times*, July 24, 1983, p. 1.

ARYAN NATIONS

Aryan Nations (AN, aka Church of Jesus Christ Christian) was one of the most prominent Christian Identity–based hate groups active in the 1980s. During that decade, AN developed a strong network comprising neo-Nazi, skinhead, Ku Klux Klan (KKK), white supremacist, and militia groups, many of which congregated and networked at the AN compound in Hayden Lake, Idaho.

The roots of the AN date back to the 1940s and the increased popularity of the Christian Identity movement in the United States. Christian Identity adherents believe that white Aryans are the "chosen people," that blacks are subhuman, that Jews are descendents of the devil, and that the world is moving toward race war. In 1970, Richard Girnt Butler, newly ordained by the American Institute of Theology (AIT), which reflects Christian Identity beliefs, took over a large Christian Identity congregation in Lancaster, California, after its leader, Wesley Swift, died. In 1973 Butler moved the congregation to a compound in Hayden Lake, Idaho, and created the Church of Jesus Christ Christian. In 1978 Butler founded the church's political arm, the Aryan Nations.

Over the following years, Butler often referred to Hayden Lake as the "international headquarters of the White race." In 1979 he began holding annual conferences that attracted members of various white supremacist groups, especially neo-Nazis and the KKK. AN even offered courses in guerrilla warfare and urban terrorism. By 1989 Butler had added Aryan Youth festivals as well, held on the weekend nearest to Hitler's birthday (April 20).

The AN gained significant public attention in the 1980s because of the actions of a splinter group called The Order (comprising several members of AN, including The Order's leader, Robert Jay Mathews, as well as members of the neo-Nazi National Alliance and some KKK groups). In a series of dramatic bank robberies, The Order stole over $4 million to fund the overthrow of the U.S. government and a race war, borrowing ideas from William Pierce's 1978 novel, *The Turner Diaries*. The Order collapsed in 1985 when 25 of its members were sent to prison.

In 1987, with many of its former members in jail, Aryan Nations began to publish a prison newsletter called *The Way*. The newsletter was used to spread Christian Identity beliefs and to connect AN with its prison faction, a prison gang known as the Aryan Brotherhood. It was also used to recruit new members, a growing concern for the organization because AN membership had begun to decline. In the early 1990s, several key members left AN. After clashing with Butler in 1993, Carl Franklin, then chief of staff and seen as the next leader of the group, left and took the security chief, Wayne Jones, with him. Others, such as Charles and Betty Tate, left to join groups elsewhere. At that time, AN had only three chapters in the United States. Despite infighting, AN began to actively recruit neo-Nazis and skinheads in an effort to increase membership. By 1994, AN had chapters in 15 states; by 1996, the organization was active in 27 states.

AN activity surged in the late 1990s. In 1997, members held rallies in several Ohio cities and distributed antiblack and anti-Semitic fliers throughout northern Kentucky and southwestern Ohio. On July 1, 1998, security guards at Hayden Lake viciously attacked Victoria Keenan and her son, Jason, when they stopped briefly in front of the compound. Two of the guards, John Yeager and Jesse Warfield, the group's security chief, served time for their roles in the attack; the ensuing civil suit destroyed the AN and its aging leader Butler.

On September 7, 2000, a jury found Aryan Nations and Butler negligent in connection with the selection, training, and supervision of the security guards and ordered AN to pay $6.3 million in damages to the Keenans. After Butler declared bankruptcy, the 20-acre compound at Hayden Lake, as well as AN's intellectual property—including the names "Aryan Nations" and "Church of Jesus Christ Christian"—were awarded to the Keenans. In March 2000, the Keenans sold the property for $250,000 to the Carr Foundation, a human rights group. Carr provided seed money to build a human rights center in nearby Coeur D'Alene in order to counter the legacy of the AN compound and of white supremacist movements in northern Idaho; the Human Rights Education Institute opened in 2006.

Following the loss of the Hayden Lake compound, Butler moved into a house in nearby Hayden, Idaho. In July 2000, Neuman Britton, of Escondido, California, was appointed the new AN leader at the Aryan Nation National Congress, held in Hayden Lake. Britton died of cancer in August 2001, leaving the group leaderless once again. In October of that year, Harold Ray Redfaeirn, of the Ohio AN chapter, was appointed the new leader. Redfaeirn appointed August "Chip" B. Kreis III as the group's minister of information. Redfaeirn and Kreis escalated the rhetoric of violence and hatred associated with AN. In the wake of the September 11, 2001, terrorist attacks, which the AN website lauded as retribution for U.S. support of Israel, Kreis wrote, "'If this beast system [the federal government] looks to us to plunder, arrest, and fill their detention camps with, then by all means fight force with force and leave not a man standing."

Under Redfaeirn's leadership, AN began to fragment. Redfaeirn expelled Butler from the organization in January 2002 and moved the group to Potter County, Pennsylvania, in part because 98 percent of that county's population is white. Potter County was also the location of Kreis's home. In May 2002, Redfaeirn fired Kreis and returned command of the AN to Butler. Kreis, however, insisted that he was still the true leader. Redfaeirn died in 2003, and Butler died the following year at the age of 86. Butler's death accelerated the splintering of the group. In 2009 the Southern Poverty Law Center, which tracks hate groups, estimated that there were 11 groups using the name "Aryan Nations," but none of them have the influence or membership of the original group.

The decline of AN was seen by many in the Christian Identity movement as exposing the limitations of high-profile organizations. While the publicity generated by AN publications and events helped recruit members, it also focused negative media, political, and police attention on the group, which became infiltrated by undercover informants working for both the police and civil rights organizations. From the 1990s onward, Christian Identity extremists have become increasingly likely to engage in so-called leaderless resistance, in which individuals or small groups act secretly and independently of each other in order to forward the movement's agenda.

Laura Lambert

See also Aryan Republican Army; Christian Identity; Order, The; *Turner Diaries, The*

Further Readings

Balch, Robert W. "The Rise and Fall of Aryan Nations: A Resource Mobilization Perspective." *Journal of Political and Military Sociology* 34, no. 1 (Summer 2006): 81–113.

Bushart, Howard L., John R. Craig, and Myra Barnes. *Soldiers of God: White Supremacists and Their Holy War for America.* New York: Kensington Books, 1998.

Federal Bureau of Investigation. "Aryan Nations Files." http://foia.fbi.gov/foiaindex/anation.htm.

Geranios, Nicholas. "Aryan Nations Revival? Maybe Not." *Deseret News,* April 25, 2009, p. B6.

Hall, Dave, and Tym Burkey. *Into the Devil's Den: How an FBI Informant Got inside the Aryan Nations and a Special Agent Got Him out Alive.* New York: Ballantine Books, 2008.

Human Rights Education Institute. http://www.hrei.org.

Morlin, Bill, and Jim Camden. "Richard Butler, Founder of Aryan Nations, Dies at 86: Racist Had Dream of a White Homeland in Northwest." *Spokesman Review,* September 9, 2004, p. A1.

Moser, Bob. "Alabama Getaway." *Intelligence Report* 119 (Winter 2004). http://www.splcenter.org/intel/intelreport/article.jsp?aid=506.

Quarles, Chester L. *Christian Identity: The Aryan American Bloodline Religion.* Jefferson, NC: McFarland, 2004.

Walters, Jerome. *One Aryan Nation under God: Exposing the New Racial Extremists.* Cleveland, OH: Pilgrim Press, 2000.

ARYAN REPUBLICAN ARMY

During the mid-1990s, the Aryan Republican Army (ARA), a six-member paramilitary cell, robbed 22 banks in the Midwest, intending to use the money to fund a white supremacist overthrow of the U.S. government.

During the ARA's short life, authorities were unaware that the thieves who had committed a slew of small-scale bank robberies in Iowa, Missouri, Ohio, and other Midwestern states had any motive other than stealing money, nor had they ever heard of the small white supremacist cell called the Aryan Republican Army. The press referred to the robbers at the "Midwest Bank Bandits."

The ARA's robberies were elaborately orchestrated—the group used the 1991 surf film *Point Break* as a template. Each heist was planned to take less than 90 seconds. One member guarded the lobby, calling out the elapsed time, while the others rifled money from the tellers' drawers. As in the movie, the robbers often wore plastic Nixon or Regan masks. They were notorious for these antics, and for their taunting of federal agents—their getaway cars were registered to FBI agents, for example. For a Christmas 1994 robbery in Ohio, one member wore a Santa Claus suit. In an April 1995 robbery in Iowa, the ARA left investigators an Easter basket holding a gold-painted pipe bomb.

The ARA focused its attacks on small-town banks and rarely stole more than $10,000 at a time, but the six were industrious, almost reaching the record of 25 banks robbed, which had been set by the legendary Jesse James. Many of their tactics were similar to those of The Order, an infamous white supremacist group of the 1980s.

The ARA had two main members, Richard "Wild Bill" Guthrie Jr. and Peter Kevin Langan. On January 19, 1996, Guthrie and Langan were charged with nearly two-dozen bank robberies. The two men, with the help of a handful of ARA "soldiers," stole more than $250,000 in just over two years. Guthrie, who was arrested in late 1996 after a high-speed chase outside of Cincinnati, entered an early guilty plea. He committed suicide in his Kentucky jail cell in July 1997, a week after promising to provide federal authorities information about other groups seeking to overthrow the government. Guthrie implicated Langan, who was arrested in 1996 and convicted in two separate federal trials in 1997; he was sentenced to life in prison without possibility of parole. Scott Stedeford, a white-power rock musician, was convicted on three bank robbery charges and six conspiracy charges in November 1996; he was sentenced to 20 years in prison. Kevin McCarthy turned state's evidence and led authorities to Michael Brescia, who spent two years in jail for his role in the robberies. In March 1998, Mark Thomas, a prominent neo-Nazi leader from Pennsylvania, pled guilty to plotting seven bank robberies. Within two years, the ARA was finished.

The ARA flourished in the antigovernment climate following the events in Ruby Ridge and Waco in the early 1990s, and some believe that Timothy McVeigh, the Oklahoma City bomber, had connections to the ARA. In addition, Brescia was once thought to be the missing "John Doe 2" suspect in the Oklahoma City bombing. Authorities have since discarded both suppositions.

Laura Lambert

See also Aryan Nations; Christian Identity; McVeigh, Timothy James; Oklahoma City Bombing; Order, The

Further Readings

Gibson, Gail. "10 Years Later, Some Seek More Answers in Bombing: Oklahoma City Survivors, Victims' Relatives Question Investigation's Conclusions." *The Sun* (Baltimore). April 19, 2005, p. 3A.

Hamm, Mark S. *In Bad Company: America's Terrorist Underground.* Boston: Northeastern University Press, 2002.

Quarles, Chester L. *Christian Identity: The Aryan American Bloodline Religion.* Jefferson, NC: McFarland, 2004.

ASAHARA, SHOKO (1955–)

Shoko Asahara is the leader of the Aum Shinrikyo cult and the mastermind of the sarin gas attack on the Japanese subway.

Asahara was born Chizuo Matsumoto, the son of a poor tatami mat maker, on March 2, 1955. Afflicted with glaucoma at birth, Asahara had only very limited vision in one eye, and his parents sent him to a school for the blind. There, his partial sight was an advantage, and Asahara used it to bully and extort money from his fellow students. An unpopular but ambitious child, he spoke to his classmates of his determination to become prime minister of Japan.

In the early 1980s, Asahara became deeply interested in spirituality. He devoted himself to both Hindu-style yoga and the daily meditation of Buddhism, and he dabbled in other religions. He was particularly intrigued by the Christian concept of Armageddon, a final battle between good and evil that will end the world as we know it. This mélange of Buddhist, Hindu, and Christian practices would become the primary ingredients of the Aum Shinrikyo cult's beliefs.

In 1984, Asahara and his wife set up a small storefront in Tokyo to teach yoga and hold religious seminars. In 1987, after a trip to India, Asahara began to claim he had attained Enlightenment—the first person to do so since the Buddha—and refer to himself as the "Venerable Master." He also claimed that by following his teachings, true believers could acquire the ability to levitate, read minds, and teleport. Intrigued by these claims, Asahara's seminars began to attract adherents, and the Aum Shinrikyo, or "Supreme Truth," cult was born.

Asahara preached that the world would soon come to an end, but by purifying themselves, cult members could save humanity from the coming horror. This message, coupled with Asahara's personal magnetism, proved an extremely potent attraction to many young Japanese, and graduates of Japan's top universities became members of the cult.

In 1990, Asahara and other cult leaders ran for seats in the Diet, or Japanese parliament. Their resounding defeat was a bitter surprise to Asahara, and his message began to change; instead of purifying themselves for the rest of humanity, it would now become the duty of the cult members to help destroy the impure and the sinful, starting with those who opposed Aum. By mid-1993, Aum had constructed an automatic weapons assembly plant and a chemical and biological weapons facility.

Asahara became increasingly paranoid, believing the CIA, the Japanese National Police Agency, and the U.S. government were attempting to kill him. In 1994 he ordered an assassination attempt on three judges whom he feared would decide a pending case against the cult. Cult members released poison gas in a residential neighborhood, killing seven people and injuring the judges. In March 1995, in an attempt to cripple the Japanese government, he ordered an attack on the Tokyo subway using sarin gas. Twelve people died in the attack, and thousands were injured. Evading capture for almost two months following the attack, Asahara was arrested on May 16, 1995.

Asahara was tried and sentenced to death in 2004, a ruling that Japan's top court upheld in 2006. However, legal proceedings continued as of 2010 and were expected to go on for several more years. Asahara continues to be regarded as the spiritual leader of Aum Shinrikyo, and cultists have purchased dozens of properties near the jail where Asahara is held, which they regard as a holy site.

Colleen Sullivan

See also Aum Shinrikyo; Biological Terrorism; Chemical Terrorism; Tokyo Subway Attack

Further Readings

Kaplan, David E., and Andrew Marshall. *The Cult at the End of the World: The Incredible Story of Aum.* London: Hutchinson, 1996.

Lifton, Robert Jay. *Destroying the World to Save It: Aum Shinrikyō, Apocalyptic Violence, and the New Global Terrorism.* New York: Henry Holt, 1999.

"Matsumoto Loses Appeal: Supreme Court Finalizes Death Sentence." *Daily Yomuri,* September 16, 2006, p. 1.

McCurry, Justin. "Ten Years on, Terror Cult Keeps Grip on Wary Japan." *The Guardian,* March 18, 2005, p. 19.

Olson, K.B. "Aum Shinrikyo: Once and Future Threat?" *Emerging Infectious Diseases* 5, no. 4 (July/August 1999): 42–47. http://www.cdc.gov/ncidod/eid/vol5no4/olson.htm.

Onishi, Norimitsu. "After Eight-year Trial, Cultist Is Sentenced to Death." *The New York Times,* February 28, 2004, p. A3.

Reader, Ian. *Religious Violence in Contemporary Japan: The Case of Aum Shinrikyō.* Nordic Institute of Asian Studies Monograph Series No. 82. Richmond, Surrey, UK: Curzon Press, 2000.

U.S. State Department. "Terrorist Groups." *Country Reports on Terrorism 2008.* http://www.state.gov/s/ct/rls/crt/2008/122449.htm.

ASYMMETRICAL WARFARE

Asymmetries in warfare refer to imbalances between opposing forces. There may be differences in the number of soldiers, equipment, firepower, morale, tactics, values, or other factors. While there has likely never been a conflict between two perfectly symmetrical forces, the term *asymmetrical warfare* is typically used to mean warfare between two forces that are not simply unequal, but that are so significantly different that they cannot make the same sorts of attacks on each other.

Guerrilla warfare, occurring between lightly armed partisans and a conventional army, is an example of asymmetrical warfare. Terrorist tactics, such as hijackings and suicide bombings, are also considered to be asymmetrical, both because they tend to involve a smaller, weaker group attacking a stronger one, and also because attacks on civilians are by definition one-way warfare. War between a country that is both able and willing to use nuclear weapons and a country that is not would be another example of asymmetrical warfare.

Victory in war does not always go to the militarily superior force: The Revolutionary War between the American colonists and the British, who at the time were a dominant military power, is a clear example of effective asymmetrical warfare. Since World War II, Western powers fighting in developing countries have sometimes been defeated by local forces, despite massive asymmetries in terms of conventional military strength. Colonial powers were forced to withdraw from Algeria, Indochina, Indonesia, and other areas, not as a result of defeat in battle, but because of the lack of will of the dominant power to sustain the war. In Vietnam, the social and political environments at home forced first the French and then the Americans to concede defeat. The insurgents in colonized countries often did not need to defeat the sometimes long-established colonizer, but merely to persuade it to withdraw from the region. Asymmetries of both power and will were operating: the colonial powers possessed superior military resources, but they were reluctant to actually use them.

After the collapse of the Soviet Union, the United States found itself with an immense infrastructure and military organized to conduct conventional war, and there was no potential enemy with equivalent military power. The Persian Gulf War, fought in 1991 as a conventional war against Iraq, showcased the military might of the United States to the world. The war was relatively short, relied heavily on technology and firepower, and was won without engaging in much ground combat. The enemy was easy to identify, hostilities generally took place away from inhabited areas, and civilian and U.S. military casualties were few. In Somalia in 1997, by contrast, the United States was involved in a complex mix of humanitarian, police, and military operations, and U.S. forces were not able to take advantage of their military superiority.

Likewise, when the United States invaded Iraq in 2003, the country's conventional forces were defeated within weeks, and the Iraqi ruler, Saddam Hussein, was captured by the end of the year. Nonetheless, a violent insurgency continued for years against U.S. forces in Iraq, unimpaired by the loss of the country's military equipment and bases, and despite the capture and eventual execution of the country's top leader—all factors that would generally cripple a conventional opponent.

The U.S. military is confident in the country's ability to prevail in any conventional conflict, but it believes that the United States is vulnerable to "asymmetrical" threats, particularly from terrorist groups. Indeed, the very superiority of the nation's conventional forces has made it more likely that it will be drawn into an asymmetrical conflict. Anyone who wishes to effectively oppose the United States with violence would be wise to avoid attempting the conventional warfare in which that country excels.

Classic war strategists such as Carl von Clausewitz (1780–1831) and Sun Tzu (sixth century BC) have stressed the importance of taking advantage of the enemy's weaknesses, and despite its strong conventional military, the United States is perceived by many to have certain weaknesses. In a 2001 report for the Strategic Studies Institute, Stephen Metz and Douglas Johnson suggested that the United States is susceptible to asymmetries of patience, preferring not to fight long wars; asymmetries of will in situations not involving vital national interests; and asymmetries of values, as the United States tends to be unwilling to accept military casualties or inflict civilian casualties. Asymmetrical strategies that could be used against the United States include limiting the fighting to urban areas, attacking the homeland, engaging in political activity designed to discourage potential allies, and using anti-access strategies, such as targeting bases, thus limiting ability to mobilize forces.

Other observers have noted that the U.S. military tends to rely heavily on technology—including advanced weaponry, body armor, and unmanned drones—rather than building up relationships with local populations whose sympathies are up in the air and who might provide valuable intelligence. Since most of United States' military armaments were designed for a conventional war, in which forces fight at some distance from each other, they can be vulnerable to attacks at close quarters, as the 2000 bombing of the USS Cole, then in port in Yemen, clearly showed.

The value of asymmetrical tactics can be seen in guerrilla warfare—indeed, guerrilla means "little war" in Spanish. Guerrilla fighters are generally fewer in number and possess fewer and less powerful weapons than the opposing force. Guerrilla tactics include ambush, avoiding open battle, cutting communications lines, and generally harassing the enemy. Guerrilla warfare has been practiced throughout history, and it includes both military operations carried out against the rear of an enemy's army and operations carried out by a local population against an occupying force. The aim of the guerrilla fighter is erosion of the enemy's will to sustain the costs of continuing the war. Henry Kissinger observed that "the guerilla wins if he does not lose. The conventional army loses if it does not win."

Although it is usually exercised by a smaller force, guerrilla fighters, especially in urban areas, can be formidable adversaries to a conventional military. Guerrilla fighters typically do not inhabit large, well-established bases, making it impossible to rely on aerial bombardment to destroy personnel and infrastructure. If the guerrillas are in an urban area, powerful conventional weapons cannot be used by their opponents, unless they are willing to inflict large numbers of civilian casualties and risk increasing popular support for the guerrillas. Small guerrilla or insurgent groups also tend to be less hierarchical, meaning that a force cannot be neutralized by the capture or death of a handful of leaders.

Groups lacking the ability to take power either militarily or politically may resort to terrorist attacks within the heart of the state. Terrorist attacks in cities attract more media coverage than those in rural areas; car bombs, assassinations, and bombs left in crowded public places are common tactics in urban terrorism.

As long as the survival of its state is not at risk, the nation under attack is politically unable to use its full military power, and thus must fight a limited war, while terrorists commit themselves and their resources to a total war. Terrorists groups are willing to rely on tactics, such as suicide bombings or targeting civilians, that the states they attack are unwilling to use. They are also quite aware of these advantages: according to Ayman al Zawahiri, a high-ranking leader of the terrorist network al Qaeda, "the way of death and martyrdom is a weapon that tyrants and their helpers, who worship their salaries instead of God, do not have."

Ellen Sexton

See also Counterterrorism; Iraq War; Persian Gulf War; Suicide Terrorism; USS *Cole* Bombing

Further Readings

Barnett, Roger W. *Asymmetrical Warfare: Today's Challenge to U.S. Military Power.* Washington, DC: Brassey's, 2003.

Clausewitz, Carl von. *On War.* Translated by Michael Howard and Peter Paret. New York: Knopf, 1993.

Laqueur, Walter. *Guerrilla Warfare: A Historical and Critical Study.* 2nd ed. New Brunswick, NJ: Transaction Publishers, 1998.

Mack, A. "Why Big Nations Lose Small Wars: The Politics of Asymmetric Conflict." *World Politics* 27, no. 2 (January 1975): 175–200.

Matthews, Lloyd J., ed. *Challenging the United States Symmetrically and Asymmetrically: Can America Be Defeated?* Carlisle Barracks, PA: U.S. Army War College, Strategic Studies Institute, 1998. http://www .strategicstudiesinstitute.army.mil/pubs/display .cfm?pubid=230.

Metz, Stephen, and Douglas V. Johnson II. *Asymmetry and U.S. Military Strategy: Definition, Background, and Strategic Concepts.* Carlisle Barracks, PA: U.S. Army War College, Strategic Studies Institute, 2001. http://www.strategicstudiesinstitute.army.mil/pubs/ display.cfm?PubID=223.

Paul, T. V. *Asymmetric Conflicts: War Initiation by Weaker Powers.* Cambridge, UK: Cambridge University Press, 1994.

Smith, James, Jerry Mark Long, and Thomas H. Johnson. *Strategic Culture and Violent Non-state Actors: Weapons of Mass Destruction and Asymmetrical Operations Concepts and Cases.* USAF Academy, CO: USAF Institute for National Security Studies, 2008. http://www.usafa.edu/df/inss/docs/StrategicCulture.pdf.

Sun Tzu. *The Art of War: The Denma Translation.* Translation, essays, and commentary by the Denma Translation Group. Boston: Shambhala, 2002.

Swabb, Erik. "Train Soldiers to Win Hearts and Minds." *Christian Science Monitor,* September 20, 2006, p. 9.

Thornton, Rod. *Asymmetric Warfare: Threat and Response in the Twenty-first Century.* Cambridge, UK: Polity Press, 2007.

ATEF, MUHAMMAD (C. 1944–2001)

A former Egyptian police officer regarded as being one of Osama bin Laden's closest advisors, Muhammad Atef (aka Abu Hafs; Abu Hafs el Masry el Khabir; Abu Khadijah; Sheikh Taysir Abdullah; Taysir) is said to have been a key planner of the September 11, 2001, attacks on the World Trade Center in New York City and the Pentagon near Washington, D.C. Atef, often described as the chief military commander of al Qaeda, died on November 15, 2001, during the U.S. bombings near Kabul, Afghanistan.

Little is known about Atef's early life. By the mid-1970s, he was a member of the Egyptian Islamic Jihad (al Jihad) and is said to have become a top lieutenant in that organization. Ayman al Zawahiri, who would later become known as the philosopher of al Qaeda, commanded the group. Islamic Jihad, which supports strict Islamic governance instead of secular government for Muslim nations, is often described as a major influence on al Qaeda.

After Egyptian president Anwar Sadat was assassinated in 1981, in a plot that al Zawahiri was involved in, Egypt cracked down on the Islamic opposition. Egyptian security officials held suspects without trial, torturing many of them, and members of al Jihad fled Egypt in large numbers. Atef went to Afghanistan, where he joined the fight against the occupying forces of the Soviet Union. In Afghanistan, Atef and his commander, Zawahiri, joined with bin Laden. The three men would become the dominant members of al Qaeda in the mid-1990s, when Zawahiri merged al Jihad with it. al Qaeda, an Arabic term meaning "the base," is an international terrorist network that uses force and violence to achieve its goal of driving the United States from all Islamic countries, especially Saudi Arabia; it also serves as an umbrella group for other militant organizations. al Qaeda carried out the September 11, 2001, attacks on the World Trade Center and the Pentagon.

In the early 1990s, Atef followed bin Laden to Sudan. According to U.S. officials, while in Africa he and other al Qaeda members gave military training to Somali tribes that were opposed to the United Nations intervention in that country. According to a U.S. indictment, tribe members trained by Atef were among those who attacked U.S. and UN troops serving in Somalia as part of Operation Rescue Hope. Hundreds of Somalis and 18 U.S. Army troops were killed in the attacks in Mogadishu in 1993.

After being expelled from Sudan in 1996, Atef, bin Laden, and Zawahiri returned to Afghanistan. All three were later indicted in the United States for involvement in the 1998 bombings of two U.S. embassies in East Africa, in which 224 people were killed and thousands wounded. According to the indictment, Atef was a major strategic commander in the attacks. He met with other al Qaeda members to plan the bombings and kept in touch with them by cellular phone. On August 7, coordinated truck bombs went off within minutes of each other at U.S. embassies in Nairobi, Kenya, and Dar es Salaam, Tanzania, cities separated by more than 400 miles. Four men with ties to al Qaeda were convicted in 2001 for various roles in the embassy bombings. Shortly after the embassy bombings, the United States declared that bin Laden and al Qaeda operatives were responsible. Atef handled media affairs for al Qaeda after the U.S. accusations, speaking by telephone and exchanging faxes with Western journalists.

In January 2001, Atef's daughter married bin Laden's son in Afghanistan, bringing the two men even closer. When U.S. forces first began bombing Afghanistan, Atef appeared in a videotaped response next to bin Laden and Zawahiri. At about six feet six inches, Atef was unmistakable. In November 2001, U.S. officials announced that Atef had been killed in an attack outside of Kabul. Their finding was partly based on overheard conversations between members of the Taliban. In the ruins of Atef's bombed house, which was destroyed by a Predator drone, U.S. forces found many al Qaeda documents, videos, and other materials.

Erica Pearson

See also al Jihad; al Qaeda; bin Laden, Osama; East Africa Embassy Bombings; September 11 Attacks; Zawahiri, Ayman al

Further Readings

Atwan, Abdel Bari. *The Secret History of al Qaeda.* Berkeley: University of California Press, 2006.

Bergen, Peter. *Holy War, Inc.: Inside the Secret World of Osama bin Laden.* New York: Free Press, 2001.

Bergen, Peter. *The Osama bin Laden I Know: An Oral History of al Qaeda's Leader.* New York: Free Press, 2006.

National Commission on Terrorist Attacks upon the United States. *The 9/11 Commission Report.* New York: Norton, 2003. http://www.9-11commission.gov.

Reeve, Simon. *The New Jackals: Ramzi Yousef, Osama bin Laden, and the Future of Terrorism.* Boston: Northeastern University Press, 1999.

Riedel, Bruce. "Al Qaeda Strikes Back." *Foreign Affairs,* May/June 2007.

Riedel, Bruce. *The Search for al Qaeda: Its Leadership, Ideology, and Future.* Washington, DC: Brookings Institution Press, 2008.

Risen, James. "The Terror Network: Bombs Have Killed 3 Qaeda Leaders U.S. Now Believes." *The New York Times,* December 13, 2001, p. A1.

Slackman, Michael. "Al Jazeera Shows Tape of bin Laden and Planners of 9/11." *The New York Times,* September 8, 2006, p. A3.

U.S. District Court for the Southern District of New York. *United States v. Usama bin Laden.* Indictment, November 5, 1998. http://www.fas.org/irp/news/1998/11/98110602_nlt.html.

Weiser, Benjamin. "Saudi Is Indicted in Bomb Attacks on U.S. Embassies." *The New York Times,* November 5, 1998, p. A1.

Wright, Lawrence. *The Looming Tower: al Qaeda and the Road to 9/11.* New York: Alfred A. Knopf, 2006.

ATLANTA CENTENNIAL PARK BOMBING

See Centennial Park Bombing

ATTA, MOHAMED (1968–2001)

Mohamed Atta helped hijack American Airlines Flight 11 and flew it into the north tower of New York City's World Trade Center on September 11, 2001, in the first in a series of attacks that left 3,000 people dead, including the 19 hijackers.

Information about Atta is somewhat sketchy, but he is believed to have been one the ringleaders, if not the primary leader, of the September 11 attacks.

Atta was born in 1968 to a relatively well-to-do family in Egypt. He grew up in Cairo, where his father was a lawyer. His family was Muslim but not especially conservative; his sisters attended college and worked. Atta studied architecture and engineering at Cairo University, receiving his degree in 1990. After graduating, Atta obtained a job, but his father felt that Atta's career would be helped if he studied abroad. In 1992, Atta, who spoke German and English as well as Arabic, moved to Hamburg, Germany, where he enrolled at the Technical University of Hamburg to study urban planning. Atta became increasingly radical in his embrace of Islam while living there. In 1998 he disappeared from Hamburg for several months, and he likely traveled to Afghanistan during this time and formed links with al Qaeda. He returned to Hamburg and finished his degree at the Technical University, graduating with high honors in 1999. Atta is also believed to have established an al Qaeda terrorist cell in Hamburg that had two of the other hijackers as members.

In June 2000, Atta, who had a travel visa for the United States, flew to Newark, New Jersey. He quickly relocated to Florida, where he began taking flight classes in July. Throughout 2000 and 2001, he practiced his flight skills. He also received large sums of money from abroad and traveled extensively in those years, including several trips overseas and much movement within the United States. Atta twice met with other hijackers in Las Vegas, Nevada, possibly finalizing the hijacking plans there. In addition, he is believed to have made practice flights to familiarize himself with the aircraft he intended to hijack. On August 28, 2001, Atta purchased two seats on Flight 11 on American Airline's website for himself and a second hijacker, Abdul Alomari.

On September 10, 2001, Atta and Alomari drove from Boston to Portland, Maine. The next day they flew from Portland to Boston, where they boarded Flight 11 along with three other hijackers. Atta and his four confederates hijacked Flight 11 shortly after the plane reached cruising altitude. His luggage was later discovered at Boston's Logan Airport; it contained a letter outlining how the hijackers should act during their attack.

Mary Sisson

See also al Qaeda; bin Laden, Osama; Hijacking; Moussaoui, Zacarias; September 11 Attacks

Further Readings

Dorman, Michael. "Unraveling 9-11 Was in the Bags: Luggage That Didn't Get Put on Hijacked Jet Provided Information about Terrorists, Say Former Investigators." *Newsday*, April 17, 2006, p. A2.

Erlanger, Steven. "An Unobtrusive Man's Odyssey: Polite Student to Suicide Hijacker." *The New York Times*, September 15, 2001, p. A1.

Finn, Peter. "A Quiet Path to Horror at World Trade Center: Emerging Details of a Hijacking Suspect's Life Indicate Rage Born in Egypt, Nurtured in Germany." *The Washington Post*, September 23, 2001, p. A14.

Lardner, George, Jr. "Atta Skillfully Evaded Authorities in the U.S.: Terrorist Ringleader Did 'Everything Right' in His Dealings with INS and Other Entities." *The Washington Post*, October 20, 2001, p. A3.

McDermott, Terry. *Perfect Soldiers: The Hijackers: Who They Were, Why They Did It*. New York: HarperCollins, 2005.

National Commission on Terrorist Attacks upon the United States. *The 9/11 Commission Report*. New York: Norton, 2003. http://www.9-11commission. gov.

Wright, Lawrence. *The Looming Tower: al Qaeda and the Road to 9/11*. New York: Alfred A. Knopf, 2006.

Yardley, Jim. "A Portrait of the Terrorist: From Shy Child to Single-minded Killer." *The New York Times*, October 10, 2001, p. B9.

ATWA, ALI (C. 1960–)

Ali Atwa (aka Ammar Mansour Bouslim; Hassan Rostom Salim), a Lebanese citizen, is perhaps best known as the would-be hijacker who was bumped from Trans World Airlines Flight 847. Atwa was included on the FBI's October 2001 list of the 22 most wanted terrorists for his role in the 1985 hijacking, which developed into a weeks-long hostage ordeal and led to the death of a U.S. Navy officer.

An alleged member of Lebanese Hezbollah during the 1980s, Atwa is thought by the FBI to be living somewhere in Lebanon. Press reports have suggested that the death of Atwa's brother during an Israeli military operation in Sidon (in Lebanon) led him to begin training to take part in the TWA hijacking. By his own admission to Greek authorities, Atwa planned on boarding TWA Flight 847 from Athens to Rome as the third hijacker on June 14, 1985. However, he was bumped, missed his flight, and was arrested.

While Atwa was left on the ground arguing with ticket agents, two hijackers took over Flight 847, brandishing a pistol and hand grenades. They forced the American pilot, John Testrake, to redirect the Boeing 727 to Beirut, where they landed and made their demands. They called for the release of hundreds of prisoners, many of them Shiite Muslims, held by Israel. One of the hijackers shot a passenger, Officer Robert Stethem, at close range and dumped his body onto the tarmac. Meanwhile, Greek authorities arrested Atwa and found forged Moroccan passports in his possession.

Atwa confessed his plans to hijack the plane. After Atwa's arrest became known, the hijackers began negotiations with Greek authorities for his release, saying, according to press accounts, that they would kill the Greek passengers on board, one every hour, until Atwa was released. The plane then flew to Algiers, continuing a bizarre air journey in which Testrake flew the plane back and forth from Beirut to Algiers, eventually logging 8,300 miles. The hijackers released some hostages at each stop. While the plane waited during its first stop in Algiers, Greek officials flew Atwa to join his cohorts in exchange for passengers. After a two-week standoff on the tarmac in Beirut, Israel released some of the Shiite prisoners. The hijackers released all of their hostages and flew to freedom in Algiers.

The U.S. indicted Atwa, along with Imad Fayez Mugniyah and Hassan Izz al Din, both also Lebanese, on July 3, 1985, on charges related to the TWA hijacking. Mugniyah was killed by a car bomb in Syria in 2008, but the other two men remain on the FBI's Most Wanted Terrorists list. A fourth man, Mohammed Ali Hamadei, was also indicted; he was later caught in Frankfurt and sentenced to life in prison by a West German court in 1989.

Lebanese officials have claimed that Atwa is not currently linked to the party structure of Hezbollah. Although Hezbollah recast itself as a legitimate political party during the 1990s, and now holds elected seats in the Lebanese Parliament, the U.S. government continues to regard it as a terrorist organization. As of 2011, the FBI was offering a reward of up to $5 million for information leading to Atwa's arrest.

Erica Pearson

See also Hezbollah; Izz al Din, Hassan; Mugniyah, Imad Fayez; TWA Flight 847 Hijacking

Further Readings

Berger, Joseph. "Hostages in Lebanon: The Course of Events; 8 Days of Mideast Terror: The Journey of Flight 847." *The New York Times,* June 22, 1985, p. A1.

Federal Bureau of Investigation. "Most Wanted Terrorists." http://www.fbi.gov/wanted/terrorists/fugitives.htm (July 2009).

Jaber, Hala. *Hezbollah.* New York: Columbia University Press, 1997.

National Commission on Terrorist Attacks upon the United States. *The 9/11 Commission Report.* New York: Norton, 2003. http://www.9-11commission.gov

Snyder, Rodney A. *Negotiating with Terrorists: TWA Flight 847.* Pew Case Studies in International Affairs, Case 333. Pittsburgh, PA: Pew Charitable Trusts, 1994.

Tucker, Neely. "$21 Million Awarded in Fatal Hijacking." *The Washington Post,* April 21, 2002, p. C1.

Wright, Lawrence. *The Looming Tower: al Qaeda and the Road to 9/11.* New York: Alfred A. Knopf, 2006.

ATWAH, MUHSIN MUSA MATWALLI (1964–2006)

Muhsin Musa Matwalli Atwah (aka Abdel Rahman; Abdul Rahman; Abdul Rahman al Muhajir; Mohammed K.A. al Namer) was an alleged member of Osama bin Laden's al Qaeda network. He was accused of involvement in the 1998 conspiracy to bomb the U.S. embassies in Tanzania and Kenya, and the FBI included him in its Most Wanted Terrorists list following the September 11, 2001, attacks on the World Trade Center in New York City and the Pentagon near Washington, D.C.

The United States indicted Atwah, an Egyptian, in 1998 on charges relating to the bombings of U.S. embassies in Tanzania and Kenya in which 224 people died. The indictment also claimed he provided military and intelligence training for members of the al Qaeda network in Afghanistan, Pakistan, and Sudan. al Qaeda, an Arabic word meaning "the base," is an international terrorist network whose goal is to drive the United States from Saudi Arabia and other Islamic countries by force. Founded by the Saudi Osama bin Laden, al Qaeda also serves as an umbrella group for other militant organizations.

The Atwah indictment included a number of other charges. He was accused of providing military training to Somali tribes during the early 1990s, thus enabling them to fight more effectively against United Nations and U.S. forces during Somalia's civil unrest. Somalis attacked peacekeepers in Mogadishu in 1993, killing 18 U.S. soldiers.

According to the indictment, Atwah did not directly take part in the plan to bomb the U.S. embassies in East Africa, but he was a member of the overall conspiracy. On August 7, 1998, in synchronized attacks 400 miles apart, two truck bombs exploded at the embassies in Nairobi, Kenya, and Dar es Salaam, Tanzania. In the wake of the bombings, the U.S. government declared bin Laden and al Qaeda operatives to be responsible. In retaliation, President Clinton ordered air attacks on al Qaeda training grounds in Afghanistan and a pharmaceutical plant in the center of Khartoum, Sudan. The air raids were met with much international criticism, and many debated whether or not the factory in Sudan had any relation to bin Laden or to chemical weapons. Of 26 men with suspected ties to bin Laden indicted in the embassy bombings, three pled guilty and cooperated with the U.S. government as witnesses, while four were convicted of conspiring in the bombings and sentenced to life in prison without parole.

Atwah was killed on April 12, 2006, in the Pakistani town of Naghar. He was targeted in a helicopter strike by Pakistani security forces, who had been informed about his location by captured militants. His death was later confirmed by DNA testing.

Erica Pearson

See also al Qaeda; bin Laden, Osama; East Africa Embassy Bombings

Further Readings

Bergen, Peter. *Holy War, Inc.: Inside the Secret World of Osama bin Laden.* New York: Free Press, 2001.

Chu, Henry, and Zulfiqar Ali. "Pakistan Attack Aimed at al Qaeda Embassies Suspect." *Los Angeles Times,* April 14, 2006, p. A5.

"A Nation Challenged: The Hunted; The 22 Most Wanted Suspects, in a Five-act Drama of Global Terror." *The New York Times,* October 14, 2001, p. 1B.

Reeve, Simon. *The New Jackals: Ramzi Yousef, Osama bin Laden, and the Future of Terrorism.* Boston: Northeastern University Press, 1999.

Smith, Martin, and Lowell Bergman. "Hunting bin Laden." *Frontline,* PBS, September 13, 2001. http://www.pbs.org/wgbh/pages/frontline/shows/binladen.

U.S. District Court for the Southern District of New York. *United States v. Usama bin Laden.* Indictment, November 5, 1998. http://www.fas.org/irp/news/1998/11/98110602_nlt.html.

U.S. District Court for the Southern District of New York. *United States v. Usama bin Laden, et al.* Indictment, April 20, 2001. http://www.uniset.ca/other/cs5/93FSupp2d484.html.

AUM SHINRIKYO

Aum Shinrikyo, a cult founded in 1985 by Shoko Asahara, perpetrated the 1995 sarin gas attack on the Tokyo subway that killed 12 people.

Aum Shinrikyo translates roughly as "Supreme Truth." The cult's major tenets are drawn from a wide spectrum of religions. Adherents believe that by withdrawing from worldly pleasures and dedicating their thoughts to the contemplation of the "Supreme Truths" as revealed by their guru, Shoko Asahara, they can become enlightened. Some commentators characterize the cult as a type of "fundamentalist" Buddhism. However, Asahara has at times described himself as an incarnation of Shiva, the Hindu god responsible for both destruction and rebirth. Aum Shinrikyo also incorporates a fervent belief in the coming of Armageddon, a term from Christian theology describing an ultimate battle between good and evil in which the known world will be destroyed and replaced by a spiritually pure world.

The organization began in 1984 with a single Tokyo storefront offering yoga classes and religious seminars. Claims that believers could attain miraculous psychic powers brought many curious people to the seminars, and the cult soon began to attract a following. In addition to the personal magnetism of Shoko Asahara, the cult's message—that only by purifying themselves could believers avert the destruction of humanity—appealed to many alienated by the industrialized, secular, and conformist society of Japan. At its peak in the mid-1990s, the cult was estimated to have 9,000 Japanese members and an unknown number of followers worldwide, with approximately 1,000 hardcore adherents living at various cult properties and compounds. Teenagers and students made up a considerable portion of the cult's membership, some of them brilliant graduates of Japan's top universities, with advanced degrees in medicine, law, and science.

The cult was a very profitable enterprise, charging high fees for initiation and for relics such as snippets of Asahara's beard and vials of his bathwater. Some initiation rituals involved ingesting Asahara's blood and taking massive doses of hallucinogenic drugs. Members were encouraged to cut off all ties to their families and donate their life savings to the cult. Dissenters were treated harshly, sometimes subjected to sleep deprivation and other torture techniques. Some runaways were kidnapped and beaten in order to return them to the fold. In 1989 cultists murdered the human rights lawyer Tsutsumi Sakamoto, along with his wife and infant son. Sakamoto had been suing the cult on behalf of members' families. An Aum member, Kazuaki Okazaki, was sentenced to death by hanging after confessing to their murders—as well as that of a potential Aum escapee—in October 1998.

As membership grew into the thousands, Aum established operations in other countries, including Australia, Sri Lanka, and the United States. Its most successful expansion was to Russia in 1992, where it attracted thousands of followers. In Japan, Aum had ventures in dozens of industries, including noodle shops and low-budget computer stores. These operations earned millions for the cult—one leader estimated that its assets were worth $1.5 billion at the time of the subway attacks.

In 1990 Asahara and several other prominent members ran, all unsuccessfully, for seats in Japan's parliament. Despite years of negative media coverage, numerous lawsuits (which the cult had fiercely contested), and public speculation about Aum's involvement in the Sakamoto family's disappearance, the crushing defeat of all of Aum's candidates

was an unexpected blow to Asahara. He began to preach that it was the duty of Aum members to hasten the coming of Armageddon, which would destroy the sinful and elevate Aum's true believers onto a higher spiritual plane.

In light of this new goal, Asahara assembled his top advisors and instructed them to begin to arm the cult. The scientific expertise of certain cultists, coupled with Aum's connections to the Russian government and underworld, proved invaluable. By mid-1993 Aum had constructed a plant to manufacture automatic weapons, as well as crude but operational chemical and biological weapons facilities, where it was able to produce botulism toxin, anthrax bacteria, sarin gas, and hydrogen cyanide.

The cult began experimenting with its new weapons. It sprayed botulism toxin in central Tokyo in 1993 during the wedding of the crown prince, but no one was harmed in the attack. The cult then released anthrax from an industrial sprayer on the roof of one of its facilities in a Tokyo suburb; the strain was nonvirulent, however, and no people were injured. After its biological arsenal failed, the cult turned to chemical weapons. Asahara ordered sarin gas used in an assassination attempt on a rival cult leader, but the attempt backfired, nearly killing one of the potential assassins. Aum then employed the gas in an attack on three judges adjudicating a property dispute Aum was involved in. On the night of June 17, 1994, cult members released the gas in a residential area of the suburb of Matsumoto. Due to a shift in the wind, the judges were only injured slightly, but seven innocent bystanders were killed and more than 150 were hospitalized.

Despite continual suspicion, Aum had been able to fend off police action through threats of costly lawsuits and accusations of religious discrimination. But in mid-March 1995, Aum received word that the National Police Agency planned to raid the cult's compound. On March 20, five cult members distributed sarin on five separate subway lines bound for the Kasumagaseki station, Tokyo's busiest. Twelve people were killed and thousands were injured. Following the attacks, hundreds of cult members were arrested, and Aum orchestrated several more terrorist attacks in response to the arrests. Asahara and the architects of the subway attack were put on trial for the murders, and several, including Asahara, have been condemned to death. Lesser figures have been sentenced to prison.

The Aum Shinrikyo religion persists despite numerous crackdowns, continuous surveillance, and the seizure of its assets by the Japanese government. Though its major beliefs remain unchanged, the cult has renamed itself Aleph, or "The Beginning." Its new leaders disavow its criminal past and insist it does not pose a threat to society, yet they continue to regard the jailed Asahara as their spiritual leader, and they look to his third daughter, Rika, as his successor. In addition, because of disagreements within Aleph, splinter groups have formed that also follow the spiritual teachings of Asahara.

Colleen Sullivan

See also Asahara, Shoko; Biological Terrorism; Chemical Terrorism; Tokyo Subway Attack

Further Readings

Ballard, Tim, Jason Pate, Gary Ackerman, Diana McCauley, and Sean Lawson. *Chronology of Aum Shinrikyō's CBW Activities.* Monterey, CA: James Martin Center for Nonproliferation Studies, 2001. http://cns.miis.edu/reports/pdfs/aum_chrn.pdf.

Juergensmeyer, Mark. *Terror in the Mind of God: The Global Rise of Religious Violence.* Berkeley: University of California Press, 2000.

Kang, Ji Hyon. "1995 Tokyo Subway Attack: The Aum Shinrikyo Case." In *A New Understanding of Terrorism: Case Studies, Trajectories, and Lessons Learned*, edited by M.R. Haberfeld and Agostino von Hassell. New York: Springer, 2009.

Kaplan, David E., and Andrew Marshall. *The Cult at the End of the World: The Incredible Story of Aum.* London: Hutchinson, 1996.

Lifton, Robert Jay. *Destroying the World to Save It: Aum Shinrikyō, Apocalyptic Violence, and the New Global Terrorism.* New York: Henry Holt, 1999.

McCurry, Justin. "Ten Years on, Terror Cult Keeps Grip on Wary Japan." *The Guardian*, March 18, 2005, p. 19.

Olson, K.B. "Aum Shinrikyō: Once and Future Threat?" *Emerging Infectious Diseases* 5, no. 4, (July/August 1999): 42–47. http://www.cdc.gov/ncidod/eid/vol5no4/olson.htm.

Onishi, Norimitsu. "After Eight-year Trial, Cultist Is Sentenced to Death." *The New York Times*, February 28, 2004, p. A3.

Reader, Ian. *Religious Violence in Contemporary Japan: The Case of Aum Shinrikyō.* Nordic Institute of Asian Studies Monograph Series No. 82. Richmond, Surrey, UK: Curzon Press, 2000.

U.S. State Department. "Terrorist Groups." *Country Reports on Terrorism 2008.* http://www.state.gov/s/ct/rls/crt/2008/122449.htm.

AUTODEFENSAS UNIDAS DE COLOMBIA

See United Self-Defense Forces of Colombia

AWDA, ABD AL AZIZ (1950–)

Abd al Aziz Awda, frequently referred to as Sheik Odeh (aka Abd al Aziz Odeh; Abdel Aziz Odeh; Abu Ahmed; Fadl Abu Ahmed; Sheik Awda; the Sheik), has been accused of directing bombings, murders, extortions, and money laundering, both within the United States and internationally, on behalf of a designated terrorist organization, the Palestine Islamic Jihad (PIJ). Along with Fathi Shaqaqi, Awda founded the PIJ in the late 1970s. Awda has served as a university lecturer and an iman (an Islamic leadership position often associated with a mosque) of the al Qassam Mosque in the Gaza Strip. He is a member of the Palestinian National Council, the highest decision-making body within the Palestine Liberation Organization (PLO). In 2010, experts believed it likely that Awda was residing in Damascus, Syria, where the PIJ was headquartered.

Awda was born on December 20, 1950 in the village of Jabalia (also spelled Jabalya). The city is located in the Gaza Strip, Palestine, and is under the jurisdiction of the North Gaza Governorate. It is adjacent to the Jabalia refugee camp. After local schooling, Awda left Jabalia and was educated in Islamic and Arabic studies in Cairo, Egypt. During that period, he and Shaqaqi, due to a widening ideological gap between the Egyptian branch of the Muslim Brotherhood, founded the more militant PIJ. Up until 1981, activities associated with the PIJ were conducted from Egypt, but in 1987 the PIJ was exiled to Lebanon, where its members received support and training from Hezbollah. In 1998 another move, this time self-initiated, was made to Damascus, the present location of the PIJ. Although the group's direct attacks against Israel have decreased since 2003, Israeli interests continue to be targets of interest. (PIJ's cofounder, Shaqaqi, was assassinated in 1995.)

Under regulations of the U.S. Office of Foreign Assets Control, Awda was identified, by the U.S. secretary of the treasury, as a Specially Designated Terrorist. He is also included on the Most Wanted Terrorists list issued by the Federal Bureau of Investigation, and he has been indicted under the Racketeer Influenced and Corrupt Organizations Act (RICO) for probable acts involving international terrorist organizations. He is wanted for allegedly conducting the affairs of a known and designated terrorist organization through a wide variety of illegal activities.

Harvey Morley

See also al Jihad; Palestine Islamic Jihad; Palestine Liberation Organization

Further Readings

Bloom, Mia. *Dying to Kill.* New York: Columbia University Press, 2005.

Cordesman, Anthony H. *The Israeli-Palestinian War: Escalating to Nowhere.* Westport, CT: Praeger, 2005.

Eubank, William, and Leonard Weinberg, "Terrorism and Democracy: Perpetrators and Victims." *Terrorism and Political Violence* 13, no. 1 (Spring 2001): 155–164.

Firestone, Reuven. *The Origin of Holy War in Islam.* New York: Oxford University Press, 1999.

Juergensmeyer, Mark. *Terror in the Mind of God: The Global Rise of Religious Violence.* 3rd ed. Berkeley: University of California Press, 2003.

AWLAKI, ANWAR AL (1971–)

An Islamic preacher who morphed from a mainstream American Muslim into one of al Qaeda's most public personalities and influential voices, Anwar al Awlaki has come to rank among America's most wanted terrorists. He has been directly linked to multiple terrorist plots in the United States and the United Kingdom, and, thanks to the Internet, his numerous sermons and propaganda videos have allowed him to spread his message around the world.

Awlaki is an American citizen. Born to Yemeni parents in Las Cruces, New Mexico, in 1971, he spent the early years of his life in the United States before his family moved back to Yemen. Over the next 11 years, the young Awlaki gained the requisite cultural experience and tools that would later help him bridge American and Arab culture.

In 1991, Awlaki returned to the United States on an education grant from the Yemeni government in order to attend college at Colorado State University. While pursuing a bachelors of science degree in civil engineering, he became active within the Muslim student association on campus. In 1994 he began preaching for the Denver Islamic Society, which he did for two years before deciding to leave Colorado and move to San Diego, California, where he began working on a graduate degree in educational leadership at San Diego State University.

While in San Diego, Awlaki assumed the role of imam at a local mosque, Masjid Ar-Ribat al Islami. It was in that role that he reportedly came into contact with two of the future 9/11 hijackers, Nawaf al Hazmi and Khalid al Mihdhar. Some reports suggest that Awlaki's relationship to the hijackers grew very close in 2000. However, although the Federal Bureau of Investigation (FBI) began investigating Awlaki's ties to terrorism as early as June 1999, they did not find sufficient incriminating evidence to take action against him.

After spending four years in San Diego, al Awlaki decided to leave in 2000, eventually settling in the Washington, D.C., metro area in January 2001. He became imam at the Dar al Hijrah mosque, located in Falls Church, Virginia, and also served as a Muslim chaplain at George Washington University. Before the 9/11 attacks, al Awlaki came into contact with another al Qaeda operative and 9/11 hijacker, Hani Hanjour. Both Hanjour and Hamzi attended Awlaki's sermons.

In the weeks after the 9/11 attacks, the FBI reportedly conducted eight interviews with

Awlaki, but they acquired no further incriminating information on any possible connection between him and al Qaeda. Nonetheless, feeling increased pressure from law enforcement, Awlaki moved to the United Kingdom in 2002, where he established a dedicated following of young British Muslims. It was during this time that he rose to prominence within the Western Islamic world. His easygoing style, colloquial use of English, and the accessible content of his lectures made him popular with diverse audiences, in spite of his lack of extensive formal religious training. British Muslims who attended his talks during this time have commented on how exciting it was for them to hear an American with his rhetorical skills.

Awlaki returned to Yemen in 2004. Although little is publicly known about his activities during this time, he was arrested in mid-2006 by Yemeni security forces. He remained imprisoned for approximately a year and a half without formal charges being issued against him. After his release, Awlaki's statements and lectures grew more openly hostile against the United States, who he says pressured the Yemeni government into arresting him. His statements also began gaining influence with Western Muslims seeking easy religious justification for plotting violence against the United States. His recorded lecture series, *Constants of the Path of Jihad,* for example, which has been widely downloaded from the Internet, helped inspire a group of men convicted of the 2006–2007 terrorist plot against the U.S. Army base at Fort Dix, New Jersey.

In December 2008, Awlaki penned an open letter of support for the Somali terrorist group called al Shabab. Written in English, Awlaki used the letter to urge Western Muslims to do whatever they could to support the organization. In January 2009, Awlaki used his website to publish another call to action to Western Muslims seeking religious justification for waging violence, titled "44 Ways to Support Jihad." Here, Awlaki argued that all Muslims are bound by religious duty to do something that supports violent Jihad.

Awlaki began regularly appearing in officially sanctioned al Qaeda media releases in 2010. In May 2010, the leader of al Qaeda in Yemen released an Internet audio statement openly supporting Awlaki as one of his own. Later that month, the Yemeni al Qaeda group released an

official interview with Awlaki, eliminating any doubt that may have existed that he had officially joined the al Qaeda organization.

The Internet has been a key tool in Awlaki's ability to spread his message and reach followers, both indirectly and directly. One of supporters was the American Army officer Nidal M. Hasan, who had attended his sermons in Virginia. On November 5, 2009, Major Hasan opened fire in the Soldier Readiness Center at the Fort Hood Army base in Texas, killing 13 people. According to reports, at least 18 e-mails had been sent between Hasan and Awlaki in the lead-up to the attacks.

In May 2010, a 21-year-old British university student, Roshonara Choudhry, stabbed a member of Parliament for his support of the war in Iraq. According to Choudhry's own confession, she had self-radicalized in large part through listening to Awlaki's speeches on the Internet. She was sentenced to 15 years in prison.

In June 2010, two American citizens, Mohamed Alessa and Carlos Almonte, sought to respond to Awlaki's call for supporting the Somali group al Shabab by attempting to travel to Somalia. According to reports, the pair had allegedly downloaded multiple videos and sermons from Awlaki on the Internet. Another American citizen, Zachary Chesser, who had downloaded videos of Awlaki and exchanged e-mails with him, was arrested in July 2010 on charges of attempting to provide material support to al Shabab.

Media reports have stated that Anwar al Awlaki was placed on the American government's official targeted killing list, as authorized by President Barack Obama and approved by the National Security Council in 2010. This designation means that, even though he is a U.S. citizen, Awlaki is considered a military enemy of the United States and not subject to America's own ban on political assassination.

Jarret Brachman

See also al Qaeda; al Shabab

Further Readings

Awlaki, Anwar al. "44 Ways to Support Jihad." http://www.nefafoundation.org/miscellaneous/FeaturedDocs/nefaawlaki44wayssupportjihad.pdf.

Barclay, Jack. *Challenging the Influence of Anwar al Awlaki. Developments in Radicalisation and Violence.* London: International Centre for the Study of Radicalisation and Political Violence, September 2010). http://icsr.info/publications/papers/1283965345ICSR_ChallengingtheInfluenceofAnwar AlAwlaki.pdf.

Carnegie Endowment for International Peace. "The Rise of Anwar al Awlaki." Discussion moderated by Christopher Boucek, June 1, 2010. Transcript available online at http://carnegieendowment.org/files/0602carnegie-awlaki.pdf.

Ayyash, Yahya (1966–1996)

The Palestinian Yahya Ayyash (aka The Engineer), a notorious Hamas commander, is said to have been as greatly loved by Palestinians as he was hated by Israelis. Ayyash achieved a near mythical status as a man who always escaped detection by Israel's intelligence service. He is said to have masterminded multiple suicide attacks in Israel that killed nearly 70 civilians and injured more than 300. Ayyash was assassinated on January 5, 1996, by a booby-trapped cellular phone allegedly planted by Shin Bet, Israel's security service. Nearly 100,000 people, about 11 percent of Gaza's population, marched at Ayyash's funeral, where he was given a 21-gun salute.

The son of a farmer, Ayyash was born in Rafat, a village in the West Bank highlands. He studied electrical engineering and chemistry at Bir Zeit University in Ramallah, Saudi Arabia. In the first large attack allegedly planned by Ayyash, in 1994, a Hamsa suicide bomber blew himself up near a bus in Afula, Israel, killing eight people. Five more attacks followed, but Ayyash continued to escape detection for more than three years. Linked to 11 suicide bombings, he became known as "the Engineer" for his skill in building bombs and planning attacks. Press accounts before his assassination reported that he earned the name "the man with seven souls" in the Palestinian territories after escaping death many times. He is even said to have posed as a Jewish settler in Israeli territory while escaping from Nablus in the West Bank to Gaza.

In late December 1995, Hamas promised Yasir Arafat and the Palestinian Authority that it would cease military operations. At that time, Ayyash was staying in Beit Lahiya in the Gaza Strip with Osama Hamad, an old friend and college roommate. Press accounts of Ayyash's murder indicate that Hamad worked for his uncle, Kamal Hamad, a contractor and suspected Shin Bet informer with close ties to the former Israeli military government. Kamal Hamad had lent his nephew a mobile phone months before the attack, saying that he wanted to be able to reach him easily. On January 4, 1996, Kamal Hamad asked for the phone, and when he returned it, he asked his nephew to leave the phone turned on at all times. The next morning, at around 9 o'clock, Ayyash's father called his son—first on the house's standard phone line and then, as the call would not go through, on the cell phone. Osama Hamad answered the cell phone and passed it to Ayyash. Hamad later said he walked away to give his nephew more privacy; he then heard an explosion and looked back to see smoke. The blast had decapitated Ayyash.

Following Ayyash's assassination, rumors circulated that he had, in fact, escaped. A loyal follower, the rumors suggested, had answered the cell phone in his place and died for his leader. In the two months following Ayyash's death, suicide bombings instigated by Hamas and Palestine Islamic Jihad in retaliation for his murder killed more than 40 people. The bombers targeted buses and bus stops in Jerusalem and Ashkelon. The international press widely reported that Kamal Hamad, who fled Gaza after the bombing, believed that the phone he gave to his nephew was rigged with a listening device, not explosives. Kamal Hamad subsequently sued Shin Bet for financial losses and the threat to his own life for playing a role in the murder.

Erica Pearson

See also Arafat, Yasir; Hamas; Iraq War; Palestine Islamic Jihad; Suicide Terrorism

Further Readings

Brown, Derek. "A War of the Shadows; Obituary: Yahya Ayyash." *The Guardian* (London), January 8, 1996, p. 11.

Cockburn, Patrick. "How the Phone Bomb Was Set Up." *The Independent* (London), January 9, 1996, p. 10.

Greenberg, Joel. "Slaying Blended Technology and Guile." *The New York Times,* January 10, 1996, p. A3.

Katz, Samuel M. *The Hunt for the Engineer: The Story of How Israel's Counterterrorist Forces Tracked and Killed the Hamas Master Bomber.* Guilford, CT: Lyons Press/Globe Pequot, 2002.

Roy, Sara. "The Reason for Rage in Gaza." *Christian Science Monitor,* January 12, 1996, p. 20.

Sayre, Edward. "Victory in Iraq May Not Stop Suicide Attacks." *Atlanta Journal Constitution,* April 1, 2003, p. A13.

BAADER, ANDREAS (1943–1977)

Andreas Baader was one of the leaders of the Baader-Meinhof Gang, also known as the Red Army Faction, a West German Marxist group active during the 1970s.

Baader was born in Munich on May 3, 1943. His father was killed on the Russian front in World War II, and he was raised by his mother and grandmother. He was an unruly child, and though intelligent, he did poorly in school. As a teenager, he became obsessed with cars and was arrested several times for driving without a license.

Baader spent most of his time hanging out in West Berlin's student bars and cafés. Handsome and charismatic, he was popular with women, though he often treated them contemptuously, using derogatory terms in conversation. In 1967 he met and became the lover of Gudrun Ensslin. Though always rebellious and prone to violence, Baader was not an intellectual, and he seems to have had no coherent political ideology before meeting Ensslin, who had long been a committed leftist and an activist. Baader's relationship with Ensslin, who was several years older than him, would prove enduring, and he came to share in her political beliefs.

Student protest was increasing in Germany in the late 1960s, just as it was in other parts of the world. Students were highly critical of U.S. involvement in Vietnam, as well as their own nation's reluctance to address its Nazi past. Ensslin, Baader, and two friends decided to strike back at what they called the fascism of the West German state by firebombing two Frankfurt department stores in April 1968. Arrested almost immediately, they were convicted in October 1968.

Released pending appeal in June 1969, Baader and two of his co-conspirators jumped bail and fled to Switzerland in November after their appeal was rejected. Within a few months, however, they were back in Berlin, and in April 1970, Baader was recaptured and imprisoned. On May 15, his comrades, executing a daring escape plan, freed Baader at gunpoint. The jailbreak became international news because of the involvement of Ulrike Meinhof, a well-known leftist journalist, and the group came to be referred to as the Baader-Meinhof Gang.

Once Baader was freed, the gang traveled to a Palestinian training camp in Lebanon for instruction in bomb making and other guerrilla techniques. After returning to Germany in August 1970, they began a series of bank robberies. Over the course of the next two years, the gang robbed dozens of banks, bombed two U.S. army bases and several German targets, killing eight people, and engaged in a number of confrontations with police in which several gang members were arrested and two police officers were killed. On June 1, 1972, the authorities discovered one of the gang's bomb-making facilities. During a two-hour standoff, the police arrested Baader, who resisted and was shot in the leg, and his two companions. Other top gang leaders, including Meinhof and Ensslin, were arrested in the following weeks.

Their trial was put off for more than three years so that the German government could construct a special terror-proof prison and courthouse in which to conduct it. The remnants of the gang made several attempts to free their leaders, while the prisoners went on hunger strikes and wrote pamphlets protesting prison conditions. After the gang member Holgar Meins died while on a hunger strike, the gang became a cause célèbre for leftists, and the famed philosopher Jean-Paul Sartre visited Baader in prison.

Baader was convicted and sentenced to life imprisonment on April 28, 1977. On October 18, 1977, after it had become clear that the latest attempt to free them had failed, Baader, Ensslin, and Jan-Carl Raspe, another member of the group, committed suicide in prison.

Colleen Sullivan

See also Baader-Meinhof Gang; German Red Army Faction; Japanese Red Army; Meinhof, Ulrike

Further Readings

Aust, Stefan, *Baader-Meinhof: The Inside Story of the R.A.F.* London: The Bodley Head, 2008.

Bauer, Karin, ed. *Everybody Talks about the Weather . . . We Don't: The Writings of Ulrike Meinhof.* New York: Seven Stories Press, 2008.

Becker, Jillian, *Hitler's Children.* Philadelphia: J.B. Lippincott, 1977.

Graham, Stephen. "Terrorism Goes Trendy in Germany." *Los Angeles Times,* December 22, 2002, p. A40.

Horchem, Hans Josef. *West Germany's Red Army Anarchists.* London: Institute for the Study of Conflict, 1974.

Huffman, Richard. "The Baader-Meinhof Gang at the Dawn of Terror." http://www.baader-meinhof.com.

Proll, Astrid. *Baader Meinhof: Pictures on the Run 67–77.* Berlin and New York: Scalo, 1998.

Schiller, Margit. *Remembering the Armed Struggle: Life in Baader Meinhof.* Darlington, NSW, Australia: Zidane Press, 2009.

Varon, Jeremy. *Bringing the War Home: The Weather Underground, the Red Army Faction, and Revolutionary Violence in the Sixties and Seventies.* Berkeley: University of California Press, 2004.

BAADER-MEINHOF GANG

The Communist group known as the Baader-Meinhof Gang (aka Red Army Faction), which was named for Andreas Baader and the leftist journalist Ulrike Meinhof, terrorized West Germany in the 1970s. The gang, which called itself the Red Army Faction (RAF), engaged in bombing campaigns and assassinations, including attacks against U.S. Army bases.

The Baader-Meinhof Gang emerged from the German student protest movement of the late 1960s. Originally focused on university reform, the student movement soon took on distinct leftist characteristics as it agitated against the Vietnam War and U.S. imperialism. Students were also highly critical of German society's reluctance to confront its Nazi past, with those on the radical fringe contending that the West German government was merely a continuation of that fascist state. It was this radical fringe that supplied most of the Baader-Meinhof Gang's members, most prominently Gudrun Ensslin, a former graduate student and longtime activist.

In April 1968, Ensslin, her lover Baader, and two accomplices, Horst Söhnlein and Thorwald Proll, moved from protest to active violence, firebombing two Frankfurt department stores. Although property was damaged, no one was hurt. Quickly arrested and convicted in October 1968, the four were released pending appeal. When the appeal was denied in November, Baader, Ensslin, and Proll jumped bail and fled to Switzerland.

Within a few months, they returned to Germany, and Baader was recaptured in April and imprisoned. On May 15, 1970, six members of the group, with the help of Meinhof, freed Baader in a daring jailbreak. After Baader's escape the group became known as the Baader-Meinhof Gang (or Group). However, they called themselves the Red Army Faction in imitation of a Japanese terrorist group, the Japanese Red Army.

Once Baader was freed, the group commenced terrorist activities in earnest, traveling to a Palestinian training camp in Lebanon for instruction in bomb making and other guerrilla skills. They returned to Germany in August 1970 and, in need of funds, began a series of bank robberies and attracted new recruits. By then the group had become the target of a massive manhunt. Three police officers were killed in a series of shootouts during 1971, and several gang members were arrested. In May 1972, they began a bombing campaign against German and American targets, setting off six bombs that killed four people and injured more than 40.

At the end of May, German police discovered the gang's bomb-making facility and staked it out. On June 1, Baader and two other men entered the building and, after a siege lasting several hours, were arrested. Over the next two weeks, lucky breaks led to the arrest of Ensslin, Meinhof, and another top gang leader. With their leadership gone, the gang was seriously incapacitated and the character of the organization was greatly altered. Several attempts, all unsuccessful, were made to free Meinhof, Baader, and the others.

The West German government, determined to both deflect criticism and prevent further terrorist attacks during the trials, built a special prison for the Baader-Meinhof prisoners, with an attached courtroom to be used solely for their trials. The trials were in fact delayed for three years during the prison's construction. During this period, members of the group went on hunger strikes to protest their solitary confinement, leading to the death of one group member. The gang also became something of a leftist cause célèbre. On May 9, 1976, just before the trial, Meinhof hung herself in her cell. On October 18, 1977, after a last-ditch attempt at getting the prisoners released had failed, the four remaining Baader-Meinhof leaders attempted suicide in their cells, with three of them succeeding in the effort. The one member who survived was released in 1994. Rumors that the prisoners had not committed suicide but been killed persisted after their deaths.

The Baader-Meinhof gang and its activities have attained an almost mythic status in Germany, while their Red Army descendants persisted in terror through the first decade of the twenty-first century. They will be remembered as one of the most feared terrorist groups in Western Europe during the turbulent 1970s.

Colleen Sullivan

See also Baader, Andreas; German Red Army Faction; Japanese Red Army; Meinhof, Ulrike

Further Readings

Ascherson, Neil. "A Terror Campaign of Love and Hate." *The Observer* (London), September 28, 2008, p. 4.

Aust, Stefan. *Baader-Meinhof: The Inside Story of the R.A.F.* London: The Bodley Head, 2008.

Bauer, Karin, ed. *Everybody Talks about the Weather . . . We Don't: The Writings of Ulrike Meinhof.* New York: Seven Stories Press, 2008.

Becker, Jillian. *Hitler's Children.* Philadelphia: J.B. Lippincott, 1977.

Eager, Paige Whaley. *From Freedom Fighters to Terrorists: Women and Political Violence.* Burlington, VT: Ashgate, 2008.

Gedye, Robin. "Baader-Meinhof Terrorist Freed after 22 Years." *Daily Telegraph,* December 2, 1994, p. 18.

Harclerode, Peter. *Secret Soldiers: Special Forces in the War Against Terrorism.* London: Cassell and Co., 2000.

Horchem, Hans Josef. *West Germany's Red Army Anarchists.* London: Institute for the Study of Conflict, 1974.

Huffman, Richard. "The Baader-Meinhof Gang at the Dawn of Terror." http://www.baader-meinhof.com.

Landler, Mark. "Germany Relives 1970s Terror As 2 Seek Release from Jail." *The New York Times,* February 7, 2007, p. A4.

Proll, Astrid, *Baader Meinhof: Pictures on the Run 67–77.* Berlin and New York: Scalo, 1998.

Schiller, Margit. *Remembering the Armed Struggle: Life in Baader Meinhof.* Darlington, NSW, Australia: Zidane Press, 2009.

Varon, Jeremy. *Bringing the War Home: The Weather Underground, the Red Army Faction, and Revolutionary Violence in the Sixties and Seventies.* Berkeley: University of California Press, 2004.

BAKUNIN, MIKHAIL (1814–1876)

Mikhail Bakunin was a Russian radical whose ideas created the theoretical foundations for anarchism and terrorism.

Born in February 1814 to members of the Russian nobility, Bakunin spent an idyllic childhood on his father's country estate. At the age of 14, he was sent to St. Petersburg to study at the Artillery School in preparation for a military career. A somewhat indifferent student, Bakunin's time in military school helped to inculcate in him the loathing for all forms of coercion and authority that would be codified in his anarchist philosophy.

After graduating, Bakunin was stationed at a remote post on the Polish frontier, where he began to study history and philosophy. Within six months, however, he decided that the army was not for him. He left his post and returned to Moscow, where he began mingling with radical students. During the early 1840s, Bakunin traveled widely in Europe, consorting with Russian expatriates, Polish nationalists, and radical European philosophers, and becoming noted for his eloquent and fiery oratory. He began to publish pamphlets and treatises outlining his new philosophy, most importantly an 1842 essay that concluded with the aphorism, "The passion for destruction is also a creative passion," perhaps his most famous saying. These activities caused the Russian government to demand that he return to Russia. When he refused, his passport was revoked, and he was tried in absentia for treason and sentenced to Siberian exile.

Already a fugitive, Bakunin achieved international infamy through his participation in the revolutions of 1848. In that year, massive revolts in several European countries brought down the French monarchy and shook the governments of Germany and Austria to their core. Bakunin flitted from disturbance to disturbance, showing up at the barricades in Paris, Dresden, Berlin, and Prague in the course of 1848–1849. His participation in the events of 1848 led to successive trials in France and Austria, and he was sentenced to death both times. The Austrian authorities, however, transferred him to Russia at the behest of the czar. For more than three years, Bakunin was imprisoned in the Peter and Paul Fortress in Moscow; while there, he wrote his enigmatic *Confession* in a plea for clemency. He was allowed to go into exile in Siberia in 1857. Four years later, he managed to escape from Siberia on a ship, returning to Europe by way of Japan and the United States.

Following his escape, Bakunin entered his most active period of revolutionary agitation, becoming the leader of the anarchist groups already active in Europe and attracting a strong following in Spain, Italy, and France. The anarchists were not the only revolutionary ideologues in the Europe of the 1860s, for this period also saw the rise of communism, with Karl Marx forming the International Workingmen's Association (the First International) in 1864 in an attempt to unite all European radicals. Bakunin and his anarchists soon entered a fierce battle with Marx for control of the European radical movement.

In 1872 Marx succeeded in expelling Bakunin and the anarchists from the International, primarily because of allegations that Bakunin had been forming secret societies within the group with the intent of taking it over. The opinions of later commentators have differed sharply on this question, but the evidence appears to support Marx's accusation. Such clandestine power plays are the antithesis of anarchist philosophy, and that Bakunin would support such a strategy highlights the complexity of his personality and his politics. Throughout Bakunin's life, his desire to personally participate in the anarchist revolution often caused him to behave in a self-contradictory manner.

His friendship and support of the Russian revolutionary Sergey Nechaev is perhaps the most striking example of the perverse effects of his radical ardor. Nechaev had cold-bloodedly murdered one of his companions while in Russia, and it was while he was on the run that he met Bakunin. Though most of their radical contemporaries reviled Nechaev and his methods, Bakunin embraced them, collaborating with him on a pamphlet called *Catechism of a Revolutionary* (or *Catechism of a Revolutionist*, 1869), discussed below. Though he eventually broke with Nechaev and renounced some of his views, Bakunin's relationship with Nechaev proved disastrous for him personally, estranging him from the movement he had helped to found. He died penniless in Bern, Switzerland, on July 1, 1876.

The Grandfather of Terrorism

It is difficult to sum up Bakunin's philosophy simply. Most of his writings are in the form of personal letters, political pamphlets responding to specific political events of the day, and fragments of uncompleted essays written on the run. In brief, Bakunin believed in a progressive notion of history; that is, he believed that historical events are not random and without purpose, but instead represent development toward a goal, and that humanity will eventually achieve a condition in which all people are self-aware and free to determine their own destinies. Bakunin believed that the desire for freedom was a primary drive in all human beings, and that any attempt to force people to behave in a manner inconsistent with their own desires was inherently evil.

Bakunin saw the state, particularly the monarchial and autocratic states of nineteenth-century Europe, as the primary obstacle to human freedom in his own time. He believed that the use of coercion by the state to maintain power over individuals was the root of all the evils of modern society. Thus, in order for people to be free, the state must be destroyed utterly. He believed that the misery inflicted on the mass of humanity by the state would inspire them to revolt, and that this revolution would come quickly, perhaps in his own lifetime. These beliefs—that individual liberty is the source of all good, that all forms of coercion are inherently evil, and that the state must be destroyed in order to bring about a utopian era of liberty—are the founding tenets of anarchism.

These tenets present a practical problem for the anarchist attempting to bring about the revolution, however. If the use of coercive power is inherently evil, how can people be convinced to revolt against the vast power of the state? Bakunin believed that the anarchist revolutionary should not attempt to organize and lead the people's revolution, for attaining a position of leadership inevitably gives one power over others, and is thus inevitably corrupting. Instead, the job of the revolutionary is merely to spark the people's revolt. Thus Bakunin, in collaboration with Nechaev, arrived at the idea of "propaganda by deed," or the use of radical violence directed at the state in order to demonstrate to the masses the vulnerability of state power.

There is some dispute about how much Bakunin and Nechaev each contributed to the composition of *Catechism of a Revolutionary*, and about whose ideas the work truly represented. The essay argues, in essence, that the ends justify the means. They believed that since the state was inherently evil, any form of attack against it was a good, no matter who was harmed. Bombings, assassinations, robbery—all were acceptable so long as they furthered the cause of revolution. The phrase "propaganda by deed" represents an important development in the formation of modern terrorism. The use of violence to send a political message, rather than as an end in itself, is one of terrorism's defining attributes.

Further, since the creation of a vast and hierarchical organization would inevitably come to involve the use of coercive power, the anarchist revolutionaries should instead form small groups, or cells, of like-minded individuals capable of acting on their own initiative. From such cells a loose network could be created, with one member of each cell reporting to a central cell or committee that could help the various small groups act in concert. The cells would necessarily be secret; only one member would be in contact with the central cell, so that if an individual member or an entire cell were discovered and arrested, the organization would persist. This idea of a cell network as the basis for the revolutionary organization's structure is another striking contribution to the development of terrorism, and it remains the primary organizational method used by terrorist groups today.

Undoubtedly the aspect of the *Catechism* that most horrified Bakunin's contemporaries, and that has caused Bakunin to be regarded as the grandfather of terrorism, is its description of the attitude of the proper revolutionary toward his fellows. The *Catechism* states that the revolutionary must completely obliterate all weaknesses within him and devote himself body and soul to the cause of revolution. No allegiances—whether to family, friends, neighbor, country, or love—must be allowed to stay his hand. He exists in society only to learn better how to destroy it.

Further, this attitude must extend not only to the members of the society that he loathes, but to his fellow revolutionaries as well. He must not hesitate to send them to their death if it furthers his cause, and in turn he must weigh the cost of rescuing them against their value to the revolution. Nor should he hesitate to use cunning and deceit if these serve his purpose; in short, the revolutionary must be both utterly dedicated and utterly ruthless in attempting to bring about revolution.

Some biographers have asserted that this aspect of ruthlessness was far more Nechaev's contribution than Bakunin's, and that it does not represent Bakunin's own revolutionary ideology. Nevertheless, it is this aspect that most perfectly encapsulates the tortuous logic of the terrorist, whose unshakable belief that he is fighting against evil leads to the commission of the most terrible crimes against humanity.

Harvey Kushner

See also Anarchism; Kropotkin, Peter

Further Readings

Bakunin, Mikhail. *Selected Writings from Mikhail Bakunin: Essays on Anarchism.* St. Petersburg, FL: Red and Black Publishers, 2010.

Goodwin, James. *Confronting Dostoevsky's "Demons": Anarchism and the Specter of Bakunin in Twentieth-century Russia.* New York: Peter Lang, 2010.

Kelly, Aileen. *Mikhail Bakunin: A Study in the Psychology and Politics of Utopianism.* Oxford: Clarendon Press, 1982.

Leier, Mark. *Bakunin: The Creative Passion.* New York: Seven Stories Press, 2009.

Masters, Anthony. *Bakunin: The Father of Anarchism.* New York: Dutton, 1974.

Nechaev, Sergey, and Mikhail Bakunin. *Catechism of a Revolutionist.* 1869. http://pages.uoregon.edu/kimball/Nqv.catechism.thm.htm

Proudman, Mark F. "Crimes of the Rich." *National Post,* September 14, 2002, p. B7.

Sonn, Richard D. *Anarchism.* New York: Twayne, 1992.

BALI NIGHTCLUB BOMBING

On October 12, 2002, a car bomb exploded outside a nightclub in the tourist district of Kuta on the Indonesian island of Bali, killing more than 200 people. Aside from the loss of life, the attack was of great significance to Southeast Asia, Australia, and the entire global community for a number of reasons. First, coming as it did 13 months after the 9/11 attacks, the Bali bombing reinforced the view that transnational terrorism was spreading to other parts of the world much faster than intelligence analysts and commentators had predicted. Second, the attack was not only the deadliest act of terrorism in the history of Southeast Asia, it also signaled that Muslim militants were extending the ideology of their fight beyond the Israeli-Palestinian problem, which the 9/11 terrorists had claimed as their driving force. Third, the Bali bombing demonstrated that al Qaeda could rely entirely on local agents to carry out its mission without direct support from Osama bin Laden. And finally, the bombing demonstrated that the earlier decision taken by some Southeast Asian extremist groups to send recruits to training camps in Afghanistan and Pakistan beginning in the mid-1980s was beginning to pay dividends. Thus, Afghanistan and Pakistan had played a greater role in shaping the perspectives of the Bali bombers than did the Middle East.

The Bali terrorists killed 202 people, of whom 152 were foreign nationals from over 20 countries, including Australia (88), the United Kingdom (24), the United States (7), Germany (6), Sweden (5), France (4), the Netherlands (4), Denmark (3), New Zealand (3), and Switzerland (3). About 240 additional people were injured.

The Bali attack actually involved the detonation of three bombs. In addition to the bomb at the Sari Club, a backpack-mounted device carried by a suicide bomber exploded in Paddy's Pub, a bar across the street from the Sari Club, minutes before the car bomb exploded; a third, smaller, device was detonated outside the United States

From left: convicted Bali bombers Ali Ghufron alias Mukhlas, Imam Samudera alias Abdul Aziz, and Amrozi bin Nurhasyim during their trials in 2003 for the nightclub bombings on the resort island of Bali in 2002 that killed 202 people. Indonesia's Supreme Court in August 2007 rejected their appeal, and the men have been quoted as saying they would not seek clemency from the president, their last avenue of appeal. (AFP PHOTO/FILES/INDAH WINARSO; AFP PHOTO/FILES/ADEK BERRY; BAY ISMOYO/AFP/Getty Images)

consulate in Denpasar. This third bomb did not cause any fatalities. The terrorists in this case targeted venues that were owned or frequented by foreigners, especially Australians. The Sari Club and Paddy's Pub were very popular with Western tourists. The message here was that the terrorists were aiming at so-called soft targets—lightly defended spots frequented by civilians.

A short time after the bombing, both Indonesian analysts and Western intelligence agencies concluded that Jemaah Islamiyah was behind the attack. Jemaah Islamiyah is a violent Islamist group that evolved from a faction of the Darul Islam political movement at the urging of Abu Bakar Bashir and the late Abdullah Sungkar. Despite his denials, Bashir is considered the spiritual head of Jemaah Islamiyah. Moreover, two of the bombers, Amrozi and Mukhlas, were Bashir's students. Like Bashir, Amrozi and Mukhlas called for an Islamic state and for the implementation of Islamic or Shariah law in Indonesia. Amrozi, Mukhlas, and Imam Samudra, who masterminded the Bali bombing, were subsequently convicted and sentenced to death. The three were killed by a firing squad on November 9, 2008. As they were executed, they shouted "Allahu Akbar," meaning "God is great."

Claims within Indonesia and Southeast Asia that Abu Bakar Bashir was the spiritual leader of Jemaah Islamiyah, and that he might have been involved in planning the Bali bombing, raised hopes in the West that he could be arrested and jailed. Although he was later charged and found guilty of involvement in the Bali attack, he was sentenced to only two and a half years imprisonment in March 2005. Then, in August 2005, as part of the tradition of remissions for Indonesia's Independence Day, his jail term was reduced by four and a half months.

Moving Forward

Despite the obvious tragedy, the 2002 Bali bombing did have a positive impact on Indonesia's ties with its neighbors. For example, Indonesia's relations with Australia had been strained severely following Australia's leadership of the International Force for East Timor (INTERFET) in September 1999. Following the Bali bombing, however, the Indonesian and Australian police forces, as well as other intelligence services, have cooperated extensively not only on terrorism matters, but also on the

illicit drug trade and human trafficking. In October 2002, just a few days after the Bali bombing, Australia committed $10 million over four years to help Indonesia build its counterterrorism capacity. Australia initially provided assistance in three broad areas: police, anti-terrorism financing, and travel security. Thus, the Bali bombing prompted the Australian government to help enhance the counterterrorism skills of the Indonesian police through programs in crisis management as well as intelligence officer and analyst training.

Moreover, as a result of the Bali bombing and subsequent terrorist attacks in Indonesia, the Australian government initiated plans to share intelligence not just with Indonesia but also with other countries in Southeast Asia interested in pursuing counterterrorism measures. In addition, through its Law Enforcement Cooperation Program (LECP), the Australian Federal Police provides a wide range of capacity-building programs to Indonesia, the Philippines, and other countries with which it signed counterterrorism agreements subsequent to the Bali bombing. Australia has also established the Jakarta Centre for Law Enforcement Cooperation in Indonesia and the Pacific Transnational Crime Coordination Centre, and it has extended similar capacity-building programs to the Philippines.

Thus, while the Bali bombing caused many deaths and extensive damage to property, it helped bring Indonesian and Australian governments closer. It also served as a wake-up call for several countries in the region and globally. In the coming years, the long-term significance of the Bali tragedy will continue to resonate as countries in Southeast Asia cooperate not only on counterterrorism measures but on other issues as well.

Samuel M. Makinda

See also Bashir, Abu Bakar; Bombings and Bomb Scares

Further Readings

Abuza, Zachary. *Militant Islam in Southeast Asia.* Boulder, CO: Lynne Rienner, 2003.

Australian Strategic Policy Institute (ASPI). *Beyond Bali: ASPI's Strategic Assessment 2002.* Barton, Australia: ASPI, 2002. http://www.aspi.org.au/htmlver/ beyondbali/index.html.

Dalpino, Catharin, E. "Second Front, Second Time: Counter-Terrorism and US Policy Toward Southeast Asia." *Cambridge Review of International Affairs* 15, no. 2 (2002): 345–354.

Lindsay, Patrick. *Back From the Dead: Peter Hughes' Story of Hope and Survival After Bali.* Milsons Point, NSW, Australia: Random House Australia, 2003.

Vaughn, Bruce, Emma Chanlett-Avery, Richard Cronin, Mark Manyin, and Larry Niksch. *Terrorism in Southeast Asia.* Washington, DC: Congressional Research Service, 2005. Order Code RL31672.

BANNA, SABRI AL (1937–2002)

Sabri al Banna, known to the world as Abu Nidal, was a terrorist mastermind whose various organizations have been responsible for an estimated 900 deaths.

Born in 1937 in the town of Jaffa, in what was then British-ruled Palestine, Banna's early years were spent in luxury. His father, Ibrihim al Banna, owned a fruit exporting business that made him one of the richest men in the country. His 18 children and several wives wanted for nothing. When Banna was nine, his father died, and the family was left in difficult financial straits, partly because of the political turmoil in the Middle East. In 1948 the Banna family was forced to flee Jaffa and the advancing Israeli army. For more than a year, they were destitute refugees, and this year of living in poverty and humiliation shaped the young Banna's worldview. In 1949 the Banna family resettled in Nablus, on the west bank of the Jordan River.

Banna's first political involvement occurred while attending college in Cairo in the mid-1950s, when he joined the Baath Party, a socialist pan-Arab and anticolonialist group whose ideas would influence his political views. In 1957, after a brief stint as a teacher, Banna moved to Saudi Arabia to work as an electrical engineer. There he joined Fatah, the organization begun by Yasir Arafat to win back Palestine from the Israelis. In 1964 Fatah united with other Palestinian groups to form the Palestine Liberation Organization (PLO). Over the next decade, Banna rose within the PLO, becoming part of Arafat's inner circle, and acquiring Abu Nidal ("father of struggle") as a nom de guerre. In 1969 Banna was sent to Sudan to recruit for Fatah.

He spent little more than a year there before being reassigned to Baghdad, which in 1970 was dominated by the Baath Party and led by Saddam Hussein.

Banna's years in Iraq and his re-immersion in Baathist ideology led to a rupture between him and Fatah leaders. Fatah and the PLO espoused a form of Palestinian nationalism that, although dependent on aid from other Arab nations, was dedicated to creating an independent Palestinian state. Banna subscribed to the Baathist belief that the boundaries between contemporary Arab states were arbitrary legacies of colonialism, and that the eventual unification of all Arab peoples in a single nation-state was the necessary and desirable way for the Arabs to assume a position of world power. Accordingly, Israel, having been imposed upon the Arabs by the West, was an obstacle to Arab unity and must be eliminated. The existence of Israel also offered an opportunity to forge Arab unity through fighting this common enemy. To Banna, the fight for the liberation of Palestine was the cornerstone in creating an Arab world power; any move from armed struggle toward political accommodation placed this goal in jeopardy, anyone who dared make such accommodations was as much his enemy as the Israelis.

In the early 1970s, Arafat began to downplay Fatah's terrorism and maneuver for political recognition; his 1974 address to the United Nations was a major step in legitimizing him on the world's stage. Banna protested strenuously, causing Fatah's leadership to question his loyalty. In 1974 Banna left the organization. Using his Iraqi base, he began forming a new terrorist group, which has operated under several names but is most widely known as the Abu Nidal Organization (ANO). In November 1974, the PLO sentenced him to death in absentia. Several commentators have suggested that the death sentence was decided on after the discovery of a plot to assassinate Arafat.

From 1974 to 1983, the ANO operated from Iraq. In return for the protection of Hussein, Banna and the ANO carried out attacks against Saddam's enemies, particularly the Syrian Baath Party, which had a long-standing rivalry with Saddam's Iraqi Baath. During these years, the group engaged in several high-profile attacks, including the attempted assassination of the Israeli ambassador to England, Shlomo Argov, in June

1982. That attack provoked Israel to invade Lebanon, where the PLO had its headquarters.

By 1983, Iraq was deeply involved in a war against Iran, and in an attempt to curry favor with the West, Saddam Hussein expelled Banna and the ANO. Banna moved the ANO to Syria, where he remained until 1985; he then moved to Libya. In 1985, while based in Libya, the ANO executed some of its most daring and despicable attacks, including the machine-gunning of El Al Airlines counters at the Rome and Vienna airports. These attacks killed 17 people, and Banna became the world's most wanted terrorist.

While in Libya, Banna began to recruit seriously. The ANO had long-established front offices in most Arab countries, and its operatives had proven their ability to strike successfully almost anywhere in the world. Banna wanted to increase ANO's number of operations. By the late 1980s, however, Banna's suspicions were overtaking his judgment. Long famous for his caution—he would only eat food prepared by his personal chef and continually circulated rumors of his own death to confuse his enemies—he began to suspect that his underlings, with the support of the new members, might be plotting to replace him. He is reported to have responded to this threat with a brutal internal purge, killing as many 150 members of ANO. This action temporarily quieted dissent but caused many senior commanders to defect in the late 1980s, leaving the ANO seriously crippled.

Banna soon faced another danger; Jordanian security forces, tiring of his threats against King Hussein, reportedly arrested several members of his family and threatened to execute them. The ANO undertook no further attacks against Jordanian targets. By the early 1990s, the Jordanian threats, combined with the previous defections and his own declining health, seriously incapacitated Banna and the ANO. The last major attack attributed to the organization was the 1991 assassination of Abu Iyad, a PLO leader and Banna's former colleague. In the late 1990s, Libya's policy toward terrorism changed significantly, and Banna was no longer welcome. In 1999 he was reported to have received medical treatment in Cairo, possibly for leukemia.

Banna was found dead in Baghdad of multiple gunshot wounds on August 16, 2002. The exact circumstances of his death remain a mystery. The Iraqi security forces who reported Banna's death claimed that he committed suicide. But documents discovered after the invasion of Iraq in 2003 indicate that the Iraqi government believed that Banna had been hired by foreign powers, including the United States, to discredit the Hussein regime. While the Iraqi government reported that Banna had committed suicide, other observers have suggested the possibility that Hussein government killed Banna.

Colleen Sullivan

See also Abu Nidal Organization; Arafat, Yasir; Fatah; Hussein, Saddam; Palestine Liberation Organization

Further Readings

Beaumont, Peter. "Abu Nidal Sows Chaos from the Grave." *The Observer,* August 26, 2002, p. 22.

Fisk, Robert. "Abu Nidal, Notorious Palestinian Mercenary, 'Was a US Spy.'" *The Independent,* October 25, 2008, p. 30.

Melman, Yossi. *The Master Terrorist: The True Story of Abu-Nidal.* New York: Adama Books, 1986.

Nasr, Kameel B. *Arab and Israeli Terrorism: The Causes and Effects of Political Violence, 1936–1993.* Jefferson, NC: McFarland, 1997.

Seale, Patrick. *Abu Nidal: A Gun for Hire.* New York: Random House, 1992.

U.S. State Department. "Terrorist Organizations." *Country Reports on Terrorism 2008.* http://www .state.gov/s/ct/rls/crt/2008/122449.htm.

BASHIR, ABU BAKAR (1938–)

The Muslim cleric Abu Bakar Bashir (aka Ustad Abu) was born in August 1938 to Yemeni parents living in Jombang, East Java, Indonesia. He has been described as the spiritual head of a militant Islamic group called Jemaah Islamiyah, which supports some of the goals of the terror group al Qaeda. While Bashir has not been found to have directly planned any of the terrorist attacks that shattered Indonesia in the early twenty-first century, he has been the ideological leader of militant Indonesian Muslims involved in terrorist bombings. As leader of the Indonesian Mujahedeen

Council, Bashir's influence has spread beyond Indonesia's borders to several Southeast Asian countries, including Malaysia, Singapore, and the Philippines.

Bashir runs the al Mukmin boarding school in Ngruki, Central Java, which he cofounded with another cleric, Abdullah Sungkar, in 1971. Sungkar died in 1999, but al Mukmin has become a venue where young Muslims are taught radical ideas, which often drive them to engage in terrorist activities. Many Jemaah Islamiyah members, including the perpetrators of the 2002 bombing on the island of Bali, studied at al Mukmin.

During the presidency of Suharto, known as the New Order administration (1967–1998), Bashir and Sungkar were arrested several times for a number of reasons. They were imprisoned without trial from 1978 to 1982. Soon after their release, the two were linked to the 1985 bomb attack on a Buddhist monument, but they fled to Malaysia.

Bashir's radicalism was reinforced in exile as he interacted with young Muslims who had trained in Afghanistan and Pakistan with a view to fight the Soviet Union's occupation of Afghanistan from 1979 to 1989. Bashir also expanded his regional base by undertaking religious teaching in Malaysia and Singapore. It was during this period that Bashir and Sungkar reorganized Jemaah Islamiyah, which had evolved from a faction of the Darul Islam political movement. Following the fall of the Suharto regime, Bashir returned to Indonesia in 1999 and renewed his call for an Islamic state and for the implementation of Shariah law.

Bashir has expressed support for Osama bin Laden, but he has denied the existence of Jemaah Islamiyah, instead making contradictory claims about the Bali bombings and other terrorist attacks. Despite admissions by his followers that they planned and carried out the 2002 Bali bombing, Bashir has claimed the CIA and Israel were behind it. At the same time, he has described the Bali bombers as the defenders of Islam and Indonesia.

In October 2004, Bashir was arrested and charged with involvement in the Marriott Hotel bombing in Jakarta in August 2003, as well as the 2002 Bali bombing. The following spring he was convicted of conspiracy for the Bali attacks but acquitted for the Marriott Hotel attacks. He was sentenced to two and a half years imprisonment, but his jail term was later reduced. He was released

in June 2006, and his conviction was overturned by the Indonesian Supreme Court. Bashir has continued to call for Shariah law to be imposed on Indonesia, and he continues to blame the 2002 Bali bombings on the Central Intelligence Agency.

Bashir remains the key inspiration to Indonesia's militants. However, Indonesian authorities have failed to find sufficient evidence to imprison him on terrorism offenses. His situation illustrates the dilemma governments face over the need to detain terrorist suspects and the imperative to respect civil liberties.

Samuel M. Makinda

See also Bali Nightclub Bombing; Religious and Spiritual Perspectives on Terrorism

Further Readings

Abuza, Zachary. *Militant Islam in Southeast Asia*. Boulder, CO: Lynne Rienner, 2003.

Australian Government, Department of Foreign Affairs and Trade. *Transnational Terrorism: The Threat to Australia*. Canberra: Commonwealth of Australia, 2004. http://www.dfat.gov.au/publications/terrorism.

Council on Foreign Relations. *Backgrounder: Jemaah Islamiyah*. Washington, DC: Council on Foreign Relations, 2009. http://www.cfr.org/publication/8948/jemaah_islamiyah_aka_jemaah_islamiah.html.

Rabasa, Angel M. *Political Islam in Southeast Asia: Moderates, Radicals, and Terrorists*. New York: Oxford University Press, 2003.

Rabasa, Angel, et al. *Beyond al Qaeda*. Part 1, *The Global Jihadist Movement*. Santa Monica, CA: RAND Corporation, 2006.

BASQUE FATHERLAND AND LIBERTY

Basque Fatherland and Liberty (Euskadi Ta Askatasuna, or ETA), a group of separatists seeking Basque independence from Spain, is responsible for a decades-old liberation campaign whose bombings and murders have left more than 800 dead. Among their most high-profile attacks were the assassination of a Spanish prime minister and the killing of 21 shoppers at a Barcelona supermarket.

Feeling that the right-wing Basque Nationalist Party (PNV) was not significantly advancing the goal of achieving Basque independence from Spain, dissidents created this extremely radical and violent faction of the Basque separatist movement in 1959. ETA's liberation campaign has long been funded by crime, including robbery, kidnapping, and extortion. They have resorted to bombings and the murder of government officials and members of political parties to advance their cause. In 1969 several prominent leaders of the ETA were arrested for their involvement in the death of a police chief. One of the ETA's best-known crimes was the murder of the Spanish prime minister, Carrero Blanco, in 1973. Blanco's assassination was a particular triumph for the ETA, as he was also formerly a top-ranking member of the Francisco Franco administration. Franco was adamantly opposed to Basque self-rule, and when he died in 1975, the activities of the ETA dramatically increased. They founded their political wing, Herri Batasuna (which later changed its name to Batasuna), in 1978, and also began to target members of the People's Party, whose founder had ties to Franco, for assassination.

Overall, the ETA has killed more than 800 people, including 21 people who were killed by an ETA bomb at a supermarket in Barcelona in 1987. Cease-fires took place during peace talks with Spain in 1988, 1995, and 1998, but the talks were unsuccessful, and in all three cases the violence escalated again.

A group similar to the ETA that exists mostly in the French provinces of the Basque region is called Enbata. They offer support to the ETA and the groups sometimes coordinate their terrorist attacks. In 2000 a Spanish group, Jarrai, and a French group, Gasteriak, united to form a youthful faction of the ETA called Haika, which has been responsible for an increase in terrorist attacks in France. Fifteen members of Haika were arrested in March 2001. Later that summer, eight members of the ETA were arrested in Spain when they were found with a car bomb that was already armed for an attack.

The September 11, 2001, attacks in the United States, while unrelated to ETA, led to a hardening of the Spanish government's stance toward the group's political wing, Batasuna. The party was banned in 2003, and since then a number of other leftist Basque nationalists parties have been banned as well because they are considered fronts for Batasuna.

Despite the harder line, the Spanish government attempted to enter into negotiations with the ETA in 2006, leading the group to declare a "permanent" cease-fire in May. That cease-fire lasted until late December, when a bomb set off by the ETA in a Madrid airport killed two people. The ETA demanded that the Spanish government lift the ban on Batasuna and move people imprisoned for ETA activities to jails in Basque territory. In addition, the organization violently opposed a high-speed rail line that was under construction and would link the Spanish capital of Madrid to cities in the Basque region. On December 3, 2008, ETA gunmen killed a businessman involved in the rail project. The group also claimed responsibility for a 2009 bombing on the island of Mallorca that killed two police officers.

In September 2010, the ETA announced that it was again observing a cease-fire and was seeking to negotiate with the Spanish government. Spanish officials responded with skepticism, pointing to ETA's numerous broken cease-fires in the past. Observers speculated that perhaps ETA was offering to negotiate because the group was too weakened to continue carrying out attacks. The former Irish Republican Army leader Gerry Adams, however, claimed that he personally had been involved in convincing ETA to negotiate, and he claimed the group's desire for peace was sincere.

Harvey Kushner

See also Basque Separatists

Further Readings

Bew, John, Martyn Frampton, and Inigo Gurruchaga. *Talking to Terrorists: Making Peace in Northern Ireland and in the Basque Country.* New York: Columbia University Press, 2009.

Burke, Jason. "Now ETA Kills in the Name of the Environment." *The Observer,* December 14, 2008, p. 40.

Clark, Robert P. *Negotiating with ETA: Obstacles to Peace in the Basque Country, 1975–1988.* Reno: University of Nevada Press, 1990.

Mulligan, Mark. "Basques Cautious over ETA 'Indefinite Ceasefire' Claim." *Financial Times,* March 27, 2006, p. 9.

Nash, Elizabeth. "Why Has the ETA Problem Flared up Again, and Can It Ever Be Resolved?" *The Independent*, June 22, 2009, p. 30.

Sullivan, J. L. *ETA and Basque Nationalism: The Fight for Euskadi, 1890–1986.* New York: Routledge, 1998.

Woodworth, Paddy. *Dirty War, Clean Hands: ETA, the GAL, and Spanish Democracy.* New Haven, CT: Yale University Press, 2003.

Zulaika, Joseba. *Basque Violence: Metaphor and Sacrament.* Reno: University of Nevada Press, 2000.

BASQUE SEPARATISTS

Basque separatists are natives of the Basque region who are campaigning for national sovereignty and cultural independence from the surrounding nations of Spain and France. Since the 1970s, the campaign has taken a both a political route and a terrorist route to achieve its goal.

The Basque people have lived in the western region of the Pyrenees Mountains between Spain and France since the Middle Ages. They speak their own language, Euskara, which is one of the oldest languages in Europe, and maintain a degree of ethnic insularity. They were independent throughout the 1700s, but around 1800 they were divided, to be partly ruled by both France and Spain. Almost immediately, a strong separatist movement was formed that still exists today. Resentful that they were no longer self-governed, the Basque separatists formed a political party called the Basque Nationalist Party (PNV), held widespread protests, and committed a variety of violent acts. Although the movement consists of Basques from both neighboring countries, the Spanish separatists were and currently are more active than the French. Spain has resisted granting full independence to the Basque Region because it contributes to the gross domestic product and offers valuable resources.

When the dictator Francisco Franco formed the Spanish Republic in 1931, he stripped those in the Basque region of many of their civil rights, including the right to use their language. After Franco's death, the Basques refused to ratify the Spanish constitution that both restored the monarchy and established democracy until Spain conceded them the right to have their own limited government. The Basque region has since elected its own parliament to govern various affairs. However, they are not completely autonomous, and many Basques still desire absolute freedom from Spain.

The Euskadi Ta Askatasuna (ETA), or Basque Fatherland and Freedom, is a terrorist group of radical separatists that have killed more than 800 people in various bombings, kidnappings, assassinations, and robberies. In particular, the ETA targets members of the People's Party and others that advocate the unity of Spain, such as King Juan Carlos. In 2000, a youth wing of the ETA called Haika was formed from a merger of the Spanish pro-Basque independence youth group Jarrai and its French counterpart, Gasteriak. Haika increased the violent activity in France, leading Spain and France to augment joint efforts to apprehend Basque terrorists. In the late 2000s, ETA turned its attention to a high-speed rail line under construction that would link Madrid and Basque territory; the group violently opposes the railroad, which it sees as eroding Basque autonomy.

Although violent groups like the ETA continue to exist, many separatist Basques are willing to pursue their goals through peaceful measures. The PNV, for example, has completely foresworn violence and has historically dominated the regional Parliament. The ETA also has a political wing, but that party was banned as a terrorist organization in 2003, and other Basque nationalist parties have been banned as well.

As a result of these actions, the PNV lost control of the regional parliament in 2009. Although it won more seats than any other party, the Basque nationalist parties it had allied with in the past had been banned or had lost so much support that the PNV could no longer put together a ruling coalition. It remains to be seen if the banning of such political parties will be accepted by Basque separatists, or if they will feel that they have been denied a political outlet for their views and will instead turn to more violence.

Harvey Kushner

See also Basque Fatherland and Liberty; Madrid Bombings

Further Readings

Bew, John, Martyn Frampton, and Inigo Gurruchaga. *Talking to Terrorists: Making Peace in Northern Ireland and in the Basque Country.* New York: Columbia University Press, 2009.

Jacob, James E. *Hills of Conflict: Basque Nationalism in France.* Reno: University of Nevada Press, 1994.

Mallet, Victor. "Security and Political Setbacks Spur Prospects for Basque Country Peace." *Financial Times,* April 13, 2009, p. 4.

Nash, Elizabeth. "Why Has the ETA Problem Flared up Again, and Can It Ever Be Resolved?" *The Independent,* June 22, 2009, p. 30.

"A New Landscape: Spain and Its Regions." *The Economist,* March 7, 2009, p. 60.

Núñez, Luis C. *The Basques: Their Struggle for Independence.* Translated from the French by Meic Stephens. Cardiff, Wales: Welsh Academic Press, 1997.

Woodworth, Paddy. *Dirty War, Clean Hands: ETA, the GAL, and Spanish Democracy.* New Haven, CT: Yale University Press, 2003.

BERENSON, LORI (1969–)

The American journalist Lori Berenson was imprisoned in Peru for alleged terrorist activity, in association with the guerilla organization known as the Tupac Amaru Revolutionary Movement (Movimiento Revolucionario Tupac Amaru, or MRTA). While supporters argued that Berenson was a political prisoner and not a terrorist sympathizer, her contact and association with members of the MRTA led a military tribunal to sentence her to life in prison for treason.

Born and raised in New York City, Berenson attended college at the Massachusetts Institute of Technology (MIT). In 1992 she moved to El Salvador as the civil war in that country was winding down. She became a secretary to a top leader of the group rebelling against the government, the FMLN, as the two sides worked toward peace.

In 1994 Berenson moved to Lima, Peru. She lived in a large house with many others in the middle-class neighborhood of La Molina. In November 1995, Peruvian police raided the house and found a supply of hidden weapons and evidence of terrorist activity. Several of the residents, including Berenson, were arrested for being alleged members of MRTA. The La Molina house was thought to be the MRTA headquarters where an attack on the Peruvian Congress was being planned. Berenson is alleged to have provided the layout of the congressional building to the MRTA. On January 11, 1996, she was convicted of treason by a panel of hooded judges in a military tribunal for her participation in the plot. (In trials involving terrorists in Peru, the judges veil their identity because they fear reprisals from the supporting terrorist organization.)

The manner in which Berenson was convicted was highly controversial. She was not allowed a jury or a personal statement, and her lawyer was not allowed to cross-examine any of the prosecution's witnesses or see their evidence. The trial lasted only minutes and resulted in the 26-year-old being sentenced to life in prison. With her parents' support, Berenson began the appeals process. She continues to maintain her innocence, claiming that she did not know her housemates were involved in the MRTA, and that she did not have any knowledge of the activities that were taking place on the floors above her room.

In March 2000 the Peruvian government agreed to set aside the life sentence and retry Berenson in a civilian court. In this second trial, Berenson was convicted of aiding the plot against the Congress by providing the layout of the building, helping to secure weapons, and renting her house to MRTA members. She was sentenced to 20 years in prison in June 2001. In 2002 the Inter-American Commission on Human Rights, part of the Organization of American States, found that Berenson's trial violated her rights and was invalid. The Peruvian government appealed the case to the Inter-American Court of Human Rights, and in December 2004 the court upheld Berenson's conviction and sentencing.

Berenson married the rebel Aníbal Apari in 2003, and she gave birth to a son, Salvador, while in prison. In May 2010 Berenson was released on parole, but she was ordered to spend the remainder of her sentence (five years) in Peru. After a strong public outcry from some sectors in Peru, however, Berenson was returned to prison in August 2010, only to be paroled again in November 2010.

Harvey Kushner

See also Tupac Amaru Revolutionary Movement

Further Readings

Berenson, Rhoda. *Lori: My Daughter, Wrongfully Imprisoned in Peru.* New York: Context Books, 2000.

Brubaker, Paul. "A Family Torn: Parents Mark
    Daughter's 10 Years in Peruvian Prison." *The Record,*
    November 10, 2005, p. L1.
Committee to Free Lori Berenson. http://www.freelori.org.
Haman, Danna. "Berenson: From Terrorist to Baker."
    Christian Science Monitor, December 27, 2005, p. 4.
"Locked-up Lori: Peru's Terrorism Trials." *The
    Economist,* December 11, 2004, p. 55.
"Lori Berenson Interview with Peruvian Times." *Peruvian
    Times,* August 19, 2010. http://www.peruviantimes
    .com/peruvian-times-interview-with-lori-berenson/
    197707.

BIN LADEN, OSAMA (1957–2011)

For much of his life, Osama bin Laden was likely the most infamous terrorist in the world. Known among his cadres as "the prince" and "the emir," bin Laden sought to overturn the current world order and replace it with one in which the Islamic world would have no borders. This Islamic polity, according to bin Laden, was to be ruled by a caliph. He also sought to encourage Muslim jihads around the world, end U.S. military operations against Iraq, destroy the state of Israel, and overthrow secular, moderate regimes in the Middle East, including Saudi Arabia and Egypt. To achieve these ends, bin Laden created a militant Islamic network called al Qaeda.

Early Years

Osama bin Laden was born on March 10, 1957, in Riyadh, Saudi Arabia. He was the 17th son of 52 children born to Mohammad bin Laden, a business mogul in Saudi Arabia. Mohammad bin Laden moved to Saudi Arabia from neighboring Yemen in 1931 and founded a construction company, the Bin Laden Group. In time, the company grew and began to do contract work for the Saudi regime, building highways and infrastructure, in addition to famous mosques in the holy cities of Mecca and Medina. When Mohammad bin Laden was killed in a helicopter crash in 1968, his inheritance, worth billions of dollars, was divided among his children.

Osama bin Laden grew up a devout Muslim. He received most of his formal schooling in Mecca

During a Sensitive Site Exploitation mission in the Zhawar Kili area of Eastern Afghanistan members of a U.S. Navy SEAL Team found valuable intelligence information, including this Osama bin Laden propaganda poster. (U.S. Department of Defense)

and in Jedda. He reportedly showed a solemn respect for Muslim practices and learned much from religious visitors to the bin Laden home during the hajj (pilgrimage) season each year. As a young man of 17, he married the first of his four wives. He then studied public management at King Abd al Aziz University in Jeddah between 1974 and 1978. While at university, bin Laden was heavily influenced by one of his professors, Sheikh Abdullah Azzam, a prominent radical Muslim. He was also said to have been influenced by Mohammed Qutb, a renowned fundamentalist thinker, and brother of the late Sayyid Qutb, arguably the most influential radical Islamic thinker in history.

When the Soviet Union invaded Afghanistan on December 26, 1979, the 22-year-old bin Laden left his wealthy existence in Saudi Arabia and joined the thousands of Muslims who answered the call for *jihad,* or holy war, to defend Afghanistan. With his inheritance, bin Laden began organizing and financing mujahideen activities for the fight against the Soviets. He purchased weapons, built training camps, dug trenches, paved roads, and developed other infrastructure. His money also provided food and medicines to fellow fighters. Reports also indicate that bin Laden fought in several battles, where he demonstrated bravery to his fellow mujahideen. More importantly, perhaps, is the fact that bin Laden founded *Maktab al Khidamat* (the Services Office) in 1984. The Services Office recruited thousands of jihad fighters from all over the world to join the war, placed them in more than a dozen "guest houses" around neighboring Pakistan, and trained them in special camps that bin Laden paid for.

When the Soviets retreated on February 15, 1989, the mujahideen, and their CIA financiers, declared victory. Indeed, many of the mujahideen of Afghanistan were bankrolled and trained by the CIA. It is unlikely, however, that bin Laden was among them. In fact, he insists he had no contact with U.S. intelligence, and numerous U.S. sources corroborate this assertion.

Building al Qaeda

On November 24, 1989, Azzam was killed by a powerful car bomb. Though crestfallen, bin Laden decided to continue the work the two had started together. With the help of careful records he kept in the training camps and guesthouses of the Services Office, bin Laden launched a militant Islamic network called al Qaeda, or "the Base." It was simply a collection of the thousands of radical Muslims that he and Azzam had financed and trained who were committed to carrying out jihad activities elsewhere around the globe. Indeed, these mujahideen returned to their homes, established secret cells, and began guerrilla campaigns against regimes they considered heretical.

With al Qaeda launched, bin Laden returned home to his native Saudi Arabia in 1990, whereupon he assumed the role of activist in opposition to the Saudi royal family. He spoke at countless mosques and other gatherings, where he was fiercely critical of governmental policies, including what he perceived to be the improper interpretation of Islam. His opposition intensified in 1991, when American troops landed in Saudi Arabia for Operation Desert Shield. Their very presence on Saudi soil offended bin Laden, who believed that

the Prophet Muhammad prohibited "infidels" from setting foot on the land of Islam's two holiest sites. "By being loyal to the U.S. regime," bin Laden said, "the Saudi regime has committed an act against Islam." Thousands of tapes of his speeches were circulated around the Saudi kingdom.

Due to rising tensions with the royal family, in April 1991, bin Laden left Saudi Arabia with his family (by then he had several wives and many children) and moved to Sudan, where a militant Islamic government had taken power two years earlier. With his inheritance, bin Laden invested heavily in the poor country, establishing several legitimate businesses, including a major construction company. Additionally, bin Laden established at least three terrorist training camps in Northern Sudan, where experts taught terrorist and guerrilla tactics to the Egyptian al Jihad and al Gama'a al Islamiyya, the Iranian-funded Hezbollah from Lebanon, and Sudan's National Islamic Front, as well as jihad groups from Yemen, Saudi Arabia, and Somalia. He sent these trained militants to the Balkans, Chechnya, and other theaters where Muslims were in conflict.

All the while, bin Laden was considered an increasingly dangerous threat to the Saudis. He formed the Advice and Reform Council, a group that condemned the Saudi regime and sought to destabilize it. In addition to several reported assassination attempts by Saudi intelligence, the Saudis froze his assets in 1993 (valued at more than $200 million). Soon after, in 1994, bin Laden renounced his Saudi citizenship, making him not only a renegade from his homeland, but also from his family, which continued to publicly distance itself from him.

At the same time, al Qaeda continued to grow. Its first attacks against America were reported at two hotels in Yemen, where bombs exploded and killed several tourists. The bombs were probably intended to kill American troops on their way to a humanitarian mission in Somalia. al Qaeda caught up with those U.S. servicemen on October 3, 1993, when 18 American soldiers were shot down over Mogadishu in Somalia. They were killed by local guerrillas trained by al Qaeda operatives. bin Laden was also said to have links to the 1993 bombing of the World Trade Center in New York City, which killed six people and wounded more than a thousand.

By early 1994, bin Laden was using the Internet and other high-tech means to plan and execute his operations, along with a complicated network of front companies and bank accounts to launder funds for continued operations. In late 1995, five Americans and two Indians were killed by a truck bomb in Riyadh, Saudi Arabia. While they were never conclusively linked to al Qaeda, bin Laden praised the four men, who were executed by the Saudis for the attacks, as "martyrs" who paved the way for other true believers.

Other attacks on non-American targets continued around the world. In December 1994, bin Laden was linked to an attempt to destroy an airplane en route to Tokyo. The attack was carried out by the Abu Sayyaf Group, a Philippine group under the aegis of al Qaeda. The following year, an assassination attempt on Egyptian president Hosni Mubarak was linked to al Qaeda. Similarly, al Qaeda/Abu Sayyaf was tied to an aborted plot to assassinate the pope. Finally, in November 1995, a car bomb planted by al Qaeda operatives rocked the Egyptian embassy in Pakistan.

bin Laden in Afghanistan

It was the attack in Riyadh, in all probability, that prompted Washington to pressure Sudan to revoke its protection of bin Laden. A year later, Khartoum yielded. In May 1996 bin Laden moved his family and hundreds of al Qaeda members to Afghanistan, where years of civil war had paved the way for the repressive fundamentalist Taliban regime, under Mullah Mohammed Omar, to rise to power. In Afghanistan, bin Laden curried favor among the Taliban by providing financial support for their radical Islamic regime and the subsequent internecine fighting that followed. He helped rebuild infrastructure that was largely destroyed after years of war against the Soviets. As a sign of respect, he was known as "Sheikh."

The operations of al Qaeda flourished in bin Laden's new headquarters. On August 23, 1996, he issued a decree declaring jihad against Americans and Jews, calling Muslims to expel them from Islamic holy lands (Saudi Arabia and Israel). Accordingly, that same year, a suspected al Qaeda attack at the Khobar Towers military complex in Dhahran, Saudi Arabia, killed 19 Americans. By then, the U.S. State Department was calling bin Laden "the most significant financial sponsor of Islamic extremist activities in the world today," due to his bankrolling of training camps in both Afghanistan and Sudan.

In 1998 bin Laden issued a fatwa, or religious proclamation, calling for the death of all Americans, both military and civilians. Later that year, bin Laden's group was conclusively linked to the bombing of two U.S. embassies in East Africa, where hundreds were killed and thousands were injured. The U.S. responded by attacking several of bin Laden's training camps in Afghanistan and a factory in Sudan thought at the time to be producing chemical weapons for al Qaeda. The attacks brought notoriety to bin Laden, who became something of a celebrity outlaw in the Muslim world.

In November 1998, the U.S. government indicted bin Laden with several charges, including complicity in the embassy bombings. Concurrently, the U.S. State Department offered a reward of $5 million for information leading to his arrest. In 1999 the FBI placed bin Laden on their Most Wanted Terrorists list. Meanwhile, rumors circulated that the Taliban was growing weary of their guest, who brought with him the consternation of the international community and the wrath of the United States. They requested that bin Laden suspend his military and political activities, and even assigned several soldiers to keep him under watch.

One year later, however, bin Laden was tied to a thwarted plot to bomb targets around the globe during the millennium celebrations on New Year's Eve 1999. On October 27, 2000, bin Laden was again suspected of masterminding the bombing of an American target; the USS *Cole* battleship, which was attacked by suicide bombers in Yemen, killing more than a dozen sailors.

What bin Laden is most known for, however, are the terrorist attacks on American soil on September 11, 2001. On that day, two hijacked commercial jets headed from Boston to Los Angeles flew into the Twin Towers of the World Trade Center. Another plane hit the Pentagon, just outside of Washington, D.C. A fourth hijacked airliner was commandeered by the passengers and crashed in western Pennsylvania. The attacks, carried out by 19 al Qaeda hijackers, killed about 3,000 people.

Following the attacks, President George W. Bush demanded that the Taliban turn bin Laden over to American authorities. The Taliban refused, requesting proof of bin Laden's involvement in the attacks. The American government did, in fact, present ample evidence to the rogue state, which still refused to hand over the suspected mastermind. Washington responded with Operation

Enduring Freedom, which began with air strikes in Afghanistan on October 7, 2001. In the fighting that followed, U.S. and friendly Afghan forces dismantled Taliban and al Qaeda strongholds throughout the country. bin Laden, however, is thought to have escaped during an especially intense battle at the Tora Bora cave complex in eastern Afghanistan.

Tora Bora is made up of a series of complex and circuitous caves. The U.S. Army was at a disadvantage in this terrain, as bin Laden had been to the caves before and was familiar with their layout. Some sources claimed that only a near miss prevented the U.S. Army from capturing bin Laden, while others asserted that there was no way to confirm the al Qaeda leader's presence at the battle at all. In 2008 a Delta Force commander appeared on the television news show *60 Minutes* under the pseudonym Dalton Fury, revealing himself as the head of the team dispatched to kill bin Laden. Amid the skirmishes, Fury believed that bin Laden had been injured but not killed, and soon thereafter escaped to Pakistan.

Speculation continued as to whether bin Laden was still alive and in hiding, or if he was in fact deceased. In 2002, Afghan President Hamid Karzai told CNN that he believed bin Laden was "probably dead." This speculation was fueled further when Pervez Musharraf, Benazir Bhutto, and Asif Ali Zardari, all former presidents of Pakistan, implied, on different occasions, the high likelihood of bin Laden's demise.

However, for every claim that bin Laden was deceased, there were rebuttals attempting to prove he could be still be alive, as well as vehement insistences from major intelligence organizations that he remained at large. A letter intercepted in 2005 between senior al Qaeda figures Atiyah Abd al Rahman and Abu Musaf al Zarqawi indicated that bin Laden might have been hiding in Waziristan. Unsubstantiated rumors also spread that there was a voice recording in which bin Laden discussed the 2010 flooding in Pakistan.

The many doubts about bin Laden's location were finally resolved on May 1, 2011, when U.S. President Barack Obama announced that bin Laden had been killed in a raid by U.S. Navy SEALs. bin Laden was shot in the head; four other men were killed, including one of bin Laden's sons, and one of bin Laden's wives was injured.

bin Laden was located in a well-protected compound in the town of Abbottabad, about an hour's drive north of Pakistan's capital, Islamabad. According to one of bin Laden's wives, the terror leader had been living there for years. Abbottabad is home to the Pakistan Military Academy, that country's equivalent of West Point; the proximity of bin Laden's hiding place to Pakistan's military establishment raised difficult questions and seemed likely to complicate the already fractious alliance between Pakistan and the United States.

The Americans took possession of bin Laden's body and buried it at sea within 24 hours, in accordance with Muslim practice. As bin Laden had not had direct operational command over al Qaeda for some time, it was unclear whether his death would have any immediate impact on the terror network. Computer disks recovered from the compound indicated that bin Laden had been considering a possible terror attack on the tenth anniversary of 9/11, but experts believed those plans were more "aspirational" than actual.

Jonathan Schanzer

See also Abu Sayyaf Group; Afghanistan War; al Qaeda; East Africa Embassy Bombings; September 11 Attacks; Taliban; USS *Cole* Bombing; Y2K Plot

Further Readings

Atwan, Abdel Bari. *The Secret History of al Qaeda.* Berkeley: University of California Press, 2006.

Bergen, Peter. *Holy War, Inc.: Inside the Secret World of Osama Bin Laden.* New York: Free Press, 2001.

Bergen, Peter. *The Longest War: Inside the Enduring Conflict between America and al-Qaeda.* New York: Free Press, 2011.

Bergen, Peter. *The Osama Bin Laden I Know: An Oral History of al Qaeda's Leader.* New York: Free Press, 2006.

bin Laden, Osama, and Bruce B. Lawrence. *Messages to the World: The Statements of Osama Bin Laden.* London: Verso, 2005.

Bodansky, Yossef. *Bin Laden: The Man Who Declared War on America.* Rocklin, CA: Prima, 1999.

Finn, Peter, Ian Shapira, and Marc Fisher. "The Hunt." *The Washington Post,* May 6, 2011. http://www.washingtonpost.com/wp-srv/projects/osama-hunt/index.html.

Griffin, David Ray. *Osama Bin Laden: Dead or Alive?* Northampton, MA: Olive Branch, 2009.

Gunaratna, Rohan. *Inside al Qaeda: Global Network of Terror.* New York: Columbia University Press, 2002.

Kepel, Gilles, Jean-Pierre Milelli, and Pascale Ghazaleh. *Al Qaeda in Its Own Words.* Cambridge, MA: Belknap of Harvard University Press, 2008.

Reeve, Simon. *The New Jackals: Ramzi Yousef, Osama bin Laden and the Future of Terrorism.* Boston: Northeastern University Press, 1999.

Riedel, Bruce. *The Search for al Qaeda: Its Leadership, Ideology, and Future.* Washington, DC: Brookings Institution Press, 2008.

Schweitzer, Yoram. "Osama Bin Ladin: Wealth plus Extremism Equals Terrorism." July 27, 1998. http://212.150.54.123/articles/articledet.cfm?articleid=40.

Wright, Lawrence. *The Looming Tower: al Qaeda and the Road to 9/11.* New York: Alfred A. Knopf, 2006.

BIOLOGICAL TERRORISM

The mail-borne anthrax attacks against U.S. citizens in the fall of 2001 demonstrated that every nation, even one as powerful as the United States, is at risk from terrorists using biological or chemical weapons. The attacks also revealed that the United States, like most other nations, did not have effective plans in place to deal with such an attack.

Terrorists have used bioweapons before. In 1984 the U.S.-based Rajneesh cult used salmonella bacteria to poison citizens by spreading the bacteria via salad bars in restaurants in an Oregon town. In 1995, the Japanese cult Aum Shinrikyo used chemical and biological weapons in attacks in and around Tokyo. Despite these attacks and repeated warnings from experts about the threat posed by biological weapons, the U.S. and other governments took little concerted action to deal with the problem prior to the fall of 2001. In the aftermath of that anthrax attack, many governments are taking steps to reduce the chances that terrorists can obtain the materials needed to make bioweapons, and to respond to outbreaks of disease if they should occur. In order to assess the magnitude of the bioterror threat, it is vital to understand how biological agents can be used as deadly tools and how terrorists might use them to instill fear or inflict heavy casualties.

Biological Weapons

Biological weapons use pathogens or organisms that cause disease in humans, other animals, or

Keala Loo, a firefighter with the Pearl Harbor, Hawaii, Fire Department Hazardous Materials Team, takes samples of a suspected biological agent in a white powder form dropped during a mock terrorist attack on Ward Field, Naval Station Pearl Harbor, on August 20, 2008, as part of an anti-terrorism field training exercise. The exercise is an integrated, quick reaction, scenario driven event to train emergency personnel in the rapid assessment of and response to escalating levels of alert. (U.S. Navy photo by Mass Communication Specialist 2nd Class Paul Honnick/Released)

plants. Pathogens include bacteria, viruses, fungi, and toxins (poisons produced by animals or plants). Crude biological weapons (or "agents") have a long history of use in warfare. In ancient times, wells were poisoned with the carcasses of dead animals, and infected corpses were thrown over the walls of besieged cities in efforts to spread sickness among defenders. During the French and Indian Wars in the 1700s, British troops gave blankets from smallpox victims to Native Americans in order to spread the disease.

The large number of casualties inflicted by chemical attacks in World War I, along with the military's general distaste for using such weapons, led to the signing of the Geneva Protocol of 1925 (officially, the Protocol for the Prohibition of the

Use in War of Asphyxiating, Poisonous or Other Gases, and of Bacteriological Methods of Warfare), a treaty prohibiting the use of both chemical and biological agents in warfare. However, that treaty did not prohibit nations from manufacturing or stockpiling such weapons, and many nations chose to do just, believing that the possession of these weapons would deter others from using them. The Japanese experimented with the use of biological weapons on a relatively small scale in World War II (Japanese forces attacked Chinese cities by dropping plague-carrying fleas from aircraft, for example), but other major combatants did not use them, possibly because they did not believe that these weapons would be decisive factors in the conflict, and possibly because they feared retaliation in kind.

The relatively crude attempts to use pathogens for military purposes throughout history were overshadowed dramatically during the Cold War period (1948–1991), when the United States and the Soviet Union exploited modern scientific knowledge and sophisticated technology to manufacture large stockpiles of deadly pathogens such as anthrax, a disease that can sicken and kill humans and livestock.

By the late 1960s, it had become apparent to military planners that biological weapons posed as much of a threat to the attacker as to the defender. An infection spread among enemy troops might easily result in the infection of friendly forces. Further, biological weapons were not regarded as posing significant threats to well-prepared military units that could be vaccinated to prevent the spread of disease. For these reasons, most nations signed a 1972 treaty known as the Biological and Toxin Weapons Convention that went beyond the Geneva Convention of 1925 by prohibiting the development, manufacture, stockpiling, and use of biological and toxin agents. Unfortunately, this treaty does not have any monitoring or verification measures to deter nations from cheating. Several countries, including Iraq and the former Soviet Union, took advantage of the loophole to continue developing these weapons secretly in violation of international law.

When the Persian Gulf War ended in 1991, UN inspectors found that Iraq had manufactured and concealed significant quantities of biological agents. Iraq may have been deterred from using biological weapons because the United States threatened overwhelming retaliation to any biological or chemical attack.

The Terrorist Connection

Prior to the Gulf War in 1991, it was not difficult to obtain starter cultures of many pathogens from supply companies specializing in their distribution to research laboratories for legitimate medical research purposes. For example, a scientist trying to develop a new disease vaccine would use the pathogen in tests. In order to obtain a quantity of the pathogen, a researcher (or a terrorist) just had to submit a purchase request on the letterhead of a laboratory or research institution. There were few rigorous procedures in place requiring the supplier to verify that the laboratory was real and the purchase request was legitimate. After UN inspectors learned that Iraq had prepared biological weapons in 1991, the United States imposed tougher restrictions on such purchases, but many other nations do not have similar safeguards in place.

Until recently, there were few procedures in place to prevent a terrorist from penetrating the facilities of a pathogen supplier by gaining employment there, posing as a repairman, or bribing an employee. Prior to the mail anthrax attacks in 2001, few universities had adequate security systems in place to prevent the theft of pathogens from their research stocks. In addition to the possibility that a disgruntled U.S. citizen might resort to bioterrorism, the reliance of U.S. universities upon foreign graduate students to staff their laboratories raised the possibility that a foreign terrorist organization could co-opt, blackmail, or threaten students to obtain pathogens for terrorist purposes.

If a terrorist can obtained a "starter" culture, it is not hard to grow rapidly multiplying bacteria. For example, a single anthrax cell takes about 20 minutes to divide. Twenty generations of such cell divisions take about seven hours and yield about 1 million anthrax bacteria. All this could take place in a flask the size of a milk bottle containing a readily available commercial growth medium, or an improvised one made from gelatin and other ingredients. A terrorist could grow bacteria and concentrate them into a wet slurry using a centrifuge process familiar to anyone who has taken high school or college chemistry. To reduce their own risk, terrorists might try to vaccinate themselves, and they would probably take precautionary doses of antibiotics.

Bioterrorist Attacks

The Japanese cult known as Aum Shinrikyo tried to use anthrax bacteria and a deadly botulinum toxin as biological weapons to attack downtown Tokyo and U.S. military installations in Japan in 1995. The cult made scientific mistakes in producing the pathogens and was not able to spread the aerosols containing them widely enough. (The cult later killed 12 persons with chemical weapons.) However, the attack did succeed in instilling fear among the population of one of the world's largest cities. Since terrorists may achieve their goals by frightening people just as effectively as by killing them, the Tokyo attack was partially successful. Investigators later learned that the Aum cult had even attempted to obtain the deadly Ebola virus from a site in Africa where an outbreak had occurred.

The use of a pathogen against unsuspecting citizens by the Rajneesh cult in a small Oregon town in 1985 provides an example of a more successful bioterrorist attack. The cult wanted its candidates to win a county election so that it could oust an incumbent town leadership that was opposing the cult's plans to expand its facilities. Cult leaders thought that if they could sicken enough of the population just prior to the election, the resulting light turnout would enable their candidates to win, giving them control of the county government.

Cult members, who at best had only modest scientific training, proceeded to use a small, makeshift laboratory to grow salmonella bacteria. Once they had an ample supply, cult members spread the bacteria in salad bars at local restaurants. The plan worked to the extent that it sickened 750 persons, but it did not reduce voter turnout enough to let the cult win control of the county government. When public health authorities investigated the disease outbreak, their first conclusion was that it was caused by inadequate sanitary measures in the restaurants. It was only much later that the real cause came to light.

One of the main lessons learned in the Oregon attack was that the pathogen was easy to grow and distribute, at least on a relatively small scale. Its production did not require a large laboratory, sophisticated equipment, or persons with advanced scientific training. Almost anyone with rudimentary knowledge of bacterial growth who could obtain a "starter culture" would be well on the way to the possession of a small but deadly stockpile. This knowledge is widely distributed, as evidenced by the popularity of home-brewed beers and wines. A second important lesson was that it can be difficult to recognize a disease outbreak as the work of terrorists.

According to the Federal Bureau of Investigation, the anthrax mail attacks of 2001 were not the work of a group, but rather that of one deeply disturbed individual. The FBI's suspect in the case, Bruce Ivins, was a trained microbiologist working for the U.S. Army who had ready access to a virulent strain of anthrax. Ivins, who had a history of mental instability, committed suicide in 2008. If he was indeed responsible, the mail attacks demonstrate how a single person in the right position can wreak considerable havoc, and also avoid prosecution for years following the attack.

Assessing Possible Terrorist Use of Viral Diseases

After the anthrax mail attacks in the United States, fears were immediately raised about the prospect that terrorists could obtain more highly infectious pathogens. Anthrax is not communicable between humans and can only be spread by direct contact with the bacteria, and it can be treated effectively with antibiotics if the infection is caught early enough. By contrast, the smallpox, or *variola,* virus causes one of the most dreaded diseases on the planet. It is highly infectious and spreads rapidly through unvaccinated populations. Since viral diseases cannot be treated with antibiotics, smallpox kills about 30 percent of those infected, leaving the survivors with disfiguring scars.

Smallpox was essentially eliminated among populations in the early 1980s. It is now only known to exist in small, closely controlled stocks in two laboratories in the United States and Russia for use in vaccine research. When smallpox was eradicated as a public health threat in the early 1980s, nations stopped vaccinating their citizens. That made sense from a public health standpoint, but while the United States and Russia were designated as the only official repositories, several other nations are suspected of possessing clandestine stockpiles of smallpox virus that might be used for biological warfare. However, since smallpox might also infect the side that uses it first, many experts at the time considered it unlikely that it would ever be used on a large scale.

The September 2001 attacks on the United States and the subsequent anthrax mailings changed that perception. Terrorists willing to commit suicide with hijacked aircraft might not shrink from using smallpox or other highly infectious agents, if they could somehow obtain them to produce fear and panic. The United States immediately announced a plan to create 200 million doses of smallpox vaccine to have available in case of an attack, and Russia and the United States took steps to heighten the security around the two laboratories possessing the last official stocks of smallpox virus. Even so, experts differ in their assessment of the ability of terrorists to make effective use of viral diseases such as smallpox, Ebola, or other deadly pathogens.

Terrorists choosing to use a noninfectious bacterial agent such as anthrax would have to spread the material directly over a large area to cause many casualties. When the United States and Soviet Union developed biological warfare capabilities during the Cold War, they had access to aircraft fitted with spray tanks, artillery shells, and missiles that could carry hundreds of small bomblets filled with pathogens. Terrorists would find it difficult to obtain those delivery systems. It was probably for that reason that the September 2001 hijackers were exploring the capabilities of agricultural crop dusters, for they would have had a difficult time distributing bacterial agents widely without such equipment. On the other hand, a small number of anthrax-contaminated letters sickened and killed only a few people but managed to disrupt the operations of government and frighten millions.

The Future of Bioterrorism

Most experts believe it would be difficult for terrorists to prepare and distribute the large quantities of pathogens needed to attack a population center. The failure of the well-funded and scientifically trained Aum Shinrikyo group to mount an effective bioweapon attack must surely have been noted by al Qaeda and other terrorist organizations. Truck, aircraft, and containership cargoes of more readily obtainable high explosives will probably seem much more attractive to terrorists than handling pathogens. Terrorist groups must also have observed that many nations are making long overdue preparations to deal with future bioterror attacks by producing and stockpiling vaccines, strengthening public health systems, and putting procedures in place to restrict access to pathogens.

Not all nations have taken these steps, however, and profound concerns about terrorist access to concealed bioweapon stockpiles in rogue states still exist. A variety of avenues for improved readiness exist. Controls and treaty verification procedures can be developed to ensure that terrorists cannot succeed in obtaining pathogens. Genetic engineering can produce disease-resistant crops, animals can be vaccinated, and improved public health procedures can limit the spread of disease should an attack take place. The international community is expected to accelerate the adoption of these measures in the future to deter biological attacks by terrorists, or to manage them should they occur.

Les Paldy

See also Agricultural Terrorism; Anthrax; Aum Shinrikyo; Chemical Terrorism; Counterterrorism; Rajneesh, Bhagwan Shree; Weapons of Mass Destruction

Further Readings

Broad, William J. "Sowing Death: A Special Report; How Japan Germ Terror Alerted World." *The New York Times,* May 26, 1998, p. A1. http://www.nytimes.com/1998/05/26/world/sowing-death-a-special-report-how-japan-germ-terror-alerted-world.html.

Center for Biosecurity. http://www.upmc-biosecurity.org/index.html.

Coen, Bob, and Eric Nadler. *Dead Silence: Fear and Terror on the Anthrax Trail.* Berkeley, CA: Counterpoint, 2009.

Cole, Leonard. *The Anthrax Letters: A Medical Detective Story.* Washington, DC: Joseph Henry Press, 2003.

James Martin Center for Nonproliferation Studies. http://cns.miis.edu.

Miller, Judith, Stephen Engelberg, and William J. Broad. *Germs: Biological Weapons and America's Secret War.* New York: Simon & Schuster, 2001.

Perez, Evan. "FBI Paints Chilling Portrait of Anthrax-Attack Suspect." *The Wall Street Journal,* August 7, 2008, p. A1.

Tucker, J. B., ed. *Toxic Terror: Assessing the Terrorist Use of Chemical and Biological Weapons.* Cambridge, MA: MIT Press, 2000

Warrick, Joby. "Suspect and a Setback in al Qaeda Anthrax Case." *The Washington Post,* October 31, 2006, p. A1.

White, Scott G. "It Happened Here: Biological Terrorism in the United States." In *A New Understanding of Terrorism: Case Studies, Trajectories and Lessons Learned,* edited by M.R. Haberfeld and Agostino von Hassell. New York: Springer, 2009.

BIRMINGHAM PUB BOMBING

The 1974 bombing of two pubs in the city of Birmingham, England, thought to be the work of the Irish Republican Army (IRA), killed 21 people. It was the most fatal attack on English soil during the 30-year struggle over the fate of Northern Ireland.

Since the late 1960s, conflict had been raging in Northern Ireland between the province's Roman Catholics, who wished Northern Ireland to become part of the Republic of Ireland, and the province's Protestants, who wished it to remain a part of the United Kingdom. Armed paramilitary groups that had sprung up in both communities were prepared to use violence to protect themselves and achieve their ends. The largest armed organization on the Republican, or Nationalist, side (that is, claiming to represent Catholics) was and is the IRA. By the start of 1974, the leaders of the IRA had come to believe that the British were growing weary of their involvement in the conflict, going so far as to declare 1974 "The Year of Victory." They felt that a serious escalation of violence would push the British into withdrawal. Accordingly, the IRA began a series of terrorist attacks on Britain's mainland.

The IRA began its bombing campaign in February 1974, when a bomb was planted on a bus in Yorkshire, England, that was transporting soldiers and their families; 12 people were killed, including two young children. Other attacks, including one at the Tower of London, followed over the course of the year, killing six and injuring

scores more. On November 21, two men hid a duffel bag containing a bomb at the Mulberry Bush, a popular pub in downtown Birmingham. They left the Mulberry Bush after a few minutes and walked to another nearby pub, Talk of the Town, where they left a second bomb. It was a Saturday night, and both bars were crowded. At 8:11 PM, a vague warning was phoned in to the Birmingham *Post and Mail* offices; the bomb at the Mulberry Bush exploded six minutes later, the Talk of the Town bomb a few minutes after that. Ten people were killed in the Mulberry Bush blast, 11 were killed in the Talk of the Town, and 168 were injured in the explosions.

Following the bombings, anti-Irish sentiment ran high in Britain, especially in Birmingham, which has a substantial Irish immigrant community. By November 24, six Irish immigrants, all longtime Birmingham residents, had been arrested and charged with the bombings. Hugh Callaghan, Paddy Joe Hill, Gerry Hunter, Richard McIlkenny, Billy Power, and Johnny Walker became known as the "Birmingham Six." In what was the largest mass-murder trial in British history, the six men were convicted on August 5, 1975, and sentenced to life imprisonment. In 1991, after a long campaign on their behalf, a court overturned all six convictions, citing police mishandling of the evidence and indications that the confessions had been coerced.

The Birmingham bombings also prompted the British legislature to pass the Prevention of Terrorism Act, a law that the home secretary described as "draconian." For instance, the act allowed a suspect to be arrested and held for up to a week without charge, and for persons suspected of being terrorists to be summarily expelled from Great Britain. Although intended as a temporary measure, the act, although it has been repeatedly amended, is still in force.

Colleen Sullivan

See also Bombings and Bomb Scares; Irish Republican Army

Further Readings

"Belfast Man Who Waited 16 Years for Justice to Be Done." *Irish Times,* May 27, 2006, p. 12.

Bew, John, Martyn Frampton, and Inigo Gurruchaga. *Talking to Terrorists: Making Peace in Northern Ireland and in the Basque Country.* New York: Columbia University Press, 2009.

CAIN Web Service. Text of the Prevention of Terrorism (Temporary Provisions) Act 1974. http://cain.ulst.ac.uk/hmso/pta1974.htm.

Campbell, Duncan. "Justice on Trial: A Lesson Paid for with Innocent Lives—and It's Not Over Yet." *The Guardian,* May 5, 2009, p. 12.

Cullen, Kevin. "British Release the Birmingham Six: After 16 Years in Prison for IRA Bombings, Their Convictions Are Reversed." *The Boston Globe,* March 15, 1991.

Holland, Jack. *Hope Against History: The Course of Conflict in Northern Ireland.* New York: Henry Holt, 1996.

McKittrick, David. *Making Sense of the Troubles.* Belfast: Blackstaff Press, 2000.

O'Brien, Brendan. *The Long War: The IRA and Sinn Fein.* 2nd ed. Syracuse, NY: Syracuse University Press, 1999.

Shanahan, Timothy. *The Provisional Irish American Army and the Morality of Terrorism.* Edinburgh: Edinburgh University Press, 2009.

Woffinden, Bob. *Miscarriages of Justice.* London: Hodder & Stoughton, 1987. Excerpted from http://www.innocent.org.uk/cases/birmingham6.

Woods, Richard, et al. "Ever-Tightening Terror Laws." *Sunday Times,* November 13, 2005, p. 13.

BLACK PANTHER PARTY

A group of revolutionary black nationalists working within the Black Power movement, the Black Panther Party (BPP) was at the vanguard of armed struggle that constituted the "New Left terrorism" of the late 1960s.

Huey Newton and Bobby Seale founded the Black Panther Party for Self-Defense in October 1966. The group, based in Oakland, California, put forth a 10-point program that demanded the following for black and oppressed communities: full employment, adequate housing, free health care, an end to police brutality and capitalist exploitation, freedom for all prisoners, reparations, and an immediate end to all wars of aggression. Of all the black nationalist and anti-imperialist movements that began in the turbulent 1960s, the BPP

was perhaps the most renowned, easily recognized by their quasi-military black berets, leather jackets, and guns.

By the mid-1960s, the predominantly white Oakland Police Department had exhibited an ever-increasing brutality against the predominantly black population of Oakland. Armed with guns and rifles (legal in California at the time), members of the early BPP visibly monitored the police. BPP members listened to police scanners and would arrive at a crime scene in order to read the alleged offender his or her rights. They stayed within the law and did not interfere with the police, standing at least 10 feet from them, but their armed presence and confrontational manner rattled lawmakers. In 1967, the "Panther Bill," a piece of anti-firearm legislation that would prevent the BPP, and others, from displaying firearms, was introduced in the California legislature. Undeterred, BPP members traveled to Sacramento that May, carrying their guns in protest.

While the BPP organized social programs and legal intimidation aboveground, it simultaneously created an underground unit that engaged in armed struggle, most notably against police. The underground BPP was decentralized, with small cells working in individual communities. Members held weapons-training classes and conducted close-order drills in public spaces while carrying guns.

After the murder of Martin Luther King Jr., in April 1968, the BPP quickly grew from a California-based organization to a nationwide group of more than 5,000 in 40 chapters. Propaganda that showed police as pigs was splashed throughout the BPP newspaper, *The Black Panther.* By September 1968, J. Edgar Hoover, the head of the FBI, believed the BPP posed "the greatest threat to internal security in the country." Indeed, the BPP was a principal focus of COINTELPRO, the government counterintelligence project that targeted New Left groups in the 1960s. By the end of 1969, more than 30 BPP members had been sentenced to death, 40 had been sentenced to life imprisonment, 55 had been charged with crimes that carried more than 30 years imprisonment, and more than 150 had become underground fugitives.

In the early 1970s, the BPP split, partly because of FBI infiltration. The "reformist" group, headed by Newton, envisioned a transformation from black revolutionaries into a legitimate social protest organization. Newton, however, had not forsaken armed struggle and violence. In 1972 he created an internal military group called the Squad, which was used to discipline BPP members internally and to commit crimes in Oakland, including extortion and murder. The other revolutionary faction, based in New York and headed by Eldridge Cleaver, continued to call for armed struggle. The still-militant factions of the New York BPP split off to form the Black Liberation Army, which continued the BPP's underground legacy well into the 1980s.

In the late 1980s, a small group in Dallas, Texas, emerged that called itself the New Black Panther Party for Self-Defense (NBPP). The NBPP promotes conspiracy theories about the 9/11 attacks and has been classified as a hate group. Despite the name, however, there is no direct connection between the NBPP and the original BPP. Although small in number, NBPP members are adept at getting themselves in the media, as evidenced by allegations of voter intimidation in Philadelphia during the 2008 presidential election. As of late 2010, the U.S. Justice Department refused to pursue any charges in the Philadelphia case, but controversy has persisted.

Meanwhile, the NBPP has been condemned by the BPP's founders, including Bobby Seale. In a formal statement, the Huey P. Newton Foundation declared, "As guardian of the true history of the Black Panther Party, the Foundation, which includes former leading members of the Party, denounces [the NBPP's] exploitation of the Party's name and history."

Laura Lambert

See also Chesimard, Joanne; May 19 Communist Organization; Symbionese Liberation Army; Weatherman

Further Readings

Austin, Curtis J. *Up Against the Wall: Violence in the Making and Unmaking of the Black Panther Party.* Fayetteville: University of Arkansas Press, 2008.

Cleaver, Kathleen, and George Katsiaficas, eds. *Liberation, Imagination, and the Black Panther Party: A New Look at the Panthers and Their Legacy.* New York: Routledge, 2001.

Foner, Philip S., ed. *The Black Panthers Speak.* New York: Da Capo Press, 2002.

Forbes, Flores Alexander. *Will You Die with Me? My Life and the Black Panther Party.* New York: Atria, 2006.

Graham, David A. "The New Black Panther Party Is the New ACORN." *Newsweek.* July 14, 2010. http://www.newsweek.com/2010/07/14/the-new-black-panther-party-is-the-new-acorn0.html.

Jones, Charles E., and Judson L. Jeffries. "Don't Believe the Hype: Debunking the Panther Mythology." In *The Black Panther Party Reconsidered,* edited by Charles E. Jones. Baltimore, MD: Black Classic Press, 1986.

Pearson, Hugh. *The Shadow of the Panther: Huey Newton and the Price of Black Power in America.* New York: Addison-Wesley Publishing Corporation, 1994.

Rhodes, Jane. *Framing the Black Panthers: The Spectacular Rise of a Black Power Icon.* New York: The New Press, 2007.

BLACK SEPTEMBER

Founded in 1970, Black September was a Palestinian militant faction. It chose its name to commemorate the violent Hashemite-Palestinian clash in Jordan in September 1970, during which the Palestine Liberation Organization (PLO) tried to seize power from King Hussein. The king ordered his military forces to forcefully confront the PLO, leading to the killing and expulsion of thousands of Palestinians and driving the PLO out of Jordan.

Black September apparently formed within Fatah, the PLO group led by Yasir Arafat (who in 1994 became the chairman of the semi-autonomous Palestinian Authority), though members of smaller Palestinian groups also joined. The urgent goal was to seek retribution by attacking Jordan's military and King Hussein, but soon thereafter the group turned its attention to attacking Israeli and Western targets worldwide. The group apparently received marching orders from the Fatah security apparatus, serving as one of its auxiliary units. However, it has also been argued that the faction eventually came to represent a radical split from the arguably more moderate Fatah.

The setup of Black September followed that of many other resistance movements. The group's members were prearranged in closed cells, which consisted of a few members. Cells were kept in the dark regarding the identity of other cells, so that the possible capture or tracking of one cell by the authorities would not jeopardize other cells. Orders were delivered by couriers, who were also kept in the dark regarding the identity of other cells and intermediaries. The group's members apparently included Palestinians residing in the Middle East, as well as Palestinians and Arabs residing abroad as students, or working as small businessmen, diplomats, and so forth.

The group's most notorious act was the attack on Israeli athletes taking part in the 1972 Summer Olympics in Munich, Germany, which resulted in the deaths of 11 Israelis and a West German policeman. In response, the State of Israel ordered Mossad (the Israeli national intelligence agency) to track and kill senior Black September and PLO operators. The Mossad conducted several operations, including the 1973 killing of Black September members in Beirut; the 1973 killing of a Moroccan waiter in Lillehammer, Norway, who, it turned out, was apparently blameless; and the 1979 killing of Ali Hassan Salameh, the "Red Prince," who is said to have masterminded several deadly Black September attacks.

Other attacks ascribed to Black September included the assassination of Jordan's prime minister following the PLO eviction from Jordan (November 1971); damaging gas and electric systems in the Netherlands and West Germany (February 1972); hijacking a Belgian aircraft flying from Austria to Israel (May 1972); sending letter bombs to Israeli diplomats, one of which killed a diplomat in London (September–October 1972); attacking the Saudi embassy in Khartoum, Sudan, where they took hostages and killed the U.S. chief of mission to Sudan, his deputy, and a Belgian diplomat (March 1973); and attacking passengers waiting to board a flight to Tel Aviv, Israel, in Athens' international airport, killing five people and wounding more than 50 (August 1973).

In the fall of 1973, the PLO apparently concluded that attacking Israeli and Western targets worldwide no longer served the cause of forming a Palestinian state, and the Black September group was dissolved. In the following years, the PLO militant operations centered on attacking Jewish targets in Israel and the West Bank and Gaza Strip territories, which Israel occupied during the Six-Day War in June 1967.

Rafael Reuveny

See also Arafat, Yasir; Mossad; Palestine Liberation Organization

Further Readings

Bar Zohar, Michael, and Eitan Haber. *The Quest for the Red Prince.* Guilford, CT: Lyons Press, 2002.

Cooley, John K. *Green March, Black September: The Story of the Palestinian Arabs.* London: Frank Cass, 1973.

Ensalaco, Mark. *Middle Eastern Terrorism: From Black September to September 11.* Philadelphia: University of Pennsylvania Press, 2007.

Hirst, David. *The Guns and the Olive Branch: The Roots of Violence in the Middle East.* New York: Thunder's Mouth Press/Nation Books, 2003.

Morris, Benny. *Righteous Victims: A History of the Zionist-Arab Conflict, 1881–2001.* New York: Vintage Books, 2001.

Reeve, Simon. *One Day in September: The Story of the 1972 Munich Olympics Massacre.* London: Faber & Faber, 2001.

Sayigh, Yezid. *Armed Struggle and the Search for State: The Palestinian National Movement, 1949–1993.* New York: Oxford University Press, 2000.

BLOODY SUNDAY

The term *Bloody Sunday* refers to the events that took place on January 30, 1972, in which 13 people were shot dead by British soldiers in the city of Derry (also known as Londonderry) in Northern Ireland. A fourteenth person died of his injuries some months later. Bloody Sunday is seen as one of the most important moments within the period of Irish conflict known as "the Troubles."

On the day in question, an anti-internment march had been organized by the Northern Ireland Civil Rights Association. The march had been banned by the authorities, but it was generally peaceful, and perhaps 20,000 men, women, and children marched. A section of the crowd later broke off from the main march and began rioting, and it was then that the elite Parachute Regiment was sent in on an arrest operation. During the next half hour, 13 people were killed by soldiers, and 17 were injured. The soldiers responsible for the shooting insisted that they had come under gun and blast-bomb attack by Republican (Nationalist) terrorists, and had only fired on those carrying weapons or evidencing a threat. However, civilian witnesses provided evidence directly refuting that given by the soldiers, and no weapons were recovered at the scene.

Bloody Sunday proved a violent watershed in the history of the conflict: for a brief period, the alienation of the Irish Catholic, Nationalist minority became almost total. News reporting of the event also radicalized feeling at home and abroad. In the Republic of Ireland, the British Embassy in Dublin was burned down by protesters, and in the North recruitment to Irish Republican paramilitary groups increased markedly. Indeed, 1972 was to be the bloodiest year of the conflict, as activity by both Irish Republican and Ulster Loyalist terrorist groups intensified.

That same year, an inquiry into the shootings in Derry was undertaken by the British government under the direction of Lord Widgery. However, the inquiry only added to the sense of grievance and injury of the Nationalist community, as it cast doubt over the innocence of some of those killed. It also neglected to consider evidence and testimony that the Nationalist community felt to be compelling. In relation to the actions of the army, Widgery could only say that the Paratroopers' firing "bordered on the reckless." In contrast, Hubert O'Neill, the coroner at the official inquest into the deaths held in 1973, stated that the shootings were "sheer unadulterated murder."

Relatives of the victims vigorously campaigned against what was seen as a government whitewash of the events of that day. Continuous political pressure and the mustering of new evidence, set against the backdrop of a developing peace process, resulted in the opening of a fresh inquest under Lord Saville in 1998. The length and cost of the inquiry proved controversial, as the hearings lasted until 2004 and cost an estimated £200 million.

The mammoth 10-volume Saville Report was finally published on June 15, 2010, and it was emphatic in concluding that those shot that day had not been presenting any form of threat. Indeed, it noted that some victims had been shot while crawling away or lying wounded on the ground. The report found no evidence of preplanning of the killings at any governmental level, but it noted that the "unjustifiable" killings were the result of a breakdown of fire discipline. The report discounted the versions of many of the soldier witnesses, some of whom it concluded had "knowingly put forward false accounts."

The day of the Saville Report's publication was one of high symbolism and emotion. The recently elected British prime minister, David Cameron, made a speech in the House of Commons, which was simultaneously relayed to a large rally in Derry, in which he stated unequivocally that the killings were "both unjustified and unjustifiable." He apologized on behalf of the government, to cheers from the watching crowd. At the rally, the innocence of each of the victims was proclaimed, and a copy of the now discredited Widgery Report was symbolically torn up.

Bloody Sunday has remained a most important part of the tapestry of memory relating to the Northern Ireland conflict. A large march forms part of an annual commemorative weekend, and the killings are commemorated by a memorial, murals, and the Museum of Free Derry. In popular culture, the events of that day have been remembered with rock and folk songs, and two films have been made depicting the events.

Kristian Brown

See also Irish Republican Army; Law and Terrorism; Media and Terrorism

Further Readings

Bloody Sunday Inquiry Website. http://report.bloody-sunday-inquiry.org.

Hayes, Patrick, and Jim Campbell. *Bloody Sunday: Trauma, Pain and Politics.* London: Pluto Press, 2005.

Walsh, Dermot. *Bloody Sunday and the Rule of Law in Northern Ireland.* Dublin: Gill & Macmillan, 2000.

BOMBINGS AND BOMB SCARES

Bombings and bomb scares are among the most popular tools in the terrorist arsenal. Thousands of bombings occur around the world each year, maiming and killing scores of people and costing millions of dollars in property damage. Bomb scares take their toll by causing the evacuation of buildings or public spaces, taking up the valuable time of security experts who must evaluate the threat, and causing hundreds of lost work hours and decreases in productivity and revenue for companies affected.

The popularity of bombs stems largely from their malleability. A bomb can weigh as much as ten tons or as little as a pound, and it can be concealed in almost anything, including a portable CD player, a duffle bag, a trash can, or a car. This variability enables the bomber to suit the bomb to his desire, whether it is to destroy a building, blow a hole in a safe, or kill dozens of people. The necessary materials for a bomb's construction can often be obtained by legal and untraceable means, and at relatively little cost. Nor do bombs of great destructive power require a vast amount of specialized knowledge to assemble. Indeed, since the advent of the Internet, almost anyone can learn simple bomb-making techniques. In addition, terrorist groups or criminal organizations will often count among their members an individual with prior military or demolition training, permitting the construction of more sophisticated devices.

Types of Bombers

The bomber's motivations may be roughly divided into two categories, the criminal and the political. All bombings are of course criminal acts, but a distinction is made between bombers for whom the crime is an end in itself and those for whom the bombing is meant to serve a broader ideological goal.

For the criminal bomber, the destruction or injury caused by the bomb enables him or her to attain some personal end, such as financial gain or revenge upon a person or institution. A bomb may also be used to cover up a crime. For instance, a bomb can make it appear that a murdered person died in an accidental fire. The criminal bomber is often a lone individual, and many such bombers suffer from some form of mental illness. Bombing has also been adopted as a tactic by criminal organizations, not only for the purpose of theft or extortion, but also as a method of assassinating rival gang leaders.

For the political bomber—the terrorist—the destructive power of the bomb is intended to

further his or her cause, especially by attracting public attention and media interest. The terrorist bomber is frequently part of a highly organized group that carries out other terrorist activities in addition to bombings. It should be noted, however, that an ostensibly terrorist group might bomb a particular target to serve a purely criminal purpose. Conversely, an individual bomber may act out of political motives. Timothy James McVeigh, the Oklahoma City bomber, targeted the Alfred P. Murrah Federal Building because it was a symbol of the federal government, which he believed to be oppressive.

The hoax bomb or bomb scare often occurs after an actual bombing, but it is usually the responsibility of a separate and unrelated individual. The bomb scare is meant to take advantage of the atmosphere of fear created by the possibility of a bombing. For the individual who causes it, the spectacle of the public response to the threat may provide a sense of power or satisfaction. Other individuals attempt to turn the precautions undertaken by authorities in the event of a bomb threat to their advantage. For instance, a student might call in a threat to his or her school in the hope that the evacuation of the building will enable them to avoid a class or a test.

Targets of Bombers

The bomber's target is dependent on his or her purpose. The target of a criminal bomber is generally specific and unique; that is, the bomb is intended to kill of injure a specific individual, or destroy a particular business, and is thus not part of an ongoing campaign. Since the criminal bomber chooses the target for personal reasons, it is often otherwise obscure. The criminal bomber may even attempt to create the impression that the bombing itself was an accident.

Since the goal of the political bomber is to create awareness of and garner support for his or her cause, the target is usually public, and sometimes famous, and the method as spectacular as possible. Furthermore, the target is intended to serve as a symbol of what the terrorist opposes; the anti-abortion group Army of God targets doctors who perform abortions and the clinics in which they take place. Unlike criminal bombers, the terrorist often aims to cause as many casualties as possible, and terrorist bombings frequently take place in crowded public spaces. Airports and aircraft, shopping districts, government buildings and corporate headquarters, train and subway stations, even movie theaters and sports arenas are potential terrorist targets.

Bomb Materials and Construction

A vast array of materials can be used to construct bombs, including black powder (gunpowder), trinitrotoluene (TNT), nitroglycerin, ammonium nitrate (a common ingredient in fertilizer), and gasoline. Dozens of widely available commercial products that have common everyday uses—household cleansers, car products, photographic chemicals—can become the basic ingredients for a bomb. Through theft or the international black market, professional terrorists or other bomb makers may be able to acquire military or industrial explosives like Semtex, the plastic explosive that was used in the 1988 Lockerbie bombing.

To construct the bomb, the explosive material is packed into a container, usually metal but sometimes glass or plastic or even cardboard. Pieces of jagged metal may also be added to the explosive material to act as shrapnel when the bomb explodes; this is often done when the purpose of the bomb is to wound as many people as possible, as it was in the case of the London nail bomber, David Copeland. A source of ignition is attached—this may be a simple fuse, a battery, or a blasting cap, as is used in controlled demolitions.

In addition, many bombers, and almost all professional terrorists, also attach a timing device to the bomb that will allow the criminal to plant the bomb and remove himself from the area of the explosion well before it occurs. Timing devices vary widely in construction and sophistication. In the 1984 Brighton bombing that nearly killed British Prime Minister Margaret Thatcher, the IRA bomber was able to plant the device weeks before it was detonated. A radio detonator is a particular type of timing device. A bomb with a radio detonator attached will not detonate unless it is sent a certain signal at a particular frequency from a radio transmitter. With this type of bomb, the bomber is able to observe the target area from afar and detonate the explosive only when and if the bomb's target is within range. Such sophisticated bombs require specialized knowledge, training, and experience to

construct, and by no means do they make up the majority of bombs used in terrorist attacks. The pipe bomb, in which a length of metal plumbing is filled with black powder, capped, and a fuse attached, is perhaps the one of the simplest and most common examples of bomb construction.

As with all technology, however, bomb design has evolved, becoming more sophisticated and more dangerous over time. The development of cell-phone bombs is a prime example. Mobile phones can serve both as bombs themselves or simply as the detonators for an explosive placed elsewhere. Perhaps most famously, in 1996, Shin Bet, Israel's security and intelligence agency, assassinated the infamous bomber Yahya "The Architect" Ayyash, using inside contacts to deliver a phone to him that was laden with explosives. Upon confirmation that Ayyash was on the phone, the device was detonated, killing him instantly.

Cell-phone detonators provide a unique and daunting challenge to counterterrorism. Not only are they omnipresent, but detonators often give no indication of what they are, appearing to function like normal cell phones. In addition to their widespread use in the Iraq conflict, cell-phone detonators were used in the Bali bombings of 2002, the Madrid attacks in 2004, and the London attacks in 2006, as well as in the unexploded mail bombs found on a Chicago-bound plane in 2010.

Cell-phone bombs are part of a larger group of bombs referred to as *improvised explosive devices* (IEDs), which are bombs that do not have specific components. As the name indicates, IEDs are usually constructed from ubiquitous parts made from objects not intended for detonation. There is no regulation on size, mass, shape, or strength that determines an IED. However, there are three general types: package, vehicle-borne (VBIEDs), and suicide bombs. Most (but not all) IEDs have certain standard parts, including a fuse, explosive material, and a detonation device with a power supply and a container. Methods of detonation also vary. One method, known as "coupling," occurs when the detonation of one device leads to the detonation of another. Coupling used to disengage machines intended to detect or defuse bombs. "Daisy chain" refers to a series of bombs that are detonated on a time delay, so that the consequent bombs will detonate upon the arrival of the rescue team. Some IEDs contain pressure-plate detonators that go off when a vehicle rolls over them. These pressure plates can often be on the surface, while the bomb is buried underground, making them undetectable—a method called "boosting." They aim to circumvent the armor that many combat vehicles have by attacking the undercarriage.

Bombs Used in Terrorism: The Lone Bomber

The Unabomber case illuminates one of the advantages of the bomb as a terrorist weapon. Theodore Kaczynski, a former Berkeley math professor, loathed technology and blamed the Industrial Revolution and its successors for all of society's ills. (He was later diagnosed as paranoid schizophrenic, although experts differ as to the extent of his irrationality.) In 1971 he withdrew from the world, building himself a cabin in the remote mountains of Montana. His extremist ideology turned violent in 1978, when he mailed his first bomb to a professor at Northwestern University. Over the next 18 years, Kaczynski was able to execute more than two dozen bombings, killing three people and injuring 23. Despite his meager means and primitive hideaway—his cabin had no electricity or running water, and most of his bombs were packaged in boxes that he built by hand—he was able to construct increasingly sophisticated and destructive devices during his terrorist career, and for a long period he was successful in frustrating the detectives sent on his trail.

Kaczynski undertook his campaign firstly as a method of striking back at technology—most of his victims were professors, often in fields like computer science, engineering, and neuroscience—but also as way of publicizing his views. In 1996 he sent a letter to federal authorities claiming he would stop his assassination campaign if his 30,000-word manifesto was printed by a major national news outlet. *The New York Times* and *The Washington Post,* acting on the advice of federal authorities, acceded to this demand.

As authorities had hoped, the publication of the manifesto did eventually result in Kaczynski's arrest, after family members familiar with his writings recognized his style. But the publication of the manifesto, and the extensive media coverage of the entire affair, granted Kaczynski and his ideas a degree of public attention he could not otherwise have hoped to attain. In this respect, then, his bombing campaign was extremely effective. That a single man working in such primitive conditions could achieve this goal is a remarkable testament to the fearsomeness of the bomb as a terrorist tool. Were it not for the simplicity and anonymity of the bomb as a weapon, Kaczynski's destructive career might well have been impossible.

Bombs Used in Terrorism: The Urban Guerrilla

Another example of the advantages of the bomb for terrorists is seen in the development of the Irish Republican Army (IRA), who used it as a primary weapon throughout the 30-year Northern Irish conflict. Northern Ireland is part of the United Kingdom and has a Protestant majority; the IRA was created in an effort to reunite the provinces of Northern Ireland with the Catholic-majority Republic of Ireland. Once violence erupted in the late 1960s, the British Army maintained a strong troop presence in Northern Ireland, in addition to the local police force, the Royal Ulster Constabulary.

Northern Ireland is quite small, and though it contains many rural areas, there is no wilderness for terrorists to retreat to, as is the case in Latin America. IRA cells were instead based in the Catholic neighborhoods, particularly the urban ghettos of Belfast and Derry. In order to operate under such conditions, IRA operatives needed to be able to melt away following each of their attacks, for if any terrorist were captured at the scene, it could mean vital intelligence leaks to the security forces. For these reasons, the IRA came to rely upon the bomb as their main tactic, particularly the car bomb.

A bomb factory could be set up in almost any location, without attracting the notice of passerby. A garage, a factory, or even a basement could serve the purpose. The weapon could similarly be transported to the scene of the attack without attracting notice, concealed in a duffle bag or a suitcase. Cars could be placed outside a target for a considerable period of time without raising police suspicion, allowing the terrorist to be far from the scene by the time of the explosion. The extensive use of bombs allowed the IRA to work for a period of decades in heavily policed, high-security urban areas with relatively little risk to its operatives.

Bomb attacks have also been particularly prevalent in the Iraq War, which has seen a mix of types of attacks, including roadside IEDs, car bombs, and suicide bombings. Bombs kill indiscriminately, and terrorists often place them in civilian areas. For just one example, in 2004 a truck bomb was detonated in the town of Tal Afar, killing 152 people. In 2007 a series of suicide bombs, including instances where fuel trucks were blown up by their drivers, killed over 500 people. The frequent use of IEDs in the Afghanistan and Iraq conflicts defined the battles in many ways. Because of the chameleon-like nature of the everyday items that make up and serve to disguise the bombs, IEDs are particularly hard to detect, making them not only a destructive weapon, but also a seemingly unavoidable one.

Bombs Used in Terrorism: The Spectacular

One of the main goals of terrorists is to attract public attention through their crimes. They therefore seek out famous or well-known targets and devastating explosions. Thus, the terrorist often seeks to create what is known as a "spectacular," an incident so shocking that its images of destruction and horror become imprinted in the minds of

viewers around the world. Bombs are one of the favorite methods of achieving such an effect.

The 1993 World Trade Center bombing is a prominent example of such an attempt. The bombers involved in that incident constructed a 1,300-pound bomb and concealed it in a Ryder moving van, parking it in an underground garage beneath one of the towers of the complex. They hoped that the explosion would cause the building's steel support beams to collapse, causing the skyscraper to fall into its twin and destroy both towers. The building was much sturdier than the terrorists had expected, however, and despite causing a 200-foot-wide crater, which in turn caused the floors to collapse above and below the level of the bomb, only six people were killed, all within the immediate vicinity of the bomb. More than 1,000 people were injured, however, and the incident highlighted the vulnerabilities of skyscrapers to terrorist attack, as it took several hours for the building to be evacuated.

Although the 1993 World Trade Center terrorists were unable to cause the thousands of casualties they had hoped for, the bombing was spectacular in the extent of the media coverage it received. Indeed, the event served as precursor to the attacks of September 11, 2001, highlighting as it did the

Afghan border policemen show U.S. Security Forces Advisory Team members several improvised explosive devices they found around the Shorabak area during a logistical assessment of the Shorabak checkpoint in Kandahar province, Afghanistan, October 31, 2010. (U.S. Army photo by Spc. Ian Schell/Released)

potential to disrupt financial markets and the intensive media coverage such an event happening in Manhattan would evoke. The 9/11 attacks brought to the fore the psychological damage that terrorist attacks also attempt to achieve. In choosing to attack buildings that not only served as business and financial centers but also dominated the city's skyline, they made sure that a symbol of their undertaking would last beyond the rescue and recovery operations, serving as a lasting reminder.

Likewise, the foiled attempt to bomb Times Square in May 2010 was clearly intended to draw attention and amplify effect. Using an IED car bomb made from, among other things, firecrackers, propane, and an alarm clock, Faisal Shahzad parked the car in Times Square before fleeing the scene and attempting to board a plane to Dubai. The device failed to detonate, however, and smoke rising from the vehicle indicated to authorities what it was. Had the bomb worked properly, its chosen location—a busy, cosmopolitan tourist area in New York City—would have guaranteed a "spectacular" result.

Preventing Bombings and Bomb Scares

Unfortunately, it is very difficult for police to prevent bomb attacks. Because the necessary materials to manufacture bombs are so common and numerous—it is estimated that nearly 4,000 different chemicals can be used to obtain an explosive reaction—it is almost impossible to track and control their sales, as is done with the chemicals used in manufacturing. Many police departments across the country have bomb squads composed of highly trained individuals who can defuse explosive devices when they are found, but bomb squads can only go into action when police have some forewarning of a potential attack. Some terrorist groups phone in such warnings before their attacks, but many do not. In addition, warnings can be used to actually increase the potential casualties from an attack, by misdirecting the police as to its location. This was precisely what happened in the 1998 bombing in Omagh, Northern Ireland.

"Jamming," the process by which a machine alters or stops the signal going to a phone, has emerged as a way to prevent cell-phone-detonated bombs from exploding. Military jammers can typically prevent phones from ringing within up to a 150-yard range. Alternately, jammers can detect a signal and call the phone early, detonating it before any targets are in proximity. However, because of the widespread use of cell phones, jamming technology cannot be applied in civilian areas, as it would disrupt all phone signals.

It is often possible to protect individual buildings or complexes from bombings, and some airports are equipped with bomb-sniffing dogs or CTX-5500 scanners to detect bombs and keep them off planes. However, the fact that bombs are so easily concealed, constructed, and transported makes it extremely difficult to protect against them in a general sense.

Colleen Sullivan

See also Afghanistan War; Bali Nightclub Bombing; Copeland, David; Counterterrorism; Forensic Science and Terrorism; Iraq War; Irish Republican Army; London Underground Bombings; Madrid Bombings; Oklahoma City Bombing; Omagh Bombing; Suicide Terrorism; Unabomber; World Trade Center Bombing (1993)

Further Readings

Brodie, Thomas G. *Bombs and Bombings: A Handbook to Protection, Security, Disposal, and Investigation for Industry, Police and Fire Departments*. 3rd ed. Springfield, IL: Charles C Thomas, 2005.

Esposito, Richard, and Ted Gerstein. *Bomb Squad: A Year Inside the Nation's Most Exclusive Police Unit*. New York: Hyperion, 2007.

Haberfeld, M. R., and Agostino von Hassell, eds. *A New Understanding of Terrorism: Case Studies, Trajectories and Lessons Learned*. New York: Springer, 2009.

Harber, David. *The Anarchist Arsenal: Improvised Incendiary and Explosives Techniques*. Boulder, CO: Paladin, 1990.

Harber, David. *Guerrilla's Arsenal: Advanced Techniques for Making Explosives and Time-delay Bombs*. Boulder, CO: Paladin, 1994.

McKittrick, David. *Making Sense of the Troubles*. Belfast: Blackstaff Press, 2000.

Mello, Michael. *The United State of America versus Theodore John Kaczynski: Ethics, Power and the Invention of the Unabomber*. New York: Context Books, 1999.

National Research Council, Committee on the Review of Existing and Potential Standoff Explosives Detection Techniques. *Existing and Potential Standoff Explosives Detection Techniques*. Washington, DC: National Academies Press, 2004.

U.S. Treasury Department. *Bomb Threats and Physical Security Planning.* Washington, DC: U.S. Department of the Treasury, Bureau of Alcohol, Tobacco and Firearms, 1998.

BOUDIN, KATHERINE (1942–)

Katherine Boudin, a member of the Weatherman terrorist group, was involved in a bomb explosion in New York City in 1970, and she was arrested and imprisoned for life for her participation in an armed robbery that left two police officers and a security guard dead.

The daughter of the attorney and civil rights activist Leonard Boudin, Katherine Boudin graduated from Bryn Mawr College in Pennsylvania. While attending law school in the 1960s, she became an activist and joined the Students for a Democratic Society (SDS), a group devoted to opposing the perceived evils of capitalist America, particularly U.S. involvement in the Vietnam War. Boudin participated in many protests and demonstrations at that time.

In 1969, Boudin joined Weatherman, the militant offshoot of the SDS. She was involved in the Days of Rage in Chicago and other violent protests, and she authored a handbook on the various ways to evade detection by the authorities. She was present at the townhouse used by Weatherman in Greenwich Village, New York City, in 1970 when a bomb that group members were manufacturing exploded. The blast killed three members of the group, but Boudin and Cathy Wilkerson managed to survive and escape from the police.

Like many other surviving members at the time, Boudin went underground to avoid being captured by the FBI. After Weatherman (by that time rechristened the Weather Underground) disbanded as an organization at the end of the Vietnam War, Boudin turned her attention toward the Black Liberation Army (BLA), an extremely violent and radical splinter group of the Black Panthers. The group was notorious for committing armed robberies in order to fund their activities. Boudin was an integral component of their largest heist ever, the robbery of a Brink's armored truck in Nanuet, New York, on October 20, 1981. She was to be the white, and therefore less suspicious, driver of their getaway vehicle, a U-Haul truck. Police stopped the vehicle on the New York Thruway because they had been alerted to look for a U-Haul. However, Boudin convinced them that hers was not the right truck. As the officers stowed their weapons, gunmen of the BLA jumped from the back of the truck and began firing with automatic weapons. Sergeant Edward O'Grady, Officer Waverly Brown, and Brink's guard Peter Paige were all killed. Boudin was apprehended, and she pleaded guilty to charges of felony murder and armed robbery in exchange for a 20-years-to-life sentence.

While in prison, she earned a master's degree in adult education and worked on AIDS prevention programs for prisons. Her son, the author Chesa Boudin, was only one year old when she went to prison in 1981, inspiring her to develop a program to help mothers behind bars parent their children. In 2001, at age 58, she had served the minimum twenty years of her sentence and was eligible for parole. On August 22, 2001, she came before the New York Board of Pardons and Paroles, but her request for parole was denied. Two years later, Boudin again became eligible for parole, and this time she was granted it in a controversial ruling. She left prison on September 17, 2003, and began working at a hospital, helping treat women infected with HIV.

Harvey Kushner

See also Black Panther Party; Dohrn, Bernardine; May 19 Communist Organization; Weatherman; Women Terrorists

Further Readings

Barron, James. "Former Radical Granted Parole in '81 Killings." *The New York Times,* August 21, 2003, p. A1.

Braudy, Susan. *Family Circle: The Boudins and the Aristocracy of the Left.* New York: Knopf, 2003.

Castellucci, John. *The Big Dance: The Untold Story of Kathy Boudin and the Terrorist Family That Committed the Brink's Robbery Murders.* New York: Dodd, Mead, 1986.

Feron, James. "Kathy Boudin Given 20 Years to Life in Prison; She Expresses Sorrow for Brink's Holdup Deaths." *The New York Times,* May 4, 1984, p. B4.

Foderar, Lisa W. "With a Bouquet and a Wave, Boudin Is Free 22 Years Later." *The New York Times,* September 18, 2003, p. B1.

Frankfort, Ellen. *Kathy Boudin and the Dance of Death.* New York: Stein and Day, 1983.

Law, Victoria. *Resistance Behind Bars: The Struggles of Incarcerated Women.* Oakland, CA: PM Press, 2009.

BRANCH DAVIDIAN COMPOUND SIEGE

In 1993, federal agents besieged the Branch Davidian Compound at Mount Carmel, 12 miles from Waco, Texas. More than 80 people, including women and children, perished during the lengthy standoff. For the far-right militia movement, Waco became a rallying cry against the perceived injustices of the U.S. government.

David Koresh had become the leader of the Branch Davidians, an offshoot of the Seventh-day Adventist Church that believed in Christ's Second Coming after an apocalypse. Koresh declared himself the "father" of all the Davidian children, insisted on Spartan living conditions, armed the compound, and began daily paramilitary training as a defensive measure to prepare for the apocalypse.

The Bureau of Alcohol, Tobacco and Firearms (ATF) believed Koresh had stockpiled illegal weapons, and on February 28, 1993, agents raided Mount Carmel. Four ATF agents and six members of the cult died in the ensuing gun battle, and many others, including Koresh, were wounded. It was the beginning of a 51-day siege.

In the first week of March, 37 people left the compound, 21 of whom were under 18. A nine-year-old girl reportedly wore a note from her mother pinned to her jacket, stating that once the children were gone, the adults would die. Federal agents continued negotiations for weeks. By mid-April, FBI agents began to clear the ground around the compound. On April 19, federal agents in armed tanks pumped tear gas into the compound. The subsequent fire, either set by the Davidians themselves or caused by the tear gas, burned the compound to the ground.

Many on the right saw the ensuing investigation as a sinister cover-up by the government. Indeed, Waco seemed to justify the militia movement's growing fears about governmental abuse of power, and it give weight to conspiracy theories claiming that the government was systematically disarming the public to prepare for a UN-led invasion, which would result in the New World Order. These speculations sprung, in part, from the 1992 government-initiated siege at Ruby Ridge, Idaho. Federal agents had issued a warrant for illegal possession of firearms for Randy Weaver, a white separatist living in rural Idaho. In the subsequent confrontation, Weaver's wife and son were killed by a U.S. marshal sniper. Much as Ruby Ridge reinforced the militia movement in Idaho, the events at Waco, which were televised, inflamed antigovernment sentiments across the country.

On the second anniversary of Waco, the Northeast Texas Regional Militia of Texarkana erected a granite headstone as a memorial. It read, "On February 28, 1993, a church and its members known as the Branch Davidians came under attack by ATF and FBI agents. For 51 days, the Davidians and their leader, David Koresh, stood proudly." Three hundred miles away, in Oklahoma City, the Alfred P. Murrah Federal Building was still smoldering from a 9 A.M. bombing that took 168 lives. The trial of the Oklahoma City bomber, Timothy James McVeigh, would later reveal that the first disaster spawned the second.

McVeigh had stopped to observe the siege at Waco while selling survivalist materials on the gun circuit. By 1993 he was already a part of an antigovernment movement based primarily on the supposed right to bear arms granted by the Second Amendment to the U.S. Constitution. In the following months, McVeigh watched conspiracy-laden videos about Waco, including *Waco: The Big Lie* and *Day 51*, which reinforced and deepened his antigovernment beliefs.

McVeigh was not the only one who committed violence in the name of Waco. In 1997, authorities received a letter taking responsibility for bombings at an abortion clinic and gay club in Atlanta, and the author mentioned retaliation for the siege at Waco as a motive. (Although it was signed "Army of God," authorities now believe the letter was from Eric Rudolph.) In 1999, prison officials intercepted letters from members of the Aryan Circle, a prison gang, that pledged violence in the name of Waco and Oklahoma City. As a result of such threats, many government officials and agencies are more vigilant each April 19.

Laura Lambert

See also April 19; McVeigh, Timothy James; Oklahoma City Bombing; Rudolph, Eric

Further Readings

Crothers, Lane. *Rage on the Right: The American Militia Movement from Ruby Ridge to Homeland Security*. Lanham, MD: Rowman & Littlefield, 2003.

Hamm, Mark S. *Apocalypse In Oklahoma: Waco and Ruby Ridge Revenged.* Boston: Northeastern University Press, 1997.

Kirk, Michael, dir. "Waco: The Inside Story." *Frontline,* PBS, August 9, 2010. http://www.pbs.org/wgbh/pages/frontline/waco.

Martin, Sheila, and Catherine Wessinger. *When They Were Mine: Memoirs of a Branch Davidian Wife and Mother.* Waco, TX: Baylor University Press, 2009.

Newport, Kenneth G. C. *The Branch Davidians of Waco: The History and Beliefs of an Apocalyptic Sect.* Oxford: Oxford University Press, 2006.

Reavis, Dick J. *The Ashes of Waco: An Investigation.* New York: Simon & Schuster, 1995.

Stern, Kenneth S. *A Force Upon the Plain: The American Militia Movement and the Politics of Hate.* New York: Simon & Schuster, 1996.

Thibodeau, David. *A Place Called Waco: A Survivor's Story.* New York: Public Affairs, 1999.

Walter, Jess. *Every Knee Shall Bow: The Truth and Tragedy of Ruby Ridge and the Randy Weaver Family.* New York: Regan Books, 1995.

Wright, Stuart, ed. *Armageddon in Waco: Critical Perspectives on the Branch Davidian Conflict.* Chicago: University of Chicago Press, 1995.

BRIGATE ROSSE

See Red Brigades

BROOKLYN BRIDGE SHOOTING

A 1994 Brooklyn Bridge shooting case, in which Rashid Baz, a Lebanese national, was convicted of shooting at a van of Jewish students, was reopened by the FBI in 1999 and reclassified as an act of terrorism.

Just before 10:30 AM on March 1, 1994, Baz, then a 28-year-old livery car driver, attacked a van on the Brooklyn Bridge that was carrying 15 Hasidic boys from Manhattan to Crown Heights, Brooklyn. Baz sprayed both sides of the van with bullets from two guns before fleeing into Brooklyn. Two of the students who were hit suffered head wounds: 16-year-old Aaron Halberstam suffered severe brain damage and died several days later, while Nachum Sosonkin, 18, underwent surgery and survived, though a bullet remained lodged in his brain. Two other students sustained minor gunshot wounds. Police arrested Baz at his uncle's home in Sunset Park, Brooklyn, the next day.

The shooting occurred less than a week after Baruch Goldstein, a Brooklyn-born Jewish settler, massacred 29 Muslims worshipping at a mosque in Hebron. The press quickly labeled Baz a "fundamentalist terrorist" who was retaliating for the attack in Hebron, and police began investigating possible links between Baz and the terrorist organization Hezbollah. After the shooting, Mayor Rudolph Giuliani placed the New York City's law-enforcement agencies on an anti-terrorist alert, although no credible threats had been issued. Concurrently, the 1993 World Trade Center bombing case was being tried in New York City. This confluence of events put a strain on New York's Arab and Jewish communities.

Baz went on trial on November 1, 1994, with angry spectators and tight security. The prosecution deemed the attack a "blind-side ambush" in which Baz, without provocation, attempted to kill all 15 boys in the van. The defense claimed that Baz's childhood in war-torn Beirut caused him to develop post-traumatic stress disorder, and that his state of mind during the attack was therefore questionable. Pretrial hearings admitted a tape of Baz's interrogation by police, in which he admitted to being "afraid," stating that the van of students had cut him off and brandished a gun at him—none of which explained why he had several illegal firearms in his car or why he had pursued the van so aggressively. (Baz did not testify on his own behalf at the trial.) On December 1, 1994, Baz was convicted on one count of second-degree murder, 14 counts of attempted murder, and one count of criminal use of a firearm; he was later sentenced to 114 years in prison. The crime was classified as a case of "road rage."

After much pressure from the Halberstam family and several political officials, including Senator Charles E. Schumer of New York, Mayor Giuliani, and First Lady Hillary Clinton, the FBI reopened the investigation in August 1999. By that December, the FBI had determined that Baz had acted alone and was not linked to any terrorist organizations. The FBI did, however, reclassify the crime as a terrorist attack, motivated by political views and a wish to retaliate against Jewish people.

Laura Lambert

See also Freelance Terrorism; Goldstein, Baruch

Further Readings

Ari Halberstam Memorial Site. http://www.arihalberstam
.com.

Dickey, Christopher. *Securing the City: Inside America's
Best Counterterror Force—The NYPD.* New York:
Simon & Schuster, 2009.

Fettmann, Eric. "Forgetting Terror: 'See No Evil' in
Hindsight." *New York Post,* March 8, 2006, p. 27.

Nagourney, Adam. "U.S. Reopens Inquiry into Yeshiva
Student's '94 Shooting Death on Brooklyn Bridge."
The New York Times, August 27, 1999, p. B9.

BRÜDER SCHWEIGEN

See Order, The

BUCKLEY, WILLIAM (1928–1985)

William Francis Buckley, the CIA station chief in
Beirut during the Lebanese War, was one of the
most crucial hostages abducted by Shiite Muslim
extremists during the hostage crisis in Lebanon.
The arms-for-hostages deal struck between Iran
and the Reagan administration was largely orchestrated to secure Buckley's release.

Buckley had been employed by the CIA from
1955 to 1957, and again from 1965 until his kidnapping in 1984. Buckley's role as station chief in
Beirut was significant. He was charged with rebuild-
ing the intelligence network in the area, which had
been shattered by the April 1983 embassy bombing. In addition, because the United States then
lacked embassies in both Iraq and Iran, Buckley
was to head all CIA operations for the northern
Persian Gulf area. In an era when simply being an
American in the Middle East was reason enough to
be kidnapped, Buckley was a prime target.

On the morning of March 16, 1984, kidnappers
seized Buckley just steps from the front door of his
apartment and stuffed him into the trunk of a
white Renault. The CIA believes that Buckley was
betrayed by a female Shiite CIA agent named
Zeynoub, whom Buckley had trained. Unbeknownst
to him, Zeynoub was also an "official" of
Hezbollah, the umbrella organization that encompassed Islamic Jihad, which had already taken
three other American hostages in exchange for
17 prisoners in Kuwait. Zeynoub and Buckley
were having an affair at the time. Three weeks
before he was taken, Buckley confided to a friend
that he suspected he might be kidnapped. By that
time, however, Zeynoub already had access to his
apartment. The decision to take Buckley came on
March 15, 1984, and he was abducted the following morning. Many Lebanese informants vanished
or were killed immediately following his abduction, and CIA agents therefore believe that Buckley
was carrying a document listing CIA assets in
Lebanon at the time of his capture.

Though there are no conclusive reports, it is
believed that Buckley was tortured repeatedly over
the next 10 months, and that the intensity and
length of these interrogations destroyed his health.
By the spring of 1985, other hostages, such as
Father Martin Lawrence Jenco and Reverend
Benjamin Weir, became aware of Buckley's presence in another cell in the room where they were
being held. On February 14, 1985, Jeremy Levin,
the bureau chief for CNN, escaped from captivity
and reported that Buckley was seriously ill, racked
by coughs and vomiting and delirious with fever.
Fellow hostages listened closely on the night of
June 3, 1985, when the coughing finally stopped.
Buckley had died in captivity.

During this time, Buckley's rescue was a top
priority for both the CIA and the Reagan administration. In August 1985, the first delivery of arms—
100 antitank missiles provided by Israel—was sent
to Iran. The following month, 408 more missiles
arrived. Father Weir was released on September 18,
1985, the first hostage to be set free under the arms-
for-hostages agreement. The CIA had requested
Buckley, not knowing he had already died.

Four months after his death, on October 4,
1985, Islamic Jihad announced Buckley's execution, claiming to have killed him in retaliation for
Israel's raid on the PLO's headquarters in Tunisia.
The United States continued to barter arms-for-
hostages, now requesting Buckley's remains along
with the remaining Americans.

On December 28, 1991, Buckley's remains were
returned to the United States and buried in Arlington
Cemetery, with full military honors. He was also
honored with a star carved in the marble memorial
wall of the CIA's main building in Langley,
Virginia.

Laura Lambert

See also al Jihad; Anderson, Terry A.; Hezbollah; Hostage Taking; Sutherland, Thomas

Further Readings

Anderson, Terry. *Den of Lions: Memoirs of Seven Years.* New York: Crown Publishers, 1993.

Arlington National Cemetery Website. "William Francis Buckley." http://www.arlingtoncemetery.net/wbuckley.htm.

Martin, David C., and John Walcott. *Best Laid Plans: The Inside Story of America's War Against Terrorism.* New York: Harper & Row, 1988.

McGovern, Glenn P. *Targeted Violence: A Statistical and Tactical Analysis of Assassinations, Contract Killings, and Kidnappings.* Boca Raton, FL: CRC Press/Taylor & Francis Group, 2010.

Walsh, Lawrence E. *Firewall: The Iran-Contra Conspiracy and Coverup.* New York: W.W. Norton, 1997.

Wroe, Ann. *Lives, Lies, and the Iran-Contra Affair.* New York: St. Martin's, 1992.

Bureau of Alcohol, Tobacco, Firearms and Explosives

Since its inception in late 1790s, the Bureau of Alcohol, Tobacco and Firearms (ATF) has undergone more changes in titles and responsibilities than any other federal agency. It was transferred to the Department of Justice under the Homeland Security Act of 2002, when "Explosives" was added to its name and mission. Despite the change, however, the bureau still uses the abbreviation "ATF." The bureau protects communities from violent criminals, criminal organizations, illegal weapons, firearms trafficking, the illegal use and storage of explosives, arson, bombings, terrorism, and the illegal diversion of alcohol and tobacco products. The ATF's *Strategic Plan—Fiscal Years 2010–2016* states, "Combating violent crime is our specialty, our niche. ATF's regulatory and enforcement missions are interwoven, providing a comprehensive approach to reducing violent crime, protecting the public, and protecting national security."

Headquartered in Washington, D.C., the ATF employs a staff of 5,000, including special agents, inspectors, auditors, and laboratory and support personnel. The ATF has four National Response Teams (NRTs), which can be deployed within 24 hours to major explosion and arson sites, as was done after bombing of the Alfred P. Murrah Federal Building in Oklahoma City in 1995, and following the September 11, 2001, attacks. Created in 1978, the NRTs partner with federal, state, and local agencies to investigate and reconstruct crime scenes, identify the origin of an explosion, conduct interviews, sift through debris for evidence, and develop a plan for further actions.

Not all ATF agents are human. Since 1990, ATF's National Canine Center in Front Royal, Virginia, has trained 272 dogs for 31 states and 13 countries. These canine agents can detect over 19,000 commercially available and home-concocted chemical compounds. Dogs have worked at the Super Bowl, the Olympics, and national political conventions, and they helped secure the Pentagon after the 9/11 attacks.

The History of the ATF

ATF traces its lineage to 1789, when Congress imposed a tax on imported liquor to raise funds to retire debts from the Revolutionary War. In 1791 a tax on domestic liquor production sparked protests and the Whisky Rebellion of 1794, but both income sources have continued to provide a steady government revenue stream into the twenty-first century. Congress created the Office of Internal Revenue within the Treasury Department in 1862. The tax enforcers transformed into a Prohibition Unit to enforce the national alcohol ban in the 1920s and then became the Alcohol Tax Unit when Prohibition ended in 1935.

The "T-men," famous for tracking down tax dodgers and moonshiners, became experts at recognizing a range of firearms and evidence tampering. The agency established a laboratory in 1886 to test the purity of margarine and, later, alcohol and tobacco. The lab developed advanced fingerprinting, arson investigation, and ballistics techniques that evolved into sophisticated modern forensic capacities such as the Integrated Ballistic Identification System. The division continued its work as part of the Internal Revenue Service (IRS) until it was separated from the IRS and became part of the Department of the Treasury in 1972. Ten years later, Congress gave ATF the authority to investigate arson cases nationwide with the Anti-Arson Act of 1982.

Bad publicity resulting from the 51-day armed standoff with the Branch Davidians at Waco, Texas, in 1993 hurt the bureau's image. However, the ATF's image been helped by its many counter-terrorism activities. For example, it was an ATF agent who identified the serial number of a truck axle, which eventually lead to the conviction of the terrorists in the first World Trade Center bombing in 1993. The bureau has also pioneered new ballistics technology, explosives identification, and methods to break up smuggling rings.

Under the Antiterrorism and Effective Death Penalty Act of 1996, the ATF established a national repository of information about arson incidents and the criminal misuse of explosives, as well as the Explosives Study Group (ESG). The ESG conducts research on the possible use and exploitation of new prevention technologies in the area of explosives, and it develops strategies for improvements in public safety. After the Oklahoma City bombing in 1995, the ESG started a campaign called "Be Aware for America," with the aim of preventing the improper sale and use of ammonium nitrate fertilizer, a component in the Oklahoma City bomb. In 2002 the ESG became the Explosives Research and Development Branch, and in 2008 ATF began construction on a new National Center for Explosives Training and Research (NCETR) at the Redstone Arsenal in Alabama.

The U.S. Bomb Data Center, managed by ATF, includes information from the ATF's Bomb Arson Tracking System (BATS) and the ATF Arson and Explosives Incidents System (AEXIS). BATS is an online case management system that provides state and local investigators current data on arson and explosives investigations across the country. It includes an Investigative Resources Library and performs trend analysis of similar motives, device components, and potential suspects. The AEXIS database includes commercially made explosives in the United States and abroad, showing patterns and trends in the usage of explosive devices in a given area or state and throughout the nation. In 1997 the ATF started an investigation of a recovered cache of explosives at a self-storage facility in Bedford Heights, Ohio, and traced it to an Armenian terrorist group that had assassinated 22 Turkish diplomats and perpetrated 160 bombings worldwide during the 1970s.

The ATF and the Homeland Security Act

The Homeland Security Act of 2002 made ATF responsible for implementing the 2002 Safe Explosives Act (SEA) and established an NCETR facility at Fort A.P. Hill in Bowling Green, Virginia. The SEA regulates how explosives are handled and stored, and it has given ATF greater capacity to regulate explosives by expanding its reach to include the intrastate manufacture, purchase, and use of explosives. The law also restricted three additional groups from gaining access to explosives: aliens, persons dishonorably discharged from the military, and individuals who have renounced their U.S. citizenship.

ATF investigations have broken up smuggling rings used to finance terrorism. Between 1999 and 2004, the number of cigarette trafficking cases jumped from a dozen to 300. Smugglers can easily make $2 million from a single truckload of cigarettes, and ATF has linked smuggling operations to al Qaeda and Hezbollah.

The transfer of ATF to the Department of Justice sparked a public turf battle with the FBI. The two investigative agencies have very different cultures and methods, and they have long been rivals. According to *The Washington Post*, "More than 30 ATF agents arrived at the smoldering Pentagon the day after September 11, 2001, to help with the largest criminal investigation in the nation's history. The FBI commander threw them off the site."

The merger between the two agencies was meant to coordinate domestic terrorism investigations. In reality, however, the change amounted to little more than a change of letterhead: ATF kept its own headquarters, offices, and management. Attorney General John Ashcroft ordered the merger of their respective bomb databases, but the FBI refused to comply. Jurisdictional boundaries became blurred, with the FBI taking the lead in explosions related to terrorism, and ATF handling all other bombings and explosions. This meant, however, that agents from both agencies might race to the scene of an attack to determine the source of the bomb. ATF agents feared the FBI would cherry-pick high-profile cases, leaving them with mundane cases. At one point the agencies were battling over which one would train bomb-sniffing dogs. The ongoing rivalry between ATF and the FBI poses a threat to national security, however, delaying efforts to create a national strategy to protect the country against terrorism.

Maria Kiriakova and Ann E. Robertson

See also Branch Davidian Compound Siege; Counterterrorism; Federal Bureau of Investigation; Hezbollah; Homeland Security; World Trade Center Bombing (1993)

Further Readings

Bureau of Alcohol, Tobacco, Firearms and Explosives. http://www.atf.gov.

Bureau of Alcohol, Tobacco, Firearms and Explosives. *Strategic Plan—Fiscal Years 2010–2016.* http://www .atf.gov/publications/general/strategic-plan.

Burgess, William J. *Piercing the Shields of Justice: Inside the ATF.* Lawrenceville, VA: Brunswick, 1996.

Markon, Jerry. "FBI, ATF Battle for Control of Cases; Cooperation Lags Despite Merger." *Washington Post,* May 10, 2008, p. A1.

Miller, Wilbur R. *Revenuers and Moonshiners: Enforcing Federal Liquor Law in the Mountain South, 1865–1900.* Chapel Hill: University of North Carolina Press, 1991.

Moore, James. *Very Special Agents: The Inside Story of America's Most Controversial Law Enforcement Agency—The Bureau of Alcohol, Tobacco, and Firearms.* Champaign: University of Illinois Press, 2001.

Vizzard, William J. *In the Cross Fire: A Political History of the Bureau of Alcohol, Tobacco and Firearms.* Boulder, CO: Lynne Rienner, 1997.

CANARY WHARF BOMBING

The 1996 bombing at Canary Wharf in East London marked the end of an 18-month Irish Republican Army (IRA) cease-fire and jeopardized the peace process in Northern Ireland.

A conflict began in the late 1960s between Northern Ireland's Protestants, who wanted the province to remain part of the United Kingdom, and Northern Ireland's Roman Catholics, who wanted it to become part of the Republic of Ireland. On August 31, 1994, after months of secret talks with the British and Irish governments, the IRA, the largest paramilitary group on the Catholic side (also called the Nationalist, or Republican, side), announced a cease-fire. In October, the major Protestant (also called Loyalist or Unionist) paramilitary groups followed suit. After 30 years of guerrilla warfare and several previous failed attempts at negotiations, these mutual cease-fires represented the best opportunity up to that point to achieve a lasting peace.

The major parties to the negotiations were all deeply suspicious of the motives of their counterparts, however. Furthermore, the government of Britain's Conservative prime minister John Major depended on his party's slim majority in Parliament, and he could not afford to lose the support of the Unionist members of Parliament from Northern Ireland. To appease the Unionists and win some assurance of the IRA's commitment to peace, Major demanded that the IRA decommission some of its arms before commencing serious talks.

IRA leaders balked, seeing this request as a confirmation of their worst fear: that the British government was merely using the negotiations as a stalling tactic in order to diminish the IRA's military capabilities. Negotiations halted for 18 months, and frustrations grew. Various envoys, including former U.S. Senator George Mitchell, tried to achieve some form of compromise. On February 9, 1996, at around 5:40 P.M., a telephone call to Scotland Yard announced the end of the IRA cease-fire and the resumption of military operations.

At 7:00 P.M., a bomb exploded at the Canary Wharf economic development site in East London's Docklands, killing two workers. The 81-acre site is home to Britain's largest office tower and is filled with offices, shops, and apartment complexes. The fertilizer-based bomb weighed several tons and was hidden in a truck. Despite the bomb's great size, fewer than 50 people were injured because police had cleared the area; property damage, however, totaled an estimated £140 million (U.S. $215 million).

Peace negotiations ceased, not to resume until 1997, when a new British prime minister, Tony Blair, took office. IRA member James McArdle was convicted for his part in the bombing and sentenced to 25 years in a 1998 trial. He has since been released, as have almost all paramilitary prisoners, under the terms of the Good Friday Agreement, which ended formal hostilities in Northern Ireland in 1998.

Colleen Sullivan

See also Bombings and Bomb Scares; Irish Republican Army

Further Readings

Campbell, Duncan. "Bomb Case Man Cleared." *The Guardian*, February 1, 1998, p. 5.

Hoge, Warren. "Notorious Killer among Inmates Freed from Ulster Prison." *The New York Times,* July 25, 2000, p. A3.

Holland, Jack. *Hope Against History: The Course of Conflict in Northern Ireland.* New York: Henry Holt, 1999.

McKittrick, David. *Making Sense of the Troubles.* Belfast: Blackstaff Press, 2000.

Moloney, Ed. *A Secret History of the IRA.* New York: W.W. Norton, 2002.

O'Brien, Brendan. *The Long War: The IRA and Sinn Fein.* 2nd ed. Syracuse, NY: Syracuse University Press, 1999.

Shanahan, Timothy. *The Provisional Irish American Army and the Morality of Terrorism.* Edinburgh: Edinburgh University Press, 2009.

Taylor, Peter. *Provos: The IRA and Sinn Fein.* London: Bloomsbury, 1997.

CARLOS THE JACKAL

See Sánchez, Illich Ramírez

CENTENNIAL PARK BOMBING

In the early morning hours of July 27, 1996, a pipe bomb exploded in Atlanta's Centennial Park, the after-hours meeting place of the 1996 Olympic Games. The bomb killed one person and injured more than 100 others.

A few minutes before 1:00 A.M., Richard Jewell, an AT&T security guard, alerted officials to a suspicious group of rowdy drunks near a sound tower in the park. Jewell had also noticed a suspicious green knapsack that had been left after the group dispersed. At 1:07 A.M. the police received an anonymous 911 call. The voice on the phone, which investigators would later identify as that of a white male with a slight southern accent, said, "There's a bomb in Centennial Park. You have 30 minutes."

Minutes later, bomb experts identified wire and a pipe bomb in the knapsack and began evacuating the area. Shortly after 1:20 A.M. the bomb exploded; investigators later discovered it to have actually been three pipe bombs filled with smokeless gunpowder, nails, and screws. Flying shrapnel caused most of the 111 injuries that night. By 2:00 A.M., all of downtown Atlanta had been sealed off.

From the start, authorities believed the bombing to be an act of domestic terrorism, partly because of the crude nature of the homemade pipe bomb, and partly because the attack did not appear to have an overtly political target. (Later reports suggested that the bomb was intentionally set to hurt the law enforcement officers assisting in the evacuation, a suggestion in keeping with the domestic terrorism hypothesis.) Early suspects included a local group of extremely violent skinheads and the Georgia Militia, a group that had been arrested in April 1996 for allegedly building pipe bombs. An eyewitness account reported four white men dressed in black acting suspiciously in the moments before the bombing.

Within three days of the bombing, however, Jewell, who had been lauded as a hero for two days following the bombing, was named as a suspect. He was also the first defendant named in a lawsuit charging that security had been slow to evacuate the area, causing extensive injuries. From August to October 1996, authorities made concerted efforts to link Jewell to forensic evidence, though hair samples and voice identification tests did not confirm his involvement. Later suspects included members of the Phineas Priesthood, who were caught in Spokane, Washington, following bombings at a newspaper, a bank, and a Planned Parenthood clinic. They, too, were cleared.

By June 1997, however, a handful of clinic and anti-gay bombings in the Atlanta and Birmingham, Alabama, areas led investigators to another suspect—Eric Robert Rudolph, a white supremacist and antigovernment and anti-abortion extremist. On October 14, 1998, more than two years after the fact, Rudolph was charged in connection with the Centennial Park bombing.

Rudolph hid out in the mountains of North Carolina for the next five years. He was finally arrested on May 31, 2003, when a police officer found him scavenging near the garbage bins of a grocery store in his hometown of Murphy, North

Carolina. Rudolph pled guilty to charges stemming from his various bombings in 2005. In a statement, he said that the purpose of the Olympic Games was "to promote the values of global socialism," and that he had hoped to force the cancellation of the event.

Laura Lambert

See also Anti-Abortion Terrorism; Bombings and Bomb Scares; Rudolph, Eric

Further Readings

Barry, Ellen, and Jenny Jarvie. "Rudolph Admits Bombing '96 Olympic Park, Clinics." *Los Angeles Times,* April 4, 2005, p. A11.

CNN Interactive. "Olympic Park Bombing: Special Section." http://www.cnn.com/US/9607/27/olympic.bomb.main.

Hull, Anne. "Olympics Bombing Suspect Caught: Also Sought in Attacks on Abortion Clinics and Gay Club, Fugitive Hid for 5 Years." *The Washington Post,* June 1, 2003, p. A1.

Schuster, Henry. *Hunting Eric Rudolph: An Insider's Account of the Five-year Search for the Olympic Bombing Suspect.* New York: Berkley Books, 2005.

U.S. Congress, Senate Committee on the Judiciary, Subcommittee on Technology, Terrorism, and Government Information. *The Atlanta Olympics Bombing and the FBI Interrogation of Richard Jewell.* Washington, DC: U.S. Government Printing Office, 1997.

Vollers, Maryanne. *Lone Wolf: Eric Rudolph; Murder, Myth, and the Pursuit of an American Outlaw.* New York: HarperCollins, 2006.

CENTRAL INTELLIGENCE AGENCY

The Central Intelligence Agency (CIA) is an independent agency of the United States government. It is responsible for amassing and assessing foreign intelligence to aid the president, the National Security Council (NSC), and other officials in making national security decisions. As of 2011, the CIA had four divisions: the National Clandestine Service, the Directorate of Intelligence, the Directorate of Science and Technology, and the Directorate of Support. The Intelligence Reform and Terrorism Prevention Act of 2004 created a new Office of the Director of National Intelligence (ODNI). This office coordinates the 17 members of the U.S. Intelligence Community, including the CIA. Its primary goal is to share and coordinate domestic, international, and military intelligence. Such information is considered to be the first line of defense against terrorism.

In 1947, as a direct result of the intelligence failure that allowed Japan's surprise attack on Pearl Harbor, President Harry S. Truman signed the National Security Act, which established the National Security Council (NSC) and the CIA. The CIA grew out of the World War II Office of Strategic Services (OSS), run by General William "Wild Bill" Donavan, who recruited from Wall Street and Ivy League schools to form an elite intelligence group based on the East Coast, with an emphasis on covert action abroad. Originally, the CIA operated only outside the United States and was prohibited from collecting intelligence about the domestic activities of its citizens. Domestic intelligence was the responsibility of the Federal Bureau of Investigation (FBI).

During its early years, most CIA operations involved supporting anti-Communist forces in foreign countries. By the 1970s, however, the CIA was working inside the United States. Throughout the 1960s and early 1970s, the CIA, through Operation CHAOS, assembled mountains of intelligence on domestic war protestors and black nationalists. The CIA justified its actions by maintaining that such antigovernment activities must be sponsored by a foreign state. Revelations about brutal CIA activities in Vietnam and assassination plots against several leaders, including Fidel Castro of Cuba and Patrice Lumumba of the Democratic Republic of the Congo, also marred the agency's reputation and indicated a need for reform.

In the post-Watergate 1970s, the U.S. Congress authorized the Church Committee in the Senate and the Pike Committee in the House of Representatives to investigate the CIA. The findings of these committees led to a series of directives. In 1976, President Gerald Ford prohibited CIA assassinations of political leaders. In 1978, President Jimmy Carter signed the Foreign Intelligence Surveillance Act, which curtailed the CIA's ability to gather foreign intelligence within the United States. Some restrictions were lifted, however, by Executive Order 12333, signed by President Ronald Reagan in December 1981. This order allowed domestic electronic surveillance and physical searches in response to a growing threat of Soviet spies within U.S. borders.

Concurrently, terrorism in the Middle East was becoming a top concern. The early 1980s saw a great number of bombings, hijackings, and kidnappings. In particular, war-torn Lebanon became a center of terrorist activity. In 1983 the entire staff of a CIA station—six operatives in total—was killed, along with 57 others, when a suicide bomber targeted the U.S. embassy in Beirut. The Beirut station chief was replaced by William Buckley, who was kidnapped by Islamic militants in 1984 and died in captivity.

These terrorist incidents led CIA director William Casey to develop the Counterterrorism Center (CTC) in 1986, with the mission to "pre-empt, disrupt, and defeat" terrorists and coordinate the intelligence community's counterterrorist activities. Although staffed with approximately 200 officers, the CTC was considered by many to be a paper-pushing outfit. The CIA's clandestine operations wing, the Directorate of Operations (DO), still controlled espionage activities overseas.

The Downfall Decade

After the fall of the Soviet Union in 1991, the CIA, long used to functioning under the Soviet threat, began to downsize operations in the Middle East, even as six new Islamic states emerged in Central Asia. By the mid-1990s, eight CIA stations in the area known as the "South Group" were closed, leaving a gaping hole in Middle Eastern intelligence, even as rumblings of fundamentalist dissent grew louder throughout the region. Like many other agencies, the CIA had begun to rely more heavily on technology, such as satellites, computers, and encryption devices. The lack of first-hand information from observers on the scene was compounded by an element of "careerism," as operatives were rewarded as much for analysis done at headquarters in Langley, Virginia, as for field-based operations abroad. Robert Baer, considered one of the best CIA operatives in the Middle East, complained, "the CIA closed down in the '90s." Baer left the agency in 1997.

In 1995 the potential for gathering first-hand intelligence—or human intelligence (HUMINT)—was further hampered by CIA blunders that involved a paid Guatemalan informant who was connected to the murders of two Americans. In response, CIA director John Deutch established a policy requiring the Directorate of Operations to approve the recruitment of sources believed to have serious criminal or abusive human rights records. According to some estimates, as much as 60 percent of the DO's contacts were lost as a direct result of this "scrub" policy.

The Guatemalan incident followed close on the heels of other blunders, including the Aldrich Ames spy scandal in 1994, reports of the endemic "malaise" at the Paris CIA station in the mid-1990s, and a failed attempt to assassinate Saddam Hussein of Iraq in 1995. Key resignations—including Baer; William Lofgren, the former chief of the Central Eurasia Division; and David Manners, the station chief in Amman, Jordan—added to the intelligence blackout in the Middle East.

By 1996 the CIA's Counterterrorism Center and the FBI had begun to exchange high-level officers to manage counterterrorism efforts in both agencies. This marked a change from previous eras, when the distinctions between the FBI and the CIA were kept clear (domestic versus foreign, law enforcement versus national security, peacetime versus wartime), but now these were blurred with respect to acts of terrorism. The joint effort included a special taskforce dedicated solely to Osama bin Laden.

After the 9/11 Attacks

The September 11, 2001, attacks on the World Trade Center in New York City and the Pentagon near Washington, D.C., tragically demonstrated the failure of U.S. intelligence. Indeed, a 2005 report by the CIA inspector general pointed to a series of systemic failures caused by a lack of information sharing and critical analysis. The CIA had been aware, for example, of the presence in the United States of some of the future 9/11 hijackers, but it never followed up on their whereabouts or activities. Michael Scheuer, the former head of the CIA's Osama bin Laden unit, claims the United States had at least 10 opportunities to assassinate bin Laden before 2001, but that the CIA and White House could not agree on the rules of engagement for such an attack. George Tenet, the

CIA director from 1997 to 2004, asked for a detailed authorization, but the White House instead gave the vague order to "apprehend with lethal force as authorized."

Beginning in October 2001, the CIA has undergone the most massive overhaul in its history. Some responsibilities were transferred to the new Office of the Director of National Intelligence. New military personnel were rushed through a four-week crash course to become part of the CIA's paramilitary division. Dozens of retired CIA operatives from the Clandestine Service Reserve were reactivated, including some who took charge of abandoned CIA stations throughout the Middle East. The CTC doubled its officer corps after 9/11 and quadrupled the number of its analysts.

Some of the CIA's activities have been highly controversial. Amnesty International, Human Rights Watch, and allied governments have condemned CIA interrogation tactics, especially the use of waterboarding (simulated drowning), which many consider a form of torture. One particularly controversial practice was extraordinary rendition, or "outsourcing torture." U.S. agents would capture suspects in one country, deny legal counsel, fly them to secret CIA prisons in countries that allowed torture, and interrogate them there. The procedure began around 1995 and accelerated in subsequent months and years. In November 2005, federal prosecutors announced that the CIA had destroyed 92 tapes of interrogations allegedly using torture, making future prosecutions difficult.

After his inauguration in January 2009, President Barack Obama surprised Congress and the CIA by appointing Leon Panetta as his CIA director. Panetta, a former congressman and Clinton-era White House chief of staff and budget director, had little intelligence experience, but he had an extensive record of successfully working with Congress. CIA staff reportedly resented the appointment; some claimed that the hiring of Panetta was an indication that Obama thought there were no qualified persons at the agency itself. Nevertheless, Panetta oversaw the agency during one of its greatest successes: a CIA-led manhunt that ultimately resulted in the killing of Osama bin Laden.

The CIA has been assigned to hunt for al Qaeda forces, manage relations with local warlords, and rebuild Afghanistan's own spy agency. Additional spies, paramilitary forces, and analysts have made the CIA's station in Afghanistan one of its largest in the world, with around 700 employees. But the agency's efforts faced several setbacks in 2009 and 2010. In December 2009 an alleged al Qaeda suicide bomber killed seven CIA agents, including the station chief, at the CIA base at Khost, Afghanistan. The man had claimed to be an al Qaeda defector, but information that he was actually plotting an attack was not shared, and security was not increased ahead of his scheduled visit. In another blow, in December 2010, Pakistan's military intelligence agency, ISI, was accused of revealing the identity of the CIA station chief in Islamabad.

As effective as high-tech operations can be, events such as 9/11 have demonstrated that there is no substitute for accurate human intelligence in the age of global terror networks. Indeed, early reports suggested that the finding of bin Laden was more due to old-fashioned intelligence work than it was to high technology.

Laura Lambert and Ann E. Robertson

See also Buckley, William; Counterterrorism; Department of Justice, U.S.; Federal Bureau of Investigation; Patriot Act; Rendition, Extraordinary; September 11 Attacks; Torture Debate

Further Readings

Baer, Robert. *See No Evil: The True Story of a Ground Soldier in the CIA's War on Terrorism.* New York: Crown, 2001.

Coll, Steve. *Ghost Wars: The Secret History of the CIA, Afghanistan, and bin Laden, from the Soviet Invasion to September 10, 2001.* New York: Penguin, 2004.

Finn, Peter, Ian Shapira, and Marc Fisher. "The Hunt." *The Washington Post,* May 6, 2011. http://www.washingtonpost.com/wp-srv/projects/osama-hunt/index.html

Gerecht, Rueul Marc. "The Counterterrorist Myth." *Atlantic Monthly,* July/August 2001.

Hersh, Seymour M. "What Went Wrong: The C.I.A. and the Failure of American Intelligence." *New Yorker,* October 8, 2001.

Monje, Scott C. *The Central Intelligence Agency: A Documentary History.* Westport, CT: Greenwood, 2008.

Scheuer, Michael. *Imperial Hubris: Why the West Is Losing the War on Terror.* Dulles, VA: Potomac Books, 2005.

CHECHEN TERRORISM

In the early twenty-first century, the Russian Federation witnessed a series of major terrorist attacks across its territory. While Vladimir Putin had made the eradication of terrorism in Russia a major political goal when he became president in 2000, it is clear that terrorist incidents in Russia have not only continued but have in fact widened from their initial loci of Chechnya, and from initial issues of secessionism to a much broader sense of instability and more general terrorist activity across the North Caucasus region and the rest of Russia.

Background

The roots and background of current terrorist activity in Russia can be traced back to the mid-1990s. Following the demise of the Soviet Union, the Chechen Republic declared its independence from the Russian Federation, which led the Russian military to conduct a campaign in Chechnya between 1994 and 1996 under the banner of reimposing constitutional order. Even in this period, Russia was already experiencing large-scale terrorist activity and hostage-taking incidents across its territory, carried out by Chechen separatist groups. These included the taking of hostages in a hospital in the southern Russian city of Budyonnovsk in June 1995, and another major hostage crisis in Kizlyar-Pervomayskoye in January 1996. Both incidents involved well over a thousand hostages. During the interwar period (1996–1999), The Russian military campaign ended with the signing of the Khasavyurt Accords on August 30, 1996, and in the period between the signing of these accords and the launch of the second military action in Chechnya in 1999, the nature of the separatist movement inside Chechnya and of terrorist activity itself, changed. The aims of actors carrying out terrorist attacks gradually shifted from seeking independence and secessionism to much more multifaceted goals.

Following the incursion of armed groups of Dagestanis, Chechens, and Arabs from Chechnya into Dagestan, in the North Caucasus, a terrorist attack on Russian military barracks, and a string of apartment bombings in Buynaksk, Moscow, and Volgodonsk in 1999, the Russian military launched a second large-scale military campaign in Chechnya in September of that year. The campaign was presented by the Russian authorities as a counterterrorist operation. This distinction between the nature of the two military campaigns in Chechnya reflected the differing aims of the two operations, with the first targeting secessionists and the second seeking to eradicate both domestic and international terrorists active in the republic. The Russian state officially ended the counterterrorist operation in Chechnya on April 17, 2009.

Since 2001, the Russian government has argued that large-scale fighting in Chechnya has ceased, prompting the authorities to introduce a policy of "normalisation" in Chechnya, aimed at the transfer of administrative control to the leadership of the Chechen Republic. However, low-intensity clashes continued, and terrorist activity spread to the other republics of the North Caucasus. Laterally, insecurity and terrorist activity in Chechnya itself has decreased significantly, particularly following the election of Ramzan Kadyrov as the Chechen president in 2007 and the creation of a more centralized power structure around him.

Terrorist Incidents in Russia, 2000–2004

In the early 2000s, and parallel to Russian counterterrorist campaigns, both in Chechnya and in North Caucasus, a wave of terrorist incidents took place in the Russian Federation. These terrorist actions were carried out by a loose alliance of Chechen and other North Caucasus groups, as well as foreign fighters, under a joint banner of jihadi resistance and Chechen independence. A series of *terakts* (a Russian amalgamation of the English term *terrorist acts*) took place across Russia, taking the form of suicide bombings, car explosions, attacks on the Russian transport systems, and large-scale hostage taking. Among the most notable were a car explosion near a McDonald's on Pokryshkina Street in Moscow on October 19, 2002; a suicide bombing during a rock festival in Tushino, Moscow, on July 5, 2003; a suicide bombing of a military hospital in Mozdok in North Ossetia on August 1, 2003; and explosions on a train between Kislovodsk and Mineral'Nye Vody, in southern Russia, on December 5, 2003, on a train in Moscow on December 9, 2003, and on the Moscow metro on February 6, 2004. The Russian authorities attributed most of these *terakts* to terrorists originating from or operating in Chechnya.

The most high-profile *terakt* in this period was the Dubrovka theater siege, which took place in the center of Moscow between October 23 and 26, 2002. A group of Chechen terrorists, under the command of Movsar Barayev, took over 900 people hostage during a performance of the musical *Nord-Ost*. The terrorists demanded the withdrawal of Russian troops from Chechnya and the granting of independence to the Chechen Republic. Russian authorities refused to negotiate with the terrorists, and they responded to an explosion inside the building by attempting to neutralize the terrorists by pumping gas into the theater. This rescue attempt resulted in the deaths of 128 people, which led to the Russian authorities being severely criticized both domestically and internationally.

From Chechnya to the North Caucasus

Between 2004 and 2005, the loci of the threat from terrorism shifted from actions primarily based in Chechnya to encompass a wider area within the North Caucasus region. The frequency of terrorist activity in the North Caucasus republics of Ingushetia and Dagestan increased, and terrorist incidents were noted in Kabardino-Balkaria and North Ossetia. This widening of terrorist activity was particularly evident in the summer of 2004, following explosions on two planes—one flying from Moscow to Volgograd and one from Moscow to Sochi—on August 24, 2004; a bomb at Rizhskaya station on the Moscow metro on August 31, 2004, and the seizing of a Ministry of Interior building in Ingushetia, in which 92 people were killed, including the acting regional interior minister, Abukar Kostoyev.

This spate of terrorist attacks across Russia culminated in the Beslan school siege between September 1 and 3, 2004, in North Ossetia. A group of militants held 1,200 people hostage, including pupils, teachers, parents, siblings, relatives, and friends, in a small school gymnasium, demanding independence for Chechnya. On September 3, Russian Special Forces stormed the building after a bomb appeared to have exploded inside and hostages began to escape through a hole

in the building. In the course of this rescue operation, 300 people died, half of them children, and many more were wounded. The subsequent official investigation into the rescue attempt was widely criticized as a cover-up of what had actually occurred during this operation. It remains unclear exactly which terrorist cell was responsible for the Beslan operation, but Shamil Basayev, an infamous Chechen leader and terrorist, subsequently claimed responsibility for the *terakt*.

This widening of terrorist activity across the North Caucasus was exemplified by the establishment of the Caucasian Front by Sheikh Abdul-Khalim, following the death of Aslan Maskhadov (the Ichkerian president, elected in 1997) in March 2005, which claimed to pursue operations in Ingushetia, Ossetia, Kabardino-Balkaria, Stavropol, Karachaevo-Cherkessia, Adygeya and Krasnodar. Subsequently, the Chechen leader Doku Umarov proclaimed himself the emir of the new "Caucasus Emirate" (an Islamic state across North Caucasus region) in October 2007. The creation of these two organizations marked a clear shift away from terrorist actions being carried out in the name of Chechen independence, and toward more diverse, though less articulated, aims. Terrorist operations were now conducted by a more radicalized, but splintered, Islamist movement, with aspirations of establishing an Islamic state or caliphate on Russian territory.

In response to this widening and intensification of terrorist activity across Russia, and in the North Caucasus in particular, Russian legislators put in place a series of new counterterrorism laws in 2002 and 2006. In addition, the National Anti-Terrorism Committee was established, with local branches throughout the Russian Federation, and a separate federal district of North Caucasus was set up in January 2010 in order to deal with ongoing socioeconomic and security issues in the region. In spite of these measures, the Russian authorities admit terrorist violence has continued to undermine the stability of the North Caucasus region.

Attacks Across Russia, 2005–2010

Alongside the widening of terrorist activity from Chechnya to the North Caucasus, terrorist attacks in the rest of Russia have also continued, despite repeated statements from the Russian authorities that the terrorist threat will be eliminated in the near future. Terrorists have carried out repeated attacks on Russian transport systems, such as the derailment of a train between Moscow and St. Petersburg on August 13, 2007, and an explosion on a bus in Togliatti, in southern Russia on August 31, 2007.

More recently, a large-scale terrorist attack took place on November 27, 2009, when an explosive device derailed a Nevsky Express train from Moscow to St. Petersburg, carrying around 700 people, causing nearly 30 fatalities. On March 29, 2010, two bomb blasts at Moscow metro stations (Lubyanka and Park Kultury), apparently detonated by two female suicide bombers from Dagestan and Chechnya, killed 34 and wounded 18 people. Both the Russian president, Dmitrii Medvedev, and FSB chief, Alexander Bortnikov, blamed this *terakt* on groups from the North Caucasus. Indeed, on March 31, 2010, Doku Umarov claimed responsibility for the attack in a video released on the Internet, as he had also done in the case of the Nevsky derailment. He stated that these attacks were carried out in revenge for the Russian operations in the North Caucasus, and he warned that such terrorist acts would intensify across Russia in the future.

Thus, despite the Russian authorities vowing to eradicate terrorist activity and passing more robust counterterrorist legislation, terrorist incidents have remained frequent occurrences in contemporary Russia. Despite the formal end of the counterterrorism campaign in Chechnya, terrorist activity continues. Whereas in the past the proclaimed aim for such terrorist actions was Chechen secessionism, terrorism is now increasingly centered around issues of Islamic radicalization and more general societal instability.

Aglaya Snetkov

See also Bombings and Bomb Scares; Jihad; Suicide Terrorism

Further Readings

Kramer, M. "Guerrilla Warfare, Counterinsurgency and Terrorism in the North Caucasus: The Military Dimension of the Russian-Chechen Conflict." *Europe-Asia Studies* 57, no. 2 (2005): 209–290.

Markedonov, Sergey. "Similar, but Different, Radical Islam Is the Universal Challenge in Chechnya, Ingushetia, and Dagestan." *Russia Profile,* July 22, 2008. http://www.cdi.org/russia/johnson/2008-137-19.cfm.

Russell, J. "The Geopolitics of Terrorism: Russia's Conflict with Islamic Extremism." *Eurasian Geography and Economics* 50, no. 2 (2009): 184–196.

Sagramoso, D. "Violence and Conflict in the Russian North Caucasus." *International Affairs* 83, no. 4 (2007).

Snetkov, Aglaya. "The Image of the Terrorist Threat in the Official Russian Press: The Moscow Theatre Crisis (2002) and the Beslan Hostage Crisis (2004)." *Europe–Asia Studies* 59, no. 8 (2007): 1349–1365.

Souleimanov, E. and O. Ditrych. "The Internationalisation of the Russian-Chechen Conflict: Myths and Reality." *Europe-Asia Studies* 60, no. 7 (2008): 1199–1222.

Trenin D. V., and A. V. Malashenko, with A. Lieven. *Russia's Restless Frontier: The Chechnya Factor in Post-Soviet Russia.* Washington, DC: Carnegie Endowment for International Peace, 2004.

CHEMICAL TERRORISM

Chemical weapons are just what the name implies—devices that use chemicals to inflict death or injury. Chemical weapons can be dispensed using bombs, artillery shells, aircraft sprayers, or even by missiles carrying hundreds of small "bomblets" that are spread over a large area when they are ejected from canisters. Chemical weapons have typically been used in large-scale warfare by organized armies. However, the prospect of the use of chemical weapons by terrorists against civilian populations is a more recent problem.

The Use of Chemical Agents in Warfare

Like their biological counterparts, chemical weapons have a long history. Early records document the use of smoke and incendiary chemicals against cities in the ancient Greek and Roman eras. The first large-scale use of modern chemical agents in warfare took place in 1915, during World War I, when the German army launched a surprise attack with chlorine gas against French troops deployed near the city of Ypres. The Germans had placed thousands of cylinders of the gas along a front several miles long. When the wind blew toward the French trenches, the Germans opened the cylinders, enabling the chlorine to be borne by that wind into the French positions. The effects were immediate and horrendous as thousands of troops choked in the deadly green cloud.

The attack touched off an immediate round of measures and countermeasures, and soon the French and their British allies were using war gases of their own against the Germans. Chemists manufactured weapons such as mustard gas (so named because of its faint odor), which burns and blisters any tissue exposed to it, and phosgene, a deadly choking gas. By the time the war ended in 1918, chemical warfare had caused more than 100,000 deaths.

Most military planners regarded chemical weapons with distaste, however, since they did not mesh well with traditional codes of arms and warfare. After the war, the general revulsion felt by many leaders toward the use of chemical weapons was reflected in the Geneva Protocol of 1925, signed by all the World War I combatants except Russia. This treaty banned the use of chemical or biological agents in warfare, but it did not ban the manufacture or possession of these weapons. Many nations continued to keep them stockpiled for possible use, and to deter their use by others. Interestingly, some groups opposed the treaty because they regarded chemical warfare as more humane than other forms of combat using high explosives and other deadly technologies that characterized modern warfare.

Italy used chemical weapons in Ethiopia in the mid-1930s, but they were not used on a large scale in World War II (if one excludes the use by the Nazis of poison gas at extermination camps such as Birkenau-Auschwitz to murder most of the Jewish population of occupied Europe). The Japanese also conducted experiments with chemical and biological weapons on prisoners of war. Most experts believe that it was only fear of massive retaliation in kind that kept these weapons from being used on a large scale in World War II, however.

Egypt used chemical weapons in Yemen in the 1960s, and Iraq used them against Kurdish dissident groups in its own territory and in the Iran-Iraq War in the early 1980s, but these weapons do not appear to have been used extensively in warfare or for the suppression of dissidents since that time. In 1993, most nations signed the Convention

on the Prohibition of the Development, Production, Stockpiling and Use of Chemical Weapons, commonly known as the Chemical Weapons Convention, or CWC. This represented a major advance because unlike the 1925 treaty, CWC requires nations to destroy their existing stockpiles under rigorous international control. CWC signatories are now engaged in that process.

Terrorists and Chemical Weapons

Treaties are signed by nation-states, however, not terrorist groups. In 1995 a Japanese terrorist group known as Aum Shinrikyo, or "Supreme Truth," attacked the Tokyo subway system with sarin, a deadly nerve gas. Twelve persons were killed and thousands more were panicked by the possibility they had been exposed to deadly gas fumes, which interfere with normal nerve and muscle functions, causing convulsions, paralysis, and death. The mechanism chosen by the terrorist group was simple: they placed plastic bags containing sarin in 15 subway stations and punctured the bags with umbrella tips, permitting the gas to escape. Even though this attack did not kill large numbers of people, it succeeded in frightening a population and disrupting normal business. It also alerted the world to the potential of a terrorist attack with chemical weapons.

Aum Shinrikyo was funded with nearly $30 million and had access to a cadre of scientifically trained people. The group's chemical weapons were produced in a small laboratory using commercially available equipment, but it was limited in its ability to produce the quantities of agent required to inflict damage on a large population. The synthesis of nerve gas is a complex chemical process involving a series of chemical reactions using toxic precursor chemicals that are difficult to handle. Synthesizing this compound requires highly competent chemists and unusual safety precautions. Such requirements will always pose major obstacles that a terrorist group would have to overcome. High explosives that are readily available on the international market, or an improvised explosive device such as the one used in the Oklahoma City bombing might seem much more practical to a typical terrorist group.

However, chemical weapons need not necessarily be manufactured by the terrorists themselves; they

A subway passenger with his mouth covered up by a handkerchief is escorted by masked policemen at Tokyo's Akasaka Station on the morning of Monday, March 20, 1995, as the station was filled by toxic fumes from sarin nerve gas. (AP Photo/ Itsuo Inouye. © 2011 The Associated Press. All Rights Reserved)

might also be obtained with the cooperation of rogue states. Nations that have signed the CWC are in the process of eliminating their chemical weapons, and their stockpiles and the incineration facilities used to destroy them are heavily guarded. While small quantities of chemical agents might be stolen or obtained through bribes, it seems unlikely that terrorists could obtain the large quantities needed to attack a large area and cause mass casualties.

Terrorist Attacks on Chemical Industries

Terrorists do not have to master advanced science to employ chemicals as weapons. The terror attacks on September 11, 2001, showed that terrorists could use hijacked airliners as cruise missiles to attack a large city. Terrorists could use this method to attack a large chemical plant and cause the release of toxic materials on a large scale. The accident at the Union Carbide plant in Bhopal in central India in 1984 killed 4,000 persons and devastated the vicinity. Railroad accidents involving shipments of tanker cars of liquefied chlorine and other chemicals have forced the evacuation of surrounding areas. Large tanker trucks carrying toxic materials have overturned with similar consequences.

Until recently, chemical plant and railroad managers devoted most of their safety planning efforts to accident prevention. The 2001 terrorist attacks on New York and Washington have forced these industries to devote more resources to protect their systems from intentional attacks. In an attempt to deter or deflect such attacks, chemical plant complexes have improved perimeter and internal security systems and begun to conduct more careful screening of personnel. Authorities have begun taking a closer look at security at the myriad small airports and flight schools in the United States, for the same suicide-attack technique used on 9/11 could conceivably be used to attack a chemical facility near a large metropolitan area. If initial fires and explosions were not contained following such an attack, they could spread rapidly through the facility and cause catastrophic releases of toxic material.

In the absence of terrorist threats, traditional measures of industrial efficiency usually lead industries to build large plants to obtain economies of scale. Such plants are usually located near population centers that can provide the thousands of employees needed to operate them. The possibility of a terrorist attack, however, may now force planners and risk managers to reconsider the benefits of scale and location in light of the potential costs. For example, an insurer may be reluctant to provide liability coverage to a large chemical facility near a metropolitan area if the probability of a major release of toxic material must be recalculated to take a possible terrorist attack into account.

Water supplies would be difficult to attack at their sources because the immense volumes of water in reservoirs would dilute a relatively small quantity of agent to the point that it was almost undetectable. Indeed, most water supplies already contain minute quantities of materials that would be toxic at higher concentrations. Furthermore, underground aquifers are not readily accessible, although the destruction of large petroleum storage facilities over aquifers would cause problems for local communities relying on those aquifers for their water supplies. Smaller quantities of water, such as supplies contained in rooftop water tanks on many large city buildings, might be easier to attack and yield more immediate results, but they would not cause large numbers of casualties. On the other hand, even a small attack on a water supply would generate panic and disruption in a community. Nevertheless, most terrorists might prefer to focus on targets that are easier to attack and whose failure would have wide repercussions, such as electric power stations serving metropolitan areas.

Food supplies are also subject to attack by chemical terrorists. The contamination of animal feedstocks and other grain supplies with chemical carcinogens would lead to the disruption of food supply chains and produce economic disorder and panicked reactions far out of proportion to the actual amount of damage. Food supplies would have to be tested over a long period to ensure that they were safe.

What is the probable future of chemical terrorism? It is not very likely that terrorists can make or dispense the large quantities of chemicals needed to cause mass casualties. Nor are they likely to have access to the weapon-delivery platforms (artillery, aircraft, missiles) available to organized military units. But attacks with smaller quantities of chemical agents can still cause wide disruption, as evidenced by the 1995 Tokyo attacks. Likewise, the anthrax letter attacks in the fall of 2001 in the eastern United States had social impacts far out of proportion to the size of the attacks or the casualties they produced. This suggests that the release of chemical agents resulting in even a few deaths or injuries in any large metropolitan area subway system would cause a chain reaction of events that would slow and disrupt commerce and other activities, further taxing already strained roadways and key transportation nodes.

Les Paldy

See also Aum Shinrikyo; Biological Terrorism; Tokyo Subway Attack; Weapons of Mass Destruction

Further Readings

Alexander, Yonah, and Milton M. Hoenig, eds. *Super Terrorism: Biological, Chemical, and Nuclear.* New York: Transnational Publishers, 2001.

Coen, Bob, and Eric Nadler. *Dead Silence: Fear and Terror on the Anthrax Trail.* Berkeley, CA: Counterpoint, 2009.

Haberfeld, M. R., and Agostino von Hassell, eds. *A New Understanding of Terrorism: Case Studies, Trajectories, and Lessons Learned.* New York: Springer, 2009.

Harris, Robert, and Jeremy Paxman. *A Higher Form of Killing: The Secret Story of Chemical and Biological Warfare.* New York: Hill & Wang, 1982.

Henry L. Stimson Center. "Chemical and Biological Weapons." http://www.stimson.org/topics/biological-chemical-weapons.

Homer-Dixon, Thomas. "The Rise of Complex Terrorism." *Foreign Policy*, January/February 2002.

Perrow, Charles. *Normal Accidents: Living With High Risk Technologies.* New York: Basic Books, 1984.

Ranstorp, Magnus, and Magnus Normark, eds. *Unconventional Weapons and International Terrorism: Challenges and a New Approach.* New York: Routledge, 2009.

Sifton, David W., ed. *PDR Guide to Biological and Chemical Warfare Response.* Montvale, NJ: Thomson/ Physician's Desk Reference, 2002.

Tucker, Johnathan B. *War of Nerves: Chemical Warfare from World War I to al-Qaeda.* New York: Pantheon Books, 2006.

CHESIMARD, JOANNE (1947–)

An African American revolutionary and writer, Joanne Chesimard was once the leader of the Black Liberation Army (BLA), a violent offshoot of the Black Panther Party. She has been living in Cuba since the mid-1980s, after escaping from the prison where she was serving a life sentence for murder.

Raised primarily by her grandparents in North Carolina, Chesimard moved to Queens, New York, when she was a teenager to live with her mother and stepfather. As a young adult, Chesimard developed strong political convictions that led to her participation in the black liberation movement and eventually to her membership in the Black Panther Party in 1970. It was around that that time she assumed the name Assata Shakur.

Between 1971 and 1973, Chesimard's involvement with the BLA became widely known, as did the various crimes, such as robberies, committed in order to fund their organization. Chesimard ran into much more serious trouble with the law on May 2, 1973. While driving on the New Jersey Turnpike with two friends, Malik Zayad Shakur and Sundiata Acoli, Chesimard was stopped by white state troopers, supposedly for a shattered headlight. Exactly how the subsequent events unfolded is still debated, but the outcome was that Malik Zayad Shakur and Trooper Werner Foerster were killed with Foerster's gun. Trooper James Harper, Acoli, and Chesimard were all wounded. The state maintains that Chesimard either fired the gun from point-blank range at Foerster, or that she was an accomplice to the shooting; defenders of Chesmiard claim the trooper was killed accidentally by his partner. Chesimard was convicted of murder and sentenced to life in prison.

With the help of four friends, who took a prison guard hostage, she managed to escape from the Edna Mahan Correctional Facility for Women on November 2, 1979. Chesimard now resides in Cuba, where she has been granted political asylum. There have been several efforts to have Chesimard extradited back to the United States to serve her full sentence, and the Federal Bureau of Investigation has offered a $1 million reward for information leading to her apprehension.

Harvey Kushner

See also Black Panther Party

Further Readings

Allen-Mills, Tony. "Bounty Hunt for U.S. Cop Killer in Cuba." *Sunday Times*, May 27, 2007, p. 27.

Austin, Curtis J. *Up against the Wall: Violence in the Making and Unmaking of the Black Panther Party.* Fayetteville: University of Arkansas Press, 2008.
Cancio Isla, Wilfredo. "U.S. Fugitive a Hero to Fidel, but a Curiosity to Many." *Houston Chronicle*, December 23, 2007, p. 21.
Federal Bureau of Investigation. *Wanted by the FBI: Domestic Terrorism—Joanne Deborah Chesimard.* http://www.fbi.gov/wanted/fugitives/dt/fug_dt.htm.
Rhodes, Jane. *Framing the Black Panthers: The Spectacular Rise of a Black Power Icon.* New York: The New Press, 2007.
Shakur, Assata. *Assata: An Autobiography.* Westport, CT: Lawrence Hill Books, 1987.
Waggoner, Walter H. "Joanne Chesimard Convicted of Killing New Jersey State Trooper." *The New York Times*, March 26, 1977, p. 1.
Williams, Evelyn. *Inadmissible Evidence: The Story of a Trial Lawyer Who Defended the Black Liberation Army.* Chicago: Lawrence Hill Books, 1993.

CHLORINE BOMBINGS, IRAQ

Chlorine bombs were first used by Iraqi insurgents on January 28, 2007, in the city of Ramadi, west of Baghdad. The bombs consisted of trucks packed with improvised explosives surrounded by chlorine cylinders, so that the poisonous gas was dispersed upon detonation of the explosives. In addition to killing many people, these bombs were intended to increase the psychological potency of insurgent operations and slow down the rescue effort by first responders, who had to deploy gas masks or wait for the poison to dissipate before they could attend to the injured. The use of chlorine bombs was an important escalation in the Iraq war, because it signaled the willingness of insurgents to experiment with chemical weapons.

Insurgents in Iraq can acquire chlorine from water and sewage treatment plants or by importing them from illicit traders in neighboring Jordan and Syria. While safe in small amounts, chlorine can cause fatalities if inhaled in large, concentrated quantities. Short of death, significant inhalation of the yellowish green gas can irritate the skin and lungs; cause vomiting and burns to the throat, nose, and eyes; and produce respiratory problems.

The main insurgent group to deploy this tactic has been al Qaeda in Iraq (AQI), an extremist

Sunni insurgent group with links to the transnational al Qaeda terrorist network. Abu Ayyub al Masri (also known as Abu Hamza al Muhajir), who led AQI from 2006 until his death in April 2010, called on scientists from the Muslim world to develop improvised weapons of mass destruction for use against the United States and its allies.

Chlorine bombings have been poorly executed in Iraq, and they have proven to be of limited military value to insurgents because the gas often burns in the explosion before it disperses in the air. Moreover, strong winds can blow the gas away from the intended targets, limiting its nefarious effects. There have been several chlorine bombings in Iraq since 2007, but while they sickened several victims, none actually produced mass casualties.

Mohammed Hafez

See also al Qaeda in Iraq; Bombings and Bomb Scares

Further Readings

Aytac, Osman, and Mustafa Kibaroglu, eds. "Defence against Weapons of Mass Destruction Terrorism." *Proceedings of the NATO Advanced Research Workshop on Defence against Weapons of Mass Destruction Terrorism.* Fairfax, VA: IOS Press, 2009.

BBC News. "Chlorine Bomb Hits Iraqi Village." *BBC News,* May 16, 2007. http://news.bbc.co.uk/2/hi/middle_east/6660585.stm.

Cave, Damien and Ahmad Fadam. "Iraqi Militants Use Chlorine in 3 Bombings." *The New York Times,* February 21, 2007.

Gregg, Heather S., Hy S. Rothstein, and John Arquilla, eds. *The Three Circles of War: Understanding the Dynamics of Conflict in Iraq.* Dulles, VA: Potomac Books, 2010.

Hafez, Mohammed M. *Suicide Bombers in Iraq: The Strategy and Ideology of Martyrdom.* Washington, DC: United States Institute of Peace, 2007.

Ranstorp, Magnus, and Magnus Normark, eds. *Unconventional Weapons and International Terrorism: Challenges and a New Approach.* New York: Routledge, 2009.

CHRISTIAN IDENTITY

Christian Identity is a theological system or ideology that has provided white supremacists with a rationale for racist, anti-Semitic, and bigoted violence. Beginning in the 1950s as a set of ideas that were marginal even among organized racists and anti-Semites at that time, its influence grew in the 1970s and 1980s to undergird Ku Klux Klan factions, Aryan Nations, Posse Comitatus, and a number of other organizations. While white-power skinheads after the 1990s have not, in the main, been Christian Identity believers, this theology has remained a potent force in the twenty-first century.

Based on a skewed reading of the Book of Genesis, Christian Identity adherents believe that only those they deem to be white people are descended from Adam. Those considered black, and other people of color, are considered to be "pre-Adamic," or "man before man," with less than fully human attributes. Within this schema, the whites of northern Europe—described as the Anglo-Saxon, Teutonic, Celtic, and Lombard peoples—are regarded as the direct biological descendants of the biblical "Tribes of Israel," and the United States of America is considered the physical embodiment of their reassembly in a promised land.

On this point, Christian Identity is derived from a nineteenth-century set of beliefs known as British Israelism. Its early proponents regarded scriptural promises of greatness believed to have been made to biblical Israel as a prophetic forecast of the power and breadth the British Empire enjoyed in the late nineteenth century. As such, it was an ideology that explained white supremacy in biblical terms, rather than simply using the language of a so-called scientific and secular racism also popular at the time.

The Christian Identity theology that appeared in the post–World War II period, by contrast, flourished in a period of decolonization in the developing world and the end of Jim Crow–style segregation in the southern United States. As such, it sought to explain the supposed fall of white power and dominance, again in scriptural terms. Several Identity preachers in the 1980s and 1990s, including Pete Peters of Colorado, traced this collapse to sins committed by white people, including interracial marriage, tolerance for homosexuality, and allowing the presence of "strangers," an Identity term for people of color. All Identity ideologues, however, placed blame on "the Jews," and on the satanic nature of their power over all earthly affairs.

Two different ideas about Jews and Satan vie for dominance among Christian Identity believers, the "two-seed" and the "one-seed" theories. The former posits that Jews are the embodiment of Satan incarnate, the offspring of a mating between Eve and the Devil (the Snake in the Garden). The latter view holds that Jews have a Satanic character, rather than being simply the Devil himself. Both points of view, however, can motivate individual believers toward violence.

Also propelling adherents are ideas about the "End Times" embedded within Identity theology. In this eschatology, believers see a period of turmoil and disaster known as the "Tribulations" before the Second Coming of Christ and the establishment of God's Kingdom. Unlike others who share this belief, known as premillennialism, Identity devotees consider the Tribulations a time of armed warfare in which they will battle satanic forces (meaning "the Jews") and win. In the parlance of a terrorist group from the early 1980s known as The Covenant, the Sword and the Arm of the Lord, believers must become "End Times Overcomers" in order to establish what they believe will be God's Kingdom on Earth. Compounding the drive toward violence and mayhem, some Identity believers think that they have already entered the Tribulations era, and that the time for guns and warfare is already upon them.

In the 1990s, during a period marked by the rise of militia movements, Christian Identity adherents created their own specific form of violent organization: the Phineas Priesthood. First elaborated by a Virginia stockbroker named Richard Kelly Hoskins in a book titled *Vigilantes of Christendom* (1990), the Phineas Priesthood was supposed to consist of Identity-inspired racist criminals in small groups of no more than six people. In the early 1990s, Byron De La Beckwith, who was convicted in 1994 of killing the NAACP leader Medgar Evers in 1963, declared himself a Phineas Priest. In 1996, a group of Identity-inspired bank bandits and bombers in Washington State, similarly described themselves as members of the Phineas Priesthood.

Using only the Bible, Christian Identity presented a complete theological system and a view of America as a sinful nation under the control of satanic Jews. In the past it has been an impetus for criminal violence with a politically defined end,

although the significance of its influence within the white supremacist underworld has waned in the twenty-first century.

Leonard Zeskind

See also Aryan Nations; Covenant, the Sword and the Arm of the Lord, The; Ku Klux Klan; Phineas Priesthood; Religious and Spiritual Perspectives on Terrorism; White Supremacy Movement

Further Readings

Aho, James A. *The Politics of Righteousness: Idaho Christian Patriotism.* Seattle: University of Washington Press, 1990.

Barkun, Michael. *Religion and the Racist Right: The Origins of the Christian Identity Movement.* Chapel Hill: University of North Carolina Press, 1994.

Levitas, Daniel. *The Terrorist Next Door: The Militia Movement and the Radical Right.* New York: St. Martin's Press, 2002.

Quarles, Chester L. *Christian Identity: The Aryan American Bloodline Religion.* Jefferson, NC: McFarland, 2004.

Zeskind, Leonard. *Blood and Politics: The History of the White Nationalist Movement from the Margins to the Mainstream.* New York: Farrar, Straus and Giroux, 2009.

CHUKAKU-HA

Chukaku-ha (aka Middle Core Faction; Nucleus Faction) is a radical Japanese leftist terrorist group best known for its 30-year struggle against the Narita Airport project. The group is believed to have about 3,500 members, of which several hundred form the active terrorist core.

Chukaku-ha was born out of the leftist student movement of 1960s Japan. From the start, Japan's student radicals focused their opposition on two issues: the perceived imperialism of Japan's government, and the close relations between Japan and the United States, particularly the continued U.S. military presence in Japan. The tendency of hardline elements within Japan's radical groups to split off and form separate groups because of ideological disputes led to increasing radicalism and created bitter rivalries. The Chukaku-ha was typical. It began in the mid-1960s as the armed wing of the Japan Revolutionary Communist League and spawned two splinter groups of its own during that turbulent decade.

Chukaku-ha participated in many demonstrations in support of various causes during the 1960s, displaying a tendency toward violence as early as 1969, when members are alleged to have killed a member of a rival student group. The organization did not find a perfect cause until the early 1970s, however, when members began to participate in demonstrations against the Narita Airport project. In 1966 the Japanese government announced the airport project without consulting or even informing the 200 farming families who would be displaced. The farmers' plight attracted substantial public sympathy and led to widespread protests, with Chukaku-ha eventually moving into the forefront of the anti-Narita struggle. In 1973 the group helped erect 50-foot steel towers next to the airport runway, thus preventing planes from taking off.

In May 1977, riots broke out at an anti-Narita protest; four people died—three policemen and a bystander. In March 1978, a week before the airport's long-delayed opening, 14 Chukaku-ha members broke into the airport's control tower. Two of them reached the control room, where they took a sledgehammer to the equipment, delaying the opening for several months. Protests have continued to cripple the facility, and 36 years later, the airport is much smaller than originally planned.

During the mid-1980s, Chukaku-ha focused its attention on opposing the proposed privatization of Japan's national rail company. During 1985 and 1986, it carried out dozens of punishment beatings of several rail executives and of union members who supported privatization; several died from their injuries. Chukaku-ha is thought to be responsible for more than 80 killings since its founding. On November 29, 1985, Chukaku-ha sabotaged two key information transmitters that controlled train scheduling and ticket ordering; millions of commuters were affected. Also in 1985, the group began experimenting with homemade rockets, launching the short-range and ineffective missiles at a U.S. Army base on the island of Okinawa. In 1986 the group made a similar attack during the G7 trade summit; at that time, experts estimated that the missiles had a two-mile range. In the G7 incident and several similar attacks, however, the aim appears to have been property damage rather than casualties.

Since 1986, Chukaku-ha has confined its activities mostly to protests, propaganda, and threats, while directing its violence toward members of rival groups. Chukaku-ha is still an active political force within Japan, however, and concerns about the group's continued terrorist capabilities led to a police crackdown and increased security during the March 2000 G8 summit.

Colleen Sullivan

Further Readings

Aldrich, Daniel P. *Site Fights: Divisive Facilities and Civil Society in Japan and the West.* Ithaca, NY: Cornell University Press, 2008.

Apter, David E., and Nagayo Sawa. *Against the State: Politics and Social Protest in Japan.* Cambridge, MA: Harvard University Press, 1984.

Jameson, Sam. "Millions Stalled as Japanese Radicals Sabotage Government Owned Rail Lines." *The New York Times,* November 29, 1985, p. 5.

McNeil, David. "Father of Narita Protest Unrelenting in Old Age." *South China Morning Post,* August 1, 2002, p. 14.

Rapoport, Carla. "Saboteurs Hit Japan Railways." *Financial Times,* November 30, 1985, p. 3.

Sato, Shigemi. "Police Crack Down on Japanese Radical Leftists Ahead of G8 Summit." Agence France Presse, March 22, 2000.

Utting, Gerald, and Joel Ruimy. "Terrorists Fire Rockets as Tokyo Summit Opens." *Toronto Star,* May 5, 1986, p. A1.

Watts, David. "Japanese Radicals Terrorize Backers of Railway Sell-off." *The Times* (London), September 3, 1986.

CICIPPIO, JOSEPH (1932–)

Joseph Cicippio was one of the last U.S. hostages to be released by the militant Islamic group that had taken him captive in Lebanon.

When he was abducted in 1986, Cicippio was the acting comptroller of the American University in Beirut. Muslim extremist groups had already abducted a handful of American University professors and staff. Because of the increasing danger to all Westerners in Beirut, Cicippio had not ventured outside of the campus for months. On the morning of September 12, 1986, gunmen, in well-orchestrated moves, grabbed Cicippio just outside the university building where he lived. Cicippio recalls that his kidnappers, posing as students, called out to him by name before taking him. His broken glasses and traces of his blood were the only evidence of his abduction.

Little was heard about Cicippio until August 1989, when a group of Shiite Muslim extremists called the Revolutionary Justice Organization announced that he was to be executed in retaliation for the arrest of Sheikh Abdul Karim Obeid. But instead of being executed, Cicippio spent the next five years in captivity, tethered by a three-foot chain.

Many initiatives for freeing the hostages converged in late 1991. The militants released Thomas Sutherland and Terry Waite on November 19, and on November 20, Abbas al Musawi, a Hezbollah leader, announced that the fate of the remaining American hostages was no longer tied to the Arabs held by Israel, thus removing a political obstacle to freeing the hostages. Iran, the principal sponsor of many of the radical Shiite groups, was using its influence to free the hostages, in hopes of eliminating the U.S. trade sanctions that were strangling its economy. Meanwhile, Giandomenico Picco, the special Middle East envoy of the UN Secretary General, was also nearing success in his negotiations with the Syrian government.

The Revolutionary Justice Organization released Cicippio on December 2, 1991, after 1,908 days of captivity. He was reunited with his Lebanese-born wife, Elham, in Damascus, Syria. U.S. military physicians found that Cicippio was in fair health, but the conditions in which he was kept would affect him for life. He suffers occasional dizziness from a blow that had left him both unconscious and with a dent in his skull, as well as permanent frostbite in his fingers from two winters spent on a partly enclosed balcony.

Cicippio returned to the United States with no job and little money. His life savings had been depleted when his wife paid ransom to conmen. Cicippio and a fellow hostage, David Jacobsen, sued Iran for $600 million in U.S. courts. The civil suit included claims of kidnapping, physical abuse, false imprisonment, inhumane medical treatment, loss of job opportunities, and pain and suffering, as well as a claim that Iran kept the Western hostages as leverage to free billions of dollars in assets frozen by the United States. Cicippio and Jacobsen thus deemed Iran's actions "commercial terrorism." Their case was dismissed in July 1994, on the grounds that the United States lacked jurisdiction.

In 1998, in a separate case, a U.S. judge ordered Iran to pay $65 million in damages to Cicippio and his wife, as well as fellow hostages David Jacobsen and Frank Reed. Cicippio's family was awarded $91 million by a U.S. judge in 2005 to compensate for the emotional distress they suffered during his imprisonment.

Laura Lambert

See also Anderson, Terry A.; Hostage Taking; Steen, Alann; Sutherland, Thomas; Waite, Terry

Further Readings

Cicippio, Joseph. and Richard W. Hope. *From Chains to Roses: The Joseph Cicippio Story.* Waco, TX: WRS Publishing, 1993.
Herbert, Keith. "Cicippio Family Awarded $91 Million." *Philadelphia Inquirer*, October 16, 2005, p. B4.
Martin, David C., and John Walcott. *Best Laid Plans: The Inside Story of America's War against Terrorism.* New York: Harper & Row, 1988.

COMMUNIST PARTY OF NEPAL (MAOISTS)

Nepal is among the world's poorest and least developed countries, with more than a third of its population living below the poverty line. Until 2008, this remote and mountainous country was one of the last absolute monarchies of the world. Given its history of poverty, oppression, and its remote geography, it is not surprising that communist ideology found a firm foothold in Nepal. The Communist Party of Nepal (Maoist), or CPN(M), aims at following the path of the Chinese Communist leader Mao Zedong and transforming the nation into a classless Marxist state.

Although the CPN(M) was founded by Pushpa Kumar Dahal—also known as Prachanda (the "terrible")—in 1994, for several years most people in the country were not even aware of the group's existence. In early 1996, CPN(M) put forward a list of 40 demands that was completely ignored by the media. However, the group soon launched a guerrilla war that shook the nation. The group destroyed buildings, stole currency, and killed civilians. The Nepali Civil War—or, as the Maoists called it, the People's War—lasted from 1996 to 2006 and resulted in the deaths of more than 12,000 Nepalis. Human rights groups were critical of the CPN(M) for their alleged use of underage soldiers, some as young as 12.

In order to capture political power and defeat the forces of the central state, the CPN(M) proposed what it called the Prachanda Path, which combined the "education" of the masses and the creation of military bases in rural areas. From these bases the CPN(M) was to capture the ultimate power in Kathmandu, the seat of the Nepalese government. The success of the CPN(M) in the villages can be attributed to its ability to deliver a modicum of governance where previously there had been none.

King Gyanendra came to power in Nepal in 2001 after a massacre that killed the reigning monarch, Gyanendra's father, King Birenda, and the majority of the royal family. As the war escalated, the Maoists began attacking the Nepalese Army. Although there were intermittent cease-fires beginning in 2002, fighting continued through 2005, when the CPN(M) sought a permanent peace accord by forming a pro-democratic alliance with several other mainstream political parties that wanted to end the Nepalese monarchy. However, the autocratic King Gyanendra lost faith in the reconciliation process, and in February 2005 he took complete control of the government by dismissing the elected parliament.

This direct challenge by the king brought the conflict to a head. The opposition political parties were finally able to drive the king out in 2008, and they declared Nepal to be a republic. The CPN(M) then became part of a coalition government. In the new government, Prachanda was elected prime minster. However, even in power, after more than a decade of fighting, the relationship between the CPN(M) and the established powers, particularly the military, is far from smooth. In May 2009 Prachanda resigned his post after he tried and failed to remove the chief of the Nepalese armed forces.

The future of the CPN(M) is uncertain. There is growing discontent within the ranks of the former revolutionaries as the Maoist militia and armed guerrillas are being assimilated into the civil society. Without marketable skills, these young men and women are increasingly depending on their weapons to earn a living, which poses a serious challenge to the Maoist's popularity among the Nepalese people.

After the fall of the Soviet Union and China's metamorphosis into a hyper-capitalistic state, many scholars believed that communism was a spent force. It was argued that communism as an ideology was dead and that capitalism had triumphed. Yet the success of the CPN(M) in Nepal and the spread of Maoist rebellion in neighboring India have inspired a reassessment.

Dipak Gupta

See also Shining Path

Further Readings

Heiberg, Marianne, Brendan O'Leary, and John Tirman, eds. *Terror, Insurgency, and the State: Ending Protracted Conflicts.* Philadelphia: University of Pennsylvania Press, 2007.

Hutt, Michael, ed. *Himalayan People's War: Nepal's Maoist Rebellion.* Bloomington: Indiana University Press, 2004.

CONTINUITY IRISH REPUBLICAN ARMY

A Northern Irish terrorist organization founded in the mid-1980s, the Continuity Irish Republican Army (IRA) emerged as the armed wing of Republican Sinn Féin in 1996.

For more than 30 years, Northern Ireland endured an armed conflict between the province's Roman Catholics (also called Republicans or Nationalists), who wanted Northern Ireland to become part of the Republic of Ireland, and the province's Protestants (also called Loyalists or Unionists), who wanted it to remain a part of the

United Kingdom. Armed paramilitary groups from both communities used violence to achieve their ends, and the most prominent of these groups on the Republican side was the Irish Republican Army (IRA). Originally formed in 1919, the IRA receded somewhat after Ireland's withdrawal from the British Commonwealth in 1949, but it was revived in 1969, when it began a terrorist campaign intended to force Britain to withdraw from Northern Ireland.

The IRA maintained a political party called Sinn Féin. Sinn Féin and the IRA refused to recognize the governments of either Northern Ireland or the Republic of Ireland as legitimate, a position stemming from ideological conflicts over the 1920 partition of Ireland. Although Sinn Féin sometimes fielded candidates in elections, these candidates refused to serve if elected. Initially, the revitalized IRA (also called the Provisional IRA or the Provisionals) took the same position, and Sinn Féin's role in the conflict was very limited.

In the mid-1980s, following the hunger strikes of 1981, in which 10 Republican prisoners starved to death in a British prison, IRA leaders began to think that greater political involvement might aid, not hinder, their struggle. At a 1986 meeting of IRA leaders, a proposal that the IRA recognize the government of the Republic of Ireland was put forth. Such recognition would allow elected Sinn Féin candidates to take office in the Dáil, the republic's legislature.

A hard-line faction of the Sinn Féin membership split with the IRA over this deviation from traditional Republicanism; the splinter group formed a political party, Republican Sinn Féin, which would adhere to the old abstentionism. During the next few years, Republican Sinn Féin gathered arms and recruits, calling its armed wing the Continuity IRA (CIRA); however, the CIRA remained inactive. The leaders of Republican Sinn Féin were allegedly threatened with death should they attempt to mount an armed campaign separate from the Provisional IRA. In late 1994, the movement toward political involvement by the Provisionals had borne fruit; the IRA called a cease-fire, and Sinn Féin leaders entered secret peace negotiations with the mainstream Nationalist parties and the British government.

By 1996, negotiations had stalled and dissatisfaction was growing within the Republican community, providing a climate in which CIRA could emerge. On July 13, 1996, CIRA made its first attack, detonating a 250-pound car bomb outside a hotel in County Fermanagh. This was followed by two more bombings in the fall of 1996. By then, the IRA had broken its cease-fire with the Canary Wharf bombing in London, and CIRA activity declined. As the IRA prepared to renew its cease-fire in the summer of 1997, CIRA escalated its attacks, planting bombs at government offices, police stations, and hotels. The CIRA is believed to have been responsible for a bomb planted outside the BBC offices in London on March 4, 2001, though some sources attribute this attack to a different splinter group, the Real IRA. No one was killed by the 17 bombings attributed to the CIRA, although dozens were injured and millions of dollars of damage was done to property.

CIRA opposed the 1998 Good Friday Accords, Northern Ireland's peace plan, and it is the only Republican paramilitary organization that did not declare a cease-fire in response to the Accords. It is believed that several Real IRA members may have joined CIRA following the 1998 cease-fire. Although its numbers are small—estimated at about 30 members—it has an unknown amount of IRA weaponry seized from arms dumps and remains a significant threat. In 2009 the group claimed responsibility for the killing of a police officer in a sniper attack in County Armagh.

Colleen Sullivan

See also Canary Wharf Bombing; Irish Republican Army; Real Irish Republican Army

Further Readings

Bums, John. F. "Police Chief in Ulster Plays Down Dissidents." *International Herald Tribune*, March 16, 2009, p. 3.

"Continuity IRA: The Struggle Goes on?" BBC News Service: Focus on Northern Ireland, March 16, 1999. http://news.bbc.co.uk/hi/english/events/northern_ireland/focus/newsid_166000/166943.stm.

Holland, Jack. *Hope Against History: The Course of Conflict in Northern Ireland.* New York: Henry Holt, 1999.

McEvoy, Joanne. *The Politics of Northern Ireland.* Edinburgh: Edinburgh University Press, 2008.

McKittrick, David. *Making Sense of the Troubles*. Belfast: Blackstaff Press, 2000.

Mitchell, Thomas G. *When Peace Fails: Lessons from Belfast for the Middle East*. Jefferson, NC: McFarland, 2010.

Moloney, Ed. *A Secret History of the IRA*. New York: W.W. Norton, 2002.

O'Brien, Brendan. *The Long War: The IRA and Sinn Fein*. 2nd ed. Syracuse, NY: Syracuse University Press, 1999.

Shanahan, Timothy. *The Provisional Irish American Army and the Morality of Terrorism*. Edinburgh: Edinburgh University Press, 2009.

Taylor, Peter. *Provos: The IRA and Sinn Fein*. London: Bloomsbury, 1997.

COPELAND, DAVID (1976–)

David Copeland is a British neo-Nazi who orchestrated a series of nail bombings in London during the summer of 1999.

Born on May 15, 1976, Copeland grew up in Yately, Hampshire, the second son of middle-class parents. An intelligent youth, he was somewhat shy and withdrawn, and of markedly slight build, a combination that made him the object of much bullying in school. He has stated that he fantasized continually about taking violent revenge on his tormentors from age 12, and some observers have suggested that his obsession with domination and violence led him to develop an interest in fascism. Whatever the case, as a teenager Copeland became fascinated with Nazism and other right-wing and racist causes. He believed in the superiority of the white race over all others and nurtured a particular, intense loathing of homosexuals.

Although he did well enough in school to go on to higher education, Copeland took a job with the London Underground. He also joined the British National Party and the National Socialist Party, two extremely right-wing groups. When he first moved from belief to action is unknown.

On April 17, 1999, Copeland planted a bomb on a street in Brixton, a mostly Afro-Caribbean neighborhood in London. The device was simple, and Copeland had to start the timer before transporting the bomb, placing himself at great risk. The sports bag containing the charge was packed with nails, bolts, and other shards of metal, and the explosion injured 40 people.

A week later, Copeland planted a second, similar device in Brick Lane, a street in a largely Pakistani and Indian immigrant neighborhood. An alert passerby noticed the suspicious bag and placed it in the trunk of his car to transport it to a police station. It exploded while inside the car, injuring 10 people.

Copeland's third and most devastating attack came on April 29. This time, instead of leaving the device in an open area, Copeland entered a gay bar, ordered a drink, and left after a few minutes. Acting on a tip, police had warned area bars of a possible attack, and several patrons noticed the suspicious gym bag. They had just gathered around the bag to examine it when it exploded. Three people were killed and 79 were injured.

The widespread use of closed-circuit television cameras in England allowed authorities to pick out the bomber from the crowd in the Brixton and Brick Lane incidents. The police released some of the closed-circuit pictures, which resulted in a tip from one of Copeland's coworkers the very afternoon of third bombing. Copeland was arrested the next day, and he confessed immediately, stating that his motive had been to spark a race war in England. Tried the following spring, he pled guilty to manslaughter with diminished capacity (claiming he was subject to paranoid fantasies and delusions), but the jury convicted him of murder. He is serving six life sentences for murder in Broadmoor Hospital, a high-security psychiatric facility. In 2007, a judge ruled that Copeland cannot be considered for parole until he completes at least 50 years of his sentence.

Colleen Sullivan

See also Bombings and Bomb Scares; Freelance Terrorism

Further Readings

BBC News. "Special Report: The Nail Bomb Terror." http://news.bbc.co.uk/hi/english/uk/newsid_332000/332807.stm.

Edwards, Richard. "Nail Bomber Must Serve 50 Years' Jail." *Evening Standard*, March 2, 2007, p. 21.

Hopkins, Nick and Sarah Hall. "David Copeland: A Quiet Introvert, Obsessed with Hitler and Bombs."

The Guardian, June 30, 2000. http://www.guardian
.co.uk/bombs/Story/0,2763,338345,00.html.

"The London Nail Bombs." *Guardian Special Report*.
http://www.guardian.co.uk/bombs/0,2759,190332,00
.html.

Pendlebury, Richard. "Five-star Broadmoor." *Daily Mail*,
October 5, 2002, p. 20.

Reynolds, Mark. "Bomber Wanted to Upset Tony Blair:
Killer Targeted Gay Pub 'Because It Was Full of Men
Hugging Each Other.'" *Daily Mail*, June 9, 2000, p. 43.

CORONADO, RODNEY (1966–)

Rodney Coronado (aka Jim Perez and Martin Rubio), a member of the Animal Liberation Front (ALF), was the first radical animal rights activist to serve time in a federal prison for actions against animal exploitation in the United States. In 1995 he was sentenced to 57 months in prison for his involvement in ALF's five-state anti-fur campaign during the early 1990s.

Coronado became involved in animal rights early in his life. He claims that a documentary film on the slaughter of harp seals converted him into an activist at the age of 12. By the age of 18, he had joined the Sea Shepard Conservation Society, an anti-whaling direct-action organization founded by Paul Watson in 1977. Watson's goal was to inflict economic damage on whaling and other marine industries. He used his boat, the *Sea Shepard*, to disrupt whaling activities, sometimes by ramming whaling boats at sea. Coronado was an engineer on the *Sea Shepard*. In November 1986 he helped sabotage a whaling station in Reykjavik, Iceland, and sink two of Iceland's four whaling ships, causing damage estimated at $2.7 million. This action, along with his role in vandalizing nine fur salons in Vancouver, earned Coronado a reputation in the animal rights community. As early as 1987, the FBI and Department of Justice had identified him as a threat.

By 1990 Coronado had become involved with the Coalition Against Fur Farms (CAFF). For nine months, he worked undercover in a fur-ranching community in Montana to gather information about industry practices. Over the next two years, Coronado's findings were used to carry out "Operation Bite Back," which used arson, destruction of property, burglary, vandalism, and theft to disrupt the fur-farming industry. In the early 1990s, ALF sabotaged fur farms and fur-animal research facilities at universities in Oregon, Washington, Utah, and Michigan, and the group brought operations at the Malecky Mink Ranch in Yamhill, Oregon, and the Northwest Fur Farm Food Cooperative in Edmonds, Washington, to an end. Although no one was injured, these acts caused several million dollars in damages. Federal investigators later linked Coronado to the site of each of these actions.

Further investigations showed that Coronado was a key organizer of each of these ALF initiatives, including an aborted proposal to free the "Silver Spring monkeys" from Tulane University in 1990 (these macaques were originally housed at the Institute of Behavioral Research in Silver Spring, Maryland). During a search of Coronado's storage locker in Talent, Oregon, investigators discovered plans to target two Montana fur farms, as well as proof that he had stolen a historical artifact—a notebook of one of Custer's soldiers—from the Little Bighorn National Park.

In July 1993 a federal grand jury in western Michigan indicted Coronado for his part in the ALF raid on Michigan State University's experimental fur farm. Coronado, who had gone into hiding after Operation Bite Back, was captured in November 1994, on the Pasqua Pueblo Indian reservation in Arizona, where he lived with his tribe, the Yaqui. On March 3, 1995, Coronado pled guilty to aiding and abetting arson and to one count of theft of U.S. government property. He served almost four years in prison.

In 2004 Coronado was arrested in Arizona for interfering with a U.S. Forest Service hunt of mountain lions in Sabino Canyon. The Forest Service had decided to shoot and trap the lions because of an increase in encounters between the lions and people in the area. Coronado attempted to stymie the hunters by digging up a trap and laying down false scent to confuse their dogs. He was sentenced to eight months in prison.

Coronado wound up on trial again in 2007, this time in San Diego, California, as the result of a speech he gave in 2003 in which he demonstrated how to build a firebomb. The speech took place shortly after an arson attack by the Earth Liberation

Front destroyed a housing complex in the San Diego neighborhood of Hillcrest.

Coronado was charged under a little-used federal law that prohibits a person from demonstrating how to make a destructive device with the intent that others commit arson. A mistrial was declared in September 2007 after a jury could not reach a verdict, but Coronado pled guilty to the charge in December in order to avoid a second charge stemming from a similar speech he gave in Colorado, as well as a charge of illegally possessing eagle feathers. In March 2008, Coronado was sentenced to a year and a day in prison, but he was released on probation in December of that year. However, he was sent back to prison in August 2010 because he "friended" a fellow activist on Facebook, thereby violating the terms of his probation. Coronado was released at the beginning of 2011 to begin his probation again.

Laura Lambert

See also Animal Liberation Front; Animal Rights Movement

Further Readings

Best, Steven, and Anthony J. Nocella II, eds. *Terrorists or Freedom Fighters? Reflections on the Liberation of Animals.* New York: Lantern, 2004.

Grossman, Ron. "Activist's Case a Free-speech Test." *Chicago Tribune,* September 9, 2007, p. 3.

Moran, Greg. "Animal Rights Activist Tells of Regret before Sentencing." *San Diego Union-Tribune,* March 28, 2008, p. 4.

Scarce, Rik. *Eco-warriors: Understanding the Radical Environmental Movement.* Chicago: Noble Press, 1990.

Soto, Onell R. "Dismissal Sought in S.D. Speech Case: Activist Indicted after Detailing Bomb Making." *San Diego Union-Tribune,* November 6, 2006, p. B1.

Tobias, Michael. "Animal Liberation." In *Voices from the Underground: For the Love of Animals.* Pasadena, CA: New Paradigm Books, 1999.

COUNTERTERRORISM

Counterterrorism is the use of personnel and resources to preempt, disrupt, or destroy the

The Metropolitan Transportation Authority has launched several security awareness campaigns that promote a toll-free number to call and provide information anonymously to the NYPD and its anti-terrorism intelligence division. (Courtesy of New York City Metropolitan Transportation Authority)

capabilities of terrorists and their support networks. Counterterrorism is inherently an offensive, as opposed to defensive, approach to a threat of terrorism. It involves diplomacy, intelligence operations, law enforcement, military operations, and counterterrorism training.

Diplomacy

The diplomatic dimension of counterterrorism traditionally is associated with foreign relations and international terrorism, but it is also applicable when fighting domestic terrorism. Diplomacy is the art of persuading others to do things that serve mutual interests. The diplomatic component of counterterrorism encompasses activities such as persuading Lebanon to close down terrorist training camps, securing Pakistan's permission to arrest and render the terrorist Ramzi Yousef to U.S. authorities, or the FBI sharing information with local police in order to prevent a terrorist attack. The use of diplomacy also involves reaching an international consensus on how to handle issues ranging from aviation security to tagging explosives to imposing sanctions on state sponsors of terrorism. Most importantly, it involves developing and implementing policy responses to terrorism or the threat of it.

Diplomacy has been used more frequently and with more success on the international front. Domestically, however, it has not been as successful. Interactions among federal, state, and local officials can be just as complicated and sensitive as any operation conducted overseas, and proper coordination among the different law enforcement agencies can play a critical role in building a prosecutable case against a terrorist. Law enforcement officials across the United States have frequently complained that federal officials, particularly the FBI, work in a vacuum, ignore local police, and refuse to share information. The cabinet-level Department of Homeland Security, established shortly after the September 11, 2001, terrorist attacks, mandated that the FBI and CIA share information with each other and with the department itself. It was hoped that such top-level coordination would translate into better interdepartmental cooperation at all levels.

Finding and arresting terrorists outside the United States is a significant undertaking. It requires the cooperation of foreign governments and coordination among a variety of agencies. The arrest of the mastermind of the 1993 World Trade Center bombing, Ramzi Yousef, is a case in point. The U.S. government first learned of his whereabouts thanks to an informant who walked into the U.S. embassy in Pakistan and told U.S. diplomats where Yousef was staying. Elements of several U.S. government agencies were involved in vetting the information provided by the source and putting in place an operation to apprehend Yousef. In addition, the United States asked for and received the full assistance of the government of Pakistan to arrest and remove Yousef from Pakistan. This type of coordination and cooperation is characteristic of what happens when things go well. But such events do not happen of their own accord; it takes preparation and often years of work to put the mechanisms in place. Securing cooperation is the nuts and bolts of diplomacy.

Intelligence Operations

Accurate intelligence also is a critical element in an effective counterterrorism policy. Intelligence, as a tool of counterterrorism, has several dimensions—field operations, covert action, technical collection, and analysis. In field operations, the objective of intelligence is to identify the members of terrorist groups, learn how they get their money, locate where they do their training and operational planning, and ultimately obtain access to the decision makers. This kind of information is essential for mounting operations to disrupt or preempt terrorist attacks. Obtaining such intelligence, however, is a daunting task.

Another facet of intelligence activities, covert action, is similar to diplomacy, only done in secret. Covert action is the use of information or disinformation to attack and weaken an opponent. The ultimate goal of such efforts is to help create an environment that supports the overall counterterrorism policy. For example, when employed against a terrorist group, covert action could encompass planting stories in the media that are designed to undermine support for that group or to build support within a country for taking action against the group.

A particular, and controversial, tactic that falls under the umbrella of covert action is that of extraordinary rendition and detention, the process by which a suspected terrorist is either abducted or transferred without legal permission to be interrogated in a country where torture is practiced. In doing this, the initiating country avoids directly violating its own laws against torture. In many instances, individuals involved in extraordinary rendition have been prosecuted and brought to trial. In 2009, for example, an Italian court convicted 23 Americans, a majority of whom were CIA operatives, of abducting a Muslim cleric in Milan. However, an equal number of cases, if not more, have been dismissed on the basis that too many covert operations would be brought to light in the course of the trial.

The technical dimension of intelligence activities includes efforts to intercept or monitor all communications by terrorists. This includes actions such as an old-fashioned wiretap to penetration of a terrorist computer. Technical intelligence activities also can be employed to disrupt terrorist communications or interfere with the transfer of financial resources.

Intelligence analysis plays an important role in identifying the structure and plans of terrorists. After field operatives gather raw data, someone has to make sense of it. A good analyst is a puzzle solver who integrates human intelligence with imagery and signal intercepts to create a picture of reality. The process is the same whether the targets are Hezbollah guerrillas in Lebanon or domestic terrorists.

When used in tandem, diplomacy and intelligence can be quite effective, as illustrated by the *Tiny Star* incident. The *Tiny Star* was a ship used by Libya in planning and carrying out a seaborne attack against Israel in 1990. After learning the details of the operation through intelligence-gathering methods, the U.S. Government dispatched briefing teams to convince skeptical allies in western Europe that Libya was in fact responsible.

Law Enforcement

Arresting, prosecuting, and incarcerating terrorists have been main objectives of U.S. counterterrorism efforts since the 1990s. In 1996, for example, the FBI, working in tandem with the U.S. State Department and the CIA, apprehended Mir Aimal Kansi and returned him to the United States. Kansi was the man responsible for murdering and wounding CIA employees on their way to work in McLean, Virginia, in 1993. In 1995 the U.S. Government apprehended the mastermind of the World Trade Center bombing, Ramzi Yousef, who was then tried and convicted on a number of charges. In addition, Sheikh Omar Abdel Rahman was convicted in 1995 for his part in a conspiracy to commit a series of terrorist acts in the New York City area.

Law enforcement offers several advantages as a counterterrorism policy and tool. Arresting and trying terrorists sends the message that people who attack the United States will be caught and punished. Second, it provides a clear demonstration of what separates a civilized government from terrorists. When terrorists are afforded the right of due process, the government prosecuting the case is

making a powerful symbolic statement about protecting its citizens and holding the terrorists accountable for their actions. Despite its theoretical advantages as an element of counterterrorism policy, however, in practice law enforcement can suffer from critical flaws that hamper its effectiveness. Internationally, there is the challenge of collecting evidence in a way that will permit it to be entered into the U.S. judicial system. Ramzi Yousef's lawyers went to great lengths to discredit the evidence gathered by Philippine police bomb technicians, for example, thought they ultimately failed to do so. There also have been several instances where intelligence operatives have identified suspects and terrorist infrastructure, only to have the resulting information be insufficient for an arrest and criminal prosecution. In the mid-1990s, for instance, Sudanese officials allegedly offered to deliver Osama bin Laden into the hands of the United States, but the offer was declined because the evidence the United States possessed was not adequate for a successful prosecution. Knowing someone is a terrorist is quite different from proving someone is a terrorist.

Domestically, law enforcement faces significant handicaps. Federal and local law enforcement must surmount major hurdles before opening an investigation on groups, be they neo-Nazis or Muslim extremists, even if they are actually planning a terrorist operation. The United States has traditionally lacked a domestic capability for gathering and collating intelligence and redistributing it to law enforcement officials nationwide.

Subsequent to the September 11, 2001, attacks on New York and Washington, the Homeland Security Act of 2002 established the Department of Homeland Security (DHS). The creation of DHS was one of the largest governmental restructurings in U.S. history. Since its inception, DHS has extended its responsibilities and goals to include various agencies under the executive branch of the U.S. government. Currently, there are 22 agencies under the DHS umbrella, with responsibilities that include but are not limited to counterterrorism, border control, immigration, transport and travel security, and emergency management. In continuance with the government's emphasis on security, most law enforcement agencies, from the Federal Bureau of Investigation (FBI) all the way down to local police departments, have some level of relationship with

DHS, providing the department with their resources, manpower, and information when needed.

Military Operations

The military component is what people generally think of when someone says, "counterterrorism." The term conjures up images of black-clad special operations forces roping down from a helicopter to launch an assault in the dead of night. The 1972 Munich Olympics taught the world that police and military teams required specialized training to confront a terrorist attack effectively. Germany's lack of preparation to manage the crisis resulted in the deaths of all Israeli hostages. In the wake of that event, the United States and Europe embarked on an extensive effort to develop counterterrorism strike forces.

While military operations have a role to play in combating terrorism, the reality is that there are a limited number of opportunities where military force can be used. Within the United States, this mission falls to local police and the FBI. U.S. military forces are proscribed from conducting domestic operations except in very special, highly restrictive situations. The biggest obstacle is that most terrorists lack the training facilities, buildings, vehicles, or aircraft that offer viable targets for a military operation. The terrorist infrastructure that existed in Afghanistan prior to 9/11 is atypical. If targets do exist, there is the more difficult challenge of securing basing rights and permission to launch operations inside a foreign country. The war in Afghanistan has demonstrated, however, that discernible terrorist targets can be effectively destroyed through military operations.

Following the defeat of the Taliban in Afghanistan, President George W. Bush launched Operation Iraqi Freedom, under the assertion that Iraq had links to al Qaeda and that it was part of an "axis of evil" with Iran and North Korea, bent on pursuing weapons of mass destruction (WMD). Though both allegations were subsequently proven false, the United States, in conjunction with Britain and several other countries, invaded Iraq in 2003. The war was successful on some fronts, particularly in the capture of the Iraqi leader Saddam Hussein. However, with the fall of Hussein's government, much of the country fell into chaos, experiencing high levels of violence due to a strong anti-American insurgency and conflict between Shiite and Sunni Muslim factions.

Training

The least understood and most important counterterrorism resource is training. In the wake of terrorist attacks such as the bombing of the U.S. embassy in Beirut in 1983, the Bureau of Diplomatic Security (DS) and the Diplomatic Security Service (DSS) were officially established in 1985. A year later, U.S. Congress enacted the Omnibus Diplomatic Security and Antiterrorism Act of 1986, which provides funds to solidify U.S. facilities overseas. In addition, the Anti-Terrorism Assistance Program (ATAP) was established in 1983. ATAP provides a proactive capability that extends U.S. force by training foreign police and senior government officials, providing them with the skills to investigate and deter terrorism. Police are trained in SWAT operations, major case management, post-blast investigation, and crisis management.

Measuring the effectiveness of such efforts is difficult, but progress has certainly been made since the 1972 Olympics. In 1992, for example, Singapore authorities who were trained by Israel and the United States stormed a hijacked airliner, killed the hijackers, and rescued all the passengers, with no fatalities. The Peruvians enjoyed a similar success in 1997, when they took down Tupac Amaru guerrillas that had taken control of the residence of the Japanese ambassador. However, the June 2002 rescue of two Americans and one Filipino, who had been kidnapped by Filipino terrorist group Abu Sayyaf more than a year earlier, did not turn out as well. Two of the hostages were killed in a shoot-out between the U.S.-trained Filipino troops and the kidnappers; the third hostage was rescued successfully.

Anti-terrorism training has also been a significant part of U.S. and the North Atlantic Treaty Organization (NATO) efforts in the wars in Afghanistan and Iraq. In 2009, NATO undertook the NATO Training Mission-Afghanistan (NTM-A), which also included the U.S.–led Combined Security Transition Command-Afghanistan (CSTC-A), to train Afghani army and police. It is hoped that these programs will help pave the way for the withdrawal of U.S. and NATO troops from Afghanistan by enabling Afghans to better manage their own security. Success in this area is reportedly mixed, however. Similarly, in Iraq, the United States Army employed the Multi-National Security Transition Command-Iraq (MNSTC-I), an operation to help train the Iraqi military and police officers in counterterrorism. Like CSTC-A, the intention was to train Iraqi forces to take over once U.S. forces leave the country.

Counterterrorism is and should be a dynamic enterprise. The threat posed by terrorists will continue to evolve and will require new and creative responses by governments at all levels. Regardless of the response, the elements of diplomacy, intelligence, law enforcement, military operations, and training will continue to be employed in a variety of manners to attacks individuals and groups engaged in terrorism.

Larry C. Johnson

See also Afghanistan War; bin Laden, Osama; Central Intelligence Agency; Criminal Prosecution of Terrorists; Federal Bureau of Investigation; Grenzschutzgruppe 9; Homeland Security; Iraq War; Kansi, Mir Aimal; Munich Olympics Massacre; September 11 Attacks; U.S. Embassy Bombing, Beirut; Yousef, Ramzi Ahmed

Further Readings

Baer, Robert. *See No Evil: The True Story of a Ground Soldier in the CIA's War on Terrorism.* New York: Crown Publishers, 2002.

Bergen, Peter L. *Holy War Inc.: Inside the Secret World of Osama bin Laden.* New York: Free Press, 2001.

Berntsen, Gary. *Human Intelligence, Counterterrorism, and National Leadership: A Practical Guide.* Dulles, VA: Potomac Books, 2008.

Bolz, Frank Jr., Kenneth J. Dudonis, and David P. Schulz. *The Counter-terrorism Handbook: Tactics, Procedures, and Techniques.* 3rd ed. Boca Raton, FL: Taylor & Francis, 2005.

Burton, Fred. *Ghost: Confessions of a Counterterrorism Agent.* New York: Random House, 2008.

Donohue, Laura K. *The Cost of Counterterrorism: Power, Politics, and Liberty.* Cambridge, UK: Cambridge University Press, 2008.

Ganor, Boaz. *The Counter-terrorism Puzzle: A Guide for Decision Makers.* New Brunswick, NJ: Transaction Publishers, 2005.

Katona, Peter, Michael D. Intriligator, and John P. Sullivan, eds. *Countering Terrorism and WMD: Creating a Global Counter-terrorism Network.* London: Routledge, 2006.

Naftali, Timothy. *Blind Sport: The Secret History of American Counterterrorism.* New York: Basic Books, 2005.

National Commission on Terrorist Attacks upon the United States. *The 9/11 Commission Report: Final Report of the National Commission on Terrorist Attacks upon the United States.* New York: W.W. Norton, 2004. http://www.9-11commission.gov.

Vise, David A. *The Bureau and the Mole: The Unmasking of Robert Philip Hanssen, the Most Dangerous Double Agent in FBI History.* New York: Atlantic Monthly Press, 2002.

Whitcomb, Christopher. *Cold Zero: Inside the FBI Hostage Rescue Team.* New York: Little, Brown, 2001.

COVENANT, THE SWORD AND THE ARM OF THE LORD, THE

The Covenant, the Sword and the Arm of the Lord (CSA) was started in Arkansas as a small fundamentalist Christian group called Zarephath-Horeb, meaning "refuge and divine inspiration," by James Ellison in 1976. Ellison eventually adopted Christian Identity, a race-based theology that claims whites are the only true descendants of God, Jews are descended from Satan, and all other races are descended from animals. The group adopted an antigovernment stance and changed its name to symbolize its paramilitary function.

Although members sold weapons, distributed hate literature, and engaged in some criminal activity, the group crossed the line into terrorism in 1983 after Gordon Kahl, a North Dakota farmer and member of the Posse Comitatus, refused to pay his taxes. After shooting and killing two federal marshals, Kahl was killed in a federal raid, making him a martyr for the extreme right. As revenge for his death, the CSA declared war on what it called the Zionist Occupied Government, or ZOG.

As part of its declaration of war, members planned to assassinate government officials, including a judge, an FBI agent, and a federal prosecutor named Asa Hutchison. A car wreck on the way to a target's house, however, was taken as a sign from

God that the plan was not ready. CSA's crimes included setting fires in an Arkansas church with a largely homosexual congregation and in a Jewish center, and bombing a natural gas pipeline. The day after the 1983 pipeline bombing, however, a CSA member, Richard Wayne Snell, killed the owner of a pawnshop, mistakenly believing he was Jewish. In 1984 Snell killed a black Arkansas state trooper, Louis Bryant, and was captured by authorities.

The CSA church, located on a 224-acre compound in rural Arkansas, eventually became a survivalist paramilitary training camp for other white supremacist groups like Aryan Nations and The Order. It was there that authorities believe David Tate, a member of The Order, was heading after gunning down Jimmie Linegar, a Missouri state trooper. On April 19, 1985, more than 200 FBI agents and other police surrounded the compound. The resulting standoff, the first of its kind in which federal authorities were up against such a well-equipped militia group, lasted four days and was resolved peacefully.

Tate was eventually located and arrested in Forsyth, Missouri. He had never made it to the compound, but four other members of The Order—two wanted on federal racketeering charges and two arrested on federal firearms violations—were there and surrendered at the same time as Ellison. Subsequent searches of the compound yielded hundreds of weapons and explosives, including the remnants of a minefield, caches of gold and neo-Nazi literature, and a 30-gallon barrel of cyanide. Ellison and his second-in-command, Kerry Noble, were sentenced in 1985 to prison on racketeering and illegal weapons charges.

Snell was executed on April 19, 1995—12 hours after a bomb exploded in the Murrah Building in Oklahoma City, killing 168 people. Members of the CSA have admitted that they had had a plan—which was later abandoned—to blow up that building. They and others have suggested that Snell may have been involved in the planning of the blast from his prison cell, but no conspiracy has been brought to light.

Nancy Egan

See also April 19; Branch Davidian Compound Siege; Ellison, James; Oklahoma City Bombing; Order, The; Patriot Movement; Posse Comitatus; Snell, Richard Wayne

Further Readings

Coulson, Danny O., and Elaine Shannon. *No Heroes: Inside the FBI's Secret Counter-terror Force*. New York: Pocket Books, 1999.

Extremism on the Right: A Handbook. Rev. ed. New York: Anti-Defamation League of B'nai B'rith, 1988.

Noble, Kerry. *Tabernacle of Hate: Why They Bombed Oklahoma City*. Prescott, Ontario: Voyageur Publishing, 1998.

Quarles, Chester L. *Christian Identity: The Aryan American Bloodline Religion*. Jefferson, NC: McFarland, 2004.

Stern, Jessica. *Terror in the Name of God: Why Religious Militants Kill*. New York: Ecco, 2008.

CRIMINAL PROSECUTION OF TERRORISTS

Two primary questions must be considered when addressing the complex concept of the criminal prosecution of terrorists. The first is definitional: What is a terrorist act or, for that matter, a terrorist? Once a determination has been made that an individual, group, or act can be so defined, the second question arises: What laws exist, at both the national and international levels, that would be applicable to any prosecutorial effort?

Creating a workable legal definition of "terrorism" is a complex question. Actions that may be associated with the overthrow of a government may be viewed as terrorism by some and as revolutionary by others. Clearly, the need to identify who is a terrorist and what is a terrorist act is a critical prosecutorial element. However, although many scholars have attempted to develop a functional definition of the term, it is rare for any individuals to agree on a single definition of terrorism. Similarly, the legal definition of terrorism varies between sources, such as the United Kingdom and the United States, the Federal Bureau of Investigation and the Central Intelligence Agency, the U.S. Department of State and the U.S. Department of Homeland Security, to name a few.

Until the events of September 11, 2001, efforts to prosecute terrorists and terrorist organizations focused primarily on the use of existing criminal procedural law—case law that includes the federal

Viktor Bout has been indicted in the United States, but his alleged arms trafficking activity and support of armed conflicts in Africa has been a cause of concern around the world. According to the federal indictment and other court documents, Bout, an international weapons trafficker since the 1990s, has carried out a massive weapons-trafficking business by assembling a fleet of cargo airplanes capable of transporting weapons and military equipment to various parts of the world, including Africa, South America, and the Middle East. The arms that Bout has sold or brokered have fueled conflicts and supported regimes in Afghanistan, Angola, the Democratic Republic of the Congo, Liberia, Rwanda, Sierra Leone, and Sudan. The United States actively pursued his extradition from Thailand on a separate set of U.S. charges, which allege that Bout conspired to sell millions of dollars worth of weapons to the Fuerzas Armadas Revolucionarias de Colombia (FARC) to be used to kill Americans in Colombia. (Drug Enforcement Administration photo)

and state statutes that are the basis for actions initiated by components of the criminal justice system. Laws pertaining to money laundering, immigration, and conspiracy, including the Racketeer Influenced and Corrupt Organizations (RICO) Act, have all used to prosecute terrorists. Additionally, the criminal justice system relies heavily on applicable sections of the U.S. Code, Section 18, pertaining specifically to terrorism and terrorist activity (18 U.S.C. 2322, 2332 a through h, 2339, and 2339A through 2339C). Several legislative packages have contributed, either directly or indirectly, to the capability of the U.S. government to prosecute terrorists. In 1996, as a direct response to the April 19, 1995, bombing in Oklahoma City, Public Law 104-132, 110 Statute 1214 was passed; its key provision focused on habeas corpus and the right, or lack thereof, of the Supreme Court to review the denial of a second filing of a habeas petition by federal courts of appeals.

Post–9/11 Legislation

On October 24, 2001, congressional leaders introduced House Resolution (HR) 3162, Public Law 107-56, 115 Statute 272. Commonly referred to as the USA PATRIOT Act (or simply the Patriot Act), the extensive legislation aimed at strengthening existing anti-terrorism law and associated procedures. Among its highlights are the expansion of law enforcement powers, the expansion of the role and function of the secretary of the treasury in counterterror efforts, modifications to the process used for gathering foreign intelligence, and an expanded definition of terrorism designed to complement the increased powers of law enforcement agencies.

Further strengthening and altering the landscape of the criminal justice system, the Patriot Act was closely followed, on November 25, 2002, by the Homeland Security Act (Public Law 107-296, 116 Statute 2135). Mirroring the reorganization under which the Department of Defense was created, the Homeland Security Act established the cabinet level position of secretary of homeland security while at the same time bringing under one administrative and operational umbrella what were once seven separate agencies; the Transportation Security Administration, U.S. Customs and Border Protection, U.S. Immigration and Customs Enforcement, the U.S. Secret Service, the Federal Emergency Management Agency, and the U.S. Coast Guard. The passage of the Intelligence Reform and Terrorism Prevention Act of 2004 (Public Law 108-458, 118 Statute 3638-3872), complemented the Homeland Security Act by further reforming the structure and composition of the intelligence community. Most significantly, the act established the position of director of national intelligence, as well as the National Counterterrorism Center, the National Counterproliferation Center, and a number of National Intelligence Centers. These new agencies reflected the perceived necessity for developing a coordinated effort for both the acquisition and analysis of intelligence information.

Two additional pieces of legislation were written to enhance the ability of the United States to prosecute terrorists under the nation's criminal laws: the Protect America Act (PAA) of 2007 and the FISA (Foreign Intelligence Surveillance Act) Amendments Act of 2008. The PAA, by removing the requirement for a warrant, allows agencies of the U.S. government to expand their surveillance of persons of interest that are believed to be affiliated with foreign entities. The FISA Amendments Act complements other pieces of legislation by (1) allowing agents of the government to conduct surveillance on people in other countries that are communicating with individuals in the United States and (2) allowing federal judges to waive lawsuits against telecommunications companies if the surveillance involved with the interception of communications, using their equipment, was authorized by the president of the United States and deemed legal. This act is highly controversial among civil liberties advocates, who consider the surveillance rules to be ripe for abuse.

Putting Legislation to Work

The government's approach, that of using every possible federal criminal justice statute to prosecute suspected terrorists, eventually turned into a more proactive approach focusing on detection and deterrence. This strategy has apparently been successful. Statistics from the Transactional Records Access Clearinghouse (TRAC), an organization that uses the Freedom of Information Act to collect data, using 2001 as the base year, illustrate an increase in conviction rates of those prosecuted as either international or domestic terrorists.

Despite these successes, additional means of prosecuting terrorists have been contemplated. Such efforts would go beyond trying suspects in criminal court and under the laws of whatever country holds jurisdiction. According to a special report written by David Scheffer for the U.S. Institute of Peace, these additional avenues include the use of U.S. military courts (already

in existence), U.S. military commissions, foreign national courts, an ad hoc UN Security Council international criminal tribunals, a similar ad hoc tribunal sponsored by the UN General Assembly, a coalition treaty-based criminal tribunal, a special Islamic court, and a UN-administered court in Afghanistan. Each possibility comes with its own particular set of challenges and questions regarding feasibility. As of 2010, the primary source for the prosecution of terrorists continued to reside with countries that were willing and able to prosecute them by applying existing applicable criminal law to each case.

Harvey Morley

See also Counterterrorism; Homeland Security; Law and Terrorism; Oklahoma City Bombing; September 11 Attacks

Further Readings

Bazan, Elizabeth B. *The Foreign Intelligence Surveillance Act: An Overview of Selected Issues.* CRS Report for Congress. Washington, DC: Congressional Research Service, July 7, 2008. http://www.fas.org/sgp/crs/intel/RL34279.pdf.

Bianchi, Andrea, ed. *Enforcing International Law Norms Against Terrorism.* Oxford: Hart Publishing, 2004.

Dershowitz, Alan. *Why Terrorism Works: Understanding the Threat, Responding to the Challenge.* New Haven, CT: Yale University Press, 2002.

Jacobson, Michael. *The West at War: U.S. and European Counterterrorism Efforts, Post 9/11.* Washington, DC: Washington Institute for Near East Policy, 2006.

Jenkins, Brian Michael. *Countering al Qaeda.* Santa Monica, CA: RAND Corporation, 2002.

Laqueur, Walter. *The New Terrorism: Fanaticism and the Arms of Mass Destruction.* New York: Oxford University Press, 1999.

National Commission on Terrorist Attacks upon the United States. *The 9/11 Commission Report.* New York: W.W. Norton, 2004. http://www.9-11commission.gov.

Reich, Walter, ed. *Origins of Terrorism: Psychologies, Ideologies, Theologies, States of Mind.* Washington, DC: Woodrow Wilson Center Press, 1998.

Wittes, Benjamin. *Legislating the War on Terror: An Agenda for Reform.* Washington, DC: Brookings Institution Press, 2009.

CYBERTERRORISM

The term *cyberterrorism* refers to the convergence of terrorism and cyberspace, particularly the politically motivated sabotage of information systems. Since the 1990s, incidents of hacking, cybercrime, and highly destructive computer viruses have been widespread, and these tools have increasingly been used for specific political ends.

Barry Collin, of the Institute for Security and Intelligence in California, coined the term *cyberterrorism* in the 1980s. In a 1997 paper, Collin described possible cyberterror scenarios. In one, a cyberterrorist hacks into the computer system of a cereal manufacturer and raises the level of iron in each box, causing innumerable children to get sick and die. In another scenario, cyberterrorists destabilize an entire country by attacking financial institutions and stock exchanges en masse.

Collin's third scenario, in which a cyberterrorist hacks into an air traffic control system, came close to reality in 1997, when a teenager gained access to a phone switch at a small Massachusetts airport and accidentally cut off all communications for the control tower for several hours. Alarming as it was, the incident was seen more as hacking gone awry than cyberterror, as the teenager lacked any political motivation.

Still, many point to destructive viruses and worms, and to denial-of-service attacks, as the seedlings for larger events. In 1999 the Melissa virus, an e-mail virus named after a Florida stripper, affected more than a million computers and caused at least $80 million in damages. (Melissa's creator, David Smith, pled guilty and was sentenced to 20 months in prison in May 2002.) In May 2000, the Love Bug virus (also called the ILOVEYOU virus) affected even the CIA and British Parliament and caused more than $10 billion in damages worldwide. The Nimda virus, discovered in 2001, has caused damages estimated at $500 million and hobbled entire businesses for days at a time.

Though viruses still constitute a threat, a more recent form of cyber attack has been the denial-of-service attack. In February 2000, Yahoo, CNN, eBay, and other e-commerce sites were flooded by e-mail messages from attacking computers, which slowed service and blocked other users from the sites, causing an estimated $1 billion in losses.

Other incidents worldwide have combined these hacking techniques with political messages. In what is believed to be the first cyber attack by terrorists against a country's computer systems, in 1998, an offshoot of the Liberation Tigers of Tamil Eelam swamped the Sri Lankan embassies with thousands of e-mails that read, "We are the Internet Black Tigers and we're doing this to disrupt your communications." In India, a group of international hackers against nuclear proliferation, called Milw0rm, hacked into the Bhabha Atomic Research Centre and posted the message, "If a nuclear war does start, you will be the first to scream," which was transposed over a photo of an atomic mushroom cloud. Similar attacks have been perpetrated against NATO sites during the conflict in Kosovo, to protest the World Trade Organization, and, particularly after the United States accidentally bombed the Chinese embassy in Belgrade, against U.S. government sites.

While denial-of-service attacks, e-mail bombs, website sit-ins, webpage takeovers, and viruses—sometimes referred to, collectively, as "hacktivism"—have not claimed lives or caused much more than nuisance and financial loss, many believe that these tactics could be used to complicate and magnify real-world attacks. Jeffrey A. Hunker, a former senior director for protection of critical infrastructure for the National Security Council, has stated that cyberattacks could act as a "force multiplier" for a bombing or attack by either by posting false information on the Internet to create panic, or by sabotaging financial, emergency, or communication networks. In 1997 the Clinton administration's Commission on Critical Infrastructure Protection concluded that electronic money transfers, the power grid, 911 services, and military command sites were also vulnerable to cyber attack. The commission's report stated, "Our dependence on the information and communications infrastructure has created new cyber-vulnerabilities, which we are only starting to understand."

In response to the commission's finding, President Clinton issued an order to create the National Infrastructure Protection Center, to protect vital national systems, such as telecommunications networks and the power grid, and to upgrade government computer security. One of Clinton's officials, Richard Clarke, continued under the Bush administration to deal directly with the threat of cyberterror. He was named special advisor for cybersecurity to the president shortly after the September 11 terrorist attacks.

By the late 1990s, the U.S. government faced daily cyber assaults on its computers and websites. Attacks against Department of Defense computers rose from less than 1,000 in 1997 to nearly 23,000 in 1999. A series of cyber attacks on high-level businesses and the Pentagon, beginning in 1998, is believed to be linked to organized crime in Russia. American hackers engaged in a "cyberwar" with their Chinese counterparts, which consisted of little more than defacing the other country's websites.

Of more concern were forays into large-scale sabotage, such as the 2000 hack into one of California's electrical transmitting stations, believed to have been perpetrated by hackers in China, and espionage-like hacks into sensitive information systems, such as the 1998 hack into NASA's Jet Propulsion Laboratory. Cyber espionage has become increasingly common as the decade has progressed.

State-Sponsored Cyberterror?

In 1996, CIA Director John Deutch warned of an upcoming "electronic Pearl Harbor." Over the next decade, however, little happened to support that claim. Skeptics began to argue that cyberterror had little appeal to traditional terrorists, due to the lack of drama and small likelihood of significant injury or death, but also because traditional terrorist tools, such as suicide bombings, were still quite effective. It appeared that hackers with the tools to disable key governmental or corporate computer systems lacked the political motivation to do so, while terrorists motivated to crumble information systems to cause chaos lacked the requisite computer skills. While it might be true that an extremist terror group like al Qaeda is not likely to pursue cyber attacks in the 2000s, another group of actors has found cyberterrorism attractive, namely national governments. Cyberterror appeals to governments precisely because it is a less dramatic form of attack. A cyber attack is unlikely to lead to mass casualties and the retaliation such casualties would cause. In addition, attracting skilled hackers is easier for a government than for a terrorist group, because the hackers are acting legally—at least by their own nation's laws.

The most enticing aspect of cyberterror for governments is its deniability. It is all but impossible to prove that a government launched a cyber attack. Even if the attack can be traced back to a particular country—and a skilled hacker can conceal an attack's geographical origin—finding the individuals responsible is very difficult, especially if the government involved is unwilling to conduct a serious investigation. The government can always claim the attack was committed by independent hackers, and since the target country cannot prove otherwise, retaliation is unlikely.

The first major incident of what is believed by most observers to have been state-sponsored cyberterror occurred in 2007, when the country of Estonia came under a massive denial-of-service attack that lasted for weeks. Estonia is very dependent on the Internet, and the attack not only shut down government websites, it also targeted private-sector websites, such as stores and banks, causing major inconveniences for Estonia's civilian population. Estonia's telephone system also proved vulnerable, and for a period of several hours Estonians could not call emergency numbers. At the time of the attack, Estonia was in the midst of a diplomatic confrontation with Russia, but the Russian government denied involvement, and Estonia has never been able to prove that it was responsible.

In August 2008, Russia's military attacked the neighboring country of Georgia. At the same time, Russian nationalists launched a website from which anyone could download a simple tool that would allow their computer to participate in a denial-of-service attack against Georgian government websites. Once again, the Russian government denied involvement, although many observers doubt that such organized campaigns could have taken place without at least the tacit permission of the Russian authorities.

Smaller attacks have been linked to North Korea and China, but in every case it has been impossible to prove government responsibility. In addition, international law is unclear as to whether a country under cyber attack can legally retaliate using other means, such as a military strike. There have been increasing calls for the international community to address the issue, as well as a campaign to make the Internet itself a less anonymous medium. At the moment, however, the penalties for cyberterrorism are basically nonexistent, making it likely that nations will continue to sponsor and engage in surreptitious cyberwarfare.

Laura Lambert

See also Asymmetrical Warfare; Liberation Tigers of Tamil Eelam; State Terrorism; State-Sponsored Terrorism

Further Readings

Aldrich, Richard W. *Cyberterrorism and Computer Crimes: Issues Surrounding the Establishment of an International Regime.* Colorado Springs, CO: USAF Institute for National Security Studies, 2000.

Alexander, Yonah, and Michael S. Swetnam, eds. *Cyber Terrorism and Information Warfare.* Dobbs Ferry, NY: Oceana Publications, 1999.

Arquilla, John, and David Ronfeldt, eds. *Networks and Netwars: The Future of Terror, Crime, and Militancy.* Santa Monica, CA: RAND Corporation, 2001.

Brenner, Susan W. "'At Light Speed': Attribution and Response to Cybercrime/terrorism/warfare." *Journal of Criminal Law and Criminology* 97, no. 2 (Winter 2007): 379–475.

Council of Europe Counter-Terrorism Task Force. *Cyberterrorism: The Use of the Internet for Terrorist Purposes.* Strasbourg, France: Council of Europe Publishing, 2007.

CSIS Global Organized Crime Project. *Cybercrime, Cyberterrorism, Cyberwarfare: Averting an Electronic Waterloo.* Washington, DC: Center for Strategic and International Studies, 1998.

McAfee, Inc. *Virtual Criminology Report 2009—Virtually Here: The Age of Cyber Warfare.* January 2010. http://resources.mcafee.com/content/NA CriminologyReport2009.

Thornton, Rod. *Asymmetric Warfare: Threat and Response in the Twenty-first Century.* Cambridge, UK: Polity Press, 2007.

Verton, Dan. *Black Ice: The Invisible Threat of Cyberterrorism.* New York: McGraw-Hill, 2003.

Yourdon, Edward. *Byte Wars: The Impact of September 11 on Information Technology.* Upper Saddle River, NJ: Prentice Hall, 2002.

DEATH SQUADS

Death squads are sometimes regarded as relics of the dictatorships that dominated much of the world in the twentieth century. But their role in carrying out killings for aims supported by the state or society is very much alive in a post–Cold War world comprising weak states, civil conflicts, and a flourishing private security sector. In every region of the world, death squads continue to be an effective form of terrorism used against targets ranging from common criminals to separatist rebels.

The criteria used to categorize armed non-state groups include their origins, composition, organization, affiliation, tactics, objectives, and adversaries. Among these characteristics, three distinguish death squads: tactics, structure, and affiliation. Most centrally, all death squads share a focus on killing targeted opponents or, less frequently, random citizens. In most cases, they have structures based on a small unit size and operational flexibility. The rationale for such tactics and structures is connected to the third distinguishing characteristic, affiliation. Minimizing size and maximizing flexibility allow their identity to be obscured, heightening the political impact of killings by magnifying their lack of predictability and obscuring links to known individuals. In fact, as Julie Mazzei points out in her book *Death Squads or Self-Defense Forces?*, the term *death squad* is adopted by a group "to insinuate virtuosity and legitimacy, and by opponents to indicate malevolence and illegitimacy."

Death squads' diversity also explains their continuing utility. With a diversity of aims, for example, many conflicts are fueled by a large number of death squads. In India, dozens of Sikh-affiliated death squads all oppose the Indian government but have very different ideologies and political goals. In Kashmir, different death squads are supported by Pakistan and other Islamic governments, with some aiming to join Pakistan and others to form an independent state.

Like other non-state armed groups, death squads are usually formed with a triad of political, economic, and security backing. Political actors provide ideological motivation and public cover, while economic actors and security officials provide material and meeting locations. By facilitating the movement of people and goods, globalization has enabled the kind of cross-border training and trafficking that sustains death squads. In particular, the huge international arms market allows many squads to acquire military-caliber weapons. Over 100,000 people were killed by military-affiliated death squads in Algeria in the 1990s, for example, many by illegally imported arms.

The most virulent death squads, though, still tend to emerge from the state's need to subcontract out killings during a period of civil war. In the 1990s, a powerful death squad known as the Tigers attacked non-Serbs throughout Bosnia, spreading widespread terror and death. Another set of genocidal death squads are Sudan's *Janjaweed* (loosely translated as "devils on horseback"), which have carried out mass killings in Darfur

153

with the support of a government whose public denials only thinly veil its support.

Even when a civil war ends, the death squads that perpetuated it often mutate into new manifestations geared toward emerging arenas of conflict. These new and more discreet forms fall into one of four major types. The first is death squads organized to kill socially marginalized people. Since 2000, the mayor of Davao in the Philippines has openly supported death squads that have summarily executed hundreds of people from among what he calls "society's garbage," including small-time drug dealers, young toughs, and street children. The city's squads are arranged into small cells and usually led by former or current police officers, who often compile lists of targets with city officials.

A second common type of contemporary death squad is organized by people or landlords to defend their communities or land in rural areas, where the state presence is thin and local powers are strong. In Guatemala, landowners formed private death squads to attack peasant union leaders and wayward employees. In Colombia, citizen groups have organized to protect their community against guerrillas and paramilitary groups.

A third type of death squad includes those involved in ongoing political disputes among sectors of the population. Throughout West Africa, for example, remnants of armed factions from civil wars carry out retribution against each other. In the Philippines in November 2009, over a hundred armed men, reportedly organized on behalf of the governor of Maguindanao province, massacred people who were perceived to be working on behalf of the governor's political opponents—in fact, the majority of the 58 victims of the Maguindanao massacre were either journalists or bystanders.

A fourth type of death squad comprises those connected to organized crime, often with deep infiltration of state agencies. Honduras, for example, has about 20 death squads with police members and organized crime connections. Some are made up of police and former military officers connected to Battalion 316, a military death squad of the 1980s, which now allegedly controls the Frontier Police, the Anti-Kidnapping Office, and the agencies that provide intelligence collection, analysis, and operational planning to anti-drug operations.

Just as most death squads typically transition from waging civil war to other kinds of conflict,

their tactical and organizational adaptability easily allows the reverse trajectory. In Indonesia, for example, death squads that terrorized the annexed nation of East Timor were connected to the Indonesian military and police and were likely modeled after anti-crime death squads. As Geoffrey Robinson describes in *"If You Leave Us Here, We Will Die": How Genocide Was Stopped in East Timor*, the Ninja gangs who harassed, kidnapped, and killed independence supporters in East Timor were linked to "the terrifying state-sponsored killing of at least 5,000 alleged petty criminals in the mid-1980s in Indonesia." While officials denied responsibility for those deaths, President Suharto later "boasted in his memoirs that the killing had been deliberate government policy—a form of 'shock therapy' to bring crime under control."

Mark Ungar

See also Ethnic Cleansing; Narcoterrorism; State Terrorism; State-Sponsored Terrorism

Further Readings

Campbell, Bruce B., and Arthur D. Brenner. *Death Squads in Global Perspective: Murder with Deniability.* New York: St. Martin's Press, 2000.

Mason, T. David, and Dale Krane. "The Political Economy of Death Squads: Toward a Theory of the Impact of State-sanctioned Terror." *International Studies Quarterly* 33, no. 2 (1989): 175–198.

Mazzei, Julie. *Death Squads or Self-defense Forces? How Paramilitary Groups Emerge and Challenge Democracy in Latin America.* Chapel Hill: University of North Carolina Press, 2009.

Robinson, Geoffrey. *"If You Leave Us Here, We Will Die": How Genocide Was Stopped in East Timor.* Princeton, NJ: Princeton University Press, 2009.

Sluka, Jeffrey A., ed. *Death Squad.* Philadelphia: University of Pennsylvania Press, 2000.

Tilly, Charles. *The Politics of Collective Violence.* Cambridge, UK: Cambridge University Press, 2003.

DECOMMISSIONING IN NORTHERN IRELAND

The decommissioning of illegal paramilitary weapons was an issue that threaded through the Northern

Ireland peace process, highlighting the potential political difficulties in dealing with the question of weaponry held by insurgent or terrorist groups. Decommissioning in this context refers to the verified disarmament or disposal of paramilitary weapons, and it became a substantive blockage at various points in an attenuated process of peacemaking.

Unionists in Northern Ireland were insistent in keeping the issue of the disarmament of paramilitary terrorist groups high up on the political agenda, because for them it constituted a key test of Irish Republican *bona fides* and peaceful intent following the cease-fire of 1994. At various stages the issue of decommissioning prevented all-party negotiations from taking place, and even after the Belfast Agreement (or Good Friday Agreement) of 1998, the decommissioning question served to undermine the functioning of the power-sharing institutions. In contrast, Irish Republicans felt that the question of decommissioning was an artificially inflated precondition that had been dropped into the developing peace process in order to prevent Republicans from engaging in political negotiations. In the early period of the peace process they felt that disarmament could be addressed only after a formalized political settlement. After the Belfast Agreement had put institutions in place, they argued that the issue should be left to the Independent International Commission on Decommissioning (IICD), rather than acting as a cause for the suspension of the workings of the agreement. In their perception, the insistence on a process of decommissioning often represented foot dragging and obstructionism by Unionists. But for Unionists, the reluctance of Republicans to even begin disarmament smacked of bad faith.

Throughout the decades-long conflict between Nationalists and Unionists in Northern Ireland, the British government had repeatedly stated that it would not talk to groups involved in, or supportive of, terrorism, although contact did in fact take place on a number of occasions. After the IRA called a cease-fire in August 1994, there was an expectation among Republicans that its political wing, Sinn Féin, would enter into negotiations. In the initial weeks of the cease-fire, British and Unionist skepticism over Republican good faith centered around a demand that Republicans clarify whether their cessation was permanent. The notion that Republicans should disarm in order to prove

their democratic credentials quickly became an assumed part of the process. For Republicans, this was a belated and purely arbitrary precondition, designed either to stymie the peace process or induce Republican surrender rather than accommodation. There is considerable documentary evidence that both the Irish government and the British government had flagged the issue of disarmament in the period 1993 to 1994, but the question of whether it was ever a precondition to negotiations is contested. By March 1995 the British government had laid down what became known as the "Washington three" test, which called for a willingness in principle to disarm, an understanding on the modalities of decommissioning, and the actual decommissioning of some weaponry as a first step toward building confidence. The result was political deadlock.

A degree of international intervention was sought, and George Mitchell, a former United States senator, was asked to chair a body reporting on arms decommissioning. The 1996 Mitchell Commission report featured a number of recommendations, including the forging of the Mitchell Principles of "democracy and nonviolence," a commitment with which negotiating parties could demonstrate their good will and peaceful intent. On arms decommissioning itself, it recommended a parallel approach, in which all-party negotiations would run alongside a process of decommissioning, but the British government appeared to downplay this aspect, instead committing itself to a process of forum elections, which would provide the basis for negotiations. Irish Republicans viewed this development as a further attempt to thwart their participation, and the IRA ended their cease-fire in February 1996.

This further deadlock was only broken in May 1997 when a new Labour government was installed after a UK general election. In July 1997 the IRA reinstated its cease-fire and, having signed up to the Mitchell Principles, Sinn Féin entered negotiations in September 1997. During these negotiations, much of the debate around decommissioning was effectively sidelined to a subcommittee. A wide-ranging peace accord, popularly known as the Good Friday Agreement, was signed in April 1998 and had the restoration of a power-sharing government in Northern Ireland at its core. The agreement also featured a section on decommissioning, which required the parties to work in good faith with the IICD, a body set up in 1997 to facilitate and monitor the process of disarmament.

But the issue of decommissioning continued to impede progress in securing the setting up of a power-sharing executive. Eventually, powers were devolved from Westminster to the Northern Ireland Executive in 1999, but a failure by Republicans to satisfy Unionists with regard to the progress of disarmament led to a series of suspensions. However, in October 2001 the IRA announced that it had begun to decommission its weapons, a process that was repeated in April 2002 and October 2003. In October 2005 the IICD announced that the IRA had completed the disarmament of all its weaponry.

Republican and Loyalist groups that had no political wings likely to be in government had largely escaped the decommissioning spotlight. But mounting government pressure, and the fact that legislation that forbade the forensic examination of decommissioned arms was fast running out, meant that the issue had to be faced. In June 2009 the Ulster Volunteer Force decommissioned its weaponry, closely followed by the Ulster Defense Association in January 2010. In February 2010 the IICD announced that three acts of decommissioning had been carried out by the dormant "Official" IRA, the Irish National Liberation Army, and a small Loyalist splinter group.

The decommissioning process in Northern Ireland revealed the difficulties that can emerge in a process of winding down illegal paramilitary activity. The long process of disarmament reflected not only problems in creating trust and choreographing move and countermove but also the symbolic importance of the weapons issue. For Republicans, the symbolic deadweight of undecommissioned weaponry could be used to reassure their base that they were remaining true to their Republican principles at a time of great political compromise; for Unionists supportive of the peace process, the ballast of decommissioned IRA guns could steady their project against charges of betrayal from within their own constituency. The reasons for the successful completion of decommissioning are several. British and Irish governmental pressure and Unionist persistence were important. So were external factors such as the September 11 attacks on the United States and Republican dalliances with the FARC paramilitary group in Colombia, which served to wear U.S. patience thin and harden international responses to those linked with terrorism.

Also of critical import was the electoral growth of Sinn Féin throughout the peace process, as well as its heightened political ambitions. The ballot box had eclipsed the bomb.

The process of decommissioning shows that in certain circumstances the issue of weaponry, particularly the disarmament of insurgent groups, can become a "wedge" issue in a peace process, representing more than issues of reciprocity or political choreography. Weaponry can acquire a symbolic value as political capital to counterbalance ideological compromise, and once it has worked its way up the hierarchy of issues, its value as a bargaining chip can also inflate, further prolonging the value of undecommissioned armament.

Kristian Brown

See also Irish National Liberation Army; Irish Republican Army; Law and Terrorism; Real Irish Republican Army; Ulster Defense Association; Ulster Volunteer Force

Further Readings

Brown, Kris, and Corinna Hauswedell. *Burying the Hatchet: The Decommissioning of Paramilitary Arms in Northern Ireland.* Bonn: Bonn International Center for Conversion, 2002.

MacGinty, Roger. "Biting the Bullet: Decommissioning in the Transition from War to Peace in Northern Ireland." *Irish Studies in International Affairs* 10 (1999): 237–247.

MacGinty, Roger. "Issue Hierarchies in Peace Processes: The Decommissioning of Paramilitary Arms and the Northern Ireland Peace Process. Lessons for Ending Civil Conflicts." *Civil Wars* 1, no. 3 (1998): 24–45.

O'Kane, Eamonn. "Decommissioning and the Peace Process: Where Did It Come From and Why Did It Stay So Long?" *Irish Political Studies* 22, no. 1 (2007): 81–101.

DEMOCRATIC FRONT FOR THE LIBERATION OF PALESTINE

In 1969, after a power struggle with his leader George Habash, Nayef Hawatmeh left the Popular Front for the Liberation of Palestine (PFLP). He and other left-wing PFLP members split to form the Democratic Front for the Liberation of Palestine

(DFLP), a marginal group that has nonetheless made multiple small attacks on Israeli targets.

The DFLP began as a Marxist-Leninist organization with the goal of creating an independent Palestinian state though a revolution of the masses. The group cultivated relationships with radical organizations and Communist parties in the Middle East. It committed its most notorious act of terror in 1974, when members attacked a school in Maalot, a town in northern Israel, and killed 20 teenagers. In 1983 the group kidnapped Sergeant Samir Assad, an Israeli soldier. Press reports later delighted in reporting that a female DFLP member had caught Assad in a "honey trap," courting him for several months until he visited her village and was taken hostage. Assad was later killed. Democratic Front members declared that he died during Israeli Air Force bombings at their base, but Israeli army pathologists reported that he had been murdered by his captors. Assad's corpse was returned to Israel eight years after he was kidnapped in return for the release of a DFLP activist. In 1991 the group split into two groups, creating a pro-Arafat faction and Hawatmeh's more radical faction.

The Democratic Front is a longtime critic of the peace process with Israel, but since Yasir Arafat signed the 1993 Oslo Accords, the group has positioned itself politically between Arafat's Fatah and more radical, rejectionist groups like Hamas and Palestine Islamic Jihad. Unlike fellow Palestinian guerrilla movements, including the PFLP, Ahmad Jibril's Popular Front for the Liberation of Palestine–General Command, and Abu Abbas's Palestine Liberation Front, the Democratic Front was not listed as an active foreign terrorist group by the U.S. State Department in its 2010 global terrorism report.

In August 2001, the group resurfaced in world headlines when members claimed responsibility for an attack on a Gaza base that killed three Israeli soldiers. Israeli officials, however, cast doubt on the claim and suggested that members of Arafat's Fatah organization were behind the raid. After the September 11, 2001, attacks on the World Trade Center in New York City and the Pentagon near Washington, D.C., an Abu Dhabi television station reported receiving a call from the Democratic Front claiming responsibility for the massacre. However, DFLP leaders denied any involvement and condemned the acts of terror. The United States later charged Osama bin Laden and his al Qaeda operatives with responsibly for the attacks.

In February 2002, five Democratic Front members were killed when their car exploded in the Gaza Strip. Palestinian security officials told the press that Israeli helicopters had fired missiles at the vehicle; Israeli officials did not comment on the Gaza explosion. The press reported that pieces of Kalashnikov rifles had been found with the men's bodies. The Democratic Front vowed retaliation for the deaths.

As relations between Fatah and Hamas have deteriorated, with Hamas taking over the Gaza Strip in 2006, the DFLP has attempted to broker peace between the two Palestinian groups, arguing that the division hurts Palestinians. At the same time, the Democratic Front has repeatedly attacked Israeli targets, including firing rockets at Israeli settlements and army posts.

Erica Pearson

See also Abbas, Muhammad "Abu"; Arafat, Yasir; Fatah; Habash, George; Hamas; Palestine Islamic Jihad; Palestine Liberation Front–Abu Abbas Faction; Palestine Liberation Organization; Popular Front for the Liberation of Palestine; Popular Front for the Liberation of Palestine–General Command

Further Readings

Drummond, James. "Almost Forgotten Name Returns to Limelight." *Financial Times* (London), August 27, 2001.

Hasso, Frances S. *Resistance, Repression, and Gender Politics in Occupied Palestine and Jordan.* Syracuse, NY: Syracuse University Press, 2005.

Mishal, Shaul. *The PLO under Arafat: Between Gun and Olive Branch.* New Haven, CT: Yale University Press, 1986.

Prusher, Ilene R. "Palestinian 'Third Way' Rises." *Christian Science Monitor*, December 13, 2005, p. 6.

Silver, Eric. "Israel Grants Amnesty to Wanted Fatah Figures." *The Independent*, July 16, 2007, p. 1.

DEMOCRATIC FRONT FOR THE LIBERATION OF RWANDA

The Democratic Front for the Liberation of Rwanda (FDLR), formerly the Army for the Liberation of Rwanda, is a guerrilla force that is leading an insurgency against the government of Rwanda, largely from bases in the neighboring Democratic Republic of the Congo.

The conflict between the FDLR and the government of Rwanda is related to deep divisions between the two ethnic groups of Rwandan society, the minority Tutsi and the majority Hutu. In the early 1990s, a Tutsi-led rebel army began attacking Rwanda from neighboring Uganda, and by early 1994 the rebel forces had taken large parts of the countryside and were approaching the capital. The Hutu-controlled government then initiated a massive genocide against Rwandan Tutsis and any Hutus believed to be collaborating with them. An estimated 500,000 people were killed. By late summer, however, the Tutsi rebels had conquered the government forces and stopped the genocide. Tens of thousands of Hutus fled into the neighboring Congo, including much of the Rwandan Armed Forces (FAR) and the civilian militias, known as the Interahamwe, that FAR had recruited to carry out the genocide.

The Rwandan government's desire to eliminate the remaining FAR and Interahamwe precipitated a complex chain of events that included the 1997 overthrow of the Congolese dictator Joseph Mobutu and the installation of the guerrilla leader Laurent Kabila in his place; the July 2001 assassination of Kabila and his replacement by his son, Joseph; and a massive war in Congo from 1998 to 2003 that involved nine African nations and killed approximately 5 million people. (Rwanda and Uganda opposed the Kabila regime and its allies in this war.) Initially, the Hutus in Congo fought against the Rwandan forces and were supported by the Kabila regime. Under the leadership of Joseph Kabila, the provisions of a peace accord signed in 1999 have begun to be enforced, and the Congolese government stopped actively supporting the Hutu rebels.

The Army for the Liberation of Rwanda (ALIR), the precursor to the FDLR, was formed in the late 1990s, apparently in an attempt to coordinate Hutu groups' efforts at defense. The ALIR leadership was mostly composed of former FAR officers, but its membership as a whole included many fighters who were not implicated in the original genocide—a large proportion were children in 1994—but who became involved in the conflict after becoming refugees. Papers seized at ALIR encampments suggest that a Christian evangelical movement may be associated with the group, but the scant evidence available precludes speculation on the ALIR's religious character.

The ALIR set up jungle training camps run by former FAR and Interahamwe members to train its new recruits. The organization issued a threat against U.S. interests in Rwanda in 1996, and three years later ALIR members slaughtered eight English-speaking foreign tourists visiting mountain gorillas in Uganda in an effort to reduce U.S. and British support for Rwanda's government.

In 2001 the ALIR merged with another Hutu group based in the Congo to form the FDLR, which largely operates in eastern Congo. Although Joseph Kabila was able to negotiate a peace with Congo's neighbors in 2003, the continued presence of the FDLR in Congo has led to repeated outbreaks of violence.

In 2008, fighting broke out in Congo between the Hutu-dominated FDLR and a Tutsi-dominated militia that was backed by the government of Rwanda. In December of that year, Congo and Rwanda struck a deal: Rwanda arrested Laurent Nkunda, the leader of the Tutsi militia, and Congolese and Rwandan forces began a joint offensive against the FDLR the following January. Whether the offensive will succeed or not is an open question; in the past, the leaders of the FDLR have found it easy to evade capture.

Colleen Sullivan

See also State-Sponsored Terrorism

Further Readings

"An Arresting and Hopeful Surprise: Congo and Rwanda." *The Economist,* January 31, 2009, p. 51.

Human Rights Watch. *Rwanda: Observing the Rules of War?* New York: Human Rights Watch, 2001. http://www.hrw.org/node/78533.

Moore, Jina. "Hutu Rebels Drop Guns, Return to Rwanda." *Christian Science Monitor,* February 20, 2009, p. 6.

Prunier, Gérard. *Africa's World War: Congo, the Rwandan Genocide, and the Making of a Continental Catastrophe.* New York: Oxford University Press, 2009.

Sanders, Edmund. "Rwanda Troops Enter Congo to Fight Rebels." *Los Angeles Times,* January 21, 2009, p. A7.

Turner, Thomas. *Congo Wars: Conflict, Myth and Reality.* London: Zed Books, 2007.

U.S. State Department. "Terrorist Organizations." *Country Reports on Terrorism 2006.* http://www.state.gov/s/ct/rls/crt/2006/82738.htm.

Vesperini, Helen. "Interahamwe: A Spent Force?" *BBC News*, July 25, 2001. http://news.bbc.co.uk/hi/english/world/africa/newsid_1456000/1456900.stm.

DEPARTMENT OF JUSTICE, U.S.

The United States Department of Justice (DOJ) is the country's primary law enforcement agency and a vital component of the U.S. counterterrorism system. As a counterterrorism tool, the criminal justice system has proven incredibly effective in both incapacitating terrorists and gathering valuable intelligence from and about terrorists. Through the office of the attorney general, the DOJ is responsible for bringing terrorists to trial.

In 1968, President Lyndon Johnson signed Executive Order 11396, which directed and authorized the U.S. attorney general to coordinate the law enforcement and crime prevention activities of all federal agencies. Thus, the DOJ is significantly involved in the domestic surveillance, arrest, detention, and trial of suspected terrorists. The prosecution of homegrown terrorists who have committed acts within the United States has, for the most part, been successful. Prosecution for attacks on U.S. targets outside of the United States or that are carried out by noncitizens who then flee the country is much more of a challenge. Suspects must be identified, located, and apprehended, often with foreign assistance. However, foreign governments that oppose the death penalty may refuse to hand a suspect over to U.S. authorities in capital cases.

Prosecuting Terrorists

Efforts to prosecute terrorists have several goals. A conviction means the terrorist remains imprisoned and is thus unable to commit further attacks. It can also have a deterrent effect, for the threat of imprisonment may keep others from committing terrorist acts. Indictments, meanwhile, alert terrorists that they are wanted, which may encourage them to go into hiding and curtail future terrorist

activities. The general publicity surrounding a trial can also stir public support for counterterrorism initiatives and influence other governments to follow suit.

In many cases, however, these supposed deterrents and checks on action do not work. For the suicide bombers of the most recent era of terrorism, issues of conviction and deterrence are irrelevant. Purported terrorists may actually seek prosecution and capital punishment as a path to martyrdom. When Zacarias Moussaoui, the alleged "19th hijacker" from the 9/11 attacks, was tried in 2002, he asked to plead guilty so he could receive a death sentence. In many cases, the prosecutions of the "underlings" who commit terrorist acts leave the masterminds, like Osama bin Laden, at large for years. One of the primary difficulties in bringing terrorists to justice, however, lies in the tensions between law enforcement and national security. The Federal Bureau of Investigation (FBI), under the auspices of the DOJ, is expected to conduct investigations and make arrests that will hold up under appeal. This means minimizing the possibility of terrorists going free because of poorly executed procedures, such as an illegal search and seizure or a failure to read a suspect his or her Miranda rights. Meanwhile, intelligence agencies, such as the CIA are unlikely to offer evidence that might jeopardize sources or intelligence strategies, because whatever is uncovered in a trial becomes a matter of public record. Once arrests are made, however, prosecution becomes the highest priority for the DOJ.

Prior to the 9/11 attacks, the United States successfully tried terrorists and their accomplices using the civilian judicial system. Timothy McVeigh was convicted in U.S. federal court for the 1995 Oklahoma City bombings, and he was put to death in 2001. Eric Robert Rudolph, who detonated bombs at the 1996 Olympic Games in Atlanta and at two abortion clinics, was convicted of murder and is serving two life sentences at the "supermax" federal prison in Colorado. The foiled "shoe bomber," Richard Reid, is confined to the same facility.

The U.S. criminal justice system provides powerful incentives for suspects to provide accurate, reliable information, and conventional court trials have brought to light significant information about the inner workings of terrorist organizations. The trial of Ahmed Ressam, who was found guilty of the Y2K plot to bomb Los Angeles International Airport on New Year's Eve 1999, gave an inside view of Osama bin Laden's terrorist training camps in Afghanistan, as did John Walker Lindh, the "American Taliban." Similarly, the trial and conviction of the terrorists who bombed the U.S. embassies in Kenya and Tanzania made the al Qaeda terrorist training manual public. The information brought out at these trials has provided substantial data about bin Laden and al Qaeda and helped U.S. law enforcement agencies to detect and disrupt planned attacks and seize the organizers. DOJ and the FBI work with other intelligence agencies to make the best use of intelligence obtained from detainees.

Military Tribunals

In the wake of the September 11, 2001, attacks, President George W. Bush declared a "war on terror." Terror suspects captured abroad were classified as enemy combatants and transported to the U.S. naval facility at Guantánamo Bay, Cuba. Bush called for prosecutions to be held in secret military tribunals rather than the civilian legal system, because military law has lower standards for evidence and does not abide by "beyond a reasonable doubt" provisions. Intelligence agencies, such as the CIA, are also more likely to offer evidence in such a trial, which has less risk of jeopardizing sources or intelligence strategies. But holding suspects in military custody leaves the door open to charges of the mistreatment of prisoners or a miscarriage of justice. One particularly controversial practice has been that of extraordinary rendition, or transporting terror suspects to be interrogated in secret facilities in countries that allow torture.

Both U.S. and international human rights groups have condemned the use of rendition, and the Bush administration was accused of voiding the constitutional rights of suspects in the name of national security. Until a June 2008 court ruling, the U.S. government could hold terror suspects without charges indefinitely. Further, without formal charges or access to U.S. courts, they could not petition for their release. As cases neared trial, defendants were often unable to see the evidence against them, because the government argued that doing so would reveal information pertaining to national security.

John Ashcroft, who served as U.S. attorney general from 2001 to 2005, embraced the Bush strategy, saying that the DOJ "must shift its primary focus from investigating and prosecuting past crimes to identifying threats of future terrorist attacks, preventing them from happening and punishing would-be perpetrators for their plans of terror." Within weeks, Ashcroft launched a law enforcement campaign targeting potential suspects that was modeled after former attorney general Robert Kennedy's tactic in defeating organized crime in the 1960s. This campaign led to more than 1,200 secret arrests and detentions of noncitizens, often on minor immigration violations. By December 2001, the DOJ had levied criminal charges against 110 individuals (60 of whom were in federal custody at the time). Likewise, the Immigration and Naturalization Service detained over 550 people. Critics denounced Ashcroft's program as a throwback to J. Edgar Hoover's campaign against domestic terrorism and subversion in the 1950s and 1960s, when Hoover served as director of the FBI.

A Change in Strategy

Within the first days of his administration in 2009, President Barack Obama ordered the secret CIA prisons closed, declared that Guantánamo would close by early 2010, and suspended the secret military commission trial system. Obama's attorney general, Eric Holder Jr., insisted that future terrorist prosecutions should take place in civilian courts, and that suspects should be accorded all of the protections guaranteed by the U.S. Constitution. Most controversially, he announced that the trial of Khalid Shaikh Mohammed, often considered the mastermind of the 9/11 attacks, would be held in a civilian court in New York City. Many survivors of the attacks strongly criticized the decision, and the city's mayor, Michael Bloomberg, flatly refused to shoulder the cost of providing security for the proceedings. Bloomberg also said he feared rioting if Mohammed was not convicted. Under Bush administration protocols, Mohammed had been subjected to waterboarding, a form of torture that simulates drowning, nearly 200 times. Any statement produced under such conditions could be thrown out of a civilian court, and foreign governments might reject convictions based on such evidence. Finding scant admissible evidence to prosecute many of the Guantánamo suspects in civilian courts, however, Obama backtracked and announced he would reform rather than suspend the commission process.

Throughout 2009 and 2010, the DOJ pursued civilian indictments against terrorism suspects, such as the 2009 Christmas Day bomber, Umar Farouk Abdulmutallab; the attempted Times Square bomber, Faisal Shahzad; and Farooque Ahmed, who planned to detonate bombs inside the Washington, D.C., metro system. By mid-2010, however, Holder conceded the occasional need to loosen the Miranda requirements for terror suspects. "We're now dealing with international terrorists," he said, "and I think that we have to think about perhaps modifying the rules that interrogators have and somehow coming up with something that is flexible and is more consistent with the threat that we now face."

Despite the Bush administration's stated preference for military-style justice and the Obama Administration's condemnation of that practice, the most successful terrorist prosecutions since 9/11 have all taken place in civilian courts, using civilian offenses such as providing material support to terrorists or receiving training from foreign terrorist organizations. Most of these suspects agreed to provide information in return for a reduced sentence. As of December 2010, more than 300 international or domestic terrorists were incarcerated in U.S. federal prisons.

Ann E. Robertson

See also Central Intelligence Agency; Criminal Prosecution of Terrorists; Federal Bureau of Investigation; Guantánamo Bay; Mohammed, Khalid Shaikh; Moussaoui, Zacarias; Patriot Act; Reid, Richard; Rendition, Extraordinary; Ressam, Ahmed

Further Readings

Ashcroft, John. *Never Again: Securing America and Restoring Justice.* New York: Center Street, 2006.
Mayer, Jane. "The Trial: Eric Holder and the Battle over Khalid Sheikh Mohammed." *New Yorker,* February 15, 2010, pp. 52–63.
U.S. Department of Justice. "The Criminal Justice System as a Counterterrorism Tool: A Fact Sheet." Washington, DC: U.S. Department of Justice, January 26, 2010. http://blogs.usdoj.gov/blog/archives/541.
Zabel, Richard B. *In Pursuit of Justice: Prosecuting Terrorism Cases in the Federal Courts.* New York: Human Rights First, 2008.

Dev Sol

See Revolutionary People's Liberation Party/Front

Dohrn, Bernardine (1942–)

A former member of the violent revolutionary organization Weatherman, Bernardine Dohrn led the "Days of Rage" riots in Chicago and was once a notorious fugitive on the FBI's Most Wanted list.

While in law school at the University of Chicago, Dohrn had the opportunity to work with Martin Luther King Jr. in efforts at alleviating poverty in Chicago. She also worked closely with the Student Nonviolent Coordinating Committee (SNCC), a civil rights group. Her activism led her to become involved with an organization called Students for a Democratic Society (SDS), an activist group originally focused on promoting civil rights and ending the Vietnam War that became increasingly radical as the 1960s progressed.

After law school, Dohrn traveled around the United States to recruit members for SDS. One of the organization's largest protests occurred at Columbia University in 1968. Students had discovered that the university was secretly doing war research for the government, and they staged a riot in protest. The police were called in to remove the protestors, forcibly when necessary. Following this event, Dohrn was elected the interorganizational secretary for the SDS. Although she was now a national officer, Dohrn didn't feel as if she was taking enough risks to further the movement.

Dohrn became one of the more militant members of the SDS. At the group's national convention in 1969, these members banded together and broke off from the SDS to form the militant faction known as Weatherman, later also known as the Weather Underground. Their first and best-known action was the rioting known as the "Days of

Rage" in the streets of Chicago. Led by Dohrn, and beginning on October 8, 1969, members of Weatherman looted downtown Chicago and engaged in a struggle with the local police force for four days.

In 1970, a bomb the group was manufacturing in a Greenwich Village townhouse exploded and killed three group members: Diana Oughton, Ted Gold, and Terry Robbins. With the FBI hot on their heels, the remaining members of Weatherman went underground and disappeared. Several members, including Dohrn, were on the FBI's Most Wanted list.

Dohrn married fellow member Bill Ayers, continued her work for the group underground, and remained one step ahead of the law for 11 years. On December 3, 1980, after having her second child and tired of hiding, she turned herself in to the authorities in Chicago. Her charges were reduced to misdemeanors and she was put on probation for three years. In the late 1990s Dohrn became the director of the Children and Family Justice Center at the Northwestern University School of Law.

Harvey Kushner

See also Boudin, Katherine; May 19 Communist Organization; Weatherman

Further Readings

Ayers, Bill. *Fugitive Days: A Memoir.* Boston: Beacon Press, 2001.

Heath, Louis G., ed. *Vandals in the Bomb Factory: The History and Literature of the Students for a Democratic Society.* Metuchen, NJ: Scarecrow Press, 1976.

Jacobs, Harold. *Weatherman.* Berkeley, CA: Ramparts Press, 1971.

Jacobs, Ron. *The Way the Wind Blew: A History of the Weather Underground.* London and New York: Verso, 1997.

Northwestern Law. "Bernardine Dohrn." http://www.law.northwestern.edu/faculty/profiles/BernardineDohrn.

Varon, Jeremy. *Bringing the War Home: The Weather Underground, the Red Army Faction, and Revolutionary Violence in the Sixties and Seventies.* Berkeley: University of California Press, 2004.

Wilkerson, Cathy. *Flying Close to the Sun: My Life and Times as a Weatherman.* New York: Seven Stories Press, 2007.

DOZIER, JAMES LEE (1931–)

General James Lee Dozier of the U.S. Army was kidnapped by the Italian Red Brigades in 1981; his eventual rescue helped bring about the downfall of the Brigade.

Dozier was born in Arcadia, Florida, in 1931, and he joined the Florida Air National Guard in 1951. His superiors recognized his potential and recommended him for West Point. Graduating in 1956, he went on to serve with the 11th Armored Cavalry Division in Vietnam, wining a Silver Star. By 1981, he had risen to the rank of brigadier general and was the NATO commander for southern Europe, based in Verona, Italy.

The Red Brigades had been active in Italy since 1970 and was known internationally for its 1978 kidnapping and murder of the Italian statesman and former premier Aldo Moro. In early 1981, U.S. army intelligence had learned that the Brigade might be planning a similar attack against a U.S. general in Italy. General George McFadden was thought to be the most likely target because the base he commanded in southern Italy housed nuclear weapons. The threat to Dozier, whose NATO position involved more tactful diplomacy than tactical deployments, was deemed slight. As a result, Dozier did not alter his daily routines, nor was his personal security detail increased.

On December 17, 1981, four members of the Red Brigades, disguised as repairmen, gained entrance to the Dozier family apartment. After a struggle, during which Dozier was beaten unconscious, they bound Dozier and his wife and stowed the general in a trunk disguised as a refrigerator carton. Leaving Mrs. Dozier locked in a utility closet, they took General Dozier to an apartment in Padua, where he would remain for 42 days.

Physically, his treatment was humane; however, his captors employed sensory deprivation techniques to disorient him and interrogated him nightly. The interrogations were aimed not only at collecting sensitive security information about U.S. military operations in Italy but also at gaining admissions that Dozier himself and the United States in general had been guilty of war crimes during the Vietnam War. Dozier revealed no secrets and refused to change his opinions and statements to suit his captors. Dozier is convinced that his discipline and persistence helped his captors see him as fellow human being and were instrumental in preserving his life.

The Red Brigades had intended the kidnapping to be part of a larger campaign, code-named "Winter of Fire." Initially, therefore, it did not negotiate with the Italian government, hoping the search for the general would cause police forces to draw their personnel from other areas of operation. The Brigade was successful in this, but almost all the planned attacks were disasters, resulting in the arrest of many key individuals, some of whom became police informants.

Coordinating their manhunt with the army's intelligence-gathering operations, the Italian police slowly began to make progress. In mid-January, more than a month into Dozier's ordeal, intercepted radio transmissions and information provided by police informants led them to the Padua apartment. On the morning of January 28, 1982, Italian commandos raided the apartment, capturing six terrorists and rescuing the general. One of the captured terrorists, Antonio Savasta, became a police informant; his revelations led to more than 200 arrests, crippling the Red Brigades. Following his release, Dozier resumed his army career, retiring with the rank of major general.

Colleen Sullivan

See also Hostage Taking; Red Brigades

Further Readings

Collin, Richard Oliver, and Gordon L. Friedman. *Winter of Fire*. New York: Dutton, 1990.

Harclerode, Peter. *Secret Soldiers: Special Forces in the War against Terrorism*. London: Cassell, 2000.

Nelan, Bruce, Barry Kalb, and Russ Hoyle. "Welcome Home, Soldier." *Time*, February 15, 1982. http://www.time.com/time/magazine/article/0,9171,925272,00.html.

Roberts, Rosemary. "A Former Hostage Tells His Story." *Greensboro News-Record*, February 27, 2004, p. A15.

Smith, Michael. *Killer Elite: The Inside Story of America's Most Secret Special Operations Team*. New York: St. Martin's Press, 2006.

EARTH FIRST!

Earth First! is one of the best-known radical environmentalist groups in the United States. It became known for the tree-spiking and tree-sitting tactics used in its campaign to save old-growth forests in the Pacific Northwest.

In 1980, Dave Foreman, an environmental lobbyist for the Wilderness Society, became frustrated with the ineffectiveness of "reform environmentalism" after a failed attempt to save 80 million acres of undeveloped land in U.S. national parks. That April, he and several colleagues, including the activist Mike Roselle, set out for the Mexican desert and formed Earth First!, using Edward Abbey's 1975 novel *The Monkeywrench Gang* as an organizational and action blueprint. The novel tells of radical Southwestern environmentalists who burned billboards, sabotaged bulldozers, and planned to blow up dams.

Earth First! announced its presence on the environmental scene in 1981, when members stood atop the Glen Canyon Dam and unfurled a 300-foot black plastic banner down its face, giving the appearance of a deep crack, in an action dubbed the "Cracking of Glen Canyon Damn." Two years later, working to save an old-growth forest in the Siskiyou National Forest in Oregon, Earth First! members set up a log roadblock to stop construction trucks. When that failed, Foreman acted as a human blockade and was dragged over 100 yards by a trucker. Meanwhile, Roselle began to organize. Soon, small, regional Earth First! chapters

sprang up all over the western United States. Like other, earlier environmental groups, Earth First! had no central authority. The chapters were connected only through the *Earth First! Journal,* published in Eugene, Oregon.

Throughout the early 1980s, Earth First! engaged in protests, propaganda, and traditional civil disobedience, using the logo of a clenched first and the slogan "no compromise in defense of Mother Earth!" Adept and media-savvy, Earth First!ers crafted pithy news bites and performed various stunts to keep its name in the news.

By 1984, members began pounding spikes into trees slated for logging; this dangerous tactic, known as "tree-spiking," was intended to damage saws and sawmill equipment. In 1987, when George Anderson, a 23-year-old mill worker, was seriously injured by an 11-inch spike, some members chose to give up this technique in favor of other "monkey wrenching" tactics described in Foreman's 1985 book *Ecodefense: A Field Guide to Monekeywrenching.*

Foreman's how-to manual included instructions for "decommissioning" bulldozers, grounding helicopters, and bringing down billboards. It also advocated pulling up survey stakes, blocking bulldozers, and tree sitting as effective ways of protecting forests and wilderness from human invasion. The ultimate goal of these tactics was to target weak links in the logging industry and make logging difficult and unprofitable.

Early on, Earth First! had adopted "deep ecology" as its governing philosophy, meaning that members conceived of environmentalism in terms of entire ecosystems. As Earth First! grew, it became infused with countercultural politics and various spiritual ideas, such as paganism. Soon, the organization was rent by factionalism. In 1987 Foreman moved away from Earth First! to form the Evan Mecham Eco-Terrorist International Conspiracy (EMETIC), which was subsequently infiltrated by the FBI. Before his arrest for conspiracy to sabotage nuclear power stations (Foreman pled guilty in 1991), Foreman told Earth First! cofounder Roselle that he was "working on something more radical."

By the 1990s, other members of Earth First! were leaving as well. In 1992, British members formed the Earth Liberation Front (ELF), believing Earth First! had become too timid and was too invested in becoming mainstream. However, while ELF and similar groups conducted underground "ecotage," Earth First! used its more moderate position to become the most recognizable group in the radical environmental movement. The group remains active, with chapters throughout North America, Great Britain, and Australia.

Laura Lambert

See also Animal Rights Movement; Earth Liberation Front; Ecoterrorism; Evan Mecham Eco-Terrorist International Conspiracy

Further Readings

Beach, Patrick. *A Good Forest for Dying: The Tragic Death of a Young Man on the Front Lines of the Environmental Wars*. New York: Doubleday, 2003.

Foreman, Dave. *Confessions of an Eco-warrior*. New York: Harmony Books, 1991.

Liddick, Donald R. *Eco-Terrorism: Radical Environmental and Animal Liberation Movements*. Westport, CT: Praeger, 2006.

Scarce, Rik. *Eco-warriors: Understanding the Radical Environmental Movement*. 2nd ed. Walnut Creek, CA: Left Coast Press, 2006.

Zakin, Susan. *Coyotes and Town Dogs: Earth First! and the Environmental Movement*. New York: Viking Penguin, 1993.

EARTH LIBERATION FRONT

In 1998, the Earth Liberation Front (ELF), an extremist environmentalist group, perpetrated one of the costliest and most sophisticated acts of "ecotage" (economic sabotage in the name of the environment) in U.S. history, thereby becoming a primary focus of the FBI.

ELF was formed in Brighton, England, in 1992, when a few members of EarthFirst! became frustrated with that group's unwillingness to break the law to achieve its goals. Modeled after Britain's Animal Liberation Front (ALF), ELF is composed of autonomous, anonymous cells that engage in direct actions to cause economic hardship to businesses and institutions that they believe are destroying the environment. Like members of ALF, the members of ELF (who call themselves "elves") take precautions against harming animals and humans during their actions. To date, they have not physically harmed anyone. Nonetheless, they have caused over $100 million in property damage, and the group's increasing reliance on explosive or incendiary devices has made ELF a significant concern.

In November 1997, a communiqué announced the presence of ELF in North America, after an attack on the Bureau of Land Management wild horse corrals in Burns, Oregon, which ELF conducted in conjunction with ALF. Most of the group's early actions, however, were against logging activities, using "monkey-wrenching" techniques borrowed from Earth First!, such as disabling heavy machinery used by loggers. The aim was to make cutting down trees unprofitable for lumber companies and, in later actions targeting suburban sprawl, to make building luxury homes less lucrative for construction companies.

On October 18, 1998, in Vail, Colorado, ELF carried out its largest-ever action, setting fire to five buildings and four ski lifts at a resort, causing more than $12 million in damage. The act of arson was committed against Vail Resorts, a large development company planning to expand operations into 2,000 acres of Rocky Mountain wilderness. This area is the habitat of the North American lynx, a threatened species. Mainstream environmentalists had protested the expansion since 1993, but by 1998 clear-cutting had begun.

Craig Rosenbraugh, then the ELF spokesperson, later delivered an ELF statement that read, "This action is just a warning. We will be back if this greedy corporation continues to trespass into wild and unroaded areas." He later stated that the

Vail arson was not an act of terrorism but "an act of love."

A federal crackdown on all forms of ecoterrorism, beginning in the late 1990s, has affected ELF. In January 2001, Frank Ambrose, an ELF member, was arrested in Indiana for timber-spiking over 100 trees. In February, three New York teenagers associated with ELF pled guilty to setting a series of fires at home construction sites that encroached on farmland in Long Island.

Another crackdown in the mid-2000s resulted in the conviction of the members of an ELF cell responsible for both the Burns, Oregon, and Vail, Colorado, attacks, as well as several more in Western states from 1996 to 2001. The cell, which called itself The Family, was allegedly led by William C. Rodgers, who killed himself in prison in December 2005. The following year, the other members of The Family pled guilty and were given prison sentences of up to 13 years. In another case, an ELF member was sentenced to 22 years in 2009 for participating in an arson attack at Michigan State University 10 years before.

The lengthy sentences were the result of guidelines that allow for "terrorism enhancements"—tougher sentences for crimes such as arson if they were motivated by a desire to intimidate society and force political change. Such "terrorism enhancements" are controversial because they provide harsh punishments for crimes even when no one is hurt. In addition, they extend the length of time a person can be prosecuted for a crime after its commission, meaning that people who have been law-abiding adults have faced harsh sentences for ELF attacks they committed as teenagers.

Nonetheless, EFL attacks themselves have been strongly criticized by environmental groups as ineffective and even counterproductive. Not only did the Vail expansion ultimately go through, but other attacks, such as the 1996 Family arson attack on a ranger station in Oregon, occurred shortly after the U.S. Forest Service had agreed to environmentalists' demands that it cancel a controversial logging project. A 2001 arson attack by The Family against a University of Washington lab they wrongly believed was genetically engineering trees destroyed endangered plants being cultivated for reintroduction into the wild.

ELF has gone increasingly underground in response to the crackdowns, although because of its decentralized structure, it is unlikely the group can completely be eradicated. ELF spokesmen have resigned, and ELF members no longer typically release explanatory statements following attacks, since such statements have been used as evidence that the attacks were designed to coerce political change.

Laura Lambert

See also Animal Liberation Front; Earth First!; Ecoterrorism

Further Readings

Liddick, Donald R. *Eco-terrorism: Radical Environmental and Animal Liberation Movements.* Westport, CT: Praeger, 2006.

Martin, Jonathan, and Mike Carter. "Arson Group Retreats Even More into Shadows." *Seattle Times,* March 18, 2008, p. A1.

Pickering, Leslie James. *The Earth Liberation Front, 1997–2002.* Portland, OR: Arissa Medai Group, 2007.

Rasmussen, Matt. "Green Rage." *Orion Magazine,* January/February 2007. http://www.orionmagazine .org/index.php/articles/article/6.

Scarce, Rik. *Eco-warriors: Understanding the Radical Environmental Movement.* 2nd ed. Walnut Creek, CA: Left Coast Press, 2006.

EAST AFRICA EMBASSY BOMBINGS

The synchronized attacks on American embassies in Kenya and Tanzania in 1998 killed 224 people, including 12 Americans stationed at the Kenya embassy, and wounded more than 4,500 innocent bystanders. The six-and-a-half-month trial that resulted from the investigation's first arrests marked the first time the United States prosecuted terrorists for crimes committed off American soil. Prior to the September 11, 2001, attacks, the embassy bombings trial revealed the fullest picture in a public forum of al Qaeda, the militant Muslim organization founded by Saudi exile Osama bin Laden, and its global conspiracy to kill Americans and destroy U.S. property.

The Attacks

The coordinated embassy bombings targeted the most visible symbols of the American presence in the capital cities of Nairobi, Kenya and Dar es

Salaam, Tanzania. On August 7, 1998, at around 10:30 A.M., a covered pickup truck loaded with TNT and aluminum nitrate exploded near the rear entrance of the U.S. embassy in downtown Nairobi, Kenya. It ripped off the back of the three-story embassy and caused tremendous structural damage to the building, which had been constructed in the 1970s to withstand an earthquake. The ruined embassy remained standing, but the seven-story office building next door, Ufundi House, collapsed into a pile of concrete rubble. One survivor would be buried in the wreckage for two days.

Around 10 minutes later, about 415 miles to the southeast, a refrigeration truck packed with TNT and oxygen and acetylene gas canisters detonated near the front gate of the U.S. embassy in Dar es Salaam. The explosion killed five security guards and six other Tanzanians working inside the charred building. Debris was thrown as far as 600 yards from the bomb crater.

Claims of responsibility for the bombings, written in Arabic, arrived on the fax machines of news media outlets in Doha, Qatar; Dubai, United Arab Emirates; and Paris, France. They stated that the bombings were intended to force the "evacuation of all American forces, including civilians, from the land of the Muslims in general, and the Arabian Peninsula in particular." Investigators would later learn that the Islamic extremists behind the blasts deliberately chose to strike in the morning when many observant Muslims would be en route to Friday prayers at a mosque, and therefore out of harm's way.

The embassy attacks came on the eighth anniversary of President George H.W. Bush's announcement of the deployment of American troops to defend Saudi Arabia, which was just five days after Iraqi president Saddam Hussein's army had invaded neighboring Kuwait in August 1990.

Within a week of the attacks, the FBI, working with Kenyan police, had arrested two suspected Nairobi embassy bombers, both with bin Laden connections. Only two months earlier, the U.S. Attorney for the Southern District of New York, Mary Jo White, had obtained a sealed terrorism conspiracy indictment against bin Laden, who had plainly declared war on the United States in a pair of fatwas, or religious decrees, that asked followers to target American military personnel and civilians.

The four men prosecuted in included the pair of Kenya embassy bombers quickly arrested in August 1998—Mohamed Rashed Daoud al Owhali, a Saudi, and Mohammed Saddiq Odeh, a Jordanian of Palestinian heritage—plus one Tanzania embassy bomber, Khalfan Khamis Mohamed, from Tanzania, arrested 10 months later in Cape Town, South Africa. When the bombings occurred, the last defendant, the Lebanese-born Wadih el Hage, was living in the United States, where he was a naturalized citizen. Hage had the longest association with bin Laden and had come under surveillance overseas. But nearly a year before the bombings, he had repeatedly lied before the New York grand jury investigating al Qaeda and protected the conspiracy.

All four defendants were shown to have ties to bin Laden. Owhali and K.K. Mohamed trained in his military camps inside Afghanistan in the 1990s, learning how to use guns and explosives, and absorbing bin Laden's brand of extreme Islamic ideology. Owhali fought alongside the Taliban and, in a personal audience with bin Laden, asked for a mission. K.K. Mohamed, however, had never met the leader or heard him speak.

Odeh, an admitted al Qaeda soldier, engaged in operations for al Qaeda as early as 1993 in Somalia, where bin Laden opposed the U.S. troop presence bolstering the United Nations mission to restore order to the civil war-torn nation. Odeh told the FBI that al Qaeda aspired to "kick out the United States by military force," because it considered the presence a "colonization" of the predominantly Muslim nation of 8 million. Odeh said he trained Somali tribes to defend themselves. The government charged that Somalis trained by al Qaeda helped shoot down U.S. Army Black Hawk helicopters and kill 18 American servicemen in an October 1993 battle in the capital city of Mogadishu.

Wadih el Hage was acquainted with bin Laden from a Peshawar, Pakistan, refugee hospital during the anti-Soviet jihad in Afghanistan, and he later served as bin Laden's personal aide when al Qaeda was based in Sudan in the early 1990s. Hage admitted conducting business transactions for bin Laden even after moving with his family to Kenya, where prosecutors said he became a facilitator of the East African cell and may have financed it with his own business ventures, such as trading in tanzanite and diamonds. Investigators wiretapped Hage's Kenya home, recoding dozens of phone calls among al Qaeda conspirators, including some received from a satellite phone owned by bin Laden. Hage left Kenya after investigators raided his home.

The Trial

The trial of the four suspects began with jury selection in January 2001. A multiracial jury of seven women and five men decided the case. The government called more than 90 witnesses and presented around 1,200 exhibits, including photos, documents, and bombing debris, in a two-month presentation. The defense case lasted only two weeks; none of the defendants testified.

One of the prosecution's burdens was to place the embassy bombings in the context of recent history and Islamic extremism. Prosecutors defined the alleged al Qaeda terror conspiracy as a decade-long plot that evolved out of Afghanistan's war with the former Soviet Union, whose military first occupied the country in 1979. Osama bin Laden and some of his followers had been among thousands of Arabs who had ventured to Afghanistan to purge the Muslim nation of Communist rule. These *mujahideen,* or holy warriors, were once considered "freedom fighters" in a Cold War battle supported by covert American aid, CIA trainers, and shipments of arms such as antiaircraft Stinger missiles. Additionally, bin Laden had donated resources from his family's multibillion dollar construction business to build roads and defensive tunnels and to finance refugee aid. After the Soviet withdrawal in 1989, the mujahideen stayed in touch through *Maktab al Khidamat,* or "the Services Office," based in the border city of Peshawar, Pakistan, and contemplated the next jihad. This was the genesis of al Qaeda.

"When the Russians decide to leave Afghanistan, bin Laden, he decided to make his own group," testified Jamal al Fadl, a former al Qaeda insider who became a top government informant and the trial's first witness. Fadl, a Sudanese man who became the third rank-and-file member to swear a *bayat,* or loyalty oath, to bin Laden, defected after embezzling money from al Qaeda. He showed up at the U.S. embassy in Eritrea in the summer of 1996, warning of Islamic militants who were training to attack.

"Maybe they try to do something inside the United States and they try to fight the United States Army outside, and also they try to make a bomb against some embassy outside," Fadl had explained, according to his testimony. Due to his paramilitary activities in Afghanistan, bin Laden was already on counterterrorism investigators' radar, and he made a government list of unindicted co-conspirators in a foiled plot to bomb New York City landmarks. That plot had been inspired by the blind Egyptian cleric Sheikh Omar Abdel Rahman, whose followers were among the bombers of the World Trade Center in 1993.

Fadl and another al Qaeda defector in the U.S. government's witness protection program, L'Houssaine Kherchtou, a Moroccan, offered an insider's account of the conspiracy behind the embassy bombings and the structure of al Qaeda. When the group was headquartered in Khartoum, Sudan, for five years starting in 1991, its business interests spanned road and bridge construction, trucking, currency exchange, a leather tannery, and exporting farm products like sesame seeds and peanuts. Prosecutors claimed these companies were fronts to provide income for the terrorist enterprise.

After returning to Afghanistan in 1996, bin Laden and his top associates communicated with the East African cell and other operatives worldwide with a laptop-sized satellite phone. The most frequent voice on the other end was an alleged founder of the East African cell, Khalid al Fawwaz, a Saudi dissident later based in London, who disseminated bin Laden's fatwas. British police arrested Fawwaz and two other alleged London cell operatives in 1998, and held them in custody for more than three years as they fought extradition to the United States and prosecution under the embassy bombings indictment.

British police also discovered what became known as "the terror manual," an 18-chapter, 180-page opus titled *Military Studies in the Jihad Against the Tyrants.* The manual, found in the Manchester home of Anas al Liby, a Libyan al Qaeda operative who had fled the UK, had instructions on writing in code, poisoning people, and blending into Western society. The manual, along with seized computer files, witness testimony, and post-arrest statements by Owhali, Odeh, and K.K. Mohamed, revealed the anatomy of al Qaeda terror cells. The organization would divide an attack into compartmentalized phases—surveillance, logistics and planning, preparation, and execution—with the group behind each phase not necessarily knowing any of the others.

Owhali told his FBI interrogator that al Qaeda chose the Kenya embassy because it was an easy target that housed a variety of U.S. government and military personnel and a female ambassador whose death would generate more attention. Owhali, who rode in the passenger seat of the Nairobi truck, was seen by an eyewitness throwing stun grenades at embassy security guards so the truck driver could get closer to the building. Owhali, expected to die in his mission, ran away from the building prior to the explosion. The driver blew himself up.

Odeh, trained in explosives, told his FBI interrogators that he felt the bombing had been a "blunder," because it had killed so many Kenyans—many in Ufundi House. Handwritten sketches bearing a striking resemblance to the embassy and roads leading to it were found by investigators in Odeh's home in the rural Kenyan coastal city of Witu. Prosecutors called him a "technical adviser" to the bombing. He stayed at a Nairobi hotel blocks from the embassy, along with other conspirators, in the days before the attacks. Clothing in the travel bag he was carrying at the time of his arrest in the Karachi airport bore traces of TNT.

K.K. Mohamed rented the Dar es Salaam house where the Tanzania embassy bomb was assembled and bought the jeep the bombers used as a utility vehicle. On the morning of the attacks, he helped the suicide driver get on his route, but he exited the passenger seat to go back and clean up the house.

After 12 days of deliberations, the jury found the four men guilty on all 302 counts brought against them, starting with having joined bin Laden's worldwide conspiracy to kill Americans. Though the U.S. sought the death penalty against the two trial defendants with the most direct roles in carrying out the embassy bombings—Owhali in Kenya and K.K. Mohamed in Tanzania—the jurors rejected a death sentence. Among their reasons, stated on the verdict form, were not wanting to make them martyrs, thus inspiring more terrorist acts, and viewing execution by lethal injection as causing less suffering than life behind bars.

The Others

Though three of the men—all but Hage—were convicted of mass murder, they were all arguably lower to midlevel players within al Qaeda in the late 1990s. Their convictions did nothing to dismantle the al Qaeda base inside Afghanistan, given safe harbor by the Taliban. Indeed, the indictment underlying their prosecution named 18 additional al Qaeda operatives, mostly fugitives at the time—including bin Laden; his top deputy, Ayman al Zawahiri; his military commander, Muhammad Atef; and the ground coordinators of the embassy bombings. Another named in the indictment, Fazul Abdullah Mohammed, is believed to be the head of al Qaeda's East African operations and to be responsible for a 2002 hotel bombing in Kenya.

When the four defendants were convicted, there were six other indicted men in U.S. or UK custody; one in particular stood out. Ali Abdelseoud Mohamed, a former Egyptian and U.S. army officer and a bin Laden associate who once provided military and surveillance training to recruits, pleaded guilty to terrorism conspiracy charges in October 2000. Mohamed told the court that he conducted surveillance of the U.S. embassy in Kenya as early as 1993. In testimony providing the first direct evidence against the terrorist leader, he noted, "bin Laden looked at the picture of the American embassy and pointed to where a truck could go as a suicide bomber."

Others named in the indictment were eventually captured or killed. Atef was killed by a U.S. drone attack outside Kabul, Afghanistan, in November 2001. Muhsin Musa Matwalli Atwah was killed by Pakistani forces on April 12, 2006. Fahid Mohammed Ally Msalam, also known as Usama al Kini, Sheikh Ahmed Salim Swedan were killed by a U.S. drone in Pakistan on January 1, 2009.

Another suspect, Ahmed Khalfan Ghailani, was captured by Pakistani forces in 2004 and turned over to U.S. custody. Ghailani was held in secret prisons run by the U.S. Central Intelligence Agency until 2006, when he was transferred to the U.S. detention facility in Guantánamo Bay, Cuba. In 2009 Ghailani was moved to New York City to face federal trial. U.S. prosecutors alleged that he bought the truck and transported the explosives used in the Tanzanian embassy bombing. He pled not guilty, telling a U.S. military tribunal in 2007 that he had not bought the truck and had thought that the boxes containing explosives held soap. (In 2010, a jury found Ghailani guilty on one count of conspiracy but not guilty of more than 200 counts of murder.) In January 2011 he was sentenced to life in prison on the conspiracy conviction.

The embassy bombings carried out by bin Laden's followers in 1998 forced the United States to reexamine embassy security abroad, just as the 1993 World Trade Center and 1995 Oklahoma City bombings forced the United States to fortify government buildings at home. But the bombings' expressed purpose remained unfulfilled long after the trial was over, for thousands of U.S. troops were still stationed on Saudi soil, and little that offended bin Laden about U.S. foreign policy, such as support for Israel or sanctions against Iraq, had changed. The embassy bombings trial in Lower Manhattan allowed the United States to claim its first courtroom victory against al Qaeda, but while the prosecution progressed throughout 2001, sleeper cells were inside the country planning and training for the suicide hijackings that would occur on September 11, again targeting the World Trade Center, just a few blocks from the courthouse.

Phil Hirschkorn

See also al Qaeda; Atef, Muhammad; Atwah, Muhsin Musa Matwalli; bin Laden, Osama; Fatwa; Ghailani, Ahmed Khalfan; Hage, Wadih el; Mohamed, Khalfan Khamis; Mohammed, Fazul Abdullah; Odeh, Mohammed Saddiq; Owhali, Mohamed Rashed al; Yousef, Ramzi Ahmed

Further Readings

Akhahenda, Elijah F. *When Blood and Tears United a Country: The Bombing of the American Embassy in Kenya.* Lanham, MD: University Press of America/ Rowman & Littlefield, 2002.

Atwan, Abdel Bari. *The Secret History of al Qaeda.* Berkeley: University of California Press, 2006.

Bergen, Peter. *Holy War, Inc.: Inside the Secret World of Osama bin Laden.* New York: Free Press, 2001.

Bergen, Peter. *The Osama bin Laden I Know: An Oral History of al Qaeda's Leader.* New York: Free Press, 2006.

Gunaratna, Rohan. *Inside al Qaeda: Global Network of Terror.* New York: Columbia University Press, 2002.

Meyer, Josh. "Top al Qaeda Suspect Caught in Pakistan." *Los Angeles Times,* July 30, 2004, p. A4.

Reeve, Simon. *The New Jackals: Ramzi Yousef, Osama bin Laden, and the Future of Terrorism.* Boston: Northeastern University Press, 1999.

Riedel, Bruce. *The Search for al Qaeda: Its Leadership, Ideology, and Future.* Washington, DC: Brookings Institution Press, 2008.

U.S. District Court for the Southern District of New York. *United States v. Osama bin Laden et al.* Indictment S(10) 98 Cr. 1023 (LBS).

Weiser, Benjamin. "Guantanamo Detainee Pleads Not Guilty in Manhattan Court." *The New York Times,* June 10, 2009, p. A25.

EAST TURKESTAN ISLAMIC MOVEMENT

The Turkestan Islamic Party (TIP) is a political separatist party of ethnic Uighurs based in Xinjiang, China. The TIP's militant wing, the East Turkestan Islamic Movement (ETIM), is reportedly associated with al Qaeda. The ETIM has been accused of numerous bombings in China and elsewhere.

Xinjiang is an autonomous region in China and is home to roughly 9 million Turkic-speaking Uighurs (or Uyghurs). Beijing's policy of settling Han Chinese in Xinjiang has been a source of tension, because Uighurs fear that they will soon be marginalized in their native territory. Politicized Uighurs claim that Han Chinese have moved into Xinjiang to exploit its oil, natural gas, and agricultural resources. Despite economic support that has turned Xinjiang into one of the most productive regions in the country, some Uighurs resent Beijing's assimilation and integration policies. Support for the separatist movement in Xinjiang among natives has grown significantly in the early twenty-first century.

In July 2009, ethnic clashes between local Uighur Muslims and Han Chinese settlers resulted in the deaths of nearly 200 people, with more than 1,700 injured. The riot was China's worst since 1949, and, indeed, ethnic and religious violence may be the biggest national challenge China faces in the near future. Wu Shimin, the vice minister of China's State Ethnic Affairs Commission, says the riot was perpetrated by the "three forces of evil": extremism, terrorism, and separatism. Meanwhile, TIP/ETIM has accused China of genocide.

While outside observers say that "genocide" is an extreme description of the situation in Xinjiang, it is true that the Chinese government restricts Islamic practices and bans practicing Muslims from most government jobs. Further, most Han employers in Xinjiang prefer not to employ Uighurs, who are perceived as untrustworthy, aggressive, and inclined toward crime. Although none of these stereotypes is fair, the perceptions themselves have worsened the gulf between the two ethnic groups. Propaganda by both nonviolent Uighur separatists and the violent ETIM has served to intensify the hatred. al Qaeda ideologues have argued that, after the defeat of the United States, the Muslims' next enemy should be China.

The ETIM was responsible for a series of bombings, both in Xinjiang and elsewhere in China, in the lead-up to the 2008 Beijing Olympics. The ETIM leadership, which is located in Waziristan, receives training, weapons, finance, and ideology from al Qaeda. Their attacks are not limited to China, however, as the ETIM has also struck in Pakistan and Afghanistan. ETIM suicide bombers trained by al Qaeda present a growing threat both to coalition forces in Afghanistan and to China's security. In addition to the ETIM, Uighur separatist groups in the United States, Canada, and Europe are working to radicalize the Uighur communities in China.

Despite its close relationship with al Qaeda, TIP/ETIM has thus far been careful not to attack the United States, largely because of the U.S. position on the Uighur detainees in Guantanamo Bay, Cuba. More than 20 Uighurs were captured by U.S. forces in Afghanistan during the first phase of the "war on terror" that began in 2001 and were sent to Guantanamo. After several years of detention, which reportedly included long episodes of solitary confinement and physical restraint, in 2008 the majority of the Uighurs were determined to no longer be "enemy combatants" and were eligible for release. Knowing that they would be executed in China, the United States found other countries to take the Uighurs, including Bermuda, Albania, and Palau. The Uighur separatists consider their lobbying campaign in Washington, D.C., where they have built multiple platforms, a success in this regard.

Nonetheless, TIP expressed displeasure in April 2009 after a TIP leader, Abdul Haq, was labeled a Specially Designated Terrorist (SDT) by the U.S. government. Although TIP/ETIM has not directly targeted U.S. interests until now, it is likely that TIP/ETIM will move in that direction in the future. After China, its tier-one target, the TIP/ETIM views Pakistan and the United States as its enemies.

The ethnic conflict in Xinjiang presents a greater challenge to the Chinese government even than Tibet. Bordering Afghanistan, Pakistan, India, Russia, Kazakhstan, and Kyrgyzstan, Xinjiang is important to China in both geopolitical and geostrategic terms. As terrorist threats are increasingly transnational, Beijing will have to take extra care to secure Xinjiang and build counterterrorism partnerships with its neighbors.

Episodic violence between the Uighur and Han communities seems likely to spread beyond Xinjiang. The Chinese hard-line approach toward Uighur separatists fails to distinguish between terrorists, supporters, and sympathizers. By the standards of most analysts, this policy stance has failed, and a long-term policy to manage and mitigate the emerging and existing drivers of separatism is needed.

Rohan Gunaratna

See also al Qaeda; Xinjiang

Further Readings

Amnesty International. *People's Republic of China: Gross Violations of Human Rights in the Xinjiang Uighur Autonomous Region.* April 1, 1999. http://www.amnesty.org/en/library/asset/ASA17/018/1999/en/6eb116ed-e285-11dd-abce-695d390cceae/asa170181999en.html.

Dwyer, Arienne M. *The Xinjiang Conflict: Uyghur Identity, Language Policy, and Political Discourse.* Washington, DC: East-West Center, 2005.

Ho, Stephanie. "China Blames Separatists for Deadly Xinjiang Riots." *VOA News* (Beijing), July 21, 2009.

Jacobs, Andrew. "Countering Riots, China Rounds Up Hundreds." *The New York Times,* July 20, 2009, p. A4.

Kaltman, Blaine. *Under the Heel of the Dragon.* Athens: Ohio University Press, 2007.

Leow, Jason, and Gordon Fairclough. "Clash at Factory Employing Uighurs Triggered Riot." *The Wall Street Journal,* July 8, 2009.

Millward, James A. *Violent Separatism in Xinjiang: A Critical Assessment*. Washington, DC: East-West Center, 2004.

ECONOMICS AND TERRORISM

Whenever major terrorist incidents happen, questions arise regarding the economic causes and consequences of these acts. The terrorist attacks of September 11, 2001, were no exception. No sooner had the dust had settled over Manhattan than studies about the human and economic costs of terrorism started to mushroom. A further immediate reaction was to trace the tragedy back to some easily understandable causes. One initial interpretation maintained that poverty constituted

Members of a combined special operations force secure a village gate during a counternarcotics operation in northern Zabul province, Afghanistan, April 10, 2010. Afghan National Army soldiers, assisted by U.S. Special Operations members, investigated the presence of drug facilities in the province. (U.S. Navy photo by Chief Mass Communication Specialist Jeremy L. Wood/Released)

one of the key triggers for the attacks. In 2002, George W. Bush, president of the United States, said, "we fight against poverty because hope is an answer to terror." That same year, Gloria Arroyo, Bush's counterpart in the Philippines, told BBC News that "terrorism and poverty are twins." But are poverty and inequality really root causes of terrorism, and how costly are terrorist attacks and counterterrorist measures?

The deterrence approach to terrorism, pioneered by the scholars Todd Sandler and Harvey E. Lapan, provides a unifying model for the analysis of these queries. It shows how terrorist organizations try to maximize the costs of their actions to the adversary in comparison to the price they have to pay for their actions. The unifying theoretical framework also allows the research community to understand how the counterterrorism policies of the target nation affect these cost-benefit calculations. This article briefly summarizes this underlying model of the analysis and discusses its main contributions to the understanding of the economic causes and consequences of terrorism.

The Costs and Benefits of Terrorism and Counterterrorism

Terrorism, especially in its transnational variant, is a complex global challenge. Both averted and realized terrorist acts are costly, sometimes exceedingly so. According to a 2004 estimate by Joshua Goldstein, the average U.S. household pays $500 per year to fight the "war on terror." The "terrorism bill" includes the costs of lives lost, of the military operations, and of the damage done to infrastructure, as well as the opportunity costs for the economic interactions that do not take place in the aftermath of a terrorist attack or because of the fear of a potential incident.

One helpful assumption for an understanding of terrorism is that both the attacker and the defender are goal oriented, and therefore are, in the economic sense, rational actors. While the terrorist organization tries to maximize the benefits attached to a particular incident in comparison to the costs of this act, the potential target attempts to increase the costs to the terrorists of an attack, hoping to induce terrorists to refrain from using force in the first place. This deterrence model has proven useful for the analysis of the actions of the perpetrators and their real or potential victims.

A key problem for deterrence is the wide range of modes of attacks from which the terrorists can choose. The pioneering article of W.M. Landes, who analyzed the impact of U.S. aircraft hijackings from 1961 to 1976 using intervention analysis, illustrates the problems that this *embarras de richesse* creates for the defender of terrorist attacks. Landes originally found that the installation of metal detectors in 1973 decreased the number of skyjackings. Subsequent empirical work, however, qualified this positive initial assessment of counter-terrorist measures. A series of articles, masterfully summarized in *The Political Economy of Terrorism* (2006) by Walter Enders and Todd Sandler, showed that terrorist organizations can quite often substitute one "instrument" of terror for a cheaper, and possibly more deadly, alternative. In this light, it is not surprising that al Qaeda switched from attacks using skyjacked airplanes as missiles to blowing up commuter trains in metropolitan areas, for the counterterrorism strategies that became effective after September 11, 2001, rendered it nearly impossible for terrorists to conduct a similar type of attack as that used on the World Trade Center and the Pentagon.

A further issue for anti-terrorist campaigns is that they are, in an economic sense, classic examples of the "free rider" problem: they constitute a public good from which each state or citizen can profit, and from whose consumption no nation or individual can be excluded. This creates a disincentive for particular individuals or nations to contribute their fair share. As is typical for joint efforts against a global or national challenge, attempts to fight terrorism are beset by so-called collective action dilemmas, which range from the underprovision of counterterrorism activities to the "free riding" of some states. This failure on the part of some states to do their share puts a larger burden on those actors that invest heavily in counterterrorism measures. The consequence of these collective action problems is that anti-terrorism activities are not as strong as they should be. Unsurprisingly, statesmen and diplomats of the nations that are highly active often condemn what they perceive to be the unfair behavior of other potential target states that do not, in the view of the activists, contribute sufficiently to the joint effort.

Terrorist organizations understand the collective action logic of counterterrorism, and they often select as a location for a terrorist act the country that is the "weakest link" in the counterterrorism alliance, and that accordingly invests relatively little in security measures. An illustrative example is that al Qaeda has chosen U.S. embassies in countries that offer relatively light protection of foreign installations and individuals in comparison to states with tougher anti-terrorism practices. Moreover, game-theoretic models suggest that in the case of global terrorism, proactive measures facilitate free rides on the efforts undertaken by the mainly targeted nation. One empirical implication of this tendency is that countries spend too little on proactive measures against transnational terrorism while spending too much on defensive measures.

Market reaction is one vivid way to assess whether counterterrorism measures are as effective as politicians make their electorates believe. An evaluation of the assassinations Israel conducted against suspected terrorists shows that the Israeli stock market declined subsequent to assassinations of senior *political* leaders, but it rose following assassinations of senior *military* leaders.

Another way of countering terrorism efficiently is by denying resources to terrorists, particularly by cutting their access to the money needed for carrying out deadly acts. Relatively little systematic research has been devoted to the issue of how terrorist organizations finance their activities, though this is not surprising in light of the difficulties in finding reliable data. The massive terrorist incidents of 2001 nevertheless sent a dire warning that fighting terrorists is not really possible without draining their human and financial resources. The majority of the studies investigating this issue have explored the resource base of Islamic terrorist groups, primarily al Qaeda. These studies estimate al Qaeda's financial flows, on average, to have been between 20 million and 50 million U.S. dollars per year from 1999 to 2006. Thus, financially, this most deadly of terrorist organizations is about the size of a midrange private-sector company. According to the scholar Friedrich Schneider, the illegal income of this transnationally active network stems from donations and, as is the case with many other terror organizations, from criminal activities such as drug trafficking. Denying terrorists the resources that they need for their operations would often be a far more effective strategy than investments in defensive measures such as harbor or airport protection. However, such alternative counterterrorism strategies would also involve policy measures, such as the legalization of drugs, that are hard to sell to the electorates of the targeted nations.

The deterrence model also explains the cycles in terrorist activities that several studies have unearthed. When the public is not alert for this danger and governments invest little in counterterrorism, the costs for attacks are small. As terrorists become more active, targeted nations protect themselves better, thereby increasing the costs to terrorists of conducting a campaign. This growing efficiency of the deterrence measures lowers the number of assaults and makes the public feel more secure. The cycle restarts when the incentives for the terrorists are sufficiently attractive to restart their "business" again.

Economic Causes of Terrorism

The study of the economic causes of terrorism has not led to any conclusive results, despite—or perhaps because of—the link that some politicians created between underdevelopment and terrorism following the attacks of September 11, 2001. Academically, the idea that poverty and inequality generate terrorism can be traced back at least to the social-scientific literature of the 1970s on deprivation and rebellion. According to this line of reasoning, the economic and political discrimination of powerful social or ethnic groups fuels unrest, political violence, and, by extension, terrorism. Another causal mechanism in support of this grievance argument hints at the opportunity costs of terrorism. Microeconomic research suggests that the more attractive the economic prospects of an individual are, the lower the risk that he or she will engage in terrorist activities or other forms of political violence. According to this adage, terrorist organizations should find more volunteers in poor countries and among the uneducated, as the underprivileged do not possess many attractive career opportunities. This opportunity-cost argument accordingly maintains that individuals for whom the opportunity costs for using violence are relatively low are more likely to join a rebel or terrorist organization.

However, several studies have shown that there is little direct connection between poverty, education, and participation in terrorism if the individual—whether as a real or potential recruit—is the unit of analysis. In 2003, Alan Krueger and Jitka Malečkova highlighted the fact that members of Hezbollah's militant wing, as well as suicide bombers from the West Bank and Gaza Strip, come predominantly from economically advantaged families and possess a relatively high level of education. These authors argue that it is the lack of political liberty, and not poverty or the lack of education, that causes terrorism.

Yet this counterargument against the received wisdom ignores the "market" that exists for activists in many deprived regions of the world. In such areas, many frustrated, disaffected, or just bored individuals volunteer to become terrorists. According to the formal argument developed by Ethan Bueno de Mesquita, this oversupply of potential attackers allows the terror organizations to carefully select the most able terrorists, who are often to be found among the better-educated militants. Other studies suggest that the content of the education the terrorists have received is relevant: according to this formulation, only indoctrination, and not education, is able to turn individuals into terrorists. Bueno de Mesquita also shows that educated volunteers are more likely to be politically motivated, and thus even more successful in committing terror acts. Against this backdrop, it does not come as a surprise that the young men selected by al Qaeda to carry out the 9/11 attacks had predominantly middle-class backgrounds. Similarly, the Marxist terrorist organizations that were active in Western Europe in the 1970s and 1980s, such as the Red Army Faction (West Germany) or the Red Brigades (Italy), hardly ever recruited volunteers from the working class they proclaimed to represent.

The question of whether economic underdevelopment is a root cause of terrorism also remains controversial in cross-country comparisons. According to the scholar James Piazza, state repression, and thus the reaction of the government to a potential rebellion, fosters terrorism. As poverty is a frequent cause of rebellion, underdevelopment could at least be indirectly linked to terrorism. Some studies, just show that the opposite might be true, to some extent. A 2004 study by S. Brock Blomberg, Gregory Hess, and Akila

Weerapana found that economic development attracts terrorist attacks, but that high income reduces the risk that a state will breed terrorism. But another wide-ranging study, "On the Origin of Domestic and International Terrorism," by Krisztina Kis-Katos, Helge Liebert, and Günther G. Schulze, argues that terrorism is more likely to originate from wealthier countries. Using a newly available data set on both domestic and transnational terrorism, the authors found evidence that terrorism increases with GDP (gross domestic product) per capita. This suggests that it is not political repression that creates terrorism. In fact, in comparison to highly autocratic regimes, states with a higher level of civil and political liberties are more prone to breed terrorism, in both its domestic and transnational variants. Future research has to show whether such discrepancies depend on the operationalization of terrorism, on the data set that is used, or on other research-design effects.

A related question is whether economic integration, often also reduced to the catchphrase "globalization," has an influence on the incidence of transnational terrorism. This question is closely connected to the poverty argument. Most social scientists agree that economic globalization in the form of increased trade and foreign investment promotes economic development. This should, in the light of the opportunity cost argument, decrease the number and intensity of terrorist incidents. In other words, the proponents of the globalization thesis believe that positive economic development removes at least one main incentive for engaging in terrorist activities, namely poverty. Studies assessing empirically the effects of economic globalization on transnational terrorist incidents find a statistical association between economic globalization and transnational terrorism. These studies show that because economic globalization promotes economic development, it can also lower the risk of the occurrence of transnational terrorism.

Although transnational terrorist incidents represent only a small percentage of overall terrorist activities, there are still very few comparative studies that explore the economic causes of domestic terrorism. The extant studies suggest that the latter form of violence is largely a development phenomenon. While armed groups rely on terrorism in rich and powerful states, they employ guerrilla tactics in economically less privileged and weaker states.

It is the extreme asymmetry of power between terrorist groups and the state that distinguishes guerrillas from terrorists. While terrorist groups are unable to control territory and lack the support of the population, guerrillas are able to control a part of the state's territory and can rely on the assistance of a considerable part of the population. Some studies, such as that by Ignacio Sánchez-Cuenca and Luis de la Calle, suggest this dichotomy could be employed to restrain civil war in developed countries. Other studies, by contrast, are more in line with the opportunity cost argument that economic growth reduces the likelihood of domestic terrorism. This raises the question of whether or not the redistribution of wealth lowers the risk of domestic terrorism. In 2010, Tim Krieger and Daniel Meierrieks showed that, at least for the case of western Europe, social welfare policies make terrorist activities less attractive. It remains to be seen whether such findings are robust across different regions and across different specifications of terrorism and social welfare spending.

Economic Consequences of Terrorist Attacks and Campaigns

Terrorism creates direct and indirect economic costs to a targeted nation. These economic repercussions can easily spill over to other countries. Most extant studies confirm that both domestic and transnational terrorist attacks are costly, but often not as grave as the panic reactions of investors following a major attack suggest. In 2007, Mikel Buesa and colleagues measured the direct economic costs of the terrorist attack on March 11, 2004, in Madrid. Direct costs arise immediately after a terrorist incident and include physical and infrastructural damages and economic losses that accrue as a result of the killing and harming of civilians, military personnel, and politicians. For example, Buesa's study estimated that the short-term economic costs of the Madrid bombings exceeded 211.58 million Euros; the direct costs were 0.16 percent of the GDP of the region around Madrid, and hardly 0.03 percent of the national GDP of Spain in that year. Other studies confirm that the direct economic costs of terrorist attacks are relatively small, short term, and transitory. In addition, markets can adapt over time to the fear that terrorist attacks create. In their 2004 article "Financial Markets and Terrorism," Rafi Eldor and Rafi Melnick analyzed of the impact of Palestinian terror attacks on stock market prices and exchange rates in Israel between 1990 and 2003. They found that these markets became desensitized to terror attacks over time and continued to function efficiently after terror incidents. There is also evidence that modern and diversified capital markets are more resilient and recover sooner than less competitive markets.

Even the overall macroeconomic effects of the attacks of September 11, 2001, were relatively small if one takes the United States of America as the frame of reference. The estimated costs of 48.7 billion U.S. dollars only represented about 0.5 percent of the U.S. GDP. Studies that focus on the short-term losses of terror attacks also underestimate the ability of a region to respond. There is quite often a "phoenix factor" in terrorism-affected areas, and the economy rebounds rather quickly after the initial shock. However, many of the negative effects of terrorism are indirect. They come, for instance, in the form of the costs of tightening security measures and insurance premiums that increase in the aftermath of a terrorist incident. It remains to be seen which terrorist attacks have a long-term crippling impact on an economy, and for which ones the negative aggregated effect was only transitory.

The effects of a terrorist campaign are much more severe and long-lasting than the impact of isolated incidents. In "The Economic Cost of Conflict: A Case Study of the Basque Country" (2003), Alberto Abadie and Javier Gardeazabal examine the GDP per capita reduction that the murderous activities of the Basque separatist organization Euskada Ta Askatasuna (Basque Fatherland and Liberty, or ETA) had on this Spanish region. They estimate that the terrorist organization provoked a GDP gap of 10 percent in comparison to an artificial region economically comparable to the Basque region. In Israel, a similar study estimated the consumption per capita gap that terrorist activities created in 2004 to be around 5 percent. Furthermore, the study estimated that the output per capita would have been around 10 percent higher for the year 2004 if Israel had not have suffered from a terrorist campaign in the previous years.

The singular experiences of Israel raise the question of whether these effects are able to be generalized across a broad set of nations affected by terrorism. In "The Macroeconomic Consequences of Terrorism," authors S. Brock Blomberg, Gregory Hess, and Athanasios Orphanides address this question in an evaluation of the macroeconomic consequences of transnational terrorism in comparison to internal conflict and external wars. They show that, on average, terrorism has a significant negative effect on economic growth. If a country suffered from transnational terrorist attacks in each year of the period examined, per capita income growth fell by 1.58 percent over the entire sample period. However, their results suggest that this effect was smaller and less incisive than that linked to internal conflicts and external wars. Concurrently, the negative effect of terrorism on economic growth is more pronounced in less developed countries. In a 2008 comparison of 18 states, Khusrav Gaibulloev and Todd Sandler found that transnational terrorism had a greater negative marginal influence on income per capita growth than domestic terrorism. Their results also showed that both transnational and domestic terrorist attacks reduce private investment but increase government spending.

Terrorism affects the different economic sectors unequally: some are directly targeted and others suffer from the aftermaths of terrorist incidents. For example, the tourism sector is often among the main economic victims of terrorism. In 1991, Walter Enders and Todd Sandler were the first to show the interrelation between transnational terrorism and tourism in Spain between 1970 and 1988; they demonstrated that transnational terrorism caused a considerable decline in the number of tourists who normally would have headed to Spain. Tourism can also be used to illustrate that terrorism, while in general being a costly collective challenge, can have redistributive effects. In a subsequent study, Sandler and his coauthors demonstrated that terrorist incidents in one country deterred tourism in neighboring countries. Other studies have found that tourists avoid high-risk countries and go instead to more secure countries.

Because terrorism affects the economy in neighboring countries, cross-border economic activities also suffer from attacks. Studies exploring the effects of transnational terrorism on international and bilateral trade indicate that the first transnational terrorist attack reduces bilateral trade about 10 percent and that a doubling of the number of terrorist attacks in a year is associated with a decrease in bilateral trade of about 4 percent. Similarly, in 1996, Enders and Sandler found for the cases of Greece and Spain that transnational terrorism reduced annual net foreign direct investment (FDI) flows in Spain by 13.5 percent and in Greece by 11.9 percent. Ten years later, however, Enders, Sachsida, and Sandler found different results when they examined the extent to which transnational terrorism altered U.S. foreign direct investment after September 11, 2001. The authors included many diversified economies in the study, which allowed resource substitution from threatened to nonthreatened sectors. Their results show that the attacks on September 11, 2001, had no long-lasting negative impact on U.S. investment flows. They found further that the attacks had a negative impact on investment in other member states of the Organisation for Economic Co-operation and Development (OECD), but that they had no effect in countries outside of the OECD. They ascribe this finding to the fact that U.S. FDI stocks in non-OECD countries are less important than those in OECD member states.

If these isolated pieces of evidence are put together, a clear image emerges. Terrorist organizations are quite often successful in their attempts to weaken the society and economy of the targeted state. This is especially the case if a network is able to unleash a terror campaign that lasts many years. However, some economic sectors are more vulnerable to terrorist attacks than others, and large diversified economies overcome terrorist attacks more easily and with only marginal losses.

Although attacks on the World Trade Center or similar symbols of global capitalism seem irrational at first, studies exploring the economics of terrorism help to reveal the logic of such assaults. Understanding the cost-benefit calculus of terror networks is mandatory not only for policymakers who try to design effective counterterrorism measures. The economic aspects of terrorism are ultimately of concern for every individual, as consumers and taxpayers have to pay the bill for deterrence efforts and the costs that terrorist attacks cause. Unfortunately, the current literature does not always offer ready-made solutions for dealing with the economic facets of terrorism. Nevertheless, it shows convincingly that building efficient deterrent mechanisms is the only way forward in the global fight against domestic and transnational terrorism.

Tahmina Sadat Hadjer and Gerald Schneider

See also Basque Fatherland and Liberty; Counterterrorism; Financing Terrorism; Madrid Bombings; September 11 Attacks

Further Readings

Abadie, Alberto, and Javier Gardeazabal. "The Economic Cost of Conflict: A Case Study of the Basque Country." *American Economic Review* 93 (2003): 113–132.

Blomberg, S. Brock, Gregory D. Hess, and Athanasios Orphanides. "The Macroeconomic Consequences of Terrorism." *Journal of Monetary Economics* 51 (2004): 1007–1032.

Blomberg, S. Brock, Gregory D. Hess, and Akila Weerapana. "Economic Conditions and Terrorism." *European Journal of Political Economy* 20 (2004): 463–478.

Bueno de Mesquita, Ethan. "The Quality of Terror." *American Journal of Political Science* 49 (July 2005): 515–530.

Buesa, Mikel, Aurelia Valino, Joost Heijs, Thomas Baumert, and Javier Gonzáles Gómez. "The Economic Cost of March 11: Measuring the Direct Economic Cost of the Terrorist Attack on March 11, 2004 in Madrid." *Terrorism and Political Violence* 19 (2007): 489–509.

Drakos, Konstantinos, and Ali M. Kutan. "Regional Effects of Terrorism on Tourism in Three Mediterranean Countries." *Journal of Conflict Resolution* 47 (2003): 621–641.

Eldor, Rafi, and Rafi Melnick. "Financial Markets and Terrorism." *European Journal of Political Economy* 20 (2004): 367–386.

Enders, Walter, Adolfo Sachsida, and Todd Sandler. "The Impact of Transnational Terrorism on U.S. Foreign Direct Investment." *Political Research Quarterly* 49 (December 2006): 517–531.

Enders, Walter, and Todd Sandler. "Causality between Transnational Terrorism and Tourism: The Case of Spain." *Studies in Conflict & Terrorism* 14 (1991): 49–58.

Enders, Walter, and Todd Sandler. *The Political Economy of Terrorism.* New York: Cambridge University Press, 2006.

Enders, Walter, and Todd Sandler. "Terrorism and Foreign Direct Investment in Spain and Greece." *KYKLOS* 49 (1996): 331–352.

Gaibulloev, Khusrav, and Todd Sandler. "Growth Consequences of Terrorism in Western Europe." *KYKLOS* 61 (2008): 411–424.

Goldstein, Joshua S. *The Real Price of War: How You Pay for the War on Terror.* New York: New York University Press, 2004.

Kis-Katos, Krisztina, Helge Liebert, and Günther G. Schulze. "On the Origin of Domestic and International Terrorism." 2010, unpublished.

Krieger, Tim, and Daniel Meierrieks. "Terrorism in the Worlds of Welfare Capitalism." *Journal of Conflict Resolution* 54, no. 6 (2010): 902–939.

Krueger, Alan B., and Jitka Malečkova. "Education, Poverty, and Terrorism: Is There a Causal Connection?" *The Journal of Economic Perspectives* 17 (Autumn 2003): 119–144.

Landes, W.M. "An Economic Study of U.S. Aircraft Hijackings, 1961–1976." *Journal of Law and Economics* 21 (1978): 1–31.

Piazza, James A. "Rooted in Poverty?: Terrorism, Poor Economic Development, and Social Cleavages." *Terrorism and Political Violence* 18 (2006): 159–177.

Sánchez-Cuenca, Ignacio, and Luis de la Calle. "Domestic Terrorism: The Hidden Side of Political Violence." *Annual Review of Political Science* 12 (2009): 31–49.

Sandler, Todd, and Harvey E. Lapan. "The Calculus of Dissent: An Analysis of Terrorists' Choice of Targets." *Synthese* 76 (1988): 245–261.

Schneider, Friedrich. "The (Hidden) Financial Flows of Terrorist and Organized Crime Organizations: A Literature Review and Some Preliminary Empirical Results." Paper presented at the EUSECON workshop, Athens, April 12–13, 2010.

ECOTERRORISM

Since the late 1980s, ecoterrorism, a blanket term referring to various forms of violence and sabotage committed in the name of the environment, has become one of the top three "single issue" domestic terrorist threats in the United States (anti-abortion and animal rights are the other main areas). The growing radical environmental movement has become a top concern of the FBI, which estimates that more than 1,200 ecoterrorist acts were committed between 1990 and the end of 2004.

Radical environmentalism went public in the United States in 1969, when a small group of environmental activists—the Don't Make A Wave Committee—boarded a rented boat they called *Greenpeace* and attempted to halt nuclear testing on the Aleutian Islands. Although this mission failed, the movement grew. Five years later, Greenpeace was known worldwide for its Save the Whales campaign, in which members in small crafts placed themselves directly between whales and whaling boats. Over the next decade, as the movement grew, Greenpeace members took on new issues, dividing the campaigns into four major categories: nuclear energy, toxic pollution, ocean ecology, and atmosphere and energy.

"Loner" environmentalists throughout the country were active in the 1970s. In Chicago, an ecological saboteur known only as the Fox targeted large-scale industrial polluters, once redirecting toxic waste into an executive's office. Minnesota's Bolt Weevils toppled more than a dozen power poles to protest a massive power line across that state, while Michigan had the "Billboard Bandits" and Arizona had the Ecoraiders. The early tactics of ecoterrorists were inspired, in part, by Edward Abbey's 1975 radical environmentalist novel *The Monkeywrench Gang*.

Growing More Radical

Earth First!, one of the most prominent radical environmental groups, also used Abbey's novel as a guidebook for action. Founded in 1980, the Arizona-based group became known for its anti-logging campaigns to save old-growth forests in the Pacific Northwest. The group's cofounder, Dave Foreman, wrote *Ecodefense: A Field Guide to Monkeywrenching*, from which individual environmentalists have learned the tools of the trade: spiking trees, disabling bulldozers and other heavy equipment, and toppling billboards and power-line towers. Activists are instructed to pull up survey stakes to halt further development into wilderness areas and to put themselves in trees to stop loggers.

Like the Animal Liberation Front (ALF), a radical animal rights group that began in England in 1976, Earth First! was decentralized and nonhierarchical. With no membership list and no formal leaders, Earth First!ers were left to conceive of and carry out their own operations, held together only by a shared philosophy of "deep ecology," the publication of the *Earth First! Journal,* and a common goal of causing significant economic damage to environmentally destructive industries. Such a loose structure makes infiltration and tracking of any group difficult. As like-minded groups with the same organizational structure began to spring up and turn more violent and destructive, authorities became alarmed and steadily more frustrated.

The latter half of the 1980s saw a new level of environmental radicalism, which brought environmental terrorism to the forefront. In the mid-1970s, the Canadian activist Paul Watson left Greenpeace to form the Sea Shepard Conservation Society, which engaged in greater levels of economic destruction in its efforts to end whale and seal hunts, drift-net fishing, and other marine industry practices. In November 1986, Watson, along with ALF activist Rodney Coronado, sabotaged a whaling station in Reykjavik, Iceland, and sank two of that country's four whaling ships. The $2.7 million in damages hobbled Iceland's whaling industry.

A year later, in the United States, while more moderate environmentalists engaged in traditional civil disobedience, a small offshoot of Earth First! calling itself the Evan Mecham Ecoterrorist International Conspiracy (EMETIC) sabotaged a ski lift at a resort that had encroached on Native America sacred grounds in Arizona. This act brought ecoterrorism to the attention of the FBI. The year 1987 was also the year the first logger was seriously injured by a tree-spike, calling even more federal attention to environmentalists, though it is not confirmed that Earth First! activists placed the spike.

Authorities spent the next 18 months and $2 million investigating EMETIC, focusing specifically on Earth First! cofounder Foreman, who headed EMETIC. By 1989, EMETIC was planning to sabotage nuclear plants in Arizona, Colorado, and California—by far the most dangerous act planned by any environmental group. On May 29, 1989, core EMETIC members were arrested trying to down a power line leading to the Central Arizona Project water pumping stations. The nearly 1,000 hours of audiotape collected by an FBI informant helped convict all those involved.

In the 1990s, just as Foreman had distanced himself from more moderate environmentalists by working with EMETIC, other environmental activists frustrated by Earth First!'s "tepid" direct action formed more dangerous offshoots. In 1992, militant members of Earth First! in England formed the Earth Liberation Front (ELF), fashioned after the Animal Liberation Front. By 1995 ecoterrorism had become the primary security priority of Scotland Yard's Special Branch, as ELF "elves" sabotaged road building with Vietcong–style *pongee* stakes. Construction equipment was routinely dismantled and set afire—the favorite form of "ecotage."

ELF arrived in North America a few years later, committing a handful of small actions in conjunction with the North American ALF. In 1998, however, ELF rose to the top of the FBI's domestic terrorist list with its arson at Vail Resorts in Colorado; damages of over $12 million made it the largest ecoterrorist act up to that time. ALF and ELF continued to cooperate and collaborate. Both groups claimed responsibility for setting fires at the Bureau of Land Management wild horse corrals in Oregon in November 1997 and, just over six months later, for setting another fire at the U.S. Department of Animal Damage Control Building in Olympia, Washington. At the time, FBI director Louis Freeh called ALF and ELF the two most active domestic terrorist organizations.

Expanding Reach and Concerns

Radical environmental groups, including Earth First!, were extremely active in Canada during the 1990s, especially in the West. In 1995, activists destroyed a logging bridge at a cost of over $2 million, and in 1997 they set off an explosion at a logging facility in Alberta that destroyed $5 million worth of equipment.

By the end of the 1990s, ecoterrorism had expanded from the traditional environmental issues of preserving trees, wilderness, and marine life to include actions against urban sprawl, the development of luxury housing and resorts on agricultural lands, and the proliferation of SUVs. In 2000, ELF claimed responsibility for more than a dozen fires at construction sites for luxury homes in Colorado, Arizona, and New York. That same year, the Anarchist Golf Association destroyed two grass seed research facilities in Oregon. Three years later, a fire set by ELF activists at a housing complex under construction in San Diego caused some $50 million in damage, making it the largest ecoterrorist attack to date.

In 2001, ELF announced through its spokesperson, Craig Rosebraugh, that it hoped to see continued activity "against capitalism and industry" that year, suggesting ever-growing links between environmentalist and other leftist social movements, such as the anti-globalization movement. Indeed, ALF's 2001 *Direct Action Report,* which tracks both ALF and ELF activities, made the connection clear: "[The] same attitude which allows the torture of animals allows the torture of humans, and allows economic policies to be imposed on 'third world' nations, policies which serve only corporations and the wealthy. . . . The root of the problem is violence, greed and arrogance."

In the wake of the September 11, 2001, attacks, both ALF and ELF were harshly criticized for maintaining their level of activism, particularly as other, more mainstream, environmental and animal rights groups curtailed their protests and activities. On September 20, 2001, the ALF bombed a primate research lab in New Mexico, and a month later the ELF set fire to a Bureau of Land Management facility in Lassen County, California, that was holding wild horses.

The continuing acts of ecoterrorism throughout the United States led to a hearing on ecoterrorism sponsored by the House Resources Subcommittee on Forests and Forest Health in February 2002. The hearing's primary focus was the activities of ELF and ALF. In his testimony, James Jarboe, the FBI's domestic terrorism section chief, claimed that more than 26 investigations related to ALF and ELF were currently under way. The committee also subpoenaed Rosebraugh, the ELF spokesperson at the time, who invoked his Fifth Amendment right against self-incrimination more than 50 times, leaving the committee with as many questions about the clandestine activities of radical environmentalists at the end of the investigation as when they began.

The mid-2000s saw a significant crackdown on ecoterrorism—one that has been criticized as a "Green Scare" by environmentalists, who liken it to the anticommunist "Red Scare" of the 1950s. Nonetheless, the effort did lead to the conviction in 2006 of the members of an ELF cell calling itself The Family, which was responsible for several high-profile ELF attacks, including the one in Vail, that caused more than $40 million in property damage.

ELF members have faced lengthy prison sentences as the result of so-called terrorism enhancements, which offer tougher sentences for crimes such as arson if they were motivated by a desire to intimidate society and force political change. In addition, prosecutors have been willing to rely on more obscure legal strategies to convict activists who they feel cross the line. Rodney Coronado, for example, pled guilty in December 2007 to charges stemming from a speech he made four years earlier, in which he demonstrated how to build a firebomb. Coronado was charged under a rarely used federal law that prohibits a person from demonstrating how to make a destructive device with the intent that others commit arson.

Laura Lambert

See also Animal Liberation Front; Coronado, Rodney; Earth First!; Earth Liberation Front; Evan Mecham Eco-Terrorist International Conspiracy

Further Readings

Bishop, Bill. "Is It the Green Scare, Eco-terrorism, or None of the Above?" *Register-Guard,* April 12, 2006, p. A1.

Foreman, Dave. *Confessions of an Eco-warrior.* New York: Harmony Books, 1991.

Grossman, Ron. "Activist's Case a Free-speech Test." *Chicago Tribune,* September 9, 2007, p. 3.

House Resources Committee, Subcommittee on Forest and Forest Health. *Oversight Hearing on Eco-terrorism and Lawlessness on the National Forests.* February 12, 2002. http://frwebgate.access.gpo.gov/cgi-bin/getdoc.cgi?dbname=107_house_hearings&docid=f:77615.pdf.

Knickerbocker, Brad. "New Laws Target Increase in Acts of Ecoterrorism." *Christian Science Monitor,* November 26, 2003, p. 2.

Knickerbocker, Brad. "A Troubling Rise in Violence for Green Causes." *Christian Science Monitor,* June 6, 2005, p. 3.

Liddick, Donald R. *Eco-Terrorism: Radical Environmental and Animal Liberation Movements.* Westport, CT: Praeger, 2006.

Martin, Jonatha, and Mike Carter. "Arson Group Retreats Even More into Shadows." *Seattle Times,* March 18, 2008, p. A1.

Rasmussen, Matt. "Green Rage." *Orion Magazine,* January/February 2007. http://www.orionmagazine.org/index.php/articles/article/6.

Scarce, Rik. *Eco-Warriors: Understanding the Radical Environmental Movement.* 2nd ed. Walnut Creek, CA: Left Coast Press, 2006.

Zakin, Susan, *Coyotes and Town Dogs: Earth First! and the Environmental Movement.* New York: Viking Penguin, 1993.

EGYPTIAN AL JIHAD / EGYPTIAN ISLAMIC JIHAD

See al Jihad

EJÉRCITO DE LIBERACIÓN NACIONAL

See National Liberation Army–Colombia

EJÉRCITO GUERRILLERO TÚPAC KATARI

See Tupac Katari Guerrilla Army

EJÉRCITO REVOLUCIONARIO DEL PUEBLO

See People's Revolutionary Army

EL RUKNS

In 1985, El Rukns (aka Blackstone Rangers), one of Chicago's most notorious street gangs, contacted the Libyan government, offering to commit terrorist acts within the United States in exchange for $2.5 million. The ensuing federal trial marked the first in which U.S. citizens were found guilty of planning terrorist acts on behalf of a foreign government in exchange for money.

El Rukns began as the Blackstone Rangers, a teenage street gang that ruled the Woodlawn district of Chicago's South Side in the 1960s. Led by Jeff Fort, the gang, which later joined with other gangs to form the Black P. Stone Nation, established its reputation for extreme violence in battles against a rival gang, the Gangster Disciples.

In 1977, Fort announced his conversion to Islam and asserted that his gang was now a black Islamic religious sect called the Moorish Science Temple of America, El Rukn tribe. (El Rukn means "the foundation" in Arabic and also refers to the cornerstone of the Kabaa in Mecca.) Fort changed his name to Malik and became the imam, or spiritual leader, of El Rukns. At approximately the same time, police and federal law enforcement agencies began cracking down on the gang. By the mid-1980s, Fort was in jail in Bastrop, Texas, on cocaine trafficking charges, and more than a dozen other gang members were serving time for serious state or federal crimes.

In October 1986 a federal grand jury returned a 50-count indictment against several members of El Rukns, including Fort, Melvin Mayes, and Trammel Davis. The indictment charged that from March 1985 until the time of the indictment, members of El Rukns had obtained explosives and weapons with the intent to kill "unspecified people" and destroy "unspecified buildings" in the United States on behalf of Libya.

The conspiracy began in March 1985, when Fort offered the group's services to the Libyan government for $2.5 million, following news that Louis Farrakhan, the head of the Nation of Islam, had received twice that amount from Libya. Members of El Rukns then traveled to Libya and Panama to negotiate. On July 31, 1985, an undercover FBI agent sold Mayes a rocket launcher for $2,000. The launcher, which had been rendered inoperative, was fixed with a radio transmitter that eventually led authorities to the El Rukns weapons arsenal. Five days later, federal agents raided two houses in Chicago's South Side and found the launcher, along with nearly three dozen other guns and grenades. Several gang members were immediately arrested; Mayes, however, remained at large.

During the trial, Davis, the former security chief for the gang, turned government witness. Authorities had recorded numerous phone calls that Fort made from jail to El Rukns headquarters in which Fort talked in elaborate code. Davis translated the code—a combination of Arabic and street slang—to reveal how Fort orchestrated the conspiracy from prison. On November 24, 1987, the jury convicted five members of El Rukns.

Mayes remained at large until March 9, 1995, when he was captured by the FBI's Chicago Joint Terrorism Task Force. By then, El Rukns had been mostly dismantled through several criminal racketeering trials. It is now primarily a prison gang.

Although the Libyan government denied involvement, and no Libyan diplomats were named in the indictment, a 1997 Department of Defense memorandum about the bombing of Pan Am flight 103 suggested that the El Rukns conspiracy was part of a larger Libyan plot to retaliate for the U.S. bombing raid on Muammar el Qaddifi's headquarters in 1986.

Laura Lambert

See also Pan Am Flight 103 Bombing; Qaddafi, Muammar el; Tripoli and Benghazi Bombing

Further Readings

"The Business of Murder Series: The Chicago Crime." *Chicago Tribune*, December 1, 2002, p. 10.
Federation of American Scientists. "Terrorism in the United States." http://www.fas.org/irp/threat/fbi_terror95/terrorin.htm.
"Qaddafi's Goons." *Time*, December 7, 1987, p. 27.
Sadovi, Carlos. "El Rukns Had Early Terror Ties." *Chicago Sun-Times*, June 11, 2002, p. 7.

ELBANEH, JABER A. (1966–)

Jaber A. Elbaneh is a Yemeni-born American Muslim who was accused by the United States of being involved with the "Buffalo Six," or "Lackawanna Six." The Lackawanna Six were a group of young men of Yemeni descent from Lackawanna, a Buffalo, New York, suburb, who sought out and received training from al Qaeda in Afghanistan in the spring of 2001 and then returned to the United States. Elbaneh, however, chose to stay with al Qaeda and was later imprisoned in Yemen for terrorist activities.

Elbaneh's family immigrated to the United States from Yemen and settled in Lackawanna when he was a child. As an adult, Elbaneh married and had seven children. Along with the "Six," he is believed to have been recruited by Kemal Derwish, an al Qaeda operative who was subsequently killed in a 2002 U.S. drone strike in Yemen.

Elbaneh is thought to have played a crucial role in financing the cell's May 2001 trip to Afghanistan to receive training. Elbaneh flew with his fellow Lackawanna residents to Karachi, Pakistan, and met with Derwish. Several weeks later, Elbaneh and his companions, along with 20 other recruits, arrived at the al Farouq training camp, an al Qaeda facility near Kandahar. The training at al Farouq included weaponry and military tactics. Early in their training, Osama bin Laden visited al Farouq and gave a speech about the alliance between al Qaeda and its mission.

While the other members of the Lackawanna cell became disenchanted with the rigors of training and were reluctant to fight, Elbaneh's commitment to jihad seemed to have been strengthened during his training. One after the other, the members of the Lackawanna cell made their way back to the United States, reportedly intending to sever their ties to al Qaeda. Only Elbaneh chose to stay. He moved to Yemen and is thought to have been part of the cell that bombed the *Limburg*, a French oil tanker, on October 6, 2002. The attack was planned by Abd al Rahim al Nashiri, who had also planned the 2000 attack on the USS *Cole*.

A criminal complaint unsealed in the United States in 2003 revealed that Elbaneh was wanted for providing material support to al Qaeda. In 2002, before he was charged for participation in the *Limburg* attack, Elbaneh was arrested by the Yemeni authorities. However, Yemen and the United States did not have an extradition treaty in place, and negotiations bore no fruit. Elbaneh was housed in Yemen's national security jail along with other al Qaeda members, and he was among two dozen inmates who escaped from the prison on February 3, 2006. The escape was led by Jamal al Badawi, an al Qaeda operative who was part of the cell responsible for the attack on the *Cole*. In 2007 a Yemeni court convicted Elbaneh in absentia for the Limburg attack and for other attacks on oil installations; the court sentenced him to 10 years in prison. He turned himself in to the Yemeni authorities in December 2007 and was imprisoned in 2008.

Lorenzo Vidino

See also al Qaeda; Training of Terrorists; USS *Cole* Bombing

Further Readings

Federal Bureau of Investigation. "Most Wanted Terrorists: Jaber A. Elbaneh." http://www.fbi.gov/wanted/terrorists/terelbaneh.htm.

Honigsberg, Peter Jan. *Our Nation Unhinged: The Human Consequences of the War on Terror.* Berkeley: University of California Press, 2009.

Temple-Raston, Dina. *The Jihad Next Door: The Lackawanna Six and Rough Justice in an Age of Terror.* New York: Public Affairs, 2007.

Ellerman, Josh (1979–)

In 1998, Josh Ellerman (aka Douglas Joshua Ellerman), a 19-year-old radical animal rights activist, received a seven-year prison sentence for his participation in an alleged Animal Liberation Front (ALF) attack. At the time, it was one of the toughest sentences ever given to an animal rights activist in the United States. His case, along with that of his brother, Clinton Colby Ellerman, marked the beginning of a crackdown on animal rights activists.

On the morning of March 11, 1997, members of ALF detonated at least five pipe bombs at the Fur Breeders Agricultural Co-op in Sandy, Utah, a plant that provided feed, materials, and live mink to hundreds of fur farms in Utah and Idaho. The ensuing blaze caused nearly $1 million in damage, but no one was injured. Such destruction of property was a hallmark of ALF, which had engaged in similar tactics during its anti-fur "Operation Bite Back" campaign in the early 1990s. Utah, which claimed the most fur farms of any state in the country, was particularly hard hit by ALF actions.

That same day, a caller to a Salt Lake City radio show claimed that the bombing was in support of animal rights and ALF, and had been committed in the name of Jeff Watkins, a "political prisoner" on a hunger strike in a New York jail. With the help of the caller, investigators later linked Ellerman to the crime. On April 20, 1997, Ellerman turned himself in. He initially faced charges that would have carried a minimum mandatory sentence of 35 years. In exchange for a reduced sentence, however, Ellerman agreed to provide "substantial" cooperation to authorities investigating ALF and other animal rights' groups. The information he provided led to several arrests and indictments, as well as sustained surveillance of Salt Lake City's "Straight Edge" community (mostly young punk rockers who eschew drugs, alcohol, smoking, casual sex, meat, and leather in favor of a pro-environment and animal rights lifestyle). Members of the Coalition to Abolish the Fur Trade (CAFT) were said to recruit Straight Edgers to become part of the illegal anti-fur crusade at concerts in Salt Lake City.

In January 1998, Ellerman pled guilty to 3 of the 16 counts on which he was indicted: maliciously damaging a building with an explosive, making a pipe bomb, and using a pipe bomb. Although he failed to appear for a pretrial hearing, he turned himself in on June 29, 1998.

On September 10, 1998, Ellerman was sentenced to seven years in prison and ordered to pay $750,000 in restitution. Concurrently, five other animal rights activists were also indicted in the bombing. Three were later found not guilty, in part because of the testimony of Ellerman and that of his older brother, Clinton Colby Ellerman. Josh Ellerman served his seven years and was last believed to be living in Utah.

Laura Lambert

See also Animal Liberation Front; Animal Rights Movement; Coronado, Rodney; Ecoterrorism

Further Readings

Kistler, John M. *Animal Rights: A Subject Guide, Bibliography, and Internet Companion.* Westport, CT: Greenwood Press, 2000.

Liddick, Donald R. *Eco-Terrorism: Radical Environmental and Animal Liberation Movements.* Westport, CT: Praeger, 2006.

Lutherer, Lorenz Otto, and Margaret Sheffield Simon. *Targeted: The Anatomy of an Animal Rights Attack.* Norman: University of Oklahoma Press, 1992.

Scarce, Rik. *Eco-warriors: Understanding the Radical Environmental Movement.* Chicago: Noble Press, 1990.

Smith, Brent. *Terrorism in America: Pipe Bombs and Pipe Dreams.* Albany: State University of New York Press, 1994.

ELLISON, JAMES

James Ellison (birth date unknown) was a preacher from Texas who in 1976 founded Zarephath-Horeb, a peaceful fundamentalist Christian group, in the Ozark Mountains of Arkansas. He eventually adopted Christian Identity, a race-based theology, and changed the name of his group to The Covenant, the Sword and the Arm of the Lord (CSA). Ellison and antigovernment Christian survivalist groups like the Christian Patriots Defense League eventually turned the CSA's 224-acre compound into a training camp for white supremacists.

By 1982, Ellison, who was now calling himself King James of the Ozarks, had about 150 followers. This number decreased dramatically that year when he announced that he would take a second (polygamous) wife. In the debate over polygamy, Ellison made clear that he would act against the wishes of the other church elders; in response, almost two thirds of the congregation defected because they regarded Ellison's actions as the adoption of a one-man ministry.

Ellison and those who stayed, particularly his second-in-command, Kerry Noble, tried for a while to underplay the group's right-wing stance. That changed, however, after the 1983 Aryan Nations World Congress, which commemorated the death of Gordon Kahl, a member of Posse Comitatus who had refused to pay his taxes. Kahl had killed two U.S. marshals, but he was considered a martyr by the extreme right because he had been killed during a skirmish with federal authorities. Ellison has often been quoted as saying at that conference that he was sorry he was not with Kahl at his death, and that he was "here to tell you that the sword is out of the sheath, and it's ready to strike. For every one of our people they killed, we ought to kill a hundred of theirs."

Ellison's terrorist activities included arson and bombings. In particular, he and his followers set fire to an Arkansas church with a largely homosexual congregation, and to a Jewish center, and they bombed a natural gas pipeline in Arkansas. He later admitted to having plans to assassinate key government officials and national personalities and to bomb the federal office building in Oklahoma City, but none of these came to fruition because of what he took to be signs from God.

In 1985, after a four-day standoff with federal authorities at the CSA compound ended peacefully, Ellison was convicted on racketeering and weapons charges. At the age of 38, he was sentenced to 20 years in prison. In 1988, he agreed to be the chief prosecution witness at the sedition trial of 14 other white supremacists, including some former CSA members. Although the defendants in that case were found not guilty, Ellison's sentence was reduced to 10 years for testifying. He was released in 1991, after serving only six years in prison, but he returned to prison briefly for violating parole. He was released again in April 1995. He reportedly moved to Elohim City, a Christian Identity camp located in Adair County, Oklahoma.

Nancy Egan

See also Christian Identity; Covenant, the Sword and the Arm of the Lord, The; White Supremacy Movement

Further Readings

Coulson, Danny O., and Elaine Shannon. *No Heroes: Inside the FBI's Secret Counter-terror Force*. New York: Pocket Books, 1999.

Extremism on the Right: A Handbook. Rev. ed. New York: Anti-Defamation League of B'nai B'rith, 1988.

Kressel, Neil J. *Bad Faith: The Danger of Religious Extremism*. Amherst, NY: Prometheus Books, 2007.

Noble, Kerry. *Tabernacle of Hate: Why They Bombed Oklahoma City*. Prescott, Ontario: Voyageur Publishing, 1998.

Quarles, Chester L. *Christian Identity: The Aryan American Bloodline Religion*. Jefferson, NC: McFarland, 2004.

Solomon, John. "Authorities Had Information before Bombing." *Columbian*, February 12, 2003, p. A6.

Stern, Jessica. *Terror in the Name of God: Why Religious Militants Kill*. New York: Ecco, 2008.

Zeskind, Leonard. *Blood and Politics: The History of the White Nationalist Movement from the Margins to the Mainstream*. New York: Farrar, Straus & Giroux, 2009.

ELN

See National Liberation Army–Bolivia; National Liberation Army–Colombia

EMPIRE STATE BUILDING SHOOTING

On February 23, 1997, Ali Hassan Abu Kamal, a 69-year-old Palestinian teacher, began shooting on the observation deck of the Empire State Building, killing one person and injuring six others before committing suicide. The attack led to tougher federal gun laws for foreign visitors and recent immigrants.

Abu Kamal arrived in the United States on December 24, 1996, on a tourist visa. After staying with friends in New York City for two weeks, he traveled to Melbourne, Florida, where, using his motel address, he obtained a temporary resident card on January 30, 1997. Taking advantage of Florida's lax gun laws, he used the card to purchase a $500 semiautomatic handgun. He received the gun in five days, and returned to New York City a week later. Law enforcement officials have speculated that Abu Kamal must have had assistance from terrorists (or sympathizers) within the United States.

Just before 5 P.M. on Sunday, February 23, Abu Kamal entered the Empire State Building and took the elevator to the 86th-floor observation deck. Security cameras later revealed he concealed the gun under a long coat, and witnesses claimed to have heard Abu Kamal mention something about Egypt before he opened fire on the crowd. After shooting seven people, he shot himself in the head.

Initially, Abu Kamal's family described him as having become "unbalanced" after losing more than $300,000 in a business deal. They claimed that the loss of his life savings caused his rampage. Investigators, however, found no evidence to support this claim. They did find two letters, one in English and one in Arabic, on Abu Kamal's body after the shooting. The English letter, titled "Charter of Honour," clearly outlined his four targets: (1) Americans, Britons, French, and all Zionists; (2) a group of his students who attacked him in 1993; (3) an Egyptian police officer and his brother in Cairo; and (4) several Ukrainian students in Gaza who had beaten his son. The letter also proved that the attack was premeditated. Abu Kamal wrote, "My restless aspiration is to murder as many of them as possible, and I have decided to strike at their own den in New York, and at the very Empire State Building in particular." Authorities did not find any connections between Abu Kamal and any pro-Palestinian terrorist groups.

In response to the shooting, New York mayor Rudy Giuliani railed against Florida's lax gun laws, citing New York's stringent requirements. Within days, Senators Edward Kennedy of Massachusetts and Richard Durbin of Illinois introduced legislation that would ban foreign visitors from purchasing and carrying guns. Existing federal law required legal foreign immigrants to prove a 90-day residency to purchase a weapon (how Abu Kamal circumvented this law remains unclear). On March 5, 1997, President Bill Clinton asked the Treasury Department to both restrict gun access by foreign visitors and to strictly enforce the existing residency requirements of federal firearms laws.

Laura Lambert

See also Freelance Terrorism; Lone-Wolf Terrorism

Further Readings

Katz, Samuel M. *Jihad in Brooklyn: The NYPD Raid That Stopped America's First Suicide Bombers*. New York: New American Library, 2005.

Kleinfield, N. R. "From Teacher to Gunman: U.S. Visit End in Fatal Rage." *The New York Times*, February 25, 1997, p. A1.

"1997 Observation Deck Shootings: Court Declines to Hear Empire State Death Case." *Newsday*, September 8, 2004, p. A30.

Purdy, Matthew. "Empire State Gunman Gave No Hint of Anger, His Hosts Say." *The New York Times*, February 27, 1997, p. B1.

Purdy, Matthew. "Empire State Gunman's Note: Kill 'Zionists.'" *The New York Times*, February 26, 1997, p. A1.

U.S. Department of Treasury, Bureau of Alcohol, Tobacco and Firearms. "Residency Requirements for Persons Acquiring Firearms (97R-687P): Temporary Rule and Proposed Rule." April 11, 1997. http://www.atf.gov/regulations-rulings/rulemakings/treasury-decisions/td-389.html.

Violence Policy Center Study. "Where'd They Get Their Guns? An Analysis of the Firearms Used in High-Profile Shootings, 1963 to 2001." February 23, 1997. http://www.vpc.org/studies/wgun970223.htm.

ETHNIC CLEANSING

First widely recognized in the 1990s during the civil war in the former Yugoslavia, the term *ethnic cleansing* has been defined as the forced removal, through violence and intimidation, of an ethnic group from a particular territory. Ethnic cleansing features in campaigns employed by diverse groups or perpetrators, ranging from official forces under the command of a government to irregular formations and paramilitaries.

In state-sponsored ethnic cleansing, official units deployed by a state or government remove targeted groups in acts of forced migration. In a second type, paramilitaries, militias, and armed bands drive out victimized groups. These two types of ethnic cleansing can overlap, but they also tend to deploy terror in different ways. Irregular forces rely more on extremely violent acts of terror, while state authorities in many instances seek to use a show of overwhelming power to quell all resistance to forced migration.

Armed bands that carry out ethnic cleansing typically employ methods that many would define as terror. These include arson attacks carried out against homes and businesses, assassinations and massacres, and rape. This style of terror dehumanizes victims and stems at least in part from the very status of irregular forces as self-constituted groupings that lack official sanction. Without any other source of authority to compel an unwanted population to leave, irregular forces make terror a central instrument of ethnic cleansing.

State-sponsored ethnic cleansing, in comparison, takes a more organized form when official state forces deport unwanted groups. Though armies are sometimes directly involved, internal security forces or police more commonly undertake such actions. These units commonly arrive at an area and tell members of an unwanted group that they must leave very shortly. The threat of force is omnipresent, but the units involved may hold back from direct violence or employ terror selectively. Should a show of overwhelming force backed by state power fail to motivate the targets of cleansing to comply with orders to vacate their homes quickly, acts of terror similar to those employed by irregular or paramilitary forces are used to accelerate the departure of the targeted group.

State-sponsored ethnic cleansing has taken place in the swiftest fashion under powerful states,

Ethnic Albanian children from Kosovo at a Turkish run refugee camp in Albania, May 5, 1999. There are several camps in Albania built and maintained by NATO allied countries to aid people fleeing Kosovo. This mission is in direct support of Operation Sustain Hope and Allied Force. (Photographer: SSGT Angela Stafford)

including Nazi Germany and the Soviet Union. Soviet security forces were particularly noteworthy for collecting and moving targeted populations with extraordinary speed. During World War II, Stalin unleashed such ethnic-cleansing operations against minorities that he saw as disloyal in the war against Nazi Germany. In particular, Stalinist ethnic cleansing targeted religious minorities, including many from the Caucasus region, including Chechens, Ingush, Karachai, Meskhetian Turks, and Kalmyks, and Soviet security forces also expelled Tatars from the Crimea. In operations that took only days, a Soviet policing organization called the People's Commissariat for Internal Affairs (known by its Russian acronym, NKVD) surrounded villages and dispatched the targeted group into trucks, from which they were transported east in trains. NKVD agents carried out both isolated shootings and more widespread massacres, but they reported relatively little immediate resistance in the face of overwhelming force. However, large numbers of people died from hunger, disease, and exposure during transit or resettlement in areas of Central Asia.

State-sponsored ethnic cleansing in the aftermath of wars typically relies more on bureaucratic operations and less on terror, based in part on the assumption that a traumatized population is more likely to be ready to leave. Turkey and Greece carried out one such vast population exchange after the new Turkish nationalist regime won the Greco-Turkish War of 1919–1922. Similarly, following World War II, the remaining ethnic Germans were moved out of much of Central and Eastern Europe by the millions in a population transfer made official by the Potsdam Accords of August 1945. Acts of revenge, theft, and intimidation, as well as a lack of medical care, meant that these transfers did not meet the standards agreed to by the victorious allies, but the element of raw terror diminished compared to the attacks and massacres carried out against ethnic Germans in the months just after the end of war.

The violence in the former Yugoslavia that made ethnic cleaning widely known in the 1990s included all the types of ethnic cleansing mentioned above, but it stands as an iconic example of ethnic cleansing by irregular forces. Especially in the early stages of the wars, regular forces or forces reconstituted from units for the former Yugoslav army carried out operations in tandem with paramilitaries. After military forces bombarded towns with heavy weapons, the paramilitaries and militias moved in and drove out targeted populations. Irregular forces repeatedly employed terror in Bosnia Herzegovina, resorting to summary executions, arson attacks, and rapes to engineer mass flight.

Contemporary investigations and reporting stressed the key role of terror in generating widespread ethnic cleansing. Terror attacks created such deep and fundamental insecurity that even Bosnian Muslims who survived assaults feared for their lives, and in many cases they fled their homes. While Bosnian Serbs generally had the upper hand in the conflict in Bosnia-Herzegovina into 1995, forces allied with other groups also carried out terror attacks with much the same goal: remaking ethnic boundaries.

Armed bands made terror central to numerous other ethnic cleansing campaigns. From the late nineteenth century up to the Balkan Wars of 1912–1913, irregulars and militias fighting in southeastern Europe carried out looting, arson, and killings that propelled civilian populations into mass flight. During World War II, ethnic warfare in Yugoslavia as well as in areas of the Eastern Front featured similar methods. Describing combat between Polish and Ukrainian forces, for example, Timothy Snyder wrote of "ethnic cleansing rampant on both sides."

A similar pattern of terror attacks carried out primarily by paramilitaries and militia groups struck other areas in the 1990s, including contested regions of the Trans-Caucasus during and after the end of the Soviet Union. Arson prompted flight by Armenians and Azerbaijanis in mixed areas where both groups lived alongside each other, and similar terror generated flows of refugees and internally displaced persons (IDPs) in Abkhazia and South Ossetia. In a 1992 report, Human Rights Watch documented summary executions, hostage taking, indiscriminate shelling, and "forcing the evacuation of civilians of the other side," carried out by both local Ossetian and Georgian combatants. Such forces also systematically burned down houses to propel civilian flight.

Similar patterns of terror employed as a means to expel an unwanted population have also taken place outside of Europe. The term *ethnic cleansing* has only been used sparingly to describe the violence and upheaval of the partition of India in 1947, but terror attacks in contested areas instilled fear among civilian populations and solidified new national boundaries. Yasmin Khan refers to a "scorched earth policy in Punjab, which would today be labeled ethnic cleansing." Militia forces attacked and burned villages or stopped trains to set fire to the railway cars, and to kill or abduct the passengers.

Perpetrators of ethnic cleansing have also employed terror in Africa and in the Middle East. In Africa, forces claiming to represent natives of particular regions have attacked immigrant populations. One such case involved the Bakossi and the Bamileke in southwestern Cameroon, while areas of West Africa, including the Ivory Coast, have seen waves of arson attacks, disappearances, and intimidation. During elections in Kenya in the 1990s, and again as recently as 2008, murders and attacks on neighborhoods prompted massive flight by targeted populations.

The extent to which forces fighting on behalf of Israel deliberately targeted civilian populations to prompt flight during the war for Palestine in 1948 remains a matter of controversy. More recent conflicts in the Middle East have not featured prominently in international discussion of ethnic cleansings and terror, but Iraq has suffered through both ethnic cleansing by the state and by irregular forces, first when Saddam Hussein targeted populations he saw as disloyal, including Kurds in the Anfal campaign of 1988, and again during the prolonged warfare following the American-led invasion in which irregular forces and sectarian militias carried out assassinations to drive out unwanted populations of Sunnis, Shiites, Kurds, or Christians, depending on the district.

The most spectacular and deadly acts of terror during ethnic cleansing are therefore likely to take place during civil wars or interethnic struggles, when varied forces, including paramilitaries, seek to create new ethnic boundaries. At the same time, such attacks and state-sponsored ethnic cleansing often converge, especially when close cooperation with armed bands that rely heavily on terror creates a level of plausible deniability for state or military authorities. The exact degree of coordination frequently surfaces as a major legal issue in investigations of terror in the aftermath of ethnic cleansing.

Benjamin Lieberman

See also Death Squads; Hussein, Saddam; Persian Gulf War; State Terrorism; State-Sponsored Terrorism

Further Readings

Atieno, Odhiambo, E. S. "Ethnic Cleansing and Civil Society in Kenya 1969–1992." *Journal of Contemporary African Studies* 22, no. 1 (2004): 29–42.

Atieno, Odhiambo, E.S. "Ethnic Cleansing in Luoland." *The Economist* 386, no. 8566 (2008): 51–52.

Bell, Andrew. *Ethnic Cleansing.* New York: St. Martin's, 1996.

Carmichael, Cathie. *Ethnic Cleansing in the Balkans: Nationalism and the Destruction of Tradition.* Routledge Advances in European Politics 8. London: Routledge, 2002.

Gutman, Roy. *A Witness to Genocide: The 1993 Pulitzer Prize–winning Dispatches on the "Ethnic Cleansing" of Bosnia.* New York: Macmillan, 1993.

Human Rights Watch. *Violations of Humanitarian Law and Human Rights in the Georgia-South Ossetia Conflict.* New York: Human Rights Watch, April 1, 1992. http://www.hrw.org/en/reports/1992/04/01/violations-humanitarian-law-and-human-rights-georgia-south-ossetia-conflict.

International Commission to Inquire into the Causes and Conduct of the Balkan Wars, and George F. Kennan. *The Other Balkan Wars: A 1913 Carnegie Endowment Inquiry in Retrospect.* Washington, DC: Carnegie Endowment for International Peace, 1993.

Khan, Yasmin. *The Great Partition: The Making of India and Pakistan.* New Haven, CT: Yale University Press, 2007.

Konings, Piet. "Autochthony and Ethnic Cleansing in the Post-colony: The 1966 Tombel Disturbances in Cameroon." *International Journal of African Historical Studies* 41, no. 2 (2008): 203–222.

Lieberman, Benjamin David. *Terrible Fate: Ethnic Cleansing in the Making of Modern Europe.* Chicago: Ivan R. Dee, 2006.

Lotnik, Waldemar, and Julian Preece. *Nine Lives: Ethnic Conflict in the Polish-Ukrainian Borderlands.* London: Serif, 1999.

Mann, Michael. *The Dark Side of Democracy: Explaining Ethnic Cleansing.* New York: Cambridge University Press, 2005.

Morris, Benny. *1948: A History of the First Arab-Israeli War.* New Haven, CT: Yale University Press, 2008.

Naimark, Norman M. *Fires of Hatred: Ethnic Cleansing in Twentieth-century Europe.* Cambridge, MA: Harvard University Press, 2001.

Pappé, Ilan. *The Ethnic Cleansing of Palestine.* Oxford: Oneworld, 2006.

Snyder, Timothy. *The Reconstruction of Nations: Poland, Ukraine, Lithuania, Belarus, 1569–1999.* New Haven, CT: Yale University Press, 2003.

Ther, Philipp, and Ana Siljak. *Redrawing Nations: Ethnic Cleansing in East-Central Europe, 1944–1948.* Lanham, MD: Rowman & Littlefield, 2001.

EVAN MECHAM ECO-TERRORIST INTERNATIONAL CONSPIRACY

In the late 1980s, the Evan Mecham Eco-Terrorist International Conspiracy (EMETIC), an Arizona-based offshoot of the radical environmentalist group Earth First!, engaged in acts of ecoterrorism against nuclear power plants. The group was eventually infiltrated and dismantled by the FBI.

EMETIC (named, sarcastically, after the conservative Republican governor of Arizona, Evan Mecham) first emerged in November 1987, when the ski lifts at the Fairfield Snow Bowl Ski and Summer Resort in Flagstaff, Arizona, were sabotaged. EMETIC claimed responsibility and called for a halt to further development of the resort, which was located on lands sacred to the Navajo and Hopi in the San Francisco Peaks. In 1988, members of the group attacked the Snow Bowl Resort again. That same year, EMETIC also sabotaged 29 power lines leading to a uranium mine (also located on land sacred to Indians) near the Grand Canyon, causing a "significant interruption of power," according to FBI reports.

No arrests were made until May 29, 1989, when two EMETIC members, Mark Davis and Marc Baker, were apprehended while using a propane torch to cut down a utility-line pole from an electrical substation in Wenden, Arizona. More than 50 armed FBI agents wearing bulletproof vests and night-vision goggles, and traveling in helicopters, on horseback, and on foot, participated in the capture. Another EMETIC member, Margaret Millet, fled the scene but was apprehended in Prescott the next day. When authorities took Dave Foreman, the cofounder of Earth First!, into custody at his home in Tucson, EMETIC was all but finished.

EMETIC was infiltrated in 1988 by an FBI mole named Michael Fain, who posed as a mentally disturbed Vietnam Veteran and self-proclaimed "redneck for wilderness." In an 18-month, $2-million operation, Fain collected more than 1,000 hours of audiotape, which helped convict EMETIC members by proving that the May 29 attack was a test run for a series of attacks on nuclear facilities in California, Arizona, and Colorado. EMETIC planned to cause severe physical and economic damage to the companies.

The grand jury indicted Davis, Baker, and Millet on counts of conspiracy, destruction of property that affected interstate commerce, destruction of an energy facility, and destruction of government property. Foreman faced charges of conspiracy for instructing EMETIC members and funding their actions. The prosecution called the group's actions ecoterrorism; the defense responded with allegations of government misconduct, coercion, and entrapment, with the intent to discredit the environmental movement. In September 1991, Davis, Baker, and Millet were all sentenced to prison, with terms ranging from one to six years. Another EMETIC member, Ilse Apslund, was sentenced to one year. Foreman pled guilty to conspiracy, but his five-year sentence was deferred.

Throughout the investigation, the FBI considered EMETIC to be a "small vanguard" of individuals committing illegal acts in the name of the environment. The audiotapes show Foreman and Earth First! were the FBI's key targets. Despite EMETIC's small membership and short lifespan, the group earned a substantial reputation and was named "mother of all ecoterrorists" by Ron Arnold, the father of the "Wise Use" movement and an opponent of environmentalists.

Laura Lambert

See also Earth First!; Ecoterrorism

Further Readings

Liddick, Donald R. *Eco-Terrorism: Radical Environmental and Animal Liberation Movements.* Westport, CT: Praeger, 2006.

Smith, Brent. *Terrorism in America: Pipe Bombs and Pipe Dreams.* Albany: State University of New York Press, 1994.

Zakin, Susan. *Coyotes and Town Dogs: Earth First! and the Environmental Movement.* New York: Viking Penguin, 1993.

FADHIL, MUSTAFA MOHAMED (1976–)

Born in Cairo, Mustafa Mohamed Fadhil is believed to have been a key member of al Qaeda, the terrorist network founded by Osama bin Laden. The United States indicted Fadhil in 1998 for his alleged role in the bombings of the U.S. embassies in Dar es Salaam, Tanzania, and Nairobi, Kenya.

According to the indictment, in 1997 Fadhil received instructions from bin Laden to militarize the East African sector of the al Qaeda group. The indictment asserts that Fadhil began plotting the bombing of the U.S. embassy in Tanzania in the spring of 1998. He is said to have rented the hideout in Dar es Salaam where he and fellow al Qaeda conspirators assembled the truck bomb. In that house, officials later found a computer that contained a document echoing bin Laden's desire to murder Americans. The document referred to "Brother Khalid," an alias reportedly used by Fadhil. The indictment also charges that Fadhil worked to prepare the truck bomb, grinding the explosives used to make the bomb, and later loaded a truck with boxes of TNT, oxygen and acetylene tanks, fertilizer, sandbags, and detonators.

On August 7, 1998, the truck exploded at the U.S. embassy in Dar es Salaam. In a coordinated attack 400 miles away, a truck bomb devastated the U.S. embassy in Nairobi, Kenya. The bombs killed 224 people. In the wake of the bombings, the United States declared that bin Laden and al Qaeda operatives were responsible. In retaliation, President Bill Clinton ordered air attacks on al Qaeda's Afghanistan training grounds and on a pharmaceutical manufacturing plant in downtown Khartoum, Sudan.

Just days before the bombing in Dar es Salaam, Fadhil flew to Pakistan. He is thought to have later fled to Afghanistan, along with many of the other 26 individuals indicted in the case. Three suspects pled guilty and cooperated with the U.S. government as witnesses, while four men linked to bin Laden were convicted of conspiring in the bombings and sentenced to life in prison without parole.

For his alleged role in the attack, Fadhil was put on the FBI's Most Wanted Terrorists list in October 2001, and the U.S. State Department offered a reward of up to $25 million for information leading directly to his apprehension or conviction. Fadhil has since been dropped from the FBI's list, however, with no explanation given. It has been rumored that he was arrested in Pakistan in 2004, and human rights groups have charged that he may have been imprisoned secretly by the United States. However, this has never been confirmed.

Erica Pearson

See also al Qaeda; bin Laden, Osama; East Africa Embassy Bombings

Further Readings

Atwan, Abdel Bari. *The Secret History of al Qaeda.* Berkeley: University of California Press, 2006.
Bergen, Peter. *Holy War, Inc.: Inside the Secret World of Osama bin Laden.* New York: Free Press, 2001.

Bergen, Peter. *The Longest War: Inside the Enduring Conflict between America and al-Qaeda.* New York: Free Press, 2011.

Bergen, Peter. *The Osama bin Laden I Know: An Oral History of al Qaeda's Leader.* New York: Free Press, 2006.

Human Rights Watch. "Ghost Prisoner." February 26, 2007. http://www.hrw.org/en/node/11021/section/1.

"A Nation Challenged: The Hunted; The 22 Most Wanted Suspects, in a Five-act Drama of Global Terror." *The New York Times,* October 14, 2001, p. 1B.

Reeve, Simon. *The New Jackals: Ramzi Yousef, Osama bin Laden, and the Future of Terrorism.* Boston: Northeastern University Press, 1999.

"Rendition: Fate Unknown; Missing Detainees." *The Guardian,* June 2, 2008, p. 9.

U.S. District Court for the Southern District of New York. *United States v. Usama bin Laden, et al.* Indictment S(2) 98 Cr. 1023 (LBS), November 4, 1998. http://www.fas.org/irp/news/1998/11/98110602_nlt.html.

FADLALLAH, SHEIKH MOHAMMAD HUSSEIN (1936–2010)

A Shiite Muslim scholar, Sheikh Mohammad Hussein Fadlallah was a religious advisor of Hezbollah, the Lebanese militant group and political party also known as Party of God. In his impassioned speeches, Fadlallah called for Lebanon to be organized as a theocratic Islamic state. He was revered in some quarters of the Middle East but highly controversial in the West because of his approval of terrorist attacks such as the 1983 bombing of a U.S. Marine compound in Beirut.

Fadlallah was born in 1936 in Najaf, the Iraqi city holy to Shiite Muslims, where his father, a religious leader from southern Lebanon, was studying. Fadlallah grew up in Iraq, and reportedly speaks with a slight Iraqi accent. While a student in Najaf, Fadlallah helped one of his professors, Muhammad Baqir al Sadr, to found the underground Dawa Party, which was later banned by Iraqi leader Saddam Hussein.

Fadlallah moved to Beirut in 1966, after he had finished his studies. He soon married Najat Noureddin, the daughter of a prominent Lebanese Islamic scholar; they had 11 children. As an imam at a mosque, Fadlallah worked to organize Islamic students, forming the Islamic Students' Union in Lebanon and writing some 40 books on Islamic law.

Fadlallah served as an important spiritual advisor to members of Hezbollah from its beginnings in the early 1980s. After the 1983 bombings of the U.S. Marine barracks and French paramilitary compounds in Beirut, both linked to Hezbollah, Christian rivals claimed that Fadlallah had blessed the two suicide drivers. Fadlallah has repeatedly denied this accusation, and followers have explained that "giving a blessing" is a largely Christian practice. Nevertheless, during the late 1980s and early 1990s hostage crisis in Lebanon, Fadlallah was said to command respect among the militants, and relatives of the hostages visited him to plead for the release of the captives.

In 1985 an explosive was planted on the path between Fadlallah's mosque and his home. The blast spared Fadlallah, who had stopped to listen to an old woman on his way home, but 80 people were killed. Press reports claimed that a group linked to the U.S. Central Intelligence Agency was responsible for the bombing.

Fadlallah's influence continued to grow in Lebanon, and he was often called the country's most respected Shiite Muslim cleric. He spoke frequently against a peace agreement with Israel and the idea of "land for peace." In 1995, when the United States declared a freeze on the assets of extremist groups that did not support the peace process, including Hezbollah, Fadlallah urged Muslims to boycott U.S. goods. As violence increased in the Middle East in 2002, Fadlallah told the Arab press that suicide bombing attacks were required in what he called a "holy war" against Israel.

Fadlallah remained ardently opposed to Israel, which bombed his house in July 2006, and deeply suspicious of the United States and other foreign powers. However, he did become more moderate in his last years, distancing himself somewhat from Hezbollah and advocating for increased dialogue among Lebanon's oft-warring political factions. He died on July 4, 2010, at age 74.

Erica Pearson

See also Hezbollah

Further Readings

Bayyant: The Website of the Religious Authority Sayyed Muhammed Hussein Fadlullah. http://english.bayynat .org.lb.

Daragahi, Borzou. "Lebanese Ayatollah Offers Advice for 'Modern Shiites.'" *Los Angeles Times*, February 6, 2008, p. A3.

Fisk, Robert. *Pity the Nation: Lebanon at War*. London: A. Deutsch, 1990.

Jaber, Hala. *Hezbollah: Born with a Vengeance*. New York: Columbia University Press, 1997.

Lally, Kathy. "How a Hero to Muslims Is a Villain to the West." *Baltimore Sun*, May 30, 2004, p. 1C.

"The Many Meanings of Jihad to 2 Prominent Muslims." *The Washington Post*, July 28, 2007, p. B9.

Norton, Augustus Richard. *Hezbollah: A Short History*. Princeton, NJ: Princeton University Press, 2007.

Reich, Walter, ed. *Origins of Terrorism: Psychologies, Ideologies, Theologies, States of Mind*. Washington, DC: Woodrow Wilson Center Press, 1998.

Sankari, Jamal. *Fadlallah: The Making of a Radical Shiite Leader*. London: Saqi Books, 2005.

Smith, Michael. *Killer Elite: The Inside Story of America's Most Secret Special Operations Team*. New York: St. Martin's Press, 2006.

Woodward, Bob. *Veil: The Secret Wars of the CIA, 1981–1987*. New York: Simon & Schuster, 1987.

Wright, Robin. *Sacred Rage: The Wrath of Militant Islam*. Updated ed. New York: Touchstone, 2001.

FALN

Between 1974 and 1983, the Puerto Rican nationalist group Fuerzas Armadas de Liberación Nacional, also known as Armed Forces of National Liberation but commonly known as FALN, perpetrated more than 130 bombings in the United States, mostly in New York City and Chicago.

Like other anti-imperialist groups founded in the late 1960s and early 1970s, including the Black Panther Party, the FALN was committed to the revolutionary ideal of "armed struggle." It wanted to win Puerto Rico's independence from the United States and end "Yankee imperialism" in the Caribbean. Along with other Puerto Rican militant nationalist groups, the FALN quickly became the second most important focus of the FBI's COINTELPRO division, which was created to investigate and infiltrate leftist groups.

Unlike other Puerto Rican nationalist groups, such as the Macheteros, the FALN focused on urban areas in the continental United States. In a communiqué on October 26, 1974, the group took credit for firebombs at five New York banks, as well as the bombings of the Newark, New Jersey, police headquarters and City Hall. Within a month, the group planted another bomb in the Bronx. When that bomb exploded, one police officer lost an eye. These early FALN attacks were typical, in that they were aimed at government and corporate offices and the police, with few civilian casualties

On January 11, 1975, a bomb went off in a restaurant in Mayaguez, Puerto Rico, injuring 10 people and killing 2 young activists and a 6-year-old child. The FALN quickly blamed the CIA for the attack. Two weeks later, on January 24, 1975, FALN members bombed the Fraunces Tavern, a historic bar and restaurant near Wall Street in lower Manhattan, killing 4 people and injuring more than 50. The group claimed responsibility in a note left in a nearby telephone booth. No one has ever been tried for the crime, the bloodiest and most infamous attack ever carried out by the FALN. The group is also the major suspect in the 1975 bombing of the Trans World Airways terminal at LaGuardia Airport in which 11 people were killed.

Over the next three years, the group set off bombs in the Chicago Loop area, a Chicago Merchandise Mart, the FBI's Manhattan headquarters, the New York Public Library, and a Mobil Oil employment office, as well as planting several pipe bombs at corporate headquarters throughout New York City and firebombs at New York's major airports. In 1978, an explosion in Queens, New York, led police to Willie Morales, a suspected FALN leader. Morales was making a bomb that accidentally detonated; he lost most of his fingers in the blast. He was arrested soon after for possession of explosive devices and jailed on Riker's Island. His lawyer, Susan Tipograph, pressed to have him transferred to the prison ward at Bellevue Hospital in Manhattan. Once there, he escaped from a window, allegedly sliding down a rope of bandages with his maimed hands. Tipograph, a major suspect because she was the last to visit Morales before his escape, was a member of the

May 19 Communist Organization, a clandestine militant group that often provided support for anti-imperialist causes, such as the FALN and the Black Liberation Army.

In September 1979, the FALN announced that it would join forces with the Macheteros and other smaller nationalist groups in Puerto Rico. On October 17, 1979, in coordinated attacks, Macheteros bombs went off in Puerto Rico, while FALN bombs struck in Chicago and New York.

FALN activities continued into the 1980s, with attacks on military recruiting offices in Chicago and the armed occupation of the Carter-Mondale and Bush-Quayle campaign offices in Chicago in 1980. In April 1980, 11 FALN members were arrested in Evanston, Illinois. These individuals, including Carlos Alberto Torres, were charged with bombing and conspiracy to bomb 28 government, military, and corporate offices in the Chicago area. Another member, Marie Haydee Beltran Torres was arrested in connection with the 1977 bombing of the Mobil Oil office in New York.

On December 10, 1980, the 12 FALN members were again indicted, this time for "seditious conspiracy" and 12 other charges. The prisoners, challenging the validity of the U.S. court system, refused to enter pleas; nevertheless, all were found guilty. One prisoner, Alfredo Mendez cooperated with the investigators in hopes of lessening his sentence. The information he supplied led to the capture, in May 1981, of Oscar Lopez Rivera, a suspected leader of FALN. Lopez was charged with seditious conspiracy and armed robbery, found guilty in July 1981, and sentenced to 55 years. In 1988 he was charged with attempting to escape and given an additional 15 years. Two former members of Weatherman, Claude Banks and Donna Willmott, were arrested in connection with this attempted escape—a testament to the enduring links between the remaining radical organizations in the 1980s.

Although FALN members conducted a few more attacks in the 1980s, including the 1982 New Year's Eve bombings at police and federal buildings in New York City, the organization began to buckle from the effects of lost leadership. In June 1983, three more FALN members—Alejandrina Torres, Edwin Cortes, Alberto Rodriguez—were arrested. All three were also members of the National Committee to Free Puerto Rican Prisoners of War (founded to support the prisoners arrested in 1980). Torres, Cortes, and Rodriquez were each accused of conspiring to free 11 Puerto Rican prisoners and of bombing two military recruiting centers in Chicago. All three were found guilty of seditious conspiracy and bomb and weapons violations.

Police estimated, even after the great number of arrests in 1980 and 1983, that the FALN retained a membership of 120, with over 2,000 supporters in New York, New Jersey, Chicago, Los Angeles, Washington, D.C., Denver, Milwaukee, Wisconsin, and El Paso, Texas. Following the August 20, 1985, FBI raids in Puerto Rico, FALN activities died down almost completely.

In 1999, President Clinton granted clemency to 12 Puerto Rican nationalists and suspected FALN members. Although they were charged with seditious conspiracy, possession of unregistered firearms, or interstate transportation of stolen vehicles, none had actually been convicted of the 130 bombings, or of any related injuries and deaths. Carlos Torres, who was not included among the FALN members given clemency in 1999, was released in July 2010.

Laura Lambert

See also Black Panther Party; Macheteros; Puerto Rican Nationalist Terrorism

Further Readings

Esposito, Richard, and Ted Gerstein. *Bomb Squad: A Year inside the Nation's Most Exclusive Police Unit.* New York: Hyperion, 2007.

Fernandez, Ronald. *Los Macheteros: The Wells Fargo Robbery and the Violent Struggle for Puerto Rican Independence.* New York: Prentice Hall, 1987.

Meyer, Josh, and Tom Hamburger. "In '99, Holder Pushed Clemency for Terrorists: FALN Members Were Linked to U.S. Bombings." *Chicago Tribune,* January 9, 2009, p. 14.

U.S. Congress. Senate Committee on the Judiciary. "Clemency for FALN Members: Hearings before the Committee on the Judiciary, United States Senate, One Hundred Sixth Congress, First Session, September 15, and October 20, 1999." Washington, DC: U.S. Government Printing Office. http://purl.access.gpo .gov/GPO/LPS9560.

Farabundo Martí National Liberation Front

The Farabundo Martí National Liberation Front (FMLN) began as an alliance of five leftist guerrilla groups that fought a 12-year civil war against El Salvador's military junta. By the twenty-first century, however, the FMLN had transformed itself into a major political party.

A military dictatorship had risen to power in El Salvador in 1929, and in January 1932 the junta put down a peasant rebellion led by Farabundo Martí, executing him and massacring between 10,000 and 30,000 of his followers. In the late 1960s, resistance to the regime began to coalesce, and by 1972 the middle-class, centrist Christian Democratic Party was poised to win that year's presidential election. The military regime engaged in electoral fraud, however, and sent Jose Duarte, the leader of the Christian Democrats, into exile. Following the election, many began to seek other methods of opposing the dictatorship.

The election scandal fostered the creation of many leftist political groups, some of which advocated open rebellion. As the decade progressed, protests, demonstrations, and terrorist attacks against the ruling elite—particularly in the form of kidnappings for ransom—escalated. The government responded with increasing repression, and by 1979 roving government death squads were killing hundreds of people each month.

At the peak of civil unrest in 1979, leftist guerrillas formed an alliance, calling the new group the Farabundo Martí National Liberation Front. Five guerrilla groups were involved in the organization, and each group's leader sat on the equivalent of an executive committee. Joint operations were discussed among these leaders, and subjects of contention were voted on. The five groups collectively had an estimated 5,000 to 10,000 fighters.

In 1981 the FMLN launched a "Final Offensive," an assault on the capital and security forces. The guerrillas anticipated that citizens would rise en masse; when they did not, FMLN fighters retreated to their strongholds in the countryside. The 1981 offensive proved that although the FMLN lacked the popular support to defeat the government, it could remain a long-term disruptive force. During the mid-1980s, helped by billions of dollars of U.S.

military and economic aid, the Salvadoran government made some tentative moves toward democratization. The FMLN began to press for political recognition rather than military victory, and it put forward its peace conditions. In 1989, another large-scale FMLN offensive finally pushed the government into negotiations. A UN-brokered peace agreement was signed in January 1992. Out of a population of 5 million, 80,000 people had been killed during the 12 years of fighting.

The immediate post-war period was a difficult time of transition for the FMLN. The five organizations had retained much of their original character and diverse political ideologies, and the FMLN's attempts to re-create itself as a political party were adversely affected by a report issued by a UN Truth Commission, which called for some of its top leaders to be banned from political office. By 1997, however, the FMLN regrouped and doubled its representation in the nation's Legislative Assembly in that year's elections, becoming a major national party. In January 2009 the FMLN won the most seats of any political party in the Legislative Assembly; two months later, the FMLN candidate, Carlos Mauricio Funes Cartagena, was elected president.

Colleen Sullivan

Further Readings

Almedia, Paul D. *Waves of Protest: Popular Struggle in El Salvador, 1925–2005*. Minneapolis: University of Minnesota Press, 2008.

Clements, Charlie. "A Salvadoran Resurrection." *The Boston Globe*, June 1, 2009, p. A11.

McClintock, Cynthia. *Revolutionary Movements in Latin America: El Salvador's FMLN and Peru's Shining Path*. Washington, DC: U.S. Institute of Peace Press, 1998.

Menzel, Sewall H. *Bullets Versus Ballots: Political Violence and Revolutionary War in El Salvador, 1979–1991*. New Brunswick, CT: Transaction Publishers, 1994.

O'Grady, Mary Anastasia. "Will El Salvador Veer Left?" *The Wall Street Journal*, December 22, 2008, p. A17.

Waller, J. Michael. *The Third Current of Revolution: Inside the "North American Front" of El Salvador's Guerrilla War*. Lanham, MD: University Press of America, 1991.

Wood, Elisabeth Jean. *Insurgent Collective Action and Civil War in El Salvador*. Cambridge, UK: Cambridge University Press, 2003.

FARC

The Fuerzas Armadas Revolucionarias de Colombia (FARC, or Revolutionary Armed Forces of Colombia) is a leftist Colombian guerrilla group that presents a grave threat to the Colombian government.

Between 1948 and 1958, Colombia saw its two leading political parties, the Liberals and the Conservatives, engage in a civil war that plunged the country into near anarchy. Indeed, this period is referred to as La Violencia, or "The Violence." During that decade and continuing into early 1960s, the Colombian Communist Party began organizing peasant militias to defend villages in the rural south. After the war ended, with the two main political parties agreeing to share power exclusively between them, the government began to act against the peasant groups, considering them to be a Communist threat to their newly formed political hegemony. In 1964, in response to the army's crackdown, the peasants formed the FARC as a coalition guerrilla force.

Throughout the mid-1970s, the FARC functioned primarily as a defensive force, providing protection for the peasantry from landowners and providing services such as schools and medical facilities that the state could not. During the late 1970s, the FARC began to expand aggressively, and by 1984 it had won some concessions from the government, one of which was allowing members of the group to run for office under the FARC banner. FARC formed a political party in November 1985, but attacks by another guerrilla group, the M-19, resulted in a crackdown by the army, and by 1986 this first attempt at peace had been abandoned by all sides. The FARC the retreated to its southern jungle strongholds and began to regroup.

During the late 1970s and early 1980s, Colombia became one of the world's centers for the growing of coca, the plant from which cocaine is derived. While the FARC did not actually traffic in the drug, it allowed coca to be grown in regions under its control, and it enforced a "tax" on coca growers. The organization also began providing a variety of services to drug traffickers, including protecting the jungle airstrips used by smugglers. Over the next 20 years, the FARC would see increasing profits from the drug trade. During the 1990s and 2000s, despite the dismantling of the largest drug trafficking cartels, cocaine production in Colombia skyrocketed. In 2010, the country provided more than 50 percent of the world's supply, and the FARC was thought to receive as much as $600 million annually from coca and heroin production.

Drugs are only one source of income for the group. FARC is also heavily involved in kidnapping for profit, a tactic begun by the National Liberation Army–Colombia (ELN) in the mid-1970s, but one that the FARC uses extensively. Targets are often wealthy businessmen or government officials, although almost anyone is potentially at risk. Western executives from international corporations operating in Colombia often fetch the highest ransoms, sometimes millions of dollars. FARC is also heavily involved in extortion, requiring an annual fee or "tax" from businesses operating in areas under its control.

These varied sources of income, particularly the huge drug profits, enabled the FARC to expand greatly during the 1980s and 1990s, transforming a force that in the early 1980s numbered a few thousand into one estimated as high as 16,000 at its peak in the early 2000s. The FARC's wealth, abetted by the collapse of Communism, made it one of the best-armed guerrilla groups in the world. It possesses highly sophisticated communications and surveillance equipment, surpassing that of the Colombian army, and can deploy heavy artillery and antiaircraft missiles against military helicopters. During the 1990s, the FARC vastly expanded its territory and controlled about 40 percent of the country, an area about the size of Switzerland.

The FARC has been responsible for most of the ransom kidnappings in Colombia. In 2007, 382 people were taken hostage, up from 232 the previous year. Most famously, FARC kidnapped a Colombian presidential candidate, Ingrid Betancourt, on the campaign trail in 2002. A severe critic of the FARC, Betancourt traveled—despite government warnings about safety—to San Vincente del Caguan, where she was captured. After six years as a jungle prisoner, she was rescued by Columbian forces on July 2, 2008, along with 14 other hostages. She received the Ordre National de la Légion d'Honneur (National Order of the Legion of Honor) shortly after her rescue. In July 2010, however, she was criticized for reports that she was seeking $6.8 million in damages for her time as a hostage. Betancourt claimed the suit was a "symbolic" move and countered accusations of irresponsible conduct by claiming the government had not provided her with enough security. Marc Gonsalves, one of the three U.S. hostages released, said governments prior to that of President Alvaro Uribe, who held that post from 2002 to 2010, gave land to the FARC and acted in cooperation with the rebels.

Drug Trade Trumps Ideology

As the FARC has become more deeply involved in the drug trade, the ideological fervor that attracted earlier recruits diminished, as did popular support for the organization. Still, the desperate poverty of much of Colombia continues to draw new members to FARC. The group's leadership appears to have abandoned the idea of a Marxist-style revolution, and their political demands now center mainly on land reform. However, within the FARC itself, rigid discipline and a degree of gender equity almost unique in Colombian society are maintained. Almost 30 percent of FARC guerrillas are women, and many have moved into midlevel command positions. The group is organized into well-defended armed camps in the remote jungle, and it is able to move troops quickly on FARC-maintained trails (government forces are reluctant to use the trails, fearing ambush). The group keeps liaisons in every large town and most villages in the areas it controls, which keeps it informed of government movements.

By 1997, faced with the growing strength of the FARC and the increase in kidnappings, extortions, and murders, a peace movement was growing in Colombia. In 1998, Andrés Pastrana was elected president, promising to begin peace talks with the guerrillas. In an effort to create stable conditions for peace negotiations, Pastrana withdrew government forces from FARC-controlled southern Colombia. This withdrawal infuriated the armed forces, however, and the FARC took advantage of the new demilitarized zone to launch new attacks, placing the peace negotiations in jeopardy almost from their start. In 2001, the U.S. government authorized a $1.3 billion military aid package to the Colombian armed forces. This aid was designated to combat drug trafficking within Colombia;

the FARC, however, saw the aid package as an attempt to move against it, and peace negotiations began to break down entirely.

In February 2002, Pastrana authorized the military to move against the rebels. In March 2002, the administration of U.S. President George W. Bush asked Congress to direct more military aid to Colombia, this time specifically to be used to combat the FARC and several other guerrilla groups. Eventually, such efforts seemed to bear fruit. In 2007, members of the FARC leadership were killed and Raul Reyes, the chief spokesman in the FARC's secretariat, was killed during a Colombian incursion into Ecuador in 2008. In March 2008 the head of the U.S. Southern Command testified that the FARC had been reduced to about 9,000 fighters.

When Juan Manuel Santos took over as president of Columbia in mid-2010, the FARC issued a video statement on the network al Jazeera, in which the group's leader, Alfonso Cano, offered to open up negotiations with the Santos administration. Santos rejected the offer, however, stating that no negotiations would take place until FARC had renounced violence and released the many hostages the group continued to hold. Meanwhile, an aggressive military campaign was undertaken against FARC. Three of the top FARC commanders—Sixto Cabana, Hugo Hernandez, and Mono Jojoy—were killed, along with dozens of other FARC members in a series of raids by Columbian security forces in late September 2010. Many observers argued that Jojoy was an irreplaceable member of the FARC, and that the group would be permanently crippled as a result.

Colleen Sullivan

See also National Liberation Army–Colombia; United Self-Defense Forces of Colombia

Further Readings

Betancourt, Ingrid. *Even Silence Has an End: My Six Years of Captivity in the Colombian Jungle*. New York: Penguin, 2010.
Chernick, Marc. "FARC-EP: Las Fuerzas Armadas Revolucionarias de Colombia-Ejército del Pueblo." In *Terror, Insurgency, and the State: Ending Protracted Conflicts*, edited by Marianne Heiberg, Brendan O'Leary, and John Tirman. Philadelphia: University of Pennsylvania Press, 2007.

Gonsalves, Marc, Keith Stansell, and Tom Howes, with Gary Brozek. *Out of Captivity: Surviving 1,967 Days in the Colombian Jungle.* New York: William Morrow, 2009.

Kirk, Robin. *More Terrible Than Death: Massacres, Drugs, and America's War in Colombia.* New York: Public Affairs, 2004.

Kline, Harvey F. *State Building and Conflict Resolution in Colombia, 1986–94.* Tuscaloosa: University of Alabama Press, 1999.

Muse, Toby. "Kidnapper Sends Letter of Apology to Candidate's Family." *USA Today,* April 16, 2008.

Otis, John. *Law of the Jungle: The Hunt for Colombian Guerrillas, Hostages, and Buried Treasure.* New York: William Morrow, 2010.

Pearce, Jenny. *Colombia: Inside the Labyrinth.* New York: Monthly Review Press, 1990.

Safford, Frank, and Marco Palacios. *Colombia: Fragmented Land, Divided Society.* New York: Oxford University Press, 2002.

FATAH

Formed by the Palestinian leader Yasir Arafat during his youth, Fatah has historically been the biggest and most influential group within the Palestine Liberation Organization (PLO).

Arafat and his colleague Khalil Wazir (later known by the *nom de guerre* Abu Jihad) founded al Fatah after leaving Egypt for Kuwait in 1957. Fatah's platform departed from the pan-Arabism of the day, and instead called on the Palestinians to lead an armed struggle for Palestine. The group began as an unnamed network of underground cells. Members published *Our Palestine: The Call to Life,* a magazine in which they called for the eradication of Israel. The magazine set forth Fatah's mission and brought in new recruits. Fatah formally organized in 1963 and set up a central governing committee.

The name Fatah is a reverse acronym for the Arabic phrase "Harakat al Tahir al Watani al Filastini" (Movement for the National Liberation of Palestine). The members reversed the initial letters of the words to form "Fatah," which also means "victory" in Arabic. Fatah gained the support of Syria and emerged from the underground in December 1964, when members blew up a water-pump installation in Israel. In the following years, Fatah members continued to infiltrate and attack Israel, entering from Lebanon or Jordan.

After Israel won the Six-Day War in 1967 and occupied the Sinai Peninsula, the Golan Heights, the Gaza Strip, and the West Bank, Fatah leaders recruited Palestinians displaced by the war. It established guerrilla-training centers in Lebanon and Jordan and increased the raids on Israel, provoking many counterattacks. Throughout the 1960s and 1970s, Fatah also offered training to terrorist groups from around the world.

In a 1968 battle in the town of Karameh, Jordan, Fatah forces held off an Israeli counterattack. As accounts of the standoff spread, al Fatah gained prestige and Arafat garnered international attention. The number of volunteer fighters also swelled. Fatah joined the PLO in 1969, and Arafat was elected chairman of the PLO's executive committee. Upon his election, Arafat reportedly declared, "Armed struggle is the only way. We reject all political settlements."

Jordan's army clashed with the PLO in the early 1970s and overpowered the group, expelling it from that country. Black September, a radical branch of Fatah, emerged in 1971. Black September was responsible for the Munich Olympics massacre in 1972, as well as other terror attacks against Israel. Meanwhile, the PLO moved its base to Lebanon, where it became embroiled in Lebanon's prolonged civil war. In 1982, after Israel invaded Lebanon, the group evacuated Beirut under international guarantees of safety.

Senior Fatah officials broke from Arafat's rule in 1983 and moved to a closer relationship with Syria. With Syrian backing, Fatah attacked Arafat and his troops in Tripoli, Lebanon. Arafat managed to keep control of the PLO, however, and he moved its headquarters to Tunisia.

In the late 1980s, Fatah developed a political wing, forming the moderate majority within the PLO. It has been criticized by militant groups such as Hamas and the former Fatah member Abu Nidal's breakaway group, the Fatah Revolutionary Council. In 1988, under the leadership of Arafat and al Fatah, the PLO accepted Israel's right to coexist with Palestine and effectively denounced terrorism.

In 1993 Arafat signed the PLO-Israel Declaration of Principles, and he brought Fatah back to the Gaza Strip after nearly three decades of exile. But as peace agreements faltered, Fatah members returned to terrorism. International leaders called upon Arafat to discipline his party, something he seemed unwilling or unable to accomplish. In the fall of 2000, a group of young Palestinians said to have grown up together in the al Fatah youth movement founded the al Aqsa Martyrs Brigades. The brigades, named for the al Aqsa Mosque in Jerusalem, became increasingly violent during 2002 and carried out many deadly suicide-bombing attacks against Israel.

The death of Arafat in November 2004 left Fatah without a leader. Even with the controversy that Arafat invited—some called him a hero, others a terrorist—he was the face of the party, as he was not only its founder but also its most well-known figure. His superior public relations skills only added to his legacy, setting a high bar for a successor that was as dynamic as he was. By this point, however, Fatah's reputation had diminished and the party was quickly losing power to Hamas. Much of the damage came from internal dissent between the younger and older leaders within the party, with the former accusing the latter of corruption.

Amid these clashes, Mahmoud Abbas was elected as the Palestinian president in 2005. Abbas, who also goes by the name Abu Mazen, was nowhere near as influential and powerful as his predecessor, yet he also came with significantly less controversy. However, where Arafat never discouraged, and indeed even facilitated, the use of violence and terrorism, Abbas has encouraged pragmatism and more official means to achieve Palestine's goals.

The death of Arafat also presented the heightened tensions between Hamas and Fatah. Fatah, damaged by in-fighting, began to lose ground, and in 2006 it lost the parliamentary election to Hamas. Even though Abbas, as president of the Palestinian Authority, still controlled foreign policy and security, Hamas controlled everything else. A tense period followed, in which Fatah leaders and commanders tried to weaken Hamas's leadership with a series of attacks and assassinations. Additionally, Abbas tried to call an early election, which Hamas, predictably, opposed.

Conflict between Hamas and Fatah continued for most of 2007, even as an agreement to share power was carved out. In June of that year, the violence reached a crescendo with a shootout between gunmen from both parties in Gaza. Abbas then attempted to fire the prime minister—Hamas leader Ismail Haniyeh—and Hamas responded by setting up its own government to run Gaza. Violence, both aimed at Israel and between the two parties, continued until a six-month cease-fire was facilitated by Egypt in mid-2008. However, on December 19, 2008, the day the cease-fire ended, the violence resumed with no less intensity that before. After Hamas fired rockets into Israel, the Israelis launched an attack on December 27 that lasted 22 days. By the time another cease-fire was finally declared on January 18, 2009, more than 1,300 Palestinians had been killed and Gaza was in shambles.

With Hamas dominant in Gaza and Fatah in charge in the West Bank, the groups' fierce opposition to each other has stood in the way of a unified, globally recognized Palestinian state. In 2009, Egypt sought to put an end to this stalemate, instigating negotiations between Hamas and Fatah that led to the decision to form committees and hold a new election in an attempt to unify the Palestinian governance.

In September 2010, negotiations between Israel and Palestine were broached, with the United States serving as a mediator. A main point of conflict has been Israel's continued construction of settlements in the West Bank, an issue that kept President Abbas from direct contact with Israel for a majority of 2009 and 2010. The Barack Obama administration attempted to secure further direct negotiations to take place in early summer 2011.

Erica Pearson

See also Arafat, Yasir; Hamas; Palestine Liberation Organization

Further Readings

Aburish, Said K. *Arafat: From Defender to Dictator.* New York: Bloomsbury, 1998.

Hart, Alan. *Arafat, a Political Biography.* London: Sidgwick & Jackson, 1994.

Kurz, Anat. *Fatah and the Politics of Violence: The Institutionalization of a Popular Struggle.* Brighton, UK: Sussex Academic, 2005.

Mishal, Shaul. *The PLO under Arafat: Between Gun and Olive Branch*. New Haven, CT: Yale University Press, 1986.

Parsons, Nigel. *The Politics of the Palestinian Authority: From Oslo to al Aqsa*. New York: Routledge, 2005.

Schanzer, Jonathan. *Hamas vs. Fatah: The Struggle for Palestine*. New York: Palgrave Macmillan, 2008.

"Talking with the PLO; The PLO: From Birth through Terrorism to Dialogue with the U.S." *The New York Times*, December 16, 1988.

Wallach, Janet, and John Wallach. *Arafat: In the Eyes of the Beholder*. Rev. ed. Secaucus, NJ: Carol Publishing Group, 1997.

FATAH REVOLUTIONARY COUNCIL

See Abu Nidal Organization

FATWA

A fatwa is a ruling or decision by an Islamic cleric. A fatwa can be a ruling on anything, and fatwas are issued by Islamic clerics all the time on everyday religious subjects, such as dress and behavior. Fatwas on everyday subjects rarely receive mention in the non-Islamic press, however. Much more controversial are fatwas calling for the death of "heretical" Muslims or non-Muslims.

The Rushdie Fatwa

One of the most famous "death" fatwas in modern times was the 1989 decree issued by the Ayatollah Ruhollah Khomeini, the then leader of the Islamic Republic of Iran, calling for the death of the British writer Salman Rushdie. The fatwa declared that Rushdie should be executed for having insulted Islam in his novel *The Satanic Verses*, published in late 1988. It also called for the death of any editor or publisher involved in publishing the novel. The fatwa read, in full:

> The author of *The Satanic Verses*, a text written, edited, and published against Islam, against the Prophet of Islam, and against the Koran, along with all the editors and publishers aware of its contents, are condemned to capital punishment. I call on all valiant Muslims wherever they may be in the world to execute this sentence without delay, so that no one henceforth will dare insult the sacred beliefs of the Muslims.

A group in Iran offered a reward for anyone, Muslim or non-Muslim, who killed Rushdie. Rushdie spent the following 10 years in hiding and received round-the-clock police protection.

On February 12, 1997, the Iranian charitable foundation, 15 Khordad, announced an increase in the reward for the murder of Salman Rushdie to $2.5 million. At the same time, the Iranian government gave its assurances that it would not send anyone to kill Rushdie, but it also said it could not revoke the fatwa.

While Rushdie himself has not been attacked, some of those associated with Rushdie's work have not escaped the fatwa. A Japanese translator of the book, Hitoshi Igarashi, and an Italian translator, Ettore Capriolo, were stabbed in their own countries in July 1991. Igarashi died immediately and Capriolo was seriously injured. The Norwegian publisher of the book, William Nygaard, was shot at three times outside his home in Oslo in 1993, but he survived the attempt on his life. No one was arrested in any of those cases.

Other Controversial Fatwas

In October 1999 a British cleric issued a fatwa calling for the death of the American playwright Terrence McNally, the author of a controversial play that portrays Jesus Christ as a homosexual crucified as the King of Queers. The Shariah (Islamic law) court of the United Kingdom issued the fatwa, saying McNally had insulted Jesus, who is a prophet in the Koran. The fatwa was signed by Omar Bakri Muhammad, an extremist cleric who at the time was a judge of the UK Shariah court.

During the Gulf War, Muhammad had issued a fatwa calling for the assassination of the former British prime minister John Major. He stated, "The fatwa is to express the Islamic point of view that those who are insulting to Allah and the Messengers of God must understand it is a crime." Muhammad has since left Great Britain and been barred from returning.

Perhaps the best-known recent fatwa was the proclamation by Osama bin Laden and four other fundamentalist figures, two from Egypt, and one each from Bangladesh and Pakistan, on February 23, 1998. That fatwa, issued in the name of the "International Islamic Front for Jihad against Jews and Crusaders" called for Muslims to "kill the Americans and their allies—civilians and military," calling it an "individual duty for every Muslim who can do it in any country in which it is possible to do it." This fatwa has since been used by various Islamic extremist groups around the world to justify attacks on military and civilian targets.

Lisa Magloff

See also al Qaeda; bin Laden, Osama

Further Readings

Appignanesi, Lisa, and Sara Maitland, eds. *The Rushdie File*. Syracuse, NY: Syracuse University Press, 1990.

Bar, Shmuel. *Warrant for Terror: Fatwas of Radical Islam and the Duty of Jihad*. Lanham, MD: Rowman & Littlefield, 2006.

Kurzman, Charles. "Pro-U.S. Fatwas." *Middle East Policy* 10, no. 3 (Fall 2003): 155–166.

Levy, Leonard Williams. *Blasphemy: Verbal Offense against the Sacred, from Moses to Salman Rushdie*. Durham: University of North Carolina Press, 1995.

Malik, Kenan. *From Fatwa to Jihad: The Rushdie Affair and Its Aftermath*. Hoboken, NJ: Melville House, 2010.

Rushdie, Salman. *The Satanic Verses*. London: Viking, 1988.

Ruthven, Malise. *A Satanic Affair: Salman Rushdie and the Rage of Islam*. London: Chatto & Windus, 1991.

Wright, Robin. *Sacred Rage: The Wrath of Militant Islam*. Updated ed. New York: Touchstone, 2001.

FEDERAL BUREAU OF INVESTIGATION

The Federal Bureau of Investigation (FBI) has two responsibilities: protecting national security and enforcing federal laws. Since late 2001, the bureau's top priority has been protecting the United States from terrorist attacks. Working with other U.S. agencies as well as international partners, the FBI uses its extensive investigative and intelligence capabilities to neutralize terrorist cells and individuals in the United States, to dismantle extremist groups in other countries, and to prevent terrorist sympathizers from raising funds or other forms of support. In addition, the FBI provides services such as crime statistics, criminal background checks, forensic capacity, and training to other government agencies and the general public.

The FBI is simultaneously part of the Department of Justice and a key component of the U.S. Intelligence Community. The bureau director is appointed by the attorney general and confirmed by the U.S. Senate. The director reports to both the attorney general and the director of national intelligence (DNI). Since 1976, directors have been limited to one 10-year term.

In December 2010 the FBI employed over 35,000 people, including over 13,500 special agents and over 20,000 analysts, linguists, technology specialists, and other support professionals. Its headquarters in Washington, D.C., develops policy and provides support to the 56 field offices and 400 satellite offices within the United States, and the 61 Legal Attache (Legat) offices abroad. In 2004 the FBI Counterterrorism Division moved to a new facility in Virginia, where it is housed alongside the CIA Counterterrorism Division and the National Counterterrorism Center (NCTC). The bureau's budget for fiscal year 2010 was $8 billion.

The FBI was reorganized in late 2001 in response to a perceived need to concentrate on counterterrorism in the wake of the September 11, 2001, attacks on the World Trade Center in New York City and the Pentagon near Washington, D.C. Five executive assistant directors, each in charge of one of the five major branches of the bureau, now report directly to the deputy director and director of the FBI. These five are responsible for the bureau's work in National Security (counterterrorism, counterintelligence, intelligence, and weapons of mass destruction), Criminal, Cyber, Response, and Services (criminal investigations, cyber issues, critical incident response, international operations,

Most Wanted Terrorists

Murder of U.S. Nationals Outside the United States; Conspiracy to Murder U.S. Nationals Outside the United States; Attack on a Federal Facility Resulting in Death

USAMA BIN LADEN

Aliases:

Usama Bin Muhammad Bin Ladin, Shaykh Usama Bin Ladin, The Prince, The Emir, Abu Abdallah, Mujahid Shaykh, Hajj, The Director

DESCRIPTION

Date(s) of Birth Used:	1957	Hair:	Brown
Place of Birth:	Saudi Arabia	Eyes:	Brown
Height:	6' 4" to 6' 6"	Complexion:	Olive
Weight:	Approximately 160 pounds	Sex:	Male
Build:	Thin	Nationality:	Saudi Arabian
		Language:	Arabic (probably Pashtu)
Scars and Marks:	None known		
Remarks:	Bin Laden is left-handed and walks with a cane.		

CAUTION

Usama Bin Laden is wanted in connection with the August 7, 1998, bombings of the United States Embassies in Dar es Salaam, Tanzania, and Nairobi, Kenya. These attacks killed over 200 people. In addition, Bin Laden is a suspect in other terrorist attacks throughout the world.

REWARD

The Rewards For Justice Program, United States Department of State, is offering a reward of up to $25 million for information leading directly to the apprehension or conviction of Usama Bin Laden. An additional $2 million is being offered through a program developed and funded by the Airline Pilots Association and the Air Transport Association.

SHOULD BE CONSIDERED ARMED AND DANGEROUS

If you have any information concerning this person, please contact your local FBI office or the nearest American Embassy or Consulate.

Prior to his death in May 2011, Osama bin Laden was number one on the Most Wanted Terrorists list issued by the FBI.

and law enforcement coordination), Human Resources, Science and Technology, and Information and Technology. The Bureau of Alcohol, Tobacco, Firearms, and Explosives was transferred from the Treasury Department to the Department of Justice in order to coordinate domestic terrorism investigations with the FBI.

Founding the FBI

The FBI began in 1908, when Attorney General Charles Bonaparte hired 10 former Secret Service agents as investigators for the Department of Justice. These detectives, designated the Bureau of Investigation, were to confine themselves to examining violations of antitrust, postal, and banking laws, as well as crimes targeting the federal government. The passage of the Mann Act (1910) and Dyer Act (1919) broadened its mission to investigating prostitution and motor vehicle theft. The World War I–inspired Espionage Act (1917) and Sedition Act (1918) further broadened the bureau's mandate.

In 1919, following a series of attempted anarchist bombings, the bureau under Director William Flynn embarked on an anti-radical campaign, investigating suspected Communists, anarchists, and foreign-born agitators. Hundreds of suspected revolutionaries were subsequently deported under the 1917 and 1918 Immigration Acts. By 1920, more than 500 special agents were working at the bureau, with roughly the same number of support staff.

Bureau investigations of dissenters within the United States continued throughout the early 1920s. Trade union and civil rights activists and political radicals were all monitored. The FBI kept close watch on both the Ku Klux Klan (KKK) and the National Association for the Advancement of Colored People (NAACP). Investigations of the KKK were initiated because southern juries refused to indict Klan members for a series of murders. The investigations ultimately led to the prosecution of KKK leader Edward Y. Clarke under the Mann Act; he was convicted in 1924.

The Hoover Years

J. Edgar Hoover, who was appointed director of the bureau in 1924, ushered in an era of massive growth and professionalization of the agency. Over a half century, Hoover's administrative skills, public relations talents, and political abilities propelled the bureau to its position as the foremost law enforcement agency in the country. Between 1924 and 1935, the bureau established an Identification Division, Technical Crime Laboratory, and National Academy. In 1935 the bureau received its current name, the Federal Bureau of Investigation, and the monitoring of politically "undesirable" individuals and groups expanded. Concerns about Fascist and Communist sabotage during the 1930s led the bureau to interpret a 1916 statute as authorizing it to conduct noncriminal investigations into the supposed activities of foreign governments, when requested to do so by the Department of State. In 1939 Hoover managed to free the FBI from the requirement of a State Department request, allowing the FBI to initiate espionage investigations on its own.

During World War II, President Franklin D. Roosevelt directed local law enforcement officials to give the FBI any information they discovered about subversive activities. Wartime investigations by the FBI were successful in identifying and convicting German agents and saboteurs, including eight Germans who came ashore in Florida and New York from enemy U-boats. (After the war, foreign intelligence became the responsibility of the newly formed CIA.)

During the Cold War era, the FBI dealt with potential threats to internal security from the U.S.S.R. and Communist sympathizers. During the 1960s it also began to focus on domestic issues such as the mistreatment of African Americans in the South and organized crime, as well as radical groups such as the Weather Underground and Black Panthers. Although the agency's successes included convictions of foreign spies, serious doubts began to be voiced about its methods, the subjects of its investigations, and the legality of its activities. Hoover authorized the first COINTELPRO (counterintelligence program) in 1956; its aim was the disruption of the Communist Party within the United States. Subsequent COINTELPROs targeted organizations ranging from the KKK to the New Left, and its operatives routinely engaged in illegal wiretapping. Only after Hoover's death in 1977 did a series of congressional hearings make the existence of these programs public knowledge.

Power Removed and Restored

In 1975, Attorney General Edward Levi issued guidelines covering the FBI's domestic security operations, which reined in the FBI's authority and ability to initiate and carry out investigations without oversight. In 1983, during the administration of President Ronald Reagan, Attorney General William French Smith rescinded the guidelines and issued his own, which again permitted the FBI to initiate domestic security and terrorism investigations to anticipate or prevent crime. Smith's guidelines permitted investigations to begin when individuals or organizations advocated crime or indicated an intent to engage in crime. The Justice Department was to be notified whenever such an investigation was begun. The Smith guidelines allowed the anti-terrorist investigations into CISPES (Committee in Solidarity with the People of El Salvador) to expand, eventually encompassing more than 100 disparate groups opposed to U.S. activities in Central America. After five years of work, however, the investigations had uncovered no evidence of terrorism and were halted. The House of Representatives then opened an investigation into the proprietary of FBI domestic surveillance practices. Testifying before a House subcommittee in September 1988, Director William Sessions conceded that the CISPES investigation was flawed because it depended on evidence from an unreliable source, the informant Frank Varelli, and that the investigation had been improperly expanded to include persons or groups only loosely connected to CISPES.

Following the collapse of the Soviet Union in 1991, domestic security and counterintelligence investigations were radically curtailed, with resources shifted to crime investigation. The FBI's counterespionage activities did, however, uncover the Russian spies Aldrich Ames in 1994 and Robert Hanssen in 2001.

During the 1980s, the term *terrorism* was increasingly used to describe what would previously have been described as internal security concerns. Following the 1979 overthrow of the shah of Iran by fundamentalist Islamic groups, the FBI gave particular attention to Islamic Americans of Middle Eastern origin. In addition, the FBI was concerned about armed Christian militia groups, violent anti-abortion activists, and white supremacists. As the 1990s saw the 1993 bombing of the World Trade Center and the 1995 bombing of the Alfred P. Murrah Building in Oklahoma City, the concerns seem to have been justified.

Terrorism and Counterterrorism

The FBI divides its investigations of terrorism into three categories: domestic, international, and weapons of mass destruction. Domestic terrorism is defined by the FBI as "Americans attacking Americans based on U.S.-based extremist ideologies." Included in this category would be the Oklahoma City bombing and the parcel bombs of the Unabomber (Theodore Kaczynski), as well as ecoterrorists and animal rights extremists. International terrorism is defined by the FBI as violent acts that are in violation of U.S. laws or that would violate U.S. laws if occurring within the United States, and that are intended to intimidate or coerce a civilian population or influence a government policy or government conduct. Weapons of mass destruction include nuclear, chemical, and biologic weapons. For example, the FBI led the investigation into anthrax-laced letters sent to members of congress and the media immediately following the 9/11 attacks.

Historically, domestic terrorists have fallen into one of three categories: right-wing terrorist groups (such as The Order), left-wing groups (including violent Puerto Rican separatists, anarchists, and extremist socialist groups), and single-interest terrorist groups (including the Animal Liberation Front and anti-abortion groups). Increasingly, however, a fourth category of domestic terrorist has sparked the concern of the FBI—that of the homegrown jihadist, such as Anwar al Awlaki, a prominent al Qaeda figure who was born in New Mexico.

International terrorists are also divided into three groups: the radical international jihad movement, formalized terrorist organizations (such as the Irish Republican Army and the Palestinian Hamas), and state sponsors of terrorism (identified as primarily Iran, Iraq, Sudan, and Libya).

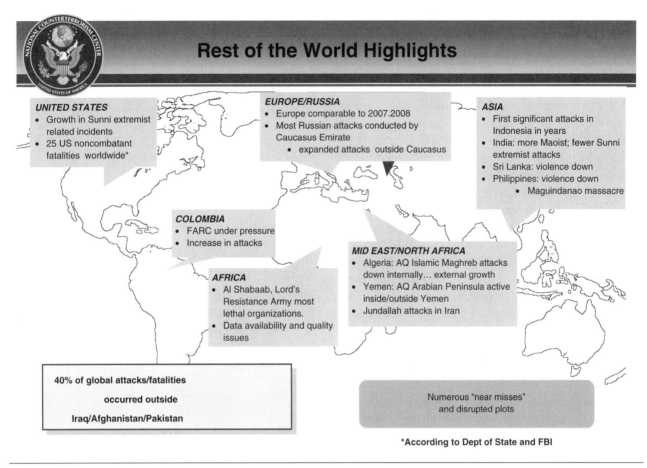

Rest of the World Highlights

UNITED STATES
- Growth in Sunni extremist related incidents
- 25 US noncombatant fatalities worldwide*

EUROPE/RUSSIA
- Europe comparable to 2007.2008
- Most Russian attacks conducted by Caucasus Emirate
  - expanded attacks outside Caucasus

ASIA
- First significant attacks in Indonesia in years
- India: more Maoist; fewer Sunni extremist attacks
- Sri Lanka: violence down
- Philippines: violence down
  - Maguindanao massacre

COLOMBIA
- FARC under pressure
- Increase in attacks

MID EAST/NORTH AFRICA
- Algeria: AQ Islamic Maghreb attacks down internally... external growth
- Yemen: AQ Arabian Peninsula active inside/outside Yemen
- Jundallah attacks in Iran

AFRICA
- Al Shabaab, Lord's Resistance Army most lethal organizations.
- Data availability and quality issues

40% of global attacks/fatalities occurred outside Iraq/Afghanistan/Pakistan

Numerous "near misses" and disrupted plots

*According to Dept of State and FBI

Figure 1   Terrorism Incidents Outside of Iraq, Afghanistan, and Pakistan in 2009

Source: National Counterterrorism Center. "Terrorism Incident Data: Country Reports on Terrorism for 2009."

FBI counterterrorist programs were centralized in 1996 at a new NCTC. The FBI has identified the use of weapons of mass destruction and cyberterrorism as emerging threats to national security. To counter the latter, the agency created the National Infrastructure Protection Center in 1998. The FBI crime laboratory collects and analyzes forensic evidence from scenes of terrorist attacks. The mobile crime laboratory has worked at the sites of the 1993 World Trade Center bombing and the 2001 terrorist attacks, the East Africa embassy bombings, and at the Khobar Towers sites. FBI laboratory work was crucial in convicting a suspect in the Pan Am Flight 103 bombing over Lockerbie, Scotland, as well as suspects in the 1993 World Trade Center bombing. In October 2001 the agency established the Most Wanted Terrorists list, which is separate from its traditional Ten Most Wanted Fugitives list.

Another weapon in counterterrorism is the Joint Terrorism Task Force (JTTF), a joint effort of the FBI and the Department of Justice. More than 100 JTFFs are spread across the United States, bringing together members of the FBI, Intelligence Community, military, federal agencies, and state and local police to break up suspected terrorist cells. The first JTFF was established in New York City in 1980, and 71 more have been established since the 9/11 attacks. JTFF operations arrested the "Virginia Jihad" network, the "Lackawanna Six," and disrupted planned attacks on Fort Dix, New Jersey, and JFK International Airport. Each year the New York City JTFF dispatches a team of more than 100 to keep order in Times Square for New Year's Eve celebrations.

In the second half of the twentieth century, presidents from both parties broadened the powers of the FBI in response to terrorist threats. President Reagan designated the FBI as the lead agency for countering terrorism in the United States. In 1984 and 1986, Congress passed laws allowing the FBI to exercise federal jurisdiction abroad in cases where a U.S. national is murdered, assaulted, or taken hostage, or when certain U.S. interests are attacked. President Bill Clinton signed the Antiterrorism and Effective Death Penalty Act in 1996; this law broadened FBI investigative powers and made the deportation of suspected terrorists easier.

The FBI and other government intelligence agencies were reorganized following the September 11, 2001, terrorist attacks. President George W. Bush signed the Patriot Act in October 2001; this legislation granted the FBI more funds, enhanced its surveillance abilities, and allowed agents access to grand jury information. FBI powers were further expanded in 2002, giving the agency greater leeway in monitoring public spaces and the Internet. The FBI reports information to the NCTC, which was established in August 2004 to integrate reports from all executive branch departments.

As part of the reorganization, the Bureau of Alcohol, Tobacco, Firearms, and Explosives was moved from the Treasury Department to the Department of Justice. The merger between the two agencies was meant to coordinate domestic terrorism investigations. Instead, however, it intensified longstanding rivalries and sparked a public turf battle. Jurisdictional boundaries blurred, with the FBI taking the lead in explosions related to terrorism and the ATF handling all other bombings and explosions. This division has meant that agents from both agencies race to the scene of an explosion to determine the source of the bomb.

Ellen Sexton and Ann E. Robertson

See also Awlaki, Anwar al; Black Panther Party; Bureau of Alcohol, Tobacco, Firearms and Explosives; Central Intelligence Agency; Counterterrorism; Department of Justice, U.S.; Oklahoma City Bombing; Pan Am Flight 103 Bombing; Patriot Act; September 11 Attacks; Unabomber; World Trade Center Bombing (1993)

Further Readings

Batvinis, Raymond J. *The Origins of FBI Counterintelligence.* Lawrence: University Press of Kansas, 2009.

Graff, Garrett M. *The Threat Matrix: The FBI at War in the Age of Global Terror.* New York: Little, Brown, 2011.

Jeffreys, Diarmuid. *The Bureau: Inside the Modern FBI.* New York: Houghton Mifflin, 1995.

Kessler, Ronald. *The Bureau: The Secret History of the FBI.* New York: St. Martin's Press, 2002.

Kessler, Ronald. *The FBI: Inside the World's Most Powerful Law Enforcement Agency.* New York: Pocket Books, 1994.

Theoharis, Athan, ed. *The FBI: A Comprehensive Reference Guide.* Phoenix, AZ: Oryx Press, 1999.

Turchie, Terry, and Kathleen Puckett. *Hunting the American Terrorist: The FBI's War on Homegrown Terror.* Palisades, NY: History Publishing, 2007.

FHIMAH, LAMEN KHALIFA

See Pan Am Flight 103 Bombing

FIGHTERS FOR THE FREEDOM OF ISRAEL

See Stern Gang

FINANCING TERRORISM

The often spectacular nature of terrorist activities sometimes obscures the simple fact that terrorist organizations need financial support to sustain operations. Without some method of securing funds, groups conducting terrorist actions would be unable to function. This funding is necessary for activities such as proselytizing, training, purchasing materials for specific operations, and obtaining basic commodities like food and lodging.

The sources of funding vary according to the political environment in which a given terrorist organization exists and the goals of the organization. For example, several groups appeared in Western Europe in the 1970s espousing a vague leftist ideology and resorting to actions like kidnapping high-ranking government and corporate officials. The relatively low cost of these operations meant that these groups did not require a large, steady supply of funding. Sometimes, these groups resorted to illegal activities like bank robbery to raise revenue. Many U.S.-based terrorist groups have resorted to bank robberies, as well; in the 1980s, for example, a white supremacist group known as The Order netted more than $3 million in a series of robberies staged to fund their right-wing revolution.

In contrast, some organizations have more precise objectives and depend on an assortment of methods to reach these objectives, including terrorism. These organizations need reliable sources of ongoing funding. For instance, the Revolutionary Armed Forces of Colombia, also known as the FARC, has been in existence since the mid-1960s. The FARC claims to represent the interests of Colombian peasants and endorses a socialist political philosophy with the goal of seizing national power. The country's illegal drug trade has proved to be a valuable source of revenue for the organization.

Ironically, one of the most expensive things a terrorist group can do is to eschew violence and become a legitimate political organization. Running candidates in elections and affecting change through the political process is far more costly (at least in terms of money) than planting bombs and the like, a fact that has complicated the transition of violent organizations like the Irish Republican Army into peaceful political parties like Sinn Féin.

Public Funding Sources

Prior to the collapse of the Soviet Union, terrorist organizations typically conducted activities within the context of the political rivalry between the Soviet Union and the United States. In this environment, terrorist groups depended heavily on state sponsorship or financial backing from a national government, because the goals of terrorist groups were almost always defined in the broad, ideological terms of the Cold War (e.g., anti-imperialism, anticolonialism). During this period, the majority of organizations using terror had as their goal either a redistribution of wealth or the attainment of basic political rights against a ruling authority.

The end of the Cold War dramatically altered the character and the prevalence of state-sponsored terrorism. Groups can no longer utilize the rivalry between superpowers as leverage for extracting revenue for their operations. To the extent that groups had relied on the Soviet Union, support from Russia has disappeared, primarily because the Russian government no longer had a political reason for underwriting groups with disruptive or subversive agendas.

A few terrorist groups have continued to receive assistance from national governments, however. Lebanon's Hezbollah has a very close financial and political relationship with Iran, for example. But this link between terrorist group and national government has become the exception rather than the rule. Unable to depend on financial support from national governments, most terrorist organizations have turned to developing their own financial sources.

Private Funding Sources

One such source involves the solicitation of contributions abroad from those sympathizing with an organization's goals. Foreign sympathizers may share the philosophical goals of the terrorist organization, or they may identify with the ethnic or religious background of the organization. Throughout the twentieth century, the Irish Republican Army regularly depended on contributions from Irish Americans. Indeed, Irish revolutionary leaders would sometimes conduct fund-raising tours in U.S. cities, much to the consternation of British authorities.

This reliance on foreign solicitations takes many forms, but an important common denominator is that the link between contributions and the terrorist organization is almost never overt. In many cases, in fact, funds are raised for purposes that have no apparent connection to terrorist activities or to terrorist organizations. Consequently, it can be difficult to establish a clear relationship between contributions and a terrorist group, which creates significant obstacles for anyone attempting to track and interrupt the flow of funds. These obstacles are augmented by the fact that countries where the sympathizers live may be reluctant to intervene and disrupt the fund-raising.

Raising money via private solicitations is an inherently unstructured, unreliable method. The features that make this approach appealing from the standpoint of avoiding detection and interference, such as decentralization and anonymity, mean that groups depending on this method can never be sure how much they will receive or when they will receive it.

Some terrorist groups have begun to use private charities to collect and remit funds. The vast majority of the work done by these charities may be legitimate, and most of the charity's donors may be unaware of any ties between the charity and terrorist groups. They also possess a high level of political insulation. Public officials and law enforcement are reluctant to accuse charities of wrongdoing, since the political repercussions of a false accusation would likely be significant. This has been a particularly thorny issue in Saudi Arabia in recent years, because groups like al Qaeda have taken advantage of the Islamic religious obligation of *zakat*, which requires that devout Muslims donate a certain percentage of their income to charity.

Related to terrorist fund-raising in both the Arab world and Asia is a mode of exchanging and transferring money known as a *hawala*. Hawalas involve a network of people with multistate contacts and established reputations. Instead of actually collecting and remitting funds from one individual to another, the hawala operator merely extends lines of credit.

Hawala operators emerged in parts of the Middle and Near East centuries ago, before banks were established. Even with the advent of banks, hawalas continue to function. They are not subject to the same record-keeping and regulatory requirements as banks, thus making them an attractive alternative to banking for anyone seeking to conceal the movement of funds. Following the September 11 attacks, hawalas came under increased scrutiny and regulation, but since the hawala system does not inherently require arduous record-keeping, there is a very real danger that a crackdown would drive the industry underground, making it even harder to track money moved that way.

Financing al Qaeda

Given the many options for funding terrorism, is it not surprising that terrorist organizations will alter their funding strategies as their situation changes. For example, the radical Islamist group al Qaeda is unique in that the initial funds for the organization came from its wealthy founder, Osama bin Laden, whose access to a portion of his family's fortune allowed him to bankroll activities in Afghanistan during that country's resistance against the Soviet Union in the 1980s. Although bin Laden was eventually cut off from his family's money, the links he created with the Afghani mujahideen helped him develop a worldwide network of allies—including many donors.

In the early to mid-1990s, bin Laden lived primarily in Sudan. There, he invested heavily in a number of business enterprises, some of which were directly related to the group's violent mission, some of which were chosen as sources of revenue, and some of which were apparently chosen to curry favor with the Sudanese government.

Nonetheless, Sudan expelled bin Laden in 1996. He returned to Afghanistan, where he was able to use his mujahideen-era contacts with donors and charities to rebuild al Qaeda. In some cases, donors gave knowingly to al Qaeda, but in other cases operatives infiltrated charitable organizations and siphoned off money. The al Qaeda network grew to include extensive training, education, and publication operations, as well as cells of operatives in many parts of the world.

al Qaeda was eventually able to fund the September 11, 2001, attack, an elaborate undertaking that is thought to have cost between $400,000 and $500,000. At least $300,000 of that money was routed via the U.S. banking system to operatives in the United States, who spent the money on food, housing, flying lessons, and airplane tickets.

Following the attack, al Qaeda's base of operations in Afghanistan was destroyed by the U.S. military, and organizations and individuals who supported the group financially or otherwise were persecuted. As a result, al Qaeda is no longer as centralized as it once was. Instead, small groups that are sympathetic to al Qaeda independently carry out attacks to support its agenda. Likewise, the funding for these attacks has changed: Instead of al Qaeda doling out money to cells, al Qaeda–linked groups are self-financing, typically relying on petty crime to fund their operations.

The Response

Prior to the 9/11 attacks, some governments had created various agreements to interrupt the flow of terrorist funds that essentially made financial transactions more transparent and outlawed certain kinds of financial activities. In 1999, for example, the UN General Assembly unanimously adopted the International Convention for the Suppression of the Financing of Terrorism. This agreement focused on the financial supporters of terrorist activities rather than either terrorists or acts of terrorism, thus allowing for greater flexibility in using criminal law to combat terrorism.

But the fact that al Qaeda was able to transfer hundreds of thousands of dollars to operatives in the United States using the country's own banking system demonstrated that the system had some significant vulnerabilities. Additional international agreements have been put into place, including agreements to freeze the funds of people and organizations linked to al Qaeda. The United States has created new law enforcement and intelligence organizations specifically to combat the financing of terror, and it has tightened regulations on both banks and other financial services, such as wire transfers.

Such measures have not ended terrorist attacks, even those from al Qaeda and its sympathizers, and they have raised concerns about the erosion of civil liberties and privacy rights. Nonetheless, learning more about how terrorist groups finance themselves has helped investigators determine how these groups operate. In addition, the efforts to counter terrorist financing will hopefully make it more difficult for such groups to launch elaborate, large-scale attacks.

Harvey Kushner

See also al Qaeda; bin Laden, Osama; Counterterrorism; Economics and Terrorism; Ecoterrorism; FARC; Irish Republican Army; Narcoterrorism; Order, The; September 11 Attacks

Further Readings

Adams, James. *The Financing of Terrorism: How the Groups That Are Terrorizing the World Get the Money to Do It.* New York: Simon & Schuster, 1986.

Biersteker, Thomas J., and Sue E. Eckert, eds. *Countering the Financing of Terrorism.* London: Routledge, 2008.

Clutterbucks, Richard. *Terrorism, Drugs and Crime in Europe after 1992.* New York: Routledge, 1990.

Day, Kathleen, and Terence O'Hara. "Obstacles Block Tracing of Terror Funding." *The Washington Post,* July 14, 2004, p. E1.

Donohue, Laura K. *The Cost of Counterterrorism: Power, Politics, and Liberty.* Cambridge, UK: Cambridge University Press, 2008.

Emerson, Steven. *American Jihad: The Terrorists Living among Us.* New York: Simon & Schuster, 2002.

Napoleoni, Loretta. *Terror Incorporated: Tracing the Dollars behind the Terror Networks.* New York: Seven Stories Press, 2005.

Rice-Oxley, Mark. "Why Terror Financing Is So Tough to Track Down." *Christian Science Monitor,* March 8, 2006, p. 4.

Roth, John, et al. *Monograph on Terrorist Financing.* Washington, DC: National Commission on Terrorist Attacks Upon the United States (9/11 Commission), 2010. http://govinfo.library.unt.edu/911/staff_statements/index.htm.

Schott, Paul Allen. *Reference Guide to Anti-money Laundering and Combating the Financing of Terrorism.* 2nd ed. Washington, DC: International Bank for Reconstruction and Development/The World Bank, 2006.

Schweitzer Glenn E., with Carole C. Dorsch. *Superterrorism: Assassins, Mobsters, and Weapons of Mass Destruction,* New York: Plenum Trade, 1998.

Walter, Ingo. *Secret Money: The World of International Financial Secrecy.* London: Allen and Unwin, 1985.

FIRST OF OCTOBER ANTIFASCIST RESISTANCE GROUP

The First of October Antifascist Resistance Group, generally known as GRAPO (from the Spanish name, Grupo de Resistencia Antifascista Primero de Octubre) is a Spanish leftist terrorist organization founded in the mid-1970s. From the beginning of its existence it has been overshadowed by the larger and more active nationalist Basque Fatherland and Liberty (Euskadi Ta Askatasuna, or ETA), and little is known about the group.

The group seems to have originated as the armed wing of the Reconstituted Communist Party, a hard-line faction that broke from the

Spanish Communist Party in 1968. It took its name from date of the revenge killing of four police officers on October 1, 1975. The four officers were murdered in retaliation for the September 1975 execution of three radical leftists by Francisco Franco's regime. GRAPO advocates a Leninist revolutionary strategy, in which a vanguard of Communist rebels acts as a catalyst for revolution by the working class. In practice its attacks, inasmuch as they seem to be directed toward a political goal, seem to center on getting amnesty for and better treatment of political prisoners. (The group did organize a bombing campaign in support of labor interests during 2000, however.) While it has engaged in several bombing campaigns, kidnappings, and robberies during its history, the group's main tactic has been assassinations, mostly of security forces and other government officials.

GRAPO was most active from 1976 to 1982, a time of great upheaval in Spain. The fascist dictatorship of General Francisco Franco had come to an end with his death in October 1975, and the country was making the difficult transition to democracy and the restoration of a constitutional monarchy. Many pro-Franco officials retained high positions in the government, however, especially the military, and political activity by radical leftists increased greatly after being suppressed for a long period. During these years, GRAPO was at its most vehement about demands for amnesty for political prisoners, a very controversial issue in Spanish politics.

Despite GRAPO's attacks on rightist figures such as military generals, speculation was widespread that the group was a tool of the extreme Spanish right. Accusers point to the timing of the group's attacks—many of the most spectacular occurred during times of political upheaval for the democratic government—and its seemingly endless funds, as well as the scheduling of its attacks, which would seem to have required an intimate knowledge of the daily agendas and security precautions of the group's high-profile victims. No evidence has come to light in support of these suspicions, but in the late 1970s, many GRAPO members were quietly released several months after being arrested without being tried.

The number of attacks attributed to GRAPO declined during the mid-1980s, after members began to serve lengthy prison sentences. The group appears to resemble the phoenix in its ability to resurrect itself. The Spanish police have announced that the group has been all but destroyed more than half a dozen times, yet it has always returned to commit more attacks. Its strength and funds have certainly been seriously diminished since its heyday, however. From a peak of about 200 members, GRAPO is now believed to have about a dozen members who are not imprisoned.

In the late 1990s, the Spanish government began secret talks with the group to convince it to lay down its arms. The talks broke down in 1998, however, over GRAPO demands that the government to reduce the prison sentences of some of its members. The government refused unless the group revealed the whereabouts of Publio Cordon, a kidnapping victim that GRAPO claims to have set free in 1995, but who has not been seen since his abduction. In November 2008, an imprisoned GRAPO member confessed that Cordon had died during his captivity, when he fell out a window during an escape attempt.

In November 2000, French police arrested seven GRAPO leaders living in hiding in that country. Officials hoped the group might finally be destroyed, but a week later GRAPO claimed responsibility for the killing of a police officer in Madrid. Another round of arrests took place in 2002, but in February 2006 a woman was shot and killed during what appeared to be a botched kidnapping attempt of her husband by GRAPO. In June 2007, six GRAPO members were arrested, including those thought responsible for the 2006 murder. Their arrests also led to the seizure of sophisticated bomb-making equipment, as well as a list of some 1,500 kidnapping targets. GRAPO members had followed and gathered detailed information on 40 of these potential victims. The group remains an enigma, and its future is a mystery.

Colleen Sullivan

See also Basque Fatherland and Liberty

Further Readings

Bew, John, Martyn Frampton, and Inigo Gurruchaga. *Talking to Terrorists: Making Peace in Northern Ireland and in the Basque Country.* New York: Columbia University Press, 2009.

De Quetteville, Harry. "Arrests Cripple Spanish Terrorists." *The Daily Telegraph*, July 19, 2002, p. 18.

McGirk, Tim. "Death Ends Hunger Strike in Spain." *The Independent*, May 26, 1990, p. 12.

Núñez, Luis C. *The Basques: Their Struggle for Independence*. Translated from the French by Meic Stephens. Cardiff, Wales: Welsh Academic Press, 1997.

"Spain: GRAPO Harvest." *The Economist*, October 20, 1979, p. 57.

Tarvainen, Sinikka. "Obscure Leftwing Terror Attacks Baffle Spaniards." *Deutsche Presse-Agentur*, July 8, 2000.

"The Terrorist Bulls Which Gored Spain's Democracy." *The Economist*, June 2, 1979, p. 41.

Wheeler, Fenton. "GRAPO Claims Responsibility for Slaying of Three Policemen." Associated Press, January 29, 1977.

FORCE PROTECTION CONDITIONS

The Force Protection Condition (FPCON) system describes progressive levels of security measures to use when military installations are threatened by a terrorist attack. The U.S. Central Command uses FPCONs to standardize threat and readiness conditions across the armed forces. FPCON levels are different from defense readiness condition (DEFCON) levels, which determine military deployment levels for incidents likely to have civilian casualties. Different locations usually have different FPCON levels, which are assigned taking into consideration the assets and infrastructures that may appeal to a terrorist group, how vulnerable the place may be to an attack, and the ability to recover and respond.

The FPCON system replaced an earlier system of "terrorist threat conditions" or THREATCONs. That terminology was changed in July 2001 to avoid confusion with the State Department's Threat Advisory System. However, many contemporary reports on the 9/11 attacks still used the term "THREATCON." The terminology became even more complicated with the establishment of the Homeland Security Advisory System in 2002, which uses five colors to indicate the danger of an attack on U.S. soil.

The first two of the five force protection threat conditions are general. The first level, FPCON (or THREATCON) Normal, means that a general threat exists but that security should be routine. FPCON Alpha—a slightly stronger, but unpredictable, terrorist threat—means that officials have not gathered enough intelligence to justify implementing the next level of security measures. Military personnel should be suspicious of strangers and alert for unidentified vehicles and abandoned packages or luggage. The military should secure all storage rooms and other areas not in regular use and increase spot checks on vehicles entering the area. This level may be maintained indefinitely.

An increased and more predictable threat leads to the third level—FPCON Bravo. All of the Alpha measures apply to this level. In addition, cars must be kept at least 25 meters from buildings, and all mail must be examined. Personnel must inspect buildings and visitors, and random patrols must check vehicles, people, and buildings. Anti-terrorist personnel must be on call.

The fourth level, FPCON Charlie, is assigned when an incident occurs or when officials gain intelligence about an imminent terrorist attack. All anti-terrorist personnel are called in to duty, access points are severely restricted, vehicles are searched, and guards are issued weapons.

The fifth and highest level, FPCON Delta, is applied to the immediate area where a terrorist attack has occurred, or when officials learn that an attack on that location is likely. More guards are called to duty at this level, and all people and vehicles in a military installation must be positively identified. The military will consult with local authorities about closing roads and facilities that could be vulnerable. The fifth level doesn't always apply to a single location. After the September 11 attacks, for example, the Pentagon declared FPCON Delta, the strongest possible level, for U.S. forces around the world, not just in New York and Washington, D.C.

Ann E. Robertson

See also Counterterrorism; Homeland Security

Further Readings

"Airman's Manual Explains THREATCON Levels." *Hilltop Times*, November 2, 2000.

Keane, Michael. *Dictionary of Modern Strategy and Tactics.* Annapolis, MD: Naval Institute Press, 2005.

Pentagon Force Protection Agency. "Antiterrorism Quick Reference Guide: Deter, Detect, Defend, and Respond." http://garrison-michigan.army.mil/sites/ptms/simplesand/antiterrorism%20attachments/AT_QuickRefGuide.pdf.

Suellentrop, Chris. "What Is THREATCON Delta?" *Slate Magazine,* September 12, 2001.

FORCE 17

In the early 1970s, Force 17 emerged as an elite personal security squad in charge of protecting Yasir Arafat and other leaders of the Palestine Liberation Organization (PLO). The group later branched out into terror attacks on Israel, although in recent years it has resumed its role of providing security to high-ranking Palestinian officials.

Theories explaining the group's name abound. It may be named for the address of its first headquarters, at 17 Faqahani Street, or for the 17 Palestinians killed in the 1968 battle of Karameh, Jordan, that brought Arafat to the world's attention. The name may also have been coined in an attempt to one-up the fearsome Lebanese Christian militia called Force 16, or in reference to the number of bows that a devout Muslim makes during daily prayers. Other theories say the name derives from the last two digits of the telephone number of its first commander, Ali Hassan Salameh, who was assassinated by the Israelis in 1979. According to another theory, the name was taken from the number of the Beirut hotel room that served as Salameh's office.

The group is said to have carried out covert attacks upon and assassinations of Palestinians opposed to Arafat's leadership. In the 1980s, Force 17 expanded its operations and attacked Israeli targets. In 1985 the group claimed responsibility for an attack that killed three middle-aged Israelis on a yacht in the marina in Lanarca, Cyprus. The PLO claimed that the Israelis were members of Mossad, Israel's secret intelligence service. Force 17 was known for recruiting foreigners to serve in its ranks, and an Englishman was one of three members convicted in the Lanarca killings. The British press reported that the man, Ian Davidson, was a carpenter who volunteered to serve "because I was sick of my empty life."

When the PLO was exiled to Tunisia, Force 17 members trained in Russia and Libya. With the establishment of the Palestinian Authority in 1994, Force 17 officially ceased to exist. It was merged into the Presidential Security force, called al Amn al Ri'asah. The terms of the Israeli-Palestinian peace agreement permitted the development of a Palestinian police force, and many Force 17 members returned to the Gaza Strip after more than a decade of exile in Tunisia. The security force is responsible for protecting the president of the Palestinian Authority and other prominent Palestinians, collecting intelligence information, and carrying out counterterrorism operations. Palestinians, however, have accused the squad of police brutality.

Despite its official dissolution, Force 17 continued to exist, more or less openly, as an organization loyal to Arafat. According to the Israeli army, Force 17 members carried out multiple attacks and drive-by shootings against Israelis during the intifada that began in 2000. The Israeli army has in turn bombed many police stations and other buildings used by the squad, which has denied all charges of recent terrorist activity. On February 13, 2001, Israeli army helicopters tracked a long-time senior officer, Masoud Ayad, as he drove his white Honda Civic along the main road in the Jabaliya refugee camp near Gaza City. As they followed Ayad, they opened fire and killed him. Ayad had been accused of being involved in mortar attacks against Israeli settlements and army positions.

Force 17 has become both larger and more acceptable to Israel in recent years due to its unswerving loyalty to the Fatah party and Palestinian President Mahmoud Abbas, who took over following Arafat's death in 2004. Both Fatah and Abbas have been weakened by political, territorial, and military losses to Fatah's main rival, Hamas, creating the need for a well-trained, disciplined, and loyal security force to protect Abbas; and Force 17 has stepped into that role. By the late 2000s, Force 17 had grown to an estimated 3,500 members, who provide protection to Abbas, patrol volatile areas, and periodically clash with Hamas forces.

Erica Pearson

See also Arafat, Yasir; Fatah; Hamas; Palestine Liberation Organization

Further Readings

Blanche, Ed. "Showdown in Gaza." *Middle East* 375 (February 2007): 6–10.

El Deeb, Sarah. "Abbas' Security Presence Expands: Tension with Hamas Prompts Call for Elite Unit." *Journal Gazette*, October 6, 2006, p. 7A.

Peralno, Kevin. "The Gangs of Gaza." *Newsweek*, June 26, 2006, p. 30.

Philps, Alan. "The Highly Trained Elite That Officially Doesn't Even Exist." *Daily Telegraph*, March 30, 2001, p. 18.

Whitaker, Brian. "Middle East Crisis: Outlawed: Enemies of Israel—Two More Groups Denounced; Bodies Linked to Arafat Join 'Terror' list." *The Guardian* (London), December 5, 2001, p. 5.

FOREIGN INTELLIGENCE SURVEILLANCE ACT

The Foreign Intelligence Surveillance Act (FISA) was passed in 1978 to provide a statutory framework for foreign and domestic intelligence electronic surveillance. Although FISA has been established law for some time, new controversies surrounding the law and its implementation have arisen in the post-9/11 United States.

Background

Following the disclosure of domestic intelligence abuses by President Richard M. Nixon in the political scandal known as Watergate, the U.S. Senate Select Committee to Study Governmental Operations with Respect to Intelligence Activities was established; it became known as the Church Committee because of its chairman, Senator Frank Church (D–ID). The Church Committee concluded, among other things, that the body of law regarding electronic surveillance was "somewhat uncertain." For example, the Fourth Amendment to the U.S. Constitution that protects against warrantless search and seizure was addressed as it applies to electronic surveillance in a 1928 U.S. Supreme Court case, *Olmstead v. United States.* The Court ruled that Fourth Amendment protection only applied to tangible things and not intangibles such as a conversation.

However, in its 1967 decision in *Katz v. United States,* the Supreme Court reversed this decision. Although the *Katz* decision held that a search warrant is required for electronic surveillance even to capture conversations without physical intrusion, the ruling recognized the president's constitutional authority to authorize warrantless surveillance and "did not extend [the requirement] to cases involving national security." Title III of the 1968 Omnibus Crime Control and Safe Streets Act regulates surveillance wiretaps in criminal investigations. The Church Committee expressed concern that Title III was not clear about a national security exception to warrant requirements for electronic surveillance.

In *United States v. United States District Court* (1972), known as the Keith case, the Supreme Court narrowed its earlier position on warrantless electronic surveillance, writing that, to satisfy the Fourth Amendment, "prior judicial approval is required for the type of domestic security surveillance involved in this case." However, the Court expressed no opinion as to "the scope of the President's surveillance power with respect to activities of foreign powers, within or without this country." Subsequent rulings further narrowed the scope of warrantless surveillance and drew a brighter line between surveillance warrants in domestic and foreign security intelligence. Nevertheless, there was little statue law supporting the federal courts. Therefore, subsequent to the Senate Watergate Report and the Church Committee Reports (the Church Committee reported on a variety of matters), the U.S. Congress passed, and President Jimmy Carter signed, FISA.

The Foreign Intelligence Surveillance Court

FISA established its own federal court, the Foreign Intelligence Surveillance Court (FISC), to review applications for surveillance warrants. The FISA application need only state facts supporting probable cause that the target of the intercept (or search) is "a foreign power, or an agent of a foreign power, and that the facilities to be monitored or searched are being used, or are about to be used, by a foreign power, or an agent of a foreign power, and to certify that a significant purpose of the surveillance is to obtain foreign intelligence information." Applications for a FISA warrant are reviewed by the FISC, which can be represented by a single judge, and a decision is made whether or not to authorize electronic surveillance or a search.

Originally, the court comprised 7 rotating U.S. district judges, but the number was expanded to 11 in 2001. Appointed by the chief justice of the U.S. Supreme Court, no FISC judge can serve more than one term of seven years. Decisions by the FISC can be appealed to a three-member FISA appellate court called the FISA Court of Review. The FISC and the Court of Review are secret courts because they commonly deal with classified materials. Thus, neither the FISC nor the Court of Review are open to the public, and the records of all proceedings are secret.

FISA and the Patriot Act

The terrorist attacks of September 11, 2001, revealed a substantial gap in FISA: warrantless electronic surveillance for national security purposes was designed for listening in on agents of foreign governments, not on subnational actors such as al Qaeda terrorists. For example, except in limited circumstances, intelligence received by warrantless electronic surveillance could not be used as evidence in a criminal prosecution (*United States v. Truong Dinh Hung*). Therefore, prior to 9/11, foreign intelligence was rarely passed to domestic criminal investigators. The two-decade practice of maintaining a procedural wall between foreign intelligence and criminal investigations doubtless contributed to the agency cooperation failures that preceded the al Qaeda attacks.

Subnational elements that threaten national security were incorporated into FISA by the United and Strengthening of America by Providing Appropriate Tools Required to Intercept and Obstruct Terrorism Act of 2001 (the USA PATRIOT Act, or, more commonly, the Patriot Act). This act removed the information-sharing wall between intelligence and investigations, but not without a procedural battle. The FISA Court of Review, in its inaugural case, ruled that utilizing intelligence gathered under FISA at criminal trial did not violate the Fourth Amendment if it was used to prosecute foreign intelligence crimes, such as espionage, international terrorism, unlawful clandestine intelligence activities, sabotage, identity fraud offenses committed for or

on behalf of a foreign power, or other ordinary crimes intertwined with a foreign intelligence activity. According to the Patriot Act, for authorization of a FISA surveillance or search application, and "to show that a person is an agent of a foreign power, the government need only relate facts demonstrating that the subject is an officer or employee of a foreign power or acts on the foreign power's behalf; or knowingly engages in clandestine intelligence-gathering activities that may involve a violation of U.S. criminal statutes; or knowingly engages in sabotage, international terrorism, or in the preparation of these activities on behalf of a foreign power."

Since the Patriot Act was enacted into law, criminal investigators have had the option of pursuing terrorists under FISA or with a federal electronic surveillance warrant under Title III. As a practical matter, federal investigators have found FISA to be more flexible in dealing with the mercurial nature of terrorists, who often change cell phones, locations, Internet accounts, and meeting locations.

NSA and the FISA Scandal

President George W. Bush authorized the National Security Agency (NSA) to conduct surveillance of domestic criminal suspects' phone calls, e-mails, and certain satellite communications as early as 2002 (if not before), and by so doing he may have violated FISA provisions. The Bush administration defended the eavesdropping, citing national security concerns. Because the charges of criminal defendants include drug and weapons charges and not exclusively violations relating to terrorism and espionage, it is anticipated that much of the information derived from this surveillance will not pass a Fourth Amendment challenge in federal court, and thus will not be usable in a criminal prosecution. In addition, it is feared that details surrounding the acquisition of the information used in prosecution may damage the FISA program. President Bush maintained that he had the legal authority under the Constitution to order surveillance of telephone calls and e-mails from inside the United States to suspected terrorists overseas as a matter of national security, but he also acknowledged that he could not ignore FISA.

Later Amendments to FISA

The short-lived Protect America Act of 2007 eased restrictions on electronic surveillance of targeted communications in which one or both parties of a conversation were outside the United States. In spite of recommendations by President George W. Bush, Director of National Intelligence Mike McConnell, and others within the Office of the U.S. Attorney General, the act was allowed to sunset. This act did not provide immunity for telecommunications companies that played a role in facilitating FISA warrants, which led to the potential for substantial civil liability in invasion of privacy litigation for firms that cooperated with FISA warrants. The FISA Amendments Act of 2008 was designed to remedy this. However, although federal statute bars suit "in any court against any provider of wire or electronic service" following a lawful warrant or court order ordering electronic surveillance, the act did not initially receive the two-thirds vote required to pass the House of Representatives. Finally, in June 2008, Congress passed the law, which prohibits civil actions against telecom firms who cooperate with FISA warrants.

A 2009 act before the 111th Congress (S. 1692, or the "USA PATRIOT Act Sunset Extension Act") was passed to prevent two provisions of the Patriot Act from sunsetting: one regarding multipoint or roving wiretaps, and one renewing the definition of what property may be searched under a FISA warrant as "any tangible thing." The third issue scheduled to sunset is part of the Intelligence Reform and Terrorism Prevention Act, known as the "lone wolf" amendment, which identifies a terrorist without necessarily linking the individual to a specific organization.

Kenneth J. Ryan

See also Counterterrorism; Criminal Prosecution of Terrorists; Federal Bureau of Investigation; Homeland Security; Intelligence Gathering; Lone-Wolf Terrorism; National Security Agency

Further Readings

Bazan, Elizabeth B., ed. *The Foreign Intelligence Surveillance Act: Overview and Modifications.* Hauppauge, NY: Nova Science Publishers, 2008.
Bulzomi, Michael J. "Foreign Intelligence Surveillance Act: Before and After the USA Patriot Act." *FBI Law Enforcement Bulletin* 72, no. 6 (June 2003). http://www2.fbi.gov/publications/leb/2003/june2003/june03leb.htm#page_26.
Foreign Intelligence Surveillance Act of 1978, P.L. 95-511, 92 Stat. 1783 (October 25, 1978), 50 U.S.C. §§ 1801 *et seq.*
Henning, Anna C. and Edward C. Liu. *Amendments to the Foreign Intelligence Surveillance Act (FISA) Set to Expire February 28, 2010.* Washington, DC: Congressional Research Service, December 23, 2009. http://www.fas.org/sgp/crs/intel/R40138.pdf.
Katz v. United States, 389 U.S. 374 (1967).
Newton-Small, Jay. "Bush's Domestic Wiretaps May Complicate Criminal Prosecutions." *Bloomberg,* December 29, 2005. http://www.bloomberg.com/apps/news?pid=newsarchive&sid=aXa1xomXvCTA&refer=us.
Olmstead v. United States, 277 U.S. 438 (1928).
United States v. Truong Dinh Hung, 629 F.2d 908 (4th Cir. 1980).
United States v. United States District Court, 407 U.S. 297 (1972).
U.S. Congress. Senate Select Committee to Study Governmental Operations with Respect to Intelligence Activities (Church Committee). *Intelligence Activities and the Rights of Americans, Book II,* April 26, 1976. Washington, DC: U.S. Government Printing Office, 1976. http://www.icdc.com/~paulwolf/cointelpro/churchfinalreportIIb.htm.

Forensic Science and Terrorism

Forensic science is traditionally that scientific discipline which determines how a crime was committed and submits those findings to courts of law. The focus is the courtroom, and forensic scientists present testimony to clarify what happened, leaving judges and juries to rule on culpability. Forensic science can be a powerful tool in counterterrorism, not only in traditional post-incident prosecution, but also in deterrence, as it adapts to situations in which there is no court. Given the increased threat of terrorism in the twenty-first century, it is incumbent upon governments to utilize their full resources in countering terrorism. Forensic science, once limited to police functions, can play a significant role.

The following discussion of forensics and terrorism relies heavily (although not exclusively) on the Israeli experience as a sort of "case study." Forensic practice, in Israeli experience, has evolved not out of theoretical philosophy, but rather is the product of experience.

Roles of Forensic Science

Dealing with terrorist cases requires absolute accuracy despite a charged political atmosphere, in which pressure to reach rapid conclusions is exerted from the public, the media (prone to making its own decisions if official statements are not made quickly enough), police investigators, and even supervisors. A classic case of error is the November 21, 1974, bombing of two pubs in Birmingham, in the United Kingdom. (A third bomb failed to detonate.) Based on erroneous forensic evidence, the "Birmingham Six" were convicted of the crime and sentenced to life in prison. After serving 16 years in prison, their verdict was finally overturned.

Another memorable case is that of the American lawyer Brandon Mayfield, who was wrongly detained after the FBI erred in linking his fingerprints to latents (undeveloped fingerprints) found on plastic bags that contained detonator caps from the March 11, 2004, Madrid train bombing.

When dealing with terrorism cases, forensic scientists have placed increased emphasis on proactive measures. One example is the suggestion made in 1992 by the Israel Police Division of Identification and Forensic Science (DIFS) to the government of Israel that, as a precautionary measure, all weapons given to the Palestinian Authority following the Oslo Accords be test-fired before transfer to the Authority. Such test-firings would aid future ballistics comparisons in the event that a weapon was misused. As events developed, the decision was fortuitous. Less than a month after the first shipment of weapons was transferred to the Palestinian Authority, an Israeli civilian was murdered in Jerusalem. Laboratory examination

Brandon Mayfield with his daughter and son outside the federal courthouse in Portland, Oregon, after he was released from custody on May 20, 2004. Mayfield, who had been arrested two weeks earlier in connection with the Madrid terror attacks, was released soon after Spanish officials said fingerprints found on a bag near the bombing site in Spain were that of an Algerian. U.S. authorities previously said the prints were Mayfield's. Mayfield settled his lawsuit against the U.S. government for $2 million in November 2006. (AP Photo/Don Ryan. © 2011 The Associated Press. All Rights Reserved)

showed beyond a doubt that the murder weapon, an AK-47, was one of the weapons given over to the Palestinian Authority.

Linking Incidents

Proactive counterterror measures are broad in scope. One of the most important things forensic scientists can do is link various incidents to help direct investigators. In 1995, for example, nine shooting incidents in northern Israel resulted in five deaths, including that of a policeman. To the surprise of investigators, forensic scientists were able to link all of the seemingly unrelated incidents.

It is routine practice to link crimes through examinations such as fingerprints, biological evidence, ballistics, handwriting, or toolmarks. In criminal cases, the focus is on individuals: once a suspect is identified, it can then be argued that the person tied to one crime in the series had at least an association with the other crimes. The ultimate goal is to "solve" as many crimes as possible by bringing the individual (or group of individuals) to justice. In counterterrorism, the basic methodology of linking cases is the same, though there are differences in the nuances of operation. In many counterterrorism cases, linkage is not to an individual perpetrator but to an organization.

In suicide bombings, for example, the bomber is but a small player in a much larger operation. In most cases it is pointless to try to link the bomber to other incidents; he or she was on a one-time mission that would end in either capture or death. The important linkage is to associate each terrorist act not to a specific individual, but to a specific organization. The next step is to search for the leadership, operations, and/or logistics units of the organization.

Detecting Trends

Another key contribution to counterterrorism operations is the detection of new trends. Over the years there have been changes in the terrorist threat and modus operandi, and forensic science is key in detection, giving the security network a basic framework in which it can build defensive measures.

During some periods, for example, there was a switch from conventional to homemade or improvised explosives. The explosive known as TATP is an example. The Explosives Laboratory of the Israel Police had identified this homemade explosive in 1980, and the information was shared with colleagues from several countries. As is well known, Richard Reid placed TATP ($C_9H_{18}O_6$) in his shoes on a flight from Paris on December 22, 2001. After the plot was foiled, the material was quickly identified based on advanced methods developed with the aid of the original Israeli report. Security forces therefore knew immediately what they were dealing with.

In the early twenty-first century, urea nitrate ($CH_5N_3O_4$) became a frequently used improvised explosive in Israel, and later in Iraq, Afghanistan, and other countries. Fortunately, in 1999 the U.S. Federal Bureau of Investigation and the UK Defense Evaluation and Research Agency published results of a joint research project on the properties of urea nitrate. This information proved to be important to the Israel Police, who soon began to receive related casework. Impetus for the research was the 1993 World Trade Center bombing, which was one of the first major incidents to employ urea nitrate.

It is common for terrorists to use bogus travel documentation, but the kind of documentation used has varied, with total forgeries, photograph substitutions, and genuine passports issued illegally all being used at one time or another. In all of these cases, it is the forensic scientist who can determine when a new trend has begun and what should be anticipated by counterterrorism forces. Based on casework experience, forensic document examiners can also recommend innovations in passport issuance procedures and technical document security.

Given this background, forensic scientists should not be seen as outside advisors to the intelligence process. Rather, to maximize benefit, they must be integral parts of the counterterrorism network.

Forensic Evidence

Not every case provides forensic evidence. Incidents can be classified as high-tech, low-tech, and no-tech. Curiously, it is the least sophisticated terrorist incident that is hardest to uncover.

The use of high-tech devices, such as missiles, weapons of mass destruction, high-quality forgeries, advanced computerization, or sophisticated explosives, requires a large technical, planning, and logistical apparatus to carry out an attack. Consequently, they bear "forensic signatures" that often assist in their decipherment, helping to thwart the terrorists' operations.

The larger the apparatus, the more intelligence possibilities there are for detection, though the indicators are not necessarily forensic. For example, the September 11, 2001, attacks did not include advanced weaponry, unless one contends that the aircraft themselves can be regarded as weapons. The high-tech aspect of the operation was in the planning and logistical apparatus, itself—the training of pilots and four virtually simultaneous attacks.

A low-tech operation, such as an attack with homemade explosives, provides fewer intelligence opportunities, though there are some. For example, the purchase or storage of starting materials for preparing improvised explosives or chemical poisons can provide intelligence leads. Identification of these starting materials is a forensic responsibility.

On July 6, 1989, an unarmed terrorist grabbed the steering wheel of a bus headed from Tel Aviv to Jerusalem, plummeting the vehicle off the highway into a valley; 13 died on the scene. This is an example of a no-tech operation. The person himself was the weapon. There were virtually no intelligence leads to pick up, and there was no "forensic signature" to mark the case. There are no scientific or technical devices known today that could detect that person's intention. Another example is driving cars into groups of people, typically queuing at roadside bus stops. Looking forward, forensic psychology could be a good avenue of research for these types of attacks.

Cooperation

Modern forensic science is based on international professional cooperation. In the early 1970s, British and Israeli forensic scientists, working separately, identified the terrorist use of Semtex, a hitherto unknown nonmilitary explosive manufactured in Czechoslovakia, with large quantities having been sold to Libya. British and Israeli scientists worked independently and produced similar results several weeks apart. Although the efforts of each group show professional productivity, how much more efficient it would have been if information exchange had avoided this duplication of work. The twenty-first century, fortunately, has seen increasing levels of international cooperation. Joint research is vital and must be expanded, and its results must be more widely shared among relevant scientists.

The rapid dissemination of forensic findings can be crucial. In June 1982, dozens of people fell sick at the Haifa University cafeteria, located on the outskirts of Israel's third largest city. Forensic analysis showed that coffee in the cafeteria had been poisoned with a large quantity of a potentially deadly agricultural pesticide put into the espresso machine. The quick forensic examination results had a twofold benefit: first, hospitals were in a much better position to render medical treatment to those who had been poisoned; and second, a new terrorist trend was identified. As later incidents were to show, once the barriers to use poison had been breached, terrorists no longer felt constrained. In several suicide bombing cases, poisons have been used in the terrorist's explosive package. There have also been cases of the poisoning of both food and water.

If for only the medical aspect, there is a basic lesson to be learned. There must be a local forensic response capability so that immediate answers can be supplied, rather than awaiting the arrival of an expert from afar. This is also true in cases of dissipating evidence such as latent fingerprints, explosive traces, gunshot residue, firearms impressions, and footwear imprints—particularly in outdoor environments.

Looking Ahead

There are many tasks awaiting forensic scientists as they confront terrorism cases. There must be an expanded use of computers and databases, and psychology is a virtually untapped resource. Biometric techniques to facilitate personal recognition must out-step the ability of terrorists to disguise themselves. New detection methods must be found to more easily locate explosives. Forensic scientists must be given the time and resources to become increasingly proactive and meet the challenges of the future.

One step to increase the role of forensic science in countering terrorism is the initiative of the University of Central Oklahoma, still under the trauma of the 1995 Murrah Building bombing. In

September 2010, the university convened the first of what hopefully will be an ongoing series of conferences where forensic scientists discuss practical applications of their know-how in thwarting the terrorist threat.

Joseph Almog and Jay Levinson

See also Biological Terrorism; Birmingham Pub Bombing; Bombings and Bomb Scares; Counterterrorism; Federal Bureau of Investigation; Madrid Bombings; Reid, Richard; September 11 Attacks

Further Readings

Almog, Joseph, and Jay Levinson. "Forensic Science and Terrorism." *Journal of Applied Security Research* 3, no. 1 (2007).

Almog, Joseph, and Jay Levinson. "Looking Backwards Part VI: No-tech Terror." *Crisis Management* 45 (2008).

Brickell, Stuart J. *The Un-fixing of the Birmingham Bombing Cover-up*. Canterbury, UK: S.J. Brickell, 1998.

Fisher, Barry A.J., William Tilstone, and Catherine Woytowicz. *Introduction to Criminalistics: The Foundation of Forensic Science*. Burlington, MA: Elsevier Academic Press, 2009.

U.S. Congress. House Committee on the Judiciary. Subcommittee on Crime, Terrorism, and Homeland Security. *Strengthening Forensic Science in the United States: A Path Forward*. Washington, DC: National Research Counsel, 2009.

Wecht, Cyril, ed. *Forensic Aspects of Chemical and Biological Terrorism*. Tucson, AZ: Lawyers and Judges Publication Society, 2004.

FORT SMITH, ARKANSAS, TRIAL

In 1987, several prominent white supremacists, including key members of The Order, the Ku Klux Klan, Aryan Nations, and The Covenant, the Sword and the Arm of the Lord (CSA), were indicted on conspiracy charges. A year later, all were acquitted, striking a major blow to government efforts to root out domestic terrorism of the far right.

More than two-dozen white supremacists were named in two separate indictments returned by grand juries in Fort Smith, Arkansas, in April 1987. Five men, including CSA member Richard Wayne Snell, were indicted for conspiring to murder a federal judge and an FBI agent. Ten others, including the chief of Aryan Nations, Richard Girnt Butler, and two top Aryan Nations leaders, Louis Ray Beam Jr. and Robert E. Miles, were indicted for conspiracy to overthrow the U.S. government by force.

The government maintained that the various conspiracies sprang from a July 1983 meeting of the Aryan Nations Congress in Hayden Lake, Idaho. There, Butler, Beam, Miles, and the late Robert Jay Mathews, founder of The Order, allegedly discussed plans to create a separate white nation in the Pacific Northwest. Some of the 119 acts said to be part of the conspiracy include the firebombing of a Jewish community center in Bloomington, Indiana, the purchase of firearms and explosives in Missouri and Oklahoma, and the theft of over $4 million from banks and armored cars in Washington State. The money was intended to fund the establishment of an Aryan nation; the bombings, murder, and sabotage were intended to disrupt society, with hopes of inciting a race war that would eventually topple the U.S. government.

The defense cast the case as a First Amendment issue, asserting that the defendants had rights of free speech and free association, and claiming that they were being persecuted by a Jewish-controlled government. In turn, the prosecution attempted to prove that Butler, Beam, Miles, Mathews, and others agreed to, and then engaged in, the conspiracies. The prosecution relied heavily on the testimony of James D. Ellison, the founder of CSA, who turned government witness to lessen his existing prison term, as well as Kerry Wayne Noble, second-in-command of the CSA.

Ellison testified that he was present at two meetings at which the conspiracies were originated and discussed. He also claimed that, in December 1983, he participated in the plan to murder H. Franklin Waters, a federal judge, and Jack D. Knox, an FBI agent. Waters and Knox were both involved in cases related to Gordon Kahl, a tax protestor who was known to several of the defendants and who had been killed by federal agents earlier that year. The plan was aborted after a traffic accident. Both Ellison and Noble testified that the white supremacist leaders planned to use the CSA compound in Arkansas for paramilitary training. Noble added that the murders would be used to incite "total insurrection across the United States."

After seven weeks of testimony and four days of jury deliberations, on April 7, 1988, the jury found all the defendants not guilty, much to the disappointment of groups such as the Anti-Defamation League of B'nai B'rith, which had lauded the initial indictments. (Many of those charged, however, were already serving prison sentences.)

The Fort Smith sedition trial followed three successful federal cases against white supremacists in the 1980s, and many had hopes that it would further hobble the movement. Critics of the government's case point to the weakness of Ellison's and Noble's testimony.

Laura Lambert

See also Aryan Nations; Covenant, the Sword and the Arm of the Lord, The; Ellison, James; Ku Klux Klan; Order, The; Snell, Richard Wayne

Further Readings

Extremism on the Right: A Handbook. Rev. ed. New York: Anti-Defamation League of B'nai B'rith, 1988.

Hamm, Mark. *In Bad Company: America's Terrorist Underground*. Boston: Northeastern University Press, 2001.

Smith, Brent *Terrorism in America: Pipe Bombs and Pipe Dreams*. Albany: State University of New York Press, 1994.

Zeskind, Leonard. *Blood and Politics: The History of the White Nationalist Movement from the Margins to the Mainstream*. New York: Farrar, Straus and Giroux, 2009.

Fraunces Tavern Bombing

In 1975, Puerto Rican nationalists bombed Fraunces Tavern, a historic bar and restaurant in New York City. The attack was one of the bloodiest ever perpetrated by the Puerto Rican nationalist group known by the acronym FALN, which eventually claimed responsibility for more than 130 bombings during the late 1970s and 1980s.

The Fraunces Tavern bombing was an early incident in the new wave of Puerto Rican nationalist terrorism that flared up in the mid-1970s. The

FALN (Fuerzas Armadas de Liberación Nacional, or Armed Forces of National Liberation) had announced its presence in October 1974, claiming responsibility for bombings in New York City and Newark, New Jersey.

The Fraunces Tavern bomb, which was placed by an unused exit door, went off during a busy lunch hour on the afternoon of January 24, 1975. Four people died in the explosion, and more than 50 others, both patrons and passers-by, were seriously injured. Investigators found that the bomb used propane gas canisters to magnify the strength of the explosion. The tavern and the adjacent New York Angler's Club sustained over $300,000 of damage.

In a communiqué left in a nearby telephone booth, FALN claimed responsibility for the attack, stating that the bombing was in retaliation for a CIA-ordered bomb that had exploded in a restaurant in Mayaguez, Puerto Rico, killing two young independence activists and a 6-year-old child and injuring at least 10 others.

Although no one has ever been formally charged with the bombing, federal investigators believe that FALN leader Willie Morales was its mastermind. Morales, who escaped from the Bellevue Hospital prison ward and fled to Cuba in 1979, said in a 1993 interview: "It may sound heartless to say it that way, but it is hard to fight a war without bystanders getting injured." Except for the Fraunces Tavern bombing, most of the 130 bombings attributed to or claimed by FALN resulted in few deaths or injuries; damage was done mostly to buildings—often banks and government offices.

The tavern itself is an icon of U.S. history. Built in 1719 on the corner of Broad and Pearl Streets in lower Manhattan, the bar was a favorite gathering place during the Revolutionary War. It was there that General George Washington bid farewell to the officers of the Continental Army in 1783. Since 1904, the Sons of the Revolution has owned and managed the establishment, which is still in operation today. The tavern's iconic status was acknowledged again after the September 11, 2001, attacks on the World Trade Center. In December 2001, a woman whose husband had been killed on September 11 held his funeral reception at the tavern, in recognition of the history of terrorism in New York City.

Laura Lambert

See also FALN; Puerto Rican Nationalist Terrorism

Further Readings

Austin, Charles. "A Terrorism Prequel." *The Record*, October 7, 2003, p. L1.

Esposito, Richard, and Ted Gerstein. *Bomb Squad: A Year inside the Nation's Most Exclusive Police Unit*. New York: Hyperion, 2007.

Fernandez, Ronald. *Los Macheteros: The Wells Fargo Robbery and the Violent Struggle for Puerto Rican Independence*. New York: Prentice Hall, 1987.

FREEDOM FIGHTERS

Much like the word *terrorist*, the term *freedom fighter* means different things to different people. This is why trying to define or classify these terms to everyone's satisfaction proves nearly impossible—and thus the adage, "One man's terrorist is another man's freedom fighter." According to that logic, one could theoretically label Yasir Arafat a freedom fighter and George Washington a terrorist. While it is conceivable that comparing the first president of the Palestinian Authority with the first president of the United States might not raise eyebrows by the twenty-second century, for now the comparison is problematic.

Nonetheless, freedom fighters and terrorists can be distinguished from each other by taking into consideration the targets of their operations. Freedom fighters predominantly concentrate on military targets, whereas terrorists deliberately target civilians; for terrorists, inspiring fear in a general population is as important, if not more so, than the particular individuals killed or injured. Still, most terrorists view themselves as freedom fighters, especially those who are fighting for national liberation or some other worthy goal. However, while one might feel that the unification of Ireland is a legitimate political objective, the actions of the Irish Republican Army in targeting civilians require that they be viewed as terrorists, not freedom fighters.

More than semantics is at stake here. The distinction between these terms is important because they can serve to subtly legitimize particular groups, especially when used by the media. In other words, describing a group as being made up of freedom fighters implies legitimate involvement with a struggle for national liberation or the like.

However, the use of the term *freedom fighter* by the media does not guarantee legitimacy of mission. For example, Hezbollah fighters, often referred to in the press as guerrilla fighters, ousted the Israeli army from southern Lebanon, ending a 22-year occupation. Yet Hezbollah is characterized by many as a terrorist organization, and it is so listed by the U.S. State Department.

It can be safely assumed that the terrorist/freedom fighter paradox will continue to provide the backdrop for debate about the legitimacy of individual and group actions. For example, some news organizations in the United States inspired a heated controversy in 2001 when it was announced that they would not use the word *terrorist* when referring to the perpetrators of the September 11 attacks. Defenders of the decision argued that it was an attempt to remain neutral by avoiding an emotionally loaded term. However, the vehemence of the reaction against this decision demonstrates how much power a simple word can wield.

Harvey Kushner

See also Arafat, Yasir; Hezbollah; Irish Republican Army; September 11 Attacks

Further Readings

Clutterbuck, Richard. *Terrorism in an Unstable World*. New York: Routledge, 1994.

Hoffman, Bruce. *Inside Terrorism*. New York: Columbia University Press, 1998.

Jordan, Michael J. "Terrorism's Slippery Definition Eludes U.N. Diplomats." *Christian Science Monitor*, February 4, 2002, p. 7.

Kushner, Harvey W. *Terrorism in America: A Structured Approach to Understanding the Terrorist Threat*. Springfield, IL: Charles C Thomas, 1998.

O'Neill, Brad E. *Insurgency and Terrorism: Inside Modern Revolutionary Warfare*. New York: Brassey, 1990.

Ward, Olivia. "A Popular, and Much Hated, Word: Who's a Terrorist Now?" *Toronto Star*, March 6, 2005, p. D1.

FREELANCE TERRORISM

The term *freelance terrorism* describes the actions of individuals or small groups who take it upon themselves to act against a target without the direct support of a terrorist organization. Their actions are largely the outcome of their own rage, although they have usually been encouraged, subliminally or otherwise, by others harboring similar hatred. Such is the case when extremist animal rights and environmental groups invite individuals visiting their websites or reading their literature to join the cause and launch an attack on the objects of their incendiary rhetoric.

Almost by definition, freelance terrorists (or "lone wolves," as they are sometimes called) are not tied to any traditional terrorist group—or to any other group, for that matter. This is not to say that at some point they might not have been a card-carrying member of some type of terrorist organization; they might even have obtained some financial support or training from such a group. In large measure, however, they take solitary action, with only their conscience to guide them. The advice and counsel of others, even those sympathetic to the cause, is for the most part absent during their freelance actions.

However, a concerned, tentative, or even frightened comrade can often stop freelance terrorism from taking place. This was most certainly the case in the summer of 1997 when someone approached an officer of the 88th Precinct in the Fort Greene section of Brooklyn, New York, and said, "My friend is going to kill people in the subway." On July 31, Gazi Ibrahim Abu Maziar and Lafi Khalil were arrested in an explosive-laden Brooklyn apartment before they could carry out a suicide attack on the subway. Abu Maziar and Khalil were later convicted and sentenced to long prison terms.

A lesson learned from this abortive suicide attempt is that more than one freelancer makes a group of freelancers more vulnerable, because the actions of one, impulsive or not, might compromise the mission of the group. An old saying attributed to organized crime members applies here: "Two can keep a secret if one is dead." Two, three, or more freelancers acting in concert are, in theory, less dangerous than the solitary freelancer acting alone, as was the case with Mir Aimal Kansi. On the morning of January 25, 1993, Kansi, a 29-year-old Pakistani wielding an AK-47 automatic rifle, shot five individuals as they sat in rush-hour traffic outside the gates of CIA headquarters in Langley, Virginia.

Other acts of international freelance terrorism took place in the United States in 1994 and 1997. In 1994 a Lebanese immigrant cab driver, Rashid Baz, "spray-fired" a Cobray M-11/9 assault pistol at a van carrying Hasidic students across the Brooklyn Bridge in New York, killing one and wounding three others. And in 1997, Ali Hassan Abu Kamal, a 69-year-old Palestinian visiting the Empire State Building, took a semiautomatic handgun from under his coat and began shooting. After the rampage was over, two were dead—including Abu Kamal, who shot himself—and six others were injured. The solitary nature of these acts can lead to confusion in the media as to the perpetrator's motivation: was Kamal merely a deranged gunman, or was he a freelance terrorist? Investigators subsequently discovered letters written by Kamal, in which he railed against Americans and Zionists, leaving little doubt as to the political nature of his assault.

In the United States, domestic terrorist leaders of various stripes have encouraged the formation of small, phantom-like cells of individuals. These cells, usually fewer than six in number, try to stay small and are wont to split apart into other cells when membership becomes too large. This technique, known as "leaderless resistance," encourages small groups with fewer members. The leaderless group can act spontaneously to commit an act of terrorism, and the group's small size makes it difficult to infiltrate.

Using the behavior of one freelancer to help predict or explain the actions of another freelancer is difficult, if not impossible, given the differences between individuals. Take, for example, the actions of Theodore John Kaczynski, the Unabomber, who killed 3 people and wounded 23 others in a nearly decade-long serial bombing campaign aimed at saving the environment from modern technology. Knowing the Unabomber's behavior would prove helpful only if other serial bombers also built 10-by-12-foot cabins without electricity or running water on the edge of the Continental Divide. Future serial bombers or freelancers might want to live the life of a hermit and decry the evils of modern technology; then again, they may not. They will have their own peculiarities and grievances, and this is why profiling is an art, rather than a science. It is also why freelance terrorism poses such a problem to the intelligence gathering and law enforcement communities.

Harvey Kushner

See also Brooklyn Bridge Shooting; Empire State Building Shooting; Kansi, Mir Aimal; Leaderless Resistance; Lone-Wolf Terrorism; Subway Suicide Bombing Plot; Unabomber

Further Readings

Fields, Gary, and Evan Perez. "FBI Hunts Lone Wolves before They Act." *The Wall Street Journal,* June 15, 2009, p. A3.

German, Mike. "Behind the Lone Terrorist, a Pack Mentality." *The Washington Post,* June 5, 2005, p. B1.

Graysmith, Robert. *Unabomber: A Desire to Kill.* New York: Berkley Books, 1998.

Katz, Samuel M. *Jihad in Brooklyn: The NYPD Raid That Stopped America's First Suicide Bombers.* New York: New American Library, 2005.

Kushner, Harvey W. *Terrorism in America: A Structured Approach to Understanding the Terrorist Threat.* Springfield, IL: Charles C Thomas, 1998.

Pressman, Jeremy. "Leaderless Resistance: The Next Threat?" *Current History* 102, no. 668 (December 2003): 422–425.

Sageman, Marc. *Leaderless Jihad: Terror Networks in the Twenty-first Century.* Philadelphia: University of Pennsylvania Press, 2008.

Frente Patriótico Manuel Rodríguez

See Manuel Rodriguez Patriotic Front

Frente Patriótico Morazanista

See Morazanist Patriotic Front

Fronte di Liberazione Naziunale di la Corsica

See National Liberation Front of Corsica

Fuerzas Armadas Revolucionarias de Colombia

See FARC

GADAHN, ADAM YAHIYE (1978–)

Adam Yahiye Gadahn, a U.S. citizen, was indicted in California on charges of treason, accused of providing "aid and comfort" to al Qaeda. He is the first person to be charged with treason against the United States since the World War II era.

Gadahn—also known as Azzam al Amriki and Azzam the American, among other aliases—was born Adam Pearlman on September 1, 1978, to parents of Jewish and Catholic heritage. He was raised in rural Riverside County, California, on a family farm. In the mid-1990s, Gadahn moved to Santa Ana in Orange County, California, to live with his grandparents. At the age of 17, he converted to Islam while studying at the Islamic Society of Orange County, located in Garden Grove, California. he describe his conversion in an essay titled "Becoming Muslim," which he posted on the website of the University of Southern California.

According to Federal Bureau of Investigation (FBI) reporting, Gadahn moved to Pakistan in 1998 and attended al Qaeda terrorist training camps in Afghanistan. He has since become known as a propagandist for the terrorist organization. In 2004 Gadahn was one of seven individuals singled out by the FBI director and the U.S. attorney general as posing a danger to U.S. interests around the world. In October 2005 a grand jury in Santa Ana, California, indicted Gadahn for his alleged involvement in terrorist activities, including making a series of propaganda videos for al Qaeda. From 2004 through 2010, at least a dozen videos have appeared in which Gadahn speaks in support of al Qaeda and promotes jihad against the United States and the West. The charges filed in the Central District of California state that Gadahn "gave al Qaeda aid and comfort . . . with intent to betray the United States."

According to the indictment, on September 2, 2006, al Qaeda's second in command, Ayman al Zawahiri, introduced Gadahn as "our brother Azzam the American" and urged Americans to listen to Gadahn. As one of al Qaeda's principal spokesmen, Gadahn's messages have been targeted toward gaining the support of English-speaking audiences in the United States and abroad. On October 11, 2006, the FBI added Gadahn to its Most Wanted Terrorists list, and the U.S. Department of State has offered a reward of up to $1 million for information leading to his arrest.

Michael Ronczkowski

See also al Qaeda; Jihad; Zawahiri, Ayman al

Further Readings

Bergen, Peter L. *The Longest War: Inside the Enduring Conflict between American and al-Qaeda.* New York: Free Press, 2011.

Gartenstein-Ross, Daveed, and Laura Grossman. *Homegrown Terrorists in the U.S. and U.K.* Washington, DC: FDD Press, 2009.

Jenkins, Brian Michael. "No Path to Glory: Deterring Homegrown Terrorism." CT-348, May 2010, Testimony presented before the House Homeland

Security Committee, Subcommittee on Intelligence, Information Sharing and Terrorism Risk Assessment, May 26, 2010.

Jenkins, Brian Michael. "Would-be Warriors: Incidents of Jihadist Terrorist Radicalization in the United States since September 11, 2001." RAND Occasional Papers Series. Santa Monica, CA: RAND Corporation, 2010.

Ronczkowski, Michael. *Terrorism and Organized Hate Crime.* 2nd ed. Boca Raton, FL: CRC Press, 2006.

U.S. Senate Committee on Homeland Security and Governmental Affairs. *Violent Islamist Extremism, the Internet, and the Homegrown Terrorist Threat.* Majority and Minority Staff Report, May 8, 2008. http://hsgac.senate.gov/public/_files/IslamistReport.pdf.

GAMA'A AL ISLAMIYYA

Gama'a al Islamiyya (aka Islamic Group) was at one time Egypt's largest militant group. During the 1990s, the group sought to violently overthrow the Egyptian government and replace it with an Islamic theocracy. The organization, formed in the late 1970s, carried out terrorist attacks on tourists and police officers. Because so many of the attacks targeted tourists, Egypt's tourism industry was severely affected.

The U.S. State Department reports that, at its height, Gama'a Islamiyya boasted membership of several thousand, as well as thousands of sympathizers. The group claimed responsibility for the 1995 attempted assassination of Egyptian president Hosni Mubarak in Addis Ababa, Ethiopia, as well as many attacks on tourist buses and a Nile cruise ship. While the group operates primarily in southern Egypt, it has support in Cairo, Alexandria, and other cities, as well as a presence in Sudan, the United Kingdom, Afghanistan, Austria, and Yemen. The Egyptian government has said that Gama'a has received financial support from Osama bin Laden as well as from Iranian and Afghan groups.

In November 1997, Gama'a Islamiyya members killed 58 foreign tourists and four Egyptians near the Valley of the Kings in Luxor. The tourists were entering the ancient Hatshepsut Temple when six gunmen disguised as police officers fired automatic rifles into the crowd. The international press reported that some of those killed had been stabbed after they were shot. In the gun battle, all of the terrorists were killed by Egyptian security forces.

When claiming responsibility for the attack, Gama'a Islamiyya maintained that it had intended only to take the tourists hostage, in an attempt to secure the release from prison of the group's spiritual leader, blind cleric Omar Abdel Rahman. (Abdel Rahman was convicted of involvement in a broad terrorist conspiracy that culminated with the 1993 World Trade Center bombing; he had fled Egypt and lived in exile in Brooklyn before his conviction.) However, witnesses reported no attempt at hostage taking, just unprovoked gunfire. The flood of travel cancellations following the attack caused an estimated $500 million in lost revenue.

Egypt immediately cracked down on Gama'a Islamiyya, and those convicted of participating in terror attacks were sentenced to death in military courts. Defendants in the trials accused the state of torture and, in support of their claims, displayed injuries to the press. According to the U.S. State Department, Gama'a Islamiyya became fractured as jailed and exiled members vied for influence and leadership. In a break with Hamza's leadership, Rifa'i Taha Musa, a former senior member of Gama'a Islamiyya, signed Osama bin Laden's 1998 fatwa against the United States. The fatwa called for attacks against U.S. civilians. Taha Musa appeared in late 2000 with bin Laden and his second-in-command, Ayman al Zawahiri, in an undated video threatening retaliation against the United States for Abdel Rahman's continued imprisonment. Taha Musa published a book supporting the use of terrorist attacks in 2001, but he disappeared several months later; his fate is unknown.

Despite Taha Musa's call to arms, and the fact that Abdel Rahman withdrew his support for the cease-fire in June 2000 from his prison cell in the United States, Gama'a Islamiyya publicly denied supporting al Qaeda and has not broken the unilaterally declared cease-fire. In 2003 most of the group's jailed leaders publicly repudiated violence and terrorism, and in return, the Egyptian government has released thousands of the group's members from jail. Gama'a Islamiyya is not believed to have engaged in any further attacks since the Luxor massacre. It is believed that those members who still support the use of violence have mostly defected to the al Qaeda network.

Erica Pearson

See also Abdel Rahman, Omar; al Qaeda; bin Laden, Osama; Fatwa

Further Readings

Abdo, Genevieve. *No God but God: Egypt and the Triumph of Islam.* New York: Oxford University Press, 2002.

Berger, Carol. "Islamic Militants Fire at Cruise Ship on Nile." *Daily Telegraph,* April 10, 1993, p. 15.

Berger, Carol. "Muslims Hang for Attacking Tourists; Egypt Faces Criticism over Repression of Opposition." *Daily Telegraph,* July 9, 1993, p. 14.

Burgat, Francois. *Face to Face with Political Islam.* London: I.B. Tauris, 2003.

El-Dakhakhny, Mohamed. "Egypt Terrorists Want Leader Back." *Chicago Sun-Times,* November 19, 1997, p. 3.

Levinson, Charles. "Once-violent Militant Group in Egypt Espouses a New Path." *The Boston Globe,* October 19, 2003, p. A3.

Lockwood, Christopher. "Massacre by the Nile: The Killers." *Daily Telegraph,* November 19, 1997, p. 3.

U.S. State Department. "Terrorist Groups." *Country Reports on Terrorism 2008.* http://www.state.gov/s/ct/rls/crt/2008/122449.htm.

Wiktorowicz, Quintan. *Islamic Activism: A Social Movement Theory Approach.* Bloomington: Indiana University Press, 2004.

GENDER-BASED TERRORISM

Gender-based terrorism refers to acts of politically motivated violence or sustained threats of violence in which victims are targeted because of their gender, and as a strategy for terrorizing a larger, target audience. The intent is to place the targeted audience in a state of chronic fear or terror so that they or their representatives accede to terrorist demands. Victims from the targeted gender may be selected randomly, opportunistically, or categorically. Thus, a particular category of women or men may be targeted based on ethnic, class, religious, or marital status, or on a behavioral category. The targeted victims are chosen for their symbolic value in transmitting a focused terror message to the target audience.

The most common acts of gender-based terrorism involve sexual violence against women or punishment of women for actual or alleged behavior, especially sexual behavior, that violates the terrorist group's norms. Both forms are sometimes referred to as sexual terrorism, sexist terrorism, or anti-female terror.

An extreme form of gender-based terrorism, sometimes referred to as "gendercide," targets a victim group for extermination. Examples of ethnic gendercides targeting male victims are the 1995 Srebrenica massacre, in which Serb troops separated out and murdered thousands of Bosnian civilian men, and the 1988 Anfal offensive, which involved the Iraqi state-sponsored killing of tens of thousands of Iraqi Kurdistan men. Acts of violence intended to exterminate women and girls, such as female infanticide or the witch hunts in early modern Europe, are called "femicide" or "gynocide."

Gender-Based Terrorism Involving Sexual Violence

Gender-based terrorism involving sexual violence frequently occurs within the context of armed conflict or civil unrest. The mass raping of civilian women during war, pervasive across time and cultures, is a leading example. War rape has historically been constructed as an unfortunate but normal part of war, as suggested, for instance, in references to the "looting and raping" by victorious soldiers, or the expression, "to the victor goes the spoils." Some war rape is opportunistic, and victims are randomly selected. However, war rape is often purposive and systematic, intended to cause terror and chaos among civilian populations in war zones. The strategy often involves raping the enemy's women in order to shame and humiliate enemy men (the target audience), and thus demoralize their war effort. As part of a genocidal strategy, mass rape may also entail the extermination of the enemy's ethnic "purity" through impregnation of their women.

In the 1990s, reports of mass raping in the Bosnia-Herzegovina and Rwanda armed conflicts gained international attention. As part of the state-sponsored genocide—also referred to as "ethnic cleansing" in Bosnia—thousands of women were rounded up and imprisoned in make-shift camps, where, during vicious interrogations, they were gang-raped and serially raped, then often murdered. In such camps, as well as in their homes and villages, some 20,000 to 50,000 mainly Muslim and Croatian women were raped over the course of this four-year war, part of a destabilizing terror strategy implemented by the Serbian army and affiliated paramilitaries. Similarly, an estimated 250,000 Rwandan women were raped during the state-supported genocide carried out by Rwandan Hutus. A strategy of ethnic cleansing by impregnation was indicated in both cases. Criminal tribunals seeking justice for both the Rwandan and former Yugoslavia war atrocities have formally identified rape as a war crime.

Strategic war rape has occurred with alarming frequency throughout the 1990s and 2000s in armed conflicts across regions, including in Afghanistan, Cambodia, Chechnya, Colombia, the Democratic Republic of the Congo, East Timor, Guatemala, Kosovo, Myanmar (Burma), Sierra Leone, and Sri Lanka. This gendered terror has been both state-sponsored and initiated by insurgent groups. Perpetrators have included government soldiers, police officers and prison guards, government-supported militias or contractors, and insurgents. In many societies, victims of war rape are ostracized and rejected by their families and communities, compounding the terror of the violent attack with the terror of abandonment.

In other war-related cases, women have been taken and held en masse as enslaved prostitutes for soldiers. A notorious example is the approximately 200,000 Asian women who were abducted and forced to service Japanese troops during World War II. These "comfort women" were shipped throughout the wide swath of Asia and the Pacific controlled by Japanese troops and listed on military supply lists under categories such as "ammunition" and "amenities." The message conveyed to the men of these largely Korean, but also Chinese, Filipina, and other Asian women, was one of Japanese masculine superiority in the Asian military arena; for women, the terror highlighted their categorical defenselessness as objects of commodified sexual violence.

Gender-Based Terrorism as Punishment for (Mis)Behaviors

Systematic acts of violence against women for perceived violations of behavioral norms that apply mainly or exclusively to women occur worldwide. Much of this gender-based terrorism is motivated by the desire to control women's sexual or reproductive behavior and is staged by extremist entities, such as fundamentalist governments, organized militias, or insurgent groups. Examples include murder or severe physical assaults on women for appearing in public unveiled or in other clothing deemed to be inappropriate, appearing in public with a nonrelative male, refusing a forced marriage, having sexual or romantic relations outside of marriage, or leaving a domestically violent husband. In accordance with certain communal laws in countries such as Afghanistan, Somalia, and Iran, women who have been raped but fail to meet the rigid standards of proof of their victimization are treated as adulterers, for which the punishment is death. The target audience of such gender-based terrorism is typically women, but the terror threat is also conveyed to their male relatives, who may be held responsible for controlling the behavior of the women in their families.

In the United States and other countries in the Global North as well as South, anti-abortion violence is another form of behavioral gender-based terrorism. Even where laws guarantee women's right to reproductive choice, extremist groups carry out or threaten violence against women seeking abortions, as well as abortion providers of both sexes. The target audiences are pregnant or potentially pregnant women, men and women who provide or support abortion services and women's right to choose, and governments that have implemented pro-choice policies.

Labeling Gender-Based Terrorism

Several authors, including Lisa Sharlach, Gus Martin, and Jacky Hardy (see Further Readings section), have noted that although the above forms of gender-based violence meet the definitional criteria of terrorism, they have not been recognized by state governments, international bodies, or the media as such. They call for a relabeling of these systematic acts of gender-based violence carried out by states or dissident groups so that their political nature might be acknowledged and confronted.

Kathryn Farr

See also Anti-Abortion Terrorism; Ethnic Cleansing

Further Readings

Farr, Kathryn. "Extreme War Rape In Today's Civil-War-Torn States: A Conceptual and Comparative Analysis." *Gender Issues* 26 (2009): 1–41.

Gendercide Watch. http://www.gendercide.org.

Green, Jennifer L. "Uncovering Collective Rape: A Comparative Study of Political Sexual Violence." *International Journal of Sociology* 34 (2004): 97–116.

Hardy, Jacky. "Everything Old Is New Again: The Use of Gender-based Terrorism against Women." *Minerva: Quarterly Report on Women and the Military,* Summer 2001.

Kimmel, Michael. "Gender, Class, and Terrorism." *The Chronicle Review,* February 8, 2002, p. B11.

Martin, Gus. "Emerging Terrorist Environments: Gender-Selective Political Violence and Criminal Dissident Terrorism." In *Understanding Terrorism: Challenges, Perspectives, and Issues,* 308–341. Thousand Oaks, CA: Sage, 2006.

Pratt, Marion, and Leah Werchick. *Sexual Terrorism: Rape as a Weapon of War in Eastern Democratic Republic of the Congo.* USAID/DCHA Assessment Report, March 2004. http://www.reformedelapnc.org/documents/Rape-in-DRC_Final-Report.pdf.

Ray, Amy E. "The Shame of It: Gender-Based Terrorism in the Former Yugoslavia and the Failure of International Human Rights Law to Comprehend the Injuries." *American University Law Review* 46 (1997): 793–840.

Sharlach, Lisa. "Veil and Four Walls: A State of Terror in Pakistan." *Critical Studies on Terrorism* 1 (2008): 95–110.

GERMAN RED ARMY FACTION

A descendant of the Baader-Meinhof Gang, the German Red Army Faction (RAF) perpetrated some of the most devastating terrorist attacks of the 1970s, and it remained a threat for more than 20 years.

The Baader-Meinhof Gang grew out of the German student movement of the 1960s. Many students believed that the West German government was fascist and corrupt, and they wanted to replace it with a Communist regime. The name "Red Army Faction" had been adopted by the members of the Baader-Meinhof Gang in honor of

the Japanese Red Army soon after its formation; however, this self-designation was at first largely ignored by the press and the public. Many of the gang's leaders were arrested in the summer of 1972, including Andreas Baader and Ulrike Meinhof, but the group was by no means destroyed.

The German RAF took on a character different from that of Baader-Meinhof. Whereas Baader-Meinhof concentrated on bank robberies and bombings, the RAF concentrated on hijackings, kidnappings, and assassinations. While Baader-Meinhof was known for its fast-living communal lifestyle, the RAF was organized into separate isolated cells. However, many RAF attacks involved demands for both Baader-Meinhof and RAF prisoners to be released. During the 1970s, some members were involved with operations by other terrorists groups, such as the Popular Front for the Liberation of Palestine (PFLP), and individual terrorists, such as Carlos the Jackal (Illich Ramírez Sánchez).

The first major attack following the capture of the Baader-Meinhof leaders was the February 1975 kidnapping of the West German politician Peter Lorenz by RAF members calling themselves the 2 June Movement. Some experts view 2 June as a splinter group of the RAF. Lorenz was released in return for five RAF prisoners. RAF's next major attack, undertaken with the aid of the PFLP, was the June 27, 1976, hijacking of an Air France flight on its way from Tel Aviv to Paris. Diverting the plane to Entebbe, Uganda, the hijackers demanded $5 million and the release of 53 terrorists and RAF leaders. The crisis was ended by a daring military operation by Israeli counterterrorism forces, in which three hostages and one Israeli soldier were killed. The success of the operation made governments much less willing to negotiate with terrorists.

On September 5, 1977, the RAF kidnapped Hanns-Martin Schleyer, a right-wing German politician, once again demanding the release of RAF prisoners, and adding the demand that the prisoners be given free passage to the country of their choice. Negotiations dragged on for five weeks while the West German government tried to find a country willing to take them. On October 14, 1977, in an effort to spur the German government into action, the RAF hijacked a Lufthansa flight and diverted it to Kuwait; five days later, a raid by Grenzschutzgruppe 9, German anti-terrorist commandos, freed the hostages. As it became clear that the government was not going to meet the terrorists' demands, several of the imprisoned Baader-Meinhof leaders committed suicide, while the RAF kidnappers killed Schleyer.

During the late 1970s and early 1980s, several important RAF members were arrested or killed in gun battles with police. From December 1984 to October 1986, the group carried out a string of attacks on U.S. Army bases and NATO facilities in Germany; concurrently, the RAF engaged in an assassination campaign against German leaders in which eight people were killed and dozens were injured. RAF continued with sporadic bombings through the 1980s, but support began to peter out with the fall of the Berlin Wall in 1989 and the subsequent reunification of Germany. During the 1990s, the group made few attacks, while several of its remaining leaders were arrested or turned themselves in. In 1998, the RAF officially announced it was disbanding.

Colleen Sullivan

See also Baader-Meinhof Gang; Grenzschutzgruppe 9; Popular Front for the Liberation of Palestine; Sánchez, Illich Ramírez

Further Readings

Aust, Stefan. *Baader-Meinhof: The Inside Story of the R.A.F.* London: The Bodley Head, 2008.

Cowell, Alan. "Red Army Faction Disbands, Saying Its Cause Is 'Now History.'" *The New York Times*, April 23, 1998, p. A9.

Crawford, David. "The Murder of a CEO: Did East Germany's Feared Secret Police Help Kill German Businessmen?" *The Wall Street Journal*, September 15, 2007, p. A1.

Eager, Paige Whaley. *From Freedom Fighters to Terrorists: Women and Political Violence.* Burlington, VT: Ashgate, 2008.

Harclerode, Peter. *Secret Soldiers: Special Forces in the War against Terrorism.* London: Cassell, 2000.

Horchem, Hans Josef. *West Germany's Red Army Anarchists.* London: Institute for the Study of Conflict, 1974.

Proll, Astrid. *Baader Meinhof: Pictures on the Run 67–77.* Berlin and New York: Scalo, 1998.

Varon, Jeremy. *Bringing the War Home: The Weather Underground, the Red Army Faction, and Revolutionary Violence in the Sixties and Seventies.* Berkeley: University of California Press, 2004.

Whitlock, Craig. "Terror Wave's Old Wounds: Parole in Germany of Red Army Leader Is Stirring Debate." *Wall Street Journal* (Europe), March 5, 2007, p. 10.

GHAILANI, AHMED KHALFAN (1974–)

Born in Zanzibar, Tanzania, Ahmed Khalfan Ghailani was alleged to be a member of the al Qaeda network and was believed to have been directly involved in the 1998 attacks on the U.S. embassies in Nairobi, Kenya, and Dar es Salaam, Tanzania. In particular, he was accused of procuring the materials for and assembling the truck bomb that devastated the embassy in Dar es Salaam. In November 2010, a jury found Ghailani guilty of conspiracy but cleared him of the murder charge; he was sentenced to life in prison.

During the late 1990s, Ghailani was allegedly a member of the Tanzanian cell of al Qaeda, which serves as an umbrella group for other militant organizations and establishes cells in areas where attacks are carried out. Ghailani allegedly worked closely with al Qaeda operatives from the Kenyan and Tanzanian cells.

In the 1998 U.S. indictment, Ghailani and a fellow al Qaeda operative, Sheikh Ahmed Salim Swedan, were charged with buying the Nissan Atlas refrigeration truck used to bomb the Dar es Salaam embassy. A few months before the attack, prosecutors argued, Ghailani also purchased the oxygen and acetylene tanks used in the bomb's construction, and then helped load all of the bomb equipment (tanks, boxes of TNT, detonators, fertilizer, and sandbags) onto the truck.

The very next day, in synchronized attacks 400 miles apart, truck bombs exploded at the embassies in Kenya and Tanzania, one bomb detonating just minutes before the other. Three suspects in the case pled guilty and cooperated with the U.S. government as witnesses. In October 2001, four men linked to bin Laden were convicted of conspiring in the bombings. All the defendants, who had pleaded not guilty, were sentenced to life in prison without parole.

In this June 9, 2009, file courtroom sketch, Guantánamo detainee Ahmed Khalfan Ghailani, left, listens as his civilian lawyer Scott Fenstermaker, right, speaks at his arraignment in U.S. Federal Court in New York. Assistant U.S. Attorney David Raskin, seated in front, and Ghailani's military lawyer Marine Col. Jeffrey Colwell, back center, are shown listening. Ghailani, the first Guantánamo detainee to face a civilian trial, was acquitted in New York City on November 17, 2010, of all but one of the hundreds of charges that he helped unleash death and destruction on two U.S. embassies in Africa in 1998. (AP Photo/Elizabeth Williams, File. © 2011 The Associated Press. All Rights Reserved)

On July 25, 2004, Ghailani was captured by Pakistani forces following a gun battle in the city of Gujrat. Pakistan turned Ghailani over to U.S. custody, and he was held in secret prisons run by the Central Intelligence Agency until 2006, when he was transferred to the U.S. detention facility in Guantánamo Bay, Cuba.

In 2009 Ghailani was moved to New York City to face federal trial as part of a drive to close the Guantánamo facility. He faced 286 charges, including murder and attempted murder, bombing, and conspiracy to use weapons of mass destruction. Ghailani, who pled not guilty, told a Guantánamo military tribunal in 2007 that he had not bought the truck, and that he thought that the boxes he transported held soap for washing horses.

Public reaction to the verdict, in which Ghailani was convicted on one count but absolved of more than 200 others, was a sort of Rorschach test regarding public opinion on using domestic courts to punish terrorists. Some pointed to the conspiracy conviction, which will keep Ghailani behind bars for the rest of his life, as evidence that the criminal prosecution can be effective. Others argued that the jury had not been presented with the most damning evidence against Ghailani because it had been thrown out by the judge, and they viewed the verdict as an embarrassing indictment of the Obama administration's determination to apply civilian law to terrorist cases.

Erica Pearson

See also al Qaeda; bin Laden, Osama; Criminal Prosecution of Terrorists; East Africa Embassy Bombings; Swedan, Sheikh Ahmed Salim

Further Readings

Bergen, Peter. *Holy War, Inc.: Inside the Secret World of Osama bin Laden.* New York: Free Press, 2001.

Farah, Douglas. *Blood from Stones: The Secret Financial Network of Terror.* New York: Broadway Books, 2004.

Khan, Kamran. "Pakistan Holds Top al Qaeda Suspect: Key Figure in 1998 Embassy Bombings Held after 10-hour Shootout." *The Washington Post,* July 30, 2004, p. A10.

Meyer, Josh. "Top al Qaeda Suspect Caught in Pakistan." *Los Angeles Times*, July 30, 2004, p. A4.

"A Nation Challenged: The Hunted; The 22 Most Wanted Suspects, in a Five-Act Drama of Global Terror." *The New York Times*, October 14, 2001, p. 1B.

Reeve, Simon. *The New Jackals: Ramzi Yousef, Osama bin Laden, and the Future of Terrorism.* Boston: Northeastern University Press, 1999.

U.S. Department of Defense. Verbatim Transcript of Open Session Combatant Status Review Tribunal Hearing for ISN 10012. http://www.defenselink.mil/news/transcript_ISN10012.pdf.

U.S. District Court Southern District of New York. *United States v. Usama bin Laden, et al.* Indictment S(10) 98 Cr. 1023 (LBS).

Weiser, Benjamin. "Guantanamo Detainee Pleads Not Guilty in Manhattan Court." *The New York Times*, June 10, 2009, p. A25.

White, Josh, and Julie Tate. "Detainee Said He Didn't Know about Bombing Plot." *The Washington Post*, March 24, 2007, p. A9.

GOLDSTEIN, BARUCH (1957–1994)

Baruch Goldstein (born Benjamin Carl Goldstein), an ultra-nationalist and member of the Jewish group Kahane Chai, massacred 29 Muslims bowed in prayer at the Ibrahimi Mosque in Hebron, a city in the West Bank, in 1994.

Born in Brooklyn, Goldstein was a serious and quiet child, graduating a year early near the top of his high school class. At Yeshiva University in Manhattan, Goldstein changed his name to Baruch and became involved in Kahane Chai, a group founded by Rabbi Meir Kahane, a militant Jewish nationalist who had argued that no Jew was safe as long as there was a single Arab in the land of Israel. Goldstein met his wife at Kahane Chai headquarters in Jerusalem, and Kahane officiated at their wedding. Kahane was assassinated in New York in 1990.

Goldstein graduated from medical school and moved to Israel in 1983, joining the Kiryat Arba settlement in the Israeli-occupied West Bank. Kiryat Arba is one of many Jewish settlements near Hebron, a town of nearly 100,000 Arabs.

Goldstein worked as an Israeli army doctor in Hebron and served for several years as a Kahane Chai representative on the Kiryat Arba local council. Admirers and friends said that his anger grew as he tended to Jewish settlers who had been shot in Arab-Israeli violence in Hebron. He and many other right-wing settlers did not support the peace talks between the Palestine Liberation Organization and the government of Prime Minister Yitzhak Rabin. In an interview on Army Radio a few months before he attacked the mosque, Goldstein complained that the army was not protecting Jewish settlers.

Before dawn on February 25, 1994, Goldstein walked into the Cave of the Patriarchs carrying an automatic weapon. At the time, Jewish settlers were allowed to carry weapons inside the holy site, held to be the burial place of Abraham. The site, called the Hebron shrine by Jews and the Ibrahimi Mosque by Muslims, is sacred to both religions and divided into separate prayer halls. Goldstein burst into the mosque and opened fire on a crowd of praying Muslims, killing 29 before the shocked crowd bludgeoned him to death. About 125 others were wounded.

During an Israeli government commission's investigation, Palestinian witnesses and army guards raised the possibility of a second gunman. However, the commission determined that Goldstein had told no one, including his wife, of his plans. The government subsequently outlawed Kahane Chai and arrested some of its leaders.

Goldstein's supporters among the Jewish settlers transformed his grave into a shrine and pilgrimage site. Many maintained that Goldstein's actions were justifiable, telling U.S. and British journalists that the doctor had possessed inside information on a large Arab attack in Kiryat Arba. No proof of this claim has been provided, however. Having passed legislation banning monuments to terrorists, the Israeli government razed the shrine to Goldstein. However, they left the controversial inscription on Goldstein's headstone, which refers to him as a "martyr" with "clean hands and heart."

Erica Pearson

See also Jewish Terrorist Groups in the United States; Kahane, Meir; Kahane Chai

Further Readings

Bronner, Ethan, and Steve Fainaru. "Life and Death of a Zealot: Hebron Gunman's Actions Present a Paradox; Goldstein Was Known as Healer." *The Boston Globe,* March 2, 1994, p. 1.

Cockburn, Patrick. "Settlers Remember 'Greatest Jew' Who Killed 29 in Mosque." *The Independent* (London), February 17, 1995, p. 12.

Foreman, David J. "The Chickens Have Come Home to Roost." *Jerusalem Post,* November 21, 2008, p. 8.

Friedman, Matt. "10 Years After Goldstein Massacre in Hebron, Legal Cases Linger On." *Jerusalem Post,* February 23, 2004, p. 8.

Haberman, Clyde. "Israel Panel Says Killer at Hebron Was Acting Alone." *The New York Times,* June 27, 1994, p. A1.

Haberman, Clyde. "West Bank Massacre: The Overview." *The New York Times,* February 26, 1994, p. A1.

GRAND CENTRAL STATION BOMBING

On September 10, 1976, terrorists calling themselves "Fighters for Free Croatia" diverted TWA Flight 355, bound for Chicago, to the Mirabel Airport in Montreal. The terrorists then instructed the pilot to radio a message directing the New York City Police Department (NYPD) to a bomb located in a Grand Central Station subway locker. Describing the bomb as a "gel" type, the terrorists threatened to detonate it if they detected any "false moves." The group also threatened to detonate another bomb located "in a highly busy location" if their demands were not published by several papers, including *The New York Times, Los Angeles Times, The Washington Post,* and *Chicago Tribune.* All of the papers published the demands.

The Federal Aviation Administration (FAA) picked up the pilot's radio message and alerted the NYPD. The city's bomb squad roped off the area identified by the hijackers and pried open 24 lockers surrounding locker number 5713, where the bomb was located. Inside that locker, the police found a sealed pressure cooker. After attempts to x-ray the bomb were unsuccessful, it was moved to the bomb squad range in Rodman's Neck, Bronx. There, four members of the bomb squad—Police Officer Brian Murray, Police Officer Henry Dworkin, Deputy Inspector Fritz Behr, and Sergeant Terence McTigue (none of whom was wearing protective gear)—placed the bomb in a dirt pit and attempted to detonate or deactivate it via remote control. After several attempts, the four men approached the bomb for inspection. It exploded, killing Murray instantly and showering shrapnel on the others, leaving McTigue with permanent injuries.

In the ensuing trial, Zvonko Busic, the leader of the group, took full responsibility for both the hijacking and setting the bomb at Grand Central Station, claiming that the others, including his wife, Julienne, were not aware of his specific plans. Busic testified that he purchased eight sticks of dynamite from a "Mafia"-type man that he met in a bar in Yorkville. He then fashioned the bomb, using instructions from *The Anarchist's Cookbook,* and placed it in the locker 48 hours before the hijacking.

The Grand Central Station bomb was meant to convince the authorities and the hijacked passengers that other devices brought onto the plane—some made from clay, and others crafted from cast-iron pots, black tape, and timers—were true bombs. Busic testified that he cautioned the police about a switch on the bomb, which he had deliberately set in the off position, rendering it inactive. He later claimed that the explosion was attributable to faulty police equipment.

In May 1977, four of the five Croatian Nationalists on trial were found guilty of air piracy. Busic and his wife were also charged in the death of Police Officer Murray and received life sentences. Two others received 30-year sentences. The fifth man, who pled guilty before the trial, also received a 30-year term. All were eventually released, the last being Busic, who was paroled and deported to Croatia in 2008.

Laura Lambert

See also Bombings and Bomb Scares; Hijacking; TWA Flight 355 Hijacking

Further Readings

Baker, Al. "U.S. Granting Parole to Croatian Hijacker." *International Herald Tribune,* July 21, 2008, p. 3.

Brockman, Richard. "Notes while Being Hijacked." *The Atlantic*, December 1976. http://www.theatlantic.com/issues/76dec/brockman.htm.

Esposito, Richard, and Ted Gerstein. *Bomb Squad: A Year inside the Nation's Most Exclusive Police Unit.* New York: Hyperion, 2007.

Gendar, Alison. "32 Years Isn't Enough." *New York Daily News*, July 25, 2008, p. 12.

Seigel, Max H. "4 Croatian Nationalists Convicted of Hijacking LaGuardia Jetliner." *The New York Times*, May 6, 1977, p. A1.

Tomasson, Robert E. "Jet out of La Guardia Is Hijacked; Bomb Left in New York Goes Off." *The New York Times*, September 11, 1976, p. A1.

GREAT EASTERN ISLAMIC RAIDERS' FRONT

The extremely anti-Semitic and anti-Christian Great Eastern Islamic Raiders' Front (IBDA-C) has allegedly been active in Turkey since the 1970s, but it was officially "founded" in 1985. With the stated aim of replacing Turkey's secular government with Islamic rule, the group has been most active in the region around Istanbul since 1993. The group's alleged leader, Salih Izzet Erdis, was arrested in 1998 and remains in prison.

The IBDA-C was first heard from in 1989 after it held demonstrations in Istanbul, and it has been aggressive since the early 1990s. Targeting Turkish secularism, the group's members have murdered scores of journalists, politicians, and academics outspoken in their defense of a secular Turkey.

Erdis, the leader of the IBDA-C, is also known by the name Salih Mirzabeyoglu and is referred to as "the commander" by IBDA-C members. He was arrested on December 29, 1998, and put on trial at the Istanbul State Security Court for "attempting to replace the Secular Constitutional order with Islamic Sheriah rules." The Turkish court sentenced him to death for "the armed attempt to overthrow the constitutional order." Two of his cohorts were sentenced to 18 years in prison. Apparently, Erdis later tried to hang himself in his cell, but a fellow inmate cut the rope.

The structure of the IBDA-C allows members to organize independently. Anyone familiar with and subscribing to the beliefs of the IBDA-C can form a group and begin to function autonomously. These cells are usually small, with four or five members that act as their own front, or team, within the organization. Some past IBDA-C fronts have been called "Ultra Force," "Altınordu," "Lazistan," and "Union of Revolutionist Sufis."

Since the early 1990s, the group has claimed responsibility for attacks on left-wing, Western, and secular targets. It published a list of Jewish targets, murdered a famous film critic, and sent a dire warning to a Turkish TV journalist, whom it accused of being "anti-Islam." Group members have also targeted banks and taverns, and even brothels and discotheques.

The number of IBDA-C members is unknown, but the IBDA-C name is well known throughout Turkey. While many have been imprisoned, the group remains active in publication and has many bookstores, websites, and printing houses, where meetings are often held. The front is suspected of the 1997 bombing of the Ecumenical Patriarchate Cathedral in Istanbul—an act strongly condemned by the United States. Its most notable attack, though, was the 1999 pipe-bomb assassination of Ahmet Taner Kislali, a former minister, professor, and respected newspaper columnist—and a firm critic of Islamic fundamentalism.

Turkish authorities have continued to arrest and try IBDA-C members, which has reduced their threat. According to Turkish officials, 20 separate operations were staged against IBDA-C in 1998 and 1999, leading to the capture of some 170 suspects and clarification of 35 acts of terror. The group still manages to make small attacks, but it is no longer believed to be capable of pulling off large, sophisticated operations. In November 2003, IBDA-C took credit for a series of deadly suicide-bombing attacks against synagogues, the British consulate, and a bank in Istanbul, but these were later found to be the work of al Qaeda.

Richard McHugh

See also Grey Wolves; Turkish Hezbollah

Further Readings

Kurkucu, Ertugrul. "The Crisis of the Turkish State." *Middle East Report*, April–June 1996, pp. 2–7.

Lapidot, Anat. "Islamic Activism in Turkey since the 1980 Military Takeover." In "Religious Radicalism in the Greater Middle East," edited by Bruce Maddy-Weitzman and Efraim Inbar, special issue, *Terrorism and Political Violence* 3 (1997): 62–74.

Smith, Craig S. "Turkish Police Arrest Suspects in Attacks on British Sites." *The New York Times,* November 22, 2003, p. A8.

Toprak, Binnaz. "Religion as State Ideology in a Secular Setting: The Turkish-Islamic Synthesis." In *Aspects of Religion in Secular Turkey,* edited by Malcolm Wagstaff, pp. 10–15. Durham, NC: Durham University, Center for Middle Eastern and Islamic Studies, 1990.

Zubaida, Sami. "Turkish Islam and National Identity," *Middle East Report,* April–June 1996, pp. 10–15.

GRENZSCHUTZGRUPPE 9

Grenzschutzgruppe 9 (GSG 9) is an elite German counterterrorist unit that was formed after the massacre at the 1972 Munich Olympics. All GSG 9 members undergo advanced counterterrorism training in areas such as building assault, hand-to-hand combat, marksmanship, and explosives. GSG 9's 1977 assault on a hijacked Lufthansa plane in Mogadishu, Somalia, brought them to world attention.

After the defeat of the Nazi regime in World War II, the West German government was reorganized. West Germany had an army, but no national police force or intelligence agency, and the national government had very little power to regulate the internal affairs of its states. In 1972, when the city of Munich hosted the Olympics, security for the games was the responsibility of the state of Bavaria (of which Munich was the capital). That security was deliberately relaxed, however, in an effort to prove to the world that Germany had moved beyond its fascist, militaristic past.

On September 5, 1972, a team of Palestinian terrorists from the Black September group entered the Olympic Village, killing two members of the Israeli Olympic team and taking nine others hostage. After hours of tense negotiations, which were televised worldwide, the Munich police made a last desperate attempt to free the hostages. The operation was a disaster, and all nine Israelis were killed.

To prevent another such catastrophe, Grenzschutzgruppe 9 was created. GSG 9 was a part of the Bundesgrenzschutz, or Federal Border Guard, one of the few German security agencies with national authority. Headed by Ulrich Wegener, who handpicked the initial 200 border guards, the group had three combat teams of 30 men, with additional members trained in logistics, support, communications, and intelligence. In later years, the GSG was expanded and divided into three divisions: GSG 9/1 (the ground forces), GSG 9/2 (trained for maritime operations), and GSG 9/3 (an aerial assault team).

On October 13, 1977, a team of Palestinian terrorists hijacked a Lufthansa flight from Majorca, eventually diverting it to Mogadishu, Somalia. They demanded the release of 13 terrorists, including the leaders of the West German Baader-Meinhof Gang, in exchange for the 90 hostages. While negotiators stalled for time, a GSG 9 team was flown to Mogadishu. At 2:07 on the morning of October 18, while the Somali Army provided a diversion, the GSG 9 team broke into the plane. Taken by surprise, the terrorists retreated to the cockpit. In less than 10 minutes, the four terrorists had been killed or wounded and all 90 hostages had been freed unharmed. The success of the operation was vital in restoring public confidence in Germany's security forces.

Following the Mogadishu raid, GSG 9 began to concentrate on counterterrorism at home, tracking down and arresting members of the German Red Amy Faction. In June 1993, the unit's reputation was somewhat tarnished by accusations that it had killed a Red Army member, Wolfgang Grams, in cold blood, but a subsequent investigation proved that he had shot himself. Even before the investigation was complete, GSG 9 was able to redeem itself in the eyes of many with its August 1993 rescue of a hijacked KLM flight from Tunis to Amsterdam, in which the commandos were able to capture the hijacker without firing a shot. The GSG 9 remains one of the best-trained and most respected counterterrorism units in the world.

Colleen Sullivan

See also Counterterrorism; German Red Army Faction; Munich Olympics Massacre

Further Readings

Hall, Allan, and David Williams. "Terrorists Planned a New 9/11 Atrocity in Germany." *Daily Mail*, September 6, 2007, p. 1.

Harclerode, Peter. *Secret Soldiers: Special Forces in the War Against Terrorism.* London: Cassell, 2000.

Tophoven, Rolf. *GSG 9: German Response to Terrorism.* Koblenz, Germany: Bernard and Graefe Verlag, 1984.

Reeve, Simon. *One Day in September: The Full Story of the 1972 Munich Olympics Massacre and the Israeli Revenge Operation "Wrath of God."* New York: Arcade, 2000.

GREY WOLVES

The Grey Wolves were the youth wing of the Milliyetci Hareket Partisi (MHP), a neo-fascist political party in Turkey. Fighting between the Grey Wolves and leftists during the late 1970s resulted in more than 5,000 deaths.

The Milliyetci Hareket Partisi (Nationalist Action Party, or Nationalist Movement Party) was founded in 1969 by Alparslan Türkes, a Turkish military officer and ardent supporter of pan-Turkism, with the idea that all Turkic-speaking peoples should be united under one political regime. Many observers compare the MHP's structure, ideology, and tactics to those of Europe's fascist regimes of the 1930s. The Grey Wolves were composed of young Turkish men, often students or rural migrants to Turkey's two largest cities, Istanbul and Ankara (the capital). The organization was run along military lines, with followers undergoing training in the martial arts and the use of various weapons and explosives. Members were fed and clothed by the MHP, and the party's willingness to provide for them, combined with the thorough political indoctrination they received, often inspired a blind devotion to the party. By the end of the 1970s, the group had tens of thousands of members.

Türkes held a series of high governmental positions in the 1970s, including the post of minister of monopolies and customs. His control of the customs department led to a profitable association between the MHP and Turkey's vast array of smugglers and drug traffickers. Türkes's position also allowed the MHP to obtain whatever weapons it needed.

As the decade progressed, Turkey's leftist groups became more politically active, and political violence worsened. It was during this period that the MHP, which was fanatically anticommunist, began to deploy the Grey Wolves in earnest. They are alleged to have been behind a May 1977 massacre at a leftist parade that killed more than 20 people and injured hundreds. In 1978 a leftist government headed by Bülent Ecevit came to power in Turkey, and the violence worsened. The Grey Wolves were used to attack the headquarters of a leftist political party, and gangs of Grey Wolves were sent into the countryside to incite riots. A December 1978 attack in the southeastern town of Kahramanmaras was typical: a bomb set off in a movie house led to several days of rioting and gun battles in the streets between the Grey Wolves and the leftists. Two hundred people were killed, with more than 1,000 wounded and more than 900 buildings destroyed. By the end of the decade, the country was near anarchy.

In September 1980, the military overthrew Turkey's government in a bloodless coup. Türkes and several dozen high-level MHP members were arrested, and the Grey Wolves reined in. Although many MHP members, including Türkes, were convicted and given stiff sentences, most served no time in prison, having been released at the conclusion of the trial. Türkes resumed his political career.

The Grey Wolves continued on the path of violence. A former Grey Wolf member, Mehmet Ali Agca, tried to assassinate Pope John Paul II in 1981; neither his motivation nor possible state sponsorship of the assassination attempt was ever fully clarified. The Grey Wolves were also linked to an attempted assassination of the Turkish prime minister in 1988 and to a series of ethnic killings in Turkey in the early 1990s, and they have been accused of inciting violence within Cypriot, German, and English Turkish expatriate communities during the 1990s.

The extent of the Turkish government's connection to and sanctioning of the Grey Wolves' activities remains unclear. In 1999, a resurgent MHP (with a new, pro-Islam stance) gained 18 percent of the vote in the Turkish parliamentary elections, winning a place in a coalition government. Just three years later, however, MHP lost its place in government, earning less than 9 percent of the vote in the 2002 national elections. MHP returned to governing after the 2007 elections, earning 14 percent of the vote.

Colleen Sullivan

Further Readings

Başkan, Filiz. "Globalization and Nationalism: The Nationalist Action Party of Turkey." *Nationalism and Ethnic Politics* 12, no. 1 (2006): 83–105.

"Going Wolfish." *The Economist,* June 12, 1999. http://www.economist.com/node/322481.

Lee, Martin A. "Turkish Dirty War Revealed, But Papal Shooting Still Obscured." *Los Angeles Times*, April 12, 1998, p. M2.

Nachmani, Amikam. *Turkey: Facing a New Millennium Coping with Intertwined Conflicts.* Manchester, UK: Manchester University Press, 2003.

Solakov, Stefan. *The Wolves of Terror.* Translated by Mark Cole. Sofia, Bulgaria: Sofia Press, 1986.

"Teens Engage in Race Warfare on Web in Germany." *Turkish Daily News,* December 19, 2007, p. 1.

Vulliamy, Ed. "Wolves on the Doorstep." *The Guardian,* December 19, 1995, p. T4.

GRIFFIN, MICHAEL FREDERICK (1962–)

In 1993, amid an increasingly violent anti-abortion movement in the United States, Michael Griffin became the first activist to murder an abortion provider, ushering in a new level of terrorism in the abortion wars.

Shortly after 10 A.M. on March 10, 1993, Dr. David Gunn arrived at the Pensacola Women's Medical Services clinic. Protestors from the anti-abortion group Rescue America had been gathered outside the clinic since 9 A.M., and as Dr. Gunn moved past the crowd, Griffin shot him three times in the back with a .38 caliber gun, shouting repeatedly "Don't kill any more babies." Dr. Gunn, then 47, was rushed to a hospital, where he died hours later.

Gunn had known he was a target. Aside from being the only individual providing legal abortions in the region, he traveled over 1,000 miles a week to work at clinics throughout Florida, Georgia,

and Alabama. In 1992 he was featured on a "Wanted" poster circulated at an Operation Rescue anti-abortion rally in Montgomery, Alabama.

The Sunday before the murder, Griffin, then a 31-year-old chemical plant employee, asked the congregation at his fundamentalist church, Charity Chapel, to pray for Dr. Gunn. Griffin and his wife, Patricia, had recently become active in the anti-abortion movement, joining the anti-abortion group Our Father's House, led by John Burt, who also headed Rescue America. Burt encouraged the Griffins' activism, showing them videos of aborted fetuses and urging him and his wife to attend protests. Allegedly, Michael Griffin also saw an effigy of Dr. Gunn hanging from a rafter in Burt's garage, bearing a quote from Genesis 9:6, "Whoso sheddeth man's blood, by man shall his blood be shed."

Immediately after shooting Dr. Gunn, Griffin approached a nearby police officer and turned himself in. As news spread, activists on both sides of the abortion debate decried Griffin and his actions. However, a small contingent of anti-abortion activists justified the murder, including the former Presbyterian minister Paul Jennings Hill. In July 1993, Hill drafted a "Defensive Action Statement," which was signed by 29 anti-abortion activists. The statement read, "We assert that if Michael Griffin did in fact kill David Gunn, his use of lethal force was justifiable provided it was carried out for the purpose of defending the lives of unborn children."

Griffin was held, without bond, at the Escambia County jail and courthouse, on an open murder count. At his trial, Griffin's lawyers presented an insanity defense, suggesting that anti-abortion propaganda caused Griffin to lose his sense of right and wrong—a defense that was ultimately not allowed because Griffin refused psychiatric examinations. On the opening day of the trial, February 21, 1994, the judge announced that Griffin would not receive the death penalty. In March, Griffin was found guilty of first-degree murder and sentenced to life in prison, with no chance for parole for 25 years.

By 1995 Griffin had denounced anti-abortion violence, claiming that a conspiracy of anti-abortion groups, police officers, and his own defense team had framed him. Anti-abortion groups, in turn, denounced Griffin as mentally unstable. Regrettably, his actions had already inspired more violence within the movement, inciting others, including Rachelle Shannon, Paul Hill, and John Salvi III, to murder.

Laura Lambert

See also Anti-Abortion Terrorism; Hill, Paul Jennings; Rudolph, Eric

Further Readings

Baird-Windle, Patricia, and Eleanor J. Bader. *Targets of Hatred: Anti-abortion Terrorism*. New York: Palgrave Macmillan, 2001.

Humphreys, Adrian. "Radical Believers: Imprisoned but Unrepentant, Killers of Abortion Doctors Say They Did God's Work." *National Post*, December 27, 2007, p. A1.

Joffe, Carole. *Dispatches from the Abortion Wars: The Costs of Fanaticism to Doctors, Patients, and the Rest of Us*. Boston: Beacon Press, 2010.

Kurst-Swanger, Karl. *Worship and Sin: An Exploration of Religion-related Crime in the United States*. New York: Peter Lang, 2008.

GUANTÁNAMO BAY

Guantánamo Bay is a large natural harbor located in southeastern Cuba. It is also the site of a leased U.S. naval base. Beginning in early 2002, the base was used to detain foreign suspected terrorists as part of the "global war on terror." The U.S. government termed these individuals "enemy combatants" and justified their detention under international law governing armed conflict, but it denied them the protections afforded by that law, most significantly those included in the 1949 Geneva Conventions. The United States insisted that these detainees were humanely treated, but their prolonged detention without trial or judicial review, coupled with widely publicized allegations of abuse, resulted in substantial criticism that eroded support for American counterterrorism efforts.

A few detainees were eventually tried by military commissions, which only fueled more controversy as observers questioned the trials' fundamental fairness. In 2008 the U.S. Supreme Court ruled that the detainees had the constitutional right to challenge their detention via petitions for writs of habeas corpus, and federal courts began reviewing the merits of individual cases. President Barack Obama committed to closing Guantánamo within a year of his January 2009 inauguration, but political opposition and a lack of consensus on viable alternatives precluded meeting that deadline. Government figures show that 779 men and boys were detained at Guantánamo during this period; fewer than 200 of these remained in U.S. custody as of mid-2010.

History

The U.S. presence in Guantánamo dates to the Spanish-American War of 1898, when some of the first American forces to land on the island encamped there. The United States effectively required Cuba to grant a lease as a condition for the post-war withdrawal of American forces, and the original 1903 agreement declares that "the United States shall exercise complete jurisdiction and control" over the base. A follow-up 1934 agreement permits the United States to maintain Guantánamo as long as it desires, subject to termination only if the base is abandoned or by mutual agreement of the two nations.

A week after the terrorist attacks of September 11, 2001, Congress authorized President George W. Bush to use military force against individuals or groups responsible for those events or aiding those who were. The United States began military operations in Afghanistan against al Qaeda and the Taliban the following month. U.S. forces captured some suspected terrorists in the course of these operations, but many of the eventual Guantánamo detainees were foreigners turned over by Afghans or Pakistanis in exchange for substantial cash rewards.

As the number of detainees held in Afghanistan increased, U.S. officials sought a secure detention facility where those suspected of having useful intelligence information could be interrogated at length. Guantánamo was ultimately selected because it was secure, remote from public view, and because it was believed that no U.S. court could exercise oversight by entertaining detainee petitions for habeas corpus. Support for this view was found in a 1950 Supreme Court decision,

U.S. Navy guards escort a detainee through Camp Delta, Joint Task Force (JTF) Guantánamo Bay, Cuba, June 10, 2008. (U.S. Army 1st Lt. Sarah Cleveland/Released)

Johnson v. Eisentrager, which appeared to draw geographic limits in denying habeas relief to foreign nationals imprisoned by U.S. forces in Germany after World War II.

The first detainees arrived at Guantánamo in January 2002. They were placed in a temporary facility called Camp X-Ray, which consisted of little more than outdoor wire cages. The world's first views of Guantánamo were Department of Defense photos showing shackled detainees clad in orange jumpsuits, blacked-out goggles, and earmuffs being forced to kneel on gravel in a barbed-wire enclosure. These images generated an immediate global public outcry and remained emblematic of Guantánamo long after the temporary cells were replaced with permanent structures based on modern civilian prison designs.

U.S. officials portrayed those detained as dangerous terrorists and leading members of al Qaeda. When early interrogation efforts failed to produce significant usable intelligence, military officials sought permission to use a series of "enhanced interrogation techniques." Lawyers in the Justice Department's Office of Legal Counsel authored several opinions, colloquially known as "the torture memos," which interpreted U.S. laws proscribing torture so narrowly as to permit a number of techniques previously considered unlawful, such

as waterboarding. The most aggressive interrogations took place at secret detention facilities operated by the Central Intelligence Agency (CIA). Secretary of Defense Donald Rumsfeld approved a more limited set of techniques for use at Guantánamo, but detainees there were subjected to extended sleep deprivation, "short shackling" for prolonged periods in painful positions without access to toilets, humiliation (including enforced nudity), and exposure to very loud music and extreme temperatures.

Judicial Review

Efforts to obtain judicial review of Guantánamo detentions began almost as soon as the camp became public knowledge. Because the detainees were initially held without charges and the government denied outside access to them, the first cases were brought by family members abroad without the knowledge or participation of those being held. In June 2004 the U.S. Supreme Court held in *Rasul v. Bush* that the federal statute governing petitions for the writ of habeas corpus applied to Guantánamo, and that federal judges could hear challenges to detentions there. In response, the government endeavored to maintain Executive Branch control over detention decisions by establishing a formal review process, consisting of an initial Combatant Status Review Tribunal (CSRT), followed by Administrative Review Board (ARB) to reconsider the continued detention of each individual. In practice, these reviews were hampered by the fact that the military officers making the review decisions often lacked access to information held by other government agencies, while the detainees, who were not represented by lawyers, could not hear or challenge any classified information against them and had little practical opportunity to obtain any exculpatory evidence on their own behalf. The U.S. government has never admitted than any detainee was held in error, but these reviews did result in some detainees being classified as "no longer enemy combatants" and approved for release or transfer to other countries.

Congress soon became involved in the process, enacting the Detainee Treatment Act of 2005, which barred torture or cruel, inhuman, or degrading treatment, but also purported to effectively deny the detainees habeas review. After the Supreme Court halted the first efforts at conducting military commission trials the following year in its *Hamdan v. Rumsfeld* decision, President Bush directed the transfer of 14 "high-value" detainees, including the alleged 9/11 mastermind Khalid Shaikh Mohammed, from CIA custody to Guantánamo. He then called upon Congress to promptly pass legislation authorizing their trial. Congress responded with the Military Commissions Act of 2006, providing statutory authority for the trials and more comprehensively foreclosing judicial review. The Supreme Court ended this back-and-forth process in June 2008, deciding in *Boumediene v. Bush* that Guantánamo detainees had a constitutional right to challenge their detentions, based on the degree of U.S. control over the base. The federal district court for the District of Columbia subsequently began hearing individual detainee's cases. By the end of May 2010, the court had ordered the release of 36 detainees while approving the continued detention of 14 others.

Military commission trials resumed at Guantánamo in early 2008, but only three were completed in the next two years. The Australian David Hicks pled guilty in exchange for his prompt return home; Salim Hamdan was convicted of several charges and given a short sentence; and the admitted al Qaeda propagandist Ali Hamza Ahmed Sulayman al Bahlul received a life sentence after refusing to mount any defense and boycotting his own trial.

Efforts to End Guantánamo Detentions

A combination of circumstances, including the fact that most of the detainees proved to be either innocent or lacking significant intelligence value, the substantial negative publicity, and the extension of federal jurisdiction over the detainees, suggested that the continued use of Guantánamo for this purpose was counter to U.S. national interests. President Bush said publicly that he would like to close the detention facility several times. While his administration never developed any formal plan for doing so, it unilaterally released or transferred the majority of those who had been detained, leaving just 242 when President Obama took office.

Obama initially directed Guantánamo's closure by January 2010, and his administration sought to purchase a surplus prison facility from the state of Illinois to house the remaining detainee population. An interagency task force was established to review the files on all remaining detainees, concluding that of the last 240 individuals, 126 could be released or transferred immediately, 36 should be criminally prosecuted, 48 should be subject to indefinite detention without trial, and 30 Yemenis should be kept in U.S. custody until the security situation in that country improved.

Political realities then intervened and kept the United States from achieving the president's goal. After years of being told that the detainees posed a major threat to American security, substantial domestic opposition developed to any efforts to move these individuals to the United States, whether for release, trial, or continued detention, and Congress refused to fund the purchase of the Illinois prison. Meanwhile, the United States found it difficult to secure any suitable foreign locations to place the detainees. As a result, the final closure of Guantánamo remained uncertain.

David Glazier

See also Criminal Prosecution of Terrorists; Intelligence Gathering; Interrogation Techniques; Law and Terrorism; Mohammed, Khalid Shaikh; Torture Debate

Further Readings

Center for Constitutional Rights. Guantanamo Bay Habeas Decision Scorecard. http://ccrjustice.org/learn-more/faqs/guantanamo-bay-habeas-decision-scorecard.

Guantánamo Review Task Force. *Final Report,* January 22, 2010. http://www.justice.gov/ag/guantanamo-review-final-report.pdf.

Marguiles, Joseph. *Guantanamo and the Abuse of Presidential Power.* New York: Simon & Schuster, 2006.

Schawb, Stephen Irving Max. *Guantánamo, USA: The Untold History of America's Cuban Outpost.* Lawrence: University Press of Kansas, 2009.

Worthington, Andy. *The Guantánamo Files.* Ann Arbor, MI: Pluto Press, 2007.

GUEVARA, ERNESTO (CHE) (1928–1967)

Che Guevara was a Latin American Marxist guerrilla who helped lead the Cuban revolution and attempted to instigate Communist revolutions in several other countries. His political theories and adventurous life have inspired many followers.

Guevara was born to middle-class parents in Rosario, Argentina, on May 14, 1928. (His birth certificate, forged to avoid scandal, states June 14, 1928.) At the age of two, Guevara developed the asthma that would haunt him throughout his life. Guevara's liberal, intellectual parents fostered his pursuit of knowledge. He excelled at school, displaying an early interest in both politics and athletics—he was a passionate rugby player, a remarkable achievement given his asthma.

After graduating from secondary school with honors, Guevara went on to medical school in 1947. In 1952, before completing his studies, he set off with a friend for several months, traveling through Argentina, Chile, Peru, Colombia, and Venezuela on a motorcycle. Traveling without much money, his journeys took him among the slums and rural villages of Latin America, where he witnessed the poverty and oppression of the people by the ruling elites and North American plantation owners.

After passing his final examinations in 1953, Guevara spent time in Bolivia and Guatemala, where in May 1954 he witnessed the CIA-sponsored coup that toppled Guatemala's leftist government. (While in Guatemala he acquired the nickname Che, which is Argentine slang for "Hey, you.") These experiences transformed him into an ardent Marxist. Expelled from Guatemala in the aftermath of the coup, he soon traveled to Mexico City, by now determined to become a revolutionary.

In 1955, Guevara met Fidel Castro, who had already made one abortive attempt to overthrow the Batista regime in Cuba. The two men became close friends, and when Castro and his ragtag band of rebels returned to Cuba in December 1956, Guevara went with them. He became Castro's second-in-command, and his ideological fervor and tactical theories (made famous in his 1960 book, *La Guerra de Guerrillas,* or *Guerilla Warfare*) shaped the Cuban Revolution. In January 1959, Castro and his followers overturned the Batista regime. Guevara spent five years in Cuba, where he took charge of economic development. His unbending radicalism and hard-line anti-American views soon irritated Cuba's Soviet supporters, however, and a rift grew between Guevara and Castro. In 1965, a frustrated Guevara left Cuba, hoping to inspire Cuban-style revolutions in other Third World countries.

The main tenets of Guevara's revolutionary theory held that a *foquista,* or *foco* (focal point), of hardened guerrillas operating in the countryside should be used to crystallize opposition to a ruling regime among the peasantry. By this method, a very small number of actual fighters could mobilize opposition without needing to confront the state military head on. Looking for a suitable country in which to try to repeat his success, he and a small band of supporters traveled first to the Democratic Republic of the Congo, which was then in the midst of a civil war. Guevara found the Congolese guerrillas undisciplined and ineffectual, and after six months he left the country. After a brief stop in Cuba, in March 1966 he traveled incognito to Bolivia to attempt another revolution.

Bolivia, too, would prove unripe for revolution. Both the local peasantry and the Bolivian Communist Party were suspicious and resentful of Guevara and his Cuban guerrillas. In addition, Guevara's asthma began to trouble him, and he spent long periods incapacitated and unable to organize his troops. Desperate, Guevara made a number of tactical errors that put the Bolivian army on his scent; as the Bolivian mission began to seem more and more futile, even Castro dropped his support. In October 1967, Guevara was captured and killed. Fearful that news of his death would spark massive unrest, the Bolivian authorities buried him in an unmarked grave. His remains were finally recovered and transported to Cuba in 1997.

After his death, and in part thanks to Cuban propaganda, Guevara became a legendary figure, a martyr to his ideals who embodied the romance of the revolution. His treatises on guerrilla warfare and communist ideology have inspired thousands of rebels in Latin America and elsewhere, and his bearded image has become a contemporary icon.

Colleen Sullivan

See also Freedom Fighters

Further Readings

Anderson, Jon Lee. *Che Guevara: A Revolutionary Life.* New York: Grove Press, 1997.

Casey, Michael. *Che's Afterlife: The Legacy of an Image.* New York: Vintage Books, 2009.

Casey, Michael. "In Argentina, Che Guevara Finally Gets More Than a Lousy T-shirt: Rebel's Birthplace Unveils a Statue of Him as It Reconsiders His Complex Legacy." *The Wall Street Journal*, June 14, 2008, p. A1.

Castañeda, Jorge G. *Compañero: The Life and Death of Che Guevara.* Translated by Marina Castañeda. New York: Knopf, 1997.

George, Edward. *The Cuban Intervention in Angola, 1965–1991: From Che Guevara to Cuito Cuanavale.* London: Frank Cass, 2005.

Guevara, Ernesto Che. *Guerrilla Warfare.* Translated by J.P. Morray. New York: Monthly Review Press, 1961.

Hart, Joseph, ed. *Che: The Life, Death, and Afterlife of a Revolutionary.* New York: Thunder's Mouth Press, 2003.

McDonnell, Patrick J. "Che's Legacy Looms Larger Than Ever." *Los Angeles Times*, October 8, 2007, p. A1.

Sinclair, Andrew. *Che Guevara.* Stroud, UK: Sutton, 1998.

GUILDFORD FOUR

The Guildford Four were three young Irish men and the English girlfriend of one of the men who were unfairly convicted of pub bombings that killed British service personnel. Their trial provides an example of how there can be a rush to judgment in a trial of persons accused of terrorism, demonstrating the need for continued protection of the civil liberties of those accused of terrorism in periods of heightened tension.

In October 1974, bombs planted by the Irish Republican Army (IRA) exploded in pubs in Guildford and Woolwich on the outskirts of London. The bombs were part of a larger IRA campaign to bring the struggle in Northern Ireland to English soil. These pubs were chosen because British military personnel frequented them when they were off duty. Seven people were killed in the blasts, including five service men and women.

Local authorities eventually arrested three young men from Northern Ireland, Gerald Conlon, Paul Hill, and Patrick Armstrong, as well as Armstrong's English girlfriend, Carole Richardson. The local police coerced confessions and used statements taken out of context from them, and these confessions became the basis for their convictions in open court. It later came to light that the police suppressed evidence that would have cast great doubt on their involvement. All four were convicted and sentenced to life in prison. British authorities later arrested Conlon's father and other relatives (the Maguire Seven) for suspected IRA activities. All seven were convicted on faulty forensic evidence.

Many prominent Britons eventually sought to free the Guildford Four when their convictions came to be seen as unfair. Their convictions were finally overturned 14 years later, when the suppressed evidence and the manipulation of their confessions came to light. A higher court ordered

Irish folk hero Gerry Conlon, released from prison after 15 years in 1989 when proven innocent of the Guildford Four's 1974 IRA bombings of two British pubs, standing beside his father Guiseppe's (who died in prison) grave at Milltown cemetery in Belfast. (Photo by Ian Cook//Time Life Pictures/Getty Images)

them freed with the notation that there was insufficient evidence to sustain a conviction, but the court did not acknowledge that the four were actually innocent.

This miscarriage of justice resulted from a number of factors. The local police were convinced that the four were guilty, so they used whatever means were necessary to get confessions and convictions. In the aftermath of the pub bombings and other IRA attacks, juries were quick to convict anyone suspected of involvement in terrorism. Further, the four suspects were marginal members of society and involved in petty crime and drugs, making it more difficult for a jury to be sympathetic. Paul Hill, who was also charged with involvement in an IRA murder of an off-duty British soldier in Northern Ireland, would not testify for fear of having any statements made in this case used against him in the second trial. Instead, he adopted the IRA tactic of refusing to recognize the authority of a British court. This stance greatly contributed to the jury's willingness to accept government claims that the defendants were members of the IRA. The IRA issued a communiqué indicating that the four were innocent,

but the authorities chose to give no credence to this claim.

Higher courts were reluctant to overturn the convictions on appeal, probably in part because reversals would cast doubt on the integrity of the court system and the judgment of the police. The desire to preserve the myth of an infallible system of justice probably played some role in the decision to release the four on the basis of insufficient evidence rather than innocence. This desire would also explain a subsequent court decision clearing the police who were involved of any misconduct.

The case of the Guildford Four demonstrated how the rights of the accused can be ignored when the charges involve terrorism in a period of public fear. Juries can be quick to convict presumed terrorists, and authorities can be inclined to protect the system against charges of error for longer than is reasonable.

James Lutz and Brenda J. Lutz

See also Birmingham Pub Bombing; Irish Republican Army; Law and Terrorism

Further Readings

Kee, Robert. *Trial and Error: The Maguires, the Guildford Pub Bombings, and British Justice*. London: Hamish Hamilton, 1986.

Lutz, Brenda J., Georgia Wralstad Ulmschneider, and James M. Lutz. "The Trial of the Guildford Four: Government Error or Government Prosecution." *Terrorism and Political Violence* 14 (Winter 2002): 113–130.

McEvoy, Joanne. *The Politics of Northern Ireland*. Edinburgh: University of Edinburgh Press, 2008.

McKee, Grant, and Ros Franey. *Time Bomb*. London: Bloomsbury, 1988.

Mitchell, Thomas G. *When Peace Fails: Lessons from Belfast for the Middle East*. Jefferson, NC: McFarland, 2010.

GUZMÁN, ABIMAEL

See Reynoso, Abimael Guzmán

HABASH, GEORGE (1926–2008)

Dr. George Habash founded the guerrilla group Popular Front for the Liberation of Palestine (PFLP) and was famous for being Yasir Arafat's main rival for many years. The fiery Marxist leader, called al Hakim, or "the Physician," by his followers, was often said to be the world's second best-known Palestinian. Later in life, poor health caused him to largely withdraw from the public arena.

Habash was born in the Palestinian town of Lydda in 1926, the son of Greek Orthodox parents. As a young medical student, Habash fled Lydda in 1948 as a refugee. (His birthplace is now part of Israel and called Lod.) Habash earned his medical degree at the American University of Beirut, and in the 1950s he was one of the founders of the Arab nationalist movement.

In 1967 Habash founded the PFLP, combining Arab nationalism with Marxist-Leninist ideology. In the early days of the Damascus-based organization, Habash became known for saying, "Fatah [Arafat's organization] represents the petit bourgeoisie. The PFLP represents the laboring classes." Habash built his Marxist-Leninist group into the second-largest faction, after Fatah, of the Palestine Liberation Organization (PLO).

Under Habash's command the PFLP became famous for a series of spectacular airplane hijackings during the 1960s and 1970s. On a single day in September 1970, PFLP members hijacked American, Israeli, British, and Swiss airliners and landed them in Amman, Jordan. The PFLP's actions sparked the expulsion of Palestinian guerrillas from their bases in Jordan and led to the fighting between Jordanian troops and Palestinians that would come to be known among Palestinians as "Black September."

Habash is known for having trained the infamous international terrorist Carlos "the Jackal" (Illich Ramírez Sánchez), and the PFLP is said to have given Carlos his first assignments. Habash made Carlos head of the PFLP's European operations section in 1973.

In 1988, Habash accepted the principle of a divided Palestine and accepted United Nations resolutions 242 and 338. However, after Arafat signed the Oslo Peace Accords with Israel in 1993, Habash and the PFLP resigned from the PLO Executive Committee in protest. In 1999, representatives of the PFLP met with Arafat for the first time since the 1993 split. Habash did not attend the meeting, saying that he refused to meet with Arafat until the Palestinian leader admitted that the November 1998 revision of the Palestinian National Charter (in which the Palestinians removed language calling for Israel's destruction) was an error.

Throughout much of his later career, Habash was plagued with health problems. In 1980 he became partially paralyzed as the result of a mistake during brain surgery. He had several serious strokes and traveled to Europe for treatment. His trip to France for medical treatment in 1992 caused a furor in that country. He was admitted to a Paris hospital and was allowed to leave France after his three-day stay, while angry opposition parties accused the governing Socialist Party of harboring a terrorist. In what became known as the "Habash affair," four senior civil servants and an advisor to President Francois Mitterand were fired. Mitterand himself told journalists that when he heard Habash had been allowed into the country he thought that those responsible had gone "mad."

Habash eventually withdrew from public view, and he stepped down from PFLP leadership in July 2000. In August 2001, Israeli forces assassinated Habash's successor, Abu Ali Mustafa, killing him as he sat in his Ramallah office. Habash died on January 26, 2008, in a hospital in Amman, Jordan, following treatment for a heart ailment.

Erica Pearson

See also Arafat, Yasir; Black September; Hijacking; Palestine Liberation Organization; Popular Front for the Liberation of Palestine; Sánchez, Illich Ramírez

Further Readings

Bailey, Clinton. *Jordan's Palestinian Challenge, 1948–1983: A Political History.* Boulder, CO: Westview Press, 1984.

Black, Ian. "Rise and Fall of the 'Wise Physician.'" *The Guardian* (London), February 1, 1992, p. 11.

Fisk, Robert. "Still Dreaming of His Homeland; Robert Fisk in Damascus Hears George Habash, Orator, Fighter and Refugee, Spell Out His Terms for a Settlement with Israel." *The Independent* (London), October 9, 1993, p. 10.

Jansen, Michael. "Habash Says PLO-Israel Peace Plan Is a Retreat from Long-term Policy." *The Irish Times,* February 16, 1994, p. 8.

Murphy, Kim. "Obituaries: George Habash, 1925–2008." *Los Angeles Times,* January 27, 2008, p. B11.

"Obituary of George Habash: Guerrilla Leader of a Marxist Palestinian Faction Which Pioneered 'Skyjacking' and Other Terrorist Tactics." *The Daily Telegraph.* January 29, 2008, p. 25.

Raab, David. *Terror in Black September: The First Eyewitness Account of the Infamous 1970 Hijacking.* New York: Palgrave Macmillan, 2007.

Sharif, Bassam Abu. *Arafat and the Dream of Palestine: An Insider's Account.* New York: Palgrave Macmillan, 2009.

HAGE, WADIH EL (1960–)

Wadih el Hage (aka Abdus Sabbur; Abd al Sabbur; Wadia; Abu Abdullah al Lubnani; Norman; Wa'da Norman; the Manager; Tanzanite), a U.S. citizen, served for several years as Osama bin Laden's personal secretary and has been called a "front man" for the leader of al Qaeda. He was indicted for his part in the August 1998 bombings of two U.S. embassies in East Africa and is serving a life sentence for conspiracy to commit terrorism.

Wadih el Hage was born in Sidon, Lebanon, to a Christian family. He grew up in Kuwait and converted to Islam as a teenager. He immigrated to the United States in 1978 and graduated from the University of Southwestern Louisiana with a degree in urban planning. During the 1980s, Hage traveled to Pakistan to join the Afghani fight against the Soviets and worked in a refugee clinic. He is thought to have first met bin Laden at this time. In 1985, after returning to the United States, he married the American April Ray, a fellow convert to Islam. The couple now has seven children. Hage and his family lived in Tucson, Arizona, and Dallas, Texas, before he accepted the position as bin Laden's personal secretary. Between 1991 and 1994, the family lived in Sudan. Hage apparently worked on several of bin Laden's farming and chemical manufacturing projects, and he may have become involved with al Qaeda at this time.

From Sudan, the Hage family moved to Nairobi, Kenya, and Hage operated the "Help Africa People" charity and a gemstone business called "Tanzanite King." Both businesses appear to have been fronts for the al Qaeda Kenyan cell, of which Hage was the leader. After an al Qaeda commander died in a 1996 ferry boat accident in Kenya, Hage allegedly investigated and sent bin Laden a report. (After his September 1998 arrest, he denied this before a New York grand jury and provoked a perjury charge.)

The FBI twice raided Hage's Nairobi home in 1997 and confiscated a computer, computer disks, notebooks, and a phone book. According to press reports, the books contained coded phone numbers of al Qaeda leaders and bin Laden's satellite telephone number. Soon after the raids, the family returned to the United States. On August 7, 1998, truck bombs exploded just minutes apart at the U.S. embassies in Nairobi, Kenya, and Dar es Salaam, Tanzania, killing 224 people. At the time of the attacks, Hage and his family were living in Arlington, Texas.

Indictment and Trial

al Qaeda soon emerged as the primary suspect in the East Africa embassy bombings, and federal officials arrested Hage in September 1998. First indicted for perjury and making false statements, he was subsequently charged with participating in the broader terrorist conspiracy and playing an active role in the al Qaeda Kenyan cell. Prosecutors also maintained that he had been involved in various shadowy groups in the United States, saying that he was friends with El Sayyid Nosair, who was later convicted of involvement in the 1993 World Trade Center bombing case and the 1990 assassination of Rabbi Meir Kahane. The admitted al Qaeda conspirator Ali Mohamed, who pleaded guilty and cooperated with U.S. investigators, said that Hage had used the "Help Africa People" charity to create false identification for al Qaeda members.

During a 1999 Manhattan federal court hearing, Hage attempted to read a letter he had sent to Judge Leonard Sand into the court record. When the judge stopped him, Hage jumped over the barrier separating him from Sand, but three U.S. marshals brought him down before he could reach the judge. Following this incident, Hage complained that he was subject to constant strip searches and harsh treatment. As the trial date neared, a psychologist hired by Hage's lawyers suggested that he had developed a mental disorder during his imprisonment and was not fit to stand trial. However, prison psychiatrists determined that he was attempting to evade prosecution. He and three other defendants linked to bin Laden went on trial for the East Africa embassy bombings in February 2001.

Hage was convicted in May 2001 of lying to a federal grand jury about al Qaeda and acting as a facilitator for the group. He and the other three defendants—Mohamed Rashed al Owhali, Mohammed Saddiq Odeh, and Khalfan Khamis Mohamed—were sentenced to life in prison without parole.

Erica Pearson

See also al Qaeda; bin Laden, Osama; East Africa Embassy Bombings; Mohamed, Khalfan Khamis; Nosair, El Sayyid; Odeh, Mohammed Saddiq; Owhali, Mohamed Rashed al

Further Readings

Akhahenda, Elijah F. *When Blood and Tears United a Country: The Bombing of the American Embassy in Kenya*. Lanham, MD: University Press of America/ Rowman & Littlefield, 2002.

Atwan, Abdel Bari. *The Secret History of al Qaeda*. Berkeley: University of California Press, 2006.

Bergen, Peter. *Holy War, Inc.: Inside the Secret World of Osama bin Laden*. New York: Free Press, 2001.

Cohen, Laurie. "FBI Links Charity, bin Laden Ex-Aide." *Chicago Tribune*, March 28, 2002, p. 1.

Gunaratna, Rohan. *Inside Al Qaeda: Global Network of Terror*. New York: Columbia University Press, 2002.

Peraino, Kevin, Evan Thomas, Gretel C. Kovach, and Mark Hosenball. "Married to Jihad." *Newsweek*, January 14, 2002, p. 40.

Reeve, Simon. *The New Jackals: Ramzi Yousef, Osama bin Laden, and the Future of Terrorism*. Boston: Northeastern University Press, 1999.

Riedel, Bruce. *The Search for al Qaeda: Its Leadership, Ideology, and Future*. Washington, DC: Brookings Institution Press, 2008.

Smith, Martin, and Lowell Bergman. "Hunting bin Laden." *Frontline*, PBS, September 13, 2001. http:// www.pbs.org/wgbh/pages/frontline/shows/binladen.

U.S. District Court for the Southern District of New York. *United States v. Usama bin Laden et al.* Indictment S(10) 98 Cr. 1023 (LBS).

Weiser, Benjamin. "Judge Upholds Conviction in Terror Case." *The New York Times*, November 3, 2005, p. B1.

Weiser, Benjamin. "Warrantless Searches of Americans Are Legal Overseas, Court Panel Rules." *The New York Times*, November 25, 2008, p. A19.

Zill, Oriana. "A Portrait of Wadih el Hage, Accused Terrorist." *Frontline*, PBS, September 11, 2001. http:// www.pbs.org/wgbh/pages/frontline/shows/binladen/ upclose/elhage.html.

HAMAS

The main Islamic movement in the Palestinian territories, Hamas ("zeal" in Arabic and an acronym for "Harakat al Muqawama al Islamiya," or

Islamic Resistance Movement; aka Students of Ayyash, Students of the Engineer, and Yahya Ayyash Units) opposes the Oslo Peace Accords and does not recognize Israel's right to exist. The military faction of the group, called the Izz ad Din al Qassam Brigades, has carried out scores of suicide bombings and terror attacks inside Israel and the occupied territories since Hamas began in 1987. The group's military wing is also said to have carried out attacks on rivals and Palestinians suspected of collaborating with Israel.

Formed in 1987 during the first intifada, or uprising, by members of the Palestinian branch of the Muslim Brotherhood, the group aims to establish an Islamic Palestinian state in place of Israel, on the land once mandated as Palestine. Hamas maintains a large social, religious, and political presence in the Palestinian territories and has built hospitals and schools there. The group also engages in political activity, with candidates running in elections for the West Bank Chamber of Commerce.

According to the U.S. State Department, which lists Hamas as a terrorist group, Hamas has an unknown number of hard-core members, plus tens of thousands of supporters and sympathizers, largely in the Gaza Strip. The group also maintained a large presence in Jordan until the fall of 1999, when King Abdullah II came into power and prohibited Hamas from operating. Jordanian authorities then arrested Hamas leaders working in the country and closed Hamas's Political Bureau offices in the capital.

The spiritual leader of Hamas, Sheikh Ahmed Yassin, was an Islamic scholar in Cairo during his youth. He was left quadriplegic after a childhood accident but rose to prominence when Hamas emerged from the Palestinian branch of the Muslim Brotherhood. Israeli forces arrested Yassin in 1989 and sentenced him to life in prison for ordering the killing of Palestinians suspected of collaborating with the Israeli army. After eight years in prison, Yassin was released in a trade with Jordan for two Israeli Mossad agents who were caught attempting to assassinate a Hamas leader in Jordan.

Yassin was famous for publicly repeating, "The so-called peace path is not peace and it is not a substitute for jihad and resistance." He was said to provide inspiration for, and promise martyrdom to, those who engaged in suicide bombings. These bombers are often young unmarried men, although women and men with families have also used themselves as human bombs for Hamas, strapping nail-filled explosives to their bodies.

As leader of the Palestinian Authority, Yasir Arafat had long been under international pressure to clamp down on Hamas and other terrorist Palestinian groups that carried out terror attacks, such as Palestinian Islamic Jihad. The Palestinian Authority's first crackdown on the group was in 1996, when it arrested some 1,000 people and shut down many Hamas institutions, including the group's weekly newspaper, *The Message*.

Although Yassin recognized Arafat and his Palestinian Authority as the only national authority in the Palestinian territories, many other Hamas leaders did not grant such recognition, saying that to recognize the Palestinian Authority was to recognize the Oslo Peace Accords.

Peace Process Halted

Hamas succeeded in bringing the peace process to a halt in the late 1990s, carrying out multiple bus bombings in 1996 that killed nearly 60 Israelis, followed by attacks in 1997 in Jerusalem that killed 15. These attacks were said to be in retaliation for the Israeli assassination of Hamas commander Yahya Ayyash, known as "the Engineer," who was killed by the blast of a tiny bomb hidden in a cellular phone.

In 2000 a sustained period of violence began that came to be known as the second intifada (uprising, or "shaking off"; the first intifada occurred in 1987). As the group's deadly attacks became increasingly frequent, Israel, the United States, and other nations called on Arafat to take greater steps to control Hamas, whose attacks are estimated to have killed 77 and wounded 547 people. After a December 2001 bus bombing that killed 10 people in Israel, Arafat ordered the closing of all Hamas and Islamic Jihad offices and arrested several Hamas political leaders and many group members. However, when the Palestinian Authority attempted to place Yassin under house arrest, riots ensued, and the Hamas spiritual leader ultimately agreed to a "voluntary" house arrest.

Hamas carried out many more attacks during the spring of 2002. For the next several years, Israel and Hamas exchanged a number of missile strikes that killed countless civilians. In 2004, Yassin was assassinated in one of these missile attacks, which also killed his bodyguards and nine bystanders. Yasir Arafat died in November of that year, and Mahmoud Abbas took control of a greatly weakened Fatah. Bringing the second *intifada* to an end in early 2005, Abbas declared that violence would cease. Ariel Sharon, prime minister of Israel, agreed to release 900 Palestinian prisoners.

In 2006, Hamas took control of Gaza after winning a majority of seats in the territory's governing body, the Palestinian National Authority. However, relations between Israel and Gaza quickly deteriorated, with Israel withholding tax revenue from the territory and sealing Gaza's borders. Hamas retaliated with violence, which incited Israeli retaliation in a vicious cycle that lasted for two years. Finally, in June 2008, both Hamas and Israel declared a six-month truce, in which the former agreed to stop the attacks—not only perpetrated by their own members but by any armed groups in Gaza—and Israel lifted its blockades.

However, in-fighting for the leadership of Palestine continued between the reigning Hamas and Fatah. In 2007 the two groups agreed to a unified Palestinian government, but it collapsed less than six months later, leading Abbas to replace the Hamas governmental presence in the West Bank with a Fatah-led faction. Meanwhile, Israel continued to attack Gaza with rockets and air assaults from late 2008 into 2009, decimating much of Gaza.

In 2010, President Barack Obama attempted to reignite peace talks with Prime Minister Benjamin Netanyahu of Israel, President Abbas, President Hosni Mubarak of Egypt, and King Abdullah of Jordan, hoping to come to an agreement over Jerusalem, the establishment of the borders of a Palestinian state, and assured Israeli security.

Erica Pearson

See also Arafat, Yasir; Ayyash, Yahya; Intifada; Mossad; Palestine Islamic Jihad; Suicide Terrorism

Further Readings

Ahmad, Hisham H. *Hamas: From Religious Salvation to Political Transformation: The Rise of Hamas in Palestinian Society.* Jerusalem: Palestinian Academic Society for the Study of International Affairs (PASSIA), 1994.

Cordesman, Anthony H. *The Israeli-Palestinian War: Escalating to Nowhere.* Westport, CT: Praeger, 2005.

Jensen, Michael Irving. *The Political Ideology of Hamas: A Grassroots Perspective.* London: I.B. Tauris, 2009.

Khalid, Harub. *Hamas: Political Thought and Practice.* Washington, DC: Institute for Palestine Studies, 2000.

Levitt, Matthew. *Hamas: Politics, Charity, and Terrorism in the Service of Jihad.* New Haven, CT: Yale University Press, 2006.

Milton-Edwards, Beverly, and Stephen Farrell. *Hamas: The Islamic Resistance Movement.* Cambridge, UK: Polity, 2010.

Nusse, Andrea. *Muslim Palestine: The Ideology of Hamas.* Amsterdam: Harwood Academic Publishers, 1998.

Shaul, Mishal. *The Palestinian Hamas: Vision, Violence, and Coexistence.* New York: Columbia University Press, 2000.

Tamimi, Azzam. *Hamas: A History from within.* Northampton, MA: Olive Branch, 2007.

Timmerman, Kenneth R. *In Their Own Words: Interviews with leaders of Hamas, Islamic Jihad, and the Muslim Brotherhood: Damascus, Amman, and Gaza.* Los Angeles: Simon Wiesenthal Center, 1994.

Wilson, Scott. "Hamas Sweeps Palestinian Elections, Complicating Peace Efforts in the Middle East." *The Washington Post,* January 27, 2006.

HANAFI MUSLIM MOVEMENT

The Hanafi Muslim Movement was founded in 1958 by Khalifa Hamaas Abdul Khaalis (born Ernest Timothy McGee). Khaalis was an African American Muslim who had joined the New York–based Hanafi Madhab Center in 1947. The center was a peaceful institution dedicated to the study and teaching of the Hanafi school of Islamic jurisprudence.

The Hanafi school was founded in eighth-century Baghdad by the noted legal scholar Abu al Hanafa. It was initially involved in developing court-of-law procedures and rules of evidence for the rapidly expanding Islamic Abbasid Empire. Considered the least "fundamentalist" of the four major schools of Islamic jurisprudence, the Hanafi legal system and interpretations of Islamic law became preeminent throughout the Ottoman Empire.

Involvement With the Nation of Islam

In 1950, Khaalis joined the Nation of Islam in an attempt to bring its teachings into line with orthodox Islam. At that time, the Nation of Islam taught a form of Islam that was considered heretical by most Muslim leaders. In 1956, Khaalis became the national secretary of the Nation of Islam.

However, Khaalis eventually fell out with the Nation of Islam over the group's refusal to adopt mainstream Islam. In 1958 he left the Nation of Islam and moved to Washington, D.C., where he opened his own Hanafi Madhab Center. At its height, during the 1960s, the center had over 1,000 members, and Khaalis led several protests for Muslim causes. The most famous member of the center was basketball star Kareem Abdul Jabbar, whom Khaalis had helped convert to Islam.

Khaalis continued to disagree with the teachings of the Nation of Islam. In 1973, five members of the Philadelphia Nation of Islam murdered Khaalis's wife, their four children, and two other Hanafi members. Khaalis was angered by the police investigation, which was, in his view, cursory. The police, he believed, did not appear interested in finding the killers.

Taking Hostages

In 1977, Khaalis and a group of his followers seized control of three Washington, D.C., buildings and took 124 people hostage. Khaalis was protesting what he felt to be the lack of progress in the investigation of his family's murder, and the group was also protesting the planned release of a movie about the life of the Prophet Mohammed (many Islamic teachings forbid the display of images of Mohammed).

The hostages in the three buildings—the B'nai B'rith building; the District Building, home to the City Council chambers; and the Islamic Center—were held for more than 30 hours. One hostage was killed during the initial takeover, and several, including Marion Berry, the future mayor of Washington, were injured. The hostages were eventually released, with the help of ambassadors from Egypt, Iran, and Pakistan, who talked Khaalis into giving himself up, at one point taking turns reading to him passages from the Koran emphasizing God's compassion and mercy.

Although the Jewish hostages were subjected to threats and anti-Semitic statements while being held, the incident did temporarily help bring the area's Jewish and Muslim communities closer. After his release, the director of the Islamic Center told the leaders of B'nai B'rith, "Now we are one." After the siege, a statement by the Hanafi Mad-hab Center threatened "all Zionist Jews and their allies" with a "bloodbath."

Khaalis and the other kidnappers were all arrested. Khaalis was sentenced to 41 to 120 years in prison; he died in custody in 2003. The Madhab Center is still in operation, teaching orthodox Hanafi Islam.

Lisa Magloff

See also Hostage Taking

Further Readings

Abdul Jabbar, Kareem, and Peter Knobler. *Giant Steps.* New York: Simon & Schuster. 2002.
"25th Anniversary of Terror." *The Washington Post,* March 9, 2002, p. A22.
Vargas, Theresa. "'Some Things You Never Forget': Thirty Years Ago, Gunmen Stormed Three D.C. Buildings, Taking 150 Hostages and One Life. Today the City Remembers That Terrifying Hint of Things to Come." *The Washington Post,* March 12, 2007, p. B1.
White, Vibert. *Inside the Nation of Islam: A Historical and Personal Testimony by a Black Muslim.* Gainesville: University Press of Florida, 2001.

HARAKAT UL-MUJAHIDEEN

Harakat ul-Mujahideen (or Harkat-ul-Mujahideen) is a large militant Sunni Muslim group that, throughout the 1990s, operated largely in the disputed states of Jammu and Kashmir on the India-Pakistan border. Reportedly, the group also had troops in such far-flung locales as Bosnia, Tajikistan, Algeria, the Middle East, Chechnya, and the Philippines. The group, headquartered in Pakistan, has recently seen its operations curtailed because of a crackdown on militant groups by Pakistan's government following the September 11, 2001, terrorist attacks on the United States.

It has been speculated that Harakat ul-Mujahideen may alter the focus of its attacks to the now hostile Pakistani regime. Before September 11, Harakat ul-Mujahideen had several training camps in Afghanistan, as well as close ties to the Taliban government of that country and the Saudi radical Osama bin Laden. Indeed, links among the three were so well established that the "American Taliban" John Walker Lindh, a U.S. citizen captured by U.S.-backed forces during the overthrow of the Taliban government in 2001, was briefly a member of Harakat ul-Mujahideen before moving to bin Laden's al Qaeda. Like al Qaeda, Harakat ul-Mujahideen is strongly anti-Western and has targeted U.S. and Western European tourists for kidnap and murder.

Harakat ul-Mujahideen was founded as Harakat ul Ansar in 1993 by the Pakistani activist Fazlur Rehman Khalil and four veterans of the war against the Soviet occupation of Afghanistan. The organization, created through the merger of two militias initially established to fight the Soviets, essentially inherited the training camps of a Sunni Muslim faction of the anti-Soviet mujahideen.

Harakat ul Ansar, which has a mostly Pakistani membership, was established to support Pakistani governance in the states of Jammu and Kashmir. The largely Muslim country of Pakistan and the largely Hindu country of India have long quarreled over which should have sovereignty in Jammu and Kashmir; armed groups within the two states also support independence. Once established, Harakat ul Ansar quickly received backing from the Pakistani government, and in 1994 the group was granted membership in a Pakistani-based umbrella association of Muslim, pro-Pakistani militant groups that operate in Jammu and Kashmir.

In September of that year, Harakat ul Ansar kidnapped two British citizens on vacation in Kashmir; the two were eventually released. The same month, group members participated in the kidnapping of four Westerners in New Delhi, India. In that case, Indian police arrested the kidnappers and freed the captives. The New Delhi kidnappings were apparently undertaken to secure hostages to trade for the release of Maulana Masood Azhar, also known as Wali Azam, a Harakat ul Ansar leader arrested in Jammu and Kashmir by India in early 1994.

In July 1995, a Harakat ul Ansar faction called Al Faran kidnapped six Westerners who were hiking through Kashmir. The kidnappers demanded the release of several jailed militants, including Azhar. One of the captives escaped, but the headless and mutilated body of a second was found a month after the kidnapping. The remaining four were never found and are believed to have been killed by their captors in the winter of 1995. Harakat ul Ansar initially denied responsibility for the kidnappings, but evidence strongly pointed to the group.

In response to the kidnappings, the United States designated Harakat ul Ansar as a terrorist organization in 1997, leading Pakistan to reduce its support of the group. Following the U.S. designation, the group changed its name from Harakat ul Ansar ("movement of helpers") to Harakat ul-Mujahideen ("movement of holy warriors"). During 1998, Harakat ul-Mujahideen was active in the fighting between Sunni and Shiite Muslims in the Punjab province of Pakistan.

Several members of Harakat ul-Mujahideen died in August 1998 when the United States launched a cruise missile attack on a bin Ladin training camp in Afghanistan. The following year, in a press conference in Islamabad, Pakistan, Khalil announced that his group would kill 100 Americans for every Muslim killed by the United States.

On December 24, 1999, a group of men believed to be members of Harakat ul-Mujahideen hijacked Indian Airlines Flight 814, which was carrying 189 people from Kathmandu, Nepal, to New Delhi. The hijackers stabbed to death a 25-year-old passenger and demanded the release of more than 30 militants, including Azhar. Eventually, the plane began to run out of fuel, and the pilot landed in Amritsar, India. A delay in refueling made the hijackers nervous, and they forced the pilot to take off. The plane was allowed to land and refuel in Lahore, Pakistan. The hijackers then forced the pilot to fly to Dubai, where the body of the stabbed passenger was unloaded, and finally to Kandahar, Afghanistan, where the plane, still filled with passengers, sat on a runway for six days while Indian authorities negotiated with the hijackers.

On December 31, 1999, an agreement was reached. India released Azhar and two other militants, including Ahmad Omar Sheikh, a Harakat ul-Mujahideen member who had been jailed for the 1994 New Delhi kidnappings. Both men were released in Kandahar, but they eventually made their way to Pakistan. Shortly after his release, Azhar founded Jaish-e-Mohammed, a rival militant group espousing an even more radical brand of militant Islam.

In December 2001, Pakistani authorities placed Azhar under house arrest as part of a crackdown on radical groups following the September 11 attacks in the United States and the suicide attack on the Indian Parliament complex in New Delhi. The New Delhi attack was linked to Jaish-e-Mohammed and another radical group, Lashkar-e-Taiba. Sheikh, who was also believed to have aligned himself with Jaish-e-Mohammed, was arrested in early 2002 in Pakistan after assisting in the abduction and murder of *Wall Street Journal* reporter Daniel Pearl. Members of Harakat ul-Mujahideen are also believed to have participated in Pearl's kidnapping and murder.

The United States has frozen Harakat ul-Mujahideen's U.S. assets. In January 2002, in a significant reversal of earlier policy, Pakistan banned the organization and arrested many members. Despite these setbacks, many observers fear that the remnants of Harakat ul-Mujahideen will join forces with surviving members of other Muslim militant organizations like al Qaeda, Jaish-e-Mohammed, and Lashkar-e-Taiba to attack Western and government targets in Pakistan and Afghanistan. In addition, another Harakat ul-Mujahideen offshoot, Harakat ul Jihad-i-Islami, which was established in 1992, became increasingly active in the 2000s and appeared to be working in concert with its sister organizations. The group, which operates mainly out of Bangladesh, is believed to be responsible for numerous bombing attacks in that country, as well as bombings in India and assassination attempts on high-ranking Pakistani officials.

Mary Sisson

See also al Qaeda; bin Laden, Osama; Jaish-e-Mohammed; Lashkar-e-Taiba; Mujahideen; Pearl, Daniel; September 11 Attacks; Taliban

Further Readings

Constable, Pamela. "'They Were on a Do-or-Die Mission': Freed Indian Hostages Recount Eight Days of Terror in Hands of Desperate Hijackers." *The Washington Post*, January 5, 2000, p. A15.

Goldenberg, Suzanne. "Terror List Angers Kashmir Fighters: Separatists Bristle at Being Linked to the Kidnapping of Westerners." *The Guardian*, October 25, 1997, Foreign Section, p. 19.

Jehl, Douglas. "Death of Reporter Puts Focus on Pakistan Intelligence Unit." *The New York Times*, February 25, 2002, p. A1.

Makkar, Sahil. "Seek Terrorists and Ye Shall (Not) Find: India's Interpol Impasse." *Eastern Eye*, August 8, 2008, p. 9.

Weaver, Mary Anne. *Pakistan: In the Shadow of Jihad and Afghanistan.* New York: Farrar, Straus and Giroux, 2002.

Wilkinson, Isambard. "Pakistan Funds Islamic Terror." *Sunday Telegraph*, May 16, 1999, International Section, p. 32.

HAWATMEH, NAYEF (~1937–)

Nayef Hawatmeh (aka Najib Hawatmeh) was one of the most powerful Palestinian terrorists during the 1960s and 1970s. He is the founder and leader of the Syria-based militant Marxist group Democratic Front for the Liberation of Palestine (DFLP).

Hawatmeh was born to a Greek Orthodox family in Salt, Jordan. He joined George Habash's Popular Front for the Liberation of Palestine, but disagreements and power struggles between the two led him to leave the Popular Front in 1969. He then formed the Democratic Front, a Marxist-Leninist organization working to create an independent, secular Palestinian state through revolution, and he brought other more radical Popular Front members into his new organization. The group, which was strongly connected with the U.S.S.R. and other Communist countries during the Cold War, has long been based in Damascus, Syria.

During the 1970s, Hawatmeh became famous for masterminding plane hijackings and other terrorist acts. In 1974, Democratic Front members attacked a school in the Israeli town of Maalot, taking the children hostage and killing more than 20. When Yasir Arafat signed the Oslo Peace Accords with Israel in 1993, Hawatmeh condemned him and famously called him "an American stooge."

Nonetheless, Hawatmeh (said to be acting in accord with Syrian leaders) soon took a more moderate tack. At the funeral of King Hussein of Jordan in February 1999, Hawatmeh shook hands with Israeli president Ezer Weizman and complimented him for being a man of peace. Weizman told Hawatmeh that the time had arrived for Israel to make peace with Syria and Lebanon. The controversial handshake was much discussed in the international press, as reporters and Israeli and Palestinian officials disagreed over who had initiated the gesture.

In August 1999, Hawatmeh met with Arafat for the first time in six years, in response to Arafat's call to strengthen the Palestinian position before upcoming talks with Israel.

Most active during the 1970s and early 1980s, the DFLP has lost much of its influence in recent years. The group now largely focuses on social and political actions. The U.S. State Department has dropped the Democratic Front from its list of active foreign terrorist groups, and in 2007, Israel allowed Hawatmeh to return to the West Bank.

Erica Pearson

See also Arafat, Yasir; Democratic Front for the Liberation of Palestine; Intifada

Further Readings

Dellios, Hugh. "Arafat, Rival Put Aside Differences; Palestinian Leaders Seek to Reconcile Factions before Key Talks with Israel." *Chicago Tribune*, August 24, 1999.

"Hawatmehh: Intifada Should Continue." *Jerusalem Post*, September 13, 1993.

Kershner, Isabel. "In Nod to Fatah, Israel Removes Militiamen from Wanted List." *The New York Times*, July 16, 2007, p. A4.

Rees, Matt. "Hopes Grow for Israeli Peace Talks with Syria." *The Scotsman*, July 21, 1999, p. 10.

Toameh, Khaled Abu. "A Dubious Pair of 'Allies' for Abbas." *Jerusalem Post*, July 16, 2007, p. 2.

HEARST, PATTY (1954–)

Patty Hearst, the heiress to the Hearst newspaper empire, is best known as a kidnapping victim turned terrorist. As a member of a small, leftist terrorist group in California, Hearst, along with her kidnappers, went to prison in 1976 for bank robbery.

The granddaughter of the legendary publishing tycoon William Randolph Hearst, Patty Hearst was raised by her parents to be privileged but not spoiled by their family's wealth. In 1974, while attending college at University of California, Berkeley, and living with her fiancé, Steven Weed, her life suddenly changed dramatically. On the evening of February 4, members of the Symbionese Liberation Army (SLA) barged into their apartment, injured Weed badly, and kidnapped Hearst. The SLA held her captive at their safe house for about two months.

Led by a man called Cinque after his escape from prison, the SLA was a radical terrorist group campaigning to overthrow the white bourgeois capitalists of America. They originally intended to exchange Hearst for the release of two SLA members jailed for the murder of the Oakland school superintendent, Marcus Foster. However, when her capture generated extensive media coverage, the SLA decided they would demand even more. In order for Hearst to be released, her father would have to organize and pay for the distribution of $70 worth of food to every poor person in California. This amount exceeded even the wealth of the Hearst family. Although he couldn't give that much, her father did donate $2 million, but the distribution locations were looted and the operation was not very successful.

It is said that the SLA then brainwashed Hearst into believing that her father was a "capitalist pig," and that he did not care enough about her or the people to comply with their demands. While keeping her locked in a closet and blindfolded, they battered her with their beliefs and condemned her for her background. It is said that several of the men also raped her. Ultimately, they gave Hearst the choice to go free or stay and fight for the cause with them. Her rationale in deciding to stay has been a cause for great debate. Some believe that Hearst was indeed brainwashed into sympathizing with her captors, while others believe that if she chose to go free they would have immediately killed her, and that she complied only to ensure her own survival. Still others believe that Hearst had prior associations with the SLA and had helped them orchestrate her own kidnapping.

Calling herself Tania, Hearst became involved in several of the SLA's activities. She issued a tape recording to the media denouncing capitalism and her family, and then participated in a bank robbery in San Francisco on April 15, 1974. On May 17 of the same year, a shootout occurred between the SLA and police at their safe house in Los Angeles. The house caught fire and six SLA members perished. Hearst and two other SLA members, Bill and Emily Harris, were not present when the shootout occurred. With the help of Kathleen Ann Soliah, the three became fugitives and lived in hiding for more than a year. The FBI was tipped off to their location, and in September 1975 they found and arrested several remaining SLA members, including Hearst. She was convicted of committing the bank robbery and of using firearms, but she only served three years of her seven-year sentence before President Jimmy Carter granted her a pardon in 1979. Released from prison, Hearst married her former bodyguard, Bernard Shaw, and moved to Connecticut, where they had two daughters.

Hearst has since written an autobiography and a novel, and she has acted in several films directed by John Waters. She was called upon to serve as a witness during the trial of Soliah (a.k.a. Sara Jane Olsen), who was apprehended in 1999 for her involvement with the SLA. On the last day before President Bill Clinton left office, he granted Patricia Hearst an absolute pardon for her role in the bank robbery. She has become a champion bulldog breeder, winning the Westminster Kennel Club show in 2008.

Harvey Kushner

See also Hostage Taking; Stockholm Syndrome; Symbionese Liberation Army

Further Readings

Graebmer, William. *Patty's Got a Gun: Patricia Hearst in 1970s America.* Chicago: University of Chicago Press, 2008.

Hearst, Patricia Campbell. *Patty Hearst: Her Own Story.* New York: Morrow Avon, 1988.

Langley, William. "Patty Hearst: Urban Guerrilla Brought to Heel." *Sunday Telegraph,* February 17, 2008, p. 28.

Maguire, John G., and Mary Lee Dunn. *The Patty Hearst Story: From Heiress to Revolutionary.* North Miami Beach, FL: Success Publications, 1974.

Payne, Leslie, Timothy Findley, and Carolyn Craven. *The Life and Death of the SLA.* New York: Ballantine, 1976.

HEZBOLLAH

Hezbollah (aka Ansar Allah; Islamic Jihad for the Liberation of Palestine; Islamic Jihad Organization; Organization of the Oppressed on Earth; Organization of Right Against Wrong; Party of God; Revolutionary Justice Organization) was responsible for some of the most infamous acts of terror during the Lebanese civil war, including the bombing of the U.S. embassy and marine barracks in Beirut, the hijacking of TWA Flight 847, and the kidnapping of Western journalists and academics. After the war's end in 1990, Hezbollah reinvented itself as a force in national politics and social programs, while simultaneously continuing to exist as one of the most active and dangerous terrorist groups in the Middle East.

Hezbollah was formed in June 1982 as a radical offshoot of the main Shiite Muslim party, Amal. At that time, Hezbollah supported the transformation of Lebanon into an Islamic state and collaborated with Palestinian terrorist groups in their fight against Israel. Many Hezbollah leaders had studied theology with Iranian clerics and maintained close ties to Iran during and after its 1979 revolution that brought the Ayatollah Ruhollah Khomeini to power. The group's first leader and secretary general, Sheikh Sobhi Tufeili, was famous for refusing to consider Lebanon as a nation-state. Tufeili was replaced in May 1991, and Israeli agents assassinated his successor, Abbas Musawi, in 1992. Contemporary Hezbollah leaders include Secretary-General Hassan Nasrallah, Deputy Secretary-General Naim Kassim, and spiritual advisor Sheikh Mohammed Hussein Fadlallah.

Hezbollah first put a representative into Lebanon's parliament in 1992. Since that time, the 128-member parliament has consistently included Hezbollah members. The party also owns or funds several hospitals, schools, cultural societies, and charities in Lebanon, and members deliver drinking water to slums, repair roads, and feed the poor. Hezbollah also runs a weekly newspaper, *Al Ahid*, a television channel, Al Manar, and a radio station, Al Nour.

Western Targets

Early on, Hezbollah targeted Western institutions and individuals. U.S. officials maintain that the former Hezbollah security chief Imad Mughniyah, who was one of the FBI's most wanted terrorists, planned the 1983 suicide truck bombings of the U.S. embassy in Beirut as well as the attacks on the French and American military headquarters in the city later that year. More than 350 people were killed in the suicide attacks, and the U.S. Marines withdrew from Lebanon soon thereafter. Mughniyah was assassinated in a car bomb in Damascus, Syria, in February 2008.

In the mid-1980s, Hezbollah began kidnapping Westerners and holding them hostage, hoping to gain more influence in regional affairs and bargain for the release of Shiites held in Israeli, Kuwaiti, or Western jails. In separate instances, militants kidnapped American, British, Irish, French, Saudi, West German, and South Korean nationals. A group called Islamic Jihad, later revealed to be a front for Hezbollah, publicly claimed responsibility for many of the kidnappings. Ten of the hostages died in captivity, including the Beirut CIA station chief, William Buckley. For nearly a decade, the kidnappers fed dictated communiqués and orchestrated images to the media.

The Associated Press journalist Terry Anderson was one of the first Americans to be kidnapped; he was seized at gunpoint in West Beirut on March 16, 1985. The former marine was held in a windowless cell, often blindfolded or chained to the floor. Brian Keenan, an Irish national, was abducted in April 1986 as he left his apartment to give a lecture at the American University in Beirut. Four armed men threw him into the back of an old Mercedes and took him to a 4-by-6-foot cell, where he was held in solitary confinement.

The English journalist John McCarthy, who had traveled to Beirut to film a news feature on

Women Hezbollah supporters pray at the grave of their slain top commander Imad Mughniyeh, during the opening of a new cemetery for their fighters who died in fighting against Israel, in a southern suburb of Beirut, Lebanon, November 12, 2010. Hezbollah leader Sheikh Hassan Nasrallah said his militant group will cut the hand of anyone who tries to arrest any member of the party and the group will not accept any accusation against any of its fighters or leaders in the 2005 assassination of former Prime Minister Rafik Hariri. (AP Photo/Hussein Malla. © 2011 The Associated Press. All Rights Reserved)

Keenan's kidnapping, was himself abducted on the way to the airport. The kidnappers later confined the two men together in a large room. Later, Keenan and McCarthy were transferred to a dungeon in the Bekaa Valley, where they were imprisoned with Anderson, American University professor Thomas Sutherland, and the American Frank Reed. It was common for the captors to beat all of the hostages on the feet, and some of them were chained for days on end.

Although the administration of President Ronald Reagan had publicly promised not to negotiate with the terrorists, officials secretly negotiated an arms-for-hostages deal with Iran. Professor David Jacobsen, Father Lawrence Martin Jenco, and Rev. Benjamin Weir were released under the arrangement. Congressional investigations into the deal, and charges that officials were channeling money from the arms sales to the Contras in Nicaragua, led to the resignation of top administration officials. On December 4, 1991, the terrorists released the last remaining captive, Anderson, bringing nearly a decade of hostage-related turmoil and fear to an end.

Although Hezbollah now denies all involvement in the kidnappings, the prisoners told the media that they believed their kidnappers were affiliated with the group. Some hostages talked about seeing pictures of Ayatollah Khomeini on the wall, reinforcing U.S. suspicions that Hezbollah remained closely aligned with Iran. One of the Shiite prisoners that the kidnappers wanted released in exchange for the Westerners was Mustafa Badreddin, the brother-in-law of Hezbollah's security chief Mughniyah. Held in a Kuwaiti jail, Badreddin and 16 other Shiite prisoners escaped during Iraq's invasion of that country.

In 1985, terrorists linked to Hezbollah hijacked TWA Flight 847, commandeering the plane as it traveled from Athens to Rome. The plane flew between Beirut and Algiers a number of times as the hijackers negotiated for the release of Shiite prisoners held by Israel. During the ordeal, a U.S. navy diver was shot and dumped onto the tarmac of the Beirut airport. Their involvement with this hijacking led the FBI to put Mughniyah, Ali Atwa, and Hassan Izz al Din on its list of most wanted terrorists.

In the early 1990s, after all other Lebanese militias had disarmed, Hezbollah continued to fight with Israeli troops stationed in southern Lebanon. At times, Hezbollah forces fired Katyusha rockets across the border, while Israel bombed Shiite villages. In 1996, Israel began a 17-day air assault to wipe out Hezbollah bases, fighters, and weaponry.

In 1992, Israeli helicopters fired on a convoy in southern Lebanon, killing Hezbollah leader Abbas Musawi. A month later, a bomb exploded in the Israeli embassy in Buenos Aires, Argentina, killing nearly 30 people. In 1999, the Argentine government issued an international warrant for Mugniyah's arrest.

After the September 11, 2001, terrorist attacks on the World Trade Center in New York City and the Pentagon near Washington, D.C., President George W. Bush had the U.S. assets of Hezbollah frozen. As the Israeli-Palestinian conflict intensified in 2002, Hezbollah once again attacked across the disputed "Blue Line," hitting Israeli villages near the Shebaa Farms.

In 2005, the billionaire Rafik Hariri, who twice served as prime minister of Lebanon, was assassinated in a car bomb. An initial UN investigation resulted in the Mehlis Report, which implicated both Syria and Lebanon officials in the killing. In order to look further into the assassination, the United Nations formed the Special Tribunal for Lebanon in March 2009. The potential indictment of Hezbollah members has sparked fears of a conflict not unlike that with Israel in 2006, when Hezbollah went to war with Israel for 34 days.

While Israel never officially declared war with Lebanon in 2006, the Lebanese government aligned itself with Hezbollah, citing the organizations' previous success in ousting Israel in its southern region. Ultimately, however, the war had a more adverse and long-lasting effect on Lebanon itself, as 1,300 people were killed, a majority of them Lebanese civilians, and the country's infrastructure and civic organization were severely crippled. However, the leader of Hezbollah, Sheikh Hassan Nasrallah, claimed a victory for his country, though he tempered his assertions with an apology to his people, stating that the group would not have engaged in the cross-border raid that incited the conflict had they known the force with which Israel would respond.

After the conflict, Hezbollah put full efforts into a reconstruction project, though mostly to benefit Hezbollah areas. The group rejoined the Lebanese government in 2008 as a full partner, and officials have claimed that Hezbollah continues to grow in power and size.

Erica Pearson

See also Anderson, Terry A.; Atwa, Ali; Buckley, William; Izz al Din, Hassan; Mugniyah, Imad Fayez; Nasrallah, Sheikh Hassan; TWA Flight 847 Hijacking

Further Readings

Anderson, Terry A. *Den of Lions: Memoirs of Seven Years.* New York: Crown, 1993.

Cambanis, Thanassis. *A Privilege to Die: Inside Hezbollah's Legions and Their Endless War against Israel.* New York: Free Press, 2010.

Dekker, Ted, and Carl Medearis. *Tea with Hezbollah: Sitting at the Enemies' Table.* New York: Doubleday, 2010.

Drake, Laura. *Hegemony and Its Discontents: United States Policy toward Iraq, Iran, Hamas, the Hezbollah and Their Responses.* Annandale, VA: United Association for Studies and Research, 1997.

Fisk, Robert. *Pity the Nation: Lebanon at War.* London: A. Deutsch, 1990.

Jaber, Hala. *Hezbollah: Born with a Vengeance.* New York: Columbia University Press, 1997.

Harel, Amos, and Avi Isacharoff. *34 Days: Israel, Hezbollah, and the War in Lebanon.* New York: Palgrave Macmillan, 2008.

Muller, Andrew. "We're Coming to Get You: The U.S. Says Hizbollah Is a Bunch of Evil Terrorists Who Should Be Destroyed. The Lebanese Set-up Insists It's Little More Than a Group of Do-gooders, and Andrew Muller Discovers That, Well, Perhaps They're Both Right." *Independent on Sunday* (London), April 7, 2002, p. 20.

Norton, Augustus Richard. *Hezbollah: A Short History.* Princeton, NJ: Princeton University Press, 2007.

Pelletiere, Stephen C. *Hamas and Hizbollah: The Radical Challenge to Israel in the Occupied Territories.* Carlisle Barracks, PA: Strategic Studies Institute, U.S. Army War College, 1994.

HIJACKING

Also known as *skyjacking,* airline hijacking was first used as an act of terrorism in the late 1960s by terrorist groups who took command of flights and held passengers and crew hostage in order to make political demands. Press reports have placed the total number of airplane hijackings throughout history at about a thousand. Although many past hijackings ended in tragedy, the scope of hijacking horrors widened on September 11, 2001, when al Qaeda operatives carried out a hijacking plot that created missiles out of commercial jet liners, destroying the World Trade Center in New York City, damaging the Pentagon near Washington, D.C., and killing thousands.

The first recorded air hijacking took place in 1931 in Peru. However, hijackings did not become well known until after World War II, when Eastern Europeans attempted to take over flights and cross over the line from Communist-controlled Europe, landing outside of the so-called Iron Curtain.

In 1961 a commercial airliner flying from Miami to Key West, Florida, was hijacked. The plane was forced to fly to Cuba, beginning the decade-long hijacking spree known as the "Cuban shuttle," as planes flying between the United States, Cuba, and Mexico were frequently hijacked by homesick Cubans or American leftists.

Although the hijacking of aircraft would soon become a common tactic for terrorist groups working to free comrades or gain publicity for a cause, many early hijackings were motivated by simple greed. In a legendary 1971 attempt, Dan "D.B." Cooper took over a Northwest Airlines plane over the Pacific Northwest of the United States. He gathered $200,000 in ransom and then parachuted out the back of the plane, never to be seen again.

The situation in the Middle East drove hijackings in the late 1960s and 1970s, as Palestinian terrorists brought notoriety to their cause. The first hijacking related to the Palestinian movement happened in July 1968, when hijackers from the Popular Front for the Liberation of Palestine (PFLP) commandeered El Al Flight 707 in Rome and forced it to fly to Algiers. Flight 707 is often referred to as the only successful hijacking attempt aboard an El Al plane.

On August 29, 1969, the Palestinian Leila Khaled, a member of the PFLP, carried out her first hijacking and captured world headlines. Khaled and a cohort stormed the cockpit of TWA Flight 840, flying from Rome to Tel Aviv. They redirected the plane to Damascus, where the passengers and crew were released unharmed.

On September 6, 1970, Khaled and other Palestinian terrorists from the PFLP carried out the first mass hijacking in history. Khaled, who underwent plastic surgery in order to pass through airport security, and a companion hijacked an El Al jet from Amsterdam, while others commandeered planes from TWA, Pan Am, and Swissair. Armed guards on board the El Al flight opened fire, taking Khaled prisoner and killing her companion. However, the other three planes were successfully hijacked and taken to an airport near Amman, Jordan. The hijackers released the hostages in exchange for Palestinian prisoners, then blew up the planes. The mass hijackings provoked Jordan's King Hussein to declare war on the Palestinian groups in Jordan.

The frequent hijackings soon caused the United States and other countries to take preventative action. In 1970, 50 countries ratified a United Nations convention calling for stricter measures for those who unlawfully seized aircraft. Airports introduced screening and other new security measures in the early 1970s, and the number of successful hijackings declined. According to press reports, between 1973 and 1979, only 1 of the 36 hijacking attempts was successful.

In order to further curtail hijacking attempts, the U.S. government put sky marshals on select flights, a program that endured through the Johnson and Nixon administrations. In 1973 the U.S. Federal Aviation Administration (FAA) instituted systematic searches of passengers and their bags. Many other countries, mostly in Europe, made similar changes to airport procedures. At a 1978 Group of Seven (G7) summit meeting, the United States, West Germany, France, Italy, Japan, Canada, and Great Britain signed a pledge to impose sanctions on countries that give sanctuary to hijackers.

However, hijackings continued throughout the political turbulence of the 1970s. On June 27, 1976, Palestinian terrorists hijacked an Air France jetliner bound from Tel Aviv to Paris and directed it instead to Entebbe, Uganda. Israeli forces carried out a famous raid to rescue the mostly Israeli hostages, killing the hijackers.

Croatian nationalists armed only with Silly Putty skyjacked an aircraft in September 1976. The hijackers displayed what they said were "five gelignite bombs" and convinced all aboard TWA Flight 355 from New York to follow their instructions. The hijackers said they had left a bomb and political tracts inside a locker in New York's Grand Central Station, and demanded U.S. newspapers publish their call for Croatian independence. Police experts opened the locker and found an actual bomb. The device was taken to a police range to be disarmed, but it exploded unexpectedly, killing a New York police officer.

In 1977, hijackers calling for the release of prisoners in West Germany commandeered a Lufthansa airliner as it left the Spanish island of Majorca for Frankfurt. The hijackers instead made stops in Rome, Cyprus, Bahrain, Dubai, and Aden, South Yemen, before landing in Mogadishu, Somalia. During the ordeal, the hijackers killed the plane's pilot and dumped his body onto the Mogadishu airport runway. The hijack attempt ended when German commandos stormed the plane, killing three hijackers and wounding the fourth.

A revisiting of the "Cuban shuttle" happened in 1980, when, according to press reports, eight U.S. domestic flights were hijacked and re-routed to Havana, Cuba. A Cuban refugee wanting to return home commandeered each plane.

In August 1980, 168 passengers took over a Braniff plane in Peru. The hijackers demanded to fly to Miami. Reportedly, after they gave up, the U.S. government agreed to expedite their immigration applications.

In 1981, three Pakistani hijackers, said to be backed by Soviet Afghanistan, forced a Pakistan International Airlines jet to fly to Kabul, where one passenger was killed. After the plane flew on to Damascus, the Pakistani Government agreed to free over 50 political prisoners, and the hostages were released.

A tragic 16-day hijacking ordeal began on June 14, 1985, when two Lebanese Shiite Muslim terrorists, later tied to the Hezbollah organization, hijacked TWA Flight 847 bound for Rome from Athens. The hijackers ordered the pilot to fly first to Algiers, but the planes low fuel supply led him to land in Beirut, where the hijackers demanded the release of hundreds of prisoners held in Israel. One of the gunmen killed Petty Officer Robert Dean Stethem at close range and dumped his body onto the Beirut tarmac. The plane flew back and forth between Algiers and Beirut for several days, until it was finally grounded in Beirut. The hijackers and their accomplices kept many of the passengers and crew hostage until June 30, when Israel agreed to release some of the prisoners.

In November 1985, Palestinians said to be linked to Abu Nidal (Sabri al Banna) captured an EgyptAir plane and forced it fly to Malta. Egyptian commandos stormed the plane, and 59 people were killed in the shootout.

While aerial hijackings are the best known, the capture of a cruise ship in 1985 is also an important moment in hijacking history. On October 7, four Palestine Liberation Front terrorists seized the Italian cruise liner *Achille Lauro* when it was traveling off of Port Said, Egypt. The hijackers held over 400 people aboard hostage for two days, and shot and killed a wheelchair-bound passenger.

Hijackings continued to occur around the world during the late 1980s and throughout the 1990s, but at a lower frequency. Many terrorist groups turned toward the more deadly tactic of destroying planes in flight, as in the tragic 1988 bombing of an American airliner over Lockerbie, Scotland.

On April 5, 1988, Shiite Muslim terrorists hijacked a Kuwait Airways plane flying from Bangkok to Mashhad, Iran. The hijackers directed the flight to Cyprus and then Algiers, demanding that Kuwait free imprisoned comrades. The terrorists killed two passengers, and then released the remaining passengers after 16 days.

A particularly harrowing hijacking took place in Karachi, Pakistan on September 5, 1986, after hijackers linked to the Abu Nidal Organization took over Pan Am Flight 73. The plane's crew were alerted, and they slipped out through an emergency exit in the cockpit. The gunmen, dressed as security personnel, held the plane on the tarmac for 16 hours, demanding a new crew to fly to Cyprus. When the plane's auxiliary power stopped working and the lights went dim, the hijackers began firing at the passengers. Pakistani security forces soon burst aboard the plane and rescued the hostages, but 22 people died in the incident.

On March 27, 1991, four Pakistani hijackers captured a Singapore Air flight en route from Malaysia to Singapore. The hijackers demanded the release of Asif Ali Zardani, the former minister Benazir Bhutto's husband. After nine hours, Singapore security forces rushed onto the plane and shot the hijackers to death. No passengers or crew

were killed in the incident. A former adviser to Bhutto's government was later arrested and accused of masterminding the hijacking.

On Christmas Eve 1994, terrorists from the Algerian group Armed Islamic Group (GIA) captured an Air France plane at the Algiers airport and flew it to Marseilles. The GIA terrorists killed three passengers before French security forces stormed the jetliner. The commandos burst into the cockpit and killed the hijackers.

Hijackers also took over a plane on Christmas Eve 1999. Terrorists from Kashmir hijacked an Indian Airlines jet en route from Kathmandu to New Delhi and forced it to fly to Kandahar. The terrorists demanded the release of their comrades and held the passengers hostage in a weeklong standoff. They released the hostage after India agreed to release the jailed fighters.

On September 11, 2001, the history of air hijacking took an unprecedented and violent turn. Terrorists, said to be working as part of the al Qaeda network, hijacked four U.S. airplanes, flying two of them into the World Trade Center towers in New York City and one into the Pentagon near Washington, D.C. The fourth plane crashed in Pennsylvania after passengers fought back and tried to take control of the aircraft. Thousands were killed aboard the airplanes, in the buildings, and on the ground. A number of new policies were put into place in response to the 9/11 hijackings, including allowing for armed air marshals onboard some flights, requirements that planes be upgraded with bulletproof cockpit doors, and increased self-defense training for flight attendants. In late 2001, when Richard Reid attempted to blow up a plane with a bomb in his shoe, he was stopped by fellow passengers, as was Umar Farouk Abdulmutallab, the so-called underwear bomber who attempted to blow up a plane on Christmas Day 2009. This suggests a new era of reduced tolerance for hijacking, not merely among airlines but among passengers as well.

Erica Pearson

Further Readings

Elias, Bartholomew. *Airport and Aviation Security: U.S. Policy and Strategy in the Age of Global Terrorism.* Boca Raton, FL: Auerbach Publications/Taylor & Francis, 2010.

Jaber, Hala. *Hezbollah.* New York: Columbia University Press, 1997.

Kushner, Harvey W. *Terrorism in America: A Structured Approach to Understanding the Terrorist Threat.* Springfield, IL: Charles C Thomas, 1998.

Oliverio, Annamarie. *The State of Terror.* SUNY Series in Deviance and Social Control. Albany: State University of New York Press, 1998.

Raab, David. *Terror in Black September: The First Eyewitness Account of the Infamous 1970 Hijacking.* New York: Palgrave Macmillan, 2007.

Seale, Patrick. *Abu Nidal: A Gun for Hire.* London: Hutchinson, 1992.

Snyder, Rodney A. *Negotiating with Terrorists: TWA Flight 847.* Pew Case Studies in International Affairs. Pittsburgh, PA: Pew Charitable Trusts, 1994.

Wallis, Rodney. *How Safe Are Our Skies? Assessing the Airlines' Response to Terrorism.* Westport, CT: Praeger, 2003.

HILL, PAUL JENNINGS (1954–2003)

On September 3, 2003, Paul Jennings Hill, a former Presbyterian minister, became the first anti-abortion terrorist to be executed for the murder of an abortion provider. Hill was also the first person to be tried under the federal Freedom of Access to Clinic Entrances Act, which was passed by Congress after the first murder of an abortion provider occurred in March 1993, when Dr. David Gunn was killed by Michael Griffin.

Hill first embraced the anti-abortion movement after graduating from the Reformed Theological Seminary in Jackson, Mississippi, in 1983. At the time, Hill contemplated assassinating a Supreme Court justice to hasten an appointment that might lead to the overthrow of *Roe v. Wade,* but because he was a minister, he decided against murder. In 1990, however, Hill voluntarily turned in his ministerial credentials, leaving him free, in his mind, to follow Griffin's lead.

Although Griffin and Hill never met, five days after Griffin shot Dr. Gunn outside the Pensacola Women's Medical Services clinic in Florida, Hill appeared on the *Donahue* television show to justify the murder of Dr. Gunn, who Hill compared to a Nazi concentration camp doctor. Within months of Dr. Gunn's murder, Hill formed Defensive Action, a small anti-abortion group that advocated violence to end abortion. He also drafted a "Defensive Action Statement," which was signed by 29 other anti-abortion activists.

Hill was quickly becoming one of the most outspoken members of the movement. His rhetoric eventually led to his excommunication from a Presbyterian church in Valparaiso, Florida, where he lived with his wife and three children. Undaunted, in December 1993 Hill appeared on *Nightline* to justify Rachelle Shannon's attempted murder of Dr. George Tiller, an abortion provider in Wichita, Kansas. Hill protested each week outside the Ladies Center in Pensacola, Florida, where 69-year-old Dr. John Bayard Britton, Dr. Gunn's successor, provided abortion services. On July 29, 1994, Paul Hill arrived at the Ladies Center just before 7:00 A.M. to join the usual Friday protests. A half-hour later, as Dr. Britton and his bodyguard, James Barrett, drove into the parking lot outside the clinic, Hill opened fire with a shotgun, killing both Britton and Barrett; Barrett's wife, June, was also struck, but she survived.

Hill claims he had decided to kill Dr. Britton just one week earlier; however, an FBI informer, Jerry Reiter, who once worked as a volunteer with the anti-abortion group Operation Rescue, claimed that Hill prophesied, months earlier, an "IRA-type reign of terror" following Griffin's murder trial.

In December 1994 Hill received two life sentences for violating federal clinic-protection laws, and he was convicted of a Florida state murder charge, for which he was sentenced to death. Unlike Griffin, who denounced anti-abortion violence after two years in jail, Hill remained unrepentant. In March 1997, following a Florida Supreme Court decision that affirmed Hill's death sentence, Hill officially waived his right to participate in the appeals process. In an interview given from the Florida State Penitentiary, Hill stated that he was convinced the he could save more babies by becoming a martyr for the anti-abortion movement than by trying to save his own life.

Hill was executed by lethal injection on September 3, 2003. The day before his execution, he held a press conference in which he told reporters that he had no remorse for committing murder, hoped that others would do as he did, and expected "a great reward in heaven" for his crime.

Laura Lambert

See also Anti-Abortion Terrorism; Griffin, Michael Frederick

Further Readings

Baird-Windle, Patricia, and Eleanor J. Bader. *Targets of Hatred: Anti-abortion Terrorism.* New York: Palgrave, 2001.

Gorney, Cynthia. *Articles of Faith: A Frontline History of the Abortion Wars.* New York: Simon & Schuster, 1998.

Kennedy, John. "Killer Hill: I Will Be Martyr." *Orlando Sentinel,* September 3, 2003, p. A1.

Kurst-Swanger, Karl. *Worship and Sin: An Exploration of Religion-related Crime in the United States.* New York: Peter Lang, 2008.

Pinkham, Paul, and Rachel Davis. "Abortion Doctor's Killer Executed by Injection." *Florida Times Union,* September 4, 2003, p. A1.

Roig-Franzia, Manuel, and Catharine Skipp. "'I Expect a Great Reward': Abortion Provider's Killer Is Unrepentant on Eve of Execution." *The Washington Post,* September 3, 2003, p. A1.

Stern, Jessica. *Terror in the Name of God: Why Religious Militants Kill.* New York: Ecco, 2008.

HIZB-UL-MUJAHIDEEN

Hizb-ul-Mujahideen is one of the largest militant Muslim groups operating in the disputed territories of Jammu and Kashmir—both of which are claimed by India and Pakistan. Hizb-ul-Mujahideen supports the integration of Jammu and Kashmir into Pakistan, a Muslim country where the group is headquartered. Hizb-ul-Mujahideen is unusual among Muslim groups in that many of its members are native Kashmiris, rather than foreign militants. Hizb-ul-Mujahideen has been linked to the vicious massacres of non-Muslims in Jammu and Kashmir in 1998 and 2000. Although the group has continued to embrace violence, it has more recently reached brief cease-fires with India.

Hizb-ul-Mujahideen was founded in the late 1980s as a militant wing of Pakistan's Jamaat-e-Islami, an Islamic political party. The group was reportedly backed by Pakistan's intelligence agency as a counterforce to the secular, pro-independence Jammu and Kashmir Liberation Front. Hizb-ul-Mujahideen members received training in terrorist camps in Afghanistan.

For years, Hizb-ul-Mujahideen operated as a sort of a local intelligence wing, assisting other militant Muslim groups whose members were largely foreign. The group attacked both Indian forces and pro-independence Kashmiri groups, especially the Jammu and Kashmir Liberation Front. Eventually Hizb-ul-Mujahideen became linked with Lashkar-e-Taiba, a radical Muslim group known for extremism and violence. Hizb-ul-Mujahideen forces took part in widespread murders of non-Muslims in Jammu and Kashmir in hopes of creating a Muslim-only state.

Two joint operations between Hizb-ul-Mujahideen and Lashkar-e-Taiba attracted especial condemnation. Twenty-three Hindus, including several women and small children, were massacred in the village of Wandhama on January 23, 1998. Two years later, during a visit of the president of the United States to South Asia, 35 Sikh men were slaughtered in Chattisinghpora.

Such violence alienated many supporters of Hizb-ul-Mujahideen. The Wandhama massacre led Jamaat-e-Islami to publicly renounce terrorism in late 1998 and apparently sever ties with the group. The leader of the Hizb-ul-Mujahideen faction involved in the massacre, Hamid Bhatt, also known as Hamid Gada or Bambar Khan, was forced out of a leadership position because he was considered to be too closely allied with the more radical foreign Muslims. On March 13, 2000, he was killed by security forces operating on information provided by an unpaid Kashmiri Muslim informant.

In late June 2000, Syed Salahuddin, the leader of Hizb-ul-Mujahideen, announced a cease-fire and suggested that the group negotiate with India. As a result, he was expelled from the leadership of a Pakistan-based umbrella organization of Muslim militant groups. The cease-fire lasted only a few weeks, however, because Salahuddin insisted that Pakistan be included in any negotiations, a condition

India found unacceptable. Nonetheless, brief negotiations did take place. Since then, India and Hizb-ul-Mujahideen have alternated between attacking each other—including a 2004 bomb attack on a bus carrying Indian security forces and their families that killed 33 people—and making proposals for further cease-fires and negotiations.

Mary Sisson

See also Lashkar-e-Taiba

Further Readings

Babington, Charles, and Pamela Constable. "Kashmir Killings Mar Clinton Visit to India; President Rebuffed on Nuclear Issue." *The Washington Post,* March 22, 2000, p. A1.

Baldauf, Scott. "Is al Qaeda Setting Up Shop in Kashmir? A Phone Call after the Mumbai Attack Trumpeted a New al Qaeda Franchise; But Police, Other Militants Are Dubious." *Christian Science Monitor,* July 18, 2006, p. 6.

Bearak, Barry. "A Kashmiri Mystery." *The New York Times Magazine,* December 31, 2001, p. 26.

Bose, Sumantra. *The Challenge in Kashmir: Democracy, Self-Determination and a Just Peace.* New Delhi: Sage, 1997.

Chopra, Anuj. "India Weighs Troop Reduction in Quieter Kashmir." *Christian Science Monitor,* April 2, 2007, p. 4.

Copeland, Jeremy. "Singh Faces First Crisis as Kashmir Bomb Kills 33." *The Independent,* May 24, 2004, p. 24.

Jamal, Arif. *Shadow War: The Untold Story of Jihad in Kashmir.* Hoboken, NJ: Melville, 2010.

Nandi, Suresh, and Harinder Baweja. "Jammu and Kashmir: A Sinister Strike." *India Today,* February 9, 1998, p. 54.

Newberg, Paula R. *Double Betrayal: Repression and Insurgency in Kashmir.* Washington, DC: Carnegie Endowment for International Peace, 1995.

Schofield, Victoria. *Kashmir in Conflict: India, Pakistan, and the Unending War.* New York: I.B. Tauris, 2010.

HOMEGROWN JIHADI MOVEMENT

Muslims in the United States and western Europe who support al Qaeda and the militant ideology it advances have become known collectively as "homegrown jihadis." Small in number and characterized by a disconnected, ad hoc structure, homegrown jihadis share an underlying commitment to a violent, extremist interpretation of Islam. The movement has evolved into a major security concern for governments and publics around the world.

The homegrown jihadi movement is part of the global movement that supports al Qaeda. However, unlike the many Middle Eastern al Qaeda recruits who venture to active war zones like Iraq and Afghanistan, homegrown jihadis in the West tend to remain in their countries of origin. They most likely have no direct connection to actual members of terrorist groups and, in many cases, have only a cursory, distorted understanding of Islam's teachings and primary texts.

Homegrown jihadis almost uniformly believe that Western governments are waging a war on Islam and that the majority of Western Muslims have become traitors to their own religion. They see themselves as an elite vanguard, defending their religion when others in their religion and their countries will not. For homegrown jihadis, debate, dialogue, and discussion, have proven ineffectual. The only remaining answer is that of violence.

Who Are the Homegrown Jihadis?

Homegrown jihadis are generally Internet-based enthusiasts and amateur operatives, and they are thus viewed as being significantly less professional than foreign jihadi operatives, who are often formally trained and battle hardened. By contrast, however, homegrown jihadis in the West tend to be loners or part of small groups of like-minded individuals.

Because homegrown jihadis emerge from domestic contexts, they have a familiarity with language, customs, and locations that makes them hard for law enforcement to spot, at least compared to foreign operatives. Generally, homegrown jihadis receive little to no formal training from external sources. In the rare cases where they do successfully travel to a foreign training location before returning back to their country of residence, training is often rushed and incomplete.

While most homegrown jihadis limit their activities to passive support for al Qaeda, including

Internet-based dialog with like-minded individuals, consumption of jihadi propaganda, and occasionally conducting activism, some do go operational. In those cases where homegrown jihadis have made it to an operational stage, they have historically done so employing low-tech means, and they have generally failed to conduct attacks that are comparable in terms of lethality or media coverage with those perpetrated by more formal organizations.

Critiques of the Term

The use of the word *homegrown* is meant to focus attention on the indigenous nature of this kind of extremist ideology. The term highlights the fact that, as opposed to terrorists who infiltrate Western countries from non-Western countries, homegrown jihadis radicalize, mobilize, and attack from within. However, the phrase "homegrown jihadi movement" is not uniformly accepted as an accurate or useful descriptor. Critics of the phrase argue that few terrorist attacks dubbed as "homegrown" ever emerge entirely from within national borders. For example, individuals may have used the Internet to access ideological content developed by foreign nationals in order to become radicalized. They may receive funding, advice, or orders from foreign sources affiliated or inspired by groups like al Qaeda.

Others take issue with the use of the label *jihadi*. For most Muslims, the religious concept of jihad is positive, referring to the peaceful struggle for religious purity. Critics suggest that using it when referring to al Qaeda inadvertently accords the terrorist group religious legitimacy.

European Jihadi

Western governments first realized the negative consequences associated with the homegrown jihadi movement in the United Kingdom. Beginning in the early 1990s, an influx of notable extremist Middle Eastern jihadi preachers sought asylum in London and the surrounding area in order to avoid prosecution on a variety of terrorism-related charges. Over the course of the decade, these charismatic hard-liners used the freedom they found in the United Kingdom to peddle their militant reading of Islam to the large, receptive audience of marginalized Muslim immigrants.

In the aftermath of the September 11, 2001, attacks on the United States, the British government began cracking down on these extremist preachers and their young, fanatical adherents. However, the jihadi movement was already firmly entrenched by that time, and a string of homegrown jihadi terrorist plots began appearing soon thereafter, most of which were plotted by British nationals taking aim at their own country.

Not all of the homegrown terror plots in Britain have been stopped, however. On July 7, 2005, a homegrown British terrorist cell conducted a coordinated bombing attack against the British public transit system. They killed 52 people and injured another 700. Homegrown jihadi plots and attacks have also appeared across most of Europe, especially in France, Germany, and Spain.

The American Homegrown Jihadi Movement

By around 2006, as an increasing number of American nationals were being arrested for plotting terrorist attacks against the United States, discussions of an American jihadi problem began appearing more regularly in public media. As plots against targets such as the Sears Tower, New York City train tunnels, Fort Dix Army base in New Jersey, American shopping malls, JFK Airport, and a New York City subway station came to light, it became clear that the United States had its own homegrown jihadi movement.

In the United States, there have been several kinds of homegrown jihadis. The first type includes those from non-Muslim backgrounds who convert to Islam. These individuals tend to be males in their late teens and early twenties who are seeking a sense of belonging and identity. They quickly embrace the hard-line, militant reading of Islam advanced by groups like al Qaeda.

While some of these homegrown jihadi converts sought to conduct terrorist attacks in the United States, others have attempted or managed to go overseas in order to join the global jihadi movement. For example, Zachary Chesser, a young man from Northern Virginia, was indicted in July 2010 on material support for terrorism charges for his attempt to aid al Shabab, a Somali terrorist group believed to be aligned with al Qaeda. Another

American, David C. Headley, who had received training from Lashkar-e-Taiba, a terrorist group associated with al Qaeda, was charged in December 2009 for his alleged involvement in a terrorism plot against a Danish newspaper. He has also been accused of conducting multiple scouting trips around Mumbai, India, in preparation for the November 2008 terrorist attacks there. Daniel Maldonado, a U.S. citizen of Puerto Rican background, was convicted of training with a foreign terrorist organization and sentenced to 10 years in prison. Maldonado had admitted to traveling to Somalia in order to join the Islamic Courts Union, an Islamist group.

The second most common type of American homegrown jihadis are U.S. nationals, many of whom are naturalized citizens, who immigrated into the country as small children or whose parents were immigrants from Islamic countries. Many of the individuals who fall into this category feel the need to find a more authentic connection to their religion and cultural heritage. Frustrated with their parents, their friends, their teachers, and their lives, these individuals are often caught between two worlds. The ideology offered by the homegrown jihadi movement offers these individuals easy answers for the questions that plague them.

There are numerous examples of homegrown jihadis who fall into this category. Samir Khan, the militant jihadi blogger turned al Qaeda propagandist, for example, was born in Saudi Arabia before his parents moved to the United States. Out of his parent's home in Charlotte, North Carolina, he blogged and ran a pro–al Qaeda magazine before being recruited into al Qaeda's franchise operation in Yemen.

Another homegrown jihadi, Nidal M. Hasan, was a U.S. Army psychiatrist who killed 13 people on the Fort Hood military base in November 2009. Hasan was born in Virginia to parents that had emigrated into the United States from Jordan. Najibullah Zazi, an Afghan-born Colorado resident, was charged in September 2009 with planning a bombing attack in the United States. Faisal Shahzad, an American who confessed to attempting to detonate a vehicle bomb in Times Square in May 2010, was a naturalized U.S. citizen who had been born in Pakistan before moving to the United States with his family.

The Homegrown Jihadi Movement's Future

The senior leadership of al Qaeda has historically been unclear about how to handle the homegrown jihadi movement, at least until 2010. Prodding Western supporters to donate money and time to the global jihadi movement, al Qaeda sought to maintain command and control over its actual operatives. Multiple statements from the top leaders of al Qaeda, including the highest-ranking American member as well as Osama bin Laden, have instructed their Western-based supporters to remain where they are and take up arms against targets in their own countries. For today's al Qaeda, the homegrown jihadi movement represents an important weapon in their global terrorist arsenal.

Jarret Brachman

See also al Qaeda; al Shabab; bin Laden, Osama; Jihad; Lashkar-e-Taiba; London Underground Bombings; Madrid Bombings; Training of Terrorists

Further Readings

Jenkins, Brian Michael. "No Path to Glory: Deterring Homegrown Terrorism." Testimony presented before the House Homeland Security Committee, Subcommittee on Intelligence, Information Sharing and Terrorism Risk Assessment on May 26, 2010. RAND Corporation Report CT-348 (May 2010). Santa Monica, CA: RAND Corporation. http://www.rand.org/pubs/testimonies/2010/RAND_CT348.pdf.

Perkins, Samuel. *Homegrown Terror and American Jihadists: Assessing the Threat.* Hauppauge, NY: Nova Publishers, 2011.

Precht, Tomas. "Home Grown Terrorism and Islamist Radicalisation in Europe: From Conversion to Terrorism." Danish Ministry of Justice (December 2007). http://www.justitsministeriet.dk/fileadmin/downloads/Forskning_og_dokumentation/Home_grown_terrorism_and_Islamist_radicalisation_in_Europe_-_an_assessment_of_influencing_factors__2_.pdf.

Silber, Mitchell D., and Arvin Bhatt. "Radicalization in the West: The Homegrown Threat." New York: New York City Police Department, 2007. http://www.nyc.gov/html/nypd/downloads/pdf/public_information/NYPD_Report-Radicalization_in_the_West.pdf.

U.S. Senate Committee on Homeland Security and Governmental Affairs. *Violent Islamist Extremism, the Internet, and the Homegrown Terrorist Threat.*

Washington, DC: U.S. Senate, May 2008. http://hsgac
.senate.gov/public/_files/IslamistReport.pdf.

Wiktorowicz, Quintan. *Radical Islam Rising*. Lanham,
MD: Rowman & Littlefield, 2005.

HOMELAND SECURITY

Homeland security is a term broadly synonymous with *domestic security* and originally intended to reflect government plans to thwart terrorist attacks against the United States from within the nation's borders, such as occurred on September 11, 2001. However, particularly since Hurricane Katrina in 2005, the term has become synonymous for preparation and response to disasters, both man-made and natural.

To differentiate terms, one must be careful not to confuse homeland security with *national security* and *national defense*, which refer to military operations that begin at U.S. borders and extend outward, such as missile defense against an enemy force or air, sea, and ground operations against enemies of the U.S. government on any front. Additional care must be taken not to immediately attribute everything relating to homeland security to the U.S. Department of Homeland Security (DHS), particularly since the states have initiatives of their own that operate independently of DHS. The term may apply to private homeland security initiatives as well, such as those by the American Red Cross and the Salvation Army.

Elements of Homeland Security

Homeland security can be organized into three categories: preparedness, incident management, and recovery. Preparedness against terrorist attacks has seemingly occupied all the attention and funds of the U.S. Congress since the 9/11 attacks. In preparation for another catastrophe, Tom Ridge spent over a billion dollars on fire apparatus, radiological protection gear, and other anticipated post-incident equipment during his tenure as secretary of homeland security (2003–2005). Though this was not necessarily money ill spent, the 9/11 Commission found that intelligence failures were responsible for the successes of the terrorist attacks, not a lack of preparedness. For example, no committee report

suggested that additional fire apparatus in New York City, Pennsylvania, or Washington would have swayed the outcome of the 9/11 attacks or mitigated the loss of life. And yet little federal funding went to intelligence operations immediately following the 2001 attacks; instead, fire departments across the United States reaped the monetary benefits of a nation mourning the loss of 341 firefighters in the collapse of the World Trade Center towers. Therefore, in the years following 9/11, the United States was better prepared to react to a cataclysmic attack but was no better prepared to proactively thwart terrorism than it had been beforehand.

However, in 2004 the federal National Counterterrorism Center (NCTC) was formed as a dedicated (i.e., task-specific), intelligence agency reporting to the director of national intelligence (DNI) and the president of the United States. The NCTC replaced its earlier iteration, the Terrorist Threat Integration Center (TTIC), created soon after 9/11. Although now a function of the DNI, it was originated in DHS but experienced difficulty finding an institutional home, moving briefly to the Federal Bureau of Investigation and the Central Intelligence Agency.

Because it is the most speculative, preparedness is the most controversial of the three categories of homeland security. Emergency managers and homeland security professionals must anticipate the next catastrophic event and move funds in the direction of proactive training and equipment acquisition. Law enforcement intelligence must be prepared to anticipate and interdict a terrorist plot with modern information collection and analysis operations. However, at present, law enforcement intelligence operations are usually poorly prepared to predict appropriate responses to natural disasters such as tornados, earthquakes, and hurricanes that occur with far greater frequency than terrorist attacks. Other facets of public safety frequently do not participate in intelligence sharing as either information providers or intelligence consumers. In the United States, public safety agencies often have no local, interagency, and coordinated mutual aid plans. Neither do they engage in collaborative planning, training, or joint operations. And, unfortunately, interagency jealousies usually prevent collaborative efforts in public safety asset and logistical management even in the worst of times.

Therefore, even a decade after the 9/11 attacks, with scarce exception, homeland security preparedness and planning remain commonly facilitated at local levels by individual agencies.

Incident management is largely a matter of public-safety asset management. The breadth of potential incidents provides homeland security managers with a spectrum of possibilities by which assets can be distributed. For example, emergency response to a mere fire is well practiced and usually well anticipated. However, if a city block is on fire, or if there is radiological contamination within a fire, or if a fire scene is an aircraft crash site, or if the scene is caused by a bombing or arson, asset management must be adjusted to accommodate variables in each scenario. Managing assets to minimize the risk while maximizing the productivity of the activity (however this might be assessed, in lives or property saved, etc.) is the job of homeland security professionals. Training and proactive crisis management preparations are key to the success of an atypical public safety response. In addition, the nature and scope of an incident will affect the number of agencies responding and could include the spectrum of public safety, from local fire and police to state and federal agencies, including the National Guard in more serious or widespread events. Doubtless, the better prepared agencies are to affect mutual aid in a common cause, the better the outcome. Unfortunately, such preparations are not commonplace.

Finally, recovery is best facilitated chronologically at the onset of incident management. Decisions made while managing an incident must be tempered with consideration toward managing recovery through asset protection. Saving lives and property can lead to difficult decisions in emergency management, particularly in managing disasters. For example, during a hurricane the decision must be made regarding when evacuation and rescue efforts will be abandoned before a hurricane strikes, and also at what point rescue efforts will resume. Amid these decisions, the number of first responders assigned to rescue tasks versus property protection duties must be determined by the emergency manager. It can be postulated that sandbagging levees to protect property against storm surge would have a lower priority than rescuing lives; therefore, more first responders would likely be assigned to rescue efforts than to sandbagging efforts. With limited assets, a homeland security manager should anticipate a low number of lives lost but a high number of destroyed homes. Therefore, recovery will be costly in terms of property lost and destroyed.

Recovery may be seen as *consequence management,* meaning preparing for the resultant effect of first responders' deployment. The more detailed that preparations are made before an incident, the more productive recovery efforts will be. Preparation is thus a category that permeates all facets of homeland security. It is not unusual for emergency managers to begin preparations for post-event training, asset distribution and management, or changes in personnel assignments while midstream in managing a catastrophe. In addition, emergency managers often prepare (or have subordinates prepare) an After Action Report (AAR) to summarize the official acts of the public safety agencies in response to a catastrophe, so that results may be scrutinized at a later date. The AAR is most efficient when written contemporaneous to the event and with an understanding that improvements can be made in the efficiency of first responders. Although the practice is not yet widespread, public safety agencies are beginning to adopt the AAR, which was originated by the military to summarize combat operations.

Homeland Security at the Federal Government Level

The U.S. Department of Homeland Security was established on January 24, 2003, approximately one year after its announced formation by George W. Bush in his annual State of the Union Address and subsequent to the signing of the Homeland Security Act of 2002. The secretary of homeland security is a cabinet-level position whose appointment is approved by the U.S. Senate. According to DHS, the secretary "has the authority to perform all functions vested in the Department, which include overseeing activities with other federal, state, local, and private entities as part of a collaborative effort to strengthen the borders, providing for intelligence analysis and infrastructure protection, improving the use of science and technology to counter weapons of mass destruction, and creating a comprehensive response and recovery system."

The DHS Preparedness Directorate (originally the Emergency Preparedness and Response Directorate), houses the Federal Emergency Management Agency (FEMA), which directs the emergency functions of a variety of other agencies, including the Federal Insurance Administration, the National Fire Prevention and Control Administration, and the Federal Preparedness Agency of the General Services Administration. From 1979 until 2005, the FEMA directorship was a cabinet-level position reporting to the president, but the FEMA director now reports to the DHS secretary.

According to DHS, the Homeland Security Act of 2002 established the Information Analysis and Infrastructure Protection (IAIP) Directorate. However, under DHS secretary Tom Ridge and IAIP undersecretary Frank Libutti, no information collection or analysis was conducted by DHS; instead, the agency's efforts (and funding) were focused on identifying critical assets and infrastructure protection. It was under this banner that DHS funded the widespread purchase of fire equipment for agencies large and small, while no

funds were made available to the states for facilitating intelligence operations. DHS priorities established by Secretary Ridge explain the movement of the Terrorist Threat Integration Center to the FBI and CIA before becoming the National Counterterrorism Center under the Office of the Director of National Intelligence.

In addition to the directorates of DHS (National Protection and Programs, Science and Technology, Directorate for Management), other sections of DHS include the Office of Policy, the Office of Health Affairs, the Office of Intelligence and Analysis (since 2007), and the Office of Operations, Coordination, and Planning. In addition, a number of federal agencies were subsumed into DHS so that operations might be coordinated at the executive level. These agencies include The Federal Law Enforcement Training Center, the Domestic Nuclear Protection Office, the Transportation Security Administration, United States Customs and Border Protection. United States Citizenship and Immigration Services, United States Immigration and Customs Enforcement, the United States Coast Guard, FEMA, and the United States Secret Service.

FEMA's Chris Geldart, director, Office of National Capital Region Coordination (far right), briefs the Department of Homeland Security (DHS) Deputy Secretary Paul Schneider (center) and the DHS secretary-designate's counselor, Rand Beers (left), on the security and safety measures in place for response as needed during the January 2009 presidential inauguration activities in Washington, D.C. (Photo by Barry Bahler/FEMA)

Homeland Security at the State Government Level

All states have some official connection to homeland security; however, the scope of the executive's authority varies widely and is often included among other duties. For example, most who are in charge of homeland security matters are merely policy advisors to the governor. Other executives who may have authority include an adjutant general or director of public safety. Meanwhile, other states seat homeland security matters with the lieutenant governor. Since 2002, when the first state directors of homeland security were named by sitting governors, there has been a dilution of homeland security responsibilities among bureaucrats, and one might have to look hard to determine who exactly is in charge of state homeland security affairs. In North Carolina, for example, the person responsible for homeland security matters is the secretary of the Department of Crime Control and Public Safety. In South Carolina, however, homeland security responsibilities are held by the chief of the Law Enforcement Division, while in Washington State the responsibility goes to the State Military Department. Similarly, in West Virginia the secretary of the Department of Military Affairs and Public Safety is the responsible party. Whereas these disparate titles are reflective of the varied roles of homeland security executives, they are also reflective of the perception of homeland security as it varies from state to state.

Cooperation and coordination among state homeland security executives is no more elevated than that of agencies on the front line. Homeland security directors meet annually in Washington, D.C., but meetings among the directors away from this event are unusual, even among states with contiguous borders. All those involved in homeland security as an industry must cooperate and coordinate at the local, state, and federal levels if the safety of America is to be assured.

Kenneth J. Ryan

See also Bureau of Alcohol, Tobacco, Firearms and Explosives; Central Intelligence Agency; Counterterrorism; Department of Justice, U.S.; Federal Bureau of Investigation; Force Protection Conditions; Law and Terrorism; National Security Agency; National Security Council

Further Readings

Bullock, Jane, George Haddow, Damon P. Coppola, and Sarp Yeletaysi. *Introduction to Homeland Security, Third Edition: Principles of All-Hazards Response.* Burlington, MA: Butterworth-Heinemann, 2009.

Howard, Russell, James Forest, and Joanne C. Moore. *Homeland Security and Terrorism: Readings and Interpretations.* New York: McGraw-Hill, 2006.

Hulnick, Arthur S. *Keeping Us Safe: Secret Intelligence and Homeland Security.* Westport, CT: Praeger, 2004.

Jackson, Brian. *The Challenge of Domestic Intelligence in a Free Society.* Santa Monica, CA: RAND Corporation, 2009.

National Commission on Terrorist Attacks Upon the United States. *The 9/11 Commission Report: Final Report of the National Commission on Terrorist Attacks Upon the United States.* New York: W.W. Norton, 2004. http://www.9-11commission.gov.

Riegle, Robert. Testimony of Director Robert Riegle, State and Local Program Office, Office of Intelligence and Analysis, before the Committee on Homeland Security, Subcommittee on Intelligence, Information Sharing, and Terrorism Risk Assessment. "The Future of Fusion Centers: Potential Promise and Dangers," 111th Congress, April 1, 2009. http://www.dhs.gov/ynews/testimony/testimony_1238597287040.shtm.

White, Jonathan R. *Terrorism and Homeland Security.* Belmont, CA: Wadsworth, 2009.

HOORIE, ALI SAED BIN ALI EL (1965–)

Ali Saed Bin Ali el Hoorie allegedly played a key role in preparing and carrying out the 1996 tanker truck bombing of the Khobar Towers military barracks in Dhahran, Saudi Arabia. The explosion, attributed to the Saudi Hezbollah group, killed 19 U.S. military personnel and wounded approximately 500. The FBI, citing his involvement in the Khobar attack, placed Hoorie on its list of most wanted terrorists.

According to the 2001 U.S. indictment, Hoorie, born in El Dibabiya, Saudi Arabia, was a member of Saudi Hezbollah (also called Hezbollah Al Hijaz) and worked as a major recruiter for the group. Saudi Hezbollah is largely made up of young men of Shiite Muslim faith who are loyal to Iran, not the Saudi government. The group is outlawed in Saudi Arabia, and its operatives often work and recruit in Lebanon, Syria, and Iran.

Hoorie worked as a liaison for Saudi Hezbollah with the Iranian embassy in Damascus, Syria. Saudi Hezbollah operatives frequently gathered at the Sayyeda Zeinab shrine in Damascus, an important religious site for Shiite Muslims. The site was also a prime recruiting area for Saudi Hezbollah, with operatives approaching men who were on religious pilgrimages.

About three years before the Khobar attack, Ahmad Ibrahim al Mughassil, the head of Saudi Hezbollah's military operations and a close associate of Hoorie, instructed him and two other group members to begin surveillance of Americans in Saudi Arabia. Mughassil eventually selected the Khobar Towers as a bombing target. The service members living in the towers were assigned to the King Abdul Aziz Airbase in Saudi Arabia, and they patrolled over the no-fly zone in southern Iraq that was declared after the Persian Gulf War. The towers housed approximately 2,000 U.S. military personnel.

During the first half of 1996, Hoorie worked to procure and stockpile explosives (many smuggled from Beirut) for the attack. He buried 50-kilogram bags and paint cans filled with explosives at various sites near the town of Qatif, not far from the Khobar Towers. Early in June 1996, Hoorie worked with Mughassil and others at a farm near Qatif to build the truck bomb. Using stolen ID, a conspirator had purchased a tanker truck from a Saudi car dealership. The men filled the truck with explosives and wired a timing device.

According to the indictment, on the evening of June 25, Hoorie rode to the Khobar Towers as passenger in the tanker truck, with Mughassil driving. They parked the truck, loaded with over 5,000 pounds of explosives, near building 131 of the high-rise barracks. Hoorie and Mughassil then escaped in a waiting car, and the truck bomb exploded within minutes.

Hoorie was one of 14 charged by the United States in the case. Eleven of the men charged in the bombing are in Saudi custody; three remain fugitives. Saudi Arabia has challenged U.S. jurisdiction in the case and has refused to extradite the men it is holding. The U.S. State Department is offering a reward of up to $5 million for information leading directly to the arrest or indictment of Hoorie.

Erica Pearson

See also Hezbollah; Khobar Towers Bombing; Nasser, Abdelkarim Hussein Mohamed al; Yacoub, Ibrahim Salih Mohammed al

Further Readings

Federal Bureau of Investigation. "Most Wanted Terrorists." http://www.fbi.gov/wanted/terrorists/fugitives.htm.

Jamieson, Perry D. *Khobar Towers: Tragedy and Response.* Washington, DC: Air Force History and Museums Program, 2008.

Melson, Kenneth E., United States Attorney. "Khobar Indictment." United States District Court, Eastern District of Virginia, Alexandria Division, May 23, 2001. http://www.usdoj.gov/opa/pr/2001/June/khobarindictment.wpd.

"A Nation Challenged: The Hunted; The 22 Most Wanted Suspects, in a Five-act Drama of Global Terror." *The New York Times,* October 14, 2001, p. 1B.

Walsh, Elsa. "Louis Freeh's Last Case." *The New Yorker,* May 14, 2001.

HOSTAGE TAKING

Hostage taking is the act of abducting or imprisoning a person for political or monetary gain; since the 1960s, it has evolved into one of the distinctive tactics of modern terrorism.

The practice of taking hostages has a long history. In ancient and medieval times, hostages (often the families of nobles) were sometimes taken by rival powers during times of peace. In war, kings and other rulers were also often captured and held hostage in exchange for ransom payments. This kind of hostage taking essentially ceased with the evolution of the modern nation-state, since the relationship of a political leader to the hostage, or of the hostage to the functioning of a state, was no longer so close or direct. Terrorism in the 1960s reverted to some of the earlier concepts, with terrorists regarding individuals as emblems of their nation and not distinguishing between combatants and civilians in planning attacks.

Hostage taking as a major terrorist tactic was encouraged in the late 1960s and early 1970s by the rise of urban guerrilla warfare and the revolutionary ideology of Dr. George Habash's Popular Front for the Liberation of Palestine (PFLP). Since the nineteenth century, guerrilla uprisings have been endemic in Latin America. For much of this time, however, the guerrillas operated in remote rural areas, and their strategies and tactics depended upon their ability to retreat into and hide in the jungle. Not until the theories of the Brazilian Communist Carlos Marighella, set forth in his *Minimanual of the Urban Guerrilla* (1969), became popular did guerrillas begin to operate in cities. Marighella's treatise discussed the three-fold purpose of terrorism: to disrupt the workings of government and civil authority; to create a climate of fear and apprehension among the populace; and to publicize the terrorists' cause. Hostage taking, especially when the victim is a high government official or industrial leader, accomplishes all these purposes.

Beginning with the abduction of the U.S. ambassador to Brazil in 1969, guerrillas across Latin America executed a daring series of kidnappings over the next several years, in particular targeting diplomats and the executives of Western companies. Governments reacted variously to the kidnappings, with some making concessions to terrorist demands, while others adamantly refused to negotiate. Still, Latin American guerrillas proved that hostage taking could be an effective and profitable terrorist tactic. Even if the hostage were rescued or killed and no ransom received, the kidnappings brought immense publicity to the terrorist group.

Latin American terrorist groups laid the groundwork, but Habash and the PFLP were the first to put the principles they had demonstrated into action in the Middle East. A Marxist, Habash's primary goal was the liberation of Palestine, and his ambition was to spark world revolution. Perhaps his most important innovation was the idea of an international terrorist front, in which terrorists from various countries and groups (many with widely varying goals and allegiances) supported each other's operations and worked together on specific attacks. During the early 1970s, at the peak of the PFLP's power, the Palestinian group was provided training and funds to terrorist groups from around the world, and in turn terrorists from Germany, Japan, Uruguay, Venezuela, Lebanon, and Turkey took part in operations to further the Palestinian cause.

The PFLP was able to seize world attention to a degree undreamed of by its Latin American counterparts. The Latin American guerrillas generally kidnapped their victims. Kidnapping offers a tactical advantage: as long as security forces are unable to locate the hostage—often extremely difficult and sometimes impossible—the government is generally compelled to negotiate in some way with the terrorists, and it may acquiesce to some of their demands. The PFLP and its associate groups, by contrast, favored much more public attacks, in which a band of terrorists would take over a given location (a building, train, or airplane) and conduct negotiations on the spot. The PFLP pioneered airplane hijacking for political purposes with its July 1968 attack on an El Al flight. Some of the many other terrorists attacks in which the PFLP was involved include a 1974 attack on the French embassy at The Hague, Netherlands, and a 1975 attack on an Organization of Petroleum Exporting Countries meeting in Austria attended by representatives of more than a dozen countries.

Because such hostage situations are public, the media can and do provide live, round-the-clock coverage, greatly increasing public awareness of the terrorists' cause. Intense media coverage also makes such attacks considerably more risky, both for the hostages and the terrorists. Although governments strive to keep the progress of negotiations secret, the heavy media coverage usually means that both resistance and acquiescence to the terrorist demands are often known instantly, and terrorists who encounter resistance often kill one or more hostages to prove their seriousness.

Another risk to the hostages is Stockholm syndrome, a psychological phenomenon named after a bank robbery in which hostages were taken in Stockholm, Sweden. In that event, after several days of imprisonment, some of the hostages came to sympathize with their captors, even defending them from the police. Psychologists believe that Stockholm syndrome may be a consequence of the hostages' desperate attempt to stay alive. What may begin as an attempt to stay on their captor's good side transmutes into complete identification with their captor. Patty Hearst is generally regarded as the most famous victim of Stockholm syndrome. In 1974, Hearst was kidnapped by members of the

Symbionese Liberation Army (SLA); after weeks of being beaten and imprisoned, she joined the SLA and helped them rob a bank.

Terrorists are also endangered by taking hostages in a public place, for the government knows the whereabouts of the hostages, and an attempt at rescue is always possible. During the initial wave of hostage takings in the late 1960s and 1970s, the responses of governments involved were often confused and inconsistent because of inexperience. (Tragedies such as the massacre of the Israeli athletes at the 1972 Munich Olympics resulted from such lack of experience.) Since the safety and release of the hostages were the paramount concerns of the authorities, governments sometimes granted huge concessions to the terrorists, including the payment of ransom, freeing of imprisoned terrorists, and safe passage for the kidnappers to a terrorist-sponsoring state. Governments soon realized that such concessions only encouraged more such attacks. By the mid-1970s, hostage negotiation protocols had begun to be developed, and governments began to deploy highly trained commando teams to rescue hostages, as occurred in an operation of the Israeli Defense Force in Entebbe, Uganda, in 1976.

These tactics had their effect, and through the 1980s and 1990s the type of spectacular attacks that the PFLP had used to capture world attention (and that had been imitated by many others) became less and less frequent. The new counterterrorist methods were not foolproof, however, and the 1979 hostage crisis in Iran revealed their shortcomings. In 1979, Iranian students overran the American embassy and subsequently held more than 400 hostages for more than 14 months. The government of Iran tacitly condoned the students' actions, and in the resulting atmosphere of mutual hostility, direct negotiations with the hostage takers could not be conducted. In the end, the United States was forced to make certain strategic concessions to win the hostages' release.

A series of abductions of journalists and other Westerners in the mid-1980s in Lebanon also demonstrated the limitations of counterterrorism. A crisp and efficient military operation like those that had freed so many other hostages was impossible in that country, torn as it was by civil war, and one of the hostages, Terry Anderson, was held for more than seven years.

In the late 1990s, guerrilla-style kidnappings once again became a favored terrorist tactic, with tourists and businesspeople being the primary targets. This wave of kidnappings further blurred the line between politics and crime. Ransom demands have always been associated with hostage taking, but groups like the Revolutionary Armed Forces of Colombia (FARC) have begun treating hostage taking less as a means of attracting publicity to their cause and more as a for-profit enterprise, generally choosing wealthier but less visible targets, such as midlevel executives and other professionals. Hundreds of people are kidnapped each year in Colombia by FARC and other guerrilla groups, and their ransoms bring millions of dollars to these groups. Almost endemic in Colombia, for-profit kidnapping has also become a worrisome occurrence in the Philippines, Kashmir, and many Latin American countries.

The 2000s saw spectacular incidents involving the seizure of enormous groups of hostages in Russia by Chechen separatists, including the taking of some 850 hostages in a Moscow theater in 2002, and the 2004 seizure of approximately 1,200 hostages, many of them children, at a school in Beslan. Both incidences ended when Russian security forces attacked the buildings where the hostages were held, but hundreds died in the process. Many experts caution that terrorists' use of a particular tactic is cyclic in nature, as governments unacquainted with past crises move into power. Given the long history of hostage taking and the many terrorist goals it can be accomplish, the tactic is certain to continue to be a threat.

Colleen Sullivan

See also Anderson, Terry A.; FARC; Habash, George; Hearst, Patty; Hijacking; Marighella, Carlos; Munich Olympics Massacre; Popular Front for the Liberation of Palestine; Stockholm Syndrome

Further Readings

Antokol, Norman; Nudell, Mayer. *No One a Neutral: Political Hostage-taking in the Modern World.* Medina, OH: Alpha Publications, 1990.
Aston, Clive C. *A Contemporary Crisis: Political Hostage-taking and the Experience of Western Europe.* Contributions in Political Science 84. Westport, CT: Greenwood, 1982.

Aston, Clive C. *Political Hostage-taking in Western Europe.* London: Institute for the Study of Conflict, 1984.

Dolnike, Adam, and Keith M. Fitzgerald. *Negotiating Hostage Crises with the New Terrorists.* Westport, CT: Praeger Security International, 2008.

Taillon, J. Paul de B. *Hijacking and Hostages: Government Responses to Terrorism.* Westport, CT: Praeger, 2002.

HUSSEIN, SADDAM (1937–2005)

Saddam Hussein was the dictator of Iraq from 1979 until the U.S. invasion of that country in 2003. He attained and maintained that position through the use of state terror, and throughout his reign he also sponsored international terrorism.

Personal History

Hussein was born on April 28, 1937, in the village of Al Auja, near the town of Tikrit, in northern Iraq. His father appears to have died before his birth, and he was raised by his mother, Subha, and stepfather, Ibrahim Hassan. The family was poor, and relations between Hussein and his stepfather seem to have been strained; Hussein did not attend school until he left home at the age of 10, when he went to live with his maternal uncle, Khayrallah Tulfah, in Baghdad. Khayrallah, a schoolteacher and former army officer, became a significant influence in his life.

A mediocre student, Hussein failed the entrance exam for the Baghdad military academy in the mid-1950s. He then worked at a series of odd jobs and became involved in the Baath Party. The Baathists were a socialist, pan-Arab group that dreamed of deposing the Western-supported monarchs who then ruled most Arab nations and uniting all Arab people in a single modern state. Hussein became a recruiter for the Baath youth wing in Iraq, leading street protests and organizing gangs.

In 1958, a coup led by General Abdul Karim Kassam overthrew the Iraqi monarchy. The Baath Party rapidly became dissatisfied with Kassam's leadership, however, and in 1959 Hussein was

A vandalized Republican Guard base wall in the vicinity of Daly Airfield, Iraq, during Operation Iraqi Freedom depicts Saddam Hussein waving. (Sgt. Mauricio Campino, USMC)

involved in attempting to assassinate Kassam. When the attempt failed, Hussein fled to Syria, where he joined other Baath exiles.

While Iraq was roiled with political turmoil, Hussein studied law in Cairo and rose within the party ranks. His cousin, General Ahmad Hassan al Bakr, was an important Baath leader, and his patronage brought Hussein a number of important positions. In 1968, Bakr led another coup, becoming president of Iraq, while Hussein became head of Iraq's security services.

Hussein then began his quest for power in earnest. He used his control of the Iraqi intelligence agencies to attach agents loyal to him to army units at every level, thus neutralizing the only segment of Iraqi society that could contend against the Baath Party. Eventually, all non-Baath leaders involved in the 1968 coup were forced to step down, and most were executed. At the same time, Hussein vastly increased membership in the Baath Party, and he made such membership a prerequisite for certain forms of employment.

Hussein then began accumulating ministerial positions. At first, he took on less glamorous jobs that other party leaders didn't want (the intelligence position being one such), but eventually he added the ministries of health and education to his portfolio, becoming Bakr's second-in-command. Hussein used his position to provide patronage to his family and to old acquaintances from Tikrit, thus creating a pool of loyalists. Hussein remained deferential to Bakr, who enjoyed all the privileges of office while being taxed with none of the work, and Bakr's faith in and reliance on Hussein increased. By the mid-1970s, Bakr was largely a figurehead; Hussein truly ran the country. In 1979, after Bakr made a belated attempt to regain power, Hussein forced him to step down and made himself president of Iraq.

Connections to Terrorism

Hussein has been likened to Joseph Stalin, and Iraq under his rule to Stalinist Russia; the comparison is apt and useful in expressing the quality of terror employed by his regime to control the people of Iraq.

Hussein apportioned power in Iraq to members of his family, with their loyalty guaranteed by his patronage and their fear. Almost every agency or department within the government reported directly to him or to a member of his family. He created many intelligence agencies, whose agents were expected to spy not only upon the Iraqi people but also on other agencies, and then report directly to Hussein. The slightest dissent or protest against his rule was considered treason and often carried a sentence of death. Iraqi security forces routinely used physical and psychological torture to extort confessions or information from prisoners, and Hussein ordered extrajudicial executions. This overarching state terror was designed to impress upon the Iraqi people that there was no alternative to Hussein's rule.

Despite Hussein's best efforts, however, two groups openly resisted his regime: Kurds and Shiite Muslims. The Shiites form the majority of Iraq's population, and their exclusion from political power by minority Sunni Muslims formed the basis of their dissent. Numerous Shiite leaders were imprisoned and executed by Hussein.

The Kurds, a mostly Muslim ethnic group with their own language and culture distinct from Arab Iraqis, have long desired a separate state. Since the

1920s, they have engaged in periodic rebellions. In the mid-1970s, Hussein began a campaign to nullify Kurdish resistance by forcibly removing Kurdish people from their homes in northern Iraq and moving them to southern Iraq. Some observers contended that the relocation campaign amounted to an attempt to eliminate the Kurds, and thus constituted genocide. During the last days of the Iran-Iraq War (1980–1988), Hussein bombed dozens of Kurdish villages with a still-unknown mixture of chemicals, possibly including the nerve agent sarin and cancer-inducing aflatoxin. Tens of thousands of people are believed to have been killed.

In addition to his actions against his own people, Hussein supported various terrorist groups. The Abu Nidal Organization (ANO) operated from Iraq from 1974 to 1983 and undertook attacks against Syria at Hussein's behest. The leader of the ANO was believed to have returned to Iraq in 1999. In the late 1980s and early 1990s, Hussein channeled funds to the Palestine Liberation Organization (PLO), but the PLO-Iraq connection was suspended in 1991.

Hussein's determination to expand his empire led to his invasion of neighboring Kuwait in 1991, and soon after to Iraq's defeat by a U.S.-led coalition in the 1991 Gulf War. However, even after this defeat, Hussein was never far from the minds of some U.S. officials. Indeed, it was not long after the terrorist attacks on September 11, 2001, that plans were being made to invade the country and depose Hussein. President George W. Bush linked Hussein's regime to a broader "war on terror," identifying Iraq, Iran, and North Korea as an "axis of evil." Suggestions that Hussein had acquired weapons of mass destruction ultimately proved to be untrue, as was the widely held belief that Hussein had some sort of involvement with the 9/11 attacks. Nevertheless, the invasion of Iraq began with U.S.-launched missile strikes in March 2003.

On December 13, 2003, it was announced that Saddam Hussein had been captured, not far from his home town of Tikrit. He was held by the United States until June 2004, when he and other former Baathist leaders were turned over to the new Iraqi government for trial. Hussein's trial began in August 2006, and in November he was convicted for crimes against humanity and sentenced to death by hanging. The sentence was carried out on December 30, 2006, and Hussein was buried in Tikrit.

Colleen Sullivan

See also Abu Nidal Organization; Biological Terrorism; Chemical Terrorism; Iraq War; Palestine Liberation Organization; Persian Gulf War

Further Readings

Aburish, Saïd K. *Saddam Hussein: The Politics of Revenge.* London: Bloomsbury, 2000.

Allawi, Ali A. *The Occupation of Iraq: Winning the War, Losing the Peace.* New Haven, CT: Yale University Press, 2007.

Coughlin, Con. *Saddam Hussein: His Rise and Fall.* New York: Ecco/HarperCollins, 2005.

Duffy, Brian, and Louise Lief. "Saddam Hussein's Unholiest Allies." *U.S. News & World Report,* January 28, 1991, p. 42.

Goldberg, Jeffrey. "The Great Terror." *The New Yorker,* March 25, 2002.

Gordon, Michael R., and Bernard Trainor. *Cobra II: The Inside Story of the Invasion and Occupation of Iraq.* New York: Vintage, 2007.

Karsh, Efraim, and Inari Rautsi. *Saddam Hussein: A Political Biography.* New York: Free Press, 1991.

Maddox, Eric. *Capturing Saddam: The Hunt for Saddam Hussein.* New York: HarperCollins, 2008.

Melman, Yossi. *The Master Terrorist: The True Story of Abu-Nidal.* New York: Adama Books, 1986.

Miller, Judith, and Laurie Mylroie. *Saddam Hussein and the Crisis in the Gulf.* New York: Random House, 1990.

Newton, Michael A., and Michael P. Sharf. *Enemy of the State: The Trial and Execution of Saddam Hussein.* New York: St. Martin's, 2008.

Seale, Patrick. *Abu Nidal: A Gun for Hire.* New York: Random House, 1992.

INSURANCE AND TERRORISM

In most industrialized countries, insurance is one of the principal tools used to manage risk. Without this mechanism for individuals and firms to transfer risks to insurance companies (who in turn transfer all or part of this exposure to reinsurance companies, to the world's financial markets, or, in some cases, to the government), people would be unable to engage in many of their normal activities.

The price of insurance can be a good signal of the level of risk of certain activities. For example, it appears sensible that a young and inexperienced driver pays a higher car insurance premium, all things being equal, than someone who has been driving for 20 years without an accident. Similarly, smokers or practitioners of extreme sports, such as rock climbing, pay an insurance premium for life coverage that is higher than others, since their risk level is higher than the average. The insured and the insurer have an *ex ante* risk-sharing arrangement: in return for the payment of a premium, the insurer indemnifies the insured if a risk described in the contract materializes. This approach, though, rests on a good knowledge of the risk associated with these insured activities (e.g., driving, staying alive) based on a large historical data set.

Terrorism: The Limit of Insurability

The insurability of terrorism risk poses several issues. In fact, while simplifying, two conditions must be verified for a risk to be judged insurable.

The first is the capacity to identify and quantify (or to estimate) the probability of occurrence of the event to be insured against, as well as the potential losses. The second is the capacity to determine an amount of premium that actually reflects the risk level, and that will be acceptable to the insurer. If these two conditions hold, the risk can then be considered insurable. It is precisely these two conditions that are problematic in the case of the risk of terrorism. As the terrorist attacks of September 11, 2001, demonstrated, large-scale terrorism has the potential to inflict truly catastrophic losses to insurers, which could lead them into bankruptcy. Moreover, there is a lot of uncertainty about what the risk actually is, because it can evolve rapidly. More specifically, since terrorists are likely to adapt their strategy as a function of their own resources and their knowledge of the vulnerability of the entity they want to attack, the nature of the risk is continuously evolving. The likelihood and consequences of a terrorist attack are influenced by a mix of strategies and counterstrategies (e.g., anti-terrorism activities by governments and potential victims of attacks) that have been developed by a range of stakeholders and shift over time. This leads to "dynamic uncertainty," which make insurance pricing a difficult task.

Even in cases where a risk is insurable, it does not necessarily mean that it will be a profitable activity for an insurance company, which can always decide not to cover it. This is notably the case if it is impossible to establish a price level at which the insurer will receive sufficient premiums to cover the inherent costs of its activities (e.g., product development, marketing, premium collection, cost of capital, claim payment), so that the product will be profitable enough to satisfy its shareholders. In some cases, the insurer can prefer not to cover certain risks, unless it is obligated to do so by law.

Terrorism Insurance Before and After 9/11

The evolution of terrorism insurance markets in the United States before and after 9/11 illustrates the insurability challenge well. Prior to September 11, 2001, terrorism coverage in the United States was included in standard commercial insurance policy packages without explicit consideration of the risks associated with these events. It was an unnamed peril on all-risk commercial and homeowners' policies covering damage to property and contents. The private insurance market had functioned effectively in the United States because losses from terrorism had historically been small and, to a large degree, uncorrelated. Attacks of a domestic origin were isolated, carried out by groups or individuals with disparate agendas, and they did not create major economic disruption or cause many casualties. Even the first attack on the World Trade Center (WTC) in 1993, which killed six people and led to over $700 million in insurance payments, was not seen as being severe enough for insurers to consider revising their view of terrorism as a peril to be explicitly considered when pricing a commercial insurance policy. Before that, the Oklahoma City bombing of 1995, which killed 168 people, had been the most damaging terrorist attack on domestic soil. However, the largest losses from these attacks were to federal property and employees and were covered by the government.

The 9/11 attacks, however, were a wake-up call for the insurance industry. On September 12, 2001, insurers found themselves with significant amounts of terrorism exposure from their existing portfolios, with limited possibilities of obtaining reinsurance to reduce the losses from a future terrorist attack. With $35 billion of insured losses (in 2001 prices), it was at that time the most costly catastrophe event in the history of insurance worldwide (it is now second to Hurricane Katrina in 2005). Reinsurers, which paid about two-thirds of this amount, decided to leave this market. As a result, primary insurers found themselves deprived of reinsurance capacity (reinsurers are the "insurers of

insurers," and are typically diversified across a large number of risk and locations around the world).

By February 2002, 45 states had authorized primary insurers to exclude terrorism risk from their insurance coverage. On September 11, 2002, America was uncovered against terrorism risk. On November 26, 2002, President Bush signed into law the Terrorism Risk Insurance Act (TRIA), which established a special public-private partnership, with insurers to provide commercial enterprises operating in the United States with up to $100 billion of coverage. The program has been extended two times since then, and it is set to expire at the end of 2014. Defining long-term-risk financing solutions is critical to assure fast economic recovery after future attacks.

Erwann Michel-Kerjan

See also Economics and Terrorism

Further Readings

Davis, Paul K., ed. *New Challenges for Defense Planning: Rethinking How Much Is Enough*. Santa Monica, CA: RAND Corporation, 1994.

Haimes, Yacov Y. *Risk Modeling, Assessment, and Management*. Hoboken, NJ: Wiley-Interscience, 2004.

Kunreuther, H., and E. Michel-Kerjan. "Challenges for Terrorism Risk Insurance in the United States." *Journal of Economic Perspectives* 18, no. 4 (2004): 201–214.

Kunreuther, H., and E. Michel-Kerjan. "Insurability of Mega-Terrorism: Challenges and Perspectives." In *Terrorism Risk Insurance in OECD Countries*. Paris: Organisation for Economic Co-operation and Development (OECD), 2005.

Lakdawalla, Darius, and George Zanjani. *Insurance, Self-Protection, and the Economics of Terrorism*. Santa Monica, CA: RAND Corporation, 2004.

Michel-Kerjan, E., and B. Pedell. "How Does the Corporate World Cope with Mega-Terrorism? Puzzling Evidence from Terrorism Insurance Markets." *Journal of Applied Corporate Finance* 18, no. 4 (2006): 61–75.

Michel-Kerjan, E., and B. Pedell. "Terrorism Coverage in the Post-9/11 Era: A Comparison of New Public-Private Partnerships in France, Germany and the U.S." *Geneva Papers on Risk and Insurance* 30, no. 1 (2005): 144–170.

Michel-Kerjan, E., and P. Raschky. *The Effects of Government Intervention in the Market for Corporate Terrorism Insurance.* Working paper. Philadelphia: The Wharton School, University of Pennsylvania, 2010.

Wills, Henry H., et al. *Estimating Terrorism Risk.* Santa Monica, CA: RAND Corporation, 2005.

Woo, Gordon. *Quantifying Insurance Terrorism Risk.* Newark, CA: Risk Management Solutions, 2002. http://www.rms.com/NewsPress/Quantifying_ Insurance_Terrorism_Risk.pdf.

INTELLIGENCE GATHERING

The targets of intelligence gathering related to terrorism are not terribly different from those related to traditional conflicts with nation-states. Intelligence services must collect information that will provide decision makers with knowledge of terrorist organizations, including their leaders, operatives, and supporters; their organizational infrastructure; and their financial and military resources. The methods employed for gathering this intelligence have not changed substantially in some time. Intelligence services seek to intercept the communications or signals intelligence (SIGINT) of terrorist networks, to capture photographic evidence (imagery intelligence, or IMINT) of terrorist activities, and to acquire human assets (human intelligence, or HUMINT) with direct knowledge of terrorist's intentions and capabilities.

Although methods and objectives of intelligence gathering remain substantially the same, terrorism does present several new and distinct challenges to intelligence communities. For example, the revolutionary development of technical systems for gathering SIGINT and IMINT in the twentieth century helped limit the fear of surprise attack. In the twenty-first century, however, these same capabilities have not had the same impact in counterterrorism efforts. Terror networks, relative to nation-states, adapt more readily to changing environments, and their size allows them to hide in the shadows, so they can more readily attack without warning. The nature of the threat thus reduces the amount of security improvement a state can buy through improvements to early warning systems. States facing substantial terrorist threats have responded with targeted operations against terrorist organizations, and intelligence gathering supports that goal.

SIGINT

Signals intelligence, or electronic eavesdropping, is the collection of signals from electronic and communications technologies. Virtually any communication system can be penetrated by a vast array of spy satellites, surveillance planes, computers, and telecom equipment around the world. Thus, the challenge for intelligence services is not access, but developing methodologies for pulling actionable intelligence from massive amounts of data. For example, al Qaeda has used both high- and low-technology means to coordinate its activities. In organizing the September 11 attacks, the terrorists exchanged hundreds of e-mails and booked airline tickets online; they also protected their communications by using public computer terminals, anonymous e-mail services, and encrypted websites.

Starting in 2005, intelligence agencies engaged in computer-to-computer signals intelligence exploration and began closely examining Internet protocol network intercepts and forensics analysis as new weapons. Traditional signals intelligence professionals had shied away from this type of intelligence gathering, but they now began to realize that the computer-to-computer intelligence gap could be filled. It is possible to target a section of the Internet—even the sections that originate in small countries—to find targets of interest online. The new technologies enabled security officials to track terrorist suspects internally, and they allowed paramilitary units to spy on terrorist computer communications.

Network forensics allows SIGINT units to capture network traffic for several requirements. Traditional data collection, alerting, and analysis help officials capture targeted e-mail, chat sessions, web pages, file transfer protocol downloads, logs, and Voice over Internet Protocol (VoIP) communications from network gatekeepers such as Internet service providers. It also provides near-real-time analysis and reporting to create actionable intelligence from network traffic. Additionally, it allows the SIGINT units to conduct relational surveys by monitoring contacts of known terrorist suspects, building orders of battle around enemy organizations.

Collectors of SIGINT have to answer several tough questions before they can turn these conversations into intelligence that is useful in counterterrorism. Who are the communicants, and do they seem knowledgeable? Where in the conversation do key words or phrases come? What is the reaction to these words? Where was the information collected? How many calls a day are there from this location, and in what languages? Is there a machine that can sort these out by language, or do you have to use a human operator? If there is such a machine, does it work in a polyglot place where one conversation often includes several languages? Such challenges do not render SIGINT capabilities obsolete in counterterrorism, but they do underscore the importance of using multiple capabilities to gather intelligence.

IMINT

Imagery intelligence includes intelligence collected by photography, infrared sensors, lasers, electro-optics, and radar sensors that reproduce images of objects optically or electronically on film or other media. Many systems collect SIGINT, including satellites and high-flying aircraft. In traditional conflicts between states, where the main threat is more quantifiable, IMINIT has an advantage over other collection methods because its uniquely compelling visual quality provides a raw, untouched feel that policy makers crave. Moreover, IMINT has a more prominent role in early warning, alerting the analysts of an adversary's troop deployments, weapons developments, or placement of weapons systems. Such advantages decrease when dealing with terrorists. Terror organizations have less infrastructure, attack from within states, and are less susceptible to surveillance by IMINT.

While IMINT has less use as defensive early-warning tool, it does have tremendous utility in offensive operations against terrorists. Satellites can produce detailed images of training camps and transmit their images almost instantaneously to paramilitary units. In addition, the capabilities of spacecraft and aircraft have evolved from being limited to black-and-white visible-light photography to being able to produce images using different parts of the electromagnetic spectrum. As a result, imagery can often be obtained under circumstances (such as darkness or cloud cover) where standard visible-light photography is not feasible.

The ability to rapidly provide imagery to a combat unit—seamlessly tied to map coordinates and other mission critical information—provides a key situational awareness. Collection teams can navigate a route with the portable immersive multi-sensor camera and at virtually any speed, and the system can capture everything around. Unmanned military vehicles have an additional capability: performing drone attacks on terrorist targets.

HUMINT

Human intelligence, or espionage, is the use of agents to steal information from targets who are trying to keep that information secret. An agent may be a defecting terrorist, a paid informant, or a family member who has access to information and is recruited to provide that information to a case officer. Case officers are paid employees of an intelligence service, such as the CIA (U.S.), MI6 (Great Britain), or Mossad (Israel). Sometimes agents willingly give information to a case officer, while at other times they do not realize they are giving information to an intelligence service.

Typically, a case officer is assigned diplomatic cover, such as performing a job at an embassy, or he or she might work in business or as a journalist, or perhaps pose as a tourist or expatriate. Contrary to popular myth, case officers do not spend the majority of their time performing paramilitary operations or dispensing exotic torture drugs to terrorism suspects. They primarily recruit agents, and their most important skill is an ability to manipulate and persuade individuals to engage in dangerous work.

One primary means of manipulation is money, and case officers look for people who have access to information and need or want significantly more money than they have. Although terrorists do not often defect for money, informants with knowledge of terrorists' activities, organization, and infrastructure regularly provide information to intelligence services. For example, Ramzi Yousef, the man responsible for the 1993 bombing of the World Trade Center, was captured thanks to an informant who was paid $2 million. Ideology is another important motivation. People will put themselves at risk for a cause. In the Middle East, for example, CIA case officers have successfully recruited Muslim agents who believe the murder of innocents is wrong—a belief that can motivate them to take grave risks to provide information to U.S. intelligence. Finally, ego can be an important motivation—agents often think they are smarter than everyone else.

When an agent offers information or services, the case officer must determine whether the agent is reliable and legitimate. The agent could be unstable or a fabricator, which can create serious problems in the future. For example, one infamous fabricator, codenamed "Curveball," played a critical role in the U.S. Intelligence Community's erroneous assessment of Iraq's biological weapons programs. The information this source provided appeared in Secretary of State Colin Powell's speech to the United Nations Security Council on February 5, 2003, causing the Bush administration much embarrassment and undermining its credibility, both domestically and internationally.

Case officers must also decide if the agent is a double agent who is approaching them to offer false information and somehow compromise operations. In late December 2009, a Jordanian case officer and seven CIA officers responsible for collecting information about militant networks in Afghanistan and Pakistan were killed by a suicide bomber. The bomber was a Jordanian double agent who had been recruited by the Jordanian intelligence service in the hope that he might deliver top members of al Qaeda. The attack at the CIA base dealt a devastating blow to operations against militants and derailed hopes of penetrating al Qaeda's upper ranks.

Espionage is dangerous work, leading some to argue that it ought to be the weapon of last resort, or at least used only when other methods of intelligence fail to produce critical information. Others consider this view naïve and say that it is wrong to put too much faith in technical means when critical information about terrorists' plans and operations often resides within the heads of human actors.

Counteroffensive Action

Although intelligence services gather data in the hopes that they can provide early warning of a terrorist attack, that is exceedingly difficult. There are literally tens of thousands of targets, including power stations, government bureaus, train stations, airports, skyscrapers, open-air markets, or sport stadiums—indeed, the list is endless. It is impossible to defend them all, especially against a determined adversary that can choose the time and place of attack. States have responded to this impossibility by responding with a mix of counteroffensive actions such as targeted killing.

Targeted killing is an unpleasant practice, and governments have often denied responsibility for specific attacks, but it can impede the effectiveness of terrorist organizations whose leadership, planning, and tactical skills are confined to a few key individuals. The methods involved have varied with the circumstances and include booby-trapped packages, drone attacks from the sky, helicopter gunships, F-16 fighter planes, car bombs, and commando operations. Israel has achieved some notable successes in this area. In the 1950s, terrorist infiltration from Egypt lessened as a result of the killing of Egyptian intelligence officers in charge of the operation. The group Black September was all but destroyed as a functioning terrorist organization in the 1970s following a Mossad campaign that hunted and killed the 13 members believed responsible for planning the terror attack that resulted in the deaths of the Israeli athletes at the 1972 Munich Olympics. The 1995 assassination of Islamic Jihad leader Fathi Shikaki undermined the effectiveness of this group for several years as successors struggled over policy and power.

The obvious revenge motivations aside, there are strong arguments supporting the effectiveness of targeted killing. Certain individual leaders have the charisma and organizational skills to keep a group together, and when they are eliminated, they are not easily replaced. There is little question that Israel's policy has hurt the capability of its adversaries to prosecute attacks. Their officials estimate they stop over 80 percent of attempts, and the incidence of poorly planned attacks indicates that there have been problems either with the organization of operations by these groups. There are, however, tradeoffs. Aside from any moral qualms, killing people and blowing things up tend to attract a lot of attention. Such actions create international incidents, expose intelligence sources, and alienate friendly countries. Intelligence services engaging in such activities must decide between taking out a terrorist target and protecting reliable sources of information.

The methods of gathering intelligence on terrorism remain, for the most part, the same as those employed against nation-states. The most powerful nations have enormous advantages over terrorists, but the weaker side sometimes does win in asymmetric conflicts. As the strongest nations of the world have combated terrorism from admittedly weaker opponent, they have learned that overwhelming force does not always spell victory in asymmetric conflicts. Thus, a terrorist can successfully defeat the early warning systems employed by states against them and achieve a tactical surprise. The long-term strategic advantages, however, remain firmly in the hands of states, which can use their superior intelligence-gathering capabilities to dismantle terror organizations.

Harold Scott

See also Asymmetrical Warfare; Black September; Central Intelligence Agency; Counterterrorism; Cyberterrorism; Interrogation Techniques; Munich Olympics Massacre; Rendition, Extraordinary; Torture Debate

Further Readings

Almog, Doron. "Cumulative Deterrence and the War on Terrorism." *Parameters* 34 (2004).

Henriksen, Thomas H. "Security Lessons from the Israeli Trenches." *Policy Review* 141 (2007).

Hulnick, Arthur S. *Keeping Us Safe: Secret Intelligence and Homeland Security*. Santa Barbara, CA: Praeger, 2004.

Lowenthal, Mark M. "Imagery's National Status Faces Questionable Future." *Signal Online*, May 1999. http://www.afcea.org/signal/articles/templates/ SIGNAL_Article_Template.asp?articleid=884 &zoneid=145.

Macdonald, Margaret S., and Anthony G. Oettinger. "Information Overload: Managing Intelligence Technologies." *Harvard International Review* 24 (2002).

Mockaitis, Thomas R., and Paul B. Rich. *Grand Strategy in the War against Terrorism*. London: Frank Cass, 2003.

Richelson, Jeffrey T. *The U.S. Intelligence Community*. Boulder, CO: Westview Press, 1999.

Interahamwe / Interhamwe

See Democratic Front for the Liberation of Rwanda

International Relations and Terrorism

The attacks on the World Trade Center and Pentagon on September 11, 2001, represented the most significant single act of international antistate terrorism in history, with roughly 3,000 people killed and damage estimates as high as $1 trillion. Until the September 11 attacks, it was generally state governments that had committed the most significant actions in terms of death and destruction, either in the repression of various partisan groups within state territory (often repressing groups that were believed to have obtained external financing or support) or in the form of state-supported terrorism against other states or against movements outside the state's borders.

Terrorism as part of a systematic and international effort to undermine, assassinate, or overthrow the leadership of both major and minor powers began to manifest itself in the late nineteenth and early twentieth centuries, with the rise of anarchist, ethno-nationalist, religious, and other left- or right-wing ideological movements. But state leaderships were generally unable to effectively coordinate action against the violent actions of such movements, either before World War I or before World War II. On the eve of World War II, the League of Nations did address the question of antistate terrorism in 1937, in the aftermath of the assassinations of King Alexander I of Yugoslavia and the French foreign minister, Louis Barthou, in 1934, but the Convention on the Prevention and Punishment of Terrorism never entered into force.

Although there was greater interstate political, military, and security coordination against terrorism during the Cold War and in its aftermath than before World War II, most efforts were piecemeal responses to individual acts of terrorism. No truly coordinated multilateral or international strategy emerged, largely because the world was divided into capitalist and communist blocs. Even after the end of the Cold War, it was not until the 9/11 attacks that states and international organizations began to more systematically address the question of terrorism.

After the September 11 attacks, the United States opted to engage in a "global war on terror," militarily intervening in Afghanistan in October 2001 and in Iraq in March 2003, while concurrently seeking international and multilateral supports from the United Nations and NATO, among other international organizations and states, in addition to nongovernmental organizations (NGOs), in an effort to deal with the questions of state-supported and antistate terrorism in all its geopolitical, socioeconomic, and ideological-cultural aspects.

Historical Background

Seen over the long term, states and international organizations have been slow to intervene collectively against acts of antistate terrorism. The state-supported terrorism of World War II had only begun to recede when modern forms of antistate terrorism began to arise at the beginning of the Cold War. At that time, both the United States and Soviet Union began to augment their nuclear weapons programs (later called the "delicate balance of terror") and engage in cloak-and-dagger operations throughout the world. Such actions helped to inspire a number of antistate groups, which were able to learn, or improvise, from CIA or KGB techniques.

During the Cold War, acts of antistate terrorism designed to overthrow state leaderships became even more systematic and international in range, particularly in areas of the world that were colonized by force. A number of these antistate or "national liberation" movements served as proxies for American, Soviet, and Chinese interests, with financing, training, or logistical support from these countries or from others. In addition, they often used a mix of unconventional guerrilla and terrorist tactics.

Despite some degree of coordination between military, police and security forces within the Western bloc, the United States generally took a fatalistic approach to the actions of terrorist groups and movements, based on the theory that not much could be done to prevent such acts of violence. It was not until the accidental confluence of the kidnapping of Israeli athletes by the Palestinian nationalist group Black September at the 1972 Munich Olympics, coupled with the November 1972 hijacking of Southern Airlines Flight 49 by three criminals who threatened to crash the plane into Oak Ridge nuclear reactor,

that American and international attention was drawn to acts of antistate terrorism. The Nixon administration responded to the latter by negotiating a deal on air hijacking with Fidel Castro that helped discourage air hijacking on both sides, indicating the necessity for even rival states to cooperate on the issue of antistate terrorism. The attack on Israeli athletes led Israel to retaliate by launching counterattacks against the Palestine Liberation Organization (PLO), whose differing factions were seen at that time as being supported by the Soviet Union, plus a number of Arab states. Operation Wrath of God sought to track down PLO members involved in the Munich attacks; Operation Spring of Youth was launched against PLO members in Lebanon. These operations then resulted in counterattacks by Palestinian groups.

In Latin America, the rise of "urban guerrillas"—once again seen as having Communist backing—in the 1960s led to efforts by many states in Central and South America to repress opposition movements through the use of "death squads" in "dirty wars" throughout the region. Secretly backed by the United States in Operation Condor, Argentina, Chile, Uruguay, Paraguay, Bolivia, and Brazil, Ecuador, and Peru, came together in 1975 in order to combat left-wing political opponents on one another's territory. This alliance was formed following the establishment of a joint revolutionary command of extreme leftwing Argentine, Chilean, Uruguayan, and Bolivian "urban guerilla" movements in 1973. The right-wing juntas in Argentina (1976–1982) and in Chile (1973–1981) were perhaps the most notorious for their repression against actual and presumed leftists. In September 1976, the Chilean government detonated a car bomb in the vehicle of a former Chilean diplomat, Orlando Letelier, in Washington, D.C. Just five days before the assassination, orders for a U.S. diplomatic demarche that was to be sent to Chile, Argentina, and Uruguay and that would have warned these states against engaging in assassination attempts against opposition figures, both within the territories of these states and abroad, were inexplicably rescinded.

In what represented the prototype of many twentieth-century guerrilla movements, the Irish Republican Army (IRA), which was first formed during the Easter Uprising of 1916, obtained the plastic explosive Semtex from Libya in the mid- to late 1980s. The explosive was to be used in terror attacks against Great Britain. The Libyan leader Colonel Muammar el Qaddafi had resumed contacts with the Provisional IRA after U.S. warplanes, stationed in the United Kingdom, had bombed Libya in 1986. (These attacks had followed U.S. allegations that Libyan agents were responsible for the bombing of a West Berlin discotheque.) Libya was likewise suspected of the bombing of Pan Am Flight 103 over Lockerbie, Scotland, in December 1988. The Lockerbie bombing may have represented an act of revenge for the U.S. air strikes on Libya in 1986. It could also have also represented revenge for the downing of Iran Air Flight 655; late in the Iran-Iraq War, the civilian airliner was accidentally shot down by the USS *Vincennes* in July 1988 over the Strait of Hormuz. The 1991 UN Convention on the Marking of Plastic Explosives for the Purpose of Detection was designed to control and limit the use of unmarked and undetectable plastic explosives and was negotiated in the aftermath of the Pan Am Flight 103 bombing.

The Iranian Revolution and International Terrorism

The 1978–1979 Iranian Revolution brought to power a militant pan-Shia Islamist movement, overthrowing the shah of Iran. The Iranian Revolution, followed by the Iran-Iraq War, tended to accentuate Sunni–Shia religious conflicts and acts of terrorism throughout the region and the world.

In 1983, the Shia Islamic Jihad (with purported links to Hezbollah and Iran) engaged in a suicide truck bombing of the U.S. Marine barracks in Beirut in an effort to impel the United States to leave Lebanon. The fact that the United States (and France, whose troops were also attacked) withdrew from Lebanon after the bombing attack may have strengthened the resolve of a number of antistate movements to pressure U.S. policy in the region by the use of extreme violence.

In 1985 and 1986, in the Iran-Contra Affair, the Reagan administration sold Iran antitank and antiaircraft missiles systems through Israel as an intermediary for use against Iraq, despite Iran's support for Hezbollah (Party of God). These efforts were taken in the effort to release American hostages taken by pro-Iranian groups, who were opposed to American military support for Saddam Hussein in the 1980–1988 Iran-Iraq War. The proceeds of these arms sales were then used to finance the Contras, a CIA-financed group opposed to the Sandinista regime in Nicaragua. Secret American actions represented an effort to circumvent the Boland Amendment, which had been placed on the 1983 Defense Appropriations Act, and which had blocked funding for the effort of American intelligence agencies to overthrow the Sandinista government by force.

Soviet Collapse and the Rise of Religious Terrorism

The Islamic Revolution in Iran was soon followed by Soviet intervention in Afghanistan in December 1979. Soviet intervention helped to spur anti-Soviet pan-Islamist mujahideen movements. At that time, the mujahideen were financially supported as "freedom fighters" by Washington and Saudi Arabia (with logistical support from Pakistan and training by the CIA), but they were seen as "terrorists" by Moscow. Soviet withdrawal from Afghanistan in the mid-1980s eventually resulted in war among rival Afghan political and religious factions until the victory of the essentially ethnic Pashtun Sunni extremist group, the Taliban, in 1996.

In the aftermath of the Soviet collapse in 1991, many left-wing revolutionary groups could no longer obtain financing and support from the Soviet Union or other state sources, and they turned to drug smuggling or other illegal activities to finance their activities. Examples include the Revolutionary Armed Forces of Colombia (FARC) and the Maoist Shining Path in Peru. Although secular antistate groups remained in the majority in many places of the world, various groups began to adopt religious ideologies, in part in an effort to combat atheistic communism. The most well known of these groups is al Qaeda, which, along with the Taliban, has thrived on the sale of opium and heroin. The terrorist network known as al Qaeda was formed in 1988 or 1989 as a kind of veterans' organization and reserve force for the training of future pan-Islamist combatants. After the assassination of one of its founders, Abdullah Azzam, in 1989, by unknown assailants, Osama bin Laden was able to take control of the group.

Once Moscow withdrew from Afghanistan, a number of al Qaeda fighters moved to struggle for jihad in Somalia, the Philippines, Bosnia (against Serbia), and Chechnya (against Russia). Afghanistan soon became a known haven for a significant number of Islamist terrorist organizations, harbored by the Taliban by 1996. In 1991, bin Laden himself had moved to Sudan, before returning to Afghanistan in 1996, where he began to more closely integrate his movement with that of the Taliban. Ironically, a number of groups, such as Hezb-e-Islami, founded by Gulbuddin Hekmatyar, who had received CIA training, plus the majority of U.S. and Saudi financial assistance, as funneled through Pakistan, began to turn against American interests.

Despite a significant number of Al Qaeda attacks during the Clinton administration, the latter was unable to convince the incoming George W. Bush administration of the significance of these new threats, as the new administration appeared to be more concerned with Saddam Hussein in Iraq. It was only after the September 11, 2001, attacks on the World Trade Center and Pentagon that the Bush administration sought both UN legitimacy and NATO military support in order to act forcefully against what it considered major threats. The Bush administration then declared a "global war on terror" (GWOT), which was granted international legitimacy on September 12, 2001, by means of UN Security Council (UNSC) Resolution 1368. This resolution characterized the September 11 attacks as a "threat to international peace and security" and reaffirmed "the inherent right of self-defense." It was presented to the UN Security Council by France, and Russian influence helped obtain the support of China. UN Resolution 1373 then established a UN Counter-Terrorism Committee and reaffirmed the need to combat by all means, in accordance with the Charter of the United Nations, threats to international peace and security caused by terrorist acts.

In effect, from 1963 to 2000, both the international and American governmental response to antistate terrorism was largely piecemeal. The UN and international law tended to focus on different actions such as plane hijacking, hostage taking, airport security, plastic explosives, theft of nuclear material, protection of maritime navigation, and the financing of terrorism, among other issues of concern, but generally only after terrorist groups had engaged in some form of violent action.

The September 11, 2001 attacks impelled a long overdue improvement in global airport security, as well as greater security coordination among the United States, Europe, and other states around the world. At the same time, the 9/11 attacks resulted in U.S.-led military intervention in Afghanistan and Iraq, as well as actions against a number of terrorist groups with global reach—which some critics have criticized as wars of "strategic choice" rather than wars of "strategic necessity" (as claimed by the Bush administration).

al Qaeda

While guerilla warfare throughout the Cold War had represented an unconventional strategy of "hit and run," al Qaeda's tactics represented an innovation involving martyrdom and "hit but not run." This approach turned commercial airliners into weapons of war.

In contrast with overseas Iranian-backed terrorism in support of such groups as Hezbollah in Lebanon, whose actions have generally been planned and controlled through Tehran, al Qaeda represented a highly decentralized, if not a spontaneous, phenomena (with possibly as many as 18,000 operatives in 60 countries). The group seeks to overthrow "corrupt" and "apostate" Muslim regimes, in part as a means to create an alliance against Israel, while simultaneously seeking to undermine American hegemony in the Middle East and the Gulf region. The offshoot al Qaeda in Iraq (AQI) has sought to destabilize the majority Shiite-led government that came to power in Baghdad after the U.S. military intervention in 2003. al Qaeda also seeks to undermine Russian hegemony over Central Asia and the Caucasus in support of Chechen independence from Moscow. (A number of Chechen groups have staged suicide attacks in Moscow and Beslan, for example, in protesting Russian control and military interventions in Chechnya.) al Qaeda likewise hopes to undermine French hegemony over North Africa, as well as Chinese control over former East Turkestan, now Xinjiang Province, in addition to seeking to infiltrate other regions with a historically strong Islamic presence, such as the Philippines.

Catastrophic Terrorism

Concurrent with the efforts of states to acquire weapons of mass destruction and nuclear weapons, antistate "terrorist" organizations and individuals have likewise attempted to obtain (and use) chemical, biological, or nuclear weapons. The Japanese sect Aum Shinrikyo, for example, used sarin nerve gas in an attack on the Tokyo subway in 1995. On the nuclear front, al Qaeda has allegedly had contacts with Pakistani nuclear scientists, and purportedly the group has sought to acquire tactical nuclear weaponry from the former Soviet Union. There is consequently a real fear that a terrorist group or other rogue elements might be able to acquire a tactical nuclear weapon, or some other weapon of mass destruction, or else seek to explode highly enriched radioactive materials with a conventional or "dirty" bomb. Another possibility is that terrorist actions could provoke nuclear-capable states into war, as almost happened in the May-July 1999 Kargil conflict between India and Pakistan. That extremely dangerous situation was defused in part due to diplomatic intervention by Washington.

The spread of nuclear capabilities to a number of states around the world raises the possibility that various terrorist groups or rogue elements in various states might soon be able acquire nuclear weapons capabilities and engage in threats of nuclear blackmail. The general situation led the administration of President Barack Obama to attempt to delegitimize nuclear weapons and press for the gradual abolishment of such weaponry. In April 2010, Obama held a Global Summit on Nuclear Security in the effort to make the Proliferation Security Initiative and the Global Initiative to Combat Nuclear Terrorism into durable international institutions. In addition, Obama hoped to strengthen the Treaty on the Non-Proliferation of Nuclear Weapons (NPT) in the 2010 NPT Review Conference as a means to stop the spread of fissionable materials that could be transformed into nuclear weaponry.

The Dilemmas of Global Terrorism

In effect, no general strategy, nor any truly effective policy, was developed to check the use of extreme violence by either antistate movements or by states themselves until after the September 11, 2001 attacks. The traditional response to antistate terrorist movements is violent repression, which, in addition to the financial costs, can carry with it tremendous costs in terms of civilian casualties (so-called collateral damage), particularly in the struggle against those terrorist organizations whose major tactic is a war of attrition in the hope they can split the population and ultimately wear the government down to achieve their goals, with as little expenditure as possible. The dilemma is that violent repression is not always successful, and the ability to repress antistate movements often depends on social and political circumstances.

One recent and apparently "successful" use of force (from the perspective of the Sri Lankan government) was the repression and capitulation of the Liberation Tigers of Tamil Eelam (Tamil Tigers), which had engaged in a long war of secession, largely in an effort to preserve power and control over Tamil language, culture, and interests. After a military campaign lasting from 1983 to May 2009, the predominantly Sinhalese Sri Lanka government defeated the Tamil Tiger opposition. Among several other Tamil organizations, the Tamil Tigers had been branded as a terrorist organization by more than 30 countries, having assassinated former Indian prime minister Rajiv Gandhi in 1991, and Sri Lankan president Ranasinghe Premadasa in 1993, in suicide–bomber attacks. The Tamil Tigers were among the first to use both men and women suicide swimmer-bombers as a techniques of assassination and attack.

The Tamil Tigers had been supported financially by the Tamil diaspora in North America, Europe, and Asia through use of the Tamils Rehabilitation Organization, which claimed to be a charitable organization, but which was nonetheless placed on the Specially Designated Nationals (SDN) list by the U.S. Treasury Department Office of Foreign Assets Control, marking the group as a supporter of terrorism. The effort of the Office of Foreign Assets Control, which lists hundreds of individuals and organizations alleged to be engaged in acts of terrorism, represents just one example of how the United States has attempted to cut off international funding of and prohibit transactions with individuals and organizations accused of engaging in terrorist actions—and to pressure other states to do the same.

The Tamil conflict also represents an interesting case study in examining why international diplomatic efforts can fail to bring peace. India and Sri Lanka tried to forge a peace agreement that would permit the Tamil Tigers a degree of autonomy, but this agreement was not accepted by all Tamil militants. In 1987, Indian peacekeepers were deployed, but they in effect became *peacemakers* in their efforts to disarm the Tamil Tigers by force until the cease-fire of 2001–2002, brokered by Norwegian mediators, was accepted. By 2005, however, the cease-fire had broken down, largely due to political divisions among the Sri Lankan leadership in response to Tamil Tiger demands for self-determination in areas where a majority of Tamils lived. The cease-fire was also hurt by concerns raised by Tamil Tigers regarding the "excessive" internationalization of the negotiation process, which the Tigers saw as strengthening the Sri Lankan government's political and economic position by means of providing international finance for development projects without adequate inclusion of Tamil Tiger interests. Following the breakdown of the cease-fire, the Sri Lankan government engaged in major military offensives in 2006, and the Tamil Tigers capitulated by May 2009. It is too early to say whether a peace settlement that can reconcile Tamils (and particularly the Tamil diaspora, who tend to support Tamil demands for secessionism) with the Sri Lankan government can be established in the long term.

Despite the capitulation of the Tamil Tigers in Sri Lanka, it appears that traditional approaches to the repression of terrorist movements *within* one state by police action or by military force have become increasingly difficult to achieve. This appears true given the new globalizing capabilities of antistate movements, coupled with their ability to utilize increasingly destructive technologies and tactics. In addition, the observation that one person's terrorist is another person's freedom fighter and that a number of antistate movements could be considered freedom fighters has raised critical political questions as to how to best determine which antistate movements may, or may not, possess a certain degree of social and political legitimacy. The answer to the latter question may then determine the best ways (through diplomacy, development assistance, co-optation, police action, use of special forces, direct military confrontation, or some combination) to best handle differing groups that threaten or use extreme violence.

With this in mind, it should be pointed out that three Nobel Peace Prize laureates were considered terrorists at one time during the careers: Menachem Begin, who was the leader of the Irgun when he fought for the independence of Israel from the British mandate; the Palestine Liberation Organization (PLO) leader Yasir Arafat, who struggled for Palestinian independence against Israel; and Nelson Mandela, the leader of the African National Congress, who struggled to abolish apartheid in South Africa. Each of these individuals believed himself to be a freedom fighter whose intent was to create a more just society. Other state leaders who were at one time considered terrorists during their careers include Jomo Kenyatta of Kenya, Archbishop Makarios in Cyprus, and Gerry Adams of Northern Ireland.

Due to the politically charged nature of the term *terrorism,* and to its increasingly globalized nature, it is not always certain that traditional military approaches can effectively attack or repress such groups, particularly those movements with strong popular or international support. These groups can often utilize the territories of neighboring states as a form of sanctuary. The Tamil Tigers, by contrast, did not possess any significant sanctuary outside of the island of Sri Lanka, and thus could be more easily contained by government military and secret police forces. Other antistate movements and groups have been able to cross borders to protect themselves, however. The Vietcong used neutral Cambodia; FARC guerrillas in Colombia have used bases in Venezuela; the Kurdistan Workers' Party (PKK) has used bases in northern Iraq for its struggle for Kurdish independence against Turkey (which has, in turn, crossed into Iraqi territory to counter the PKK); the Basque ETA in Spain has used sanctuaries in France; Hezbollah has been supported by Iran and Syria in its struggle against Israel in Lebanon; and so on.

In contemporary circumstances, U.S.-led forces rapidly incapacitated the Taliban in October–November 2001, yet they began to lose control over much of Afghanistan by 2006, in large part because the United States had focused most of its financial resources and military and counterterrorist capabilities on intervention in Iraq in 2003. In effect, most militant Afghan groups of Pashtun origin have opposed American backing for the leadership of Hamid Karzai, who was placed in power in Kabul in December 2001 under the UN-sponsored Bonn accords, in large part due to their perception of a lack of strong Pashtun participation in that government (despite the fact that Karzai himself is of Pashtun origin).

Toward the end of the Bush administration in 2008, and at the beginning of the Obama administration, the United States began to widen the war by countering al Qaeda and the Taliban in their hiding places in southern Afghanistan and in northwest Pakistan by the use of unmanned aerial vehicles (UAVs) or drone missiles that can strike when not expected, in addition to engaging in Special Forces operations. The Obama administration has also raised troop deployments to engage in counterinsurgency. Concurrently, while Pakistan has attempted to eliminate Al Qaeda and Taliban forces in northern Pakistan, Al Qaeda and a number of anti-Pakistan Taliban groups have sought to destabilize Islamabad by attacking police and military-intelligence compounds of the Pakistani Inter-Services Intelligence (ISI). In its crackdown on the Taliban, Pakistan has thus far tended to distinguish between those Taliban who oppose the Afghan leadership, while repressing only those groups who oppose Islamabad. In the meantime, the Afghan government and the United States have entered into a dispute as whether or not to negotiate with those elements of the Taliban, such as Mullah Mohammed Omar, who have thus far opposed the United States and the Afghan government. The United States has preferred to try to co-opt Taliban militants, bring them over to the side of the Afghan government, and then attempt to deal with the Taliban leadership from a "position of strength." The dilemma, however, is that it is not clear the United States and NATO can or will obtain a position of strength in the near future. As it appears difficult to see how these apparently intractable conflicts can be ended by the complete defeat of any one side, as has appeared to be the case with the Tamil Tigers, the question remains as to whether a resolution to these complex conflicts can ultimately be found through complex behind-the-scenes negotiations that will ultimately lead to reconciliation and power sharing, while simultaneously engaging in the use of force.

Another issue is that violence wielded by state leaderships (no matter how extreme) is often considered more legitimate (as was the case with the Sri Lankan government) than violence wielded by antistate movements, as the latter generally possesses no legal basis, or formal recognition by third parties. At the same time, however, violence wielded by "national liberation" groups has often been perceived as legitimate in the eyes of many developing countries or those states or populations (including diasporas) that believe in the cause of those antistate groups or political movements.

In April 1998, for example, the Arab League issued a Convention for the Suppression of Terrorism, which "rejects all forms of violence and terrorism and advocates the protection of human rights," but which likewise affirms "the right of peoples to combat foreign occupation and aggression by whatever means, including armed struggle, in order to liberate their territories and secure their right to self-determination, and independence and to do so in such a manner as to preserve the territorial integrity of each Arab country." On the one hand, from the Arab League perspective, armed struggle is legitimate for national self-determination (but not for "terrorism"); on the other hand, such struggle must preserve the territorial integrity of each Arab country. While justifying the Palestinian struggle, the latter statement in effect condemns the Kurdish struggle for national self-determination from Iraq, among other independence struggles within the Arab world.

The question raised here is whether or not it is possible to find political compromises that lie between demands for complete self-determination and demands to sustain a state's territorial sovereignty—among other apparently incompatible demands. In this respect, the conflict in Northern Ireland now appears to be one of the few conflicts involving acts of terrorism and counterterrorism that has more or less ended with a negotiated compromise between both sides, indicating that not all such conflicts are entirely intractable. With the Clinton administration working to facilitate an accord in the background, the conflict in Northern Ireland began to wind down following the 1998 Good Friday Agreement and the establishment of a power-sharing government by 2007. At the same time, however, the mix of the use of force and diplomacy that helped reach an accord with the majority of the Republican and Unionist parties helped splinter the Irish Republican movement between those willing to accept compromise and those who want to continue the struggle, such as the smaller hard-core factions that call themselves Real IRA and Continuity IRA. The resolution of the Irish struggle could nevertheless serve as a possible model for other conflicts for negotiated compromise and power sharing. Such an option failed in Sri Lanka, but it might not fail in other circumstances.

In addition to the essentially peaceful political resolution of the violent struggle against apartheid in South Africa (in which Nelson Mandela and the African National Congress had once been accused of engaging in acts of terrorism), and which did result in a power-sharing arrangement, another type of international diplomatic reconciliation took place between Libya, Britain, France, and the United States. In 1999, Britain opened its embassy in Libya and restored diplomatic relations, as did the United States in 2006 under the George W. Bush administration, thus taking Libya off the American list of state sponsors of terrorism.

Britain and the United States claim that Libyan leader Muammar el Qaddafi has changed his ways, that his government no longer intends to support international terrorism or develop nuclear weaponry, and that Tripoli has started to open to international trade and investment, particularly in the energy sector. (It appears dubious, however, that Qaddafi has ceased to repress his domestic political opposition.) The process of international reconciliation was assisted by the fact that Qaddafi had agreed to compensate victims for some of Libya's previous acts of terrorism, including the bombing of Pan Am Flight 103 over Lockerbie, Scotland.

Another reason that it is very difficult to coordinate international policy toward both antistate terrorist movements and state-supported terrorist actions is that it is very difficult to decide which groups might be fighting for a just or justifiable cause, and which groups might not be. In addition, it is difficult to determine whether certain groups or states might be willing to accept political compromise. The latter political dilemma is, at least in part, due to the fact that a number of states continue to engage in repression and acts of terrorism, while democratic states themselves are not necessarily immune to engaging in acts of violence, or even state-supported terrorism, in the effort to protect or assert their interests. In the realm of geopolitics, this dilemma may ultimately require finding ways to make multilateral political arrangements and diplomatic compromises among both conflicting states and antistate actors in a number of key hot spots throughout the world.

International Organizations and Terrorism

In this respect, in its 2006 Summit, NATO (which formally committed itself to peacekeeping and peacemaking in Afghanistan in 2003) declared that terrorism, coupled with the spread of nuclear weapons, is likely to remain the principle threat to the alliance for the next 10 to 15 years. As part of its campaign against international terrorism, NATO reached out to its former rival Russia to form the NATO-Russia Council in 2002, and the organization developed an action plan in 2004 in which NATO, Russia, and other partners could find areas of cooperation (despite their geopolitical disputes over the prospects of NATO enlargement to Georgia and Ukraine, and the August 2008 Georgian-Russian conflict).

By 2007, after giving support to the United States after the attacks on September 11, 2001 (but arguing largely for legal reasons for a "fight against terrorism," as opposed to a "war on terror"), the European Union (EU), in response to the attacks on the Madrid train system in 2004 and London Underground in 2005, developed its own counterterrorism strategy that covers four areas: prevention, protection, pursuit, and response. In 2001 the Shanghai Cooperation Organization (SCO) led by China and Russia, signed a convention that defined and interlinked terrorism, separatism, and extremism. One of the main aims of the Russian-led Collective Security Treaty Organization (CSTO) has been to coordinate approaches to international terrorism, collective security, foreign policy, and other issues. The question remains as to whether NATO, the EU, the CSTO, and the SCO can ultimately cooperate on a number of questions concerning terrorism, separatism, and extremism, due to their differing political perceptions and interests.

By 2006 the United Nations General Assembly began to develop a global strategy to deal more effectively with the origins and roots of terrorism. Then, in September 2008, all 192 member states confirmed their commitment to the principles of the strategy and pledged to pursue its implementation.

The strategy spells out concrete measures for UN Member States to address the conditions conducive to the spread of terrorism, to prevent and combat terrorism, and to strengthen their individual and collective capacity to do so, while concurrently protecting human rights and upholding the rule of law.

From this perspective, new policy approaches to acts of antistate and state-supported terrorism appear necessary and require more coordinated and multilateral diplomatic actions, particularly when military actions fail to bring about desired results and might prove counterproductive by potentially working to widen the conflict. Such diplomatic approaches might provide development and educational assistance through bilateral cooperation, from nongovernmental organizations, and from the United Nations or other international organizations, as a means to change social conditions and prevent human rights violations that help to foster recruits for antistate violence. Also needed is greater multilateral state cooperation in areas of police and intelligence, financial controls, immigration and border controls, and cooperation against the trafficking of drugs and illegal goods, in addition to efforts to prevent the spread of weapons of mass destruction, if not eliminate the ultimate nuclear "terror" altogether.

Hall Gardner

See also al Qaeda; Central Intelligence Agency; Counterterrorism; Department of Justice, U.S.; Freelance Terrorism; Hezbollah; Hostage Taking; Irish Republican Army; Law and Terrorism; Liberation Tigers of Tamil Eelam; London Underground Bombings; Madrid Bombings; Mossad; Nuclear Terrorism; Pan Am Flight 103 Bombing; Qaddafi, Muammar el; September 11 Attacks; State Terrorism; State-Sponsored Terrorism; Suicide Terrorism; Tokyo Subway Attack; United Nations; Weapons of Mass Destruction

Further Readings

Alexander, Yonah, and Michel S. Swetnam. *Usama bin Laden's al Qaida: Profile of a Terrorist Network.* Ardsley, NY: Transnational Publishers, 2001.

Beckman, James. *Comparative Legal Approaches to Homeland Security and Anti-terrorism.* Aldershot, UK: Ashgate, 2007.

Clarke, Richard A. *Against All Enemies: Inside America's War on Terror.* New York: Free Press, 2004.

Coll, Steve. *Ghost Wars: The Secret History of the CIA, Afghanistan and bin Laden, from the Soviet Invasion to September 10, 2001.* New York: Penguin, 2004.

Crenshaw, Martha. "The Logic of Terrorism: Terrorist Behavior as a Product of Strategic Choice." In *Terrorism and Counter-terrorism,* edited by Russell D. Howard and Reid R. Sawyer. 2nd ed. Dubuque, IA: McGraw-Hill, 2006.

Crocker, Chester. "The Place of Grand Strategy, Statecraft, and Power in Conflict Management." In *Leashing the Dogs of War,* edited by Chester Crocker, Fen Osler Hampson, and Pamela Aall. Washington, DC: United States Institute of Peace, 2007.

Ferguson, Niall. "Clashing Civilizations or Mad Mullahs: The United States between Formal and Informal Empire." In *The Age of Terror: America and the World after September 11,* edited by Strobe Talbott and N. Chanda. New York: Basic Books, 2001.

Gardner, Hall. *American Global Strategy and the "War on Terrorism."* Aldershot, UK: Ashgate, 2005.

Gardner, Hall. "From the Egyptian Crisis of 1882 to Iraq of 2003: Alliance Ramifications of British and American Bids for 'World Hegemony.'" *Sens Public* 3 (March 2005). http://www.sens-public.org/spip.php?article114.

Géré, François. "Suicide Operations: Between War and Terrorism." In *The History of Terrorism,* edited by Gérard Chaliand and Arnaud Blum. Berkeley: University of California Press, 2007.

Hoffman, Bruce, William Rosenau, Andrew J. Curiel, and Doron Zimmerman. *The Radicalization of Diasporas and Terrorism: Proceedings of a Joint Conference by the RAND Corporation and the Center for Security Studies, ETH Zurich, 2007.* Santa Monica, CA: RAND Corporation, 2007. http://www.rand.org/pubs/conf_proceedings/2007/RAND_CF229.pdf.

International Crisis Group. "Tamil Diaspora Groups Should Move Away, Once and for All, from the Failed Agenda of LTTE." February 2010. http://transcurrents.com/tc/2010/02/crisis_group_full_report_the_s.html.

League of Arab States. "The Arab Convention for the Suppression of Terrorism." Cairo. April 1998. http://www.ciaonet.org/cbr/cbr00/video/cbr_ctd/cbr_ctd_27.html.

Naftali, Timothy J. *Blind Spot: The Secret History of American Counterterrorism.* New York: Basic Books, 2005.

Obama, Barack. "Remarks by President Barack Obama, Hradcany Square, Prague, Czech Republic."

Washington, DC: White House, Office of the Press Secretary, April 5, 2009. http://www.whitehouse.gov/the_press_office/Remarks-By-President-Barack-Obama-In-Prague-As-Delivered.

United Nations. "Convention on the Marking of Plastic Explosives for the Purpose of Detection." March 1, 1991. http://treaties.un.org/doc/db/Terrorism/Conv10-english.pdf.

United Nations. "UN Action to Counter Terrorism: Global Counter-terrorism Strategy." http://www.un.org/terrorism/strategy-counter-terrorism.shtml.

United Nations. "UN Action to Counter Terrorism: Implementing the Global Counter-terrorism Strategy." Fact Sheet, March 2009. http://www.un.org/terrorism/pdfs/CT_factsheet_March2009.pdf.

United Nations. "UN Action to Counter Terrorism: International Legal Instruments to Counter Terrorism." http://www.un.org/terrorism/instruments.shtml.

United Nations Security Council. Resolution 1371. September 28, 2001. http://www.unodc.org/pdf/terrorism/Global/en/1r1373en.pdf.

U.S. Department of Treasury. Office of Foreign Assets Control. "Iraq: What You Need to Know about U.S. Sanctions." ftp://ofacftp.treas.gov/fac_bro/iraq.pdf.

Uyangoda, Jayadeva. "Ethnic Conflict in Sri Lanka: Changing Dynamics." Policy Studies 32. Washington, DC: East West Center, 2007. http://www.eastwestcenter.org/fileadmin/stored/pdfs/PS032.pdf.

Wiktorowisz, Quintan. "A Geneology of Radical Islam." In *Terrorism and Counter-terrorism*, edited by Russell D. Howard and Reid R. Sawyer. 2nd ed. Dubuque, IA: McGraw-Hill, 2006.

Wright, Lawrence. *The Looming Tower: Al-Qaida and the Road to 9/11.* New York: Knopf, 2006.

INTERNET

See Cyberterrorism

INTERROGATION TECHNIQUES

Acquiring information from an adversary has evolved into an art form. The variables in interrogation techniques are as diverse as its venues. Methods used in interrogation typically vary according to three factors: whether or not an adversary is in custody; whether or not an adversary is to be charged with a crime; and whether or not an adversary is on a nation's own soil. The methods vary because the law pertaining to each situation is different.

Black's Law Dictionary defines interrogation as "questioning a person arrested or suspected to seek solution of a crime." However, this definition does not apply well to all situations, and it particularly does not fit an intelligence-seeking interrogation by a non-law-enforcement agency such as the Central Intelligence Agency or the U.S. Army. For example, is any questioning regarding a criminal act necessarily interrogation, regardless of whether or not a person suspected of a crime is in custody? What if a person in custody is suspected of committing a crime such as a terrorist act, but no criminal charges will be sought? According to legal principles and terms of art in law enforcement and intelligence operations, the answers are murky. The following entry assesses the standard and broadly accepted aspects of interrogation; more controversial practices are discussed in a separate entry (see Torture Debate).

Criminal Interrogation

In the United States, those who are suspected of domestic violations are protected by a labyrinth of laws. Even with the best of law enforcement intentions, the courts may rule that the confession of a criminal suspect (including a terrorist) is inadmissible because of a change in law since the time of arrest. Often, however, law enforcement errs on the side of caution and goes beyond minimum requirements in interrogation law in order to avoid later complications in court. The game of criminal interrogation has become an exercise in guile and trickery, in which law enforcement officers often utilize methods of misdirection and deception to acquire incriminating statements from criminal defendants. Going beyond these limits—into the realm of physical intimidation, for example—may violate a suspect's civil rights, meaning that any information gained would not be admissible in court. Furthermore, interrogators who cross the line may face federal criminal charges as well.

The first thing to remember about interrogating terrorist suspects is that in most venues there is not a specific crime called *terrorism*. In the criminal justice system, this term more often appears as a motive or aggravating factor in the commission of a crime, such as murder, arson, hijacking, kidnapping, and so on. In domestic terror cases, U.S. law must be used to prosecute those charged as criminal suspects. There is no constitutional exception in criminal law for the treatment of terrorist suspects as criminal defendants, although crossing an international border to commit an act of terrorism may be perceived by the U.S. Department of Defense (DOD) and the U.S. Department of Justice (DOJ) as an act of war, as occurred in the jurisdictional debate over 2009 Christmas bomber Umar Farouk Abdulmutallab. Abdulmutallab is accused of attempting to explode an incendiary device onboard a commercial airliner flying over Detroit. He was immediately arrested and advised of his "Miranda rights" by the FBI, a move that inspired some controversy afterward. If intelligence agents seek information from a suspect that will not used at a criminal trial, Miranda rights are not necessary before interrogation. However, once a suspect is warned that anything he or she says can be used as evidence in court, intelligence agents may be bound to comply with Miranda. Once a suspect is in custody and under interrogation, and Miranda has been invoked, that person is entitled to have an attorney present during any questioning. Further fueling the controversy over Abdulmutallab is the question of whether or not the DOD has any jurisdiction in domestic terror. This question arises because the contemporary "war on terror" is not fought against state actors but against individuals and groups. Therefore, terrorists as criminal suspects, apprehended inside U.S. borders and charged with law violations, are protected by the U.S. Constitution.

In interrogating a criminal suspect such as a terrorist, domestic law enforcement must apply the provisions of the U.S. Supreme Court's ruling in *Miranda v. Arizona* (1966). According to *Miranda*, a suspect in custody who is being questioned regarding participation in a criminal act is protected by the Fifth, Sixth, and Fourteenth Amendments to the Constitution. Therefore, suspects must be informed that they cannot be forced to provide self-incriminating testimony, and that they have the right to remain silent, because anything one says to law enforcement officers during interrogation can be repeated by the police in court. In addition, a person may have an attorney

present during questioning and, once formally charged with a crime, if a suspect cannot afford an attorney, the court will appoint one to serve as counsel on the defendant's behalf.

It is important to understand that in its *Miranda* decision, the Supreme Court wrote that custody and interrogation are both required for a suspect to be informed of so-called Miranda rights before interrogation. This was affirmed in *Oregon v. Mathiason* (1977). In that case, a criminal suspect was interviewed by a law enforcement officer, but the suspect was never in custody. The Supreme Court ruled that, although law enforcement asked questions regarding the guilt of the suspect, because he was never in custody, Miranda rights were not required.

There are circumstances in which law enforcement may deliberately choose not to interrogate a person under the cover of *Miranda*, such as if the person questioned is not under any suspicion of wrongdoing; if the crime involves public safety, such as the location of a terrorist bomb or discarded weapon; if a suspect is not in custody during the time of questioning; or if the information sought is not intended to be used as evidence in a criminal prosecution. The last of these possibilities opens the door to acquiring information for intelligence analysis purposes alone, which is vital in counterterrorism.

Interrogation for Counterterror Intelligence

Intelligence is broadly defined as "analyzed information." The prototypical intelligence agency, or the intelligence arm of a law enforcement agency, collects raw information, processes (translates) and analyzes it with other information, and then disseminates the resultant intelligence product to policymakers for action. Because the information will never be used as evidence in court, there is far less consideration regarding the interrogators' acquisition methods. Information acquired by stealth and guile, through intercepts and espionage, and through clandestine and covert operations are all fair game for intelligence agencies.

Nevertheless, interrogations must be conducted within the scope of U.S. law if the questioning occurs inside U.S. borders. Once outside the country, however, there is no constitutional restraint on U.S. agents. Within the four intelligence varieties—foreign, defense, criminal, and commercial/ industrial—only those involved in domestic information collection need be concerned with domestic interrogation conforming to U.S. law. Agencies collecting information outside U.S. borders have often done so with impunity and without regard to the laws of the foreign nation involved. Therefore, U.S. intelligence agencies have participated in information collection activities outside the United States that might be considered civil rights violations if the same conduct had occurred inside U.S. borders.

Since 1999, to avoid political complications and accusation of human rights violations, U.S. intelligence agencies (and those of its allies in the "war on terror") have begun to adopt stricter interrogation policies. As an example, the U.S. Army recommends that it is beneficial to know as much about a person as is practical before that person is subjected to an interrogation designed to acquire information for intelligence analysis. In its field manual titled *Intelligence Interrogation*, the Army notes that "people tend to: talk, especially after a harrowing experience; show deference when confronted with superior authority; rationalize acts about which they feel guilty . . . ; cooperate with those who have control over them; appreciate flattery and exoneration from guilt; resent having someone or something they respect belittled . . . ; respond to kindness and understanding; and cooperate readily when given material rewards." A successful interrogator most often will utilize direct, incentive, emotional, fear (escalating or de-escalating), and ego approaches to motivate the interrogated to provide information.

Interrogation Methods

It is not unusual for someone to withhold information from a government interrogator, whether or not the subject is the focus of an investigation. There are a number of practical methods by which information can be sought and misinformation can be detected. Interpretations of body and eye movements are one such method. For example, an interrogator may observe fluttering eyelids associated with a person's answer, which is a signal of deception. Other subtle deception clues include covering one's mouth while speaking, looking up when answering, looking away when answering, or leaning away from the interrogator, to name a few.

Verbal clues also can indicate deception. For example, phrases that begin with "honestly,"

immediately suggest deception shall soon follow. A successful interrogator pays close attention to details offered, especially in regard to time line, days and dates, names and relationships, and who participated in what. In intelligence collection, organizational details are often sought, such as structure (hierarchy) and systems (operations) details. Because any of these details can be complicated, the successful interrogator will note any inconsistencies, which can be used in confronting the subject at a later point.

Rationalization works well in disarming a subject psychologically. An interrogator can suggest that he understands why a person would join an organization, commit a crime, affiliate with a terrorist organization, and so on. Once the subject is comfortable with the interrogator as a like-minded individual, he is more likely to cooperate. This is a common facet of criminal interrogations, particularly in crimes of violence. The U.S. Army also suggests that rationalization is valuable in interrogating terrorists.

The weakest link in a multiple subject interrogation is nearly always the youngest and most inexperienced of the lot. Whereas an experienced terrorist may have training in counterintelligence, perhaps offering bad information to an interrogator, a younger, less experienced terrorist may be more likely to yield to the pressure of a professional interrogation. However, interrogators will often have to rely on trial and error in order to determine which member of a group is the weakest link.

Several machines are useful in lie detection during interrogation, although experienced interrogators usually prefer to use the devices as a method to eliminate truthful suspects, rather than identify a deceptive suspect. The polygraph, which has been in use for a century, measures respiration, blood pressure, and galvanic skin response. In addition, the voice stress analyzer (VSA), originally believed to be superior to the common lie detector, has come to the fore since the 1960s. Measuring "microtremors" in voice patterns, and how they vary in truthful versus deceptive answers, the VSA relies on how stress alters physiological patterns of the body. This concept operates much in the same way that polygraphs rely on stress-related variables. However, the singularity of measurement in the VSA (i.e., voice microtremors alone) is frequently criticized as being insufficient to produce a reliable result. Although the debate rages on as to which device is more effective, neither is sufficiently reliable to consistently produce scientific results that can be used as evidence in court.

Kenneth J. Ryan

See also Counterterrorism; Department of Justice, U.S.; Forensic Science and Terrorism; Law and Terrorism; Rendition, Extraordinary; Torture Debate

Further Readings

Alexander, Matthew, with John R. Bruning. *How to Break a Terrorist: The U.S. Investigators Who Used Brains, Not Brutality, to Take Down the Deadliest Man in Iraq.* New York: Free Press, 2008.

Bybee, Jay S., Assistant Attorney General. "Memorandum for Alberto R. Gonzales, Counsel to the President, Re: Standards of Conduct for Interrogation under 18 U.S.C. §§ 2340–2340A." August 1, 2002. http://news .findlaw.com/nytimes/docs/doj/bybee80102mem.pdf.

Lippman, Matthew. *Criminal Procedure.* Thousand Oaks, CA: Sage, 2011.

Meydani, Assaf. "The Interrogation Policy of the Israeli General Secret Service: Between Law and Politics." *International Journal of Intelligence and CounterIntelligence* 21, no. 1 (Spring 2008).

Miranda v. Arizona, 384 U.S. 436 (1966).

New York v. Quarles, 467 U.S. 649 (1984).

Sosa v. Alvarez-Machain, 542 U.S. 692 (2004).

U.S. Department of the Army. *FM-34–52: Intelligence Interrogation.* Washington, DC: U.S. Department of the Army, 1992. http://www.fas.org/irp/doddir/army/ fm34-52.pdf.

U.S. Department of the Army. *U.S. Army Intelligence and Interrogation Handbook.* Guildford, CT: Lyons Press, 2005.

INTIFADA

The word *intifada* is Arabic for "shaking off," but in the context of the Israeli-Palestinian conflict, it has come to mean "uprising." Between 1987 and 2005, two intifadas aimed to create a Palestinian state. The first began in December 1987 and ended with the September 1993 signing of the Oslo Accords, which provided a framework for peace negotiations between Israel and the Palestinians. The second ("al-Aqsa") intifada began in September 2000. Although no single event signaled its end, most analysts agree that it had run its course by late 2005.

The proximate causes of the first intifada were intensified Israeli land expropriation and settlement construction in the West Bank and Gaza after the electoral victory of the right-wing Likud party in 1977; increasing Israeli repression in response to heightened Palestinian protests since 1982; the emergence of a new cadre of local Palestinian activists who challenged the leadership of the Palestine Liberation Organization (PLO)—a process aided by Israel's stepped-up attempts to repress political activism and break the PLO's ties to the occupied territories in the early 1980s; and, in reaction to the 1982 Israeli invasion of Lebanon, the emergence of a strong peace camp on the Israeli side, which many Palestinians thought provided a basis for change in Israeli policy. With motivation, means, and perceived opportunity in place, only a precipitant was required for collective action. This took the form of a fatality involving a military vehicle that was rumored to be an act of Israeli revenge for a stabbing a few days earlier.

Most of the Palestinian rioting took place during the intifada's first year, after which a shift occurred, from throwing rocks and Molotov cocktails to attacking with rifles, hand grenades, and explosives. The shift occurred mainly because of the severity of Israeli military and police repression, which intensified after Palestinian attacks became more violent. According to data from B'Tselem, the Israeli Information Center for Human Rights in the Occupied Territories, 1,265 deaths due to collective violence occurred during the 69 months of the first intifada, nearly 90 percent of them Palestinian.

Pragmatism crystallized alongside the violence. In 1988 the PLO accepted American conditions for opening a dialogue: the rejection of terrorism, recognition of Israel's right to exist, and the acceptance of UN Security Council Resolution 242, calling for Israel's withdrawal to its pre-1967 borders. With the intifada proving to be politically and economically damaging to Israel, a new Israeli government was elected in 1992 with a mandate to sue for peace. The United States pressured both sides to come to the bargaining table, and negotiations resulted in the signing of the Oslo Accords in

1993. The accords reiterated the PLO's 1988 commitments, while Israel recognized the PLO as the Palestinian people's legitimate representative, agreed to withdraw in stages from the West Bank and Gaza, and allowed the creation of a Palestinian Authority (PA) to govern those areas. Outstanding matters were to be settled over the next five years.

Just as the PLO turned to pragmatism, however, a new organization, Hamas, turned in the opposite direction, articulating a vision of an Islamic state in all of historic Palestine. In 1993, Hamas rejected the Oslo Accords and, in a move to scuttle peace talks, initiated a series of suicide attacks against Israeli targets. Twenty such bombings occurred between 1993 and 1997, killing 175 Israelis and their attackers. Israel retaliated, but in a focused way. Some 635 fatalities due to collective violence were recorded in the 84 months between the signing of the Oslo Accords and the beginning of the second intifada, just 40 percent of the monthly fatality rate during the first intifada. The ratio of Palestinian to Israeli deaths was a relatively low 1.6 to 1, and talks continued.

Israel continued to build settlements in the occupied territories during the Oslo lull, and the Palestinians tried to force the issue by importing arms and building up security forces, in violation of the terms of the accords. As a result, talks broke down in 2000 in a wave of frustration and mutual recrimination. Shortly afterward, the prime ministerial candidate Ariel Sharon visited the esplanade of al Aqsa Mosque as an assertion of Israel's sovereignty over Islam's third holiest site. Rioting broke out, Israeli police responded with lethal force, and unrest quickly spread throughout the occupied territories. The second intifada had begun.

The second intifada was much more violent than the first, and the ratio of Palestinian to Israeli deaths due to collective violence was much less skewed. Over 64 months, 4,361 fatalities were registered, for a monthly fatality rate 3.7 times higher than that during the first intifada. The ratio of Palestinian to Israeli deaths was 3.4 to 1, largely because 138 suicide bombings took the lives of 657 Israelis and their attackers.

In March 2002, following an especially horrific suicide bombing that killed 30 people and injured 140, the Israeli army launched Operation Defensive Shield. Some 20,000 troops reoccupied the West Bank and part of Gaza in order to "crush all forms and all elements of the terrorist infrastructure," in the words of the defense minister. A year later, Israel started building a physical and electronic separation barrier in the West Bank to prevent suicide attacks. Completion of a similar barrier in Gaza in 1996 ensured that only a fifth of the suicide attacks were launched from Gaza during the second intifada, and the new barrier soon proved similarly effective in the West Bank. Also helping to suppress the uprising were some 210 state-directed assassinations of Palestinian military operatives and political leaders.

Although the violence had nearly petered out by 2005, the conditions causing it had in some respects worsened. Israeli settlement activity in the West Bank continued, and tight controls were placed on the movement of Palestinian goods and people, stifling economic growth. Negotiations were at a standstill. In addition, the Palestinian Authority lost support amid charges of widespread corruption. Many Palestinians now turned to Hamas, which won the 2006 legislative elections and took power by force in Gaza in 2007. The two intifadas resulted in the deaths of more than 5,000 Palestinians and 1,400 Israelis.

Robert J. Brym and Bader Araj

See also Arafat, Yasir; Hamas; Palestine Liberation Organization

Further Readings

Beitler, Ruth Margolies. *The Path to Mass Rebellion: An Analysis of Two Intifadas.* Lanham, MD: Lexington Books, 2004.

Jamal, Amal. *The Palestinian National Movement: Politics of Contention, 1967–2005.* Bloomington: Indiana University Press, 2005.

Kurz, Anat N. *The Palestinian Uprisings: War with Israel, War at Home.* Tel Aviv: Institute for National Security Studies, 2009.

IRANIAN HOSTAGE CRISIS

Beginning in late 1979, Iranian radicals held 52 Americans hostage for a grueling 444 days. Americans hungry for news of the hostages

294 Iranian Hostage Crisis

watched television reports and taped statements from the captives, and their safety and return became a national focus. The inability of the administration of President Jimmy Carter to quickly master the crisis is often cited as a main cause for Carter's loss to Ronald Reagan in the 1980 presidential elections.

The crisis developed in the midst of Iran's Islamic revolution, after the U.S.-supported Shah Muhammad Reza Shah Pahlevi fled the country in January 1979. Ayatollah Ruhollah Khomeini, living in exile in Paris, returned to Tehran in February, and anti-American sentiment reached a fever pitch. The hostage crisis began soon after the United States permitted the shah to enter the country for cancer treatment in October 1979.

On November 4, a crowd of about 500 radical students occupied the U.S. embassy in Tehran, taking embassy employees hostage. The students soon had the backing of Khomeini and most of the government, and they demanded concessions from the United States and Iran's former monarch. After capturing approximately 90 people inside the embassy, the captors freed most of the women, non-Americans, and blacks. They held the remaining 52, many of them elderly diplomats, hostage until January 1981.

Television screens across the United States broadcast images of the hostages nearly every night and showed video messages released by the kidnappers. Soon after the hostages were taken, the ABC television network began a nightly report called *America Held Hostage;* the show's name was changed in the spring of 1980 to *Nightline.* The hostages were often shown handcuffed and blindfolded, growing thinner as the ordeal continued. Two Christmases in a row, Kathryn Koob, director of the Iran-America Society, looked into the cameras to send a message home and gathered enough wry humor to report that she had finally solved her weight problem.

According to the captives' later testimony, many were tied to chairs, blindfolded, for weeks at a time. They worked to keep records of their days and even fashioned a coffee stove from a discarded tin can. At times they were separated into small groups and not allowed to communicate; at least one hostage attempted suicide.

In the winter of 1979, Penelope Laingen, the wife of hostage Bruce Laingen, tied a yellow ribbon around a tree in the front yard of her Maryland home. Millions across the nation followed suit, hanging yellow ribbons as symbols of solidarity with the hostages and hoping for the prisoners' safe release. However, Carter's diplomatic attempts and economic sanctions (halting oil imports from Iran and freezing Iranian assets in the United States) failed to bring the captives home.

Desperate Times

As the crisis dragged on, the administration called on the military. The United States launched a failed airborne commando raid called Operation Eagle Claw in April 1980 that ended in disaster after a rescue plane and a helicopter collided during a sandstorm in the Iranian desert. Eight people were killed in the accident. Without enough spare helicopters to continue, mission leader Colonel Charles Beckwith aborted the mission. The hostages later told the press that their treatment worsened thereafter. Carter took full responsibility for the disastrous attempt; Secretary of State Cyrus Vance, who had opposed the mission, resigned in its wake. Beckwith wrote in his memoirs that he had recurring nightmares after the failed mission.

In Iran, hard-line anti-Western clerics gained influence over moderates during the hostage crisis and justified the situation by documenting what they saw as U.S. actions hostile to Iran. The students who had captured the embassy published classified documents that revealed U.S. intelligence activities in Iran. In 1980, the shah died in exile in Egypt. After Iraq invaded Iran in September 1980, starting the eight-year Iran-Iraq War, the Iranian government became more receptive to resolving the hostage situation. The United States had broken diplomatic ties with Iran because of the ongoing crisis, and negotiations for release were brokered through Algeria. Iran demanded $24 billion in exchange for the hostages' release, later dropping that figure to $20 billion, and then $8 billion.

After months of talks, the hostages were released on January 20, 1981—the day of Reagan's inauguration as president. The captives, who had been held for one year and 79 days, were released after the United States unfroze $8 billion in Iranian assets. The hostages were brought to the U.S. Air Force hospital in Wiesbaden, Germany, for medical assessment and treatment before being flown home.

In 1991, eight of th... ...es signed a letter
demand... ...gress investigate
...aign delayed the
...gressional task

Erica Pearson

Claw

...e First Battle
...w York:

...n
New York:

...e Iran Crisis and
...h Radical Islam.
...ersity Press, 2005.

Holt, Pat M. ... ...esmanship; Lessons from
    Iranian Hostage Crisis." *Christian Science Monitor*,
    August 2, 1985.
Kennedy, Moorhead. *The Ayatollah in the Cathedral.*
    New York: Hill & Wang, 1986.
McFadden, Robert D., Joseph B. Treaster, and Maurice
    Carroll. *No Hiding Place: The New York Times*
    Inside Report on the Hostage Crisis. New York:
    Times Books, 1981.
Sick, Gary. *All Fall Down: America's Tragic Encounter*
    with Iran. New York: Random House, 1985.
Smith, Michael. *Killer Elite: The Inside Story of*
    America's Most Secret Special Operations Team. New
    York: St. Martin's Press, 2006.
Wells, Tim. *444 Days: The Hostages Remember.* New
    York: Harcourt Brace Jovanovich, 1986.

IRAQ WAR

The Iraq War is an armed conflict that began in
2003 with a U.S.-led invasion of Iraq to remove
the regime of President Saddam Hussein. It became
a large-scale campaign to establish a new Iraqi
political order in the midst of terrorism, insurgency, and civil war. It is generally identified as a
component campaign of the "global war on terror" that President George W. Bush initiated after
the terrorist attacks on the United States of
September 11, 2001. The U.S. combat role ended
in September 2010, and a full withdrawal of
American troops is mandated by the end of 2011,
according to an agreement between the United
States and the Iraqi government.

Origins of the War

The origins of the Iraq War are complex and
remain somewhat murky. U.S. military involvement with Iraq dates to the Iraqi invasion of
Kuwait in 1990. Backed by a United Nations-
authorized coalition, the United States defeated
Iraqi military forces and liberated Kuwait after six
weeks of aerial bombardment and a 100-hour
ground campaign known as Operation Desert
Storm in February 1991. Controversially, Saddam
Hussein was left in power, and international forces
did not come to the aid of Kurdish and Shia rebels
who rose up against the regime at the urging of
American leaders. However, his government was
subjected to intrusive UN weapons inspections to
ensure the dismantling of Iraq's nuclear, chemical,
and biological weapons programs; the imposition
of coalition-enforced no-fly zones over northern
and southern Iraq to prevent the Iraqi military
from threatening its own Kurdish and Shia Arab
populations; and a crippling regime of economic
sanctions that strangled Iraqi trade.

The harsh peace terms were clearly meant to
undermine Saddam Hussein's government, but the
Iraqi dictator maintained a strong grip on power
and continually challenged the international
resolve to contain him. Iraq periodically ejected
UN weapons inspectors and subverted the sanctions through black market oil sales. The United
States responded with aerial bombardment campaigns in 1993, 1996, and 1998, as well as regular
targeting of Iraqi air defense systems within the
area of the no-fly zones. However, it was unable to
compel the return of weapons inspectors after
1998, and the international sanctions regime
appeared to be gradually unraveling.

The international community's weakening
resolve to keep the pressure on Saddam's government led to substantial frustration in the United
States. Prominent national security leaders, mainly
Republicans but also many Democrats, argued for
more forceful policies and actions against the
Saddam Hussein regime. In 1998, the U.S. Congress

passed the Iraq Liberation Act, which stated an official U.S. policy preference for regime change in Iraq. The election of George W. Bush as president of the United States brought into power a number of policymakers who had served in government during the 1991 war and believed that it had been a mistake to leave Saddam in power.

After the September 11, 2001, terrorist attacks, Iraq returned to the center of the foreign policy debate. Despite a lack of Iraqi links to the al Qaeda terrorist group that carried out the attacks, senior Bush administration officials began to consider military action to remove Saddam Hussein as part of the military response. Although the United States first took action against Afghanistan, where the al Qaeda leadership had sought sanctuary with the support of the Taliban regime, the administration began to shift its focus elsewhere. In his 2002 State of the Union address, President Bush referred to Iraq as part of an "axis of evil," along with Iran and North Korea, aggressive rogue states that sponsored international terrorism and pursued the development of weapons of mass destruction. A steady drumbeat for military action against Iraq developed over the course of 2002. In a commencement speech at West Point, the president announced that the United States could not afford to wait for threats to develop, but would act preventively. The administration's National Security Strategy, released in September, repeated the declaration that the United States would use force against potential threats. Statements such as these were widely interpreted as justifications for targeting Iraq.

The primary case for war was Iraq's continued flouting of UN resolutions requiring it to submit to inspections of its dismantled weapons of mass destruction (WMD) facilities. The Bush administration pressed for enforcement of these resolutions as well as a new one explicitly authorizing the use of force if Iraq did not comply. U.S. and British intelligence reports emphasized Iraq's WMD capabilities, even though evidence was lacking: the reports largely assumed that Iraq's capacity to produce these weapons had not been affected by the years of sanctions and periodic bombings since 1998. The U.S. and British governments seemed interested in playing up fears about Iraqi capabilities as much as possible, and they resisted dissenting opinions that these were overstated. In

February 2003, Secretary of State Colin Powell presented the U.S. case against Iraq using this intelligence, much of which was subsequently found to have been false. Hans Blix, the chief UN weapons inspector, acknowledged that Iraq was being less than fully cooperative, but he noted that his inspectors had found no evidence of "proscribed activities" in their final rounds of inspections.

Yet the Bush administration's approach to generating American public support for a confrontation with Iraq also relied on other justifications. One was the false argument that Iraq had played a role in the September 11 attacks. There was little hard evidence to support this argument, other than an intelligence report of uncertain accuracy about a meeting in Prague between the lead hijacker, Mohamed Atta, and an Iraqi intelligence agent. Nonetheless, President Bush and other officials continually conflated the threat posed by al Qaeda with the threat posed by Saddam Hussein, generally invoking the prospect that Saddam would provide WMD to al Qaeda for use against the United States. Despite the lack of evidence, substantial segments of the U.S. population accepted at face value the claim that Iraq had some hand in the September 11 attacks and was linked to Osama bin Laden. Additionally, some elements of the administration argued that removing Saddam Hussein would help create a flourishing democracy in Iraq that would exert a powerful demonstration effect on the rest of the region. The assumption was that democracy would spread pro-U.S. sympathies and lead to a decline of terrorism in the region.

Despite the controversy surrounding the case for military action, it enjoyed substantial U.S. public support. In October 2002, the U.S. Congress passed a resolution authorizing the use of force against Iraq with fairly significant levels of bipartisan support (the resolution passed the House of Representatives 297–133 and the Senate 77–23). The administration's aggressive case eventually produced public approval of military action by a majority (near 60 percent) of the American public.

Gathering international support, however, proved to be a difficult matter. In early 2003, the United States and United Kingdom argued for a new UN resolution authorizing the use of force, but it was steadfastly refused in the Security Council by France, Russia, and China. (Resolution

1441, finding Iraq in breach of its obligations to disarm, was the seventeenth UN resolution against Iraq and had been passed in November 2002.) Other NATO allies, notably Germany, also vigorously opposed attacking Iraq. Global public opinion was strongly against war, with major protests across major world cities involving millions of people. The U.S. argument was undermined in March 2003 when chief weapons inspector Hans Blix reported that his team had not found evidence corroborating U.S. intelligence about Iraqi WMD and requested several additional months for more inspections before any new action was taken.

The Bush administration, however, had clearly already decided to take military action. After Blix's report, it declared that "diplomacy has failed" and that it would lead a "coalition of the willing" against Iraq. It warned the UN inspectors to leave in advance of military action. On March 18, 2003, President Bush issued a public ultimatum giving Saddam Hussein and his sons 48 hours to leave Iraq or face "military conflict commenced at a time of our choosing."

The Invasion and Aftermath

The military conflict began on March 20, 2003, with a series of missile strikes near Dora Farms, Baghdad, intended to "decapitate" the regime, based on intelligence about Saddam Hussein's whereabouts. However, the strikes failed to eliminate Saddam.

The invasion of Iraq, code-named Operation Iraqi Freedom, began on the morning of March 20. The military operation had been planned through extensive consultation between Defense Secretary Donald Rumsfeld and Central Command (CENTCOM) commander General Tommy Franks. Rumsfeld wanted the invasion to demonstrate the U.S. military's "transformation" into a nimble, flexible force capable of achieving rapid, decisive battlefield results. He had pushed Franks hard to reduce the number of ground forces used in the invasion far below those estimated in previous war games and contingency plans, and to emphasize speed above all else, bypassing potential nests of resistance to seize Baghdad and topple the regime. The invasion was spearheaded by the U.S. 1st Marine Division and the U.S. Army's 3rd Infantry Division, which swept from Kuwait

Thirty-foot-tall bronze sculptures of former Iraqi dictator Saddam Hussein sit on the grounds of the Republican Palace in the international zone located in Central Baghdad, Iraq. The sculptures once sat atop the towers in the palace but have since been removed, following the overthrow of the Saddam Hussein regime. Photograph taken during Operation Iraqi Freedom, October 2005. (DoD photo by Jim Gordon, CIV)

toward Baghdad while encountering limited resistance. British and other coalition forces took control in southern Iraq, while U.S. special operations forces in the north cooperated with the Kurdish *peshmerga* militia to eliminate strongholds of the Sunni militant group Ansar al Islam. Meanwhile, the United States initiated a major aerial bombardment campaign intended to "shock and awe" the Iraqis into surrender.

It quickly became clear that the Iraqis were not going to fight conventionally. The main source of resistance came from the Fedayeen Saddam, an elite paramilitary unit that conducted guerrilla-style attacks against the invading forces' less secure supply lines and rear areas. Most Iraqi forces simply melted away into the population, with some continuing to fight in civilian clothes. U.S. forces reached Baghdad in early April 2003 and captured it, after meeting resistance in initial forays into the city. However, there had been no decisive engagement with the Iraqi military, and the regime's leadership had fled to Sunni strongholds to the north. Despite ongoing harassing attacks, President Bush declared the end to major combat operations on May 1, 2003.

The fall of Baghdad revealed the key weakness in U.S. planning: there was no strategy for postwar Iraq. Under Rumsfeld's leadership, the Defense

Iraqi and Peshmerga army soldiers work together, searching locals who drive through Checkpoint 13, near Sinjar Sub-District, Iraq, March 4, 2010. Security measures were increased with the onset of the Iraqi election, which was happening in a few days. (U.S. Army photo by Spc. Jillian Munyon/Released)

Department had monopolized all planning for the conflict, but it had failed to develop sufficient preparations for what would happen after the invasion. The initial assumption was that Iraqi exiles would quickly take over the establishment of a democratic government and that the Iraqi population would react to the fall of the Saddam Hussein regime peacefully. U.S. forces had no specific direction for action after the fall of Baghdad; the plan assumed that they would be rapidly withdrawn over a period of weeks or months.

These best-case assumptions proved false, and the lack of planning proved damaging. Postwar management and reconstruction was handled in an ad hoc fashion. The Defense Department established the Office of Reconstruction and Humanitarian Assistance (ORHA) in January 2003 under the leadership of retired general Jay Garner. Yet ORHA never received sufficient personnel or resources and did not arrive in Iraq until late April 2003. It was promptly replaced by the Coalition Provisional Authority (CPA), headed by Ambassador L. Paul Bremer. The CPA would be responsible for governing Iraq until preparations for elections and an Iraqi government could be completed. Meanwhile, U.S. military forces were reorganized

under Combined Joint Task Force-7 (CJTF-7), led by Lieutenant General Ricardo Sanchez.

Insurgency and Civil War

Continuing low-level violence in Iraq grew into a full-blown insurgency over the course of 2003. Several factors contributed to this development. The relatively small number of U.S. ground forces in Iraq and the invasion plan's emphasis on driving to Baghdad as quickly as possible left swathes of the country, particularly in Sunni-dominated provinces in the north and west that had been strongholds of Saddam Hussein's Baath Party, unsecured. The invading forces had also not secured the vast stores of armaments Saddam had scattered around the country, and hundreds of thousands of tons of munitions were subsequently looted. A collapse of civil order, and a general failure of coalition efforts to restore it, allowed Iraqis to loot government buildings, banks, museums, and numerous other facilities in Baghdad, weakening the foundations for future governance and demonstrating America's lack of control.

Perhaps most important, though, were the CPA's first two orders. CPA Order 1 dissolved the

Baath Party and ordered that the future Iraqi government be purged of any former Baath Party members. Yet under Saddam's regime, Baath Party membership was a prerequisite for career advancement in virtually any advanced education or skilled profession. The de-Baathification order effectively banned any skilled Iraqi administrators from returning to their positions, leaving Iraq's civil institutions stripped of any human capital or capacity. Order 2 disbanded all elements of the Iraqi national security infrastructure, putting hundreds of thousands of armed men with military skills out of work. The Iraqi army had been expected to serve as a stabilizing force in most postwar planning, and U.S. officers were already in talks with Iraqi counterparts to bring back their soldiers to help maintain order; these efforts were undercut by the CPA.

The insurgency initially grew in the concentrated Sunni heartland, roughly bounded by the cities of Tikrit in the north (Saddam's home city), Ramadi in the west, and Baghdad in the east. This area also contained hotbed cities such as Samarra and Fallujah. Insurgent tactics initially consisted of crude roadside bombs, but the rapidly developed into more sophisticated and lethal methods. The capabilities of insurgent forces were first demonstrated in a major way in the August 2003 bombing of the United Nations mission in Baghdad, which killed the UN special representative Sergio Viera de Mello. The U.S. military response was to conduct sweeps and night raids for suspected insurgents, rounding up large numbers of Iraqi men without a developed means for determining who was actually an insurgent. At the same time, U.S. policymakers from President Bush to Ambassador Bremer refused to acknowledge the existence of an insurgency at all, referring instead to "former regime elements" or "dead-enders" perpetrating the violence. This narrative was largely undermined by the fact that even the capture of Saddam Hussein in December 2003 failed to slow the rising violence.

The insurgency comprised a wide variety of groups. The smallest and most virulent were the hard-core jihadists who identified with al Qaeda and eventually came to be known as "al Qaeda in Iraq" (AQI). AQI included both homegrown Iraqi jihadists as well as foreign fighters; its most prominent lead, Abu Musab al Zarqawi, was a Jordanian national. The larger body of insurgents, including

former regime loyalists, was divided among a myriad of Sunni nationalist groups like the 1920 Revolution Brigades. Others fought on the orders of local community leaders. Sunni insurgents initially established a haven in the city of Fallujah, west of Baghdad. The city became the focus of resistance to the United States and the fledgling interim government in 2004, when four American contractors were murdered while driving through the area. An outraged Bush administration ordered a Marine assault to retake the city, but it then ordered a halt a few days afterward when several Iraqi political leaders threatened to resign in the uproar surrounding the images of U.S. forces attacking the city. Fallujah was ultimately taken in heavy fighting in November 2004.

At the same time, Shia militia groups were forming and beginning to take up arms against Coalition forces. The Badr Corps was an Iranian-trained group associated with the Supreme Council for Islamic Revolution in Iraq (SCIRI), which at the time was the most well-organized Shia party. Increasingly significant though was the Mahdi Army (*Jaysh al Mahdi*, or JAM), a growing organization of fighters loyal to the upstart firebrand Shia cleric Muqtada al Sadr, the son of a renowned ayatollah assassinated by Saddam Hussein's government. Sadr initiated two significant uprisings against coalition forces in April and August 2004, revealing the mass appeal the junior cleric had among the poorer segments of the Shia population.

The United States failed to develop a coherent strategy to manage the insurgency and the challenge of militia politics. The CPA turned over sovereignty to an interim Iraqi government led by Ayad Allawi in June 2004, and Sanchez's CJTF-7 was replaced by a more substantial U.S.-led military command called Multinational Force-Iraq (MNF-I), led by General George Casey. Casey, working with ambassador John Negroponte and later Zalmay Khalilzad, came to the conclusion that the U.S. presence (including abuses such as occurred at the Abu Ghraib prison) was aggravating Iraqi resistance, and that the appropriate course of action was to transition control to the Iraqis as quickly as possible. The result was a rush to Iraqi elections, the adoption of a constitution in 2005, and an effort to train thousands of Iraqi security forces, though without sufficient vetting. U.S. security operations continued with only limited successes. Some U.S. commanders began to grasp counterinsurgency principles and apply them (most notably at Tal Afar, where the 3rd Armored Cavalry Regiment under Colonel H.R. McMaster secured what had once been an AQI stronghold). Yet without an overarching strategy, these successes remained isolated and failed to spark wider security gains.

U.S. strategy also failed to account for the emerging Shia-Sunni civil war that finally exploded into the open with the February 2006 bombing of the Shia al Askari shrine in Samarra. Bombings against Shia civilian targets by AQI served as provocations that prompted Shia-dominated Iraqi security forces and militias to crack down on Sunnis, frequently torturing and killing innocents. This struggle had been largely concealed, but after the Samarra bombing moderate voices were drowned out in favor of extremists urging retaliation and revenge. The cycle of violence accelerated through 2006, with thousands of Iraqi civilians being killed each month.

Yet U.S. leaders insisted that the transition strategy was continuing to go as planned, despite mounting evidence of Iraqi government and security forces' unreliability and, sometimes, complicity in atrocities. For the first half of 2006, the Iraqi political system was deadlocked over the selection of a prime minister after the December 2005 elections. The eventual pick was Nouri Kamal al-Maliki, a relatively little-known leader from the small Dawa Shia Islamist party. He was the compromise candidate, but the United States regarded him as weak and unwilling to stand up to the militant Shia factions and their militias that were wreaking havoc across Baghdad. The Iraqi government's lack of capacity led populations to associate more closely with militias or insurgent groups for protection, further increasing the polarization between Sunni and Shia communities. The United States seemed incapable of preventing Iraq from spinning out of control as public support for the war collapsed, culminating in the November 2006 Democratic landslide in midterm elections and President Bush's replacement of Defense Secretary Rumsfeld with Robert Gates.

The Surge and the U.S. Withdrawal

Against the advice of many of his confidantes, President Bush responded in January 2007 with a decision to adopt a new strategy with a "surge" of more troops into Iraq. He selected General David Petraeus, who had led a successful occupation effort in 2003 in northern Iraq as commander of the 101st Airborne Division and organized the writing of a new army counterinsurgency doctrine in 2006. Petraeus, with his deputy Lieutenant General Raymond Odierno, organized a new military approach that focused on clearing and holding neighborhoods and the surrounding suburbs of Baghdad. With the additional troops, the United States was able to forcibly impose a modicum of order in Baghdad neighborhoods while pursuing AQI and other insurgent and militia forces outside the city.

The troop surge was not the sole reason for the reduction in violence. Arguably, the most significant factor was the fact that AQI had alienated many of its supporters among the Sunni Arab population with its heavy-handed efforts to impose control over them. AQI's abuses, such as the murder of uncooperative sheikhs' families, produced a backlash that began in Anbar province in late 2006. This "Anbar Awakening" consisted of tribal fighters turning on AQI fighters with the support of U.S. forces. General Petraeus and his subordinates recognized the significance of this development and encouraged the spread of the Awakening movement into Baghdad in the form of U.S.-sponsored "concerned local citizens" or "Sons of Iraq" militias who manned roadblocks and provided neighborhood security. The Sons of Iraq groups were formed in an ad hoc fashion, but the ultimate goal was to transition them to Iraqi government control and into permanent Iraqi security-force positions.

The other significant factor was Muqtada al Sadr's order for his militia to stand down in August 2007. This occurred after a clash between JAM and the Badr Corps at a Shia shrine in which several worshippers were killed, provoking a popular backlash against militia violence. The JAM's marginalization as a political force was completed when U.S.-supported Iraqi military operations asserted government control over Basra in the south and the Sadr City neighborhood of Baghdad.

The American public's increasing antipathy toward the war spiked amid the high casualties of the surge, and substantial polarizing attention was directed upon General Petraeus's and Ambassador Ryan Crocker's testimony before Congress in September 2007 to report on the campaign's progress. But as security improvements took hold in late 2007 and 2008, U.S. attention drifted away from Iraq and increasingly shifted to the worsening situation in Afghanistan. The Bush administration negotiated two key agreements regarding the future U.S. relationship with Iraq. The Status of Forces Agreement (SOFA) set the conditions for the withdrawal of the American military presence, mandating joint-only operations, a pull-back from Iraqi cities in June 2009, and a final withdrawal of all American forces by the end of 2011. President Barack Obama, elected in 2008, largely accepted the contours of this agreement, setting out guidance for a drawdown to 50,000 troops by August 2010 prior to the 2011 withdrawal.

The second agreement is the Strategic Framework Agreement, which lays out areas for U.S.-Iraqi cooperation on security, political and economic development, and numerous other issues. The U.S. relationship with Iraq will increasingly be politically, rather than militarily, driven. Iraq's politics continue to remain unstable and prone to violence, but as of late 2010, the country did not appear likely to lapse back into major insurgency or civil war.

Brian Burton

See also al Qaeda in Iraq; Chlorine Bombings, Iraq; Hussein, Saddam; September 11 Attacks; Zarqawi, Abu Musab al

Further Readings

Allawi, Ali A. *The Occupation of Iraq: Winning the War, Losing the Peace.* New Haven, CT: Yale University Press, 2007.

Baker, James A. and Lee Hamilton, et al. *The Iraq Study Group Report: The Way Forward—A New Approach.* New York: Vintage, 2006.

Byman, Daniel L. "An Autopsy of the Iraq Debacle: Policy Failure or Bridge Too Far?" *Security Studies* 17, no. 4 (October 2008): 599–643.

Gordon, Michael R., and Bernard Trainor. *Cobra II: The Inside Story of the Invasion and Occupation of Iraq.* New York: Vintage, 2007.

Hashim, Ahmed S. *Insurgency and Counterinsurgency in Iraq.* Ithaca, NY: Cornell University Press, 2006.

Iraqi women approach the entrance of a voting station in Faisalia, a neighborhood in Mosul, Iraq, January 31, 2009. (U.S. Air Force photo by Staff Sgt. JoAnn S. Makinano/Released)

Kahl, Colin H., Michele A. Flournoy, and Shawn Brimley. *Shaping the Iraq Inheritance.* Washington, DC: Center for a New American Security, 2008.

Mansoor, Peter R. *Baghdad at Sunrise: A Brigade Commander's War in Iraq.* New Haven, CT: Yale University Press, 2008.

Packer, George. *The Assassins' Gate: America in Iraq.* New York: Farrar, Straus and Giroux, 2005.

Ricks, Thomas E. *Fiasco: The American Military Adventure in Iraq.* New York: Penguin, 2006.

Ricks, Thomas E. *The Gamble: General David Petraeus and the American Military Adventure in Iraq, 2006–2008.* New York: Penguin, 2009.

IRGUN ZVAI LEUMI

The main Jewish underground militant group during Israel's formation, the Irgun Zvai Leumi (aka Etzel; IZL) is famous for blowing up the British administration headquarters in the King David Hotel in Jerusalem, killing 91 people.

Formed in 1931, the Irgun revolted against British rule over Palestine, demanding that the British leave the country and calling for the establishment of a Jewish state. The Irgun and other militant Zionist factions began a fierce armed struggle against Britain in British-ruled Palestine as it became clear that the Balfour Declaration of 1916, which promised the Jewish people a national home in Palestine, was being ignored. In 1939 the British signed what is known as the "White Paper," which limited total Jewish immigration into the territory to 75,000 through 1944.

In 1943, Menachem Begin, a former Polish soldier and Zionist youth movement leader, became leader of the Irgun. Begin would later become prime minister of Israel, and he was awarded the Nobel Peace Prize in 1978 for his work toward peace in the Middle East.

During World War II, the Irgun believed Germany to be a greater enemy of the Jewish people and ceased attacks on British military installations. Some Irgun supporters even joined the British army. However, not all Irgun members were in agreement about this temporary peace with the British. Avraham Stern declared the British to be the ultimate enemy and led a more extreme splinter group called Lehi, or the Stern Gang, to carry out attacks on British targets even as the fight against the Nazis raged.

After World War II, British troops blocked the arrival of Jewish Holocaust survivors seeking a refuge in Palestine. The Irgun resumed its attacks on the British and carried out what is now perhaps the best-known Jewish strike against the British administration in Jerusalem. On July 22, 1946, Irgun operatives set out disguised as hotel workers to place bombs hidden in milk churns inside the King David Hotel, where much of the British administration in Palestine was based. According to Begin and other Irgun commanders, the group made three phone calls to people inside the hotel before the blast in hopes of minimizing casualties. The British denied that they were warned. In any case, the staff of the government secretariat and military command remained in their rooms; the blast killed 91 people: 41 Arabs, 28 Britons, 17 Jews, and 5 others.

After the King David bombing, Irgun continued to fight against British forces, often brutally retaliating for attacks on Irgun operatives. In response to the executions of its men by the British, the Irgun captured and executed two British sergeants in 1947, leaving their bodies hanging on a tree. The British instituted a manhunt, and offered a £10,000 reward for Begin, dead or alive. A 1947 Irgun raid on a British prison in the fortress of Acre led to a spectacular escape, as more than 200 people broke free, including 41 Irgun and Stern Gang members. In a controversial attack in 1948, more than 200 Palestinians were killed by Irgun forces at the village of Deir Yassin.

The Irgun emerged from the underground in May 1948, after the proclamation of the state of Israel. Begin and the Irgun kept fighting independently, however, until June. After the Irgun arms ship *Altalena* was shelled by Israeli artillery on June 22, Begin accepted the authority of Israel's first prime minister, David Ben-Gurion. He transformed the Irgun into a political movement, the Herut, or Freedom, Party.

Erica Pearson

See also King David Hotel Bombing; Stern Gang

Further Readings

Begin, Menachem. *The Revolt.* New York: Nash Publishing, 1977.

Cesarani, David. *Major Farran's Hat: The Untold Story of the Struggle to Establish the Jewish State.* Cambridge, MA: DaCapo Press, 2009.

Duffy, Judith. "MI5 Feared Attacks by Jewish Terrorists." *Sunday Herald,* March 5, 2006, p. 17.

The Irgun Site. "Introduction." http://www.etzel.org.il.

Perlmutter, Amos. *The Contradictory Career of the Former Prime Minister of Israel: The Life and Times of Menachem Begin.* New York: Doubleday, 1992.

IRISH NATIONAL LIBERATION ARMY

The Irish National Liberation Army (INLA) is a Marxist terrorist group formed in 1974 with the purpose of fighting for a united Ireland.

In the late 1960s in Northern Ireland, a conflict erupted between the province's Roman Catholics (also called Republicans or Nationalists), who wanted Northern Ireland to become part of the Republic of Ireland, and the province's Protestants (also called Loyalists or Unionists), who wanted it to remain a part of the United Kingdom. The resurgence of violence in the 1960s brought about a revival of the Irish Republican Army (IRA), a paramilitary group originally formed in 1919. The modern IRA split into two factions in late 1969. One, calling itself the Provisional IRA, went on to become the largest and most powerful of the Republican paramilitary groups; it is the Provisional IRA most people think of when they think of the IRA.

The other faction, calling itself the Official IRA, was less ideologically committed to armed struggle. The leaders of the Officials were leftists with Marxist inclinations; they believed that Protestant and Catholic working-class solidarity could overcome sectarian interests. The Officials were thus much more open to political solutions and inter-community dialogue. In 1972 the Officials declared a cease-fire, hoping to parlay their military strength into open political power.

Dissatisfied with the Official's continuing cease-fire, in December 1974 a small faction of Official members, who shared the group's Marxist beliefs but lacked their leadership's faith in the political process, formed the Irish National Liberation Army. The political wing of the INLA, founded simultaneously, was called the Irish Republican Socialist Party. At the height of its power in the mid-to-late 1970s, the INLA was estimated to have more than 100 members. It sometimes carried out attacks using the cover names People's Liberation Army, People's Republican Army, and the Catholic Reaction Force.

The Officials were displeased with the INLA's defection from its ranks, and a feud erupted between the two groups in early 1975. The first death attributed to the INLA was that of an Official IRA leader, Paul Crawford, in April 1975. In the years following, the INLA would be involved in several more vicious feuds, both with other paramilitary forces and within the group itself.

The INLA was responsible for several significant terrorist attacks, including the 1979 car bombing in a parking lot of the House of Commons that killed Airey Neave, a prominent Unionist member of Parliament, and the 1982 bombing at the Droppin' Well disco, which killed 17 people, 11 of them British soldiers. The INLA was also very involved in the 1981 prison hunger strikes led by IRA member Bobby Sands; of the 10 men who died, three were INLA members. In December 1997, three INLA prisoners obtained a gun and assassinated Billy "King Rat" Wright, leader of the Loyalist Volunteer Force, in the courtyard of the Maze Prison. Wright's death led to riots and a string of revenge killings both inside prison walls and beyond them.

On August 22, 1998, following the Omagh bombing by a splinter group called the Real IRA, the INLA declared a cease-fire. (Government security forces allege that INLA and Real IRA provided mutual aid, and they believe that the INLA provided the vehicles that the Real IRA used in the Omagh bombing.) The INLA largely maintained a cease-fire starting in 1998. In the fall of 2009, one of the founding members announced a permanent end to its violent activities, stating that the INLA "has concluded that the armed struggle is over." The INLA turned over its weapons in February 2010. The group is thought to be responsible for between 125 and 150 deaths between its founding and the cessation of violence.

Colleen Sullivan

See also Continuity Irish Republican Army; Decommissioning in Northern Ireland; Irish Republican Army; Real Irish Republican Army

Further Readings

Dixon, Paul. *Northern Ireland: The Politics of War and Peace.* New York: Palgrave, 2001.

Holland, Jack. *Hope against History: The Course of Conflict in Northern Ireland.* New York: Henry Holt, 1999.

Holland, Jack, and Henry McDonald. *INLA: Deadly divisions.* Dublin: Torc, 1994.

McEvoy, Joanne. *The Politics of Northern Ireland.* Edinburgh: Edinburgh University Press, 2008.

McKittrick, David. "The Afterlife of the IRA." *The Independent,* November 8, 2008, p. 22.

McKittrick, David. *Making Sense of the Troubles.* Belfast: Blackstaff Press, 2000.

Moriarity, Gerry. "Man Who Killed Billy Wright Dies of Cancer." *Irish Times,* June 30, 2008, p. 6.

O'Kane, Eamonn. "Decommissioning and the Peace Process: Where Did It Come from and Why Did It Stay So Long?" *Irish Political Studies* 22, no. 1 (2007): 81–101.

O'Regan, Michael, and Gerry Moriarty. "INLA 'Has Ended Armed Struggle' Says Statement from Organisation." *Irish Times,* October 12, 2009.

IRISH REPUBLICAN ARMY

The Irish Republican Army (IRA) is a terrorist organization originally formed in 1919 and revived in the late 1960s with the aim of reuniting the Republic of Ireland with Northern Ireland, a province of the United Kingdom.

Origins

When the IRA was originally formed, all of Ireland was a British colony. The majority of Ireland's population was Roman Catholic, Celtic, and nationalist—that is, desirous of independence. In the northeastern part of the country, however, the majority of the population was Protestant, of British or Scots descent, and intent on remaining part of Great Britain.

Under the leadership of Michael Collins, the IRA successfully instigated the Anglo-Irish War (1919–1921). The peace treaty that followed called for Ireland's partition: 26 Irish counties would become the largely independent Irish Free State, while the remaining 6 northeastern counties (Amtrim, Down, Fermagh, Armagh, Derry, and Tyrone) would become the province of Northern Ireland (also called Ulster) and be governed by a special parliament in Belfast.

A great number of IRA members were dissatisfied with the treaty—they wanted all 32 counties to be included in the Irish Republic. A civil war between the pro- and anti-treaty forces was fought during 1922–1923. The pro-treaty forces were victorious, but the IRA remained viable, although membership and activities gradually declined. The contemporary IRA regards itself as a continuation of the organization begun in 1919, with the same goal—a 32-county Irish Republic.

Revival of the IRA

Catholics were widely discriminated against in Protestant-dominated Northern Ireland, most notably in the arrangement of voting districts, distribution of public housing, and employment, particularly in the civil service. In 1967, inspired by the civil rights movement in the United States, the Northern Ireland Civil Rights Association (NICRA) was formed to agitate on behalf of Catholic rights.

Many Protestants (also called Unionists or Loyalists) felt that NICRA's protest marches and sit-ins were merely a covert method of stirring up Republican sentiment. They began to organize counter marches and protests. During 1968–1969, marches by both sides sparked riots. On August 12, 1969, a Protestant march in the city of Derry incited a three-day riot. The violence spread throughout the province and was particularly vicious in Belfast, where six people died and Catholic homes were burned. British troops were called in to restore the peace.

The IRA made a lackluster showing as a Catholic defense force during the riots; Indeed, the Catholic population warmly welcomed the British troops, viewing them as their only protection from the Protestant mobs and local police force, the Royal Ulster Constabulary (RUC). A crisis ensued within the IRA's depleted ranks. At a meeting of the leadership in late 1969, the organization split. One faction became the Official IRA, which was dedicated to accumulating political power that could be openly exercised. The Official IRA declared a cease-fire in 1972 and has largely been inactive since then (the cease-fire spawned the Irish National Liberation Army).

The second faction called itself the Provisional IRA, because its leadership and structure had not been formally codified. The Provisionals (also known as Provos or the PIRA) were committed to a military struggle as the only solution to Northern Ireland's conflict. They adopted many of the same structures as the 1919 IRA, instituting a governing body called the Army Council, organizing their forces into brigades (one for each county), which were further subdivided into battalions and companies, and associating with a political party called Sinn Féin, which had been associated with the original IRA.

Viewing the British military presence in Northern Ireland as the most important obstacle to Irish reunification, the Provisionals targeted British military installations and soldiers, the RUC and Northern Irish politicians, Loyalist paramilitary forces, and sites in mainland England in an effort to force the British to withdraw. Although the IRA viewed itself as choosing legitimate military and economic targets, in truth its campaigns killed far more civilians than security forces.

Rise of the Provisionals, 1969–1974

After its formation, the Provisional IRA began to set itself up as a Catholic defense force. Catholic neighborhoods in Derry and Belfast had become "no go" areas after the riots; neither the British Army nor the RUC was allowed inside them, a prohibition enforced by IRA snipers. Instead, the Provisionals patrolled the Catholic neighborhoods, conducting punishment beatings of petty criminals, and occasionally executing them.

During this period, the relationship between the British Army and Catholic residents deteriorated severely and IRA membership soared for two reasons: the 1971 introduction of internment without trial, meaning a suspect could be arrested and held for months without charge; and the events of January 30, 1972, a day known as "Bloody Sunday." On that day, members of the British Parachute Regiment opened fire on a crowd of unarmed civil rights demonstrators in Derry, killing 14.

Indeed, 1974 proved to be the worst year of the conflict, with 479 people killed and more than 5,000 injured. In March 1972, the IRA detonated the world's first car bomb in Belfast. On March 22, 1972, the British government suspended the Northern Irish Parliament at Storemont and instituted direct rule from London. The IRA regarded the move as a clear indication that it was winning and escalated the violence.

In 1973 the British government made its first attempt to establish peace, initiating secret talks with the IRA and public discussions with more moderate Unionist and Nationalist political parties. The result was the Sunningdale Agreement (which contained many of the same provisions as the Good Friday Accords of 1998). Protestant Unionists despised the agreement, however, and the Ulster Worker's Council launched a massive strike, effectively crushing Sunningdale.

The IRA did not see the agreement's failure as a setback. Ignoring the massive Unionist opposition, they felt the agreement's failure would make Britain more inclined to withdraw. Declaring 1974 the "Year of Victory," the IRA began a bombing campaign in Britain itself, hoping it would push the British to withdraw. Forty-three people were killed in the attacks on England's soil, 21 of those in the November 1974 Birmingham Pub bombing. The campaign, however, had the opposite effect. Following the pub bombings, the British Parliament passed the Prevention of Terrorism Act, which gave the police sweeping new powers.

In the years that followed, the British government began to change its anti-terrorism tactics. It abolished internment and launched a new "criminalization" strategy—reducing its military presence by restoring civil authority in the form of the RUC and treating terrorist offenses as criminal acts to be handled by criminal courts, not as a form of political rebellion to be put down militarily.

The Long War

By this time, the IRA had settled in for a war of attrition, known informally as the "Long War." Informants within the IRA ranks enabled the British to foil several attacks during 1975 and 1976. In response, the IRA undertook serious reforms, abolishing the structure of brigades and battalions, instead establishing small independent terrorist cells that were much more difficult to penetrate.

In support of criminalization, in 1976 the British government revoked certain special privileges that

IRA and other paramilitary convicts had enjoyed owing to their status as political prisoners. Republican prisoners launched a protest, eventually known as the Dirty Protest or the Blanket Protest, because of the prisoners' refusal to wear prison uniforms or empty their cells' chamber pots. The British government of Prime Minister Margaret Thatcher refused to negotiate with the prisoners.

In March 1981, after the failure of the Dirty Protest, Bobby Sands, an IRA member being held in the Maze Prison, began a hunger strike. He was soon joined by dozens of Republican prisoners, and the hunger strike began to attract international attention. In April, Sands was elected to Parliament, representing West Belfast. By September, however, he and nine other prisoners had died, and the British government acquiesced to some of the prisoners' demands. The political successes of the hunger strike, particularly the election of Sands, would prompt the IRA to become politically involved, using Sinn Féin to field candidates in elections; in the 1982 and 1983 elections, Sinn Féin secured more than 40 percent of the nationalist vote.

Militarily, the IRA began to suffer from the defections of the "supergrasses," a succession of captured IRA men who informed on their comrades in exchange for sentencing leniency. From 1982 to 1986, when the British security force relied most heavily on this tactic, hundreds of IRA men were arrested and convicted based solely on information supplied by supergrasses. However, the lack of corroborating evidence in many of the cases eventually led to most of the supergrass convictions being overturned.

Although the supergrass cases damaged the IRA's military capabilities severely, it was still able to carry out one of the most spectacular attacks in the conflict's long history, the October 1984 Brighton bombing, which killed five people and very nearly killed Prime Minister Margaret Thatcher and her entire cabinet.

Between August 1985 and September 1986, the IRA received approximately 150 tons of weapons and explosives in four shipments from Libya. Using the new arms supply, the IRA began attacking RUC stations in the rural counties of Armagh, Fermagh, and Tyrone. The aim was to drive security forces from the countryside, and thus establish a secure area from which to attack the cities.

However, British counterintelligence was able to thwart the campaign by ambushing an IRA active service unit on May 8, 1987, at the RUC station in Loughgall, County Armagh. Eight IRA members were killed, the most casualties the IRA suffered in a single attack.

From Stalemate to Peace, 1993–1998

Recognizing that the armed campaign had come to an impasse, IRA members began to seek a political solution. Beginning in 1988, the leader of Sinn Féin, Gerry Adams, started meeting with John Hume, leader of the Social Democratic and Labour Party, a nonviolent Irish nationalist group. In September 1993, Hume and Adams released a joint statement outlining the IRA's position on peace.

The British government, however, could not openly negotiate with the IRA, because the IRA had not declared a cease-fire and was conducting a bombing campaign in London at the time. In addition, it had already detonated a one-ton bomb in central London's financial district in April 1992, causing an estimated £750 million ($1.32 billion) in damage. Prime Minister John Major did begin talks with the Irish government and Unionist politicians, talks that resulted in the December 1993 Downing Street Declaration, a document that established important principles for opening peace talks.

In August 1994 the IRA declared a cease-fire. This preliminary move would allow Sinn Féin to participate in peace talks. Major's government then asked the IRA to begin a limited decommissioning, or disarmament, as a good-faith gesture. The IRA refused. For the next 18 months, negotiators fruitlessly tried to achieve some kind of compromise. On February 9, 1996, the IRA declared its cease-fire over and detonated a truck bomb at London's Canary Wharf, killing two people and causing millions of dollars of damage.

Not until the summer of 1997, after the election of Tony Blair as prime minister, did peace negotiations resume. (The Real IRA split from the Provisionals at this time.) On April 12, 1998, negotiations culminated in the Good Friday Agreement, which called for a new Northern Irish Parliament in which Catholics and Protestants shared power, a joint commission to oversee affairs between Northern Ireland and the Republic of Ireland, extensive reforms in the RUC, the early release of paramilitary convicts, and the eventual decommissioning of IRA weapons.

In the years since the Good Friday Agreement, the issue of decommissioning has several times threatened to destroy the peace; only in October 2001 did the IRA agree to begin destroying its arms. In 2002 it was revealed that at least 15 IRA members had made visits to Colombia, allegedly to train members of the Marxist terrorist group Revolutionary Armed Forces of Colombia (FARC). Meanwhile, the IRA has been implicated in several murders since 1998. Sporadic violence continues, and dissident IRA factions opposed to the Good Friday Agreement have attempted to rekindle the violence. Despite the fragility of peace in Northern Ireland, so far the cease-fire has held. In 2005 the IRA announced that it was permanently abandoning military operations, and three years later, the Independent Monitoring Commission, which monitors the peace process in Northern Ireland, found that the IRA's Army Council was no longer operational.

Colleen Sullivan

See also Birmingham Pub Bombing; Bloody Sunday; Bombings and Bomb Scares; Continuity Irish Republican Army; Decommissioning in Northern Ireland; FARC; Irish National Liberation Army; Real Irish Republican Army; Red Hand Defenders; Ulster Defense Association; Ulster Freedom Fighters; Ulster Volunteer Force

Further Readings

Bew, P., and G. Gillespie. *Northern Ireland: A Chronology of the Troubles, 1968–1999.* Dublin: Gill and Macmillan, 1999.

Dixon, Paul. *Northern Ireland: The Politics of War and Peace.* New York: Palgrave, 2001.

English, Richard. *Armed Struggle: The History of the IRA.* New York: Oxford University Press, 2003.

Holland, Jack. *Hope against History: The Course of Conflict in Northern Ireland.* New York: Henry Holt, 1999.

Independent Monitoring Commission. http://www.independentmonitoringcommission.org.

Kee, Robert. *Ireland: A History.* London: Sphere, 1982.

LaFranchi, Howard, and Mark Rice-Oxley. "The IRA Pledges a Farewell to Arms." *Christian Science Monitor,* July 29, 2005, p. 1.

McEvoy, Joanne. *The Politics of Northern Ireland.* Edinburgh: Edinburgh University Press, 2008.

McKittrick, David. *Making Sense of the Troubles.* Belfast: Blackstaff Press, 2000.

Mitchell, Thomas G. *When Peace Fails: Lessons from Belfast for the Middle East.* Jefferson, NC: McFarland, 2010.

Moloney, Ed. *A Secret History of the IRA.* New York: W.W. Norton, 2002.

O'Brien, Brendan. *The Long War: The IRA and Sinn Fein.* 2nd ed. Syracuse, NY: Syracuse University Press, 1999.

O'Brien, Brendan. *Pocket History of the IRA: From 1916 Onwards.* Dublin: O'Brien Press, 2000.

Shanahan, Timothy. *The Provisional Irish Republican Army and the Morality of Terrorism.* Edinburgh: Edinburgh University Press, 2009.

Sutton, Malcolm. *Bear In Mind These Dead . . . An Index of Deaths from the Conflict in Ireland, 1969–1993.* Belfast: Beyond the Pale Publications, 1994.

Taylor, Peter. *Loyalists: War and Peace in Northern Ireland.* New York: TV Books, 1999.

Taylor, Peter. *Provos: The IRA and Sinn Fein.* London: Bloomsbury Publishing, 1997.

ISLAMIC ARMY FOR THE LIBERATION OF HOLY PLACES

Possibly based in Germany, the Islamic Army for the Liberation of Holy Places (or Holy Sites) is a mysterious terrorist group that has claimed responsibility for bombings later proven to be the work of al Qaeda operatives; it is sometimes called al Qaeda's military wing.

The group was unknown until the U.S. embassy bombings in East Africa in 1998. On August 7, 1998, car bombs exploded nearly simultaneously at the U.S. embassies in Dar es Salaam, Tanzania, and Nairobi, Kenya. The blasts killed 224 people and destroyed both embassies. The Islamic Army for the Liberation of Holy Places subsequently sent statements to Arab news organizations claiming responsibility for the attacks. Many experts cautioned that the Islamic Army could be a new group trying to make a name for itself by taking responsibility for an action in which it had no part.

U.S. investigators soon declared that Osama bin Laden's al Qaeda network was responsible for the attacks and indicted 26 people. al Qaeda, an Arabic word meaning "the base," is an international network that employs violence to attempt to drive the United States from Saudi Arabia and other Islamic countries. The group uses a long list of pseudonyms in addition to Islamic Army for the Liberation of Holy Places, including Islamic Salvation Foundation, The Group for the Preservation of the Holy Sites, The World Islamic Front for Jihad against Jews and Crusaders, Osama bin Laden Network, and Osama bin Laden Organization.

The name Islamic Army for the Liberation of Holy Places surfaced again in April 2002, when a truck carrying natural gas crashed into a synagogue on a Tunisian resort island. The crash killed 17 people at the Ghriba Synagogue on the island of Djerba, a Jewish pilgrimage site and popular tourist destination.

The synagogue president and Tunisian officials at first called the crash an accident. However, the Islamic Army for the Liberation of Holy Places soon claimed responsibility, faxing a statement with corroborating details to two Arabic newspapers in London. The statement said that attack was in retaliation for Israeli crimes against Palestinians. The synagogue bombing is said to have been the first al Qaeda attack outside of Afghanistan since the September 11, 2001, attacks on the World Trade Center and the Pentagon. The Tunisian blast, like the Tanzanian embassy attack, used a truck filled with butane gas. Tunisian officials later said that the 24-year-old truck driver, Nizar Newar, had links to Islamic militant cells around the world.

Erica Pearson

See also al Qaeda; bin Laden, Osama; East Africa
　　Embassy Bombings; September 11 Attacks

Further Readings

Hedges, Chris. "Explosion at Synagogue Tied to Jihad;
　　Arrest Made." *The New York Times*, April 24, 2002.
Johnson, Ian. "In Europe and Asia, More Hints of al
　　Qaeda Ties." *The Wall Street Journal*, April 19, 2002.
McNeil, Donald G., Jr. "Family of Driver Killed at
　　Synagogue Denies a Link to Terrorism." *The New
　　York Times*, April 18, 2002.
Trounson, Rebecca, and Dexter Filkins. "Islamic Groups
　　Target U.S. with New Threats." *Los Angeles Times*,
　　August 20, 1998, p. A1.

ISLAMIC GREAT EASTERN RAIDERS

See Great Eastern Islamic Raiders' Front

ISLAMIC GROUP

See Gama'a al Islamiyya

ISLAMIC JIHAD FOR THE LIBERATION OF PALESTINE

See Hezbollah

ISLAMIC MOVEMENT OF UZBEKISTAN

The Islamic Movement of Uzbekistan (IMU, aka Islamic Party of Turkestan) is a coalition of fundamentalist Islamic militants from Uzbekistan and other Central Asian countries that oppose President Islom Karimov's secular government and work to establish an Islamic theocracy.

Founded in 1999, the IMU seeks to destabilize both the country of Uzbekistan and the surrounding region. Although it is not the only group to oppose the current government of Uzbekistan, it is the only group that has resorted to terrorism to achieve its goals. The change of name to the Islamic Party of Turkestan in June 2001 may have indicated an expansion of the original goal of establishing an Islamic state in Uzbekistan to the creation of Islamic states throughout Central Asia. The group has been active throughout Central Asia, especially in Afghanistan and Pakistan. IMU, as well as its offshoot, Islamic Jihad Union, has cooperated with the radical Islamic organizations al Qaeda and the Taliban.

The IMU initially conducted only small-scale armed attacks—car bombings and hostage taking—and initially it operated only in the Ferghana Valley on the Uzbek-Kyrgyz border. However, it soon became active in Kyrgyzstan, Tajikistan, Afghanistan, Pakistan, and throughout Uzbekistan. IMU members have been known to carry out their attacks in the open, withdrawing to villages and disguising themselves as locals rather than retreating to the mountains following an attack. The group is considered responsible for at least five car bombings in Uzbekistan in February 1999 and a number of hostage takings in 1999 and 2000. Among those taken hostage were four U.S. mountain climbers, four Japanese geologists, and eight Kyrgyzstani soldiers.

In November 2000, Uzbek courts sentenced the IMU leaders Tahir Yuldashev and Juma Namangani to death in absentia for the February 1999 bombings. Both Yuldashev and Namangani fled the country in 1999 for Afghanistan, where they recruited and trained militants under shelter of the Taliban. Namangani was killed in Afghanistan in 2001, and Yuldashev was killed in a U.S. drone strike in southern Waziristan in August 2009.

In the wake of Yuldashev's death, Abu Usman Adil emerged from a power struggle within the IMU to take over as its leader. Since then, IMU forces have concentrated on fighting U.S. forces and their allies in Afghanistan, working in concert with al Qaeda and the Taliban. Security officials believe that the IMU continues to control the drug trade between Afghanistan and Central Asia, using the profits to finance its operations. The group also receives support from other fundamentalist Islamist groups throughout Central and South Asia.

In the spring of 2004, an offshoot of the IMU, Islamic Jihad Union (originally Islamic Jihad Group), conducted a series of suicide bombings in Tashkent, the capital of Uzbekistan, that killed more than 45 people. Three years later, German authorities arrested three members of Islamic Jihad Union on charges of plotting a massive bomb campaign against U.S. interests in Germany; a fourth would-be bomber was later arrested in Turkey. All four confessed their role in the plot in 2009.

Richard McHugh

Further Readings

Abdurasulov, Abdujalil. "Afghan, Pakistani Conflicts Spilling into Central Asian States?" *Christian Science Monitor*, July 30, 2009, p. 6.

Jones, Seth G. *In the Graveyard of Empires: America's War in Afghanistan*. New York: W.W. Norton, 2010.

Rand, Robert. *Tamerlaine's Children: Dispatches from Contemporary Uzbekistan*. Oxford, UK: Oneworld Publications, 2006.

Rashid, Ahmed. "Interview with Leader of Hizb-e Tahrir." *Central Asia–Caucasus Institute Analyst*, November 22, 2000. http://www.cacianalyst.org/?q=node/248.

Rashid. Ahmed. *Jihad: The Rise of Militant Islam in Central Asia*. New Haven, CT: Yale University Press, 2002.

U.S. State Department. "Terrorist Groups." *Country Reports on Terrorism 2008*. http://www.state.gov/s/ct/rls/crt/2008/122449.htm.

Whitlock, Craig. "Germany Says It Foiled Bomb Plot." *Washington Post*, September 6, 2007, p. A1.

ISLAMIC RESISTANCE MOVEMENT

See Hamas

ISMOIL, EYAD

See World Trade Center Bombing (1993)

IZZ AL DIN, HASSAN (1963–)

For his alleged role in the 1985 hijacking of Trans World Airlines Flight 847, Hassan Izz al Din (aka Ahmed Garbaya; Sa-id; Samir Salwwan), a native of Lebanon, was placed on the FBI's list of most wanted terrorists. A hijacker convicted in the TWA case testified that Izz al Din killed a U.S. Navy diver during the two-week ordeal.

The FBI believes that Izz al Din returned to Lebanon after the hijacking. While he was tied to the Shiite Muslim militant group and political party Hezbollah during the 1980s, Lebanese officials have claimed that he is not currently linked to Hezbollah's party structure. (Although the U.S. government continues to regard Hezbollah as a terrorist organization, the group recast itself as a legitimate political party during the 1990s and holds elected seats in Lebanon's Parliament.)

According to U.S. officials, Izz al Din was one of the two hijackers who took over Flight 847 from Athens to Rome on June 14, 1985. The two men's weapons included a pistol and hand grenades they had smuggled through Athens airport security. The hijackers redirected the Boeing 727 to Beirut. After the plane landed, the hijackers called for the release of hundreds of prisoners, many of them Shiite Muslims, held by Israel. Mohammed Ali Hamadei, who was sentenced to life in prison in 1989 by a West German court for his role in the hijacking, testified that at this point Izz al Din shot U.S. Navy diver Robert Stethem and dumped his body onto the tarmac.

The plane eventually logged 8,300 miles, flying between Beirut and Algiers. The hijackers released some of the 153 passengers and crew held hostage each time the plane landed. Eventually, the plane stayed in Beirut while negotiations were under way. On June 30, the last of the hostages was released after Israel agreed to free 300 prisoners. The hijackers had also negotiated a flight to Algiers and freedom for themselves. The United States indicted Izz al Din, Hamadei, Imad Fayez Mughniyah, and Ali Atwa on July 3, 1985, on charges related to the hijacking. Hamadei was later caught in Frankfurt and sentenced to life in prison, while Mughniyah was killed by a car bomb in Syria in 2008.

Izz al Din has avoided capture for decades. Press reports in 1994 told of failed U.S. efforts to kidnap him from his Beirut home and bring him by speedboat to a U.S. warship in the Mediterranean. As of 2010, Atwa also remained on the FBI's Most Wanted Terrorists list. The U.S. State Department has offered a reward of up to $5 million for information leading to Izz al Din's arrest or conviction.

Erica Pearson

See also Atwa, Ali; Hezbollah; Mughniyah, Imad Fayez; TWA Flight 847 Hijacking

Further Readings

Berger, Joseph. "Hostages in Lebanon: The Course of Events; 8 Days of Mideast Terror: The Journey of Flight 847." *The New York Times,* June 22, 1985, p. A1.

Federal Bureau of Investigation. "Most Wanted Terrorists." http://www.fbi.gov/wanted/terrorists/fugitives.htm.

Jaber, Hala. *Hezbollah.* New York: Columbia University Press, 1997.

"A Nation Challenged: The Hunted; The 22 Most Wanted Suspects, in a Five-act Drama of Global Terror." *The New York Times,* October 14, 2001, p. 1B.

Snyder, Rodney A. *Negotiating with Terrorists: TWA Flight 847.* Pew Case Studies in International Affairs 333. Pittsburgh, PA: Pew Charitable Trusts, 1994.

Tucker, Neely. "$21 Million Awarded in Fatal Hijacking." *The Washington Post,* April 21, 2002, p. C1.

Jaish-e-Mohammed

Jaish-e-Mohammed (JEM, aka Mohammed's Army) is a militant Islamist group based in Pakistan. The JEM was founded in the late 1990s by Maulana Masood Azhar, a former leader of the ultra-fundamentalist Islamist group Harakat ul-Mujahideen.

Azhar was active in the Harakat ul-Mujahideen throughout the 1980s and 1990s. He spent time training with al Qaeda and fighting in Afghanistan during the Soviet occupation, and later he organized groups that fought alongside al Qaeda against U.S. troops in Somalia and Yemen.

The main aim of Harakat ul-Mujahideen, however, was to reunite Kashmir with Pakistan, and the group was responsible for numerous attacks on Hindus and Indian army troops in Kashmir. Pakistan's intelligence service is believed to have supported both Harakat ul-Mujahideen and other terrorist groups in their operations in Kashmir. Azhar was arrested by the Indian authorities in 1994 in connection with several attacks and held in a Jammu jail.

Azhar's supporters made several attempts to free him, including the 1994 kidnapping of U.S. and British nationals in New Delhi and the July 1995 kidnapping of Westerners in Kashmir. In 1999, members of Harakat ul-Mujahideen hijacked an Indian Airlines jet and flew the plane to Afghanistan. They demanded the release of Azhar in exchange for the 155 passengers and crew. The Indian government agreed to their demands and flew Azhar to Afghanistan; all the hostages were then freed and returned to India.

On his release, Azhar announced the formation of the Jaish-e-Mohammed and organized recruitment drives throughout Pakistan. About three-quarters of the members of Harakat ul-Mujahideen joined the new group. The JEM is based primarily in Peshawar and Muzaffarabad, Pakistan, but members are active primarily in Kashmir. Until the United States invaded Afghanistan in 2001, the JEM also maintained training camps in that country and was heavily supported by the Taliban and pro-Taliban groups in Pakistan.

In July 2000 the JEM launched a rocket grenade attack on the chief minister of Kashmir at his office in Srinagar. In December 2000, JEM militants threw grenades at a bus stop in Kupwara, India, injuring 24, and at a marketplace in Chadoura, India, injuring 16. JEM militants also planted two bombs that killed 21 people in Qamarwari and Srinagar.

The JEM was responsible for the October 1, 2001, suicide bomb attack on the Jammu and Kashmir Assembly in Srinagar that left 31 people dead, including members of the Indian Parliament. On October 11, 2001, Britain, Pakistan, and the United States froze JEM's assets. The next day, the group announced that it had renamed itself Tehrik al Furqan, and it moved all of its assets into new accounts. Azhar remained in charge of the new organization, which declared "the opening of jihad against the United States."

With the fall of the Taliban and a suicide attack on the Indian parliament by the JEM and another militant group, Lashkar-e-Taiba, in late 2001, Pakistani government support for the JEM temporarily evaporated. Pakistani officials put Azhar under house arrest in December 2001 and banned the JEM and other extremist groups the following month.

Declaring the Pakistani government to be in thrall to the West, the JEM then turned against the government of Pakistan. The group is suspected of having been involved in the January 2002 kidnapping and murder, in Pakistan, of the American journalist Daniel Pearl. Ahmad Omar Sheikh, charged with masterminding the abduction and murder, is a close friend and associate of Azhar. Nonetheless, Azhar was released from detention that December, indicating the ambivalent relationship the Pakistani government has with the militant Islamic groups that operate in Kashmir. Despite the putative ban, the JEM has operated openly in some parts of Pakistan, and it has continued to attack targets in Kashmir and India.

In addition, the JEM has targeted Western powers and is thought to have allied with al Qaeda. In August 2006, Rashid Rauf, who is related to Azhar by marriage and is believed to have been active in both the JEM and al Qaeda, was arrested in Pakistan. Rauf is believed to have been the ringleader of an aborted plot to bomb several airplanes simultaneously, using liquid explosives. Rauf escaped custody in 2007. He was reportedly killed by a U.S. missile strike in Pakistan the next year.

In 2009, four men were arrested in New York City for allegedly planning to blow up a synagogue in the Bronx, and for intending to fire surface-to-air missiles at military planes. One of the men, James Cromitie, reportedly told a police informant that he desired to do "something to America," and that he hoped to join the JEM.

Lisa Magloff

See also Afghan Arabs; al Qaeda; Harakat ul-Mujahideen; Lashkar-e-Taiba; Pearl, Daniel

Further Readings

Chand, Attar. *Pakistan Terrorism in Punjab and Kashmir.* Columbia, MO: South Asia Books, 1996.

Gall, Carlotta, et al. "Pakistan Confirms Many Details About Key Figure under Arrest." *The New York Times,* August 17, 2006, p. A15.

Ganguly, Sumit. *Conflict Unending: India-Pakistan Tensions since 1947.* New York: Columbia University Press, 2001.

Giyas-Ud-Din, Peer. *Understanding the Kashmiri Insurgency.* New Delhi: Anmol Publications, 1997.

Kumar, D. P. *Kashmir: Pakistan's Proxy War.* New Delhi: Har-Anand Publications, 1995.

Solomon, Jay, et al. "Battle Ground: Despite U.S. Effort, Pakistan Remains Key Terror Hub." *The Wall Street Journal,* July 22, 2005, p. A1.

JAMAAT UL FUQRA

Fuqra is an Arabic word that translates as "the impoverished." Jamaat ul Fuqra (Community of the Impoverished) was founded in 1980 by the Pakistani cleric Sheikh Mubarak (Shah) Ali Gilani and advocates the purification of Islam by force and violence. Although active in the guerrilla war in Kashmir, Jamaat ul Fuqra has maintained a low profile in Pakistan, especially during its early years. In the United States, however, its members have been more active, committing at least 13 murders and fire bombings over the years.

Jamaat ul Fuqra in the United States

Court documents link Jamaat ul Fuqra to Muslims of the Americas, a tax-exempt group that Sheikh Gilani established in the United States in 1980. Almost all of the U.S.-based ul Fuqra members are American citizens.

During the 1980s, Jamaat ul Fuqra members in the United States attacked a variety of targets that they saw as enemies of Islam, including Hindus and Muslims they regarded as heretics. The group is believed to be responsible for firebombing Hare Krishna temples in Denver and Philadelphia, and for the January 1990 murder of Rashad Khalifa, a Tucson, Arizona, Muslim cleric. Jamaat ul Fuqra and its members have been investigated for a number of alleged terrorist acts, including murder and arson in New York, Detroit, Philadelphia, Toronto, Denver, Los Angeles, and Tucson.

During the 1980s and 1990s, ul Fuqra members in the United States purchased isolated rural compounds, where they lived communally and engaged in paramilitary exercises. The discovery in 1989 of guns, explosives, pipe bombs, military training manuals, false identification documents, and workers compensation claim forms in a storage locker in Colorado eventually led to the arrest of several members of the group. A two-year investigation resulted in the indictment of several members by a Colorado grand jury in 1992 on racketeering charges, including theft, mail fraud, murder, arson, and forgery.

In 2001, several members of an ul Fuqra commune in Virginia were arrested on fraud and weapons charges. The group was believed to be filing fraudulent workers compensation claims and sending the proceeds to Gilani in Pakistan. In California, a member was arrested for the murder of a Fresno County deputy sheriff in August 2001. Five months later, the Fresno school district revoked a charter for a school run by a member of Muslims of the Americas, citing (among other infractions) the inability of the charter school to account for $1.3 million in state money.

In January 2002, *Wall Street Journal* reporter Daniel Pearl was kidnapped in Pakistan while investigating a connection between Jamaat al Fuqra and the failed shoe bomber Richard Reid. Pearl's family told the authorities that he was scheduled to meet with Gilani before he disappeared. Pearl was murdered by his abductors. Gilani was arrested by Pakistan but was later released, and he is not believed to have been a part of Pearl's abduction and murder.

Lisa Magloff

See also Pearl, Daniel; Reid, Richard

Further Readings

Chand, Attar. *Pakistan Terrorism in Punjab and Kashmir.* Columbia, MO: South Asia Books, 1996.

Emerson, Steven. *Jihad Incorporated: A Guide to Militant Islam in the U.S.* Amherst, NY: Prometheus, 2006.

Ganguly, Sumit. *Conflict Unending: India-Pakistan Tensions since 1947.* New York: Columbia University Press, 2001.

Jalalzi, Musá Khan. *Sectarianism and Politico-Religious Terrorism in Pakistan.* Rev. ed. Lahore: Tarteeb Publishers, 1993.

Margolis, Eric S. *War at the Top of the World: The Struggle for Afghanistan, Kashmir, and Tibet.* New York: Routledge, 2000.

Seper, Jerry, and Steve Miller. "Militant Muslims Seek Virginia Base." *Washington Times,* July 1, 2002, p. A1.

JAPANESE RED ARMY

The Japanese Red Army (JRA) was a 1970s terrorist group famous for its actions on behalf of Palestinian nationalism, including a 1972 massacre at Israel's Ben Gurion Airport.

The Japanese Red Army arose from the Japanese student protest movement of the mid-to-late 1960s. Protests were directed not only at the Japanese government, which students felt was corrupt, but also at the U.S. military presence in Japan and against the Vietnam War. As the decade progressed, rampant factionalism overtook the Japanese student movement, with intergroup violence often more deadly and more frequent than student clashes with the police. The Japanese student movement was also marked by a certain militarism, and students often arrived at protests equipped with color-coded helmets and staves strikingly similar to the helmets and batons of the riot police. The end of the decade saw hundreds of student groups, many of which espoused radical strains of Marxism. The Red Amy was one such group.

By 1969 the JRA had come to accept that student protests were not swaying public opinion in conservative Japan, and that they were not likely to in the immediate future. Inclined to radical action rather than political persuasion, the JRA decided to align with the international communist movement. In March 1970, six JRA members hijacked a Japan Airlines plane and forced it to take them to North Korea, where the hijackers freed the hostages and surrendered themselves to the Communist North Korean government.

The successful hijacking left a void within the JRA leadership, and the group soon split into two factions. The first, under Tsuneo Mori, decided to remain in Japan and ally itself with another radical student group, the Keihin Anti-Treaty Joint Struggle. The new organization, called the United Red Army (URA), went into hiding in the Japanese countryside in the winter of 1972. It then conducted a brutal internal purge, in which 12 of the group's few dozen members were killed by their comrades. As the purge was winding down in mid-February, area police became aware of the group's presence and members fled their hideout. Five URA members invaded an inn and took the innkeeper hostage; a weeklong siege ensued. Police raided the building on February 28; one officer was killed, the innkeeper was freed, and the terrorists surrendered. This episode put an end to Mori's JRA faction.

The second JRA faction, which had no more than a few dozen members, was led by Fusako Shigenobu. This group left Japan in 1971 and went to Lebanon to support the Palestinian cause. In Lebanon they became protégés of the Popular Front for the Liberation of Palestine (PFLP). In May 1972, three JRA members attacked the Ben Gurion Airport near Tel Aviv, gunning down passengers in the terminal and attempting to blow up a plane. Twenty-three people were killed, and more than 80 were injured.

In July 1973 the JRA and Palestinians hijacked a Japan Airlines plane flying out of Amsterdam. The plane eventually landed in Libya, where the hostages were released and the plane destroyed. In February 1974, JRA and PFLP members blew up a Shell oil rig in Singapore; a second team attacked the Japanese embassy in Singapore, after which the Japanese government acceded to their demands and both groups of terrorists were allowed safe passage to Yemen.

In September 1974 the JRA attacked the French embassy in The Hague, the Netherlands. Negotiations stalled at first, but after Carlos the Jackal (Illich Ramírez Sánchez) orchestrated an attack on a Paris café on the JRA's behalf, the French ambassador and the other hostages were released in exchange for several JRA members who had been arrested in Europe. Once again the terrorists escaped to the Middle East.

In August 1975 the JRA attacked the U.S. and Swedish consulates in Kuala Lumpur, Malaysia, taking over 50 hostages. As in The Hague attack, the hostages were released in exchange for imprisoned JRA members, and the terrorists allowed to fly to Syria. The last major attack by the JRA was the September 1977 hijacking of another Japan Airlines plane. The plane, flying out of Bombay, India, was forced to land at Dacca, Bangladesh. During the ensuing standoff, elements in the Bangladeshi army attempted a coup d'état, which resulted in considerable confusion, but eventually the government restored control, and the JRA freed the hostages in exchange for a prisoner.

In the hostage takings in 1974 and 1977, the JRA had also demanded and received large ransoms. By the early 1980s, however, the JRA was seriously short of funds, and the country where they had found permanent refuge, Lebanon, was embroiled in civil war. Little was heard from them for several years. Between 1985 and 1987, several prominent former JRA members were arrested on charges of smuggling and trafficking in false passports. In April 1988, Yu Kikumura, a JRA member, was arrested in New Jersey with bomb-making materials; on April 15, a U.S. officers' club in Naples, Italy, was bombed, killing five people, in what was believed to be a JRA attack. The group's surprising resurgence resulted in strict security during the 1988 Olympics in Seoul, South Korea.

The JRA seemed once again to fade into oblivion until 1997, when five JRA members were deported from Lebanon to Japan. On November 8, 2000, JRA leader Shigenobu was arrested in Japan (she had entered the country on a false passport). Shigenobu announced in April 2001 that the group was disbanding. Nonetheless, in February 2006, Shigenobu was sentenced to 20 years in prison for her role in The Hague attack. Recent years have also seen the trial and sentencing of a number of other JRA members who had been freed from prison in the 1970s in response to the group's hostage-taking operations.

Colleen Sullivan

See also Kikumura, Yu; Popular Front for the Liberation of Palestine; Sánchez, Illich Ramírez; Shigenobu, Fusako

Further Readings

Farrell, William. *Blood and Rage: The Story of the Japanese Red Army.* Lexington, MA: D.C. Heath, 1990.

McCurry, Justin. "Founder of Japan's Red Army in Final Appeal for Freedom." *The Guardian,* December 13, 2008, p. 32.

Steinhoff, Patricia G., and Yoshinori Ito. *Rengo Sekigun to Oumu Shinrikyo.* Tokyo: Sairyusha, 1996.

JEWISH TERRORIST GROUPS IN THE UNITED STATES

The few organized Jewish terrorist groups outside of Israel operate mainly in the United States. They were most active during the 1970s and 1980s and were responsible for numerous bombings directed at Soviet personnel and institutions, as well as individuals doing business with the Soviet government.

The Jewish Defense League

The Jewish Defense League (JDL) was founded in 1968 by Meir Kahane, an orthodox Brooklyn rabbi. The group's original function was to protect elderly Brooklyn residents from street attacks. Kahane, however, was outspoken, even strident, and the JDL soon became known for its confrontational style.

Focusing mainly on the treatment of Jews in the Soviet Union, who were often jailed and refused exit visas, the JDL decided that violence was necessary to draw attention to the plight of Soviet Jewry. The goal was to strain U.S.-Soviet relations, for Kahane reasoned that Moscow would need to respond to the pressure by allowing more Soviet Jews to immigrate to Israel.

The JDL began a series of demonstrations against Soviet offices and personnel in 1969, including physical attacks and harassment. While the majority of JDL members participated in peaceful political demonstrations, Kahane later publicly admitted that some members "bombed the Russian mission in New York, the Russian cultural mission here [Washington] in 1970, and the Soviet trade offices."

JDL members were also implicated in two high-profile murders. Jerome Zeller was indicted for the 1972 bombing of the office of agent Sol Hurok, which killed his receptionist and injured 12 others. In 1992, Kahane admitted that he too had had a part in that attack. Two other JDL members, Robert Manning and his wife Rochelle, were indicted for the 1985 bombing death of Alex Odeh, the regional director of the American-Arab Anti-Discrimination Committee (ADC) in Santa Ana, California.

According to a 1985 Justice Department report, the FBI also suspected Manning and several other JDL members of being involved in a yearlong series of violent incidents that year. These included the August house-bomb slaying of Tscherim Soobzokov, a suspected Nazi war criminal, in Paterson, New Jersey; the August 16 attempt to bomb the Boston offices of ADC, in which two policemen were severely injured; the September bombing at the Brentwood, Long Island, home of the alleged Nazi

Elmars Sprogis, in which a 23-year-old passerby lost a leg; and setting fire to the ADC office in Washington, D.C., on October 29.

Manning and his wife were arrested in Israel on March 24, 1991, and charged in a separate suit involving the 1980 letter-bomb murder of Patricia Wilkerson, a secretary in California. Manning was extradited to the United States on condition that he not be tried in the Odeh murder and the other cases, because the events occurred after he became an Israeli citizen. However, on October 13, 1994, Robert Manning was found guilty of complicity in the Wilkerson murder.

A 1985 Justice Department study of terrorist acts in the United States between 1981 and 1984 found that of 18 incidents initiated by so-called "Jewish terrorist elements," 15 were perpetrated by the JDL. In a 1986 study of domestic terrorism, the Department of Energy concluded: "For more than a decade, the Jewish Defense League (JDL) has been one of the most active terrorist groups in the United States."

Kahane moved to Israel in 1971, where he won a following among that country's extreme right. He established a political party, Kach, which eventually won several seats in the Knesset, or Israeli Parliament. Kahane was assassinated in New York in 1990. El Sayyid Nosair, an Egyptian-born Muslim who was a naturalized U.S. citizen, was accused of the murder and acquitted by a Manhattan jury, but he was later sentenced to a life term after being convicted in a new trial.

During the 1990s, Jewish terrorist acts were infrequent. In December 2001, however, two top leaders of the JDL were arrested and charged in Los Angeles with a plot to bomb the King Fahd Mosque in Culver City, California, the Muslim Public Affairs Council (MPAC), and the office of Congressman Darrell Issa, an Arab American. On November 4, 2002, one defendant, Irv Rubin, the chairman of the JDL, slit his throat and threw himself off a ledge in his prison; he died of his injuries nine days later.

The second defendant, Earl Krugel, the Western regional director of the JDL, pled guilty to bombing charges in February 2003 and received a sentence of 20 years in prison. As part of Krugel's plea deal, he agreed to assist with the investigation into the Odeh murder. Krugel was himself murdered in an Arizona prison on November 4, 2005, by another inmate.

The Jewish Armed Resistance

Throughout 1976 and 1977, a group calling itself the Jewish Armed Resistance (JAR) took responsibility for a spate of bombings of Soviet targets in the United States. In January 1976, a pipe bomb exploded in front of the Polish consulate in New York City. After the explosion, a man called two wire services and took responsibility for the bombing, claiming he represented, "the voice of Jewish Armed Resistance."

Over the next two years, JAR, which also acted under the name Jewish Armed Resistance Strike Group, claimed responsibility for a number of terrorist acts, including firing shots at the Soviet U.N. Mission residence, bombing a building housing the Soviet airline offices, firebombing two vehicles at Kennedy Airport, and firebombing the national headquarters of the Communist Party USA and a Russian bookstore.

In 1977 the group claimed responsibility for setting fire to a New York area bank, saying the arson was a political protest. That same year, the JAR also took responsibility for bombing a Jewish center in California, claiming in a letter that the center was too liberal. However, as protests against the JAR from Jewish rabbis and Jewish social action groups mounted, the group became considerably less active and eventually seemed to disappear.

Other Groups

During the 1980s, other Jewish groups mounted a few isolated attacks on Soviet targets. In 1983 a group calling itself the United Jewish Underground took responsibility for the pipe bombing of a car belonging to a Russian diplomat. In 1984 a Soviet residential compound in Brooklyn was bombed by a group calling itself Jewish Direct Action.

Lisa Magloff

See also Kahane, Meir; Kahane Chai; Nosair, El Sayyid; Odeh, Mohammed Saddiq

Further Readings

Friedman, Robert I. *The False Prophet: Rabbi Meir Kahane.* Brooklyn, NY: Lawrence Hill Books, 1990.

Friedman, Robert I. "How Shamir Used JDL Terrorism." *The Nation,* October 31, 1988.

Guiccione, Jean. "JDL Chief Dies." *Los Angeles Times,* November 15, 2002, p. B1.

Halsell, Grace. *Prophecy and Politics: Militant Evangelists on the Road to Nuclear War.* Westport, CT: Lawrence Hill, 1986.

Hoffman, Bruce. *Terrorism in the United States and the Potential Threat to Nuclear Facilities.* Santa Monica, CA: RAND Corporation, 1986.

Karp, Yehudit. *The Karp Report: Investigation of Suspicions Against Israelis in Judea and Samaria.* Jerusalem: Israeli Government, 1984.

Keller, Karen. "Pipe Bomb Mystery, 24 Years Later: Quest Still on for Killer of Dad, a Former Nazi." *The Record,* March 15, 2009, p. L1.

Kirkorian, Greg. "Evidence Emerges in '85 Santa Ana Slaying: Official Say the Findings Shed New Light on Bomb Plot That Killed Arab American Alex Odeh." *Los Angeles Times,* October 11, 2007, p. B1.

"The Manning File: Evidence Against Extradition." *The Jerusalem Torah Voice and Investigative Report,* June 1992. http://www.torah-voice.org/manning.htm.

Rosenthal, Richard. *Rookie Cop: Deep Undercover in the Jewish Defense League.* Wellfleet, MA: Leapfrog, 2000.

Twair, Pat, and Samir Twair. "Accused Letter-Bomb Murderer Extradited to U.S. from Israel." *Washington Report,* September/October 1993, p. 60.

U.S. Department of Justice. *FBI Analysis of Terrorist Incidents and Terrorist Related Activities in the United States, 1985.* Washington, DC: National Criminal Justice Reference Service, 1985.

JIBRIL, AHMED (1938?–)

Ahmed Jibril is the militant Palestinian leader of the Syrian-sponsored terrorist group known as Popular Front for the Liberation of Palestine–General Command (PFLP–GC). He is a master bomb maker and is considered by many to be one of the most dangerous terrorists of the late twentieth century.

It is believed that Jibril was born in Yazur, south of Tel Aviv, although some accounts list his birthplace as Ramallah, Iraq, or even Syria. In any case, his family later moved to Syria, and Jibril joined the Syrian army in 1956, rising to the rank of captain before being expelled as a troublemaker and suspected Communist in 1958. Jibril briefly worked with Yasir Arafat's Fatah movement in its early days, but he left to cofound the Palestine Liberation Front (PLF). With Syrian support, the PLF carried out assassinations as well as multiple terror attacks against Israel. Jibril served as a commander and became particularly known for training others in terror techniques.

In 1968 Jibril and George Habash formed the Popular Front for the Liberation of Palestine (PFLP). Jibril soon broke away from the group, however, as tensions developed between Syria and Habash. In 1968 Jibril founded the separate, pro-Syrian group PFLP–General Command, claiming that fighting, not politics, was the way to achieve Palestinian goals.

The PFLP–GC carried out many attacks and kidnappings during the 1970s and 1980s, including the 1970 bombing of Swissair Flight 330, and numerous attacks on Israeli civilian targets, such as school buses and apartment buildings. In May 1985, Jibril negotiated with Israel for the release of more than 1,000 Palestinian prisoners in exchange for three Israeli soldiers the PFLP–GC had taken hostage while fighting in Lebanon. The trade became known as the "Jibril exchange."

Jibril also orchestrated Operation Kibya, referred to as Night of the Hang Gliders. On November 25, 1987, four heavily armed PLFP members hang glided into Israeli territory. Three of the terrorists experienced mechanical problems and did not get far, but the fourth, Khaled Aker, managed to penetrate the Israeli Defense Force's Camp Gibor and kill six soldiers before being shot himself. The spectacular attack made a terror icon of Jibril and inspired the first Intifada ("throwing off"), a period of intense violence against Israel. The Night of the Hang Gliders has such symbolic weight that the Israeli military traditionally makes a point of striking PFLP–GC targets every November 25.

The explosion of Pan Am Flight 103 over Lockerbie, Scotland, in 1988, struck many intelligence officials as the work of Jibril and the PFLP–GC. From his Damascus headquarters, Jibril denied any involvement. However, the type of bomb used appeared to investigators to be a Jibril trademark, leading many to suspect that Jibril had, at the very least, trained the bombers. Investigators thought it more likely still that Jibril had orchestrated the entire attack, possibly as revenge for the 1988 downing of Iran Air Flight 655 by the United States. Scotland later indicted two employees of

Libyan Arab Airlines for the Pan Am attack, in which a total of 270 people died.

In 1989, during the international uproar about Salman Rushdie's novel *The Satanic Verses*, Jibril told the press that he and his group were ready to murder Rushdie for heresy, as called for by Iranian religious leader Ayatollah Ruhollah Khomeini.

Rumors have abounded since the 1990s that Jibril has experienced health problems. Along with a concerted effort by the Israeli military to eliminate the PFLP–GC, this illness seems to have led the group to scale back its activity. In the twenty-first century, the PFLP–GC has turned its attention to supporting Hezbollah in its efforts to attack Israel from Lebanon, where the PFLP–GC has several bases. Jibril's son, Jihad Jibril, played an important role in this campaign until he was killed by a car bomb in Beirut in 2002.

Erica Pearson

See also Arafat, Yasir; Fatah; Fatwa; Habash, George; Intifada; Pan Am Flight 103 Bombing; Popular Front for the Liberation of Palestine; Popular Front for the Liberation of Palestine–General Command

Further Readings

Asser, Martin. "The Palestinian Connection." *BBC News Online*, May 4, 2000. http://news.bbc.co.uk/hi/english/world/middle_east/newsid_736000/736490.stm.

Black, Robert, and John P. Grant. *The Lockerbie Trial.* Edinburgh, UK: Dunedin Academic Press, 2010.

Katz, Samuel M. *Israel Versus Jibril.* New York: Paragon House, 1993.

Milne, Seumas. "Lockerbie: Theories and Evidence." *The Guardian* (London), December 20, 1993.

O'Sullivan, Arieh. "Ahmed Jibril's Son Killed in Beirut Blast." *Jerusalem Post*, May 21, 2002, p. 1.

U.S. State Department. "Terrorist Groups." *Country Reports on Terrorism 2008*. http://www.state.gov/s/ct/rls/crt/2008/122449.htm.

Walker, Christopher. "Palestinian Group Offers to Fight for Gaddafi." *The Times*, April 17, 1992.

JIHAD

Although the Arabic term *jihad* is often interpreted as "holy war," the word is derived from a word root meaning "to strive" or "to make an effort." The word *jihad* is commonly followed by the Arabic expression *fi sabil Illah,* meaning "in the path of God." The concept of jihad is often defined as a struggle against injustice or ungodliness, stemming from the injunction in the Koran (the Islamic holy book) to "command the right and forbid the wrong."

The form that jihad should take—violent war or peaceful striving—has been the subject of much discussion and disagreement by Islamic scholars throughout history. The Koran and the hadiths (reports on the sayings and acts of the prophet Mohammed) refer to four ways by which the duty of jihad can be fulfilled: by the heart, the tongue, the hand, and the sword.

Jihad is seen by some Muslims as primarily a struggle against evil and injustice within oneself. One hadith recounts how Muhammad, after a battle, said "We have returned from the lesser jihad (*al jihad al asghar*) to the greater jihad (*al jihad al akbar*)." When a follower asked, "What is the greater jihad?," Mohammed replied, "It is the struggle against oneself." This view of jihad was predominant in Sufism, an extremely influential form of Islamic spirituality. To this day, many Muslims conceive of jihad as a personal rather than a political struggle.

However it is understood, jihad is considered by most Muslims to be one of the primary duties of Islam. Sayyid Abul Ala Maududi (1903–1979), the founder of the Jamaat-e-Islami Party in Pakistan and a leading fundamentalist scholar, described jihad as, "just as much a primary duty of Muslims as daily prayers and fasting. One who shirks it is a sinner. His very claim to being a Muslim is doubtful. He is clearly a hypocrite who fails in the test of sincerity and all of his (religious observances) are a sham, a worthless hollow of devotion."

In past centuries, Islamic jurists described jihad as a general obligation of the Muslim community. In this view, Muslims are required to participate in violent jihad only when Islam comes under attack. The Islamic legal philosopher Ibn Taymiyah (1268–1328), however, took a more confrontational position. He declared that a ruler who fails to enforce Shariah (Islamic law) rigorously in all its aspects, including the performance of jihad, forfeits his right to rule. Most jurists at the time tolerated Muslim rulers who violated the Shariah for the sake of the community, preferring tyranny over disorder, but Ibn Taymiyah insisted that waging jihad is a requirement for a Muslim ruler.

Interpretations of Jihad

Beginning in the twentieth century, some Islamic thinkers sought to reconcile Islam with the interdependence of modern nation-states, which required adherence to non-Islamic international laws and treaties. One scholar, Muhammad Shaltut, a former rector of Al Azhar University in Cairo, described Shariah's emphasis on international peace and the legitimate right of self-defense through jihad as similar to the principles of the United Nations.

Modern Islamists, particularly Islamic extremists, describe jihad differently. Maududi presented jihad not merely as warfare to expand Islamic political dominance, but also to establish Islamic rule. For Maududi, jihad was akin to a war of liberation; Islamic rule meant freedom and justice. Maududi's ideas were very influential in the development of modern Islamist ideas of jihad. Thus, in the twentieth century, jihad became associated more with Islamic liberation movements and the fight against colonialism. This approach allowed any resistance, even by non-Muslims, to Zionism and Israel (and more recently the United States and Jews everywhere) to be termed *jihad.*

For Islamist thinkers such Maududi, Hassan al Banna (1906–1949) and Sayyid Qutb (1906–1956), jihad includes the overthrow of governments, even Muslim governments, that fail to enforce Shariah. Significantly, Islamists consider jihad to be a mandatory and individual duty for all Muslims, rather than a duty of the state. This view sanctions terrorism as a legitimate form of jihad.

Iranian Shia revolutionaries had a similar perspective. Ayatollah Ruhollah Khomeini (1903–1989), the leader of the Iranian revolution, argued that Muslim jurists "by means of jihad and enjoining the good and forbidding the evil, must expose and overthrow tyrannical rulers and rouse the people so the universal movement of all alert Muslims can establish Islamic government in the place of tyrannical regimes."

Other modern Islamic thinkers apply the term jihad to political and social action to establish justice, not only to warfare. For example, President

Habib Bourguiba of Tunisia once described the struggle for economic development in Tunisia as a jihad against poverty.

The Meaning of Jihad Today

A war jihad can be called for by any Islamic leader, but individual Muslims must decide whether to answer the call to arms. Most calls for jihad tend to appeal mostly to Islamist extremists and do not result in total war within or between countries. However, America's wars in Afghanistan and Iraq have led many Muslims to rethink jihad. While most do not see jihad as a violent struggle, more and more Muslims would argue that all Muslims have a duty to defend Islam. The increase in terrorist acts against American and Israeli civilians reflects this widened, violent interpretation of jihad. More Muslims now consider some form of jihad—violent or nonviolent—to be an obligation of the faith. Therefore, modern Muslims can mean many things by jihad—the extremists' idea of warfare, Ibn Taymiyah's revolt against an impious ruler, the Sufi's moral self-improvement, or the modern concept of political and social reform.

Terrorist organizations often take advantage of the disagreements over the types of jihad to insist to less sophisticated Muslims that war is the only acceptable form of jihad. The different interpretations of jihad have also caused confusion in the West. For example, in 1997, when Yasir Arafat called for a "jihad for Jerusalem," he intended his Muslim audience to hear a call to arms while simultaneously assuring his Western supporters he intended only a peaceful struggle.

Usually, however, the meaning of the word jihad is clear from its usage. When Sufis discuss spiritual jihad, they use the term "greater jihad." Advocates of a jihad on social issues, like Bourguiba's war on poverty, clearly do not intend to use violence to improve education and development. When the World Islamic Front for Jihad against Jews and Crusaders, backed by Osama bin Laden, called for a jihad in 1998, its aim was clearly violent.

Lisa Magloff

See also Afghanistan War; al Jihad; al Qaeda; bin Laden, Osama; Homegrown Jihadi Movement; Iraq War; Islamic Army for the Liberation of Holy Places

Further Readings

Bonney, Richard. *Jihad: From Qur'an to Bin Laden.* New York: Palgrave Macmillan, 2004.

Bostom, Andrew G., ed. *The Legacy of Jihad: Islamic Holy War and the Fate of Non-Muslims.* Amherst, NY: Prometheus Books, 2005.

Cook, David. *Understanding Jihad.* Berkeley: University of California Press, 2005.

Dajami-Shakeel, Hadia, and Ronald A. Messier, eds. *The Jihad and Its Times.* Ann Arbor: University of Michigan Center for Near Eastern and North African Studies, 1991.

Devji, Faisal. *Landscapes of the Jihad: Militancy, Morality, Modernity.* Ithaca, NY: Cornell University Press, 2005.

Kelsay John and James Turner Johnson, eds. *Cross, Crescent, and Sword: The Justification and Limitation of War in Western and Islamic Tradition.* New York: Greenwood Press, 1990.

Kelsay, John, and James Turner Johnson, eds. *Just War and Jihad: Historical and Theoretical Perspectives on War and Peace in Western and Islamic Tradition.* New York: Greenwood Press, 1991.

Lewis, Bernard. *The Political Language of Islam.* Chicago: University of Chicago Press, 1988.

Peters, Rudolph. *Jihad in Classical and Modern Islam.* Princeton, NJ: Markus Weiner, 1996.

Renard, John. "*Al Jihad al Akbar*: Notes on a Theme in Islamic Spirituality." *Muslim World* 78 (1988): 225–242.

JIHAD GROUP

See al Jihad

JUSTICE DEPARTMENT

The emergence of the Justice Department, a small, extremely violent animal rights group active in England and North America, demonstrated a significant philosophical change within the extreme wing of the animal rights movement. The group went beyond the financial sabotage carried out by groups such as the Animal Liberation Front (ALF) to actually threatening and harming individuals— a tactic similar to that employed by the Unabomber.

Since its inception in October 1993, the England-based Justice Department has specialized in directly targeting individuals involved in industries that use and may abuse animals. Its first act was to mail devices—such as razor-tipped mousetraps—to "blood-sports" supporters (i.e., hunters).

The Justice Department seemed to have declared war in 1994. That year the traditional Boxing Day (December 26) hunts in Sussex saw over 30 bomb attacks against them, including two bomb hoaxes; responsibility for the attacks and hoaxes was claimed by the Justice Department. The group targeted Prince Charles with a razor-tipped mousetrap after he took his two sons on their first hunts in October. Finally, the Justice Department shut down several ferries involved in the meat industry's live export sector.

In 1996 the Justice Department became active in Canada. In January, group members mailed 65 envelopes containing razor blades tainted with rat poison to big-game hunting guides throughout British Columbia and Alberta. Borrowing a tactic from another extremist animals rights group, Britain's Animal Rights Militia, in November 1997 the Justice Department began a contamination hoax in the eastern United States, claiming to have injected toxic substances into Thanksgiving turkeys at large chain supermarkets.

The Justice Department's most significant acts occurred in the fall of 1999, with two large-scale razor-blade campaigns in North America. The first wave, in August, against the fur industry, involved over 100 envelopes with rat-poisoned razorblades. The second, in October, targeted more than 80 scientists and researchers at major U.S. universities that conducted AIDS and cancer-related research on primates. The Justice Department indicated that the razorblades had been contaminated with AIDS-infected blood. The envelopes also contained four typewritten lines: "You have been targeted and you have until autumn 2000 to release all your primate captives and get out of the vivisection industry. If you do not heed our warning, your violence will be turned back upon you." (A similar message had been included in the anti-fur campaign.) Although no one was hurt by the razorblades, the FBI and Americans for Medical Progress (AMP) officially recognized the mailings as an act of domestic terrorism.

With passage of Terrorism Act 2000 in Great Britain, the Justice Department became the first-ever animal rights group to join the company of the Irish Republic Army as a domestic terrorist group. Since then, the number of attacks explicitly committed by the Justice Department have significantly declined. But because the organization, like the ALF, operates in a loose, anonymous, and decentralized cell structure, it has been difficult for authorities to infiltrate. In addition, the loose structure of extremist animal rights groups means that membership among them is fluid, so that the same individuals may be committing acts under the name of more than one group.

Laura Lambert

See also Animal Liberation Front; Animal Rights Movement; Unabomber

Further Readings

Best, Steven, and Anthony J. Nocella II, eds. *Terrorists or Freedom Fighters? Reflections on the Liberation of Animals.* New York: Lantern, 2004.

Guither, Harold D. *Animal Rights: History and Scope of a Radical Social Movement.* Carbondale: Southern Illinois University Press, 1998.

Liddick, Donald R. *Eco-terrorism: Radical Environmental and Animal Liberation Movements.* Westport, CT: Praeger, 2006.

Scarce, Rik. *Eco-warriors: Understanding the Radical Environmental Movement.* Chicago: The Noble Press, 1990.

KACZYNSKI, THEODORE J.

See Unabomber

KAHANE, MEIR (1932–1990)

Brooklyn-born Rabbi Meir Kahane was a radical ideologue and founder of Kach, the militant nationalist and outlawed political party in Israel that advocates violence against Arabs. Kahane was assassinated on November 5, 1990, in New York City.

Kahane developed and disseminated his beliefs that Greater Israel, including the occupied West Bank, was given to the Jews by God and that all Arabs should be expelled from the land. In the 1960s, Kahane formed the anti-Arab Jewish Defense League (JDL), a forerunner of Kach and Kahane Chai. He used the slogan "Never Again!" (in reference to the Holocaust) when recruiting for the league. Kahane moved to Israel in 1971 and founded the Kach Party. Kach means "thus" or "this is the way" in Hebrew. After he won a seat in the Israeli Parliament in 1984, Kahane is said to have submitted a bill to Israel's Parliament to completely separate Jews and non-Jews in Israel. The government of Israel declared the Kach Party racist and ineligible to field candidates in 1988.

Kahane was assassinated on the evening of November 5, 1990. In a meeting room of the Marriott Halloran House Hotel in midtown Manhattan, Kahane gave a speech calling for the forcible expulsion of native Palestinians from Israel to an audience of about 100; he was answering questions when a man approached and shot him in the neck with a handgun. Kahane was mortally wounded, and the gunman fled the scene. Egyptian-born El Sayyid Nosair was arrested a few blocks away.

Kahane's funeral was marked by violence; a mob of his supporters stabbed an Arab gas station attendant and stoned camera crews, shouting "Kill the Arabs" and "Kill the Media." Nosair was tried and found not guilty on the murder charge, but he was later convicted on weapons charges. When the not guilty verdict was read, teenage followers of Kahane shouted "Death to Nosair!" and clashed with Nosair's supporters in the hallways of the court.

In Kahane's absence, the Kach Party withered. However, Kahane's son Binyamin founded the group Kahane Chai, or "Kahane Lives" to pursue his father's goals. Kahane's teachings, also called Kahanism, remain influential among right-wing Jewish settlers in the West Bank. After a Kahane disciple, Dr. Baruch Goldstein, massacred 29 praying Muslims in a Hebron mosque in February 1994, the Israeli government voted to outlaw Kach, Kahane Chai, and any organization following Kahane's teachings under Israel's 1948 Prevention of Terrorism Ordinance. The ban also criminalized giving financial or verbal support to these groups.

In December 2000, Binyamin Kahane was also assassinated, shot by Palestinian gunmen in a drive-by shooting. Five years later, Eden Natan-Zada, a devotee of Kahane, opened fire on a bus in an Arab section of Israel, killing four people.

Erica Pearson

See also Goldstein, Baruch; Jewish Terrorist Groups in the United States; Kahane Chai

Further Readings

Ben-David, Caley. "The Life of Meir Kahane: A Cautionary Tale." *Jerusalem Post*, October 23, 2002, p. 6.

Cordesman, Anthony H. *The Israeli-Palestinian War: Escalating to Nowhere*. Westport, CT: Praeger, 2005.

Goodstein, Laurie. "Rebirth of the 'Tough Jew': The Ideas of Racist Rabbi Meir Kahane Are Flourishing in New York." *Toronto Star*, March 11, 1994.

Haberman, Clyde. "Israel Votes Ban on Jewish Groups Linked to Kahane." *The New York Times*, March 14, 1994, p. A1.

Kressel, Neil J. *Bad Faith: The Danger of Religious Extremism*. Amherst, NY: Prometheus Books, 2007.

Miller, Marjorie. "Jewish Extremists Commemorate Kahane." *Los Angeles Times*, November 13, 1995. http://articles.latimes.com/1995-11-13/news/mn-2621_1_rabbi-meir-kahane.

Perelman, Marc. "Secret FBI Files Reveal Hoover's Obsession with Militant Rabbi." *Forward*, February 24, 2006, p. 1.

Rempel, William C. "NY Trial in Rabbi's Death Planted Explosive Seed." *Los Angeles Times*, July 4, 1993. http://articles.latimes.com/1993–07–04/news/mn-9960_1_abdul-rahman.

Sprinzak, Ehud. *The Ascendance of the Israeli Radical Right*. London: Oxford University Press, 1991.

Stern, Jessica. *Terror in the Name of God: Why Religious Militants Kill*. New York: Ecco, 2008.

KAHANE CHAI

A Jewish nationalist group banned in Israel, Kahane Chai spreads the anti-Arab ideology of the late Rabbi Meir Kahane. Right-wing Jewish people in the West Bank largely support the group, particularly those from Airyat Arba in Hebron. Kahane Chai is listed as a terrorist group by the U.S. State Department.

Rabbi Kahane founded the right-wing nationalist Kach Party in Israel in the 1970s and disseminated his violent, anti-Arab ideas until he was assassinated in New York City in 1990. After Kahane's death, the rabbi's son Binyamin gathered together Kach members and Kahane supporters to found the Kahane Chai or "Kahane Lives" group. The group's stated goal is to restore the biblical state of Israel, replacing democracy with theocracy. Its rallying cry is often, "Rabbi Kahane was right!"

Baruch Goldstein, the Brooklyn-born doctor who massacred 29 praying Muslims at a Hebron mosque in February 1994, was a staunch Kahane Chai supporter and close follower of the rabbi. The group was outlawed in Israel after making public statements in support of Goldstein's bloody attack. Under the provisions of the 1948 Prevention of Terrorism Ordinance, the Israeli cabinet banned Kach, Kahane Chai, and any organization following Kahane's teachings. The Israeli government vote also made it a crime to financially or verbally support such groups.

Many members of Kahane Chai are the children of Holocaust survivors. The group is largely based in Israel and the territories, but it maintains a presence in the United States, mainly in Brooklyn, New York. In the mid-1990s, the group ran a summer training camp, called "Camp Meir," in the Catskill Mountains in New York state.

Kahane Chai often organizes protests against the Israeli government, and its members harass and threaten Palestinians in Hebron and the West Bank. The group has issued many death threats, according to the U.S. State Department. In July 1993, Israeli authorities charged four teenage Kahane Chai members with a grenade attack in the Old City of Jerusalem that killed one Arab merchant and wounded nearly a dozen others. According to press reports, Kahane Chai members have carried out a long list of unsophisticated attacks, such as throwing eggs at the Israeli ambassador in a Queens synagogue, beating Palestinian demonstrators in front of the White House, and punching and kicking a U.S. journalist visiting a settlement in the occupied territories. But the group's members are also capable of more significant harm: In 1995, Yigal Amir, a Kahane sympathizer, assassinated Israeli Prime Minister Yitzhak Rabin.

On December 31, 2000, Palestinian gunmen assassinated Binyamin Kahane, killing him and his wife in a drive-by shooting. The mid-2000s nonetheless saw an uptick in activity by Kahane Chai as

Israel moved to end its occupation of the Gaza Strip in September 2005. Israel's withdrawal from Gaza, in particular the dismantling of Jewish settlements, was unacceptable to Kahane Chai members because it reduced the size of Israel's territory, rather than expanding it to its historical, biblical limits. In 2004, Israeli police detained several Kahane Chai members for making threats against the Israeli political leaders responsible for the withdrawal.

On August 4, 2005, an Israeli soldier and deserter named Eden Natan-Zada opened fire on a bus in the Israeli Arab town of Shfaram; he killed four people before being lynched by the crowd. Zada had ties with Kahane Chai, as well as the Jewish Legion, a paramilitary organization of Jewish settlers. Authorities believe that Zada's attack was an attempt to stop the withdrawal from Gaza; it led instead to the banning of the Jewish Legion in early 2006 because the group was considered to be a front for Kahane Chai.

Erica Pearson

See also Goldstein, Baruch; Jewish Terrorist Groups in the United States; Kahane, Meir

Further Readings

Cordesman, Anthony H. *The Israeli-Palestinian War: Escalating to Nowhere.* Westport, CT: Praeger, 2005.

Farrell, Stephen. "Israeli Killer Was Recruited to Terror over the Internet." *The Times* (London), August 6, 2005, p. 40.

Goodstein, Laurie. "Rebirth of the 'Tough Jew': The Ideas of Racist Rabbi Meir Kahane Are Flourishing in New York." *The Toronto Star,* March 11, 1994.

A crowd surrounds the bus where a soldier, identified by the military as 19-year-old Eden Natan-Zada, boarded and opened fire, killing the driver and three passengers and wounding 13, in the northern Israeli town of Shfaram, August 4, 2005. An angry crowd then killed the gunman. (AP Photo/Ancho Ghosh © 2011 The Associated Press. All Rights Reserved.)

Gutman, Matthew. "7 Kahane Chai Members Held for Threats." *Jerusalem Post*, June 7, 2004, p. 2.

Katz, Yaakov. "Police Raid Jewish Legion Offices: Group Suspected of Being Associated with Outlawed Kach Movement." *Jerusalem Post*, January 9, 2006, p. 5.

King, Laura, and Maher Abukhater. "Four Slain Arabs Buried in Israel: After a Radical Jew's Bus Attack, Some Call for Harsher Punishment on Those Who Incite Violence before This Month's Gaza Pullout." *Los Angeles Times*, August 6, 2005, p. A6.

Lueck, Thomas J. "Group Grew Out of Militancy." *The New York Times*, December 13, 2001. http://www.nytimes.com/2001/12/13/us/group-grew-out-of-militancy.html.

Murphy, Deane. "Terror Label No Hindrance to Anti-Arab Jewish Group." *The New York Times*, December 19, 2000. http://www.nytimes.com/2000/12/19/nyregion/terror-label-no-hindrance-to-anti-arab-jewish-group.html.

Sprinzak, Ehud. *The Ascendance of the Israeli Radical Right.* London: Oxford University Press, 1991.

Stern, Jessica. *Terror in the Name of God: Why Religious Militants Kill.* New York: Ecco, 2008.

U.S. State Department. "Terrorist Groups." *Country Reports on Terrorism 2008.* http://www.state.gov/s/ct/rls/crt/2008/122449.htm.

KAMAL, ALI HASSAN ABU

See Empire State Building Shooting

KANSI, MIR AIMAL (1964–2002)

In 1993, Mir Aimal Kansi (or Kasi), a Pakistani national, attacked the CIA headquarters in Langley, Virginia, killing two people; he was executed in 2002.

Born in 1964 to a wealthy family in Quetta, Pakistan, Kansi inherited about $100,000 after his father's death. Reportedly involved in a militant nationalist group in Pakistan, Kansi traveled to the United States in 1991, entering the country on a business visa. On January 25, 1993, he stepped out of his car near the CIA gates in Langley. While morning commuters waited at a traffic light outside CIA headquarters, Kansi used

an AK-47 assault rifle to shoot through car windows, walking between the lanes and spraying bullets left and right. He first shot Frank Darling, a 28-year-old CIA communications worker, in the back. Darling's wife, Judy Becker-Darling, also worked at the CIA and was riding to work with her husband. She crouched on the floor when Kansi returned to the car and shot Darling again. He also shot and killed Lansing Bennett, a 66-year-old CIA analyst and physician, and wounded three others.

Kansi fled to Pakistan the next day; he evaded capture for over four years. He spent much of that time in Afghanistan. At first, the U.S. government did not label the CIA killings an act of international terrorism, reportedly to minimize problems with Pakistan. Judy Becker-Darling publicly spoke about what she saw as the CIA's indifference to her husband's death, and she became a gun control activist. Originally, the government offered a $100,000 reward for information leading to Kansi's capture, later raising the amount to $2 million.

On June 17, 1997, Kansi was arrested in a Punjab hotel room and then extradited to the United States, where he was tried in Virginia. Prosecutors in his trial said that his actions aimed to protest and take revenge for U.S. involvement in Muslim countries. Kansi did not testify at his trial, but he wrote a series of letters to a reporter at Salon.com, explaining that he had intended to assassinate either CIA director James Woolsey or the former director Robert Gates.

The jury found Kansi guilty on November 10, 1997, and began deliberating their recommendation on his sentence. The next day, four auditors from the U.S. oil company Union Texas were shot, along with their Pakistani driver, in Karachi, Pakistan. Because the jury was still deliberating, they were sequestered to shield them from news of the Karachi shootings. The jury recommended the death penalty, and the judge sentenced Kansi to death on January 24, 1998.

Kansi was executed by lethal injection on November 14, 2002, in Virginia. Although he apologized to the families of the people he killed, he maintained that his attack on the CIA building was a legitimate response to U.S. policies toward the Muslim world. Following his death, Kansi's body was shipped to Pakistan for burial; the flight carrying his corpse was greeted by more than

2,000 Pakistanis, many of them chanting anti-American slogans.

Erica Pearson

See also Lone-Wolf Terrorism

Further Readings

Glod, Maria, and Eric M. Weiss. "Kasi Executed for CIA Slayings." *The Washington Post,* November 15, 2002, p. A1.

Melillo, Wendy. "Kasi Jurors Recommend Death Penalty; Decision Cites 'Vileness' of Shootings outside CIA." *Washington Post,* November 15, 1997.

O'Harrow, Robert, Jr., and Bill Miller. "CIA Suspect Left Trail of Conflicting Personal Data." *The Washington Post,* February 18, 1993.

Stein, Jeff. "Convicted Assassin: 'I Wanted to Shoot the CIA Director.'" Salon.com, January 22, 1998. http://www.salon.com/news/1998/01/22news_kasi.html.

Weiner, Tim. "Killer of Two at C.I.A. Draws Death Sentence." *The New York Times,* January 24, 1988. http://www.nytimes.com/1998/01/24/us/killer-of-two-at-cia-draws-death-sentence.html.

KHALED, LEILA (1944–)

A member of the Popular Front for the Liberation of Palestine (PFLP), Leila Khaled became famous in the late 1960s and early 1970s for being one of the few Arab women publicly involved in terrorist activities.

One of 13 children, Khaled was only four years old when her family was forced to leave her birthplace of Haifa in Palestine due to the creation of the Israeli state in 1948. They settled in a refugee camp in Tyre, Lebanon. She and her siblings shared the belief that Palestine should be liberated and the refugees should be allowed to return home. While she was a teenager, she joined the Arab Nationalist Movement to fight for her beliefs. In 1963, to help her struggling family, Khaled became an English teacher in Kuwait. It was there that she became a member of the political group that would lead to her fame, the PFLP, created by George Habash and Wadi Haddad.

The Israeli defeat of the Arabs in 1967 was the impetus for Khaled's move to Jordan to join the resistance. She was trained by Haddad to hijack airplanes. On August 29, 1969, Khaled and a colleague hijacked TWA Flight 840 en route from Rome to Tel Aviv. No passengers were harmed, but the case attracted extensive media coverage because female hijackers were not common, especially not ones with a conservative Arab background. Khaled became well known as a terrorist to some, and as a hero to others. In a famous picture of her from that time, she is seen holding a gun and wearing a ring made of a hand-grenade pin and a bullet.

Before attempting her second hijacking, Khaled underwent several cosmetic surgeries so that she would be unrecognizable. On September 6, 1970, she and Patrick Arguello hijacked an El Al jet flying from Amsterdam to New York. No passengers were harmed, but security guards on the plane opened fire and killed Arguello. The plane landed at London's Heathrow Airport, where Khaled was arrested and detained in the Ealing police station for 23 days. Prime Minister Edward Heath set her free in exchange for the release of 56 hostages taken

Leila Khaled, 24, a member of the Marxist-oriented Popular Front for the Liberation of Palestine (PFLP), a radical Palestinian faction, is shown in Amman, Jordan, in 1970. (AP Photo/Hagop Toranian. © 2011 The Associated Press. All Rights Reserved.)

in a PFLP hijacking that occurred after Khaled's arrest. Since 1970, Khaled has taken a less prominent role in the Palestinian struggle to regain their homeland. She was associated with the Palestine Liberation Organization (PLO) until 1982. As of 2010, she was living in Amman, Jordan, with her second husband and two sons, and she remained an ardent supporter of the Arab movement.

Harvey Kushner

See also Habash, George; Palestine Liberation Organization; Popular Front for the Liberation of Palestine; TWA Flight 840 Hijacking; Women Terrorists

Further Readings

BBC News Online. "Transcripts: The Guerrilla's Story." January 1, 2001. http://news.bbc.co.uk/hi/english/in_depth/uk/2000/uk_confidential/newsid_1090000/1090986.stm.

Gonzalez-Perez, Margaret. *Women and Terrorism: Female Activity in Domestic and International Terror Groups*. New York: Routledge, 2009.

Khaled, Leila. *My People Shall Live: The Autobiography of a Revolutionary*. Edited by George Hajjar. London: Hodder and Stoughton, 1973.

O'Farrell, John. "Guerilla in Our Midst; Lelia Khaled, Ex-Hijacker and Pin-up for Palestinian Radicals, Is Beamed into a Belfast Republican Festival." *Financial Times*, September 17, 2005, p. 8.

Raab, David. *Terror in Black September: The First Eyewitness Account of the Infamous 1970 Hijacking*. New York: Palgrave Macmillan, 2007.

"Revolution Is Not Just for the Single." *The New York Times*, November 27, 1970, p. 54.

Sjoberg, Laura, and Caron E. Gentry. *Mothers, Monsters, Whores: Women's Violence in Global Politics*. London: Zed Books, 2007.

KHOBAR TOWERS BOMBING

Nineteen U.S. service members were killed when a truck bomb destroyed their high-rise air force barracks in Dhahran, Saudi Arabia, on June 25, 1996. Bombers pulled a tanker truck stuffed with explosives up next to the dormitory and then jumped into waiting vehicles, escaping just before the detonation. About 500 people were injured in the explosion.

The towers housed the 2,000 U.S. military personnel assigned to the King Abdul Aziz Airbase in Saudi Arabia. The service members were at the airbase near Dhahran in order to mount patrols over the no-fly zone in southern Iraq that was declared after the Persian Gulf War.

The tanker truck that pulled up to Khobar Towers just before 10 P.M. on the evening the attack carried 5,000 pounds of explosives—an even larger cache than that used by Timothy McVeigh to blow up Oklahoma City's federal building. The intense explosion, so loud it was heard some 20 miles away, left a crater 85 feet wide and 35 feet deep.

FBI director Louis Freeh traveled several times to Saudi Arabia to interview suspects held in Saudi jails, and he publicly claimed that the Clinton administration was not doing enough to pursue evidence involving the Iranian government. U.S. officials built a case charging leaders of the Iranian-backed Saudi Hezbollah terrorist group, and as the fifth anniversary of the bombing grew near, the U.S. indicted 14 men in the attack. The 46-count indictment, announced on June 21, 2001, charged 13 Saudi Shiite Muslims and one Lebanese man in the bombing plot. According to the indictment, the bombing plot had been in the works for more than three years by Saudi Hezbollah members, who wanted to oust Americans from Saudi Arabia. The bombers transported the explosives from Beirut and stuffed them into a tanker truck.

At a news conference announcing the indictment, Attorney General John D. Ashcroft said that Iranian government officials "inspired, supported and supervised members of Saudi Hezbollah" in the attack. However, no Iranian officials were actually charged in the indictment.

Iran denied any role in the bombing, and Saudi Arabia challenged U.S. jurisdiction in the case, as the act took place in Saudi Arabia and 13 of the men charged were Saudi citizens. Eleven of the suspects are in Saudi custody, while the rest remain fugitives. Saudi officials have stated that it is impossible to extradite the men now in their custody and that the Saudi Arabian government will try them instead.

Four of the men indicted by the United States in the Khobar case, Abdelkarim Hussein Mohamed al Nasser, Ahmad Ibrahim al Mughassil, Ali Saed bin Ali el Hoorie, and Ibrahim Salih Mohammed al Yacoub, remained on the U.S. Federal Bureau of Investigation's list of most-wanted terrorists as of 2010.

Erica Pearson

See also Bombings and Bomb Scares; Hezbollah; Hoorie, Ali Saed bin Ali el; Mughassil, Ahmad Ibrahim al; Nasser, Abdelkarim Hussein Mohamed al; Yacoub, Ibrahim Salih Mohammed al

Further Readings

Federal Bureau of Investigation. "Most Wanted Terrorists." http://www.fbi.gov/wanted/terrorists/fugitives.htm.

Jamieson, Perry D. *Khobar Towers: Tragedy and Response*. Washington, DC: Air Force History and Museums Program, 2008.

Rizen, James, and Jane Perlez. "Terrorism and Iran: Washington's Policy Performs a Gingerly Balancing Act." *The New York Times,* June 23, 2001, p. A6.

U.S. District Court for the Eastern District of Virginia, Alexandria Division. *United States v. Ahmed al-Mughassil, et al.* Indictment, June 21, 2001 (Khobar Indictment). http://fl1.findlaw.com/news.findlaw.com/cnn/docs/khobar/khobarindict61901.pdf.

Walsh, Elsa. "Louis Freeh's Last Case." *The New Yorker,* May 14, 2001.

KIKUMURA, YU (1952–)

Yu Kikumura was a member of the Japanese Red Army (JRA) who was apprehended on the New Jersey Turnpike in 1988 with bombs and bomb-making materials. He may have been planning to bomb targets in New York City.

Kikumura was born on the island of Kyushu, Japan, on July 18, 1952. Little is known of his early life, although he has stated that he was politically influenced by his father, a labor organizer and political activist. In the late 1960s, he participated in the Japanese student protest movement, although he has claimed that his involvement was slight. He is known to have lived in London and Athens for a number of years during the 1970s.

At some point, he became a member of the JRA, a radical Marxist terror group that conducted many hijackings and terrorist attacks during the 1970s. Realizing the difficulty of fomenting a Communist revolution in Japan, a large number of the group's members, led by Fusako Shigenobu, left that country in 1971 and moved to Lebanon. There they became protégés of the Popular Front for the Liberation of Palestine (PFLP), a Middle Eastern Marxist group that was affiliated with many Western terrorists groups during the 1970s. Kikumura may have been trained in the manufacture and use of explosives at a PFLP training camp during this time.

In April 1986 the U.S. government bombed Libya in retaliation for Colonel Muammar el Qaddafi's role in the La Belle disco bombing in West Berlin, in which an American serviceman was killed. In response, the JRA planned a campaign of reprisals against U.S. targets. In May 1986, Kikumura was arrested in Amsterdam, after airport security discovered more than a kilogram of plastic explosives and several detonators concealed in his luggage. After Kikumura spent four months in prison, a Dutch judge ruled that the search of his luggage had been conducted illegally, and he was freed and deported to Japan. Kikumura traveled extensively on a false passport during the next year. He left Madrid, Spain, days after a cache of bombs believed to be intended for the U.S. embassy was discovered, but no connection between Kikumura and the Madrid bombs could be proved.

On March 8, 1988, Kikumura entered the United States. He spent the next several weeks crisscrossing the country collecting bomb materials. On April 12, a New Jersey state trooper searched Kikumura's car while he was parked at a rest stop. Three bombs, consisting of shrapnel and gunpowder encased in fire extinguishers, were discovered, along with bomb-making materials and maps of New York City, including the subway system.

Two days later, on the anniversary of the Libyan bombings, a USO canteen in Naples, Italy, was bombed by the JRA. Kikumura's thwarted attack may have been planned to coincide with the Naples bombing. An ambiguous mark on one of his maps led investigators to believe that he intended to bomb a naval recruitment office in Manhattan. In February 1989, Kikumura was tried in the United States and sentenced to 30 years in prison for terrorist activities. In 1991 this sentence was reduced to 21 years and 10 months.

Kikumura was released from prison on April 18, 2007. He flew to Japan the next day, where he was arrested and eventually given a two-year suspended sentence for using forged official documents, a charge that stemmed from his having a fake international driver's license when he was arrested in 1988.

Colleen Sullivan

See also Japanese Red Army; Popular Front for the Liberation of Palestine; Qaddafi, Muammar el; Shigenobu, Fusako

Further Readings

Dickey, Christopher. *Securing the City: Inside America's Best Counterterror Force—the NYPD.* New York: Simon & Schuster, 2009.

Farrell, William. *Blood and Rage: The Story of the Japanese Red Army.* Lexington, MA: D.C. Heath, 1990.

Hanley, Robert. "Man Is Arrested Carrying Bombs on Jersey Pike." *The New York Times,* April 14, 1988, p. B4.

"Japanese Terrorist Arrested at Home after U.S. Prison Term." *The Daily Yomiuri,* April 20, 2007, p. 1.

Kessler, Robert E., and Scott Ladd. "Sentence Ends Political Thriller; Prisoner Tied to Japan Terrorist Organization." *Newsday,* February 12, 1989, p. 7.

Sullivan, Joseph F. "Man Who Carried 3 Pipe Bombs Has Sentence Reduced by 8 Years." *The New York Times,* March 2, 1991, p. 26.

KILBURN, PETER (1924–1986)

Peter Kilburn, a librarian at the American University in Beirut, is believed to have been the first American hostage to be executed during the Lebanon hostage crisis.

Kilburn, who had worked for the American University library for more than 20 years, was reported missing after he failed to show up for work on December 3, 1984. He was last seen alive on November 30, 1984. Unlike most hostage takings, no group claimed responsibility for Kilburn's disappearance. During the 16 months Kilburn was

"missing," his name was notably absent from the various videos, letters, and messages sent by American hostages to their families and the U.S. government.

Little is known about the conditions in which Kilburn was held or how he was abducted. Some have suggested that he was kidnapped because he hired a Christian over two Shiites for a library position at the university. Later CIA intelligence indicated that "thugs" more interested in money than political causes abducted Kilburn, and that he was to be "sold" to the highest bidder.

In the summer of 1985, a Canadian of Armenian descent who claimed to be a representative of the group holding Kilburn claimed that Kilburn's freedom could be purchased for $500,000. That figure later jumped to $3 million once the Canadian offered proof, in the form of Kilburn's American University identification card. By March 1986, the CIA and FBI had planned an elaborate "sting" operation in which the kidnappers were to be paid with chemically treated bills that would dissolve a few days after the swap. Ross Perot, the Texas billionaire, supplied the $100,000 to be paid to the Canadian intermediary, and the altered money was delivered to Europe. However, in the midst of these transactions, a Libyan intelligence agent in Lebanon paid to have Kilburn murdered, based on rumors that the United States was planning a military strike against Libya's leader Muammar el Qaddafi for his role in the La Belle disco bombing in West Berlin.

On April 17, 1986, two days after the United States bombed Libya, the bodies of Kilburn and two British schoolteachers, John Leigh Douglas, and Philip Padfield, were found in the hills of East Beirut. They had been shot in the back of the head. Farid Fleihan, Kilburn's longtime friend and physician at American University hospital, identified Kilburn's body in Beirut. A later autopsy at Bethesda Naval Hospital revealed no signs of torture or mistreatment.

The Arab Fedayeen Cells (or Arab Revolutionary Cells), a pro-Libyan group of Palestinians affiliated with the terrorist Abu Nidal, claimed responsibility for these deaths. A note found with the bodies described the men as "two British intelligence agents" and a "CIA agent" who were killed in response to the U.S. air strikes against Libya, and Britain's cooperation in that action.

Kilburn's body was returned to the United States on April 20, 1986, and buried later that month in the army cemetery in San Francisco's Presidio. Six years later, the United States offered up to $2 million for aid in capturing the individuals involved in Kilburn's death, as well as the deaths of Walter Higgins, a colonel in the U.S. Marines, and William Buckley, the Beirut CIA station chief.

Laura Lambert

See also Abu Nidal Organization; Buckley, William; La Belle Discotheque Bombing; Qaddafi, Muammar el

Further Readings

Martin, David C. and John Walcott. *Best Laid Plans: The Inside Story of America's War against Terrorism.* New York: Harper & Row, 1988.

Smith, Michael. *Killer Elite: The Inside Story of America's Most Secret Special Operations Team.* New York: St. Martin's, 2006.

KING DAVID HOTEL BOMBING

On July 22, 1946, the primary Jewish underground militant group, Irgun Zvai Leumi, blew up the southern wing of the King David Hotel in Jerusalem, in what was then British-ruled Palestine.

Zionists clashed many times with the British during the mid-twentieth century. The Balfour Declaration of 1916 promised the Jewish people a national home in Palestine. However, the 1936 Arab Revolt led Britain to retreat from this commitment, and in 1939 the British enacted the so-called White Paper, which limited Jewish immigrants to 75,000 over the next five years. During World War II the Irgun suspended attacks against the British in Palestine, concentrating instead on fighting the Germans, and many Irgun supporters joined the British Army. However, a more extreme splinter group called Lehi, or the Stern Gang, continued attacking the British in Palestine.

Most of the British Administration in Palestine was based in the King David, a seven-story luxury hotel. The Irgun strike force set out disguised as hotel workers on the morning of July 22, riding in a van loaded with seven milk churns filled with explosives and detonators. They entered the hotel, brought the churns in through the hotel's side gate,

and placed them next to supporting pillars in the hotel restaurant. The timers on the bombs were set for 30 minutes.

The Irgun leader, Menachem Begin, who became Israel's prime minister in 1977, has publicly stated that the Irgun placed three phone calls to various parties before the blast, issuing a warning to minimize casualties. However, the British have long denied that they were warned before the explosion. If the calls were made, they were ignored, for the staff of the government secretariat and military command remained in their rooms. Ninety-one people were killed in the blast: 41 Arabs, 28 Britons, 17 Jews, and 5 others. In the face of this and other attacks, Britain soon turned over the administration of Palestine. The last British High Commissioner, General Sir Alan Cunningham, sailed from Haifa in May 1948. In 1995, in a controversial move, the Jerusalem Municipality chose to name a street "Gal Boulevard," after Joshua "Gal" Goldschmidt, one of the planners of the King David Hotel attack.

Erica Pearson

See also Bombings and Bomb Scares; Irgun Zvai Leumi; Stern Gang

Further Readings

Begin, Menachem. *The Revolt.* New York: Nash Publishing, 1977.

Evron, Yosef. "Clearing the Debris from a Decades-old Explosion." *Jerusalem Post,* July 19, 2002, p. 9A.

La Guardia, Anton. "The Violent Birth of a Jewish State." *The Daily Telegraph,* April 18, 1998, p. 20.

KLINGHOFFER, LEON

See Achille Lauro Hijacking

KNEECAPPING

Kneecapping is a form of physical attack developed by the Red Brigades in Italy. Members of the group would approach a victim and shoot him in one or both knees. In addition to being physically damaging and excruciatingly painful, the technique was especially effective because it required the assailant to get very close to the victim, demonstrating how vulnerable a person could be. The assailants would get away after the attack, providing evidence of the government's inability to protect people. Further, the group opted to undertake the more difficult task of getting close to a victim rather than shooting him at a distance with a rifle because it demonstrated the abilities of the group. Because the Red Brigades were "only wounding" the victims, even if they were likely to be crippled as a consequence of the attack, the group avoided the negative publicity that would have come with murders. A wounded person also provided continuing publicity for the group.

The Red Brigades may have borrowed this technique from criminal groups in Italy (and elsewhere) that developed kneecapping as a mechanism for extorting money from individuals or for collecting debts. Thus, while it was not an original technique, it was still effective in terms of spreading fear among the target audience and demonstrating the weaknesses of the government. Such audacious attacks also suggested that the Red Brigades could strike at will. While terrorist groups actually pick the more vulnerable targets rather than the well-guarded ones, the appearance that the group could strike at will was very effective.

The Red Brigades eventually escalated their attacks and launched more deadly assaults when they failed to achieve their goals with these assaults. Other groups, however, adopted the use of kneecapping. Both the Irish Republican Army and the Protestant groups in Northern Ireland began using the technique. Although at times they used it against political targets on the other side, Irish groups principally used kneecapping against their own people, as one means on a graduated scale of violence to maintain control within their own communities. The leftist Revolutionary Organization 17 November in Greece also adopted the technique against its opponents on a selective basis. While the Northern Irish groups may have adopted the technique independently of the Red Brigades, the Greek leftists appear to have copied the idea from their Italian compatriots.

The kneecapping technique was effective in its initial stages. It provided great publicity to the Italian Red Brigades, and it proved to be a useful technique for other groups in the right circumstances. There have been very few long-lasting groups, however, that have been able to rely only on kneecapping and similar kinds of assaults. They either escalate to more violent tactics or disappear from the scene when limited violence is ineffective in achieving the objectives of the group.

James Lutz and Brenda J. Lutz

See also Irish Republican Army; Red Brigades; Revolutionary Organization 17 November

Further Readings

Barr, R.J., and R.A.B. Mollan. "The Orthopaedic Consequences of Civil Disturbance in Northern Ireland." *Journal of Bone and Joint Surgery* 71, no. 5 (1989): 739–744. http://www.jbjs.org.uk/cgi/reprint/71-B/5/739.pdf.

Drake, Richard. *The Revolutionary Mystique and Terrorism in Contemporary Italy*. Bloomington: Indiana University Press, 1989.

Silke, Andrew. "Rebel's Dilemma: The Changing Relationship between the IRA, Sinn Fein, and Paramilitary Vigilantism in Northern Ireland," *Terrorism and Political Violence* 22, no. 1 (1999): 1–20.

KORESH, DAVID

See Branch Davidian Compound Siege

KOSOVO LIBERATION ARMY

The Kosovo Liberation Army (KLA) emerged in 1996 and instigated a war between Kosovo and Serbia in the hope of winning Kosovo's independence.

Kosovo, which borders on Albania, was a province of Serbia, which itself was a part of the former Yugoslavia. Kosovo was once the center of Serbian culture and society, but over the past several hundred years its population has changed. Today, more than 90 percent of its people are of Albanian ethnicity, most of them Muslim. Serbs still consider Kosovo an integral part of their country.

In Communist Yugoslavia, which united several Balkan provinces (including Serbia), Kosovo was considered to be a part of Serbia but was administered autonomously. In 1989, during the death throes of the Communist government, Slobodan Milosovic was elected president of Serbia on a nationalist platform. One of his first actions was to strip Kosovo of its independence, replacing Albanian officials with Serbian ones and closing Albanian-language schools. The reaction of the Kosovo Albanians was to boycott all Serbian institutions in a form of peaceful protest, setting up their own shadow government. These tactics did not gain the hoped-for attention and support of the international community, however. After the 1995 Dayton Peace Accords (which resolved a separate war between Serbia and Bosnia) failed to address Kosovo's independence, many Kosovo Albanians began to look for other solutions.

In this atmosphere, the Kosovo Liberation Army emerged. In 1996 and 1997, the KLA, which was originally composed of a few hundred Albanian Muslim veterans of the Bosnian war, attacked several Serbian police stations and wounded many officers. The KLA made its first public statement on December 1, 1997, during a funeral service for an Albanian teacher killed by Serbian police. The speech was a call to arms outlining the KLA's position and objectives. (Prior to this appearance, some observers suspected that the KLA was actually a Serbian tool—an indirect way of stirring up ancient ethnic tensions that would allow Milosovic to move against Kosovo's Albanian population.)

The KLA's stated objectives were the secession of Kosovo from Serbia and the eventual creation of a "Greater Albania," encompassing Kosovo, Albania, and the ethnic Albanian minority of neighboring Macedonia. The KLA found great moral and financial support among the Albanian diaspora, and it used the money it received to purchase weapons, which were then smuggled over the porous Albania-Kosovo border. As the KLA became better armed, its attacks became more effective; the Serbian president of the University of Pristina, Kosovo's capital, narrowly escaped assassination in January 1997.

In response, the Serbian government began a crackdown against the Kosovo Albanian population, raiding villages and expelling people from their homes. Massacres by the Serbian police were reported, and suspects taken into police custody were often beaten and tortured to extort confessions. The crackdown on the Kosovo Albanian population only increased support for the KLA, which attracted thousands of new recruits and was removed from the United States' list of terrorist groups in 1998. Throughout that year, the KLA escalated its attacks and Serbia followed suit with reprisals. By the end of 1998, the KLA had killed scores of police; the Serbian government had sent 40,000 troops to the region; and an estimated 200,000 Kosovo Albanian refugees had fled into neighboring countries.

The mounting refugee crisis began to attract serious international attention. In February 1999, the allied governments of the North Atlantic Treaty Organization (NATO), led by the United States, forced the Serbian government and the KLA into truce negotiations in Rambouillet, France. The KLA was prevailed upon to sign the treaty, but the Serbian government refused. In March 1999, NATO commenced air strikes on Serbian forces. The air campaign lasted for 11 weeks. During the campaign, an estimated 1.5 million Albanian refugees are believed to have left the area, about 85 percent of Kosovo's total population. The KLA ranks also expanded, and by the end of the campaign some observers estimated that the organization had about 20,000 troops, several thousand of whom were well-trained former soldiers. The KLA forces on the ground played an important role—especially during the campaign's final weeks, when the organization was at full strength. By engaging Serbian troops, they were able to concentrate the Serbian forces so that NATO air strikes were much more effective. Between 25 and 50 percent of the Serbian equipment is thought to have been destroyed during the campaign.

Following the war, the United Nations sent a multinational peacekeeping force of 50,000 into the region. All Serbian government forces were removed, and many Kosovo Serbs left as well. In contrast, almost all the Kosovo Albanian refugees returned; the population of the province is now believed to be about 95 percent Albanian. The presence of the UN forces quickly quelled the retaliatory violence perpetrated by returning refugees on their former Serb neighbors. The KLA submitted to demilitarization, and several of its most important leaders went on to form political parties. The KLA parties won 37 seats in Kosovo's first parliamentary elections in November 2001, and former KLA members now largely compete against each other for high political office.

During the Rambouillet negotiations, the international community had hoped to re-establish Kosovo's autonomy, but not full independence, as it was believed an independent Kosovo would tend to destabilize the entire region and lead to further war. Kosovo declared itself an independent nation in February 2008, but many countries have not recognized it as such, considering it to still be a province of Serbia.

The exact status of the now defunct KLA has likewise generated significant controversy. Following demilitarization, the combat wing of the KLA became the Kosovo Protection Corps (KPC), an emergency-response organization largely staffed by ex-KLA fighters. In January 2009, despite Serbian objections, the KPC took on security duties and became the Kosovo Protection Force.

The Serbian government argued that the KLA was a terrorist group, and that its former leaders should be tried for crimes committed during and after the war against Serbia. Individual KLA members have been tried and convicted for war crimes, both by Kosovo courts and by the United Nations International Criminal Tribunal for the former Yugoslavia (ICTY), located in The Hague. But the ICTY, which began indicting Kosovar Albanians in 2003, has consistently found that while some KLA members did commit atrocities, the KLA itself did not make a policy of targeting civilians or engaging in war crimes.

As a result, higher-ranking KLA leaders who have been tried by the ICTY have largely been acquitted. These include Fatmir Limaj, a KLA commander who as of 2010 was minister of transportation and telecommunications in Kosovo, and Ramush Haradinaj, a KLA commander who became prime minister in 2004 but stepped down the next year to stand trial. Others, such as Agim Ceku, a former KLA military head and a former prime minister of Kosovo, as well Hashim Thaci, a former KLA political head who became prime minister in 2008, have never been indicted by the ICTY, although they are considered war criminals by Serbia.

Colleen Sullivan

See also State Terrorism

Further Readings

Bilefsky, Dan. "Ex-Soldier May Go from The Hague's Docket to Kosovo's Ballot." *The New York Times,* July 12, 2008, p. A6.

Chifflet, Pascale. "The First Trial of Former Members of the Kosovo Liberation Army: *Prosecutor v. Fatmir Limaj, Haradin Bala, and Isak Musliu.*" *Leiden Journal of International Law* 19 (2006): 459–476.

Daalder, Ivo H., and Michael E. O'Hanlon. *Winning Ugly: NATO's War to Save Kosovo.* Washington, DC: Brookings Institution Press, 2000.

Human Rights Watch. *Under Orders: War Crimes in Kosovo.* New York: Human Rights Watch, 2001.

Koktsidis, Pavlos-Ioannis, and Casper Ten Dam. "A Success Story? Analysing Albanian Ethno-nationalist Extremism in the Balkans." *East European Quarterly* 42, no. 2 (June 2008): 161–190.

Layne, Christopher. *Blunder in the Balkans: The Clinton Administration's Bungled War against Serbia.* Washington, DC: Cato Institute, 1999.

Perry, Henry, Jr. *The Kosovo Liberation Army: The Inside Story of an Insurgency.* Urbana: University of Illinois Press, 2008.

Rieff, David. "Kosovo's Humanitarian Circus." *World Policy Journal* (Fall 2000).

Taylor, Scott. *An Uncivil War: The Violent Aftermath of the Kosovo Conflict.* Ottawa, Ontario: Esprit de Corps Books, 2002.

United Nations International Criminal Tribunal for the former Yugoslavia. http://www.icty.org.

KROPOTKIN, PETER (1842–1921)

A Russian geographer and revolutionary, Peter Kropotkin published a large body of work promoting anarchism, though he was ultimately disappointed in the economic and social outcomes of Russia's 1917 revolution.

Born in Moscow to a noble family, Kropotkin held the title of prince. When he turned 15, he joined the elite Corps des Pages of St. Petersburg so that upon graduation he could become a page to Czar Alexander II. In the 1860s he chose to work in Siberia helping implement Alexander's social reforms. In 1867 he studied the geography of Eastern Siberia and was offered the position of secretary of the Imperial Geographical Society. Kropotkin turned down the job, renounced his aristocratic heritage, and devoted himself to instigating Russian revolution.

Kropotkin developed a theory of anarchist communism, a system in which goods and services could be distributed freely and equally with the cooperation of every member of society. Kropotkin was also a proponent of "propaganda by deed," a theory of Mikhail Bakunin that argued individuals should undertake violent actions in order to inspire revolutionary fervor in the general population. In the early 1870s, Kropotkin joined the revolutionary First International Workingmen's Association.

He was arrested for openly criticizing the Russian government but then managed to escape to Switzerland. His extreme socialist views made him unpopular in Switzerland as well, and in 1881 he moved to France. The French authorities arrested Kropotkin in 1883 for sedition. While in prison, he wrote a book on his anarchist views called *Paroles d'un revolte* (*Words of a Rebel*, 1885), in which he often explained his views from a scientific standpoint. After he was released and had moved to England, he wrote another book called *In Russian and French Prisons* (1887). In this work, he called for more humane treatment of prisoners. Over the next few years, he was an active participant in the international socialist movement and authored many more books, including *Conquest of Bread* (1892), *Fields, Factories, and Workshops* (1899), *Mutual Aid* (1902), and *The Great French Revolution 1789–1793* (1909).

Now known around the world for his political views, Kropotkin returned home to Russia after the revolution took place in 1917. He soon became dismayed with the authoritarian regime of the Bolsheviks, however, and he felt that the revolution ultimately failed. He remained in Russia until his death on February 8, 1921. He left *Ethics, Origin and Development* unfinished, but it was published after his death.

Harvey Kushner

See also Anarchism; Bakunin, Mikhail

Further Readings

Cahm, Caroline. *Kropotkin and the Rise of Revolutionary Anarchism, 1872–1886.* Cambridge, UK: Cambridge University Press, 1989.

Kropotkin, Peter. *The Black Flag: Peter Kropotkin on Anarchism.* St. Petersburg, FL: Red and Black Publishers, 2010.

Marshall, Peter. *Demanding the Impossible: A History of Anarchism.* Oakland, CA: PM Press, 2010.

McKay, Iain. "Mutual Aid: An Introduction & Evaluation." *Anarcho-Syndicalist Review* 52 (Summer 2009): 25.

Miller, Martin Alan. *Kropotkin.* Chicago: University of Chicago Press, 1976.

Woodcock, George, and Ivan Avakumovic. *Peter Kropotkin: From Prince to Rebel.* Montreal: Black Rose Books, 1990.

KU KLUX KLAN

The Ku Klux Klan is the oldest organized hate group in the United States, dating back more than 135 years to the Reconstruction era following the end of the Civil War. Although the Klan's original intent was to assert the supremacy of the white race over the newly freed black slaves, over the decades the organization widened the scope of its hatred to include Roman Catholics, Jews, immigrants, and homosexuals. The KKK has been a model for other extremist groups in the country, who have emulated Klan practices of intimidation and violence.

The Historical Klan

Accounts vary, but many believe that six Confederate soldiers formed the KKK on Christmas Eve 1865, in Pulaski, Tennessee. (Other accounts place the founding in May or June 1866.) In its early years, the group was considered to be a social organization; however, the KKK soon began to terrorize local freed slaves. Klansmen would don white flowing robes and pointed hats, sometimes cloaking their horses in white sheets as well to affect the appearance of Confederate soldiers risen from the dead, and would raid the homes of blacks in the middle of the night.

Scholars believe that the Klan formed initially in response to white anxiety over the weak Reconstruction governments in the South and the possibility of insurrection on the part of newly freed slaves. Klansmen attacked black freedmen and their white Republican supporters alike, as well as assailing "carpetbaggers" from the North. Their intimidation was intended to keep black men and Republicans from voting, thus maintaining white political power in the South. In short, the Klan hoped to uphold southern culture and politics as it existed before the Civil War, and it was willing to take violent measures to succeed.

In 1867, the disparate chapters of the Klan, which had taken root throughout Tennessee, Mississippi, and Alabama, held their first national convention in Nashville, and they elected as their national leader, or Grand Wizard, General Nathan Bedford Forrest, a former Confederate cavalry leader. This convention established the elaborately named organizational hierarchy, including Grand Cyclops, Magi, and Night Hawks, who governed over dominions and dens, and the concept of the Klan as an "invisible empire" was born.

As the Klan grew, it was plagued by infighting, which continued to be part of the group's turbulent history. By 1869, Forrest officially "disbanded" the organization. Even the individual KKK chapters had nearly died off by the 1870s, due to a confluence of several factors, including national anti-Klan legislation in 1870 and 1871, "Jim Crow" laws that neatly reestablished segregation in the South, and internal dissension over the use of violence.

The Modern Klan

After lying dormant for more than 40 years, the Klan's "second era" began in 1915, when William J. Simmons, a former minister, resurrected the Klan at Stone Mountain, Georgia—an event marked by a cross burning, soon to become the Klan's calling card. Scholars attribute the renewed interest in the Klan to the release and popularity of D.W. Griffith's 1915 film, *Birth of a Nation*, which was based on a book by Thomas Dixon called *The Clansman* (1905) and credited the Klan with the preservation of the southern way of life.

Within a decade, the Klan reached the height of its power, rapidly spreading nationwide. In its second incarnation, the Klan opposed immigration, mostly of Jews and Catholics, and benefited from a growing Protestant fundamentalism and the patriotic fervor generated by World War I. By the mid-1920s, membership had developed from approximately 10,000 to between 4 and 5 million, and Klan leaders attained high political offices, becoming governors, senators, and representatives.

Scandal soon rocked the organization, however. After David C. Stephenson, a Klan leader in the Midwest, was convicted for the rape and mutilation of a woman, evidence emerged that led to the indictments of the governor of Indiana and the mayor of Indianapolis, both Klan supporters. Once again, upper-class and more mainstream Klansmen distanced themselves from such violence. During the Great Depression (1929–1941), the Klan also lost its core dues-paying members, mostly from the lower and middle classes, to poverty.

The Klan re-emerged in the 1950s, fighting racial desegregation and terrorizing blacks and civil rights workers with cross burnings, beatings, bombings, death threats, and murder. In 1963 the Klan members Robert Chambliss, Bobby Frank Cherry, Herman Frank Cash, and Thomas E. Blanton Jr. bombed the Sixteenth Street Baptist Church in Birmingham, Alabama, killing four young girls. This incident is widely considered to be the lowest point of the civil rights struggle. Klan members were also behind the murders of the civil rights activists Medgar Evers in June 1963; James Chaney, Andrew Goodman, and Michael Schwerner in June 1964; and Viola Liuzzo in March 1965.

By the mid-1960s, the federal government began to intervene. The FBI added the KKK to the organizations targeted by the COINTELPRO counterintelligence program. This federal program aimed to "disrupt and neutralize" both left- and right-wing extremist groups. The House Un-American Activities Committee also investigated the Klan. This government involvement and the KKK's persistent factionalism caused a membership decline in the 1970s.

Violence Reemerges

Significant violence occurred in 1979, when Klansmen killed five anti-Klan demonstrators in Greensboro, North Carolina, and again in 1981, when Klansmen lynched Michael Donald, a black teenager, in Mobile, Alabama. The 1980s and 1990s, however, were marked by mostly sporadic, isolated violence. In the early 1990s, the Texas Knights of the White Camellia Ku Klux Klan engaged in extensive racial intimidation in Vidor, Texas, to prevent the desegregation of a federal housing project. Klan groups are also believed to be behind a rash of nationwide church burnings that began in January 1995.

At the same time, several organizations, the Southern Poverty Law Center among them, worked successfully against the Klan in the courts, dismantling the United Klans of America in 1987 for the Donald lynching, and the Invisible Empire, Knights of the Ku Klux Klan in 1993 for attacking civil rights activists in Forsyth, Georgia. Arrests of Klan members continued throughout the late 1990s and 2000s, including an April 1997 arrest of three Klan members for conspiracy to blow up a natural gas refinery in Fort Worth, Texas, and several arrests in February 1998 for plots to poison water supplies, rob banks, plant bombs, and commit assassinations. In July 1998, the Christian Knights of the Ku Klux Klan were found to have participated in a conspiracy to burn a black church.

In March 2006, six members of the Nation's Knights of the Ku Klux Klan pled guilty in North Carolina to running an illegal gun-selling operation, which was created to finance a plan to blow up a county courthouse. In 2008 a teenager in Kentucky was awarded $2.5 million in a civil suit involving one branch of the Klan, whose members had attacked the boy, breaking his jaw and arm and cracking several of his ribs, because they believed (mistakenly, as it turned out) he was an undocumented immigrant. That same month, a woman was shot and killed in Louisiana during a botched initiation into the Sons of Dixie Knights; four people were charged in the case, and two pled guilty.

By the twenty-first century, the Klan had dissolved from one large organization into independent chapters and splinter groups; the Anti-Defamation League has estimated an overall membership of about 5,000. It is not believed that the Klan has any central leadership at this point. While some factions are openly racist and follow the Christian Identity movement, others have tried to mainstream themselves, cloaking racism as "civil rights for whites." Contemporary Klan propaganda typically moves beyond mere racism to also exploit concerns about immigration, crime, the 2008 financial crisis, or even gay marriage. The Internet has aided Klan recruitment efforts: Klan chapters maintain websites with propaganda, historical accounts, and membership applications, as well as links to other Klan chapters. Some Klan spokesmen predicted a race war after the election of Barack Obama, the first black president of the United States, and indeed the U.S.

Justice Department expressed concerns over a possible rise in violence from hate groups. However, groups such as the Southern Poverty Law Center hold out hope that civil actions such as the victory in Kentucky will decimate the Klan financially and impede its ability to organize in any substantive way.

Laura Lambert

See also Christian Identity; Lynching; Sixteenth Street Baptist Church Bombing; White Supremacy Movement

Further Readings

Chambers, David M. *Hooded Americanism: The History of the Ku Klux Klan.* New York: Franklin Watts, 1981.

Dobratz, Betty A., and Stephanie L. Shanks-Meile. *White Power, White Pride! The White Separatist Movement in the United States.* Baltimore: Johns Hopkins University Press, 1997.

Durham, Martin. *White Rage: The Extreme Right and American Politics.* New York: Routledge, 2007.

May, Gary. *The Informant: The FBI, the Ku Klux Klan, and the Murder of Viola Liuzzo.* New Haven, CT: Yale University Press, 2005.

Newton, Michael. *The Ku Klux Klan: History, Organization, Language, Influence, and Activities of America's Most Notorious Secret Society.* Jefferson, NC: McFarland, 2007.

O'Donnell, Patrick, ed. *Ku Klux Klan: America's First Terrorists Exposed.* West Orange, NJ: Idea Man Productions, 2006.

Stanton, Bill. *Klanwatch: Bringing the Ku Klux Klan to Justice.* New York: Grove Weidenfeld, 1991.

Zeskind, Leonard. *Blood and Politics: The History of the White Nationalist Movement from the Margins to the Mainstream.* New York: Farrar, Straus and Giroux, 2009.

KURDISH HEZBOLLAH

See Turkish Hezbollah

KURDISTAN WORKERS' PARTY

The Kurdistan Workers' Party (Partiya Karkerên Kurdistan, or PKK) was founded to establish a

Kurdish state and self-rule in southeastern Turkey, an area that is predominantly Kurdish. Established in 1978 by Abdullah Ocalan, the PKK began its terrorism campaign by focusing on Turkish security forces and civilians in the early 1980s. The sometimes intensely bloody conflict has continued into the 2010s.

PKK's history is inextricably linked with the plight of the Kurds, the world's most numerous stateless people. Largely Muslim, Kurds number between 15 million and 20 million, have their own language and culture, and live in an area known as Kurdistan, a mountainous region that lies within portions of Turkey, Iran, Iraq, Syria, and Armenia.

Demonstrators shout slogans outside the Celio military hospital in downtown Rome to protest against the arrest of Kurdistan Workers' Party's (PKK) leader Abdullah Ocalan, November 14, 1998. Ocalan was arrested in Rome after stepping off a plane from Moscow and was facing extradition to Turkey. The PKK has been fighting for autonomy in southeastern Turkey since 1984. Nearly 37,000 people have died in the conflict. (AP Photo/Marco Ravagli.© 2011 The Associated Press. All Rights Reserved.)

Nearly 11 million Kurds live in Turkey and represent roughly 20 percent of that country's population. Turkey is home to the highest concentration of Kurds anywhere.

After World War I, the breakup of the Ottoman Empire formed new nation-states, but no separate Kurdistan. Thus, the Kurds, who were until then nomadic, could no longer keep to their ancient migratory ways. Although the 1920 Treaty of Sevres promised independence, the Kurds were never granted nationhood. In 1923, Turkey refused to honor that provision of the treaty, and the Kurds remained an ethnic group within Turkey. Kurd revolts in the 1920s and 1930s were met by the Turkish government with mass executions and village burnings.

The founder and leader of the PKK, Abdullah Ocalan, was born in 1948 in southeastern Turkey, near the Syrian border. While attending the university at Ankara, he studied political science and developed, many believe, what would become the thinking behind the PKK. He dropped out of school, wrote a manifesto on the subject of Kurdish liberation, and in 1978 he formed the PKK as a terrorist group to help establish a Kurdish state. Today, many of the Kurdish people refer to him as "Apo," the Kurdish word for "uncle."

Although Ocalan left Turkey for exile in 1980, he directed the PKK from Syria and other countries, and he has orchestrated most PKK plots. The PKK held its first congress in July 1981, and it later established a "Presidential Council," comprising 10 senior commanders, to run the group's day-to-day operations. In 1984 the PKK began to use terror (usually serial kidnappings and bombings) to spread its message. Some of the first targets were police stations and other state buildings in Turkey's southeastern provinces, but the campaign eventually turned against civilians, most of them Kurds, whom the PKK accused of conspiring with the state.

The Turkish government fought back. Between 1984 and 1999 (with 1991 and 1993 seeing the peak of PKK activity), nearly 40,000 people died as a result of PKK violence and government retaliation. In 1999 Ocalan was apprehended in Kenya and returned to Turkey, where he was sentenced to death. (The sentence was commuted to life in prison in 2002.) The day he was sentenced, riots, demonstrations, and occupations of embassies occurred throughout Europe. From prison, however, Ocalan announced a cease-fire and asked all PKK forces to abandon Turkey. In February 2000, the PKK officially ceased its 15-year revolution and agreed to the political program put forward by the imprisoned leader.

Although many believed that Ocalan's imprisonment would end the PKK, which strongly venerated him, the group, although weakened, did not disappear. Ocalan is still considered the PKK's leader, and the organization has moderated its views somewhat in keeping with his. For example, the organization now seeks greater autonomy for Turkish Kurds, rather than outright independence. Following his arrest, however, Ocalan's leadership became largely symbolic, and day-to-day leadership of the PKK was taken over by members operating from bases in neighboring Iraq. Under their leadership, the PKK announced an end to its cease-fire with Turkey in 2004. PKK guerrillas then commenced a variety of attacks on Turkish forces, slipping back over the poorly controlled border with Iraq to regroup. In addition, an offshoot of the PKK called the Kurdistan Freedom Falcons conducted a series of bomb attacks in popular tourist areas that targeted civilians in an attempt to cripple Turkey's tourism industry.

In 2008 the group was believed to have 4,000 to 5,000 active members (down from 10,000 earlier in the decade), 3,000 to 3,500 of whom were based in the Kurdish region of Iraq. The large PKK presence in Iraq has caused a great deal of diplomatic tension between that country and Turkey, with the Turkish government accusing the largely autonomous Kurdish regional government in Iraq of tolerating the PKK, and the Iraqi government responding that it lacked the resources to eliminate the group.

By late 2007, Turkey was regularly conducting air strikes against PKK bases in Iraq, and in February 2008, Turkey launched a weeklong military incursion into that country. Turkey's incursion into Iraq generated protests from both the national and regional governments. Following Turkey's withdrawal, Iraq pledged to work more closely with Turkey to crack down on the PKK, which continues to conduct attacks in Turkey. In addition to the military maneuvers, in November 2009 the Turkish government proposed a reconciliation plan that would eliminate restrictions currently in place regarding the use of the Kurdish language. It is hoped that this might reduce the appeal of militant groups like the PKK.

Richard McHugh

See also Ocalan, Abdullah

Further Readings

Arsu, Sebnem. "Turkey Plans to Ease Restrictions on Kurds and Help End Decades of Conflict." *The New York Times,* November 14, 2009, p. A4.

Bird, Christiane. *A Thousand Sighs, A Thousand Revolts: Journeys in Kurdistan.* New York: Ballantine Books, 2004.

Chailand, Gerard, ed. *A People without a Country: The Kurds and Kurdistan.* Rev. ed. London: Olive Branch Press, 1993.

Mango, Andrew. *Turkey and the War on Terror: For Forty Years We Fought Alone.* London: Routledge, 2005.

Olson, Robert. *The Kurdish Question and Turkish-Iranian Relations: From World War I to 1998.* Costa Mesa, CA: Mazda Publishers, 1998.

Partlow, Joshua. "A Kurdish Society of Soldiers." *The Washington Post,* March 8, 2008, p. A1.

Romano, David. *The Kurdish Nationalist Movement: Opportunity, Mobilization and Identity.* Cambridge: Cambridge University Press, 2006.

Shishkin, Phillip. "Destabilizing Force: In Northern Iraq, a Rebel Sanctuary Bedevils the U.S." *The Wall Street Journal,* October 2, 2006, p. A1.

La Belle Discotheque Bombing

On April 5, 1986, a bomb packed with nails exploded at the La Belle disco in West Berlin, killing two U.S. soldiers and a Turkish woman and injuring 229 people. The four-pound bomb exploded at 1:40 A.M. on the crowded dance floor; the flying nails caused such grave injuries that dozens of the victims lost their limbs.

President Reagan quickly accused Libya of the bombing of La Belle, a popular nightspot for U.S. soldiers stationed in West Berlin. Citing intercepted communications between the Libyan embassy in East Berlin and Tripoli, Libya, Reagan ordered U.S. air raids on Libya. One of the U.S. bombs dropped 10 days after the La Belle attack hit Libyan leader Muammar el Qaddafi's home and killed one of his children.

The case went unsolved for years, until the collapse of the Berlin Wall allowed German investigators to discover a wealth of evidence in former East Germany. Files seized from the headquarters of the Stasi, the East German secret police, led to the arrest of five suspects in 1996. More than 15 years after the bombing, a German court convicted a former Libyan diplomat and three accomplices on murder charges in the La Belle bombing.

During the four-year trial, prosecutors showed that the diplomat, Musbah Eter, worked with the Palestinian Yasser Chraidi, an employee of the Libyan embassy in East Berlin, to carry out the attack. The men recruited Ali Channa, a German man of Lebanese descent, and his wife, the German Verena Channa, to carry out the bombing. The Channas were paid about $7,000 for their roles in the attack, according to prosecutors.

Mrs. Channa actually planted the bomb, carrying the explosives into the nightclub in her knapsack. Mrs. Channa's sister went with her to the nightclub and left with her five minutes before the blast, but claimed to have known nothing of the plot. Mrs. Channa was imprisoned for 14 years on the charge of murder, while the others were sentenced to between 12 and 14 years in jail for attempted murder.

The German court also ruled that Libya was involved in the La Belle bombing, but that no evidence proved the direct involvement of Qaddafi. Prosecutors had charged that Qaddafi called for a terrorist attack against the United States in retaliation for the March 1986 sinking of two Libyan ships in the Gulf of Sidra, presenting radio messages between Tripoli, Libya, and the East Berlin Libyan embassy. "Expect the result tomorrow morning. It is God's will," read a message sent on the night of the attack. Hours after the bombing, another cable reported, "at 1:30 A.M., one of the acts was carried out with success, without leaving a trace." These messages were originally intercepted by the U.S. National Security Agency, which ran an eavesdropping station in West Berlin to monitor East Berlin diplomatic communication. In August 2008, Libya, which since 2003 has been attempting to improve its international relations, agreed to pay $283 million to the victims of the La Belle bombing.

Erica Pearson

339

See also Bombings and Bomb Scares; Qaddafi, Muammar el; Tripoli and Benghazi Bombing

Further Readings

Arnold, Guy. *The Maverick State: Gaddafi and the New World Order.* New York: Cassell, 1997.

Burton, Fred. *Ghost: Confessions of a Counterterrorism Agent.* New York: Random House, 2008.

Davis, Brian Leigh. *Qaddafi, Terrorism, and the Origins of the U.S. Attack on Libya.* New York: Praeger, 1990.

Kim, Lucian. "Berlin Disco Terror Trial Nears End." *Christian Science Monitor*, November 2, 2001, p. 6.

"United States and Libya Sign Agreement to Resolve Pan Am Flight 103 and Other Claims." *American Journal of International Law* 102, no. 4 (October 2008): 892–893.

Laden, Osama bin

See bin Laden, Osama

LaGuardia Airport Bombing

On December 29, 1975, a bomb exploded at New York City's LaGuardia Airport, killing 11 and injuring more than 75. The crime, considered to be one of the most lethal bombings of its time, as well as one of the first major terrorist attacks on an airport, remains unsolved more than 25 years later.

The bomb detonated at 6:30 P.M. on a busy, post-holiday Monday night, shattering the 30-foot-tall plate-glass windows of the lower-level baggage claim area shared by TWA and Delta. The explosion blew a 10-by-15-foot hole through the eight-inch-thick reinforced concrete ceiling, also damaging the ceiling on the floor above. The terminal's luggage carousels and huge metal doors lay mangled following the explosion.

The blast touched off a two-alarm fire and triggered the airport sprinkler system. Firefighters, who battled rush-hour traffic, suppressed the fire within an hour. The damage (estimated at $750,000) included burned walls and injuries from shards of glass that had rained down over an area

longer than a football field. In addition, pieces of a nearby bank of 12 metal storage lockers flew, like shrapnel, hundreds of feet. While the bombing had come without warning, at approximately 7:30 P.M. an anonymous caller claimed that another bomb was in the American Airlines baggage claim area, adding to the chaos. This claim, like the many others that plagued airports and bus terminals nationwide in the days that followed, proved to be false.

By New Year's Eve, investigators had reconstructed most of the explosion. The bomb had been placed in one of the 12 parcel lockers located between two luggage carousels, and had not come in on an inbound flight. The reconstructed bank of 24-hour lockers, painstakingly pieced together from bits of metal found in the debris, revealed facts about the bomb, but little about who placed it. Initial guesses had put the power of the explosion at 15 sticks of dynamite. Later estimates rose to 25 sticks, or approximately 12.5 pounds of explosives. This was one-and-a-half times the amount of explosives used in the Fraunces Tavern bombing in January 1974, which had claimed four lives.

Many believed that the Puerto Rican independence group who claimed responsibility for the Fraunces Tavern bombing, the Fuerzas Armadas de Liberación Nacional (FALN), was also responsible for the LaGuardia bomb. However, neither the FALN nor any other prominent terrorist group came forward to claim responsibility for the bombing. In fact, the Palestine Liberation Organization (PLO), which was mentioned early on in AP and UPI news reports, emphatically denied involvement and denounced the attack. In May 1976, a Cuban American charged with six other bombings in Miami, Florida, was sought in connection with the case, but was not charged. It is now thought that Croatian nationalists were the perpetrators, though no one has ever been brought to justice in the case.

Laura Lambert

See also FALN; Grand Central Station Bombing; TWA Flight 355 Hijacking

Further Readings

Kihss, Peter. "LaGuardia Blast Yields No Leads in Investigation." *The New York Times*, December 31, 1975, p. 1.

McFadden, Robert D. "14 Killed, 70 Hurt at LaGuardia by Bomb in Baggage-claim Area; Airport Is Closed until Tonight." *The New York Times,* December 30, 1975, p. 1.

Naftal, Timothy. *Blind Spot: The Secret History of American Counterterrorism.* New York: Basic Books, 2005.

LASHKAR-E-TAIBA

Lashkar-e-Taiba (Army of the Pure) is a notoriously violent militant Muslim group that initially operated in the Indian state of Jammu and Kashmir, on the Pakistan-India border, but by 2010 had expanded its reach further into India. Jammu and Kashmir is claimed by both India, a largely Hindu country, and Pakistan, a largely Muslim country, and the dispute has given rise to many armed groups within Jammu and Kashmir.

Lashkar-e-Taiba is rabidly pro-Pakistan, and it is one of the largest groups operating in Jammu and Kashmir. The group opposes any concessions to India, with its leaders expressing the desire to drive Hindus out of much of India once they have been eliminated from Jammu and Kashmir. The group has taken part in several massacres targeting non-Muslim civilian populations in Jammu and Kashmir in an effort to create a Muslim-only state. Following a cease-fire accord between India and Pakistan in 2003, Lashkar-e-Taiba was believed to have moved most of its operations to Pakistan's northwest, an area bordering Afghanistan over which the central government does not have control. The organization has also increasingly focused its violence on India itself.

Lashkar-e-Taiba arose in the early 1990s as a militant wing of Markaz-ud-Dawa-wal-Irshad, an Islamic fundamentalist organization influenced by the Wahabi sect of Sunni Islam. Many of Lashkar-e-Taiba's members are Pakistani or Afghani. The group, headquartered in Pakistan, is believed to have had ties with Afghanistan's Taliban government and with the wealthy Saudi extremist Osama bin Laden. Fighters from Lashkar-e-Taiba and another militant Muslim group, Hizb-ul-Mujahideen, were killed in August 1998 when American cruise missiles fell on bin Laden's training camps in Afghanistan, and a senior official of bin Laden's al Qaeda organization was captured in a Lashkar-e-Taiba safe house in Pakistan in March 2002.

Lashkar-e-Taiba made its first incursions into Jammu and Kashmir in 1993. In the late 1990s, Lashkar-e-Taiba received greater funding from Pakistan and began operating in the Jammu region, which has large numbers of non-Moslem minorities. Working in conjunction with Hizb-ul-Mujahideen, Lashkar-e-Taiba began a program of ethnic cleansing, slaughtering Hindus and Sikhs.

Infamous for their brutality, Lashkar-e-Taiba attacks were often aimed at unarmed civilians. Children as young as one year old were among 23 Hindus killed at Wandhama in 1998. The group massacred 25 members of a wedding party in Doda later that same year. Beginning in 1999, Lashkar-e-Taiba conducted a series of suicide attacks against Indian security forces, often targeting seemingly secure headquarters. In such attacks, Lashkar-e-Taiba forces have been outnumbered and eventually killed, but not before killing Indian troops and causing extensive damage. In March 2000, 35 Sikhs were killed in Chattisinghpora; five months later, Lashkar-e-Taiba members staged eight attacks that left roughly 100 people dead, most of them Hindu civilians.

In 2000, Lashkar-e-Taiba had a falling out with Hizb-ul-Mujahideen, which had declared a short-lived cease-fire with India. The group lost more allies in 2001, after the September 11, 2001, attacks on the United States led to the removal of the Taliban government in Afghanistan by American-led military forces.

On December 13, 2001, Lashkar-e-Taiba undertook a daring suicide attack on India's parliament complex in the capital, New Delhi, in conjunction with Jaish-e-Mohammed, another militant group. In response, the United States froze the U.S. assets of Lashkar-e-Taiba, calling it a terrorist organization. Under pressure from the United States to crack down on terrorist groups and to avoid a war with India, the government of Pakistan banned the group and arrested its leader, Hafiz Muhammed Saeed, but he was released a few months later.

Targeting Mumbai

Lashkar-e-Taiba operatives continued their attacks, which were primarily aimed at Indian security forces, throughout the 2000s. In 2006, however, the group staged a considerably more deadly attack against civilians in Mumbai (formerly Bombay), India's most populous city. On July 11, 2006, several bombs tore through Mumbai's commuter-train system during the evening rush hour, killing more than 180 people. The bombs were all placed in first-class train compartments in an apparent effort to target India's professional class. Following the attack, which India linked to Lashkar-e-Taiba, Pakistan once again detained Saeed, and once again released him, claiming that India's investigation was biased.

Two years later, on the evening of November 26, 2008, 10 Lashkar-e-Taiba gunmen landed boats in Mumbai, spread out to popular tourist destinations, and began shooting people. The gunmen, who were well armed and well trained, eventually met up in two luxury hotels and a Jewish center, where they took hostages and held off Indian police and military for three days. More than 170 people died in the attacks, including nine of the attackers. One was captured alive, however, and confessed that he was a member of Lashkar-e-Taiba, that he had trained in Pakistan, and that the attackers had come to Mumbai by boat from Karachi.

In the past, Pakistan had been reluctant to appear to cave in to Indian pressure over Lashkar-e-Taiba's activities, but the solidity of the evidence, combined with pressure from the United States and the United Nations, spurred the country to raid Lashkar-e-Taiba camps and arrest several operatives linked to the Mumbai siege. Pakistan also made public in July 2009 an investigation that reached largely the same conclusions as India's, acknowledging that Lashkar-e-Taiba had indeed planned and launched the attack from Pakistan.

The trial of those Lashkar-e-Taiba operatives detained in Pakistan began in October 2009; as of January 2011, it remains unfinished due to various delays and controversies, including accusations that one of the defense lawyers had a fake law degree. The Pakistan government has not conclusively linked Saeed with the attack, however, and he claims to have renounced violence. He has nonetheless been repeatedly placed under house arrest.

While Pakistan's crackdown on Lashkar-e-Taiba may well hamper the group's activities, the organization remains a threat, in particular because it has been reaching out to militant Muslims worldwide. Several people trained in Lashkar-e-Taiba camps have been arrested or linked to terror

attacks in Great Britain, and in March 2010 the Chicago resident David C. Headley pled guilty to U.S. criminal charges that he traveled to India to pick out targets for the 2008 Mumbai attack.

Mary Sisson

See also bin Laden, Osama; Hizb-ul-Mujahideen; Jaish-e-Mohammed; Mumbai Attack, 2008; September 11 Attacks; State-Sponsored Terrorism

Further Readings

Allen, Mike. "Bush Orders Two More Groups' Assets Frozen." *The Washington Post,* December 21, 2001, p. A24.

Anand, Goota, et al. "Alleged Terrorist Group Steers Young Men to Fight—Mumbai Suspect, Ex-recruits Describe How Pakistan-based Lashkar-e-Taiba Gave Them the Motivation and Skills to Kill." *The Wall Street Journal,* December 8, 2008, p. A6.

Babington, Charles, and Pamela Constable. "Kashmir Killings Mar Clinton Visit to India; President Rebuffed on Nuclear Issue." *The Washington Post,* March 22, 2000, p. A1.

Bearak, Barry. "A Kashmiri Mystery." *The New York Times Magazine,* December 31, 2001, p. 26.

Behera, Navnita Chadha. *Demystifying Kashmir.* Washington, DC: Brookings Institution Press, 2006.

Haqqani, Husain. "The Ideologies of South Asian Jihadi Groups." *Current Trends in Islamist Ideologies* 1 (April 2005). http://www.carnegieendowment.org/files/Ideologies.pdf.

King, Laura. "Mumbai Attacks Put Focus on Pakistani Militant Group." *Los Angeles Times,* December 5, 2008, p. A1.

Margolis, Eric S. *War at the Top of the World: The Struggle for Afghanistan, Kashmir, and Tibet.* Rev. ed. New York: Routledge, 2002.

Polgreen, Lydia, and Souad Mekhennet. "Militant Network Is Intact Long after Mumbai Siege." *The New York Times,* September 30, 2009, p. A1.

Sappenfield, Mark. "New Template for Terror?" *Christian Science Monitor,* December 3, 2008, p. 1.

Schofield, Victoria. *Kashmir in Conflict: India, Pakistan and the Unfinished War.* London: I.B. Tauris, 2000.

Swami, Praveen. *India, Pakistan and the Secret Jihad: The Covert War in Kashmir, 1947–2004.* London: Routledge, 2007.

Whitlock, Craig, and Rajiv Chandrasekaran. "Pakistan Detains Islamic Militants: Arrests May Calm Tensions with India." *The Washington Post,* January 1, 2002, p. A1.

LAUTARO YOUTH MOVEMENT

Named for a famous Araucanian Indian warrior, the Lautaro Youth Movement (MJL, aka Lautaro Faction of the United Popular Action Movement and Lautaro Popular Rebel Forces) is a militant Chilean leftist group that became active in the 1980s. Now said to be largely disbanded, the MJL has been linked to bank robberies, the killing of policemen, and attacks on Mormon churches.

The movement was formed as a splinter group of the political party United Popular Action Movement (Movimiento de Accion Popular Unitario, or MAPU). The breakaway group called itself the Lautaro Faction of the MAPU, and it developed a separate youth movement, the MJL, and a militia, the Lautaro Popular Rebel Forces. A major goal of the MJL and its sister organizations was to overthrow the regime of the Chilean dictator Augusto Pinochet.

After Chile returned to democracy in 1990, the MJL continued its violent activities. But in 1990, a foiled rescue attempt turned tragic for the MJL. On November 14, guards transferred Marco Ariel Antonioletti, a top MJL militant, from the public jail to a hospital for treatment. International human rights groups have said that Antonioletti had been beaten and tortured by the police and was taken to be treated for his injuries. An MJL commando team burst into the hospital and began firing at the guards and police officers watching Antonioletti. The officials returned fire, and the gunfight left four guards and one police officer dead. Marcela Rodriguez, the MJL member known in the right-wing Chilean press as the *mujer metralleta,* or "machine gun girl," was in charge of taking Antonioletti from the hospital and driving him to a safe haven. However, in the exchange of bullets, Rodriguez was shot in the back and gravely wounded. Her companions fled, and she was arrested. Police later shot Antonioletti in the forehead, killing him.

Paralyzed by her injuries, Rodriguez underwent multiple surgeries. In 1999, despite being confined to a hospital bed, Rodriguez was sentenced to 20 years in prison. Appeals for her pardon by various human rights groups and the Chilean Catholic Church moved the Chilean government to allow her to serve her sentence outside of the country.

Many top leaders of the MJL are in prison, and its members have scattered. MJL members imprisoned in Chile's high-security prisons have engaged in hunger strikes, demanding better conditions for prisoners.

Erica Pearson

See also Manuel Rodriguez Patriotic Front; Movement of the Revolutionary Left

Further Readings

Coad, Malcolm. "Hospital Gunfight Halts Plan to Free Chile's Prisoners." *The Guardian* (London), November 16, 1990.

Ensalaco, Mark. *Chile under Pinochet: Recovering the Truth*. Philadelphia: University of Pennsylvania Press, 2000.

Long, William R. "Terror Attacks Send Jitters Through Chile." *Los Angeles Times*, May 6, 1991.

National Consortium for the Study of Terrorism and Responses to Terrorism. "Terrorist Organization Profile: Lautaro Youth Movement." http://www.start.umd.edu/start/data_collections/tops/terrorist_organization_profile.asp?id=4107.

LAW AND TERRORISM

The mobilization of a society against terrorism inevitably affects the laws of that society. This entry will examine the potential strategic approaches, the principles and policies affecting those strategies, and a number of recurrent specific measures that commonly appear in the counterterrorism codes of many states. The focus is mainly on national laws, but international law, which is becoming increasingly prominent, will also be discussed.

Legal Strategies and Counterterrorism

There are three dominant legal stances taken by states facing a terrorism problem. One is to do nothing. Before the attacks of September 11, 2001, this stance was adopted by many states. In this approach, terrorism is viewed as simply a form of organized crime, and while more threatening than common thefts or assaults, the view is that a robust criminal law and criminal justice system can handle terrorism.

At the other end of the scale, a state may perceive terrorism as an existential threat—a threat to its fundamental constitutional values or its territorial integrity. In these circumstances, a military response will be considered, with the purpose being to apply maximum force and eradicate the enemies of the state. The adoption of this stance was evident in the declaration on September 16, 2001, by President George W. Bush of "the first war of the twenty-first century." Generally, however, a military response is avoided within the domestic sphere because of fears that the military will exert a dominant political influence, and because of the inevitable brutality of military operations (such as the 1972 attack on unarmed protesters in Northern Ireland known as Bloody Sunday).

Powerful states, such as the United States, France, and the United Kingdom, tend to adopt a third approach that mixes the foregoing themes. On the one hand, their prime reliance is on criminalization, to be achieved not only by reliance on existing laws but also by adaptations that produce a legal code geared to battling terrorism. This approach, which was adopted in the United Kingdom as long ago as the Diplock Report in 1972, is likely to predominate within the domestic sphere. However, these nations are also willing to commit their military forces, especially outside their own borders, and to apply all elements of national power, including diplomatic, intelligence, and economic resources.

This entry principally examines specialized counterterrorism laws, which represent the most prominent and important trend in the domestic sphere. The sections below analyze the justifications for distinct counterterrorist laws and the necessary safeguards, as well as typical examples of their content.

Principles and Policies for "Special" Counterterrorism Laws

Implicit in legislation such as the UK's Terrorism Act 2000 and the Uniting and Strengthening America by Providing Appropriate Tools Required to Intercepting and Obstructing Terrorism Act (USA PATRIOT Act) of 2001 is the assertion that legislation against political violence is needed now

and forever. Sunset clauses may attach to some provisions, but they are often extended and much of the legislation (including the Antiterrorism and Effective Death Penalty Act of 1996) has no expiration date. This resort to an ongoing and distinct anti-terrorist code within a "militant" democracy can be justified at three levels.

The first level of justification concerns the powers and duties of states. As Justice William O. Douglas stated in *Terminiello v. Chicago* (1949), democracy is not "a suicide pact." In principle, it is justifiable for liberal democracies to defend the security and safety of both the nation and the public. This approach is reflected in the war powers granted to the U.S. Congress and president under the U.S. Constitution (Article I, Section 8, Clause 11, and Article II, Section 2, Clause I), as well as internationally by the UN Universal Declaration on Human Rights (UDHR), Article 30 (prohibiting the engagement in any activity or performance of any act aimed at the destruction of rights and freedoms), and in the power of derogation in time of emergency threatening the life of the nation under Article 4 of the UN International Covenant on Civil and Political Rights (ICCPR). Aside from the power to take action, there is a state responsibility to act against violence in order to safeguard the protective right to life of citizens (UDHR, Article 3). In addition, various United Nations instruments forbid the harboring or condoning of terrorism (UN General Assembly Resolution 40/61 of December 9, 1985; Resolution 49/60 of December 9, 1994; and UN Security Council Resolution 1373 of September 28, 2001).

The second level of justification for special laws is more morally grounded. This argument points to the illegitimacy of terrorism as a form of political expression. Many of its emanations are almost certainly common crimes, crimes of war, or crimes against humanity, even if the political cause of the terrorist is deemed legitimate.

Third, terrorism may be depicted as a specialized form of criminality that presents peculiar complications in terms of policing and criminal process. Paramilitary groups can typically hinder the reestablishment of public safety and democratic processes because of their sophistication, the transnational scale of their activities, and the difficulty of obtaining assistance from paramilitary-affected communities because of the impact of intimidation, or even because of the popularity of the group. Terrorism therefore demands a specialized response to overcome the complications posed for normal detection methods and processes within criminal justice.

However, while specialized laws have an allure, they also entail many dangers. First, there is a pressure to respond quickly to any incident, which can produce ill-considered, "panic" legislation. Second, fear is consciously or unconsciously amplified so as to justify a reaction. The poor design of legislation arising from these two factors may result in ineffective or merely symbolic legislation, or, even worse, in inappropriate or excessive legislation. A third danger is that "emergency" laws regularly linger beyond the original emergency. Fear and risk are endemic, not transitory, so normality is hard to reassert.

The fourth hazard is that the executive branch of the state will become unduly dominant. People expect action, not words, and the ability to take action is held by the executive, not the courts or the legislature. In addition, the executive has the most detailed information and intelligence, and thus appears better placed to act. Fifth, emergencies are the time of greatest threat to individuals and to the rights of individuals. These rights, unfortunately, are often depicted as obstacles to public safety and security. Sixth, even if the legislature does provide new laws, sweeping though they may be, there remains the grave danger that the executive or the security forces will exceed them. This can cause harm to those affected, and the state's international reputation may be damaged, making interstate cooperation less viable. Seventh, special laws provide a dangerous precedent that may result in contagion. For example, special powers may be adapted to unintended situations, or there may be an adoption within "normal" laws of measures that become commonplace incursions onto liberty.

Eighth, security laws tend not to be applied fairly. Ethnic minorities or aliens will suffer most, either through the discriminatory implementation of the laws or through the higher chances of abuse and error that accompany them. Thus, miscarriages of justice will occur, such as the cases of the Birmingham Six or the Guildford Four—two incidents of wrongful arrest that occurred during the "Troubles" in Northern Ireland. The legislation may also trigger disaffection and discontent among targeted communities, as happened to the Irish in the late twentieth century, and as is happening to some Muslim communities in the twenty-first century.

Balance and Limits

As already discussed, it is rational to react to the consequences of terrorism and to the costs of upholding rights in changed circumstances. It is rational to give reassurance to the public in times of crisis. What is less rational is the common assertion that security and liberty are "balanced" in a causal relationship, with the assumption being that greater security demands less liberty. Especially if security is considered in a broader sense of requiring "human security" from state repression as well as terrorism, as under the UN Global Counter-Terrorism Strategy of 2006, then security becomes an aspect of the exercise of individual rights, just as individual rights protection becomes an aspect of security.

In reality, experienced commentators in the field of anti-terrorism laws have long eschewed any simplistic balance. An example is Lord Lloyd, who was asked by the UK government to review anti-terrorism laws. In his 1996 report, Lloyd set out four principles against which the laws should be judged: (1) legislation against terrorism should approximate as closely as possible ordinary criminal law and procedure; (2) additional statutory offenses and powers may be justified, but only if they are necessary to meet the anticipated threat, and they must then strike the right balance between the needs of security and the rights and liberties of the individual; (3) the need for additional safeguards should be considered alongside any additional powers; and (4) the law should comply with obligations in international law. Likewise, the guiding principles behind the UK's National Security Strategy comprise "human rights, rule of law, legitimate and accountable government, justice, freedom, tolerance, and opportunity for all," while a main objective of the U.S. National Security Strategy of 2006 is to "Champion Aspirations for Human Dignity."

Building up these precepts, the normative setting to be observed by special laws against terrorism should be understood as requiring "constitutionalism," which has three parameters. The first parameter is a determination to ensure that states do not ride roughshod over individual rights in their efforts to combat terrorism. While episodes of official angst may arise regarding the imputed hindrance of rights on the effectiveness of terrorism operations, few states have denied their obligation to take account of human rights, even under the challenge of supreme emergencies. Thus, the principle here advanced, but not always observed in reality, is that the rights of individuals must be respected according to the traditions of the domestic jurisdictions and the demands of international law.

In enforcing this precept within a domestic setting, there is a special role for the courts as the prime deliberative forum in law. The judge's perspective, based within individual rights, need not cause constitutional conflict with policy formation by the legislature or policy action by the executive. Nevertheless, many judges will tend to be hesitant about overstepping the mark and running into public opprobrium for undue "activism." Thus, judges are often perceived during an emergency as being "deferential" to the predilections of the other branches of state. This deference tends to be affected by a number of variables. First, the longer the terrorism persists, the less there is a sense of emergency in which decisive executive responses must be allowed at all costs. As the conflict matures, more information emerges and expertise is no longer confined to those with access to intelligence and diplomatic sources.

Another variable is that the judges often feel more comfortable with issues that fall clearly within their expertise, such as issues of due process rather than substantive rights. It follows that many of the cases arising from Guantánamo Bay, such as *Rasul v. Bush* (2004), *Hamdan v. Rumsfeld* (2006), and *Boumediene v. Bush* (2008), have been depicted as debates around habeas corpus and jurisdiction, rather than about substantive liberty and discrimination.

The third variable is that some rights are more highly protected than others in international law, even in the extremes of a terrorist emergency. In response to terrorist threats, some governments, and even some academics, will occasionally inquire, "Why *not* torture terrorists?" However, the prohibition on torture and inhuman or degrading treatment is absolute (as under the UDHR, Article 5).

The disregard of this rule under the rubric of the U.S. "war on terror," as set out in special rules of interrogation and reflected in the harsh conditions applied at Guantánamo Bay, undermines the moral standing of the United States. This has been recognized in the policies of President Obama, who in 2009 announced the immediate end of the special interrogation regime and the intended closure of Guantánamo Bay. Rights to liberty and due process may be termed "fundamental" rather than absolute. In other words, restrictions on these rights can be allowed, but only for limited and permitted purposes, such as for the sake of the rights of others, and only if proportionate to those purposes.

Other rights (such as privacy, freedom of expression, and freedom of assembly) are more provisional and, except under the more absolutist stance of the U.S. Constitution's First Amendment right to free speech, may in most countries be proportionately balanced not only against other rights but also against wider societal interests.

Regarding the demands of international law, three impacts have occurred. The first has already been mentioned—the prioritization accorded to absolute rights. The second impact is the setting up of supranational review mechanisms. Examples include the work of the UN Committee against Torture and the UN Special Rapporteur on the promotion and protection of human rights and fundamental freedoms while countering terrorism. In some regions, judicial scrutiny can be applied. By far the most advanced and powerful international human rights jurisdiction is exercised by the European Court of Human Rights, which operates under the terms of the Council of Europe. It has shown some indulgence toward states that are assailed by terrorism, but it has also set some firm lines against abusive interrogation methods (in *Ireland v. United Kingdom* [1978]), against excessive police detentions (*Brogan v. United Kingdom* [1988]), and against excessive stop and search powers (*Gillan and Quinton v. United Kingdom* [2010]).

The third impact tends, to some extent, in the opposite direction. There is recognition that serious campaigns of terrorism can justify a state's "derogation" from rights (such as under the ICCPR, Article 4). Yet even this resort to emergency powers can still be subject to international judicial review, and some states also allow domestic judicial review. In 2004, the United Kingdom's highest court concluded, to the consternation of the government, that detention without trial of persons suspected of al Qaeda involvement could no longer be justified, though the derogation that allowed it was upheld in *A v. Secretary of State for the Home Department* (2004). The derogation notice was withdrawn in 2005.

The second parameter of constitutionalism demands "accountability," which includes attributes such as information provision, open and independent debate, and an ability to participate in decision making. These attributes run counter to the idea that a dictatorial regime is best suited to respond to a crisis, and instead seek to ensure the continuance of public and partisan scrutiny as provided by the legislature. This process can be aided by the willingness of the executive to publish information about its actions and intentions. Equally, the legislature must recognize that extra efforts are needed to achieve detailed scrutiny. Among the techniques found helpful has been the involvement of specialist committees to call in papers and witnesses. In the United Kingdom, for example, most observers feel that the parliamentary Joint Committee on Human Rights has performed sterling work. Another helpful mechanism is the appointment of independent reviews of terrorism policy and laws, as conducted by the 9/11 Commission in the United States or Lord Carlile in the United Kingdom.

The third and broadest parameter of constitutionalism demands "constitutional governance." This aspect includes the subjection of governmental action to a lawfulness requirement that terrorism laws "indicate with reasonable clarity the scope and manner of exercise of the relevant discretion conferred on the public authorities." Next, the constitutional mode of governance demands respect for "meta-norms"—tenets of national constitutional law and also international law. The norms must reflect the need for rationality and proportionality, including the overall purpose of the restoration of fundamental features of constitutional life. These considerations of constitutional governance also point toward the delineation of special powers in advance of an emergency.

In addition to these three principled concerns, questions of policy relevance and impact must be considered. Legislation should meet demands of efficacy and efficiency, and these attributes should

be judged in the light of the overall domestic counterterrorist strategy. Indeed, these tests ought to be the first to be applied, for if a measure does not sensibly advance the chosen strategy, there is no point in applying further tests.

Specific Counterterrorist Measures in Domestic Law

Specific counterterrorism powers speak to the need for criminalization and control. Where there is sufficient evidence of criminal activity, then a criminal prosecution is a legitimate and morally desirable response. The objective of criminalization is to modify the criminal law or criminal process, or both, so as to make it more likely that that a prosecution will be successful against terrorists. Many states adopted this objective following the 9/11 attacks, but countries with an enduring history of terrorism have longer-standing legislation (such as France's Loi no. 86-1020 of September 9, 1986, and the UK's Terrorism Act 2000).

Within a counterterrorist code, one tactic of criminalization will be the creation of specialist offenses, relating to, for example, membership of proscribed (banned) organizations, other forms of material support (under 18 USC 2339A and 2339B), such as terrorist training and recruitment and the possession of materials; incitement to terrorism (an offense found in the UK's Terrorism Act 2006, Section 1, and in Israel's 1948 Prevention of Terrorism Ordinance, Section 4); and various regulations concerning mass destruction materials. Complex legislation also responds to terrorist financing and property, such as under Title III of the USA PATRIOT Act (2001), and in the UK's Terrorism Act 2000, Part III; Anti-terrorism, Crime and Security Act 2001, Parts I and II; and Counter-Terrorism Act 2008, Part V.

Counterterrorist law may next introduce deviations from the ordinary criminal judicial processes in order to assist the prosecution in handling terrorist cases. In Northern Ireland, for example, non-jury trials—(called Diplock courts in honor of the report that suggested them) are held under the Justice and Security (Northern Ireland) Act 2007, Sections 1–9. National security courts sometimes impose limits on disclosure of evidence or of the identities of witnesses. They may also involve military tribunals, as occurred in the past in the

Republic of Ireland under the Offenses against the State Act, 1939, and in Turkey under Article 143 of the Constitution. Similarly, the Military Commissions Act of 2009 keeps open the possibility of military trials for foreign detainees at Guantánamo Bay.

In order to find the evidence on which to base criminalization, extra investigative powers are often granted to the police or security services. Typically, these include powers relating to electronic surveillance and data mining, such as under the USA PATRIOT Act, Title II, which adapts for terrorism investigation purposes the very broad powers already granted under the Foreign Intelligence Surveillance Act of 1978, which were designed for espionage investigation purposes. Individual countries have also instituted extensive police search powers of property; in the United Kingdom, this was enacted in the Terrorism Act 2000, Schedule 5. In Canada, under the Anti-Terrorism Act of 2001, coercive investigative hearings were allowed until the measure expired in 2007. Up until 2010, the UK police were permitted by the Terrorism Act 2000, Section 44, to stop and search any person or vehicle, even without reasonable suspicion, in order to search for articles that could be used in relation to terrorism. In New York City, a similar police power to carry out random searches without probable cause on the subway was upheld by the U.S. Court of Appeals for the Second Circuit in *MacWade v. Kelly* (2006).

These special policing powers may also be turned against individuals. One commonly encounters modifications to the "normal" power to arrest, detain, and question a suspect. Some of the most extensive modifications have been enacted in the United Kingdom, where the power to arrest, without warrant, a suspected terrorist (under the Terrorism Act 2000, Section 41) deviates from the traditional power in that it allows an arrest on a broad suspicion of "terrorism," rather than for a specific offense. The permitted length of pre-charge detention is also considerably longer than the norm of four days: detention can last up to 28 days (subject to approval by a judicial authority after 48 hours), as set out in the Terrorism Act 2006, Section 23. Once a suspect has been detained, it is common to specify diminutions in the suspect's right to have someone notified of their detention and to speak with a lawyer. Following

abusive treatment of terrorist suspects in Northern Ireland in the 1970s, these rights have been more clearly granted and observed in UK legislation, but variant treatment applies elsewhere. For instance, in France, access to a lawyer during the police *garde à vue,* under Article 706-88 of the Code of Criminal Procedure, was limited to 30 minutes, a level declared unconstitutional by the Conseil d'État in July 2010.

Another area where individuals are affected by search and detention relates to border control. For example, as part of its counterterrorist strategy, the United States implemented heightened screening upon arrival for air passengers, additional pre-travel screening for passengers traveling from visa-waiver countries, and the subjection of nationals from specified countries to the national security entry/exit registration system. In the United Kingdom, police, immigration, and designated customs officers have expanded powers to stop, search, question, and detain passengers at ports and borders under the Terrorism Act 2000.

When criminal prosecution becomes problematic, owing to the scarcity of evidence or to the sensitivity of evidence (e.g., if said evidence involves secret agents, informants, or surveillance techniques), the legal focus switches toward "control" measures. These are a response to the growing emphasis upon anticipatory risk, but they evade the principled restraints of criminal law in terms of admissibility of evidence and standard of proof. The fear of mass-casualty terrorism has escalated the use of preventive and preemptive interventions, on the basis that terrorism is too dangerous to require the post-attack compilation of evidence.

These powers are often among the most controversial within counterterrorist laws. Not only do they evade normal due process controls, they are granted to the executive rather than the judiciary. Examples include the power to proscribe (ban) organizations and to treat their members automatically as "terrorists." For example, the United Kingdom's Terrorism Act 2000 has allowed the banning of over 40 groups, including al Qaeda and the Irish Republican Army.

In addition, some states hold terrorist suspects without trial. Some of the measures that allow this are based on security legislation, such as under the Malaysian Internal Security Act 1960, but a more recent trend has been to divert immigration and

Terrorism Act 2006

CHAPTER 11

TERRORISM ACT 2006

PART 1

OFFENCES

Encouragement etc. of terrorism

Preparation of terrorist acts and terrorist training

Offences involving radioactive devices and materials and nuclear facilities and sites

Increases of penalties

PART 2

MISCELLANEOUS PROVISIONS

Detention of terrorist suspects

23 Extension of period of detention of terrorist suspects

(1) Schedule 8 to the Terrorism Act 2000 (c. 11) (detention of terrorist suspects) is amended as follows.

(2) In sub-paragraph (1) of each of paragraphs 29 and 36 (applications by a superintendent or above for a warrant extending detention or for the extension of the period of such a warrant), for the words from the beginning to "may" substitute—

"(1) Each of the following—

(a) in England and Wales, a Crown Prosecutor,

(b) in Scotland, the Lord Advocate or a procurator fiscal,

(c) in Northern Ireland, the Director or Public Prosecutions for Northern Ireland,

(d) in any part of the United Kingdom, a police officer of at least the rank of superintendent, may".

(3) In sub-paragraph (3) of paragraph 29 (period of extension to end no later than 7 days after arrest)—

(a) for "Subject to paragraph 36(3A)" substitute "Subject to sub-paragraph (3A) and paragraph 36"; and

(b) for "end not later than the end of" substitute "be".

(4) After that sub-paragraph insert—

"(3A) A judicial authority may issue a warrant of further detention in relation to a person which specifies a shorter period as the period for which that person's further detention is authorized if—

(a) the application for the warrant is an application for a warrant specifying a shorter period; or

(b) the judicial authority is satisfied that there are circumstances that would make it inappropriate for the specified period to be as long as the period of seven days mentioned in sub-paragraph (3)."

(5) In paragraph 34(1) (persons who can apply for information to be withheld from person to whom application for a warrant relates) for "officer" substitute "person".

(6) In paragraph 36 (applications for extension or further extension), omit the words "to a judicial authority" in sub-paragraph (1), and after that sub-paragraph insert—

"(1A) The person to whom an application under sub-paragraph (1) may be made is—

(a) in the case of an application falling within sub-paragraph (1B), a judicial authority; and

(b) in any other case, a senior judge.

(1B) An application for the extension or further extension of a period falls within this sub-paragraph if—

(a) the grant of the application otherwise than in accordance with sub-paragraph (3AA)(b) would extend that period to a time that is no more than fourteen days after the relevant time; and

(b) no application has previously been made to a senior judge in respect of that period."

asylum laws for this purpose, given that many of the current suspects are foreigners. Examples include, in Canada, the Immigration and Refugee Protection Act of 2001, the procedures of which were struck down in *Charkaoui v. Canada* (2007). In the United Kingdom, detention under the Anti-Terrorism, Crime and Security Act 2001, Part IV, was declared to be incompatible with human rights on grounds of discrimination by the House of Lords in *A v. Secretary of State for the Home Department* (2004). The UK system was repealed in 2005, and the Canadian system has fallen into disuse. However, detention without trial remains in the extraordinary circumstances of Guantánamo Bay. Even in the United Kingdom, the repeal of detention without trial was not the end of the story. Another executive measure, under the Prevention of Terrorism Act 2005, replaced detention with new executive restrictions on movement, residence, contacts, activities, and communications by way of control orders imposed by the home secretary.

Not only do these executive orders often have a grievous impact on the rights of the individual, but the procedures by which they are applied also deviate from the norms of due process. Often, details of the case against the suspect may be withheld from them and their lawyer on the basis of the sensitive nature of the evidence. The situation is sometimes ameliorated by the operation of a "special advocate," but this device is not a panacea, and the suspect must be informed of the "essence of the case against him," according to the 2009 decision in *Secretary of State for the Home Department v. AF (no. 3)*.

The Role of International Law

International law suffered a very hesitant introduction into the field of terrorism. It remained narrowly based at first, so that there were conventions dealing with specific aspects of terrorism (hijacking, hostage-taking, attacks on diplomats, etc.), but no general coverage. The explanations for this included respect for the internal sovereignty of other states and, in some cases, a positive endorsement of justified militancy against colonial, alien, or racist occupation, terms that were frequently applied to conflicts relating to Palestine, among others.

The body of international law on terrorism began to expand in the 1990s. By then, Cold War rivalries, largely expressed through client states and insurgency groups, were on the wane. In addition, the savagery of modern weapons and the potential vulnerability of technologically networked global systems meant that every state was placed in harm's way from terrorism. As a result, more ambitious international law began to emerge, signaled by two conventions in particular. One was the 1997 UN International Convention for the Suppression of Terrorist Bombings, and the other was the 1999 UN International Convention for the Suppression of the Financing of Terrorism. Even so, the international community is still unable to agree on a general definition of terrorism, or on a general convention against it, and terrorism has not yet been included as an offense that can be brought before the International Criminal Court.

Contrary to contemporaneous claims, the 9/11 attacks did not "change everything," but they did give further impetus to the international implementation of specific measures. The most notable change was the passage of UN Security Council Resolution (UNSCR) 1373, which condemned terrorism in general terms and set up the Counter-Terrorism Committee to implement and monitor compliance with international law. The UN has given the most attention to countering the financing of terrorist groups, with measures such as the seizure and freezing of assets of listed persons and entities under UNSCR 1267 relating to the Taliban and al Qaeda. There are also multilateral international agreements relating to the retention and transfer of financial data, such as the EU-U.S. SWIFT II agreement of 2010.

Terrorism has certainly moved up the list of international priorities, though new problems have emerged, especially in terms of the new international order being used as an excuse for the repression of political dissent rather than combating terrorism.

Genevieve Lennon and Clive Walker

See also Birmingham Pub Bombing; Bloody Sunday; Counterterrorism; Criminal Prosecution of Terrorists; Foreign Intelligence Surveillance Act; Forensic Science and Terrorism; Guildford Four; Homeland Security; International Relations and Terrorism; September 11 Attacks; Torture Debate

Further Readings

Ackerman, B. *Before the Next Attack.* New Haven, CT: Yale University Press, 2006.

Bonner, D. *Executive Measures, Terrorism and National Security.* Aldershot, UK: Ashgate, 2007.

Donohue, L.K. *The Cost of Counterterrorism: Power, Politics, and Liberty.* Cambridge, UK: Cambridge University Press, 2008.

Duffy, H. *The "War on Terror" and the Framework of International Law.* Cambridge: Cambridge University Press, 2005.

Ginbar, V. *Why Not Torture Terrorists?* Oxford: Oxford University Press, 2008.

Gross, O., and F. ni Aolain. *Law in Times of Crisis.* Cambridge, UK: Cambridge University Press, 2006.

National Commission on Terrorist Attacks upon the United States. *The 9/11 Commission Report: Final Report of the National Commission on Terrorist Attacks upon the United States.* New York: W.W. Norton, 2004. http://www.9-11commission.gov.

Posner, E.A., and A. Vermeule. *Terror in the Balance.* Oxford: Oxford University Press, 2008.

Thiel, M., ed. *The "Militant Democracy" Principle in Modern Democracies.* Aldershot, UK: Ashgate, 2009.

Walker, C. *The Law and Terrorism.* Oxford: Oxford University Press, 2011.

LEADERLESS RESISTANCE

Leaderless resistance is a strategy advocated and used by some militant antigovernment groups in the United States. Each member is free to engage in whatever actions, and at whatever time or place, he or she believes appropriate to further the organization's aims. The organization neither issues direct orders nor coordinates actions, thus avoiding legal responsibility for any criminal activity of individual members. Members act independently and secretly, in isolation from the group and from each other.

The American militia leader and Ku Klux Klansman Louis Beam wrote and published a widely circulated essay advocating leaderless resistance as a strategy to counteract the destruction of hierarchical U.S. militias by law enforcement agencies. The essay, originally published in 1994 in *Seditionist,* a white supremacist magazine, was later widely distributed on the Internet. Beam's vision was one where "all individuals and groups operate independently of each other, and never report to a central headquarters or single leader for direction or instruction." Beam recognized fairly early the opportunities the Web offered for dissemination of information and communication with far-flung fellow believers. In 1984 he created a bulletin board system for the terrorist group Aryan Nations.

Jeffrey Kaplan, an expert on religious violence and terrorism, traces the development of leaderless resistance to California in the early 1970s, where Joseph Tommasi, the leader of the small National Socialist Liberation Front, was frustrated by the failure of the radical right to build a revolutionary majority. Tommasi was determined "to act resolutely and alone" against the state. The willingness to act alone was in contrast to the prevailing organization of contemporary terrorist groups, where a rigid, centralized command-and-control structure existed, with a top council directing the activities of individual cells and columns.

Radical right-wing authors have helped spread the concept of leaderless resistance. In 1989, William Pierce wrote a sequel to his more famous *Turner Diaries,* called *Hunter,* in which the hero, acting alone, sets out to assassinate the enemies of the white race. A year later, another radical right author, Richard Kelly Hoskins, wrote a fantasy entitled *Vigilantes of Christendom,* which features an order of assassins called the Phineas Priesthood. Thus inspired, some right-wing radicals and pro-life activists have styled themselves "Phineas priests." David Lane, a founding member of The Order, a white nationalist group, advocated a strict division between the political arm and the armed wing of an organization, thus freeing the political wing to disseminate propaganda and recruit new members without engaging in illegal activities. Lane envisioned the armed wing recruiting from the political wing, but, once active, having each member sever all connection with the political wing. These "Wotans" would act independently and secretly "to hasten the demise of the system."

Timothy McVeigh appears to have been an example of leaderless resistance. McVeigh acted without direct orders from any organization in blowing up the federal office building in Oklahoma City in 1995. However, McVeigh was not a member of any right-wing militia group when he carried out the bombing, though his knowledge of leaderless resistance is unknown. Literature found in his car advocated the creation of a mass revolutionary movement rather than individual acts of violence. He does seem to have acted in response to the vitriolic propaganda of the radical right on his own initiative, independently developing and carrying out his own strategy. His actions were thus consistent with the concept of leaderless resistance.

The Earth Liberation Front (ELF) uses an extreme form of leaderless resistance. No formal membership exists, and anyone believing in the aims of the ELF can carry out a terrorist act on his or her own initiative. A website offers advice on acts of economic sabotage and lists actions already taken. The site does not actually advocate criminal activity, and so operates within the letter of the law. Followers can use the Internet to communicate with each other anonymously.

A major feature of leaderless resistance is the isolation of the individual actor from the organization. The individual is not controlled by the organization and may be out of touch with the group's ideology, particularly as it evolves. Following the Oklahoma City bombing, many members left the militias in disgust; some approached law enforcement agencies and even testified in court.

Networks

Terrorism experts see a revolution taking place among terrorist groups. They have noted a movement away from the hierarchical structure common in the 1960s and 1970s, and toward a flatter, networked structure like that of more recently founded groups, such as Hamas and al Qaeda. Characteristics of these networked terrorist groups include decentralization and delegation of decision-making authority, as well as loose lateral ties between dispersed groups and individuals. Networked organizations share some of the characteristics of leaderless resistance and can be thought of as an intermediate form on the continuum between the traditional hierarchical terrorist organization and the anarchy of leaderless resistance.

Kaplan calls leaderless resistance a strategy adopted in despair, when victory is seen as impossible. It may also be attractive to those for whom the immediate disruption of normal activities is the desired outcome, such as anti-abortion militants. In addition, it may be particularly appealing to U.S. militants in its focus on the autonomous,

independent individual, rather than the group. The concept of leaderless resistance is particularly dangerous because it may provide unstable individuals already stimulated by hate propaganda with added motivation to commit violent acts.

Ellen Sexton

See also al Qaeda; Earth Liberation Front; Freelance Terrorism; Hamas; Homegrown Jihadi Movement; McVeigh, Timothy James; Order, The; Phineas Priesthood

Further Readings

Arquilla, J., and D. Ronfeldt, eds. *Networks and Netwars: The Future of Terror, Crime and Militancy.* Santa Monica, CA: RAND Corporation, 2001.

Barcott, Bruce. "From Tree-hugger to Terrorist: How Critter Became Part of a Shadowy, Increasingly Violent Radical Environmental Movement." *New York Times Magazine*, April 7, 2002, pp. 56–59, 81.

Beam, Louis. "Leaderless Resistance." *The Seditionist* 12 (February 1992). http://www.louisbeam.com/leaderless.htm.

Chalk, Peter. "U.S. Environmental Groups and 'Leaderless Resistance.'" *Jane's Intelligence Review*, July 1, 2001. http://www.rand.org/hot/op-eds/070101JIR.html.

German, Mike. "Behind the Lone Terrorist, a Pack Mentality." *The Washington Post*, June 5, 2005, p. B1.

Joyce-Hasham, Mariyam. "Emerging Threats on the Internet." Royal Institute of International Affairs Briefing Paper, new series. London: Royal Institute of International Affairs, July 15, 2000.

Kaplan, Jeffrey. "Leaderless Resistance." *Terrorism and Political Violence* 9, no. 3 (1997): 80–95.

Pressman, Jeremy. "Leaderless Resistance: The Next Threat?" *Current History* 102, no. 668 (December 2003): 422–425.

Sageman, Marc. *Leaderless Jihad: Terror Networks in the Twenty-first Century.* Philadelphia: University of Pennsylvania Press, 2008.

Stern, Kenneth. *A Force upon the Plain: The American Militia Movement and the Politics of Hate.* Norman: University of Oklahoma Press, 1996.

LIBERATION TIGERS OF TAMIL EELAM

The Liberation Tigers of Tamil Eelam (LTTE) is a Marxist Tamil separatist group that began fighting the government of Sri Lanka in 1978. Often referred to simply as the "Tamil Tigers," the LTTE made a number of grim contributions to the history of terrorism, including the invention of the suicide bomb jacket and pioneering the use of women as suicide bombers. After a 26-year battle with many human rights violations committed by both sides, the LTTE issued a statement in 2009 that the group would be laying down its arms.

Sri Lanka is an island nation located off the southeast coast of India. Sinhalese Buddhists compose about 75 percent of the island's population, while Hindu Tamils, concentrated in the north and east of the country, make up roughly 15 percent. In the early 1970s, following a Marxist-led student rebellion, the Sri Lankan government began to place special emphasis on Sinhalese unity and cultural cohesion. For instance, the 1972 constitution named Sinhala and Buddhism as Sri Lanka's official language and religion, respectively. However, the government's efforts at overcoming divisions within the Sinhalese community only exacerbated existing ethnic tensions between the Sinhalese and the Tamils. The resurgence of Sinhalese chauvinism sparked a comparable rise in Tamil separatism, with calls for the establishment of a Tamil homeland, called Eelam. In 1978 a radical faction of Tamils led by Velupillai Prabhakaran founded the Liberation Tigers of Tamil Eelam (LTTE) in the hope of gaining total independence.

Over the course of its existence, the LTTE was considered one of the most effective guerrilla forces operating in the world, fighting a government force approximately 10 times larger than itself for a generation. Initially, the LTTE exclusively employed hit-and-run guerrilla tactics in its fight against the government, but as the force grew larger, it began to operate in the traditional division-brigade-battalion structure used by most armed forces. Extremely well equipped, with heavy artillery (including antiaircraft rockets and grenade launchers), the LTTE even had its own small navy, the Sea Tigers, which they used for smuggling as well as attacks.

Several unusual attributes of the LTTE attracted international interest. The LTTE had a large number of women in every division, many of whom rose to command positions. Its use of child soldiers in combat, some as young as 12, brought condemnation by the United Nations. But perhaps most

unusual was the LTTE's Black Tiger division, a specially trained squad used for terrorist attacks, including suicide bombings. Black Tiger assassins killed dozens of Sri Lankan politicians, including then-president Ranasinghe Premadasa in 1993; Industry Minister C.V. Goonaratne in 2000; Foreign Minister Lakshman Kadirgamar in 2005; and several other members of parliament in 2008. In 1991 a LTTE suicide bomber murdered the prime minister of India, Rajiv Ghandi. At all levels, LTTE members showed an unusual willingness to die for their cause. Fighters were issued cyanide caplets, which were worn on a chain around their necks, and many chose to swallow the capsule rather than be taken prisoner. The LTTE was equally careless of others' lives; in addition to the suicide bombings, the organization sometimes massacred innocent villagers to draw army forces away from the scene of its operations.

From 1978 to 1983, the LTTE carried out sporadic attacks against the Sri Lankan police and armed forces, but the group was not supported by the vast majority of Tamils. At the time, LTTE probably had, at most, a few hundred members. All this changed in July 1983, after an attack by the LTTE on a Sri Lankan army convoy sparked days of rioting across the country. Hundreds of Tamils were killed, and tens of thousands were forced to flee for their lives. The riots radicalized the Tamil community, and the LTTE soon had hundreds of recruits. By 1985, according to some estimates, the organization had 5,000 active members and an additional 5,000 sympathizers and supporters. The riots also sparked the growth of more than a dozen other Tamil insurgent groups, with which the LTTE would become bitter rivals during the next few years. Indeed, some of the LTTE's most brutal attacks were made against these rival groups and their sympathizers.

The LTTE was helped in its rise to power by the clandestine aid of the Indian government, which was motivated by a number of complex political considerations, not least the hope of appeasing its own 50 million–strong Tamil population. The Indian government allowed Tamil insurgents (though not, initially, the LTTE) to operate camps in southern India, and provided military training and weapons to thousands of insurgents. (The LTTE also received significant funding from a large Tamil diaspora throughout the world, especially in

Britain and Canada.) With Indian training and arms, the Tamil insurgents from various groups soon controlled large sections of Sri Lanka's northern peninsula and most of Jaffna, the capital of the Northern Province.

In April 1987 the government struck back, orchestrating a huge counterattack that retook most of the peninsula and bottled up the rebels in Jaffna. Alarmed by these developments, the Indian government airdropped relief supplies into Jaffna, then offered its services to help broker a peace agreement. The Sri Lankan government, afraid of displeasing (and possibly being invaded by) its much larger neighbor, agreed, and the Indians sent 10,000 troops to form the Indian Peace-Keeping Force (IPKF). The rebels and the government proved utterly unable to reach a compromise, however, and the LTTE, which was the most hard-line of the rebel groups, began to eliminate rival organizations and consolidate power. The Sri Lankans asked the IPKF to stop the violence, and the IPKF expanded to 80,000 men as India discovered the tenacity and fighting capabilities of the guerrillas.

The IPKF pulled out of Jaffna in 1990, leaving the city to the Tigers. For the next five years, a military stalemate ensued, while the Tigers set up a para-state in the Northern Province, operating schools, hospitals, courts, and other government facilities. In 1995 another government counterattack succeeded in expelling the rebels from Jaffna and in securing large parts of the peninsula. The LTTE was not destroyed, however, and in 1999 it engaged in a series of battles that brought the port of Trincomalee and the Elephant Pass (the only land route into the Northern Province) under its control. The LTTE's position was greatly strengthened by these conquests.

In the mid-1990s, a newly elected president, Chandrika Kumaratunga, along with the rest of the Sri Lankan government, struggled to develop a peace plan they hoped would acceptable to the Sinhalese majority and the Tamils—and to the rebels in particular. Violence lessened in the early years of the twenty-first century, and a cease-fire was reached in 2002. As part of the compromise, the LTTE dropped its demand for a separate Tamil state, while the government lifted its ban on LTTE membership. The cease-fire lasted less than two years, however. It was broken in the summer of 2004, when four policemen were killed in a suspected LTTE suicide bomb. The tsunami in December of that year killed more than 30,000 people but interrupted the conflict only briefly. According to Preeti Bhattachrji, writing for the Council on Foreign Relations, by 2006 fighting between Tamil rebels and the Sri Lankan military was at its highest level since before the cease-fire. More than 13,000 people, 9,000 of them civilians, were killed in 2009 alone. The United Nations has accused both sides of war crimes, estimating that more than 265,000 Sri Lankans were forced to flee the violence.

In May 2009 the Sri Lankan government claimed that it had finally defeated the LTTE. The military retook the rebel-held parts of the country and killed Prabhakaran, either in a protracted firefight (according to the government), or when he tried to surrender (according to LTTE supporters). Regardless, Defense Secretary Gotabaya Rajapaksa announced on Sri Lankan television, "We have successfully ended the war." But without some genuine rapprochement between the Tamil and Sinhalese ethnic groups, instability and violence seem doomed to continue. One British supporter told London's *Independent* newspaper, "The original Tamil Tigers were like the Palestine Liberation Organization. What will come next is a Tamil Tiger Hamas."

Colleen Sullivan

See also Narcoterrorism; Women Terrorists

Further Readings

Bhattacharji, Preeti. "Liberation Tigers of Tamil Eelam." Washington, DC: Council on Foreign Relations, May 20, 2009. http://www.cfr.org/publication/9242/liberation_tigers_of_tamil_eelam_aka_tamil_tigers_sri_lanka_separatists.html.

Bose, Sumantra. *States, Nations, Sovereignty: Sri Lanka, India, and the Tamil Eelam Movement.* New Delhi, India: Sage, in association with the Book Review Literary Trust, New Delhi, 1994.

Bullion, Alan J. *India, Sri Lanka and the Tamil Crisis, 1976–1994: An International Perspective.* London: Pinter, 1995.

Denish, Roy. "Sri Lanka: The Tiger Blitzkrieg." *India Today,* November 22, 1999, p. 54.

Jayasinghe, Christine. "Sri Lanka: Calling a Truce." *India Today,* March 11, 2002, p. 50.

Jesse, Neal G., and Kristen P. Williams. "Sri Lanka: A Protracted Rebellion." In *Ethnic Conflict: A Systematic Approach to Cases of Conflict.* Washington, DC: CQ Press, 2010.

Marks, Thomas A. *Maoist Insurgency since Vietnam.* London: Frank Cass, 1996.

Prakesh, Sanjiv. "Sri Lanka: A Peace Offering." *Defense & Foreign Affairs,* February 1988, p. 30.

Richardson, John. *Paradise Poisoned: Learning about Conflict, Terrorism, and Development from Sri Lanka's Civil Wars.* Kandy, Sri Lanka: International Centre for Ethnic Studies, 2005.

"Sri Lanka Faces a Critical Strategic Watershed." *Defense and Foreign Affairs Strategic Policy,* October 2001, p. 30.

"Sri Lanka Says Leader of Rebels Has Died." *The New York Times,* May 18, 2009, p. A4.

Swamy, M.R. Narayan. *The Tiger Vanquished: LTTE's Story.* New Delhi, India: Sage, 2010.

"Tamil Tigers Break U.N. Pledge on Child Soldiers." *The Independent* (London), February 4, 2000. http://www.independent.co.uk/news/world/asia/tamil-tigers-break-un-pledge-on-child-soldiers-724701.html.

"Tamil Tigers: Defeated at Home, Defiant Abroad." *The Independent* (London), May 23, 2009. http://www.independent.co.uk/news/uk/home-news/tamil-tigers-defeated—at-home-defiant-abroad-1689766.html.

Yapa, Vijith, and David Orr. "Tamil Raid Kills 1,000 troops." *The Times* (London), November 4, 1999.

LIBY, ANAS AL (1964–)

Anas al Liby (aka Nazih Abdul Hamed al Raghie), born in Tripoli, Libya, is often described as the computer wizard of Osama bin Laden's al Qaeda network. He was indicted in December 2000 for conspiring to kill Americans in the East African embassy attacks in 1998. He has also been linked to the Libyan Islamic Group, the militant anti-Qaddafi organization.

The international terror network al Qaeda, which planned and carried out the September 11, 2001, attacks on the World Trade Center and the Pentagon, has also worked against non-Islamic governments in the Middle East. However, the extent of Anas al Liby's recent involvement with the group is unclear. Testimony in the East African embassy bombings trial suggested that Liby quarreled with bin Laden over financial matters and

split with him in the late 1990s. The U.S. indictment in that case charges that Liby discussed the possibility of an attack on the U.S. embassy in Nairobi, Kenya, with co-conspirator Ali Mohamed in 1993. Mohamed, who cooperated with U.S. prosecutors, described Liby's involvement during his own guilty plea in October 2000. Mohamed also said that he and Liby reviewed other possible targets in Nairobi. The indictment also charges that Liby conducted visual and photographic surveillance of the Kenyan embassy.

In 1995 Liby relocated to Britain. The FBI maintains that he was granted political asylum, while British officials have said that his immigration status was never determined. al Liby was living in relative obscurity in England when bomb-laden cars exploded at the U.S. embassies in Nairobi, Kenya, and Dar es Salaam, Tanzania, on August 7, 1998. The bombs exploded just minutes apart, killing a combined total of 224 people and turning both embassies into partial ruins.

After Liby was indicted by the United States, British police raided his Manchester apartment to find that he had fled. However, they discovered a computer with a terrorist training manual called *Military Studies in the Jihad Against the Tyrants.* The manual included tutorials on car bombing, sabotage, torture, and disguise.

Anas al Liby was reported captured on several different occasions—first by U.S. forces in January 2002 during an assault on the al Qaeda cave systems in eastern Afghanistan, and then in Sudan later that year. Reports of his capture have led some human rights groups to allege that he may be held in a secret prison. Officially, however, as of 2010 he remained on the FBI's list of most wanted terrorists.

Erica Pearson

See also al Qaeda; bin Laden, Osama; East Africa Embassy Bombings

Further Readings

Bergen, Peter. *Holy War, Inc.: Inside the Secret World of Osama bin Laden.* New York: Free Press, 2001.

Burke, Jason, Martin Bright, Anthony Barnett, Nick Paton Walsh, and Burhan Wazir. "Investigation: The UK Connection." *The Observer,* January 20, 2002.

Federal Bureau of Investigation. "Most Wanted Terrorists." http://www.fbi.gov/wanted/terrorists/fugitives.htm.

"A Nation Challenged: The Hunted; The 22 Most Wanted Suspects, in a Five-act Drama of Global Terror." *The New York Times*, October 14, 2001, p. 1B.

Smith, Martin, and Lowell Bergman. "Hunting bin Laden." *Frontline*, PBS, September 13, 2001. http://www.pbs.org/wgbh/pages/frontline/shows/binladen.

LINDH, JOHN WALKER (1981–)

A young American convert to Islam, John Phillip Walker Lindh became known as the "American Taliban" after being captured fighting alongside Taliban forces in Afghanistan in November 2001. Brought back to the United States to stand trial, Lindh pled guilty to supplying services to the Taliban and agreed to serve a 20-year sentence.

Lindh was born in 1981 in a suburb of Washington, D.C. At the age of 10, he moved with his parents and two siblings to San Anselmo, an affluent community in the San Francisco Bay area. He attended private schools and cultivated various interests, including one for hip-hop. Browsing the internet for more information on this musical genre he became enthralled by websites on Malcolm X and, subsequently, Islam. By the age of 16, Lindh had converted to Islam and changed his name to Suleyman al Faris.

Feeling that local mosques could not fulfill his desire to live in an Islamic environment, the 17-year-old Lindh traveled to Yemen, where he enrolled in a school to study Arabic. He soon became dissatisfied by the school's lack of focus on Islam, however, and he went to live on the campus of Al Iman University, an institution on the outskirts of Sana'a headed by the Yemeni Islamist leader Abdul Majid al Zindani.

After spending some months in a madrassa near the Afghan border, in the spring of 2001 Lindh got in contact with leaders of Harakat ul-Mujahideen, a Pakistan-based jihadist group with close links to the Taliban and al Qaeda. Lindh underwent paramilitary training in a Harakat ul-Mujahideen camp and then traveled to Afghanistan to fight alongside the Taliban.

In May 2001, Lindh reported to Taliban recruiters in Kabul, who assigned him to al Qaeda's al Farouq camp. Lindh spent six weeks at al Farouq, where he briefly met Osama bin Laden and other al Qaeda leaders. Asked to conduct operations against the United States and Israel, Lindh chose instead to join Taliban forces fighting against the Northern Alliance in northern Afghanistan. A few weeks before the September 11 attacks, Lindh reached the front lines in the Takhar province with a handful of foreign fighters.

In November 2001, under heavy bombardment from U.S. airplanes, Lindh and many of his comrades surrendered to the Northern Alliance warlord Abdul Rashid Dostum. They were detained at the Qala-i-Jangi fortress, and some of the prisoners started a bloody rebellion that killed, among others, CIA operative Mike Spann, the first known U.S. victim in Afghanistan. Lindh, though injured, survived and was taken into custody by U.S. forces. After being treated by the U.S. military, on January 23, 2002, Lindh arrived back in the United States where he was indicted on a number of charges, including conspiring to kill Americans. He eventually pled guilty to one of the charges—supplying services to the Taliban—and was sentenced to 20 years in a federal penitentiary.

As the first American arrested in the "war on terror," Lindh attracted enormous public attention. While some considered the "American Taliban" a traitor who had consorted with both the Taliban and al Qaeda, others thought of him as a naïve young man who happened to be in the wrong place at the wrong time. Lindh has since publicly expressed regret for his actions and condemned al Qaeda.

Lorenzo Vidino

See also Afghanistan War; al Qaeda; bin Laden, Osama; Harakat ul-Mujahideen; Homegrown Jihadi Movement; Training of Terrorists

Further Readings

Kukis, Mark. *My Heart Became Attached: The Strange Journey of John Walker Lindh*. Washington, DC: Brassey's, 2003.

Liptak, Adam. "John Walker Lindh's Buyer's Remorse." *The New York Times*, April 23, 2007. http://select.nytimes.com/2007/04/23/us/23bar.html.

U.S. District Court for the Eastern District of Virginia. *United States v. John Phillip Walker Lindh,* Criminal No. 02-37-A. Indictment, February 5, 2002. http://news.findlaw.com/hdocs/docs/lindh/uswlindh 020502cmp.html.

LOCKERBIE BOMBING

See Pan Am Flight 103 Bombing

LONDON NAIL BOMBING

See Copeland, David

LONDON UNDERGROUND BOMBINGS

On July 7, 2005, London was hit by four bombs that killed 52 people, in addition to the four suicide bombers. The series of attacks echoed those in Madrid, 16 months earlier. The bombers had planned to destroy four trains in the London Underground (subway), and to detonate their devices within a minute of each other, just before 9 AM, at the height of the rush hour. However, one bomber had a problem with the technology, and chose instead to destroy a London bus, detonating his device nearly one hour later. Some 700 people were injured by the bombers, who were all Britons who professed to be Muslims. Echoing the attacks of September 11, 2001, which were soon referred to as simply "9/11," the London bomb attack became known after its date, as "7/7."

The attack was a shattering blow, not only to those whose relatives and friends were killed on the day, but to the country at large. Britain was in the midst of a wave of euphoria, because the previous day the International Olympic Committee had announced that London had won the competition to host the 2012 Olympic Games. In addition, the G8 leaders were meeting in Scotland that day, with hopes of real advances for Africa's development, a cause with a high degree of public interest.

The four bombers—Mohammad Sidique Khan (age 30), Shehzad Tanweer (22), Germaine Lindsay (19), and Hasib Hussain (18)—were all Britons, and their actions drew attention to the dangers of "homegrown terrorism," Native-born perpetrators, or "homegrown jihadis," are often harder for counterintelligence agencies to track than foreign-born terrorists. Charles Clarke, the home secretary at the time, referred to the bombers as "clean skins," although it subsequently emerged that Khan had been scrutinized by the British intelligence service, MI5, at one point. Khan, the leader, lived in Dewsbury with his wife and young child, and he was a respected member of the local community, working as a teacher. Both Tanweer and Hussain lived in the nearby and larger city of Leeds, while Lindsay lived in Buckinghamshire, outside London, with his pregnant wife. Khan, Tanweer, and Hussain had left Leeds before 4 AM by car, and had driven to Luton. They met up with Lindsay at the Luton rail station, and then all four continued to London by train.

The reasons for the attacks were explained by two of the bombers in so-called martyrs videos. Mohammed Sidique Khan's video was released first, and in it he declared, "Our drive and motivation doesn't come from tangible commodities that

This is a video grab taken from the pan-Arab television TV channel Al Jazeera and aired on September 1, 2005, that allegedly shows Mohammed Sidique Khan, one of the suicide bombers of the July 7, 2005, attacks in London. al Qaeda claimed responsibility for the July 7 bombings in London and threatened more attacks in Europe, Al-Jazeera reported. (AP Photo/Al Jazeera. © 2011 The Associated Press. All Rights Reserved.)

this world has to offer. Our religion is Islam, obedience to the one true God and following the footsteps of the final prophet messenger. Your democratically elected governments continuously perpetuate atrocities against my people all over the world. And your support of them makes you directly responsible, just as I am directly responsible for protecting and avenging my Muslim brothers and sisters. Until we feel security you will be our targets and until you stop the bombing, gassing, imprisonment and torture of my people we will not stop this fight." Khan delivered his speech in his broad regional accent, aurally underscoring the Britishness of the bombers.

In another video, Tanweer spoke to the group's demands: "What have you witnessed now is only the beginning of a string of attacks that will continue and become stronger until you pull your forces out of Afghanistan and Iraq." That the bombers were British but would nonetheless bomb their fellow citizens became a focal point of the media coverage. The bombers, it was pointed out, not only had British citizenship, they behaved like Britons in their everyday lives. Tanweer, for example, spent the day before his suicide playing cricket, and on the way to Luton, he argued over his change while buying gas for the car.

The fear that there might be other cells of bombers was realized two weeks later. On July 21, four more bombers set out to kill on the London transport system. Three were on Underground trains and a fourth was on a bus, in an attempt to exactly match the first attack. However, only the detonator caps fired, and the bombs themselves did not go off. There were no injuries (though one induced asthma attack was reported), and by July 29, the police had arrested all the suspects. (However, July 22, police had shot and killed Jean Charles de Menezes, mistakenly suspecting him of being one of the bombers.) On July 9, 2007, four defendants, Muktar Ibrahim, Yassin Omar, Ramzi Mohammed, and Hussain Osman, were found guilty of conspiracy to murder and were sentenced to a minimum of 40 years imprisonment.

The individuals killed in the 7/7 attacks represented contemporary London in many ways. Among the victims were individuals who had come from many countries—including Iran, Israel, Nigeria, and Poland—to live and work in London. Victims included both Christians and Muslims, as well as those of no religion. They are honored in a permanent memorial in Hyde Park, London, made of tall stainless steel pillars, each individually finished and arranged in groups according to the different locations of the deaths, with a form that symbolizes the random nature of the loss of life.

Stuart Croft

Each of the 52 stainless steel columns represents a victim of the July 7, 2005, London bombings and is inscribed with the date, time, and location of the bomb that took their lives. The columns are arranged into four clusters representing the four different locations of the bombings. A plaque at the rear of the memorial lists the names of the victims in full. The memorial was designed by architectural studio Carmody Groake and was unveiled on the fourth anniversary of the bombings, July 7, 2009. (Photo: Hahnchen)

See also Homegrown Jihadi Movement; Madrid Bombings; September 11 Attacks; Suicide Terrorism

Further Readings

"7/7 Five Years On." Special issue, *International Affairs* 86, no. 4 (June 2010).

UK House of Commons. *Could 7/7 Have Been Prevented?* Report of the House of Commons Intelligence and Security Committee. London, 2009. http://www.cabinetoffice.gov.uk/media/210852/20090519_77review.pdf.

UK House of Commons. *Report of the Official Account of the Bombings in London on 7th July 2005.* London: The Stationery Office, May 11, 2006. http://news.bbc.co.uk/1/shared/bsp/hi/pdfs/11_05_06_narrative.pdf.

Zimonjic Peter. *Into the Darkness: 7/7.* London: Vintage, 2008.

LONE-WOLF TERRORISM

Lone-wolf terrorism, also called *lone-offender terrorism*, has emerged in the twenty-first century as one of the foremost security concerns for law enforcement and counterterrorism communities. In testimony to the U.S. Congress in 2010, both the director of the Federal Bureau of Investigation (FBI) and the director of the Central Intelligence Agency (CIA) highlighted this threat during the homeland security review. CIA Director Leon Panetta put it plainly: "It's the lone-wolf strategy that I think we have to pay attention to as the main threat to this country."

Very little research exists on the lone-offender problem, and it can be difficult to define these cases in a way that makes them distinct. Most experts tend to agree that the "lone wolf" characterization applies to attacks that are conceived and carried out by one person, without the direction of any larger, organized group. There are differences of opinion, however, about cases that reach beyond that scope. There are two key points of debate. The first is whether to include cases in which there was a single attacker, and where the planning and execution of the attack was supported by a small number of other people, but where the individuals involved were not under the direction or influence of an organized group or network. The 1995 Oklahoma City bombing perpetrated by Timothy James McVeigh is a good example of this scenario. The second type of cases are those in which there was a single attacker, but the planning and execution were in fact supported by members of an organized group or network. An example is the 2009 "underwear bomber" case, in which Umar Farouk Abdulmutallab attempted to blow up Northwest Airlines Flight 253. Ultimately, it may be that support from an organized group or network will be the key distinguishing factor, more so than whether a few other unaffiliated persons were involved. The challenge in this distinction is that the concept of what constitutes an "organized group or network" continues to evolve.

Certain persons who commit acts of terrorism may be—or may claim to be—inspired by al Qaeda–affiliated leaders, for example, even though they have never had support from or contact with any group members prior to their attack. Other actors may seek support or endorsement from al Qaeda leaders, and they may then be vetted, trained, and equipped by the organization, but they are then deployed in their attack to act alone. These two types of cases may differ from one another. The former may be more like public-figure attackers, representing a diverse group who find personal meaning in planning and executing an attack, while the latter may simply reflect a tactic used by violent extremists to maximize operational security and minimize the chance of pre-attack detection by using a single actor.

In the 1990s, Dr. Robert Fein and Bryan Vossekuil led the Exceptional Case Study Project (ECSP), an operational exploration of the thinking and behavior of persons known to have attacked, or tried to attack, a prominent public official or public figure in the United States since 1949. Given the nature of public-figure assassination, the ECSP findings are inextricably intertwined with the lone-offender issue. In fact, a number of the public-figure attackers in the ECSP study had previously considered a lone-offender type of attack.

Offenders in the ECSP study ranged in age from 16 to 73 and were often well educated. Most were described as social isolates, and they often had histories of transience and harassing others, but only half had known histories of violence. Most attackers had interests in militant or radical ideas and groups but were not active members, and they had histories of weapon use. Many had histories of serious depression or despair and had attempted or considered suicide. Motives were often complex and multifaceted, including desires to achieve notoriety and fame or to avenge a perceived wrong. About half of ECSP offenders had multiple targets or "directions of interest" throughout the course of deliberating about an attack.

In a 2007 report on lone-wolf terrorism for the COT Institute for Safety, Security and Crisis Management, the scholar Ramon Spaaij identified 72 likely incidents of lone-wolf terrorism occurring worldwide between 1968 and 2007. The largest proportion (42%) of these cases came from the United States, and their incidence appears to have increased since the mid-1980s. The motivations varied widely, but the most common were white supremacy (nine incidents), Islamist fundamentalism (five incidents) and anti-abortion activism (four incidents). In both European and non-European incidents, the targets of the attacks were primarily civilians. Most of the attackers were characterized as "loners" and had few friends, appearing not even to "fit in" with existing extremist groups and movements. Quite a few of these lone-wolf offenders were known to have histories of psychological problems, particularly depression, though this was not systematically assessed in all cases.

The finding that psychological disturbance was fairly common among the lone offenders is an interesting point of distinction in the study of terrorist psychology, since most terrorists are believed not to be mentally ill. The COT study suggests that psychological disturbance may be more common among loner offenders than among other terrorists. Of note, however, is that the nature of the disorders typically did not cause them to become cognitively disorganized, and in most cases they did not they fully lose contact with reality.

The rise in lone-offender violence may also reflect a resurgence of "leaderless resistance," a tactic long employed by violent extremist movements and reinvigorated in the U.S. white supremacy movement by Louis Beam. The concept of leaderless resistance suggests that violent action against a state is most effectively deployed by independent "cells" in which, as Beam put it, "all individuals and groups operate independently of each other, and never report to a central headquarters or single leader for direction or instruction." Beam goes on to assert, "It is the duty of every patriot to make the tyrant's life miserable. When one fails to do so he not only fails himself, but his people." This mindset shifts both agency and accountability from the group to the individual or autonomous collective. It is under this banner than many of the lone-wolf attacks stemming from the white supremacy and anti-abortion movements have occurred.

Randy Borum

See also Anti-Abortion Terrorism; Homegrown Jihadi Movement; Leaderless Resistance; McVeigh, Timothy James; Oklahoma City Bombing

Further Readings

Beam, Louis. "Leaderless Resistance." *The Seditionist* 12 (February 1992). http://www.louisbeam.com/leaderless.htm.

Fein, Robert, and Bryan Vossekuil. "Assassination in the United States: An Operational Study of Recent Assassins, Attackers, and Near Lethal Approachers." *Journal of Forensic Sciences* 44 (1999): 321–333.

Hewitt, C. *Understanding Terrorism in America: From the Klan to al Qaeda.* London and New York: Routledge, 2003.

Spaaij, Ramon. *Lone-wolf Terrorism.* The Hague, Netherlands: COT Institute for Safety, Security and Crisis Management, 2007.

Spaaij, Ramon. "The Enigma of Lone Wolf Terrorism: An Assessment." *Studies in Conflict & Terrorism* 33, no. 9 (2010): 854–870.

LONG, WILLIAM ANDREW, MURDER OF

A military recruiter and private in the U.S. Army, William Andrew Long of Conway, Arkansas, was killed on the morning of June 1, 2009, by Abdulhakim Mujahid Muhammad outside the Army-Navy Career Center, a recruiting station in Little Rock.

Muhammad, a 23-year-old man originally from Nashville, opened fire on Private Long, also 23 years old, and another recruiter, 18-year-old Private Quinton Ezeagwula, from his black pickup truck. Long and Ezeagwula, both Arkansas natives and recent graduates of basic training, worked in Little Rock as part of a recruiting program designed to promote the Army in recruits' home regions. Muhammad killed Long and wounded Ezeagwula before fleeing the scene. He was caught and arrested just a few minutes later in a nearby shopping center. The police confiscated a handgun, a .22 caliber rifle, and a Russian made SKS semiautomatic rifle from his truck. Authorities believe that Muhammad acted alone, not as part of a terrorist group or larger conspiracy, and that he was familiar with the layout of the recruiting station because of its close proximity to his Little Rock home.

During his lengthy interview with police, Muhammad said he was upset about the wars being conducted by the United States in Afghanistan and Iraq, and more specifically about the killing of Muslims in those countries. Mohammad, who was born Carlos Bledsoe, told police that he had converted to Islam during his teenage years. He became a deeply observant Muslim during his time in college and traveled to Yemen to study Arabic, marrying a Yemeni woman while in that country. He claimed in a note to the judge presiding over his case that he had been a member of al Qaeda in the Arabian Peninsula, but investigators do not believe this statement to be true.

Muhammad had reportedly been under investigation by a Federal Bureau of Investigation (FBI) joint terrorism task force after his travel to Yemen and subsequent arrest there for using a Somali passport. An agent with the FBI interviewed Muhammad, once in Yemen and once in Nashville, after his release. However, Muhammad was not believed to be a threat at that time.

Army recruiting officials reported that they were not able to recall any fatal attacks on recruiting offices within the few years prior to the incident, but there had been a number of bomb threats and acts of vandalism committed against recruiting offices. In 2008 a bomb was detonated at a recruiting station in Times Square, shattering its glass facade but failing to injure anyone. Further, in March 2009, vandals broke windows and splattered paint on the walls of the Marine Corps recruiting office in Berkeley, California, causing $5,000 in damage. This vandalism occurred on March 19, the sixth anniversary of the beginning of the Iraq War. A report issued by the not-for-profit Move America Forward in 2008 suggested that bomb threats and incidents of vandalism were on the increase, as were threats to military recruiters, citing that there had been 50 such attacks between 2003 and 2008.

Muhammad was charged with one count of capital murder and 15 counts of terrorist acts, one each for Long and Ezeagwula, and 13 more for the others in the recruiting office who were otherwise endangered by the shots he fired. Muhammad's trial was set for February 2011. Prosecutors anticipated trying the case as a straightforward case of murder, and they did not intend to hash out any of Muhammad's religious or political convictions.

Marie Palladini

See also Criminal Prosecution of Terrorists; Iraq War; Leaderless Resistance; Lone-Wolf Terrorism

Further Readings

Barnes, Steve, and James Dao. "Gunman Kills Soldier Outside Recruiting Station." *The New York Times*, June 2, 2009, p. A16.

Dao, James. "A Muslim Son, a Murder Trial and Many Questions." *The New York Times*, February 17, 2010, p. A11.

Gartenstein-Ross, Daveed, and Laura Grossman. *Homegrown Terrorists in the U.S. and U.K.* Washington, DC: FDD Press, 2009.

Sageman, Marc. *Leaderless Jihad: Terror Networks in the Twenty-first Century.* Philadelphia: University of Pennsylvania Press, 2008.

LORD'S RESISTANCE ARMY

The Lord's Resistance Army (LRA) has waged a war of attrition against the government and peoples of Uganda since the late 1980s. Unlike most antistate terrorists, the LRA has been largely devoid of any national vision or unifying social objective. Civilians in Uganda have become targets, booty of war, or liabilities to be minimized in the LRA's pursuit of wealth and power.

Background

Historically, the British colonial enterprise in Uganda was met with resistance from indigenous communities, most notably the Acholi of northern

Uganda. The Acholi are Luo in language and custom, and are closely related to the Alur and other Luo groups in Sudan. Numerous factors in the north, including the Acholi's active resistance to colonial rule, the harsh physical environment, and the region's pastoralist livelihood system, made it difficult for the British to "civilize" the Acholi. Therefore, peoples in the north were officially stigmatized as backwards, primitive, warlike, and comparatively less evolved than peoples of the south, who were more cooperative and thus more civilized. As a result, in comparison to the north, southern Uganda received more economic and infrastructure development and colonial civil service jobs and the relative power attached to them went to southerners. The warlike, "backwards" northerners were used as laborers or conscripted into the colonial army. Serving in the King's African Rifles, they became instruments of suppression and internalized contempt for the people. Large segments of the army under the British were Acholi.

The colonially created socioeconomic divisions and belligerence between north and south were institutionalized even further after independence. During the military dictatorship of General Idi Amin (1971–1979), the social fabric of Uganda was decimated. The situation was exacerbated during the war to overthrow Amin and the resultant conflicts among competing parties to fill the power vacuum left in the wake of his removal. Two of the main parties were the National Resistance Movement (NRM) headed by Yoweri Museveni, consisting primarily of peoples from the south and the west of the country, and the Uganda People's Democratic Army headed by General Tito Okello, consisting primarily of Acholi and other northern peoples.

Regional antagonisms between the northern and southern parts of the country were further aggravated when Museveni came to power after defeating the Acholi general Tito Okello in 1986. Acholi political and sectarian leaders revolted, invoking Acholi nationalism and historical resistance to marginalization. Many of Okello's Acholi soldiers fled north to their home districts along the Sudanese border. Some of the fleeing soldiers crossed into Sudan and joined up with other opponents of Museveni to form a rebel alliance.

The Creation of the LRA

In 1986 a spirit medium named Alice Lakwena established the Holy Spirit Movement, a resistance group that claimed to be inspired by the Holy Spirit of God. Lakwena preached that the Acholi could overthrow the government of Uganda if they followed her messages from God. In 1997 the Holy Spirit Movement was defeated by government troops and Lakwena escaped into exile in Kenya. Joseph Kony, a relative of Lakwena's who also had a reputation as a spirit medium, assumed leadership of the movement.

The son of subsistence farmers, Kony was born in 1961 in the village of Odek, in northern Uganda. He learned to be a healer and spirit medium from his older brother, Benon Okello. His father was a lay apostle in the Catholic Church, and Kony served as an alter boy for several years. Kony first appeared on the Ugandan national stage in 1986 as the leader of the United Holy Salvation Army (UHSA), one of many premillennialist Christian groups that sprang up in northern Uganda at the end of the twentieth century.

By 1988, with the addition of remnants from the defeated Uganda People's Democratic Army (UPDA), the UHSA was becoming a formidable resistance movement. Among the remnants of UPDA was Commander Odong Latek, who convinced Kony to adopt standard military tactics, as opposed to previous methods that involved attacking in cross-shaped formations and depending on oil or holy water to ward off bullets and evil spirits.

Being an amorphous amalgam of different groups and interests, the LRA has been known by a number of different names, including the Lord's Army (1987–1988) and Ugandan Peoples' Democratic Christian Army (1988–1992). The group finally settled on the current name, the Lord's Resistance Army. Preaching a message similar to Lakwena, Kony has insisted that he receives messages from God, and he has proclaimed that the Lord's Resistance Army is fighting in the name of God to overthrow the government of Uganda and establish a government with the Ten Commandments as its constitution.

The strategy of the Lord's Resistance Army has been to use terror to render the country ungovernable, disrupting life and normal social function, spreading fear and insecurity, and causing the

Oyet Christopher, 11, left, and Innocent Okot, 12, right, study math in Gulu, Uganda, in June 2003. They are two of the estimated 20,000 children who would leave their homes in the countryside each night to sleep in the northern Ugandan town, where they are safe from Lord's Resistance Army rebels known for abducting children, turning the boys into fighters and using the girls as concubines. Innocent was abducted once and spent seven months in the bush before managing to escape. (AP Photo/ Vanessa Vick. © 2011 The Associated Press. All Rights Reserved.)

national government to appear weak and unable to protect its citizens. People in the northern districts of Gulu, Kitgum, and Pader have been terrorized in this manner since the 1980s. More than a million Acholi have had to move to protected camps.

The LRA has also become infamous for its reliance on child soldiers, as the group has forced more than 30,000 boys and girls into combat operations. Children are put on the front lines of combat, and are even forced to kill, mutilate, and rape family members, schoolmates, neighbors and teachers. Because the casualty rates among child soldiers are very high, new soldiers are acquired by raiding schools. One of the earliest mass abductions occurred in 1987 when the LRA attacked the Sacred Heart Girls Secondary School, an all-girls boarding school, in the town of Gulu.

The LRA has been responsible for violent incidents both in Uganda and in neighboring countries. For example, in January 1997 the LRA attacked Lamwo, in northern Uganda, killing more than 400 people and displacing as many as

100,000. In May 2002 the LRA attacked Eastern Equatoria in Sudan, killing 450 people and abducting an unspecified number. On July 25, 2002, 48 people were hacked to death near the town of Kitgum in northern Uganda; newspaper reports said elderly people were killed with machetes and spears, and babies were smashed against trees. On December 25, 2008 the LRA attacked a church in Faradje, Democratic Republic of the Congo (DRC), killing 189 people and abducting 120 children. Following this, the LRA attacked three more communities in the DRC: 75 people were killed in Dungu, 48 were killed in Bangadi, and 213 were killed in Gurba. In December 2009, the LRA massacred 312 people in Makombo, DRC. Victims were hacked or beaten to death and more than 80 boys and girls were abducted.

On July 8, 2005, the International Criminal Court (ICC) issued warrants against Joseph Kony, his deputy, Vincent Otti, and LRA commanders Raska Lukwiya, Okot Odhiambo, and Dominc Ongwen. According to Chief Prosecutor Luis Moreno Ocampo, the men have been indicted on 12 counts of crimes against humanity, including murder, enslavement, sexual enslavement, and rape, and on 21 counts of war crimes, including murder, cruel treatment of civilians, intentionally directing an attack against a civilian population, pillaging, inducing rape, and forced enlisting of children into the rebel ranks.

In 2006 a team of U.S.-trained Guatemalan Special Operations soldiers were sent to assassinate Joseph Kony. They were unsuccessful and were themselves killed by LRA fighters. On August 28, 2008, the United States placed Kony on its list of Specially Designated Global Terrorists.

The LRA has become a problem throughout the Great Lakes Region of East and Central Africa, including the countries of Burundi, DRC, Rwanda, Tanzania, and Uganda. Exploiting the inability of the DRC, South Sudan, and the Central African Republic (CAR) to control their frontiers, small mobile bands of fighters have attacked unprotected villages to pillage food and clothing and abduct recruits. Killings and mutilations have been part of the strategy to terrorize the population and discourage anyone from cooperating with the Ugandan or other national armies.

As of this writing, the LRA was scattered over several states and districts in the Great Lakes region, with the bulk of forces in CAR. They were under constant pursuit and the leadership core appeared to be growing thin. Despite these organizational stresses, LRA fighters have remained a danger and a source of fear and terror capable of inflicting great suffering and pain. In March 2010 it was reported that Kony was in the southern Darfur region of Sudan, seeking support from his former patrons in the Sudanese government. There have been many attempts at negotiating a peace settlement, but thus far all have failed.

Ikaweba Bunting

See also Religious and Spiritual Perspectives on Terrorism

Further Readings

Allen, Tim, and Koen Vlassenroot. *The Lord's Resistance Army: Myth and Reality.* London: Zed Books, 2010.

Amnesty International. *Uganda: "Breaking God's Commands": The Destruction of Childhood by the Lord's Resistance Army.* London: Amnesty International, September 17, 1997. http://www.amnesty.org/en/library/info/AFR59/001/1997/en.

Doom, Ruddy, and Koen Vlassenroot. "Kony's Message: A New *Koine?* The Lord's Resistance Army in Northern Uganda." *African Affairs* 98 (1999): 5–36. http://afraf.oxfordjournals.org/content/98/390/5.short.

Drogin, Bob. "Christian Cult Killing, Ravaging in New Uganda." *Seattle Times,* April 1, 1996. http://community.seattletimes.nwsource.com/archive/?date=19960401&slug=2321945.

Eichstaedt, Peter. *First Kill Your Family: Child Soldiers of Uganda and the Lord's Resistance Army.* Chicago: Lawrence Hill Books, 2009.

Engeler, Elain. "UN: Ugandan Rebel Attacks May Have Been War Crimes." *Seattle Times,* December 21, 2009. http://seattletimes.nwsource.com/html/nationworld/2010558643_apununlordsresistancearmy.html.

Human Rights Watch. *The Scars of Death: Children Abducted by the Lord's Resistance Army in Uganda.* New York: Human Rights Watch, September 1, 1997. http://www.hrw.org/en/reports/1997/09/18/scars-death.

International Crisis Group. *Great Lakes: A Regional Strategy beyond Killing Kony.* Africa Files, April 28, 2010. http://www.africafiles.org/article.asp?ID=23487.

Mutibwa, Phares. *Uganda since Independence: A Story of Unfulfilled Hopes.* Trenton, NJ: Africa World Press, 1992.

LOW-INTENSITY WARFARE

See Asymmetrical Warfare

LOYALIST VOLUNTEER FORCE

The Loyalist Volunteer Force (LVF) is a Protestant Unionist paramilitary group responsible for a number of sectarian killings in Northern Ireland.

A splinter group of the larger Ulster Volunteer Force (UVF), the LVF broke with its parent organization in 1996 in a dispute related to the Drumcree Protests of that year. For more than 30 years, beginning in the late 1960s, Northern Ireland's Roman Catholic minority, who wished the province to become part of the Republic of Ireland, and its Protestant majority, who wished it to remain a part of Great Britain, were engaged in a bloody conflict. In late 1994 the major armed paramilitary groups representing both Protestants (also called Loyalists or Unionists) and Catholics (also called Nationalists or Republicans) declared cease-fires because they wished to participate in peace negotiations. By 1996, however, the negotiations had stalled.

Protestant frustration and suspicion at the lack of progress was aggravated in June by the banning of the Orange Order's July 12 March (a parade in Belfast that commemorates a 1690 Protestant victory over Catholics), the route of which passed through a Catholic neighborhood. Thousands of Loyalists assembled at a church in Drumcree for a protest lasting several days. Billy "King Rat" Wright, the UVF representative in Portadown, threatened violent reprisals if the march was not allowed. The leadership of the UVF had forbidden Wright to break its cease-fire, as this would have resulted in the organization's suspension from peace talks, but on July 8 a Catholic taxi driver named Michael McGoldrick was found murdered a few miles from Drumcree. Many observers believed the shooting to be the work of Wright's men.

Following McGoldrick's murder, Wright broke with the UVF, taking most of the organization's Portadown membership with him, and formed the rival LVF. The LVF has been linked to more than a dozen murders, and, as with other Loyalist paramilitary groups, most of its victims have been Catholics targeted at random. The LVF has also been implicated in a string of deaths thought to be the result of disputes over drugs.

In the spring of 1997, Wright was arrested on charges of intimidating a witness. On December 27, 1997, while in prison, he was shot to death by members of the Irish National Liberation Army, a Republican paramilitary group. His murder sparked a series of vengeance killings among the prisoners and led to two civilian deaths, as members of the LVF avenged, as best they could, their leader. With the death of the charismatic and popular Wright, a serious blow was dealt to LVF, and no new leader has yet emerged.

In 1998 the LVF declared a cease-fire because it wanted to participate in the early release program for paramilitary prisoners set up under the Good Friday Accords, which ended the overall conflict. Despite the cease-fire, however, the LVF is thought to be operating still, using the cover name "Red Hand Defenders" for sectarian attacks. A spokesperson for the Red Hand Defenders claimed responsibility for the murder of a Catholic postman, Daniel McColgan, on January 12, 2002, and issued a threat declaring all Catholic civil servants and teachers to be legitimate targets; the threat was retracted several days later. Many observers believe that the Red Hand Defenders consists primarily of members of the LVF and the Ulster Defense Association, another Unionist group. In August 2002, someone claiming to be an LVF operative made a death threat to Neil Lennon, a soccer player who was about to become the first Catholic to captain the Northern Ireland team. Although the LVF leadership disavowed responsibility for the threat, Lennon resigned from the team.

The LVF has also become involved in bloody fights with other Unionist groups, primarily over control of the drug trade. From mid-2002 to early 2003, the LVF backed Johnny "Mad Dog" Adair, a former commander of the Ulster Defense Association, as he attempted to take over the UDA; police finally ended the turf war by arresting Adair. In 2004 and 2005, the LVF and UVF engaged in a violent feud that killed four people. The two groups finally declared a truce on October 30, 2005, and the LVF announced that it would order all of its military units to stand down.

Colleen Sullivan

See also Irish Republican Army; Red Hand Defenders; Ulster Defense Association; Ulster Volunteer Force

Further Readings

Bardgett, Graham. "Loyalists in Peace Move." *Daily Mirror,* October 31, 2005, p. 16.
Bryan, Dominic. *Orange Parades: The Politics of Ritual, Tradition and Control.* London: Pluto Press, 2000. Excerpt on Drumcree controversy available online at http://cain.ulst.ac.uk/issues/parade/bryan/bryan00.htm.
Cusack, Jim, and Henry McDonald. *The UVF.* Dublin: Poolbeg, 1997.
Holland, Jack. *Hope against History: The Course of Conflict in Northern Ireland.* New York: Henry Holt, 1999.
Hundley, Tom. "Loyalist Gangs in Belfast Wage Bloody Turf War." *Houston Chronicle,* January 26, 2003, p. 21.
Jesse, Neal G., and Kristen P. Williams. "Northern Ireland: Protestants, Catholics, and the 'Troubles.'" In *Ethnic Conflict: A Systematic Approach to Cases of Conflict.* Washington, DC: CQ Press, 2010.
McEvoy, Joanne. *The Politics of Northern Ireland.* Edinburgh, UK: University of Edinburgh Press, 2008.
McKay, Susan. *Northern Protestants: An Unsettled People.* Belfast: Blackstaff Press, 2000.
McKittrick, David. *Making Sense of the Troubles.* Belfast: Blackstaff Press, 2000.
Mitchell, Thomas G. *When Peace Fails: Lessons from Belfast for the Middle East.* Jefferson, NC: McFarland, 2010.
Taylor, Peter. *Loyalists: War and Peace in Northern Ireland.* New York: TV Books, 1999.

LYNCHING

Lynching is the extrajudicial killing of an individual by a mob. It can include hanging, castration, burning, and other forms of torture. Lynching has been employed throughout American history as far back as the colonial period—primarily, although not exclusively, as a form of racial control. The extreme violence of the act, combined with its deliberate use to inspire fear among a wider populace, qualifies lynching as an act of terrorism.

Until the birth of the anti-lynching movement in the early twentieth century, lynching was used as a common way of intimidating African Americans and other minorities. The word *lynch* is derived from a Quaker judge from Virginia named Charles Lynch, who imprisoned British loyalists during the period leading up to the Revolutionary War. During that period, the practice was a widely accepted precursor to the establishment of courts and proper law enforcement agencies.

In time, lynching was increasingly used by whites against blacks for purposes of racial intimidation and control. A sort of mythology was created in order to justify the violence, in which any successful black landowners, businessmen, or professionals who were perceived as a threat to white supremacy were killed and made into an "example." The organization most widely credited for its frequent use of lynching as a means of control is the Ku Klux Klan, an ultra-racist white supremacist group that came to power during the Reconstruction era.

In 1979 the Tuskegee Institute determined that during the 86-year period between 1882 and 1968, 4,742 blacks were lynched. During the late nineteenth century, an average of 139 lives were taken each year, and 75 percent of the victims were black. White mobs assumed the role of judge, jury, and executioner, often with the support of local law enforcement officials. Newspapers described the events in graphic detail, using divisive language that reinforced the idea that blacks were less than human, making the actions of lynch mobs seem less reprehensible. The practice of lynching lasted well into the twentieth century as a commonplace tool for white control, with a brief upsurge in the 1960s in opposition to the civil rights movement.

Some incidents of lynching were not racially motivated; for example, lynching was a common practice by both the Union and Confederate armies during the Civil War as a form of military reaction to dissenters on both sides. During the conflict, when a man or a boy was hanged, it was almost always because of a war-related offense, as executioners were often members of county militias. White men and boys were also lynched in the years following the Civil War, with the greatest contributing factor being the lingering suspicions of perceived Confederate or Union opponents. Immediately following the war, the majority of people lynched were southern blacks, who were seen as becoming increasingly "uppity," with their newfound freedom from the bonds of slavery. Julius E. Thompson, the author of *Lynchings in Mississippi: A History, 1865–1965* (2006), has estimated that in the late 1860s in Mississippi, perhaps two or three blacks a week were killed, resulting in between 400 and 600 blacks killed during a four-year period.

The post-Reconstruction era was characterized by the Supreme Court's reversal of the Civil Rights Act of 1875, opening the door for greater violence against blacks, particularly in the South. The "New South" and its racist policies, known as "Jim Crow" laws, made it clear to blacks that their only way to escape violence from white Americans was to organize more effectively. The result was a growth in black-led groups with leaders such as Bishop Henry McNeal Turner, a bishop of the African Methodist Episcopal (AME) Church, and T. Thomas Fortune, a well-known black journalist. Religious officials were frequent leaders of the anti-lynching movement, as churches appealed to the religious conscience of sympathetic whites. However, perhaps the most influential early African American leader in the anti-lynching movement was the journalist Ida Wells, who vehemently and persistently pushed passive blacks into action.

However, the progress made by anti-lynching crusaders during the early twentieth century was curbed by the "Red Summer" of 1919, in which many whites attempted to relegate blacks to their pre–World War I position in society. Interestingly, the increased antiblack violence led to greater support among sympathetic whites, who perceived the issue, in some instances, as putting white society and values themselves on trial. Others worried about the potential destabilization of the social order if extralegal actions continued to run unpunished and unabated.

Lynching declined during the early 1920s, largely because of national support for anti-lynching reform, spearheaded by the National Association for the Advancement of Colored People (NAACP). The NAACP's political efforts were focused on support for the legislation known as the Dyer Bill, proposed by Representative L.C. Dyer of Missouri. The bill was passed the U.S. House of

Representatives, but it was defeated by a white Southern Democrat filibuster in the U.S. Senate.

In an effort to involved women in the anti-lynching movement, the Anti-Lynching Crusaders were created on July 15, 1922, and led by Mary B. Talbert, the president of the National Association of Colored Women. The organization consisted mostly of black women, but managed to attract some 200 white members. The group had moderate success in raising money in support of the Dyer Bill and various other activities, but with the Senate failing to follow the House of Representatives in passing the bill, the group disbanded after existing for only five months. With the failure of the Dyer Bill, the NAACP chose instead to focus on individual cases of lynchings and state-level legislation, in an attempt to approach the issue from a different perspective and garner more national attention and support.

When President Herbert Hoover was elected in 1929, he inherited the wavering loyalty of blacks to the Republican Party following the presidency of Warren Harding and the failure of the Dyer Bill. The new president did not consider the lynching issue to be politically important, a stance reflected by his support of the "lily-white" faction of the Republican Party in the South, which sought to remove blacks from elected and appointed offices. Both he and his successor, Franklin D. Roosevelt, failed to pass nationwide legislation outlawing lynching.

The decline in lynching in the mid- to late twentieth century is attributable to a number of factors, including the Great Migration of southern blacks to Northern urban centers starting around 1915, and economic developments nationwide that lessened the importance of southern agriculture, an industry that had served as a motivating factor for white violence. However, the civil rights movement and the revitalization of African American unity saw a rise in lynchings, with 21 African Americans killed between 1961 and 1965, without a single person convicted of the crimes. Organizational aspects and certain tactics of the anti-lynching movement were adopted by the civil rights–era movement for equality, even though many of the early attempts against lynching were largely unsuccessful.

In the twenty-first century, lynching is extremely rare in developed countries, but it continues to be used as a form of control and extrajudicial justice in some countries. In Mozambique, 78 people were lynched in 2009; 51 of the incidents resulted in homicides. This was a decrease from 2008, however, during which 68 homicides were recorded. The motivations for the mob violence in these cases were attributed to misinformed individuals who question why certain people have attained wealth or to anger at alleged criminals being released from jail without being convicted. In a similar incident, Iraqi police were charged in 2007 for the lynching of a failed suicide bomber, an instance in which the officers beat to death a known terrorist. In all these cases, individuals decided to take the law into their own hands, much like white American mobs in earlier eras.

Jonathan Martin

See also Ku Klux Klan; White Supremacy Movement

Further Readings

Allen, James, Hilton Als, John Lewis, and Leon F. Litwack. *Without Sanctuary: Lynching Photography in America.* Sante Fe, NM: Twin Palms, 2000.

Frazier, Harriet C. *Lynchings in Missouri, 1803–1981.* Jefferson, NC: McFarland, 2009.

Grant, Donald L. *The Anti-lynching Movement: 1883–1932.* San Francisco: R and E Research Associates, 1975.

Sims, Angela D. *Ethical Complications of Lynching: Ida Wells's Interrogation of American Terror.* New York: Palgrave MacMillan, 2010.

Thompson, Julius E. *Lynchings in Mississippi: A History, 1865–1965.* Jefferson, NC: McFarland, 2006.

Wells-Barnett, Ida B. *Southern Horrors: Lynch Law in All Its Phases.* 1892. http://www.gutenberg.org/files/14975/14975-h/14975-h.htm.

MACDONALD, ANDREW

See Turner Diaries, The

MACHETEROS

Los Macheteros—Spanish for "the Machete Wielders" (and also known as Boricua Popular Army; Ejercito Popular Boricua; EPB Movimiento Popular Revolucionario; Partido Revolucionario de Trabajadores Puertorriquenos)—was one of the more successful and dangerous Puerto Rican militant nationalist organizations. A splinter group of the FALN, another nationalist organization, the Macheteros emerged in the late 1970s and is believed to be responsible for numerous attacks on Puerto Rico's military and government, as well as one of the largest bank robberies in U.S. history.

On August 24, 1978, the Macheteros issued its first communiqué, claiming responsibility for the death of a Puerto Rican police officer, Julio Rodriguez Rivera, who had been shot and killed at a beach in Naguabo. The act was in retaliation for the murder by police of two *independentistas,* Arnaldo Dario Rosado and Carlos Soto Arrivi, at Cerro Maravilla, Puerto Rico, in July 1978.

Unlike the FALN, which primarily bombed public buildings, banks, and government offices, the Macheteros concentrated on bombing military sites, including military recruiting stations, defense contractors, and post offices where men registered for the draft, as well as attacking military personnel. The message of the group was clear: Puerto Rico was a country occupied militarily by the United States.

In October 1979 the Macheteros took responsibility for several bombings of federal installations in Puerto Rico; no one was hurt in these incidents. That December, group members fired automatic weapons at a bus carrying 18 U.S. Navy personnel, leaving 2 sailors dead and 10 injured. This was a combined attack, also involving the Organization of Volunteers for the Puerto Rican Revolution and the Armed Forces of Popular Resistance, in retaliation for the death of the Puerto Rican independence fighter Angel Rodriguez Cristobal. Cristobal had been found hanged in federal prison in Tallahassee, Florida, in what the Puerto Rican groups believed was a CIA action.

Throughout the early 1980s, the Macheteros engaged in two or three actions per year, often in retaliation for navy maneuvers on the Puerto Rican island of Vieques, or for police and government actions against a squatter village, Villa Sin Miedo (Town Without Fear). As a calling card, members would leave a machete with a flag near the scene of the attack, contacting UPI reporters the next day to officially claim responsibility.

On September 12, 1983, the birthday of Pedro Albizu Campos, a Puerto Rican nationalist leader, the Macheteros carried out its first action in the continental United States, robbing more than $7 million from a Wells Fargo depot in West Hartford, Connecticut. On September 13, the Macheteros claimed responsibility in a communiqué sent to the

Hartford Courant. Macheteros had named the action *agila blanca* (white eagle) to commemorate Jose Maldonado, who, during the Spanish-American War, had led a number of Puerto Rican patriots in a skirmish against the invaders from the north. Most of the money disappeared with Victor Manuel Gerena, a Machetero who worked at the Wells Fargo depot as a guard. Gerena fled first to Mexico, and then to Cuba, where he remains in exile. (It is believed that the group had significant ties to Cuba, with many of its members trained there.) Once out of the United States, the money was used to fund nationalist activities, including a toy giveaway in Hartford and Puerto Rico.

In August 1985, investigators apprehended 13 suspects in the robbery—11 in Puerto Rico, one in Massachusetts, and one in Dallas. Four others, including Gerena, were indicted. Juan Segarra Palmer and Filiberto Ojeda Rios, two of the group's founders, were the first to be tried. Ojeda Rios was tried in absentia, however, because he jumped bail in 1990. Eventually, all were found guilty on charges connected to the robbery and sentenced to more than 35 years in prison. Most were released in 1999, when President Bill Clinton commuted the sentences of 16 Puerto Rican nationalist prisoners.

In 2005, Ojeda Rios was tracked down in Hormigueros, a small town in western Puerto Rico. On September 23, 2005, he was killed in a shoot-out with FBI agents. Ojeda Rios's death sparked tremendous controversy because, after shooting him, the agents waited a day before entering the house, ensuring the fatality of his wounds. The FBI maintains that the delay was necessary because its agents were waiting for specialized teams to check the house for explosive booby-traps.

On February 7, 2008, FBI agents in Puerto Rico arrested Avelino Gonzalez-Claudio, the third founder of the group, on charges stemming from the 1983 robbery. He was moved to Connecticut, where he was tried, and in 2010 he was sentenced to seven years in federal prison. As of 2010, Gerena remained on the FBI's "most wanted" fugitives list, and the agency offered a $1 million reward for information leading directly to his arrest.

Laura Lambert

See also FALN; Puerto Rican Nationalist Terrorism

Further Readings

Fernandez, Ronald. *Los Macheteros: The Wells Fargo Robbery and the Violent Struggle for Puerto Rican Independence.* New York: Prentice Hall, 1987.
Heine, Jorge, and Juan M. García-Passalacqua. *The Puerto Rican Question.* New York: Foreign Policy Association, 1984.
Hewitt, Christopher. *Understanding Terrorism in America.* New York: Routledge, 2003.
Levinson, Nan. "La Mordaza." In *Outspoken: Free Speech Stories.* Berkeley: University of California Press, 2003.
Mahony, Edmund H. "Revolutionary to the End." *Hartford Courant,* November 20, 2005, p. A1.
Smith, Brent L. *Terrorism in America: Pipe Bombs and Pipe Dreams.* Albany: State University of New York Press, 1994.

MAD BOMBER

See Metesky, George

MADRID BOMBINGS

On March 11, 2004, a series of 10 bombs detonated aboard four commuter trains in Madrid, Spain. The trains connect Alcalá de Henares (home to Latin American and eastern European immigrant communities) to the southeast part of the city. Four bombs exploded at 7:39 A.M. at Atocha station on train 21431; simultaneously, three bombs exploded just outside Calle Tellez station on train 17305. A few minutes later, two additional bombs exploded on train 21435 at El Pozo del Tío Raimundo station. At 7:42, one further explosion occurred on train 21713 at Santa Eugenia station. In all, 191 people died (177 at the scene and 13 in the hospital) and more than 1,800 were injured—the highest total in the history of terrorist attacks in Spain. According to the police, the bombs aboard the Atocha and Téllez trains were intended to cause an even higher number of victims by bringing down the roof of Atocha station.

One hour after the attack, Spanish prime minister José María Aznar declared that the Basque separatist group Euskadi Ta Askatasuna (ETA, or

Rescue workers line up bodies beside a bomb-damaged passenger train at Atocha station following a number of explosions on trains in Madrid on March 11, 2004, just three days before Spain's general elections, killing more than 191 rush-hour commuters and wounding more than 1,800 in Spain's worst terrorist attack. (AP Photo/Denis Doyle. © 2011 The Associated Press. All Rights Reserved.)

Basque Fatherland and Liberty) was surely responsible for the bombings. The ETA has a long tradition of staging terrorist attacks as part of its campaign for Basque independence from Spain, and two similar abortive attempts made it reasonable that ETA might be involved.

However, a sports bag containing an unexploded bomb and a cell-phone configured in Arabic were found near the sites of the explosion; the implications of the Arabic cell phone were initially ignored by Spanish authorities. Additional clues caused international public opinion to focus on the al Qaeda hypothesis. Some pointed to the high symbolic nature of the date: the attacks occurred exactly 912 days after the attacks of September 11, 2001 (9/11), meaning that there were 911 days in between the two events. Moreover,

the ETA, which usually claims responsibility for its actions, strongly denied any responsibility.

Nevertheless, the Spanish foreign minister, Ana Palacio, sent a message to all Spanish embassies declaring again that ETA was without any doubt responsible for the attacks. On Sunday, March 14, the day of Spain's national elections, an editorial published in *El País* stated, "The prime minister gave his word to the heads of the media so that they would present the attacks as the work of the ETA terrorist group." The initial ETA hypothesis also gained support from the United Nations. At the request of the Spanish government, the UN Security Council passed Resolution 1530 condemning the attacks and accusing ETA of responsibility for the attacks.

Just a few days later, however, the Spanish ambassador had to submit an apologetic letter, explaining the new progress of the investigation, and the likely involvement of al Qaeda. Four days after the attacks, on March 16, *The Washington Post* reported that "the Spanish government knew early on that there was evidence pointing to Islamic terrorism, but they instructed the police to keep quiet about it and instead pushed the idea that ETA was behind it." On March 18, the Inter Press Service published an article titled "Spanish Reporters: Government Silenced the Truth About the Attack," where it was argued that the EFE, a group representing reporters and editors at Spain's state-run news agency, knew very early on about the Arabic cell phone, as well as other evidence that pointed toward al Qaeda.

In April 2006, 29 suspects were charged with involvement in the attacks. The trial began on February 15, 2007. Evidence presented at the trial indicated that the linking of the attacks with ETA had been inaccurate, and indeed, in August 2007, al Qaeda pridefully claimed responsibility for the slaughter. On October 31 the Audiencia National de Espana delivered its verdicts, and "local cells of Islamic extremists inspired through the Internet" were found guilty. Twenty-one of the defendants were sentenced to death.

It is worth noting that shortly after the March 11 attacks, on April 2, there was a failed bombing attempt on high-speed AVE (Alta Velocidad Española) train. A railway worker found the bomb in a blue plastic bag on the railway track between Madrid and Seville, averting a disaster potentially even greater than that of March 11. The perpetrators of that failed attack remain unknown.

Anna Lisa Tota

See also al Qaeda; Basque Fatherland and Liberty; Basque Separatists; bin Laden, Osama; Bombings and Bomb Scares; September 11 Attacks

Further Readings

Bergen, Peter I. *The Longest War: Inside the Enduring Conflict between America and al-Qaeda.* New York: Free Press, 2011.

Collins, Randall. "Rituals of Solidarity and Security in the Wake of Terrorist Attack." *Sociological Theory* 22, no. 1 (2004): 53–87.

Martin, Gus. *Essentials of Terrorism: Concepts and Controversies.* 2nd ed. Thousand Oaks, CA: Sage, 2011.

Tilly, Charles. "Terror, Terrorism, Terrorists." *Sociological Theory* 22, no. 1 (2004): 5–13.

Tuman, Joseph S. *Communicating Terror: The Rhetorical Dimensions of Terrorism.* London: Sage, 2003.

Vidino, Lorenzo. *Al Qaeda in Europe: The New Battleground of International Jihad.* Amherst, NY: Prometheus Books, 2006.

MANUEL RODRIGUEZ PATRIOTIC FRONT

Founded in 1983 as the armed wing of the Chilean Communist Party, the Manuel Rodriguez Patriotic Front (Frente Patriótico Manuel Rodríguez, or FPMR) was formed to carry out armed attacks against members and institutions of the brutal regime of Augusto Pinochet. The Pinochet regime dealt severely with the FPMR and other dissident groups and is said to have tortured *frentistas,* as FPMR members are called. After the regime fell in 1990, the group, named for a hero of Chile's war of independence against Spain, continued its attacks on civilians and international targets.

In the late 1980s, the FPMR splintered into two factions, one of which became a political party in 1991. The other dissident faction continued its terrorist activity, and the U.S. State Department considered this group to be a terrorist organization for many years.

The flag of the FPMR

In 1991 the FPMR carried out two famous operations. On April 1, the group assassinated the right-wing senator Jaime Guzman, killing him as he left a Catholic University campus in Santiago. On September 9, three hooded FPMR members kidnapped Cristian Edwards, whose family runs Chile's most prominent newspaper. Edwards was wrapped in a sleeping bag and taken to a FPMR hideout. His captors kept Edwards for 145 days in a small room without natural light, playing music continually. After his family paid $1 million in ransom, the FPMR freed him. Edwards has since kept a low profile and moved to the United States.

The dissident wing of the FPMR has also attacked international targets, including U.S. businesses and Mormon churches. In 1993, FPMR operatives bombed two McDonald's restaurants and attempted to bomb a Kentucky Fried Chicken. In December 1996, four FPMR members managed a spectacular escape from a Chilean high-security prison; the facility had been widely considered escape-proof. FPMR operatives on the outside hijacked a helicopter that had been rented by tourists and flew it over the prison. They then dropped a 15-meter rope with a basket attached into the prison yard. As guards began to shoot, the four escapees climbed into the basket and were lifted to safety. Landing the helicopter in a park in south Santiago, Chile's capital, they escaped in waiting vehicles. Chile mounted a massive police search, but the FPMR members had fled. Some of them went to Cuba, where they received asylum. One of the fugitives, Patricio Ortiz Montengro, fled to Switzerland and requested political asylum. Extradition requests were denied because the Swiss government was not assured that Ortiz would be safe if returned to Chile.

On December 11, 2002, *frentistas* kidnapped the Brazilian publicist Washington Olivetto as he rode home from work in Sao Paulo. The kidnappers, disguised as police officers, stopped Olivetto's driver and forced their way into his car. The FPMR held Olivetto for 53 days in a small, windowless room located in the countryside near São Paulo. Again, music blared 24 hours a day. Olivetto attempted to determine how much time had passed by counting the number of albums played. Shortly after Olivetto's family agreed to pay $10 million in ransom, the landlord who rented to the kidnappers told the police he had suspicions about his strange young tenants. The Brazilian police soon freed Olivetto.

After his release, Chilean experts suggested that the dissident branch of the FPMR carried out the Olivetto kidnapping in an attempt to gain enough funds to regroup as an armed force. In any case, the FPMR has been essentially inactive since that time. In November 2004, Sergio Galvarino Apablaza, the FPMR commander accused of ordering the Guzman assassination and the Edwards kidnapping, was arrested in Argentina. The Chilean government requested his extradition, but Apablaza applied for and, in September 2010, received political asylum in Argentina.

Erica Pearson

See also Lautaro Youth Movement

Further Readings

Ensalaco, Mark. *Chile under Pinochet: Recovering the Truth*. Philadelphia: University of Pennsylvania Press, 2000.

Muñoz, Heraldo. *The Dictator's Shadow: Life under Augusto Pinochet*. New York: Basic Books, 2008.

O'Grady, Mary Anastasia. "Don't Count on Argentina to Help Fight Terror." *Wall Street Journal*, July 8, 2005, p. A11.

MARIGHELLA, CARLOS (1911–1969)

Carlos Marighella, one South America's most famous revolutionaries, founded and controlled the *Ação* Libertadora Nacional (Action for National Liberation, or ALN). His writings include essays on revolutionary methods and the *Minimanual of the Urban Guerrilla* (1969), a handbook for urban warfare that has influenced terrorists the world over since its publication.

Marighella was born on December 5, 1911, in the Bahia state of eastern Brazil. His father, Augustus, was an Italian immigrant, and his mother, Marialva, was an Afro-Brazilian and a descendent of slaves. At the age of 19, Carlos joined the Brazilian Communist Party (PCB) as an organizer and activist. He spent most of the years during World War II in jail. When he was released in 1952, he joined the Central Committee of the Communist Party, and in 1953 he traveled to China and met with Mao Zedong.

By 1963, Brazil had experienced a military coup and become a totalitarian state. By 1965, two-thirds of Brazil's population was living in cities—a major change for this vast nation. The populace had never embraced the military leaders, however, preferring a traditional civilian government. Partly in response to the military dictatorship, a number of small urban terrorist groups formed, composed of activists, students, artists, and Communist dissenters.

The Communist Party had been forced underground by the government. Marighella began to disagree with the PCB, and he was thrown out of the party in August 1967. He then formed the ALN in 1968. Many others, mostly radical intellectuals, left the Communist Party with Marighella; these individuals formed the core of the ALN, a group that eventually grew to nearly 200. Throughout 1968 and 1969, the ALN brought guerrilla warfare into the cities with a series of bombings, bank assaults, kidnappings, ambushes, assassinations, and acts of sabotage. Ambassadors were kidnapped and security forces were murdered. The government struck back after each incident—sometimes arresting thousands in citywide raids. Brazil's rulers even created a Department of Social and Political Order to handle this onslaught of urban terrorism. The violence had two outcomes: it created exactly the chaos that the terrorists wanted, but it also brought about their demise.

In June 1969, Marighella wrote his *Minimanual of the Urban Guerrilla*. The ALN read it live over Brazilian radio, and the document, published as a book and translated into many languages, became a popular discussion of and guide to urban warfare for militant groups worldwide. The book explains the reason and strategy for urban terrorism: "It is necessary to turn political crisis into armed crisis by performing violent actions that will force those in power to transform the military situation into a political situation. That will alienate the masses, who, from then on, will revolt against the army and the police and blame them for this state of things."

On November 30, 1969, Marighella was killed in a police ambush; the ALN subsequently collapsed. Within two years, much of the urban terrorism in Brazil ceased, with most of the terrorists either dead or jailed.

Richard McHugh

Further Readings

Burton, Anthony. *Urban Terrorism: Theory, Practice, Response*. London: L. Cooper, 1975.

Caine, Philip. "Urban Guerrilla Warfare." *Military Review*, February 1970.

Joes, Anthony James. *Urban Guerrilla Warfare*. Lexington: University Press of Kentucky, 2007.

Marighella, Carlos. *Minimanual of the Urban Guerrilla*. 1969. Reprint. Chapel Hill, NC: Documentary Publications, 1985.

Moss, Robert. *Urban Guerrilla Warfare*. London: International Institute for Strategic Studies, 1971.

MARZOOK, MOUSA MOHAMMED ABU (1951–)

The Hamas political leader Mousa Mohammed Abu Marzook lived in the United States for more than a decade before an Israeli warrant for his arrest led to his being taken into custody in 1995. Amid much controversy, he was held by the U.S. government for several years without being charged. He was finally deported to Jordan in 1997.

Marzook was born in a Gaza refugee camp and studied at Helwan College of Engineering and Technology in Cairo. He traveled to the United States in the early 1980s and earned a master's degree in industrial engineering at Colorado State University. He received his Ph.D. in engineering from Columbia State University in Louisiana in 1991.

Marzook apparently first joined the Palestinian militant group Hamas in 1992, when he became head of the organization's political bureau. Soon after, Marzook moved to a suburban neighborhood outside of Washington, D.C., with his wife and family. Four of his six children were born in the United States.

In 1995, Marzook was detained at New York's Kennedy Airport after returning from the Middle East. His name had been added to a list of suspected terrorists after Israel issued a warrant for his arrest for conspiracy to kill Israeli citizens. Israeli officials said that hundreds of thousands of dollars were transferred from Marzook's account into the bank account of a Chicago auto dealer, Muhammad Hamid Khalil Salah, who was later arrested in Israel for distributing money to the military wing of Hamas. Israel called for Marzook's extradition, saying he was tied to 10 violent Hamas attacks between 1990 and 1994.

Marzook admitted to leading Hamas's political bureau, but he maintained that Hamas keeps political and military functions separate. He repeatedly denied any involvement with Hamas's military wing and compared himself to Gerry Adams, leader of Sinn Fein, the legal political wing of the Irish Republican Army. For nearly two years, U.S. authorities held Marzook in solitary confinement at the Metropolitan Correction Center in New York City without charging him with a crime. Marzook first appealed the Israeli extradition request, but he waived his right to an extradition hearing in January 1997, saying he had lost faith in the U.S. justice system. However, Israel dropped the request for Marzook's extradition in April 1997, saying that trying Marzook in Israel would provoke further violence. The following month the United States deported Marzook to Amman, Jordan. He was rearrested in Jordan but soon left the country and moved to Damascus, Syria, where he continued to serve as a deputy of the Hamas political bureau in that country.

In 2004 Marzook was indicted by the United States on racketeering charges, accused of "playing a substantial role in financing and supporting international terrorism." Two other men, Abdelhaleem Hasan Abdelraziq Ashqar, of Alexandria, Virginia, and Muhammad Hamid Khalil Salah of Chicago were arrested and indicted on the same charges. Ashqar and Salah pled not guilty, and in

February 2007 they were found innocent of the racketeering charges but convicted on lesser charges involving obstruction of justice and criminal contempt. As of 2010, Marzook was still a deputy with Hamas, periodically offering the group's perspective on current events to Western newspapers.

Erica Pearson

See also Hamas

Further Readings

Curtiss, Richard H. "An American Dreyfus Affair: The Case of Mousa Abu Marzook." *Washington Report on Middle East Affairs* 25, no. 8 (1997): 19.

Hall, Charles W., and Robert O'Harrow Jr. "Virginia Man Suspected of Terrorism Known for Anonymity." *The Washington Post,* August 8, 1995.

Lancaster, John. "Freedom Suits Hamas Leader; Fresh from U.S. Jail, Abu Marzook Minds His Step in Jordan." *The Washington Post,* May 9, 1997.

Lancaster, John, and Charles W. Hall. "U.S. Is Asked to Turn Over Terror Suspect; Israel Wants Marzook for Activities in Hamas." *The Washington Post,* July 29, 1995.

Marzook, Mousa Abu. "Hamas' Stand." *Los Angeles Times,* July 10, 2007.

Marzook, Mousa Abu. "What Hamas Is Seeking." *The Washington Post,* January 31, 2006. http://www .washingtonpost.com/wp-dyn/content/article/2006/ 01/30/AR2006013001209.html.

MASRI, ABU AYYUB AL (1957–2010)

Abu Ayyub al Masri (aka Abu Hamza al Muhajir) was relatively unknown before he became the leader of al Qaeda in Iraq (AQI) in 2006. Much of his biography is sketchy and often contradictory. Arabic sources describe him as an "intellectual" with little expertise in military warfare, yet he took charge of the Defense Ministry of the Islamic State of Iraq, established by al Qaeda in 2006. Unquestionably, Masri led a secretive life, and until 2005 he did not appear on any terrorist watch lists. Observers agree that his mysterious

background was a factor in his selection by al Qaeda leader Osama bin Laden as the new AQI leader in 2006, following the killing of Abu Musab al Zarqawi.

It appears that al Masri's penchant for religious extremism developed early in his formative years. After beginning his university studies in Egypt in pharmacy, he transferred to commerce, only to give that up and travel to Saudi Arabia, where he earned a bachelor's degree in Shariah Islamic Studies from the prestigious Medina University in 1985. Married, and with one child, he moved his family to Jordan, where he deepened his understanding of Islam by studying 'ilm al kalam (religious sciences) and Salafism under noted religious scholars, including theologian and Salafi scholar Muhammad Nasiruddin al Albani. At this juncture, al Masri began to develop his own religious Salafi intellect. He published several essays on religious sciences and *jahiliyah* (ignorance of divine guidance) and was the imam (leader of Islamic religious worship) of a major mosque in Jordan, a distinction that would enable him to further expand his understanding of the religion as a trusted Islamic scholar. But for unspecified reasons, Masri left Jordan to return to Egypt for a short time.

Subsequently, Masri traveled to Pakistan to earn a master's degree in religious sciences from a university in Peshawar. There, he continued preaching in mosques and gathered a following impressed by his intellect. Upon graduation, he resumed his travels, shuttling among the United Arab Emirates, Egypt, and Pakistan, eventually settling in Iraq in 2001. In Iraq, Masri worked closely with al Zarqawi as an al Qaeda recruiter. This marked his official affiliation with the group, but it is unclear whether he held any higher positions, particularly in his area of expertise: indoctrination.

At the time of Masri's appointment to head AQI, the group was in deep crisis, and its image had been sullied on all fronts, especially among the Sunni population, tribal leaders, and allies. AQI's indiscriminate attacks against civilians and Shia religious sites were intended to spread violence throughout the country and drag the Shia population into an all-out war against its Sunni counterpart. The attacks proved counterproductive, however, and Sunni tribal leaders turned against

AQI, forging stronger ties with the United States, and culminating in the establishment of the Sunni Awakening movement in Anbar Province in preparation for an eventual American withdrawal. Moreover, the Shia religious establishment condemned AQI's terrorist activities and reigned in extremist Shia groups to preempt any escalation of violence that would be detrimental to the establishment's political interest. Meanwhile, the United States had successfully imprisoned or killed several key AQI leaders, most notably Zarqawi.

It was in this context that Masri became the favored successor to Zarqawi. Both bin Laden and Ayman al Zawahiri, al Qaeda's second-highest leader, sought to avoid any repeat of the 1988 Afghan scenario, when the Soviet Union withdrew from the country and al Qaeda found itself with no role in the country. Masri's intellect, obscure background, and connections to foreign recruits positioned him as the best fit to bring order to AQI and prepare it for a prominent role in post-independence Iraq. But judging by his performance over four years—notably his inability to lead AQI and unite all Sunni extremists, his dismal record in the battlefield, and his frustrated attempts to change AQI's image in the country—Masri failed on all accounts. He proved to be, in the words of many specialists, an "amateur" and a powerless leader, and he was killed by U.S. forces in 2010.

Hamoud Salhi

See also al Qaeda; al Qaeda in Iraq; bin Laden, Osama; Iraq War; Zarqawi, Abu Musab al; Zawahiri, Ayman al

Further Readings

"al-Qaida Interview with Abu Hamza al Muhajar in Iraq, October 24, 2008." NEFA Foundation. http://www.nefafoundation.org/miscellaneous/nefaabuhamza1008.pdf.

Fishman, Brian. "After Zarqawi: The Dilemmas and Future of al Qaeda in Iraq." *Washington Quarterly* 29 (Autumn 2006): 19–32.

Fishman, Brian. *Dysfunction and Decline: Lessons Learned from Inside al Qaeda in Iraq.* West Point, NY: Harmony Project, The Combating Terrorism Center, 2009.

Kaplan, Eben. *Backgrounder: Abu Hamza al Muhajir, Zarqawi's Mysterious Successor (aka Abu Ayub alMasri).* Washington, DC: Council on Foreign Relations, June 13, 2006. http://www.cfr.org/publication/10894/abu_hamza_almuhajir_zarqawis_mysterious_successor_aka_abu_ayub_almasri.html.

Shafey, Mohammed al. "al Qaeda's Leader in Iraq: Abu Hamza al Muhajar; 'More Violent Than Zarqawi.'" *Asharq al Awsat*, June 13, 2006. http://www.aawsat.com/english/news.asp?section=1&id=5293.

MATHEWS, ROBERT JAY (1953–1984)

In 1984, Robert Jay Mathews was killed in a confrontation with federal agents on a remote island in Washington State's Puget Sound. Few outside the white supremacist and Christian Identity movements had heard of Mathews before his death, though he was the founder of The Order, one of the most infamous white supremacist groups of the 1980s.

Mathews embraced right-wing ideologies early in life. At the age of 11, he joined the local John Birch Society in Phoenix, Arizona. By high school, he was attending tax resistance seminars held by the Arizona "Patriot" Marvin Cooley, who occasionally appointed Mathews sergeant-at-arms for meetings. At 19, Mathews formed the Sons of Liberty, a paramilitary group comprised mostly of Mormons and survivalists who trained in the nearby desert. By 1973, however, the Sons of Liberty was foundering. Mathews left Arizona and the tax rebellion movement and moved to the rural community of Metaline Falls, Washington.

In Metaline Falls, Mathews joined the neo-Nazi National Alliance and began a reading program in "racial progress" that included Oswald Spengler's *Decline of the West* and William Simpson's *Which Way Western Man?* His education later included *The Road Back,* a terrorist instruction manual, *Essays of a Klansman* by Louis Beam, and William Pierce's novel *The Turner Diaries,* which portrays the violent overthrow of the U.S. government and a race war that establishes an "Aryan" world.

By the early 1980s, Mathews had also connected with the nearby Aryan Nations compound in Hayden Lake, Idaho. He shared the Aryan

Nations' goal of establishing a separate white nation in the Pacific Northwest. (Richard Girnt Butler, the head of Aryan Nations, said Mathews was "of the highest idealism and moral character.") At the Aryan Nations compound, Mathews began to form the inner circle of what would become known, variously, as Bruder Schweigen, the Silent Brotherhood, or The Order.

Mathews's vision of The Order was inspired, in part, by the violent crimes of the far left, such as the 1981 failed Brinks armored truck robbery in New York, attempted by members of the Black Liberation Army and May 19 Communist Organization. The Order was also modeled closely on the fictional organization in *The Turner Diaries*.

From 1983 to 1984, The Order counterfeited money and stole nearly $4 million to fund the coming race war. Members of the group bombed a synagogue in Boise, Idaho, and a pornography shop in Spokane, Washington. In June 1984, The Order murdered Alan Berg, a Jewish radio talk show host in Denver, Colorado. By November 1984, however, authorities had caught up with Mathews in Portland, Oregon, with the help of an FBI informant, Thomas Allen Martinez. Mathews was wounded in a gunfight before escaping.

In early December, police located Mathews on a Whidbey Island, in Puget Sound. Two hundred officers surrounded the house where Mathews was hiding, and he held them at bay for 36 hours with a machine gun. On December 7, 1984, Mathews died in a blaze set by a flare dropped from a helicopter by the FBI. For many on the racist right, he died a martyr.

Laura Lambert

See also Order, The; Patriot Movement; *Turner Diaries, The*

Further Readings

Flynn, Kevin, and Gary Gerhardt. *The Silent Brotherhood: Inside America's Racist Underground.* New York: The Free Press, 1989.
"The Murder of Alan Berg: 25 Years Later." *Denver Post*, June 18, 2009, p. A1.
Zeskind, Leonard. *Blood and Politics: The History of the White Nationalist Movement from the Margins to the Mainstream.* New York: Farrar, Straus and Giroux, 2009.

MAY 19 COMMUNIST ORGANIZATION

The May 19 Communist Organization, a clandestine Marxist-feminist revolutionary group with roots in the Weather Underground, participated in an 1981 armored car robbery that renewed interest in the remnants of the New Left terrorism.

By the mid-1970s, the infamous group of armed white revolutionaries known as Weatherman had split into bickering factions. One faction advocated a return to more traditional forms of political protest, while the other faction, which eventually took the name Weather Underground Organization (WUO), continued to advocate terrorist activity in the name of black liberation and anti-imperialism. This struggle included bombings and potential assassinations of political figures.

On November 20, 1977, after infiltrating the WUO, the FBI sent several members to jail for plotting to bomb the offices of California state senator John Briggs. Those who remained, including Kathy Boudin, a founder of Weatherman, came together to form the May 19 Communist Organization, named in honor of the birthday of both Malcolm X and Ho Chi Minh. In New York, the May 19 Organization, comprising mostly white, middle-class women, joined forces with the Black Liberation Army (BLA), the violent offshoot of the New York Black Panther Party. Their mutual goals were the establishment of a "New Afrika" in the southern United States and the socialist overthrow of the U.S. government. The BLA planned to partly fund its mission by an "expropriation of funds," or robbing rich American institutions, such as banks, and giving the money to Third World peoples. The women of the May 19 Organization functioned as the effort's public face, renting and driving the getaway cars, securing safe houses, and purchasing weapons, while the BLA took care of the violence.

On October 20, 1981, the two groups robbed a Brinks armored car in Nanuet, New York. Several BLA members, led by Mutulu Shakur (Jeral Wayne Williams), seized $1.6 million and killed one guard before escaping in a rented truck driven by Boudin and David Gilbert, another ex-Weatherman. When police stopped the truck, the armed BLA members in the back opened fire, killing two police officers. Boudin, Gilbert, Judy Clark, and Samuel Brown were immediately apprehended.

The investigation into the Brinks robbery revealed the link between the May 19 Organization and the BLA, as well alliances with other radical groups, including the Republic of New Africa and, subsequently, FALN, the radical Puerto Rican independence group. May 19 members were suspected and later charged with assisting the prison escapes of two prominent revolutionaries: Assata Shakur (Joanne Chesimard), the BLA radical serving a life sentence for killing a New Jersey state trooper in 1973, and Willie Morales, a leader of FALN. These unique collaborations triggered new concerns about "urban terrorism," which led the administration of President Ronald Reagan to reopen investigations, dormant since the mid-1970s, of the radical Left.

In February 1983, May 19 members Silvia Baraldini and Michelle Miller were jailed for refusing to testify against FALN. That September, three more May 19 members, Linda Evans, Marilyn Buck, and Laura Jane Whitehorn, pleaded guilty to charges relating the 1983 bombing of the U.S. Capitol and other Washington, D.C., targets. In 1985, Elizabeth Duke, head of the May 19 Organization in Austin, Texas, was indicted on federal charges for her suspected involvement in several bombings, including a 1982 New Year's Eve bombing in New York City that injured two police officers. These May 19 members are still considered political prisoners by those who share their beliefs.

Laura Lambert

See also Black Panther Party; Boudin, Katherine; Chesimard, Joanne; Weatherman

Further Readings

Braudy, Susan. *Family Circle: The Boudins and the Aristocracy of the Left.* New York: Alfred A. Knopf, 2003.

Castellucci, John. *The Big Dance: The Untold Story of Kathy Boudin and the Terrorist Family That Committed the Brink's Robbery Murder.* New York: Dodd, Mead, 1986.

Frankfort, Ellen. *Kathy Boudin and the Dance of Death.* New York: Stein and Day, 1983.

Jacobs, Ron. *The Way the Wind Blew: A History of the Weather Underground.* New York: Verson, 1997.

MAYES, MELVIN

See El Rukns

McVeigh, Timothy James (1968–2001)

Timothy James McVeigh was condemned to death for bombing the Alfred P. Murrah Federal Building in Oklahoma City, on April 19, 1995. One hundred and sixty-eight people, including 19 children, were killed, and more than 500 were injured. At the time, the bombing was the worst act of terrorism on U.S. soil.

Early Life

McVeigh grew up in the small, predominantly white, blue collar, and overwhelmingly Christian town of Lockport, outside Buffalo, New York. His parents separated when he was 11, and McVeigh lived with his father while his two sisters lived with his mother. At the age of 13, his grandfather gave him his first gun. When McVeigh graduated from high school, with honors, he was already a considerable gun enthusiast and budding survivalist.

After brief attendance at a business school, McVeigh joined the army in May 1988. He received basic training at Fort Benning, Georgia, where he befriended Terry Lynn Nichols and Michael Fortier, then joined the 1st Infantry Division at Fort Riley, Kansas. When the Gulf War broke out in 1990, McVeigh was deployed to the Gulf, where he was assigned to a Bradley Fighting Vehicle. He distinguished himself as the best shot in his platoon and was awarded a Bronze Star on his return. He was invited to join the Green Berets, but his brief three-day stint with that elite unit was followed by his resignation from the army after 43 months of service.

In 1993, McVeigh began to travel state-to-state selling antigovernment literature and survival items on the gun show circuit. He also traveled to Waco to protest the government siege of the Branch Davidian complex, believing that the members of the Bureau of Alcohol, Tobacco and Firearms (ATF) were violating the Davidians' Second Amendment rights. McVeigh watched the final fiery standoff, on April 19, 1993, on television. This moment solidified McVeigh's hatred of the federal government and initiated his quest to stop the ATF.

Planning the Attack

Over the following months, as new gun laws further enraged McVeigh, he plotted to blow up the Alfred P. Murrah Federal Building in Oklahoma City, which he mistakenly believed housed the ATF. His plan was taken almost directly from the plot of *The Turner Diaries,* a 1978 novel that described not only a full-scale race war, but also the plight of Earl Turner, who truck-bombed the FBI headquarters in Washington, D.C., in protest of gun control laws. McVeigh had been pushing the book on family and friends since he first read it, just after high school.

Evidence and testimony later showed that McVeigh and his former army buddy, Terry Nichols, bought and stole bomb-making materials, including ammonium nitrate fertilizer and racing car fuel, and stored them in lockers rented under various aliases. McVeigh and Nichols also robbed a gun collector, Roger Moore, of guns, gold, silver, and jewels to fund their conspiracy. In December 1994, McVeigh drove Michael Fortier, another former army friend, past the Murrah Building, explaining his plans as well as his getaway route.

In early 1995, McVeigh and Nichols traveled to Kingman, Arizona, where Fortier lived with his wife, Lori. She later testified that McVeigh showed her how he planned to position the explosives, demonstrating with cans of soup. She also helped make the fake Robert Kling driver's license that McVeigh used. Within months, McVeigh would act on his plan: drive a rented truck filled with over 4,000 pounds of explosives to the Murrah Building on a workday morning, park it, and calmly walk away.

The Investigation

McVeigh was arrested 80 minutes after the truck-bomb exploded at the Alfred P. Murrah Federal Building. Oklahoma state trooper Charlie Hanger stopped a yellow 1977 Mercury Grand Marquis driving north on Interstate I-35. At first, it seemed to be a routine traffic stop—the Marquis had no license plates. The driver, McVeigh, emerged from the car, and when Hanger asked to see his license, he noticed a gun bulging from inside the driver's windbreaker. Hangar confiscated the gun, a 9mm Glock, and handcuffed McVeigh before taking him to the Noble County jail in Perry, Oklahoma. McVeigh was booked on four misdemeanor charges: unlawfully carrying a weapon; transporting a loaded firearm in a motor vehicle; failing to display a current license plate; and failing to maintain proof of insurance. The address on McVeigh's driver's license was the Decker, Michigan, family farm of Terry Lynn Nichols.

As McVeigh waited in jail for his bail hearing, federal investigators pieced together the evidence that would eventually lead to McVeigh's arrest on federal charges. Hours before McVeigh might have been released from jail on $500 bail, he was arrested by the FBI.

Investigators at the scene linked mangled pieces of the rented Ryder truck used for the bomb to a rental company in Junction City, Oklahoma. From employee descriptions emerged the sketches of John Doe 1, who used the alias "Robert Kling" to rent the truck, and John Doe 2. The manager of a nearby motel confirmed that a man resembling John Doe 1, but using the name Timothy McVeigh, had rented a room and parked both a Ryder truck and a yellow Grand Marquis.

Indictment, Trial, and Sentence

When the three indictments came down in August 1995, Fortier, who could have been indicted on conspiracy charges, pled guilty to lesser charges, including charges that he knew and concealed McVeigh's plan, as well as possession and transportation of illegal firearms, in exchange for his testimony against McVeigh and Nichols. (He was released from prison in January 2006.) Both McVeigh and Nichols faced eight counts of first degree murder for the deaths of federal officials killed in the blast, as well as one count each for conspiracy to use a weapon of mass destruction, the use of a weapon of mass destruction, and destruction by explosive.

Opening statements began on April 24, 1997, after several pretrial decisions by the court, including attempts to move the case to Denver, try McVeigh and Nichols separately, and allow for the death penalty. Over the next few weeks, the prosecution called more than 130 witnesses, including McVeigh's sister, Jennifer, and the Fortiers, who provided some of the most damning evidence. (Jennifer McVeigh and Lori Fortier were both given immunity in exchange for their testimony.) Although no one could place McVeigh at the Murrah Building, substantial evidence, including explosive residue found on his clothes, confirmed his involvement.

The defense, in turn, tried to discredit the prosecution's main witnesses, focusing on Michael Fortier, who had previously lied to federal authorities and the press about his knowledge of the bombing. The defense did reveal several weaknesses in the prosecution's case, particularly that no fingerprints were found on the Ryder truck rental agreement or on the truck's key (found in an alley in Oklahoma City), and that no explosive residue was found in the lockers allegedly used for storage. Other gaps included an unidentified severed leg discovered in the rubble and the persistent phantom of a John Doe II; these led to extensive conspiracy theories, including improbable suggestions that the government orchestrated the bombing to discredit the militia movements growing throughout the country.

On June 2, 1997, after four days of deliberation, the jury found McVeigh guilty on all 11 counts. Eleven days later, the same jury condemned McVeigh to death by lethal injection. U.S. District Judge Richard P. Matsch, who would later preside over the trial of Terry Lynn Nichols, formally sentenced McVeigh on August 14, 1997. McVeigh, who did not testify on his own behalf, expressed no remorse at any time. At his sentencing, he quoted the late Supreme Court justice Louis Brandeis: "Our government is the potent, the omnipresent teacher. For good or for ill, it teaches the whole people by its example."

After losing his first appeal, and forgoing all subsequent appeals, McVeigh was transferred to the federal Bureau of Prisons men's execution facility at the U.S. penitentiary at Terre Haute, Indiana. While incarcerated at the state-of-the-art federal prison known as Supermax, in Colorado,

McVeigh had shared facilities with Ramzi Yousef, who had been convicted for the 1993 World Trade Center bombing; Ted Kaczynski, the Unabomber; and Luis Felipe, founder of the notorious Latin Kings New York street gang. Their shared unit was nicknamed "Bombers Row."

On June 5, 2001, the three-judge panel of the 10th U.S. Circuit Court denied McVeigh's final request for a stay of his scheduled May 16 execution. After a short delay caused by the FBI's failure to turn over 4,000 pages of documents to McVeigh's defense team during the trial, McVeigh was put to death, via lethal injection, just after 8 AM on June 11, 2001. He spoke no final words, but, in a handwritten statement, quoted from the poem *Invictus:* "I am the master of my fate. I am the captain of my soul."

Laura Lambert

See also Bombings and Bomb Scares; Branch Davidian Compound Siege; Nichols, Terry Lynn; Oklahoma City Bombing; *Turner Diaries, The*; Unabomber; Yousef, Ramzi Ahmed

Further Readings

Axtman, Kris. "Oklahoma City Moves Past Its Infamous Bombing: The Release of Michael Fortier Friday Caused Few Ripples in the Revitalized City, Despite His Role in the 1995 Terror Attack." *Christian Science Monitor,* January 23, 2006, p. 2.

Hersley, Jon, et al. *Simple Truths: The Real Story of the Oklahoma City Bombing Investigation.* Oklahoma City: Oklahoma Heritage Association, 2004.

Kellner, Douglas. *Guys and Guns Amok: Domestic Terrorism and School Shootings from the Oklahoma City Bombing to the Virginia Tech Massacre.* Boulder, CO: Paradigm Publishers, 2008.

Michel, Lou, and Dan Herbeck. *American Terrorist: Timothy McVeigh and the Oklahoma City Bombing.* New York: ReganBooks, 2001.

Serrano, Richard A. *One of Ours: Timothy McVeigh and the Oklahoma City Bombing.* New York: Norton, 1998.

MEDIA AND TERRORISM

Terrorism differs from other forms of violence or crime in that it is aimed at people other than its victims. Most violence is committed for its own sake. An ordinary murderer, for example, wants the victim dead, and usually does not want anyone to know who is responsible. A terrorist attack, by contrast, uses violence to influence others. The victim may be chosen at random, and the terrorists committing the act of violence generally want people to know that they are responsible. A repressive government might assassinate a relative of a political activist in order to intimidate him and other dissidents. A regional separatist group might bomb a police station in order to show authorities that their hold on that region is tenuous. A small fringe group might kidnap a celebrity in order to attract attention to their cause.

In each of these cases, the victim—the relative, the police officers, the celebrity—is not the real target of the terrorist attack. Instead, the target is a group or groups—enemies, potential supporters, the general public—who essentially form an audience. One highly effective way to reach an audience is through the modern media network of television, radio, newspapers, magazines, the Internet, and books. The rise of satellite television, all-news channels, and Internet video has meant that modern media can now reach a worldwide audience almost instantly.

Terrorists often create their own media outlets. Pamphlets, books, videotapes, and audiotapes have all been circulated by terrorist organizations seeking support. Groups that have relatively stable control over a particular territory often have their own radio stations or newspapers. Further, the Internet has given terrorists a new forum in which to advertise their views and make contacts with potential recruits. Such terrorist-generated media poses fairly straightforward issues for authorities. With the appropriate legal backing, law enforcement officers can shut down websites and radio stations, and they can seize flyers or tapes. The main challenge is finding out who is producing and distributing the material or broadcasts.

A more complex set of issues is created by the mainstream media's coverage of terrorist activities. In any country with a reasonably free press, terrorist attacks are almost certain to attain widespread coverage—even if the group is tiny and its attacks cause relatively little damage. Not only is the attack itself covered as an event, but media outlets often run pieces on the group responsible that

detail the group's agenda. The response of authorities to terrorist attacks can be subject to highly critical coverage. At the same time, the publicity resulting from terrorism can be a boon to a cause. Terrorist acts committed by Palestinians in the early 1970s, for example, riveted world attention on an issue—the displacement of Arabs by the founding of the state of Israel—that had for decades had largely been ignored by the international community.

Such terrorism was nothing new, but advances in media technology meant that by the early 1970s it was occurring on a global stage. For example, the 1972 Olympic Games held in Munich, Germany, were the first to be televised live around the world, thanks to the now commonplace use of satellites to broadcast television signals. During the games, a radical splinter group of the Palestine Liberation Organization called Black September raided the compound housing Israeli athletes. The group killed two athletes and took nine hostage; those nine were killed during a botched getaway. The horrific events were broadcast worldwide as they happened, making a formerly obscure group instantly famous, or infamous. The group was even featured fictitiously plotting a blimp attack on the Super Bowl in the 1976 movie thriller *Black Sunday*.

But such media attention doesn't always benefit the group or its cause. Simply because the public now knows about a group does not mean that its cause will be embraced. Support for the Palestinian cause is tepid in the United States, for example, despite the relatively heavy coverage Middle Eastern terrorism receives in the U.S. media. In addition, disseminating information about terrorists through the media can lead to their apprehension. In 1995, for example, *The New York Times* and *The Washington Post* printed the manifesto of the Unabomber, an ecoterrorist who for years had mailed bombs to people, killing three. The publication of the manifesto generated tremendous controversy, but among its readers was David Kaczynski, who realized that his brother, Theodore, probably wrote it. Kaczynski contacted the Federal Bureau of Investigation, and the Unabomber, who had eluded authorities for 18 years, was arrested in Montana in 1996.

Indeed, not all terrorists seek media attention in the first place. State terrorism, for example, is usually conducted in secret. In countries where the government relies on terrorism to maintain power, the media is usually tightly controlled and prevented from publishing or broadcasting accounts of terrorist acts committed by government agents. Instead, the perpetrators rely on word of mouth to spread the news among dissidents. Consider, for example, the more than 13,000 people killed or "disappeared" during Argentina's "Dirty War" in the 1970s.

Extremely radical groups dedicated to the elimination of a particular enemy tend to be more or less indifferent to how the public perceives them, especially if they consider the average consumer of the mainstream media as the enemy. The 1990s saw the rise of such groups, which conduct attacks designed to maximize casualties and do not take credit for them. But many terrorist groups deliberately seek media coverage and attempt to manipulate that coverage so they will appear in a positive light. Attacks by these groups may be designed to attract the maximum of publicity but result in relatively few casualties, since large numbers of casualties will turn public opinion against the group. Some groups have demonstrated considerable savvy in seeking media attention. In the 1970s, the left-wing Red Brigades of Italy habitually released communiqués to newspapers on Wednesdays and Saturdays, because they knew the Thursday and Sunday editions of Italian newspapers have a wider circulation. The communiqués were released to several newspapers to create a competitive pressure to publish, and they were released late in the day in order to give reporters less time to solicit a critical response from people opposed to the Red Brigades.

The Red Brigades also engaged in another common tactic for manipulating the media: attacking critical reporters and editors. Especially in Latin America and Africa, journalists are likely targets for assassination, kidnappings, and beating by terrorists, and terrorist groups have bombed newspapers and occupied television and radio stations. In some cases, as with the execution of *The Wall Street Journal* reporter Daniel Pearl by radical Muslims in Pakistan in early 2002, reporters are slain because their nationality or religious affiliation essentially places them in the enemy camp. Opposition journalists are often a target for state terrorism.

As such tactics suggest, most terrorists read newspapers, watch television, and listen to the radio, just as ordinary people do. That means terrorists can take advantage of information that is published or broadcast, including information on how authorities plan to combat terrorism. Live coverage of terrorist attacks can feed valuable information to the terrorists conducting the attacks. In at least one hijacking, a hostage was killed because radio broadcasts revealed he was surreptitiously aiding authorities, and in other cases media reports of police activities during hostage situations have put lives at risk.

Media coverage may even influence what types of terrorist attacks take place. Terrorism tends to go through trends or phases: first kidnapping will be common, then airplane hijackings, and then suicide bombs. Media coverage of, say, a hijacking may plant the idea in the minds of other terrorists that they too should conduct a hijacking rather than a bank robbery. The real anthrax attacks of 2001 were doubtless a spur to a variety of hoax attacks against abortion clinics and other targets. Of course, media coverage may only be one of many factors because terrorist groups often share information and receive similar training from a common source.

The willingness of terrorists to take advantage of the media has led some observers to the conclusion that the media contributes to the problem of terrorism. The harshest critics charge that media outlets deliberately cover terrorist attacks in a way that will lead to more attacks. These critics allege that the media and the terrorists benefit each other, since ratings and sales go up when terrorism occurs. Consequently, media reports portray the terrorists positively, as dashing freedom fighters, for example, thus encouraging future attacks.

Studies of media coverage of terror attacks lend little authority to this criticism, however. Media reports of terrorist attacks tend to use either neutral or condemning language, rarely expressing support. In addition, media reports are more likely to condemn attacks if they occur in the same country where the outlet is based, suggesting that any popular support for terrorist groups in a country where attacks take place is for reasons other than positive portrayals of terrorism in the local media.

Other critics say that media outlets inadvertently encourage attacks because they help publicize the cause of a terrorist group. Since terrorists are trying to send a message, the thinking goes, media outlets merely assist them when they cover terrorism. In some cases, those messages may go beyond publicizing a group's goals. Following the September 11, 2001, attacks by al Qaeda on the United States, the group released several videotapes of its leader, Osama bin Laden, which raised concerns among U.S. officials that the tapes contained coded instructions intended for al Qaeda operatives.

But even if there are no secret messages, critics argue that the guarantee of widespread coverage encourages groups to resort to terrorism in order to put their cause in the public eye. Coverage of repeated attacks emphasizes the impotence of authorities in ending terrorism and the power of the terrorist group. Such thinking led British prime minister Margaret Thatcher to declare in 1985 that democracies "must find a way to starve the terrorists and hijackers of the oxygen of publicity on which they depend."

Forcing a halt to media coverage of terrorism is a controversial idea, however. Some argue that if the media chooses to ignore a terrorist group, the group may conduct bigger, more deadly attacks that cannot be ignored. And while spreading the news about an attack likely spreads a sense of terror among the general public, if the public believes that media outlets are holding back and that the news is even worse, genuine panic can emerge. The media can also be used by authorities to publicize potential threats as well as arrests made and plots foiled, thus communicating to the public and the terrorists that the government is in control of the situation.

Preventing media coverage of terrorism while retaining the press freedoms seen as crucial to maintaining a democratic society is a tricky business. In the 1970s and 1980s, Great Britain combated terrorism by Irish nationalists by barring broadcasts featuring people who supported Irish terror groups. These measures were controversial and largely ineffective in preventing terrorist attacks. Indeed, some have argued that by curtailing press freedom, governments can do as much damage to democracy as terrorists can.

Mary Sisson

See also al Qaeda; bin Laden, Osama; Counterterrorism; Hostage Taking; Irish Republican Army; Munich Olympics Massacre; Palestine Liberation Organization; Pearl, Daniel; Red Brigades; September 11 Attacks; State Terrorism; Unabomber

Further Readings

Alali, A. Odasuo, and Kenoye Kelvin Eke, eds. *Media Coverage of Terrorism: Methods of Diffusion.* Newbury Park, CA: Sage, 1991.

Alexander, Yonah, and Richard Latter, eds. *Terrorism and the Media: Dilemmas for Government, Journalists and the Public.* Washington, DC: Brassey's, 1990.

Giroux, Henry A. *Beyond the Spectacle of Terrorism: Global Uncertainty and the Challenge of the New Media.* Boulder, CO: Paradigm, 2006.

Kavoori, Anandam P., and Todd Fraley, eds. *Media, Terrorism, and Theory: A Reader.* Lanham, MD: Rowman & Littlefield, 2006.

Nacos, Brigitte L. *Mass-mediated Terrorism: The Central Role of the Media in Terrorism and Counterterrorism.* 2nd ed. Lanham, MD: Rowman & Littlefield, 2007.

Palmer, Nancy, ed. *Terrorism, War, and the Press.* Cambridge, MA: The Joan Shorenstein Center on the Press, Politics and Public Policy, 2003.

Picard, Robert G. *Media Portrayal of Terrorism: Functions and Meaning of News Coverage.* Ames: Iowa State University Press, 1993.

Schmid, Alex P., and Janny de Graaf. *Violence as Communication: Insurgent Terrorism and the Western News Media.* London: Sage, 1982.

MEINHOF, ULRIKE (1934–1976)

The left-wing journalist Ulrike Meinhof was known for her affiliation with the West German Red Army Faction (RAF), often referred to in the media as the Baader-Meinhof Gang, after its two most prominent members.

Meinhof's parents were killed when she was young, and she was raised in West Germany by her foster mother, Renate Riemack, who was a socialist and profoundly influenced Meinhof's political views. As a college student, Meinhof married Klaus Rainer Rohl and became an editor and journalist for his left-wing student newspaper. They had twin girls together but then separated in the late 1960s.

At that time, Meinhof was becoming more involved in the radical left student movement. She joined the Red Army Faction after she interviewed their leader, Andreas Baader, while he was in prison for arson. The aims of the RAF were to revolutionize the working people, to convert the capitalist society, and to eliminate the U.S. presence in West Germany, which they believed to be the cause of many injustices. They committed several bank robberies, murders, kidnappings, and bombings to forward their cause.

Meinhof became infamous on May 14, 1970, when she helped free Baader from prison in Berlin. After this event, journalists began calling RAF the Baader-Meinhof Gang. This name stuck, and has led to the frequent incorrect assumption that Meinhof was a co-leader of the group. In fact, the other leader was not Meinhof but Baader's girlfriend, Gudrun Ensslin.

Meinhof evaded the law for two years after she aided Baader's escape. In these years, she continued to rob banks and bomb buildings before being caught and sentenced to prison in 1972. While incarcerated, she grew increasingly depressed and on May 9, 1976, Ulrike Meinhof committed suicide.

Harvey Kushner

See also Baader, Andreas; Baader-Meinhof Gang

Further Readings

Aust, Stefan. *Baader-Meinhof: The Inside Story of the R.A.F.* London: The Bodley Head, 2008.

Bauer, Karin, ed. *Everybody Talks about the Weather . . . We Don't: The Writings of Ulrike Meinhof.* New York: Seven Stories Press, 2008.

Becker, Jillian. *Hitler's Children: The Story of the Baader-Meinhof Terrorist Gang.* 3rd ed. Collingdale, PA: Diane Publishing, 1998.

Colvin, Sarah. "'Wenn deine Identität Kampf ist': Violence, Gendered Language and Identity in the Writing of Ulrike Marie Meinhof." In *Violence, Culture and Identity: Essays on German and Austrian Literature, Politics and Society,* edited by Helen Chambers. Oxford: Peter Lang, 2006.

Landler, Mark. "German Radical's Daughter Seeks Brain Kept after Suicide." *The New York Times,* November 12, 2002, p. A8.

Schiller, Margit. *Remembering the Armed Struggle: Life in Baader Meinhof.* Darlington, NSW, Australia: Zidane Press, 2009.

Varon, Jeremy. *Bringing the War Home: The Weather Underground, the Red Army Faction, and Revolutionary Violence in the Sixties and Seventies.* Berkeley: University of California Press, 2004.

METESKY, GEORGE (1904–1994)

During the 1940s and 1950s, George Metesky, known at the time only as the "Mad Bomber," set more than 30 bombs in the New York area. The 16-year hunt for the Mad Bomber was solved using one of the first applications of criminal profiling.

Metesky's first bomb was found on November 16, 1940, on a window ledge of the Consolidated Edison building on West 64th Street. The small, crudely made pipe bomb never exploded. A note on the outside of the bomb read, "Con Edison crooks, this is for you!" Police believed that the note's placement suggested it was never intended to detonate.

After a cursory investigation of disgruntled employees and other possible suspects, the police dropped the case. Nearly a year later, in September 1941, another unexploded bomb was found on 19th Street, a few blocks from the Con Edison office at Irving Plaza. The bomb, which was similar in construction to the November 1940 bomb, was found in an old sock, with no note. The following December, shortly after the bombing of Pearl Harbor, a letter bearing the same block-style handwriting of the initial note arrived at police headquarters. The bomber claimed he would stop his activities for the duration of the war. He also wrote, "I will bring the Con Edison to justice. They will pay for their dastardly deeds," and signed the letter, "F.P."

Though threatening letters continued to plague Con Ed, police, and others, "F.P." did not set another bomb until March 29, 1950, when a third hoax bomb was discovered in Grand Central Station. The following month, a bomb exploded in a phone booth inside the New York Public Library, followed by another bomb at Grand Central Station. Over the next five years, nearly 30 more bombs were planted throughout New York—at locations including Penn Station, the Port Authority Bus Terminal, the Brooklyn Paramount Theater, Radio City Music Hall, as well as in phone booths throughout the city—nearly half of which exploded, ultimately causing more than a dozen injuries but no deaths.

Frustrated after 16 years of investigation, Inspector Howard Finney of the New York City Crime Lab turned to Dr. James A. Brussel, a private psychiatrist who had performed counterintelligence profiling work during World War II and the Korean War. Using police evidence, including handwriting analysis, Brussel developed an elaborate profile: he predicted that the Mad Bomber was (1) a foreign-born male of eastern European descent; (2) between 40 and 50 years of age; (3) an unmarried loner living with female relatives; (4) a clean-shaven, neatly dressed man with an athletic build; and (5) a textbook paranoid. Most famously, Brussel also predicted that the bomber would be wearing a double-breasted suit, and that it would be buttoned.

After local newspapers published summaries of the Mad Bomber's profile, police were inundated with false leads. The bomber continued his activities, even calling Dr. Brussel to threaten him. Meanwhile, Con Ed expanded its search of personnel files of disgruntled employees to the years before its major mergers in the 1930s, and found the file of George Metesky, of Waterbury, Connecticut, who blamed his bout with tuberculosis on his former employer, which later became part of Con Ed.

In January 1957, Metesky, who fit Brussel's profile in every detail, confessed to planting 32 bombs, admitting that "F.P." stood for "fair play." Four months later, he was committed to the Matteawan Asylum for the Criminally Insane. Upon his release in 1973, he moved home to Connecticut, where he remained until he died, in 1994.

Laura Lambert

See also Bombings and Bomb Scares; Forensic Science and Terrorism

Further Readings

Brussel, James A. *The Casebook of a Crime Psychiatrist.* New York: Bernard Geis Associates, distributed by Grove Press, 1968.

Ewing, Charles Patrick, and Joseph T. McCann. *Minds on Trial: Great Cases in Law and Psychology.* New York: Oxford University Press, 2006.

Nash, Jay Robert. *Bloodletters and Badmen.* New York: M. Evans, 1995.

Schauer, Frederick. *Profiles, Probabilities, and Stereotypes.* Cambridge, MA: Belknap Press of Harvard University Press, 2003.

Zonderman, Jon, *Beyond the Crime Lab: The New Science of Investigation.* Rev. ed. New York: Wiley, 1999.

MIDDLE CORE FACTION

See Chukaku-ha

MILLENNIUM BOMB PLOT

See Y2K Plot

MILLER, FRAZIER GLENN (1941–)

During the 1980s, Frazier Glenn Miller (aka F. Glenn Miller Jr.; Glenn Miller), a former U.S. army officer, was the leader of the Carolina Knights of the Ku Klux Klan (CKKKK) and, later, the White Patriot Party (WPP), a paramilitary offshoot of the CKKKK.

Miller was discharged from the army in 1979 for distributing racist literature. In November of that year, he allegedly helped instigate an attack on an anti-Klan rally and march in Greensboro, North Carolina, in which five demonstrators, all members of the Communist Workers Party, were gunned down by Klansmen and American Nazis. When all of the accused were acquitted on April 15, 1984, Miller, already a vocal public figure in North Carolina, called the Klansmen and Nazis "heroes" who acted in "self-defense," and claimed that the verdict was a victory for "all patriotic, anti-communist, freedom-loving Christian people."

In the mid-1980s, Klan activity throughout the country was declining. Under Miller's leadership, however, the CKKKK raised its profile, becoming one of the most active Klan groups. In 1983, Bobby Person, a black prison guard in rural Moore County, North Carolina, filed a civil rights suit against Miller and the CKKKK. Person was working to become the first black sergeant at the local prison in Moore County, and he was being harassed by the CKKKK.

The case came to trial with Morris S. Dees, an anti-Klan activist lawyer from the Southern Poverty Law Center in Alabama, representing Person. In addition to harassment, charges related to the CKKKK's paramilitary activities had been added. During the trial, Miller maintained that group members were only involved in "self-defense," that they were training men, women, and children how to safely shoot and maintain firearms, and that they rarely practiced outdoor maneuvers. On January 17, 1985, the case was settled out of court, with terms that called for no monetary settlements, but the end of all paramilitary activity by the CKKKK.

Miller subsequently disbanded the CKKKK and formed the White Patriot Party (WPP), a para-military group that embraced Christian Identity–type racist beliefs. The WPP's goal was to create a white "Southland" in the southern United States by 1992; such a settlement had been described by William Pierce in his race-war novel, *The Turner Diaries* (1978).

In 1986 Miller and other WPP members were arrested for conspiracy to murder Dees and for continuing to conduct paramilitary operations in North Carolina. Testimony in the case revealed that Miller accepted $200,000 in stolen funds from Robert Mathews, the founder of The Order, and that active-duty military personnel were involved in training members of the WPP. Miller was sentenced to six months in prison in July 1986 for disobeying the court order prohibiting him from operating the WPP.

While free on bond and awaiting appeal, Miller went underground. In April 1987, he mailed nearly 5,000 letters to other white supremacists, issuing a declaration of "total war" against the federal government, which Miller referred to as ZOG (Zionist Occupational Government), and urging others to take up arms against nonwhites, civil rights activists, and judges.

Miller was captured in May 1987 in Ozark, Missouri. Federal agents staged a predawn raid, firing tear-gas canisters into Miller's mobile home. At the same time, other WPP members—Robert Jackson and Lawrence Sheets (both wanted in North Carolina for failing to appear to testify in a conspiracy case), and Tony Wydra—were arrested. Wydra was later released without being charged.

Miller became an FBI informant, testifying against his fellow white supremacists at the Fort Smith, Arkansas, conspiracy trial. After the trial, he entered the federal witness-protection program. Although his cooperation with federal authorities has made him suspect in many white supremacist circles, in the 2000s Miller became more public as

a racist activist. He is a frequent contributor to Vanguard News Network, an anti-Semitic and racist website, and helped run VNN's print publication, *The Aryan Alternative*. Miller is also a frequent write-in candidate for Congress in Missouri.

Laura Lambert

See also Fort Smith, Arkansas, Trial; Ku Klux Klan; Mathews, Robert Jay; Order, The; *Turner Diaries, The*; White Patriot Party; White Supremacy Movement

Further Readings

Quarles, Chester L. *The Ku Klux Klan and Related American Racialist and Antisemitic Organizations: A History and Analysis.* Jefferson, NC: McFarland, 1999.
Stanton, Bill. *Klanwatch: Bringing the Ku Klux Klan to Justice.* New York: Grove Atlantic, 1991.
Zeskind, Leonard. *Blood and Politics: The History of the White Nationalist Movement from the Margins to the Mainstream.* New York: Farrar, Straus and Giroux, 2009.

Milliyetci Hareket Partisi

See Grey Wolves

Mivtzah Elohim

See Wrath of God

Mogadishu, Attack on U.S. Soldiers

See al Qaeda; bin Laden, Osama

Mohamed, Khalfan Khamis (1973–)

Khalfan Khamis Mohamed was the first person convicted of a direct role in the August 7, 1998, bombing of the United States embassy in Dar es Salaam,

Tanzania. On May 29, 2001, a federal jury in New York found him guilty of participating in the attack and of murdering the 11 people killed as a result of the explosion.

Mohamed was one of four defendants who went on trial in Manhattan federal court in January 2001 for the Tanzania blast and the coordinated, more lethal bombing of the U.S. embassy in Nairobi, Kenya, where 213 people were killed. He and his codefendants were all found to be part of a worldwide terrorist conspiracy led by the Saudi exile Osama bin Laden and carried out by his Islamic militant organization, al Qaeda.

Mohamed, who was 25 at the time of the embassy bombings, grew up in mud-walled house on the rural island of Zanzibar, Tanzania, one of seven children of a farmer who grew sweet potatoes, lemongrass, and coconuts. Fatherless at seven, Mohamed never finished high school, and at 17 he moved to live and work with one of his brothers, who owned a grocery store in Dar es Salaam. There, through a mutual friend, Mohamed met an al Qaeda member who recruited him for religious and weapons training in Afghanistan. Mohamed underwent 10 months of training in 1994, but he was not invited to officially join the group. Mohamed returned to Tanzania in 1995, was sent on a training mission for "Muslim brothers" in Somalia in 1997, and was tapped for his job the following spring.

Trial testimony and physical evidence showed that in the summer of 1998 Mohamed rented the house in the Ilala district of Dar es Salaam, a half-hour drive from the embassy, where the bomb components were assembled and loaded into a used 1987 Nissan Atlas refrigeration truck. Using a flour mill, Mohamed helped grind the TNT, and with others, he loaded 20 wooden crates of the explosive powder onto the truck, along with 15 cylinders of acetylene and oxygen to enhance the explosion. Using money given to him by a cell leader, Mohamed had also purchased the Suzuki Samurai pickup truck that the conspirators used to ferry bomb-making materials to the house.

A defense attorney once referred to Mohamed's role as a "gopher," stating that he didn't even know the target until five days beforehand. On the day of the attacks, Mohamed helped the Nissan bomb truck embark on its journey, riding in the passenger seat next to the Egyptian suicide driver.

Once the truck got to the main road, Mohamed exited to return to the bombmaking house and clean it up. He heard the news of the explosion on TV, and left Dar es Salaam the next day by bus.

Using a Tanzanian passport bearing a friend's name, Mohamed settled in Cape Town, South Africa, and obtained a temporary residency permit after he applied for political asylum. He worked in a hamburger restaurant and lived with its owners, impressing them as a hardworking and pious young man. His year on the run ended when FBI agents traced the passport application back to him. Agents were waiting for Mohamed on October 5, 1999, when went to renew his South African residential papers.

Mohamed essentially confessed to his role in the terror conspiracy during two days of interrogation. "He felt it was his obligation and duty to kill Americans," FBI agent Abigail Perkins testified at trial. Although Mohamed never met bin Laden or heard him speak, he considered him his jihad leader and shared his views. Perkins said that Mohamed "really didn't like the fact that soldiers were in Saudi Arabia, in the Holy Land" and he felt the United States, as a superpower, could make peace in Palestine.

Mohamed said that because soldiers were "such a hard target to get to," U.S. government buildings were targeted, and although no Americans were killed in the Tanzania blast, he considered it a success. "Bombings were the only way that America would listen and that it also kept the Americans busy investigating," Perkins recalled Mohamed saying. Had he not been caught, Mohamed told Perkins, "He would have continued in his efforts to kill Americans."

Pursuing the death penalty, prosecutors focused on the impact of the Tanzania embassy bombing on the victims' families and on Mohamed's potential future dangerousness, even behind bars. Prosecutors tried to link him to a pretrial jailhouse stabbing by his one-time cellmate that left a corrections officer critically wounded.

The jury deadlocked on the death sentence sought by prosecutors, imposing on Mohamed a life sentence in prison without the possibility of parole. On their verdict form, most jurors agreed with defense attorneys that Mohamed was not a leader of the terror conspiracy and was only a minor participant in the bomb plot. Jurors also believed that an execution would have made Mohamed a martyr and could have been used to justify future terrorist acts.

Phil Hirschkorn

See also al Qaeda; bin Laden, Osama; East Africa Embassy Bombings; Odeh, Mohammed Saddiq

Further Readings

Bergen, Peter. *Holy War, Inc.: Inside the Secret World of Osama bin Laden.* New York: Free Press, 2001.

Gunaratna, Rohan. *Inside al Qaeda: Global Network of Terror.* New York: Columbia University Press, 2002.

Reeve, Simon. *The New Jackals: Ramzi Yousef, Osama bin Laden and the Future of Terrorism.* Boston: Northeastern Press, 1999.

Stern, Jessica. *Terror in the Name of God: Why Religious Militants Kill.* New York: Ecco, 2008.

Weiser, Benjamin. "A Jury Torn and Fearful in 2001 Terror Trial." *The New York Times,* January 5, 2003, p. 1.

MOHAMMED, FAZUL ABDULLAH (1972 OR 1974–)

Fazul Abdullah Mohammed is believed to be one of the leading operatives of Osama bin Laden's al Qaeda network in East Africa. An explosives and computer expert, he was added to the FBI's list of most wanted terrorists for his involvement in the 1998 bombings of two U.S. embassies in East Africa.

Mohammed was born in the Cormoros Islands, a tiny former French colony off the coast of East Africa. As a teenager, he received a scholarship for a fundamentalist Islamic education in Pakistan and left the Cormoros. According to the 1998 U.S. indictment in the embassy bombings, he attended al Qaeda's paramilitary training camp in Afghanistan in 1991 and 1992. The international terror network al Qaeda serves as an umbrella group for other militant organizations, and establishes cells in areas where attacks are carried out. Group members manage the cells and recruit individuals to perform administrative and other tasks. According to the indictment, Mohammed worked for Wadih

el Hage, the leader of the Nairobi cell in Kenya. He and other al Qaeda members also allegedly provided military training to Somali tribes opposed to the United Nations intervention in Somalia's civil war in 1993.

The indictment also claims that in late 1996 or early 1997, Mohammed began sending coded messages to co-conspirators in the embassy bombings plot. He and Hage carried funds from bin Laden to Kenya. He later rented the Nairobi villa at 43 New Runda Estates, where the bomb was assembled and where final preparations for bombing the embassy were made. On August 7, 1998, Mohammed left the villa in a pick-up truck, driving just ahead of the bomber to lead the way to the U.S. embassy. In a synchronized attack 400 miles away, a bomb-laden car also approached the U.S. embassy in Dar es Salaam, Tanzania. The bombs exploded just minutes apart, killing a total of 224 people.

Shortly following the embassy bombings, the U.S. government declared that bin Laden and al Qaeda operatives were responsible. As retaliation, President Bill Clinton ordered air attacks on al Qaeda training grounds in Afghanistan and a pharmaceutical plant in the center of Khartoum, Sudan. Three suspects indicted in the embassy bombings case pled guilty and cooperated with the U.S. government as witnesses. This resulted in the conviction of Wadih el Hage and three other men linked to bin Laden for conspiracy in the bombing at their October 2001 trial in U.S. District Court in New York City. All of the defendants who pled not guilty were sentenced to life in prison without parole.

Mohammed, however, fled to the Cormoros Islands the week following the attacks. He then flew on to Dubai, and by 2001 he was back in Kenya. In July 2002, Mohammed was arrested by Kenyan police (who did not know his true identity) in connection with an armed robbery, but he escaped.

On November 28, 2002, two surface-to-air missiles were fired at an Israeli airliner filled with tourists as it took off from Mombassa, Kenya. The missiles narrowly missed, but that same day a suicide bomber attacked a resort near Mombassa that is popular with Israeli tourists: 15 people died, most of them Kenyans. Mohammed is believed to have been one of the masterminds of the Mombassa attacks. He is thought to be hiding in Somalia, a country with a nonexistent central government that shares a long, porous border with Kenya.

Mohammed was a target of a pair of U.S. air strikes in Somalia in January 2007, but he was not killed in the attacks. He returned to Kenya in August 2008, reportedly to seek medical treatment for a kidney ailment, sparking a sizeable but unsuccessful manhunt. He remains at large. The U.S. State Department is offering up to $5 million for information leading to Mohammed's arrest or conviction.

Erica Pearson

See also al Qaeda; bin Laden, Osama; East Africa Embassy Bombings; Hage, Wadih el

Further Readings

Bergen, Peter. *Holy War, Inc.: Inside the Secret World of Osama bin Laden.* New York: Free Press, 2001.

England, Andrew. "Kenya Terrorist Attacks in '98 and '02 May Be Linked." *Chicago Tribune,* March 23, 2003, p. 18.

Federal Bureau of Investigation. "Most Wanted Terrorists." http://www.fbi.gov/wanted/terrorists/fugitives.htm.

Gordon, Michael R., and Mark Mazzetti. "U.S. Used Base in Ethiopia to Hunt al Qaeda in Africa." *The New York Times,* February 23, 2007, p. A1.

Reeve, Simon. *The New Jackals: Ramzi Yousef, Osama bin Laden, and the Future of Terrorism.* Boston: Northeastern University Press, 1999.

U.S. District Court for the Southern District of New York. *United States v. Usama bin Laden, et al.* Indictment S(2) 98 Cr. 1023 (LBS), November 4, 1998. http://www.fas.org/irp/news/1998/11/98110602_nlt.html.

MOHAMMED, KHALID SHAIKH (1965–)

Born in Kuwait, Khalid Shaikh Mohammed (aka Ashraf Refaat Nabith Henin; Khalid Adbul Wadood; Salem Ali; Fahd bin Abdallah bin Khalid) was the mastermind behind the September 11, 2001, attacks on the World Trade Center and the Pentagon. Before 9/11, the CIA did not have strong intelligence connecting him to al Qaeda, but after the attack he was regarded as al Qaeda's terrorist operations chief. At the time of his capture in 2003, he was plotting further attacks against the United States and Great Britain. In 2006 he was moved to the U.S. military prison at Guantánamo Bay, Cuba.

Mohammed is a bomb expert who earned a degree in mechanical engineering from North Carolina A&T University in 1986 before going to Afghanistan to fight the Soviets. He is believed to have received most of his terrorist training in Afghanistan. He first came to international attention for his participation in Ramzi Yousef's foiled 1995 conspiracy called "Project Bojinka." This deadly and wildly ambitious plot aimed to blow up nearly a dozen American airplanes with virtually undetectable bombs made of inexpensive digital watches and liquid explosives hidden in contact lens solution bottles. Mohammed was put on the FBI's list of most wanted terrorists for his role in the plot. The conspirators were based in Manila, the Philippines, and they targeted airliners flying to the United States from Southeast Asia.

In 1996, the United States indicted Mohammed for his involvement in Project Bojinka, accusing him of helping finance the conspiracy. Prosecutors referred to Project Bojinka as a conspiracy for "48 hours of terror in the sky." Mohammed and other conspirators allegedly plotted to blow up 11 American commercial jets and, according to a *New York Times* report, crash a plane into CIA headquarters and kill the president of the United States with a deadly gas released into the air. Philippine officials found out about the plot on January 6, 1995, when a fire started in the Manila apartment where Yousef, who had fled to the Philippines in 1993, and Abdul Hakim Murad were building bombs. When Murad returned to the apartment, he was arrested. Yousef fled the country but was finally captured in Pakistan in February 1995 and extradited to the United States.

In addition to taking part in and financing Project Bojinka, Mohammed was also accused of participating in the December 1994 bombing of Philippine Airlines Flight 434 from the Philippines to Tokyo. The explosion killed a Japanese passenger and wounded 10 others, but the plane was able to make an emergency landing in Guam. Murad's confession indicates that Yousef boarded the plane in Manila carrying liquid nitroglycerin in a bottle normally used for contact lens solution. He mixed the bomb solution, containing only about 10 percent of the explosives planned for use in Project Bojinka, in the plane's restroom and taped it under his seat in the economy section. Yousef then left the plane at its first layover, in the southern city of Cebu. The bomb exploded during the second leg of the plane's journey to Tokyo. Project Bojinka called for similar actions carried out by five bombers spread across Asia, who would plant similar bombs on U.S. airplanes flying multi-stop routes.

Mohammed brought his plan to use aircraft as missiles in order to attack symbolic targets in the United States to Osama bin Laden in 1996. It is believed that bin Laden approved the plan at some point in late 1998 or early 1999. Mohammed, along with bin Laden and Muhammad Atef, began assembling the hijacker teams. In early December 1999, Mohammed held an instructional meeting with three al Qaeda operatives who would carry out the 9/11 attacks, during which he gave the trainees background about American culture and the English language.

After 9/11 and before his 2003 capture, Mohammed was involved in other plots against the United States. According to a 2006 press release from the director of national intelligence, a plot to crash planes into several West Coast targets was disrupted in mid-2002. As operational commander of al Qaeda, Mohammed was also behind the failed shoe-bombing plot meant to happen aboard an American Airlines flight from Paris to Miami on December 22, 2001.

In early 2002 Mohammed met with a naturalized American citizen, Iyman Faris, about two attacks al Qaeda was planning in New York and Washington, D.C. He instructed Faris to study the viability of an attack on the Brooklyn Bridge using gas cutters on the bridge's famous suspension cables, and to buy equipment to use in the derailment of a train in the Washington, D.C., area. Faris determined the Brooklyn Bridge plot was not feasible, and the plan fell apart fully upon Mohammed's capture.

Mohammed also claimed to have beheaded *The Wall Street Journal* reporter Daniel Pearl in 2002. Pearl had been kidnapped in Karachi, Pakistan by a militant group calling itself The National Movement for the Restoration of Pakistani Sovereignty. Mohammed confessed to the murder under CIA interrogation, saying, "I decapitated with my blessed right hand the head of the American Jew, Daniel Pearl, in the city of Karachi, Pakistan." An extensive report on Pearl's murder, released by the Center for Public Interest in January 2011, confirmed that Mohammed had, indeed, killed Pearl.

In early 2003 Mohammed was plotting an attack on London's Heathrow Airport, but the plot was disrupted by the United States and its allies. Soon after, on March 1, 2003, he was captured by U.S. and Pakistani officers in Rawalpindi, Pakistan. During his CIA interrogation at a "black site" prison, and before his transfer to Guantánamo Bay, Mohammed was subjected to waterboarding more than 180 times. Waterboarding, a technique that involves simulated drowning, was approved by the Bush administration for use against certain high-value prisoners. While torture of prisoners is prohibited by the Geneva Conventions, waterboarding is not specifically mentioned. Although condemned as torture by many, the Bush administration maintained that it was not torture and interrogated Mohammed accordingly. Comments made by Mohammed about a "courier" working for Osama bin Laden helped lead investigators to bin Laden's hiding place inside Pakistan; the al Qaeda founder was killed by U.S. forces in May 2011.

On February 11, 2008, Mohammed and four others were charged under the military commission system with the attacks of September 11, 2001. At a pretrial hearing, Mohammed admitted his role in 31 different plots against the United States, including 9/11. The military trial began on June 5, with the U.S. government seeking the death penalty and Mohammed handling his own defense. Mohammed attempted to plead guilty in December 2008, but his case was transferred from military to civil jurisdiction in early 2009.

In November 2009, the U.S. attorney general, Eric Holder, announced that Mohammed and his four co-conspirators would be transferred to the United States and tried in a civilian court in New York. In January 2010, military charges against Mohammed were officially dropped by the Pentagon, clearing the way for civilian trials to proceed. Attorney General Holder assembled a team of civilian prosecutors to build a criminal case against Mohammed independent of the tainted CIA interrogations. In April 2011, however, Holder announced that due to restrictions imposed by

Congress, Mohammed would be prosecuted in a military tribunal rather than in a civilian setting.

Erica Pearson

See also al Qaeda; bin Laden, Osama; Criminal Prosecution of Terrorists; Pearl, Daniel; September 11 Attacks; Torture Debate; Yousef, Ramzi Ahmed

Further Readings

Federal Bureau of Investigation. "Most Wanted Terrorists." http://www.fbi.gov/mostwant/terrorists/fugitives.htm.

Fouda, Yosri, and Nick Fielding. *Masterminds of Terror: The Truth behind the Most Devastating Attack the World Has Ever Seen.* New York: Arcade Publishing, 2003.

GlobalSecurity.org. "Khalid Shaikh Mohammed: 9/11 Mastermind." http://www.globalsecurity.org/security/profiles/khalid_shaikh_mohammed.htm.

Miniter, Richard. *Mastermind: The Many Faces of the 9/11 Architect, Khalid Shaikh Mohammed.* New York: Sentinel HC, 2011.

"A Nation Challenged: The Hunted; The 22 Most Wanted Suspects, in a Five-act Drama of Global Terror." *The New York Times,* October 14, 2001, p. 1B.

Nomani, Asra Q., Barbara Feinman Todd, Katie Balestra, and Kira Zalan. *The Truth Left Behind: Inside the Kidnapping and Murder of Daniel Pearl.* New York: The Pearl Project of the Center for Public Integrity, January 2011. http://www.washingtonpost.com/wp-srv/world/documents/daniel-pearl-project/index.html.

Paddock, Richard C., and Josh Meyer. "Suspect's Role in '95 Plot Detailed; Inquiry: Khalid Shaikh Mohammed, Alleged Sept. 11 Mastermind, Was a Financial Conduit in the Plan to Blow Up U.S. Jets, Philippine Official Says." *Los Angeles Times,* June 7, 2002. http://articles.latimes.com/2002/jun/07/world/fg-khalid7.

Reeve, Simon. *The New Jackals: Ramzi Yousef, Osama Bin Laden, and the Future of Terrorism.* Boston: Northeastern University Press, 1999.

Satloff, Robert B. *War on Terror: The Middle East Dimension.* Washington, DC: Washington Institute for Near East Policy, 2002.

Wallace, Charles P. "Weaving a Wide Web of Terror; The Plan, Officials Say, Was to Blow Up 11 U.S. Airliners in One Day. The Probe into the Foiled Plot Points to the Accused Mastermind of the Trade Center Blast and to a Network of Muslim Veterans of the Afghan War." *Los Angeles Times,* May 28, 1995, p. A1.

MORAZANIST PATRIOTIC FRONT

A Honduran terrorist group, the Morazanist Patriotic Front (Frente Patriótico Morazanista, or FPM), now largely inactive, attacked U.S. military targets in Honduras several times during the early 1990s.

During the early 1980s, the Reagan administration began to actively support a counterinsurgency against the socialist Sandinista government of Nicaragua. Neighboring Honduras provided a natural base to provide training and deliver arms and funds to the insurgents, known as Contras. Through the first half of the decade, the United States vastly increased its military presence in Honduras. Some Hondurans resented the U.S. military presence, feeling that their country was becoming a client state of the United States. In this climate, the Morazanist Patriotic Front emerged. A leftist and extremely nationalist organization, the group's goal was the removal of all U.S. military forces from Honduras, as well as the expulsion of the remaining Contras. The U.S. State Department believes FPM may have received support from the Nicaraguan and Cuban governments.

FPM's first known attack was on a U.S. military convoy in April 1989; the convoy, while engaged in exercises with the Honduran military, was forced to turn back. In July of that year, the group bombed a disco frequented by soldiers in La Cieba, Honduras; seven soldiers were injured. In March 1990, four FPM guerrillas machine-gunned a bus carrying U.S. personnel, injuring eight soldiers. The group has also claimed involvement in an attack on a Peace Corps office in December 1988, and in another military bus bombing in February 1989 that wounded three soldiers.

In February 1990 the Sandinista government in Nicaragua was replaced with a U.S.-backed government, which demobilized the Contras in June. The FPM now had no possibility of support from the Nicaraguan government. In addition, the United States had begun a gradual withdrawal from the region, and by the following year the FPM appeared to have disbanded. However, two bombings in the Honduran capital of Tegucigalpa in 1992 and 1994 have been linked to the group. No one was hurt in either bombing, but both bombs were accompanied by propaganda critical of the U.S. and Honduran military presence. The recent stability in Honduras, coupled with U.S. disengagement, appears to have substantially lessened the threat of violence by the FPM.

Colleen Sullivan

Further Readings

Childress, Michael T. *The Effectiveness of U.S. Training Efforts in Internal Defense and Development: The Cases of El Salvador and Honduras.* Santa Monica, CA: RAND Corporation, 1995.
National Consortium for the Study of Terrorism and Responses to Terrorism. "Terrorist Organization Profile: Morazanist Patriotic Front (FPM)." http://www.start.umd.edu/start/data_collections/tops/terrorist_organization_profile.asp?id=4132.

MORO ISLAMIC LIBERATION FRONT

The Moro Islamic Liberation Front (MILF) is a Muslim military group in the southern Philippines. MILF was created in 1981 when it split off from the Moro National Liberation Front (MNLF), a Muslim separatist group that waged a 24-year guerrilla war against the Philippine government to achieve an independent Islamic state. The MILF split from the MNLF in response to the latter's acceptance of the Philippine government's 1987 offer of semi-autonomy for the southern, largely Muslim region of Bangsamoro. The MILF refused to go along with the MNLF and continued its insurgency campaign, while the MNLF continued to negotiate with the government over the next decade. As of September 2010, the stated goal of the MILF was no longer independence from the Philippines but rather the creation of an Islamic "substate" within the country, with status akin to that of a U.S. state.

Background and History of Philippine Muslim Insurgency

The MNLF traces it origins to a 400-year conflict between Muslims and Christians in the Philippines. Sixteenth-century Spanish colonizers converted the majority of the country's native inhabitants to Christianity. However, the southern islands of the archipelago had a large Muslim community (today estimated at 5 percent of the country's total population) that did not convert. The Spaniards called these people "Moros" (as in Moor, or Muslim) and they became a despised and often persecuted minority. Violent clashes between Moros and colonial administrators (first Spanish, and later American) were frequent.

In the 1950s and 1960s, the Philippine government began to encourage Christians to migrate to the southern island of Mindanao, the second-largest island of the Philippines and one of the richest in natural resources. Mindanao's Muslim inhabitants, however, are among the country's poorest. By the late 1960s, on many islands and on parts of Mindanao itself, Christians had become the majority population. Many Muslims felt that the government—in encouraging the Christian migration—was deliberately attempting to push them out of their homes.

The MNLF was founded by Nur Misuari as a Muslim advocacy group in the late 1960s. In 1972, Philippine president Ferdinand Marcos declared martial law and attempted to disarm the Muslim population. Misuari and the MNLF went to war against the government, hoping to establish an independent Muslim state.

During the early 1970s, the MNLF army was 50,000 strong, while the Philippine army numbered about 60,000. By 1972, Marcos had vastly expanded the armed forces in response to the secessionist threat, committing about 80 percent of the country's troops to Mindanao and the surrounding islands. During those bloody years, tens of thousands of people were killed and the MNLF made substantial territorial gains. In 1976 the rebels and the government signed a Libyan-brokered truce under which the MNLF would integrate its forces with the Philippine army and the Muslim provinces would become economically and politically autonomous but remain part of the Philippines.

Once the agreement was signed, Marcos did nothing to implement it. In 1978, dissatisfaction with the accord caused a split within the MNLF; Misuari's second-in-command, Hashim Salamat, formed the Moro Islamic Liberation Front (MILF). Salamat's group of 10,000 to 15,000 men was more Islamist in outlook. The MILF rejected limited autonomy, holding out for complete independence. Operating separately, the two groups continued attacking government forces throughout the late 1970s and early 1980s, but neither the government nor the rebels was able to gain the upper hand.

In 1986, Marcos, widely regarded as corrupt, was overthrown by the Philippine military and presidential candidate Corazon Aquino, the widow of a martyred opposition leader. Aquino began negotiations with the MNLF, and violence decreased briefly. In 1989, the Autonomous Region in the Muslim Mindanao (ARMM) was created and plebiscites were held in various provinces to determine what territory the ARMM would include. Lanao del Sur, Maguindanao, Sulu, and Tawi-Tawi were the only areas that voted for inclusion, and conflicts over which provinces would become autonomous soon stalled negotiations. The MNLF wanted to place many areas with clear Christian majorities under Muslim control. Nothing substantive was accomplished until 1993, when Aquino's successor, Fidel Ramos, succeeded in drawing the MNLF to the negotiating table.

In 1996 an agreement was signed giving Misuari control over four majority-Muslim provinces on Mindanao, with the possibility of more provinces opting for autonomy in three years. MNLF members laid down their arms, and the Ramos government hoped that Misuari could persuade the MILF to do likewise. The MILF declined to disarm, however, and over the next few years, Misuari would prove to be a better guerrilla than politician. In the meantime, promised aid for economic development in Mindanao and other Muslim provinces was not forthcoming. Continued dissatisfaction lent support to the MILF, which stepped up its attacks.

In 1998 the former action movie star Jose Estrada was elected president of the Philippines. He underestimated the strength of the guerrillas, however, and his tough talk about eliminating the rebel threat soon undid all the peace efforts of his predecessor's administration. Clashes between the army and the MILF drove 80,000 people from their homes in 1999. Escalating violence forced a tactical reconsideration, but Estrada's administration was inconsistent in its approach to the MILF. At first, the government attempted to initiate negotiations with the group under a tentative cease-fire agreement reached in 1997; however, the army continued operations during negotiations, and, in

response, Salamat refused to meet with Estrada. Estrada then authorized the army to begin an all-out campaign against the rebels, increasing military manpower and funds to the region.

In July 2000 the army captured Camp Abubakar, a compound that housed both rebel headquarters and three Muslim villages with schools and other services run by the MILF. Estrada celebrated the victory by trucking in beer and barbeque for the troops. Islam prohibits both alcohol and pork, and Muslims saw the victory party as a slap in the face. Salamat then called for a jihad against the government. The capture of Camp Abubakar was only the first of several advances by government troops, and the MILF was forced to retreat to the hills. Once again, however, the government was unable to eliminate the guerrilla threat. In 2001 Estrada was ousted by his vice president, Gloria Arroyo, who initiated peace talks with the guerrillas. In June 2001 the MILF and Arroyo signed a peace agreement and began talks to determine the limits of autonomy for the southern Muslims.

MNLF Resurgence

During 1999 and early 2000, MNLF members had been growing steadily more displeased with Misuari's leadership. In March 2000, a breakaway faction of young MNLF members, estimated at 200 former guerrillas, launched a surprise attack on a Mindanao army post, killing several soldiers. The group failed to inspire a mass revolt in the MNLF and was quickly disbanded. Rumblings about replacing Misuari grew steadily louder during this time, however, and in November 2001, with his loss in the upcoming presidential elections a near certainty, Misuari resigned as president of the autonomous Muslim provinces and once again called for war.

His rebellion was short-lived; by December 2001, Misuari had fled to Malaysia, where he was arrested, deported back to the Philippines, and put under house arrest in Manila. In April 2008 the former rebel leader Muslimin Sema replaced Misuari as MNLF chairman, promising to continue the peace process with the Philippine government.

Post-9/11 MILF Activity

By early 2002, both the MNLF and the MILF had signed peace agreements with the government.

However, conditions in the Muslim homeland remained among the worst in the country, and the activities of a separate al Qaeda–linked Muslim terror group, Abu Sayyaf, continued to threaten the peaceful development of the region. Following the terrorist attacks on the World Trade Center and the Pentagon on September 11, 2001, the U.S. government pledged $100 million in aid to the Philippines and sent Special Forces troops to the country to help train the Philippine army to combat terrorism, causing controversy in the Philippines. MILF leaders claimed that the troops would be deployed against them. The MILF denied any ties to al Qaeda or Osama bin Laden, but it was reported that hundreds of MILF members attended al Qaeda training camps in Afghanistan.

Peace negotiations with the Philippine government and a cease-fire were threatened after the bombing at the Davao City Airport in March 2003, which the government blamed on MILF operatives. The MILF also denied responsibility for a 2006 bomb attack on Andal Ampatuan, the governor of Maguindanao Province. Fighting between the MILF and police erupted after this incident and a cease-fire agreement was signed a few weeks later.

In June 2007, while MILF was involved in peace talks with the government, the Italian priest Giancarlo Bossi was kidnapped on Basilan Island by a group of Islamic militants believed to be members of either Abu Sayyaf or the MILF. A group of marines searching for the priest were seized by the rebels, and 14 of them were killed, most by beheading. The MILF acknowledges that some of its members were involved in the clash, but only because their stronghold was attacked first, in violation of the cease-fire agreement. The MILF denied, however, having anything to do with either the beheadings of the marines or the kidnapping of Father Bossi.

In August 2008, the Supreme Court of the Philippines threw out a proposed peace agreement between the government and the MILF that would have expanded the boundaries of the ARMM. The court deemed the agreement unconstitutional because the territorial expansion would lead to the ARMM's "eventual independence," thus violating the country's "physical and territorial integrity."

In September 2010, Mohagher Iqbal, the chief negotiator for the MILF, informed reporters that the MILF would no longer be demanding independence from the Philippines, but would instead pursue the creation of a "substate arrangement" that would operate under a unitary government. The region's cyclic history of violence and chronic underdevelopment makes it fertile ground for further rebellion, however. It remains to be seen whether the current negotiations between the MILF and the Philippine government will allow the religious and political détente to flower into a lasting peace.

Colleen Sullivan

See also Abu Sayyaf Group; Alex Boncayao Brigade; New People's Army

Further Readings

Aglionby, John. "Basilan Is Home to Separatist Violence and Kidnappings." *The Guardian*, January 12, 2001. http://www.guardian.co.uk/uk/2001/jan/12/philippines.

Banloi, Rommel C. *Philippine Security in the Age of Terror: National, Regional, and Global Challenges in the Post-9/11 World*. Boca Raton, FL: CRC Press, 2009.

Clifford, Mark L. "Conflict: The Philippines." *BusinessWeek*, July 11, 1997, p. 37.

Davis, Anthony. "Rebel without a Pause." *Asiaweek*, April 3, 1998, p. 30.

Espinosa-Robles, Raissa. "Lone Fighter." *Asiaweek*, November 30, 2001, p. 28.

Majul, Cesar Adib. *Muslims in the Philippines*. Quezon City: University of the Philippines Press, 1999.

Steinberg, David Joel. *The Philippines: A Singular and Plural Place*. 4th ed. Boulder, CO: Westview Press, 2000.

Teves, Oliver. "Philippine Muslim Rebels Drop Independence Demand." Associated Press, September 23, 2010. http://www.boston.com/news/world/asia/articles/2010/09/23/philippine_muslim_rebels_drop_independence_demand.

Weymouth, Lally. "Terrorist Cells All Over." *Newsweek*, February 11, 2002, p. 36.

MOSSAD

The *Mossad Merkazi Le-modiin U-letafkidim Meyuhadim*, or Central Institute for Intelligence and Special Operations, is Israel's secret foreign intelligence service. Mossad agents have hunted down Nazi war criminals and coordinated countless sophisticated assassination attacks on Arab guerrilla leaders and German and Iranian nuclear scientists.

Mossad was founded in 1951 by Isser Harel, who served as director of the organization until 1963. Mossad is complemented by the Shin Bet, Israel's internal intelligence service. Israel's government describes Mossad's and Shin Bet's assassinations of leaders of groups such as Hamas and Palestine Islamic Jihad as counterterrorism, while Arab leaders have accused the agency of "state terrorism."

Mossad made its reputation as a fierce spy corps with the May 11, 1960, kidnapping of the Nazi war criminal Adolf Eichmann from his home in Buenos Aires, Argentina. Eichmann was brought to Israel to stand trial and was found guilty of—and executed for—crimes against humanity. In 1976, Mossad agents also staged an impressive rescue of hostages aboard an Israeli airliner that had been hijacked to Entebbe, Uganda. In the early part of the 1970s, however, Mossad agents bungled the planned assassination of the alleged organizer of the murders of the Israeli team at the 1972 Munich Olympics, mistakenly attacking a Moroccan waiter in Norway.

In 1986, Mossad agents carried out another famous mission, as a blonde agent identified only as "Cindy" brought the nuclear technician Mordechai Vanunu from London to Italy on a holiday. Vanunu, an Israeli citizen, was then drugged and taken to Israel to be tried for leaking Israeli nuclear secrets to the British press. He was sentenced to 18 years in prison.

Mossad agents often targeted members of the Palestine Liberation Organization (PLO) during the 1980s. In 1988 they assassinated a top PLO leader, Abu Jihad, who was a cofounder of Yasir Arafat's Fatah movement.

In Mossad's first few decades, its agents were often said to be the best spies in the world, but the agency made a number of blunders in the late 1990s. Headlines compared the agency to the Keystone Kops, and high-ranking Mossad officials resigned. In 1997 in Amman, Jordan, Mossad agents tried to assassinate Hamas member Khaled Meshal with a poison injection in broad daylight. They aimed poorly, however, and were arrested

after a foiled attempt at flight. The captured agents were later exchanged for prominent Islamic leaders held by Israel.

Further problems ensued when a routine wiretap was discovered in Bern, Switzerland. Another Mossad agent was put on trial for fabricating information that nearly led to a declaration of war between Israel and Syria. In 1998, two agents were caught in Cyprus with surveillance tapes and charged with spying. As the number of mistakes rose, the agency's head, Danny Yatom, was forced to resign, and British-born Ephraim Halevy, who was previously Israel's diplomatic envoy to the European Union, was appointed as his replacement.

In summer 2000, Mossad advertised for new recruits in Israel's newspapers for the first time, asking qualified applicants to fax resumes and identification numbers. In April 2001, another ad sought electronics engineers and computer scientists for the technology division. This advertising campaign provoked much surprised discussion in the press, as Mossad had historically been so secretive that it had never released a telephone number. In the twenty-first century, the once ultra-secret agency got its own website, which includes pages on the organization's mission, history, a job application form, and a contact form. The site does not list a physical address, telephone number, or email address.

Since 2001, Mossad agents have been credited with a series of assassinations of individuals connected to terrorist organizations, and of scientists involved in Iran's nuclear program. The Hezbollah mastermind Imad Fayez Mugniyah died in a car bomb attack in Syria in 2008. Known as the "bin Laden of the 1980s," Mugniyah orchestrated many of the kidnappings of British officials in Lebanon, and before 9/11, according to the *Daily Mail,* he "was responsible for the deaths of more Westerners than any other terrorist leader." Mossad was also blamed for the mysterious death of the Iranian nuclear physicist Ardeshire Hassanpour in February 2007. On November 29, 2010, motorcycle riders slapped car bombs onto two vehicles during rush-hour traffic in Tehran, killing Majid Shahriari, and narrowly missing Fereydoun Abbasi. All three men were leading figures in Iran's nuclear program.

Following the July 7, 2005, terrorist attacks on the London transit system, Mossad agents reportedly passed information to MI5, the British intelligence service, about a suspected al Qaeda member known as "Mustafa." The man had visited England just before the attack and departed soon after. Mossad later identified him as Azhari Husin, a member of Jemaah Islamiyah, a terrorist group based in Southeast Asia.

The Hamas military commander Mahmoud al Mabhouh was found dead in his Dubai hotel room in January 2010. He appeared to have passed away in his sleep—his clothes were neatly folded, he was in bed, a bottle of heart medication on his nightstand, and the room was locked from the inside. But hotel security cameras revealed a different, much more elaborate scenario. A reported Mossad hit team had injected him with a paralyzing drug and smothered him. The 26 people on the hit team—many seen on the surveillance cameras—subsequently vanished. At least a dozen had traveled to Dubai on forged British passports, leading to a diplomatic row between London and Tel Aviv.

After the failures of the 1990s, Mossad began to reclaim its reputation for sophisticated, stealth attacks. Indeed, when sharks began attacking tourists at a resort on the Red Sea in December 2010, officials accused Israel of trying to sabotage the Egyptian tourism industry. Much of the credit for a reinvigorated Mossad has been given to Meir Dagan, who was appointed director in 2002. His predecessor, Ephraim Halevy, had prioritized maintaining good relations with other intelligence agencies, but Dagan seemed to prefer expediency over diplomacy, as Mossad's increasing use of fake Western passports confirmed. His term ended in 2009, but Prime Minister Binyamin Netanyahu extended it by a year. The *Israel Hayom* noted on November 30, 2010, that Dagan "will be leaving an organization that is far sharper and more operational than the organization he received, and all of the accusations from Tehran yesterday are a good indication of that." Dagan was replaced by Tamir Pardo, who previously had served as deputy chief of the agency, on January 1, 2011.

Ann E. Robertson

See also Counterterrorism; Fatah; Hamas; Mugniyah, Imad Fayez; Munich Olympics Massacre; Palestine Liberation Organization

Further Readings

Black, Ian, and Benny Morris. *Israel's Secret Wars: The Untold History of Israeli Intelligence.* London: Hamish Hamilton, 1991.

Jones, George. *Vengeance: The True Story of an Israeli Counter-terrorist Team.* New York: Simon & Schuster, 2005.

Melman, Yossi. *Every Spy a Prince: The Complete, History of Israel's Intelligence Community.* New York: Houghton Mifflin, 1990.

Ostrovsky, Victor, and Claire Hoy. *By Way of Deception: A Devastating Insider's Portrait of Mossad.* New York: St. Martin's, 1990.

Thomas, Gordon. *Gideon's Spies: The Secret History of the Mossad.* 5th ed. New York: St. Martin's, 2009.

MOUSSAOUI, ZACARIAS (1968–)

Zacarias Moussaoui (aka Abu Khalid al Sahrawi; Shaqil) was the first person to be convicted in the United States on charges stemming from the September 11, 2001, attacks that destroyed New York City's World Trade Center and part of the Pentagon near Washington, D.C., even though he was in prison in Minnesota when the attacks occurred. Moussaoui, a radical Muslim with ties to al Qaeda, is believed to have been a last-minute recruit who was supposed to fill in for another would-be hijacker on September 11. Moussaoui has claimed that he was actually supposed to take part in an attack on the White House slated to happen after September 11. Whatever the original plan, Moussaoui was never able to participate in any attack, because he was jailed in August 2001 for overstaying his visa.

Moussaoui was born in 1968 in St. Jean de Luz, France, the son of a Moroccan couple who married when Moussaoui's mother was 14 years old. His parents divorced when he was young, and Moussaoui's mother worked to support her four children, eventually buying a home in Narbonne. She raised her sons and daughters to share housework, a practice that was criticized by some of her more conservative relatives.

Moussaoui moved to London in the early 1990s. He received a master's degree in economics from Southbank University and fell in with radical Muslims, eventually becoming estranged from his immediate family. Nonetheless, he made several visits to France and was outspoken enough about his views to attract the attention of French authorities, who put him under surveillance. He traveled to Pakistan and Afghanistan more than once, training at an al Qaeda camp in 1998. He occasionally attended the same mosque in Brixton, England, as Richard Colvin Reid, who in December 2001 attempted to blow up an airliner by igniting explosives hidden in his shoes.

In fall 2000, Moussaoui contacted Airman Flight School in Norman, Oklahoma, inquiring about taking flight lessons. Around the same time, Ramzi bin al Shibh, a member of al Qaeda living in Germany, abandoned his efforts to get an entrance visa to the United States. These facts initially led investigators to conclude that Moussaoui was a replacement for bin al Shibh. Later, the National Commission on Terrorist Attacks on the United States reported that Moussaoui may have been trained as a potential replacement for Ziad Jarrah, a hijacker who seriously considered dropping out of the plot but eventually carried through with the attack.

Moussaoui entered the United States on a student visa in February 2001. From late February to late May 2001, Moussaoui took flight lessons at Airman on small planes. He was reportedly a dreadful pilot, and after being told that he would need more lessons, he quit the school. Moussaoui left Norman in August and moved to Minneapolis, Minnesota, where he attended the Pan Am International Flight Academy. His behavior soon attracted attention. He paid thousands of dollars of fees in cash, he was extremely evasive, and he adamantly insisted that he be taught to fly a large passenger plane even though he had not mastered flying a small plane. Instructors became suspicious and contacted the Federal Bureau of Investigation. Moussaoui was arrested on August 16, 2001, and held on immigration charges.

In December 2001, Moussaoui was formally charged with six charges of conspiracy related to the September 11 attacks in a federal court in Alexandria, Virginia. In March 2002 the U.S. government announced that it would seek the death penalty for Moussaoui. As a French citizen, Moussaoui was eligible to be tried before a special military tribunal empowered to charge foreign terrorists, but he was instead indicted in a civilian court.

Moussaoui initially represented himself in his case. His behavior was so erratic, however, that the judge forced him to accept legal representation. Nonetheless, he frequently made threatening outbursts and rambling speeches in court. Despite questions about his mental health, he was found competent to plead guilty to all six counts on April 22, 2005 (although he later tried to withdraw the plea). In May 2006 a jury sentenced Moussaoui to life in prison; he is serving that sentence in the Supermax top-security federal prison in Colorado.

Mary Sisson

See also al Qaeda; Atta, Mohamed; bin Laden, Osama; Hijacking; September 11 Attacks

Further Readings

Chrisafis, Angelique. "'Zacarias Was the Child I Never Had a Problem With.'" *The Guardian*, April 21, 2006, p. 12.

Daley, Suzanne. "Mysterious Life of a Suspect from France." *The New York Times*, September 21, 2001, p. B1.

Doyle, Pat. "Suspect Was a 'Hardheaded' Student Pilot: Zacarias Moussaoui Didn't Leave Much of a Trail for Investigators." *Star Tribune*, September 18, 2001, p. 15A.

Fallis, David S., and Lois Romano. "Between Two Worlds: Suspect Chafed at Western Ways, Alienated Fellow Muslims." *The Washington Post*, September 29, 2001, p. A19.

Lewis, Neil A. "Moussaoui Tells Court He's Guilty of a Terror Plot." *The New York Times*, April 23, 2005, p. A1.

Markon, Jerry, and Timothy Dwyer. "In Closing, Moussaoui Trial Rests on His Lies." *The Washington Post*, March 30, 2006, p. A5.

McDermott, Terry. *Perfect Soldiers: The Hijackers: Who They Were, Why They Did It*. New York: HarperCollins, 2005.

Moss, Michael. "A Traveler with Strong Views on the Right Kind of Islam and No Fear of Sharing Them." *The New York Times*, December 12, 2001, p. B6.

Moussaoui, Abd Samad. *Zacarias, My Brother: The Making of a Terrorist*. New York: Seven Stories Press, 2003.

National Commission on Terrorist Attacks on the United States. http://www.9-11commission.gov.

U.S. District Court for the Eastern District of Virginia, Alexandria Division. *United States v. Zacarias Moussaoui*. Indictment, December 11, 2001. http://www.justice.gov/ag/moussaouiindictment.htm.

Movement of the Revolutionary Left

The militant Movement of the Revolutionary Left (Movimiento Izquierda Revolucionaria, or MIR) began as a Marxist-Leninist group in Chile dedicated to popular revolution. Founded by Miguel Enriquez, a young medical student in Concepcion, the MIR held its first meeting in August 1965.

The group, made up primarily of young students associated with the Young Socialist Party, grew in influence, first in Chile's provinces, and later among university students in the capital, indigenous people, industrial workers, and miners. At its strongest in 1970, the MIR had some 40,000 members.

In the mid-1960s the MIR organized the poor and homeless to take over land as squatters and to work cooperatively to build houses. By 1969 the MIR had also developed an underground structure of armed groups across the country. These groups began to rob banks, and there were heated discussions among the established Chilean Left about the MIR's evolution and tactics. Enriquez publicly claimed that the robberies funded the group's social programs, and it was reported that the MIR gave stolen money directly to the poor.

When the Socialist Salvador Allende was elected president in 1970, the MIR made an informal union with his Popular Unity Party. As the threat of a military coup increased, the MIR worked against Allende's wishes to build up an armed popular force to fight Chile's army. After the 1973 military takeover in which Allende was killed, General Augusto Pinochet's death squads hunted down suspected MIR members, torturing and killing them in detention centers, and many MIR members were murdered or exiled. Enriquez was killed in October 1974. Andres Pascal Allende, nephew of the late president, assumed leadership of the MIR and continued to operate a small underground network inside Chile.

During the 1980s, the group carried out bombings and attacked targets related to the military government. The MIR claimed responsibility for the January 1988 killing of the high-ranking police-squad chief Julio Benimeli, by setting a booby trap with six TNT charges inside a small house. "The formation of an armed people's power is needed to overthrow the dictatorship and win freedom," read part of the communiqué the group released after the blast.

In December 1989, the MIR kidnapped the millionaire Brazilian businessman Abilio Diniz, abducting him in a fake ambulance. Asking a ransom of $30 million, 10 MIR members held the supermarket magnate prisoner for six days in a tiny room dug at the bottom of a well. The kidnappers equipped the room with a mattress and a portable toilet, and they piped in fresh air with hoses. When police burst into the house where the abductors were staying, all 10 surrendered. Officials said that the group had kidnapped Diniz to get funds to support the MIR. After Pinochet was overthrown in 1990, the MIR greatly reduced its activities.

Erica Pearson

See also Lautaro Youth Movement; Manuel Rodriguez Patriotic Front

Further Readings

Brazao, Dale. "Brazil Probes Canadians' Terror Links." *The Toronto Star,* December 31, 1989.
Constable, Pamela, and Arturo Valenzuela. *A Nation of Enemies: Chile under Pinochet.* New York: W.W. Norton, 1991.
Ross, Jen. "In Chile, Hope Is Reborn in 30-Year Quest for Justice." *The Washington Post,* July 18, 2004, p. A22.
U.S. State Department. "Chile Human Rights Practices, 1992." *1993 U.S. Dept. of State Department of State Dispatch,* March 1993.

Movimiento de Liberación Nacional

See Tupamaros

Movimiento Revolucionario Túpac Amaru

See Túpac Amaru Revolutionary Movement

MSALAM, FAHID MOHAMMED ALLY (1976–2009)

Born in Mombasa, Kenya, Fahid Mohammed Ally Msalam was believed to be a member of the al Qaeda network. He was said to have been directly involved in the 1998 attack on two U.S. embassies in East Africa, working closely on the bombing in Dar es Salaam, Tanzania. He was included on the FBI's Most Wanted Terrorists list for his role in the bombings, which killed 224 people.

According to the FBI, Msalam was an al Qaeda member who worked in the past as a clothing vendor. In 1998 the United States indicted Msalam and 26 others with alleged links to bin Laden for the East Africa embassy bombings. According to the indictment, as early as 1996, Msalam showed co-conspirators TNT and detonators that he had obtained in Tanzania. Prosecutors say his fingerprints were also found on a magazine inside a gym bag that contained clothing with traces of TNT. Msalam was accused of buying the vehicle used as a bomb by the conspirators in Dar es Salaam, and of purchasing the truck used in the Nairobi bombing with fellow al Qaeda operative Sheikh Ahmed Salim Swedan.

The indictment charged that Msalam then helped to prepare the Dar es Salaam bomb truck, loading it with oxygen and acetylene tanks, TNT boxes, detonators, fertilizer, and sandbags before fleeing to Pakistan on August 6, 1998. On August 7, 1998, in synchronized attacks 400 miles apart, the truck bombs exploded at the embassies in Kenya and Tanzania, one bomb detonating just minutes before the other.

The U.S. government declared that bin Laden and al Qaeda operatives were responsible for the bombings. Officials at the Karachi, Pakistan, airport detained the al Qaeda operative traveling with Msalam on August 6, but Msalam managed to slip through their net.

Following the September 11, 2001, attacks by al Qaeda on the United States, Msalam is thought to have been put in charge of the organization's operations in the Afghani province of Zabul, and to have also provided support for operations in East Africa. In 2007 he was given a leadership role for al Qaeda in Pakistan, helping coordinate attacks with Pakistani militants. He is believed to have organized a suicide-bombing attack on the former Pakistani prime minister Benazir Bhutto in Karachi in October 2007. While the prime minister survived that attack, more than 140 people died, and she was later assassinated. Msalam is also thought to have organized the bombing of a hotel in Islamabad in September 2008 that killed more than 50 people.

On January 1, 2009, Msalam was killed in Pakistan, along with Sheikh Ahmed Salim Swedan, who was also wanted in connection to the 1998 embassy attack. Both men were believed killed by missiles fired by a U.S. drone.

Erica Pearson

See also al Qaeda; bin Laden, Osama; East Africa Embassy Bombings; Swedan, Sheikh Ahmed Salim

Further Readings

Bergen, Peter. *Holy War, Inc.: Inside the Secret World of Osama bin Laden.* New York: Free Press, 2001.

"A Nation Challenged: The Hunted; The 22 Most Wanted Suspects, in a Five-act Drama of Global Terror." *The New York Times*, October 14, 2001, p. 1B.

Reeve, Simon. *The New Jackals: Ramzi Yousef, Osama bin Laden and the Future of Terrorism.* Boston: Northeastern University Press, 1999.

Schmitt, Eric. "2 Qaeda Leaders Killed in U.S. Strike in Pakistan." *The New York Times*, January 9, 2009, p. A7.

Shah, Saeed, and Harroon Siddique. "Al Qaeda Chief Killed in Pakistan, U.S. Claims." *The Guardian*, January 10, 2009, p. 24.

Smith, Martin, and Lowell Bergman. "Hunting bin Laden." *Frontline*, PBS, September 13, 2001. http://www.pbs.org/wgbh/pages/frontline/shows/binladen.

U.S. District Court for the Southern District of New York. *United States v. Usama bin Laden, et al.* Indictment S(2) 98 Cr. 1023 (LBS), November 4, 1998. http://www.fas.org/irp/news/1998/11/ 98110602_nlt.html.

Warrick, Joby. "Jan. 1 Attack: CIA Killed Two Leaders of Al Qaeda." *The Washington Post*, January 9, 2009, p. A12.

MUGHASSIL, AHMAD IBRAHIM AL (1967–)

In June 2001, the U.S. indicted the Saudi national Ahmad al Mughassil (aka Abu Omran) for his role in coordinating and carrying out the 1996 bombing of the Khobar Towers military barracks (which housed about 2,000 U.S. Air Force personnel) in Dhahran, Saudi Arabia. The explosion killed 19 American service members and wounded approximately 500. Mughassil is one of the FBI's most wanted terrorists.

U.S. officials charge that Mughassil, born in Qatif-Bab al Shamal, Saudi Arabia, is the leader of the military wing of the Saudi Hezbollah terrorist group. Saudi Hezbollah, also called Hezbollah al Hijaz, is largely made up of young Shiite Muslim men who profess loyalty to Iran instead of the Saudi government. Saudi Hezbollah is outlawed in Saudi Arabia, and Mughassil often met with the head of Saudi Hezbollah, Abdelkarim Hussein Mohamed al Nasser, and other organization leaders in Lebanon, Syria, or Iran.

According to the 2001 indictment, Mughassil was in charge of planning and directing terror attacks against the U.S. presence in Saudi Arabia. He also worked as a recruiter for Saudi Hezbollah, arranging for military training for new members in camps in Lebanon and Iran.

About three years before the Khobar attack, Mughassil ordered Saudi Hezbollah members to find possible terrorism targets in Saudi Arabia. His goal, according to U.S. officials, was to expel the U.S. military from Saudi Arabia. The service members living in Khobar Towers were assigned to the King Abdul Aziz Airbase in Saudi Arabia, and they patrolled over the no-fly zone in southern Iraq that was declared after the Persian Gulf War.

In early June 1996, according to the U.S. indictment, Mughassil and his co-conspirators worked at a farm in the Qatif area of Saudi Arabia to build the truck bomb used in the Khobar attack. A tanker truck, which had been purchased using stolen identification from a Saudi Arabian car dealership, was filled with explosives and wired with a timer. On the evening of June 25, al Mughassil drove the truck, now loaded with more than 5,000 pounds of explosives, and parked it near building no. 131 of the high-rise air force barracks. He and a passenger then jumped into a waiting car and drove away. The truck bomb exploded within minutes. The enormous blast, heard 20 miles away, destroyed the north side of the building.

Mughassil was 1 of 14 charged on June 21, 2001, in the Khobar Towers case. Eleven of the 14 are in Saudi custody, while 3, including Mughassil, remain

fugitives. Saudi Arabia has challenged U.S. jurisdiction in the Khobar case and refused to extradite the men, as the attack happened on Saudi soil and was committed mostly by Saudi citizens.

Three others indicted in the Khobar case, Nasser, Ibrahim Salih Mohammed al Yacoub, and Ali Saed bin Ali el Hoorie, are also on the FBI's Most Wanted Terrorists list. The U.S. State Department is offering a reward of up to $5 million for information leading directly to the arrest or indictment of Ahmad Ibrahim al Mughassil.

Erica Pearson

See also Hezbollah; Hoorie, Ali Saed bin Ali el; Khobar Towers Bombing; Nasser, Abdelkarim Hussein Mohamed al; Yacoub, Ibrahim Salih Mohammed al

Further Readings

Federal Bureau of Investigation. "Most Wanted Terrorists." http://www.fbi.gov/wanted/terrorists/fugitives.htm.

Jamieson, Perry D. *Khobar Towers: Tragedy and Response.* Washington, DC: Air Force History and Museums Program, 2008.

"A Nation Challenged: The Hunted; The 22 Most Wanted Suspects, in a Five-act Drama of Global Terror." *The New York Times*, October 14, 2001, p. 1B.

U.S. District Court for the Eastern District of Virginia, Alexandria Division. *United States v. Ahmed al-Mughassil, et al.* Indictment, June 21, 2001 (Khobar Indictment). http://fl1.findlaw.com/news.findlaw.com/cnn/docs/khobar/khobarindict61901.pdf.

Walsh, Elsa. "Louis Freeh's Last Case." *The New Yorker*, May 14, 2001.

MUGNIYAH, IMAD FAYEZ (1962–2008)

Deemed "the ultimate faceless terrorist" in press accounts, Imad Fayez Mugniyah (aka Mr. Haij) eluded the FBI for 25 years. According to U.S. officials, he was tied to the hijacking of a commercial jet, four mass bombings, and the abductions of six American, one British, and five French hostages. Mugniyah was at times described as the senior intelligence officer of Hezbollah, at others as Hezbollah's security chief or operations chief.

Born in Tir Dibba in the hills of southern Lebanon overlooking the Mediterranean Sea, Mugniyah was forced to leave his town for the slums of southern Beirut when Israel began attacking Palestinian guerrillas in Lebanon in the late 1970s. The death of his brother, who was shot by Lebanese Army troops in the Muslim suburbs of Beirut, was a turning point in Mugniyah's life.

He joined the Palestine Liberation Organization (PLO) as a teenager, did extremely well in military training, and was placed in Force 17, Yasir Arafat's personal security detail. After Israel invaded Lebanon in 1982, driving out the PLO, Mugniyah joined a small Shiite Muslim–based militia that would later fuse with similar groups to become the Iran-backed Shiite Muslim Hezbollah terror group. Mugniyah operated almost exclusively in Lebanon, and many of the terrorist acts he was charged with committing were aimed at ending Israel's presence in Lebanon, Gaza, and the West Bank and putting an end to U.S. involvement in the Middle East. U.S. intelligence officials said Mugniyah planned the 1983 suicide bombings of the U.S. embassy in Beirut and similar attacks on the Marine Corps barracks and French paratroopers headquarters in Beirut later that year. More than 350 people died in the 1983 Beirut attacks. He was also said to have played a role in the kidnapping and eventual death in captivity of Beirut CIA station chief William Buckley in the 1980s.

The United States indicted Mugniyah for involvement in the 1985 hijacking of TWA Flight 847 in which a U.S. Navy diver was shot at close range and then dumped onto the tarmac of Beirut International Airport. When Flight 847 was finally grounded in Algiers, the passengers and crew were held hostage for more than two weeks until Israeli officials partly acceded to the hijackers' demands for the release of hundreds of prisoners, many of them Shiite Muslims.

Mugniyah was also implicated in a chain of hostage takings in Lebanon from 1984 to 1991. Mugniyah's brother-in-law, Mustafa Badreddin, was jailed in Kuwait awaiting execution after being tried in 1984 for the 1983 Beirut bombings. The hostages were taken in an attempt to barter for Badreddin's freedom. Badreddin later escaped from jail during Iraq's invasion of Kuwait.

In 1999 the Argentine government issued an international warrant for Mugniyah's arrest in connection with the 1992 bombing of the Israeli embassy in Buenos Aires, which killed 29 people. The embassy was bombed one month after Israeli forces killed Hezbollah leader Abbas Musawi, his family, and his bodyguards. Argentine officials further implicated Mugniyah in the 1994 bombing of a community center that killed 85 in Buenos Aires. Still, Mugniyah eluded capture for decades and was rumored to have had extensive plastic surgery to change his appearance.

According to a report published in *The Washington Post,* just five months after the hijacking of TWA Flight 847, Lebanese security officials traced Mugniyah to Paris. He was staying in a luxury hotel across the street from the U.S. embassy. The Lebanese told U.S. officials of Mugniyah's presence. However, instead of releasing him into U.S. custody, French agents met with him several times over six days to broker an agreement. They eventually released Mugniyah in return for the freedom of a French hostage. According to further press accounts, Mugniyah also narrowly evaded capture when U.S. officials heard of his plans to stop over in Saudi Arabia during a flight from Khartoum, Sudan to Tehran, Iran. Saudi authorities did not respond to U.S. pressure to take Mugniyah into custody and refused to allow the plane to land. Mugniyah flew safely to Tehran.

In the late 1990s, Hezbollah curtailed its attacks abroad to focus on the Middle East. Mugniyah reportedly led Hezbollah armed forces during their surprisingly successful campaign against Israel in Lebanon in 2006. On February 12, 2008, Mugniyah was killed in a car bombing in Damascus, Syria. Although both Israel and the United States applauded his death, neither country claimed responsibility, and the possibility remains that Mugniyah was killed by Syria, by Iran, or by rival elements in Hezbollah.

Erica Pearson

See also Arafat, Yasir; Force 17; Hezbollah; TWA Flight 847 Hijacking; U.S. Embassy Bombing, Beirut; U.S. Marine Barracks Bombing, Beirut

Further Readings

Boustany, Nora. "'We Are . . . Doing Whatever Is Being Asked of Us.'" *The Washington Post,* October 17, 2001, p. A30.

Bruce, Ian. "Face of Terror before bin Laden." *The Herald* (Glasgow), October 12, 2001, p. 6.

Cody, Edward. "Anti-terror Efforts Revive Interest in an Old Enemy; FBI List Includes Lebanese Suspect in Past Attacks on U.S." *The Washington Post*, October 31, 2001, p. A11.

Daragahi, Borzou, and Sebastian Rotella. "Hezbollah Warlord Was an Enigma: The Death of Imad Mughinyah, Alleged Mastermind of Many Terrorist Attacks, Was as Mysterious as His Life." *Los Angeles Times*, August 31, 2008, p. A1.

Fiaola, Anthony. "Justice Delayed in Argentine Attack: Trial of 20 Suspects Begins Seven Years after Fatal Bombing of Jewish Center." *The Washington Post*, September 25, 2001, p. A19.

Jaber, Hala. *Hezbollah*. New York: Columbia University Press, 1997.

"A Nation Challenged: The Hunted; The 22 Most Wanted Suspects, in a Five-act Drama of Global Terror." *The New York Times*, October 14, 2001, p. 1B.

Norton, August Richard. *Hezbollah: A Short History*. Princeton, NJ: Princeton University Press, 2007.

Shadid, Anthony, and Alia Ibrahim. "Bombing Kills Top Figure in Hezbollah." *The Washington Post*, February 14, 2008, p. A1.

Wright, Robin. "Shadowy Lebanese; On the Trail of a Deadly Terrorist." *Los Angeles Times*, November 26, 1988.

MUJAHIDEEN

The mujahideen were a loose alliance of Afghan traditionalists who in the late 1970s rebelled against the Soviet-backed government of Afghanistan. The mujahideen overthrew the government in 1992 before being largely conquered themselves by the Taliban a few years later.

The mujahideen emerged in 1978, after the leftist People's Democratic Party of Afghanistan (PDPA) seized power in a military coup. The PDPA allied itself with the Soviet Union and quickly began reshaping Afghan society along Marxist lines. The effort quickly provoked a backlash, as tribal leaders saw their authority threatened and many Muslims saw an effort to destroy Islam. By the end of 1978, rebellion had broken out, and by summer 1979, the mujahideen controlled much of the countryside.

In late December 1979, Soviet forces entered Afghanistan to defend the PDPA government. Although the Soviets initially tried to broker a compromise, the invasion threw more popular support behind the mujahideen. Roughly 6 million Afghans fled to the neighboring countries of Pakistan and Iran; once there, they established bases of operation from which to attack Soviet forces. The invasion also prompted countries hostile to the Soviet Union—including the United States, Pakistan, Iran, Saudi Arabia, China, and Egypt—to support the mujahideen with arms and training. The United States alone spent more than $2 billion on weapons and supplies for the mujahideen during the 1980s.

The mujahideen consisted of dozens of factions that had little in common besides wanting to rid Afghanistan of the Soviets and the PDPA government. Afghans of different ethnic groups and with different approaches to Islam found themselves in different factions, and each faction found different foreign backers. Among the various factions were Islamic fundamentalist groups, who were soon joined by fundamentalists from other countries. The Saudi billionaire Osama bin Laden joined the mujahideen in the late 1970s or early 1980s. In the mid-1980s he helped found an organization that recruited thousands of people from around the world to come to Afghanistan and fight; this organization would ultimately become al Qaeda ("the Base"). By the end of the decade, Afghanistan was home to terrorist training camps for al Qaeda and other Islamic terror groups.

By the late 1980s, the war in Afghanistan had become extremely unpopular in the Soviet Union. In 1988, the Soviet Union, United States, Pakistan, and Afghanistan reached an agreement ending all foreign intervention in Afghanistan, and the Soviet Union withdrew its forces the next year. The mujahideen did not stop fighting, however. The 1988 agreement left the PDPA government in power, and both the United States and Soviet Union continued to send arms. In 1992 the mujahideen lay siege to the capital of Kabul, overthrowing the PDPA in April.

Following the overthrow of the PDPA, many of the foreign mujahideen returned to their home countries, establishing or joining Islamic terrorist groups. The Afghan mujahideen promptly began fighting among themselves, further decimating a country ravaged by decades of war. Two years after the fall of the PDPA, a new group, the Taliban, emerged, promising to rid the country of the mujahideen. The Taliban quickly swept through the country, seizing Kabul from a mujahideen faction in 1996.

Mary Sisson

See also al Qaeda; bin Laden, Osama; Taliban

Further Readings

Crile, George. *Charlie Wilson's War: The Extraordinary Story of the Largest Covert Operation in History.* New York: Atlantic Monthly Press, 2003.

Gall, Sandy. *Behind Russian Lines: An Afghan Journal.* New York: St. Martin's Press, 1983.

Gall, Sandy. *Afghanistan: Agony of a Nation.* London: The Bodley Head, 1988.

Giustozzi, Antonio. *War, Politics, and Society in Afghanistan 1978–1992.* Washington, DC: Georgetown University Press, 2000.

Urban, Mark. *War in Afghanistan.* New York: St. Martin's Press, 1988.

MUJAHIDEEN-E-KHALQ ORGANIZATION

In the 1960s, years before Shah Reza Pahlavi was overthrown in Iran, college-educated children of Iranian merchants formed the Mujahideen-e-Khalq (MEK), also known as the Muslim Iranian Student's Society, National Liberation Army of Iran (NLA), National Council of Resistance (NCR), and People's Mujahideen of Iran (PMOI). With an ideological blend of Marxism and Islam, the MEK originally sought to work against Western cultural and economic influences that the group's founders felt pervaded their country. After the revolution of 1979, the MEK developed into Iran's largest and most active armed dissident group, opposing the mullahs' control of the country.

Although the U.S. State Department has declared the MEK to be a terrorist organization, others consider it to be a grassroots movement opposing a tyrannical theocracy. The MEK was also described at one time as a group of stooges for Saddam Hussein's military government in Iraq, where its organization of several thousand fighters was based.

During the 1970s, the MEK worked to overthrow the Shah and his backers. The group engaged in terror attacks against Western interests in Iran, killing several U.S. military personnel and civilians; the group also supported the takeover of the U.S. embassy in Tehran in 1979. After the Shah fled in January 1979 and Ayatollah Ruhollah Khomeini returned from French exile during the Islamic revolution, the MEK fought against the ayatollah's supporters in street battles in an enduring struggle for power over governmental control.

During the 1980s, Iranian security forces persecuted the MEK's leaders and forced them to flee to France. MEK members and other dissidents were killed or abducted, and many were tortured; at one point the MEK accused the government of holding up to 140,000 political prisoners. By 1987 most MEK leaders had resettled in Iraq, where the group remained until the U.S. invasion in 2003. According to the U.S. State Department, the MEK was largely supported by Iraq during that period, and it fought on the Iraqi side in the 1980–1988 Iran-Iraq War. The group also depended on front organizations to raise donations from expatriate Iranians.

In the 1990s the MEK carried out and claimed responsibility for a number of attacks in Iran, including a bombing in a Tehran public building that killed two children. In April 1992, in a large-scale attack, the MEK targeted Iranian embassies in 13 different countries. When the U.S. State Department first designated the armed wing of the MEK, the National Liberation Army, a terrorist organization in 1997, more than 100 members of Congress signed a statement criticizing the administration of President Bill Clinton, claiming that the administration was labeling a group of freedom fighters as terrorists. In 1998 a member of the MEK tried to gain access to a United Nations meeting attended by world leaders, including President Clinton and President Mohammad Khatami of Iran. He was foiled by a routine screening of his application.

In February 2000 the group claimed that it had launched over 12 attacks against Iran, as part of what it called Operation Great Bahman. Later that year, the MEK regularly accepted responsibility for mortar attacks and hit-and-run raids along the Iraq-Iran border; these attacks targeted Iranian military, police, and government units. It also accepted responsibility for six mortar attacks on government and military buildings in Tehran.

During this period, the MEK received the majority of its funding from the Saddam Hussein regime in Iraq. Hussein also provided the MEK with weapons, bases, and protection within his country. After Iraq was invaded and Hussein was overthrown by the United States in 2003, MEK members surrendered to the coalition forces and were held in a special prison, Camp Ashraf, and promised protection under the Geneva Convention. However, the new Iraqi government announced in 2009 that members of MEK would soon have to return to Iran or to some third country. Although the MEK still receives some support from Iranian expatriates, membership in the group is believed to have dwindled, despite public statements of support from some on the American political right.

Erica Pearson

See also Hussein, Saddam; Iranian Hostage Crisis; Iraq War

Further Readings

Aghababaei, Hussein, and Hassan Rezaei. "Iran: Borders of an Islamic Republic in the Middle East." In *Border Security in the Al Qaeda Era*, edited by John A. Winterdyk and Kelly W. Sundberg. Boca Raton, FL: CRC Press/Taylor & Francis Group, 2010.

Amjad, Mohammed. *Iran: From Royal Dictatorship to Theocracy*. New York: Greenwood Press, 1989.

Axworthy, Michael. *A History of Iran: Empire of the Mind*. New York: Basic Books, 2008.

Buchan, James. "Princess Leila of Nowhere." *The Irish Times,* June 16, 2001, p. 61.

Davies, Charles, ed. *After the War: Iran, Iraq, and the Arab Gulf.* Chichester, UK: Carden Publications, 1990.

Fletcher, Holly. *Backgrounder: Mujahadeen-e-Khalk (MEK)*. Washington, DC: Council on Foreign Relations, April 18, 2008. http://www.cfr.org/publication/9158/mujahadeenekhalq_mek_aka_peoples_mujahedin_of_iran_or_pmoi.html.

Limbert, John W. *Negotiating with Iran: Wrestling with the Ghosts of History*. Washington, DC: United States Institute of Peace, 2009.

MUMBAI ATTACK, 2008

On November 26, 2008, 10 armed gunman from the Muslim extremist group Lashkar-e-Taiba (Army of the Pure) attacked various targets in the Indian city of Mumbai (formerly Bombay). The attack, which left more than 230 people injured and more than 170 dead, including 9 of the 10 terrorists, was the result of years of planning. The gunmen were well equipped and remarkably well trained. They broke into small teams that simultaneously attacked targets and eventually occupied a number of buildings. The terrorists, who fought to the death, were able to hold off Indian police and commando forces for up to three days.

The attacks were planned and carried out by Lashkar-e-Taiba, which began as a pro-Pakistan militia in the border state of Jammu and Kashmir. Officially a part of India, Jammu and Kashmir is claimed by both India and Pakistan. The two countries reached a cease-fire in 2003, at which point Lashkar-e-Taiba began to increasingly focus its violence on India itself. The Pakistani group is fanatically pro-Muslim with the expressed goal of driving out or conquering India's large Hindu population.

Mumbai was apparently an enticing target even before 2008. The city, situated on a peninsula between two bays, is India's most populous, and it houses the country's high-profile financial, film,

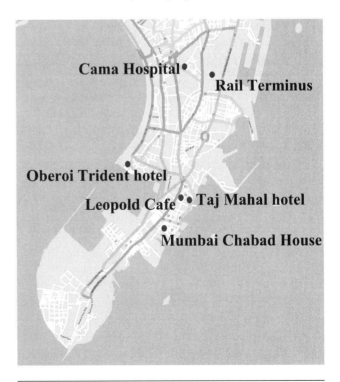

Map showing the locations of the four attacks in Mumbai, November 26, 2008.

and television industries. In 2006, Lashkar-e-Taiba staged a bomb attack on the commuter-train system of Mumbai that killed more than 180 people.

The Attack

On November 22, 2008, ten Lashkar-e-Taiba gunmen boarded a ship in Karachi. The organization apparently decided to approach Mumbai by sea because security along the coast was lax. Once in Indian waters, the men hijacked a fishing boat, killed its crew, and forced its captain to sail them to Mumbai. After killing the captain, the men landed in small boats on the evening of November 26, 2008. The men then broke up into five two-man teams to conduct their attacks.

The first team attacked the Leopold Café, a restaurant and bar in southeast Mumbai that is popular with both foreign tourists and wealthy Mumbaikars. The two men opened fire on the café, killing several people. They then went to the nearby Taj Mahal Palace and Tower, a large luxury hotel, where they met a second two-man team that had gone directly to the hotel. The four men attacked the Taj Mahal with bombs, grenades, and guns, destroying the first floor restaurant. They went from room to room in the hotel, taking some guests hostage and executing others. The third two-man team traveled to the Oberi and Trident hotels, two large hotels that occupy a single complex in southwest Mumbai. The men took hostages and holed up on a high floor of the Oberi hotel, firing down on police.

The fourth team attacked a building called Naiman House, which was apparently selected because it contained a Jewish center. Unlike the other targets, Naiman House was not a notable landmark—indeed, it was somewhat difficult for visitors to find. The fact that the terrorists were able to go directly to it indicated that a significant amount of advance planning went into the attack. Likewise, the teams at the Taj Mahal and the Oberi/Trident complex were apparently quite familiar with the layout of the hotels, which put them at a considerable advantage when repelling attacks by Indian forces.

While the first four teams set up fortified positions within buildings and settled in for a siege, the last two-man team opened fire and threw grenades at the Chhatrapati Shivaji Terminus, a historic railway station that is one of the busiest in India, killing dozens of people. They then attempted to enter and kill patients at a nearby hospital before police drove them out. They slaughtered a group of policemen and stole their car, then engaged in a car chase through Mumbai, hijacking a new car before they were stopped by a police roadblock. One man was killed in the ensuing gun battle, but the second, Ajmal Amir Kasab, was captured alive; he was the only terrorist to survive the operation.

The Response

In India, it is not uncommon for police to be completely unarmed or armed only with batons, and many were killed in the initial attack by the gun-wielding Lashkar-e-Taiba operatives. The nation's elite commando forces were stationed in New Delhi, where they typically protect high-ranking government officials, and it took them several hours to reach Mumbai, time the terrorists used to fortify their positions. Even the commandos proved to be relatively poorly equipped, and faulty bulletproof vests and a lack of night-vision gear resulted in many casualties and hampered efforts to retake the Taj Mahal, the Oberi/Trident complex, and Naiman House.

The Lashkar-e-Taiba gunmen were, in contrast, quite well prepared. In addition to guns, grenades, and other explosives, the men were outfitted with digital maps, GPS devices, and cell phones. During the attacks, the terrorists called handlers in Lashkar-e-Taiba who gave them information gleaned from media coverage of the attack, directions regarding which hostages to kill, and encouragement to fight to the death.

The teams were also well trained in urban warfare, particularly in the art of occupying a building and holding off a much larger force. They set themselves up on higher floors in order to have better sightlines on the forces below them. The team in Naiman House blew the doors off the building's elevator and used the shaft for cover. The terrorists booby trapped dead bodies with explosives to ambush Indian forces. They claimed to have taken hostages, although in most cases the hostages were executed long before the final attack. As a result, it took two days for Indian forces to retake the Oberi/Trident complex and Naiman House. The four men in the Taj Mahal

Members of the National Students Union of India (NSUI) hold placards during a protest against the recent attacks in Mumbai on December 10, 2008. The NSUI condemned the November 26 terror attacks and collected blood from Hindu, Muslim, Christian, Sikhs, and all other communities to be mingled and sent to the prime minister of Pakistan. (SAJJAD HUSSAIN/AFP/Getty Images)

were able to hold out for fully 60 hours before they were all killed and the hotel retaken.

The Aftermath

The relationship between India and Pakistan has been rocky since the latter's founding in 1947, and the Mumbai attack made it far worse—indeed, some argue that the primary purpose of the attack was to foment conflict between the two countries. Pakistan initially denied that the attack could have been planned on its soil, while some in India charged that the Pakistani government masterminded the attack.

Despite a troop build-up on the India-Pakistan border, the evidence indicating Lashkar-e-Taiba's involvement eventually spurred Pakistan to acknowledge the organization's role and arrest several members. Their trial began in October 2009, and as of January 2011 it remains unfinished. While relations have improved, Pakistan has resisted Indian requests that the leader of Lashkar-e-Taiba, Hafiz Muhammed Saeed, be extradited to India for trial, stating that there is not enough evidence linking him to the attack. Nonetheless, Saeed has been repeatedly put under house arrest in Pakistan.

The lone surviving gunman from the Mumbai attack, Kasab, repeatedly confessed his involvement in the attack and then retracted his confessions. In his confessions, he said that the men underwent lengthy training in Pakistan, involving weapons, boat handling, and the use of GPS and other electronic devices. In May 2010, Kasab was convicted and sentenced to death by an Indian court for his role in the attack.

More details regarding the planning of the attack became known in March 2010, when a U.S. citizen named David C. Headley pled guilty to charges of having traveled to Mumbai on behalf of Lashkar-e-Taiba to pick out targets for attack. Headley made five extensive trips to Mumbai from 2006 to mid-2008. He selected the location where the gunmen should land their boats to launch their attack, as well as other details.

While the November 26, 2008, attack actually killed fewer people than Lashkar-e-Taiba's bomb attack on Mumbai two years before, the later attack, stretching as it did over days, generated much greater publicity. The fact that so few men could hold off India's military and law enforcement for so long outraged Indians and generated the impression that the country's government was not able to protect its populace. India's minister for home affairs resigned shortly after the attack as a result.

But while India was not necessarily as prepared as it could have been for such an attack, observers note that any counterterrorism force would have a difficult time combating a well-trained terrorist force that has taken hostages and fortified a position in an easy-to-defend location, such as a building. The years of planning that went into the 2008 Mumbai attack make it less likely that such attacks will become common; however, when they occur, they will likely be very difficult to counter swiftly and without extensive loss of life.

Mary Sisson

See also Asymmetrical Warfare; Lashkar-e-Taiba

Further Readings

Baweja, Harinder, ed. *26/11 Mumbai Attacked*. New Delhi: Roli Books, 2009.

BBC News. "Mumbai Attacks." http://news.bbc.co.uk/2/hi/in_depth/south_asia/2008/mumbai_attacks/default.stm.

Bose, Mrityunjay. *War Zone Mumbai*. New Delhi: Pentagon Press, 2009.

Haqqani, Husain. *Pakistan: Between Mosque and Military*. Washington DC: Carnegie Endowment for International Peace, 2005.

"India Not Satisfied with Progress in Mumbai Trial in Pak: PM." *Times of India,* January 7, 2011. http://timesofindia.indiatimes.com/india/India-not-satisfied-with-progress-in-Mumbai-trial-in-Pak-PM/articleshow/7234911.cms.

Mir, Amir. *True Face of the Jihadis*. Lahore, Pakistan: Mashal Books, 2004.

Polgreen, Lydia, and Souad Mekhennet. "Militant Network Is Intact Long After Mumbai Siege." *The New York Times*, September 30, 2009, p. A1.

Rabasa, Angel, et al. *The Lessons of Mumbai*. Santa Monica, CA: RAND Corporation, 2009.

Riedel, Bruce. "The Mumbai Massacre and Its Implications for America and South Asia." *Journal of International Affairs* 63 (Fall/Winter 2009): 111–126.

Trofimov, Yaroslav, et al. "India Security Faulted as Survivors Tell of Terror." *The Wall Street Journal,* December 1, 2008, p. A1.

MUNICH OLYMPICS MASSACRE

Before the 1972 Munich Olympics, security for major international events was often lax, and terrorism was generally not a major concern among civilians. Much of this changed in 1972, when a group of Palestinian terrorists kidnapped nine Israeli athletes at the Olympic Games in Munich, Germany.

The hostage drama, which resulted in the death of 11 athletes, took place almost entirely under the glare of the media cameras. The world watched, horrified, as terrorism was brought into their homes for the first time. Neither security considerations, media coverage of terrorist incidents, nor the way the Western world views terrorism, has ever been the same since.

The Beginning

At around 5:00 A.M. on September 5, 1972, five terrorists hopped over the six-foot, six-inch fence surrounding the Olympic Village in Munich. Although they were seen by several people, athletes routinely hopped the fence and no one thought it was odd. Once inside, they were met by three more terrorists who had obtained credentials to enter the village.

The terrorists first knocked on the door of the 33-year-old Israeli wrestling coach Moshe Weinberg. Weinberg opened the door, saw the attackers and shouted, "Boys get out!" He and weightlifter Joseph Romano attempted to block the door while other Israeli athletes escaped. The terrorists fired through the door, mortally wounding Weinberg and killing Romano.

The noise of the shots alerted the Olympic Village to news of the attack. Although some Israeli athletes escaped by climbing out windows, the terrorists managed to capture nine more people before armed German police officers sealed off the area. Once the siege began, the terrorists announced that they were members of a Palestinian terrorist organization called Black September. At 9:35 AM the terrorists issued their demands. They set a noon deadline for the release of 200 Arab prisoners being held in Israeli jails, and they demanded safe passage out of Germany. They threatened to begin killing the athletes if their demands were not met.

Negotiations dragged on for hours as the deadline was set back to 1 P.M., then 3 P.M., then 5 P.M., and finally cancelled. During the standoff, a great number of people became involved in the negotiations, including A.D. Tuney, the Egyptian mayor of the Olympic Village. The West German chancellor, Willy Brandt, consulted by phone with Prime Minister Golda Meir of Israel. The Israeli government announced that it would stand by its policy of never dealing with terrorists and would not negotiate. At 9 P.M., Brandt phoned President Anwar

Sadat of Egypt. The Egyptian prime minister, Aziz Sidky, took the call, told Brandt, "We don't want to get involved in this," and hung up.

The Germans decided that the terrorists would kill their hostages if their demands were not met, so the decision was made to allow the terrorists to leave West Germany in exchange for the hostages' release. Meanwhile, Avery Brundage, the president of the International Olympic Committee, decided to allow the Games to continue during the siege. The public could watch the hostage drama unfolding on one TV channel, while athletes competed on another.

The Air Field

Although several plans were proposed, terrorists and police eventually agreed to a plan whereby the terrorists would be flown by helicopter to the military airbase at Furstenfeldbruck, 15 miles away. There they would be met by a Lufthansa 737. The Tunisian government agreed to let a plane carrying the hostages and terrorists fly to Tunisia. Once in Tunisia, the hostages would be let go. West German negotiators would accompany the terrorists to the airfield to ensure their safety. Shortly after 10 P.M., the terrorists and hostages, followed by hundreds of media cameras, emerged from the building and walked to the helicopters. The Israeli hostages were bound, blindfolded and tied close together. The German counterterrorist team had not dealt with such well-trained terrorists before and were not prepared. The German snipers had no radios with which to communicate with each other, and no night-vision goggles to help them see at night. This failure was to lead to disaster.

The German helicopter pilots had been told the police would try to rescue the Israelis once they had landed at the airbase, but after landing the terrorists told the pilots to stand in front of their aircraft, breaking an earlier promise that West Germans would not be involved as hostages. Two terrorists then walked the 170 yards to the plane for an inspection, bringing two hostages with them. As they were returning to the helicopters, German sharpshooters opened fire. In the ensuing firefight, the two terrorists and their hostages were killed. The remaining terrorists leaped from the helicopters, then turned and fired into one helicopter and

tossed a hand grenade into the second, killing all of the hostages. The firefight continued, but with the hostages dead, the police did not hold back and it was all over in a few minutes. In all, 11 athletes, 5 terrorists and 1 policeman were killed. Three of the terrorists were captured.

Despite much criticism, Brundage decided to go ahead with the Games. The remaining 11 members of the Israeli team, however, did not stay for the end of the Games.

The Aftermath

Although the 1972 Olympic Games ended, the story of the Munich massacre continued for another 30 years, and its impact continues today. On October 29, 1972, just over a month after the Games, a Lufthansa jet was hijacked by Palestinian terrorists demanding the release of the three captured Munich terrorists. The Germans capitulated and the terrorists were released.

Prime Minister Golda Meir of Israel then gave instructions for Israeli agents to hunt down and kill all those responsible for the Munich massacre. She told the Israeli Knesset on September 12, "We have no choice but to strike at the terrorist organizations wherever we can reach them. That is our obligation to ourselves and to peace. We shall fulfill that obligation undauntedly." At least eight Palestinian terrorists connected with Munich were assassinated in the following months, including the three released by West Germany.

In 1999, Abu Daoud, a member of the Palestine National Council, admitted in his autobiography, *Palestine: From Jerusalem to Munich*, that he had been responsible for planning the Munich operation. Daoud (whose real name is Mohammed Daoud Machmoud Auda) had earlier admitted that Black September was a cover for Fatah, Yasir Arafat's faction of the Palestine Liberation Organization (PLO). Daoud wrote in his autobiography that he had briefed Arafat before the attack, and Arafat had sent him off on the mission with the words, "Allah protect you." Daoud wrote that he had no regrets over the deaths, but did regret that instead of rousing sympathy for the PLO cause, they caused only revulsion.

Besides Daoud, at least one other PLO terrorist linked to the Munich attack was given a position in the Palestinian Authority (PA)—Amin al Hindi, who headed Arafat's General Intelligence Service. Israel objected in 1995 when Arafat tried to appoint another Munich suspect, Mustafa Liftawi (Abu Firas), as PA police chief in Ramallah.

The families of the victims were initially paid $1 million in compensation by the German government, but they later sued, saying that the German police had bungled the rescue attempt by stationing only five poorly equipped snipers at the airfield. The German government has always denied responsibility for the deaths, arguing that they had done everything they could, and the lawsuit brought by the families was rejected by several German courts, most recently in 1999.

The Munich Olympics marked the end of naivete in planning security for large, international proceedings. Never again would police find themselves so unequipped or have such a lax attitude about security precautions for major events. Watching the events on TV also brought terrorism that much closer to home for many ordinary people, creating, for the first time, an awareness of the price paid for poor planning and inadequate protection.

Lisa Magloff

See also Arafat, Yasir; Black September; Fatah; Palestine Liberation Organization

Further Readings

Daoud, Abu. *Palestine: From Jerusalem to Munich.* Paris: Anne Carriere Editions, 1999.

Klein, Aaron J. *Striking Back: The 1972 Munich Olympics Massacre and Israel's Deadly Response.* New York: Random House, 2005.

Reeve, Simon. *One Day in September: The Full Story of the 1972 Munich Olympics Massacre and the Israeli Revenge Operation "Wrath of God."* New York: Arcade Publishing, 2000.

Serge, Groussard. *The Blood of Israel: The Massacre of the Israeli Athletes, the Olympics, 1972.* New York: William Morrow, 1975.

NARCOTERRORISM

The word *narcoterrorism* was coined in 1983 by Peru's President Belaúnde Terry to describe attacks on the anti-narcotic police in that country. Even as use of the word has spread, experts are arguing about its definition. Some claim that narcoterrorism designates too broad a range of activities to be definitive for a particular form of terrorism. This article will consider narcoterrorism to mean forms of terrorism that are linked to the production of illegal drugs, either through the use of drug profits to fund political violence or the use of violence and terror to protect and preserve illegal drug production.

These two purposes may, of course, overlap. A group using illegal drug profits to fund an armed political campaign will need to preserve the lawlessness and atmosphere of fear necessary for large-scale illegal drug production. Any large drug-trafficking group will also need to influence the political climate of the country where it operates so that the general population fears the traffickers. Terrorism is effective in accomplishing these goals.

Origins of Narcoterrorism

During the tumultuous 1960s, the United States and many other Western countries saw attitudes toward recreational drugs change significantly, and use of illegal drugs increased steadily in the industrialized world. Drug sales are believed to generate $40 billion dollars or more in revenue per year in the United States alone, and this figure does not include profits from money laundering and other services necessary for drug trafficking. Countries that are the source of most illegal drugs are often extremely poor, their governments are often weak, and their civil and social structures are often chaotic. In such conditions, drug traffickers have been able to attain tremendous power and influence.

Political activism and rebellions also increased during the 1960s, with some student and revolutionary movements giving rise to terrorist groups, many of which are still operating today. During the Cold War (1948–1991), terrorist groups, particularly those that advocated communism, often received funds in secret from various state sponsors. During the 1980s, however, state sponsorship of terrorism began to decline, and with the collapse of the Soviet Union and other Communist states in eastern Europe during the early 1990s, this source of funds for terrorists dried up almost completely. In a world dominated by a sole superpower and becoming ever more interconnected via globalization, the international community found cooperation (e.g., passing economic sanctions) against terrorist-sponsoring states easier. In response, terrorist groups turned to other sources of revenue, such as kidnappings, hostage taking, bank robbery, and drug trafficking. Drug trafficking is quite possibly the most profitable and reliable of these revenue sources, and terrorist groups throughout the world engage in it.

The Narcoguerrilla

Narcoterrorism was first recognized in Latin America, and the Revolutionary Armed Forces of Colombia (known by its Spanish acronym, FARC) provides a typical example. Coca, the main ingredient of cocaine, is indigenous to Colombia. As cocaine consumption increased worldwide during the 1970s, coca became a major cash crop for many Colombian peasants, one whose profit margin was vastly superior to every other. This decade also saw the rise of the FARC. The group's goal—to inspire a Marxist revolt among the Colombian peasantry—is political and originated independent of drug trafficking. As with any guerrilla army or rebel group, however, one of the FARC's goals was to drive government armed forces from its areas of operation, and the group had some success in this regard in the remote Colombian countryside.

When the FARC was firmly in control of remote areas and effectively replacing government authority, it began to traffic in drugs. Initially, this may have grown out of its assertion of control: FARC exacts "taxes," or extortion payments, from every landowner or business in the areas it controls. Thus, coca-growing peasants were no different from coffee-growing peasants, and coca traffickers were no different from coffee exporters. The revenues FARC received from drug traffickers and growers were considerably higher than those realized from legal industries, however. The guerrillas quickly moved from taxing the traffickers to offering to protect coca markets, labs, and airstrips from government attack. For the narcoguerrilla, the illegal nature of both the drug trade and the rebellion were complementary; untrammeled by national or international law, guerrillas can openly offer traffickers their services, and traffickers are happy to pay richly for that protection.

Drug profits allowed FARC to expand aggressively throughout the 1980s and 1990s, and the group recruited more troops and equipped them better than their army counterparts. At the same time, its reliance on drug money unmoored it from the causes and grievances that had inspired its formation. As the FARC no longer had to depend on popular support to survive, it quickly lost it. However, the incredible wealth the group realized from its participation in the drug trade (revenues are estimated to be between $300 million and $1 billion yearly) allowed it to continue to attract recruits and expand its territory. By the late 1990s, the group controlled almost 40 percent of Colombia's land area.

The FARC is a premier example of the unique danger of narcoterrorism, as it demonstrates the potential for drug profits to turn a rebellion into a self-perpetuating criminal enterprise. Several attempts at negotiation with the group have failed. Few political concessions can induce a group to lay down its arms once it is no longer reliant on the support of some part of the populace. The FARC's decline during the 2000s resulted from increased pressure by Colombian security forces and a successful defection campaign.

The case of the FARC, while prominent and extreme, is one of many. Colombia's National Liberation Army (ELN) and United Self-Defense Forces (AUC) have exhibited a growing dependence on drug profits, as did the Shining Path in Peru and dozens of smaller groups in Southeast Asia, including the Liberation Tigers of Tamil Eelam in Sri Lanka, which was finally defeated in 1999 after more than 30 years of fighting. The Taliban in Afghanistan also used drug profits as a major source of funds for several years; in the months before its downfall, the regime had banned poppy cultivation in an effort to improve its reputation and secure aid money. Following the Taliban's retreat after the U.S.-led intervention, poppy growing burgeoned. (The Northern Alliance forces, which were allied with the United States, had been even more dependent on drug revenues for funds.) Given the extremely close relations between the Taliban and al Qaeda forces in Afghanistan and Pakistan, drug money is possibly a major source of revenue for al Qaeda as well.

Terrorism as an Outgrowth of Criminal Violence

The second type of narcoterrorism grows out of drug trafficking itself. Just as the vast profits generated by the drug trade tend to transform political rebellions into criminal enterprises, they tend to create criminal empires with evolving political agendas.

Any legal multibillion-dollar industry, particularly one dominated by a few key firms, will attempt to influence political policies that affect the industry. However, legitimate businesses are often restrained by law from exercising certain types of political influence. The illegality of drug trafficking makes bribery necessary, and corruption of the government is inevitable. Drug traffickers may begin by buying the silence of local officials—village mayors, local police, even army lieutenants—in areas of production. As a cartel becomes more influential, it is able to buy the influence of ever more powerful officials, including senators and congressmen, the chief of the national police, and army generals. If an official cannot or will not be corrupted, drug traffickers usually resort to violence against them or their families. Bribery and violence are typical of most organized crime syndicates; however, as they serve merely to enable drug traffickers to operate and not to influence politics, many experts do not classify them as terrorist acts.

If a cartel becomes large enough and powerful enough, its interests may come to be affected by a vast array of political issues not specifically related to drug production. In the late 1980s and early 1990s, the Medellin cartel of Colombia engaged in a series of spectacular political assassinations in an effort to change Colombia's extradition laws. Culminating with the August 1989 murder of Luis Carlos Galan, a popular presidential candidate, the violence of the cartel's campaign and the cartel's demonstration that even the country's highest officials were not safe prompted a series of concessions. Colombia's government amended its extradition laws and offered amnesty to drug dealers who would lay down their arms. The head of the Medellin cartel, Pablo Escobar, negotiated a 1991 surrender that included a specially built prison to house him, a say in the choice of his guards, and various other concessions that, many observers believe, allowed him to run the cartel from inside prison as effectively as he had outside it.

In 2010, Mexico's long-simmering drug war finally received increased attention as violence spilled across the border into the United States. Overall, as many as 30,000 people have died in horrendous violence between competing cartels, terrorist groups such as FARC, and Mexican authorities. In 2007, gas lines in central Mexico were blown up by the group Popular Revolutionary Army (EPR), using explosives believed to have

been stolen by the group several years earlier. The following year, 10 people were killed and at least 100 injured when hand grenades were lobbed into a crowded plaza in the city of Morelia during an Independence Day celebration; several members of the group Los Zetas were arrested for the attack. In July 2010 a car bomb in Ciudad Juárez, which is near El Paso, Texas, targeted Mexican security forces, killing three and wounding nine others. Car bombs had been used in Mexico before, usually by one drug cartel against another; the 2010 attack was startling to many observers because it was believed to be the first such attack on Mexican police.

Despite the Mexican government's insistence that the term *narcoterrorism* does not apply to the current violence in their country, outside observers are not so sure. The argument over whether or not these acts constitute terrorism is not merely semantic: designating groups such as the EPR as terrorists would give law enforcement greater latitude, including enabling them to freeze a groups' financial assets, which can be considerable in some cases.

Combating Narcoterrorism

One problem that confronts security forces when fighting narcoterrorism is its dual nature: Narcoterrorism bridges fundamental divisions between the criminal and the political, and between the domestic and the foreign. Law enforcement agencies combating criminal violence within a country (U.S. examples would be local and state police and the FBI) do not usually share information or conduct investigations in conjunction with agencies that monitor outside threats to a country (military intelligence, the CIA, and the State Department in the United States). This lack of coordination and reluctance to share information leads to inefficiency, hampers the ability to gather and integrate intelligence, and interferes with making arrests.

The terrorist attacks of September 11, 2001, and the continuing "war on terror" led to efforts to remove bureaucratic obstacles in the fight against narcoterrorism. However, narcoterrorism is the product of a marriage of convenience between two larger social problems—the tremendous appetite of Western societies for illegal drugs, and the political grievances of various groups—whose solutions, are very different.

Colleen Sullivan

See also al Qaeda; Economics and Terrorism; FARC; Financing Terrorism; Liberation Tigers of Tamil Eelam; National Liberation Army–Colombia; Shining Path; Taliban; United Self-Defense Forces of Colombia; Zetas, Los

Further Readings

Bowden, Charles. *Murder City: Ciudad Juarez and the Global Economy's New Killing Fields.* New York: Nation Books, 2010.

Davids, Douglas J. *Narco-terrorism: A Unified Strategy to Fight a Growing Terrorist Menace.* Ardsley, NY: Transnational Publishers, 2002.

Dorn, Nicholas, Karim Murji, and Nigel South. *Traffickers: Drug Markets and Law Enforcement.* London and New York: Routledge, 1992.

Ehrenfeld, Rachel. *Narco-terrorism.* New York: Basic Books, 1990.

Grayson, George W. *Narco-violence and a Failed State?* Piscataway, NJ: Transaction Publishers, 2010.

Grillo, Ioan. "Terror Bloodies Mexico Celebrations." *Time,* September 16, 2008. http://www.time.com/time/world/article/0,8599,1841623,00.html.

Jamieson, Alison, ed. *Terrorism and Drug Trafficking in the 1990s.* Aldershot, UK, and Brookfield, VT: Dartmouth, 1994.

McCoy, Alfred W., Cathleen B. Read, and Leonard Palmer Adams. *The Politics of Heroin: CIA Complicity in the Global Drug Trade.* Rev. and exp. ed. New York: Lawrence Hill Books, 1991.

Smith, G. Davidson. *Terrorism and the Rule of Law: Dangerous Compromise in Colombia.* Commentary No. 13. Ottawa: Canadian Security Intelligence Service (CSIS), October 1991. http://www.csis-scrs.gc.ca/pblctns/cmmntr/cm13-eng.asp.

Thompson, Barnard. "The Drug War in Mexico: By Any Other Name It's Terrorism." Mexidata.Info, August 9, 2010. http://www.mexidata.info/id2755.html.

U.S. Department of Justice, Drug Enforcement Administration. "Target America: Traffickers, Terrorists, & Your Kids, a National Symposium on Narco-terrorism, December 4, 2001." Arlington, VA: Drug Enforcement Administration. http://www.targetamerica.org/downloads/symposium_transcript.pdf.

NASRALLAH, SHEIKH HASSAN (1960–)

Sheikh Hassan Nasrallah became general secretary of the Lebanese Shiite Muslim movement Hezbollah in 1992, and he presided over Israel's 2000 withdrawal from southern Lebanon. Nasrallah has been described by some as Hezbollah's most diplomatic leader, and he has guided the organization into a more political role in Lebanon. For example, Hezbollah provides needed social services for Lebanon's Shia population. However, Nasrallah has also supervised the group's violent activities.

The son of a poor vegetable vendor and a descendant of the Prophet Muhammad, Nasrallah fled his home in East Beirut in 1975 at the start of the Lebanese civil war. He later traveled to Iraq to study theology in the holy Shiite city of Najaf. Like many Shiite leaders, Nasrallah left Iraq by a decree of President Saddam Hussein. When he was 21, Nasrallah helped found the militant Lebanese Shiite movement Hezbollah, or "Party of God." During the 1980s, when Hezbollah made headlines by taking a number of Western hostages, Nasrallah served as a commander in Lebanon's Bekaa region.

When the Lebanese civil war ended in the early 1990s, most of the country's militias disarmed; Hezbollah, however, continued to fight Israeli troops occupying southern Lebanon. In 1992, Israeli forces assassinated Nasrallah's predecessor, Abbas Musawi, along with his wife and five-year-old son. Hezbollah members then elected Nasrallah to head the party. Under Nasrallah's leadership, Hezbollah grew into a great political force, holding seats in the Lebanese Parliament and managing schools, hospitals, and various media outlets. In 1997, Nasrallah's 18-year-old son Muhammad Hadi was killed in a fight with Israeli soldiers inside southern Lebanon. After his son's death, Nasrallah told a Beirut crowd that he thanked God for choosing his son to be a martyr.

When the Israeli forces withdrew from southern Lebanon in May 2000, Nasrallah publicly announced that his Hezbollah fighters had won the only Arab victory in the 50-year conflict with Israel. The withdrawal led to a significant increase in the popularity of Hezbollah in general, and of Nasrallah

Hezbollah supporters listen to their leader Sheik Hassan Nasrallah address a speech through a video link to mark the end of Hezbollah's construction arm planting of 1 million trees in the southern suburb of Beirut, Lebanon, on October 9, 2010. (AP Photo/Hussein Malla. © 2011 The Associated Press. All Rights Reserved.)

in particular, among the Shia. However, although Hezbollah has achieved some success as a political party, including winning representation in Lebanon's parliamentary elections, Nasrallah himself has stayed above the fray. The terrorism analyst Walid Phares has described Nasrallah as a "messianic figure, much higher than any official in Lebanon." Nasrallah's position on terrorism in general has proved a bit paradoxical: he has condemned both al Qaeda and the Taliban to Western reporters, but he has also met with leaders of Hamas.

Erica Pearson

See also Hamas; Hezbollah

Further Readings

Dekker, Ted, and Carl Medearis. *Tea with Hezbollah: Sitting at the Enemy's Table*. New York: Doubleday, 2010.

Drake, Laura. *Hegemony and Its Discontents: United States Policy toward Iraq, Iran, Hamas, the Hezbollah and Their Responses*. Annandale, VA: United Association for Studies and Research, 1997.

Fisk, Robert. *Pity the Nation: Lebanon at War*. London: A. Deutsch, 1990.

Jaber, Hala. *Hezbollah: Born with a Vengeance*. New York: Columbia University Press, 1997.

Kaplan, Eben. *Backgrounder Profile: Hassan Nasrallah*. Washington, DC: Council on Foreign Relations. August 11, 2010. http://www.cfr.org/publication/11132/profile.html.

Noe, Nicholas, ed. *The Voice of Hezbollah: The Statements of Sayyed Hassan Nasrallah*. New York: Verso, 2007.

Norton, Augustus Richard. *Hezbollah: A Short History*. Princeton, NJ: Princeton University Press, 2009.

Nasser, Abdelkarim Hussein Mohamed al

On June 21, 2001, Abdelkarim Hussein Mohamed al Nasser (birth date unknown) was indicted in the United States for his role in coordinating the 1996 bombing of the Khobar Towers, a high-rise U.S. military barracks in Dhahran, Saudi Arabia. The FBI lists Nasser as one of its "most wanted terrorists."

The indictment asserts that Nasser, who was born in Al Ihsa, Saudi Arabia, was the head of Saudi Hezbollah in the 1990s. That group is largely made up of young Shiite Muslim men who are loyal to Iran, not the Saudi government. Saudi Hezbollah, also called Hezbollah al Hijaz, is outlawed in Saudi Arabia, forcing Nasser to meet other organization leaders in Lebanon, Syria, or Iran.

Saudi Hezbollah operatives frequently gathered at the Sayeda Zeinab shrine in Damascus, Syria, an important religious site for Shiite Muslims. The site was also a prime recruiting place for Saudi Hezbollah, and its operatives often approached men there on religious pilgrimages.

According to the indictment, Nasser's military operations chief, Ahmad Ibrahim al Mughassil, planned and carried out much of the attack on the Khobar Towers in an attempt to force the U.S. military from Saudi Arabia. Weeks before the attack, Nasser led a meeting at the Sayyeda Zeinab shrine to discuss the final plans for the truck bomb assault. On the evening of June 25, 1996, Mughassil and fellow a Saudi Hezbollah member, Ali Saed bin Ali el Hoorie, drove a truck carrying more than 5,000 pounds of explosives to the Khobar Towers; they parked the truck and quickly drove off in a waiting getaway car. Minutes later, the truck exploded, killing 19 U.S. service members and wounding another 500 people.

Eleven of the 14 men charged with the bombing are in Saudi custody. Saudi Arabia has challenged U.S. jurisdiction because the attack was on Saudi soil and was committed largely by Saudi citizens. The Saudi government has declared that it will not extradite these men.

Three other men indicted in the Khobar case, Ahmed al Mughassil, Ali el Hoorie, and Ibrahim Salih Mohammed al Yacoub are also on the FBI's most wanted list. The U.S. State Department is offering an award of up to $5 million for information leading directly to the arrest or indictment of Abdelkarim al Nasser.

Erica Pearson

See also Hezbollah; Hoorie, Ali Saed bin Ali el; Mughassil, Ahmad Ibrahim al; Yacoub, Ibrahim Salih Mohammed al

Further Readings

Jamieson, Perry D. *Khobar Towers: Tragedy and Response*. Washington, DC: Air Force History and Museums Program, 2008.

"A Nation Challenged: The Hunted; The 22 Most Wanted Suspects, in a Five-act Drama of Global Terror." *The New York Times,* October 14, 2001, p. 1B.

Strobl, Staci, and Jon R. Lindsay. "Lost in Transition: Khobar Towers and the Ambiguities of Terrorism in the 1990s." In *A New Understanding of Terrorism: Case Studies, Trajectories and Lessons Learned,* edited by M.R. Haberfeld and Agostino von Hassell. New York: Springer, 2009.

U.S. District Court for the Eastern District of Virginia, Alexandria Division. *United States v. Ahmed al-Mughassil, et al.* Indictment, June 21, 2001 (Khobar Indictment). http://fl1.findlaw.com/news.findlaw.com/cnn/docs/khobar/khobarindict61901.pdf.

Walsh, Elsa. "Louis Freeh's Last Case." *The New Yorker,* May 14, 2001.

NATIONAL LIBERATION ARMY– BOLIVIA

The National Liberation Army–Bolivia (ELN) was a Communist terrorist group that is now believed to be defunct.

Bolivia, bordering on Brazil, Peru, Chile, Argentina, and Paraguay, occupies a central place in Latin American history. The country has experienced more than 200 coups in its 157 years as a nation. Because of its strategic location and chronic political instability, the Marxist revolutionary Che Guevara chose Bolivia in 1966 as the place to attempt to repeat the successes of the Cuban revolution.

Guevara's *foquista* revolutionary theory held— and his experiences in Cuba taught him—that a mobile band of hardened guerrillas operating in the countryside could become the *foco,* or focal point, of peasant opposition to the government. Guevara arrived in Bolivia in March 1966 with a group of about 20 Cubans and established a camp in the southern jungle, naming his new group the National Liberation Army. (A different National Liberation Army was founded in 1964 in Colombia, where it is still operative.) Guevara hoped that a successful Communist revolution in Bolivia would ignite continent-wide wars of liberation.

Guevara's group was joined by about 20 Bolivian Communists, but the Bolivian Communist Party favored open political efforts over armed struggle and refused to back his group. In addition, the largely Cuban forces seem to have frightened the local peasants rather than inspiring them to rebellion. Within weeks, Guevara's camp was discovered by the Bolivian armed forces, and the revolutionaries were forced to go on the run. Guevara's health and that of his men declined rapidly in the jungle. After months of hardship, during which the force was split in two and suffered many casualties, Guevara and the remnants of the ELN were captured and executed by the Bolivian armed forces in October 1967.

A few of the group's members escaped the final military ambush, and for the next several years strived to reestablish the ELN; Nestor Paz Zamora, brother of future Bolivian president Jaime Paz Zamora, was killed fighting for the ELN during this period. By the early 1970s, however, the group had been effectively crushed by the Bolivian military.

In the late 1980s, a group calling itself the Nestor Paz Zamora Commission and claiming to be a wing of the ELN, carried out several attacks in Bolivia. These attacks included the 1990 kidnapping and murder of Jorge Lonsdale, president of Coca-Cola's Bolivian division, and an October 1990 attack on a U.S. Marines residence in Bolivia's capital, in which a Bolivian police officer was killed. This reincarnation of the ELN ceased operating sometime in the 1990s.

Colleen Sullivan

See also Guevara, Ernesto (Che); National Liberation Army–Colombia

Further Readings

Anderson, Jon Lee. *Che Guevara: A Revolutionary Life.* New York: Grove Press, 1997.
"Kidnapped Executive Slain by Bolivia Rebels." *The New York Times*, December 6, 1990, p. A12.

National Consortium for the Study of Terrorism and Responses to Terrorism. "Terrorist Organization Profile: National Liberation Army (Bolivia)." http://www.start.umd.edu/start/data_collections/tops/terrorist_organization_profile.asp?id=237.

NATIONAL LIBERATION ARMY–COLOMBIA

Founded in 1965, the National Liberation Army–Colombia (Ejército de Liberación Nacional, or ELN) is a Marxist terrorist group that has conducted a guerrilla war of almost 40 years against the Colombian government.

The founders of the ELN were student activists inspired by the success of the 1959 Cuban Revolution. Most important among them was Fabio Vasquez, the founder of the MOEC, a students, workers, and peasants union. Many MOEC members would become ELN members. Most of the ELN's first leaders received military training in Cuba in the early 1960s; returning to Colombia, they attempted to apply Fidel Castro and Che Guevara's *foquista* tactics to Colombia.

The ELN first attacked on January 7, 1965, when 27 ELN guerrillas held the town of Simacota for two hours. The organization remained obscure until November 1965, when Camilo Torres, a former priest well known in Colombia for his political activism, joined the organization. Despite Torres's death in action the following February, he attracted many other recruits. In 1973 the organization suffered a major setback, when a carefully planned army operation, code-named Operation Anori, succeeded in killing several hundred ELN fighters and nearly wiping out the group. After a 1978 defection resulted in the arrest of the majority of the organization's leaders, many thought the ELN was finished.

The dedication of the organization's grassroots workers had been underestimated, however. At first the ELN had ignored political work in favor of military action; after the losses of the 1970s, however, low-level organizers working independently in several areas chose to continue their efforts to gain political support among the peasants and urban poor. As the Colombian regime of the time was particularly repressive and economic conditions were bad, they soon found support. By 1983 the ELN had regrouped and had enough recruits to once again begin guerrilla operations. The new leadership was organized as a national council of nine members led by another former priest, Manuel Perez.

Between 1984 and 1986, the ELN enjoyed a brief truce with the Colombian government, but bad faith on both sides stalled negotiations. After breaking the truce, the ELN began a new strategy— focusing its attacks on the Colombian oil industry, one of the country's top revenue generators. Over the next several years, the group attacked the country's oil pipelines thousands of times; the damage cost hundreds of millions of dollars and forced the government to deploy a significant percentage of its armed forces to protect the pipes. The ELN also engaged in kidnapping for ransom; early targets were oil executives, but as kidnapping has been adopted by other guerrilla groups and ordinary criminals, almost anyone is now at risk. Colombia has the world's highest kidnapping rate.

The ELN is believed to receive millions of dollars in extortion payments from oil companies to protect their pipelines and ransom their executives. Unlike the Revolutionary Armed Forces of Colombia (FARC), Colombia's larger guerrilla organization, the ELN's leadership has generally not engaged in drug trafficking. This abstention coupled with the extremely strict discipline imposed by the ELN may be what has prevented it from expanding as much as the FARC did. Nevertheless, ELN grew from a few hundred members in the early 1980s to over 6,000 in 2003.

At the turn of the 20th century, the ELN withstood a number of challenges to its power. In 1998, to facilitate peace negotiations, Colombia's president, Andreas Pastrana, withdrew government forces from a FARC-controlled area covering about 40 percent of the country. Pastrana hoped that successful negotiations with FARC would force ELN to fall into line. Instead, ELN demanded a similar autonomous area, engaging in a series of spectacular kidnappings in 1999 to demonstrate its power. In the fall of 2000, the government moved to grant such an area, but before the government forces could withdraw, ELN found itself faced with a new threat—the United Self-Defense League of Colombia (AUC), a right-wing paramilitary organization that opposed any negotiations with the guerrillas and that believed it could defeat the ELN militarily. By April 2001, a string of AUC victories left ELN scrambling to regain control of its territory. Peace negotiations between FARC and the government broke down, and the government resumed military operations against the guerrillas. In 2002, the Bush administration asked Congress to increase the U.S. military aid package to Colombia to help that country combat the guerrillas.

Meanwhile, talks between the ELN and the Colombian government continued sporadically, with representatives from first Mexico, then Cuba, and then Norway, Spain, and Switzerland acting as mediators at various points. However, ELN kidnappings continued, and by 2007 the talks had broken down yet again. In 2008, ELN leader Carlos Marin Guarin (a.k.a. "Pablo" or "Pablito") was captured in January 2008, and a weakened ELN reportedly sought to partner with the FARC later that year. However, in October 2009, Guarin escaped from prison and returned to lead the group. Shortly after Guarin's escape, 10 members of a Colombian football (soccer) team were kidnapped, probably by the ELN; they were found, dead of multiple gunshot wounds, two weeks later in Venezuela.

By 2010 the Colombian government had made significant inroads against rebels, with many FARC leaders killed or arrested. The ELN was estimated to have 1,500 members or less as of 2010, and some in Colombia believe them to no longer to be a threat. However, in their analysis of ELN, the International Crisis Group warned that the group has come to the brink of extinction before and yet still managed to reconstitute itself.

Colleen Sullivan

See also FARC; Guevara, Ernesto (Che); United Self-Defense Forces of Colombia

Further Readings

Bouvier, Virginia M. *Colombia: Building Peace in a Time of War*. Washington, DC: United States Institute of Peace, 2009.

Bruce, Victoria, and Karin Hayes. *Hostage Nation: Colombia's Guerrilla Army and the Failed War on Drugs*. New York: Alfred A. Knopf, 2010.

Hanson, Stephanie. *Backgrounder: FARC, ELN: Colombia's Left-wing Guerrillas.* Washington, DC: Council on Foreign Relations. August 19, 2009. http://www.cfr.org/publication/9272/farc_eln.html.

Hrsistov, Jasmin. *Blood and Capital: The Paramilitarization of Colombia.* Athens: Ohio University Press, 2009.

Kline, Harvey F. *Democracy under Assault.* New York: Westview Press, 1995.

Kline, Harvey F. *State Building and Conflict Resolution in Colombia, 1986–94.* Tuscaloosa: University of Alabama Press, 1999.

McDermott, Jeremy. "Rebel Leader's Daring Escape Is Blow to Colombia's Government." *The Scotsman.* October 26, 2009. http://news.scotsman.com/world/Rebel-leader39s-daring-escape-is.5764841.jp.

Safford, Frank, and Marco Palacios. *Colombia: Fragmented Land, Divided Society.* New York: Oxford University Press, 2002.

Wilson, Scott. "Colombian Right's 'Cleaning' Campaign; Takeover in Major City Illustrates Political Side of Drug War." *The Washington Post*, April 17, 2001, p. A1.

NATIONAL LIBERATION FRONT OF CORSICA

The National Liberation Front of Corsica (Front de Libération Nationale de la Corse, or FLNC) is the largest and most violent of the Corsican nationalist movements. Formed in 1976 from two smaller groups seeking self-government for Corsica through force, the FLNC has engaged in more than 20 years of violence. The group has been responsible for thousands of bomb attacks on property of non-Corsican settlers, police stations, government offices (in both Corsica and France), and other symbolic targets of the "colonial state" in Corsica. Successive French governments have denied Corsica any distinctive regional autonomy, never recognized inhabitants of Corsica as a distinct nationality, and never given official status to the Corsican language. As a result, the FLNC claims to be fighting French "internal colonialism."

Corsica has always expressed discontent with French rule, even before its annexation in 1769. Although the Paris-based government provides funds for public services and infrastructure, a wide economic gap between the island and the mainland still remains. This, coupled with the settling of non-Corsicans on the island, has continued to fuel Corsican nationalism.

During the 1980s the FLNC split into two groups: the Canal Historique (Historical Faction) and the Canal Habituel (Usual Faction). A series of new, smaller divisions formed, and a number of other terrorist organizations followed, most of which lasted only a few years. The FLNC-Canal Historique and the FLNC-Canal Habituel thus remained the most important terrorist organizations; the latter, however, ended activities in 1997.

In the 1990s the FLNC became more violent. Dozens of people were killed, including mayors, policemen, and other state workers. The violence culminated in the 1998 assassination of Prefect Claude Erignac, the highest representative of the French Republic on the island. The assassination was highly publicized and criticized so strongly that the FLNC publicly denied—and abjured—the attack.

In 1999, the FLNC-Canal Historique merged with some of the other underground organizations, taking the name "FLNC" again. With an estimated 600 members (organized horizontally into independent cells), the FLNC remains most active in Corsica, only occasionally bombing a building in mainland France. Although it has carried out 200 to 800 bombings a year, the FLNC has caused few deaths. The group funds itself through armed robberies of banks and extortion of what it refers to as "revolutionary taxes." Most Corsicans wish to protect Corsican identity and stimulate peaceful economic growth; only a small minority supports the radical autonomists, but the "see nothing, say nothing" attitude is generally accepted.

Despite the frequent bombings, the FLNC is considered relatively unthreatening. Thus, the French government has had little incentive to come to the bargaining table. In the early 2000s, however, the French government took a more conciliatory approach, providing new aid for infrastructure development and for the teaching of the Corsican language in primary schools.

In 2003, Corsicans voted in a referendum on whether to merge the island's three governmental councils into a single assembly. The measure, which was designed to give Corsica a more unified and autonomous government, was regarded as insufficient by militants and was narrowly defeated in July. Two days before the vote, police arrested Yvan Colonna, the suspected gunman in the Erignac assassination, who was eventually sentenced to life in prison.

Shorty after the referendum and arrest, the FLNC announced that it would no longer abide by a cease-fire that had been established in January. The announcement was followed by a series of bomb attacks in Corsica and southern France, including one in Nice that injured 16 people. The FLNC announced another cease-fire in November 2003; this held until the spring of 2005 and the arrest of Charles Pieri, who is believed to be the group's commander, on charges of racketeering and financing terrorism. Pieri was sentenced to ten years in prison in May 2005. Despite Pieri's imprisonment, the FLNC has continued to carry out bombings in Corsica, in particular targeting vacation homes owned by wealthy non-Coriscans.

Richard McHugh

Further Readings

Chrisafis, Angelique. "Island Attacks: Corsican Separatists' Violent Protest at Rising House Prices." *The Guardian,* August 28, 2006, p. 20.

Savigear, Peter. *Corsica: Regional Autonomy or Violence?* London: Institute for the Study of Conflict, 1983.

Sciolino, Elaine. "In Blow to Paris, Corsica Rejects French Restructuring Plans." *The New York Times,* July 7, 2003, p. A4.

U.S. State Department, Office of the Coordinator for Counterterrorism. *Patterns of Global Terrorism 1997: Europe and Eurasia Overview.* http://www.fas.org/irp/threat/terror_97/eurasia.html.

Webster, Paul. "Corsicans Divided After Paris Offers Separatists a Crumb of Independence: France Is Offering More Autonomy but Will It Advance or Retard Self-rule?" *The Guardian,* July 4, 2003, p. 18.

NATIONAL SECURITY AGENCY

The National Security Agency (NSA) was established by a secret memorandum, National Security Council Intelligence Directive (NSCID) No. 9, signed by President Harry S. Truman on October 24, 1952. A separate and extremely secretive agency within the Department of Defense, headquartered at Fort George G. Meade, Maryland, the NSA is a cryptologic organization, arguably the world's best at making and breaking codes and ciphers, as well as one of the leading centers of foreign-language analysis within the U.S. government. Neither the number of employees nor the agency's budget can be publicly disclosed, but some analysts estimate that its yearly budget is as high as $10 billion. NSA does not disclose sources or methods of intelligence and never comments on media speculations about actual or possible intelligence issues. Many Washingtonians jokingly claim that "NSA" stands for "No Such Agency."

The NSA works closely with the Central Security Service (CSS), the umbrella organization for the codemaking and codebreaking units of the U.S. Army, Navy, Air Force, Marine Corps, and Coast Guard. The CSS was established by presidential directive in 1972, and the NSA director is also the chief of the CSS. NSA staff and CSS personnel work closely together in facilities around the world to maintain a smooth, integrated information flow to relevant policymakers.

The NSA's civilian and military employees include physicists, engineers, mathematicians, analysts, computer scientists, and linguists. They are charged with two sensitive activities within the U.S. intelligence community: signals intelligence (SIGINT), or gathering information that foreign adversaries prefer to remain confidential, and information assurance, or protecting U.S. information from interception or tampering. The SIGINT and information assurance missions combine to facilitate Network Warfare, a military function. The NSA uses bomber planes, sea vessels, submarines, and satellites to gather information, operating a global network of ground stations to intercept diplomatic, military, scientific, and commercial satellite communications.

Signals Intelligence

SIGINT is collected from many sources, such as communications, radar, and other electronic systems. SIGINT protocols are used to encrypt U.S. transmissions and decode intercepted enemy communications. The data are used to protect troops and assist allies, as well as for counterintelligence, including the detection of espionage, sabotage, terrorism, and related hostile activities of foreign powers. NSA supplies SIGINT to the White House, U.S. military commands, government officials, allies, and government contractors.

The United States has a long history of successfully using SIGINT. Both sides used SIGINT in the Civil War, and SIGNIT-captured information played a critical role in the U.S. decision to participate in World War I. During World War II, the Marine Corps and Army used Native Americans to create a code based on the Navajo language. Neither Germany nor Japan were able to decipher transmissions by the Navajo "code talkers." One of the most successful NSA operations was the VENONA Project, which collected and decrypted Soviet KGB and GRU messages during the 1940s. This project provided extraordinary insight into Soviet attempts to infiltrate the highest levels of the U.S. government. During the Cuban Missile Crisis in 1962, SIGINT provided the only in-depth information about the Cuban military build-up to senior policymakers and military officials. The NSA had Osama bin Laden's electronic communications under constant surveillance starting in 1995.

Revelations in the 1970s about the NSA interception of the communications of political activists (operations SHAMROCK and MINARET) led to new rules for U.S. intelligence agencies. Foreign surveillance operations are regulated by the Foreign Intelligence Surveillance Act (FISA) of 1978, and by Executive Order 12333 (1981), with full consideration for the privacy rights of U.S. citizens.

After the September 11, 2001, attacks on the World Trade Center and the Pentagon, the intelligence community was criticized for security failures. The NSA admitted that its electronic intelligence and cryptologic tools picked up massive amounts of information, but that little human intelligence (HUMINT) had been deployed to translate intercepted communications and provide insight into the social and cultural context of the terrorists. Since 9/11, SIGINT has often discovered suspicious "chatter" (talk, text, and electronic postings) that led to heightened security levels. In February 2010, for example, the Department of Homeland Security reported intercepted messages from al Qaeda sources concerning ways to bypass airport security scanners. Similar chatter led to the discovery of suspicious packages from Yemen aboard UPS and FedEx cargo airplanes in October 2010.

On December 16, 2005, *The New York Times* revealed that President George W. Bush had allowed the NSA to eavesdrop on communications within the United States. Until then, the FBI had been responsible for domestic surveillance. Bush had also exempted the NSA from first obtaining warrants from the Foreign Intelligence Surveillance Court (FISC), as required for the FBI. Critics saw the new form of wiretapping as unconstitutional, as it violated the constitutional right to privacy by allowing unlawful searches. The White House defended its stance on national security grounds, but in January 2007, executive-branch officials agreed to process electronic eavesdropping requests through the FISC. The NSA also amended its mission statement in hopes of allaying concerns about domestic spying practices: "Through carrying out its mission, NSA/CSS helps save lives, defend vital networks, and advance our Nation's goals and alliances, while strictly protecting privacy rights guaranteed by the U.S. Constitution and laws."

In the post–Cold War era, the United States has become highly dependent on networked information systems to conduct essential activities, including military operations and government business. As a result, the notion of "information assurance" has come to the fore, and the NSA has concentrated its resources in areas such as network security, vulnerability analysis, data and fiber optic communications, and biometrics in an effort to protect national communications, transportation and transportation infrastructures, and financial transactions from disruption by a physical or electronic attack.

In December 2010 the NSA announced a major shift in its operating principles. Instead of working to keep hostile forces away from sensitive U.S. data, the NSA would now assume that its security at some point will be breached and pursue ways to minimize the damage. Debora Plunkett, head of the NSA Information Assurance Directorate, explained,

There's no such thing as "secure" any more. The most sophisticated adversaries are going to go unnoticed on our networks. We have to build our systems on the assumption that adversaries will get in. We have to, again, assume that all the components of our system are not safe, and make sure we're adjusting accordingly.

Some analysts speculated that the reorientation was at least partly influenced by the massive amounts of confidential information made public by the website WikiLeaks.

As the Internet and social media become more and more pervasive, the NSA will face increasing challenges to safeguard U.S. information and collect foreign information that will strengthen U.S. national security. Officials recognize this increasing vulnerability and have responded by creating cybersecurity divisions within the National Security Council and other security agencies.

Maria Kiriakova

See also bin Laden, Osama; Central Intelligence Agency; Counterterrorism; Federal Bureau of Investigation; Foreign Intelligence Surveillance Act; Homeland Security; September 11 Attacks

Further Readings

Aid, Matthew. *The Secret Sentry: The Untold History of the National Security Agency.* New York: Bloomsbury, 2010.

Bamford, James. *Body of Secrets: Anatomy of the Ultra-Secret National Security Agency: From the Cold War through the Dawn of a New Century.* New York: Random House, 2001.

Black, Tricia E. "Taking Account of the World as It Will Be: The Shifting Course of U.S. Encryption Policy." *Federal Communications Law Journal* 53, no. 2 (March 2001): 289–314.

Durrett, Deanne. *Unsung Heroes of World War II: The Story of the Navajo Code Talkers.* Lincoln, NE: Bison Press, 2009.

Federation of American Scientists. "National Security Agency." http://www.fas.org/irp/nsa.

Hallett, Nicole. "Protecting National Security or Covering Up Malfeasance: The Modern State Secrets Privilege and Its Alternatives." *Yale Law Journal* 117, no. 82 (2007). http://www.yalelawjournal.org/the-yale-law-journal-pocket-part/constitutional-law/protecting-national-security-or-covering-up-malfeasance:-the-modern-state-secrets-privilege-and-its-alternatives.

Keefe, Patrick Radden. *Chatter: Dispatches from the Secret World of Global Eavesdropping.* New York: Random House, 2005.

Risen, James and Eric Lichtblau. "E-mail Surveillance Renews Concerns in Congress." *The New York Times,* June 17, 2009.

NATIONAL SECURITY COUNCIL

After World War II, the United States emerged as the leading Western power. To meet the administrative demands of this new role, President Harry Truman approved a massive reorganization of the U.S. security system. The Security Act of 1947 (PL 235-61 Stat. 496; U.S.C. 402) created the Department of Defense, the U.S. Air Force, the Central Intelligence Agency, and the National Security Council. The NSC is an advisory body to the president on national security and foreign policy matters, and it coordinates such policies among the branches of the government involved in domestic, foreign, and military policies relating to national security. The critical task of the NSC is to coordinate the policy process so that all agencies get a full and fair hearing, enabling the president to make clear foreign policy decisions in a timely manner.

Every president has used the NSC to install a system of national security policymaking and coordination that reflects his personal management style and that responds to prevailing political pressures, congressional demands, and bureaucratic rivalries. Statutory members of the NSC include the president, the vice president, the secretary of state, the secretary of defense, and the chairman of the Joint Chiefs of Staff. The heads of other executive departments and agencies, new positions such as secretary of homeland security and director of national intelligence, as well as other senior officials, are invited to attend meetings of the NSC when appropriate. The NSC professional staff includes other members of the military, foreign policymakers, and research institutions and has vacillated between 36 and 200 members. President George W. Bush's first national security advisor, Condoleezza Rice, reduced her staff to about one-third of that of her predecessor. Working groups or subcommittees are usually established to deal with new security threats or specific parts of the globe. Each incoming president also reorganizes the NSC in line with his foreign policy goals.

The national security adviser is not a statutory member of the NSC, but typically participates in meetings. The position of the assistant to the president for national security affairs (the formal title of the national security adviser) was created under President Eisenhower in 1953 and has changed from being a clearance coordinator across departments to being the president's personal confidant and spokesperson. He or she funnels security-related information from the Department of State, Department of Defense, CIA, and other agencies to the president. The adviser is appointed by the president and does not need congressional approval. Most of those who have held this position have been either academics or military officers. Two of the most prominent national security advisers—Henry Kissinger and Zbigniew Brzezinski—were foreign-born. Rice, a professor at Stanford University, was the first woman appointed to this post.

The NSC traditionally has had to coordinate terrorism and counterterrorism responsibilities spread across a range of departments. The FBI played the "lead agency" role in responding to domestic terrorists, the Federal Emergency Management Agency (FEMA) handled disaster recovery efforts, and the Pentagon focused on military solutions, while the State Department had responsibility for attacks against U.S. citizens or facilities abroad. Foreign terrorist groups and events were views as regional problems. Irish terrorism was handled by the British desk at the State Department, for example, while Palestinian groups were assigned to the Middle East division.

With the spread of terrorist attacks on American diplomats, tourists, and airliners, and especially after the massacre of Israeli athletes at the Munich Olympic Games in 1972, the White House started to build a more comprehensive and coordinated approach. The Working Group on Terrorism (WGT), a subcommittee of the NSC, was created to provide the United States with a more efficient governmental structure for coordinating and implementing anti- and counterterrorism policies among more than 30 federal agencies, departments, and offices.

WGT agency members were guided by three major goals: containment of terrorism while minimizing open conflict with foreign states, avoiding the loss of American lives, and defeat of terrorism. The use of military force as the means of active defense against terrorism was promulgated in the National Security Decision Directive (NSDD) 138, signed by President Reagan in 1984. NSDD 138 also redirected the focus of American foreign policy into a more systematic and stronger effort to combat international terrorism.

The shape of the WGT has evolved in response to events. Through different administrations it has been renamed, redivided, and reconstituted under a variety of names, including the WGT, the Interdepartmental Group on Terrorism (IGT), the Executive Committee on Terrorism (ECT), the Special Coordination Committee (SCC), and the Special Situation Group (SSG).

In the wake of the bombings of the World Trade Center in 1993, it became apparent that international terrorism had spread to American soil. In May 1998, President Bill Clinton issued Presidential Decision Directive (PDD) 62 on combating terrorism and responding to attacks involving the use of the unconventional means (weapons of mass destruction or advanced computer technology). PDD 62 established the Office of the National Coordinator for Security, Infrastructure Protection and Counter-Terrorism within the NSC to oversee a broad variety of relevant policies and programs covering such topics as counterterrorism, protection of critical infrastructure, and preparedness and consequence management for weapons of mass destruction.

Richard A. Clarke led the NSC Counterterrorism Security Group for much of the 1990s. He was appointed to the CSG in 1992 by President George H.W. Bush, and then named National Coordinator for Security, Infrastructure Protection and Counter-Terrorism by President Clinton in 1998. He initially served President George W. Bush as a "counterterrorism czar" until 2002, when Bush named him the first head of an NSC committee on cybersecurity. Clarke has been a vocal critic of President George W. Bush, insisting that the president ignored warnings about al Qaeda and did not even request a briefing on that organization until a few days before the 9/11 attacks.

After 9/11, President Bush reconstituted the NSC and formed various Policy Coordination Committees (NSC/PCC), including the Committees on Counter-Terrorism and National Preparedness; on Proliferation, Counterproliferation, and Homeland Defense; on Intelligence and Counterintelligence; and on Records Access and Information Security. The Homeland Defense Council, established in October 2001, later formed the core of the new Department of Homeland Security, established in 2002.

After his inauguration in 2009, President Barack Obama appointed Major-General James L. Jones

President Barack Obama holds a strategy review on Afghanistan in the Situation Room of the White House, September 30, 2009. (Official White House Photo by Pete Souza)

as his first national security advisor. Under Obama, the NSC was intended to play a significant role in domestic as well as international issues, and the Homeland Security Council and NSC staffs merged. Experts hope that departmental boundaries can be harmonized so that various interests and foreign partners are grouped similarly in every agency. To bring greater order to the decision-making process, Interagency Policy Committees managed the creation and implementation of national security policies across multiple agencies. Obama has expanded the membership of the NSC, including Cabinet secretaries, and has added new issues to the NSC's areas of concern, such as pandemics.

Maria Kiriakova

See also Central Intelligence Agency; Counterterrorism; Federal Bureau of Investigation; Homeland Security

Further Readings

Brzezinski, Zbigniew K. *Power and Principle: Memoirs of the National Security Adviser, 1977–1981.* New York: Farrar, Straus and Giroux, 1983.
Brzezinski, Zbigniew K. *In Quest of National Security.* Boulder, CO: Westview Press, 1988.
Clarke, Richard A. *Against All Enemies.* New York: Free Press, 2004.
Inderfurth, Karl F., and Loch K. Johnson, eds. *Fateful Decisions: Inside the National Security Council.* New York: Oxford University Press, 2004.
Jenkins, Brian M. "Defense against Terrorism." *Political Science Quarterly* 101, no. 5 (1986): 773–786.
Lord, Carnes. *The Presidency and the Management of National Security.* New York: Free Press, 1988.
Prados, John. *Keepers of the Keys: A History of the National Security Council from Truman to Bush.* New York: William Morrow, 1991.
Rothkopf, David J. *Running the World: The Inside Story of the National Security Council and the Architects of American Power.* New York: Public Affairs, 2005.
Sarkesian, Sam C. *U.S. National Security: Policymakers, Processes, and Politics.* London: Lynne Rienner, 1989.
U.S. Department of State, Bureau of Public Affairs, Office of the Historian. *History of the National Security Council, 1947–1997.* August 1997. http://clinton2.nara.gov/WH/EOP/NSC/html/History.html.

NEW PEOPLE'S ARMY

The New People's Army (NPA) is the Maoist-inspired, armed wing of the Communist Party of the Philippines; it has been fighting a guerrilla war against the Philippine government since 1968.

Communism has been well established in the Philippines since the Huk Rebellion in the early 1950s. By the mid-1960s, however, Philippine Communism was in decline. Following the election of Ferdinand Marcos as president in 1965, a group of young Communists, many of them former student radicals, broke away from the old Philippine Communist Party to form the Communist Party of the Philippines (CPP) in 1968. The CPP at once began to recruit and organize clandestinely, and it founded the NPA in the same year. Members of NPA believe in a Maoist "people's war" strategy, in which the revolution is led by rural peasantry, with "liberated zones" controlled by the guerrillas established in the countryside until major cities are encircled by besieging guerrilla forces. The guerrilla siege cuts off supplies and prompts collapse and surrender.

The CPP laid extensive groundwork for the movement, giving the NPA a strong and resilient base of support that served it well in later years. For instance, rather than recruit directly into the NPA (or the party itself), citizen militias would first be set up in sympathetic villages. The cream of the militia corps would then be selected for recruitment into the NPA, and only after a number of neighboring villages had established such militias would they be selected to field a NPA Fighting Front, which might include several dozen guerrillas, although sizes varied widely. A local Fighting Front was, in turn, under the control of its district command, of which there were several on each island.

In 1972, partly in response to the NPA threat and partly in response to the threat of the Moro National Liberation Front (MNLF), President Marcos declared martial law across the country and began to greatly increase the size of the armed forces, which more than doubled in numbers. The crackdown, combined with an economy that worsened throughout the decade (compounded by the massive corruption of the Marcos regime) worked to increase support for the guerrillas. By the mid-1980s, the NPA had an estimated 26,000 members active throughout the country, in particular on the island of Luzon, the country's largest and home to the capital, Manila.

The NPA, however, was unsuccessful in establishing true "liberated zones" in its areas of operation,

and the army was still able to move freely about the country. Frustrated with its inability to achieve strategic parity with the army, the NPA began to use other strategies, one of which was the establishment of an urban terror division called the Alex Boncayao Brigade in the early 1980s. Its leadership also began to break into factions. The NPA's internal problems, in part, prevented it from being a major player in the 1986 Philippines rebellion that replaced Marcos with Corazon Aquino.

Aquino began peace talks with the guerrillas, in the hope that the prospect of an amnesty would undermine their support, and a two-month cease-fire was declared in December 1986. Hard-liners within the NPA used the cease-fire as an opportunity to eliminate their political rivals and consolidate their support; war resumed more fiercely than ever the following year. The injustice and corruption of the Marcos regime had been a major factor in attracting recruits to the NPA; when the guerrillas saw their party resisting the democratic Aquino with the same fervor, many of them abandoned it. Between 1986 and 1995, NPA membership dropped from about 26,000 to about 6,000, and the Philippine army began to gain ground.

While it seems clear that the NPA no longer poses a significant threat to Philippine democracy, the army has been unable to eliminate the NPA, nor has a lasting cease-fire been negotiated. In the early 2000s, the NPA staged something of a comeback, increasing membership, stepping up assassinations of government officials, and eventually becoming listed as a terrorist organization by both the United States and the European Union. By 2006 the Philippine army was suffering more casualties in its fight against the NPA than the organization itself.

In response, President Gloria Macapagal Arroyo stepped up funding for the fight against the NPA, pledging to defeat the organization by the end of her term in 2010. The effort has seen some results, and by mid-2009 the NPA's membership was believed to be fewer than 5,000. Whether or not it could be eliminated completely remained to be seen.

Colleen Sullivan

See also Alex Boncayao Brigade; Moro Islamic Liberation Front

Further Readings

Chapman, William. *Inside the Philippine Revolution: The New People's Army and Its Struggle for Power.* New York: Norton, 1987.

Marks, Thomas A. *Maoist Insurgency since Vietnam.* London: Cass, 1996.

"More AFP Men Killed Than NPA Guerrillas." *Filipino Reporter* 34, no. 30 (July 7–July 13, 2006): 24.

"PGMA, DND Chief Cite AFP for Its Accomplishments vs NPA." *Filipino Express* 23, no. 23 (June 5–June 11, 2009): 25.

Tan, Abby. "Manila Focuses on Rising Foe: Communist Guerrillas." *Christian Science Monitor,* September 5, 2002, p. 7.

New Terrorism, The

One of the biggest challenges facing international counterterrorism professionals is the ever-evolving typology of terrorism. While nationalist and anticolonial movements characterized twentieth-century terrorism, the terrorism of the twenty-first century is significantly different in nature. Modern-day terrorism, typified by the al Qaeda network, has truly distinguished itself from its predecessors. A loose cell-based organizational structure, a religious motivation, and asymmetrical tactics are just some of the characterizations of this new terrorism.

Late-twentieth-century terrorism was primarily shaped by nationalist and anticolonial movements. From the Front de Libération du Québec, a Quebecois separatist group, and the Euskadi Ta Askatasuna (Basque Fatherland and Liberty, or ETA), to the Front de Libération Nationale, a socialist anticolonial party in Algeria, and the Irish Republican Army, these groups typify the old hierarchical, top-down terrorism, whose activities were primarily directed at government forces. While the terrorist groups of the twenty-first century have adopted some of the characteristics of their predecessors, they have also evolved into an even more menacing threat—that of an amorphous, indistinct, and broad movement. While it is not the only terrorist group operating today, al Qaeda is perhaps the best personification of the evolution of the terrorist threat to where it currently stands.

Prior to the attacks of September 11, 2001, al Qaeda represented a unitary organization, in many ways similar to other nationalist and anticolonial groups. However, as Bruce Hoffman explains in *Inside Terrorism* (2006), since 9/11 the group "has transformed itself from a bureaucratic entity that could be destroyed and an irregular army that could be defeated on the battlefield to the clearly less powerful, but nonetheless arguably more resilient, amorphous entity it is today." In the past, terrorist groups were recognizable mostly as collections of individuals belonging to an organization with a well-defined command and control apparatus. Today's groups, however, are more loosely or indirectly linked through networks of both professionals and "amateurs."

Nowhere is this cell-based structure more evident than in the rise of the homegrown jihadi movement. Homegrown jihadis are motivated by a shared sense of enmity and grievances toward the West. They may have no formal connections with al Qaeda, but they are nonetheless prepared to carry out attacks in solidarity with the group's radical jihadist agenda. As FBI director Robert Mueller recognized in testimony before the Senate Committee on Homeland Security in September 2009, "the emergence of individuals and groups inspired by al-Qaeda rhetoric but sometimes lacking the capabilities to launch a spectacular, large-scale attack poses a growing Homeland challenge." What links these groups, more than anything else, is a shared radical Islamist ideology.

In particular, 2009 saw a spike in domestic terrorism plots thwarted within the United States. Demonstrative is the case of Najibullah Zazi, a 25-year-old man who was born in Afghanistan and moved to the United States as a teenager. He lived in Colorado, but then trained in al Qaeda camps and traveled to New York City with the intention of blowing up the city's subway system around the anniversary of 9/11. Following his capture, Zazi pled guilty to the charges. Explaining his justification for the attempted attack, he stated, "It meant that I would sacrifice myself to bring attention to what the U.S. military was doing to civilians in Afghanistan." Similarly, the shooting by Major Nidal Hassan at Fort Hood, Texas, which killed 13, demonstrated that the threat of domestic radicalization is not simply a problem for American civilians, but also for military personnel.

Indeed, one of the distinctive features of twenty-first-century terrorism is its shifting ideological foundation, particularly the rise of Islamist ideology. The principle of jihad is the ideological bond that unites this amorphous movement, transcending its loose structure, diverse membership, and geographical separation. In a 2008 report titled *The Evolving Threat of Terrorism in Policymaking and Media Discourse,* the COT Institute for Safety, Security and Crisis Management defined this ideology as "Islamist-inspired terrorism drawn on a totalitarian, anti-modernist and anti-Western version of Islamism which has its conceptual origin in modern Islamist thinkers such as Hassan al-Banna, Sayyid Maududi and especially Sayyid Qutb." In 1928, Hassan al Banna founded the Muslim Brotherhood, an Islamic revivalist organization whose Palestinian branch is Hamas, which the United States has designated as a foreign terrorist organization. Similarly, Qutb, another leader of the Muslim Brotherhood, has provided modern ideological justification for the replacement of failed Arab regimes with truly Islamic governments. While this ideology may not be the only driving force behind modern-day terrorism, it cannot be denied that it represents a significant component of this new terrorism.

Perhaps more demonstrative of the evolution of terrorism is the means by which radical Islamist ideology is spread. Although groups such as al Qaeda consistently demonstrate an aptitude for adapting to changing technologies, the accessibility of the Internet has significantly expanded the opportunities for terrorists to secure publicity and spread propaganda, as well as revolutionizing the process of enlistment. The sermons of radical imams such as Anwar al Awlaki calling for acts of terrorism can be found throughout the World Wide Web. Awlaki's popularity derives from his articulate, well-educated English and the clarity with which he presents jihad and violence to young Western audiences.

More than simply an evolving organizational structure or a growing Islamist ideology, the new terrorism can be characterized by a shift toward more asymmetrical tactics. Whether it is the rise in the use of suicide bombers or attempts to acquire weapons of mass destruction, modern-day terrorist groups have evolved from attacks on government and military personnel to deliberately targeting civilian populations.

Although suicide terrorism is not a new phenomenon, its increase as a tactic has its point of departure in modern-day terrorism. Favored primarily by Islamic terrorists, the use of suicide bombers has risen significantly since 2000. According to the *Report on Terrorism* put together by the United States' National Counterterrorism Center, suicide attacks were used approximately 1,600 times against both military and civilian personnel between 2005 and 2008, primarily in Afghanistan and Iraq.

The threat posed by the new terrorism is truly unique compared to any threats encountered during the twentieth century. This amorphous enemy, motivated primarily by Islamist ideology and well versed in the use of asymmetrical tactics will pose a significant challenge to international counterterrorism experts well into the twenty-first century.

Steven Emerson

See also al Qaeda; Awlaki, Anwar al; Homegrown Jihadi Movement; Lone-Wolf Terrorism

Further Readings

Hoffman, Bruce. *Inside Terrorism.* New York: Columbia University Press, 2006.

Reich, Walter. *Origins of Terrorism: Psychologies, Ideologies, Theologies, States of Mind.* Baltimore, MD: Johns Hopkins University Press, 1998.

Sageman, Marc. *Understanding Terror Networks.* Philadelphia: University of Pennsylvania Press, 2004.

Staun, Jørgen, Kasper Ege, and Ann-Sophie Hemmingsen. *The Evolving Threat of Terrorism in Policymaking and Media Discourse.* The Hague, Netherlands: COT Institute for Safety, Security and Crisis Management, 2008. http://www.transnationalterrorism.eu/tekst/publications/WP2%20Del%202.pdf.

NICHOLS, TERRY LYNN (1955–)

In 1998, a federal jury found Terry Lynn Nichols guilty in the April 19, 1995, bombing of the Alfred P. Murrah Federal Building in Oklahoma City, Oklahoma.

On the date of the attack, Nichols was hundreds of miles away at his home in Herington, Kansas. On April 21, 1995, Nichols voluntarily went in for questioning at the Herington Police headquarters, claiming he had heard on the news that he was a material witness. (James Nichols, Terry's brother, was also held as a material witness, but all charges against James were later dropped.) Two hours into the questioning, a warrant was issued for the arrest of Terry Nichols, although he was questioned for seven more hours before being arrested in connection with the bombing.

On May 10, 1995, Nichols was formally charged with the bombing, and three months later, both Nichols and Timothy McVeigh were indicted by a federal grand jury. The indictments were identical, charging each man with conspiracy to use a weapon of mass destruction, the use of a weapon of mass destruction, destruction by explosives, and eight counts of first-degree murder for the deaths of federal employees in the Murrah Building.

Nichols went on trial three months after McVeigh had been convicted and condemned to death. The prosecution used much of the same evidence and called many of the same witnesses, but the case lacked some of the key elements that had contributed to McVeigh's conviction, such as a strong antigovernment motive and significant physical evidence. The government alleged that Nichols, using the alias "Mike Havens," purchased forty 50-pound bags of ammonium nitrate fertilizer—the main ingredient in the Oklahoma City bomb—from a farm co-op in McPherson, Kansas, on September 30, 1994.

From that date forward, the prosecution linked Nichols to several key stages in the plot, including renting storage lockers and stealing 299 sticks of Tovex explosives, 544 blasting caps, and detonating cord from a quarry in Marion, Kansas, on October 1, 1994. Fingerprint evidence found on a receipt in Nichols's wallet confirmed that Nichols and McVeigh were together on April 13, 1995. Other circumstantial evidence connected Nichols to the robbery of a gun collector in Arkansas, which the prosecution claimed was to fund the bombing conspiracy. The prosecution also suggested that Nichols drove McVeigh from Junction City, Oklahoma, to Oklahoma City on April 16, 1995, to drop off the getaway car. Nichols's wife, Marife Nichols, could not testify to his whereabouts on April 18; his former wife, Lana Padilla, testified that Nichols had left a package with her, to be opened in the event of his death while away in the Philippines. In this package, she found a letter written to McVeigh in which Nichols urged McVeigh to "Go for it!"

On December 24, 1997, the federal jury found Nichols guilty on one count of conspiracy and eight counts of involuntary manslaughter. Unlike McVeigh, he was spared the sentence of death because of a deadlocked jury. On June 4, 1998, U.S. District Judge Richard P. Matsch sentenced Nichols to life in prison without possibility of parole, as well as to 48 years for the deaths of eight federal employees.

Over the next several years, Nichols lost a series of appeals, including efforts to block a trial for state charges, which included 161 counts of first-degree murder for which Nichols could have still received the death penalty. The state trial took place in 2004, and although the jury convicted Nichols on all murder charges, as well as conspiracy and arson charges, the jury members disagreed on whether or not to give him the death penalty. Because Oklahoma requires the unanimous agreement of a jury to enact the death penalty, it was no longer an option. On August 9, 2004, District Judge Steven Taylor sentenced Nichols to 161 consecutive life sentences without possibility of parole.

Laura Lambert

See also McVeigh, Timothy James; Oklahoma City Bombing

Further Readings

Hersley, Jon, et al. *Simple Truths: The Real Story of the Oklahoma City Bombing Investigation.* Oklahoma City: Oklahoma Heritage Association, 2004.

Hoberock, Barbara, and Rod Walton. "Jurors Find Nichols Guilty." *Tulsa World,* May 27, 2004, p. A1.

Michel, Lou, and Dan Herbeck. *American Terrorist: Timothy McVeigh and the Oklahoma City Bombing.* New York: ReganBooks, 2001.

Moreno, Sylvia. "Nichols Gets 2nd Life Sentence." *Chicago Tribune,* August 10, 2004, p. 10.

Nichols, James D., and Robert S. Papovich. *Freedom's End: The Oklahoma Conspiracy.* Decker, MI: Freedom's End, 1997.

Sherrow, Victoria. *The Oklahoma City Bombing: Terror in the Heartland.* Berkeley Heights, NJ: Enslow, 1998.

Nidal, Abu

See Banna, Sabri al

9/11 Commission

The National Commission on Terrorist Attacks Upon the United States, more commonly known as the 9/11 Commission, was one of the most influential bipartisan study groups in modern American history. The commission was composed of five Republicans and five Democrats. Their report served as the basis for a major reform of the United States intelligence community, marking the most far-reaching changes since the creation of the modern national security bureaucracy at the start of the Cold War in the late 1940s.

A commission was widely called for by the public and many in Congress in the wake of the September 11, 2001, attacks on New York and Virginia by al Qaeda terrorists. At first the Bush administration was hesitant about such a review, but President George W. Bush and the Congress created the Commission with Public Law 107-306 on November 27, 2002. The Commission was initially to be chaired by former secretary of state Henry Kissinger and former U.S. senator George Mitchell, but each of them declined. Former New Jersey governor Thomas Kean and former congressman Lee Hamilton subsequently agreed to chair and vice chair the study. A staff of experts led by Philip Zelikow prepared the report after interviewing 1,200 individuals and studying thousands of classified and unclassified reports. Nineteen days of public hearings were held. The commission's report, titled *The 9/11 Commission Report: The Final Report of the National Commission on Terrorist Attacks Upon the United States,* was delivered in July 2004.

The report details the planning and execution of the al Qaeda attacks, the response of the intelligence and policy communities to the intelligence warnings of an attack in the months preceding them, and the response of the national security system to the attacks when they occurred. The Commission concluded that the Central Intelligence Agency (CIA) and the Federal Bureau of Investigation (FBI) had inadequately assessed the threat posed by al Qaeda and had not taken sufficient steps to disrupt its planning. The report says the most important failure in both the intelligence and policy communities was one of imagination, in understanding the depth of the threat al Qaeda posed.

The 9/11 Commission Report narrates in detail the development of al Qaeda, its evolution into the organization that carried out the 9/11 attacks, and the central leadership role played by Osama bin Laden. The report discusses al Qaeda's attacks on American targets before September 11, 2001, with a special focus on August 1998 attacks on the American embassies in Kenya and Tanzania and the attack on the USS *Cole* in Aden, Yemen, in September 2000. The Commission also studied foiled al Qaeda attacks like the so-called Millennium Plot to attack Los Angeles in 1999. Much of the data on al Qaeda's planning and execution of the 9/11 and other attacks derives from the statements of captured al Qaeda operatives detained after 9/11.

The Commission also carefully assessed the role of foreign states in the plot and the attack. Significantly, it concluded that Iraq had no role in the events of September 11, 2001, and was not involved in the al Qaeda plot. It noted that 15 of the 19 hijackers were Saudi citizens but found no evidence of Saudi government participation in the attack. The Commission assessed that Pakistan plays a central role in the development of Islamist extremism and urged the administration to take steps to strengthen democracy there. It applauded the administration for its intervention in Afghanistan after 9/11 and urged a fully resourced effort to build a stable government in that country. The Commission reviewed evidence of Iran's involvement with al Qaeda and suggested more intelligence collection and analysis were needed in this area.

The report concluded with a series of recommendations for reforming and restructuring the American intelligence community and other national security agencies to deal with the threat of twenty-first-century terrorism. It called for the creation of a national intelligence director with authority over all agencies in the intelligence community; this suggestion led to the creation of the Office of the Director of National Intelligence (ODNI).

THE
9/11
COMMISSION
REPORT

FINAL REPORT OF THE NATIONAL COMMISSION ON TERRORIST ATTACKS UPON THE UNITED STATES

Front cover of *The 9/11 Commission Report*

It also called for the creation of a National Counterterrorism Center (NCTC) to replace the Terrorist Threat Intelligence Center, which had been created soon after 9/11; the NCTC was duly created in the aftermath of the report.

The Commission also recommended extensive changes in the manner in which the CIA and FBI conduct their work. The CIA was mandated to put a higher emphasis on human intelligence collection programs and to expand its analytical capabilities. More language training was recommended. The FBI was encouraged to develop new analytical skills and develop an analytical cadre to match its traditional field agent structure.

The Commission's extensive public hearings were widely watched across the nation. President George W. Bush and Vice President Richard Cheney refused to testify under oath and were interviewed privately together by the commission. Former president William Clinton and former vice president Al Gore also declined to testify under oath and were interviewed separately in private.

The public hearings included testimony from Secretary of State Colin Powell, Secretary of Defense Donald Rumsfeld, Director of Central Intelligence George Tenet and the White House counterterrorism expert Richard Clarke. National Security Advisor Condoleezza Rice testified in public but not under oath.

The Commission's work and its final report received a generally positive response from both Republicans and Democrats. The report itself became a best-seller and was lauded for the quality of its prose. *The New York Times* even cited its "uncommonly lucid, even riveting" style, unusual for a government report by a large number of experts. However, the report was criticized by some for not assigning blame for any individual failures.

Since the report's publication in 2004, considerable new scholarship has expanded on its analysis of the development of al Qaeda, al Qaeda's strategies and objectives on 9/11, the errors in the intelligence community's handling of the threat warning in the spring and summer of 2001, and the effectiveness of the Bush administration's strategy in Afghanistan. Some of these studies are cited in the recommendations for Further Readings below.

Bruce Riedel

See also al Qaeda; Central Intelligence Agency; Counterterrorism; Federal Bureau of Investigation; Homeland Security; Intelligence Gathering; September 11 Attacks

Further Readings

Clarke, Richard. *Against All Enemies: Inside America's War on Terror*. New York: Free Press, 2004.

Coll, Steve. *The Bin Ladens: An Arabian Family in the American Century*. New York: Penguin, 2008.

National Commission on Terrorist Attacks Upon the United States. *The 9/11 Commission Report: Final Report of the National Commission on Terrorist Attacks Upon the United States*. New York: W.W. Norton, 2004. http://www.9-11commission.gov.

Riedel, Bruce. *The Search for al Qaeda: Its Leadership, Ideology and Future*. Washington, DC: Brookings Institution Press, 2010.

Wright, Lawrence. *The Looming Tower: Al Qaeda and the Road to 9/11*. New York: Knopf, 2006.

Nosair, El Sayyid (1956–)

El Sayyid Nosair is serving a life sentence in prison for participating in a conspiracy that involved, in part, the February 1993 bombing of the World Trade Center in New York City. Six people were killed and 1,000 more were injured in that attack. Nosair has also been found guilty of the 1990 murder of the militant Zionist Rabbi Meir Kahane.

Like his spiritual leader Sheikh Omar Abdel Rahman, Nosair was not actually charged with the 1993 blast; he was instead convicted on racketeering charges. Prosecutors claimed that the 1993 bombing and the earlier assassination of Kahane were two acts in a larger conspiracy.

Born in Egypt, Nosair immigrated to the United States and found a job as a maintenance worker in Jersey City, New Jersey. He attended the Jersey City mosque of Sheikh Omar Abdel Rahman, the spiritual leader of the Egyptian Islamic militant group Gama'a al Islamiyya.

According to prosecutors, on November 5, 1990, Nosair attended a speech given by Kahane in the Marriott Hotel ballroom. As Kahane finished his speech, Nosair shot him and dashed from the hotel, firing all the while. He ran into the street and shot an older man and a postal police officer. The officer fired back, hitting Nosair in the neck. Soon arrested, Nosair denied involvement in the killing. According to press reports, after Nosair's arrest, federal agents raided his apartment and found many incriminating items, including an Abdel Rahman sermon that urged his followers to attack "the edifices of capitalism."

At his first trial, Nosair was acquitted of state murder charges but convicted of related gun-possession and assault charges; he was sentenced to seven years in the Attica Correctional Facility for the gun offense. While in Attica, according to prosecutors, Nosair encouraged visitors to continue with the holy war against the United States, and even called upon his supporters to assassinate the judge who sent him to prison.

After the 1993 bombing of the World Trade Center, investigators found that many of the major suspects in the case had closely watched Nosair's trial and contributed money for his defense. Prosecutors carefully constructed a huge terrorism and conspiracy case involving Abdel Rahman, Nosair, and other supporters. The indictment tied together a three-year string of terrorist incidents, including an alleged plot to blow up the George Washington Bridge, the Lincoln and Holland Tunnels, the United Nations building, and other Manhattan landmarks.

In the larger conspiracy trial, prosecutors brought up Nosair's involvement in Kahane's murder, maintaining that it was part of Abdel Rahman's conspiracy to undermine the U.S. government. In this second trial, Nosair was convicted of Kahane's murder. Nosair's cousin, Ibrahim el Gabrowny, was also convicted of taking part in the conspiracy.

The issue of double jeopardy was not pertinent to Nosair's second trial because he was charged with the new crime of federal racketeering, and prosecutors proved that he took part in a broader conspiracy against the United States.

Erica Pearson

See also Abdel Rahman, Omar; Kahane, Meir; World Trade Center Bombing (1993)

Further Readings

Cohen, Patricia. "Nosair Loses Suit against Postal Cop Who Shot Him." *Newsday,* September 2, 1993.

Dickey, Christopher. *Securing the City: Inside America's Best Counterterror Force—the NYPD.* New York: Simon & Schuster, 2009.

Grunwald, Michael, and T.R. Reid. "U.S. Tries to Link N.Y., Africa Bombs; Prosecutors Say bin Laden Aide Got Guns for Trade Center Plotter." *Washington Post,* September 24, 1998, p. A29.

Hurtado, Patricia. "Terror Sheik Gone for Life: Rahman, 9 Others Get Stiff Sentences in NYC Bomb Plot." *Newsday,* January 18, 1996, p. A5.

Kocieniewski, David. "Witness Recalls Kahane Slaying." *Newsday,* February 9, 1995, p. A7.

Smith, Greg B. "Terrorist Aided Kahane Killer's Defence." *Toronto Star,* October 10, 2002. p. A10.

Tyre, Peg, and Nadia Abou el Magd. "Agent Ties Nosair to Death Plot." *Newsday,* March 9, 1995, p. A19.

Usborne, David. "New York's Terrorist Sheikh Jailed for Life." *The Independent* (London), January 18, 1996, p. 11.

NOVEMBER 17

See Revolutionary Organization 17
   November

NUCLEAR TERRORISM

A nuclear explosion and its incendiary and blast effects would cause physical destruction on a vast scale. The detonation of even a small nuclear weapon in a densely populated area would probably kill tens of thousands of people and seriously wound even more. The radiation released immediately in a nuclear explosion and the radioactive fallout of ash and debris that would probably follow would also cause serious damage to exposed individuals. What is the likelihood, however, that terrorists could obtain and use nuclear weapons? What are some of the ways that terrorists might choose to attack nuclear targets in a highly developed country that made extensive use of nuclear power plants? These are some of the more important questions that any analysis of terrorism needs to address.

Nuclear Weapons

Nuclear weapons are devices that release energy stored in the atomic nucleus, the central, positively charged core of all atoms. The first nuclear weapons used uranium, a dense metal mined from the earth in many parts of the world, and plutonium, a man-made metal produced by irradiating uranium in nuclear reactors. The nuclei of these atoms can be made to fission, or divide, liberating vast quantities of energy in the process. Each fission also releases a few neutrons. If there is a sufficiently large mass of uranium or plutonium present, called a "critical mass," those extra neutrons stimulate more nuclei to fission in an explosive chain reaction in which energy released by vast numbers of fissioning nuclei is transformed into heat, radiation, and shock waves. This vast release of energy creates a nuclear explosion.

Fortunately, it is not easy to make a nuclear weapon, despite the fact that numerous books, articles, and websites purport to give information about how it can be done. The most difficult part of making a nuclear weapon involves obtaining the necessary fissionable material, an isotope (or variety) of uranium known as U-235 (because the total number of protons and neutrons in its nucleus is 235). It is very difficult to separate the lighter variety, the U-235 needed to make bombs, from the heavier variety, U-238. Bomb-builders who have obtained U-235 can then make a bomb from it directly, or they can use it to build a nuclear reactor that uses neutrons to irradiate U-238 and make plutonium-239 (Pu-239), another bomb material that fissions readily. The bomb dropped on Hiroshima in August 1945 used U-235, and the one employed at Nagasaki several days later used Pu-239.

The project to build the first U.S. nuclear weapons during World War II was a massive undertaking requiring the full resources of a powerful nation. Could terrorists do it? What is the probability that they have both the skills and technology needed to take the next step? Could they make a fission bomb or perhaps even a thermonuclear weapon? Several possible scenarios will be considered.

A Terrorist Threat Assessment

It can be said with complete confidence that a terrorist organization that did not have the support of a government could not produce the fissionable uranium or plutonium for a fission bomb from raw materials. Nor would it be possible for a group of non-state actors to take irradiated nuclear fuel from a reactor and extract plutonium from it. The technologies involved are too complex, dangerous, and expensive for a small group to master.

Suppose, however, that terrorists could somehow obtain the fissionable uranium or plutonium in either metallic or powder form through theft, purchase, or bribery. In that case, a group that had access to scientific and engineering expertise—including nuclear physicists, electrical engineers, skilled machinists, and explosives experts—could probably make a nuclear device with an explosive yield approaching that of the weapons used against Japan in World War II. Such a device would probably not be small enough to be dropped from any aircraft that terrorists could commandeer or be launched as a missile warhead, but it would be deliverable by truck, railcar, or ship.

The threat posed by the existence of many tons of uranium and plutonium in the stockpiles of nuclear-weapon states is one of the most dangerous threats faced by governments attempting to block terrorists from acquiring nuclear weapons. Such stockpiles are heavily guarded, but in tests carried out in the United States, highly trained paramilitary strike forces succeeded in about 50 percent of the trials in penetrating security barriers at national laboratories and production facilities to seize dangerous quantities of nuclear materials.

The problem of fissionable material stockpile security is particularly acute in Russia, where low salaries, poor morale among scientific workers, and deteriorating physical security systems at weapons laboratories such as Sarov and Zelenogorsk have produced a situation where this material may be at risk. There have been enough reports of thefts of small quantities of fissionable materials from Russia to indicate that the problem is a real one. The United States and other nations have responded to this threat by providing assistance to Russia to improve facility security and provide more employment support for weapons scientists. It has also arranged to purchase fissionable material from Russia and Kazakhstan that might otherwise have been diverted from legitimate custody. In September 2000, the United States and Russia signed the Plutonium Management and Disposition Agreement (PMDA), by which each nation agreed to dispose of at least 34 metric tons of surplus weapons-grade plutonium. This commitment was officially reaffirmed by both governments in 2010.

Terrorist Theft of Intact Nuclear Weapons

Of course, if terrorists obtained a functioning nuclear weapon through force, theft, or bribery, that would pose an immediate threat of the greatest magnitude. Nuclear weapons themselves are kept under very high security conditions in all countries possessing them. They are also equipped with various safety and security features to keep them from being used by unauthorized persons. Information regarding their locations, and the security procedures associated with them is highly classified.

There is relatively little public information available from countries other than the United States about any tests that have been conducted to penetrate security screens and seize an intact weapon. National authorities in declared nuclear-weapon states assert that their weapons are under tight control. During the 2001 war in Afghanistan, however, press reports circulated suggesting that U.S. officials were poised to intervene in Pakistan in the event that fundamentalist groups aligned with terrorists succeeded in overthrowing the Pakistani military government and threatened to seize Pakistan's small stockpile of nuclear weapons. The unofficial Pakistani response was that its government was in no danger and that its nuclear weapons were under tight control.

The United States and Russia once possessed stockpiles of small nuclear weapons, sometimes called "suitcase bombs," that could be carried by one or two men. Such weapons would obviously be very attractive to terrorists and were presumably tightly guarded. Several years ago, a Russian general testified to the U.S. House of Representatives that about 40 of these weapons could not be accounted for in the Russian inventory. His claim was denied by Russian authorities, but the lack of international access to information about the Russian nuclear stockpile leaves analysts uneasy about the prospects that such weapons might have been procured by terrorists. One can only conclude that as long as nuclear weapons exist in national stockpiles, there is a small probability that terrorists could somehow obtain one as a result of a security system failure.

Attacks on Nuclear Reactors

While terrorists might find it difficult to make a nuclear weapon, even if they could obtain the necessary uranium or plutonium, and though they would face even more difficulty if they tried to obtain a complete weapon, there are other forms of attack that are well within their means. The large number of nuclear power reactors in the United States, Europe, and Asia presents terrorists with an array of attractive targets. An attack on one of these reactors that succeeded in releasing large quantities of radioactive materials would threaten the downwind populations as well as those in the immediate vicinity. The accident at the Chernobyl Nuclear Power Plant in Ukraine is a case in point. That accident released vast quantities of radioactive nuclear materials and forced the permanent evacuation and abandonment of a large swath of land in the vicinity. Radioactive fallout from the accident was detected throughout Europe in regions where wind carried the particulate matter released in the plant explosion.

Terrorists might try to attack reactors in several ways. An armed group might try to force its way into the plant to take over the system and damage it intentionally, causing a release of radioactive materials. Since the instrumentation systems that control such plants are complex, such an effort would require considerable knowledge of nuclear engineering and plant design to succeed. The terrorists would also have to overcome intrinsic safeguards built into the system to prevent accidents. Most nuclear plants have taken steps to upgrade physical security systems to minimize the probability that attackers could penetrate them. Some legislators want federal security guards at all reactor sites and nuclear weapons laboratories, where guards are now usually provided by private security services.

In the aftermath of the 9/11 attacks, authorities recognized the need to pay more attention to the possibility of terrorist suicide attacks on nuclear plants using aircraft. Most nuclear reactors are shielded by containment vessels (the domes often seen at nuclear plants). These reinforced concrete domes are several feet thick and designed to contain an internal explosion so that radioactive debris does not escape into the atmosphere. Domes have been tested against the impact of light aircraft, but no tests have ever been conducted with heavy aircraft like the ones used to attack the World Trade Center in New York. Many experts doubt that the typical containment vessel would be able to withstand such an impact. There are still questions about what would happen if an aircraft did penetrate one of these domes. It is not known whether this would result in the release of nuclear material from the reactor core, or what the magnitude of the release might be. Such questions require extensive computer modeling using probabilistic risk assessment techniques to model the attack and make estimates of resulting damage.

Other attack scenarios at nuclear plants involve strikes against storage sites for spent nuclear fuel. Spent fuel is highly radioactive, and its release would pose a serious threat to surrounding populations. Spent-fuel sites are usually not as heavily protected as reactor cores and are perceived to be more vulnerable. Experts are trying to address this problem, which may eventually be solved by creating a national storage site in a secure location that would accept spent fuel from reactor facilities.

Nations are responding to terrorist threats against reactors by trying to model various attack scenarios and devise appropriate responses. France was reported to have placed surface to air antiaircraft missile batteries near some of its most sensitive nuclear facilities to guard against the possibility of suicide air attack. The United States has established "no-fly zones" over reactors, but it is not clear how effective such zones would be in the absence of round-the-clock combat air patrol or the installation of antiaircraft missile batteries.

Attacks With Improvised Radiological Weapons

A radiological weapon is an improvised device designed to spread radioactive nuclear material over a wide area. A typical device might use an explosive charge attached to a container of radioactive material that had been obtained either legally or illegally. Such devices, referred to as "dirty bombs," would not require a great deal of technical sophistication, and it is apparent that terrorists are able to use commercial or military explosives. They might also make improvised explosives from readily obtainable materials of the type used in the Oklahoma City attack.

The magnitude of the damage inflicted by such an attack would depend on the quantity and radioactive half-lives of the materials released, and on local wind and weather conditions. Most assessments suggest that the effects of such an attack would be relatively small because the terrorists would not be able to obtain the large quantities of long-lived radioactive materials needed to contaminate more than a few city blocks or so. Nevertheless, it is easy to imagine that the explosion of a radiological weapon in a densely populated area would cause panic and flight.

Recent terrorist attacks and the declared intentions of groups such as al Qaeda demonstrate that nations must increase their vigilance over nuclear weapons, nuclear reactors, and related systems. They will also have to come to terms with the need to reduce nuclear weapon stockpiles and negotiate strong treaty agreements that will make it more difficult for terrorists to obtain nuclear weapons, fissionable materials, or the technologies needed to make them.

In the twenty-first century, the most immediate threat may exist from nuclear-armed nations that are sympathetic to radical movements. This is why, for example, the political stability of Pakistan is of such great significance to the United States and the rest of the world. Should the Taliban, for example, manage to take over the Pakistani government, al Qaeda would find itself with a nuclear-armed ally. Likewise, given its history of religious extremism and sympathy to anti-Western terrorists, Iran's apparent determination to have its own nuclear weapon is an issue of utmost concern.

Les Paldy

See also al Qaeda; Counterterrorism; International Relations and Terrorism; September 11 Attacks; State Terrorism; Taliban

Further Readings

Allison, Graham. *Nuclear Terrorism: The Ultimate Preventable Catastrophe.* New York: Henry Holt, 2004.

Falkenrath, Richard, Robert D. Newman, and Bradley A. Thayer. *America's Achilles Heel: Nuclear, Biological, and Chemical Terrorism and Covert Attack.* Cambridge, MA: Belfer Center for Science and International Affairs, 1998.

Ferguson, Charles D. *Preventing Catastrophic Nuclear Terrorism.* CSR No. 11. New York: Council on Foreign Relations, 2006.

Ferguson, Charles D., and William C. Potter. *The Four Faces of Nuclear Terrorism.* New York: Routledge, 2005.

Langewiesche, William. *The Atomic Bazaar: Dispatches from the Underground World of Nuclear Trafficking.* New York: Farrar, Straus & Giroux, 2007.

Laqueur, Walter. *The New Terrorism: Fanaticism and the Arms of Mass Destruction.* New York: Oxford University Press, 1999.

Levi, Michael. *On Nuclear Terrorism.* Cambridge, MA: Harvard University Press, 2009.

Mueller, Robert. *Atomic Obsession: Nuclear Alarmism from Hiroshima to Al Qaeda.* New York: Routledge, 2009.

National Nuclear Security Administration. "Plutonium Disposition." http://nnsa.energy.gov/aboutus/ourprograms/nonproliferation/programoffices/fissilematerialsdisposition/plutoniumdisposition.

"Nuclear Reactors as Terrorist Targets." *The New York Times,* January 21, 2002, p. A14.

Ranstorp, Magnus, and Magnus Normark, eds. *Unconventional Weapons and International Terrorism: Challenges and a New Approach.* New York: Routledge, 2009.

Serber, Robert, and Richard Rhodes, eds. *The Los Alamos Primer: The First Lectures on How to Build an Atomic Bomb.* Berkeley: University of California Press, 1992.

U.S. Congress, Office of Technology Assessment. *Proliferation of Weapons of Mass Destruction: Assessing the Risks.* OTA-ISC-559. Washington, DC: U.S. Government Printing Office, 1993.

Ocalan, Abdullah (1948–)

Abdullah Ocalan, the leader of the left-wing guerrilla unit known as the Kurdistan Workers' Party (PKK), was born in 1948 in southeastern Turkey, near the Syrian border. He is generally considered to be the strongest advocate and fighter for Kurdish sovereignty and has been labeled a hero by some Kurds, a terrorist by most international intelligence sources, and a "baby killer" by the Turkish government.

Raised by his peasant family in Omerli, Ocalan had vague political aspirations as a youngster. He tried to enter the Turkish military but was refused, a decision he claims was related to his Kurdish ancestry. Later, Ocalan was accepted into Ankara University, where he studied political science and first began to embrace Marxism and voice left-wing sentiments. He organized student movements and was jailed for distributing leftist brochures. He then dropped out of Ankara University, returned to southeastern Turkey, and began to advocate for a Kurdish state.

In 1977, Ocalan and two comrades wrote a manifesto, "The National Road to the Kurdish Revolution." This document would become the blueprint for and the beginning of the PKK. In 1980 a military coup in Turkey forced Ocalan and some of his cohorts to flee to Syria, where they began forming and training the ranks that would later be known as the PKK. On August 15, 1984, the PKK began its armed campaign for a Kurdish state with an attack on a pro-government village in southeastern Turkey.

Ocalan, whose surname means "avenger" in Turkish, is usually referred to as "Apo," Kurdish for "uncle." His leadership between 1984 and 1999 resulted in a terribly bloody outcome for the PKK and Turkey. Ocalan is alleged to have ordered the murder of uncountable civilians, the kidnapping of Western tourists, and the murder of many comrades who challenged his beliefs. In the overall war, Turkish officials claim that nearly 40,000 people died as a result of PKK offensives and government retaliation.

In 1999, Ocalan was apprehended in Kenya and brought back to Turkey, where he was tried and sentenced to death for treason and sedition. The day he was sentenced, riots broke out, demonstrations were held in Turkey and Europe, and Turkish embassies throughout Europe were invaded. These actions were orchestrated by some of the 850,000 Kurds living in Turkey and the various countries of Europe. Ocalan appealed for the overturn of the death penalty and announced a cease-fire, ordering all PKK forces to leave Turkey. In February 2000, the PKK officially foreswore its 15-year revolution and agreed to the political program proposed by its imprisoned leader. In 2002 PKK had nearly 10,000 active members and supporters throughout Europe.

In October 2002, Turkey commuted Ocalan's sentence to life in prison, following the country's abolition of the death penalty to bring its laws in line with the requirements of the European Union, which Turkey wished to join. Nonetheless, in 2003, the European Court of Human Rights in Strasbourg, France, found that Ocalan's 1999 trial was unfair, claiming that Ocalan's defense was improperly restricted. Turkey appealed the ruling, but in 2005 the European Court upheld the ruling and recommended a retrial, which Turkey refused to hold.

Many believed that Ocalan's imprisonment would end the PKK, but that was not the case. The PKK called off its cease-fire and resumed attacks in 2003. Although reduced in size, in 2008 the group was believed to have 4,000 to 5,000 active members, many of whom are based in the Kurdish region of Iraq.

Richard McHugh

See also Iraq War; Kurdistan Workers' Party

Further Readings

Chailand, Gerard, ed. *A People without a Country: The Kurds and Kurdistan.* London: Interlink Publishing Group, 1993.

Gunter, Michael M. *The Kurds and the Future of Turkey.* New York: St. Martin's, 1997.

Ocalan, Abdullah. *Prison Writings: The Roots of Civilisation.* Translated by Klaus Happel. London: Pluto Press, 2007.

Olson, Robert. *The Kurdish Question and Turkish-Iranian Relations: From World War I to 1998.* Costa Mesa, CA: Mazda, 1998.

Schleifer, Yigal. "European Push for Retrial of Kurdish Leader Roils Turkey." *Christian Science Monitor,* May 18, 2005, p. 7.

ODEH, MOHAMMED SADDIQ (1965–)

Mohammed Saddiq Odeh was one of the first two people convicted of a direct role in the August 7, 1998, terrorist bombing of the United States embassy in Nairobi, Kenya. On May 29, 2001, a federal jury in New York found him guilty of participating in the attack and of murdering the 213 people, including 12 Americans, killed as a result of the explosion. Prosecutors had not sought the

death penalty against Odeh, but the trial judge sentenced him to life in U.S. prison without the possibility of parole.

Odeh, a Jordanian and Kenyan national of Palestinian heritage, was one of four defendants who went on trial in Manhattan federal court in January 2001 for the Kenya bombing and the coordinated but less lethal bombing of the U.S. embassy in Dar es Salaam, where 11 people were killed. He and his codefendants were all found to be part of a worldwide terrorist conspiracy led by the Saudi exile Osama bin Laden and carried out by his Islamic militant organization, al Qaeda. Odeh, who underwent weapons and explosives training at al Qaeda camps inside Afghanistan in 1992, admitted to being a "soldier" of the group who had sworn a loyalty oath, or *bayat,* to bin Laden.

Odeh was born in Saudi Arabia in 1965 and grew up in Jordan. He studied engineering and architecture at a university in Manila starting in 1986, and it was in the Philippines that he was exposed to radical Islam and gained interest in the anti-Soviet jihad in Afghanistan. In 1990, he went to join the mujahideen fighting the Soviets. With the Afghan conflict winding down, Odeh was among the militants dispatched to Somalia in 1993 to train native Somalis who, like al Qaeda, considered the U.S. military presence there "colonization," although the mission began as part of a United Nations peacekeeping operation. Somali fighters killed 18 U.S. Army Rangers in an October 1993 battle in the capital city of Mogadishu.

In 1994, Odeh settled near the Somalia-Kenya border in the coastal city of Mombassa, where he supported himself and al Qaeda with a fishing boat supplied by the group. Odeh met and married a Kenyan woman and fathered two children, one of whom was born after his arrest and he never saw.

Odeh was put in custody on the day of the embassy bombings. He had fled Kenya the night before on a flight to Karachi with another conspirator, who passed Pakistani immigration officials without incident. But at Karachi airport, just hours before the explosions, officials detected that Odeh's Yemeni passport was fake (the picture didn't resemble Odeh), and they detained him.

In his post-arrest statements to the FBI, Odeh said he felt a moral responsibility for the embassy bombings because he was a paid member of al Qaeda. He denied a role in the plot, but various pieces of evidence implicated him. Clothes inside his carry-on luggage were laced with TNT residue. In the days before the attack, Odeh had stayed a mile from the target at the same downtown Nairobi hotel as other bombing conspirators and registered under the name in his fake passport. Further, his fingerprint was found on the East Africa cell-leader's hotel room door.

Prosecutors described Odeh as a "technical adviser" to the Kenya bombing. In his mud-walled, thatched-roof home in rural Witu, Kenya, investigators found two handwritten sketches of the embassy compound and the roads surrounding it. They also found an Arabic ledger detailing his fishing expenses; it had one entry listing $1,400 in weapons and artillery for "work," a code word for jihad. Odeh told the FBI other al Qaeda code words were "tools" for weapons, "papers" for fake documents, "soap" for TNT, and "potatoes" for grenades.

During his interrogation, Odeh told FBI agent John Anticev that he thought the bombing was a "blunder," because it killed so many Kenyan civilians who did not work in the embassy. "The people who drove the truck should have gotten it into the building or died trying," Anticev recalled Odeh telling him.

Odeh also explained that al Qaeda cells were split into planning and execution phases, with members of one group not necessarily knowing the other. For example, there was no evidence that Odeh ever met Mohamed al Owhali, his trial codefendant, who had helped assemble the Nairobi bomb truck and rode in it to the embassy. Odeh told Anticev that the cell's planning group assessed a target's construction and vulnerabilities, probed for security weaknesses, and determined what kind of explosives were needed. If proper on-site surveillance could not be conducted, Odeh said operatives might set up a food cart, taxi stand, or barber shop as a covert observation post. Odeh later told a former CIA analyst who interviewed him in jail that al Qaeda sometimes recruited nonmembers to assist in low-level logistical tasks.

After his convictions, Odeh's defense attorneys said Odeh "did not join al Qaeda to follow Mr. bin Laden or take orders from anyone blindly," but as a way to "change oppressive circumstances" for Muslims. The attorney offered a political explanation for the embassy bombings: in Odeh's view,

American support for Israel and the U.S. troop presence "in the holy lands of Saudi Arabia, the Persian Gulf, and the Horn of Africa constitutes provocation." On October 18, 2001, U.S. District Judge Leonard Sand imposed the life sentence on Odeh mandated by his 213 murder counts.

Phil Hirschkorn

See also al Qaeda; bin Laden, Osama; Mujahideen; Owhali, Mohamed Rashed al; World Trade Center Bombing (1993)

Further Readings

Bergen, Peter. *Holy War, Inc.: Inside the Secret World of Osama bin Laden.* New York: Free Press, 2001.

Gunaratna, Rohan. *Inside al Qaeda: Global Network of Terror.* New York: Columbia University Press, 2002.

Hirsch, Susan F. *In the Moment of Greatest Calamity: Terrorism, Grief, and a Victim's Quest for Justice.* Princeton, NJ: Princeton University Press, 2006.

Hurtado, Patricia. "Failed Prison Break Detailed: '98 Bombing Suspect Testifies." *Newsday,* September 7, 2002, p. A17.

Reeve, Simon. *The New Jackals: Ramzi Yousef, Osama bin Laden and the Future of Terrorism.* Boston: Northeastern Press, 1999.

Stern, Jessica. *Terror in the Name of God: Why Religious Militants Kill.* New York: Ecco, 2008.

OKLAHOMA CITY BOMBING

The 1995 bombing of the Alfred P. Murrah Federal Building in Oklahoma City, Oklahoma, is among the worst acts of domestic terrorism committed on U.S. soil. Although the two main suspects in the bombing, Timothy James McVeigh and Terry Lynn Nichols, were both tried and found guilty, questions about a larger conspiracy remain.

On April 19, 1995, at 9:02 A.M., a rented Ryder truck carrying a 4,000-pound fertilizer bomb exploded in front of the Murrah Building in Oklahoma City. The bomb destroyed over one-third of the nine-story building, including a daycare center located on the second floor. In all, 168 people, including 19 children and 8 federal employees, perished; over 500 more were injured.

Two days later, McVeigh, then 26, was charged in connection with the bombing. Amid throngs of spectators yelling "baby killer!" and "murderer!" authorities led McVeigh out of the Noble County Jail in Perry, Oklahoma, where he had been held on misdemeanor charges unrelated to the bombing. That same day, Nichols, then 39, turned himself in to the police in Herington, Kansas, where he was held as a material witness before being formally charged in connection with the bombing. A third possible suspect, identified only as John Doe No. 2 from a police sketch, remained at large.

Rescue workers and investigators continued to comb the rubble for nearly a month. On May 23, 1995, 150 pounds of dynamite were used to implode what remained of the building. By then, preliminary hearings had already begun. In late August 1995, a federal grand jury indicted McVeigh and Nichols on murder and conspiracy

On April 26, 1995, search-and-rescue crews work to save those trapped beneath the debris, following the Oklahoma City bombing. (FEMA News Photo)

charges. Two years would pass before either would go to trial.

The Trial

Opening statements for *United States v. McVeigh* began on April 24, 1997, in a Denver, Colorado, courtroom. The government presented several points: McVeigh's antigovernment beliefs; his anger over the government-initiated sieges in Waco, Texas, and Ruby Ridge, Idaho; forensic evidence; telephone and rental records; John Doe No. 1 sightings; the facts of McVeigh's initial traffic arrest on Interstate 35; and key testimony from McVeigh's army buddy Michael Fortier, his wife, Lori, and McVeigh's sister, Jennifer. Jennifer McVeigh testified to Timothy's ascent from antigovernment protest to "direct action," while Michael and Lori Fortier, who traded their testimony for lesser charges and immunity, respectively, told the court of McVeigh's plan, hatched, the government asserted, in September 1994, as well as their roles in aiding his efforts. The judge also allowed highly emotional testimony from survivors and victims' family members, which often brought the jury of seven men and five women to tears.

McVeigh's defense team, in the months preceding the trial, launched a large and expensive independent investigation focusing on the possibility that the conspiracy included many more individuals, not just McVeigh and Nichols. Stephen Jones, McVeigh's chief defense counsel, made an early assertion that the two men, if guilty, did not have the resources to carry off the bombing on their own. The defense suggested possible links with Islamic militants based in the Philippines, neo-Nazis, Iraq, and Elohim City, the nearby Christian Identity compound. Jones also claimed that the government, through its various agencies, was suppressing evidence that proved it knew of the planned attack beforehand and could have prevented it. These claims, which were suppressed in court but made known through public records and in Jones's book, *Others Unknown* (1998), have been the basis for the persistent conspiracy theories surrounding the Oklahoma City bombing.

The most alarming connections alleged by the defense's investigation, especially in light of the September 11, 2001, terrorist attacks, involved

Nichols's repeated trips to the Philippines. Nichols first traveled to the Philippines in 1990 to meet his mail-order bride, Marife Torres. Nichols returned several times, ostensibly researching "business opportunities." Before his final trip, in November 1994, Nichols gave his former wife, Lana Padilla, a package to be opened in the event of his death. Padilla opened the package soon after Nichols departed, finding therein a significant amount of cash, stolen valuables, wigs, a life insurance policy, and a letter from Nichols to McVeigh. That letter urged McVeigh to "Go for it."

Terrorist Connection?

Further investigation into Nichols's Philippine trips revealed a meeting, in the early 1990s, between an American, known only as "the Farmer," and several now-imprisoned terrorists—including Ramzi Yousef, Wali Khan Amin Shah, and Abdul Hakim Murad—in which bomb-making and other terrorist activities were discussed. An incarcerated informant and former member of the terrorist group Abu Sayyaf identified "the Farmer" as Terry Nichols. Jones's investigation also placed Osama bin Laden in the Philippines in the early 1990s, and Nichols was also in the Philippines at that time. One of Jones's hypotheses was that McVeigh and Nichols took the fall for a larger conspiracy, much as the Arab men who rented the Ryder truck used in the 1993 World Trade Center bombings were convicted while Ramzi Yousef escaped.

The defense also made significant links between McVeigh and neo-Nazi elements in the United States, most of whom were connected to Elohim City, a white supremacist compound near the Oklahoma-Arkansas border. In the early 1980s, members of The Covenant, the Sword and the Arm of the Lord (CSA), including a man named Richard Wayne Snell, plotted to blow up the Murrah Building in retaliation for the death of Gordon Kahl, a member of the white supremacist group Posse Comitatus who was killed in a shootout with federal agents in 1983. This plot, however, was never implemented. Snell was later sentenced to death and executed for two separate, unrelated murders. His execution fell on April 19, 1995, the day of the Oklahoma City bombing, as well as the second anniversary of the raid on Waco. April 19 is also the date of the Battle of

Lexington and Concord, where citizen militia groups attacked the English government in 1775, now celebrated as Patriot's Day.

The defense also made much of McVeigh's phone call to Andreas Carl Strassmeier, a German neo-Nazi living in Elohim City. Although McVeigh maintained, after his conviction, that he had met Strassmeier at a gun show and was calling to inquire about places to hide after the bombing, the defense claimed that the connections were much deeper. Strassmeier had roomed with a man named Michael Brescia, a member of the Aryan Republican Army, and was strongly suspected by the authorities of being John Doe No. 2. Strassmeier was also allegedly connected to Dennis Mahon, a Klansman who ran paramilitary training at Elohim City. Mahon was fervently antigovernment, had allegedly received money from the Iraqi government for several years following the Gulf War, and was identified by Interpol as an international terrorist.

Elohim City also produced a possible defense witness named Carol Howe, a paid informant for the Bureau of Alcohol, Tobacco and Firearms (ATF) who knew both Mahon and Strassmeier. Howe provided the ATF with information suggesting that both men had contemplated or threatened direct action against the government, including blowing up federal buildings in Oklahoma City and Tulsa. The prosecution, led by Beth Wilkinson, repeatedly asserted that neither Strassmeier nor Mahon was considered to be a suspect. Jones hoped to reveal FBI or government negligence for not pursuing these leads.

Inadmissible Evidence

Judge Richard P. Matsch eventually ruled that the evidence relating to Mahon, Strassmeier, Elohim City, and Howe was "not sufficiently relevant to be admissible," thus eliminating the basis of Jones's wider conspiracy argument. (Jones had abandoned the Philippines-based conspiracy argument when his main informant changed details of his story.) The defense team then focused on discrediting the Fortiers' testimony and revealing the holes in the FBI investigation, including an unidentified and unaccounted for leg found in the rubble, which Jones asserted was that of the "real" bomber, as well as suggestions that the FBI's forensic methods were insufficiently rigorous.

On June 13, 1997, McVeigh was sentenced to death by lethal injection. In August, after McVeigh's well-publicized complaints about Jones's competency, Jones stepped down as the lawyer for the appeals process. McVeigh would eventually decline to move forward with his appeals, and he was sent to a prison in Terre Haute, Indiana, to await execution.

Nichols on Trial

Terry Lynn Nichols went on trial in November 1997. He faced the same charges as McVeigh, and much of the same evidence and testimony was used in his trial. However, because Nichols was at home in Kansas when the bombing occurred, and because he lacked the motive that the prosecution had established for McVeigh, Nichols was found guilty on only one charge of conspiracy and on eight charges of involuntary manslaughter. In April 1998, Nichols rejected an offer of leniency in exchange for more information about the bombing because he could still be prosecuted by the state of Oklahoma for murder.

On December 31, 1998, after a year and a half of investigation, a grand jury discounted all theories presented by McVeigh's original defense team, including the existence of John Doe No. 2, wider foreign involvement, and speculation that the federal government had prior warning about the bombing and chose not to act.

McVeigh was executed on June 11, 2001. In 2004, Nichols was tried by the state of Oklahoma on 161 counts of murder, as well as conspiracy and arson charges. During his trial, He defense attorneys also alleged that he was set up to take the blame for the bombing, although the judge in the case refused to allow testimony linking the attack to Elohim City, ruling that there was no substance to such allegations. Nichols was convicted and sentenced to 161 consecutive life sentences without possibility of parole.

Today, a reflecting pool surrounded by 168 chairs, 149 for each of the adult victims and 19 smaller chairs for the children, is the memorial to those killed in the Oklahoma City bombing. The Survivor Tree, an American elm that somehow withstood the explosion, overlooks the scene. A nearby museum features evidence from the attack.

Laura Lambert

See also April 19; Branch Davidian Compound Siege; Covenant, the Sword and the Arm of the Lord, The; McVeigh, Timothy James; Nichols, Terry Lynn; Snell, Richard Wayne; World Trade Center Bombing (1993); Yousef, Ramzi Ahmed

Further Readings

Crothers, Lane. *Rage on the Right: The American Militia Movement from Ruby Ridge to Homeland Security.* Lanham, MD: Rowman & Littlefield, 2003.

Hamm, Mark S. *Apocalypse in Oklahoma: Waco and Ruby Ridge Revenged.* Boston: Northeastern University Press, 1997.

Hersley, Jon, et al. *Simple Truths: The Real Story of the Oklahoma City Bombing Investigation.* Oklahoma City: Oklahoma Heritage Association, 2004.

Hoffman, David. *The Oklahoma City Bombing and the Politics of Terror.* Venice, CA: Feral House, 1998.

Jones, Stephen. *Others Unknown: The Oklahoma City Bombing Case and Conspiracy.* New York: Public Affairs, 1998.

Michel, Lou, and Dan Herbeck. *American Terrorist: Timothy McVeigh and the Oklahoma City Bombing.* New York: ReganBooks, 2001.

Oklahoma City National Memorial and Museum. http://www.oklahomacitynationalmemorial.org.

Serrano, Richard A. *One of Ours: Timothy McVeigh and the Oklahoma City Bombing.* New York: Norton, 1998.

U.S. Congress, House International Relations Committee. *The Oklahoma City Bombing: Was There a Foreign Connection?* Chairman's Report: Oversight and Investigations Subcommittee of the House International Relations Committee, December 26, 2006. http://rohrabacher.house.gov/UploadedFiles/Report%20from%20the%20Chairman.pdf.

Wright, Stuart A. *Patriots, Politics, and the Oklahoma City Bombing.* Cambridge, UK: Cambridge University Press, 2007.

OMAGH BOMBING

One of the deadliest single bombings during the 30 years of conflict in Northern Ireland, the 1998 bombing in the village of Omagh, County Tyrone, Northern Ireland, killed 29 people and seriously threatened the peace process.

From the late 1960s until 1998, Northern Ireland was the scene of a civil conflict between members of its majority-Protestant community, who wished Northern Ireland to remain a part of Great Britain, and its minority-Catholic community, who wished the province to become a part of the Republic of Ireland. Late in 1997, the Irish Republican Army (IRA) and various Protestant paramilitary groups declared a cease-fire. On April 10, 1998, delegates representing the major parties to the conflict signed the Good Friday Accords, a document laying out the necessary steps to peace and the order in which they should be taken.

A number of IRA members disagreed with the decision to declare a cease-fire, and they were disgusted by the Good Friday Accords, which required the IRA to seek a political solution to the conflict through its representative political party, Sinn Féin. These members split with the group and formed a competing organization, the Real IRA.

On August 15, 1998, members of the Real IRA are believed to have driven from the Republic of Ireland across the border to Omagh, County Tyrone, Northern Ireland. Omagh, a small town with a largely Catholic population, had long housed a British Army garrison. Sometime early that morning, a 500-pound car bomb was parked in the town's market square, an area sure to be crowded with shoppers, as that Saturday was the final day of an annual town festival.

Around 2:30 P.M. a call was placed to Omagh's police force warning them of a bomb. The police believed it was near the town's courthouse, a building at the opposite end of the main street from the market square. Police rushed to clear the area, tragically directing people toward the market. Shortly after 3:00 P.M., the car bomb exploded, utterly destroying two buildings nearby. More than 200 people were injured, and 29 were killed, with one victim dying several months later of his injuries. The dead included nine children and three generations of one family.

The attack was the most deadly single bombing in Northern Ireland, and it immediately put the peace accords into jeopardy. Although suspicion quickly fell on the Real IRA, many Unionist politicians declared that the IRA's failure to disarm—its reluctance to do so had been a major obstacle throughout the peace process—had allowed the atrocity. Providing some reassurance about the IRA's commitment to the peace process, Gerry Adams, president of Sinn Féin, made an unprecedented declaration

condemning the bombings. Previously, the IRA's position was that civilian deaths were regrettable but justified. In the days following the bombing, the British Parliament passed harsh new anti-terror laws that allowed suspects to be convicted on the word of a senior police officer, and the Real IRA issued an apology for the bombing, insisting that civilians had not been the target.

In December 2001, Nuala O'Loan, the ombudsman for Northern Ireland's new security force, issued a report severely criticizing the conduct of the Royal Ulster Constabulary (RUC), in particular the officers of its Special Branch, in the days before the bombing. The report maintains that a highly regarded police informant warned his Special Branch handlers that a bombing was being planned somewhere in Northern Ireland for August 15. It further alleges that a warning was received by the RUC that a mortar attack on police headquarters in Omagh was also planned for that date. The report implies that if these two pieces of information had been given to local police, the tragedy might have been averted.

August 15, 1998, photo of Royal Ulster Constabulary police officers and firefighters inspecting the damage caused by a bomb explosion on Market Street in Omagh, County Tyrone, Northern Ireland. Relatives of the Omagh bomb victims won a landmark multimillion pound civil action against four men they blamed for the atrocity in which 29 people died. Real IRA leader Michael McKevitt and three other men—Liam Campbell, Colm Murphy, and Seamus Daly—were found to be responsible for the terrorist attack by a judge in a landmark civil case brought by victims' families at Belfast High Court. (Paul McErlane/ Press Association via AP Images. © 2011 The Associated Press. All Rights Reserved.)

The victims' families expressed outrage at these conclusions, outrage that was only heightened when the only person convicted in connection with the Omagh bombing, Republic of Ireland citizen Colm Murphy, had his conviction overturned and a retrial ordered in 2005 because law enforcement officials tampered with interview notes and perjured themselves. A second suspect, Sean Holey, Murphy's nephew, was acquitted in 2007, with the judge once again strongly criticizing law-enforcement's handling of evidence from the attack.

Frustrated by the criminal courts, the families of the victims took the case to civil court, suing Murphy, Seamus Daly, Liam Campbell, and the founder of the Real IRA, Michael McKevitt, for their involvement in the bombing. On June 8, 2009, a judge found that the four men were liable for the attack and awarded the relatives £1.6 million.

Colleen Sullivan

See also Continuity Irish Republican Army; Irish Republican Army; Real Irish Republican Army

Further Readings

BBC News, World Edition. "In Depth: The Omagh Bomb." http://news.bbc.co.uk/2/hi/in_depth/northern_ireland/2000/the_omagh_bomb/default.stm.

Holland, Jack. *Hope against History: The Course of Conflict in Northern Ireland.* New York: Henry Holt, 1999.

McKittrick, David. "Justice at Last for the 29 Victims of the Omagh Bombing." *The Independent,* July 9, 2009, p. 2.

McKittrick, David. *Making Sense of the Troubles.* Belfast: Blackstaff Press, 2000.

O'Brien, Brendan. *The Long War: The IRA and Sinn Fein.* 2nd ed. Syracuse, NY: Syracuse University Press, 1999.

Taylor, Peter. *Provos: The IRA and Sinn Fein.* London: Bloomsbury, 1997.

Ware, John. "Garda Still Has Questions to Answer over Omagh Failures." *Belfast Telegraph,* December 24, 2007, p. 1.

OMEGA 7

Omega 7 was an anticommunist Cuban terrorist group that engaged in more than 30 attacks against Cuban-linked targets in the 1970s and 1980s.

The 1959 overthrow of Cuba's Batista regime by Fidel Castro and his Communist guerrillas initiated a massive exodus of refugees with links to the old regime. These exiles were welcomed in the United States, where they established large Cuban enclaves in several cities, most visibly in Miami. The U.S. government strongly opposed the Castro regime, and in the early 1960s it began training a guerrilla force with the intent of overthrowing the Communist government. The 1961 Bay of Pigs invasion was a fiasco, however, and the United States declined to involve itself in further military operations. By the early 1970s, some members of the Cuban American community had grown dissatisfied with only politically opposing Castro. With the support of the larger Cuban political organizations, a Cuban refugee named Eduardo Arocena began to recruit a small elite force, many of them veterans of the 1961 invasion, that would assassinate and bomb people and institutions deemed to be pro-Castro.

Founded on September 11, 1974, Arocena's group became known as Omega 7, after the original number of members, who were drawn from the Movimiento Insurreccional Martiano (MIM) and the Cuban Nationalist Movement (CNM). Omega 7 appears to have never had more than 20 members. Most of its financial support came from these groups and wealthy Cuban businessmen. However, in 1981 Arocena and a few other Omega 7 members were paid by a Cuban marijuana trafficker to conduct surveillance and other activities (the group, however, did not sell or transport any drugs). As it operated with the tacit approval of many within the Cuban exile community, the FBI found the group extremely difficult to infiltrate. Indeed, for several years, the FBI thought "Omega 7" was a cover name for the larger CNM, an impression that the CNM actively fostered.

The organization made its first attack in 1975, bombing the Venezuelan consulate in New York City on February 1. Over the next seven years, its targets included Soviet businesses and ships, Latin American embassies, and pro-Castro Cuban exiles and businesses in New York, New Jersey, Washington, D.C., and Florida. In the more than 30 attacks attributed to Omega 7, two people were killed and a few injured, and property damage was extensive. Its most devastating attacks were against the Cuban Mission to the United Nations. On March 25, 1980, the group attached a radio-controlled bomb to the car of Dr. Raúl Roa Kouri, the Cuban ambassador to the United Nations. In parking the car, however, the bomb was loosened from the undercarriage, and Arocena decided not to detonate it. An Omega 7 gunman killed a Cuban attaché, Felix Garcia Rodriguez, on September 11, 1980.

Law enforcement agencies were beginning to close in following the group's bombing of the Cuban consulate in Montreal in December 1980. By 1981, dissension began to fracture the Omega 7 group. Chafing under Arocena's leadership, several members allied themselves with the more moderate Cuba Independiente y Democrática (CID). In September 1982, FBI agents investigating the bombing in Montreal approached Arocena, asking him to give information about the group's activities. Apparently convinced that his comrades were informing on him in an attempt to oust him from the leadership, Arocena agreed to be interviewed by the FBI. He admitted to being "Omar," his *nom de guerre* as Omega 7's leader, and implicated himself and several colleagues in the murder of Rodriguez and the attempted murder of Dr. Kouri. After five days, Arocena fled New York for Miami, where he resumed his anti-Castro activities. Found and arrested on July 22, 1983, he is currently serving a life term in federal prison. Information Arocena provided led to the capture and arrest of several other group members, and to the dissolution of the group.

Colleen Sullivan

See also Arocena, Eduardo

Further Readings

Elfrink, Tim. "Let Terrorist Eduardo Arocena Go: *El Exilio* Wants Him out of Jail." *Miami New Times,* September 25, 2008. http://www.miaminewtimes. com/2008-09-25/news/let-terrorist-eduardo-arocena-go.

Federal Bureau of Investigation. "Cuban Information Archives: Omega 7." http://cuban-exile.com/menu1/ !group.html.

Lubasch, Arnold H. "Cuban Exile Group Reportedly Planned to Kill Castro on His '79 U.N. Trip." *The New York Times,* September 22, 1983, p. B1.

Treaster, Joseph B. "Suspected Head of Omega 7 Terrorist Group Seized." *The New York Times,* July 23, 1983, p. 1.

Treaster, Joseph B. "Weapons Seized in Apartment of Omega 7 Suspect." *The New York Times,* July 24, 1983, p. 1.

OPERATION EAGLE CLAW

In 1980, after nearly six months of failed diplomatic negotiations for the release of American hostages held at the U.S. embassy in Tehran, Iran, President Jimmy Carter approved a military rescue. This mission, known as Operation Eagle Claw, failed in its first stages, but profoundly influenced the military structure of Special Operations Forces.

On November 4, 1979, 3,000 militant students stormed the U.S. embassy in Tehran, taking 66 Americans hostage. The siege came two weeks after Carter had allowed the former shah of Iran, who was deposed during the Iranian revolution in 1978, into the United States for cancer treatment. Iran's new fundamentalist leader, Ayatollah Ruhollah Khomeini, called for the United States to return the shah, as well as for the end of Western influences in Iran.

By mid-November, 13 women and African Americans had been freed; however, the remaining 53 hostages waited out five months of failed negotiations. At the time, U.S. military forces, though trained for a possible conventional war with the Soviet Union, were ill-prepared for a terrorist siege. Carter, inexperienced in foreign affairs, relied on Zbigniew Brzezinski, his national security advisor, who favored force, and Secretary of State Cyrus Vance, who favored diplomacy, to shape his foreign policy. When diplomacy failed on April 16, 1980, Carter approved a military rescue operation.

Three branches of the service—army, air force, and marines—were to be involved in the rescue. The two-day plan called for helicopters and C-130 air force planes to land 250 miles from Tehran on a salt flat in the Dasht-e-Kavir desert (code-named Desert One), where the helicopters would refuel from the C-130s and pick up combat troops. The helicopters would then transport troops to the mountain location from which the actual rescue mission would launch the following night. Starting on April 19, forces were deployed throughout Oman and the Arabian Sea; on April 24, Operation Eagle Claw began.

Eight navy helicopters left the USS *Nimitz* just after 7 P.M. En route, two helicopters experienced mechanical failure and could not continue, and the entire group was hindered by a low-level dust storm (*haboob*) that reduced visibility to one mile. Six helicopters landed at Desert One just after 1 AM, more than 90 minutes late. There, another helicopter was deemed unfit for service and the mission, which could not be accomplished with only five helicopters, was aborted. As the forces were leaving, a helicopter collided with a C-130 and exploded, destroying both aircraft and killing five members of the air force and three marines. Remaining personnel were quickly evacuated by plane, leaving several helicopters, equipment, weapons, maps, and the dead behind. Iranian intelligence discovered this material, which led to the near-capture of other Special Operations Forces on the ground in Tehran.

Operation Eagle Claw helped transform U.S. military internal operating procedures. After investigations concluded that the weaknesses of Operation Eagle Claw arose from a lack of coordination between the military services, evidenced in part by compartmentalized training and inadequate equipment maintenance, the military embraced the "joint doctrine" under which it currently operates. Operation Eagle Claw also led to a rebirth of the Special Operations Forces, including the development of elite counterterrorism forces such as Seal Team Six.

Laura Lambert

See also Counterterrorism; Iranian Hostage Crisis

Further Readings

Acree, Cliff M. *The Iranian Hostage Rescue Mission: What Went Wrong?* Norfolk, VA: Armed Forces Staff College, 1984.

Campbell, James L. *Downfall at Desert One: The Cost of Operational Security in the Iran Rescue Operation.* Newport, RI: Naval War College, 1990.

Christopher, Warren, et al. *American Hostages in Iran: The Conduct of a Crisis.* New Haven, CT: Yale University Press, 1985.

Coker, Christine. "Planning in Hostage Rescue Missions, US Operation Eagle Claw and UK Operation Barras." *Military Technology* 30, no. 9 (2006): 66–69.

Jordan, Hamilton. *Crisis: The Last Years of the Carter Presidency.* New York: Putnam, 1982.

Kyle, James H., and John Robert Eidson. *The Guts to Try: The Untold Story of the Iran Hostage Rescue Mission by the On-scene Desert Commander.* New York: Orion Books, 1990.

Smith, Michael. *Killer Elite: The Inside Story of America's Most Secret Special Operations Team.* New York: St. Martin's, 2006.

Zimmerman, Dwight Jon, and John D. Gresham. *Beyond Hell and Back: How America's Special Operations Forces Became the World's Greatest Fighting Unit.* New York: St. Martin's, 2007.

ORANGE VOLUNTEERS

Relatively little is known about the Orange Volunteers, a Northern Irish terrorist organization that has claimed responsibility for a number of attacks on Roman Catholics beginning in 1998.

From the late 1960s until 1998, Northern Ireland, a province of Great Britain, experienced a steady and violent conflict between Catholics, who wanted Northern Ireland to become part of the Republic of Ireland, and Protestants, who wanted it to remain a part of the United Kingdom. Both communities fostered armed paramilitary groups that were prepared to use violence to achieve their ends. In the early 1970s, a Protestant paramilitary group known as the Orange Volunteers, led by the former British soldier Bob Marno, was formed. Members claimed responsibility for some murders of Catholics between 1974 and 1977, but the Orange Volunteers were principally known for its association with the 1974 Ulster Worker's Council (UWC) strike. This strike had caused the failure of the Sunningdale Agreement, the first serious peace attempt between Northern Ireland and Great Britain.

Before the strike, the UWC was a largely unknown organization with little political power. The council engaged paramilitaries from the Ulster Volunteer Force (UVF), the Ulster Defense Association (UDA), and the Orange Volunteers to compel workers to stay home during the strike's early days. (Once the strike seemed to be having an effect, most workers stayed home voluntarily.)

After the strike, the Orange Volunteers faded from public view, and many believed the organization to be defunct by the 1980s.

In late 1997, peace negotiations had again begun in Northern Ireland, with all parties—the governments of Britain and Ireland, the major political parties, and paramilitaries—involved; the negotiations covered a provision that persons imprisoned for terrorist activities on behalf of the paramilitary groups would be released gradually. On April 10, 1998, preliminary negotiations were concluded and The Good Friday Agreement was signed. The agreement laid out a plan to achieve political stability in Northern Ireland, and this plan included a provision for the release of prisoners.

Hard-line factions in both Loyalist organizations (representing Protestants; also called Unionists) and the Republican organizations (representing Catholics; also called Nationalists) split over the Good Friday peace plan and formed their own groups. Members of the re-formed Orange Volunteers (at first believed to be a separate splinter group of one of the larger Loyalist organizations) gave a televised interview to the journalist Ivan Little in November 1998, stating that they were taking up arms for the express purpose of killing newly released Republican prisoners. Comments by the group during the interview and references made to the biblical Book of Revelations may indicate that the group has some connection to fundamentalist Protestants and with the Protestant fraternal organization the Orange Order. The Orange Volunteers have been linked to about a dozen sectarian attacks on Catholic homes, mostly with mortar and pipe bombs, and to violent Loyalist protests at Drumcree centered around a route for a Protestant march in 1999 and 2000. In February 2001, the group issued a "Back to War" statement, once again declaring its intention to murder released Republican prisoners. They have also threatened to bomb Dublin, the capital of the Republic of Ireland. They have been linked to the September 2001 murder of Northern Irish journalist Owen Martin O'Hagan. The group was declared illegal in Great Britain and Ireland in 1999 and was placed on the U.S. State Department's list of terrorist organizations in 2001.

Many observers now believe that the Orange Volunteers is merely a cover name employed by dissatisfied members of one of the larger Loyalist groups—possibly the Ulster Defense Association or the Loyalist Volunteer Force, both of which have observed a cease-fire since 1994 and 1998, respectively. After remaining fairly quiet for a number of years, the Orange Volunteers began to make news again in 2008, when the group claimed responsibility for setting fire to a clubhouse in County Tyrone. The Orange Volunteers have also issued death threats against Irish Catholic politicians such as Gerry Adams, Alex Maskey, and Caitriona Ruane.

Colleen Sullivan

See also Irish Republican Army; Loyalist Volunteer Force; Red Hand Defenders; Ulster Defense Association; Ulster Freedom Fighters; Ulster Volunteer Force

Further Readings

BBC News. "The Search for Peace: Orange Volunteers." http://news.bbc.co.uk/hi/english/static/northern_ireland/understanding/parties_paramilitaries/orange_volunteers.stm.

Bruce, Steve. *The Red Hand: Protestant Paramilitaries in Northern Ireland.* Oxford: Oxford University Press, 1992.

Henry, Lesley-Anne. "As the Halls Burn, Relations Suffer." *Belfast Telegraph,* November 21, 2008, p. 12.

Holland, Jack. *Hope Against History: The Course of Conflict in Northern Ireland.* New York: Henry Holt, 1999.

Kaufmann, Eric P. *The Orange Order: A Contemporary Northern Irish History.* Oxford: Oxford University Press, 2007.

McKay, Susan. *Northern Protestants: An Unsettled People.* Belfast: Blackstaff Press, 2000.

Scottish Loyalists. "Orange Volunteers 'Back to War' Statement, 4-Feb-01." http://www.scottishloyalists.com/paramilitaries/ovolunteers.htm.

Ryder, Chris. *The RUC 1922–1997: A Force under Fire.* London: Mandarin, 1997.

Taylor, Peter. *Loyalists: War and Peace in Northern Ireland.* New York: TV Books, 1999.

ORDER, THE

Best known for the assassination of Alan Berg, a Jewish radio talk show host, the white supremacist group known as The Order planned to start a revolution against the U.S. government. Although its founder, Robert Jay Mathews, preferred the name *Bruders Schweigen*, meaning "Silent Brotherhood," the group's organization and activities were so closely modeled on the fictional group called The Order in William Pierce's *The Turner Diaries* (1978) that several of its members as well as authorities adopted this name.

In the 1970s, Mathews became involved with the tax protest movement, which sees taxation as a design of the federal government to take money from white Christian Americans and put it in the hands of Jews. He became somewhat disenchanted with the movement when he was arrested in 1973 for falsifying tax forms, because he received no support from his associates in the movement during the period between his arrest and trial. However, Mathews stayed involved with white supremacists through meetings of the Aryan Nations and the National Alliance. In October 1983 at his family compound in Metaline Falls, Washington, he and eight other men—some Neo-Nazi militants and others participants in the racist Christian Identity movement—took an oath to work toward a white supremacist society, and The Order was born.

To finance their group, members of The Order turned to crime; initially they targeted pimps, drug dealers, and anybody else they judged had no morals, convincing themselves they were doing God's work. Their first heist was at a pornographic video store, where the total take was $369.10. After that disappointing start, they escalated to counterfeiting and bank robbery. In December 1983, several members began "the revolution" by passing phony money in stores near Spokane, Washington. One member, Bruce Pierce (no relation to William Pierce), was discovered passing bad currency and arrested. Released on bail, he became a fugitive, continuing to work with The Order until his capture in 1985.

From shortly after Pierce's arrest in December 1983 through the summer of the following year, the group engaged in a very profitable crime spree. They pulled off two bank robberies that netted them $24,952 and $3,600, respectively. Finding those funds insufficient to bankroll a full-scale revolution, they invested in a more sophisticated counterfeiting scheme. For this, they recruited Robert Merki, a counterfeiter who had been

arrested and fled while released on bail. They also chose to engage in a more daring and elaborately schemed source of income: armored car robbery. Their first attempt took place in March and earned them $43,000. For the second armored car robbery, in April, they first set off a bomb in a pornographic movie house in Seattle in order to create a diversion for police. The take was $230,379 in U.S. currency, plus checks and some Canadian currency.

In July a third armored car robbery, in Ukiah, California, netted them $3.8 million. The money was divided among the members for salary and various enterprises. One member, Randall Rader—a survivalist trainer formerly of The Covenant, the Sword, and the Arm of the Lord (CSA)—was given enough money to build and outfit a militia training camp in Priest River, Idaho. Richard Scutari, the group's security expert, was given money to invest in security equipment. Allotments were also dispersed to various heads of right-winged extremist groups, including William Pierce of the National Alliance and Glenn Miller of the White Patriot Party.

In April 1984, shortly after the Seattle armored car robbery, Pierce and another Order member, Jack Kemp, decided to go out on their own and commit a crime without first telling their associates. They drove to Boise, Idaho, and planted a homemade bomb in an empty synagogue. The resulting blast did little damage and ultimately angered the other members. Mathews was especially angry, as he saw the action as an unnecessary risk, considering little damage had been done and nobody was hurt or killed.

Then in May, The Order committed its first murder. Walter West, an Aryan Nations member, had become a security threat. It was believed he was drinking and talking about The Order's activities in local bars. West was killed and buried in a wooded area by four members—Kemp, Randy Duey, David Tate, and James Dye.

The following month, Mathews enlisted his lover's mother, Jean Craig, to track the Denver radio show host Alan Berg, and to prepare a detailed dossier of the popular radio personality's habits and movements. Berg was targeted because he was Jewish and a vocal opponent of right-wing extremism. Informants later confirmed that David Lane drove Mathews, Pierce, and Scutari to Berg's home, where Pierce shot Berg several times with a machine gun. The Order had an assassination list that included Morris Dees, the cofounder of the Southern Poverty Law Center, and Norman Lear, a producer of television programs that often showed blacks in a positive light. None of these other assassinations were carried out.

While seemingly a huge success, in the long term the Ukiah robbery proved a failure in one respect. Mathews made a crucial error, dropping the gun he was using in the back of the armored car. The gun, found at the scene by police, was traced to another member of The Order, Andrew V. Barnhill. That put the FBI on a trail that led to several members, forcing the group underground.

Their ultimate downfall began when Thomas Martinez, a member of the group, was arrested in Philadelphia for passing counterfeit money that Lane had brought to him shortly after the Berg assassination. When it came time for his trial, Martinez cooperated with authorities, and in November 1984 he tricked Mathews into meeting with him in Portland. Gary Yarbrough was also at the meeting. Wanted by the FBI for shooting at several agents, a search of Yarbrough's home turned up the gun that was used in the Berg assassination. At the Portland meeting, the FBI captured Yarbrough as he tried to climb out the back window of his motel room. Mathews managed to escape.

Several members of The Order fled with Mathews to Whidbey Island in Puget Sound, where they composed a declaration of war on the United States government. The FBI eventually tracked them to the island but not before most of them managed to escape. Duey, Merki, and Merki's wife Sharon, however, remained there with Mathews and eventually surrendered to the FBI. Mathews died after a two-day standoff when the house he was in went up in flames from a flare.

Over the next several months, authorities captured all but one member of The Order. Most were taken without incident, including Pierce and Lane, who were captured in March and April of 1985. Tate, however, killed a state trooper during a traffic stop. Authorities believed Tate was headed to the CSA compound in Arkansas, so they laid siege to the compound. As it turned out, Tate was not there, but he eventually surrendered at a park not far away. Four other Order members, however, surrendered with the CSA after a four-day standoff. Almost a year later, in March 1986, Richard

Scutari, the last Order member brought to justice, was captured.

Eventually 11 members negotiated plea bargains, and 10 were convicted of racketeering and conspiracy in a trial that set legal precedent: It was the first time the Racketeer Influenced and Corrupt Organizations (RICO) Act was used in a political case. (Until then, it had been used mostly to prosecute organized crime figures.) Sentences ranged from 30 to 150 years. One member, Bill Soderquist, was granted complete immunity for his cooperation. Martinez was sentenced to probation and was eventually paid $25,000 for his role in the investigation.

In the fall of 1987, Lane, Scutari, Pierce, and Craig were prosecuted for civil rights violations for their roles in the Berg slaying. Lane and Pierce were convicted, while Scutari and Craig were found not guilty. Then, in 1988, 14 people involved in the white supremacist movement—including five members of The Order—faced federal sedition charges in the federal government's Operation Clean Sweep. All were acquitted in that trial.

Nancy Egan

See also Covenant, the Sword and the Arm of the Lord, The; Law and Terrorism; Mathews, Robert Jay; Scutari, Richard; *Turner Diaries, The*; White Supremacy Movement

Further Readings

Durham, Martin. *White Rage: The Extreme Right and American Politics*. New York: Routledge, 2007.
Flynn, Kevin, and Gary Gerhardt. *The Silent Brotherhood: Inside America's Racist Underground*. New York: Free Press, 1989.
Martinez, Thomas, and John Guinther. *Brotherhood of Murder*. New York: McGraw-Hill, 1988.
Singular, Stephen. *Talked to Death: The Life and Murder of Alan Berg*. New York: Beech Tree Books, 1987.
Zeskind, Leonard. *Blood and Politics: The History of the White Nationalist Movement from the Margins to the Mainstream*. New York: Farrar, Straus and Giroux, 2009.

ORDINE NUOVO

On December 12, 1969, a bomb exploded in the Banca Nazionale dell'Agricoltura in Milan's Piazza Fontana, killing 16 and wounding 90.

Authorities later determined that Ordine Nuovo, an Italian right-wing neofascist group also known as Armed Revolutionary Nuclei, was responsible for the attack. The bombing marked the beginning of Ordine Nuovo's "strategy of tension"—a series of public bombings intended to destabilize Italy and diminish support for the Communist Party. The group's terror-bombing campaign would continue for more than a decade.

The origins of Ordine Nuovo are still in dispute. Among of the fiercest advocates for fascism in Italy, Ordine Nuovo was organized around 1960 by a journalist named Pino Rauti. The group was long mired in controversy over an alleged connection to the CIA. Informants have testified that Rauti and many other Italian fascists were actually "rehabilitated" Nazi collaborators tapped by the CIA for a NATO "stay behind" anticommunist terror network, known as "Gladio."

Ordine Nuovo's terror campaign began with the 1969 Piazza Fontana bombing and continued with a number of similar attacks throughout Italy in the 1970s and early 1980s. In July 1970, Ordine Nuovo bombed a Rome-Messina train, leaving six people dead and nearly 100 wounded. Four years later, members of the group threw grenades into an antifascist march in Brescia, killing eight activists. Its most infamous and horrific attack occurred on August 1, 1980, when an offshoot of Ordine Nuovo, the Armed Revolutionary Nuclei (ARN), bombed the Bologna train station. More than 80 civilians died.

On June 30, 2001, three members of Ordine Nuovo received life sentences for planting the Piazza Fontana bomb in 1969. Some prosecutors and families of the victims maintain that this was a political sentencing; one of the original suspects, Giuseppe Pinelli, died after falling out of a police-house window during questioning. Another suspect, Pietro Valpreda, spent only three years in prison before being set free. Rauti is now the head of another neofascist group, Fiammi Tricolore (Tricolor Flame), which is popular with both skinheads and neo-Nazis.

Richard McHugh

Further Readings

Jones, Tobias. *The Dark Heart of Italy*. London: Faber and Faber, 2003.

Levy, C. *Gramsci and the Anarchists*. Oxford: Berg, 1999.

Linklater, Magnus. "Expect Dirty Tactics in New Hundred Years War on Terror." *Scotland on Sunday*, March 14, 2004, p. 15.

Woolf, S. J., ed. *Fascism in Europe*. London: Methuen, 1981.

OWHALI, MOHAMED RASHED AL (1977–)

Mohamed Rashed al Owhali (aka Mohammed Akbar; Abdul Jabbar Ali Abdel-Latif; Khalid Salim Saleh Bin Rashid) is known for being the failed martyr who ran from the bomb-laden truck in front of the U.S. embassy in Nairobi, Kenya, just before it exploded. A member of Osama bin Laden's al Qaeda network, Owhali was later captured and convicted of playing a direct role in the 1998 U.S. embassy bombings in East Africa; he is now serving a life sentence in the United States.

Mohamed al Owhali was born in Liverpool, England, where his wealthy Saudi father was a student. He formed radical ideas as a teenager, listening to audiotapes of conservative clerics and reading religious magazines. After high school, Owhali studied at Imam Muhammad Ibn Saud University in Riyadh, Saudi Arabia. After graduating from college, Owhali and a group of friends left for Afghanistan to join the fight against the Soviets. In Afghanistan, Owhali studied military and covert operations. He also met al Qaeda leaders and fought with the Taliban against the Northern Alliance in 1996.

Owhali was later recruited for the attack on the U.S. embassies in Nairobi and Dar es Salaam. In July 1998 he used a Yemeni passport to travel to Kenya, just a week before the bombing. In his confession, he said that the operation was planned so that he and a fellow driver would die as martyrs. On August 7, 1998, Owhali rode in the cab of the Toyota truck carrying the bomb to the U.S. embassy compound in Nairobi. As the truck neared the embassy, he threw a grenade at the guard stationed outside. Once the truck pulled up alongside the embassy, he decided that his death was not necessary for the mission to be accomplished. Just before his partner detonated the bomb from inside the cab, Owhali ran from the embassy compound.

The blast partially demolished the embassy. At the same time, 400 miles away in Dar es Salaam, another bomb exploded at the U.S. embassy there. In total, the two blasts killed 224 people. Owhali, who had cuts and abrasions all around his hands and face and a large wound on his back, was left without money or plane tickets, as he had been expected to die in the bombing. He went to a local hospital to get treatment, and while he was in the hospital bathroom, he threw away the keys from the padlock on the back of the bomb truck and three bullets from a gun he had left in the truck. Two days later, Kenyan officials found and arrested him. He was later tried with three others in a New York court. During the trial, the prosecuting attorney showed a photograph, taken after the bombing, of Owhali, his hands clasped together in the boxer's symbol of victory.

In June 2001 a jury sentenced the 24-year-old Owhali to life in prison. Several jurors said that they had decided against the death penalty because executing him could have given him the status of a martyr.

Erica Pearson

See also al Qaeda; East Africa Embassy Bombings; Odeh, Mohammed Saddiq

Further Readings

Akhahenda, Elijah F. *When Blood and Tears United a Country: The Bombings of the American Embassy in Kenya.* Lanham, MD: University Press of America/ Rowman & Littlefield, 2002.

Avalon Project. *Documents on Terrorism: Criminal Complaint against Kenya Bombing Suspect Al-'Owhali; August 26, 1998.* http://avalon.law.yale .edu/20th_century/t_0024.asp.

Jenkins, Brian Michael. *Countering Al Qaeda.* Santa Monica, CA: RAND, 2002.

PBS/Frontline. "FBI Executive Summary: Bombings of the Embassies of the United States of America at Nairobi, Kenya and Dar es Salaam, Tanzania, August 7, 1998." http://www.pbs.org/wgbh/pages/frontline/ shows/binladen/bombings/summary.html.

"Suicide Bomber Who Flunked Martyrdom." *Financial Times* (London), November 29, 2001.

Swanson, Stevenson. "Embassy Bomber Gets Life; 10 on Jury Feared Creating a Martyr." *Chicago Tribune,* June 13, 2001.

PADILLA, JOSÉ (1970–)

An American-born convert to Islam, José Padilla became known in the U.S. media as the "Dirty Bomber." He was accused by the U.S. government in 2002 of being tasked by al Qaeda's leadership to detonate nuclear materials inside the United States. Subsequent investigations revealed that Padilla had indeed consorted with al Qaeda's mastermind Khalid Shaikh Mohammed and discussed attacking the United States, but his plan involved blowing up apartment buildings using natural gas. Initially detained in a Navy brig as an enemy combatant, Padilla was later charged in a civilian court for his role in a South Florida–based recruitment network and sentenced to 17 years in jail.

Born in Brooklyn in 1970, José Padilla moved as a child to Chicago, where he grew up in an underprivileged neighborhood with his mother and four siblings. As a teenager he joined a gang and was frequently involved in criminal activities. At age 14 he served his first stint in jail after he and a friend killed a Mexican immigrant they had tried to rob. He was placed in juvenile detention until he was 19.

Shortly after his release, Padilla relocated to South Florida, where he served additional time for other felonies. At 21 he obtained a job at a local fast-food outlet and, together with his Jamaican girlfriend (soon to be his wife), became interested in Islam. Upon converting he abandoned his criminal life and immersed himself in religious studies. While attending the Masjid al Iman mosque in downtown Fort Lauderdale, Padilla met Adham Hassoun, the head of the Florida chapter of Benevolence International Foundation, an al Qaeda–linked charity shut down by U.S. authorities after 9/11. Hassoun was also at the center of a nationwide network that recruited for various jihadist causes throughout the 1990s.

In 1998 Padilla left his wife and moved to Egypt, ostensibly to study Arabic and live in an Islamic environment. He married a local woman, but soon began spending extensive time in Yemen, where he met an al Qaeda recruiter who sponsored him to travel to Afghanistan. There, in the fall of 2000, he completed basic training at al Qaeda's al Farouq training camp under the name Abdullah al Espani (Abdullah the Hispanic).

At al Farouq, Padilla met Muhammad Atef, then al Qaeda's military commander. Atef became a mentor for the young American militant and tasked him with a mission to return to America and blow up apartment buildings using natural gas. Padilla accepted and went on to train with an explosives expert at a site near Kandahar Airport. However, disagreements between Padilla and his designated accomplice, fellow Florida resident Adnan Shukrijumah, brought the plan to a halt.

A few weeks later, in the wake of the 9/11 attacks, U.S. forces attacked Afghanistan and Atef was killed in the bombing of his hideout. Padilla barely escaped with his life and fled to Pakistan. Near the Afghan-Pakistani border Padilla met the senior al Qaeda official Abu Zubaydah, who had assumed the role of coordinating the activities of the al Qaeda militants fleeing Afghanistan after the

U.S. invasion. Padilla presented Zubaydah with a plan to detonate explosives wrapped in uranium (a "dirty bomb") on U.S. soil. Zubaydah was skeptical about the feasibility of the plan but nevertheless referred Padilla to Khalid Shaikh Mohammed, the mastermind of the 9/11 attacks and al Qaeda chief of operations.

Mohammed was reportedly similarly skeptical about the plot, but suggested that Padilla and an accomplice, the Ethiopian native Binyam Mohamed, travel to the United States. They were instructed to rent several apartments in high-rise buildings that had gas stoves. The plan was for the men to detonate bombs in the buildings after having left the gas on in order to enhance the explosions that would follow. After receiving extensive training in communication security by Mohammed, his nephew and close associate Ammar al Baluchi, and 9/11 planner bin al Shibh, Padilla and Mohamed were reportedly given $20,000 each and dispatched to the United States.

Binyam Mohamed was arrested in Pakistan and later transferred to the Guantánamo Bay detention center. Padilla was arrested upon entering the United States at Chicago's O'Hare International Airport in May 2002. Accused of planning to carry out a dirty-bomb attack inside the country, he was designated an enemy combatant. Padilla was detained in solitary confinement in a Navy brig in South Carolina for three and half years without charges being filed against him.

After extensive legal wrangling, the U.S. government was forced to move Padilla's case to the civilian court system, and in November 2005 a federal grand jury in Miami returned an indictment charging Padilla and four other defendants with various conspiracy charges, including providing material support to terrorists. Transferred from the custody of the Defense Department to that of the Justice Department, Padilla was tried neither for his role in the dirty-bomb plot nor for the apartment plot. Instead, authorities charged him, Hassoun, and three others with being part of a "North American support cell" that between 1993 and 2001 sent "money, physical assets and mujahideen recruits to overseas jihad conflicts." Padilla was found guilty by a federal jury, and in January 2008 he was sentenced to 17 years and 4 months in prison.

Padilla's case is remembered mostly for two reasons. First, the charge that he was involved in a plot with al Qaeda's upper echelons to detonate radioactive material on U.S. soil attracted enormous attention from the media. Later, his case became controversial because of his designation as an "enemy combatant." While the designation was applied by the Bush administration to hundreds of foreign nationals, Padilla was the only U.S. citizen to be considered as such and consequently deprived of due process guarantees.

Lorenzo Vidino

See also al Qaeda; Atef, Muhammad; Bombings and Bomb Scares; Homegrown Jihadi Movement; Law and Terrorism; Mohammed, Khalid Shaikh; Zubaydah, Abu

Further Readings

DeMarzo, Wanda. "Ex-mosque Leader Says Suspect Wasn't Radical in Broward." *Miami Herald*, June 17, 2002.

Emerson, Steven. *Jihad Incorporated: A Guide to Militant Islam in the U.S.* Amherst, NY: Prometheus, 2006.

Sontag, Deborah. "Terror Suspect's Path from Streets to Brig." *The New York Times*, April 25, 2004.

U.S. District Court for the Southern District of Florida. *United States v. Adham Amin Hassoun, et al.* Case No. 04-60001-CR-COOKE, Superseding Indictment, November 17, 2005. http://openjurist.org/476/f3d/1181/united-states-v-hassoun.

Wilgoren, Jodi. "From Chicago Gang to Possible al Qaeda Ties." *The New York Times*, June 11, 2002. http://query.nytimes.com/gst/fullpage.html?res=9800E EDB1E3DF932A25755C0A9649C8B63.

PALESTINE ISLAMIC JIHAD

A tiny but fiercely militant Islamic group, Palestine Islamic Jihad (PIJ) is made up of a handful of loosely affiliated factions, the largest of which was led by Dr. Fathi Shaqaqi until his assassination in 1995. Although PIJ has become well known for its violent tactics and its opposition to a negotiated peace with Israel, the group, headquartered in Syria, is relatively small and mysterious; it is said to receive financial assistance from Iran. Attacks by the group are sometimes claimed by its armed wing, al Quds Brigades.

Palestine Islamic Jihad was founded in Egypt in the late 1970s by three Palestinian students. Shaqaqi, Abdul Aziz Odeh, and Bashir Moussa, all Sunni Muslims who are said to have been inspired by the Shiite groups that came to power during Iran's Islamist revolution in 1978–1979. PIJ has focused primarily on terror attacks against Israel. Shaqaqi had publicly stated that PIJ shares a name and ideology with many other Islamic jihad groups (in Egypt, Lebanon, and Turkey, for example), though the groups have little contact with one another. Many of the groups, like PIJ, have material and ideological ties to Iran.

After the assassination of President Anwar Sadat of Egypt in 1981, the Egyptian government cracked down on Islamic terrorists. Shaqaqi, Odeh, and Moussa were expelled from the country and they returned to Palestine. During the 1980s, the group began organizing in territories occupied by Israel. PIJ carried out its first successful military operation in 1987, assassinating an Israeli military police captain. Shaqaqi and Odeh were later deported to Lebanon, after which they found refuge in Damascus, Syria, where they plotted multiple bombing attacks on Israeli military and civilian targets.

The PIJ strongly opposed the Arab-Israeli peace process and continued to attack Israel as negotiations intensified. In 1995 the PIJ blew up a military bus stop near Netanya, killing 19 in an attack that press reports said seemed timed to cause the maximum number of casualties. Just months later the group took responsibility for a suicide nail bomb in Tel Aviv that killed 13. In October 1995, on the evening before U.S. secretary of state Warren Christopher's trip to Damascus, assassins thought to be working for Israel's intelligence service Mossad gunned down Shaqaqi on the Mediterranean island of Malta.

After Shaqaqi's death, an academic working in the United States, Ramadan Abdullah al Shallah, became PIJ's new leader. Shallah left his post at the University of South Florida to take command of the group. According to the U.S. State Department, PIJ has never specifically attacked U.S. interests, despite a July 2000 public threat to carry out attacks if the U.S. embassy was moved from Tel Aviv to Jerusalem. The PIJ has continued to work to stall the peace process, initiating several attacks against Israel, including suicide bombings and numerous rocket attacks. PIJ has worked increasingly closely with Hamas, sparking rumors in 2009 (which the group denied) that it might merge with the larger organization.

The Sami al Arian Case

The departure of Shallah in 1995 from the University of South Florida to lead PIJ caused tremendous controversy in the United States. Two years later, federal immigration agents arrested one of Shallah's Palestinian academic colleagues, Mazen al Najjar. While he was never charged with a crime, al Najjar was held in jail without bail for three-and-a-half years on secret evidence suggesting that he was a threat to national security. Finally, a judge ruled that his detention was unconstitutional, and he was released in late 2000, only to be arrested again in November 2001. He was finally deported to Lebanon in September 2002, because he had overstayed a visa that had been issued 20 years before. He later moved to Egypt.

The following year, al Najjar's brother-in-law, colleague at the University of South Florida, and close friend Sami al Arian was arrested along with three other men for providing assistance and leadership to PIJ. At the time of his arrest, the U.S. attorney general characterized Arian as the U.S. leader of PIJ.

The al Arian case was regarded as a test case for the Patriot Act of 2001, which was adopted to strengthen the United States' ability to fight terrorism following the September 11 attacks. The act made it legal to admit material gathered under the 1978 Foreign Intelligence Surveillance Act as evidence in a criminal case; previously such material was inadmissible. Despite the new law, on December 6, 2005, al Arian was acquitted on 8 of the 17 counts against him, including conspiracy to commit murder, and the jury deadlocked on the other 9 counts. His codefendants were acquitted of most or all of the charges against them.

In April 2006, Sami al Arian reached a deal with prosecutors, pleading guilty to two charges: one of assisting people (including al Najjar) who he knew to be in PIJ, and one of concealing his knowledge of their links to the organization. He was given a 57-month sentence, with time off for time served, followed by deportation.

Instead, however, his sentence was extended because he refused to testify in another case in

Virginia, claiming that his plea agreement permitted him to do so. Criminal contempt charges were filed against him, but a judge ordered him released on bail in July 2008. Instead of being released, al Arian was incarcerated by immigration authorities. He was finally released on bail in September 2008, five years after he was initially jailed, with his contempt case still pending. However, Florida prosecutors acknowledged that when they reached their plea agreement with Arian in 2006, they too understood it to exempt him from having to testify in other cases.

While Ramadan Abdullah al Shallah's taking the helm of PIJ caused tremendous concern in the United States that the country was harboring terrorists, the cases of al Najjar and al Arian have led to equally vigorous protests that the government has run roughshod over people's rights in its post–September 11 enthusiasm to quash terrorism.

Erica Pearson

See also Hamas; Hezbollah; Patriot Act

Further Readings

Bhatia, Shyam. "Shadow of Mossad over Shooting in Malta." *The Observer,* October 29, 1995.

Fisk, Robert. "Suicide Bombing of Israeli Café Heralds Fresh Wave of Attacks." *The Independent,* August 13, 2001, p. 1.

Gellman, Barton. "Two-stage Bombing Kills 19 at Israeli Military Bus Stop." *The Washington Post,* January 23, 1995, p. A1.

Kushner, Harvey. *Holy War on the Home Front: The Secret Islamic Terror Network in the United States.* New York: Sentinel, 2004.

Laughlin, Meg. "Al Arian Walks out of Prison." *St. Petersburg Times,* September 3, 2008, p. A1.

Leby, Richard. "Talking out of School: Was an Islamic Professor Exercising His Freedom or Promoting Terror?" *The Washington Post,* July 28, 2002, p. F1.

Richey, Warren. "Failed Case Seen as Blow to Terror War." *Christian Science Monitor,* December 8, 2005, p. 3.

Sachs, Susan. "Terrorism Inc.; Islamic Jihad Founder Admits Funding by Iran." *Newsday,* April 11, 1993, p. 7.

U.S. State Department. *Country Reports on Terrorism 2008.* http://www.state.gov/s/ct/rls/crt/2008/122449.htm.

PALESTINE LIBERATION FRONT– ABU ABBAS FACTION

The Abu Abbas–led faction of the Palestine Liberation Front (PLF), which has had headquarters in Lebanon, Tunisia, and Iraq, first became known for using hang gliders and hot air balloons in bizarre terror attacks against Israel. The group later came to world attention during the 1985 hijacking of the cruise ship *Achille Lauro,* in which a disabled, elderly New Yorker was killed and his body dumped overboard.

During the mid-1970s, the PLF was formed by men who broke from the Popular Front for the Liberation of Palestine–General Command (itself a breakaway faction of George Habash's original Popular Front for the Liberation of Palestine). The PLF, which began as a secular, Marxist group, later split into three factions: pro-Syrian, pro-Libyan, and pro-Yasir Arafat and his Palestine Liberation Organization (PLO). Each faction kept the original "Palestine Liberation Front" name and claimed to be the main organization. The pro-PLO faction, which has the most members and eventually absorbed one of the other splintered groups, was led by Muhammad "Abu" Abbas. Because Abbas's faction was critical of both Syria and Libya, Iraq also backed the group, but it was mostly identified with Arafat and the PLO. Abbas, who had been deputy general secretary of the PLF before it split into three groups, remained loyal to Arafat during the 1980s, when many others began to defect. Abbas became a member of the PLO Executive Committee in 1984.

Unique Invasion Methods

During the late 1970s and early 1980s, Abbas became famous for planning numerous unorthodox attacks on Israel, many of which were foiled. In 1979, a four-member PLF crew, carrying machine guns and shoulder-launched grenades, paddled a rubber dinghy from Lebanon to invade Israel via the Mediterranean Sea. According to press reports, the squad landed in the Israeli town of Nahariya and held a family hostage inside their home. They killed the father, his daughter, and a police officer, and injured four others.

Two years later, two PLF members left Lebanon in hang gliders, attempting to fly over the electronic fence at the border into the Haifa area of Israel. The PLF operatives were apparently planning to continue gliding for as far as possible and, once over the border, throw bombs and grenades from the air. Israeli forces captured the gliders at the border. In just over a month, Abbas's men attacked again by air, this time aboard a hot air balloon. As the floating balloon neared the Israeli border, the army shot it down. The two PLF operatives fell to their death.

As provocative and unconventional as these attacks were, international attention was only gained when PLF members hijacked a cruise ship. On October 8, 1985, off Port Said, Egypt, PLF members from the Abbas faction took control of the *Achille Lauro* cruise ship as it sailed toward Israel. They held hundreds of passengers hostage for two grueling days, during which the hijackers demanded the release of 50 Palestinians held in Israel and threatened to blow up the ship. As the ship sailed along the Syrian coast, the hijackers shot and killed a U.S. citizen, Leon Klinghoffer. The men then threw his body overboard.

During the hijacking, the PLF accepted responsibility for the attack. This caused confusion in the press and illustrated just how splintered the Palestinian national movement had become, as reporters attempted to pin down which faction of the PLF—pro-Syrian, pro-Libyan, or pro-PLO— was responsible. Some speculated that the attack had been a Syrian attempt to sabotage Arafat's progress toward diplomatic agreements. After the ship docked in Cairo, Egyptian officials granted Abbas and his men safe passage to Tunisia in return for the hostages' release. However, U.S. Air Force fighter jets forced the Egyptair plane carrying the PLF members to land in Sicily, where Italian authorities arrested three of the hijackers. These same officials refused to turn Abbas and two colleagues over to the U.S. Marines, however; instead, they helped them flee to the former Yugoslavia.

Although an Italian court later tried him in absentia and sentenced him to life in prison, Abbas was never imprisoned in Italy. The press teemed with stories of his narrow escapes from the law. After the Italian conviction, the U.S. Justice

Achille Lauro was seized by a commando of the Palestine Liberation Front of Abu Abbas who organized the hijacking off the Egyptian coast on October 7, 1985, taking its 450 passengers hostages. A handicapped Jewish American passenger, Leon Klinghoffer, was killed by commando chief Majid al-Molki and thrown overboard. (Mike Nelson/AFP/Getty Images)

Department dropped its international warrant for Abbas's arrest, saying that the prosecutors did not have enough evidence to try him in a U.S. court. In many interviews, Abbas maintained that the hijacking was a mistake, and that he had instead plotted for his men to travel incognito aboard the *Achille Lauro* and then invade Israel when the ship docked at the Israeli town of Ashdod. He did, however, later admit that his operatives had killed Klinghoffer.

The PLF moved its base of operations to Iraq following the *Achille Lauro* hijacking. Like Arafat, Abbas supported Iraq's Saddam Hussein during the Gulf War (1990–1991), declaring "my enemy's enemy is my friend." (Hussein had threatened to attack Israel many times, famously stating that Iraq could "burn half of Israel.")

Negotiations Thwarted

In May 1990, in the midst of diplomatic negotiations between the PLO and the United States, a 17-member PLF squad once again attempted to invade Israel by sea. In five speedboats, PLF operatives traveled to beaches near Tel Aviv and Ashdod. Israeli defense forces stopped the attack before it began, killing four PLF members and arresting 12 others. Although Arafat quickly asserted that he had played no part in the raid, Washington terminated its 18-month discussion with the PLO.

Under pressure from the United States, Libya later expelled more than 100 PLF members and closed down several of the group's training camps. Abbas claimed that the aborted raid was in retaliation for the killing of Palestinian workers in Tel Aviv by an Israeli gunman. Israeli officials countered that the raid had been planned for a long time and could not be a response to the workers' deaths. An Israeli military court later tried the captured PLF members and sentenced them to 30 years in prison for attempted murder, membership in a terrorist group, and possession of firearms.

Abbas left the PLO a year after the failed raid. He moved the PLF toward the mainstream in 1993 when he supported the Oslo Accords, and he publicly embraced the peace process in 1996. Two years later, Israeli officials allowed him to enter the country and travel to the Gaza Strip, where, in a Palestinian National Council meeting, he voted to revoke the parts of the PLO's charter that call for Israel's destruction. He then returned triumphantly from exile to establish himself and the PLF in Gaza City, commuting between Gaza and his old base in Baghdad.

Although Abbas said that the new path of the PLF would be a political one, in November 2001 Israeli security forces arrested at least 15 PLF members suspected of plotting further attacks. According to Israeli officials, the men were planning to plant bombs at Ben-Gurion Airport and in Tel Aviv and Jerusalem.

As the peace process with Israel broke down, Abbas moved back to Baghdad, where he was arrested in 2003 by U.S.-led forces. He died of a heart attack on March 8, 2004, while in U.S. custody there. Following his death, the PLF elected Omar Shibli, also known as Abu Ahmed Halab, as secretary-general of the group. According to the U.S. Department of State, which considers the PLF a terrorist group, in 2008 the organization had somewhere between 50 and 500 members. While the group has largely been quiet since the early 1990s, it took credit for two attacks on Israeli targets in March 2008.

Erica Pearson

See also Abbas, Muhammad "Abu"; Achille Lauro Hijacking; Palestine Liberation Organization; Popular Front for the Liberation of Palestine; Popular Front for the Liberation of Palestine–General Command

Further Readings

"Abu Abbas." *The Daily Telegraph*, March 11, 2004, p. 25.

"Abu Abbas: Maverick Palestinian Guerilla Leader." *The Herald*, March 11, 2004, p. 18.

Abukhalil, Asad. "Arab Israeli Conflict." In *The Middle East*, edited by Robin Surrat. 9th ed. Washington, DC: CQ Press, 2000.

Associated Press. "Abbas Interview in Algeria." *The New York Times*, May 21, 1986, p. A12.

Berger, Joseph. "Hijacking at Sea: Even with a Name, It's Hard to Know Who the Hijackers Are." *The New York Times*, October 9, 1985, p. A9.

Bohn, Michael K. *The Achille Lauro Hijacking: Lessons in the Politics and Prejudice of Terrorism*. Washington, DC: Brassey's, 2004.

Burns, John F. "Mideast Tensions; Iraqi President Renews Threat to Attack Israel." *The New York Times*, October 10, 1990, p. A11.

Cockburn, Patrick. "Leader of 'Achille Lauro' Hijack Turns to the Ballot-box." *The Independent* (London), May 27, 1998. http://www.independent.co.uk/news/leader-of-achille-lauro-hijack-turns-to-the-ballotbox-1157499.html.

Dudkevitch, Margot. "Iraq-backed Terror Cell Nabbed in West Bank." *Jerusalem Post*, November 26, 2001, p. 3.

National Consortium for the Study of Terrorism and Responses to Terrorism. "Terrorist Organization Profile: Palestine Liberation Front." http://www.start.umd.edu/start/data/tops/terrorist_organization_profile.asp?id=157.

Sennott, Charles M. "Plotter Recast as Proponent of Mideast Peace." *The Boston Globe,* June 26, 1998, p. A1.

U.S. State Department. "Terrorist Organizations." *Country Reports on Terrorism 2008.* http://www.state.gov/s/ct/rls/crt/2008/122449.htm.

Vulliamy, Ed. "A Threat from the Angry Outsider: Abu Abbas, the Leader of the Palestine Liberation Front Wanted in the West for Murder, Is Promising to Wreak Worldwide Vengeance on the US If It Dares to Wage War on His Iraqi Benefactor." *The Guardian* (London), December 18, 1990.

PALESTINE LIBERATION ORGANIZATION

The Palestine Liberation Organization (PLO) is basically an umbrella organization that coordinates various Palestinian terrorist groups, professional unions and syndicates, and civilian groups. The PLO has built a network of embassies across the world and claims to be the sole representative of the Palestinian people. When PLO chairman Yasir Arafat signed the Oslo Peace Accords in 1993, the organization returned from exile in Tunisia to the West Bank and Gaza Strip. Throughout PLO history, cohesion between the many factions has been fragile, and many of its various terrorist groups have quarreled with and split from the organization, some later returning and some remaining independent.

Early Years

When the PLO was formed under the chairmanship of Ahmad Shuqairi at an Arab summit meeting in Cairo in 1964, it was said to be largely a token organization controlled by Egypt. The dynamics of the organization changed after the resounding Arab defeat in the Six-Day War (1967). Shuqairi came under attack for opposing the commando raids that groups such as Arafat's Fatah were carrying out against Israel. Shuqairi was forced to resign in December 1967, amid the growing popularity and power of these guerrilla factions. Yahya Hamuda replaced him as the PLO's acting chairman until the July 1968 Palestine National Council session brought large political gains to Fatah and the group Popular Front for the Liberation of Palestine (PFLP). Arafat was elected to replace Hamuda less than a year later, during the fifth meeting of the Palestine National Congress, the group's parliamentary body.

The PLO made Jordan its base during its early years, setting up outposts in the Palestinian refugee camps and crossing the border to raid Israeli settlements. During the late 1960s and early 1970s, many of the Palestinian groups also engaged in terror attacks in other countries to gain international attention for the cause. (Infamously, during the 1972 Olympic Games in Munich, 11 Israeli team members were killed in an attack linked to Black September, an extremist group within Fatah.) The PLFP, led by George Habash, became notorious for airline hijackings. These attacks caused problems between King Hussein of Jordan and the PLO, as the king felt the groups were undermining his authority.

In September 1970 the PFLP hijacked four planes in a single day, forcing them to land outside of Amman, the capital of Jordan. After all the hostages were released, the king ordered his army to attack Palestinian guerrillas and camps in Jordan. After 10 days of fighting, the Palestinians were defeated. This setback, known as "Black September" (from which the Black September Organization took its name), left Lebanon as the sole base from which the PLO could launch raids and attacks on Israel.

Gaining Ground

Even after being expelled from Jordan, the PLO continued to grow, establishing social and charity networks and creating the Palestinian Red Crescent Society, a health program. Many Arab states supplied the PLO with funds and diplomatic backing, and at an Arab League summit in Rabat, Morocco, in October 1974, the 20 Arab League heads of state unanimously recognized the PLO as the "sole legitimate representative of the Palestinian People."

A month later, the PLO and its chairman made history: Yasir Arafat addressed the United Nations General Assembly in New York City on November 13, 1974, saying, "Today I have come bearing an olive branch and a freedom fighter's gun. Do not let the olive branch fall from my hand. I repeat, do not let the olive branch fall from my hand." The General Assembly later voted, 105–4, with 20 abstentions, to grant the PLO observer status at the UN; the four "no" votes were cast by Israel, the United States, Bolivia, and the Dominican Republic. In 1976 the Arab League made the PLO the 21st full member of the league. Despite greater international recognition, the PLO was not invited to the 1979 Camp David negotiations between Egypt and Israel mediated by President Jimmy Carter. The resulting Camp David Accords called for talks on Palestinian self-rule in the occupied territories. The United States had maintained its policy of refusing to negotiate with the PLO until the organization recognized Israel's right to exist and accepted the UN Security Council Resolutions that renounced terrorism.

Lebanon

The PLO's presence in Lebanon was straining a country already on edge, as a conflict between Maronite Christian militias, government troops, and PLO-supporting Muslim groups was becoming more pronounced. In an attempt to defuse the violence in the region, the 1969 Cairo Agreement recognized Lebanese military control over the country but also allowed the PLO to maintain a political and military presence in specified areas of southern Lebanon, including the refugee camps. Conditions in Lebanon remained unstable, however, and civil war broke out in April 1975. The PLO did not immediately join in the fighting, but it did so several months later on the side of the Lebanese National Movement (LNM), a group of leftist and Arab nationalist organizations. As the power of the PLO-LNM allied forces began to grow, Lebanon's president, Sulayman Franjiyyah,

a right-wing Maronite, called upon Syria to intervene. This intervention was supposed to restore the balance and prevent the left-wing forces from taking over the government.

When Syria entered Lebanon, PLO forces returned to the south of the country. The PLO continued to carry out raids on Israel, however. Israel, in turn, began arming Lebanese Christian militias, aiding the Free Lebanon Militia and the Maronite Lebanese Forces. Israeli forces invaded Lebanon in March 1978, only to retreat three months later. Fighting between Israel, Syria, Lebanese militias, and the PLO continued, halted by a PLO-Israeli cease-fire on July 24, 1981.

Nearly a year later, on June 6, 1982, Israel thundered into Lebanon, driving PLO forces back into Beirut. Israel besieged that city eight days later. The siege continued until the end of the summer, when the PLO evacuated Beirut in an internationally brokered agreement. Just two weeks after the PLO forces left Beirut, a Maronite militia allied with Israel killed hundreds of Palestinian refugees in the city's Sabra and Shatila refugee camps. Many Palestinians held Arafat and other PLO leaders responsible for leaving Palestinians in the camps unprotected.

Throughout the PLO's history, many leaders of Arab nations have attempted to take control. In 1983, a PLO-Syria feud grew heated, with President Assad of Syria supporting a mutiny against Arafat's leadership of Fatah and the PLO. The "coup" was unsuccessful, however, and Arafat regrouped in Tunis, Tunisia. After leaving Lebanon, the organization was under a great deal of pressure to officially acknowledge Israel and accept the existing UN resolutions on the Arab-Israeli conflict in exchange for Palestinian self-rule.

Many of the different groups within the PLO were more radical about these issues than Arafat's Fatah movement, causing groups within the PLO to quarrel among themselves. In 1982, Palestinian terrorist groups affiliated with the PLO included Fatah, the Popular Front for the Liberation of Palestine (PFLP), the Democratic Front for the Liberation of Palestine (DFLP), al Sa'iqa, the Arab Liberation Front (ALF), the Popular Front for the Liberation of Palestine–General Command (PFLP–GC), the Palestine Liberation Front (PLF), and the Palestinian Popular Struggle Front (PPSF). In the years following, these groups split into various factions and alliances, and in 1985 many more split from the PLO.

In September 1985, members of Arafat's personal security squad, Force 17, killed three Israelis on a hijacked yacht in Lanarca, Cyprus. The PLO claimed that the men were agents for Mossad, the Israeli intelligence agency. Israel responded by bombing PLO headquarters in Tunis, killing 65.

Peace Negotiations

Arafat and the PLO began to negotiate more successfully for peace as the 1980s drew to a close. The first Palestinian intifada, or organized uprising, in the occupied territories also broke out during this time. As the intifada continued, Arafat convened a meeting of the Palestinian National Council in Algiers. On November 15, 1988, the PLO proclaimed its support in principle of the establishment of an independent Palestinian state and announced the recognition of UN Resolution 242, effectively recognizing Israel's right to coexist with Palestine. At the meeting the group also accepted a declaration rejecting terrorism. One month later, Arafat officially accepted UN Resolutions 242 and 338. Arafat also spoke before a special session of the UN General Assembly in Geneva, calling on Israel to join peace talks. The following day, President Ronald Reagan responded by making the first diplomatic contact between the United States and the PLO.

As diplomatic talks began, violent acts called Arafat's authority and desire for peace into question. Forces working for Abu Abbas, the leader of a faction of the PLF and a member of the PLO's executive council, were unsuccessful in their attempt to raid a Tel Aviv beach in May 1990. The United States broke off talks with the PLO after the Tel Aviv attack, saying that Abbas, who had also masterminded the 1985 *Achille Lauro* hijacking, in which an elderly New Yorker was shot and dumped from his wheelchair into the sea, needed to be disciplined for the acts. During the Persian Gulf War, Arafat and the PLO vocally supported Saddam Hussein, the president of Iraq, causing further distance between the PLO and the United States.

The United States did not restore contacts with the PLO until President Bill Clinton re-opened the dialogue in 1993. In the early 1990s, 11 meetings of bilateral peace negotiators took place between Israel and its bordering Arab states. When these talks reached a stalemate in 1993, PLO officials took part in secret, direct meetings with Israeli diplomats in Oslo, Norway; these meetings ultimately led to the signing of the 1993 PLO-Israel Declaration of Principles. Arafat and Israeli Prime Minister Yitzhak Rabin signed the declaration in Washington, D.C., on September 13, shaking hands on the White House lawn.

In 1994, in accordance with the Oslo Accords, the PLO leadership returned from nearly 30 years in exile to the West Bank and Gaza Strip. They were mandated to establish the Palestinian Authority (PA), the first Palestinian government in modern history. Two years later, the Palestinian people held their first national elections and Arafat was elected president of the PA.

In 1998, during negotiations at the Wye River Plantation in Maryland, Arafat and Israeli prime minister Benjamin Netanyahu signed an agreement guaranteeing Palestinian control of an additional 13 percent of land in the West Bank. However, in July 2000 President Clinton was unable to broker a final peace settlement at Camp David. Violence has since escalated in the region. A second intifada broke out in the fall of 2000; Palestinian suicide bombings by the PLO-associated al Aqsa Martyrs Brigades wracked the Holy Land for more than four years. More than 5,000 Palestinians and 1,000 Israelis were killed before the second intifada ended and something resembling stability was restored in Gaza.

Clashes With Hamas

The largest faction within the PLO, Fatah has been at odds with Hamas for several years. Sparked when Hamas won the majority of parliamentary seats in the Palestinian National Authority in 2006, among Palestinians the conflict is referred to as *wakseh*, a word that means humiliation and ruin. Following Arafat's death in November 2006, tensions rose between the parties, heightened by a ceasing of foreign aid until Hamas recognizes Israel's right to exist. The situation was further exacerbated when Fatah officials refused to obey Hamas commands. Mahmoud Abbas, the leader of Fatah, moved for a general election, the validity of which Hamas called into question, citing it as an attempted coup. This led to fighting at the end of 2006, continuing into 2007, in the Gaza Strip.

Finally, Hamas took control of Gaza, while Fatah commandeered the West Bank, establishing separate governments following the dissolution of the unified party. Fighting between the two factions continues, as do attempts at a negotiated settlement.

Erica Pearson

See also al Aqsa Martyrs Brigades; Arafat, Yasir; Democratic Front for the Liberation of Palestine; Fatah; Palestine Liberation Front–Abu Abbas Faction; Popular Front for the Liberation of Palestine; Popular Front for the Liberation of Palestine–General Command

Further Readings

Aburish, Said K. *Arafat: From Defender to Dictator.* New York: Bloomsbury, 1998.

Hart, Alan. *Arafat, A Political Biography.* London: Sidgwick & Jackson, 1994.

Laqueur, Walter, and Barry Rubin, eds. *The Israel-Arab Reader.* Rev. ed. New York: Penguin, 2008.

Mishal, Shaul. *The PLO under Arafat: Between Gun and Olive Branch.* New Haven, CT: Yale University Press, 1986.

Mussalam, Sami. *The PLO: The Palestine Liberation Organization, Its Function and Structure.* Brattleboro, VT: Amana Books, 1988.

Pradhah, Bansidhar. *From Confrontation to Hostile Intimacy: PLO and the US.* New Delhi: Sehyog Prakashan, 1994.

Sharif, Bassam Abu. *Arafat and the Dream of Palestine.* New York: Palgrave, 2009.

Surratt Robin, ed. *The Middle East.* 9th ed. Washington, DC: CQ Press, 2000.

Wallach, Janet, and John Wallach. *Arafat: In the Eyes of the Beholder.* Rev. ed. Secaucus, NJ: Carol Publishing Group, 1997.

PAN AM FLIGHT 73 HIJACKING

The takeover of a Pan American World Airways jumbo jet in the predawn hours of September 5, 1986, developed into a tragic 16-hour ordeal. Hijackers linked to the extremist group known as the Abu Nidal Organization killed 22 hostages during the standoff at the Karachi International Airport in Pakistan.

As the last busload of passengers was boarding a flight to Frankfurt, Germany en route to New York, four men dressed as security personnel took over the plane. According to a 1991 US indictment, they had passed through Karachi Airport security in a van outfitted to look like a security vehicle. The hijackers stopped the van at the bottom of the plane's stairs, ran up firing shots, and commandeered the aircraft. Flight attendants on board alerted the crew, who escaped through an emergency exit in the cockpit. The 379 passengers aboard were held hostage as the hijackers demanded a new crew to fly them to Cyprus, in order to free "friends" in prison there. To enforce the demand, the men selected and executed an American citizen, Rajesh Kumar. They also threatened to blow up the aircraft with all passengers on board.

Many of the deadlines set by the hijackers went unheeded as they pursued discussions with Pakistani police about whether they would release all passengers before flying on, or just women and children. Then, at about 8 P.M., the plane's auxiliary power stopped working and the lights dimmed. The hijackers rounded up passengers in a huddle in the center of the plane, and when the plane turned completely dark, they fired on the passengers with machine guns and grenades. Twenty-one passengers were killed and many others were injured in this assault. Some passengers, however, were able to force open the left and right escape doors and flee the aircraft as Pakistani commandos stormed the plane and fired on the hijackers. They killed one of the gunmen and captured the other three.

The U.S. indicted six men linked to the Abu Nidal Organization in 1991 on murder charges. Two U.S. citizens, Kumar and Surendra Patel, were among those killed in the attack. In late September 2001, Pakistan released Zayd Hassan Safarini, who had spent 14 years in a Pakistani jail for murder in the Pan Am 73 hijacking, into U.S. custody to stand trial in the United States. Safarini pled guilty to 95 charges, including murder, air piracy, and terrorism, on December 16, 2003, and was sentenced to three consecutive life sentences, as well as 25 years in prison. He is currently incarcerated in a federal prison in Colorado.

Erica Pearson

See also Abu Nidal Organization; Hijacking

Further Readings

Kushner, Harvey W. *Terrorism in America: A Structured Approach to Understanding the Terrorist Threat.* Springfield, IL: Charles C Thomas, 1998.

Leonning, Carol D. "Airline Hijacker Pleads Guilty: Pan Am Flight 73 Terrorist Will Receive Life Sentence." *The Washington Post,* December 17, 2003, p. A14.

Leonning, Carol D. "A Day of Horror in 1986 Is Relived: Flight 73 Testify at Sentencing for Hijacker." *The Washington Post,* May 13, 2004, p. A2.

Seale, Patrick. *Abu Nidal: A Gun for Hire.* London: Hutchinson, 1992.

PAN AM FLIGHT 103 BOMBING

On December 21, 1988, Pan American World Airways Flight 103 from London to New York exploded 31,000 feet above the small town of Lockerbie, Scotland, killing 270 people. The crash provoked one of the longest criminal investigations in Scottish history, and led to an eight-year diplomatic game of cat and mouse in which the United Nations imposed sanctions on Libya.

Just after 7 P.M. that December night, the Boeing 747 crash-landed onto the little Scottish town, destroying 21 houses in Lockerbie. The youngest person killed in the explosion was just two months old, while the oldest was 82 years of age. All 259 passengers, hailing from 21 nations, were killed, along with 11 people on the ground; 189 of those killed were American citizens.

The bombing took place four months after an Iranian Airbus was shot down by the American military cruiser *Vincennes.* Iranian government officials and Middle East terrorist groups had issued threats of revenge in wake of the July 1988 Airbus disaster, in which 290 people were killed. U.S. officials originally suspected that Iran had paid the Popular Front for the Liberation of Palestine–General Command to carry out the bombing. The organization denied any involvement in the crime.

The Scottish investigation, which lasted three years, would later point to different culprits. Investigators sifted through 4 million pieces of wreckage, scattered throughout 845 square miles of countryside, and cataloged more than 15,000 items of personal effects. A one-pound Semtex bomb placed inside a Toshiba radio-cassette recorder was found to have caused the disaster. The bomb was inside a brown Samsonite suitcase in the plane's cargo hold. Investigators traced the owner of every piece of luggage on board the flight, except for the brown suitcase.

Computer records at the Frankfort airport in West Germany, where the flight originated, showed that the brown Samsonite suitcase traveled aboard Pan Am Flight 103 without an accompanying passenger. Investigators determined that the luggage had been transferred from an Air Malta flight that had recently arrived in Frankfort from Malta's Luqa airport.

Abdel Basset Ali al Megrahi and Al Amin Khalifa Fhimah both worked for the state-owned Libyan Arab Airlines at the time of the disaster. Megrahi worked as an operations manager, while Fhimah held the position of security manager. The Libyan Arab Airlines and Air Malta desks were located side by side, and they shared luggage loading belts. Inside the brown suitcase that housed the Semtex bomb, investigators also found articles of clothing that were traced to a Malta shop. In a piece of much-contested evidence, the shop owner told investigators that he remembered selling the clothes to a man who resembled Megrahi.

The United States and Scotland issued an indictment in 1991 charging Megrahi and Fhimah, both Libyan nationals, with the bombing of Pan Am 103. French officials also announced that the two men were suspects in the 1989 bombing of a French jet over Niger that killed 171 people. Colonel Muammar Qaddafi and Libyan officials refused to hand the two over to stand trial, however, arguing that the men would not be treated fairly in a trial in either Scotland or America. This refusal led the United Nations (UN) in April 1992 to adopt resolutions calling for sanctions prohibiting military sales to Libya and banning airline traffic from taking off or landing in Libya. The UN increased the severity of the sanctions in November 1993, freezing Libya's overseas assets and forbidding the sale of oil equipment to the country.

Libyan officials first indicated that they might consent to a trial in a third country in 1994. However, it wasn't until August 1998 that Libya finally agreed to hand over Megrahi and Fhimah for a trial in the Netherlands under Scottish law. Libyan officials haggled over the deal for months afterward. South African President Nelson Mandela

The Justice Department released this photo on November 14, 1991, showing the reconstruction of Pan Am Flight 103, the Boeing 747 that exploded over Lockerbie, Scotland, in 1988, killing 270 people. The Justice Department announced that two Libyan intelligence officials were indicted in connection with the explosion. (AP Photo/Barry Thumma. © 2011 The Associated Press. All Rights Reserved)

helped broker the final agreement, and the two suspects were handed over to UN representatives on April 5, 1999. The UN then immediately lifted the sanctions on Libya. Four years later, Libya took formal responsibility for the bombing and offered to pay compensation to the families of those killed.

The trial of Megrahi and Fhimah, held in the former airbase Camp Zeist in the Netherlands, lasted nine months. Megrahi was convicted of the mass murder of 270 people, and sentenced to life in prison, but Fhimah was acquitted. In their 82-page written decision, the judges in the Lockerbie case admitted that the prosecution's case had "uncertainties and qualifications," but voted unanimously for Megrahi's conviction. They concluded that the prosecution had not proved Fhimah's guilt in the bombing beyond a reasonable doubt.

The results of the trial are still debated, and some say that it has raised as many questions as it has answered. Megrahi and his defense team appealed the decision, and they later claimed they had fresh evidence in the case. The evidence was reported to have been the statements of a Heathrow Airport security guard, who told police that Pan Am's baggage area was broken into just 17 hours before Flight 103 exploded, which might cast doubt on the prosecutors' case showing the Malta airport as the place where the Lockerbie bomb began its journey.

Megrahi lost his appeal in March 2002, but he then undertook a second appeal. In June 2007, the Scottish Criminal Cases Review Commission ruled in a largely classified report that Megrahi's trial may have been unfair, and it allowed the appeal to continue. Megrahi dropped his appeal in 2009, however, shortly before the Scottish government ordered his release on August 20 for "humanitarian" reasons—Megrahi had been diagnosed with cancer and was not expected to live more than a few months. He flew to Libya that day, where he was greeted by cheering crowds. His release unleashed a storm of criticism in Great Britain and the United States, with charges in the press that Megrahi was released to help British firms gain access to Libya's petroleum reserves.

Erica Pearson

See also Bombings and Bomb Scares; Popular Front for the Liberation of Palestine–General Command; United Nations

Further Readings

Adler, Jerry, and Allan Gerson. *The Price of Terror: One Bomb, One Plane, 270 Lives: The History-making Struggle for Justice after Pan Am 103.* New York: HarperCollins, 2001.

Cohen, Susan, and Daniel Cohen. *Pan Am 103: The Bombings, the Betrayals, and a Bereaved Family's Search for Justice.* New York: New American Library, 2000.

Cowell, Alan. "Lockerbie Ruling Raises Questions on Libyan's Guilt." *The New York Times,* June 29, 2007, p. A1.

Cowell, Alan, and A. G. Sulzberger. "Libyan Jailed in Bombing of Jetliner Arrives Home." *The New York Times,* August 21, 2009, p. A4.

Dornstein, Ken. *The Boy Who Fell out of the Sky: A True Story.* New York: Random House, 2006.

Ferguson, Ian, and John Ashton. *Cover Up of Convenience: The Hidden Scandal of Lockerbie.* Edinburgh: Mainstream Publishing, 2001.

Johnson, Simon. "We Caved In to Libya over Lockerbie Bomber, Says Straw." *Daily Telegraph,* August 31, 2009, p. 1.

Slevin, Peter. "Libya Accepts Blame in Lockerbie Bombing: Letter on Flight 103 Is Bid to Ease Sanctions." *The Washington Post,* August 17, 2003, p. A1.

Sutherland, Lord, Lord Coulsfield, and Lord Maclean. "Pan Am 103–Lockerbie Verdict: Opinion of the Court, Case No: 1475/99." Terrorism Central. http://www.terrorismcentral.com/Library/Legal/HCJ/Lockerbie/LockerbieVerdict.html.

Wallis, Rodney. *Lockerbie: The Story and the Lessons.* Westport, CT: Praeger, 2000.

PATRIOT ACT

The Uniting and Strengthening America by Providing Appropriate Tools Required to Intercept and Obstruct Terrorism Act, or USA PATRIOT Act of 2001 was enacted by Congress in response to the September 11 terrorist attacks and signed into law by President George W. Bush on October 26, 2001. Often referred to simply as the Patriot Act, it was passed in the Senate by a vote of 98–1 and in the House of Representatives by a vote of 357–66.

The Original Act

In his remarks on signing the Patriot Act, President Bush called it "an essential step in defeating terrorism, while protecting the constitutional rights of American citizens," adding that it gave "intelligence and law enforcement officials important new tools to fight a present danger." Generally speaking, the Patriot Act is a complex statute covering a wide range of law. It created new crimes and new penalties, and it contains many provisions enabling U.S. government and law enforcement agencies to better coordinate their information exchange and working procedures. The Patriot Act is divided into 10 sections, called "Titles," and contains hundreds of individual changes in U.S. law. The titles indicate the scope of the act:

Title 1. Enhancing Domestic Security Against Terrorism

Title 2. Enhanced Surveillance Procedures

Title 3. International Money Laundering Abatement and Anti-Terrorist Financing Act of 2001

Title 4. Protecting the Border

Title 5. Removing Obstacles to Investigating Terrorism

Title 6. Providing for Victims of Terrorism, Public Safety Officers, and Their Families

Title 7. Increased Information Sharing for Critical Infrastructure Protection

Title 8. Strengthening the Criminal Laws Against Terrorism

Title 9. Improved Intelligence

Title 10. Miscellaneous

The Patriot Act contains several key provisions that enhance governmental counterterrorism efforts. For example, it authorizes the president to freeze assets under U.S. jurisdiction of any person, organization, or country when U.S. national security is threatened. The act authorizes federal officers who acquire foreign intelligence information to consult with other federal law enforcement officers and encourages federal intelligence officials to "establish and maintain intelligence relationships" with anyone "for the purpose of engaging in lawful intelligence activities." Similarly, the Patriot Act requires heads of federal law enforcement agencies to disclose foreign intelligence information obtained in the course of a criminal investigation to the director of central intelligence.

The Patriot Act has also had significant impact in the area of criminal law and procedure, anti–money laundering measures, and immigration policy. In the area of criminal law, the act prohibits terrorist attacks against mass transportation systems and harboring terrorists; gives the United States jurisdiction over crimes committed at U.S. facilities abroad; and considers terrorism to be "racketeering activity" so it can be prosecuted under the 1970 Racketeer Influenced and Corrupt Organizations (RICO) statute. Additionally, it created penalties for terrorist conspiracies such as attempting to provide material support for terrorism or knowingly possessing a biological agent that is not for research or other peaceful purposes.

With regard to criminal procedures, the Patriot Act allows the sharing of grand jury information regarding foreign intelligence with federal government and law enforcement officials. It also allows for roving wiretaps under the Foreign Intelligence Surveillance Act (FISA), the seizure of voicemail messages pursuant to a search warrant (instead of under wiretapping procedures), for law enforcement to subpoena additional subscriber records from service providers (contact and payment information), and for law enforcement to delay notice that may be required to give a search warrant if a "court finds reasonable cause to believe" that providing that notice may adversely affect the search.

The Patriot Act also expanded U.S. money laws. Securities brokers and dealers now have to file "Suspicious Activities Reports" with the Treasury Department (prior to the act this was required only of bankers). U.S. anti–money laundering laws are now applicable to credit unions as well as individuals or "any network of people" who facilitate the transfer of money "outside the conventional financial institutions systems." The act prohibits establishing a "correspondent account" in the United States for a foreign "shell bank" (a bank without a physical presence), and "bulk cash smuggling" (the transport of more than $10,000 into or out of the United States). It also requires financial institutions to obtain more detailed background information on their clients and to compare names of potential clients with the names on terrorist or suspected terrorist lists provided by the U.S. government.

In the area of immigration and border protection, the Patriot Act allows the State Department and the Immigration and Naturalization Service access to criminal history and other records held by the Federal Bureau of Investigation. It denies admission to the United States to an alien who is a member or representative of a terrorist organization, or to an alien who through his "position of prominence" in a foreign country has endorsed or persuaded others to endorse terrorism that undermines U.S. counterterrorism efforts, and it mandates the attorney general to maintain custody of an alien involved in terrorism until that person is removed from the United States.

The Patriot Act contains many miscellaneous provisions, such as authorizing payments to individuals who furnish information leading to the prevention of terrorism or disclose the identity of someone "who holds a key leadership position in a terrorism organization." It prohibits a state from issuing a license to operate a motor vehicle transporting hazardous material unless the secretary of transportation determines that the individual does not pose a security risk warranting the denial of the license.

Because it was enacted soon after the September 11, 2001, attacks, critics argue that insufficient thought was given to the constitutionality and effect of some of the act's provisions. Because it gives the government unprecedented power to monitor individuals' activities, some say it is an infringement of the Bill of Rights, that it particularly violates the rights of noncitizens, and that it aims to silence political dissent. Additionally, critics believe that the original act's "sunset provision," a clause stating that certain provisions would be in force only through 2005, essentially acknowledged concerns that the act is of dubious constitutionality.

Reauthorization

The USA PATRIOT Act has been reauthorized by two bills: the USA PATRIOT and Terrorism Prevention Reauthorization Act of 2005, and the USA PATRIOT Act Additional Reauthorizing Amendments Act of 2006. The 2005 act reauthorized provisions in the original act as well as in the Intelligence Reform and Terrorism Prevention Act (IRTPA) of 2004, and it created new provisions regarding seaport security, the financing of terrorism, and the death penalty for terrorists, among a number of other additions. It also reauthorized all but two provisions of the controversial Title II that were scheduled to expire. Not reauthorized were section 206, which allowed for roving wiretaps, and section 215, which granted the federal government access to records under FISA. For civil libertarians, section 215 was one of the most controversial sections of the entire act because it seemed to permit the federal government to access the library records of ordinary Americans. These two sections were rescheduled to sunset on December 31, 2009. The 2006 act introduced minor amendments to the 2005 act.

In February 2010, President Barack Obama signed legislation that would extend three controversial provisions in the Patriot Act that were set to expire for another year: the aforementioned sections 206 and 215, as well as a related counterterrorism provision (section 207) regarding surveillance of "lone-wolf terrorists" that had been sunsetted in the original act but that was later enhanced by IRTPA in 2004.

Criticism and Challenges

The Patriot Act has been controversial from its inception, with critics from both the left and the right of the American political spectrum arguing that the act was an overreach on the part of the federal government into the private lives of American citizens. After its enactment, organizations such as the American Civil Liberties Union and prominent individuals such as former Democratic vice president Al Gore, as well as conservative activists such as Grover Norquist, publicly voiced their fears of the encroachment of a Big Brother–style government.

Supporters of the Patriot Act argued that its new measures had been considered at length by the government and should have been enacted long before September 11, 2001. Some were even concerned that the new provisions designated in the act were not extensive enough to prevent terrorist threats. Still, the propriety or constitutionality of certain provisions have in the intervening years been reviewed by Congress and have begun to be tested in the courts.

In 2003, for example, Sami Omar al Hussayen, a computer science Ph.D. student from Saudi Arabia who was attending the University of Idaho, was charged by federal prosecutors under section 805 of the Patriot Act with three counts of providing "expert advice and assistance" to terrorists. Hussayen had served as webmaster for several Islamic organizations whose websites included links to sites that praised suicide bombings in Chechnya and Israel. As a "technical editor," his lawyers argued, he could not be held criminally liable for what others wrote. He was acquitted of all three terrorism charges. Moreover, the provisions of the Patriot Act under which he was charged were ruled unconstitutional by a federal court in Los Angeles in 2004. In September 2009 the Ninth Circuit Court of Appeals in Boise, Idaho, ruled that former attorney general John Ashcroft could be sued and held personally responsible for the wrongful detention of a U.S. "terror" witness (detained during the Hussayen case), calling the government's assertions of this power "repugnant." The case will likely ultimately be considered by the Supreme Court.

The USA PATRIOT Act will continue to be debated, challenged, and amended as the United States moves further away from the frenzied days during which it was originally conceived, in the immediate aftermath of the attacks of September 11, 2001.

Richard Horowitz and Tim Anderson

See also Counterterrorism; Criminal Prosecution of Terrorists; Financing Terrorism; Foreign Intelligence Surveillance Act; September 11 Attacks

Further Readings

Baker, Stewart A. *Patriot Debates: Experts Debate the USA Patriot Act.* Chicago: American Bar Association, 2005.

Congressional Research Service. "The USA PATRIOT Act, a Legal Analysis." CRS Report for Congress, April 15, 2002. http://www.fas.org/irp/crs/RL31377.pdf.

Frieden, Terry. "Antiterrorism Bill Gives Authorities 'New Tools.'" CNN.com, October 26, 2001. http://www.cnn.com/2001/US/10/26/rec.anti.terrorism.bill.

Smith, Cary Stacy. *The Patriot Act: Issues and Controversies*. Springfield, IL: Charles C Thomas, 2010.

PATRIOT MOVEMENT

The *Patriot movement* refers to a loose collection of extreme right-wing movements, groups, and individuals in the United States that broadly share a number of antigovernment and conspiratorial views. Arising in the 1970s, the movement reached a peak of activity in the 1990s following the controversial standoffs at Ruby Ridge, Idaho, and Waco, Texas, generating a number of criminal and terrorist acts, including the bombing of the Alfred P. Murrah Federal Building in Oklahoma City on April 19, 1995. The Patriot movement is still quite active in the United States, and criminal activity associated with it remains common.

Origins

Right-wing extremists in the United States have had a long history of domestic terrorism, as well as other ideologically based criminal activity. Much of this activity originated from white supremacist convictions, ranging from Klan violence during the civil rights era to neo-Nazi and skinhead violence in later decades. The rise of the Patriot movement in the United States is significant in that, though the movement cannot be divorced from white supremacy, its ideology is primarily antigovernment rather than racist in nature. Its adherents believe that the U.S. government (federal, state, and local) is illegitimate and they rationalize taking action, including violent action.

The Patriot movement began in the 1950s and 1960s, stemming from right-wing opposition to the federal income tax. Tax protesters did not merely want income tax laws reformed or repealed, they believed the government was taxing individuals selectively and unfairly, and that they could rightfully avoid paying taxes. Tax protesters generated a number of justifications for their claims of immunity, believing that the judicial system was also corrupt for not upholding their arguments in court.

The first group to popularize the notion of the government illegitimacy due to its income tax policy, and which was in large part responsible for the birth of the Patriot movement, was the Posse Comitatus. The Posse was created in 1970 by Henry "Mike" Beach in Oregon and William Potter Gale in California (each claimed to have originated the idea) and spread across the country during the following decade. Initially it was most popular in the Pacific Northwest and in Wisconsin, but by the early 1980s, much Posse activity occurred in the Great Plains. The Posse Comitatus (Latin for "power of the county") claimed that the county level of government—because it was closest to the people—was preeminent, and that counties could essentially ignore federal and state laws, taxes, regulations, and court orders with which they did not agree. The county sheriff was the key authority within the county, but the sheriff's role was not so much to enforce the law as to obstruct it, insuring that "unconstitutional" state and federal laws were not enforced. Any sheriff who enforced those laws could be hanged by the Posse.

The Farm Crisis and the 1980s

Throughout the 1970s, the Posse Comitatus exhibited low levels of activity, with only occasional standoffs (to oppose a repossession, for instance) or assaults on public officials. In the 1980s, however, the Posse swelled in popularity because of the serious farm crisis that gripped the country. Right-wing extremists targeted desperate farmers for recruitment at the same time that the government was largely indifferent to their plight. The Posse received national attention in 1983, when Posse activist Gordon Kahl killed two U.S. marshals attempting to arrest him. A nationwide manhunt ensued, which ended several months later in Arkansas with another gun battle that killed Kahl and a local sheriff. The Kahl shootouts, however, were only two of a number of violent incidents that occurred around the country, especially in the farm belt.

In addition to violence, Posse adherents also adopted what has come to be called "paper terrorism." Paper terrorism is the use of bogus legal filings, documents, or financial instruments, or the misuse of legitimate items in order to harass or intimidate public officials, law enforcement officers, or private citizens and businesses. Common paper terrorism tactics included bogus liens, false IRS 1099 forms, and fictitious financial instruments billed as sight drafts or "public office money certificates."

The Posse was the most active antigovernment group in the 1980s, but it spawned a host of offshoots and imitators, including "schools of common law" as well as fictitious "townships." These groups, which shared the Posse's view of an illegitimate government established by conspiracy, became the backbone of what would eventually be called the Patriot movement. Joining them were tax protesters, or "tax patriots," as well as others who frequently identified themselves as "Christian Patriots." The latter often included white supremacists. Especially prominent was the religious sect Christian Identity, whose adherents believe that whites of European descent are descendants of the ancient Israelites of the Bible, while Jews are descended from a physical relationship between Eve and Satan, and nonwhites are "mud peoples," the product of a creation prior to that which created Adam and Eve.

Posse Comitatus founder William Potter Gale was a leading Identity adherent, as was John Harrell, an Illinois millionaire who held gatherings and "freedom festivals" of his Christian Patriots Defense League (CPDL) in Illinois and Missouri. On the Missouri-Arkansas border another group of Identity advocates established a compound called The Covenant, the Sword, and the Arm of the Lord. The movement lost steam in the late 1980s as the farm crisis eased somewhat, and some Patriot leaders died, were imprisoned, or simply dropped out of the movement. However, within a few years, the movement experienced a resurgence in numbers and activity, thanks to new energy and recruits.

Resurgence in the 1990s

The end of the Cold War prompted many on the far right to look for enemies other than the Soviet Union, and they found those foes in their own government. However, a distinct series of events catalyzed the Patriot movement and gave it new life and a new sense of urgency. The election of Bill Clinton and the Rodney King riots in 1992 were causal factors, as was the North American Free Trade Agreement (NAFTA). Even more important were two gun control measures, the Brady Law (1994) and the Assault Weapons Ban (1994).

Overshadowing all of these, however, were the deadly standoffs involving federal agents at Ruby Ridge, Idaho, in 1992, and Waco, Texas, in 1993, which convinced many on the Far Right that the federal government would stop at nothing to stamp out dissent or nonconformity, especially if it involved race or firearms. Many groups saw a resurgence in numbers, which also resulted in growth of extremist-related criminal activity. For example, the Aryan Republican Army, a small group of white supremacists, stole several hundred thousand dollars from over 20 banks in the Midwest in the mid-1990s to finance racist causes. While Christian Identity still played an important role, the Patriot movement in the 1990s attracted many people who were not racist, and even some who claimed to be anti-racist, particularly in the militia movement. The focus then became overwhelmingly antigovernment in nature. Although very loosely organized, three main submovements dominated the Patriot movement: the militia movement, the sovereign citizen movement, and the tax protest movement.

The Militia Movement

The militia movement is the youngest major rightwing movement, solidifying in the wake of the Branch Davidian standoff at Waco, Texas, in 1993. Pioneers of the movement, such as Linda Thompson of Indiana and John Trochmann of Montana, argued that the people needed to arm and organize themselves to prevent future incidents such as the Waco standoff. They practiced and justified paramilitary activity, claiming to be the statutory militia established in federal and state law. Trochmann's Militia of Montana was the first such group, but it was quickly followed by others as the movement spread across the country. By the summer of 1994, militia groups had formed in at least 25 states, particularly active in Michigan, Texas, Ohio, Montana, and Florida.

The militia movement focuses primarily on two issues. The first is opposition to gun control; militia adherents believe that there is a deliberate plan to disarm all Americans. The second is the "New World Order" conspiracy theory, according to which the U.S. government, in collaboration with organizations like the United Nations, is aiming to establish concentration camps and a foreign military presence in the United States in preparation for the inevitable takeover of the country. Throughout the 1990s, militia members trained and amassed stocks of weapons, including illegal weapons or explosives, in order to fight back. In 1995 an Oklahoma militia leader, Ray Lampley, and several followers were arrested for conspiring to blow up government buildings and other targets. The following year, militia members of the Georgia Republic Militia, the Arizona Viper Militia, the Washington State Militia, and the West Virginia Mountaineer Militia were arrested on weapons, explosives, or conspiracy charges. Moreover, members of militia groups continued to be arrested for incidents ranging from murder and attempted murder to planned acts of domestic terrorism to a variety of illegal weapons and explosives charges. Militia groups frequently engaged in confrontations with law enforcement, in which adherents would identify "victims" of government and show up in numbers to "protect" those persons. These acts justified public concerns about the movement.

The militia movement reached a peak of popularity after the Oklahoma City bombing. Although the event was initially linked to militia groups, the men convicted of the bombing were not affiliated with any militias. Timothy McVeigh, though part of the Patriot movement, didn't belong to any particular group, and Terry Nichols was essentially a "sovereign citizen." However, the multiple arrests in 1996 caused the more timid to drop out of the movement, while the lack of a militia response to standoffs in Montana and Texas in 1996 and 1997 caused many radical members to leave because they felt the movement was not aggressive enough. The decline in numbers continued after 2000.

The election of an African American, Barack Obama, as president of the United States in 2008 appears to have reinvigorated the militia movement, at least the more racist and anti-immigrant elements of it. Overall, however, levels of militia activity were lower in 2010 than in 1996, though arrests and incidents continued.

The Sovereign Citizen Movement

"Sovereign citizens" (also called "constitutionalists" and "freemen") are the direct descendants of the Posse Comitatus, imbibing its antigovernment ideology as well as its employment of paper terrorism tactics. Sovereign citizens also believe in a twisted interpretation of the Fourteenth Amendment that claims it created a new class of citizenship that people could voluntarily join, but only at the expense of all their rights. The government therefore "tricked" people into becoming Fourteenth Amendment citizens by having them sign "contracts" (such as Social Security cards, drivers' licenses, and birth certificates) to receive privileges that would put them under the jurisdiction of the government. They also believe that because these contracts were made without one's knowledge, one can tear them up and no longer be subject to the "illegitimate" federal or state governments, and thus to any laws of those governments.

Throughout the 1990s, a common sovereign citizen activity was the creation of fictitious financial instruments, such as check-like documents labeled as money orders, sight drafts, or comptrollers' warrants. These were used to pay off debts, to purchase cars and boats, or fraudulently sold to others for use as currency. Groups ranging from the Montana Freemen to Family Farm Preservation to the Republic of Texas put out several billion dollars (face value) of these instruments. Following the Montana Freemen standoff in 1996, in which about two dozen sovereign citizens held off the FBI for 81 days before surrendering, a nationwide crackdown on the bogus money orders temporarily put an end to the activity. However, within a few years another scheme, "Redemption," which involved the creation of bogus sight drafts, swept the sovereign citizen movement.

Although paper terrorism tactics are the weapon of choice of sovereign citizens, violence is also common, as indicated by the 1997 Republic of Texas standoff in which members of the group took neighbors hostage in retaliation for the arrest of a fellow member. There have also been a number of violent incidents stemming from traffic stops, where sovereign citizens have shot or assaulted police officers who pulled them over, as well as threats to and attacks on judges and prosecutors.

The Tax Protest Movement

The tax protest movement is one of the most active right-wing movements and is often a source of recruitment for the extreme right, due to its lure of income tax avoidance. Some of the largest Patriot groups have been tax protest groups, including Your Heritage Protection Association (YHPA), the Pilot Connection Society, and the Save-A-Patriot Fellowship. The YHPA grew to nearly 19,000 members in the early 1980s before its leader, Armen Condo, was convicted of mail and tax fraud. A number of tax protest groups have met similar fates for marketing bogus trusts, fraudulent "untax kits," or other tax evasion devices.

While most of the criminal activity associated with the movement consists of tax evasion–related charges, the movement also generates a number of violent extremists. In the 1990s, tax protesters attacked IRS buildings and offices with mortars, shotguns, bombs, and gas, and several IRS offices have been burned down. In 1995, Charles Polk was arrested (and later convicted) for plotting to blow up an IRS office in Austin, Texas.

The movement received an unexpected boost when IRS enforcement budgets were reduced following highly publicized congressional hearings in the late 1990s on alleged IRS wrongdoings. As a result, many tax protesters came to believe they could be open about their activities without risk of prosecution. Unlike many other right-wing movements, most of which are strapped for cash, prominent tax protest groups were able to place full-page color ads in national newspapers, and some tax-preparation offices specialize in filing fraudulent returns in keeping with various tax-protest ideologies.

As a result, the federal government has once again begun cracking down on tax protestors, with fines for frivolous tax returns increasing tenfold by 2007, and the U.S. Department of Justice initiating a "National Tax Defier Initiative" in 2008. It is believed that, at this point, many of the people who participate in tax-protest schemes are not so much ideologues as opportunists attracted by the idea of saving money; increasing the costs of tax evasion may significantly reduce the movement's appeal.

Mark Pitcavage

See also Covenant, the Sword, and the Arm of the Lord, The; McVeigh, Timothy James; Oklahoma City Bombing; Posse Comitatus

Further Readings

Aho, James A. *The Politics of Righteousness: Idaho Christian Patriotism*. Seattle: University of Washington Press, 1990.

Churchill, Robert H. *To Shake Their Guns in the Tyrant's Face: Libertarian Political Violence and the Origins of the Militia Movement*. Ann Arbor: University of Michigan Press, 2009.

Corcoran, James. *Bitter Harvest: The Birth of Paramilitary Terrorism in the Heartland*. New York: Viking, 1990.

Crothers, Lane. *Rage on the Right: The American Militia Movement from Ruby Ridge to Homeland Security*. Lanham, MD: Rowman & Littlefield, 2003.

Durham, Martin. *White Rage: The Extreme Right and American Politics*. New York: Routledge, 2007.

Gallaher, Carolyn. *On the Fault Line: Race, Class, and the American Patriot Movement*. Lanham, MD: Rowman & Littlefield, 2003.

Levitas, Daniel. *The Terrorist Next Door: The Militia Movement and the Radical Right*. New York: Thomas Dunne, 2002.

Mulloy, D. J. *American Extremism: History, Politics and the Militia Movement*. London: Routledge, 2004.

Neiwert, David A. *In God's Country: The Patriot Movement and the Pacific Northwest*. Pullman: Washington State University Press, 1999.

Noble, Kerry. *Tabernacle of Hate: Why They Bombed Oklahoma City*. Prescott, ON: Voyageur Publishing, 1998.

Pitcavage, Mark. "Camouflage and Conspiracy: The Militia Movement from Ruby Ridge to Y2K." *American Behavioral Scientist* 44 (February 2001): 957–981.

Ridgeway, James. *Blood in the Face: The Ku Klux Klan, Aryan Nations, Nazi Skinheads, and the Rise of a New White Culture*. New York: Thunder's Mouth Press, 1990.

Snow, Robert L. *The Militia Threat: Terrorists among Us*. New York: Plenum Trade, 1999.

Southern Poverty Law Center. "SPLC Report: Return of the Militias." http://www.splcenter.org/news/item.jsp?aid=392.

Van Dyke, Nella, and Sarah A. Soule. "Structural Social Change and the Mobilizing Effect of Threat: Explaining Levels of Patriot and Militia Organizing in the United States." *Social Problems* 49, no. 4 (November 2002): 497–520.

Wright, Stuart A. *Patriots, Politics, and the Oklahoma City Bombing.* Cambridge, UK: Cambridge University Press, 2007.

Zeskind, Leonard. *Blood and Politics: The History of the White Nationalist Movement from the Margins to the Mainstream.* New York: Farrar, Straus and Giroux, 2009.

PEARL, DANIEL (1963–2002)

Daniel Pearl, a reporter for *The Wall Street Journal,* was investigating terrorist groups in Pakistan when he was kidnapped and later murdered by Islamic extremists.

Pearl was born in Princeton, New Jersey, in 1963. He began his career as a journalist at a string of regional East Coast papers, joining *The Wall Street Journal* in 1990. As a foreign correspondent for the *Journal,* Pearl filed many stories about the Middle East, writing about pearl divers in the Persian Gulf and describing how Osama bin Laden used the gem trade to finance his military activities. Taking on the post of South Asia bureau chief for the *Journal* in 2000, he moved to Bombay with his wife, Mariane.

At the time of his kidnapping, Pearl was in Karachi researching the links between bin Laden's al Qaeda network and Richard Reid, the so-called shoe-bomber. Reid, a British-born Islamic militant, was arrested in December 2001 aboard a Paris-Miami flight for allegedly trying to ignite explosive materials concealed in the heels of his sneakers. On January 23, 2002, Pearl went to meet with contacts who had promised to arrange a meeting with radical Islamic leader Sheikh Mubarak (Shah) Ali Gilani. Pearl was never seen alive again.

A previously unknown group, the National Movement for the Restoration of Pakistani Sovereignty, had abducted Pearl. The group sent emails to various news agencies calling for the release of Pakistani prisoners among the Taliban and al Qaeda detainees held at the U.S. military base in Guantánamo Bay, Cuba. The emails included attached photos of Pearl in chains and with a gun to his head. The group, reportedly linked to the outlawed Pakistani group Jaish-e-Mohammed, threatened to kill Pearl and accused him of being a spy for the United States and for the Mossad, Israel's foreign intelligence agency.

Pearl was confirmed dead by the U.S. State Department on February 22, 2002, after a Pakistan-based journalist obtained a videocassette showing Pearl being murdered (he was decapitated) and brought it to the U.S. embassy in Pakistan. His body was discovered that May. Pearl was survived by his wife, who was seven months pregnant at the time of his death. In his memory, Pearl's family set up the Daniel Pearl Foundation to combat cultural and religious hatred.

Ten days before Pearl's death became known, Pakistani officials arrested British-born Islamic militant Ahmed Omar Saeed Sheikh and later accused him of masterminding the kidnapping. According to press reports, Pakistani police had also detained Gilani after Pearl's disappearance but released him because they found nothing to connect him with the incident. During the spring of 2002, a special anti-terrorism court in Pakistan put Sheikh, Salman Saqib, Fahad Naseem, and Sheikh Mohammed Adeel on trial for Pearl's murder; all four pleaded not guilty. The prosecution detailed how the terrorists had trapped Pearl—the kidnappers pretended to be arranging interviews for him but instead plotted his abduction. The press and public were banned from the trial, which was first held inside the central jail of the port city of Karachi and then moved 100 miles inland for security. A Pakistani journalist who helped Pearl in his attempts to set up an interview with Gilani identified Sheikh as the man who (using the pseudonym Chaudry Bashir) met with the two journalists and promised to arrange the interview.

During the murder trial, the defendants and their supporters reportedly intimidated witnesses, lawyers, and officials. The chief prosecutor said that he felt his life was in danger, and all of the defendants are said to have shouted insults at witnesses. In July 2002, all four men were found guilty. Sheikh was sentenced to death, while the other three received life sentences. All four have filed appeals, which have been repeatedly delayed.

Seven others were also charged by Pakistan with Pearl's kidnapping, and others linked with it have been arrested but not charged in the case, apparently because of concerns that information obtained from their arrests could potentially be used to overturn Sheikh's conviction. The man suspected of picking up Pearl and driving him to the nursery where he was held and killed, Amjad Hussain Farooqi, was himself killed in a shootout with Pakistani security forces on September 26, 2004. Farooqi had also planned two assassination attempts on the president of Pakistan. In July 2005, Pakistani police apprehended Hashim Qadeer, who is believed to have introduced Pearl to Sheikh.

Sheikh is still believed to have organized Pearl's kidnapping, but information uncovered by the arrests indicate that the crime also involved members of a number of different militant Islamic organizations that operate in Pakistan, including Jaish-e-Mohammed, Harakat ul-Mujahideen, and al Qaeda. Khalid Shaikh Mohammed, a captured al Qaeda operative, told U.S. interrogators that he personally had murdered Pearl. An extensive report released by the Center for Public Integrity in January 2011, confirmed that Mohammed killed Pearl; researchers used a technique called "vein matching" to link the veins in Mohammed's hand to the veins in a hand seen decapitating Pearl in the video of his murder.

Erica Pearson

See also al Qaeda; Harakat ul-Mujahideen; Hostage Taking; Jaish-e-Mohammed; Jamaat ul Fuqra; Mohammed, Khalid Shaikh; Reid, Richard

Further Readings

Daniel Pearl Foundation. http://www.danielpearl.org.

Jackson, Harold. "Daniel Pearl: Fine Reporter and Sensitive Observer of Islam." Obituary. *The Guardian* (London), February 23, 2002. http://www.guardian.co.uk/news/2002/feb/23/guardianobituaries.pakistan.

LeVine, Steve. "A Murder's Aftermath: Killing of Pearl Fit into Pakistani Web of Radical Islam." *The Wall Street Journal*, January 23, 2003, p. A1.

Mydanis, Seth. "Trial Witness Tells of Pearl's Safety Concerns." *The New York Times*, April 25, 2002.

Nomani, Asra Q., Barbara Feinman Todd, Katie Balestra, and Kira Zalan. *The Truth Left Behind: Inside the Kidnapping and Murder of Daniel Pearl*. New York: The Pearl Project of the Center for Public Integrity, January 2011. http://www.washingtonpost.com/wp-srv/world/documents/daniel-pearl-project/index.html.

Pearl, Daniel. *At Home in the World: Collected Writing from* The Wall Street Journal. Edited by Helene Cooper. New York: Simon & Schuster, 2002.

Pearl, Mariane. *A Mighty Heart: The Brave Life and Death of My Husband, Danny Pearl*. New York: Scribner, 2003.

PEOPLE AGAINST GANGSTERISM AND DRUGS

Formed in 1996 as a grassroots attempt to combat gang fighting and drugs in Cape Town, South Africa, People Against Gangsterism and Drugs (PAGAD) later adopted antigovernment and anti-Western ideologies and used terror to spread its message. It declared a jihad (holy war) against Cape Town's gangs and is believed to have murdered about 100 people. Although PAGAD's initial objective was to serve as a broad-based anti-crime group, it has adopted a paramilitary style and is thought to have ties with Islamic extremists in the Middle East. PAGAD now views the South African government as a threat to Islamic values and to Muslims in South Africa.

For many years, criminal gangs and drug dealers troubled the impoverished communities on the outskirts of Cape Town. A mix of citizens, populist moderate Muslim leaders, and Islamic extremists formed what became known as PAGAD and set about to destroy the area's gangs and drug sellers. Led by Abdus Salaam Ebrahim, the group operates in small cells. PAGAD first made headlines in 1996 when the group beat and later murdered and set afire Rashaad Staggie, leader of a notorious criminal gang in South Africa.

As a consequence, people viewed PAGAD less favorably and the government was unsure how to respond to such vigilantism. Speculation arose that PAGAD had either merged with—or been infiltrated by—Qibla, a militant Shiite Muslim group that formed in South Africa in 1980. Qibla (originally called the Qibla Mass Movement) was heavily influenced by the 1979 Iranian revolution and sought to transform South Africa into a Muslim theocracy, under the slogan "One Solution, Islamic Revolution." Both PAGAD and Qibla are believed to receive support from Islamic extremists in the Middle East.

PAGAD shifted its focus in the late 1990s: members have attacked South African authorities, moderate Muslims, synagogues, gay nightclubs, tourist attractions, and Western-associated restaurants, and they are the chief suspects in the 1998 bombing of the Cape Town Planet Hollywood. After a series of pipe-bomb attacks on the homes of academics, businesspeople, and police, South African authorities have taken a strong stand against PAGAD. The government links PAGAD—and Qibla—to hundreds of bombings and violent crimes in the Western Cape since the mid-1990s. From 1997 to 2002, at least 60 people have been killed and 125 injured at the hands of PAGAD.

South African authorities cracked down on PAGAD in 2002, convicting three PAGAD leaders on charges of public violence stemming from the Staggie killing in May. In December of that year, two PAGAD militants, Ebrahim Jeneker and Abdullah Maansdorp, were give three life sentences stemming from a campaign of violence against the drug trade in the spring of 1999 that resulted in three deaths.

The convictions led to a dwindling of activity, but in 2009, PAGAD again made headlines when the organization attempted to march against the home of a known drug dealer in Lentegeur, a suburb of Cape Town. Police arrested 58 marchers, and serious violence was averted.

Richard McHugh

Further Readings

Bangstad, Sindre. "Hydra's Heads: PAGAD and Responses to the PAGAD Phenomenon in a Cape Muslim Community." *Journal of Southern African Studies* 31, no. 1 (March 2005): 187–208.

De Vries, Lavern, and Jade Witten. "People Against Gangsterism and Drugs (PAGAD) Has Flooded Mitchells Plain with Flyers Questioning the Ability of the Area's Police and Its Station Commissioner to Deal with Drugs and Crime." *The Argus*, August 18, 2009, p. 1.

Esack, Farid. "Taking On the State: PAGAD and Islamic Radicalism." *Indicator SA* 13, no. 4 (Spring 1996).

Said, Edward W. *Covering Islam: How the Media and Experts Determine How We See the World*. London: Vintage, 1997.

PEOPLE'S REVOLUTIONARY ARMY

The People's Revolutionary Army (Ejército Revolucionario del Pueblo, or ERP) was a leftist guerrilla organization active in El Salvador's 12-year civil war (1980–1992); it also played a leading role in the Farabundo Martí National Liberation Front (FMLN).

El Salvador had been ruled by a military dictatorship since 1929. The army, which served the interests of the 14-family oligarchy that controlled the Salvadoran economy, ran the country. Elections were held, but true changes in leadership came only through internal coups. In the late 1960s, however, resistance to the regime began to coalesce, and by 1972 the middle-class, centrist Christian Democratic Party appeared certain to win that year's presidential election. The army responded with widespread election fraud and exiled Jose Duarte, the Christian Democrat's leader. Many political dissidents, having lost faith in the electoral process, began to look for other methods of opposing the dictatorship.

The ERP was founded in late 1972 by leftist dissidents, many of them former students at the National University of El Salvador, a Marxist stronghold. The ERP was aligned with communists, but unlike other leftist groups it emphasized action over dogma. ERP leaders were far more concerned with overthrowing the dictatorship while the time was ripe than with the political character of the government that would replace it; they were also not opposed to working with El Salvador's moderate middle class. In 1975 the ERP came to widespread attention when its leadership assassinated Roque Dalton, a Salvadoran poet who had advocated a more strictly Marxist-Leninist, long-term political approach.

By the late 1970s, the ERP had established a base of operations in the eastern province of Morazán. It was also involved in terrorist activities in the capital, San Salvador, kidnapping businessmen and political leaders, orchestrating bombings, and attacking security forces. At the peak of civil unrest in 1979, leftist guerrillas formed an alliance to better pool their resources, calling the new group the Farabundo Martí National Liberation Front (FMLN). Of the five guerrilla groups involved, ERP was the second largest and believed by many to have the best-trained guerrillas. ERP's leader, Joaquin Villalobos, became one of the most prominent spokesmen for the FMLN.

In 1981, ERP guerrillas were an essential component of the FMLN's "Final Offensive," an assault on the capital and security forces planned in accordance with the ERP's direct, action-oriented revolutionary vision. When the "Final Offensive" failed to inspire a mass uprising of the populace, the guerrillas withdrew to the countryside. A stalemate ensued until 1989, when another large-scale FALN offensive pushed the government into negotiations; a peace agreement was signed in January 1992. After the war, the ERP and particularly its flashy commander, Villalobos, emerged as a moderate, center-left political force, while the FMLN has become a potent force in El Salvador's government. In 2009, Carlos Mauricio Funes Cartagena, an FMLN member, was elected president.

Colleen Sullivan

See also Farabundo Martí National Liberation Front

Further Readings

McClintock, Cynthia. *Revolutionary Movements in Latin America: El Salvador's FMLN and Peru's Shining Path*. Washington, DC: United States Institute of Peace Press, 1998.

Menzel, Sewall H. *Bullets versus Ballots: Political Violence and Revolutionary War in El Salvador, 1979–1991*. New Brunswick, NJ: Transaction Publishers, 1994.

Wade, Christine. "El Salvador: The Success of the FMLN." In *From Soldiers to Politicians: Transforming Rebel Movements after Civil War*, edited by Jeroen de Zeeuw. Boulder, CO: Lynne Rienner, 2008.

Waller, J. Michael. *The Third Current of Revolution: Inside the 'North American Front' of El Salvador's Guerrilla War*. Lanham, MD: University Press of America, 1991.

PERSIAN GULF WAR

The 1991 Persian Gulf War, in which a U.S.-led international coalition expelled an invading Iraqi army from Kuwait, is a watershed in post–Cold War international relations and the development of modern terrorism.

History of the Conflict

Prior to the conflict, Iraq and Kuwait had a long-standing border dispute that had caused tension between the two countries for decades. In particular, Iraq accused Kuwait of drawing oil from fields on the Iraqi side of the border. Following the Iran-Iraq War (1980–1988), Iraq was heavily in debt and desperate to increase its oil revenue. At this time, the price of oil declined, and Iraq accused Kuwait of deliberately manipulating world oil markets to Iraq's disadvantage. Experts now believe that President Saddam Hussein of Iraq acted against Kuwait in the hope of annexing the country and its oil fields, thereby making up Iraq's shortfall in oil revenues. Anti-Kuwaiti rhetoric became more and more evident and shrill in the Iraqi press and in official statements in months leading up to Iraq's August 2, 1990, invasion of Kuwait.

Foreign policy experts in the U.S. government were preoccupied in the late 1980s and early 1990s with the fall of Communism in Europe and the geopolitical implications of the end of the Cold War; in comparison, the Iraq-Kuwait border dispute seemed minor. Following the hardships of the Iran-Iraq War, most analysts expected Iraq to begin to rebuild its economy and society. That the U.S. government would not countenance an Iraqi invasion in the volatile Gulf region was considered self-evident, and Iraq's anti-Kuwaiti rhetoric was perceived as blustering.

Taken by surprise, the U.S. government now questioned assumptions it had made about the Iraqi regime. If Hussein had been so foolish as to invade Kuwait, he might also attempt to invade Iraq's other neighbors—in particular, oil-rich Saudi Arabia. Such instability in the region could drive up world oil prices and be a serious risk to the U.S. economy. The United States began to assemble a coalition to prevent further invasion and put pressure on Iraq to withdraw from Kuwait.

The United States was not alone; the United Nations passed a resolution condemning the invasion and calling for an immediate withdrawal, and within a week it had passed a resolution calling for an economic embargo against Iraq. Both resolutions passed almost unanimously. At the same time, the U.S.–led coalition, which included several Arab nations, began sending troops to Saudi Arabia. Eventually, more than 300,000 troops would participate in "Operation Desert Shield," with the United States supplying most of the military personnel and other coalition members supplying the funds. Over the next few months, as diplomatic efforts and an embargo failed to compel an Iraqi withdrawal, President George Bush successfully lobbied the UN to approve the use of force against Iraq. The UN passed a resolution on November 29, 1990, demanding that Iraq withdraw before January 15, 1991, or face the prospect of war. The coalition forces then doubled the number of troops they had in the region.

Iraq did not respond to the UN ultimatum, believing the threat of war to be a bluff. On January 16, 1991, Operation Desert Shield became Operation Desert Storm; led by the U.S. Air Force, the coalition forces began a campaign of air bombardment that decimated Iraqi defenses over the next several weeks. On February 23, after additional U.S. demands for unconditional withdrawal from Kuwait had been refused by Iraq, the coalition forces began a ground campaign. After just four days of fighting, the majority of the Iraqi army had either surrendered or fled, and Kuwait was in the hands of Allied forces.

Effects of the Persian Gulf War on International Relations and Terrorism

The period between the fall of the Berlin Wall in 1989 and the final dissolution of the Soviet Union in December 1991 was a time of great uncertainty for governments around the world, as Cold War political alignments, which had first been formed in 1945, began to disintegrate. How the dissolution of the Communist bloc would affect the rest of the world was a matter of great debate. Could one superpower survive without the other? For instance, without the fear of the Soviets, would former allies prove more intractable when considering U.S. demands? Now that the Cold War arms race was over, could a rising economic power such as Japan or Germany become a counterweight to the United States? What would be the role of the United Nations, now that the opposing interests of

the United States and the Soviet Union no longer worked to impede Security Council resolutions?

The important role that the United Nations had played showed that the international community could act in concert over issues of mutual concern. But the blueprint for international action provided by the Persian Gulf War was by no means universally applicable. In some ways, the Persian Gulf War was a simple conflict; Iraq's actions were clearly illegal, aggressive, and destabilizing to the region. The country had no strong allies to support its claims, while its actions posed a threat to the vital interests of several other nations. Achieving an international consensus to support action against Iraq, while a daunting task, was considerably simpler than achieving such a consensus in future conflicts—the Balkan wars of the mid-1990s being an example.

In addition, the vigorous diplomacy of the Bush administration had been instrumental in securing the unanimity necessary to pass the UN resolutions. The Persian Gulf War revealed the extent of U.S. power, both politically, in its ability to rally the world behind the anti-Iraqi operation, and militarily, in the devastating firepower that it was able to supply so readily and that had concluded the conflict so rapidly and decisively.

This revelation had its dark side, however, as those individuals and groups that opposed U.S. hegemony and the values that it represented—democracy, capitalism, and individual liberty—made the United States the target of their attacks. As the war against Iraq showed, a nation-state could not risk an open attack against the vital interests of the United States without fear of military reprisal. Independent terrorist organizations, however, were not so constrained.

An upsurge in anti-U.S. demonstrations, and in terrorism directed at U.S. targets, became immediately evident at the beginning of the military buildup in the Gulf known as Operation Desert Shield. The period of military action, from mid-January 1991 to the end of February, saw hundreds of terrorist incidents against U.S. and coalition targets across the globe. Despite exhortations from Saddam Hussein to fellow Arabs to rise up in support of him, the terrorism was not more pronounced in the Middle East than elsewhere. The anticipated surge in activity of Palestinian terrorist groups that had the support of Iraq did not come to pass, perhaps because Yasir Arafat's vocal support of Hussein led to a drop in funding from Saudi Arabia and Kuwait.

Meanwhile, analysts were surprised to discover instead an upswing in the activity of European leftist terrorist groups that many had thought defunct. Most of these incidents involved small bombs intended to inflict property damage, and the wave of terrorist activity subsided almost immediately after the war ended, with the number of incidents for the rest of 1991 fewer than the same period in 1990. Several incidents could be attributed to Iraqi agents, however, and the Persian Gulf War only increased Iraq's support of international terrorism.

Since the Gulf War, the vast majority of significant incidents of international terrorism have been directed against U.S. targets, with the September 11, 2001, attacks on the World Trade Center and the Pentagon being the most prominent.

Lasting Problems

The antipathy between Iraq and the United States, culminating in the U.S. invasion of Iraq in 2003 to oust Saddam Hussein, was one of the most lasting effects of the Persian Gulf War. The surrender agreement between Iraq and the United Nations, signed at the end of the war, required Iraq to allow international inspectors to evaluate its weapons programs and determine whether it was attempting to manufacture or maintain weapons of mass destruction. Iraq's noncompliance was a regular diplomatic, economic, and military irritant, leading the Bush administration to argue that Iraq had weapons of mass destruction and might use them against the United States. (However, said weapons, if they ever existed, have never been recovered.)

The United States also maintained no-fly zones over parts of northern and southern Iraq that the Iraqi army was forbidden to enter. These zones were intended to protect the Kurds and Shia Muslims who live there, who had been targeted by Hussein in the past. To maintain these no-fly zones, the United States maintained military bases in Saudi Arabia that were established during the Gulf War. The Saudi government, concerned about the threat of Iraqi invasion, supported these bases. Others in the region, however, came to view the use of non-Muslim forces to defend a country with the holiest of Islam's sites as an insult. The

removal of U.S. military presence within Saudi Arabia was a primary goal of Osama bin Laden and his al Qaeda organization when it was founded in the early 1990s.

Colleen Sullivan

See also al Qaeda; bin Laden, Osama; Hussein, Saddam; Iraq War; United Nations

Further Readings

Aburish, Saïd K. *Saddam Hussein: The Politics of Revenge.* London: Bloomsbury, 2000.
Garrity, Patrick J. "Implications of the Persian Gulf War for Regional Powers." *The Washington Quarterly* 16, no. 3 (1993): 150.
GulfLINK: Office of the Special Assistant for Gulf War Illness. http://www.gulflink.osd.mil/index.jsp.
PBS/Frontline. *The Gulf War: An In-depth Examination of the 1990–1991 Persian Gulf Crisis.* http://www.pbs.org/wgbh/pages/frontline/gulf.
U.S. State Department. *Patterns of Global Terrorism.* Annual Report. Washington, DC: U.S. Government Printing Office. http://www.state.gov/s/ct/rls/pgtrpt.

PHINEAS PRIESTHOOD

The name "Phineas Priesthood" comes from a 1990 book called *Vigilantes of Christendom: The Story of the Phineas Priesthood* by Richard Kelly Hoskins. Hoskins, a Christian Identity adherent and prolific writer, used the story from Chapter 25 of the Book of Numbers to glorify the biblical character Phineas, a descendent of Aaron. In essence, God was displeased that some Israelite men were having sex with "the daughters of Moab" and practicing foreign religions. So God told Moses to kill the transgressors. But before Moses could act, Phineas, javelin in hand, "went after the man of Israel [named Zimri] into the tent, and thrust both of them through, the man of Israel, and the [Midianite] woman through her belly. So the plague was stayed from the children of Israel."

The point of the story, as Hoskins retold it, was the virtue of vigilantism in service of white racial purity. Hoskins wrote: "As the kamikaze is to the Japanese/As the Shiite is to Islam/As the Zionist is to the Jew/So the Phineas priest is to Christendom. . . .

[I]t makes little difference whether you agree or disagree with the Phineas Priesthood. It is important that you know that it exists, is active, and in the near future may become a central fact in your life."

The term *Phineas Priesthood* is more a concept than an organization, although there is an agreed-upon Phineas symbol—a P with a horizontal line through it. Since the book's publication, various white supremacists, as well as anti-abortion and anti-homosexual extremists, referred to the Priesthood concept in justifying their acts of violence. In 1994, for example, Paul Hill, an anti-abortion extremist, murdered the abortion provider Dr. John Britton and his bodyguard, James Barrett. Hill spoke of the virtue of such "Phineas actions."

In 1996, Peter Langan and Richard Guthrie were arrested. They were part of a group called the Aryan Republican Army, which sought to pay for a white supremacist revolution through numerous bank robberies in the early to mid-1990s. Langan had made a video promoting the group, in which he held up a copy of Hoskins book and called it "an effective handbook for revolution."

Most notoriously, in April 1996, three white supremacists from the Idaho panhandle, Charles Barbee, Robert Berry, and Verne Jay Merrell, calling themselves the Phineas Priesthood, planted a pipe bomb at the local Spokane newspaper, and while police were responding to that, they robbed a bank. A few months later they bombed an area Planned Parenthood office, then held up the same bank.

The importance of the Phineas Priesthood concept is its overlap with those of "leaderless resistance" and "lone wolves." The idea is that large groups, such as the traditional Ku Klux Klan of the 1960s, were too easily infiltrated by law enforcement, and that small cells acting independently, or even individual actors driven by an overarching white supremacist ideological zeal, could be more effective. The concept of the Phineas Priesthood adds octane to this strategy, by linking acts of violence with the recasting of a troubling story from the Hebrew bible as something noble and to be emulated.

Kenneth Stern

See also Anti-Abortion Terrorism; Christian Identity; Hill, Paul Jennings; Leaderless Resistance; White Supremacy Movement

Further Readings

Bushart, Howard L., John R. Craig, and Myra Barnes. *Soldiers of God: White Supremacists and Their Holy War for America.* New York: Kensington Books, 1998.

Levitas, Daniel. *The Terrorist Next Door: The Militia Movement and the Radical Right.* New York: Thomas Dunne Books/St. Martin's Griffin, 2002.

Sharpe, Tanya Telfaire. "The Identity Movement: Ideology of Domestic Terrorism." *Journal of Black Studies* 30, no. 4 (2000).

Zeskind, Leonard. *Blood and Politics: The History of the White Nationalist Movement from the Margins to the Mainstream.* New York: Farrar, Straus and Giroux, 2009.

PIERCE, WILLIAM L.

See Turner Diaries, The

PLO

See Palestine Liberation Organization

POPULAR CULTURE, TERRORISM IN

Popular culture and terrorism have an intricate, interconnected, and even interactive relationship. Certainly popular culture plays a critical role in shaping American attitudes toward terrorism—after all, it is through movies, television shows, books, and video games that the vast majority of people are exposed to terrorism. These various elements of popular culture can reflect, frame, and reconstruct past and contemporary acts of terrorism to create mass shared experiences. Among the questions explored here with regard to the intersection of popular culture and terrorism are how much popular culture affects American attitudes about the terrorist threat; how the depiction of terrorist themes has developed over time; and what impact the "war on terror" has had both on popular culture and the public's response to it.

Before 9/11

There are notable differences in the ways terrorists and counterterrorism fighters were portrayed before 9/11 by mass culture and they ways they have been portrayed since. Terrorists of the 1970s and early 1980s were often driven by a nationalist or leftist ideology, had stronger or more easily identifiable ties with countries and governments of the former Soviet bloc or Latin American countries, and were not necessarily depicted as completely unsympathetic villains. Examples of this type of portrayal include the Palestinian terrorists from *Black Sunday* (1977), the Lebanese terrorists from *The Delta Force* (1986), and the left-wing guerrillas in *Salvador* (1986).

After the dissolution of the Soviet Union and the end of the Cold War, characters of Middle Eastern descent and individuals with close ties to the Middle East slowly replaced the Soviets in the role of global foreign villains, but their depictions tended to be fairly complex, not easily reducible to stark black-and-white portrayals. This was also true of "villains" more generally, including Oliver Lang (played by Tim Robbins), the antigovernment terrorist plotter from *Arlington Road* (1999), and Malli (Ayesha Dharker), the hired assassin from the Indian film *The Terrorist* (1998). The 1990s also saw shifts in the overall nature of "counterterrorist heroes," who displayed much less aggressive militarism than images of terrorism fighters in the 1980s. For example, the 1980s film heroes Major Scott McCoy (Chuck Norris) from *The Delta Force* (1986) and John McClane (Bruce Willis) in *Die Hard* (1988) assumed much more showy and violently antagonistic postures than did Thomas Devoe (George Clooney) in *The Peacemaker* (1997), President James Marshal (Harrison Ford) in *Air Force One* (1997), or captain Riley Hale (Christian Slater) in *Broken Arrow* (1996).

Real-world conflicts involving terrorism have often been used as the basis or the backdrop for cinematic drama. The conflict in Northern Ireland, for example, inspired a number of dramatic films that tackled the knotty and seemingly intractable ethno-political struggle that plagued Ireland, Northern Ireland, and England between the late 1960s and the late 1990s. Films like *The Crying Game* (1992), *In the Name of the Father* (1993), *The Devil's Own* (1997), and *The Boxer* (1997) dramatized the violent struggle among paramilitary and security forces, politicians, and political activists on both sides, as well as the profound and often horrific results wrought by the seemingly endless cycles of violence. *The Crying Game,* in particular, is notable for its nuanced and sympathetic portrayal of an IRA terrorist who is unable to bring himself to carry out the murder of a fleeing British soldier whom he and his fellow "freedom fighters" have been holding hostage.

Terrorism as a tool of white supremacy and neo-Nazism in America is another topic that has provided much fodder for the movies. America's history of racial violence and terrorist activity against blacks by the Ku Klux Klan has been explored in films like *Mississippi Burning* (1988), which was based on the murders of three civil rights workers in Neshoba County, Mississippi, in 1964. Although the film was criticized by historians for its fictionalization of the events surrounding the murders, it was highly praised by film critics upon its release. (The same story had previously been made into a TV movie called *Attack on Terror: The FBI vs. the Ku Klux Klan* in 1975.) Other films in this category include *Betrayed* (1988), loosely based upon the murder in 1984 of radio DJ Alan Berg by a white supremacist group known as The Order; *Rosewood* (1997), a dramatization of the 1923 Rosewood Massacre in Florida that stemmed from the violent actions against local blacks of a group of white vigilantes; and *Ghosts of Mississippi* (1994), a treatment of the trial of the white supremacist Bryan De La Beckwith, the killer of civil rights leader Medgar Evers.

Filmmakers have also taken on stories involving American neo-Nazism. One of the most celebrated by critics is *American History X* (1998), which tells the story of two brothers, one of whom is drawn into the neo-Nazi movement in Venice Beach, California, and ultimately murders two black gang members and is sent to prison. *The Believer* (2001), also acclaimed by critics, dramatized the story of the neo-Nazi skinhead (and Jew) Daniel Burros, who in his rejection of his faith as a young man in the 1960s moved in the opposite direction, became violently anti-Semitic, and began to advocate the murder of Jews.

The Post–9/11 Era

The terrorist attacks of September 11, 2001, and the wars in Afghanistan and Iraq have provided

Hollywood much fodder for dramatic, often horrific depictions of the terrorist threat from radical Islamists, and of the counterterrorist fight against that threat. The stories have evolved over time from more simplistic treatments of "good guys" versus "bad guys" into more nuanced accounts that highlight the complexity of the fight, which has involved massive civilian casualties, torture, the use of fear by the government as a political tool, the exigencies that come with fighting a war against non-state actors, and the questionable rationalization that the ends justify the means. Early post–9/11 images of terrorists were mostly focused on religion-inspired terrorism, where terrorists were depicted as unsympathetic, often irrational individuals with ties to radical religious leaders and organizations. Typical examples of this portrayal are Mohammad Hassain (played by Anthony Azizi) from ABC's television drama *Threat Matrix* (2003) and Yussef Nasseriah (Alki David) from TNT's short-lived drama series *The Grid* (2004). Other films and television shows have used metaphor and allegory to reflect the issues that have arisen during the war on terror.

The events of September 11 had a major impact on the tone and tenor of much popular culture in the subsequent months and years. One of the first terrorism-related films to be released in theaters after 9/11 was *Collateral Damage,* which starred Arnold Schwarzenegger as a Los Angeles firefighter seeking to avenge the deaths of his wife and son at the hands of a Colombian terrorist who was targeting a CIA officer. Completed before September 11, the film was re-edited in the wake of the attacks and the release date was also pushed back from October to February of 2002. Although in all other respects the film was a conventional, pre–9/11 terrorism-themed Hollywood thriller featuring easily discerned good guys and bad guys—in the mold of *Speed* (1994), *Passenger 57* (1992), *The Siege* (1998), and *Con Air* (1998)—*Collateral Damage* signified a new sensitivity, at least in the short term, in Hollywood's approach to depictions of terrorism.

The 2002 film *The Sum of All Fears* walked a similarly tricky line with its story about a neofascist plot to detonate a nuclear bomb at a football stadium in Baltimore. Based on Tom Clancy's 1991 novel of the same name, the film is a so-called techno-thriller, a hybrid genre that combines action, technology, and science fiction and that

often features male American heroes who use advanced technology to violently respond to terrorist threats against the country, indulging the belief in American technological superiority. Interestingly, although the terrorists in the book were Muslim extremists, they were changed to neo-Nazis for the film in order for it to have more international appeal and not alienate a major segment of the world market, and—according to the film's screenwriter—to avoid the cliché of the Arab terrorist. (As the film critic Roger Ebert put it in his review, "Best to invent villains who won't offend any audiences.") Though the film was a box office success, the critical reception it received showed a pronounced post–9/11 unease with the depiction of a large-scale terrorist event taking place on U.S. soil, regardless of the background of the perpetrators. In his review of the film, for example, the critic Richard Roeper remarked, "there's something cringe-inducing about seeing an American football stadium nuked as pop entertainment."

Nonetheless, American popular culture in the years after 9/11 did not shy away from dramatizing the war on terror, and some of these attempts proved to be quite popular. The Fox television drama *24* (2001–2010), for example, brought the techno-thriller to the small screen. Like Clancy's hero Jack Ryan Jr. in the novel *The Teeth of the Tiger,* *24*'s Jack Bauer (Kiefer Sutherland) can be viewed as a typical 9/11-era counterterrorism fighter—patriotic, almost superhumanly committed, and willing to break the rules if necessary. Bauer is a federal agent with the fictional "Counter Terrorist Unit," a government agency tasked with preventing attacks against the homeland. The hook of the series results mainly from Bauer's clock-racing attempts to thwart assassination plots against political leaders, biological and chemical weapons strikes, anti-American conspiracies, and cyber attacks. While the show developed a big audience worldwide, over its seven seasons it came under increasing criticism for what some commenters described as its glorification and justification of torture as a legitimate tool for fighting terrorism.

The Sci-Fi Channel's reboot of *Battlestar Galactica* also waded into themes from the war on terror in its story about a civilization of humans fighting a cybernetic race known as Cylons. In the three-hour movie (2003) that opened the series, the Cylons launched a catastrophic 9/11-style attack on their human creators, destroying their home planets and much of the human population and forcing the 50,000 survivors to flee aboard a fleet of spacecraft, the titular *Galactica* being the only surviving military craft. From this premise, and through the use of allegorical elements in the story, the creators of the show delved into thorny terrorism-related themes such as torture, religious fundamentalism, human rights, and racial/ethnic profiling, garnering much critical and popular acclaim during its five-year run.

One film that blended the history of a counter-terrorist fight from 1972 with a resonant post-9/11 treatment of the moral conflicts surrounding the pursuit of terrorists was *Munich* (2005), directed by Steven Spielberg. The movie tells the story of the Israeli retaliation plot, eventually known as Operation Wrath of God, against Black September, a Palestinian terrorist group that kidnapped and murdered 11 Israeli athletes and a German police officer during the 1972 Olympics in Munich, Germany. The film was generally well-received by critics, though its depiction of the Israeli plot to assassinate Black September members who allegedly took part in the Munich attack has also been hotly debated. Although many reviewers commended *Munich*'s nuanced characters, many also raised objections, with some feeling that the film is overly generous in its depiction of the assassins' self-doubt, and others bristling at what they saw as the film's moral equivalence between the Israeli assassins and the Palestinian killers being hunted. Still others disputed the history as the film presented it. Despite—or perhaps because of—the controversies stemming from the film, however, it performed well at the box office and received much attention during award season.

Not all of Hollywood's attempts to dramatize terrorism-related stories in the decade following 9/11 were embraced by a seemingly ambivalent American public, however. Although 9/11 movies based on actual events, such as Oliver Stone's *World Trade Center* and Paul Greengrass's *United 93*, were well received by critics and the public, other, fictional films tackling terrorism and war-on-terror issues, such as *Rendition* (2006), *Lions for Lambs* (2007), and *Vantage Point* (2008), went largely uncelebrated by the press and unnoticed by moviegoers; some films, such as Brian De Palma's *Redacted* (2007), about a massacre in

Iraq committed by U.S. Marines, stirred up considerable controversy. Even *The Hurt Locker* (2009), a film about a U.S. Army bomb-defusing team in Iraq, and the winner of the 2009 Oscars for Best Picture and Best Director (for Kathryn Bigelow), struggled at the box office.

Interactivity

One element of popular culture that experienced exponential growth in the first decade of the twenty-first century, and that continues to take up a larger and larger piece of the pop culture pie, is gaming—and in the post-9/11 world, games involving counterterrorism plots have become especially popular. Many of these are directly based on popular techno-thriller novels such as those by Tom Clancy. The obvious difference between films, television shows, and novels that depict terrorist fighting and video games that do the same is the interactive nature of gaming, which allows players to take part in covert counterterrorism operations that resemble footage from Afghanistan and Iraqi operations against religious insurgents in the Middle East. These techno-war counterterrorism games, such as *Call of Duty: Modern Warfare*, often put the player in the position of "first-person shooter," supplied with countless technologically advanced weapons of war while the local "savages" use only primitive weaponry and primeval violence. The "special ops" themes have proven very profitable for the industry, and their popularity points to how such games strongly resonate among gaming fans, who are drawn in by the allure of becoming virtual military heroes and virtual special ops operatives in the war on terror.

One development in the landscape of popular culture that has come to great prominence in the post–9/11 world is the widespread ability of the public to upload, access, and comment on videos on video-sharing sites like YouTube. The rise of YouTube as a repository for conspiracy videos related to terrorism reflects not just an interest in the topic on the part of pop culture consumers, it also highlights the attraction of interactivity and under-the-radar (i.e., outside mainstream media) message dissemination. Videos on topics such as the New World Order (the belief in the emergence of a one-world government), the Illuminati (the Enlightenment-era secret society), and the so-called

9/11 Truth Movement (the belief that the attacks of September 11, 2001, were an "inside job") have never been easier for consumers to access and spread through e-mail and social media sites. Conspiracy movements such as the Three Percenters and the Oath Keepers can disseminate their recruitment videos widely and build their movements digitally with much less legwork than ever before. Likewise, terrorist sympathizers—be they homegrown jihadists or white supremacists—can also post their videos and seek recruits through social media.

Pop Culture, Terrorism, and Public Anxiety

Another way of looking at the interaction of popular culture and terrorism, especially in the post-9/11 context, is to examine the extent to which depictions of political violence in popular culture influence society's general anxiety level over the possibility of a terrorist act occurring. One can argue that terrorism is modern society's biggest nightmare, and that its reoccurring depiction in popular culture is harmful because it creates fears and insecurity through excessive and exaggerated depictions of the threat society actually faces from terrorist acts. Moreover, some argue that the depiction of terrorism in popular culture creates a kind of anxiety loop: by creating further insecurity in society through the outsized depiction of terrorist acts, creators of pop culture media can trigger more consumption of this kind of cultural content in the manner of a compulsion, and this, in turn, can further raise the level of fear in a repetitive loop.

On the other hand, some critics suggest that post-9/11 depictions of terrorism actually serve a useful purpose in American society. In this view, looking at fictional images of terrorist acts allows American society to "cure" itself of the psychological effects stemming from the events of 9/11, which are viewed by many as an authentic cultural trauma that introduced new insecurities into the post–Cold War world and challenged the idea of American power. Popular culture can allow people to face these perceived vulnerabilities, which can help mitigate the insecurity and renew American society's faith in itself. The process of mitigation is sometimes achieved through the reintroduction of traditional cultural storylines (sometimes referred to in the literature as "mythologies" and "mythos"), such as that of the white male hero saving a helpless female victim from aboriginal "savages," the conservative frontier narrative depicting a battle of "us versus them," or even the fantastical myth of the American superhero fighting—and beating—the evil villain. Various studies argue that in post-9/11 popular culture these mythologies have often been reintroduced to re-narrate this collective insecurity to recover a sense of national pride and potency.

One example of this traditional narrative in a post-9/11 context is the film *Superman Returns* (2006), which takes place in the aftermath of the attacks. The movie offers its audience psychological recovery through what one scholar has termed a triumphant "spectacle of heroism" in the figure of Superman, the anthropomorphized stand-in for the United States. *Superman Returns* unspools an idealized narrative of national recuperation and spectacular victory against the enemy (Superman's arch-nemesis Lex Luthor) in scenes such as Superman's rescue of an airliner that is about to crash into a baseball stadium. In the world of *Superman Returns*, and other films like it, spectacular destruction is met with a spectacular, and morally unambiguous, response.

Conclusion

Unlike the news media, where images of the war on terror are often sanitized, remote, and abstract, popular culture has a unique opportunity to dramatize the violence, human suffering, and complex geopolitical maneuverings surrounding the issue of terrorism and American counterterrorist operations, not to mention the significant ethical and moral questions involved. Thus, it is fair to say that recent popular-culture images covering the counterterrorism fight have contributed to a critique of the "war on terror" in unflinching and visceral ways. However, it is also true that the degree of popular-culture critique is often mitigated by the need to remain entertaining in order to remain popular. There is a recognizable tension within popular forms of entertainment when they engage in cultural and political critique.

Tim Anderson and Olga B. Semukhina

See also Counterterrorism; Media and Terrorism; September 11 Attacks; Torture Debate

Further Readings

Altheide, D. *Terrorism and the Politics of Fear.* Lanham, MD: Rowman & Littlefield, 2006.

Brabazon, T. *Thinking Popular Culture: War, Terrorism, Writing.* Burlington, VT: Ashgate, 2008.

Brottman, M. "The Fascination of the Abomination." In *Film and Television after 9/11,* edited by W.W. Dixon, pp. 163–177. Carbondale: Southern Illinois University Press, 2004.

Castonguay, J. "Intermedia and War on Terror." In *Rethinking Global Security. Media, Popular Culture, and the "War on Terror,"* edited by A. Martin and P. Petro, pp. 151–178. New Brunswick, NJ: Rutgers University Press, 2006.

Dixon, W.W. *Film and Television after 9/11.* Carbondale: Southern Illinois University Press, 2004.

Forest, J.J. *Teaching Terror: Strategic and Tactical Learning in the Terrorist World.* Lanham, MD: Rowman & Littlefield, 2006.

Hoskins, A., and B. O'Loughlin. *Television and Terror: Conflicting Times and the Crisis of News Discourse.* Hampshire, UK: Palgrave Macmillan, 2007.

Jenkins, P. *Images of Terror: What We Can and Can't Know about Terrorism.* New York: Aldine de Gruyter, 2003.

Martin, A., and P. Petro, eds. *Rethinking Global Security. Media, Popular Culture, and the "War on Terror."* New Brunswick, NJ: Rutgers University Press, 2006.

Schopp, A., and M.B. Hill, eds. *The War on Terror and American Popular Culture.* Teaneck, NJ: Fairleigh Dickinson University Press, 2009.

Tuman, J.S. *Communicating Terror: The Rhetorical Dimensions of Terrorism.* Thousand Oaks, CA: Sage, 2003.

Zizek, S. *Welcome to Desert of the Real.* London: Verso, 2002.

POPULAR FRONT FOR THE LIBERATION OF PALESTINE

Founded in 1967 by George Habash after Israel captured the West Bank in the Six-Day War, the Popular Front for the Liberation of Palestine (PFLP) embraces a blend of Marxist-Leninist ideology and Arab nationalism. The group, which became notorious during the 1970s for hijacking civilian airliners, is a leading faction in the Palestine Liberation Organization (PLO). The U.S. State Department lists the Popular Front as a terrorist group.

In August 1969, PFLP members Leila Khaled and Salim Issawi took over a TWA Rome-to-Tel Aviv flight and directed the plane to Syria, where the passengers and crew were released unharmed. With the plane emptied, the hijackers blew up the cockpit. Khaled, then just 25, became infamous, being referred to as the "girl terrorist" and "deadly beauty" by the press. She subsequently had plastic surgery to disguise her well-known face, and took part in the Popular Front's next, and most daring, round of hijackings. On September 6, 1970, PFLP members hijacked four planes in a single day, all bound for New York City. After all hostages were released safely, King Hussein of Jordan declared war on the Palestinian groups operating in Jordan. In the battles known as "Black September," the Jordanian Army crushed the Palestinian fighters.

The group renounced hijacking and largely dropped from the headlines for several decades. Members became involved in a variety of social projects, including working to provide a network of Palestinian health-care clinics. Although the group moved part of its headquarters from Syria to the West Bank during the mid-1990s, Habash continued to lead the group from his base in Damascus. According to the U.S. State Department, Syria not only provided a haven for Habash and other Popular Front members, but it has given the group logistical support.

In 1993, the Popular Front, a longtime opponent of peace negotiations, broke from the PLO to oppose the signing of the Declaration of Principles signed by the PLO and Israel. The PFLP joined the Alliance of Palestinian Forces, but it split from this umbrella organization in 1996 because of ideological differences. During the same year, Habash commanded his members to refrain from taking part in the Palestinian legislative council elections. Although PFLP members sit on the PLO's Executive Committee, the group is not part of the Palestinian Authority.

In July 2000, an ailing Habash, who had led the Popular Front for three decades, stepped down; he died in 2008. The group's 800-odd members elected Habash's deputy Mustafa Zibri, widely known as Abu Ali Mustafa, as the new secretary-general. In the intifada that began later that year, the Popular Front took responsibility for roadside bombs and mortar attacks. In many interviews, Mustafa told the press that Israel was an "illegitimate entity."

Israeli minister Ephraim Sneh was, in turn, widely quoted as saying that Mustafa was taking the Popular Front "back into what it was in the 1960s, 1970s and 1980s—an active and deadly terrorist organization." In August 2001, Israeli forces assassinated Mustafa, firing laser-guided missiles into his Ramallah office. Israeli officials stated that he was killed to prevent the Popular Front from carrying out bombing attacks.

Two months later, the Popular Front retaliated and assassinated right-wing Israeli cabinet minister Rehavam Zeevi, who had advocated the killing of Palestinian political leaders and the expulsion of all Palestinians from the West Bank and Gaza. Israel accused Mustafa's successor, Ahmed Saadat, of orchestrating the crime, and pressured the Palestinian Authority to arrest him. Yasir Arafat banned the group's military wing and arrested Saadat in January 2002. (Saadat was seized by Israeli authorities in 2006.) That very week, the military arm of the PFLP, named the Martyr Abu Ali Mustafa Brigade for its late leader, threatened to kill Palestinian Authority officials if Saadat and other Popular Front prisoners were not released from Palestinian Authority jails. At the same time, however, Popular Front political leaders were distancing themselves from the group's military arm in public statements, although they did not go so far as to threaten the lives of fellow Palestinians.

The military wing of the PFLP continues to contribute to the region's escalating violence, conducting numerous suicide bombings and rocket attacks against Israeli targets. At the same time, the PFLP has attempted to foster dialog between Fatah, the largest PLO faction, and Hamas, which have engaged in an armed struggled for control of Palestinian territory since 2006.

Erica Pearson

See also Habash, George; Hamas; Khaled, Leila; Palestine Liberation Organization; TWA Flight 840 Hijacking

Further Readings

Goldenberg, Suzanne. "Attack on Afghanistan: Profile: Far-right Leader Who Fell Victim to His Own Ideas: Minister Fought for Strategy of Assassination." *The Guardian* (London), October 18, 2001, p. 7.

Hockstader, Lee. "Israel Kills Palestinian Activist; Missiles Fly Through Windows of Building Housing Americans." *The Washington Post,* August 28, 2001, p. A1.

Joffe, Lawrence. "Abu Ali Mustafa: Palestinian Leader Who Rejected Peace Accords." Obituary. *The Guardian* (London), August 28, 2001, p. 14.

Khaled, Leila. *My People Shall Live: The Autobiography of a Revolutionary,* edited by George Hajjar. London: Hodder and Stoughton, 1973.

Lybarger, Loren D. *Identity and Religion in Palestine: The Struggle Between Islamism and Secularism in the Occupied Territories.* Princeton, NJ: Princeton University Press, 2007.

Raab, David. *Terror in Black September: The First Eyewitness Account of the Infamous 1970 Hijacking.* New York: Palgrave Macmillan, 2007.

Reeves, Phil. "Arafat Angers Allies by Arresting PLO Official." *The Independent* (London), January 17, 2002.

U.S. State Department. "Terrorist Organizations." *Country Reports on Terrorism 2008.* http://www .state.gov/s/ct/rls/crt/2008/122449.htm.

Usher, Graham. "PFLP Threatens to Kill Arafat Aides If Leader Is Not Freed." *The Guardian* (London), January 18, 2002, p. 14.

Wilson, Scott. "Palestinians Captured in Israeli Raid on Prison." *The Washington Post,* March 15, 2006, p. A13.

POPULAR FRONT FOR THE LIBERATION OF PALESTINE– GENERAL COMMAND

In 1968, Ahmad Jibril led a number of discontented members of the Popular Front for the Liberation of Palestine (PFLP) to form a separate group. Claiming to focus more on fighting and less on politics, they created the Popular Front for the Liberation of Palestine–General Command (PFLP–GC).

According to the U.S. State Department, PFLP–GC operatives carried out dozens of attacks in Europe and the Middle East during the 1970s and 1980s. They also engaged in various kidnappings. In May 1985, according to press reports, Israel exchanged 1,150 Arab prisoners for three Israelis held by the PFLP–GC. As of 2010, The State Department continued to list the PFLP–GC as an active foreign terrorist organization in its report on global terrorism.

Jibril, a former captain in the Syrian army, originally based the group in Damascus. Although its headquarters remains in Syria, the PFLP–GC is now also closely tied to Iran. According to the State Department, the group receives logistic and military support from Syria, and financial support from Iran. Press reports in the mid-1990s disclosed that the PFLP–GC began to set up training camps in several areas of Iran.

After Pan Am Flight 103 exploded over Lockerbie, Scotland, on December 21, 1988, killing 270 people, U.S. officials originally suspected that PFLP–GC operatives were paid by Iranian officials to carry out the crime. The Pan Am bombing happened just four months after a U.S. military cruiser accidentally shot down an Iranian Airbus, killing 290. After the Airbus disaster, Iranian government officials and affiliated militant groups had issued threats of revenge. Jibril denied any involvement in the Lockerbie bombing, and a lengthy criminal investigation carried out by Scottish officials later pointed to two Libyan Arab Airlines employees.

When Salman Rushdie published his novel *The Satanic Verses* in 1988, Jibril made headlines by publicly declaring that the PFLP–GC was prepared to carry out the Iranian religious leader Ayatollah Ruhollah Khomeini's fatwa against the author. Recently, the group has focused on guerrilla attacks in southern Lebanon and small-scale attacks in Israel, the West Bank, and the Gaza Strip, often working in cooperation with Hezbollah. Rocket attacks launched into Israel from Lebanon by the PFLP-GC resulted in a number of retaliatory air strikes by Israeli jets in the mid-2000s.

Erica Pearson

See also Pan Am Flight 103 Bombing; Popular Front for the Liberation of Palestine

Further Readings

Claiborne, William, and Jonathan C. Randal. "Life in the Shattered South: A Gangland Chicago in the Levant." *The Washington Post,* March 15, 1981, p. A21.

Fisk, Robert. "Jibril Protests Too Much in Face of Time and History." *The Independent,* January 10, 1990, p. 11.

Myre, Greg. "Israel Aims Airstrikes at Militants in Lebanon." *International Herald Tribune,* May 29, 2006, p. 4.

U.S. State Department. "Foreign Terrorist Organizations." http://www.state.gov/s/ct/rls/other/des/123085.htm.

POPULAR LIBERATION ARMY

The Popular Liberation Army (aka People's Liberation Army, Ejército Popular de Liberación, or EPL), also known as the People's Liberation Army, is a Marxist guerrilla group that has been fighting the government of Colombia since the mid-1960s.

The 1960s were a time of great upheaval in Colombia, resulting in the formation of several active resistance forces; the best known are the Revolutionary Armed Forces of Colombia (FARC) and National Liberation Army (ELN). Unlike the ELN and the FARC, which although communist in ideology have operated independently of any political faction, the EPL was founded in 1967 as the armed wing of an existing political party, the Marxist-Leninist Communist Party (ML-CP), a breakaway faction of the Colombian Communist Party. Thus, the EPL was the instrument of its party, not an independent entity. During the EPL's early years, it adhered strictly to party dogma, which may have made it more receptive to political solutions to Colombia's ongoing conflict.

The ML-CP advocated a strict Maoist strategy in which revolution was to originate among guerrilla fighters and peasants in the countryside, who would then encircle major cities with "liberated" territory, thus gradually choking off government support until besiegement caused collapse. This strategy prompted the EPL to infiltrate local unions and worker's rights groups to indoctrinate the peasantry. While the EPL infiltrated these groups effectively, its recruitment efforts met largely with failure. By 1975, disagreements within the EPL leadership over strict adherence to Maoist strategy began a period of infighting that limited the group's ability to fight on the outside. In 1980 the EPL announced that it had abandoned Maoism, and it began to attract new members in its northeastern area of operation. By the early 1980s, the group was estimated to have about 1,500 active members.

In 1982, Colombia's president, Belisario Betancur, initiated peace negotiations with the guerrillas. The EPL and another guerrilla group, the M-19, were the most receptive; in August 1984 the EPL signed a peace accord with the government. Many in the government and the army were opposed to Benatacur's peace initiative, however, and right-wing paramilitary death squads began to form. The EPL and other guerrilla groups that had tried to enter politics found their activists the targets of assassination, and neither the army nor the larger guerrilla groups were honoring the cease-fire. After the November 1985 assassination of EPL's leader Oscar Calvo, the group abandoned the now-collapsed peace process.

This was a heavy blow to the EPL, as it had been one of the initiative's most ardent supporters. Former sympathizers felt betrayed by the EPL's political capitulation and began to support the FARC and the ELN, both of which were seen as rightly mistrustful of the government. The EPL attempted to reestablish itself as a guerrilla force, copying the FARC and ELN tactics of kidnapping and attacks on the oil industry, but the group never truly recovered. In 1989–1990, the EPL once again entered talks with the government. An amnesty offer induced 1,800 EPL guerrillas to lay down their arms in March 1991, seemingly finishing the organization.

A hard-core group of dissidents refused to participate in the amnesty, however. During the 1990s they, along with members of FARC and ELN, attacked and killed members of the Hope, Peace, and Liberty Party, the nonviolent political party formed by those members of EPL who had disarmed. In the following decade, however, the Colombian government clamped down on guerrilla organizations, rending the already-small dissident branch of the EPL largely defunct.

Colleen Sullivan

See also FARC; National Liberation Army–Colombia; United Self-Defense Forces of Colombia

Further Readings

Forez-Morris, Mauricio. "Joining Guerrilla Groups in Colombia: Individual Motivations and Processes for Entering a Violent Organization." *Studies in Conflict & Terrorism* 30, no. 7 (July 2007): 615–634.

Jaramillo, Daniel Garcia-Pena. "Colombia: In Search of a New Model for Conflict Resolution." In *Peace, Democracy, and Human Rights in Colombia*, edited by Christopher Welna and Gustavo Gallon. Notre Dame, IN: University of Notre Dame Press, 2007.

Kline, Harvey F. *Democracy under Assault.* New York: Westview Press, 1995.

Kline, Harvey F. *State Building and Conflict Resolution in Colombia, 1986–94.* Tuscaloosa: University of Alabama Press, 1999.

Rojas, Christina, and Judy Meltzer. *Elusive Peace: International, National, and Local Dimensions of Conflict in Colombia.* New York: Palgrave Macmillan, 2005.

Safford, Frank, and Marco Palacios. *Colombia: Fragmented Land, Divided Society.* New York: Oxford University Press, 2002.

POSSE COMITATUS

The Posse Comitatus, meaning "Power of the County," was founded in 1969 by an Oregon dry-cleaner, Henry L. Beach. Members believe that the only legitimate authority in the United States is the county sheriff, and that any power above that level is illegal. They object to, and sometimes refuse to pay, federal taxes. Influenced by the racist, anti-Semitic theology of Christian Identity, the Posse preaches that the founders of the country intended a Christian republic, and that desegregation laws wrongly encourage "race mixing." Group members establish churches to which they deed their properties and claim religious tax exemptions. Fearing the government's takeover by a Jewish-led, communist conspiracy, many stockpile weapons and food supplies and train in weapons use and military tactics. Some, like Gordan Kahl, who shot two federal marshals at a roadblock in 1983, have resorted to violence.

The group first attracted the FBI's attention in 1975 when plans to assassinate "money czar" Nelson Rockefeller were unearthed. The resulting investigation uncovered chapters of the organization in 23 states and an estimated 12,000 to 50,000 members. The group accumulated its largest membership gains during the farm crisis of the 1980s. When, after years of struggling, farmers were forced to sell some or all of their farms on the auction block, the Posse convinced many of them to blame their troubles on the federal government and the banking system, both allegedly controlled by Jews.

Throughout the 1980s, Posse members engaged in a wide range of subversive activities aimed at the state and federal governments. Several state officials received letters of "asseveration" from members claiming they were no longer U.S. citizens. Many others filed "pro-se" lawsuits against the Federal Reserve and other banks in efforts to reclaim taxes and interest they already paid and to clog up the courts with cases. Still others, like James Wickstrom, the leader of a Wisconsin branch, formed their own municipalities. Wickstrom was later imprisoned for conspiring to distribute $100,000 in counterfeit money that he planned to use to set up a militia training camp.

Some incidents turned violent. In one case, a member shot three undercover federal agents who were buying guns from him. In Oregon, the FBI thwarted a plot to firebomb the homes of four judges who had presided over members' trials. In another case, a California branch leader, William Potter Gale—credited with bringing Christian Identity tenets into the Posse movement—and several associates, were arrested for making death threats to a judge and IRS agents.

The Posse gained widespread notoriety in the 1983 case involving Gordon Kahl. In North Dakota, U.S. Marshals set up a roadblock to arrest Kahl for a probation violation having to do with an earlier tax evasion case. A gunfight resulted that left two marshals dead, and another marshal and two police officers wounded. Five other people, including Kahl's wife and son, were arrested in connection with the murders, but Kahl became a fugitive, eventually making his way to another member's house in Arkansas. After a four-month manhunt, he shot and killed a sheriff. Authorities responded by firing back with guns and teargas, igniting stockpiled ammunition. Kahl was killed and his charred body was later identified through dental records.

Kahl's death made him a martyr for the Far Right. It also alerted officials to the Posse's true potential, influencing law enforcement and legislation in several states. Officials believe that the Posse, like other militia groups, lost its impetus after the 1995 bombing of the Alfred P. Murrah Federal Building in Oklahoma. However, the group and its rhetoric have inspired successors. In 1996, members of the Posse-inspired Family Farm Preservation were charged with passing approximately $80 million in counterfeit money orders in an effort to disrupt the federal monetary system. They were found guilty of conspiracy and mail fraud.

Nancy Egan

See also Oklahoma City Bombing; Patriot Movement

Further Readings

Albrecht, Mike. "The Roots of Posse Comitatus." *Bismarck Tribune,* February 11, 2003, p. 1.

Bennett, David H. *The Party of Fear: From Nativist Movements to the New Right in American History.* New York: Vintage Books, 1990.

Corcoran, James. *Bitter Harvest. Gordon Kahl and the Posse Comitatus: Murder in the Heartland.* New York: Viking, 1990.

Levitas, Daniel. *The Terrorist Next Door: The Militia Movement and the Radical Right.* New York: Thomas Dunne Books, 2002.

Wright, Stuart A. *Patriots, Politics, and the Oklahoma City Bombing.* Cambridge, UK: Cambridge University Press, 2007.

PUERTO RICAN NATIONALIST TERRORISM

Puerto Rican nationalist terrorism was one of the four major domestic terrorist threats that faced the United States in the latter part of the twentieth century, along with right-wing groups, militia groups, and single-subject special interest groups (e.g., anti-abortion militants, radical environmentalists, the animal rights movement).

Militant Puerto Rican nationalism dates to the 1930s, when Pedro Albizu Campos became president of the Puerto Rican Nationalist Party (NPPR), a political group advocating that Puerto Rico become a free and independent republic. The charismatic and Harvard-educated Campos injected the movement with a "radical nationalism," calling for "direct action" to achieve the goal of national sovereignty. Faced with repression by the government of Puerto Rico, he pledged that for every nationalist killed, a continental American would die—a promise he kept. Police fired into a student protest at the University of Puerto Rico in October 1935; in response, in February 1936, members of the NPPR assassinated Colonel Frank Riggs, Puerto Rico's police commander.

Momentum Lost and Regained

The cycle of nationalist uprisings, government repression, and nationalist retaliation continued through the 1930s. Campos was arrested in March 1936, and Puerto Rico witnessed massive demonstrations after his conviction, culminating in what is known as the Ponce Massacre in February 1937, when police killed 30 civilians and wounded over 150 others. That June, nationalists tried to kill both the judge who presided over Campos's trial and Puerto Rico's resident commissioner. However, without Campos's leadership, internal strife caused the movement to lose much of its momentum.

The 1940s were marked by less militant political actions. By 1945 a good portion of the nationalist party had drifted toward the moderate "commonwealth" status, helping elect Luis Munoz Marin, leader of the Popular Democratic Party, as the first governor of Puerto Rico in 1948. Marin went to Washington, having formulated a "temporary" commonwealth status for Puerto Rico in exchange for a ratified constitution for Puerto Rico. By the end of the decade, Campos was released from jail, and extreme nationalism began to resurface.

On October 30, 1950, U.S. forces put down uprisings of over 2,000 nationalists all over Puerto Rico. Two days later, nationalists struck, for the first time, on continental U.S. soil. Oscar Collazo and Griselio Torresola, two NPPR members, tried to assassinate President Harry S. Truman. As the two men approached Blair House, Truman's temporary residence, a gunfight erupted between them and Truman's guards, leaving Torresola and one police officer dead. Investigators found a letter from Campos on Torresola's body, and though the letter did not refer explicitly to the assassination, it was enough to convict Campos a second time. On March 4, 1954, militant nationalists struck again, carrying Puerto Rican flags and armed with guns, they stormed the U.S. House of Representatives, wounding five members of Congress before running out of ammunition. By the end of the 1950s, as in the 1930s, the nationalist movement had again lost momentum, splitting into student organizations and "grouplets" like Accion Patriotica Revolucionaria (APR) and Movimiento 27 de Marzo.

FALN and More

The antiwar and anti-imperialist movements that marked the late 1960s, coupled with the demise of consensus on Puerto Rico's commonwealth status, led to a revival of militant Puerto Rican nationalism in the 1970s. In October 1974, Fuerzas Armadas de Liberación Nacional (FALN) announced its presence in the United States with a communiqué claiming responsibility for bombings in New York City and Newark, New Jersey. In January 1975, the FALN perpetrated one of its bloodiest attacks, the bombing of Fraunces Tavern, in which four died and more than 50 were injured. As FALN continued to bomb, in August 1978, another militant nationalist group, the Macheteros ("Machete Wielders" in Spanish), sent its first communiqué, claiming responsibility for the death of a police officer in Puerto Rico. The two groups joined forces in September 1979, in solidarity for Puerto Rican independence by any means necessary. That October, FALN and the Macheteros detonated bombs in Puerto Rico, New York, and Chicago.

While the FALN conducted bombings in the continental United States, focusing on government and public buildings in New York and Chicago, the Macheteros focused their activities on the islands of Puerto Rico, bombing U.S. military installations and draft offices and attacking military personnel. The Macheteros were joined by other, smaller militant groups. In December 1979, the Macheteros, the Organization of Volunteers for the Puerto Rican Revolution, and Armed Forces of Popular Resistance jointly attacked a U.S. Navy bus: two sailors died and 10 were injured. In January 1981, yet another nationalist group, the Revolutionary Commandos of the People, bombed post offices where men registered for the draft. In the subsequent communiqué, the Revolutionary Commandos, who claimed that they did not want to hurt postal employees or destroy correspondence with their protest, tried to downplay the seriousness of its actions by citing the smallness of the bombs.

By the early 1980s, several members of the FALN and the Macheteros were already serving lengthy prison sentences. Willie Morales, the alleged leader of the FALN, had been convicted of possession of explosive devices in 1978—his "bomb factory" had exploded in Queens, New York, maiming both his hands. (He later escaped prison and fled to Cuba.) In April 1980, 11 FALN members were captured in Evanston, Illinois. Three more FALN members were arrested in June 1983, in Chicago, marking the end of the FALN bombings, but not the organization.

Macheteros on the Mainland

On September 12, 1983, the Macheteros struck for the first time outside of Puerto Rico, stealing over $7 million from a Wells Fargo depot in Hartford, Connecticut. The theft, one of largest cash robberies in U.S. history, elicited a strong response from federal authorities. On August 30, 1985, over 200 FBI agents were deployed in San Juan, Puerto Rico, to disassemble the Macheteros.

At the time of the Wells Fargo robbery, only eight groups merited full-investigation status by the FBI. Five of these were Puerto Rican—FALN, the Macheteros, FARP (Armed Forces of Popular Resistance), MLN (Movement for National Liberation), and COR (Committee of Revolutionary Workers)—the other three groups were the Arizona chapter of the Knights of the Ku Klux Klan, the May 19 Communist Organization, and the Jewish Defense League. However, by 1987, which is often cited as the end of the threat of Puerto Rican nationalist terrorism, most key members were behind bars or living in exile.

In 1999, President Bill Clinton commuted the sentences of 16 Puerto Rican nationalists amid great controversy and a Senate measure (passed 95–2) that condemned the clemencies as "deplorable." (President Jimmy Carter faced little opposition when, in 1979, he granted clemency to the nationalists who attempted to assassinate Truman in 1950 and those who stormed the House of Representatives in 1954.) The release of these nationalists re-ignited the debate about whether the Puerto Rican nationalists should be considered terrorists or patriots, criminals or political prisoners.

Laura Lambert

See also FALN; Fraunces Tavern Bombing; Macheteros

Further Readings

Esposito, Richard, and Ted Gerstein. *Bomb Squad: A Year inside the Nation's Most Exclusive Police Unit.* New York: Hyperion, 2007.

Fernandez, Ronald. *Los Macheteros: The Wells Fargo Robbery and the Violent Struggle for Puerto Rican Independence.* New York: Prentice Hall, 1987.

Morris, Nancy. *Puerto Rico: Culture, Politics, and Identity.* Westport, CT: Praeger, 1995.

QADDAFI, MUAMMAR EL (1942–)

Muammar el Qaddafi has been the leader of Libya since 1969. He has often used his position to support insurgencies and terrorist groups throughout the world.

Qaddafi's exact birth date is unknown. A Bedouin, he was born in a tent in the Libyan desert near the town of Surt. He grew up in the traditional tribal, nomadic way of his people; throughout his life Qaddafi has extolled and romanticized tribal values and castigated the soullessness of modern industrial cities.

Qaddafi has always been fiercely proud and independent—traits for which the Bedouins are noted. Ambitious and intelligent, Qaddafi, from his earliest youth, abhorred all forms of foreign domination and "imperialism" in Libya. As a teenager, he came to admire Gamal Abdel Nasser, the president of Egypt from 1956 to 1970, and he was inspired by the 1952 revolution and coup that brought Nasser to power. Qaddafi believed in and endorsed Nasser's pan-Arabist philosophy.

In 1961 Qaddafi enrolled in the Libyan military academy in the city of Benghazi. While there, he helped found the Free Officers Movement, a group of young military men who wanted to overthrow the Western-supported King Idris I. He graduated in 1965 and quickly rose within the military ranks. In September 1969, Qaddafi and the Free Officers participated in a bloodless coup that exiled Idris. Some historians believe Qaddafi was the guiding spirit behind the coup, while others feel that he merely took advantage of it to achieve power. Whatever the case, by 1970 Qaddafi had taken control of the Revolutionary Command Council and become the leader of Libya. (Qaddafi has bestowed on himself and later discarded dozens of honorary titles; most Libyans refer to him as "the leader.")

Almost immediately after assuming power, Qaddafi banned alcohol and expelled the Italian community (a colonial remnant), and he forced the British, French, and Americans to withdraw from the military bases they had established on Libyan soil. Despite his claims of fealty to Islamic virtues, Qaddafi also cracked down on Sanusi sect, a politically influential system of Islamic schools and monasteries. By the mid-1970s, following the socialist philosophy discussed in his *Green Book*, Qaddafi had instituted an unusual system of government in Libya. In brief, each town and village formed people's councils to decide local government policy; delegates from these local councils were sent to larger regional bodies, who in turn sent delegates to the national ruling body. Laws were enforced by the Revolutionary Command Council, of which Qaddafi was the head. This system is called the *Jamahiriya*, or "state of the masses," but the term has been criticized as merely being a new name for a totalitarian consolidation of power. Supporters, however, describe it as an effective method of involving the Libyan people in the political life of the state, which is important in a country with a tiny educated elite and a short history of political participation, having had no national political bodies until after World War II.

Qaddafi's experiences shaped his extreme view of international relations. His beliefs and statements have often appeared inexplicable to outside observers; many have characterized him as eccentric, and some have gone so far as to call him mad. Yet certain predominant themes and motivations can be discerned in even his most seemingly bizarre actions. He has many times described the globe as being divided into "imperialists"—that is, the West, and particularly the United States—and "revolutionaries," or the struggling nations of the Third World. He believes that the latter need to unite to overthrow the former, as he himself ousted the Libyan monarchy. He has supported the Palestinians in the struggle against Israel and has attempted to develop strategic alliances with other Arab states in line with the concepts of Nasser. In the early twenty-first century, he turned his attention to Africa, extolling similar unification and mutual aid plans to other North and sub-Saharan African nations in his travels around the continent. In February 2009 he was elected chairman of the African Union at a summit in Ethiopia, where he championed the pursuit of a "United States of Africa."

Qaddafi and Terrorism

During much of his time as leader, Qaddafi has seen terrorism as a legitimate means to accomplish the overthrow of imperialists. Libya's sponsorship of international terrorism since Qaddafi's assumption of power has included dozens of groups in as many countries; a partial list includes the Irish Republican Army, the Red Brigades of Italy, the Japanese Red Army, the Sandinistas of Nicaragua, the Armenian Secret Army for the Liberation of Armenia, the Baader-Meinhof Gang of Germany, the Abu Nidal Organization, the Palestine Liberation Organization, the Popular Front for the Liberation of Palestine, and the Moro National Liberation Front of the Philippines. Libya has not only provided groups such as these with funds, it has also sent them arms—in some cases tons of weaponry—and allowed them to establish training camps in Libya.

Qaddafi's sponsorship of terrorism has extended beyond the patronage of foreign groups. He has ordered the assassination of Libyan dissidents in

Muammar Qaddafi, the Libyan chief of state, attends the 12th African Union Summit in Addis Ababa, Ethiopia, February 2, 2009. Qaddafi was elected chairman of the organization. (U.S. Navy photo by Mass Communication Specialist 2nd Class Jesse B. Awalt/Released)

other countries. In 1984 an English policewoman was killed when shots were fired from inside Libya's embassy in London into a crowd of demonstrators. Libyan intelligence operatives are believed to have been involved in the bombing of a Berlin nightclub in 1986 and the bombing of Pan Am Flight 103 over Lockerbie, Scotland, in 1988. Libyan links to terrorism, particularly attacks on U.S. targets, have often made Qaddafi and his regime the target of U.S. reprisals. Since the Berlin bombing, Libya has been sanctioned by the United Nations, while the United States cut off all diplomatic relations with the country and imposed its own, more stringent sanctions. In 1986, the administration of President Ronald Reagan bombed several Libyan targets in retaliation for the Berlin nightclub bombing. Qaddafi's compound was hit in the bombing, and while he escaped, several family members and associates were killed, including his daughter. He has since had the site made into a national shrine. The incident heightened Qaddafi's reputation in the Middle East, however, for he was seen as having courageously and successfully defied the most powerful nation in the world.

Qaddafi's Pivot

In the final decade of the twentieth century, it appeared that Libya and Qaddafi might be turning away from terrorism. U.S. and international sanctions took a severe toll on the Libyan oil industry, and with the fall of Communism in the Soviet Union and other countries, Qaddafi's revolutionary rhetoric lost much of the appeal it had held in the 1970s. In 1999, Libya expelled the Palestinian terrorist Abu Nidal and turned over to a Scots court two former intelligence officers wanted in the Lockerbie bombing. (The two were convicted and sentenced to life in prison in 2001.) Also in 1999, Libya made a public declaration of its commitment to fighting al Qaeda. Following the attacks of September 11, 2001, Qaddafi strongly denounced the attacks and the Muslim extremists that carried them out.

In May 2002, Libya offered $2.7 billion—an unprecedented amount—in compensation to the families of the victims of the Lockerbie bombing. The money was predicated upon the lifting of sanctions, and in September 12, 2003, the UN Security Council lifted sanctions against Libya. On May 15, 2006, the United States announced that it would remove Libya from the State Department's list of state sponsors of terrorism and renew full diplomatic relations with the country. Then in October 2008, Libya paid $1.5 billion into a U.S. compensation fund for relatives of terror attacks in which Tripoli had been blamed, including the 1986 Berlin discotheque bombing and the 1989 UTA Flight 772 bombing. (The final 20 percent of the Lockerbie money was also part of this payout.)

In 2004, following the 2003 invasion of Iraq and the overthrow of Saddam Hussein by U.S. forces, Qaddafi announced Libya's decision to abandon its weapons of mass destruction program. President Bush claimed that this development was a direct result of the U.S. invasion, but

there is some disagreement over the truth of this declaration, with many commentators pointing out that Libya and U.S. representatives had been engaging in diplomatic relations in the years leading up to the invasion, and that by renouncing its nuclear program, Libya was just seeking to build on the foundation that had already been laid.

From Revolutionary to Statesman?

In a 2009 profile of Qaddafi, the *Daily Telegraph* diplomatic editor David Blair highlighted Qaddafi's transformation from terrorist radical to "eccentric statesman," describing his relationship with the western world as "entirely benign." However, Qaddafi's behavior in the first decade of the twenty-first century was not quite as conciliatory as that characterization suggests. For example, the Lockerbie bomber Abdel Basset Ali al Megrahi, convicted in 2003, was released from a Scots prison in 2009 on compassionate grounds, as he was supposedly suffering from colon cancer and was expected to live only a few months. Secret U.S. embassy cables leaked late in 2010 indicate that Qaddafi had put severe pressure on Britain to release Megrahi. Allegedly, Qaddafi made explicit threats to stop all trade deals with Britain and begin a campaign of harassment against British embassy staff. Qaddafi subsequently received much criticism from Western leaders for this lobbying effort and for harboring a known terrorist.

Moreover, on September 23, 2009, during his first-ever visit to the United States, Qaddafi addressed the 64th session of the UN General Assembly and delivered a rambling 94-minute speech in which he floated conspiracy theories about the origin of swine flu (a military laboratory creation) as well as the deaths of John F. Kennedy, Martin Luther King Jr., and former UN Secretary-General Dag Hammarskjöld. He went on to assert that the 15-member UN Security Council, and especially its five veto-holding members—Britain, China, France, Russia, and the United States—"should not be called the Security Council, it should be called the 'Terror Council.'"

Antigovernment protests erupted across Libya in early 2011, and the Qaddafi regime's reaction was swift and violent. Reports from several sources indicate that Qaddafi brought in foreign mercenaries to kill protesters. In March 2011, the UN Security Council declared a "no-fly zone" over Libya in the hope of protecting the antigovernment rebels. As of publication it remained uncertain whether Qaddafi would be able to hold on to power.

Regardless of the outcome, Qaddafi will remain a controversial figure on the world stage. On the one hand, he made definitive steps to return his country to the world community, publicly and vehemently criticizing al Qaeda, renouncing Libya's nuclear program, and owning up to his country's past terrorist acts. Simultaneously, however, he defended the Taliban in Afghanistan, lobbied aggressively for the release of a convicted terrorist, and is suspected by human rights organizations of engaging in political assassination and mass murder. Summing up this seeming contradiction of impulses, in February 2010, Qaddafi defended the notion of armed struggle, saying of Libya, "we reject terrorism and we do not abandon jihad."

Colleen Sullivan and Tim Anderson

See also Abu Nidal Organization; Banna, Sabri al; La Belle Discotheque Bombing; Pan Am Flight 103 Bombing; State-Sponsored Terrorism; Training of Terrorists

Further Readings

Arnold, Guy. *The Maverick State: Gaddafi and the New World Order*. London: Cassell, 1996.

Blair, David. "Profile: Muammar Gaddafi, Libyan Leader at Time of Lockerbie Bombing." *Daily Telegraph*, August 13, 2009. http://www.telegraph.co.uk/news/uknews/6022449/Profile-Muammar-Gaddafi-Libyan-leader-at-time-of-Lockerbie-bombing.html.

El-Kikhia, Manour O. *Libya's Qaddafi: The Politics of Contradiction*. Gainesville: University Press of Florida, 1997.

"Libya—Protests and Revolt (2011)." *The New York Times*. http://topics.nytimes.com/top/news/international/countriesandterritories/libya/index.html.

Sicker, Martin. *The Making of a Pariah State: The Adventurist Policies of Muamar Qaddafi*. New York: Praeger, 1987.

Tremless, George. *Gaddafi: The Desert Mystic*. New York: Carroll & Graf, 1993.

RAJNEESH, BHAGWAN SHREE (1931–1990)

In 1984, disciples of the Indian guru Bhagwan Shree Rajneesh used salmonella bacteria to poison 750 people in rural Oregon.

Rajneesh, an Indian philosophy professor turned spiritual guru, left his commune in Poona, India, in 1981 and traveled to the United States, where he established a commune on a 64,000-acre ranch in the high desert of Wasco County, Oregon. In a short time, the commune, called Rajneeshpuram, developed into a small city, complete with sewer and water systems, a paved airstrip, a 44-acre reservoir, a shopping mall, and its own "peace" force that carried assault weapons and patrolled the commune 24 hours a day.

As the commune's population swelled to over 4,000, one hundred times that of the local community of Antelope, tensions mounted. Some of Rajneesh's followers moved into Antelope and took over the city council, changing the city's name to Rajneesh. Antelope's population had dropped to 17 when the commune began to unravel.

The major disputes between Rajneeshpuram and the surrounding communities were over Oregon's land-use laws, which prohibited building a city on land that was zoned for agriculture. In 1984, Rajneesh's followers pushed for a special election, ostensibly to change the zoning laws; what they planned was to take control of Wasco County's affairs. Rajneesh's followers imported thousands of homeless people to vote, in hopes of winning the election. Rajneesh's chief aide, Ma Anand Sheela, masterminded a plan that would have guaranteed their success.

In September 1984, followers of Rajneesh sprinkled the bacteria *Salmonella typhimurium* on salad bars in 10 restaurants in Wasco County. Within two weeks, 751 residents became violently ill, suffering from acute stomach pains, fever, chills, headaches, bloody stools, and vomiting. Investigators quickly linked the symptoms to salmonella poisoning and traced the poisoning to local salad bars.

Initially, it was thought that food-handlers had contaminated the food. Suspicions that members of Rajneeshpuram had poisoned residents to skew the voting were raised, but they were quickly dismissed because the elections were not until November, and any debilitation from salmonella poisoning would not last that long. Investigators did not consider that the attack was just a practice run. Reportedly, Sheela ultimately planned to contaminate the county's water supply.

The Oregon State Health Department's chief epidemiologist, along with the FBI and the Centers for Disease Control and Prevention (CDC) took a full year to determine that the salad bar had been deliberately contaminated with the salmonella bacteria. When investigators finally raided Rajneeshpuram, they found proof in the commune's laboratory, registered as Pythagoras Clinic, where another follower, Ma Anand Puja, grew the *Salmonella typhimurium* cultures.

In 1986 Sheela was convicted of masterminding the salmonella poisoning, as well as the poisoning of two Wasco County officials, the attempted poisoning of Swami Devaraj (Rajneesh's physician), setting fire to a county office, and arranging more than 400 sham marriages. Two other commune members, both British women, were later jailed for conspiracy to kill the Oregon attorney general, Charles Turner, a long-time enemy of Rajneeshpuram. Rajneesh, who had fled the commune in 1985, was later arrested on immigration fraud charges and deported; he returned to Poona, where he changed his name to Osho and established another commune. He died of heart failure in January 1990.

Laura Lambert

See also Biological Terrorism

Further Readings

Gordon, James S. *The Golden Guru: The Strange Journey of Bhagwan Shree Rajneesh.* Lexington, MA: Stephen Greene Press, 1987.

Guest, Tim. *My Life in Orange: Growing Up with the Guru.* New York: Harcourt, 2005.

Lindholm, Charles. "Culture, Charisma, and Consciousness." In *Psychological Anthropology: A Reader on Self in Culture,* edited by Robert A. LeVine. Oxford: Wiley-Blackwell, 2010.

McCormack, Win, ed. *The Rajneesh Chronicles.* Portland: New Oregon Publishers, 1987.

Milne, Hugh. *Bhagwan: The God That Failed.* New York: St. Martin's, 1986.

Urban, Hugh B. "Osho, from Sex Guru to Guru of the Rich." In *Gurus in America,* edited by Thomas A. Forsthoefel and Cynthia Ann Humes. SUNY Series in Hindu Studies. Albany: State University of New York Press, 2005.

REAL IRISH REPUBLICAN ARMY

The Real Irish Republican Army is a splinter group of the Irish Republican Army (IRA); it was responsible for the 1998 Omagh Bombing in County Tyrone, Northern Ireland. Although the majority of the combatants in the conflict in Northern Ireland have accepted the terms of the peace laid out in the 1998 Good Friday Agreement, the Real IRA has continued its attacks.

Beginning in 1969, the IRA carried out various terrorist attacks and assassinations, attempting to compel the British Army to withdraw from Northern Ireland. The IRA also wanted to reunite Northern Ireland with the Republic of Ireland. In the summer of 1997, after several years of secret peace talks and two previous cease-fires, the Irish Republican Army's governing body, the Army Council, met to discuss whether the IRA should again declare a cease-fire to enable delegates from its political arm, Sinn Féin, to join the proposed public peace negotiations. The Army Council debated fiercely about the proposed cease-fire, because of British government expectations that the IRA would decommission, or disarm, as a precondition of joining the peace talks. A majority of the leadership voted to call the cease-fire, but a small group of dissenters, led by Michael McKevitt, walked out.

McKevitt and the others considered decommissioning to be a betrayal of the IRA's goals that would lead to the defeat of its ideal of a united Ireland. (The IRA considered itself to be the lawful army of the Irish Republic, as envisioned in the declaration of Easter 1916, which first proclaimed the Irish Republic. Decommissioning would thus suggest that its existence as a standing army of a sovereign state was not legitimate.) McKevitt and his colleagues established a political party, The 32-County Sovereignty Committee, led by Bernadette Sands-McKevitt (the sister of Bobby Sands, an IRA terrorist and martyr), and an armed wing called the Real IRA, or sometimes the True IRA, reflecting their belief that their organization has not deviated from the original Republican ideal. The Real IRA is estimated to have between 30 and 50 members, almost all of whom are former IRA members with expertise and experience in the arts of war, including bomb making.

The Real IRA immediately began bombings and attacks on British soldiers and Northern Irish police officers. Between the fall of 1997 and the summer of 1998, the Real IRA is believed to have been involved in eight bombings or attempted bombings. On August 15, 1998, Real IRA members left a 500-pound car bomb in the market square of Omagh, a town in Northern Ireland. A warning was phoned to the police 10 minutes before the bomb exploded, but the police response to this warning was tragic. Whether the warning was deliberately misleading, or whether the police misunderstood it, the result was that the police cleared the area near the town's courthouse and directed people toward the market square, where the bomb had been planted. The explosion killed 29 and injured over 200, making it the deadliest single bombing in Northern Ireland's 30-year conflict. The bombing was condemned by the IRA; several days later, the Real IRA issued an apology, stating that the death of innocent civilians had not been its intent.

In September 1998, the Real IRA declared a ceasefire, but the group did not keep to it for long. Some sources believe that Real IRA members were involved in a bombing in London in March 2001; others attribute the attack to the Continuity IRA, saying that the Real IRA has suffered defections to that group. A few months later, three Real IRA members, Fintan Paul O'Farrell, Declan John Rafferty, and Michael Christopher McDonald were arrested for a bombing conspiracy that involved seeking funding from Iraq; the men were convicted in May 2002 and given 30-year sentences.

In the summer of 2002, security experts in Britain warned that the Real IRA might be planning a new bid to sabotage the peace process. By 2009, however, the peace process had taken hold and governance of the six counties of Northern Ireland had become increasingly independent from England. Not coincidentally, experts reported that dissident groups in general had become increasingly active that year, and the Real IRA likewise stepped up its attacks, with minor attacks in London and more significant ones in Northern Ireland itself.

In March 2009 the group claimed responsibility for the murder of two soldiers stationed at the Massereene army base in Antrim, Northern Ireland. Two republican dissidents, Colin Duffy and Brian Shivers, were arrested for the shootings, and a woman named Marian Price was also arrested on suspicion of involvement. (Price is a longtime IRA supporter; she and her sister Dolours Price were convicted of setting a bomb that killed one person and injured more than 200 in 1973.) The Real IRA also claimed responsibility for a detonating a bomb in Belfast on April 12, 2010; the bomb was placed inside a taxi parked just outside the Northern Irish headquarters of the MI5, Britain's intelligence agency.

Despite extensive investigations into the Omagh bombing, no Real IRA member has been successfully prosecuted for involvement; only one man, Sean Hoey, was prosecuted, and he was acquitted in 2007. However, in 2009 the families of the Omagh victims won a largely symbolic civil suit against Michael McKevitt and four other suspected Real IRA members. McKevitt, believed to have been the leader of the IRA at the time of the Omagh attack, is already serving time in prison on other terrorism charges.

Colleen Sullivan

See also Continuity Irish Republican Army; Decommissioning in Northern Ireland; Irish Republican Army; Omagh Bombing; Women Terrorists

Further Readings

CAIN Web Service. "Conflict and Politics in Northern Ireland (1968 to the Present)." http://cain.ulst.ac.uk.

Chick, Kristen. "Real IRA Bombing Meant to Derail Last Step of N. Ireland Peace." *Christian Science Monitor*, April 11, 2010. http://www.csmonitor.com/World/terrorism-security/2010/0412/Real-IRA-bombing-meant-to-derail-last-step-of-N.-Ireland-peace.

Edwards, Ruth Dudley. *Aftermath: The Omagh Bombing and the Families' Pursuit of Justice*. London: Random House UK, 2010.

Holland, Jack. *Hope Against History: The Course of Conflict in Northern Ireland*. New York: Henry Holt, 1999.

McGrattan, Cillian. *Northern Ireland 1968–2008: The Politics of Entrenchment*. London: Palgrave Macmillan, 2010.

McKittrick, David. *Making Sense of the Troubles*. Belfast: Blackstaff Press, 2000.

O'Brien, Brendan. *The Long War: The IRA and Sinn Fein*. 2nd ed. Syracuse, NY: Syracuse University Press, 1999.

Simpson, Mark. "Second Shooting 'Feels Like Déjà Vu.'" BBC News, March 10, 2009. http://news.bbc.co.uk/2/hi/uk_news/northern_ireland/7934762.stm.

RED ARMY FACTION

See Baader-Meinhof Gang; Japanese Red Army

RED BRIGADES

The Red Brigades, founded in 1969 in Milan, were a Marxist terrorist group active in Italy throughout the 1970s.

Since World War II, in which communist-led resistance fighters contributed decisively to the Allied victory in Italy, the Italian Communist Party has been a potent force in that country's politics. By the late 1960s, the party was more interested in attaining parliamentary power than in fomenting revolution, and when student protests swept across Italy, the party did little to aid the protesters. Former students and factory workers who had abandoned the official Italian Communist Party founded the Red Brigades. They claimed to follow pure Marxist-Leninist doctrine, in which a small group of revolutionaries inspires massive worker uprisings through attacks on the political structure.

The Red Brigades began by distributing pamphlets and releasing statements that attacked the government and Italian industrialists. In the early 1970s, they orchestrated a series of bank robberies and bombings, but they did not emerge as a significant force until members kidnapped prosecutor Mario Sossi in 1974. Sossi was released unharmed in exchange for eight imprisoned Red Brigades members. The group then began to concentrate on kidnappings as its main tactic, snatching business leaders and government officials. If demands were met, the hostages were often released unharmed; if they were not, the victims were usually executed.

In 1978, the Red Brigades seized their most famous victim, Aldo Moro, the reformist leader of the scandal-plagued Christian Democrat Party, which had ruled Italy since the end of World War II. On the morning of March 16, 1978, the day Moro was to announce that the Italian Communist Party would become part of a new governing coalition, he was kidnapped by the Red Brigades, who saw his attempts to bring the communists into government as a threat to the revolution. For 55 days, Moro was held in a secret location. The Red Brigades released his increasingly desperate pleas for the government to attempt to secure his release,

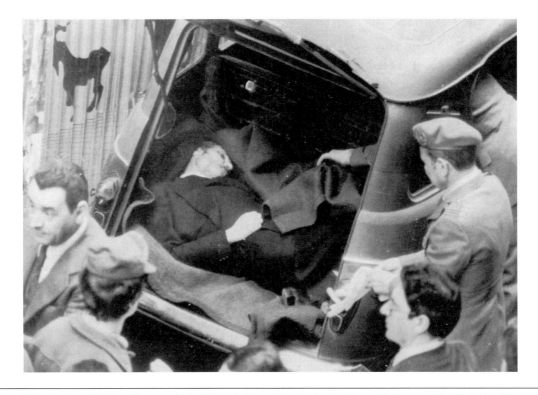

The bullet-riddled body of Italian Premier Aldo Moro is found in the back of a vehicle near his Christian Democrat Party headquarters in Rome, Italy, on May 9, 1978. Moro was kidnapped March 16 in central Rome by Red Brigade terrorists. (AP Photo/Gianni Giansanti. © 2011 The Associated Press. All Rights Reserved)

but the prime minister refused to negotiate. Thousands of police conducted the most intensive investigation in modern Italian history, but turned up nothing. On May 9, 1978, Moro's body was found in the trunk of a car in Rome. The case remains a seminal event in Italian politics, in part because of the lengthy series of criminal trials that followed, but also because of the many conspiracy theories that sprung up around Moro's abduction and murder.

When Moro was kidnapped, the Red Brigades were at the peak of their power, with an estimated 1,500 active volunteers. The volunteers were organized into columns—areas of the country overseen by a single individual who served on the Executive Committee, the Brigades' ruling body—with each column further subdivided into four- or five-person cells, or "brigades." Moro's murder soured the public on the brigadiers, however, and a reorganized police force finally began to make progress against the group.

During the autumn of 1981–1982, after a number of arrests had hurt the group's operational capacity, the executive committee decided to strike back with a daring series of attacks code-named "Winter of Fire." The first attack, the kidnapping of Brigadier General James Dozier, a NATO official, was executed successfully. While Dozier was being held hostage, however, the Brigades' other operations were complete disasters, resulting in dozens of arrests. Some of those arrested became police informants, eventually providing information that led police to Dozier. After 42 days of captivity, Dozier was freed in a commando raid that helped restore the credibility of the Italian police.

Captured in the Dozier rescue was Antonio Savasta, the top commander of the Red Brigades in northern Italy. While in police custody, Savasta called on his comrades to lay down their arms and provided more than 200 names to the police. His information decimated the Red Brigades. The group made one more high-profile attack, assassinating Leamon Hunt, the director of a Sinai peacekeeping force, but it soon split in two. In 1989, two key remaining Red Brigades leaders were arrested in Paris. The information they provided led to the arrest of scores of other terrorists, which seemingly put an end to the organization.

In the early twenty-first century, however, the Red Brigades' splinter groups—the Revolutionary Proletarian Initiative Nuclei (NIPR) and the New Red Brigades/Communist Combatant Party (NR/BCC)—claimed responsibility for three attacks: an April 2002 bombing in Rome, and the killings of Massimo D'Antona in May 1999 and Marco Biagi in March 2002. Both men were government advisors helping to reform Italy's labor laws, a project that has caused much controversy in Italy. The clear links between the two murders (the same gun was used both times), coupled with the bombing attack, raised fears that a revival of the Red Brigades was imminent.

In November 2002, police in Argentina arrested Leonardo Bertulazzi, a suspected leader of the Red Brigades. In October 2003, Italian police raids in Rome, Florence, Pisa, and Sardinia, led to the arrest of six more alleged members, four of whom were sentenced to life imprisonment in June 2005. Two additional members connected to the 1978 assassination of Moro were arrested in Cairo, Egypt, in January 2004. In 2007, Marina Petrella, a former member of the group, was arrested in Paris after 20 years on the run. While it is possible that other isolated Red Brigades cells exist, any threat they may pose is thought to relate to possible criminal activity, rather than meaningful political action.

Colleen Sullivan

See also Dozier, James Lee

Further Readings

Center for Defense Information. "In the Spotlight: New Red Brigades/Communist Combatant Party (BR/PCC)." March 23, 2005.

Collin, Richard O., and Gordon L. Friedman. *Winter of Fire: The Abduction of General Dozier and the Downfall of the Red Brigades.* New York: Dutton, 1990.

Drake, Richard. *The Aldo Moro Murder Case.* Cambridge, MA: Harvard University Press, 1995.

Harclerode, Peter. *Secret Soldiers: Special Forces in the War against Terrorism.* London: Cassell, 2001.

HistoryOfWar.org. "The Red Brigade Terrorist Group." http://www.historyofwar.org/articles/weapons_red_brigades.html.

Kennedy, Frances. "Italy Fears Revival of Red Brigades after Government Aide Is Shot Dead." *The Independent* (London), March 21, 2002, p. 3.

Lutz, James M., and Brenda J. Lutz. *Global Terrorism.* 2nd ed. New York: Routledge, 2008.

"The Red Brigades: A Manifesto." In *Voices of Terror: Manifestos, Writings, and Manuals of Al Qaeda, Hamas, and Other Terrorists from around the World and throughout the Ages,* edited by Walter Laqueur, pp. 469–479. New York: Reed Press, 2004.

"Red Brigades Woman Held in Paris." BBC News, August 23, 2007. http://news.bbc.co.uk/2/hi/europe/6960084.stm.

Sciascia, Leonardo. *The Moro Affair and the Mystery of Majorana.* New York: NYRB Classics, 2004.

Red Hand Commandos

See Ulster Volunteer Force

Red Hand Defenders

The Red Hand Defenders (RHD), believed to be a cover organization for members of the Ulster Defense Association (UDA) and the Loyalist Volunteer Force (LVF), is a Northern Irish terrorist organization that has claimed responsibility for a number of attacks on Roman Catholics, beginning in 1998. The image of the "red hand" comes from the coat of arms of an ancient Irish family; in modern times it was adopted by Protestants as a symbol of the northern county of Ulster.

Beginning in the late 1960s, Northern Ireland was the scene of a 30-year conflict between the province's Catholics, or Republicans, who wanted Northern Ireland to become part of the Republic of Ireland, and the province's Protestants, or Loyalists, who wanted it to continue as part of the United Kingdom. Both Protestants and Catholics fielded armed paramilitary groups that used violence to achieve their ends. In April 1998, the governments of Britain and Ireland signed a peace accord known as the Good Friday Agreement. The agreement laid out a plan to achieve political stability in Northern Ireland and included a provision that persons imprisoned for terrorist activities on behalf of the paramilitary groups would be released on a specific timetable.

Extreme members of both Loyalist and Republican organizations refused to recognize the Good Friday Agreement and split from the larger paramilitaries, forming their own terrorist groups. When the Red Hand Defenders emerged in 1998 and first began to claim responsibility for the bombings and sectarian killings, many observers believed them to be a splinter group. The Red Hand Defenders have claimed responsibility for several sectarian murders, mortar bomb attacks on Catholic homes, and the attempted bombing of a pub that served both Catholics and Protestants.

The Red Hand Defenders' most prominent victim was the human rights lawyer Rosemary Nelson, who defended both Protestants and Catholics and had filed hundreds of briefs charging Northern Ireland's police force, the Royal Ulster Constabulary (RUC), with brutality. Nelson claimed she had received death threats from RUC officers. On the early afternoon of March 15, 1999, she returned to her car after dropping off her daughter at school; a bomb attached to the undercarriage exploded, blowing off Nelson's lower legs and trapping her in the car. She died two hours later. A spokesperson for the RHD called local newspapers to claim responsibility. However, the sophistication of the device and Nelson's antagonistic relationship with the RUC led some to question the claim and to further speculate that the RHD was merely a cover name used by members of the larger Loyalist groups. Suspicion fell on the Ulster Defense Association (UDA), which was associated with a group called the Red Hand Commandos in the 1970s, and the Loyalist Volunteer Force (LVF), the last Loyalist organization to declare a cease-fire.

In January 2002, the Red Hand Defenders claimed responsibility for the killing of a Catholic postman, Daniel McColgan; other sources have implicated the UDA in the attack. The RHD then issued a warning to Catholic civil servants and teachers, stating that they were now considered legitimate targets. The murder and subsequent announcement are believed to be related to a dispute between Protestant residents of the Glenbryn neighborhood and Catholic parents whose children attend the nearby Holy Cross primary school. On January 16, 2002, the Red Hand Defenders announced they were revoking the warning, apparently in response to public condemnation by the UDA leadership. A further announcement was made that the group would disband, but just a few months later it claimed responsibility for a nail-bomb attack on the home of a prominent Republican.

In February 2003 the RHD distanced itself from the UDA by claiming responsibility for the murder of a senior UDA member, John Gregg. (Gregg was best known for his attempt to assassinate Sinn Féin leader Gerry Adams in the 1980s.) The RHD also continued with sporadic shootings of Catholics and bombing attacks on public places throughout the first decade of the twentieth century. Despite divisions in the Loyalist movement that suggesting weak leadership and organizational structure, those operating under the RHD banner have remained a threat to the peace process.

Colleen Sullivan

See also Decommissioning in Northern Ireland; Loyalist Volunteer Force; Orange Volunteers; Ulster Defense Association; Ulster Volunteer Force

Further Readings

Bruce, Steve. *The Red Hand: Protestant Paramilitaries in Northern Ireland.* Oxford: Oxford University Press, 1992.

Holland, Jack. *Hope Against History: The Course of Conflict in Northern Ireland.* New York: Henry Holt, 1999.

Lavery, Brian. "A Catholic Mailman Is Slain as Ulster Violence Continues." *The New York Times*, January 13, 2002, p. 6.

McKay, Susan. *Northern Protestants: An Unsettled People.* Belfast: Blackstaff Press, 2000.

Ryder, Chris. *The RUC 1922–1997: A Force under Fire.* London: Mandarin, 1997.

Spencer, Graham. *The State of Loyalism in Northern Ireland.* New York: Palgrave Macmillan, 2008.

Taylor, Peter. *Loyalists: War and Peace in Northern Ireland.* New York: TV Books, 1999.

Wood, Ian S. *Crimes of Loyalty: A History of the UDA.* Edinburgh: Edinburgh University Press, 2006.

REHABILITATION OF TERRORISTS

As of 2010, there were more than 100,000 convicted and suspected terrorists languishing in penitentiary and detention centers around the world, from Europe to the Middle East to Asia. Although vocational and educational programs exist to rehabilitate criminals, there are very few initiatives to rehabilitate terrorists. Despite significant study into terrorist mindsets and the ideologies driving them, terrorist rehabilitation remains the exception worldwide and has not become the norm.

Egypt pioneered the idea of religious rehabilitation in the 1990s. Scholars at al Azhar University and other counselors, as well as the historical leadership of Gama'a al Islamiyya (Islamic Group) in Egypt, began to influence detainees and inmates to abandon violence and build peace. Programs for rehabilitating communist terrorists in Malaysia and Singapore were developed in the 1960s and 1970s, but these were not elaborate. Communism in Asia was not a global threat, and religion was not the basis for the ideological mindset in that era.

After realizing the scale of the threat following the al Qaeda attacks on the United States on September 11, 2001, a number of countries—including Singapore, Saudi Arabia, Iraq, Uzbekistan, Indonesia, and Malaysia—developed national rehabilitation programs. Since then the process of detainee and inmate rehabilitation has been gaining popularity worldwide. As a new frontier in counterterrorism practice, rehabilitation programs have provided degrees of success in countries that have adopted them. Some programs, such as those in Singapore, have been developed with community participation. Clerics and scholars have volunteered to counsel detainees and other well-meaning individuals, and institutions have provided for the detainee families. In such counterterrorism and extremism initiatives, the participation of the community is an important first step in the right direction.

In the early twenty-first century, the world's most comprehensive terrorist rehabilitation program was established in Saudi Arabia, where the Saudi Interior Ministry spent 1.7 billion riyals to construct five modern high-tech security prisons. Ultimately, nine centers for rehabilitation were established. In addition to special facilities for housing families and meeting visitors, high-tech classrooms and libraries for reading and studying were built. A special committee oversaw specialists in security, sports, Islamic law, social science, and psychology, drawn from government and universities.

The program prepares militant jihadis to engage gradually with the rest of society. The compounds, each with a capacity for 1,200 people, support reintegration back to Saudi society. The "beneficiaries," as they are called, are able to swim and play football, table tennis, and TV games. In an air-conditioned tent converted into a dining hall that serves traditional food, they engage in dialogue.

Why Rehabilitate?

Many believe that rehabilitation should become a complementary strategy in the ongoing fight against terrorism and extremism. However, many terrorists who are arrested are treated either as criminals or as prisoners of war. Unlike common criminals, though, terrorists carry an ideology. The mind is the most powerful weapon the terrorist possesses, and by unlocking the mind, a terrorist can be made to reflect on and reexamine his own ideas and thoughts.

Terrorist rehabilitation is based on the theory that mere punishment through imprisonment is not enough to permanently reform terrorists and facilitate their reintegration into society. Particularly for Islamic terrorists, ideological debate and religious counseling sessions are very important components of the rehabilitation program. This is because their behavior and way of thinking are based on an incorrect understanding or a misinterpretation of Islamic concepts. Hence, counseling sessions serve to provide them with a correct understanding of Islam and its leading concepts. This correct understanding will not only forestall future criminal acts but will also convince them that such behavior is inappropriate and misguided. Ideally, this will bring about genuine feelings of remorse and repentance, and thus permanently remove the source of motivation for their involvement in terrorist activities.

The four principal modes of rehabilitation are: religious rehabilitation, psychological rehabilitation, social and family rehabilitation, and educational and vocational rehabilitation.

Religious Rehabilitation. Militant jihadis have misused Islam to influence and convince the larger Muslim community that the United States and its allies are deliberately attacking Islam and killing Muslims. According to this line of thinking, a religious obligation binds Muslims to attack the United States. Through the imposition of an extremist and militant interpretation of Islam, the terrorists are committed to reestablishing the caliphate. Such religiously inspired messages are therefore best countered by Islamic religious teachers and scholars, as they will have the understanding, knowledge, and authority to correct misconceptions of Islamic teachings.

Psychological Rehabilitation. Psychological rehabilitation is necessary to ensure that a terrorist renounces his or her violent ideology and adopts a moderate viewpoint. By showing the beneficiaries that they can benefit from both denouncing a violent ideology and adopting a pro-social behavior and ideology, their reasons to fight will be nullified.

Social Rehabilitation. Social rehabilitation addresses the concerns of the terrorist's family. The detention of the male terrorist who is the head of a family can throw the family into financial instability, as he is often the sole breadwinner. Thus, social rehabilitation in the form of assistance must be rendered to the families traumatized by the detention of their loved one: this assistance can take the form of providing an alternative livelihood for the family, school for the children, and housing. Thus, family rehabilitation becomes a part of social rehabilitation. Families should receive community assistance to carry on with their lives.

Vocational Rehabilitation. In order to facilitate the detainees' reintegration back into society, they need to be guided and prepared through the development of skills and educational attainment. Vocational rehabilitation imparts skills useful to detainees and inmates upon release. Unlike the other modes of rehabilitation, however, certain types of vocational rehabilitation may create a security risk. Detainees and inmates are not taught certain skills, such as electronics, for example, as a capability in such a field could be used to build circuitry for bombs. Former terrorists must therefore be taught skills that will allow them to find suitable and stable employment and prevent them from returning to arms.

The global campaign against terrorism has been dominated by an overwhelming kinetic response. The lethal operations have temporarily disrupted terrorist operational infrastructures but have not disrupted the conceptual infrastructures driving extremism and terrorism. Although the operational capabilities of terrorist groups have been reduced in some theaters, the motives and intentions of the terrorists to fight back have grown, protracting the fight.

In some countries, soft power has been cast aside in favor of hard. The combination of the two types—sometimes referred to in the counterterrorism business as "smart power"—is used by very few nations. While the use of operational measures should not be disregarded, an equal amount of attention has not been given to the strategic fight, to the battle of ideas. Ideology is the foundation of the terrorist movement, and if the environment remains permissive, ideology remains the lifeblood of contemporary terrorist groups and movements. Terrorist ideologies can only be delegitimized by ideological and theological refutation. To safeguard the next generation of youth from the lure of fighting and the appeal of extremist ideology, counter-ideology must be incorporated into the counterterrorism toolbox.

Rohan Gunaratna

See also Counterterrorism; Criminal Prosecution of Terrorists; Law and Terrorism; Religious and Spiritual Perspectives on Terrorism; Training of Terrorists

Further Readings

Blaydes, Lisa, and Lawrence P. Rubin. "Ideological Reorientation and Counterterrorism: Confronting Militant Islam in Egypt." *Terrorism and Political Violence* 20, no. 4 (October 2008): 461–479.
"1.7 Billion Riyals to Develop Saudi Prisons and Rehabilitation Centres for Terrorists." *Arabian Business*, April 27, 2008. http://www.arabianbusiness.com/arabic/517622?refresh=1&r=1.
Shefali Rekhi. "Spiritual Rehab for Terrorists." *Straits Times* (Singapore), March 8, 2009.

REID, RICHARD (1973–)

On December 22, 2001, an al Qaeda member named Richard Colvin Reid (aka Abdel Rahim; Abu Ibrahim) became known as the "shoe bomber" after attempting to destroy an airplane carrying almost 200 people by setting fire to explosives hidden in his sneakers.

Reid was born in London in 1973, the only son of an English mother and Jamaican father who divorced in 1984. His father spent most of Reid's childhood in prison; Reid himself dropped out of school in 1989, and within a year he was arrested for a mugging. Reid spent the next six years in and out of jail.

In 1995 Reid was released from prison and embraced Islam, changing his name to Abdel Rahim. Initially his conversion seemed a positive step, and Reid stayed out of trouble with the law. By late 1997, however, Reid had apparently fallen in with more radical Muslims, including Zacarias Moussaoui, who is believed to have been slated to take part in al Qaeda's attack on the United States on September 11, 2001. Reid became more combative and militant in his views, eventually becoming estranged from family members who would not convert to Islam.

In 1998, Reid disappeared from London. He is believed to have traveled to Pakistan, and then to Afghanistan, where he received terrorist training at al Qaeda camps. In the summer of 2001, he returned to England, but in mid-July 2001 he left again, traveling from London to Israel, then to Egypt, Turkey, Pakistan, and perhaps Afghanistan. In December 2001 he returned to Europe, flying to Brussels and obtaining a new British passport in an apparent attempt to conceal his recent travels. Investigators believe Reid traveled so extensively to help al Qaeda identify targets for attacks.

Later in December, Reid purchased an expensive pair of basketball sneakers, using cash, then took a train to Paris, where he paid $1,800 in cash for a round-trip ticket to Antigua on a plane that stopped in Miami, Florida. Reid was scheduled to leave on December 21, 2001, but he had paid cash for the tickets and had no luggage, thus instigating an extensive security check at the airport, and he missed the flight. That evening, he went to an Internet café and sent an e-mail to a recipient in Pakistan, asking what he should do. The correspondent replied that Reid should try again, and the next day he successfully boarded American Airlines Flight 63, flying from Paris to Miami. Roughly 90 minutes after the plane took off, a flight attendant smelled sulfur and realized that Reid had lit a match. She made him put it out, but he lit another and attempted to set fire to the tongues of his sneakers. When she tried to make him stop, Reid attacked her, knocking her down, and then bit another attendant. Passengers quickly responded, holding Reid down, tying him up with belts and cords, and dousing him with water. A doctor on board eventually injected him with sedatives.

After Reid was subdued, the flight was redirected to Boston, Massachusetts, where investigators examined his shoes and discovered that the soles were packed with enough plastic explosives to punch a hole through the side of the plane. The conjecture was that Reid acted alone, but his e-mails and other evidence revealed his considerable connections to al Qaeda.

In 2002 Reid was charged before a federal court in Boston, and he pled guilty to eight criminal counts. On January 31, 2003, he was sentenced by District Court Judge William Young to life in prison without parole on three counts, including one of attempted use of a weapon of mass destruction against U.S. nationals outside the United States, and two of interference with a flight crew using a dangerous weapon. Reid is held in the same "supermax" prison in Colorado that is home to the Unabomber, Theodore Kaczynski; 9/11 conspirator Zacarias Moussaoui; Olympics bomber Eric Rudolph; and al Qaeda bomber Ramzi Yousef.

Mary Sisson

See also Airport Security; al Qaeda; Moussaoui, Zacarias; September 11 Attacks

Further Readings

Bayles, Fred. "Shoe-bomb Suspect's Travel Suggests Financial Help." *USA Today*, December 31, 2001, p. 4A.

Burlingame, Debra. "Revenge of the 'Shoe Bomber.'" *The Wall Street Journal*, July 29, 2009. http://online.wsj.com/article/SB10001424052970203609204574317090690242698.html.

Canedy, Dana. "A 'Strange' Traveler Acted, and the Passengers Reacted." *The New York Times*, December 24, 2001, p. A1.

Elliott, Michael. "The Shoe Bomber's World." *Time*, February 16, 2002.

Hoge, Warren. "Shoe-bomb Suspect Fell in with Extremists." *The New York Times*, December 27, 2001, p. B6.

Reid, T. R., and Keith B. Richburg. "Shoe Bomb Suspect's Journey into al Qaeda: Search Continues for Reid's Mysterious Handlers." *The Washington Post*, March 31, 2002, p. A9.

Shenon, Philip. "Terrorism Warning for Airlines Focuses on Shoes and Clothing." *The New York Times*, December 6, 2003. http://www.nytimes.com/2003/12/06/us/terrorism-warning-for-airlines-focuses-on-shoes-and-clothing.html.

RELIGIOUS AND SPIRITUAL PERSPECTIVES ON TERRORISM

This entry will cover the religious connections and justifications for terroristic violence as they exist in major world belief systems. The primary focus is on the monotheistic systems (Judaism, Christianity, and Islam), but dualistic systems, such as Zoroastrianism and Manichaeism, as well as Hinduism and Buddhism are also discussed.

Religion and violence have been closely linked since the beginnings of recorded history. In general, prior to the rise of the monotheistic faiths, that link has presupposed that the god of a given group would fight on the group's behalf. Victory in battle was seen as validation of a god's potency, as well as reason to abandon the belief or worship of the defeated deity. Examples of this type of religion-violence connection are legion, stemming from the great empires of the ancient world, such as the Egyptians, the Assyrians, the Babylonians, the Persians, the Hellenistic kingdoms, and the Roman Empire. The most common form of attack against religious institutions on the part of these empires would be the ritual temple desecration, in which a victorious or defiant enemy would defile the sanctities of its opponent's belief system. This desecration would have a dual effect: It would demonstrate the absolute impotence or worthlessness of the sanctuary or pantheon in question, and it would present a challenge that could not be ignored by those adhering to that sanctuary or pantheon. (Additionally, as temples served as banks during this period, it usually gained the attacker large amounts of ready cash.) Forms of ritual desecration or even terror would more than occasionally cause a total capitulation on the part of those adhering to the desecrated sanctuary's pantheon.

With the rise of the monotheistic religions, however, this paradigm was no longer necessarily operative. During the period of the destruction of the First Temple (586 BCE) by the Babylonian Empire (cf. II Kings 25), the Jews were among the first who did not accept that the destruction of their sanctuary did not mean the defeat of their god, as described in 2 Chronicles 36:15–19. Instead, the Jewish chroniclers of the Bible proclaimed that God himself was responsible for the destruction of the sanctuary in Jerusalem because of the misdeeds of the people. It was through this mechanism that the Jews, and beyond them the two larger monotheistic faiths of Christianity and Islam, began to distinguish between sanctuary and deity—the sanctuary could be destroyed, but the divinity survived.

Monotheistic Belief Systems

Without a doubt, monotheistic systems contain within them a strong imperative for violence. This violence, while comparatively muted in the case of Judaism as a result of its non-missionary imperative, occurs in both Christianity and Islam as a result of their global mission. It is significant, however, that in neither Christianity nor Islam is conquest seen as a necessary precondition for conversion. Rather, in both cases, violence is closely linked to either a just or divinely sanctioned war or to removing impediments to conversion and proselytization. The absolute nature of the monotheistic belief system requires that, there being only one deity and one path leading to salvation, all other forms of worship must be satanic and deceptive by their very nature. Fighting those belief systems, therefore, could be logically construed an act of worship in and of itself. In general, this line of thinking is the one taken for granted by monotheistic theologians and the warriors they have justified.

Judaism

Judaism, as it is described in the Hebrew Bible (Old Testament), is strikingly similar to the belief systems of the ancient Near East. Its god is singular (not part of a pantheon) and jealous of his prerogatives, but given reciprocity he fights on behalf of the Israelites and, later, the Jews descended from them (cf. Joshua 10:14). Although the virtues of peace are frequently extolled in the Bible, none

of the major royal or prophetic figures is said to have rejected violence per se or upheld pacifism as a virtue (other than in places where the Jewish people were actually helpless and could not fight anyway). In these ways, the Jewish belief system was similar to those around it, though in the biblical account the deity progressively becomes hostile toward the holy sanctuary and the elites that surround it. This fact enabled the Jewish people to survive not one but two destructions of their sanctuary in Jerusalem, along with a number of desecrations (such as that carried out by Antiochus Epiphanes in 167 BCE, which led to the Maccabean revolt, and that by Pompey the Great in 70 BCE).

Because of the loss of their sanctuary in 70 CE, and their independence shortly thereafter, the Jewish people developed theories of violence different from those of the other monotheistic religions. Violence was applied in theoretical terms primarily toward those non-Jewish figures who persecuted the Jewish people, and in practical terms toward those Jews who aided or abetted them. This policy led to the development of the so-called *din moser* (law of a traitor, who turns over Jews to an oppressor) and its counterpart the *din rodef* (the law of attacking an oppressor or a murderer [*Sanhedrin,* viii:7]).

Messianic violence is described by the great philosopher and community leader Maimonides (d. 1206) in his "Book of Kings" (the *Mishneh Torah*), where he states that the messiah will conquer the land of Israel to its ancient boundaries (including the present-day regions of Syria and parts of Egypt) and wage war. One of the signs of the true messiah will be his victory in battle. Success on the battlefield, as in Islam, is one of the characteristics of God's support and favor of the messianic figure.

Contemporary Jewish radicals utilize these theoretical discussions to carry out violence. For example, Yigal Amir, who assassinated Prime Minister Yitzhak Rabin of Israel in 1995, sought support from prominent radical rabbis, claiming that he was carrying out the punishment of the *din rodef*. Occasionally, the story of Phineas, who is said to have used a spear to kill an Israelite man and a Midianite woman who were worshipping false gods in the midst of the people and causing a plague, as chronicled in Numbers 25:6–13, is also used as a basis for radical action by ideologues from the Gush Emunim (the right-wing settler movement in Israel). In general, Jewish justifications for violent and terroristic action are just now being translated from theory to practice by the exigencies of the state of Israel.

Christianity

Christianity has always been schizophrenic with regard to the justification of violence. On the one hand it is heir, through the Bible, to the Jewish tradition of historically violent monarchs and prophets, and the god that supported them, but on the other it portrayed itself as a religion of universal love and was itself persecuted for the first three centuries of its existence. For these reasons, while Judaism has largely existed as a pacifistic tradition (since the destruction of the Second Temple), and Islam has been closely associated with conquest and jihad (see below), Christianity has swung between the two extremes and supports adherents of equal conviction who can advocate either complete pacifism or violent militancy—or, as in most cases, a mixture of both.

Nor is there a good example from Jesus as he is portrayed in the New Testament. While an emphasis is usually placed upon his pacifistic side, with its doctrine of universal love, he is also said, in Matthew 10:34, to have "not come to bring peace, but a sword," and to have reacted violently upon occasions, such as against the money changers in the Temple (Matthew 21:12–13). If this latter instance is to be taken as normative, then the Christian would have a strong precedent for conducting violence against perceived injustices. Moreover, the apocalypse of Revelation contains a number of descriptions of Jesus as a warrior (including Revelation 1:16, 12:5, 19:11–21) that would indicate that any pacifism during his earthly ministry will not be carried over into the end of the world. It is not surprising, therefore, to find that historically Christian apocalyptic movements have been violent and purificationist, in anticipation of the slaughter described in Revelation.

The most important innovation for Christianity after the New Testament period was that of St. Augustine (d. 430 CE). Following centuries of persecution, Augustine developed the doctrine of "just war" as part of an official theology, as Christians were responsible for the governing of the Roman Empire. Prior to the time of Augustine, Christians had been quite hostile to the military, and many Christian soldiers refused to fight (and were martyred for their beliefs). Augustine needed to elucidate under what circumstances Christians could fight, particularly as their pagan opponents decried Christianity as being the factor responsible for the destruction of Rome by barbarian tribes (many of whom, ironically, were Christian as well).

Augustine's doctrine allowed for the necessity of war, but only in order to protect a defenseless third party or to protect the Roman civilization, which he saw as a value (as opposed to the destruction and lawlessness of barbarians). The doctrine of the "just war" continued to influence Christianity, but there were elements that never fully accepted it, ideal though it was for an imperial system. For example, Warren Treadgold writes in his *History of Byzantine State and Society* (1997) that when the Byzantine emperor Nicephorus II Phocas (d. 969) sought to turn Christian soldiers killed in the warfare against Muslims during the 10th century into martyrs, the patriarch of Constantinople, Polyeuktos, refused, even though he was threatened with death for this refusal.

In the Western church, however, as a result of the Muslim invasions of western Europe (8th–10th centuries) a much more aggressive interpretation of the just war developed during the period of the Crusades (1096–1351), and the papacy was able to utilize this interpretation to raise mass numbers who attacked the Muslims on a number of different fronts. While the most prominent and obvious of these was the First Crusade (1097–1099) directed at reestablishing Christian control over Jerusalem, the Crusades in Sicily (1050–1100) and the *Reconquista* in Spain (culminating in the Battle of Las Navas de Tolosa in 1212, in which the Muslims suffered a crushing defeat) were part of the same process. The religious basis of the First Crusade is revealed in the words of Fulcher of Chartres, who documented it and stated that the Crusaders were to be compared with the Israelites and the Maccabees who fought against injustice. The anonymous *Gesta Francorum* (ca. 1100) likewise sees the Crusaders as following the words of Jesus in Matthew 16:24, "if anyone would come after me, he must deny himself and take up his cross and follow me," which is cited at the beginning of the chronicle.

Following the Crusades, for the most part, religious justifications of violence followed the patterns established by Augustine and amplified by the Crusaders. By the colonial period a number of colonial religious movements such as the Boer community in South Africa, modeled themselves closely upon the Israelites, utilizing the biblical narratives to justify their expansion. Contemporary Christian radicals who utilize violence have done so usually under the influence of racist "identity" movements (e.g., the Church of Jesus Christ Christian, the Aryan Nations, and so forth) or as part of the fulfillment of an apocalyptic purificationist narrative (such as the Lord's Resistance Army in Uganda).

Islam

Islam, which developed as a bedrock, "no compromises" monotheism, initially went through a pacifistic period during its earliest incarnation in the pagan town of Mecca, but during the period following the Prophet Muhammad's *hijra* to the oasis of Medina in 622 CE, it became increasingly militant. By the first major battle at Badr in 624, God (Allah) was said to be participating in the warfare on the side of the believers (Koran 8:17). In general, this divinely sanctioned warfare came to be called *jihad*, although the term is little used in the Koran and does not appear to have become common until after the great conquests of the seventh and eighth centuries. *Jihad* means "struggle" with the implication of "spiritual struggle," and has developed both a militant warfare aspect as well as a inner spiritual struggle aspect (common among Sufis).

As jihad was developed by Muslim jurisprudents and theologians, it is waged by the authority of a legitimate representative of God (such as the caliph or the consensus of the scholars), using tactics that are mandated and regulated by the Koran and Shariah (divine law), against an enemy who is non-Muslim and patently unjust, for the benefit of the Muslim community overall, or in its defense. Obviously, the battles fought by Muhammad against his pagan opponents are seen by Muslims as being the best examples of jihad. In most cases those battles could be seen as defensive, and as compensation for the losses the Muslims had incurred when they had fled from Mecca to Medina. There is less clarity, however, with regard to Muhammad's warfare against the Jewish tribes of Medina, who are usually described as having broken their covenants with him, or against the numerous Bedouin tribes around Medina, who threatened the Muslim community by sometimes siding with the pagans of Mecca. The battles of the final years of Muhammad (630–632) are difficult to justify as anything other than offensive warfare. Following Muhammad's death, the assassination of prominent figures, such as Ali ibn Abi Talib (d. 661), the fourth caliph and son-in-law of Muhammad, was justified using Koranic verses (his assassin is said to have recited 2:205, "and some people sell themselves for the sake of Allah's favor," as he stabbed Ali).

The concept of jihad gained its definition from the patently offensive campaigns of the great Islamic conquests (approx. 634–732), during the course of which the Muslims came to dominate the entire Middle East and part of the Mediterranean basin, as well as substantial sections of Central Asia, India, and Africa. During this period and throughout the high Muslim culture (until 1300), jihad is described in adulatory terms. Fantastic rewards are developed for the martyr involving forgiveness of sins, a central location in paradise, marriage to the houris (women of paradise), and intercession of the martyrs on behalf of others in order to encourage fighters in jihad.

Extensive legal discussion of jihad also dates from this period, and it is in this discussion that one finds the closest analogue to the Christian ideal of "just war." Jihad is described here as a process, involving the ritual summoning of the enemy to Islam, a lengthy discussion of possible tactics (together with rejection of those that would sully the name of Islam), as well as the responsibilities of Muslims toward the fighting of jihad. These responsibilities are divided into two categories: the *fard 'ayn* (specific obligation), which is in effect when a Muslim region is attacked by non-Muslims, and obligates all Muslims to participate in the jihad; and the *fard kifaya* (general obligation), which is in effect during other times and requires that jihad be fought at some place in the Muslim world, but that not every Muslim needs to fight. Additional discussion focuses upon the captives, the division of the spoils, and the administration of the captured territories. Because in general Muslims were on the offensive (or at least not on the defensive) during the formative period of Muslim law, there is little discussion concerning what one should do if Muslims are not victorious or consistently lose while fighting a jihad.

During the contemporary period, jihad has come into prominence as a method by which radical Muslims (usually called Salafi-jihadis) apply violence against their opponents. Jihad in these cases differs somewhat from the classical paradigms in that there is no obvious replacement mechanism for the caliph in the declaration of jihad. In general, during the classical period after the destruction of the caliphate in 1258, Muslim scholars held that only agreement and consensus of the scholars had the right to declare jihad and make it legitimate. This axiom is rejected by contemporary radicals, who see the scholarly elites as being wholly subservient to corrupt or non-Muslim regimes. In many cases, contemporary jihad swirls around the question of who has the authority: the traditional scholarly elites or the mujahideen fighting in the field?

Tactics and methodology have changed as well. Even in classical times, tactics that were not legitimate in *fard kifaya* situations frequently became so when jihad was *fard 'ayn*. Therefore, a great deal of the discussion concerns the question of whether sections of the Muslim world are "under occupation" at the present time. If this question is answered in the affirmative, then radicals argue that tactics such as indiscriminate bombing of civilians (exemplified by suicide attacks) become legitimate. While this argument gains them some sympathy with regard to certain situations, such as the Israeli-Palestinian conflict and the conflict in Chechnya (in southern Russia), the idea that the rest of the Muslim world is "under occupation" because of non-Muslim economic or cultural domination has not been broadly accepted. Jihad against what radical Muslims consider to be their apostate governments is mandated by the classical doctrine of *al-amr bi'l-ma'ruf wa'l-nahy 'an al-munkar* (enjoining the good and forbidding the evil), which allows Muslims to proactively confront practices inside their own societies deemed to be non-Muslim.

The use of suicide attacks is one of the major differences between classical and contemporary waging of jihad. Prior to the invention of explosives, the suicide attack was not prominent in Muslim warfare. There was, however, the category of the "single fighter who charges a large number," which today would be defined as a "suicidal attack." (A suicidal attack is one in which the combatant has a chance of surviving; the suicide attack is one in which the first casualty is the combatant, who has no chance of surviving other than by some malfunction of the explosive.) Classical acceptance of the "suicidal attack" as a legitimate form of jihad has stilled debate to a large extent as to whether suicide attacks are acceptable (and not a form of suicide, which is prohibited by Koran 4:29).

The indiscriminate killing of civilians, especially women and children, and even doubly Muslim women and children has been a controversial by-product of suicide attacks. This "collateral damage" is legitimized by citing the example of Muhammad, who is said to have employed mangonels (catapults) to cast rocks over the town walls during the siege of the town of al-Ta'if (630). A great many modern tactics involving the killing of innocents are justified using this example (including the use of weapons of mass destruction), as radicals point out that the rocks thus lobbed would not discriminate between fighters and non-fighters. However, this argument has not won broad acceptance beyond radical circles, and the killing of innocents remains an issue that causes Muslims to turn away from radical movements (such as in Iraq, Pakistan, and Saudi Arabia).

While in Christianity there is not a strong need to justify every act of violence through biblical texts or precedents, in Islam—both in its conservative and its radical varieties—there is an absolute need to find such justification. The battles of the Prophet Muhammad are seen as normative and paradigmatic throughout Muslim history, and contemporary radicals will always attempt to portray their warfare as following his example. Just as in Christianity, Islamic apocalyptic literature is violent, and the messianic figure, the Mahdi, both in his Sunni and Shiite versions, is a warrior. The ideal of the apocalyptic future is to usher in the messianic, utopian society, in which the entire world will be dominated by Islam, if not entirely converted to it.

Non-Monotheistic Systems

Major dualistic systems such as Manicheanism and Zoroastrianism are largely pacifistic (Zoroaster's original revelations were pacifistic; later Persian practice was militaristic). However, they do contain within them extensive descriptions of eschatological violence. Other major belief systems, such as Hinduism and Buddhism, have a much more ambivalent attitude toward connecting religion and violence. In the Hindu text the *Bhaghavad Gita,* a conversation occurs between a noble warrior, Arjuna, and his chariot driver (who is Krishna) during the course of a battle. Much of the text covers the question of the ethics of violence. In general, however, Hinduism developed as an almost pacifistic belief system during the period of Muslim and British domination until Indian independence in 1947. However, Hindu radicals utilize the example of the sixteenth- and seventeenth-century Hindu warrior hero Shivaji (who fought against the Muslims) in order to justify contemporary *hindutva,* the aggressive policy of Hinduizing the multi-religious country of India in order to bring it in accord with the classical mythos of the Aryan warriors who invaded the subcontinent during the first millennium BCE.

Buddhism, in many of its manifestations, has been pacifistic, and yet in Mahayana Buddhism there is reference to the process of self-sacrifice: "O Beflowered by the King of Constellations! If there is one who, opening up his thought . . . if he can burn a finger or even a toe as an offering to a Buddhastupa, he shall exceed one who uses realm or walled city, wife or children or even all the lands, mountains, forests, rivers, ponds and sundry precious objects in the whole thousand-millionfold world as offerings" (translation by Leon Hurvitz). This aggressive and self-sacrificing ethos is the one to which the militant order of Zen Buddhism (prominent in Japan) harks back. Its most violent offshoot, the Amida Tong, was a medieval group of assassins that believed their killings would bring them union with the Buddha. Other strands of Buddhism have not exhibited this type of militancy. But even in those comparatively pacifistic systems the urge to martyrdom remains latent (as among the Vietnamese Buddhist monks who immolated themselves publicly in 1963).

Conclusion

As can be seen by the above examples, the monotheistic faiths, especially those of a universalistic message such as Christianity and Islam, are the ones where religion and violence are most likely to be linked. In fairness, however, this link also appears at least passively in Buddhism (another missionary faith) and other nonconversionary faiths. Links between religion and violence have both an official legitimizing aspect, in which ruling elites will seek to solidify their political legitimacy through the application of violence, as well as a popular sanctifying aspect, in which the common people will seek redemption through engagement of the other (a perceived "enemy of God") in warfare. Therefore, violence is highly useful to a religious system. It enables the creation of group identity and could even be seen as one of the foundations of the nation-state. In the form of a crusade or a jihad, it can serve as an outlet for the violent and disorderly members of the society, as well as the terrorization of its opponents, and perhaps their eventual capitulation.

In contemporary political and religious systems, religion and violence continue to enjoy a close link. Even in states where the political order is largely secular, resorting to violence is usually justified in terms laid down by St. Augustine (the "just war"), and during times of national crisis, God is said to be fighting on the side of the country in a manner not dissimilar to that of the national god (or pantheon) operative in pre-monotheistic times.

David B. Cook

See also Jihad; Lord's Resistance Army; White Supremacy Movement

Further Readings

The Bible. New International Version.

Cook, David. *Understanding Jihad.* Berkeley: University of California Press, 2005.

Epstein, Isidore, trans. *Babylonian Talmud.* London: Soncino, 1962.

Fakhry, Majid, trans. *The Qur'an: A Modern English Version.* London: Garnet, 1997.

Hill, Rosalind, trans. *Gesta Francorum.* Oxford: Oxford University Press, 1962.

Hurvitz, Leon, trans. *Scripture of the Lotus Blossom of the Fine Dharma (The Lotus Sutra).* New York: Columbia University Press, 1976.

Johnson, James Turner. *The Holy War Idea in Western and Islamic Traditions.* University Park: Pennsylvania State University Press, 2002.

Kelsay, John, and James Turner Johnson, eds. *Just War and Jihad*. Westport, CT: Greenwood Press, 1991.

Krey, August, trans. *The First Crusade: The Accounts of Eyewitnesses and Participants*. Princeton, NJ: Princeton University Press, 1921.

Maimonides. *Mishneh Torah*. Translated by Eliyahu Tager. New York: Moznayim, 1986.

Nelson, Eric, "Buddhism and War: A Review of Two Books." *Journal of Military Ethics* 2, no. 3 (2003): 252–255.

Schaff, Philip, ed. "St. Augustine: The City of God." in *The Nicene and Post-Nicene Fathers*. Grand Rapids, MI: W. Eerdmans, 1988.

Stroble, James. "Buddhism and War: A Study of the Status of Violence in Early Buddhism." 1991. http://www2.hawaii.edu/~stroble/BUDDWAR.HTM.

Treadgold, Warren. *A History of Byzantine State and Society*. Palo Alto, CA: Stanford University Press, 1997.

Victoria, Brian Daizen. *Zen War Stories*. London: Routledge, 2003.

RENDITION, EXTRAORDINARY

To better understand the concept of *extraordinary rendition*, it is best to first understand the meaning of the term *rendition*, which is defined in *Black's Law Dictionary* as the "return of a fugitive to the State in which he is accused of having committed a crime." In the United States, rendition is based on the legal concept of *extraterritorial jurisdiction*, which presupposes that some persons who are in other countries fall under the reach of the U.S. government (e.g., a U.S. soldier in a foreign land). As U.S. law has evolved, extraterritorial jurisdiction has come to mean that the American government has authority over any person in a foreign land who is a suspect in a U.S. criminal proceeding. Although this may appear to have immediate negative consequences in international law, rendition has become an accepted and often cooperative practice in many nations. However, the practice of extraordinary rendition, meaning the forcible taking of a person from one jurisdiction to another for interrogation by extreme measures or torture, is a matter of hot debate in political circles, both inside and outside the United States.

The precedent in law dates to 1886, when a detective working on behalf of the U.S. government delivered an extradition order to the government of Peru, demanding that Peru give over a criminal suspect, Frederick Ker, for return to the United States. After several months of fruitless waiting, on his own initiative the detective located and apprehended Ker and returned him to the United States to stand trial. In the proceeding that followed, Ker asserted that he was denied constitutionally guaranteed due process because the government failed to follow its own extradition laws. Upholding Ker's conviction, the U.S. Supreme Court wrote, "forcible abduction is [not a] sufficient reason why the party should not answer when brought within the jurisdiction of the court . . . and [defendant Ker] presents no valid objection to his trial in such court." More than half a century later, a criminal suspect was apprehended by government agents in Chicago and forcibly returned to stand trial in Michigan. In its 1952 decision in *Frisbie v. Collins*, the U.S. Supreme Court affirmed its decision in *Ker v. Illinois*, thwarting federal kidnapping charges brought by the defendant (Frisbie) against those who had abducted him. Combining these two decisions, the Ker-Frisbie doctrine was created. This doctrine states that abduction rather than extradition to deliver a defendant before a court is insufficient reason to dismiss a criminal case.

In a more recent case, *Sosa v. Alvarez-Machain, et al.*, the Ker-Frisbie doctrine was further narrowed. An agent of the Drug Enforcement Agency (DEA) was working undercover in Mexico when he was kidnapped by drug lords and tortured to death. During this time, the plaintiff, Humberto Alvarez-Machain, a physician, was tasked with keeping the agent alive to endure more torture. Ultimately, Mexican agents killed the drug lords, but Alvarez-Machain escaped. A warrant charging the doctor with murder was issued in the United States. Soon thereafter, Mexican mercenaries kidnapped Alvarez-Machain and returned him to the United States to stand trial. Acquitted of the charge, Alvarez-Machain filed a civil suit against the DEA under the Federal Tort Claims Act for, among other things, violation of the "headquarters doctrine," which states that an agency is liable for the unlawful conduct of its agents when they are acting in an official capacity. In 2004 the U.S. Supreme Court, reversing a Ninth Circuit decision, that found for Alvarez-Machain, writing that an exception to the headquarters doctrine applied in *Sosa v. Alvarez-Machain, et al.*, because the injury to Alvarez-Machain occurred outside the United States. This being the case, according to the U.S. Supreme Court, government agents are generally immune from civil or criminal litigation for their official conduct abroad, even if the conduct originates at home.

During the Clinton administration, the practice of extraordinary rendition was first utilized, but sparingly. Typically, the Central Intelligence Agency would kidnap a terrorist suspect abroad and take that person to another country to be interrogated. The interrogation could include extreme measures, meaning torture, and perhaps death, for the terrorist suspect. Not yet having the *Sosa v. Alvarez-Machain* decision to serve as a guide, President Clinton acknowledged that in all likelihood such covert operations were illegal but necessary.

Two things happened during the presidency of George W. Bush to accelerate the use of extraordinary rendition. First, the terrorist attacks of September 11, 2001, brought urgency to the interrogation of terrorist suspects, as another attack was feared to be imminent. A global sweep of terrorist suspects began, and scores of defendants were tried in criminal courts at home and abroad. Nevertheless, many suspected terrorists were outside the reach of any criminal court and enjoyed asylum in nations friendly to their cause. Second, with the U.S. Supreme Court decision in *Sosa v. Alvarez-Machain*, the legal concerns of the Clinton administration disappeared and the CIA was free to conduct abductions in foreign lands for the purpose of interrogation elsewhere. The practice of extraordinary rendition then accelerated to unprecedented levels.

Condoleezza Rice, the secretary of state under George W. Bush, stated, "Rendition is necessary to save lives," and that terrorist suspects had been neither transported nor tortured by U.S. agents (which did not preclude the possibility that suspects had been tortured at the behest of the U.S. government). Since the expanded use of extraordinary rendition began, secret prisons of renditioned terrorist suspects have been discovered in several nations allied to the United States. Although President Barack Obama suspended extraordinary rendition by executive order in 2009, the practice was subsequently resumed.

Kenneth J. Ryan

See also Central Intelligence Agency; Counterterrorism; Interrogation Techniques; Law and Terrorism; Torture Debate

Further Readings

Central Intelligence Agency. "Management of Public Diplomacy Relative to National Security." National Security Directive NSD-77, January 14, 1983.

Clinton, William J. "Presidential Decision Directive 39: U.S. Policy on Counterterrorism," version U, June 21, 1995.

Federal Tort Claims Act, 28 U.S.C. § 1346.

Frisbie v. Collins, 342 U.S. 519 (1952). http://supreme .justia.com/us/342/519/case.html.

Kelemen, Michele. "Rice Defends U.S. Tactics on Terrorism Suspects." National Public Radio, December 5, 2005. http://www.npr.org/templates/ story/story.php?storyId=5039601.

Ker v. Illinois, 119 U.S. 436 (1886). http://supreme.justia .com/us/119/436/case.html.

Miller, Greg. "Obama Preserves Renditions as Counter-Terrorism Tool." *Los Angeles Times*, February 1, 2009. http://articles.latimes.com/2009/feb/01/nation/ na-rendition1.

Murphy, Sean D. *U.S. Practices in International Law.* Vol. 2, 2002–2004. Cambridge, UK: Cambridge University Press, 2006.

Nolan, Joseph R., and Jacqueline M. Nolan-Haley, *Black's Law Dictionary.* St. Paul, MN: West Group, 1990.

Scheuer, Michael (a.k.a. Anonymous). *Imperial Hubris: Why the West Is Losing the War on Terror.* Washington, DC: Brassey's, 2004.

Sosa v. Alvarez-Machain, et al., 542 U.S. 692 (2004). http://supreme.justia.com/us/542/692/case.html.

RESSAM, AHMED (1967–)

Ahmed Ressam, an Algerian terrorist, was captured at the U.S.-Canadian border on New Year's Eve 1999. He was on his way to blow up Los Angeles International Airport (LAX), a plan that came to be known as the "Y2K plot," or the "Millennium plot." Since his capture, Ressam, hoping to reduce his prison sentence, has provided key testimony against others in the Y2K plot, as well as Osama bin Laden's terrorist network, al Qaeda, and its training camps.

Ressam, the eldest of seven children, grew up in a small, poor town west of Algeria called Bou Ismail. In 1984, while in Paris to receive treatment for an ulcer, Ressam read books that had been banned in his homeland about the onset of military dictatorships and ruined hopes for democracy in Algeria after it gained independence from France. On his return, according to his brother, he expressed bitterness against the Algerian government and began to take up militant Islamic causes. After failing to pass a college entrance exam, Ressam headed for France in 1992 in an attempt to find work. That year, civil war broke out in Algeria after its military government blocked an Islamic fundamentalist party that won the national elections.

After living illegally in France for two years, Ressam emigrated to Canada in 1994, using a false passport. When he was found out, Ressam asked for political asylum, claiming that he had been tortured in Algeria for his politics, and he was allowed to settle in Canada. He stayed in Montreal until 1988, living off welfare payments and petty theft, while residing in an apartment later identified as the headquarters of a cell of the Armed Islamic Group (GIA), an Algerian terrorist organization.

During this time, Ressam, along with his friend Mokhtar Haouari, also made money trafficking in false identification documents. Ressam would later become Benni Antoine Norris, complete with a Canadian passport, Montreal driver's license, insurance card, several bankcards, and a Costco membership card.

In March 1998, Ressam traveled to Peshawar, Pakistan, where he was approved by Abu Zubaydah, a top bin Laden associate, to attend bin Laden's terrorist training camps, known colloquially as "Jihad University." Over the next several months, at Khalden Camp, Ressam was instructed in using explosives, handguns, machine guns, and small rocket launchers, all provided by the ruling Taliban. He was taught how to disrupt government infrastructure through sabotage, and he was schooled in ways to work unnoticed. In another camp, in Deronta, Afghanistan, he was taught how to use cyanide and other poisons, and how to construct bombs from small electronic devices. Ressam then became part of a European-based Algerian terrorist cell with five other men, who all agreed to travel to Canada, where they would rob banks to fund their ultimate plot—a terrorist attack on the United States.

When Ressam left Afghanistan in February 1999, he was carrying hexamine fuel tablets, a chemical booster for explosions, glycol, and $12,000; the details of the attack were still to be determined. His flight stopped briefly in Los Angeles before arriving in Vancouver, and it was then that he decided to target Los Angeles International Airport (LAX). He later testified that LAX was "sensitive politically and economically."

After two members of his cell were stopped at immigration in Great Britain, Ressam went on alone. Beginning in August 1999, he began to carry out the plot. Over the next several months, he found others to help him and gathered the bomb-making materials that would later be found hidden in the trunk of his rental car as he tried to enter the United States from Victoria, Canada.

Ressam was arrested on December 14, 1999, after trying to flee U.S. Customs agents at Port Angeles, Washington. On April 6, 2001, he was convicted on nine counts, including conspiracy to commit an international terrorist act, smuggling explosives, and lying to customs officials. According to Attorney General John Ashcroft, Ressam was the first person convicted under the Terrorism Transcending National Boundaries statute (18 U.S.C. § 2332b).

Ressam then agreed to testify against others involved in the plot, including Haouari, who was convicted in July 2001 and sentenced to 24 years in prison on January 17, 2002. Ressam's sentencing, originally scheduled for February 2002, was postponed so that he could testify against individuals apprehended in the wake of the September 11, 2001, attacks. On July 27, 2005, U.S. District Court Judge John C. Coughenour sentenced Ressam to 22 years in prison, a comparatively light sentence given the charges. But after Ressam reneged on an agreement to cooperate with investigators, a three-judge panel of the Court of Appeals for the Ninth Circuit said a "substantial reduction" in his sentence was undeserved. The court then restored the minimum 65-year sentence called for in federal sentencing guidelines.

Laura Lambert

See also al Qaeda; Armed Islamic Group; bin Laden, Osama; Moussaoui, Zacarias; Y2K Plot; Zubaydah, Abu

Further Readings

AbuKhalil, As'ad. *Bin Laden, Islam, and America's New "War on Terrorism."* New York: Seven Stories Press, 2002.

Bergen, Peter. *Holy War, Inc.: Inside the Secret World of Osama bin Laden.* New York: Free Press, 2001.

Kershaw, Sarah. "Terrorist in '99 U.S. Case Is Sentenced to 22 Years." *The New York Times,* July 28, 2005.

Mahajan, Rahul. *The New Crusade: America's War on Terrorism.* New York: Monthly Review Press, 2002.

PBS/Frontline. "Trail of a Terrorist." *Frontline,* October 25, 2001. http://www.pbs.org/wgbh/pages/frontline/shows/trail.

Preschel, Jill. "22 Years for Millennium Bomb Plot." CBS News, July 27, 2005.

Schwartz, John. "Appeals Court Throws Out Sentence in Bombing Plot, Calling It Too Light." *The New York Times,* February 2, 2010. http://www.nytimes.com/2010/02/03/us/03bomber.html.

Steinhauer, Jennifer. "Court Vacates Term of Algerian in Bomb Plot." *The New York Times,* January 17, 2007. http://www.nytimes.com/2007/01/17/us/17bomber.html.

Terry, Lynne. "Would-be Millennium Bomber Ahmed Ressam Appeals Ruling on Sentence." *Oregonian,* March 17, 2010. http://www.oregonlive.com/news/index.ssf/2010/03/would-be_millennium_bomber_ahm.html.

REVOLUTIONARY ARMED FORCES OF COLOMBIA

See FARC

REVOLUTIONARY JUSTICE ORGANIZATION

See Hezbollah

REVOLUTIONARY ORGANIZATION 17 NOVEMBER

The Revolutionary Organization 17 November (RO-17N, or 17N) is a Greek terrorist group that carried out dozens of operations and whose members eluded capture for more than 25 years, until many of the group's members were convicted of terror-related crimes in 2003.

17N took its name from the events of November 14–17, 1973, when a student protest against Greece's military dictatorship was met with excessive police force, resulting in the death of 34 protestors. The military junta subsequently fell and was replaced by a civilian government in 1974.

No member of 17N had ever been arrested and interrogated until July 2002, and most of the information about the group's goals and leadership was gleaned largely from communiqués released by 17N after its attacks. The leadership of 17N hoped that the fall of the junta would bring about a Marxist, or at least a socialist, revolution. The election of the moderate, somewhat conservative Konstantinos Karamanlis as prime minister disillusioned members of the group, and they set about making 17N a vanguard whose violent attacks on the repressive establishment would, according to Leninist theory, spark a communist revolution.

Although the members of 17N were Marxist, their ideology had a distinctly nationalist flavor. The group advocated the closing and repatriating of U.S. military bases in Greece, opposed Greek membership in the European Union, and frowned on closer ties between Greece and Turkey. (Turkey ruled Greece for several hundred years; the continuing animosity between the two nations has led them to the brink of war many times.) Given the extreme difficulty police had in penetrating the organization, experts believed that it was probably extremely small, perhaps having as few as a dozen members. However many their number, 17N demonstrated thoroughly professional organization throughout its existence. The group's operations were noted for their careful planning and execution, and its members were known for their coolness under pressure.

17N's first attack was the assassination of CIA station chief Richard Welch in Athens on December 23, 1975. Over the next five years, the group attacked noted Greek political figures. Following each attack, 17N claimed responsibility and provided details about the crimes to prove its culpability. In 1981, following the election of a socialist government in Greece, 17N seemed to have briefly suspended operations, but it resumed them in 1983 after the Greek government agreed to let the U.S. military bases remain on Greek soil. In response, the group assassinated Captain George Tsantes of the U.S. Navy. In 1985, 17N detonated its first car bomb, killing one police officer and injuring 14. Following a raid on a Greek military museum in 1990, which netted the group two rocket launchers, many of its attacks used rockets.

After resuming operations in 1983, 17N mounted more than 100 attacks against U.S. and Greek government targets and Western businesses in Greece; more than 20 people were killed in these attacks. 17N increased its activity during the Persian Gulf War and the NATO air strikes in Kosovo. In 1997 a Kurdish member of 17N alleged that the group was connected to leftist Greek political parties. That no member of the group was ever arrested during these years gives some credence to the speculation that 17N may have been protected by elements within the Greek government. Over the years, however, as some of its operations failed, the group seemed to lose some of its fervor.

The first break in the investigation came on June 29, 2002, when Greek police arrested Savvas Xeros, believed to be 17N's commander, after he had been injured while attempting to plant a bomb. The arrest of Xeros led the police to a cache of weapons and documents, including a Colt .45 pistol used in several of 17N's attacks. Hundreds of people were subsequently questioned. The Greek police believed that the capture of 17N's arsenal would be a crushing blow to the organization. In December 2003, a Greek court convicted 15 members, five of whom were given multiple life terms, while four other alleged members were acquitted for lack of evidence.

An attack in May 2004, at a courthouse in Larissa, Greece, wounded one civilian and caused minor damages to the facility. While no group claimed responsibility for the attack, authorities suspected 17N. In December 2005, under a new Greek law, a group appeals trial opened for the 15 convicted members and two of the previously acquitted members. At the conclusion of the trial in May 2007, 13 of the 17 members of 17N were found guilty of terrorism.

Colleen Sullivan

Further Readings

Beyer, Cornelia and Michael Bauer, eds. *Effectively Countering Terrorism: The Challenges of Prevention, Preparedness and Response.* Eastbourne, East Sussex, UK: Sussex Academic Press, 2009.

Dolnik, Adam. *Understanding Terrorist Innovation: Technology, Tactics and Global Trends.* London: Routledge, 2007.

Kassimeris, George. *Europe's Last Red Terrorists: The Revolutionary Organization 17 November.* New York: New York University Press, 2001.

Naxos, Shyam Bhatia, and Leonard Doyle. "Poison Bomber Offers Secrets for Sanctuary." *The Observer,* September 28, 1997, p. 1.

REVOLUTIONARY PEOPLE'S LIBERATION PARTY/FRONT

The Revolutionary People's Liberation Party/Front (Devrimci Halk Kurtulus Partisi/Cephesi, or DHKP/C), also known as Dev Sol (Revolutionary Left), was formed in 1978 as an offshoot of the Turkish People's Liberation Party/Front, with the goal of establishing a communist social order in Turkey. In the 1990s, the DHKP/C was the most active of the left-wing Marxist-Leninist terrorist groups in Turkey. With intensely xenophobic roots, the group is both anti–United States and anti-NATO.

According to Turkish sources, Dev Sol assassinated many Turkish officials and the country's former prime minister, Nihat Erim, in 1980. After this, Dev Sol did not step up its efforts until the late 1980s, when the group attacked Turkish security and military officials. In 1990, the group focused its attention on foreigners in or around Turkey, and in the ensuing two years, Dev Sol murdered two U.S. military contractors, wounded a U.S. Air Force officer, and launched rockets at a U.S. consulate in Istanbul, all in retaliation for U.S. involvement in the Persian Gulf War.

On July 12, 1991, 11 Dev Sol terrorists were killed during a string of Turkish National Police (TNP) raids in Istanbul. As a result, that date became a hostile DHKP/C anniversary of sorts, and for the next two years the group attempted attacks on U.S. targets in Turkey on or near that date.

After some infighting in 1994, the group changed its name to DHKP/C. In its first major act under its new moniker, the DHKP/C murdered a prominent Turkish businessman. In response to the growing terrorism problem, the Turkish government conducted raids against Dev Sol safe houses and enacted new anti-terrorist legislation. Largely because of such raids, DHKP/C attacks have decreased significantly since 1991. In light of some failed attempts at forming an alliance with the Kurdistan Workers' Party (PKK), another of Turkey's active terrorist groups, it is thought that support for the DHKP/C could be waning.

The group's leader, Dursun Karataş, was arrested and jailed after the events of 1980, and he remained in jail for nearly 10 years. He eventually escaped and fled to Europe, but in the mid-1990s he was arrested by French authorities. He served a minimal jail term in France, but was never extradited to Turkey, and he died in the Netherlands in August 2008.

In June 1999, Turkish officials circumvented a DHKP/C attempted assault on the U.S. Consulate during a presidential visit to Istanbul. Two years later, the DHKP/C added suicide bombings to its portfolio, with successful attacks against Turkish police in January and September 2001. The DHKP/C has typically used improvised explosive devices against official Turkish targets and soft U.S. targets of opportunity. Beginning in 2003, attacks against U.S. targets were probably undertaken in response to Operation Iraqi Freedom.

In March 2008, three DHKP/C members were arrested in Istanbul while preparing terrorist attacks, probably against U.S. commercial interests and the Turkish prime minster, Recep Erdogan. While operations against the group and arrests of its members have weakened its capabilities, the DKHP/C probably has several dozen terrorist operatives inside Turkey, with a large support network throughout Europe. After Karataş died, the Turkish press reported the onset of a leadership struggle within the organization. By 2009 the DHKP/C was operating in very limited capacity against Turkish targets. In April of that year, two DHKP/C members attempted to assassinate the former Turkish justice minister Hikmet Sami Türk, but the two were apprehended.

Richard McHugh

See also Kurdistan Workers' Party

Further Readings

Alexander, Yonah, and Edgar H. Brenner. *Turkey: Terrorism, Civil Rights, and the European Union.* New York: Routledge, 2008.

Alexander, Yonah, and Dennis A. Pluchinsky. *Europe's Red Terrorists: The Fighting Communist Organizations.* Oxford: Frank Cass, 1992.

"Foiling a Deadly Plot." *Time,* August 5, 1991, p. 43.

Østergaard-Nielsen, Eva. *Transnational Politics: Turks and Kurds in Germany.* London: Routledge, 2003.

Pelton, Robert Young. *The World's Most Dangerous Places.* New York: Harper Resource, 2000.

REVOLUTIONARY UNITED FRONT

The Revolutionary United Front (RUF), an infamously brutal guerrilla unit in Sierra Leone, sought to create instability in the region and overthrow the government. Formed in 1990, the group later financed itself through control of the country's diamond resources, and for 11 years it carried out extremely violent attacks on civilians that are said to have claimed about 200,000 lives. The group was especially notorious for recruiting children into its ranks, raping women and girls, and dismembering its victims. In 2002, UN military efforts finally disabled the group and restored peace in Sierra Leone.

The RUF's roots date back to the early 1990s. Foday Saybana Sankoh was a former student activist who in the 1970s had spent time in exile in Libya, where he came under the philosophical influence of Muammar Qaddafi. While in Liberia in 1991, Sankoh aligned himself with a Liberian guerrilla unit, the National Patriotic Front for Liberia (NPFL), and their leader, Charles Taylor. Taylor, who later would become president of Liberia following an eight-year terror campaign, had tried a few months earlier to invade Sierra Leone. He and Sankoh founded the RUF to carry out attacks on towns along Sierra Leone's eastern border. At that time, the Sierra Leone government and military were quite weak, and within a month the RUF had not only taken control of a sizeable region of the eastern part of the country but were also on track to overtake the government.

The nation's economy was in shambles by 1992, and a small military group unconnected to

A Sierra Leonean whose two hands were hacked off by terrorist rebels helps another place a sling on his functionless hands, which were similarly hacked off at the wrists, but later sewn back for cosmetic reasons only, at the Camp for War Wounded and Amputees in Freetown, the Sierra Leonean capital, September 1, 1999. (AP Photo/ Brennan Linsley. © 2011 The Associated Press. All Rights Reserved)

the RUF staged a coup. The RUF continued its campaign against this new military junta, murdering and dismembering unarmed civilians. The atrocities rippled throughout the country, and thousands fled to neighboring Guinea.

By 1994 the RUF had systematically eliminated many rural workers in the country's diamond-mine areas, and by year's end, thousands had been murdered and half of the country's nearly 5 million people had been displaced. The strength of the government's army was dwindling, and the RUF successfully continued to exploit many of the diamond mines.

By early 1995, the RUF had commandeered nearly all of the country's economic resources, and it had kidnapped, drugged, and enlisted hundreds of young men against their will. The RUF had some 4,000 members in its ranks, and it moved within several miles of Freetown, the capitol. At this time no one really understood the RUF's mission, what they stood for, or who Sankoh was. An RUF manifesto, titled "Footpaths to Democracy: Toward a New Sierra Leone," gave people their first vague idea of the group's goals.

The government enlisted the help of Executive Outcomes (EO), a South African security firm that had once assisted the Angolan government in its fight against the UNITA rebels. The EO troops

first arrived in May 1995, and within days they had beaten back RUF forces from Freetown. They regained control of the diamond mines shortly thereafter.

EO continued their assault on the RUF, and by 1996 the RUF was weakening and called for a cease-fire. Peace talks began in Abidjan and went on for nearly a year, during which time RUF attacks continued. The RUF asked the newly elected president, Ahmed Tejan Kabbah, to expel the EO from the country in exchange for a peace agreement, and both sides accepted. But in May 1997, soldiers attacked a jail in Freetown and released some 600 criminals and former coup organizers, and Kabbah fled the country.

Some of those freed from the prison then formed the Armed Forces Revolutionary Council (AFRC), and this group invited the RUF to join them against the government. In the period that followed, the country fell into complete chaos. Banks and other government institutions closed down, while rape, murder, and general lawlessness brought the economy to a standstill. The Economic Community of West African States (ECOWAS) sent its military arm, ECOMOG—a force comprising thousands of soldiers from Nigeria, Ghana, Guinea, and Gambia—to combat the AFRC and the RUF. The ECOMOG offensive pushed the groups out of Freetown in a bloody battle that left many civilians dead. President Kabbah then came back to Freetown and took control of the country, while ECOMOG forces pursued AFRC/RUF groups around the country.

When nearly 50 RUF terrorists were arrested and sentenced to death, including Sankoh, the RUF undertook its most bloody endeavor to date, "Operation No Living Thing." They abducted, dismembered, and murdered thousands of people in a ruthless sweep across the country. In January 1999, the AFRC/RUF attacked Freetown again, and nearly 6,000 civilians were killed before ECOMOG could force them out. By May, a cease-fire was in place, and by July, a peace deal had been cut between the government and the RUF, in exchange for the release of Sankoh and the promotion of some rebels into government ranks.

UN peacekeeping troops arrived in November and December to monitor the peace agreement, and by the following April they had come under attack in the eastern region of the country, with hundreds of them taken hostage. By May 2000,

Britain sent 800 paratroopers to help evacuate its citizens and rescue UN workers. Sankoh was then recaptured.

By March 2001, UN troops were deploying to rebel-heavy areas, and the overall disarmament of RUF forces began in May. The new, British-trained Sierra Leone army regained control of rebel territory, and by January 2002 the UN declared that all 45,000 fighters had been disarmed. Further, the UN set up a separate war-crimes court, which indicted five alleged leaders of the RUF—Sankoh, Sam Bockarie, Issa Hassan Sesay, Morris Kallon, and Augustine Gbao—for war crimes, crimes against humanity, and other serious violations of international humanitarian law. The indictments against Sankoh and Bockarie were withdrawn on December 8, 2003, due to their deaths—Sankoh of a stroke while awaiting trial, and Bockarie in a shootout with Liberian forces. On February 25, 2009, Sesay and Kallon were found guilty on 16 counts, while Gbao was found guilty on 14 counts.

Richard McHugh

See also Lord's Resistance Army; Qaddafi, Muammar el

Further Readings

Abdullah, Ibrahim. "Bush Path to Destruction: The Origin and Character of the Revolutionary United Front/Sierra Leone." *Journal of Modern African Studies* 36, no. 2 (1998): 223.

Denov, Myriam S. *Child Soldiers: Sierra Leone's Revolutionary United Front.* Cambridge, UK: Cambridge University Press, 2010.

Gberie, Lansan. *A Dirty War in West Africa: The RUF and the Destruction of Sierra Leone.* Bloomington: Indiana University Press, 2005.

Stewart, Ian. *Freetown Ambush: A Reporter's Year in Africa.* London: Vision, 2003.

REWARDS FOR JUSTICE

The Rewards for Justice program, administered by the Bureau of Diplomatic Security in the Department of State, was created in 1984 by the U.S. Congress as part of the Act to Combat International Terrorism. The monetary rewards are an incentive to potential informants to provide law enforcement agencies with information about any terrorist act, whether planned or carried out, against U.S. citizens. Acts and people that the Rewards for Justice program has specifically targeted include: the 1994 genocide in Rwanda; Serbian leaders Radovan Karadzic and Ratko Mladic; Eric Rudolph, for the 1996 Olympic bombings in Atlanta; and the kidnapping and murder of the journalist Daniel Pearl in Pakistan. A flight instructor named Clarence Prevost was reportedly paid $5 million from the program for testifying against Zacarias Moussaoui in 2006. The largest payout was $30 million, paid to an individual who pinpointed the locations of Uday and Qusay Hussein, the sons of Saddam Hussein, who were subsequently killed in a U.S. military strike in 2003.

At least $80 million has been paid to more than 50 tipsters since the program's inception. Information about most of these cases is classified. One significant catch was Ramzi Ahmed Yousef, later convicted of the 1993 World Trade Center bombing, who was arrested on the basis of information provided in exchange for $2 million. In October 2001, the Patriot Act increased the amount that could be paid to an individual to more than $5 million, while up to $25 million can be given for information leading to the capture of Osama bin Laden and other al Qaeda leaders. In the wake of the September 11, 2001, attacks on the World Trade Center in New York City and the Pentagon, outside of Washington, D.C., additional money for the program was collected by public donations to the nonprofit Rewards for Justice Fund, established by the businessmen Scott Case and Joe Rutledge. The Air Transport Association of America and the Airline Pilots Association also pledged $1 million each to be distributed as supplemental awards for cases involving aviation. In the four months following September 11, 2001, the program received 24,000 tips.

Following the nomination of a potential recipient by a U.S. investigating agency, an interagency committee evaluates the information provided, decides if a reward is appropriate, and determines how much is to be paid. Both the secretary of state and the attorney general must approve the committee's decision. The amount of the reward is based on the value of the information, the risk faced by the informer, and the degree of his or her cooperation.

Publicity for the program has included advertisements in local languages placed in both foreign and U.S. media, posters, matchbook covers, and an Internet site. The advertising firm Ogilvy & Mather Worldwide worked pro bono to create a new advertising campaign. The national campaign was launched in December 2001, with media sources within the United States running the ads free as public service announcements. Undersecretary of State for Public Diplomacy and Public Affairs Charlotte Beers oversaw the campaign.

The campaign has generated some controversy, however. It has been accused of creating misleading and inaccurate advertisements—notably a poster with a photograph of the terrorist Mohamed Atta and unattributed text describing the activities of the suspected conspirator Zacarias Moussaoui. One critic claimed that a noncitizen offering information was detained by the Immigration and Naturalization Service rather than rewarded, while the Zionist Organization of America has complained that Palestinian killers of U.S. citizens in Israel are not named on the program's website.

The State Department has called the program "one of its most valuable U.S. Government assets in the fight against international terrorism," but many critics charge that Rewards for Justice is ineffective. The program is not well advertised in the Arab world, some argue, and even if it is known, many people there distrust the United States and are skeptical that they would ever actually receive any money.

Ellen Sexton

See also Counterterrorism; Intelligence Gathering; Patriot Act; September 11 Attacks; Yousef, Ramzi Ahmed

Further Readings

Hewitt, Steve. "American Counter-terrorism through the Rewards for Justice Program, 1984–2008." In *International Terrorism Post-9/11: Comparative Dynamics and Responses*, edited by Asaf Siniver. London: Routledge, 2010.

Lee, Chisun. "In the Crosshairs." *Village Voice*, January 29, 2002, pp. 45–47.

Radler, Melissa. "State Dept. Not Publishing Names of U.S. Citizen's Killers." *Jerusalem Post*, March 6, 2002, p. 4.

Rewards for Justice Program. http://www.rewards forjustice.net.

Whitlock, Craig. "Bounties a Bust in Hunt for Al-Qaeda." *The Washington Post,* May 17, 2008. http://www.washingtonpost.com/wp-dyn/content/article/2008/05/16/AR2008051603921.html.

Reynoso, Abimael Guzmán (1934–)

Manuel Rubén Abimael Guzmán Reynoso (aka Presidente Gonzalo; Comrade Gonzalo) was the founder and leader of the Sendero Luminoso, or Shining Path, a terrorist organization in Peru.

The illegitimate son of a wealthy Peruvian businessman, Guzmán was born in December 1934 in Arequipa, Peru. His mother, Berenice Reynoso, died when he was five, and he is generally known by the name of his father, Guzmán. He excelled as a student but showed little interest in politics until his late teens, when he began associating with leftist intellectuals. He became the protégé of the painter Carlos de la Riva, an ardent admirer of Joseph Stalin; Guzmán joined the Peruvian Communist Party in the late 1950s.

In 1962 Guzmán was appointed to the post of professor of philosophy at San Cristobal del Huamanga University in Ayacucho, a remote, desperately poor province inhabited mostly by Peruvian Indians. There, Guzmán began to hold weekly political discussions with students and colleagues; he was a passionate speaker, and his tirades against the injustices of Peruvian society and the need for Indian peasants to rebel found a receptive audience. Many students were of Indian heritage, and often the first in their families to obtain an education. By the late 1960s, the discussion group had become a political faction calling itself the Communist Party of Peru.

Guzmán studied the theories of Mao Zedong, which held that a successful communist revolution did not require an industrialized, urban proletariat. Instead, an agrarian, preindustrial society could be transformed into a modern communist society by making the peasantry politically conscious. Between 1965 and 1967, Guzmán visited China several times and saw the Cultural Revolution unfold. Seeing Mao's theories put into practice radicalized Guzmán, and he returned to Peru convinced that a rapid, violent revolution was necessary to destroy Peru's existing government and culture and institute a peasant dictatorship.

Under Guzmán's leadership, by the mid-1970s the Communist Party of Peru had begun to transform itself into a guerrilla army—the Sendero Luminoso, or Shining Path, a name taken from a quotation by the Peruvian Marxist Jose Carlos Mariátigua. Early adherents from San Cristobal became Guzmán's top commanders and closest advisors, with his wife, Augusta, assuming a leading role. Guzmán ran the organization with an iron hand; new recruits were required to sign a loyalty oath not to the Shining Path, but to Comrade Gonzalo, the *nom de guerre* Guzmán had chosen for himself. As the organization's power increased, Guzmán's revolutionary fervor began to assume legendary proportions, and his followers regarded him as the "Fourth Sword" of communist thought, after Marx, Lenin, and Mao. His ability to inspire complete devotion in his followers, especially in his officers—college-educated, middle-class intellectuals—was crucial to the Shining Path's success.

The Shining Path began military operations in Ayacucho in 1980, rapidly winning peasant support. Guzmán's tight-knit, hierarchical organization easily resisted infiltration by the military. Guzmán regarded anyone with the slightest connection to the state as a potential target, and the Shining Path did not hesitate to torture and kill anyone it perceived as an enemy, including civilians. By the late 1980s, in part because of lucrative connections to the drug trade, the group controlled the majority of Peru's countryside.

In 1988 Guzmán decided to focus on Peru's urban coast, particularly the capital, Lima. For four years, the Shining Path made steady gains as its bombing campaigns and assassinations immobilized the capital, and the country was brought close to anarchy. In 1992, Peru's president suspended the constitution and declared a state of emergency, effectively placing the country under martial law. In September 1992, Guzmán and 14 other top Shining Path commanders were captured and quickly received life sentences from a military court.

The dictatorial control Guzmán exerted over the Shining Path proved to be the movement's Achilles heel. With no clear second-in-command to take over leadership, the organization rapidly disintegrated. In 1993 Guzmán helped negotiate a peace agreement with the government that provided amnesty for former Shining Path fighters. Guzmán's conviction was overturned by a constitutional court in 2003, and he was retried by a civilian court, which likewise sentenced him to life in prison in 2006. As of 2010, Guzmán was in solitary confinement in a specially built naval prison in El Callao, west of Lima, but he continued to appeal his sentence.

According to Peru's Truth and Reconciliation Commission, 54 percent of all deaths in Peru's 20-year conflict were caused by the Maoist Shining Path insurgency, 30 percent by Peru's armed forces, and most of the rest by government-backed peasant militias.

Colleen Sullivan

See also Shining Path

Further Readings

"Abimael Guzmán's Lawyers File Claim with Inter-American Commission on Human Rights, Shining Path Founder Hopes for Retrial." *Andean Air Mail & Peruvian Times,* December 14, 2008.

Chernick, Marc. "PCP-SL: Partido Comunista de Perú-Sendero Luminoso." In *Terror, Insurgency, and the State: Ending Protracted Conflicts,* edited by Marianne Heiberg, Brendan O'Leary, and John Tirman. Philadelphia: University of Pennsylvania Press, 2007.

Federation of American Scientists. "FAS Project on Peru: The Sendero Files." http://www.fas.org/irp/world/para/docs/sf1.htm.

Kirk, Robin. *The Monkey's Paw: New Chronicles from Peru.* Amherst: University of Massachusetts Press, 1997.

Masterson, Daniel. "In the Shining Path of Mariategui, Mao Tse-tung, or Presidente Gonzalo? Peru's Sendero Luminoso in Historical Perspective." In *Revolution and Revolutionaries: Guerilla Movements in Latin America,* edited by Daniel Castro. Lanham, MD: SR Books, 2006.

McClintock, Cynthia. *Revolutionary Movements in Latin America: El Salvador's FMLN and Peru's Shining Path.* Washington, DC: United States Institute of Peace Press, 1998.

RIYADH, SAUDI ARABIA, BOMBING

On November 13, 1995, bombers parked a car filled with explosives next to a building that housed U.S. military trainers in the busy commercial district of Riyadh, Saudi Arabia's capital. The car exploded, killing at least six people. The Saudi government later arrested, tried, and beheaded four Saudi men for their involvement in the case. Before their execution, the men claimed to have been influenced—although not necessarily assisted—by Osama bin Laden and al Qaeda.

The American service members working in the building were in Riyadh as part of a U.S. Army–run program that trained members of the Saudi National Guard to use U.S.-made tanks and other weapons. The building, a converted apartment complex in the prosperous business and shopping district of al Olaya, served as headquarters for the training mission. The United States had built up its forces in the region after the 1991 Persian Gulf War, and the bombing attack was apparently the work of Saudi militants who violently opposed such a large foreign and Western presence.

At about 11:30 A.M., just as the snack bar inside the complex began to fill up, the car bomb exploded. The blast took off the entire wall of the three-story building and shattered windows nearby. Among the dead were a U.S. Army sergeant and four American civilians; at least 60 people were injured. Saudi officials arrested four militant Saudi Muslims; after a trial in which they were found guilty, they were beheaded, according to the dictates of Islamic law. Press accounts indicated that each man confessed.

A very similar bombing at the Khobar Towers high-rise military barracks in Dhahran in eastern Saudi Arabia followed the Riyadh attack. On June 25, 1996, 19 U.S. service members were killed when a car bomb exploded near the towers housing the 2,000 U.S. military personnel assigned to the King Abdul Aziz Airbase in Saudi Arabia.

Erica Pearson

See also Khobar Towers Bombing

Further Readings

Champion, Daryl. *The Paradoxical Kingdom: Saudi Arabia and the Momentum of Reform.* New York: Columbia University Press, 2005.

Hegghammer, Thomas. *Jihad in Saudi Arabia: Violence and Pan-Islamism Since 1979.* New York: Cambridge University Press, 2010.

Jehl, Douglas. "Bomb in Saudi Arabia Felt round the Persian Gulf." *The New York Times,* November 16, 1995, p. A3.

Lancaster, John. "Five Americans Killed by Car Bomb at Military Building in Saudi Capital; Suspicion Falls on Domestic Militants, Hostile Gulf Neighbors." *Washington Post,* November 14, 1995.

RUDOLPH, ERIC (1966–)

Eric Robert Rudolph spent years on the FBI's Ten Most Wanted list for his role in a two-state bombing spree from 1996 to 1998, including the first fatal bombing of a U.S. abortion clinic, in Alabama; a series of bombings in the Atlanta area; and the Centennial Park bombing during the 1996 Summer Olympics in Atlanta, Georgia. He was finally captured in 2003.

Initially, the Atlanta-area bombings were believed to be part of the growing anti-abortion violence throughout the southern United States. In the early morning hours of January 16, 1997, two bombs exploded at the Sandy Springs Professional Building, just north of Atlanta, injuring seven. The first bomb blasted through the operating and waiting rooms of the abortion clinic; the second, authorities believed, was deliberately timed to injure rescue workers rushing to the scene. A month later, two similarly manufactured bombs exploded in midtown Atlanta's Other Side Lounge, a gay/lesbian nightclub, injuring four.

On February 24, 1997, media outlets received a letter claiming responsibility that was signed by the "Army of God," a shadowy anti-abortion group active since 1982. In it, the bomber railed against abortion, the "agents of the so-called federal government," and the "sodomites" at the Other Side Lounge. The sign-off threatened, "Death to the New World Order."

Not until June 1997 did authorities link the two bombings to the 1996 Centennial Park bomb, which killed two people and injured more than 100 during the Summer Olympics in Atlanta. Six months later, after another deadly explosion at the New Woman All Women Health Care center in Birmingham, Alabama, in which a security guard was killed and a nurse was gravely injured, investigators announced they finally had a suspect—Eric Robert Rudolph.

Rudolph's gray 1989 Nissan pickup truck was quickly linked to the scene of the Birmingham clinic bombing. Although Rudolph was initially sought only as a material witness, when hunters in the woods near Murphy, North Carolina, found Rudolph's abandoned pickup, the investigation intensified. Shortly thereafter, the FBI searched Rudolph's storage facility in Marble, North Carolina, and found a book titled *How to Build Bombs of Mass Destruction*.

On February 14, 1998, Rudolph was named as a suspect in the Birmingham clinic bombing. By May, he was on the FBI's Ten Most Wanted list. Five months later, Attorney General Janet Reno charged him with all three Atlanta-area bombings. By that time, Rudolph had long been hiding in the caves and mines of the Nantahala National Forest in North Carolina, using survivalist skills learned in his 18-month stint in the U.S. Army. In July 1998 he was rumored to have left $500 in exchange for a six-month supply of food and a pickup truck (later abandoned) taken from the home of his girlfriend's father. Members of the Southeast Bomb Task Force—a collaboration between the FBI, the Bureau of Alcohol, Tobacco and Firearms, the Department of Justice, and local trackers—searched the Great Smoky Mountains for signs of Rudolph.

As the investigation progressed, authorities found links between Rudolph and Christian Identity—a quasi-neo-Nazi movement that is both anti-gay and anti-abortion. However, investigators believed Rudolph had more in common with anti-government terrorists such as Timothy McVeigh than with the anti-abortion activists that came before him, such as Michael Griffin or Paul Hill.

On May 31, 2003, Rudolph was captured in Murphy, North Carolina, after nearly five years on the run. As part of a plea bargain, Rudolf pled guilty to four attacks, including the 1996 Olympic blast. In a 2005 statement, he declared, "Abortion is murder. And when the regime in Washington legalized, sanctioned and legitimized this practice, they forfeited their legitimacy and moral authority to govern." While offering an apology to the victims, saying that he did not intend to harm "innocent civilians," he maintained that his cause to anger and embarrass a government that permits women to have abortions was just. Rudolph pled guilty to all charges so as to avoid the death penalty, and he was sentenced to four consecutive life terms, which he serves at the supermax prison in Florence, Colorado, which also holds the Unabomber, Theodore Kaczynski; the 9/11 co-conspirator Zacarias Moussaoui; the Oklahoma City bombing conspirator Terry Lynn Nichols; the would-be terrorist José Padilla; the failed shoe bomber, Richard Reid; and Ramzi Yousef, who planned the first World Trade Center bombing in 1993.

Laura Lambert

See also Anti-Abortion Movement; Army of God; Centennial Park Bombing; Christian Identity; Griffin, Michael Frederick; Hill, Paul Jennings; McVeigh, Timothy James

Further Readings

Baird-Windle, Patricia, and Eleanor J. Bader. *Targets of Hatred: Anti-abortion Terrorism*. New York: Palgrave Macmillan, 2001.

Federal Bureau of Investigation. "The Pursuit and Capture of Eric Rudolph: An Interview with FBI Exec Chris Swecker." http://www.fbi.gov/news/stories/2005/may/swecker_051605.

Gorney, Cynthia. *Articles of Faith: A Frontline History of the Abortion Wars*. New York: Simon & Schuster, 1998.

Schuster, Henry, with Charles Stone. *Hunting Eric Rudolph*. New York: Berkeley Books, 2005.

Vollers, Maryanne. *Lone Wolf: Eric Rudolph and the Legacy of American Terror*. New York: HarperPerennial, 2008.

Walls, Kathleen. *Man Hunt: The Eric Rudolph Story*. St. Augustine, FL: Global Authors Publications, 2003.

S

SALAFIST GROUP FOR PREACHING AND COMBAT

See al Qaeda in the Islamic Maghreb; Armed Islamic Group

SALAMEH, MOHAMMAD

See World Trade Center Bombing (1993)

SAN DIEGO, DANIEL ANDREAS (1978–)

In 2009, Daniel Andreas San Diego became the first American to be added to the FBI's Most Wanted Terrorists list. He was sought in connection with acts of environmental terrorism committed in 2003. San Diego was known to have connections to an animal rights extremist group known as the Revolutionary Cells—Animal Liberation Brigade (RCALB).

San Diego was born in Berkeley, California, in 1978, and he grew up in the San Francisco area. He attended Terra Linda High School in San Rafael, California, and later attended classes at the College of Marin in Kentfield, California. His father was a city manager for Marin County. San Diego worked for a time as a computer network specialist, and he traveled internationally and was a skilled sailor. His multiple tattoos make reference to environmental causes.

The bombings in question occurred in 2003 at corporations in the San Francisco area with ties to Huntingdon Life Sciences (HLS), a British-based research company that performs laboratory tests on animals. HLS had been the focus of strong activism by a campaign called Stop Huntingdon Animal Cruelty (SHAC) since 1999. SHAC was formed by a group of activists dedicated to ending laboratory testing on animals. The campaign extended to companies that did business for HLS, which is why the two corporations in California were targeted. The first bombing was on August 28 at the Chiron Life Sciences Center, a biotechnology firm in Emeryville, California. Two bombs were set off one hour apart, at 2:55 A.M. and 4:00 A.M., outside Chiron office buildings. The second bombing occurred a month later, on September 26 at 3:22 A.M. at the Shaklee Corporation in Pleasanton, California. An improvised explosive device loaded with nails was set off outside the commercial office building. Shaklee makes eco-friendly products such as vitamins and shampoos, but it is a subsidiary of Yamanouchi Pharmaceutical Co. Ltd., which has ties to Huntingdon Life Sciences. No people were injured in any of the bombings.

San Diego allegedly posted a claim of responsibility for the bombings on the Internet, stating they were done in the name of "animal rights." San Diego disappeared in October 2003, though he was

525

Maliciously Damaging and Destroying, and Attempting to Destroy and Damage,
by Means of Explosives, Buildings and Other Property; Possession of a Destructive
Device During, in Relation to, and in Furtherance of a Crime of Violence

DANIEL ANDREAS SAN DIEGO

Aliases:
Andreas San Diego, D. Andreas San Diego, "Andreas"

DESCRIPTION

Date(s) of Birth Used:	February 9, 1978	**Hair:**	Brown
Place of Birth:	Berkeley, California	**Eyes:**	Brown
Height:	6'0" (1.80 m)	**Complexion:**	Light
Weight:	160 pounds (73 Kg)	**Sex:**	Male
		Race:	White
		Citizenship:	American

Scars and Marks: San Diego has the following tattoos: a round image of burning hillsides in the center of his chest with the words "It only takes a spark" printed in a semicircle below; burning and collapsing buildings on the sides of his abdomen and back; and a single leafless tree rising from a road in the center of his lower back. These tattoos may have been significantly altered or covered with new tattoos.

Remarks: San Diego has ties to animal rights extremist groups. He is known to follow a vegan diet, eating no meat or food containing animal products. In the past, he has worked as a computer network specialist and with the operating system LINUX. San Diego wears eyeglasses, is skilled at sailing, and has traveled internationally. He is known to possess a handgun.

CAUTION

Daniel Andreas San Diego is wanted for his alleged involvement in the bombing of two office buildings in the San Francisco, California, area. On August 28, 2003, two bombs exploded approximately one hour apart at the Chiron Corporation in Emeryville. Then, on September 26, 2003, one bomb strapped with nails exploded at the Shaklee Corporation in Pleasanton. San Diego was indicted in the United States District Court, Northern District of California, in July of 2004.

REWARD

The FBI is offering a reward of up to $250,000 for information leading directly to the arrest of Daniel Andreas San Diego.

SHOULD BE CONSIDERED ARMED AND DANGEROUS

Daniel Andreas San Diego's "Most Wanted Terrorists" poster (FBI.Gov, Most Wanted Terrorists list) under surveillance as a suspect in the bombings. He was indicted in the U.S. District Court for the Northern District of California in July 2004. The FBI has offered a reward of up to $250,000 for information leading to San Diego's arrest.

Brent Smith and Paxton Roberts

See also Animal Liberation Front; Animal Rights Movement; Bombings and Bomb Scares; Earth Liberation Front; Ecoterrorism

Further Readings

Liddick, Donald R. *Eco-terrorism: Radical Environmental and Animal Liberation Movements.* Westport, CT: Praeger, 2006.

Lovitz, Dara. *Muzzling a Movement: The Effects of Anti-terrorism Law, Money, and Politics on Animal Activism.* Brooklyn, NY: Lantern Books, 2010.

Manes, Christopher. *Green Rage: Radical Environmentalism and the Unmaking of Civilization.* Boston: Little, Brown, 1990.

Romero, Frances. "Top 10 Notorious Fugitives: Daniel Andreas San Diego." *Time*, March 15, 2010. http://www.time.com/time/specials/packages/article/0,28804,1971762_1971761_1971731,00.html.

SÁNCHEZ, ILICH RAMÍREZ (1949–)

The Venezuelan-born Ilich Ramírez Sánchez, widely known as Carlos the Jackal, was involved in some of the most spectacular terrorist incidents of the 1970s and 1980s. He eluded police capture for more than 20 years.

Ilich Ramírez Sánchez was born on October 12, 1949. His parents presented a study in contrasts: his mother, Elba Maria Sánchez, was a deeply religious woman who enjoyed high society; his father, José Altagracia Ramírez Navas, was a fervent Marxist. He named his sons Vladimir, Ilich, and Lenin, after V. I. Lenin, the leader of the 1917 Russian Revolution. From the moment they were born, José Ramírez intended his sons to be revolutionaries. Despite his Marxist beliefs, José Ramírez maintained a successful law practice, and the family was well off and moved in the upper circles of Venezuelan society.

Sánchez attended Fermin Toro Lycée, a secondary school famous for its leftist radicalism. He participated in street demonstrations and riots in the streets of Caracas in the mid-1960s and is rumored to have taken guerrilla training in Cuba in 1966. Later that year, concerned about rising violence and political unrest in Venezuela, his mother took her sons to London to continue their schooling. In 1968, José Ramírez arranged for Sánchez to attend Patrice Lumumba Friendship University in Moscow.

Lumumba University was not a typical center of academics, as its purpose was to train future terrorists and revolutionary leaders for the Third World. Subjects included communist doctrine and covert operations. Discipline was strict, and Carlos chafed under it, slighting his studies in favor of partying and womanizing. In early 1970 he was forced to leave Moscow.

Terrorism Training

While at the university, Sánchez had become engaged in the Palestinian cause after meeting Muhammad Boudia, a fellow student and member of the Popular Front for the Liberation of Palestine (PFLP). Wadi Haddad and George Habash had created the PFLP after the crushing defeat of a joint Arab army by Israel in the 1967 Six-Day War. Determined to strike back at Israel, in 1968 the PFLP abandoned conventional military tactics, taking up bombings, assassinations, and civilian airline hijackings. Its techniques contributed significantly to the development of modern terrorism, and radical groups began to look to the PFLP as a model. The PFLP welcomed them, allowing terrorists from around the world to attend its training sessions. Habash hoped to use these foreigners to advance the Palestinian cause in the West.

After his expulsion from Lumumba, Sánchez traveled to Lebanon to attend a PFLP training camp. He attended two three-month training sessions during 1970 and 1971, becoming one of Habash's most prized students. It was Habash who, in 1971, gave him the alias "Carlos."

Terrorist Actions

In the fall of 1971, Carlos traveled to London to begin work for the PFLP. His friend Boudia was now in charge of PFLP operatives in Europe. At first, Carlos stuck to collecting intelligence, compiling a 500-person hit list for PFLP. In June 1973, Israeli agents killed Boudia, and Carlos was named PFLP co-commander in Europe, along with Muhammad Moukharbal. Carlos made his first foray into active terrorism in December 1973 with the attempted assassination of Joseph Edward Sieff, a British Jewish businessman.

Carlos and Moukharbal next arranged the August 3, 1974, bombing of four news outlets deemed to be pro-Israeli. Car bombs were placed outside the company's Paris headquarters, set to detonate at 2 A.M., though one of the bombs, placed outside the Maison de Radio, failed to go off. No one was injured in the blasts.

Acting on the advice of Wadi Haddad, during 1974 and 1975 Carlos began working with other terrorist groups. In September 1974, Carlos consulted with the Japanese Red Army (JRA) on its planned assault on the French embassy in The Hague. The JRA succeeded in capturing the embassy, but negotiations with the French government were stalled. To prod the French to again negotiate, Carlos is believed to have slipped into a Paris café called the Drugstore, situated in a crowded shopping area, and thrown a hand grenade from the second-floor balcony into the crowd below. Thirty-three people were injured and two were killed in the attack, and the French government acceded to the JRA's demands soon afterward. The grenade used in the attack was later discovered to have been stolen by Baader-Meinhof Gang, a group of West German terrorists, from a U.S. Army base in Germany. Carlos is also believed to have aided the Latin American terror coalition Junta de Coordinación Revolutionaria with its assassination of the Uruguayan attaché to France in December 1974.

In January 1975, Carlos made two attempts to launch rockets at El Al flights on the runway of France's Orly Airport. In the first attack, Carlos and his accomplice got off two shots, which missed, before making their escape. Carlos returned with three Palestinian accomplices six days later to try again. This time, the terrorists managed to fire a single rocket before being confronted by security officers. During the gun battle, while his companions retreated into an airport bathroom and took hostages, Carlos managed to slip away. (The hostages were released unharmed and the Palestinians were later flown to Baghdad.)

In June 1975, Lebanese security officials detained Moukharbal, later turning him over to the Direction de la Surveillance du Territoire (DST), France's intelligence agency. Once captured, Moukharbal informed on his comrades, agreeing to lead the police to the home of one of Carlos's many girlfriends. On the night of June 27, Moukharbal and three DST officers arrived at the apartment during a party and attempted to question Carlos. After arguing briefly with the police officers, Carlos excused himself to use the bathroom. He returned with an automatic pistol, and within seconds had killed Moukharbal and two of the DST officers.

OPEC Attack

Eluding a massive dragnet, Carlos first returned to PFLP headquarters in Lebanon, and then went on to East Germany. He later went to Hungary to plan his next operation, which was to be his most audacious: an attack on the annual Organization of Petroleum Exporting Countries (OPEC) meeting in Vienna. The attack began at 11:30 A.M. on December 19, 1975. Carlos and his five accomplices entered the OPEC headquarters and methodically shot their way through security. Three people were killed in the initial assault, and several were wounded. When police arrived, Carlos had taken more than 80 meeting attendees hostage, including the oil ministers of 11 countries. After 36 hours of negotiations, the Austrians agreed to all of Carlos's demands, including flying the terrorists and their hostages to the country of their choice. In return, upon their departure for the airport, Carlos was to release 40 of the hostages, retaining the oil ministers and their entourages. The terrorists left Austria and flew to Algiers, where the non-Arab ministers were released.

What happened next is a matter of some debate. Some sources suggest that Wadi Haddad's original plan had been to fly each of the ministers to his country's capital, where he would be released for ransom, and that the Algerian government participated with full knowledge of the plan. Carlos and his fellow terrorists next traveled to Tripoli, Libya, where the Libyan minister was released. They then returned to Algiers, where the rest of the hostages were released on December 24.

It is unknown whether Carlos and the PFLP received any ransom, and if so, from whom and in what amount. Some sources suggest that a ransom of up to $50 million was paid for the Syrian and Saudi Arabian ministers, and that a significant amount of it went to the PFLP. However, Carlos, Wadi Haddad, and George Habash may have retained a large portion for their personal use. After releasing the hostages, Carlos and his accomplices were offered political asylum by Algeria. Once again he had escaped the grasp of the police.

The OPEC attack was the last terrorist attack led by Carlos personally. His movements after 1975 are a matter of speculation, but he is believed to have returned to Lebanon and become part of the PFLP leadership; he is also thought to have been involved in planning the 1976 Entebbe, Uganda, hijacking.

The Terrorist as an Anachronism

The PFLP never trusted Carlos absolutely, however, and after the death of Wadi Haddad in 1978 he drifted away from them. Intelligence sources believe, and he himself has claimed, that he became something of a "professional revolutionary," hiring out his services and expertise to the highest bidder. Between 1976 and 1985 Carlos is known to have

operated out of East Germany and (then communist) Hungary. In 2010, newly available files of the Stasi, East Germany's feared security force, revealed that there had been a pact between Carlos and the Stasi, who furnished him with apartments, medical services, cars, and other services whenever he was in East Berlin. Carlos also may have operated terrorist training camps in Iran in the early 1980s, working with Imad Mugniyah.

In January 1982, Carlos's wife, the German terrorist Magdalena Kopp, was arrested in Paris. Carlos bombed several French targets in an effort to force her release, but was unsuccessful. In 1984 Carlos unwisely allowed himself to be interviewed and photographed by a Lebanese journalist; he later tried and failed to prevent the article from being printed. Soon after publication, the magazine's Paris offices were bombed, injuring 64 people and killing 1, and the writer of the article disappeared. This incident and a New Year's Eve 1984 bomb attack

This is a copy of a passport that was found in a London flat on July 2, 1975, among an arms cache belonging to a man named "Carlos" and believed to be connected with the deaths of two French counter-espionage agents in Paris. This Chilean passport carried the name Adolfo Bernal. The photograph, however, was of a man known to his friends as Carlos Martinez or "Carlos the Jackal" (real name: Ilich Ramírez Sánchez) and similar to the terrorist hunted by French police. (AP Photo/prb/gdn. © 2011 The Associated Press. All Rights Reserved)

are the last terrorist acts in which Carlos is believed to have been involved.

In 1985 Carlos left Hungary for Prague, and he is known to have been living in Syria in the late 1980s. Terrorist organizations in the Middle East had begun to change, however, becoming more Islamic and Arab-centric, and they wanted to nothing to do with a Marxist Westerner. By 1991, with the Soviet Union dissolved and the Gulf War having rearranged Middle East alliances, Carlos could find no place to hide and no regime that wanted him. He had become an anachronism.

Carlos spent the early 1990s being hustled from one Arab state to another on a series of false diplomatic passports. In 1993 he ended up in Sudan, where an Islamic fundamentalist regime had come to power. In 1994 the French made a secret deal with the Sudanese, and Carlos was extradited to France, where he was tried for the 1975 murder of three policemen. He is currently serving a life sentence and is said to have converted to Islam. Active even while incarcerated, he wrote an autobiography in 2003, titled *Revolutionary Islam*, and he brought suit against a French production company shooting a documentary film about him in 2010.

In 2005 the European Court of Human Rights heard a complaint from Carlos about "inhuman and degrading treatment" while in solitary confinement, but the court rejected the claim. In 2007 a new trial was ordered for Carlos for a series of bombings in France during the 1980s that left at least 11 people dead. He is believed to have killed more than 80 people and been responsible for the deaths of hundreds more during his career.

Colleen Sullivan

See also Japanese Red Army; Popular Front for the Liberation of Palestine

Further Readings

Cody, Edward. "Carlos the Jackal, Imprisoned for Life, Looks in Lawsuit to Protect His Image." *The Washington Post*, January 26, 2010. http://www.washingtonpost.com/wp-dyn/content/article/2010/01/25/AR2010012503690.html.

Follian, John. *Jackal: The Complete Story of the Legendary Terrorist, Carlos the Jackal*. New York: Arcade Publishing, 2011.

Paterson, Tony. "Rescued from the Shredder, Carlos the Jackal's Missing Years." *The Independent*, October 30, 2010. http://www.independent.co.uk/news/world/europe/rescued-from-the-shredder-carlos-the-jackals-missing-years-2120492.html.

Smith, Colin. *Carlos: Portrait of a Terrorist*. London: Deutsch, 1976.

Tuman, Joseph S. *Communicating Terror: The Rhetorical Dimensions of Terrorism*. 2nd ed. London: Sage, 2010.

Waugh, Billy, with Tim Keown. *Hunting the Jackal: A Special Forces and CIA Soldier's Fifty Years on the Frontlines of the War against Terrorism*. New York: HarperCollins, 2004.

Yallop, David. *To the Ends of the Earth: The Hunt for the Jackal*. London: Jonathan Cape, 1993.

SAYERET MATKAL

Sayeret Matkal (aka General Staff Reconnaissance Unit 269; "The Unit"), the most elite commando unit of the Israel Defense Force (IDF), was founded in 1957 by Avraham Arnan, who petitioned the IDF General Staff for a combat unit in enemy territory to conduct top secret intelligence gathering missions. The unit has carried out many counterterrorist operations since its founding.

Sayeret Matkal has had tremendous influence on the IDF and is known for several spectacular hostage rescues. In 1972 the unit freed hostages on a Sabena airliner at the Tel Aviv Airport. Commandos disguised as maintenance personnel took control of the airliner from members of Abu Nidal's Black September Organization during "Operation Isotope."

In a 1976 mission the Sayeret Matkal worked with other Israeli Defense Force units to free hostages from an Air France plane that had been hijacked by Palestinian terrorists and flown to Entebbe, Uganda. The unit used a black Mercedes that was a perfect copy of the Ugandan leader Idi Amin's personal car, and the ruse fooled the local troops. Rescue force leader Lt. Col. Yonatan Netanyahu, brother of former Israeli Prime Minister Benjamin Netanyahu, was killed as he brought the hostages to safety.

On May 15, 1974, a Sayeret Matkal hostage rescue mission at an Israeli school went horribly wrong. Members of Nayef Hawatmeh's Democratic Front for the Liberation of Palestine had taken over the school in the northern town of Ma'alot, and dozens of teachers and students were taken hostage.

When Sayeret Matkal stormed the school, Democratic Front members began firing at the hostages. At least 20 people, many of them children, were killed. Some were killed or wounded in the exchange of fire between Sayeret Matkal and the Democratic Front.

The unit has also engaged in many counterterror attacks and assassinations. In 1973, the Sayeret Matkal commando Ehud Barak (who would serve as Israel's prime minister from 1999 to 2001) led a raid into Lebanon dressed as a woman. The unit assassinated three Palestinian leaders during the mission, called Operation Spring of Youth. Barak, who joined the unit while still in his late teens, rose to the leadership of Sayeret Matkal. Benjamin Netanyahu, who also later served as prime minister of Israel, served under Barak in Sayeret Matkal.

The unit is credited with the 1988 assassination of PLO second-in-command Khalil Wazir, known as Abu Jihad. He was gunned down inside his Tunis home. However, Abu Jihad's assassination has also been attributed to the Mossad, Israel's secret service.

In July 1989, Sayeret Matkal reportedly kidnapped Hezbollah's spiritual leader Sheikh Abdul Karim Obeid from his southern Lebanon home. According to press reports, five Sayeret Matkal members were killed in 1992 at the Tse'elim base when a rehearsal of the assassination of Iraqi President Saddam Hussein turned deadly. In that instance, a guided missile was accidentally fired on the base.

Sayeret Matkal was at the center of a different kind of controversy in 2003, when 13 of its members presented the prime minister with a resignation letter, saying that they refused to continue assisting "the reign of oppression in the territories." The letter was widely condemned by the Israeli military, and the 13 were expelled from the unit.

In 2006, during the Second Lebanon War, Sayeret Matkal undertook Operation Sharp and Smooth, intended to disrupt weapons smuggling. The operation was discovered, however, and one member was killed and two others wounded. The following year, Sayeret Matkal was believed to be involved reconnaissance missions in Syria, including the collection of soil samples, that preceded Operation Orchard, the bombing of a Syrian nuclear reactor.

Erica Pearson

See also Counterterrorism; Mossad

Further Readings

Bruck, Connie. "The Commando: Ehud Barak Took Huge Risks and Trusted No One: Now He Is Alone." *New Yorker*, April 17, 2000.

Goodman, Hirsh. "How the Israelis Snatched the Sheik." *U.S. News & World Report*, August 14, 1989.

Pedahzur, Ami. *The Israeli Secret Services and the Struggle against Terrorism*. New York: Columbia University Press, 2010.

Zonder, Moshe. *Sayeret Matkal*. Jerusalem: Keter, 2000.

SCUTARI, RICHARD (1947–)

The head of security for the white supremacist group known as The Order, Richard Scutari was the last to be brought to justice after a FBI investigation led to the group's downfall.

Born on April 30, 1947, Scutari lived in Port Jefferson, New York, until 1956, when his family moved to Florida. He dropped out of high school to join the navy, where he learned how to dive. After leaving the military, he worked as a diver until 1979, when he started a construction business with his brother. He joined the American Pistol and Rifle Association (APRA), a survivalist gun club, and while attending a national meeting in 1980 he was introduced to the race-based theology known as Christian Identity.

Scutari started a local unit of the APRA, and throughout the early 1980s he taught shooting and combat in Port Salerno, Florida. In 1982 he was invited to the compound of The Covenant, the Sword, and the Arm of the Lord (CSA), a survivalist group that practiced Christian Identity, to teach hand-to-hand combat. That same year, his construction business failed. In 1983, when Andrew Barnhill offered him a month's salary to come to Washington State and join him in The Order, he accepted.

The Order's founder, Robert Jay Mathews, used Scutari's knowledge of the voice stress analyzer to interview potential recruits and screen for informants. Mathews assigned him the code name "Mr. Black" and made him the head of internal security. Although Scutari joined the group relatively late, informants later testified that he participated in much of its criminal activity, including the June 1984 assassination of Alan Berg, a Denver radio talk show host. Scutari and Mathews served as lookouts while Order member Bruce Pierce did the actual shooting and David Lane drove the getaway car. Scutari also took part in the robbery of an armored car in Ukiah, California, that netted the group $3.8 million.

As head of security, Scutari developed a system of rules, code names, and contact telephone numbers. With his share of the Ukiah robbery money, he purchased sophisticated equipment, including a second voice stress analyzer, surveillance equipment, and telephone scramblers. Often ridiculed by other Order members because of his swarthy complexion, he eventually became Mathews's most trusted confidant and adviser.

Scutari tried to convince Mathews to drop Thomas Martinez as a member when Martinez refused to take a voice stress test. Martinez claimed it was too dangerous to meet with Scutari and Mathews because he was under surveillance. In fact, Martinez was cooperating with federal agents and feared he wouldn't be able to pass the test. Fortunately for him, Mathews did not take Scutari's advice. Martinez later played a crucial role in the downfall of both Mathews and The Order.

In November 1984, with the FBI on their trail, Scutari, Mathews, and other members of The Order fled to Whidbey Island off the coast of Washington State. Although Mathews was killed during a stand-off with authorities on the island, Scutari and other members had earlier managed to escape the FBI's net. Eventually making the FBI's "Most Wanted" list, Scutari was the last Order member to be taken into custody. He was arrested on March 1986, while all the others had been arrested by April 1985. Scutari was traced through an alias while working as a garage mechanic in San Antonio, Texas. Although Scutari had previously vowed that he would not be taken alive, he was arrested without incident.

Scutari pled guilty to most of the charges against him but denied any involvement in the Berg assassination. He was sentenced to 60 years in prison for robbery, racketeering, and conspiracy. After his involvement in a violent incident during a prison football game, Scutari was transferred to the federal supermax prison in Florence, Colorado. Scutari has converted to Odinism, a white supremacist religion based on Nordic myths. He has remained active in the white supremacist movement, writing articles and granting interviews to the like-minded, and continuing to maintain that he is a political prisoner.

Nancy Egan

See also Christian Identity; Mathews, Robert Jay; Order, The; *Turner Diaries, The*; White Supremacy Movement

Further Readings

Extremism on the Right: A Handbook. Rev. ed. New York: Anti-Defamation League of B'nai B'rith, 1988.

Flynn, Kevin, and Gary Gerhardt. *The Silent Brotherhood: Inside America's Racist Underground*. New York: Free Press, 1989.

"Richard Scutari." Anti-Defamation League. http://www .adl.org/learn/ext_us/scutari.asp.

"White Supremacist on Most-wanted List." *The New York Times*, October 1, 1985, late city final edition. http://www.nytimes.com/1985/10/01/us/around-the-nation-white-supremacist-on-most-wanted-list.html.

SENDERO LUMINOSO

See Shining Path

SEPTEMBER 11 ATTACKS

On September 11, 2001, 19 members of al Qaeda hijacked four passenger airplanes in the United States. Two of the planes were deliberately crashed into New York City's World Trade Center, one was flown into the Pentagon, near Washington, D.C., and one crashed into a field in western Pennsylvania. The attacks, which killed approximately 3,000 people, targeted two potent symbols of U.S. military and economic might: the Pentagon, which houses the nation's military leadership, and the World Trade Center, which symbolized U.S. global financial power. The United States responded with a military campaign in Afghanistan to destroy the al Qaeda network, whose leader, Osama bin Laden, had found sanctuary in that country with the radical Islamic Taliban government.

The September 11 attacks were extraordinarily deadly. Instead of killing dozens, a more typical toll for a terrorist attack, they killed thousands. They also demonstrated the perils of the nation's relatively relaxed approach to security, as the terrorists took over the airplanes using knives and box cutters that were in their carry-on baggage.

Plotting and Paying

The attacks took years to plan and between $400,000 and $500,000 to execute, all provided by al Qaeda. The plot originated with Khalid Shaikh Mohammed, a jihadist born in Kuwait who had had a hand in earlier terrorist activity in the Philippines and who had helped financially with the bombing of the World Trade Center in 1993. That attack, carried out by Mohammed's nephew, Ramzi Yousef, killed 6 people and injured more than 1,000. It had also convinced Mohammed that bombs could be problematic and that a new form of attack should be employed for maximum devastation. He also claims that he and Yousef had begun entertaining the idea of using airliners as weapons when they were plotting attacks in the Philippines.

In 1996, during a meeting in Tora Bora, Afghanistan, Khalid Shaikh Mohammed brought his idea of using hijacked airliners as missiles to destroy American targets to bin Laden. According to Mohammed, the 1998 bombings of the U.S. embassies in Nairobi and Dar es Salaam provided a turning point in the plotting of 9/11, because they removed any doubt that bin Laden was serious about attacking the United States. Mohammed was given the green light for the 9/11 operation in late 1998 or early 1999. After bin Laden approved the operation, he, Mohammed, and the alleged al Qaeda military chief Muhammad Atef came up with a list of targets—bin Laden wanted to hit the White House and the Pentagon, Khalid Shaikh Mohammed wanted to strike the World Trade Center, and all three men wanted to hit the Capitol building.

The hijackers, 15 of whom were citizens of Saudi Arabia (as was bin Laden), and other conspirators were apparently brought together by their embrace of radical Islam and their hatred of the United States. Most of the hijackers, perhaps all, spent time in al Qaeda training camps in Afghanistan, and some may have met there.

Three of the hijackers—Mohamed Atta, Marwan al Shehhi, and Ziad Jarrah—came to Afghanistan via Hamburg, Germany, where as students they had formed a radical Islamist cell dedicated to violent jihad against the United States. They left Germany for Afghanistan in late 1999 and, following instructions given by a contact in Germany, met Atef and bin Laden and were quickly brought into the operation, with Atta designated as an operational leader. The 9/11 plot was once believed to have originated

with the Hamburg cell, but it is now believed that Atta, Shehhi, and Jarrah were not involved in the initial planning and were only brought in after meeting Atef and bin Laden, who believed that, on top of the men's anti-American fervor, their fluency in English and familiarity with life in the West made them very attractive candidates for the operation.

In late 1999, Atta, Shehhi, and Jarrah all reported their travel documents missing to the German police and were issued new ones; they then applied for travel visas to the United States. Investigators believe that reporting the documents stolen was a ploy to get "clean" travel documents, ones without visa stamps indicating that the men had traveled to Afghanistan.

By mid-2000, Atta, Shehhi, and Jarrah had all received the appropriate visas and had moved to the United States. Ramzi bin al Shibh, another aspiring jihadist from the German contingent, encountered difficulties, however. From May to October 2000, he applied four times for a visa to enter the United States, but his request was denied each time. In December 2000, bin al Shibh traveled to London, apparently to meet with Zacarias Moussaoui, a French-born ethnic Moroccan living in London, who had reportedly trained at an al Qaeda camp in Afghanistan in 1998. Moussaoui was able to obtain the proper visas and entered the United States in February 2001.

Atta, Shehhi, and Jarrah began meeting with Hani Hanjour, Nawaf al Hazmi, and Khalid al Mihdhar, all of whom lived in California. Mihdhar had been photographed speaking to a suspect in the October 2000 bombing of the American naval destroyer Cole in Yemen. In August 2001, Mihdhar and Hazmi were placed on a U.S. Federal Bureau of Investigation terrorist-alert list as associates of bin Laden. Nevertheless, the two were able to leave and reenter the United States at will before being placed on the list, and they were able to buy plane tickets in late August 2001 without triggering any security alerts.

Funding

Beginning in summer 2000, Atta and Shehhi began to receive large sums of money wired to them, from bin al Shibh or from a source in the United Arab Emirates. During this period, the six men lived in different parts of the United States and moved frequently. They attended flight schools in various states, purchased instruction videos on how to fly large aircraft, and made several trips out of the United States, apparently to contact al Qaeda cells abroad. Atta also made inquiries into starting crop-dusting companies in Florida; later, Moussaoui would do the same in Oklahoma.

By mid-2001, the rest of the hijackers—Abdulaziz al Omari, Wail al Shehri, Waleed al Shehri, Satam al Suqami, Fayez Ahmed Banihammad, Ahmed al Ghamdi, Hamza al Ghamdi, Mohand al Shehri, Salem al Hazmi, Majed Moqed, Ahmed al Haznawi, Saaed al Ghamdi, and Ahmed al Nami—had entered the United States.

This group did not seek flight instruction, since their role in the operation would be as "muscle." Their job would be to overpower the passengers and crew, enabling the pilot hijackers to take control of the cockpit. Instead of enrolling in flight school, they joined gyms and purchased knives. Several opened bank accounts in Florida, and one, Fayez Ahmed Banihammad, also opened a bank account in the United Arab Emirates. Ahmed gave power of attorney over that account to Mustafa Ahmed al Hawsawi, who is believed to have handled much of the finances linked to the attack. Hawsawi sent credit and automatic teller cards to Banihammad.

Putting the Plan Into Action

The hijackers continued to move around, meeting together as a group at least once in Las Vegas. They lived cheaply, with one exception: Periodically some of the hijackers would take a first-class plane flight, apparently as practice runs for the September 11 attacks.

On August 17, 2001, Moussaoui was arrested in Minnesota. Moussaoui, who had more than $30,000 in cash when he entered the United States the previous February, had attended the Airman Flight School in Norman, Oklahoma. He was an exceptionally poor student, and eventually left Airman. After being wired $14,000 by bin al Shibh in Germany, Moussaoui moved to Minneapolis, Minnesota, and began attending Pan Am International Flight Academy.

At Pan Am, Moussaoui quickly attracted the notice of his teachers. He was secretive about his background, and he had paid the $6,300 fee in cash. Obviously incompetent even with small air-planes, Moussaoui nevertheless insisted that he learn to fly a Boeing 747. His instructors contacted

the FBI, and on August 16 Moussaoui was arrested. His arrest, however, did not derail the plot. Federal investigators found no evidence of wrongdoing, except that Moussaoui had overstayed his visa. He was jailed on immigration charges, and the plan proceeded without him.

In late August, the hijackers bought first-class tickets aboard four flights: American Airlines Flight 11, United Airlines Flight 175, American Airlines Flight 77, and United Airlines Flight 93.

Investigators believe that the hijackers traveled first class to be closer to the cockpits. The flights were apparently chosen with great care. They were all nonstop, cross-country flights and thus had full fuel tanks; they took off at about the same time; and they were all either Boeing 767 or Boeing 757 models, which have similar cockpit designs. The terrorists, who had purchased instruction videos on flying such airplanes, knew enough about them to disable the transponders on two of the planes to prevent them from being tracked from the ground.

In the days preceding the attacks, the hijackers wired money to the United Arab Emirates. Investigators believe that these were excess funds that were returned to al Qaeda. Ramzi bin al Shibh left Germany for Spain, then disappeared after the attacks until he was captured by the FBI on September 11, 2002, in Karachi; Hawsawi left the United Arab Emirates for Pakistan on the day of the attack; he was captured on March 1, 2003, in Pakistan. In the United States, the hijackers split up into small groups and traveled to different cities, apparently to avoid notice.

September 11

On the morning of September 11, 2001, Flight 11 and Flight 175 both departed from Logan Airport in Boston—Flight 11 at about 8 A.M., Flight 175 about 15 minutes later. Atta, Omari, Suqami, Wail al Shehri, and Waleed al Shehri were aboard Flight 11. On Flight 175 were Shehhi, Banihammad, Mohand al Shehri, Ahmed al Ghamdi, and Hamza al Ghamdi. Just before Flight 11 took off, Atta used his cell phone to call Shehhi, and the two conversed briefly.

Shortly after the two airplanes reached cruising altitude, the hijackers struck. As far as can be determined from cell-phone calls made by crew members and passengers, the hijackers attacked crew members and passengers with knives and box

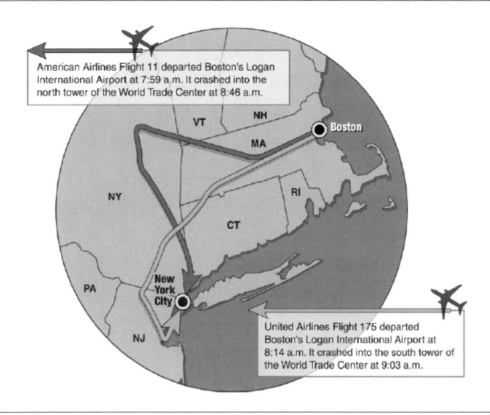

Flight paths of the two airplanes that crashed into the Twin Towers of the World Trade Center in New York City. (FEMA.gov)

Urban search-and-rescue specialists continue to search for survivors among the wreckage at the World Trade Center in New York City, September 13, 2001. (Photo by Andrea Booher/FEMA News Photo)

cutters, wounding those who resisted. They forced open the cockpit doors and disabled or killed the pilots. Then the hijackers with flight training took over the planes, while the rest of the team kept the passengers and crew at bay.

Instead of heading to Los Angeles, the planes turned south, flying toward New York City and the World Trade Center. At 8:48 A.M., Flight 11 flew into the north tower of the 110-story World Trade Center from the north. At 9:06 A.M., Flight 175, approaching from the south, crashed into the south tower.

The towers initially withstood the impact of the crashes. But the fuel in the jets poured into the buildings and ignited. Thousands of workers in the lower floors began evacuating, but those in the upper floors were trapped by the intense heat and choking smoke. Some managed to telephone relatives before they perished. Eyewitnesses on the ground saw people jump from windows to their death to escape the flames.

Jet fuel burns at temperatures high enough to soften steel, and the building's steel supports

collapsed. Just before 10:00 A.M., the south tower collapsed, killing all but a handful of the office workers and rescue personnel inside. Less than 30 minutes later, the north tower went down. Several nearby buildings were seriously damaged, with one collapsing completely, and the subway, train, telephone, and electricity systems in the area all suffered heavy damage. More than 2,900 people died in the attack, including hundreds of rescue workers and the 147 passengers and crew on Flights 11 and 175, but the fire was so hot and the destruction so complete that incomplete remains of only 1,845 people were recovered as of June 2010.

The Pentagon

At about the time Flights 11 and 175 were hitting the World Trade Center, Hanjour, Mihdhar, Moqed, Nawaf al Hazmi, and Salem al Hazmi were hijacking Flight 77 somewhere west of Indiana. The flight had departed Dulles International Airport in Virginia for Los Angeles at about 8:20 A.M. After disabling the transponder, the hijackers turned the

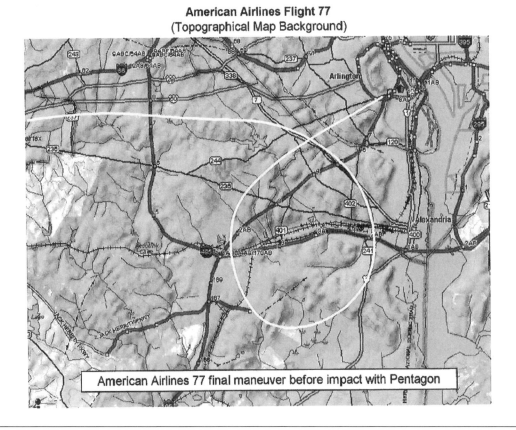

American Airlines Flight 77
(Topographical Map Background)

American Airlines 77 final maneuver before impact with Pentagon

Flight path of the airplane that crashed into the Pentagon in Virginia, near Washington, D.C. (Map courtesy of National Transportation Safety Board)

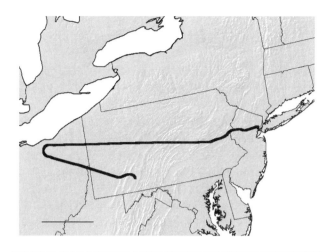

Flight path of the fourth hijacked airplane. United Airlines Flight 93 departed from Newark International Airport at 8:01 A.M. The plane crashed in an open field near Stony Creek Township, Pennsylvania, at 10:10 A.M. (Map courtesy of National Transportation Safety Board)

plane east toward Washington, D.C. By 9:30 A.M., federal authorities realized that the third hijacked plane was flying toward Washington. The White House and the Capitol were evacuated, and military planes were sent to intercept the hijacked airliner.

Minutes later, however, Flight 77 crashed into the southwest side of the Pentagon in nearby Arlington, Virginia. The impact and resulting fire destroyed parts of three of the Pentagon's five concentric rings, killing 125 people in the building and all 59 passengers and crew on board the plane.

The toll could have been far greater. That area of the Pentagon, which contained the offices of army and navy operations personnel, was under renovation, and many of the offices were empty. The renovations had fortified the building to withstand a bomb attack, so the damage to the building was not as great as it might have been. None of the U.S. senior military leaders were lost.

The Fourth Airplane

Flight 93 was the latest of the four flights, leaving Newark International Airport in New Jersey for San Francisco at 8:45 A.M. Unlike the other hijacked planes, Flight 93 had only four terrorists aboard: Jarrah, Haznawi, Saeed al Ghamdi, and Nami. Investigators believe that first bin al Shibh, and then Moussaoui, had been slated to be the fifth member of the hijacking team.

The flight traveled its normal route until it reached Ohio. It then turned back, presumably to strike another target in the Washington, D.C., area. Despite the smaller team, the Flight 93 hijackers were no less aggressive. At least one passenger was stabbed to death in the course of the hijacking, and the hijackers told the passengers they had a bomb on board.

Flight 93 was the last flight to be hijacked, however, and that worked against the terrorists. Several passengers on the flight had cell phones that they used to call family members and authorities, who told them what had happened to the other hijacked planes. Two passengers told family members that the passengers had decided to attack the hijackers and attempt to retake the plane.

At around 10:00 A.M., Flight 93 crashed into an empty field in western Pennsylvania. The passengers' resistance cost them their lives—all 40 passengers and crew were killed—but they did not act in vain. Unlike the other hijacked planes, Flight 93 destroyed no buildings and caused no fatalities on the ground.

All air traffic was ordered grounded; planes landed at the nearest airports and remained there, and thousands of passengers were stranded. The investigation began immediately. Officials at Boston's Logan Airport discovered that Atta's luggage did not make it on to Flight 11. The luggage contained Atta's will, flight-instruction videotapes, and a five-page handwritten letter instructing the hijackers on how to comport themselves. Copies of the letter were found in a car registered to Nawaf al-Hazmi parked at Dulles Airport, and in the wreckage of Flight 93.

The War on Terrorism

Soon after the attacks, U.S. President George W. Bush declared a "war on terror," warning countries that harbored terrorists that they would face the full power of the U.S. military. The United States charged al Qaeda with responsibility for the attacks and demanded that the Taliban turn over bin Laden and the al Qaeda leadership and dismantle the terrorist training camps in Afghanistan. The Taliban denied that bin Laden was responsible. In October, the United States launched an attack on the Taliban and terrorists within Afghanistan; its allies were Great Britain and anti-Taliban forces in Afghanistan.

The Taliban government quickly collapsed and many al Qaeda leaders, although not bin Laden, were captured or killed. Authorities in several countries arrested alleged members of al Qaeda, but the international network was not eradicated. The role bin Laden played in enabling the attacks appeared to be confirmed by videotapes in which he said that the September 11 attacks had been even more destructive than he had hoped they would be.

In response to both attacks, security was considerably tightened on airplanes, in buildings, and in public areas. U.S. authorities detained hundreds of people whose actions or immigration status made them appear questionable, and President Bush created special military tribunals to try foreign nationals accused of terrorism. Such measures led to intense debates between those who considered them necessary and those who considered them an overreaction. Despite campaign promises to the contrary, President Barack Obama largely kept in place the Bush-era policies related to the detention of suspected terrorists after he took office in 2008. After a manhunt of almost 10 years, bin Laden was finally killed by U.S. Navy SEALs in May 2011.

By December 2001, various detainees had been cleared, and only one, Moussaoui, faced charges stemming from the attacks. Moussaoui, a French citizen, faced charges in a civilian rather than a military court. In a federal court in Virginia, Moussaoui was charged on six counts of conspiracy in the attacks; four of those counts carried the possibility of the death penalty. In May 2006, Moussaoui was convicted and sentenced to life in prison without the possibility of parole.

Attorney General Eric Holder likewise intended for Khalid Shaikh Mohammed and his co-conspirators to be tried in a civilian court in New York. However, in April 2011, Holder announced that Mohammed would be tried in a military court. The change was due not only to staunch opposition but also to intense uneasiness on the part of the general public with the idea of allowing the mastermind of the 9/11 attacks to face trial just blocks from the towers he helped destroy.

Mary Sisson

See also Airport Security; al Qaeda; Anthrax; Atta, Mohamed; bin Laden, Osama; Hijacking; Mohammed, Khalid Shaikh; Moussaoui, Zacarias; Taliban

Further Readings

Bergen, Peter. *Holy War, Inc.: Inside the Secret World of Osama bin Laden.* New York: Free Press, 2001.

Bergen, Peter. *The Longest War: Inside the Enduring Conflict between America and al-Qaeda.* New York: Free Press, 2011.

Bergen, Peter. *The Osama bin Laden I Know: An Oral History of al Qaeda's Leader.* New York: Free Press, 2007.

Clarke, Richard. *Against All Enemies: Inside America's War on Terror.* New York: Free Press, 2004.

Griffith, Victoria, et al. "The Hijackers' Tale: How the Men of September 11 Went Unnoticed." *Financial Times,* November 30, 2001, p. 11.

Gunaratna, Rohan. *Inside al Qaeda: Global Network of Terror.* New York: Columbia University Press, 2002.

Kleinfield, N. R. "U.S. Attacked: Hijacked Jets Destroy Twin Towers and Hit Pentagon in Day of Terror." *The New York Times,* September 12, 2001, p. A1.

Mahajan, Rahul. *The New Crusade: America's War on Terrorism.* New York: Monthly Review Press, 2002.

National Commission on Terrorist Attacks upon the United States. *The 9/11 Commission Report: Final Report of the National Commission on Terrorist Attacks upon the United States.* New York: W.W. Norton, 2004. http://www.9-11commission.gov.

Reeve, Simon. *The New Jackals: Ramzi Yousef, Osama bin Laden and the Future of Terrorism.* Boston: Northeastern University Press, 1999.

Riedel, Bruce. *The Search for al Qaeda: Its Leadership, Ideology, and Future.* Washington, DC: Brookings Institution Press, 2008.

Snow, Donald. *September 11, 2001: The New Face of War?* New York: Pearson Higher Education, 2001.

Talbott, Strobe, and Nayan Chanda. *The Age of Terror: America and the World after September 11.* New York: Basic Books, 2001.

Wald, Matthew L. "Controllers Say Flow of Information on Hijacked Planes' Course Was Slow and Uneven." *The New York Times,* September 13, 2001, p. A5.

Wright, Lawrence. *The Looming Tower: al Qaeda and the Road to 9/11.* New York: Alfred A. Knopf, 2006.

Zernike, Kate, and Don Van Natta Jr. "Hijackers' Meticulous Strategy of Brains, Muscle and Practice." *The New York Times,* November 4, 2001, p. A1.

17 NOVEMBER

See Revolutionary Organization 17 November

SHAKUR, ASSATA

See Chesimard, Joanne

SHALLAH, RAMADAN ABDULLAH (1958–)

Dr. Ramadan Abdullah Shallah, a former part-time professor at the University of South Florida in Tampa, made national headlines in 1995 when he left his job in the United States to lead the militant group Palestine Islamic Jihad (PIJ). The PIJ was founded in Egypt in the late 1970s by Palestinian students but is now based in Syria.

Born in 1958 in the Gaza Strip, which was then under Egyptian administration, Shallah taught economics at the University of Gaza in the mid-1980s. He attended university in Zagazig, Egypt, and received a doctoral degree in Islamic and Middle Eastern studies from England's University of Durham in 1990, writing many articles on the economics of Middle Eastern countries. He speaks Arabic, Hebrew, English, and a little Yiddish.

Shallah arrived in Tampa, Florida, in 1991 and spent four years teaching political science at the University of South Florida. He was a well-liked professor, known for being a soft-spoken intellectual. He also worked for a think tank called World Islamic Studies Enterprise. In several controversial articles, the *Tampa Tribune* called the think tank a terrorist front, and its founder, Sami al Arian, was called the group's front man. The FBI arrested al Arian on racketeering charges for alleged involvement with the PIJ. After several years of detention, al Arian was indicted on multiple counts in 2003; the trial was underway when he pled guilty on one count of conspiracy.

Shallah did not publicly claim any link to the PIJ during his academic career, and his possible covert actions are unknown. The PIJ is a loosely knit, mysterious group known for its violence and its opposition to peace negotiations with Israel.

In October 1995, gunmen said to be working for Israel shot down the PIJ leader, Dr. Fathi Shaqaqi, in the Mediterranean island of Malta. The group then named Shallah its new leader. The following spring, an unknown group called War Purgers sent a bomb threat to the University of South Florida's campus newspaper. The letter demanded a public apology for Shallah's treatment and threatened to bomb a building and kill a professor. In response, the university moved up the date of final exams to enable students to be off campus by the date set in the letter. No attacks occurred, and a student pleaded guilty to making the threats in December 1996.

As Middle East violence began to escalate in 2000, the PIJ carried out many suicide bombings and other attacks against Israelis, and Shallah publicly endorsed the bombings. In December 2001, the Palestinian leader Yasir Arafat called for a stop to the attacks. Shallah told the London newspaper *El Hayat* that he would not follow Arafat's demand, and that he planned to direct his organization to continue carrying out the bombings. In 2002 the group took responsibility for a bus bombing in which 17 Israelis were killed.

Shallah and al Arian and were among eight people indicted in February 2003 on 53 charges of racketeering and conspiracy to murder, maim, or injure persons outside the United States. According to reports, the PIJ has grown increasingly close to Hamas, as the two groups' methods and long-term goals have converged. In a 2009 interview, Shallah stated, "I cannot speak for Hamas. But I will never, under any conditions, accept the existence of the state of Israel. . . . Never. Ever. I hope that is clear enough."

Under the Rewards for Justice program, the United States has offered $5 million for the capture of Shallah, now based in Syria and on the FBI's Most Wanted Terrorist list.

Erica Pearson

See also Hamas; Palestine Islamic Jihad; Rewards for Justice

Further Readings

Atran, Scott, and Robert Axelrod. "Interview with Ramadan Shallah, Secretary General, Palestinian Islamic Jihad." *Perspectives on Terrorism: A Journal of the Terrorism Research Initiative* 4, no. 2 (May 2010): 3–8. http://www.terrorismanalysts.com.

Emerson, Steven. *Jihad Incorporated: A Guide to Militant Islam in the US.* Amherst, NY: Prometheus Books, 2006.

Fechter, Michael. "Court Hands Al-Najjar 1 Victory but Says He Can Be Kept in Jail." *Tampa Tribune,* November 30, 2001, p. 10.

"Islamic Jihad Says Suicide Attacks on Israelis Will Go On." *AP Worldstream,* December 23, 2001.

"Jihad's New Man May Have Tampa Ties." *St. Petersburg Times,* October 31, 1995, p. 1A.

Niebuhr, Gustav. "Professor Talked of Understanding but Now Reveals Ties to Terrorists." *The New York*

Times, November 13, 1995. http://www.nytimes
.com/1995/11/13/us/professor-talked-of-
understanding-but-now-reveals-ties-to-terrorists.html.

Sachs, Susan. "Terrorism Inc.; Islamic Jihad Founder Admits
Funding by Iran." *Newsday,* April 11, 1993, p. 7.

SHIGENOBU, FUSAKO (1945–)

A wing of the Japanese Red Army (JRA) founded by Fusako Shigenobu was responsible for a series of terrorist attacks, including a 1972 attack on Ben Gurion Airport (now Lod Airport) in Tel Aviv.

Born in Tokyo, Japan, Fusako Shigenobu was an active student member of the Red Army Faction (Sekigun-ha) in the 1960s, while she was working part-time for the Kikkoman Corporation and going to night school at Meiji University. The Red Army, a radical leftist group, wanted to drive out the democratic government and end American involvement in the country so that Japan could become a communist state. The group split into several factions, and in 1971 Shigenobu left Japan to travel in Europe, where she came into contact with members of the Popular Front for the Liberation of Palestine (PFLP). She and a handful of followers went to Lebanon to join forces with the PFLP, foreshadowing the origination of the Japanese Red Army (Nihon Sekigun).

The early actions of Shigenobu's faction included kidnappings, murders, and hijackings, mostly on behalf of the PFLP. The deadliest attack was a machine gun and grenade attack at the Ben Guiron Airport in Tel Aviv in 1972. The JRA killed 26 people in the attack, including 16 Americans. Then, in 1974, the JRA invaded the French Embassy in The Hague, took the French ambassador and 10 others hostage, and demanded the release of several incarcerated Red Army members. Shigenobu was thought to be the mastermind of the plan, causing authorities to add her to the international list of wanted terrorists.

One infamous story about Shigenobu involves her ordering the murder of a fellow JRA member who was considered overly "bourgeois." The condemned woman, who was pregnant at the time, was reportedly buried alive. The incident solidified Shigenobu's reputation as a leader of the JRA.

The JRA was responsible for many terrorist attacks in the 1970s and 1980s, including the takeover of the U.S. embassy in Kuala Lumpur in 1975, the hijacking of a flight bound from Japan to Paris in 1977, and the seizure of the U.S. and British embassies in Rome in 1987. Four of the terrorists involved in the hijacking of a Japan Airlines plane in 1970 are believed to be in North Korea, which granted them asylum. The question remains one of several issues hindering the normalization of diplomatic relations between Pyongyang and Tokyo. The activities and strength of the JRA decreased in the 1990s due to the fall of the Soviet Union, the advancements made toward peace in the Middle Eastern conflict, and the capture of many members.

By the late 1990s, police had been tipped off that Shigenobu had returned to Japan and was consorting with other members of the group in order to strengthen their support bases. On November 8, 2000, the 55-year-old Shigenobu was finally apprehended in Osaka, Japan, and brought to Tokyo for trial. In a statement made from prison, she proclaimed that she would continue to pursue the goals of the JRA, but now through a legitimate political party instead of a terrorist organization. In February

Japanese Red Army founder Fusako Shigenobu, shown in this undated photo, was sentenced to 20 years by Tokyo District Court on February 23, 2006, for kidnapping and attempted murder in a 1974 attack on the French Embassy in The Hague. Shigenobu was arrested in Japan in November 2000 after more than 25 years on the run, part of it in the Middle East. (AP Photo/Kyodo News. © 2011 The Associated Press. All Rights Reserved)

2006, she was sentenced to 20 years in prison for her involvement in the 1974 kidnapping of French embassy workers in The Hague. Shigenobu underwent surgery for cancer in 2009.

Harvey Kushner

See also Black September; Japanese Red Army

Further Readings

Craig, John S. "The Japanese Red Army's Black Widow—Fusako Shigenobu." Associated Content, January 2, 2009. http://www.associatedcontent.com/article/1355527/the_japanese_red_armys_black_widow.html.

Farrell, William Regis. *Blood and Rage: The Story of the Japanese Red Army*. New York: Free Press, 1990.

"Japanese Red Army Leader Arrested." BBC News, November 8, 2000. http://news.bbc.co.uk/2/hi/asia-pacific/1012780.stm.

Morgan, Robin. *The Demon Lover*. New York: Washington Square Press, 1989.

SHINING PATH

The Shining Path, or Sendero Luminoso, is a communist guerrilla group founded in Ayacucho, Peru; in 1980, it began a terrorist campaign that almost brought down of the government of Peru.

The Shining Path takes its name from Peruvian Marxist leader Jose Carlos Mariategui, who once stated "Marxism-Leninism will open the shining path to revolution." The group's ideology, however, is Maoist. (Marxism posits that society must develop a group of urban, industrialized, class-conscious workers, the proletariat, before a communist revolution can be successful. Maoism, named for Chinese communist leader Mao Zedong, holds that an agrarian, preindustrial society can be transformed directly into a communist one by indoctrinating the peasantry and using them to spur revolution.) Inspired by China's Cultural Revolution, the group sought to destroy Peru's government and cultural institutions and create a perfect communist society, which would be led by a peasant dictatorship. Like the Khmer Rouge of Cambodia, the Shining Path regards civilian casualties as not only inevitable but desirable in furthering revolution, and it has specifically targeted doctors, relief workers, educators, and clergy in some of its campaigns.

At its peak, the group's structure was strictly hierarchical, with local cells or bands of guerrillas reporting to a regional council, which in turn reported to a central committee of up to 19 members. The group's founder and leader, Abimael Guzmán Reynoso, dictated the central committee's actions. A cult of personality existed around Guzmán, known to his followers as Comrade Gonzalo. The depth of devotion he inspired in his followers gave the group a quasi-religious character. Many Shining Path members believed they would inevitably be killed in action, and they considered themselves honored to die for the cause.

Sendero's origins can be traced to San Cristobal de Huamanga University, a local university in the remote, poverty-stricken, and mountainous province of Ayacucho, Peru. A philosophy professor at the university, Guzmán began holding informal political discussions with students and fellow teachers in the early 1960s. Reforms of the Peruvian educational system had led to increased university enrollment, especially in the provinces. A significant portion of these new students was of native Indian heritage, and many were the first in their families to have a chance for higher education.

From these early discussion groups would emerge the core of the Sendero leadership. By the late 1960s, the group had attracted a number of followers and formed a Maoist political party, the Communist Party of Peru. Guzmán's ideas were evolving and becoming progressively more radical; he began to advocate a bloody military uprising as the only legitimate form of revolution. In response, in the mid-1970s the group began to purchase weapons and train members in guerrilla warfare.

In May 1980, the Shining Path began its attacks in the Ayacucho area, burning the ballot boxes used in the presidential election. The group began to infiltrate Indian villages, often tailoring its operations to gain local support. For example, the group assassinated certain hated landowners and local criminals. The government first regarded the rebellion as insignificant and waited more than two years to crack down on the Shining Path. In December 1982 the government declared Ayacucho to be an emergency zone, and the military was sent to restore control at the beginning of 1983.

The guerrillas had by then established a base of operations and developed grassroots support, while Peru's political instability and worsening economic crisis rendered the government's moves ineffective. Unable to infiltrate the small, tightly organized terrorist cells, the military's attempts at repression—thousands of people accused of sympathizing with the guerrillas disappeared from military bases during the 1980s—only strengthened support for the Shining Path. As the organization grew, it gained control of coca-producing areas. The group demanded and received millions of dollars in protection fees from drug traffickers, and these funds enabled it to further expand its territory.

In 1988 Guzmán announced that the Shining Path, with an estimated 10,000 active members and more than half the population living in areas under its control, would now move in a new direction and bring the revolution from the countryside into the cities, in particular the capital, Lima. The ongoing violence in the countryside had driven an estimated 100,000 migrants from their Andes villages to Lima's ever-expanding slums on the outskirts of the capital. Home to the poorest of Lima's 7 million residents, these slums proved fertile ground for the Shining Path, which plastered revolutionary slogans on walls, distributed propaganda, set up soup kitchens, and began an extensive bombing campaign in the capital. By 1992 the group's campaign had brought the country to the brink of anarchy.

Responding to the almost daily terrorists attacks that had paralyzed the capital, in April 1992, President Alberto Fujimori closed the congress, suspended the constitution, and gave the military sweeping powers to arrest and detain citizens, effectively putting the country under martial law. In September of that year, army commandoes raided a Sendero hideout and arrested 15 top commanders, including Guzmán.

Guzmán's arrest was a crushing blow to the Shining Path. Disorganization and desertion followed. The Fujimori government then passed a series of amnesty laws for former guerrillas, which led to the almost complete disintegration of the Shining Path by the mid-1990s.

People carry coffins containing the remains of the victims of a 1984 massacre during a funeral ceremony in Putis, Peru, on August 29, 2009. According to Peru's government-appointed truth commission, Peru's military massacred 123 people in the village of Putis in 1984, the largest mass slaying of the bloody standoff between Maoist Shining Path guerrillas and security forces. (AP Photo/Martin Mejia. © 2011 The Associated Press. All Rights Reserved)

In the 2000s, however, Sendero began staging a comeback. Attacks on an army barracks and police outpost during summer 2001 were attributed to Shining Path members, and the group retains strong links to the cocaine and heroin trades in the Andes. The group was implicated in a foiled plot to bomb the U.S. embassy in Lima in November 2001, causing the U.S. State Department to issue an advisory warning to U.S. travelers to avoid Peru. Peruvian authorities continued operations against the Shining Path in 2002, and Comrade Artemio, believed to be one of the group's active leaders, offered a truce to Peru's government.

The Shining Path, whose rebellion claimed nearly 70,000 victims according to a 2003 Truth and Reconciliation Committee report, resurfaced in 2008, when at least 26 people were killed by the group. Emerging from remote mountain reaches and swooping into isolated coca-producing hamlets to extort taxes from farmers, the rebels have contended with the military for control over territories and land, fueled by profits from Peru's thriving cocaine trade. In 2010 an alleged Shining Path leader named Teodoro Penadillo Carmen, also known as Comrade Rayo, was arrested in Lima, just days after several other members were killed by the military in an operation near the Huallaga River. Both the Peruvian and U.S. governments have offered rewards for information about Shining Path leaders still at large.

Colleen Sullivan

See also Reynoso, Abimael Guzmán

Further Readings

Collyns, Dan. "Peru Struggles with Its Dark Past." BBC News, December 10, 2007. http://news.bbc.co.uk/2/hi/americas/7132375.stm.

Gregory, Kathryn. *Backgrounder: Shining Path, Tupac Amaru*. Washington, DC: Council on Foreign Relations, August 27, 2009. http://www.cfr.org/publication/9276/shining_path_tupac_amaru_peru_leftists.html.

Kirk, Robin. *The Monkey's Paw: New Chronicles from Peru*. Amherst: University of Massachusetts Press, 1997.

McClintock, Cynthia. *Revolutionary Movements in Latin America: El Salvador's FMLN and Peru's Shining Path*. Washington, DC: United States Institute of Peace Press, 1998.

Palmer, David Scott. *The Shining Path of Peru*. New York: St. Martin's, 1994.

Rochlin, James F. *Vanguard Revolutionaries in Latin America: Peru, Colombia, Mexico*. Boulder, CO: Lynne Rienner, 2003.

Stern, Steve J., ed. *Shining and Other Paths: War and Society in Peru, 1980–1995*. Durham, NC: Duke University Press, 1998.

Strong, Simon. *Shining Path: Terror and Revolution in Peru*. New York: Times Books, 1992.

SIKH TERRORISM

Terrorist acts by militant Sikhs, members of a religion that began in northern India in the 1500s, reached a peak in the 1980s with the assassination of Prime Minister Indira Gandhi of India and the bombing of Air India Flight 182. Militants have attacked the Indian government because Sikhs want an independent homeland. In addition, many acts of Sikh terrorism were committed as revenge for a 1984 attack by the Indian military on the Golden Temple in Amritsar, the holiest of Sikh shrines. Militant Sikhs have also targeted moderates and critics in the Sikh community and members of nontraditional or minority Sikh sects.

The vast majority of Sikhs live in India, although substantial Sikh communities can be found in the United States, Canada, and Great Britain. Most Sikhs in India live in the northwestern state of Punjab, where they constitute a narrow majority. For the first half of the nineteenth century, this area was an independent Sikh kingdom, until it was conquered by the British in 1849. When India and Pakistan became independent nations in 1947, Sikhs agitated for the creation of either an independent Sikh state or an autonomous Sikh entity within India. Although no such state was created, the borders of Punjab were eventually redrawn to create a Sikh-majority state. A Sikh political party, the Akali Dal, was created to promote greater political autonomy for Sikhs.

No single group has come to dominate militant Sikhism—by 1990 even the Panthic Committee, an umbrella organization of Sikh militants, had splintered into three factions. But radical Sikh groups generally trace their roots to a single individual, Jarnail Singh Bhindranwale. Bhindranwale, the leader of a Sikh fundamentalist sect and a fiery orator, who rose to prominence in the mid-1970s. In 1977, a party coalition, including the Akali Dal, came to power in Punjab, defeating India's then-dominant Congress Party, led by Indira Gandhi. In an effort to gain popularity among Sikhs, the Congress Party began to support Bhindranwale.

In 1978, followers of Bhindranwale battled with members of a small Sikh sect, and at least 18 people died in the fighting. Bhindranwale and his followers gathered arms and turned their religious center into a fortress. On September 9, 1981, the chief editor of a chain of newspapers harshly critical of Bhindranwale was assassinated, and police arrested Bhindranwale at his fortress. Bhindranwale's followers embarked on a month-long campaign of violence to obtain his release, attacking Hindus, derailing trains, and even hijacking an Air India plane.

Bhindranwale was released from prison on October 14, 1981. He appeared so powerful that even the Akali Dal attempted a rapprochement. Bhindranwale was able to assume effective control of the All-India Sikh Students Federation, a large youth organization. In April 1983 a high-ranking police officer was assassinated in front of the Golden Temple in broad daylight, apparently on Bhindranwale's orders. Once again, however, he was not prosecuted.

Murders of individuals rapidly gave way to massacres. In October 1983, six Hindu bus passengers were slaughtered by Sikh militants, leading the Indian government to impose emergency rule in Punjab. To avoid arrest, Bhindranwale moved himself and his followers into the Golden Temple.

While Bhindranwale usually insisted that his goal was simply to ensure that Sikhs were treated fairly in Indian society, many of his followers stated that their goals included the establishment of an independent Sikh nation, usually called Khalistan, which translates as "land of the pure." Some nonviolent groups also supported the establishment of Khalistan, but for the rest of 1983 and the first half of 1984, violence continued in Punjab, generally targeted against Bhindranwale's Sikh rivals and critics, as well as Hindus. Indian government officials became convinced that Bhindranwale was directing assaults out of the Golden Temple. In early June 1984, India launched Operation Bluestar, a military assault against the temple as

well as other Sikh places of worship throughout Punjab. The assault killed hundreds, including Bhindranwale and the leader of the All-India Sikh Students Federation, Bhai Amrik Singh.

Intended to put an end to Sikh terrorism, Operation Bluestar had the opposite effect. Many militants were killed or arrested in the assault, but so were many unarmed religious pilgrims who had come to the Golden Temple to worship. That the Indian government launched a military attack on a deeply sacred place profoundly offended many Sikhs. Sikh attacks on Hindus in Punjab escalated, with Indian officials becoming targets and violence spilling over the state's borders. On October 31, 1984, Gandhi, who had ordered the attack on the Golden Temple, was gunned down by two of her Sikh bodyguards as she walked from her home to her office in New Delhi.

The assassination led to anti-Sikh riots and a major government crackdown on Sikh militants that was widely criticized for its brutality. Events the following year raised the specter of a global network of Sikh terrorists. In June 1985, members of the militant organization Babbar Khalsa International living in Canada planted bombs on two Air India jetliners, killing more than 300 people. In mid-1988, outdoor markets in New Delhi were bombed. That year, an estimated 2,500 people were killed either by Sikh militants or Indian security forces, a toll that was matched or exceeded in each of the next three years.

By the early 1990s, however, many Sikh militant leaders had been captured or killed by Indian security forces. While the threat of Sikh terrorism seemed largely contained, Pakistan's Inter-Services Intelligence (ISI), which has been accused of supporting armed separatists in Indian-administered Kashmir and the northeastern region of the country, has promoted various militant groups, including the International Sikh Youth Federation (ISYF), believed to be the most active Sikh militant group based in Pakistan. In 2005, reports surfaced of a possible revival of Sikh militancy in Punjab, with signs of training programs having been established in Pakistan. Two bomb attacks in October 2007 heightened concerns that Sikh terrorism had returned: three people were killed when a bomb exploded at a Muslim shrine in Rajasthan, and just days later a bomb went off in a crowded cinema in Ludhiana, killing six. Meanwhile, the Indian government has continued to accuse Pakistan's ISI of providing assistance to Sikh militants.

Mary Sisson

See also Air India Flight 182 Bombing; Lashkar-e-Taiba

Further Readings

Das, Dilip K., and Peter C. Kratcoski. *Meeting the Challenges of Global Terrorism: Prevention, Control, and Recovery.* Lanham, MD: Lexington Books, 2003.

Deora, Man Singh, ed. *Aftermath of Operation Bluestar.* New Delhi: Anmol Publications, 1992.

Grossman, Patricia. *Punjab in Crisis: Human Rights in India.* New York: Human Rights Watch, 1991.

Kalbag, Chaitanya. "Bhindranwale Legacy: The Saint's Son." *Outlook India,* October 19, 2009.

O'Connell, Joseph T., et al. *Sikh History and Religion in the Twentieth Century.* Toronto: University of Toronto, 1988.

SIXTEENTH STREET BAPTIST CHURCH BOMBING

On September 15, 1963, a bomb exploded in a basement lounge of the Sixteenth Street Baptist Church in Birmingham, Alabama, killing four girls and injuring more than 20 others. Although authorities had sufficient evidence to prosecute several members of the Ku Klux Klan shortly after the bombing, nearly 40 years passed before all the suspects were brought to trial.

The church bombing occurred just 18 days after civil rights leaders had led the March on Washington, D.C., where Dr. Martin Luther King Jr. gave his "I Have a Dream" speech. In the 1960s, Birmingham was at the center of the civil rights struggle in the South, and the church was a vital part of Birmingham's African American community, serving both as the headquarters for local civil rights efforts and a frequent meeting place for activists.

Between 1947 and 1965, Birmingham experienced a series of more than 50 racially motivated bombings. Indeed, it was referred to as "Bombingham" following a particularly concentrated wave of bombings in the spring of 1963. One repeatedly bombed neighborhood became known as

"Dynamite Hill." Bomb threats at the Sixteenth Street Baptist Church were an "everyday occurrence," according to Rev. John H. Cross.

At 10:22 A.M. on Sunday, September 15, 1963, a dynamite bomb exploded while church members were readying themselves for the 11 A.M. service. Four girls—11-year-old Denise McNair, 14-year-old Carole Robertson, 14-year-old Cynthia Wesley, and 14-year-old Addie Mae Collins—were preparing for Sunday school in the church basement. All four were killed in the blast. Although Reverend Cross urged church members to return to their homes, many took to the streets, throwing rocks at passing cars driven by whites. By the end of the day, riots and fires had broken out throughout the city and two other black teenagers were dead.

On September 18, 1963, Martin Luther King Jr. gave the eulogy at the funeral of three of the girls, saying, "The deaths may well serve as the redemptive force that brings light to this dark city." The public outcry about the Sixteenth Street Church bombing was enormous. The bombing and the nation's horrified reaction made passage of the Civil Rights Act of 1964 much easier for members of Congress. This legislation ended lawful segregation in the South.

Investigations and Trials

Initially, after local authorities tried and failed to convince the public that the bombing was the work of "unknown black perpetrators," Robert "Dynamite Bob" Chambliss, a member of the Ku Klux Klan, was charged with illegal possession of dynamite. The charge was later dropped, making clear that local authorities would not pursue the case. The FBI then became involved. By 1965, a memorandum sent to J. Edgar Hoover, the director of the FBI, identified four Klansmen—Chambliss, Bobby Frank Cherry, Herman Frank Cash, and Thomas E. Blanton Jr.—as the key suspects. The Birmingham FBI office recommended prosecution. Hoover, however, twice blocked prosecution attempts, claiming that the chance of conviction would be "remote." In 1968 the FBI closed the case.

In 1971 the Alabama attorney general, Bill Baxley, reopened the case, and the FBI, following Hoover's death in 1972, contributed some

Civil rights leader Rev. Dr. Martin Luther King Jr. is followed by Rev. Fred Shuttlesworth, left, and Ralph Abernathy as they attend funeral services at the Sixth Avenue Baptist Church for three of the four black girls killed in a church explosion in Birmingham, Alabama, on September 18, 1963. (AP Photo. © 2011 The Associated Press. All Rights Reserved)

additional evidence. In September 1977, Chambliss was indicted on four counts of first-degree murder.

During the ensuing trial, Chambliss's niece, Elizabeth Cobbs, testified about her uncle's Ku Klux Klan activities. Cobbs stated that Chambliss was a member of "Klavern 13," also known as the "Cahaba Boys," a secretive militant group of Klansmen that had terrorized the black community in Birmingham for years and was suspected of many of the area bombings. Another witness placed Chambliss in a parked car across the street from the church in the hours before the explosion. On November 18, 1977, Chambliss, then 73 years old, was convicted of murder in the death of Denise McNair and sentenced to life in prison.

Although Baxley repeatedly asserted that others involved in the bombing would face prosecution, the case languished for more than two decades. In 1980, the Justice Department concluded that Hoover had actively blocked evidence that could have been used to convict the Klansmen in 1965, but no new charges were filed. Chambliss died in jail in 1985, never having publicly admitted to his role in the bombing. Three years later, the case was

briefly reopened when Gary Tucker, a suspect who was dying of cancer, admitted that he had helped set the bomb. Again, however, no new charges were filed. In 1994 another key suspect, Herman Frank Cash, died.

In July 1997, the FBI once again opened the investigation. A federal grand jury in Jefferson County, Alabama, began hearing evidence in October 1998. On May 4, 2000, Bobby Frank Cherry, in jail in Texas for raping his stepdaughter, turned down a deal in which he would receive probation in exchange for pleading guilty of transporting explosives across state lines. On May 17, 2000, he was extradited to Alabama, where he and Thomas Blanton Jr. surrendered to authorities. Both were indicted on four counts of first-degree murder and four counts of "universal malice."

A year later, Blanton was tried, convicted, and sentenced to life in prison for first-degree murder. Blanton's conviction relied heavily on dozens of conversations between Blanton and Mitchell Burns, a former Klansman turned FBI informant. These conversations were secretly recorded with a microphone planted by the FBI in Blanton's house in 1964. In May 2002, Cherry, at age 71, became the last Klansmen to be convicted for what is considered by many to be the worst incident in the civil rights struggle. He died while imprisoned in 2004. Meanwhile, additional investigations of Klan-related or civil rights era murders remained active. Authorities believe the chance to prosecute these crimes is running out, as many date back more than 40 years, and most of the accused were middle-aged men at the time of the crimes and are now near the end of their lives.

Laura Lambert

See also Ku Klux Klan

Further Readings

Anderson, Susan W. and Jacquelyn D. Hall. *The Past on Trial: The Sixteenth Street Baptist Church Bombing, Civil Rights Memory, and the Remaking of Birmingham.* Chapel Hill: University of North Carolina Press, 2008.

Hamlin, Rev. Dr. Christopher M. *Behind the Stained Glass: A History of the Sixteenth Street Baptist Church.* Birmingham, AL: Crane Hill Press, 1998.

Sikora, Frank. *Until Justice Rolls Down: The Birmingham Church Bombing Case.* Tuscaloosa: University of Alabama Press, 1991.

SKINHEADS

In the late 1980s, shaven-headed youths called "skinheads" espoused white supremacist and neo-Nazi ideologies and became the media's latest folk devil. Racist skinheads appeared as the villains in movies, police dramas, and TV talk shows, going so far as breaking one host's nose in a 1988 brawl on the *Geraldo Rivera Show.* The characterization of skinheads as "racist terrorists" can be misleading, as skinheads come in many varieties and engage in various levels of skinhead activity. Nevertheless, since the 1980s, skinheads have routinely been linked to hate crimes, political extremism, and bias-motivated terror.

The lifestyle known as "skinhead" emerged from the plethora of British youth subcultures in the late 1960s. Amid well-documented groups, such as mods and rockers, skinheads appeared as, essentially, a working-class response to the more middle-class hippies. Their style and ideology were designed to be polar opposites of those of the hippies (long hair/shaved head, feminine/masculine, classless/class identified, etc.). Much of their taste in clothing and music came directly from classmates from the Caribbean. The skinheads adopted the styles and love of ska music of the black "rude boys."

The black roots of skinhead style were tested in the 1970s when British unemployment skyrocketed. Skinhead youth saw recent Indian and Pakistani immigrants as cultural interlopers and as competitors for jobs and a place in the economic sun. Neofacist political movements, such as the National Front, began indoctrinating skinheads into racist ideologies that included blacks as targets. Skinhead violence moved from "hippie-bashing" to "Paki-bashing," and then to attacking anyone and anything that seemed to threaten white working-class masculinity. Skinhead music, often called "Oi! music," moved toward racist themes. Popular bands such as Skrewdriver attracted skinheads with themes of racially returning Britain to the world dominance it enjoyed as a colonizing power in previous centuries.

By the mid-1980s, skinheads were becoming more common in North America, where they were usually seen as a subgroup of the punk-rock subculture. As the American economy went into decline in the late 1980s and early 1990s, skinheads were quickly recruited by racist and neo-Nazi groups, like the Ku Klux Klan, the White Aryan Resistance (WAR), and the New Order. Reports of skinhead violence against homosexuals, leftists, Jews, the homeless, and ethnic minorities made national news. Most noteworthy was the murder of an Ethiopian university student by three skinheads in Portland, Oregon, in 1988. In 1990 a civil court determined that the skinheads had been directed to murder by WAR, a group based in southern California. Tom and John Metzger, the leaders of WAR, were ordered to pay the victim's family $12.5 million.

By the early 1990s, the Anti-Defamation League of the B'nai B'rith believed approximately 3,500 racist skinheads were active in the United States. The Southern Poverty Law Center (SPLC) charted a rise in skinhead groups and skinhead crimes in the United States in the 1990s. With the collapse of the Soviet Union in 1991, skinhead terror arose in eastern Europe, where its targets were recent immigrants and the Roma (gypsies).

A connection with racial terrorism does not exist among all skinheads. The 1990s saw the growth of the SHARP subculture in the United States. SHARPs (Skinheads Against Racial Prejudice) are similar to the original nonracist skinheads of the 1960s. They feel that the skinhead subculture has been hijacked by racists and the media, and they often use violence to purge the skinhead scene of Nazis and other undesirables. As their styles are similar, racist and antiracist skinheads are easily mistaken for each other.

Skinheads and racial terrorism are linked by religion, subcultural solutions, hate crimes, and intimidation. The majority of skinheads seem to be attracted by the subculture's rebellious style or political expression, though a core element of the subculture sees itself as a movement dedicated to a massive social revolution and the end of America as it currently exists. This desire for radical change is based on the idea that the American government is not controlled by the American people, but by a secret cabal of Jewish elders whose primary goal is the destruction of the white race. This "Zionist Occupation Government," or "ZOG," is believed by the skinheads to use the dominant institutions, including the media, to undermine the power of northern Europeans, referred to as "Aryans."

Subcultural Solutions

For many, the appeal of the skinhead subculture arises from its goals. The skinhead creed can influence terrorist behavior on local levels and more generally in the wider population. The research of Randy Blazak has shown how skinhead "problem solving" operates on two levels. On the immediate local level, skinheads create a gang-like protective subculture that provides emotional and ideological resources to marginalized youth. This can include the commission of hate crimes. For example, criminal acts committed against minority groups can solve the problem of harassment of a white youth by minorities, or it can limit job competition from minorities.

On a more global level, skinheads are often portrayed as foot soldiers in a future racial holy war. They are street warriors who are to agitate against minorities, feminists, homosexuals, and "race-traitors," pushing toward a "final conflict," in which North America and northern Europe will be purged of all enemy elements. This militaristic vision is often attractive to young men looking to assert a type of masculinity they feel has been lost.

Skinheads have been linked to hundreds of racist, sexist, anti-Semitic, and homophobic attacks since the mid-1980s. Although individuals are the victims, terror is the larger goal. The criminologists Jack Levin and Jack McDevitt point out that the ultimate goal of hate crimes is to terrorize entire communities. The victim is a relatively random representative of a target group and meant to be a symbol. When two skinheads murdered a gay man in Sylacauga, Alabama, in 1999, the message was to all gay men to be on notice, just as Klan cross burnings were meant for all African Americans. The criminologist Mark Hamm points out that the three players in a hate crime are the perpetrator, the audience the perpetrator is performing the crime for (for example, fellow skinheads), and the group the victim belongs to (not the actual victim).

Groups like the Nazi Low Riders in California or the Hammerskins in Texas have been described as instituting a "reign of terror" in local communities. Skinheads use their aggressive ideology, imposing image, and history of violence to threaten those who oppose them. Their speech and music, which is constitutionally protected, is filled with messages about burning down synagogues, killing "race-traitors," and starting Rahowa, an acronym for "racial holy war." Skinheads claim to be proud of their race but often use aliases and rarely meet in public. One of the most powerful skinhead groups, the Aryan Brotherhood, primarily recruits among white prison inmates.

Randy Blazak

See also Aryan Nations; Ku Klux Klan; White Supremacy Movement

Further Readings

Blazak, Randy. "White Boys to Terrorist Men: Target Recruitment of Nazi Skinheads." *American Behavioral Scientist* 44, no. 6 (February 2001).
Hamm, Mark. *American Skinheads: The Criminology and Control of Hate Crimes.* Westport, CT: Praeger, 1995.

King, John. *Skinheads*. London: Jonathan Cape, 2008.

Levin, Jack, and Jack McDevitt. *Hate Crimes: The Rising Tide of Bigotry and Bloodshed*. New York: Plenum, 1993.

Moore, Jack B. *Skinheads: Shaved for Battle: A Cultural History of American Skinheads*. Bowling Green, OH: Bowling Green State University Press, 1993.

Perry, Barbara. *In the Name of Hate: Understanding Hate Crimes*. New York: Routledge, 2001.

Southern Poverty Law Center Intelligence Project. *Skinheads in America: Racists on the Rampage*. Montgomery, AL: Southern Poverty Law Center, 2009. http://www.splcenter.org/get-informed/publications/skinheads-in-america-racists-on-the-rampage.

SNELL, RICHARD WAYNE (1931–1995)

Richard Wayne Snell, a key figure in the far-right Christian Identity movement and one-time member of a right-wing religious paramilitary group called The Covenant, the Sword, and the Arm of the Lord (CSA), was executed on April 19, 1995, a significant date among white supremacist and right-wing groups. (April 19, 1995, was also the date of the Oklahoma City bombing.) At the time of Snell's death, some Christian Identity adherents believed he was to be the second coming of Christ.

Snell was on death row for murdering two men—Louis Bryant, a black Arkansas state trooper, and William Stumpp, the owner of a Texarkana pawn shop. In 1984 Bryant stopped Snell for a traffic violation near DeQueen, Arkansas. Snell shot Bryant once as he approached the car, and again as Bryant lay on the ground. Police chased Snell to Broken Bow, Oklahoma, where a gun battle erupted in which Snell was wounded. When Snell was finally captured, police searched Snell's car and found firearms, silencers, and hand grenades, as well as the gun used in the 1983 murder of Stumpp. Snell had shot Stumpp after mistakenly identifying him as Jewish (Stumpp was Episcopalian). Although Snell later claimed he shot Bryant in self-defense, he was convicted on both counts and sentenced to death for Stumpp's murder.

Snell had a long history of involvement with crime and was deeply connected to right-wing and militia circles. During the 1980s he acted as an "emissary" who passed information from group to group. During a 1998 trial of 15 white supremacists in Fort Smith, Arkansas, James Ellison, a former CSA leader turned government informant, testified about links between Snell, the CSA, and other prominent white supremacist groups, including Posse Comitatus, Aryan Nations, and The Order.

Ellison also testified that Snell and the CSA plotted to blow up the Alfred P. Murrah Federal Building in Oklahoma City in October 1983, a decade before Timothy McVeigh blew up that building. After a meeting of white supremacists at the Aryan Nations compound in Hayden Lake, Idaho, members of the CSA sought to retaliate against the government for the death of Gordon Kahl, a member of Posse Comitatus who was shot to death in a 1983 gun battle with federal agents in Smithville, Arkansas. The plan involved using rocket launchers to topple the Murrah Building. CSA members had even scouted the building.

Though Snell and McVeigh had never met, many believe that the date of Snell's execution, April 19 (also known as "Militia Day"), and the Oklahoma City bombing were intimately linked. Snell's behavior in jail also suggested his knowledge of an attack. He had repeatedly predicted that an explosion or bombing would occur on the date of his execution. The morning of April 19, Snell watched the live coverage of the Oklahoma City bombing from his cell on death row, laughing and chuckling, according to prison officials. According to witnesses to the execution, later that evening, as Snell was strapped to the gurney, he said, "Governor Tucker, look over your shoulder. Justice is on the way." Snell was executed by lethal injection at 9 P.M., just 12 hours after the attack.

Robert G. Millar, Snell's religious advisor and the leader of Elohim City, a right-wing religious compound near the Oklahoma-Arkansas border, witnessed his execution and brought Snell's body back to Elohim City for burial. Millar kept Snell's casket open for three days, in the event the he might rise again as the Christian Identity messiah.

Laura Lambert

See also April 19; Christian Identity; Covenant, the Sword and the Arm of the Lord, The; McVeigh, Timothy James; Oklahoma City Bombing

Further Readings

Bushart, Howard L., John R. Craig, and Myra Barnes. *Soldiers of God: White Supremacists and Their Holy War for America*. New York: Kensington Books, 1998.

Dyer, Joel. *Harvest of Rage: Why Oklahoma City Is Only the Beginning*. Boulder, CO: Westview Press, 1998.

Extremism on the Right: A Handbook. Rev. ed. New York: Anti-Defamation League of B'nai B'rith, 1988.

Zeskind, Leonard. *Blood and Politics: The History of the White Nationalist Movement from the Margins to the Mainstream*. New York: Farrar, Straus and Giroux, 2009.

SPECIAL AIR SERVICE REGIMENT

The original Special Air Service Regiment (SAS) was established in Great Britain during World War II. Created by David Stirling in 1941, the SAS was conceived as a desert raiding force, operating behind German lines in North Africa to wreak havoc on the enemy's supply lines. Disbanded in 1946, only to be revived in 1947 in the form of 21st Battalion, Army Air Corps SAS, it was deployed in the Korean War in 1950 and to what is now Malaysia from 1950 to 1955, where it gained much expertise in jungle warfare. A similar elite commando group was developed by the Australian army in 1957, and many other elite commando units, including the U.S. Navy SEALs, are modeled after the British SAS.

Great Britain

Great Britain's SAS is widely considered to be the best in the world in ending hijack and hostage situations with minimum loss of innocent lives. Its prowess was made known to the world in May 1980, when the SAS rescued 19 hostages held in the Iranian embassy in London in a matter of minutes. *Time* magazine named Great Britain's SAS the world's toughest anti-terrorist commando unit.

The SAS is organized into four "sabre" squadrons—A, B, D, and G—with 60 soldiers in each. Each sabre squad rotates through counterterrorism duties every six months. In addition, squadrons specialize in intelligence gathering, forward air control, behind-the-lines sabotage, close protection, and training foreign militaries. Soldiers are usually deployed in four-man patrols, and each member has a primary area of expertise: communications, medical, linguistics, forward air control, or demolition.

SAS candidates undergo a grueling screening process. They must pass endurance tests, jungle training, and escape, evasion, and tactical questioning. Only about 10 percent of any training class passes the screening. Women cannot serve in the SAS.

The British SAS grew out of the Long Range Desert Group, which was active in the North African desert during World War II. Stirling transformed the group into the military arm of the British security forces, encompassing high-level land, air, and water operations, with communication, medical, and survivalist skills.

Since World War II, the unit has put down insurgencies in British-held Malaya, taken part in the Falklands War in the 1980s, and engaged the Irish Republican Army (IRA) in Ulster, killing more than two dozen IRA members during the 1970s and 1980s. SAS troops took part in the UN coalition deployed to Bosnia in the 1990s and later returned to help in the hunt for war criminals.

Task Force Black, the SAS operation in Iraq, ran from 2003 to 2009. Altogether, the 150 men who served in the task force killed or captured approximately 3,500 insurgents. General Stanley McChrystal, who headed the Joint Special Operations Command in Iraq and later commanded NATO forces in Afghanistan, praised the professionalism of the SAS forces saying they were "essential. Could not have done it without them," in regard to defeating the Sunni insurgency in Iraq, winning control of Baghdad, and neutralizing suicide bombers.

Many of the SAS forces that served in Iraq moved on to Afghanistan in 2009. There they focused on assassinating as many senior Taliban as possible. McChrystal pointed out several unique SAS skills: "They understand the sweep of history. They know the history of British forces not just in Afghanistan but the history of British successful counter-insurgencies. . . . There's a particularly strong understanding of things beyond tactics." The SAS paid a high price for its vaunted service in Afghanistan. The almost daily operations left 70 troops incapacitated or dead, making the campaign the SAS's worst in terms of losses in 60 years.

SAS personnel guard members of the British royal family when they travel to dangerous locations. When Prince Harry deployed to Afghanistan in 2008, a special six-person SAS detail was assigned to protect him because al Qaeda had announced its desire to assassinate such a high-profile target. Even upon his return to England, SAS details were often added to the prince's regular Scotland Yard protection when new specific threats emerge.

Australia

The Australian SAS, whose history can be traced to the 1940s when Australian soldiers were part of the Allied Intelligence Bureau (AIB), was formed in July 1957 when Major W. Cook formed a "Special Forces" unit modeled after the British SAS. Its first mission, in February 1965, was to quell insurgencies in Borneo. The Australian SAS also spent more than six years in Vietnam, where members earned the name *ma rung* or "phantoms of the jungle," for their stealthy maneuvers. The SAS forms a significant part of Australia's armed forces.

After Vietnam, the SAS took on dual roles: "green" for standard army responsibilities; "black" for counterterrorist actions. Each unit spends one rotation in "black," during which they are permanently on-call. Each of the three SAS squadrons is composed of three troops: a boat troop with expertise in submarine operations; an airborne troop with specialized parachuting capabilities; and ground specialists for jungle warfare and long-range desert reconnaissance. Australian SAS personnel are nicknamed "chicken stranglers" for their ability to live off the land in enemy territories.

SAS units often cross-train with other elite counterterrorism outfits, including the British SAS, U.S. Navy SEALs, and Germany's Grenzschutzgruppe 9 (GSG-9). They worked alongside U.S. forces in Somalia in the 1990s, as well as during Operation Desert Storm and Operation Enduring Freedom, and they have permanent assignments at the U.S. Army base in Fort Bragg, North Carolina, and the Little Creek Naval Amphibious Base in Virginia. Since its inception, the unit has maintained a close relationship to the British SAS, on which it is modeled. The two SAS forces have engaged in various joint operations, including in Northern Ireland and Bosnia.

The SAS was the first allied force to have soldiers on the ground in Afghanistan, fielding up to 1,100 personnel in the first six months of Operation Enduring Freedom. However, Australian military leaders have been known to complain that the U.S. seeks them out for troops, but not advice. They believe they have valuable insight into Islamist terrorism, due to long-time contact with neighboring predominantly Muslim countries such as Malaysia and Indonesia. The SAS earned the respect of the United States and other NATO coalition members by infiltrating an al Qaeda training camp at Shah-i-Kot in 2005 and capturing senior Taliban insurgent commander Mullah Faqir in April 2010.

Ann E. Robertson and Laura Lambert

See also Counterterrorism; Grenzschutzgruppe 9

Further Readings

Cross, Roger T., and Avon Hudson. *Beyond Belief: The British Bomb Tests: Australia's Veterans Speak Out.* Kent Town, South Australia: Wakefield Press, 2005.

Elite UK Forces. http://www.eliteukforces.info.

Horner, David. *SAS: Phantoms of War: A History of the Australian Special Air Service.* St. Leonards, NSW, Australia: Allen & Unwin, 2002.

Horsfield, B. *"Warrior Monks": Notes on Professional Communication, Culture, and Training in the Australian Special Air Service Regiment.* Thousand Oaks, CA: Sage, 2000.

Jones, Tim. *SAS: The First Secret Wars: The Unknown Years of Combat and Counter-insurgency.* New York: I.B. Tauris, 2005.

Mackenzie, Alastair. *Special Force: The Untold Story of 22nd Special Air Service Regiment (SAS).* London: I.B. Tauris, 2010.

Special Warfare Network: Counterterrorism, Australia. http://www.specwarnet.net/oceana/sasr_ct.htm.

Spence, Cameron. *All Necessary Measures.* New York: Penguin, 1999.

United Kingdom Special Air Service. http://www .specwarnet.net/europe/sas.htm.

SPECIAL OPERATIONS WING

The U.S. Air Force fields four Special Operations Wings (SOWs) to provide unconventional warfare tactics and other support services for counterter-rorism operations. It is the U.S. Air Force counter-part of the Navy SEAL and Army Ranger special forces units. During wartime, the SOW divisions report to the Air Force Special Operations Command (AFSOC) at Hurlburt Field, Florida.

The 1986 Defense Authorization Act called for the creation of a unified command for special opera-tions. As a result, the 23rd Air Force was assigned to the new U.S. Special Operations Command estab-lished April 1987 at Florida's McDill Air Force Base. Over the next three years the non–special-operations functions of the 23rd Air Force were assigned to other units. On May 22, 1990, the 23rd Air Force was redesignated as a separate new entity: AFSOC.

AFSOC has two active-duty wings, one reserve wing, and one National Guard wing, as well as a menu of specialized groups and squadrons. The two active-duty wings are the 1st Special Operations Wing, based at Hurlburt Field, and the 27th SOW, which works out of Cannon Air Force Base in New Mexico. The 919th SOW, located at Duke Field in Florida, bears the distinction of being the only SOW in the Air Force Reserve, and has about 1,300 reservists. The 193rd SOW is part of the Air National Guard.

The 1st SOW mission focus is unconventional warfare, including counterterrorism, search and rescue, aviation assistance to developing countries, personnel recovery, psychological operations, and deep battlefield resupply. It specializes in low-level, high-speed missions. The 1st SOW also brings distinctive intelligence capabilities to the fight, including intelligence, surveillance and reconnaissance, predictive analysis, and targeting expertise. The 1st SOW fleet consists of 75 aircraft and 8,700 personnel. In line with its motto, "Keeping the Air Commando promise to provide reliable, precise Air Force special operations air power.... Any Time, Any Place," the 1st SOW has played a major role in the global war on ter-ror, logging over 48,000 combat sorties and more than 150,000 combat hours by late 2009. The 1st SOW has units based in Florida and Nevada. (The 1st was known as the 16th SOW prior to November 16, 2006.)

The 27th SOW is based at Cannon Air Force Base in New Mexico. Its primary mission is specialized and contingency operations using advanced aircraft and refueling tactics to provide

intelligence, surveillance and reconnaissance, and close air support for Special Operations forces. The unit traces its origins to the 27th Bombardment Group in 1940. As the Air Force has reorganized over the years, the 27th designation has been used for other units at various locations, such as the 27th Fighter Wing, based in Nebraska in 1947. As part of the Base Realignment program, in 2007 the Cannon AFB 27th Fighter Wing changed its mis-sion, becoming the 27th SOW. Cannon AFB has 3,300 military and 600 civilian personnel.

The 919th SOW provides and maintains the MC-130E Combat Talon 1 and the MC-130P Combat Shadow special operations aircraft, which are designed for covert operations. It also provides 60 percent of the AFSOC's helicopter aerial fueling training. This SOW has a long history of foreign deployment. Personnel participated in the 1989 invasion of Panama, the 1991 Gulf War, Operation Uphold Democracy in Haiti in 1994, and the sub-sequent wars in Afghanistan and Iraq. During the Gulf War, the 919th were the first forces to enter enemy air space, where they successfully disman-tled two radar stations. Thanks to their work, naval forces were able to conduct a successful air raid with no casualties. The 919th employs some 1,300 reservists.

The 193rd SOW is the most deployed Air National Guard unit in the United States, partici-pating in 12 to 15 exercise or real-world deploy-ments annually. It took part in the 1983 invasion of Grenada, as well as operations in Panama, the Gulf War, and Haiti. The primary mission of the 193rd is to provide an airborne broadcast platform for a range of contingencies, including foreign conflict or national disasters in the United States. This unique mission, designated "Commando Solo," uses six EC130E/RR aircraft specially con-figured as flying radio and television stations. The broadcasts are psychological operations (psyops), part of an information war tailored to specific cir-cumstances. The crew of a Commando Solo air-craft is able to broadcast AM and FM radio signals and on local TV channels; it also drops leaflets, radios, and food rations. Commando Solo can monitor, jam, and allegedly alter other existing transmissions.

In the Gulf War, SOW broadcasts became known as the "Voice of the Gulf" and included prayers from the Koran, testimonials from well-treated Iraqi

U.S. military personnel assigned to the 4th Psychological Operations Group, 193rd Special Operations Wing, Pennsylvania Air National Guard (ANG) broadcast television and radio programming from onboard an ANG EC-130J Hercules "Commando Solo" aircraft, in support of Operation Iraqi Freedom. (PH1 [SW] Aaron Ansarov, USN)

prisoners, instructions on how to surrender, and information on future bombing campaigns. About three-quarters of all Iraqi soldiers who surrendered were thought to have been influenced by these broadcasts. In Afghanistan, where TVs, radios, and electricity are scarce and many people are illiterate, the 193rd dropped hand-crank-generated radios and food rations. The goal was to convince the population that the war on terror was against Osama bin Laden and al Qaeda, not the Afghan people.

The 193rd returned to Haiti following the January 2010 earthquake. With nearly all Haitian broadcasting services inoperable, the SOW took the lead telling informing the world what was happening on the ground. Voice of America broadcasts from EC-130J aircraft provided updates and government bulletins to the disoriented population. At one point the Toussaint Louverture Airport in Port-au-Prince was in danger of becoming overwhelmed. The 193rd broadcast warnings that if the airport was swamped, relief operations would have to stop. Thanks to these broadcasts, many worst-case scenarios were averted.

In June 2010 the Pentagon announced that psyops would be referred to as "military information support operations," or MISOs. Officials hoped to increase public recognition and understanding of its information and influence activities. MISO encompasses all efforts to influence foreign audiences.

Ann E. Robertson

See also Counterterrorism

Further Readings

Air Force Special Operations Command. http://www
    .afsoc.af.mil/index2.shtml.
Hebert, Adam J. "The Air Commandos." *Air Force
    Magazine* 88, no. 3 (March 2005).
Kodosky, Robert J. *Psychological Operations American
    Style: The Joint United States Public Affairs Office,
    Vietnam and beyond.* Lanham, MD: Lexington, 2007.
Pushies, Fred J. *The Complete Book of U.S. Special
    Operations Forces.* St. Paul, MN: MBI, 2004.
Pushies, Fred, J. *Deadly Blue: Battle Stories of the U.S.
    Air Force Special Operations Command.* New York:
    American Management Association, 2009.
Schanz, Marc V. "The New Way of Psyops." *Air Force
    Magazine* 93, no. 11 (November 2010).

STATE TERRORISM

Terrorism is often thought of as the province of relatively small nongovernmental groups that, more often than not, exist despite the best efforts of governments to destroy them. Indeed, some observers define terrorism specifically to exclude violence conducted by governments, arguing that when nations engage in violence and killing as a means of reaching a particular political end, it should be called oppression, not terrorism. At the other extreme, some argue that nations are the deadliest of terrorists. The average country, they note, has considerably greater military and financial resources than the average terrorist group, and some states regularly use violence for political ends. Such violence, these observers argue, should be considered terrorism.

Defining state terrorism is complicated because all nations rely on violence to some degree. War, for example, is a violent and deadly way for countries to settle their differences. War can be very one-sided, as when a powerful country launches attacks on a much smaller, weaker neighbor to force it to adopt policies that benefit the attacker. All functioning governments have systems of law enforcement that rely on various forms of violence to maintain order, including armed police, imprisonment, forced labor, and the physical mutilation or killing of certain criminals.

So how does state terrorism differ from other forms of state violence? One difference is the predictability of ordinary warfare and law enforcement. Wars are rarely unexpected and are generally preceded by a long period of escalating disagreements and failed negotiations. Often, a country declares war before conducting an attack, publicizing its grievances and explaining the rationale for the decision to wage war. Although they are not always honored, rules of war have been established—unarmed civilians, for example, are not supposed to be targeted by the military—and deliberate violations of these rules are considered war crimes.

Ordinary law enforcement is likewise designed to be predictable. Laws are written, and what constitutes a violation usually is apparent. If a law is violated, certain protocols must be followed regarding the capture of the suspect, the determination of guilt, and the choice of punishment. Law enforcement may involve violence, but a functional legal system enables individuals to avoid that violence by not committing the crimes that trigger it. In an ideal law-enforcement system, law-abiding individuals would never wonder whether they will be arrested, imprisoned, beaten, mutilated, or killed by state officials, because they would know what constitutes a crime, and that such punishments will only be given to those who commit criminal acts.

Secrecy

State terrorism, in contrast, is marked by secrecy. Governments often deny responsibility for acts of terror, or they deny that an act of terrorism has even taken place. For example, during the 1970s and 1980s, several right-wing regimes in Latin America began "disappearing" citizens. People were taken into custody and were never heard from again, with the government denying all knowledge of their whereabouts. Most of the people who were "disappeared" were later found to have been executed and their bodies hidden.

Secrecy is such a part of state terrorism that covert acts by government officials in societies that are generally open—such as the secret U.S. campaign to assassinate Cuban leader Fidel Castro in the 1960s—can generate tremendous controversy when they are uncovered. Groups that oppose state terrorism, like the human rights group Amnesty International, have found that publicizing the details of specific acts of state terrorism can be effective in stopping such acts.

Governments that engage in terrorism operate in secrecy, but that secrecy is usually not complete. The "disappeared" people of Latin America, for example, were often openly taken into custody by easily identified state officials. Such quasi-secrecy is essential to creating an atmosphere of terror. Latin Americans knew that something bad was happening to the "disappeared" people, and that their governments were responsible, but the details were left to the imagination.

The very unpredictability of state terrorism generates escalating fear. In a country where the state relies on terror to maintain control, people are unsure of what actions might result in their being detained, tortured, or killed, although they may have a broad notion of what groups are vulnerable. This unpredictability is often deliberate. When the

Nazis took over Germany in the 1930s, for example, they randomly arrested 1 lawyer out of every 10. Some of the arrested lawyers were then executed. Arresting and murdering lawyers for no discernible reason was designed to instill fear in the remaining lawyers so they would not challenge the Nazi regime.

Terrorizing a population is also a goal of non-state terrorism. A non-state group, however, usually relies on terror to publicize its goals or to punish perceived enemies. State terrorism, however, usually has one goal: the strengthening of government control through the complete intimidation of a population. Thus, if people are unsure of what actions might lead to unspeakable torture and even death, they will avoid actions not specifically sanctioned by the government, thereby policing themselves more closely than could the government.

Accordingly, state terrorism is especially appealing to authoritarian regimes that wish to exercise a great deal of control over how people act and think. State terrorism also appeals to governments that have only tenuous control over their populations. The white-minority government that ruled South Africa until the early 1990s is one example. That government engaged in arbitrary detention, torture, and executions for decades. In some cases, such as the Soviet Union, a newly established government will rely heavily on state terrorism, but then eventually rely on it less as the rulers become more established and secure.

Even well-established governments have adopted policies of state terrorism, especially directed against unpopular minorities that are viewed with suspicion by the general populace. While state terrorism is embraced as a way to strengthen government, as South Africa demonstrated, state terrorism can backfire badly, leading not only to international and domestic condemnation but also to the establishment of non-state terrorist groups determined to fight violence with violence.

Mary Sisson

See also State-Sponsored Terrorism

Further Readings

Bianchi, Andrea, ed. *Enforcing International Law Norms against Terrorism.* Oxford, UK: Hart Publishing, 2004.

Byman, Daniel. *Deadly Connections: States That Sponsor Terrorism.* Cambridge, UK: Cambridge University Press, 2007.

Herman, Edward S. *The Real Terror Network: Terrorism in Fact and Propaganda.* Boston: South End Press, 1982.

Köcher, Hans, ed. *Terrorism and National Liberation: Proceedings of the International Conference on the Question of Terrorism.* Frankfurt: Verlag Peter Lang, 1988.

Lebovic, James H. *Deterring International Terrorism and Rogue States: US National Security after 9/11.* New York: Routledge, 2006.

Martin, Gus. *Essentials of Terrorism: Concepts and Controversies.* 2nd ed. Thousand Oaks, CA: Sage, 2011.

Schmid, Alex P., and Albert J. Jongman. *Political Terrorism: A New Guide to Actors, Authors, Concepts, Data Bases, Theories and Literature.* Amsterdam: North-Holland Publishing, 1988.

STATE-SPONSORED TERRORISM

Although terrorism is widely condemned, many countries have given assistance to terrorist groups in the form of money, weapons, training, or providing bases for operations. Every year, the U.S. State Department releases a list of countries that support terrorism, and those countries face stiff sanctions. If a country's support for terrorist groups is not extensive enough for it to be placed on the list, the United States may impose sanctions nonetheless. The United States declared a "war on terrorism" following the September 11, 2001, attacks on the World Trade Center and the Pentagon.

During the Cold War, a decades-long period of conflict with the former Soviet Union following World War II, the United States provided extensive aid to anti-Soviet and anti-Communist groups in many countries. Likewise, the former Soviet Union was extremely open about its support for leftist groups—so much so that it was criticized for claiming to extensively support groups to which it gave little practical assistance. Some linguistic finesse was necessary: neither country claimed to support "terrorism," arguing instead that they were assisting, in the terminology preferred by the United States, "freedom fighters," or armed liberation movements that represented the true will of a given population. Many of these groups, however, would fit into contemporary definitions of terrorists.

The coinage of the phrase "freedom fighters" points to one reason why countries support terrorist groups: supporting terrorist movements, especially those with some popular backing, can actually enhance another nation's standing. The communist government of Cuba, for example, obtained international notice by openly promising to "export the revolution"—that is, to foster and support communist groups in other nations. Muslim governments in Iran and Afghanistan have made much the same promise to militant Muslim groups. While such proclamations can lead to international condemnation and trade sanctions, they can also establish a nation as an ideological leader, a country willing to make sacrifices to help support and export a certain political philosophy.

"Exporting the revolution" can also be a profitable business. Cuba routinely required leftist groups to pay for Cuban soldiers and civilians sent to help, and Bulgaria's government was once notorious for its willingness to sell weapons to terrorist groups at a hefty profit. However, the primary reason countries support terrorist groups is neither prestige nor profits. Instead, a nation almost always supports terrorist groups that share a common enemy with the state, especially when peaceful reconciliation is impossible but war is also not an option. During the Cold War, for example, the United States and the Soviet Union were implacable foes, divided by deep ideological differences. Both countries had extensive arsenals of nuclear weapons, meaning that an outright war could have very well led to global annihilation. Instead of making peace or waging war, both countries supported terrorist groups that operated in other countries and that were in ideological alignment with one or the other of the superpowers.

Obviously, adopting this kind of policy involves risks: if a country supports a group that conducts direct attacks against a second country, the second country may take military action against the first. Thus, during the Cold War, the United States and the Soviet Union did not support terrorist groups that conducted operations in the other's country. Instead, they would generally support insurgent groups operating in a third country. Thus, the Soviet Union would support an insurgency in countries where the government was seen as friendly to the United States. The United States would then provide arms and assistance to the government to help put down the Soviet-backed insurgent groups. An armed conflict, or "proxy war," often resulted within the third nation. Supporting terrorism can sometimes lead to outright war. In the 1990s, Pakistan supported militant Muslim groups in the disputed state of Jammu and Kashmir, which is largely controlled by India. These groups attacked Indian targets, raising the hostility level between the two countries to the point of battle between Pakistani and Indian troops.

Terrorist groups can be very hard to control. Pakistan essentially lost control over many of the militant groups operating in Jammu and Kashmir, which then became more radical and more violent and eventually viewed the government of Pakistan as yet another enemy. Likewise, while the anti-Soviet mujahideen, supported by the United States in the 1980s, successfully defended Afghanistan following a Soviet invasion, the country subsequently became a haven for groups like al Qaeda that considered the United States to be just as much of an enemy to its radical Muslim agenda as the Soviet Union.

The methods terrorist groups use can make state sponsorship of terrorism extremely controversial, even in the sponsoring state. In the early 1980s, for example, the anti-Communist Nicaraguan Contras were linked to torture, rape, and assassinations. U.S. support of the Contras became so controversial that Congress essentially outlawed such aid, and the decision by members of the administration of President Ronald Reagan to continue support in spite of the congressional ban led to a major scandal.

Terrorist groups often find they have little influence with sponsor nations. Because terrorism is so controversial, state sponsorship often vanishes when it becomes public knowledge, or when a new administration comes to power. Even states that are very open to supporting terrorism may not be willing or able to provide the amount of funding needed, especially if the state is trying to support several groups to advance its specific ideology. As a result, most well-established terrorist groups find other sources of funds, from narcotics to kidnap-and-ransom schemes to networks of private supporters.

A state's sponsorship of a terrorist group can also create public-relations problems for the group if it is seen as simply the pawn of that country. Indeed, a common tactic of governments battling terrorist groups is to emphasize any support by foreign states, implying both that the group is operating at the behest of foreign powers and that it lacks popular support in the country where it operates.

Nonetheless, state support can be crucial to a terrorist group and can transform a relatively ineffective organization into a serious threat. Nations can often provide great sums of money that groups need to buy equipment and supplies, and they also have well-developed militaries that can train and provide expertise to terrorists. A state can give away or sell weaponry and explosives that ordinarily would be very hard for a private group to obtain. Such gifts can be crucial to the success of a terrorist group. The United States provided the mujahideen with antiaircraft missiles, while Libya provided the Irish Republican Army with the plastic explosive Semtex, significantly increasing the military capabilities of both groups.

States can also do a great favor to terrorist groups by providing them with a haven where members of the group can plan attacks without fear of arrest, and where they can flee and regroup after attacks. Afghanistan came to play such a role for al Qaeda under Taliban rule. These havens also provide groups an opportunity to interact and form networks to share information and carry out coordinated attacks. Such networking is sometimes explicitly encouraged by supportive governments.

The issue of safe havens can be complicated, however, because a country can provide havens to terrorists passively or even inadvertently simply by not arresting members of terrorist groups. Countries with lax banking laws can become financial havens as well, allowing groups to hold and channel money.

Discouraging Support

Because state support can be so important to terrorist groups, international efforts to curb such support have a long history. During the Cold War, however, such efforts were hindered because the United States and the Soviet Union were supporting a variety of armed groups in many countries. In the 1970s and 1980s, therefore, international treaties designed to curb terrorism focused on certain actions—including hijacking, the taking of hostages, and violence against diplomats, but excluding bombings and assassinations—that all parties could agree were "terrorism," not "freedom fighting." Despite these limitations, the treaties did encourage the international community to act in coordination to condemn countries that were seen as supporting terrorism. The dissolution of the Soviet Union and the end of the Cold War in the early 1990s largely put an end to superpower support for armed groups, and by the end of the decade, states that supported terrorism risked being treated as international pariahs.

How best to deter states from supporting terrorist groups is still under debate. The United States has taken a relatively confrontational approach, occasionally launching military attacks against governments it considers especially flagrant in their support for terrorism, and readily imposing trade sanctions and other restrictions on such governments. U.S. officials argue that such actions help isolate states that contribute to the problem of terrorism, and that they deter other states from considering support for terrorism.

European countries, in contrast, have generally taken a more conciliatory approach, preferring to maintain diplomatic and trade relations intact with countries that support terrorism. Such engagement, they argue, is in the long run more likely to turn countries away from such policies. Further, it avoids the risk of retaliatory terrorism that often follows an attack. However, all opponents of state-sponsored terrorism have focused on the importance of international cooperation, of attempting to create a global culture in which supporting terrorism is unacceptable.

Mary Sisson

See also Financing Terrorism; Mujahideen; September 11 Attacks; State Terrorism

Further Readings

Becker, Tal. *Terrorism and the State: Rethinking the Rules of State Responsibility.* Portland, OR: Hart Publishing, 2006.

Byman, Daniel. *Deadly Connections: States That Sponsor Terrorism.* Cambridge, UK: Cambridge University Press, 2007.

Han, Henry H, ed. *Terrorism and Political Violence: Limits and Possibilities of Legal Control.* New York: Oceana Publications, 1993.

Köcher, Hans, ed. *Terrorism and National Liberation: Proceedings of the International Conference on the Question of Terrorism.* Frankfurt: Verlag Peter Lang, 1988.

Lebovic, James H. *Deterring International Terrorism and Rogue States: US National Security after 9/11.* New York: Routledge, 2006.

Levitt, Geoffrey M. *Democracies against Terror: The Western Response to State-sponsored Terrorism.* New York: Praeger, 1988.

Tanter, Raymond. *Rogue Regimes: Terrorism and Proliferation.* New York: St. Martin's, 1998.

Wright, Thomas C. *State Terrorism in Latin America: Chile, Argentina, and International Human Rights.* Lanham, MD: Rowman & Littlefield, 2007.

STATUE OF LIBERTY BOMBING

On June 3, 1980, a bomb exploded in the museum at the base of the Statue of Liberty. Initially, at least five separate terrorist groups took responsibility, but within days the bombing was attributed to the Croatian Freedom Fighters.

The bomb, which was placed in a wooden exhibit case in the museum's Story Room, exploded at 7:25 P.M., an hour after the last ferry full of visitors left Liberty Island. Although a dozen residents and five workers were still on the island, no one was injured. The explosion damaged a large section of the room's ceiling, as well as some contents of the exhibit case, including a first publication of Emma Lazarus's poem "The New Colossus," which includes the lines, "Give me your tired, your poor / Your huddled masses yearning to breathe free." Damages exceeded $15,000.

The bombers left no note at the scene, and federal authorities had few initial leads. Within hours of the bombing, however, members of Omega 7, an anti-Castro terrorist group; the Fuerzas Armadas de Liberación Nacional (FALN), a Puerto Rican independence group; the National Socialists, a Nazi group; the Jewish Defense League; and the Palestine Liberation Army had all contacted newspapers and authorities claiming responsibility and, in some cases, threatening more violence. Investigators suspected that Omega 7 was responsible because the group had cited Lazarus's poem in its protests related to immigration policies and a recent wave of Cuban refugees.

Two days later, however, *The New York Times* and NBC received letters from the Croatian Freedom Fighters, written in Croatian, taking responsibility for the bomb. The letters made no specific demands, but urged the worldwide community to recognize the plight of the people of Croatia, who had lost their autonomy to Yugoslavia in 1971. A similar letter had been sent to *The Washington Post* a day earlier, in which the Croatian Freedom Fighters had claimed responsibility for the June 3 bombing of the home of a Yugoslavian ambassador, Vladimir Sindjelic, in Washington, D.C., and had demanded for the creation of a Croatian state.

The Croatian Freedom Fighters had also been responsible for several other bombings in the New York area. In December 1979, the group bombed a Yugoslav-owned travel agency in Astoria, Queens, followed by a St. Patrick's Day bombing of a Yugoslav bank, Yugobanka, on Fifth Avenue in Manhattan. The group also claimed responsibility for bombs at the United Nations and Grand Central Station in 1978. During the late 1970s, the FBI placed the Croatian Freedom Fighters among the top three most active militant foreign nationalist groups within the United States, along with the FALN and Omega 7.

The museum bombing was part of a series of political protests staged at the Statue of Liberty. In 1980, two men scaled the statue, using climbing equipment, to protest the treatment of a convict during a criminal trial in California. In 2000, activists protesting the U.S. bombing tests on the island of Vieques draped the statue in the Puerto Rican flag. After the closing of Liberty Island and the statue due to security concerns following the 9/11 attacks, they reopened in late 2001 and 2004, respectively. The Statue of Liberty's crown was reopened to the public with considerable fanfare on July 4, 2009.

Laura Lambert

See also FALN; Omega 7

Further Readings

Baker, Al. "Fire Alarm Prompts Visitors to Flee the Statue of Liberty." *The New York Times,* July 21, 2010. http://www.nytimes.com/2010/07/22/nyregion/22statue .html.

Chan, Sewell. "Statue of Liberty's Crown Will Reopen July 4." *The New York Times,* May 8, 2009. http:// cityroom.blogs.nytimes.com/2009/05/08/statue-of- libertys-crown-will-reopen-july-4.

"Croatians Are Suspected in Blast at Statue of Liberty." *The New York Times,* June 6, 1980, p. B3.

Khiss, Peter. "Statue of Liberty Bomb Caused Only Minor Damage to Three Museum Items: Room in the Base of the Statue." *The New York Times,* June 5, 1980, p. B3.

Montgomery, Paul L. "Statue of Liberty Is Site of a Blast in Exhibit Room." *The New York Times,* June 4, 1980, p. B2.

Roach, John. "Statue of Liberty Facts: July 4th Reopening and More." *National Geographic News,* July 2, 2009. http://news.nationalgeographic.com/ news/2009/07/090702-statue-of-liberty-facts.html.

STEEN, ALANN (1940–)

Alann Steen, a professor of journalism at Beirut University College, was one of the last American hostages to be released in Lebanon.

Steen was abducted during the series of kidnappings of Western foreigners that followed Terry Waite's final trip to Beirut. Waite, the Anglican envoy and hostage negotiator, had been sent to Lebanon to secure the release of several Western hostages. Steen's was the tenth kidnapping in two weeks.

On January 24, 1987, a Saturday afternoon, gunmen dressed in the olive-colored uniforms of the Lebanese police carried out a mass kidnapping on the Beirut University College campus. Four gunmen drove into the campus in a Nissan patrol jeep, claiming to have been assigned to provide protection for all foreign professors. Once inside, they asked the university staff to congregate in the ground floor of the living quarters. Steen, along with three others—Jesse Turner, a professor of math and computer science; Robert Polhill, a business studies professor; and Mithileshwar Singh, an Indian business professor with an American passport—were taken at gunpoint. Female professors and university staff were not abducted.

The group Islamic Jihad for the Liberation of Palestine claimed responsibility for the kidnappings. (Islamic Jihad for the Liberation of Palestine was considered separate from Islamic Jihad, the extremist group that had kidnapped other Americans to be used as bargaining chips for the release of 17 Iraqi and Lebanese prisoners in Kuwait.) Investigators later found that Imad Mugniyah and Abdul Hadi Hamadi had orchestrated the mass kidnapping, bribing the police and other guards.

In the weeks following Steen's abduction, Islamic Jihad for the Liberation of Palestine repeatedly threatened to execute Steen and the others unless 400 Palestinian prisoners held in Israel were released. Steen's photograph often accompanied such statements, which were delivered to one of the Western news agencies in Beirut and to the Beirut paper *an-Nahar.* He was also used to deliver a six-minute statement on videotape, released in late February. In the statement, deemed the captives' "last message," Steen, unshaven and weary, announced that he, Polhill, Turner, and Singh would be executed at midnight unless the Palestinian prisoners in Israel were released. Hours before the deadline, the Islamic Jihad for the Liberation of Palestine released a written statement reiterating the threat. At midnight, however, the kidnappers, citing the televised pleas of the hostages' wives, abandoned their execution plans. Later that week, the Islamic Jihad for the Liberation of Palestine again issued threats against the prisoners' lives, as retribution against the defenders of Salman Rushdie, the author of the novel *The Satanic Verses.* The kidnappers did not follow through on these threats.

According to fellow hostage Terry Anderson, Steen did not fare well in the hands of his kidnappers. Steen was falsely identified by his kidnappers as a "spy" and was beaten severely, including repeated kicks to the head that left him with brain injuries and periodic convulsions. The kidnappers finally called in a Hezbollah doctor to prescribe medicine to keep him alive.

Steen was released on December 3, 1991, and driven to Damascus, Syria, where previous American hostages had been released to U.S. authorities. The White House thanked the UN Secretary General, and the governments of Iran, Syria, and Lebanon, for Steen's release, which came just one day after Joseph Cicippio, abducted in September 1986, was freed. Terry Anderson, the last American hostage, would be freed the following day, December 4, marking the end of the Lebanon hostage crisis for Americans.

Laura Lambert

See also Anderson, Terry A.; Cicippio, Joseph; Hostage Taking; Waite, Terry

Further Readings

Anderson, Terry. *Den of Lions: Memoirs of Seven Years.* New York: Crown, 1993.
Fisk, Robert. *Pity the Nation: Lebanon at War.* London: A. Deutsch, 1990.
Steen, Alann. "Coming Home." Gordon Hadley Memorial Lecture, Humboldt State University, February 20, 2008. Video available at http://humboldt-dspace.calstate.edu/handle/2148/306.

STERN GANG

In the years immediately before and after 1948, the year Israel became an independent nation, Avraham Stern's extremist Jewish nationalist group used terror tactics to fight against British control of Palestine. British detractors called the group the Stern Gang, while members called their organization Lehi, a Hebrew acronym for Lohamei Herut Israel (Fighters for the Freedom of Israel). The gang was the smallest and fiercest of the underground groups fighting the British.

In 1940, Stern and other members of the Jewish group Irgun Zvai Leumi broke away to form Lehi because they disagreed with the Irgun leaders' decision to stop the struggle against the British and join the war effort against the Nazis. (Irgun, led by Menachem Begin, is most notorious for placing bombs in Jerusalem's King David Hotel in 1946, killing many British administrators.) Stern and his colleagues considered the British Empire to be the enemy of the Jewish people. Subscribing to the philosophy of "my enemy's enemy is my friend," they even attempted to win support from Benito Mussolini and Adolf Hitler for Palestine as a place of refuge for European Jews.

Beginning in 1940, Lehi waged a campaign against the British that included assassinations, bank robberies, and bombings. While the British were the gang's primary targets, Jews and Arabs also died in their attacks. Mainstream Zionists condemned the group, and British detectives hunted Stern, killing him in 1942. After Stern's death, Yitzhak Shamir took control of the gang, along with his colleagues Nathan Friedman Yellin and Yisrael Scheib. Shamir, who was elected prime minister of Israel in 1983, took the *nom de guerre* "Micail" in honor of IRA leader Michael Collins.

Shamir was a man of many disguises, including bearded Orthodox Jew, Polish soldier, and blind man. He was caught three times by the British, escaped from prison in 1942, and was deported to prison in Eritrea in 1943. He escaped from the Eritrean prison camp by digging a tunnel. While Shamir was in Eritrea, his cohorts in Palestine hunted down Sergeant T.G. Martin, the British policeman who had identified him, following him to a tennis court, where they shot him to death.

According to Shamir's own account, the Stern Gang tried to assassinate Sir Harold MacMichael, the British high commissioner in Palestine, several times, failing at each attempt. The group was successful, however, with a 1944 plot to murder Lord Moyne, the British minister resident in the Middle East.

In 1948, after the Israeli War of Independence was virtually finished, the group assassinated Count Folke Bernadotte, a Swedish diplomat appointed by the United Nations to mediate the dispute between Arabs and Israelis. Just three years earlier, Bernadotte had secured the release of 21,000 prisoners bound for extermination by the Nazis. After being appointed the UN troubleshooter in the Middle East, Bernadotte, the former president of the Red Cross and a nephew of the king of Sweden, raised the idea of ceding Jerusalem to the Palestinians. According to statements made by former gang members, four Stern Gang men attacked Bernadotte in his car and then shot and killed both him and his French aide-de-camp.

Israel subsequently outlawed the group, and after 1949, members of both Lehi and Irgun drifted into fringe politics and relative obscurity until Begin rose to prominence as a national politician.

He became Israel's prime minister in 1977 and paved the way for Shamir, who was elected in 1983.

Erica Pearson

See also Irgun Zvai Leumi; King David Hotel Bombing

Further Readings

Heller, Joseph. *The Stern Gang: Ideology, Politics, and Terror, 1940–1949*. London: Frank Cass, 1995.

Marton, Kati. *A Death in Jerusalem*. New York: Pantheon Books, 1994.

Shamir, Yitzhak. *Summing up: An Autobiography*. London: Weidenfeld & Nicholson, 1994.

STOCKHOLM SYNDROME

The Stockholm syndrome is a common psychological response that occurs among hostages, as well as other captives, wherein the captive begins to identify closely with the captors and their agenda and demands.

The name of the syndrome refers to a botched bank robbery in Stockholm, Sweden. In August 1973, two men held four bank employees of Sveriges Kreditbank in an 11-foot by 47-foot bank vault for six days. During the siege, one female captive initiated sexual relations with her captor. Their relationship persisted after the bank robber was tried and convicted.

Stories of this seemingly incongruous bond between captive and captor resurfaced repeatedly in subsequent hostage situations. The most infamous case is that of Patricia Hearst. In 1974, 10 weeks after being taken hostage by the Symbionese Liberation Army, Hearst helped her kidnappers rob a California bank and reportedly became the lover of one of the kidnappers.

During the hostage crises in Iran and Lebanon, the Stockholm syndrome worked its way into the public imagination. The syndrome was cited when the hostages from TWA Flight 847, upon their release, were openly sympathetic to the demands of their kidnappers. Fellow Lebanon hostages believed that Terry Anderson, Terry Waite, and Thomas Sutherland all suffered from the syndrome when, upon their release, they claimed they had been treated well by their captors, though they had often been held in solitary confinement, chained up in small, unclean cells. Similar responses were exhibited by the hostages held at the Japanese embassy in Peru in 1996, and by two European women who were held hostage for 71 days in Costa Rica that same year.

Psychologists who have studied the syndrome believe the bond is initially created when a captor threatens a captive's life, deliberates, and then chooses to not kill the captive. The captive's relief at the removal of the death threat is transposed into feelings of gratitude toward the captor for giving him or her life. In nearly all cases, the victim is also unable to escape and is isolated from the outside world. As the Stockholm bank robbery incident proves, it takes only three to four days for this bond to cement, proving that, early on, the victim's need to survive trumps the urge to hate the person who created the situation.

The survival instinct is at the heart of the Stockholm syndrome. Victims live in enforced dependence and interpret rare or small acts of kindness in the midst of horrible conditions as good treatment. They often become hypervigilant to the needs and demands of their captors, making psychological links between the captors' happiness and their own. Indeed, the syndrome is marked not only by a positive bond between captive and captor, but also by a negative attitude on behalf of the captive toward authorities who threaten the captor-captive relationship. The negative attitude is especially powerful when the hostage is of no use to the captors except as leverage against a third party, as has often been the case with political hostages.

By the 1990s, psychologists expanded their understanding of the Stockholm syndrome from hostages to other groups, including battered women, concentration camp prisoners, cult members, prisoners of war, procured prostitutes, incest victims, and abused children. Over time, however, the term has lost some of its initial significance. Twenty years after the term was coined, it has been employed to describe situations as varied as Patty Hearst's kidnapping by the Symbionese Liberation Army in 1974, Arab-Israel relations, and, cynically, the response of moviegoing audiences to a season of bad movies.

Laura Lambert

See also Hearst, Patty; Hostage Taking; Symbionese Liberation Army

Further Readings

Bolz, Frank, Jr., Kenneth J. Dudonis, and David P. Schulz. *The Counter-terrorism Handbook: Tactics, Procedures, and Techniques.* New York: Elsevier, 1990.

Crelinsten, Ronald D., and Denis Szabo. "A Phenomenological Analysis of Hostage-taking." In *Hostage-taking.* Lexington, MA: Lexington Books, 1979.

Dolnik, Adam, and Keith M. Fitzgerald. *Negotiating Hostage Crises with the New Terrorists.* Westport, CT: Praeger, 2007.

Hero, Eneli. *The Stockholm Syndrome: Towards an Integrated Approach.* Copenhagen: University of Copenhagen, Institute of Psychology, 2006.

Miller, Abraham H. *Terrorism and Hostage Negotiations.* Boulder, CO: Westview Press, 1980.

Ochberg, Frank M., and David A. Soskis, eds. *Victims of Terrorism.* Boulder, CO: Westview Press, 1982.

Reich, Walter, ed. *Origins of Terrorism: Psychologies, Ideologies, Theologies, States of Mind.* Washington, DC: Woodrow Wilson Center Press, 1998.

SUBWAY SUICIDE BOMBING PLOT

In the early morning hours of July 31, 1997, police, acting on a tip, raided a Brooklyn, New York, apartment, capturing two Palestinian men who were allegedly planning an attack on the Atlantic Avenue subway and Long Island Rail Road stations.

At 10:45 P.M. on July 29, 1997, Abdel Rahman Rosabbah, a recent immigrant from Egypt, approached two Long Island Rail Road police officers and tried to explain, in broken English, that friends of his were plotting to kill people on the subway. When officers heard the word "bomb," they brought Rosabbah to the 88th Precinct, in Fort Greene, Brooklyn.

Just over 24 hours later, at approximately 4:30 A.M. on July 31, members of New York's Emergency Services Unit stormed into a shabby two-floor apartment building on 4th Avenue, near the Gowanus section of Park Slope. When the officers entered a bedroom, 24-year-old Ghazi Ibrahim

Abu Maizar tried to detonate a nearby pipe bomb. Before the bomb could be fully armed, an officer shot him twice in the leg. Another man, Lafi Khalil, who allegedly reached for an officer's gun, was shot five times before being subdued. Both were taken to the hospital. The bombs in the apartment, which were fashioned from four lengths of pipe, were dismantled and taken to the police range in Rodman's Neck, in the Bronx. (Investigators suggested that the bombs could have killed anyone within a 25-foot radius.) Police also found anti-Semitic materials, bomb-making instructions, immigration papers for Abu Maizar, which stated he was accused of being a terrorist in Israel and that he was seeking political asylum, as well as what was deemed an unsigned suicide note. The note called for the release of several jailed Islamic militants, including Ramzi Yousef and Eyad Ismoil, who were about to go on trial for the 1993 World Trade Center bombing, as well as the jailed cleric, Sheikh Omar Abdel Rahman. Police also found detonators and harnesses, but no timing device. The bomb was designed to detonate when its four switches were flipped. All evidence indicted that a suicide bombing was planned.

Initially, investigators looked for links between the two men and other Middle Eastern terrorist organizations. The arrests came two days after a double suicide bombing in Jerusalem, for which the militant Islamic organization Hamas claimed responsibility. Hamas denied any connection with the two men, however, stating that their enemies were Israeli Zionists, not Americans. One of the men, Lafi Khalil, had the name of a known member of a terrorist organization in his address book, but no links were ever discovered.

Abu Maizar and Khalil were both arraigned in their hospital beds. On August 19, 1997, they were indicted on federal conspiracy and weapons charges. A year later, during the opening remarks of the trial, Abu Maizar's defense claimed that he and his associates were actually trying to defraud the government of reward money offered by the State Department for information related to terrorist bombings, not kill innocent people. A copy of the "suicide note" that had been mailed to the State Department on July 29 was the defense's main evidence. However, Abu Maizar later testified that he planned to kill as many Jews as possible in a suicide attack—but not on a subway. He also claimed that Khalil knew nothing of the planned attack.

On July 23, 1998, Abu Maizar was found guilty, and in March 1999 he was sentenced to life in prison. Kahlil, who was acquitted of conspiracy charges, was sentenced to three years in prison in December 1998 for immigration fraud.

Laura Lambert

See also Abdel Rahman, Omar; Hamas; World Trade Center Bombing (1993); Yousef, Ramzi Ahmed

Further Readings

Barry, Dan. "Bombs in Brooklyn. The Overview/Bomb Suspect Was Detained by U.S. but Released." *The New York Times,* August 2, 1997, p. 1.

Macfarquhar, Neil. "Bombs in Brooklyn. The Suspects: Little Interest in Politics or Religion, Families Say." *The New York Times,* August 2, 1997, p. 24.

McFadden, Robert D. "Suspects in Bomb Plot Took Two Paths From the West Bank." *The New York Times,* August 3, 1997, p. 29.

Morrison, Dan. "Subways Were a Target/Feds: 2 Planned Suicide Attack on City." *Newsday,* August 1, 1997, p. A5.

SUICIDE TERRORISM

Suicide terrorism involves the intentional sacrifice of one's life in order to facilitate an act of terror. Until the late twentieth century, most terrorists took advantage of technological developments that allowed them to kill from afar. In contemporary times, however, suicide terrorism has been on the increase for a number of reasons. A suicide attacker can effectively commit large-scale damage without the need for expensive technologies. A single suicide terrorist can easily and cheaply place him or herself deep inside enemy territory and deliver the payload directly to the target. Most importantly, the dramatic and, to most people, perverse nature of suicide terrorism is so extreme that the mere thought of a suicide attack is enough to instill fear in the general populace.

Terrorists have long understood that their lives were at risk. For example, the Russian anarchists and revolutionaries of the nineteenth century

understood that their makeshift bombs might explode in their hands, and many penned farewell notes to friends and loved ones. During World War II, Japanese pilots flew kamikaze missions against U.S. military assets in the Pacific. Although these attacks where aimed at military targets, and as such not acts of terrorism against civilians, they did demonstrate a willingness to use suicide as a weapon.

Suicide terrorism, in the sense we think of it today, dates to the early 1980s, when young Hezbollah terrorists in Lebanon came under the control of Sheikh Mohammed Fadlallah. His apocalyptic preaching attracted young followers who, like Fadlallah, believed that the enemies of Islam could be destroyed through martyrdom and suicide missions. In 1983, Hezbollah launched a devastating suicide bombing campaign against U.S. interests in the region. The first suicide bomber drove an explosive laden van into the side of the U.S. embassy in Beirut, killing many people and injuring many more. Six months later another suicide bomber attacked the U.S. embassy and U.S. Marine barracks in Beirut, Lebanon, causing massive loss of life.

Shortly thereafter, suicide terrorism was employed by the Liberation Tigers of Tamil Eelam (LTTE), better known as the Tamil Tigers, a terrorist group waging war against the government of Sri Lanka. Tamil Tigers are believed to have designed the suicide bomber jacket that is now a common feature of such attacks the world over. They used suicide terrorists to kill Indian prime minister Rajiv Gandhi in 1991 and Sri Lankan president Ranasinghe Premadasa in 1993. A Tiger suicide bomber killed 100 people in an attack on a bank in Colombo, Sri Lanka, in 1996.

In 1994, Hamas, which means "zeal" in Arabic, began using suicide terrorism against Israel. At about the same time, the al Qaeda network, under the leadership of Osama bin Laden, began planning suicide missions against U.S. embassies in Kenya and Tanzania in 1998, as well as the USS *Cole* in Yemen in 2000. Also in 2000, the second Palestinian uprising, or *intifada,* saw suicide attacks move to the forefront as the terrorist weapon of choice.

The most egregious act of suicide terrorism occurred on September 11, 2001, when 19 hijackers commandeered four planes, flying two into the

World Trade Center in New York and one into the Pentagon. The fourth plane crashed in an open field in Pennsylvania after a struggle between passengers and terrorists. These suicide missions managed to take the lives of 3,000 individuals.

Religion and Suicide Terrorism

Religiously sanctioned suicide attacks are not unique to the modern period or confined to the Middle Eastern region. Similar types of assaults are known to have occurred over a span of several centuries in three little-known Muslim communities of the Indian Ocean region: those of the Malabar coast of southwestern India; Atjeh in northern Sumatra; and Mindanao and Sulu in the southern Philippines. Although these earlier suicide attacks in Asia were not undertaken with the same political awareness that characterizes the organizers of the incidents in Beirut and Israel, they represent essentially the same phenomena: Muslims who thought they had no other means of fighting against a superior military power used suicide terrorism as a form of protest against Western authority, colonial rule, or occupation.

It can be argued that today's suicide bombers are merely performing acts of martyrdom that first took place 13 centuries ago after the death of Muhammad. The Prophet's death in 632 left Muslims without a leader to watch over the faith. Several followers met to rectify this by selecting a caliph, a temporal authority to guide the community, but religion soon gave way to politics. Within 40 years after the Prophet's demise, various caliphs had managed to assassinate their way to power, and Islam had divided into two sects. The orthodox Sunnis accepted the reign of temporal leaders, whereas the Shiites believed that their imams were the divinely inspired and infallible descendants of Muhammad.

In 680, Husayn ibn 'Ali and his wife Fatima (the daughter of Muhammad), marched on the Sunnis in what Husayn hoped would be a gesture of reconciliation. According to legend, Husayn dreamt that no reconciliation was possible, and that he and his followers would die in a battle with the Sunnis. Husayn disregarded the premonition, and he and his family marched to their deaths near the village of Karbala, which is today in Iraq. To this day, especially in Iraq and Iran, passion plays and mass processionals are performed each year in commemoration of Husayn's martyrdom. These events are sometimes marked by rites of self-flagellation in which young men scrape their backs with hooks to draw blood, especially on Ashura, the 10th day of the month of Muharam, the anniversary of Husayn's death.

These rituals are clearly not suicide; indeed, Islam forbids the taking of one's own life. Rather, they symbolize the readiness to summit to the will of Allah, with the understanding that rewards will come after death. Islam emphasizes that life on earth is merely a transition to a better life. A suicide bomber is making a transition that will put him or her alongside the other heroes of Islam.

Members of such groups as the Arous ad-Damm, the "Brides of Blood," are sworn to avenge the death of Husayn through their own martyrdom, but they do not actively pursue suicide. The choice is not theirs, just as it was not Husayn's: Allah selected Husayn for martyrdom. Here is the intimate link between the practice of martyrdom in Islam—expressed in the act of suicide—and the official structure of Islam as a political entity. Given no distinction between church and state in Islam, an act of religious devotion, such as suicide, can become an instrument of state policy for militant Muslims.

Viewing suicide as a form of religious devotion can help Westerners make sense of the apparently bizarre actions of these suicide bombers. Consider, for example, the affable smile worn on the face of the bomber as he made his way into the compound to blow up the U.S. embassy in Beirut in 1983. This smile, known as the *bassamat al Farah*, or "smile of joy," symbolizes the joy of martyrdom. The notion of joy in the act of suicide is also evident in the videotape left behind by a 17-year-old female suicide bomber, San'ah Muheidli, who in 1983 drove her yellow Mercedes Benz laden with explosives into an Israeli military convoy in southern Lebanon, killing two soldiers and herself. On the tape, San'ah instructs her mother not to mourn her untimely death but, "Be merry, to let your joy explode as if it were my wedding day." A suicide bomber's death is described by Islamic militants as "the martyr's wedding," an occasion of joy and celebration.

Religious fervor may also explain, at least in part, the spate of more than 75 suicide bombings that rocked Israel after the start of the second intifada. Some of these suicide bombers are inspired to commit the ultimate sacrifice by the prodding of their spiritual handlers. These suicide bombers leave for their missions directly from their mosques, after completing many days of mental preparation, such as chanting aloud the relevant scriptures from the Koran. A favorite verse reads: "Think not of those who are slain in Allah's way as dead. No, they live on and find sustenance in the presence of the Lord."

So strong is their belief that bombers are able to walk among the enemy without exhibiting the slightest anxiety. In 1996, Israeli television reported that a suicide bomber dressed in an Israeli army uniform mingled with soldiers at a bus stop and hitchhiking post in coastal Ashkelon before setting off an explosion, killing two Israeli soldiers and himself. Witnesses to other bombings have told the authorities that they never suspected the bomber on the bus was a suicide terrorist on a mission.

It is important to understand the role religious inspiration plays in precipitating the actions of suicide terrorists. It would be naïve to think of these suicide terrorists as mere religious fanatics blindly following a spiritual leader. However, it would be equally foolish to dismiss the impact of incendiary clerics on the minds of impressionable youngsters, as well as people of all ages.

Profile of a Suicide Bomber

Before the attacks of September 11, the stereotype of a suicide bomber was that of an angry young Islamic male driven by visions of paradise to kill infidels. On his way to heaven, this zealot, who had few opportunities on Earth, provides economic support for his family through an annuity commonly paid to the families of suicide terrorism by supporting organizations or countries. The suicide bomber's own personal reward is said to include the services of 72 virgins that await his arrival in a glorious afterlife filed with golden houses and clear-running steams.

The events of September 11 awakened the world to a new type of suicide bomber. Mohamed Atta, who is believed to have flown American Airlines Flight 11 into the north tower of the World Trade Center, was an educated young man

from a well-to-do family. Atta and the other 18 suicide hijackers rendered past profiles inaccurate: some were highly educated, others had the wherewithal to achieve, and still others were married with children. Clearly, their ages, educational levels, and marital statuses were well outside the previous experience with suicide terrorists.

The typical suicide bomber has historically been male, but this stereotype was shattered in 2002. According to Hamas, women could not be suicide bombers because traveling outside the home without male accompaniment violated Islamic law. But Sheikh Ahmed Yassin, the founder and spiritual leader of Hamas, did state, "We will start using women when we have run out of men." As the violence of the second intifada intensified, Palestinian nationalism became as strong a motivation for martyrdom as Islamic radicalism.

Supposedly driven by nationalist fervor, a Fatah spin-off, the secular al Aqsa Martyrs Brigades, embraced suicide bombing as a method capable of inflicting pain against the Israelis. A female unit was formed. Wafa Idriss, a divorced 26-year-old ambulance worker from a Ramallah refugee camp, became the first female suicide bomber, blowing herself up in Central Jerusalem in January 2002. Shortly thereafter Dareen Abu Aisheh, a student at Nablus University who had been rejected by Hamas and joined the al Aqsa Brigades, detonated herself at a checkpoint near Jerusalem. Ayat al Akhras, an 18-year-old secretary and member of the Brigades, blew herself up in a supermarket in Kiryat Hayovel.

Young, educated males and females, individuals of economic means, and older individuals with families are now suicide terrorists. Moreover, many suicide terrorists do not appear to be solely motivated by a distorted religious belief in the value of martyrdom; politics may play a role in inspiring their actions, and they use their bodies accordingly.

Trends and Future Threats

Suicide bombings have become increasingly common in the wake of the 9/11 attacks. Their effectiveness in generating shock and media attention has only increased the number of attacks. The second intifada in Palestine, sparked by a visit to

Vests waiting to be outfitted with explosive devices intended for use by suicide bombers. These vests were found by Marines from Explosive Ordnance Disposal, Combat Service Support Company 117, Regimental Combat Team 7, 1st Marine Division, in a schoolyard located in the Baghdad suburb of Ziona. These devices were to be used to inflict civilian and coalition forces casualties during Operation Iraqi Freedom. (Photo by MSGT Howard J. Farrell, USMC)

the al Aqsa Mosque by Israeli Prime Minister Ariel Sharon, was infamous for the use of suicide attacks, with more than 40 incidents occurring during the four-year span that preceded the Gaza war. The use of suicide terrorism was also a prominent aspect of local resistance to the U.S. presence in both Afghanistan and Iraq. Since the U.S. invasion in 2003, over 1,500 suicide bombings have occurred in Iraq, at locations ranging from public areas like mosques and markets to vehicles such as cars and buses.

Because suicide terrorism employs humans as the bomb-delivery system, the bombs themselves are less easily detected and can be brought closer to heavily populated areas than traditional types of explosives. For that reason, the use of women and children as suicide bombers is of growing concern to counterterror experts. The use of child soldiers and bombers in the Palestine-Israel conflicts and the use of women in the Iraq wars have appalled human rights' groups and the public.

Though practiced frequently by al Qaeda and various Palestinian terror groups, suicide terrorism is not limited to one culture, country, or demographic. The more successful these tactics appear, the more likely they are to be used. In December 2010, two people were wounded during a suicide bomb attack in a busy shopping area in Stockholm, Sweden. Experts fear that it is only

A U.S. Air Force Explosive Ordnance Disposal Team and U.S. Army Soldiers from the 278th Regimental Combat Team inspect the area around a detonated suicide bomber's vehicle-borne explosive device in Tuz, Iraq, on June 17, 2005, during Operation Iraqi Freedom. The suicide bomber killed himself and injured four civilians and three Iraqi police officers. (U.S. Air Force photo by Staff Sgt. Suzanne M. Day/Released)

a matter of time before the trend spreads to North America.

Harvey Kushner

See also al Aqsa Martyrs Brigades; bin Laden, Osama; East Africa Embassy Bombings; Hamas; Iraq War; Liberation Tigers of Tamil Eelam; September 11 Attacks; U.S. Embassy Bombing, Beirut; U.S. Marine Barracks Bombing, Beirut; USS *Cole* Bombing

Further Readings

Berko, Anat. *The Path to Paradise: The Inner World of Suicide Bombers.* Westport, CT: Praeger Security International, 2009.

Eager, Paige Whaley. *From Freedom Fighters to Terrorists: Women and Political Violence.* Burlington, VT: Ashgate, 2008.

Glucklich, Ariel. *Dying for Heaven: Holy Pleasure and Suicide Bombers.* New York: HarperOne, 2009.

Hafez, Mohammed M. *Suicide Bombers in Iraq: The Strategy and Ideology of Martyrdom.* Washington, DC: United States Institute of Peace, 2007.

Kobrin, Nancy Hartevelt. *The Banality of Suicide Terrorism: The Naked Truth about the Psychology of Islamic Suicide Bombing.* Dulles, VA: Potomac Books, 2010.

Kushner, Harvey W. "Suicide Bombers: Business as Usual." *Studies in Conflict & Terrorism* 19 (1996): 329–337.

Pape, Robert Anthony. *Dying to Win: The Strategic Logic of Suicide Terrorism.* New York: Random House, 2005.

Rappaport, David. "Fear and Trembling: Terrorism Three Religious Traditions." *American Political Science Review* 78 (September 1984).

Taheri, Amir. *Holy Terror.* Bethesda, MD: Adler & Adler, 1987.

Wright, Robin. *Sacred Rage.* New York: Touchstone, 1986.

SUTHERLAND, THOMAS (1931–)

Dr. Thomas Sutherland, a Scots-born American professor, was held hostage for nearly six-and-a-half years during the hostage crisis in Lebanon.

Sutherland and his wife, Jean, moved to Beirut in the summer of 1983 to work at the American University, then one of the most prestigious educational institutions in the Middle East. Sutherland, who had taught animal sciences at Colorado University for 26 years, signed a three-year contract as dean of faculty for agriculture and food science; his wife was to teach English at the school. When the Sutherlands arrived to take up their posts, Western staff and professors at American University were already becoming targets of radical Shiite Muslim fundamentalists.

The first of these targets was Malcolm Kerr, the president of American University. Kerr was assassinated on January 18, 1984. Professor Frank Reiger was abducted the following month. Concerned for his own safety, but not intimidated, Sutherland remained at the university. Over a year later, on May 28, 1985, radical Shiite gunmen seized David P. Jacobsen, the director of the American University hospital. Two weeks later, two cars forced Sutherland's limousine to stop, and he was abducted at gunpoint within minutes of his return from the United States.

Sutherland believes his kidnapping was a case of mistaken identity, that the gunmen who seized him were actually seeking the new American University president, Calvin Plimpton, whose limousine Sutherland was using. Regardless, on June 9, 1985, Sutherland became the seventh American and the twelfth Western foreigner to disappear in Lebanon.

Sutherland spent much of his initial time as a hostage in solitary confinement. His captors interpreted a flier for a conference on basic Islam found in his briefcase as proof that Sutherland was a "spy." They interrogated him relentlessly. Finally, by the end of the summer, Sutherland was allowed to join the other hostages: Jacobson, Terry Anderson, Rev. Robert Weir, and Father Lawrence Martin Jenco. Sutherland was chained to the floor, like the others. Sutherland became extremely depressed, and he spoke of suffocating himself with a garbage bag. In late 1986, when he was moved to a tiny, solitary, underground cell, Sutherland attempted suicide three times. He spent the last portion of his 2,354 days of captivity with Anderson.

Sutherland was freed on November 18, 1991, along with Terry Waite, the Anglican envoy and hostage. Their release, the first following the Iran-Contra arms-for-hostages debacle in the United

States, marked the beginning of the end of the Lebanon hostage crisis for the United States. Within a month, Anderson, the last American hostage, would be released. (Two German aid workers remained.) Upon release, Sutherland was flown to the U.S. military base in Wiesbaden, Germany, to be treated for a peptic ulcer, before joining his family in California for his first Thanksgiving in six years.

In 1993 Sutherland traveled to Beirut with NBC and the BBC to shoot a film about his captivity. He was the first hostage to return. In June 2001, following Anderson's $341 million lawsuit the year earlier, the Sutherlands—Thomas, Jean and their three daughters—won a $353 million judgment against Iran.

Laura Lambert

See also Anderson, Terry A.; Buckley, William; Hezbollah; Hostage Taking; Mugniyah, Imad Fayez

Further Readings

Anderson, Terry. *Den of Lions: Memoirs of Seven Years.* New York: Ballantine, 1994.
Sutherland, Tom, and Jean Sutherland. *At Your Own Risk: An American Chronicle of Crisis and Captivity in the Middle East.* Golden, CO: Fulcrum Publishers, 1996.

SWEDAN, SHEIKH AHMED SALIM (1969–2009)

Sheikh Ahmed Salim Swedan (aka Ahmed the Tall; Sheikh Ahmad Salem Suweidan) was alleged to have bought both trucks used in the 1998 bombings of the U.S. embassies in Tanzania and Kenya. For his role in the bombings, which killed 224 people, he was placed on the FBI's list of "most wanted terrorists," where he stayed until his death in 2009.

Swedan, born in Mombasa, Kenya, was believed to have been a member of the al Qaeda network. According to the FBI, Swedan managed a trucking business in Kenya before becoming involved in al Qaeda's East African cells. A 1998 U.S. indictment charges that Swedan and fellow al Qaeda members bought a 1987 Nissan Atlas truck in Tanzania and

a Toyota Dyna truck in Kenya several months before the bombings. An African poultry farmer who had lived near Swedan in Kenya testified about the Toyota in the bombings case, saying that he told Swedan in jest that he would sell him his pickup truck for $10,000. As this was twice what he had bought it for, the farmer was surprised when Swedan agreed. The man never saw his neighbor again.

According to the indictment, Swedan then made alterations to the back of the Toyota and arranged for mechanical and welding work on the Nissan. Members of al Qaeda later filled the trucks with oxygen and acetylene tanks, fertilizer, sandbags, boxes of TNT, and detonators, transforming the trucks into moving bombs. On August 2, 1998, Swedan fled for Pakistan. Five days later, in synchronized attacks 400 miles apart, the truck bombs exploded at the U.S. embassies in Kenya and Tanzania, one bomb detonating just minutes before the other. The U.S. government declared that Osama bin Laden and al Qaeda operatives were responsible. President Bill Clinton then ordered air attacks on al Qaeda training grounds in Afghanistan and on a pharmaceutical plant in Khartoum, Sudan. Swedan allegedly fled to Afghanistan, as did many of the other 26 individuals indicted in the embassy bombings case. Three of the suspects pled guilty and cooperated with the U.S. government as witnesses. In October 2001, four men linked to bin Laden were convicted of conspiracy in the case. All of the defendants, who pled not guilty, were sentenced to life in prison without parole. In January 2009, Swedan and his aide, Usama al–Kini, were killed in Pakistan close to the Afghan border by a U.S. missile attack.

Erica Pearson

See also al Qaeda; bin Laden, Osama; East Africa Embassy Bombings

Further Readings

Bergen, Peter. *Holy War, Inc.: Inside the Secret World of Osama bin Laden.* New York: Free Press, 2001.
"A Nation Challenged: The Hunted; The 22 Most Wanted Suspects, in a Five-act Drama of Global Terror." *The New York Times,* October 14, 2001, p. 1B.

Nelson, Dean. "Pakistan: Al-Qaeda Leaders Killed in U.S. Strike." *The Telegraph,* January 9, 2009. http://www .telegraph.co.uk/news/worldnews/asia/pakistan/ 4207565/Pakistan-Al-Qaeda-leaders-killed-in-US- strike.html.

Reeve, Simon. *The New Jackals: Ramzi Yousef, Osama bin Laden and the Future of Terrorism.* Boston: Northeastern University Press, 1999.

Smith, Martin, and Lowell Bergman. "Hunting bin Laden." *Frontline,* PBS, September 13, 2001. http:// www.pbs.org/wgbh/pages/frontline/shows/binladen.

SYMBIONESE LIBERATION ARMY

The Symbionese Liberation Army (SLA), a small group of multiracial militant revolutionaries based in California during the 1970s, owes nearly all its notoriety to the kidnapping and subsequent indoctrination of Patty Hearst, the newspaper heiress. Founded in the Berkeley California area in 1973 by Donald DeFreeze, known to the group as General Field Marshal Cinque Mtume, much of the short life of the group was lived in the media spotlight, making SLA one of the more infamous revolutionary groups of the era, though one of the least respected politically.

The SLA began as a collaboration between convicts and prison activists. Led by DeFreeze, an escaped convict and initially the only black member of the group, the seven other members, who were white middle-class men and women, adopted Swahili names and took up arms for the self-styled Symbionese Federation. The group's motto, "Death to the fascist insect that preys upon the life of the people," was included on each of their communiqués.

The SLA's first significant action, on November 6, 1973, was the assassination of Marcus Foster, the first black superintendent of schools in Oakland. Foster was working to improve education in Oakland, but because his plan included mandatory ID cards, the SLA targeted him as a "fascist." By murdering a prominent black leader, the SLA alienated the Black Panther Party and other revolutionary leftist groups (though the SLA was later hailed by the waning Weather Underground). In January 1974, when SLA members Russell Little and Joseph Remiro were arrested for Foster's murder, the group began to plan another violent act.

On February 4, 1974, Patty Hearst, then a sophomore at the University of California, Berkeley, was kidnapped from her apartment by three SLA members. Three days later, the SLA sent a communiqué denouncing the "establishment" and claiming Hearst as their "prisoner of war." On February 12, KPFA Radio aired a tape in which Hearst demanded that her family distribute food to the poor in exchange for her release. Ten days later, the Hearsts funded a program, "People In Need," which eventually supplied food to over 30,000 people, at the cost of $2 million. Patty Hearst then denounced her parents as "pigs" and joined the SLA, taking on the revolutionary name "Tania," after Che Guevara's companion.

With Hearst as Tania, the SLA robbed a branch of the Hibernia Bank on April 15, 1974, where Hearst's transformation to a revolutionary was captured by the surveillance camera. The group then fled to southern California. On May 16, Hearst and Bill and Emily Harris, known then as Teko and Yolanda, attempted to rob a sporting goods store in Inglewood, California. The following day, police blasted 5,000 rounds into the SLA hideout in South Central Los Angeles, which then went up in flames. Six SLA members—DeFreeze, Angela Atwood, Nancy Ling Perry, Willie Wolfe, Patricia Soltysik, and Camilla Hall—were killed. Hearst and the Harrises watched the events on television from a motel room in Anaheim.

The remaining SLA members robbed two more banks—one in Sacramento, on February 25, 1975, and another in Carmichael, California, on April 21, 1975. Myrna Lee Opsahl, a bank customer, was shot and killed in the latter robbery; Emily Harris subsequently admitted to having fired the shot that killed Opsahl. That September, in San Francisco, Hearst, the Harrises, and two minor SLA members were captured. All were tried, convicted, and served prison sentences for their SLA-related activities. Upon release, they all returned to relatively mainstream lives.

Kathleen Soliah, also known as Sara Jane Olson, had joined the SLA after the police shoot-out in Los Angeles. She remained a fugitive until she was apprehended in 1999, when she was charged with planting bombs under police cars in August 1975. In January 2002, two days before Soliah was sentenced for the bomb charges, she and the four remaining SLA members—Bill Harris, Emily Harris, Michael Bortin, and James Kilgore—pled guilty to second-degree murder in the Opsahl case. After serving sentences ranging from six to eight years, the SLA members were eventually released on parole, with Emily Harris and James Kilgore as the last released, in 2009.

Laura Lambert

See also Black Panther Party; Hearst, Patty; Weatherman

Further Readings

Baker, Marilyn, with Sally Brompton. *Exclusive! The Inside Story of Patricia Hearst and the SLA*. New York: Macmillan, 1974.

Bloomekatz, Ari B. "Last Captured SLA Member Is Released from Prison." *Los Angeles Times*, May 11, 2009. http://articles.latimes.com/2009/may/11/local/me-kilgore11.

Findley, Tim, and Les Payne. *The Life and Death of the SLA*. New York: Ballantine Books, 1976.

Graebner, William. *Patty's Got a Gun: Patricia Hearst in 1970s America*. Chicago: University of Chicago Press, 2008.

McLellan, Vin, and Paul Avery. *The Voices of Guns*. New York: G.P. Putnam's Sons, 1977.

TALIBAN

The Taliban is a religious and military movement that seized control of large portions of Afghanistan in the mid-1990s. While the Taliban was initially seen as a stabilizing force in war-torn Afghanistan, the movement's embrace of a radical form of Islam quickly made it a pariah in the international community. The Taliban's hosting of the terrorist organization al Qaeda eventually led to its ouster by the United States in late 2001, following the attacks of September 11. Since 2004, however, the Taliban has managed to mount a successful insurgency campaign against both Western forces and the Afghan government, extending its reach not only into the formerly peaceful northern region of Afghanistan but also into the tribal regions of northwestern Pakistan.

Coming to Power

The Taliban emerged in the southern Afghan district of Kandahar in 1994. Two years before, the mujahideen—a loose alliance of Afghan ethnic and religious groups, plus foreigners who had come to defend Islam—had ousted the Soviet-backed People's Democratic Party of Afghanistan (PDPA) after more than a decade of war. But peace did not follow victory. Mujahideen warlords began fighting over the control of Afghanistan. While some areas, such as the western city of Herat, were relatively stable, the

Afghan capital of Kabul was attacked ceaselessly for two years as various factions fought for control of the city.

The district of Kandahar was also in chaos. There, the mujahideen warlords acted more like bandits than would-be governors, attacking civilians as well as each other. In the summer of 1994, a former mujahideen fighter named Mohammed Omar decided to rid Afghanistan of the mujahideen warlords and restore unity under Islam. At the time, Omar was living at a madrassa, or Islamic religious school, in the village of Singesar. A reclusive man who would not allow himself to be photographed, Omar would eventually become the ultimate leader of the Taliban, given the title Commander of the Faithful. His background, and the religious philosophy of the madrassas, would strongly shape the Taliban's agenda.

Omar was a member of the Pashtun ethnic group. Roughly half the Pashtuns lived in southern Afghanistan, and the other half lived in neighboring Pakistan. National lines had been muddled following the Soviet invasion of Afghanistan in 1979 to shore up the PDPA government. Many Afghan Pashtuns fled to Pakistan, where they lived in refugee camps and among Pakistani Pashtuns. Most Pashtuns follow the Sunni sect of Islam, which is the dominant sect in Afghanistan.

The madrassas could also be found on both sides of the Afghan-Pakistani border. Students at the madrassas received an education that was primarily religious. The madrassas had been greatly influenced by the Deobandi movement, a Sunni religious movement that emphasizes strict observance of religious ritual.

The madrassas of Afghanistan and Pakistan not only supplied the Taliban with a leader, but also with soldiers—most of them Afghan, but many Pakistani. Even the Taliban's name reflected its roots in the madrassas: The word *Taliban* is a Persian pluralization of the Arab word *talib,* which means religious student. The Taliban was largely dominated by the Pashtuns, and it was exclusively Sunni, to the detriment of Afghanistan's Shiite Muslim minority. The Deobandi influence was expressed by the Taliban's strident emphasis on the observance of religious customs, whether or not that observance was sincere or even voluntary.

In October 1994, Omar and his growing group of comrades seized a village and an arms depot. A month later, the Taliban—now with almost 3,000 fighters—routed an attack on a Pakistani convoy, then swept into the provincial capital of Kandahar and seized the city.

While supporters of the Taliban tended to credit the group's remarkable success to divine favor, popular discontent with the mujahideen, and the genius of Omar, critics noted the contribution of other factors. Almost from its inception, the Taliban received aid from Pakistan and from mujahideen warlords—including ones the Taliban would later overthrow—who apparently believed that the Taliban would serve to weaken rivals.

As a result, the Taliban were almost always better trained than their foes and had enough money on hand to purchase support from key warlords. Success created more success: Seizing Kandahar gave the Taliban access to heavy weaponry, including airplanes, helicopters, and tanks, once owned by the warlords who held the city. Nonstudents soon joined, and despite the Taliban's emphasis on Islam and on destroying the mujahideen, its leadership ranks soon included former warlords and PDPA officers.

By 1995, the Taliban had tens of thousands of fighters and the increased support of Pakistan, which was apparently both responding to pressure by its Pashtun population and eager to have influence within Afghanistan. In March, the Taliban tried to take Kabul to the north but were defeated. Turning west, Taliban forces took Herat in September 1995, then returned to Kabul, finally seizing the national capital the following year.

The mujahideen withdrew to the north, eventually forming the rival Northern Alliance. The Taliban attacked the north repeatedly—in 1997 they came so close to success that Pakistan, Saudi Arabia, and the United Arab Emirates recognized it as the government of Afghanistan—but were never able to eradicate the mujahideen, a fact that would come back to haunt the Taliban.

Running Afghanistan

The Taliban's successful conquest of much of Afghanistan was initially greeted with equanimity by the United States. It was hoped that the Taliban would restore stability to the country and close down the terrorist training camps that had been established by radical Muslims in Afghanistan during the war against the Soviets. The Taliban's strict religiosity was initially seen in a positive light as well. Some observers believed that the Taliban would stamp out Afghanistan's thriving opium-poppy industry, and its leadership's hostility toward Shiite-dominated Iran dovetailed neatly with the United State's poor relations with that country.

But the poppy trade for the most part continued. The Taliban's hostility toward Iran went beyond poor relations, leading to the murder of several Iranian diplomats in 1998. In addition, the Taliban routinely persecuted and periodically massacred Shiites, especially those of the Hazara ethnic group.

In urban areas where the Taliban's grip on power was especially strong, the Taliban outlawed a variety of activities considered un-Islamic, including music, television, movies, kite-flying, and chess. Men were required to wear long beards; those whose beards were of insufficient length could be jailed until their beards grew out. Such rules were enforced by the religious police, part of the Taliban's Ministry for the Promotion of Virtue and Suppression of Vice.

The Taliban's treatment of women attracted especial condemnation. The Taliban forbade girls from attending school and forbade women from working. Women's bath houses—often used as a source of hot water in wintertime—were closed. Women were forbidden from going out in public without male relatives, and they were forced to wear a burqa, a garment that covered the entire body. Religious police publicly beat women who strayed from such rules.

Foreigners were not exempt from harassment and persecution by the Taliban. Indeed, the Taliban's willingness to target diplomats and aid workers triggered a number of international incidents. Even Pakistan soon found that it had little control over a movement it had helped build.

The Taliban and bin Laden

A significant reason for this was that the Taliban had found another source of funds—the wealthy Saudi radical Osama bin Laden, who had helped recruit foreign fighters for the mujahideen during the Soviet occupation of Afghanistan. In 1996, bin Laden returned to Afghanistan after the United States forced Sudan to expel him following attacks on U.S. military personnel in Saudi Arabia by his al Qaeda terrorist network. While bin Laden originally entered Afghanistan at the invitation of a mujahideen warlord, he soon made common cause with the Taliban, reportedly helping finance the final takeover of Kabul. His acceptance by the Taliban seriously strained relations with Pakistan and Saudi Arabia, but the wealth bin Laden commanded meant that the Taliban still had access to considerable funds, making support from other nations less crucial.

The drawbacks of such an arrangement became clear in August 1998, when terrorists linked to al Qaeda bombed U.S. embassies in Kenya and Tanzania. In response, the United States bombed an al Qaeda camp in Afghanistan. At the end of 1999, the United States discovered an al Qaeda plot to attack the country on New Year's Eve; the U.S. government warned the Taliban that it would pay the price for any al Qaeda attacks. But the Taliban continued to support al Qaeda and other radical Muslim groups. Military training camps in Taliban-controlled territory were used by a variety of terrorists and separatists groups, and bases in Afghanistan were even used to help launch an Islamic military movement in Tajikistan in early 2001.

On September 11, 2001, 19 al Qaeda operatives hijacked four planes in the United States, crashing two of them into the Twin Towers of New York City's World Trade Center and one into the Pentagon outside Washington, D.C. The attacks killed about 3,000 people.

Demands by the United States that the Taliban turn over bin Laden and the rest of al Qaeda's leadership were denied, with the Taliban insisting that bin Laden was their guest and not responsible for the attacks. After a period of fruitless negotiations, the United States and Great Britain began bombing Afghanistan in early October, and the United States put a bounty of $25 million on Omar's head, as well as on bin Laden's. Using Northern Alliance troops on the ground, the U.S.-led assault quickly overwhelmed Taliban forces, taking Kabul in November and Kandahar in December. On December 22, 2001, Hamad Karzai was sworn in as chairman of a U.S.-backed interim government created to replace the Taliban.

Into Pakistan

In the wake of their ouster from Afghanistan, Taliban leaders found a safe haven in the Pakistani city of Quetta, near the border with Afghanistan. There, the Taliban regrouped and continued as a guerrilla warfare operation, supplying men and weapons for the fighting in southern Afghanistan. Their resurgence was largely funded through the opium trade and foreign donations, and it was bolstered by foreign recruits from Chechnya, Pakistan, Uzbekistan, and various Arab countries. The Taliban were also assisted, in effect if not intent, by Hamid Karzai's corrupt and inept administration. Many Afghanis learned to distrust the government and turned to the Taliban for services, especially after Karzai's reelection in 2008, which was widely considered a sham. Many Afghan civilians began to prefer the Taliban's enforcement of strict Islamic law to the corrupt bureaucracy of the government.

Independent Pakistani branches of the Taliban began to spring up in 2002 in Pakistan's tribal border region. The Pakistani Taliban allied with al Qaeda to plan and finance attacks against the government of Pakistan, and these attacks grew in ferocity and complexity toward the end of the decade. In February 2009 the Pakistani government announced it would accept a system of Islamic law in the Swat Valley, a Taliban-controlled tribal area—a decision that was seen by analysts as a capitulation to the insurgents. Violence continued, however. In October 2009 a series of well-planned attacks on police and government installations took place that killed at least 40 people across Pakistan.

In late 2008 and early 2009, the Pakistani Taliban commanders and a six-member Afghani team dispatched to Waziristan by Mullah Omar formed a united council and vowed to put aside their differences and join together in the fight against American-led forces in Afghanistan. The Taliban also teamed up with Pakistani militants in the country's populous Punjab Province and carried out a series of deadly attacks.

In 2009 Omar moved to the Pakistani city of Karachi with the help of the Pakistani Inter-Services Intelligence Directorate (ISI) to escape attacks from unmanned U.S. drones. For many years the ISI had offered money, supplies, and guidance to the Taliban in Afghanistan as a way of influencing a friendly government in Afghanistan following the eventual departure of U.S. forces. But as the Pakistani Taliban, which was increasingly seen as indistinguishable from the Taliban in Afghanistan, pushed further into Pakistan, the country's military and political leaders, with strong pressure from the United States, took on a full-scale military operation to push the Taliban back. Omar's deputy, Abdul Ghani Baradar, who was largely seen as a powerful force behind the Taliban's resurgence in Afghanistan, was captured by the ISI in February 2010, signaling a shift in Pakistani strategy, though an ambiguous one, with some seeing it as a sign that Pakistan was turning against the Afghan Taliban and others considering it just a tactical move made in advance of the U.S. departure from Afghanistan and meant to marginalize Karzai and bolster Pakistan's future negotiating position with the rebel leadership.

An Expanded Presence and Influence in Afghanistan

In the second half of the 2000s, the Taliban proved itself to be a resilient insurgency. The year 2006 was one of the bloodiest of the new millennium, with suicide attacks reaching record levels and the number civilian deaths higher than any year since 2001. Both records were then broken in 2007.

Pfc. Dalton Martin of Tactical Command Post, HQ Company, 2-502 Infantry, 101st Airborne Division, keeps watch as two men and woman pass by during a joint patrol with the Afghan Army in Zhari district, Kandahar province, southern Afghanistan, on August 25, 2010. Soldiers in Zhari operate in a district that is the birthplace of the Taliban movement and holds many well-armed insurgents who blend in with a support network providing them with explosives and safe havens. (AP Photo/Brennan Linsley. © 2011 The Associated Press. All Rights Reserved)

In 2009 President Barack Obama announced a build-up of 30,000 troops to reverse the Taliban's gains and force it to the negotiating table. The Taliban showed its determination to cause havoc on January 18, 2010, when Taliban gunmen and suicide bombers launched a coordinated assault on Kabul that targeted a shopping center, a movie theater, and a hotel, killing 12, injuring 71, and creating a sense of chaos in the capital.

In 2010, U.S. troops stepped up operations in Kandahar Province, a Taliban stronghold, and successfully forced the Taliban to give up their hold on all the districts around the city of Kandahar by the end of the year. Many Taliban commanders took refuge in Pakistan. The advances in the south, however, have come at the expense of the north, which in 2010 experienced a stronger insurgency than in the past, with armed groups attacking and terrorizing local people, government officials, and diplomats, highlighting the inability of the government to secure and protect the region.

By the end of 2010, the Taliban was also stronger in eastern Afghanistan, where the government was a particularly weak presence. Insurgent leaders have largely filled the void left by the government and are in very regular contact with the local people, providing services, settling disputes, and dictating school curriculums.

American progress in southern Afghanistan remained tentative at the beginning of 2011, and U.S. losses in the north and east were worrisome. Certainly the Taliban exerted more power in Afghanistan in early 2011 than they did in the first few years after the 9/11 attacks and the invasion by coalition forces. The U.S. fight against the Taliban continues, and many security and military experts worry about the organization's increasing foothold in Pakistan, a nuclear country.

Mary Sisson and Tim Anderson

See also Afghanistan War; al Qaeda; bin Laden, Osama; East Africa Embassy Bombings; Mujahideen; Riyadh, Saudi Arabia, Bombing; September 11 Attacks; Taliban Code of Conduct

Further Readings

Crews, Robert D., and Amin Tarzi, eds. *The Taliban and the Crisis of Afghanistan.* Cambridge, MA: Harvard University Press, 2009.

Ellis, Deborah. *Women of the Afghan War.* Westport, CT: Praeger, 2000.

Maley, William, ed. *Fundamentalism Reborn? Afghanistan and the Taliban.* New York: New York University Press, 1998.

Marsden, Peter. *The Taliban: War, Religion and the New Order in Afghanistan.* London: Zed Books, 1998.

Rashid, Ahmed. *Taliban: Militant Islam, Oil and Fundamentalism in Central Asia.* 2nd ed. New Haven, CT: Yale University Press, 2010.

Rohde, David, with Dexter Filkins and Eric Schmitt. "Taliban Give Way in Final Province Where They Ruled." *The New York Times,* December 10, 2001, p. A1.

"Times Topics: Taliban." *The New York Times.* http://topics.nytimes.com/top/reference/timestopics/organizations/t/taliban/index.html.

Zaeef, Abdul Salam. *My Life with the Taliban.* New York: Columbia University Press, 2010.

TALIBAN CODE OF CONDUCT

In 2009 the Afghan Taliban leadership, exiled in Pakistan, issued a "code of conduct," known formally as the "Taliban 2009 Rules and Regulations Booklet." The booklet provided guidance to local, regional, and provincial Taliban commanders, who enjoyed some autonomy in deciding which operations to conduct and running their territory of control. The booklet aimed to consolidate command and control of the Taliban movement and introduce discipline among the rank and file.

Comprising 11 chapters and 59 articles, the code was prepared by the advisory council of the Islamic Emirate of Afghanistan. Although most Taliban fighters are illiterate, the "code" is issued to every fighter as a 64-page pocket book. It is available in Pashtu, Urdu, Arabic, and English, and it is likely the booklet will be translated to other languages as more nationalities fight alongside the Afghan Taliban. The Taliban leadership has insisted that not only its fighters but also foreigners that fight in Afghanistan should adhere to its "code."

The booklet marked an attempt to create an internal disciplinary system through which the Taliban could enforce its own laws of war. To increase legitimacy, the code departed from an earlier 2006 code and contains rules similar to the International Humanitarian Law. The text states, for example, that "all mujahideen must do their best to avoid civilian deaths and injuries and damage to civilian property." Nevertheless, the code does not forbid suicide operations, and indeed it provides strict guidelines as to who might undertake such operations, and under what circumstances.

Beyond its immediate guidelines on behavior, the code also sheds considerable light on the structure and aims of the Afghan Taliban, which is seeking to recover its "Islamic Emirate of Afghanistan" regime of 1996–2001 by continuing to fight against coalition and Afghan forces and the Afghan government. The code was thus calibrated to achieve the next step for the Taliban: to win the hearts and minds of the Afghan populace. Historically regarded as a dogmatic group impervious to external developments, the exiled leadership of the Afghan Taliban apparently hoped the new code would help to transform the ruthless group into a more populist movement.

With the orientation of Afghan and coalition forces changing in Afghanistan, the Afghan Taliban will ensure compliance to the code or risk alienation. Yet the code will probably not be followed, most notably by Pakistani Taliban, whose oath of allegiance pledged to Mullah Omar is symbolic, not functional. The Afghan Taliban wants to exercise control over the two-dozen Pakistani Taliban factions mounting deadly attacks against Pakistani targets, but the bulk of these factions are not expected to heed the advice.

The Pakistani Taliban itself remained fragmented in 2010, with factions willing to cease attacks inside Pakistan termed "soft Taliban" and others insistent on attacks known as "hard Taliban." As of 2010, the Afghan Taliban's influence over Pakistani Taliban appeared to be dwindling, and it seemed likely that the code would be followed only by the Afghan Taliban itself, rather than the majority of the groups active in region.

Rohan Gunaratna

See also al Qaeda; Bombings and Bomb Scares; Taliban

Further Readings

Rashid, Ahmed. *Taliban: Militant Islam, Oil, and Fundamentalism in Central Asia.* 2nd ed. London: I.B. Tauris, 2010.

"Taliban 2009 Rules and Regulations Booklet." SITE Monitoring Service, September 10, 2009.

Zaleef, Abdul Salam. *My Life with the Taliban.* New York: Columbia University Press, 2010.

TAMIL TIGERS

See Liberation Tigers of Tamil Eelam

TEHRIK-I-TALIBAN PAKISTAN

Tehrik-i-Taliban Pakistan (TTP), also known as the Pakistani Taliban, is a coalition of militant Islamist groups based in the border region of Pakistan and Afghanistan. The group is distinct from the Taliban that controlled large portions of Afghanistan from the mid-1990s until it was ousted by U.S. forces in late 2001, but the TTP does have close links with and similar aims as that group, as well as the terrorist network al Qaeda. Although a relatively new group, the TTP has carried out deadly attacks throughout Pakistan and even launched an attack against the United States.

The TTP seeks to establish areas independent of the Pakistani government that will operate under Shariah, or Islamic law. To that end, the group has repeatedly attacked Pakistani military and police forces, and it has been linked to the assassination of former Pakistani Prime Minister Benazir Bhutto. The group is rabidly pro-Sunni Muslim, and it has conducted deadly attacks against Pakistan's religious minorities.

The TTP also has a strong anti-U.S. bent, which has become more intense since a U.S. drone killed Baitullah Mehsud, the group's founder, in August 2009. In response, the TTP has targeted U.S. personnel in the region and financed a failed car bombing in New York City on May 1, 2010. The organization has promised to carry out more attacks against U.S. and European targets.

The Forming of the TTP

Following the September 11, 2001, attack on the World Trade Center orchestrated by al Qaeda, U.S. forces invaded Afghanistan and overthrew the

Taliban government there, which had supported the terrorist network. Many Taliban and al Qaeda militants found a haven in the northwest region of Pakistan. This region functions primarily under tribal leadership and is autonomous from the central Pakistani government.

Pakistan has long been home to a variety of Islamic militant groups, and once the ousted Afghan Taliban made its home in northwest Pakistan, the area became even more of a magnet for militants. Many of these militants remained largely focused on the political situation in Pakistan, not Afghanistan, and as a result they were never been fully incorporated into the Afghan Taliban. These militants consolidated control over the northwest border area of Pakistan by executing more moderate tribal leaders there.

The Pakistani militants in the region became informally known as the Pakistani Taliban, and in December 2007 the TTP announced its existence under the leadership of Baitullah Mehsud, an established militia leader from South Waziristan who had close ties to al Qaeda. Despite the formality of the announcement, most observers believe that the TTP is more of a loose federation of militia groups, rather than a tightly organized operation under the strict control of one person. Nonetheless, by forming a coalition and coordinating action, the Islamic groups in the region have been able to carry off an extremely ambitious series of attacks.

The announcement of the founding of the TTP was followed two weeks later by the assassination of Bhutto. Bhutto, who was prime minister of Pakistan from 1988 to 1990 and from 1993 to 1996, was the first woman to serve in such a position in an Islamic country, and she vocally opposed legal restrictions on women's behavior that are generally supported by militant Islamists. Bhutto was assassinated in a gun and bomb attack on December 27, 2007, while campaigning for another term as prime minister. While the TTP denied having a role in the assassination, the government of Pakistan maintains that Baitullah Mehsud was involved in the planning of the attack.

Despite that charge, the Pakistani government initially exhibited a willingness to negotiate with the TTP, which had effective control over sizeable areas of northwest Pakistan. Although negotiations led to the occasional brief cease-fire, throughout 2008 the TTP carried out a series of suicide bombings and attacks aimed at Pakistani forces in the northwest region. As a result, in August 2008 the Pakistani government banned the group.

A month later, the TTP carried out a suicide bombing at a hotel in Islamabad, the capital of Pakistan, killing more than 50 people. The bombing marked the beginning of a series of attacks in Pakistan's major cities outside the northwest region. These attacks were typically aimed at Pakistan's armed forces, its police, or its foreign population, and they had the goal of forcing Pakistan to withdraw its forces from the northwest.

The strategy apparently backfired, as Pakistan's government became more convinced that the TTP posed a threat to its survival and increased its cooperation with the United States, which has been fighting Islamic militants in the region since 2001. The government allowed the United States to conduct a series of drone attacks in its northwest region, and on August 5, 2009, a drone killed Mehsud.

Escalation

By the end of August 2009, a new leader of the TTP had emerged: Hakimullah Mehsud, another member of the Mehsud clan of South Waziristan. Before the founding of the TTP, Hakimullah Mehsud had made a name for himself as a brash and aggressive militia leader, and under his leadership the coalition became even more violent.

Following the death of Baitullah Mehsud, the TTP stepped up its suicide bombings and attacks against government targets across Pakistan. A particularly brutal series of attacks in October 2009, including a 22-hour siege at the Pakistani army's headquarters in Rawalpindi, left more than 160 people dead. In December 2009 the TTP attacked a mosque popular with military personnel in Rawalpindi during Friday prayers, killing more than 35 people. While such attacks have generally focused on military or government targets, they have indiscriminately killed many civilians, and in the deeply Islamic country of Pakistan, the mosque attack was considered especially shocking.

The TTP also began to aggressively target Muslims who are not members of the Sunni sect. On May 28, 2010, during Friday prayers, the group stormed two mosques in Lahore that are

Seeking Information Against International Terrorism

Rewards for Justice

Home
Program Overview
Rewards Paid
FAQ

Reward Offers

Wanted for Terrorism
Acts of Terror
Regime Elements
War Crimes

Fighting Terrorism

Terrorism Financing
WMD Terrorism
Submit a Tip

Links

Department of State
Diplomatic Security
FBI Most Wanted
RFJ Fund

Search the RFJ Site:

Google™ Custom Search

[Search]

Languages

english
français
español

中

deutsch

Wanted
Wali Ur Rehman
Up to $5 Million Reward

Place of Birth : South Waziristan, Pakistan
Hair : Black
Eyes : Brown
Complexion : Olive
Sex : Male
Nationality : Pakistani
Characteristics : Full beard, mustache.
Status : Fugitive

Wali Ur Rehman is second in command and chief military strategist of Tehrik-e-Taliban Pakistan (TTP). He commands TTP members. He has participated in cross-border attacks in Afghanistan against U.S. and NATO personnel, and is wanted in connection with his involvement in the murder of seven American citizens on December 30, 2009, at Forward Operating Base Chapman in Khost, Afghanistan.

The TTP's primary purpose is to force withdrawal of Pakistani troops from the FATA of Pakistan, which is located along the Pakistan-Afghanistan border; to expel Western interests from Pakistan; and to establish Sharia – or Islamic law – in the tribal territories.

The TTP has had alleged roles in, or claimed responsibility for, a number of acts of violence, including the September 2008 bombing of the Marriott Hotel in Islamabad, which resulted in the deaths of more than 50 people and another 300 wounded, including several Americans. These attacks are often coordinated with other insurgents or terrorist groups, including the Taliban and al-Qaeda.

TTP continues to plan and carry out attacks against the interests of the United States from the FATA. Most recently, the TTP has claimed responsibility for the failed bombing of Times Square in New York City on May 1, 2010.

Reward poster for Wali Ur Rehman. (RewardsforJustice.net)

used by Ahmadi Muslims, killing more than 90 people. In September 2010 the group bombed religious processions of Shiite Muslims in Lahore and Quetta, killing more than 80 people.

In perhaps its most ambitious undertaking, the TTP began to target the United States, a significant change from its previous domestic focus. In December 2009 a TTP operative set off a suicide bomb at a U.S. Central Intelligence Agency base in Khost, Afghanistan, killing seven Americans. In a

video released after the attack, Hakimullah Mehsud and the operative, who the CIA was attempting to recruit as a double agent, discuss the planned bombing and claim that it was in retaliation for the death of Baitullah Mehsud.

On May 1, 2010, a car bomb ignited but failed to fully detonate in the busy Times Square neighborhood of New York City; the resulting smoke drew the attention of the authorities, but no one was injured. Two days later, U.S. law-enforcement officials arrested Faisal Shahzad, a Pakistan-born U.S. citizen. Investigations revealed that Shahzad had traveled to Pakistan in 2008, hoping to join a militant group. He eventually was accepted by the TTP, which decided to take advantage of Shahzad's U.S. passport and send him back to the United States to conduct an attack. Shahzad returned to the United States in early 2010, where he received financing from the TTP that allowed him to carry out the failed attack.

In response, the U.S. Department of State designated the TTP as a foreign terrorist organization on September 1, 2010. Through its Rewards for Justice program, the department also offered a $5 million reward for information leading to the death or capture of Hakimullah Mehsud or the TTP's second in command, Wali Ur Rehman. It was widely rumored that Mehsud had died from injuries sustained in a January 2010 drone attack, but the reward offered for his capture suggests that the U.S. government believe him to still be alive.

Mary Sisson

See also Afghanistan War; al Qaeda; Taliban

Further Readings

Abbas, Hassan. "A Profile of Tehrik-i-Taliban Pakistan." *CTC Sentinel* 1, no. 2 (January 2008). http://www.ctc .usma.edu/sentinel/CTCSentinel-Vol1Iss2.pdf.

Elliot, Andrea. "A Bloody Siege, a Call to Action, a Times Sq. Plot." *The New York Times,* June 23, 2010, p. A1.

Fair, C. Christine. "Pakistan's Own War on Terror: What the Pakistani Public Thinks." *Journal of International Affairs* 63, no. 1 (Fall/Winter 2009): 39–55.

Franco, Claudio. "The Tehrik-i-Taliban Pakistan." In *Decoding the New Taliban: Insights from the Afghan Field,* edited by Antonio Giustozzi. New York: Columbia University Press, 2009.

"Hakimullah Mehsud." Rewards for Justice (U.S. Department of State). http://www.rewardsforjustice .net/index.cfm?page=Mehsud&language=english.

Mir, Amir. *The Talibinisation of Pakistan from 9/11 to 26/11.* New Delhi: Pentagon Security International, 2009.

Perlez, Jane. "Pakistan Attacks Show Tightening of Militant Links." *The New York Times,* October 16, 2009, p. A1.

THREATCON

See Force Protection Conditions

TOKYO SUBWAY ATTACK

In 1995, members of the Aum Shinrikyo cult attacked Tokyo's Kasumigaseki subway station in an attempt to cripple the government of Japan.

The Aum Shinrikyo cult believes that Armageddon, an ultimate battle between good an evil that will annihilate the world as it exists and bring forth a new and pure spiritual one, is imminent, and that it is their duty to hasten this battle and expunge the impure and sinful from the Earth. In light of these views, Aum began to collect and create weapons of mass destruction in the early and mid-1990s.

The cult tested its new arsenal several times during 1993 and 1994, secretly releasing botulism toxin, anthrax, and poison gas in and around Japan; one of these tests, a June 1994 release of sarin gas in the town of Matsumoto, killed seven people. Sarin, a nerve gas developed in Germany during World War II, is colorless, odorless, and tasteless. A single drop on the skin is enough to kill an adult. The first symptoms are nosebleeds and nausea; if enough sarin is inhaled, the victim will begin to convulse and eventually collapse into a coma and die.

By early 1995 continuing allegations created mounting pressure on law enforcement to move against the cult; in mid-March the cult was tipped off that a massive police raid was planned for the 21st of the month. Cult leaders decided to launch a coup against Japan's government, using sarin. They chose the Kasumigaseki subway station, in the heart of Tokyo, because it is the city's busiest subway station, and because it is the closest station to National Police Agency headquarters and hundreds of other vital government offices. The cult hoped to kill thousands of ministers and police officers on their way to work, throwing the government into disarray and allowing Aum to take over.

On the morning of March 20, 1995, at approximately 7:45, five cult members boarded five different subway lines, all heading toward Kasumigaseki station. Each man carried a package of liquid sarin wrapped in newspaper, and an umbrella. At 8 A.M., as the trains approached Kasumigaseki, each man punctured his package with the sharpened tip of the umbrella and left the train. The liquid immediately began to evaporate. Sarin is very dense, and if it is not lifted by strong air currents, it will remain close to the ground. The inefficient method of distribution chosen by the terrorists, evaporation, probably averted a much greater tragedy. As it was, thousands of commuters collapsed on the train and the adjacent platforms, turning Kasumigaseki and other nearby stations into bedlam. Twelve people were killed and thousands injured.

The attack and its violent aftermath gripped the nation. In the weeks after the incident, police raided Aum Shinrikyo compounds and arrested hundreds of members. These arrests provoked violent reprisals, including an assassination attempt on the chief of the National Police Agency. The incident shattered Japan's peaceful view of itself as the world's safest industrialized nation, and it sparked reforms in the criminal justice system. It also highlighted the immense vulnerabilities of a modern city to terrorism, even if the terrorists have access to only crude weapons and very simple means of distributing them.

In 2004, Aum Shinrikyo leader Shoko Asahara was found guilty of orchestrating the Tokyo subway attacks and sentenced to death; he was in custody, awaiting execution, as of 2010. Aum Shinrikyo continued to operate in Japan under the name of Aleph, and in 2005, Japanese authorities estimated that it had about 1,600 members. However in 2007 some of those members split off into a new group, called Hikari no Wa, which does not worship Asahara.

Colleen Sullivan

See also Asahara, Shoko; Aum Shinrikyo; Biological Terrorism; Chemical Terrorism

Further Readings

Fletcher, Holly. *Backgrounder: Aum Shinrikyo*. Council on Foreign Relations, May 28, 2008. http://www.cfr.org/publication/9238/aum_shinrikyo.html.

Kaplan, David E., and Andrew Marshall. *The Cult at the End of the World: The Incredible Story of Aum*. London: Hutchinson, 1996.

Lifton, Robert Jay. *Destroying the World to Save It: Aum Shinrikyo, Apocalyptic Violence, and the New Global Terrorism*. New York: Henry Holt, 1999.

Metraux, Daniel A. "Religious Terrorism in Japan: The Fatal Appeal of Aum Shinrikyo." *Asian Survey* 35, no. 12 (December 1995): 1140–1154.

Murakami, Haruki. *Underground: The Tokyo Gas Attack and the Japanese Psyche*. New York: Vintage, 2001.

Reader, Ian. *Religious Violence in Contemporary Japan: The Case of Aum Shinrikyo*. Nordic Institute of Asian Studies Monograph No. 82. Richmond, Surrey, UK: Curzon Press, 2000.

TORTURE DEBATE

In order to subvert terrorist plans, it is necessary to collect information about terrorists and their organizations, plans, membership, and objectives. Terrorists usually do not give up this information freely, and often the threat of death is insufficient to compel a suspected terrorist to provide information to interrogators—indeed, death may have an ideological appeal to certain religiously centered terrorists. However, the dread of torture is so powerful that rational persons have committed suicide, even *en masse,* rather than be captured by those who might use torture against them. Therefore, the question has often arisen as to whether torture and the threat of torture are acceptable alternatives in a free democracy to acquire information from terrorism suspects. Societies in many forms, in contemporary and ancient times, have utilized torture and the threat of torture as a powerful tool in extracting information from adversaries, and surely the twenty-first-century United States is counted among them.

Torture is defined as an act that is a "cold-blooded, calculated intent to inflict extreme and prolonged pain." Interrogators of many cultures have regarded its use as a reasonable and accepted means for extracting information from a reluctant victim. Its priority as a methodology for acquiring information has frequently made torture and the threat of torture a principal tool of interrogation. During the Renaissance, those who were about to be interrogated were first shown torture devices and asked to confess before being subjected to any pain. Indeed, many confessed without being tortured, as the mere threat of torture caused sufficient fear in the victim to induce compliance with the interrogator.

Methods of torture are as varied as the imaginations of those who commit the acts. From the mechanical age of torture during the Renaissance to the horrors of Gestapo interrogations during World War II, and to contemporary uses of electric shock and waterboarding, man's ingenuity in inflicting pain on his fellow man appears boundless. Specifics of the debate on what acts are or are not torture will not be addressed here. That debate is more fitting for the courts, and there have been dozens of books written on the topic. However, in opening the torture debate, it should be noted that evidence collected over history has shown that inflicting pain or the threat of inflicting pain can compel nearly anyone to say nearly anything. Doubtless this includes suspected terrorists past, present, and future.

There is considerable question as to the usefulness of information extracted under torture. U.S. Central Intelligence Agency (CIA) officials have reported that information collected under torture is notoriously unreliable. There is considerable evidence that an interrogator can induce a confession from someone who is not guilty or extract some other fictitious admission merely so the victim can stop the torture. In other words, torture does not guarantee veracity. As such, any information obtained under torture is immediately suspect and likely tainted, if nothing else, by the inferences of the interrogator during questioning. If this is so, then it begs the question, why torture at all?

The torture debate in the United States is multifaceted and radically polarized, but it can generally be separated into two distinct groups: pro- and anti-torture. Pro-torture advocates believe that it is a necessary evil to save American lives. However, even though several U.S. presidents are on the record saying this very thing, the CIA doubts this has ever happened. The anti-torture believers hold that no violation of human rights is ever justifiable, even if it means the doom of civilization as we know it. However, the CIA has reported results using "extreme measures" (the CIA term-of-art for torture) in identifying terrorists and terrorist plots.

However, the debate is not quite this simple, since some argue that torture should be utilized under certain conditions, even in a free democracy. This argument suggests that the conditions predicating torture are the real variables in the debate, rather than merely whether or not torture is permissible. For example, some argue that if a terrorist possesses information that by its disclosure might save lives, then it is permissible to utilize torture to extract the information by force Strong evidence suggests that this is the policy of the United State and a number of its allies.

Because of a U.S. Supreme Court ruling in *Sosa v. Alvarez-Machain, et al.* (2004), the CIA and its agents may be immune from domestic prosecution for acts of violence against others abroad while acting on behalf of the U.S. government. The Court ruled that acts of torture of U.S. agents or those who act on behalf of the U.S. government abroad are not punishable by American courts, generally speaking, because the conduct occurred outside the jurisdiction of the United States; therefore, any act of torture that occurs abroad should be litigated in the foreign jurisdiction wherein the conduct occurred, not the United States. Opponents of this interpretation of the law suggest that *Sosa* narrowly regarded rendition cases in which extradition from a foreign power was unlikely (aligning *Sosa* with the rendition policies of the previous four presidents), and that *Sosa* does not apply broadly to all conduct issues of U.S. agents abroad. However, the practice of extraordinary rendition—in which the CIA forcibly seizes terror suspects to be tortured, or to be tortured to death—has been condoned in policy by Presidents Clinton, Bush, and Obama. Condoleezza Rice, the secretary of state under President George W. Bush, speaking about the practice of extraordinary rendition, noted, "It's not illegal."

Often included among the arguments that promote torture by cloaking the conduct is the "secret intelligence option," meaning that information gathered through torture would remain secret and never surface in any official proceeding, such as a criminal trial or military hearing. Therefore, information extracted by torture for the purposes of intelligence analysis would never surface at any proceeding in which the victim would be likely to testify. Thus, the interrogators' conduct—no matter how egregious—remains secret and beyond the scrutiny of oversight. This out-of-sight, out-of-mind viewpoint suggests that illegal or unethical conduct is permissible if it never officially comes to light.

In a general sense, those who condone torture as a means to extract information from terror suspects usually suggest that the ends justify the means, and that in order to stop the murder of innocents by terrorists, any act against them is reasonable. The argument by proponents of torture is that ethical behavior has a "terrorist exception" that permits unethical measures against suspects, or that because terrorists have no conventional rules, no conventional rules are needed against them. Beyond this there lies the supposition that, given the interrogation of a terrorist suspect, violating international law is also acceptable practice because the terrorists are themselves lawless. Therein is the crux of the anti-torture proponent's argument: if the United States chooses to ignore international law regarding basic human rights, then what other international laws does the United States choose to ignore?

Amnesty International has championed the anti-torture cause for 40 years. According to noted attorney Alan Dershowitz, "once torture has been legitimized, even on a small scale, the use of torture, cruel, inhuman and degrading practices inevitably expands to include countless other victims, and ultimately erodes the moral and legal principles on which society depends." Anti-torture proponents warn that this ethical erosion likewise erodes the civil rights of those at home by establishing an unsustainable double standard of permissibility. Critics say that, in time, conduct permitted abroad will come home to roost in the United States. Amnesty International writes that torture is a problem, not a solution, and that its influence serves to corrupt a free society, citing Israel as proof. Israel approved the use of torture in questioning nearly any criminal suspect, and ultimately torture was used against those whose crimes were no more serious than throwing stones. Israel finally banned the practice in 1999, but not before it had become routine to torture its own citizens for insignificant crimes.

The CIA became embroiled in a scandal involving alleged videotaping of interrogations that involved waterboarding of terrorist suspects. At the forefront of the scandal is the allegation that the CIA destroyed videotaped evidence of torture, which in law suggests knowledge of guilt. If, in fact, the CIA engaged in torture and videotaped the interrogations, then why were the tapes destroyed if they enjoyed immunity from prosecution under *Sosa*? The apparent answer is that CIA officials had knowledge that their acts were outside U.S. law, and that they feared that participants might face criminal penalties in the future. The reasoning behind the destruction of evidence is speculated to be that it was considered preferable to face federal charges for obstruction of justice than for crimes against humanity.

Extremists on both sides of the torture debate have escalated the argument, suggesting that someone who does not support the torture of terrorist suspects is anti-American, or that one who does support torture is anti–human rights. Although this polarization serves to focus the respective viewpoints, it is not particularly helpful in resolving the issue. Ultimately, a free society will impose its will on that of the government. In time, therefore, torture will either be common here and abroad, or it will cease to exist as a matter of policy and law. The middle ground is unacceptable to all sides.

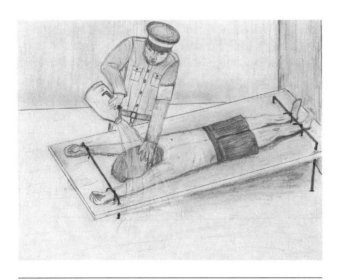

An illustration of the waterboarding technique used as a form of torture. (Artwork provided by Lori Young)

Kenneth J. Ryan

See also Central Intelligence Agency; Intelligence Gathering; Interrogation Techniques; Rendition, Extraordinary

Further Readings

Amnesty International. "Counter Terror with Justice Campaign." http://www.amnestyusa.org/ctwj.

Central Intelligence Agency. "National Security Directive NSD-77: Management of Public Diplomacy Relative to National Security," January 14, 1983.

Clinton, William J. "Presidential Decision Directive 39: US Policy on Counterterrorism," Version U, June 21, 1995.

Federal Tort Claims Act, 28 U.S.C. § 1346.

Miller, Greg. "Obama Preserves Renditions as Counter-Terrorism Tool." *Los Angeles Times*, February 1, 2009. http://articles.latimes.com/2009/feb/01/nation/na-rendition1.

Scheuer, Michael (a.k.a. Anonymous). *Imperial Hubris: Why the West Is Losing the War on Terror.* Washington, DC: Brassey's, 2004.

Seibel, Mark, and Warren P. Strobel. "CIA Official: No Proof Harsh Techniques Stopped Terror Attacks." McClatchy Newspapers, April 24, 2009. http://www.mcclatchydc.com/2009/04/24/66895/cia-official-no-proof-harsh-techniques.html.

Sosa v. Alvarez-Machain, 542 U.S. 692 (2004). http://supreme.justia.com/us/542/692/case.html.

Whips, Heather. "Torture Has a Long History . . . of Not Working." *Live Science*, October 19, 2007. http://www.livescience.com/history/071019-torture-history.html.

TRAINING OF TERRORISTS

Terrorist activities—be it carrying out operations, managing an organization, or surviving the pressure of surveillance and security—require capabilities that most people do not naturally possess. Terrorist training is the process through which people acquire, improve, or maintain the skills and knowledge needed for terrorist activities.

For an existing terrorist group, training is frequently handled formally by the organizations' leadership and is designed to achieve specific group goals. It can occur when an individual first joins the group, or in some situations even before the person officially does so. Training new recruits is the process through which organizations seek to transfer group knowledge and ideology, as well as build skills in the military or other roles the recruits will be expected to fulfill within the organization.

But training can be aimed at current members as well. In that case, the goal of training is not to create an entirely new terrorist, but to hone the skills and knowledge of current operatives and maintain or strengthen the capabilities of the organization as a whole. If a terrorist group wants to stage a type of attack that it has not done before, it may need to teach new tactics or instruct members in the use of particular weapons. Training also serves a critical maintenance function: if individuals' skills are not kept fresh through constant use, training can help to prevent their loss through unlearning and the "rusting away" of expertise.

Structured training processes also help terrorist organizations manage their members and gather information to shape their plans. When going through a training process is a requirement before acceptance into an organization, groups with a surplus of potential members can assess interested recruits and decide whom they want to accept. Training is also a chance for group leaders to assess existing group members, for performance in training can inform them about specific individuals' skills and fitness for particular roles within the group, or for specific types of missions.

Training and Ideology

When considering terrorist training efforts, pictures of individuals learning how to shoot or build bombs, or even just engaging in physical fitness training to make themselves better fighters immediately come to mind. This sort of functional content—teaching new and existing group members skills they can use in operations—is indeed a central part of terrorist training. Although there are differences among different terrorist groups, the functional areas that are covered in most training regimens cover topics such as how to maintain and use firearms, the construction and use of improvised explosive devices, military tactics, operational security and counterespionage, intelligence collection, and how to stage specific types of terrorist operations relevant to the group (e.g., kidnapping, hijacking, or bombing operations). For clandestine groups that almost always are under direct pressure from military, intelligence, or law enforcement agencies, learning techniques for secure communication and how to remain hidden from surveillance is also a prominent goal of most organized training efforts.

Though skills are a major component, a central element of organized group training frequently focuses on ideology—on not just the how but the "why" of being a terrorist. Generally labeled "indoctrination," to distinguish it from the teaching of functional skills, ideological training is intended to build or maintain group members' commitment to the cause around which the group is organized, as well as their commitment to the group itself. Though such ideological indoctrination is often associated with religiously driven groups—notably al Qaeda—it has also been important for nationalist groups, such as the Irish Republican Army (IRA) in Northern Ireland, and for political terrorists, such as the left-wing groups that operated in Europe during the 1970s and 1980s. Building such commitment is important to clandestine organizations, both to motivate members to act to advance the group's goals and to build their resistance to being subsequently turned against the group.

Tools and Resources

As part of their efforts to teach recruits and members, terrorist organizations across the spectrum—from the highly delocalized environmentalist terrorist groups to more hierarchical groups like the IRA to hybrids like al Qaeda—have developed manuals and curricula to provide a basis for their training efforts. For al Qaeda, such training resources range from medium-length articles or videos exchanged via Internet sites to documents reaching into the thousands of pages that describe the management and execution of terrorist activities from the strategic down to the very tactical level. For its members, the IRA wrote *The Green Book*, a manual that covered a variety of military and ideological topics relevant to the organization and its goals.

Though many different terrorist groups have crafted training manuals to support their efforts, there are limits to what can be taught through the printed word or, in the Internet era, through online video and other interactive methods. While information that has been captured in a book or other form is easy to transfer from one person to another (e.g., a new recruit can be handed a rifle and instructions for how to maintain, load, and fire it), there are other types of knowledge and expertise that are more difficult to pass on. Just because someone can learn from a book how to use a rifle, that does not mean the person will be able to hit a target. Transferring that sort of expertise or tacit knowledge usually requires hands-on teaching. The other alternative is a training program in which recruits can learn skills for themselves through trial and error (e.g., extensive target practice with a firearm), which allows them to "fill in the blanks" between what they can be taught and the full set of skills needed to apply it.

Since the success of terrorist activities can depend significantly on the skills of individual operatives, groups seek out training and knowledge sources that can provide necessary expertise and tacit knowledge. This includes recruitment of individuals with the needed skills that can then be passed on to others. For example, the IRA actively sought out individuals with military experience, and Aum Shinrikyo, the Japanese group that built an extensive chemical and biological weapons acquisition effort, recruited individuals with technical knowledge.

In other cases, groups have sought out training from outside sources. The operatives for the September 11, 2001, attacks were trained in flight schools, for example, because al Qaeda decided that getting training from commercial sources was necessary to build its capabilities for that operation. State sponsors have provided training to terrorist groups across the political and ideological spectrum, sometimes out of sympathy with the groups' causes or simply in pursuit of other state interests. Terrorist groups have also provided training to each other. Such assistance has been driven by sympathy or common goals, but also by groups selling their services to raise funds or gain access to other resources.

Centralized Versus Decentralized Training

Terrorist training is often associated with physical terrorist training camps, such as those maintained by al Qaeda during Taliban rule in Afghanistan.

Centralized locations present a number of advantages, including the ability to filter potential recruits and build a common set of skills among group members who, for a global group like al Qaeda, might be operating in countries throughout the world. Groups that have controlled territory at different points in their life cycle have centralized training activities. The Tamil Tigers in Sri Lanka, for example, maintained a structured training effort in which building up knowledge about the capabilities of its individual members was done in a very systematic way.

But in the training of terrorists, centralized training camps are likely more the exception rather than the rule. For smaller terrorist organizations, such infrastructure is unnecessary, and centralization presents serious risks for groups of all sizes. Centralized training camps represent potential targets for counterterrorist action, and if the camps are monitored, they could provide information on many members of the group. As a result, terrorist training is often done in a more decentralized way; the IRA, which had centralized management, carried out much of its training in small groups in locations that were not dedicated to that function.

Perhaps the most extreme example of decentralized terrorist training is the use of the Internet and online resources by contemporary terrorist groups. Though the use of the Internet by al Qaeda and related jihadist terrorist groups has received a great deal of attention, groups ranging from white supremacists and neo-Nazis to the Earth Liberation Front use the Internet as a conduit for their messages and to provide resources and training to potential group members. Some have even characterized the Internet as a "virtual training camp" where an individual's computer takes on some of the previous functions of physical locations. As technology has improved, the use of Web video has provided groups with ways of transmitting footage of actual attack operations to other group members (or potential members) who may be hundreds or even thousands of miles away. The Internet has also made it possible to disseminate resources such as manuals to a global audience, providing a virtual library for the aspiring terrorist.

Though the Internet clearly does represent a major change in the ability of terrorist organizations to disseminate information for training (as well as for propaganda and other purposes), whether it represents a revolution or an evolution in terrorist training activities is still an open question. Supporting the former conclusion, the decentralization and global reach of the Internet has made it possible for groups to reach individuals who might never have traveled to physical training camps. This has made the Internet absolutely central to self-radicalization and creating a greater potential for "lone wolf" terrorist operations by individuals sympathetic with, but potentially unconnected to, existing terrorist groups. But supporting the latter conclusion, real questions have been raised about the quality of the training information that is being disseminated online. It is unclear, that is, whether manuals purporting to teach aspiring jihadists how to use chemical and biological weapons actually contain much useful information at all. While online methods may be very good for transmitting certain kinds of information, such as recipes for explosives, the Internet is less able to transmit the tacit expertise needed to follow those recipes safely and effectively. For groups that only rely on online training of dispersed group members, this can constrain the sophistication of their operations to simple tactics that do not require much expertise.

Finally, though a terrorist group may want to implement a training program in a specific way—to teach their operatives to be effective members of the organization with the skills they think they need to achieve their goals—the practical constraints of operating clandestinely can often constrain how training can be done in practice. Though training that involves providing direct experience to members in using weapons—such as target practice with firearms or testing out their bomb designs—may be desirable, it is not always possible for many groups. Extensive training activities and live-fire training certainly risk attracting attention to a group. Similarly, though rehearsing future attacks in great detail might increase the chance the attack team will execute them well, doing so also risks compromising details of the attack to observant authorities. Such risks emphasize the importance of groups having access to safe havens where they can carry out such training efforts with less risk of compromise and discovery.

Brian Jackson

See also al Qaeda; Bombings and Bomb Scares; Homegrown Jihadi Movement; Irish Republican Army; Liberation Tigers of Tamil Eelam; Lone-Wolf Terrorism; Taliban Code of Conduct

Further Readings

Byman, Daniel. *Deadly Connections: States That Sponsor Terrorism.* Cambridge, UK: Cambridge University Press, 2005.

Cragin, Kim, et al. *Sharing the Dragon's Teeth: Terrorist Groups and the Exchange of New Technologies.* Santa Monica, CA: RAND Corporation, 2007.

Forest, James J.F., ed. *The Making of a Terrorist: Recruitment, Training, and Root Causes.* Vol. 2, *Training.* Westport, CT: Praeger Security International, 2006.

Jackson, Brian A., et al. *Aptitude for Destruction.* Vol. 2, *Case Studies of Learning in Five Terrorist Organizations.* Santa Monica, CA: RAND Corporation, 2005.

Lia, Brynjar. "Doctrines for Jihadi Terrorist Training." *Terrorism and Political Violence* 20, no. 4 (2008): 518–542.

Stenersen, Anne. "Chem-bio Cyber Class: Assessing Jihadist Chemical and Biological Manuals." *Jane's Intelligence Review,* September 2007, pp. 8–13.

Stenersen, Anne. "The Internet: A Virtual Training Camp?" *Terrorism and Political Violence* 20, no. 2 (2008): 215–233.

TRIPOLI AND BENGHAZI BOMBING

Following the deadly 1986 bombing of a Berlin nightclub, President Ronald Reagan accused Libya of planning the attack and ordered a "counterterrorist" military mission. In a controversial operation, U.S. planes bombed Libya, hitting the cities of Tripoli and Benghazi. It was the first time the United States had bombed another country to, as Reagan officials announced, preempt terrorist acts.

Relations between the United States and Libya had been strained long before the air strike. In March 1986, U.S. Navy bombers destroyed two Libyan patrol boats in the Gulf of Sidra in a brief exchange of fire. Less than a month later, a knapsack packed with nails and explosives detonated in the crowded West Berlin discotheque La Belle, a popular nightspot for American soldiers. The April 5 blast killed two U.S. soldiers and a Turkish woman and injured more than 200 people—62 Americans among them.

Reagan announced in a televised news conference on April 9 that the United States suspected Libyan participation in the bombing and that the U.S. military was prepared to attack if evidence directly linking Libya to the attack was found. Reagan also called Libyan president Muammar el Qaddafi the "mad dog of the Middle East." On April 14, Reagan announced both that the U.S. government had irrefutable evidence that the Libyan government had been behind the La Belle attack and that he had ordered a massive bombing raid on Tripoli and Benghazi.

American planes flew from aircraft carriers and U.S. bases in Great Britain to attack their targets, hitting Qaddafi's home and headquarters, a naval academy, and air bases in Benghazi. The planes, reportedly by accident, also hit a residential neighborhood in Tripoli and a row of houses in Benghazi. At least 15 people were killed in the raid, including Qaddafi's infant daughter. Several Tripoli farms were also mistakenly hit, and farmers lost a great deal of livestock. One Libyan farmer told *The New York Times,* "Tell Reagan thank you very much for killing all my chickens."

During the attack, Libyan forces shot down one U.S. F-111 bomber, killing the two crewmen on board. All Arab nations condemned the U.S. strike, as did many western European countries. The U.S. planes were forced to fly a circuitous route because France refused to allow the bombers into its airspace.

Well over a decade later, a German court convicted a former Libyan diplomat and three accomplices for their roles in the La Belle bombing. Prosecutors in the 2000 trial also revealed the evidence that had led the Reagan administration to attack Libya, presenting incriminating radio messages sent between Tripoli and the Libyan embassy in East Berlin. A message sent on the night of the La Belle bombing read, "Expect the result tomorrow morning. It is God's will." Another, sent hours after the bombing, reported, "at 1:30 AM, one of the acts was carried out with success, without leaving a trace."

Erica Pearson

See also La Belle Discotheque Bombing; Qaddafi, Muammar el

Further Readings

Anderson, Lisa. "Rogue Libya's Long Road." In "Iran: Looking Ahead," special issue, *Middle East Report* 241 (Winter 2006): 42–47.

Arnold, Guy. *The Maverick State: Gaddafi and the New World Order.* New York: Cassell, 1997.

Davis, Brian Leigh. *Qaddafi, Terrorism, and the Origins of the U.S. Attack on Libya.* New York: Praeger, 1990.

Kempster, Norman. "Cables Cited as Proof of Libyan Terror Role." *Los Angeles Times,* April 15, 1986.

Solomon, Andrew. "Circle of Fire." *The New Yorker,* May 8, 2006, pp. 44–47.

Wilson, George C., and David Hoffman. "U.S. Warplanes Bomb Targets in Libya as 'Self-defense' against Terrorism." *Washington Post,* April 15, 1986, p. A1.

TUPAC AMARU REVOLUTIONARY MOVEMENT

The Tupac Amaru Revolutionary Movement (Movimiento Revolucionario Túpac Amaru; MRTA) is a Peruvian Marxist guerrilla organization founded in 1983. The group took more than 600 people hostage at the Japanese embassy in Lima, Peru, in 1996.

Emerging from the factionalism of the Peruvian left, a small group of Marxists radicals founded the Tupac Amaru Revolutionary Movement with the aim of ridding Peru of foreign "imperialists," overthrowing the government, and establishing a Marxist regime. The group takes its name from Tupac Amaru II, a member of the Inca royal house who led a vast Indian uprising in Peru in the 1780s. Inspired by the Cuban Revolution, its leaders particularly admired the politics and tactics of Che Guevara, and the group often staged attacks on the

anniversaries of his birth and death. Even at its peak, however, the MRTA was estimated to have fewer than 1,000 members, and it was always overshadowed by the much larger and notably more brutal Maoist guerrillas known as Sendero Luminoso, or Shining Path.

The MRTA launched its first attack in Lima, the capital, in early 1984, spraying the U.S. embassy with machine gun fire. In its early years, the movement cultivated something of a Robin Hood image—members sometimes hijacked produce trucks and distributed the food to slum dwellers. The group's typical targets were banks and government institutions, and bombings were often timed for the early morning to minimize risk of civilian casualties. The MRTA also sought publicity for its attacks by painting slogans on slum dwellers' walls and leaving propaganda pamphlets at bombsites.

In 1988 the MRTA moved to expand from its base in the slums of the coastal cities into the countryside. Shining Path depended on the peasant villages of the Andes highlands for its power base. In order to compete, the MRTA likewise had to gain the support of the peasants. The character of the MRTA thus began to change: violent clashes with rival guerrillas and the military became more frequent, and the group became involved in drug trafficking. The MRTA was not able to seriously challenge Shining Path for control of the countryside, however, and its newly violent reputation diminished the organization's standing in the leftist circles of the capital.

In July 1990 the MRTA conducted its most successful operation, tunneling into a newly built maximum-security prison from the outside, freeing its leader, Victor Polay, and 47 others. Polay was recaptured in June 1992, and subsequent arrests and assaults by the military greatly diminished the organization's power and effectiveness. New laws allowing amnesty for former guerrillas further reduced membership.

Lori Berenson, an American notoriously connected with MRTA, was arrested in 1995 in Lima. In early 1996 Berenson was charged with treason and sentenced to 20 years in a Peruvian prison. She was released on parole in 2010, but the government ordered her to spend the remainder of her sentence in Peru.

On December 17, 1996, 14 members of the MRTA invaded the Japanese embassy, blowing a hole through a wall during a reception and taking more than 600 guests hostage, including many prominent Peruvian government leaders and business people, and more than 30 ambassadors. The group demanded the release of 400 of its imprisoned members in exchange for the release of the hostages. While stating his desire for a peaceful resolution, President Alberto Fujimori refused to negotiate with the terrorists. A four-month standoff ensued, during which the MRTA gradually released all but 72 of the hostages. On April 22, 1997, the military stormed the embassy, rescuing all but one of the remaining hostages and killing all 14 MRTA members. These deaths, particularly the death of the MRTA leader Nestor Cerpa in the raid, all but crushed the organization.

Colleen Sullivan

See also Berenson, Lori; Guevara, Ernesto (Che); Shining Path

Further Readings

Alegria, Claribel, and Darwin Flakoll. *Tunnel to Canto Grande*. Translated by Darwin Flakoll. Willimantic, CT: Curbstone Press, 1996.

Baer, Suzie. *Peru's MRTA: Tupac Amarú Revolutionary Movement*. New York: Rosen, 2003.

Burt, Jo-Marie. "'Quien Habla es Terrorista': The Political Use of Fear in Fujimori's Peru." *Latin American Research Review* 41, no. 3 (2006): 32–62.

McClintock, Cynthia. *Revolutionary Movements in Latin America: El Salvador's FMLN and Peru's Shining Path*. Washington, DC: United States Institute of Peace Press, 1998.

Richardson, Louise. *What Terrorists Want: Understanding the Enemy, Containing the Threat*. New York: Random House, 2006.

Sims, Calvin. "Mythology Surrounds Rebel Leader." *The New York Times*, December 23, 1996, p. A9.

Torrens, James. "Getting Out Alive: An Interview with Juan Julio Wicht." *America* 177, no. 6 (September 13, 1997): 11–17.

U.S. Department of State. "Tupac Amaru Revolutionary Movement (MRTA)." In *Background Information on Foreign Terrorist Organizations*, 1999. http://www.state.gov/s/ct/rls/rpt/fto/2801.htm.

TUPAC KATARI GUERRILLA ARMY

The Tupac Katari Guerrilla Army (Ejército Guerrillero Túpac Katari, or EGTK) was an Indian terrorist group that operated in Bolivia during the early 1990s.

Sharing a border with Brazil, Peru, Chile, Argentina, and Paraguay, Bolivia occupies a central place in both the South American continent and in Latin American history. Like its neighbors, the majority of its population is Indian or of Indian descent, and a substantial proportion of them live in poverty. Land reform is a major political issue. Bolivia is also one of the world's major producers of cocaine, and narcotrafficking and the corruption and lawlessness it engenders remain problems. A nation for 157 years, Bolivia's government has seen more than 200 coups in that time. Despite its chronic political instability, however, Bolivia has for the most part escaped the lengthy and traumatic guerrilla warfare that has plagued its neighbors—with the short and ineffective career of the National Liberation Army–Bolivia (founded by Che Guevara in 1966), being the exception.

The Tupac Katari Guerrilla Army was founded in Bolivia in the early 1990s. Starting on July 4, 1991, it carried out more than 40 attacks around the country, with the most devastating being a series of bombings of electricity pylons and oil pipelines near La Paz, the capital; two EGTK members were killed while trying to dynamite an electricity pylon in April 1992. The group's robberies are believed to have netted it more than $500,000.

In April 1992, more than a dozen of the group's leaders were arrested and jailed. The arrests seem to have crushed the fledgling group, and though intelligence reports predicted a resurgence in its activity in 1997, no new bombings occurred. After his release in 1997, one of the group's leaders, Álvaro García Linera, went on to become vice president of Bolivia, serving under president Evo Morales in 2006.

Little is known about the group's motivations or ideology. They were named after Tupac Katari, a member of Inca royalty who rebelled against the Spanish in the eighteenth century. The similarities between their methods of attack and that of the

Peruvian terrorist group the Shining Path, as well as the fact that the EGTK first made itself known when Shining Path activity on the Peru-Bolivia border was increasing, led to much speculation about the existence of links between the two groups. While imprisoned, however, the EGTK's leader denied any such connection. Stricter border controls and the arrest of the Shining Path's leader in September 1993 would seem to have put an end to any possibility of aid or support from that group, and the EGTK appears unlikely to pose a threat to Bolivia in the future.

Colleen Sullivan

See also National Liberation Army–Bolivia; Shining Path

Further Readings

"Bolivian Police Focus on Tupac Katari Guerrilla Group; Army to Fight 'Terrorism.'" *BBC World Monitoring Report*, April 3, 1992.

Books LLC. *History of Bolivia: Simón Bolívar, Túpac Amaru, Tupac Katari Guerrilla Army, Military Career of Simón Bolívar, Bolivian Gas Conflict, Tiwanaku.* Books LLC, 2010.

Brooke, James. "Relief at Guerrilla's Capture in Peru Turns to Fear." *The New York Times*, September 20, 1992, p. 17.

Loveman, Brian, and Thomas M. Davies, eds. *Che Guevara: Guerrilla Warfare.* 3rd ed. Wilmington, DE: Scholarly Resources, 2001.

Nash, Nathaniel C. "Bolivians in Fear as Maoist Rebels Slip in from Peru." *The New York Times*, September 5, 1992, p. 1.

Romero, Simon. "The Saturday Profile: An Urbane Bolivian Politician Who Tries to Bridge 2 Worlds." *The New York Times*, October 7, 2006. http://www .nytimes.com/2006/10/07/world/americas/07garcia .html?ref=americas&pagewanted=print.

Tupamaros

Uruguay's Tupamaros, or the Movimento de Liberación Nacional (MLN), was founded in 1962 by Raúl Sendic, Julio Marenales, and Jorge Maner Lluveras. The Tupamaros were of purely Uruguayan origin, and they were completely funded and staffed from within Uruguay, instead of receiving material support from foreign armed groups. The group eventually evolved into part of a legal coalitional political party, and the former Tupamaros member José Mujica was elected president of the country in 2009.

Although the label of "terrorist" is typically applied to groups that target civilians, the Tupamaros used violence sparingly, especially in the beginning. In fact, the Tupamaros effectively used propaganda to increase public support and undermine a regime that, in their view, supported the interests of a dominant oligarchy as opposed to the national interest. Notable actions in the late 1960s and early 1970s included the release of regular communiqués, posters and leaflets, to the media and the public, and the use of temporary takeovers of businesses and radio stations to deliver speeches.

The Tupamaros supported their activities through theft, robberies, and kidnapping people for ransom. They also kidnapped officials, diplomats, and prominent businessmen and landowners for trial in their own courts. Dan Mitrione, an American who was working as an advisor to the Uruguayan police, was kidnapped and later killed because he was believed to have introduced torture techniques to the police. Most kidnapping victims were held for months, tried, and released. Often, taped recordings of the mock trials were released to the press, in an attempt to discredit the government and build broad support for the Tupamaros.

The group's efforts at attracting broader public sympathy were successful, particularly their attempts at portraying the state as corrupt and ineffective. Early on, for example, the Tupamaros were successful at evading arrest. Often, even if suspected Tupamaros were arrested, many were released without being charged. Of those jailed, over 180 were freed through spectacular jail and prison breaks. Some politicians even agreed with the Tupamaros' policy proposals, albeit not their tactics.

By April 1972 the Tupamaros had begun a new offensive against the police and the armed forces, including a group of anti-Tupamaro commandos, known as Caza Tupamaros. In the process, they released well-documented charges of the use of torture and other extrajudicial human rights abuses by the Uruguayan government. The Tupamaros issued death threats against members of Caza Tupamaros, and four were killed within hours. By May the conflict had devolved into a flurry of bombings and violence. In response, the military assumed control of the counterinsurgency and effectively quelled the Tupamaro activity by the fall of 1972. However, the National Assembly was dissolved in 1973 and the country was ruled by the military until a transition to democracy began in 1984.

After the restoration of democracy, traditional candidates succeeded in presidential elections until the 2004 election Tabaré Vázquez of the left-wing Frente Amplio (Broad Front) coalition. The Frente Amplio alliance includes former Tupamaros such as Nora Castro, who became the leader the Chamber of Deputies, and José Mujica, who became leader of the Senate. Mujica, who was imprisoned during the military regime, assumed the office of the presidency in March 2010.

Jennifer Holmes

Further Readings

Generals and Tupamaros: The Struggle for Power in Uruguay 1969–1973. London: Latin America Review of Books, 1974.

Gillespie, Charles G. *Negotiating Democracy: Politicians and Generals in Uruguay.* Cambridge, UK: Cambridge University Press, 1991.

Holmes, Jennifer S. *Terrorism and Democratic Stability Revisited.* Manchester, UK: Manchester University Press, 2008.

Labrousse, Alain. *The Tupamaros: Urban Guerrillas in Uruguay.* London: PenguinBooks, 1970.

Porzencanski, Arturo. *Uruguay's Tupamaros.* New York: Praeger, 1973.

TURKISH HEZBOLLAH

Formed in southeastern Turkey in the 1980s, Turkish Hezbollah (aka Kurdish Hezbollah), one of Turkey's more active Islamic terror groups (unrelated to Lebanon's Hezbollah), seeks to overthrow the constitutional and secular government of that country and establish a strict Islamic theocracy. Targeting civilians—mainly Kurds and Kurdish sympathizers—in southeast Turkey, Turkish

Hezbollah is responsible for hundreds of murders. The group has earned a reputation for brutality, and many of its victims were tortured before they died.

Turkish Hezbollah (founded at the height of an armed separatist Kurdish rebellion in the 1980s) focused its early attacks on those who sympathized with the rebel Kurds and on the Kurdistan Workers' Party (PKK), the country's largest pro-Kurd terror organization, and one largely opposed to the establishment of a strict Islamic state. At the time, the Turkish government was accused of fostering, or even forming, Hezbollah to act against the PKK as a counter-guerrilla group, a claim the government unequivocally denied. Nevertheless, Hezbollah was thought to have infiltrated state institutions. Turkish security officials maintained that Hezbollah members had been trained in—and financed by—Iran to subvert Turkey's secular government, and that Hezbollah was formed as early as 1979 as the Iranian Revolution began supporting terror as a means of establishing Islamic states throughout the region. The group used mosques and bookstores for recruitment and maintained safe houses throughout Turkey.

Experts believe that Turkish Hezbollah's roots go back to the Kurdish Islamic movement of the early 1980s. At that time, the PKK was a significant problem for the Turkish government, so any terror action against the PKK was basically ignored. Hezbollah was able to operate with great freedom, and it often carried out brutal attacks in broad daylight. Between 1991 and 1995, at the height of the conflict between Hezbollah and the PKK, some 700 people were killed.

In addition to the murders of hundreds of civilians in the 1990s, Turkish officials say Hezbollah may be responsible for the murders of several leading Turkish academics and journalists who supported a secular government. Beginning in 1995, the Turkish government arrested and tried scores of Hezbollah members. Just before 2000, the group began infiltrating Istanbul and cities of western Turkey, murdering and often robbing to fund their cause. When one militant used a stolen credit card, Turkish security officials were able to trace it to Hezbollah, and a massive attack on the organization was launched. Nearly 100 Hezbollah militants were arrested in southeastern Turkey, and on January 17, 2001, the organization's leader, Huseyin Velioglu, was killed in a shoot-out.

That same day, two other Hezbollah leaders were arrested, leading to the discovery of the bodies of hundreds of Hezbollah victims, which had been buried in safe houses. The corpses showed evidence of having been tortured and buried alive; many had broken bones. Videotapes recovered by Turkish authorities revealed these torture sessions, and they even documented some of the executions. Grisly findings were made in various Turkish cities, including Adana, Antalya, Diyarbakir, Ankara, Konya, and Tarsus. These victims puzzled Turkish security officials because many were Kurds, themselves enemies of the state.

Hezbollah membership is unclear, though one Turkish security official claimed they had seized documents suggesting around 20,000 members. The anti-Hezbollah operation of 2000, though, was a severe blow to the group. Thousands of Hezbollah sympathizers were taken into custody in security raids and questions about the group's structure, strategy, system of education, and finances were answered. Since this operation, Turkish Hezbollah has not posed any threat to Turkey.

Richard McHugh

See also Kurdistan Workers' Party

Further Readings

Lapidot, Anat. "Islamic Activism in Turkey since the 1980 Military Takeover." In "Religious Radicalism in the Greater Middle East," edited by Bruce Maddy-Weitzman and Efraim Inbar, special issue, *Terrorism and Political Violence* 3 (1997): 62–74.

Olson, Robert. *The Kurdish Question and Turkish-Iranian Relations: From World War I to 1998.* Costa Mesa, CA: Mazda Publishers, 1998.

Orttung, Robert, and Andrey Makarychev, eds. *National Counter-terrorism Strategies: Legal, Institutional, and Public Policy Dimensions in the US, UK, France, Turkey, and Russia.* NATO Security through Science Series E: Human and Societal Dynamics, Vol. 14. Amsterdam: IOS Press, 2006.

Richardson, Louise. *What Terrorists Want: Understanding the Enemy, Containing the Threat.* New York: Random House: 2006.

Shah, Niaz A. *Self-defense in Islamic and International Law.* New York: Palgrave Macmillan, 2008.

TURNER DIARIES, THE

An apocalyptic tale of genocide, *The Turner Diaries* has been referred to as "the bible of the racist right," "the handbook for white victory," and "the blueprint for revolution." William L. Pierce, the head of the National Alliance—a neo-Nazi group—published the book in 1978 under the pseudonym Andrew Macdonald. It had first appeared in serial form in the National Alliance's publication, *Attack!*

A former physics professor at Oregon State University, Pierce was a follower of George Lincoln Rockwell, the founder of the American Nazi Party. Although Pierce claimed to doubt the book's impact, *The Turner Diaries* has been credited with influencing the terrorist and criminal activities of groups and individuals like The Order and, most notably, Timothy McVeigh. The publication and distribution of the book by Lyle Stuart, a large publishing house, shortly after McVeigh's arrest in 1995, sparked a heated public debate about censorship.

The Story

The novel is written in the form of the diaries of a one-time electrical engineer, Earl Turner, supposedly unearthed near Revolutionary Headquarters in the one-hundredth year of the New Era. In the book's foreword, Turner is described as one of the "men and women whose struggle and sacrifice saved our race in its time of greatest peril." The diaries describe a society that has completely deteriorated because of the powerlessness of its white citizens, as well as Turner's patriotic fight to take the country back from a government dominated by Jews, blacks, and other minorities. Turner begins as a rank-and-file member of a group called "the Organization" and is later invited to join a secret elite faction called "the Order," which wages a war of political terrorism on the System. These acts of terrorism are designed to instigate a further crackdown on basic freedoms, thus creating an even more repressive environment, so that the Organization will gain sympathy and converts.

Turner's adventures begin on September 16, 1991, about two years after the notorious gun raids, in which the government, through the enforcement of the Cohen Act, confiscates every-one's guns. Resisters are forced underground, but key members, called "legals," remain functioning in society and gathering information. To fund its operations, the Organization commits only "socially conscious" crimes—those against Jews or other minorities. Turner's unit is assigned a larger undertaking when the System begins issuing pass-ports to all citizens. To thwart the System's plans, the unit blows up FBI headquarters in Washington, D.C. The blast kills approximately 700 people and, because of the damage done to the FBI's infra-structure, causes a temporary halt in the issuing of passports.

Although he regrets the loss of innocent life, Turner laments, "There is no way we can destroy the System without hurting many thousands of innocent people—no way. It is a cancer too deeply rooted in the flesh. And if we don't destroy the System before it destroys us—if we don't cut this cancer out of our living flesh—our whole race will die." Eventually the Organization takes over much of the West Coast by force. Those who survive are then subjected to the "day of the rope," in which blacks as well as whites characterized as "race trai-tors" are hanged. "Race traitors" are those whites who either support minorities through their views and work or—particularly offensive to the Organization—are part of interracial relationships. Despite the looting and the cannibalism of desperate blacks, the landscape begins to take on a utopian character when surviving whites clean up their homes and property. The farms that have been neglected because of the migrant workers' expulsion are eventually tended by young white children, eager to do their part for the region's recovery.

Turner's last entry records his acceptance of a suicide mission in which he will blow up the Pentagon with a nuclear weapon. He has accepted the mission willingly as punishment for his betrayal of the Order while being tortured by an Israeli police official and his "Negro assistants." Turner's death, as noted in the epilogue, marks "the day of the Martyrs" in the New Era.

Violent Influence

The book is written in the style of an adventure novel with elements—including a love interest—clearly intended to appeal to a wide audience. Seemingly effective, it is believed to have inspired white supremacists' crimes in the United States and abroad, including those of Buford Furrow, who wounded five people, three of them children, in 1999 at a Los Angeles area Jewish community center. He also killed a Filipino postal worker. He later remarked that his actions were "a wake up call to America to kill Jews." In addition, dur-ing the 1998 rampage that killed James Byrd Jr., one of the most vicious hate crimes in Texas his-tory, John William King declared, "we're going to start *The Turner Diaries* early." In London, David Copeland, who killed three people and wounded dozens of others in the 1999 Soho pub bombings, was also believed to have been influ-enced by the novel.

The book was also a likely inspiration for the 1980s crime wave initiated by a group calling itself The Order. The Order replicated many of the crimes committed by its fictional counterpart, including robbery, counterfeiting, and murder. Other white supremacists refer to the day in 1984 that the real-life leader of The Order, Robert Jay Mathews, died in a fiery standoff with federal authorities as "Martyr's Day."

The novel received more widespread attention after the arrest of McVeigh for the April 19, 1995, bombing of the Alfred P. Murrah Federal Building in Oklahoma City, Oklahoma. McVeigh had used an ammonium nitrate fertilizer bomb in a truck much like the one described in the book. The time of the Oklahoma bombing was 9:04 A.M., just 11 minutes earlier than the time in the fictional account. When McVeigh was arrested, pages from the book were found in the front seat of his car. At his trial, witnesses confirmed that McVeigh was fascinated by the book and recommended it to friends.

By 1995 an estimated 200,000 copies had been sold, mostly through mail order by antigovernment groups. In 1996 a mainstream New York publisher announced that it would print 50,000 copies and release the book for distribution. Many organiza-tions, the Southern Poverty Law Center and the Simon Wiesenthal Center among them, objected and appealed to bookstores to "make an informed decision" about stocking the book. Canadian Customs declared the book's importation illegal under part of its Criminal Code that prohibits the importation of hate propaganda. In the United States, however, the publisher and the American Booksellers Association maintained that even objectionable material is protected by the First Amendment. The publisher, who had also published *The Anarchist's Cookbook*, took on *The Turner Diaries* on the condition that a foreword would be added condemning the book's racist views, and that one dollar from every sale would be given to a gun control organization. The author received 5 percent of the sales revenues before his death in 2002. By 2000, approximately 500,000 copies had been sold, but by 2010 the work was primarily circulated online.

Nancy Egan

See also Christian Identity; Copeland, David; Mathews, Robert Jay; McVeigh, Timothy James; Oklahoma City Bombing; Order, The; White Supremacy Movement

Further Readings

Barkun, Michael. *Religion and the Racist Right: The Origins of the Christian Identity Movement.* Chapel Hill: University of North Carolina Press, 1994.

Brodie, Renee. "The Aryan New Era: Apocalyptic Realizations in the Turner Diaries." *Journal of American Culture* 21 (Fall 1998): 13–22.

Coates, James. *Armed and Dangerous: The Rise of the Survivalist Right.* New York: Hill & Wang, 1987.

Kossof, Julian. "Is This the *Mein Kampf* of the 21st Century?" *The Times* (London), July 2, 2000.

Macdonald, Andrew. *The Turner Diaries.* Hillsboro, WV: National Vanguard Books, 1978.

Stewart, Richard. "Trio Charged in Jasper Slaying; Suspects Linked to Hate Groups." *Houston Chronicle,* June 10, 1998.

Swain, Carol Miller. *The New White Nationalism in America: Its Challenge to Integration.* Cambridge, UK: Cambridge University Press, 2002.

Zeskind, Leonard. *Blood and Politics: The History of the White Nationalist Movement from the Margins to the Mainstream.* New York: Farrar, Straus and Giroux, 2009.

TWA FLIGHT 355 HIJACKING

Shortly after Trans World Airlines Flight 355 left New York's La Guardia Airport on September 10, 1976, Croatian nationalists skyjacked the aircraft by displaying what they claimed were "five gelignite bombs." The Boeing 727's crew and the 81 passengers bound for Chicago followed the hijackers' instructions, unaware that the so-called bombs were in fact made of Silly Putty.

The group of hijackers, led by the Croat Zvonko Busic and his American wife, Julienne Busic, a former TWA stewardess, took the plane on a bizarre transatlantic journey. Stopping in Montreal, the hijackers sent word that they had left another bomb and two political tracts in a subway locker at Grand Central Terminal in Manhattan. They demanded that four U.S. newspapers and the *International Herald Tribune* publish their appeal for Croatian independence, and that leaflets proclaiming their message be airdropped over New York, Montreal, and Chicago.

Police experts did find an actual bomb in the Grand Central Terminal locker. After the device was taken to a police range to be disarmed, it exploded unexpectedly, killing New York City police officer Brian J. Murray. The FBI complied with the hijackers' instructions, and sent the Croatian manifesto to the press. The *Washington Post, Los Angeles Times,* and *Chicago Tribune* all published the tract.

Stopping in Newfoundland to refuel, the hijackers allowed 35 passengers to get off the plane, giving first priority to children, the ill, and those with pending business. "They were so polite it was ridiculous," passenger James Perkins told *Newsweek* in an article published 10 days after the ordeal. The hijackers landed the 727 at the Charles de Gaulle Airport outside Paris, where French officials slashed the jet's tires. After Julienne Busic spoke with the U.S. Ambassador, Kenneth Rush, and confirmed the publication of the group's manifesto, the hijackers surrendered.

The group freed all of the hostages and revealed that the bombs they carried were fake. They had been smuggled though security with the aid of Julienne Busic's outdated TWA pass. All five hijackers were flown to the United States and convicted in 1977 in U.S. federal court on charges of air piracy. The Busics were also convicted of homicide and sentenced to mandatory life terms. Zvonko Busic served 32 years in federal prison before being paroled and returning to Croatia in 2008. Julienne Busic was paroled from prison in 1989, and she was later hired as an advisor at the Croatian Embassy in Washington, D.C. As of

2011, she had relocated to Rovanjska, Croatia, and written several books.

Erica Pearson

See also Airport Security; Grand Central Station
    Bombing; Hijacking

Further Readings

Alpern, David M. "A Skyjacking for Croatia."
    Newsweek, September 20, 1976.
Baker, Al. "Croatian Leader of 1976 Hijacking Is
    Granted Parole, but Faces Deportation." *The New
    York Times,* July 19, 2008. http://www.nytimes.com/
    2008/07/19/nyregion/19parole.html.
Binder, David. "A Strange Bond: Officer's Widow and Air
    Hijacker." *The New York Times*, December 19, 1994.
Busic, Julienne Eden. *Lovers and Madmen: A True Story
    of Passion, Politics, and Air Piracy.* San Jose, CA:
    Writers Club Press, 2000.
Busic, Julienne Eden. *Your Blood and Mine.* Raleigh, NC:
    Lulu Enterprises, 2010.
Harding, John. *Flying's Strangest Moments:
    Extraordinary but True Stories from Over 1100 Years
    of Aviation History.* London: Anova, 2006.

TWA Flight 840 Hijacking

The hijacking of Trans World Airlines Flight 840 brought the Palestinian guerrilla Leila Khaled, who became an icon in the Arab world, to international attention.

On August 29, 1969, Khaled and Salim Issawi, hijackers for the Popular Front for the Liberation of Palestine (PFLP), took over the Rome-to-Tel Aviv flight. Khaled had boarded Flight 840 wearing a wide-brimmed hat, a book called *My Friend Ché* (about her hero Che Guevara) in hand. Not long after takeoff, she and Issawi, armed with grenades, jumped from their first-class seats and stormed the cockpit. By Khaled's account, she pulled the safety pin from her grenade and offered it to the pilot as a souvenir; he declined. They re-routed the plane to Damascus, Syria. Khaled forced the pilot to fly low over Haifa, the town (now a part of Israel) that she and her family fled from in 1948 to become refugees in Lebanon. After landing in Damascus, Issawi and Khaled evacuated the passengers and crew and blew up the plane's cockpit. The hijackers were arrested and held in Syria for five weeks, and then released.

A photo of the 25-year-old Khaled, snapped the day of the hijacking, captured the world's imagination. The 1970s press often referred to her as "girl terrorist" and "deadly beauty." The hijackers used the takeover of Flight 840 and Khaled's instant notoriety to bring attention to their Marxist-Leninist organization, the PFLP, which was founded in 1967 following Israel's capture of the West Bank in the Six-Day War.

After hijacking Flight 840, Khaled underwent many plastic surgery operations, altering her face so that she could slip through airport security undetected. In 1970 she hijacked (with the Nicaraguan Patrick Arguello) an El Al jet from Amsterdam, charging the cockpit midflight, grenades in hand. Armed guards opened fire, killing Arguello, and they captured Khaled. The plane landed at Heathrow Airport, and Khaled was held in England for 28 days, until being released in exchange for western hostages held by the PFLP.

Following the September 6, 1970, El Al hijacking, Jordan erupted in violence. On the same day as Khaled's attempt, Palestinian hijackers took three other planes. King Hussein of Jordan cited these incidents and declared war on the Palestinian groups in Jordan, creating the fighting that has become known as "Black September."

In 2006, Khaled's story was documented by Swedish filmmaker Lina Makboul in a film called *Leila Khaled, Hijacker,* which won the best film award at India's Tri-Continental Film Festival, and Sweden's Nöjesguiden Gothenburg Festival.

Erica Pearson

See also Black September; Hijacking; Khaled, Leila; Popular
    Front for the Liberation of Palestine; Women Terrorists

Further Readings

Cragin, Kim, and Sara A. Daly. *Women as Terrorists:
    Mothers, Recruiters, and Martyrs.* Santa Barbara, CA:
    ABC-CLIO, 2009.
Khaled, Leila. *My People Shall Live: The Autobiography
    of a Revolutionary*, edited by George Hajjar. London:
    Hodder and Stoughton, 1973.
Macdonald, Eileen. *Shoot the Women First.* London:
    Fourth Estate, 1991.
Ness, Cindy D. *Female Terrorism and Militancy: Agency,
    Utility, and Organization.* New York: Routledge, 2008.

Richardson, Louise. *What Terrorists Want: Understanding the Enemy, Containing the Threat.* New York: Random House, 2006.

Struck, Doug. "Palestinian Hijacker-turned Housewife Regrets Nothing; Former Revolutionary Maintains Extremism but Rhetoric Has Lost Appeal." *Baltimore Sun,* October 31, 1995, p. 7A.

Viner, Katherine. "I Made the Ring from a Bullet and the Pin of a Hand Grenade." *The Guardian* (London), January 26, 2001, p. 2. http://www.guardian.co.uk/world/2001/jan/26/israel.

TWA FLIGHT 847 HIJACKING

On June 14, 1985, two gunmen used hand grenades and a pistol to overpower a commercial jet bound for Rome from Athens. The 153 passengers and crew members aboard Trans World Airlines Flight 847, many of them Americans, were caught in a 16-day showdown as the plane flew back and forth between Beirut and Algiers.

The hijackers, who were later tied to the Shiite Muslim militant group and political party Hezbollah, burst into the cockpit and ordered pilot John Testrake to fly to Algiers. The image of one of the hijackers holding a gun to the Testrake's head was shown on TV screens around the world. The Boeing 727's low fuel supply would only take the aircraft as far as Beirut, however. There, the hijackers refueled and issued their first demands. They called for the release of 766 prisoners in Israel, many of them Shiites, and a moratorium on oil and arms deals between the United States and its Arab partners. During this first stop in Beirut, the gunmen shot Petty Officer Robert Dean Stethem at close range and dumped his body to the tarmac.

Testrake flew the plane back and forth between Beirut and Algiers for the next two and a half days. Other accomplices joined the hijackers as the ordeal progressed. A number of the hostages, many of them women and children, were released sporadically during the plane's several stops. Finally, the flight engineer faked engine failure, and the hijacking exploit was grounded. The plane landed for a final time in Beirut, and hijacking accomplices took the passengers from the plane to guarded houses in the city. The crew members were kept hostage on the grounded plane for the next two weeks, surrounded by gunmen. On June

30, after Israel agreed to release 300 prisoners, the hijackers freed the remaining hostages and flew back to Algiers, avoiding arrest.

Mohammed Ali Hamadei was arrested in 1987 in West Germany and later sentenced by a German court to life in prison for hijacking flight 847 and murdering Stethem. Hamadei remains the only person tried in the case, although U.S. officials have released the names of other suspects. In 2005, Hamadei was released on parole from federal prison. Imad Fayez Mugniyah, at times described as Hezbollah's senior intelligence officer and at others the group's security or operations chief, was indicted in the case, as was fellow Lebanese Hassan Izz al Din. American officials further contend that Mugniyah was involved in the 1983 bombing of the U.S. Marine Corps barracks in Beirut as well as the kidnap, torture, and killing of the CIA station chief William Buckley in the 1980s. Mugniyah was killed by a car bomb in Damascus, Syria, in 2008. As of 2010, Izz al Din remained at large.

According to his own admission to Greek authorities, a third man was supposed to take part in the hijacking. Ali Atwa was waiting to board Flight 847 but was relegated to standby, bumped, and left behind. He was arrested in Athens, and found to be carrying forged Moroccan passports.

TWA pilot John Testrake is held hostage by an unidentified hijacker at the airport in Beirut, Lebanon, on June 19, 1985. (Nabil Ismail/AFP/Getty Images)

Greek officials later freed him to join those on the hijacked plane in exchange for hostages. Atwa, Izz al Din, and Hamadei all appear on the FBI's Most Wanted Terrorists list.

Erica Pearson

See also Airport Security; Atwa, Ali; Hezbollah; Hijacking; Izz al Din, Hassan; Mugniyah, Imad Fayez

Further Readings

Bernstein, Richard. "Germany Frees '85 Hijacker Who Killed American Sailor." *The New York Times,* December 21, 2005. http://www.nytimes.com/2005/12/21/international/europe/21germany.html.

Dominus, Susan. "The Lives They Lived: The Peacemaker of Flight 847." *The New York Times,* December 25, 2005. http://www.nytimes.com/2005/12/25/magazine/25derickson.html.

Jaber, Hala. *Hezbollah.* New York: Columbia University Press, 1997.

Oliverio, Annamarie. *The State of Terror.* SUNY series in Deviance and Social Control. Albany: State University of New York Press, 1998.

Richardson, Louise. *What Terrorists Want: Understanding the Enemy, Containing the Threat.* New York: Random House, 2006.

Snyder, Rodney A. *Negotiating with Terrorists: TWA Flight 847.* Pew Case Studies in International Affairs Case 333. Pittsburgh, PA: Pew Charitable Trusts, 1994.

U

ULSTER DEFENSE ASSOCIATION

The Ulster Defense Association (UDA) was the largest of Northern Ireland's Loyalist paramilitary organizations. It engaged in sectarian assassinations and bombings in Northern Ireland beginning in 1972, and it was an important factor in politics and peace negotiations during the conflict in Northern Ireland until the group officially disbanded in 2007.

For more than 30 years, Northern Ireland was torn by a conflict between the province's Roman Catholics (also known as Republicans or Nationalists), who wanted Northern Ireland to become a part of the Republic of Ireland, and its Protestants (also called Loyalists or Unionists), who wished it to remain part of Great Britain. Catholic and Protestant paramilitary organizations were formed, and both employed terror to achieve their ends.

As the violence escalated in the late 1960s, many people came to believe that Northern Ireland's security forces, the Royal Ulster Constabulary (RUC) and the British army, could no longer protect them. The Provisional Irish Republican Army (PIRA or, more commonly, the IRA) had patrolled Catholic neighborhoods since the organization's re-formation in 1969. Protestants, however, had no equivalent organization, though local vigilante groups had sprung up, particularly in the working-class neighborhoods of Belfast and Derry. In May 1971 the leaders of several local vigilante groups organized a series of community meetings, and the result was the formation of the Ulster Defense Association, a group committed to combating the IRA and protecting Protestants.

The group was organized along British military lines: each of Northern Ireland's six counties had a brigade, and the brigades were subdivided into battalions and companies. The governing body was called the Inner Council; initially, this was a large committee comprising several dozen local leaders, but by 1974 a Supreme Commander, Andy Tyrie, had been elected. He and his deputies would lead the organization for the next 15 years. Although estimates vary, some sources believe the UDA had about 30,000 members in the mid-1970s, when the violence in Northern Ireland was at its peak. The primary method of attack by the UDA was sectarian assassination, or killing members of the Catholic community at random in reprisal for IRA attacks. Its first campaign, begun in the spring of 1972, killed more than 80 people by the end of the year.

Because they feared a Protestant backlash, the police and other security forces were loathe to acknowledge that the murders were a deliberate sectarian campaign. In turn, the UDA was reluctant to publicly accept responsibility because the organization would then have been declared illegal and many of its members arrested. Their solution was to use a cover name, the Ulster Freedom Fighters (UFF), to claim responsibility for any attacks. Many UFF attacks were deliberately brutal. Stabbing was preferred to shooting, and the bodies of some victims were mutilated and burned in an effort to terrorize the Catholic community and thus diminish support for the IRA.

Strikes

In 1974 the British government attempted to implement the December 1973 Sunningdale Agreement, a peace plan that contained many of the provisions of the current Good Friday Agreement. Protestants were strongly opposed to the plan, and on May 14, a heretofore unknown group, the Ulster Worker's Council, called a general strike. The UDA and other Loyalist paramilitaries threw their support behind the strike. UDA members used intimidation, threats, and street blockades to force Protestant workers to stay home during the strike's early days. Their tactics were effective, and public utilities and private businesses across the province were shut down for more than a week. Following the strike's success, the Sunningdale Agreement was abandoned. In May 1977 the UDA tried a similar tactic in an attempt to restore a separate, Protestant-controlled Parliament in Northern Ireland, but it failed in this effort.

After the failure of the 1977 strike, the UDA entered a period of relative decline. While the number of sectarian assassinations decreased, the UDA's planning and tactics grew increasingly sophisticated. In 1984, a UFF gunman nearly killed Gerry Adams, the president of Sinn Féin, the IRA's political arm.

Scandal and More Murder

In 1989 the UDA was embroiled in a scandal when it came to light that Northern Ireland's security forces had been sharing intelligence on Republican activists. The UDA had used the information it received to plan assassination campaigns. Nonetheless, during the early 1990s, the UDA stepped up its sectarian campaign against Catholics. Indeed, 1991 was the first year in which Loyalist forces killed as many people as Republicans. As a result of the investigation following the scandal, and because of its renewed activity against Catholics, the UDA was banned by the government in 1992. In 1994 the UDA and other Loyalist paramilitaries declared a cease-fire, as did the IRA, as a move toward peace. Negotiations then stalled for months. The IRA broke its cease-fire in February 1996 and resumed it in September 1997; the UDA broke its cease-fire late in 1997 and resumed it in January 1998. The UDA's political arm, the Ulster Democratic Party (UDP), was a signatory to the April 1998 Good Friday Agreement.

After the signing of the Good Friday Agreement, also known as the Belfast Agreement, many Unionists grew increasingly dissatisfied with the peace process. The UDA disbanded the UDP in the fall of 2001. While the UDA never openly declared its cease-fire over, sectarian attacks from 1998 onward by groups calling themselves the Orange Volunteers and the Red Hand Defenders were believed by many to be linked to the UDA. On October 12, 2001, the British government declared that it considered the UDA to have broken its cease-fire. Attacks by the Red Hand Defenders led some observers to believe that the UDA was once again actively recruiting and might be planning a full-scale military campaign, but in 2007 the UDA released an official statement renouncing violence. Following in the footsteps of other Irish terror groups, the organization declared that they believed the war between Catholics and Protestants was over, and that their list of potential targets would be destroyed. In January 2010 the UDA officially disarmed and issued a statement of regret for its role in the violence.

Colleen Sullivan

See also Irish Republican Army; Orange Volunteers; Real Irish Republican Army; Red Hand Defenders; Ulster Freedom Fighters; Ulster Volunteer Force

Further Readings

CAIN Web Archive. "Sunningdale Chronology." http://cain.ulst.ac.uk/events/sunningdale/chron.htm.

Dixon, Paul. *Northern Ireland: The Politics of War and Peace.* New York: Palgrave, 2001.

Holland, Jack. *Hope against History: The Course of Conflict in Northern Ireland.* New York: Henry Holt, 1999.

McEvoy, Joanne. *The Politics of Northern Ireland.* Edinburgh: Edinburgh University Press, 2008.

McKay, Susan. *Northern Protestants: An Unsettled People.* Belfast: Blackstaff Press, 2000.

McKittrick, David. *Making Sense of the Troubles.* Belfast: Blackstaff Press, 2000.

Mitchell, Claire. *Religion, Identity, and Politics in Northern Ireland.* Burlington, VT: Ashgate, 2006.

Mitchell, Thomas G. *When Peace Fails: Lessons from Belfast for the Middle East.* Jefferson, NC: McFarland, 2010.

Taylor, Peter. *Loyalists: War and Peace in Northern Ireland.* New York: TV Books, 1999.

"War Ends for Militant Group in Northern Ireland." *The New York Times,* November 12, 2007.

Wood, Ian S. *Crimes of Loyalty: A History of the UDA.* Edinburgh: Edinburgh University Press, 2006.

ULSTER FREEDOM FIGHTERS

The Ulster Freedom Fighters (UFF) was a Northern Irish Loyalist paramilitary group that claimed responsibility for dozens of assassinations believed to have been carried out by members of the Ulster Defense Association (UDA) before it disbanded in 2007.

In Northern Ireland, beginning in the late 1960s, a bloody conflict was waged between the province's Roman Catholics (also called Republicans or Nationalists), who wanted Northern Ireland to become a part of the Republic of Ireland, and its Protestants (also called Loyalists or Unionists), who wanted it to remain part of Great Britain. Armed paramilitary groups sprung up in both communities. One such Loyalist group, the Ulster Defense Association, began a campaign of sectarian assassinations in the spring of 1972, killing Catholics at random in reprisal for attacks by the Irish Republican Army (IRA). By the end of the year, more than 80 people had been killed.

The Northern Irish police and British government were initially reluctant to acknowledge the murders as politically motivated sectarian attacks. They did not want to give the IRA a propaganda victory, and they feared provoking a Protestant backlash that could destroy the delicate peace negotiations then under way. For its part, the UDA could not claim responsibility for the attacks without the organization being declared illegal and having many of its members arrested.

At a meeting in May 1973, UDA leaders decided that a shadow organization called the Ulster Freedom Fighters would be created within the UDA. The UDA could continue its attacks, but the UFF would claim responsibility. The

Mural in Kilcooley, a housing estate situated in Bangor, County Down, Northern Ireland.

UFF would also streamline the UDA's terrorist operations. The UDA was structured like the British Army; the UFF, in contrast, would be composed of small, hard-to-penetrate cells of four or five individuals. The most reliable members of the Belfast death squads that had committed the previous murders were chosen as UFF commanders. On June 26, 1973, a man claiming to be "Captain Black" of the UFF called a Belfast newspaper and claimed responsibility for the murder of the Catholic politician Paddy Wilson and his companion, marking the first public use of the UFF name.

The UFF was banned as a terrorist organization in November 1973, while the UDA remained legal until 1992. Despite the banning, the UFF claimed responsibility for or was implicated in hundreds of deaths over the next 25 years. The UFF was also involved in the assassinations and attempted assassinations of several prominent Republican activists, including the murder of the lawyer Pat Finucane in 1989, and the attempted murders of Bernadette Devlin McAliskey in 1981 and Gerry Adams, the leader of Sinn Féin (the IRA's political arm) in 1984. The UFF was also implicated in a 1989 scandal that involved members of Northern Ireland's security forces who had passed on secret police intelligence about Republicans to Loyalist paramilitaries for use in planning assassinations.

In January 1998, the UFF and the UDA declared a cease-fire in compliance with the Good Friday Agreement. A series of attacks beginning in 1998 by groups calling themselves the Red Hand Defenders and the Orange Volunteers are believed to have been carried out by former UDA/UFF members. On October 12, 2001, the British government declared that it no longer considered the UDA and the UFF to be honoring the cease-fire, although the group itself had not announced the cease-fire to be at an end. In 2007, shortly after an official statement released by the UDA renouncing violence, the group was ordered to stand down, and along with its parent group, the UFF began disarming in 2009.

Colleen Sullivan

See also Irish Republican Army; Orange Volunteers; Red Hand Defenders; Ulster Defense Association; Ulster Volunteer Force

Further Readings

CAIN Web Archive. "Ulster Freedom Fighters and Ulster Defense Association Profile." 2002. http://cain.ulst.ac.uk/othelem/organ/uorgan.htm.

Holland, Jack. *Hope against History: The Course of Conflict in Northern Ireland.* New York: Henry Holt, 1999.

McKay, Susan. *Northern Protestants: An Unsettled People.* Belfast: Blackstaff Press, 2000.

McKittrick, David. *Making Sense of the Troubles.* Belfast: Blackstaff Press, 2000.

Mitchell, Claire. *Religion, Identity, and Politics in Northern Ireland.* Burlington, VT: Ashgate, 2006.

Taylor, Peter. *Loyalists: War and Peace in Northern Ireland.* New York: TV Books, 1999.

"UFF Given the Order to Stand Down." BBC News, November 12, 2007.

Wood, Ian S. *Crimes of Loyalty: A History of the UDA.* Edinburgh: Edinburgh University Press, 2006.

ULSTER VOLUNTEER FORCE

The Ulster Volunteer Force (UVF) was a Loyalist paramilitary organization that carried out numerous bombings and assassinations in an attempt to ensure continued rule by the Protestant majority in Northern Ireland. The group officially disbanded in 2007, but authorities suspect that some remnant of the UVF may remain operational.

Beginning in the late 1960s in Northern Ireland, Roman Catholics (also called Republicans or Nationalists) and Protestants (also Loyalists or Unionists) battled for control of the region. Catholics wanted Northern Ireland to become a part of the Republic of Ireland, while Protestants wanted it to remain part of Great Britain. Paramilitary organizations formed within each group, and both factions employed violence to achieve their ends.

The Ulster Volunteer Force took its name from a private army set up in 1912 by Sir Edward Carson. The modern UVF was formed in 1966 by Augustus Andrew "Gusty" Spence and several friends who feared that the paramilitary Nationalist group known as the Irish Republican Army (IRA) was again becoming active in Northern Ireland. (The IRA is believed to have had only a few dozen members in the mid-1960s.) Spence and his fellow

UVF members vowed to kill IRA men or their sympathizers.

The UVF's first action was the attempted fire-bombing of a Belfast pub on May 7, 1966; Matilda Gould, a 76-year-old Protestant, was killed. Over the next weeks, the group killed two Roman Catholics, neither of whom was a member of the IRA. Following the murders, the leaders of the UVF were arrested, and in October 1966, Spence and two others were sentenced to 20 years in prison. The UVF remained active, however, embarking on a bombing campaign in 1969.

While Spence and his cohorts were imprisoned, a conflict began to take shape within Northern Ireland. A Catholic civil rights movement had sparked violent confrontations between protesters and police, and in August 1969, British troops had been called in to keep the peace. By early 1970, the IRA had been revitalized and was patrolling Catholic neighborhoods and attacking British troops. Many Protestants now viewed Spence as prophetic, and UVF membership soared.

While other Protestant paramilitary organizations concentrated on killing Catholics in Northern Ireland, the UVF concentrated its efforts in the Republic of Ireland, much as the IRA had begun carrying out bombings in England. On May 17, 1974, the UVF planted three car bombs in and around Dublin. These bombs exploded almost simultaneously around 5:30 P.M., and a fourth bomb detonated in County Monaghan about an hour later. Thirty-three people were killed, the highest number of casualties in a single day during the 30 years of conflict.

In the mid-1970s, the UVF organized street gangs in Belfast that murdered Catholics. The methods of the most vicious of these gangs, the Shankill Butchers, have been likened to those of Jack the Ripper. By 1979 many gang members, including most of the Butchers, had been arrested and jailed. During the 1980s, the UVF suffered heavily from the work of informants used by the security forces. Dozens of UVF members were arrested and imprisoned, though many convictions based solely on informant information were later overturned.

Spence, whose years in prison caused him to reconsider the use of violence, led the UVF toward peace in the early 1990s. On October 13, 1994, the UVF declared a cease-fire prior to opening peace negotiations with the government. The group leadership also issued a statement in which it expressed sorrow and regret about the 28 years of violence. In 1996, the UVF's continued commitment to peace negotiations prompted some of its members to break with the organization, forming the Loyalist Volunteer Force (LVF). In April 1998, the Progressive Unionist Party, the UVF's political arm, signed the Good Friday Agreement, which marked a formal end to the long conflict.

Despite the peace accord, however, the UVF continued to be involved in murderous feuds with its rival LVF and sections of the Ulster Defense Association. Unionists have not always been happy with the progress of peace in Northern Ireland, and an increase in violence by Loyalists in the mid-2000s placed the UVF cease-fire in jeopardy. In 2005 the UVF was officially declared an enemy of peace by the British government after the group broke from their 1994 cease-fire agreement. The group officially disbanded in 2007 and disarmed in 2009. However, in the spring of 2010, Bobby Moffett, a Belfast man well known in Loyalist circles, was murdered on Shankill Road. Both local police and the Independent Monitoring Commission, a group overseeing the cease-fire, stated they believed the UVF was responsible, but the group has never officially taken credit for the killing.

Colleen Sullivan

See also Irish Republican Army; Loyalist Volunteer Force; Orange Volunteers; Red Hand Defenders; Ulster Defense Association; Ulster Freedom Fighters

Further Readings

CAIN Web Archive. "Ulster Volunteer Force Profile." 2002. http://cain.ulst.ac.uk/othelem/organ/uorgan.htm.

Cusack, Jim, and Henry McDonald. *The UVF*. Dublin: Poolbeg, 1997.

Holland, Jack. *Hope against History: The Course of Conflict in Northern Ireland*. New York: Henry Holt, 1999.

McKay, Susan. *Northern Protestants: An Unsettled People*. Belfast: Blackstaff Press, 2000.

McKittrick, David. *Making Sense of the Troubles*. Belfast: Blackstaff Press, 2000.

Mitchell, Claire. *Religion, Identity, and Politics in Northern Ireland*. Burlington, VT: Ashgate, 2006.

Taylor, Peter. *Loyalists: War and Peace in Northern Ireland.* New York: TV Books, 1999.

"Ulster Group No Longer Part of Cease-fire, Britain Says." *The New York Times,* September 14, 2005. http://www.nytimes.com/2005/09/14/world/europe/14iht-ireland.html.

Wood, Ian S. *Crimes of Loyalty: A History of the UDA.* Edinburgh: Edinburgh University Press, 2006.

UNABOMBER (1942–)

The Unabomber, named for his initial attacks on universities and airlines, (the "un" in his FBI code name was short for university, and "a" referred to airlines) was responsible for placing or mailing 16 package and letter bombs that resulted in three deaths and nearly two dozen injuries in the United States. After one of the longest and most expensive manhunts in the nation's history, the FBI seized Ted Kaczynski, a Harvard-educated mathematician-turned-recluse, who later pled guilty for the attacks.

The Unabomber addressed his first package bomb, crudely made with plumbing pipe and electrical wire from a lamp, to a professor at the University of Illinois. The package was found in a university parking lot on May 24, 1978, and sent back to the return address, at Northwestern University, where the bomb exploded, injuring one person. Although no link was made to Kaczynski at the time, later reports suggest that professors at both universities had rejected Kaczynski's attempts to publish a treatise he wrote against technology and modernization.

The Unabomber struck three more times in the Chicago area—at Northwestern University, the cargo compartment of American Airlines Flight 444, and the home of the president of United Airlines—before expanding his scope to universities throughout the country, including two bombs mailed to the University of California, Berkeley. (Kaczynski had been an assistant math professor at the campus in the late 1960s.) Investigators knew that these bombings were linked because the perpetrator engraved the initials "FC" on parts of the bomb or spray-painted them nearby. Otherwise, the Unabomber never left a trace.

In 1985 the Unabomber's attacks increased and became more dangerous. He bombed a computer room at UC–Berkeley that May, and he sent another bomb to the Boeing Company in Auburn, Washington, the following month (the Boeing bomb was safely disarmed). In November, a package bomb exploded at a University of Michigan professor's home, injuring two people. Finally, on December 11, 1985, the Unabomber's most lethal bomb to date was placed in the parking lot of a computer store in Sacramento, killing the owner, Hugh Scrutton. For the first time in his seven-year bombing spree, the Unabomber had claimed a life.

Two years later, a police sketch gave the country the only image of the Unabom suspect—a mustached man in a hooded sweatshirt, wearing aviator glasses. The bombings immediately stopped. For six years, the Unabomber remained inactive.

Out of the Shadows

In June 1993, shortly after the 1993 World Trade Center bombing, the Unabomber reemerged, sending a letter-bomb to the home of a University of California geneticist, Dr. Charles Epstein, followed three days later by a bomb to David Gelernter, a computer science professor at Yale University. Both men were seriously injured. Breaking his silence, the Unabomber sent a letter to *The New York Times,* claiming that the bombings were the work of an anarchist group. More than 125 investigators from three different federal agencies were immediately committed to the case.

In December 1994 a package bomb killed Thomas J. Mosser at his home in New Jersey. Mosser was an advertising executive at Young & Rubicam, the parent company of the public relations firm Burson-Marsteller. An FBI investigation into the group Earth First! later found that Kaczynski had attended a meeting of several hundred environmentalists at the University of Montana, Missoula. At that meeting, speakers erroneously suggested that Burson-Marsteller designed the public relations campaign for Exxon following the massive Exxon-Valdez oil spill in Prudhoe Bay, Alaska. One month later, Mosser was dead.

The Unabomber's final attack came five days after Timothy McVeigh's bombing of the Murrah Building in Oklahoma City. On April 24, 1995, a package-bomb sent to the offices of the California Forestry Association killed Gilbert Murray, a timber lobbyist and the association's president. That same day, in a letter to *The New York Times,* the Unabomber explained that he was targeting scientists and engineers, especially those involved with computers and genetics. He called for the "destruction of the worldwide industrial system."

Five months later, *The Washington Post* and *The New York Times* copublished the Unabomber's 35,000-word manifesto, "Industrial Society and Its Future," following his promise to stop his attacks if the work were published. In that document, the Unabomber railed against technology, consumerism, advertising, "oversocialization," the government, and corporations—all in relation to the individual's loss of freedom. "Industrial-technological society cannot be reformed in such a way as to prevent it from progressively narrowing the sphere of human freedom," he wrote. The manifesto also presented justifications for his violence: "In order to get our message before the public with some chance of making a lasting impression, we had to kill people."

Calls poured in to the FBI, but the real break in the investigation came when David Kaczynski recognized the similarities between the Unabomber's manifesto and the writings of his older brother Ted, a brilliant mathematician who had left a tenure-track position at Berkeley's math department to live a solitary life in a remote mountain cabin. Although torn, David Kaczynski nevertheless contacted the FBI. By February 1996, investigators began staking out the one-room cabin near Lincoln, Montana, where Ted Kaczynski had lived in self-imposed exile for over 25 years.

On April 3, 1996, FBI agents, disguised as local mountain men, seized Ted Kaczynski. Inside his cabin, they found a fully constructed, unaddressed package bomb, countless bomb-making materials, the two typewriters that were used to write the Unabomber letters and the manifesto, as well as 22,000 pages of personal notes—in English, Spanish, and mathematical code—that linked Kaczynski to 18 years of bombings. He was indicted in Sacramento for the murders of Scrutton and Murray and the attacks against Epstein and Gelernter, and in New Jersey for the murder of Mosser.

The Washington Post contains the Unabomber's manifesto, September 19, 1995. At the request of Attorney General Janet Reno and the FBI, the *Post* published the unedited 35,000-word manifesto of the Unabomber, Theodore J. Kaczynski, in the hope of ending his 17-year letter bomb campaign. (Photo by Evan Agostini/Liaison, Getty Images News)

Kaczynski's trial, which began in November 1997, encountered significant delays and difficulties. The judge twice rejected Kaczynski's motions to fire his lawyers (in favor of a team who would defend the bombings based on a political argument), and he later denied Kaczynski's request to represent himself. Kaczynski did not want his defense to be based on the claim of mental illness. The psychiatric evaluation performed by Dr. Sally Johnson was inconclusive—Kaczynski was found to be mentally competent to stand trial, but it was also determined that he was probably a paranoid schizophrenic.

On January 22, 1998, Kaczynski, in a plea bargain, pled guilty to 13 federal bombing offenses and was sentenced to life in prison without possibility of parole. He was placed at the federal "supermax" prison in southern Colorado, where for a time he shared one-hour workouts with Ramzi Yousef (found guilty of the 1993 World Trade Center bombing) and McVeigh.

Laura Lambert

See also Bombings and Bomb Scares; Earth First!; Ecoterrorism; McVeigh, Timothy James; Oklahoma City Bombing; Yousef, Ramzi Ahmed

Further Readings

Chase, Alston. *A Mind for Murder: The Education of the Unabomber and the Origins of Modern Terrorism.* New York: W.W. Norton, 2004.

Gibbs, Nancy, et al. *Mad Genius: The Odyssey, Pursuit, and Capture of the Unabomber Suspect.* New York: Warner Books, 1996.

Graysmith, Robert. *Unabomber: A Desire to Kill.* Washington, DC: Regnery, 1997.

Kaczynski, David. "Missing Parts." In *Brothers: 26 Stories of Love and Rivalry,* edited by Andrew Blauner. San Francisco: Jossey-Bass, 2010.

Kaczynski, Theodore. *Technological Slavery: The Collected Writings of Theodore J. Kaczynski, a.k.a. "The Unabomber."* Port Townsend, WA: Feral House, 2010.

Kaczynski, Theodore. *The Unabomber Manifesto: Industrial Society and Its Future.* Minneapolis, MN: Filiquarian Publishing, 2005.

McFadden, Robert D. "Prisoner of Rage—A Special Report: From a Child of Promise to the Unabom Suspect." *The New York Times,* May 26, 1996.

http://www.nytimes.com/1996/05/26/us/prisoner-of-rage-a-special-report-from-a-child-of-promise-to-the-unabom-suspect.html.

Mello, Michael. *The United State of America versus Theodore John Kaczynski: Ethics, Power and the Invention of the Unabomber.* New York: Context Books, 1999.

Unconventional Warfare

See Asymmetrical Warfare

United Freedom Front

In 1987, the United Freedom Front (UFF, aka Ohio Seven; Sam Melville/Jonathan Jackson Unit [SMJJU]), a clandestine, militant anti-imperialist group, faced one of the longest seditious conspiracy trials in U.S. history. While all members were acquitted of the conspiracy charges, most were sent to prison on related charges, including bombing corporate buildings and military installations between 1982 and 1984 and the death of a New Jersey state trooper.

The UFF carried out more than 10 bombings in the New York metropolitan area during the early 1980s. In May 1983, explosions rocked military reserve centers in Nassau County and Queens. These bombings came a few months after the UFF attacked an IBM office in Harrison, New York, the South African embassy office in Elmont, Long Island, and a federal building on Staten Island that housed the FBI and an army-navy recruiting office.

By the end of 1983, the group had claimed responsibility for bombing another recruiting office in Long Island, as well as two undetonated bombs housed in attaché cases with "bomb" stenciled on the outside that were found at the offices of the Honeywell Corporation in Long Island City, Queens. The UFF would contact local authorities before the blasts to make sure no one was hurt, then call news organizations to claim the acts and spread various anti-imperialist messages, such as "U.S. Out of El Salvador," "Death to Apartheid," "Viva El Salvador." The group's actions were often compared to those of another group from the 1960s, the Weather Underground.

During 1984 the UFF attacked the New York City corporate offices of Motorola, IBM, GE, and Union Carbide to protest U.S. military and corporate involvement in Central and Latin America, specifically Nicaragua and El Salvador, and to protest apartheid in South Africa. UFF's final act was the September 26, 1984, bombing of the South African consulate on Park Avenue in Manhattan.

Two months later, authorities in Ohio raided the homes of Thomas and Carol Ann Manning, Raymond Luc Levasseur and Patricia Gros, and Jaan Karl Laaman and Barbara Curzi-Laaman. Thomas Manning, Levasseur, and Laaman were arrested on charges related to the death of Philip Lamonaco, a New Jersey state trooper, and a series of bank robberies in New England. Authorities also found copies of UFF communiqués, handwritten descriptions of the GE and IBM buildings bombed by the UFF, and bomb-related devices similar to those found at the Honeywell site.

On March 12, 1985, the Mannings, Levasseur, Gros, Laaman, Curzi-Laaman, and a man named Richard Williams—now known as the Ohio 7—were indicted for the UFF bombings. Evidence also linked them to a series of eight bombings in the 1970s in New England, claimed by the Sam Melville/Jonathan Jackson Unit (SMJJU).

The four-and-a-half month federal trial was held in Brooklyn, New York. All charged, except Gros, who was tried separately, were found guilty on at least two counts. In May 1986, the U.S. attorney's office in Boston, Massachusetts, indicted the Ohio 7, plus a man named Christopher King (a.k.a. Kazi Toure), on charges of seditious conspiracy and racketeering. This indictment encompassed the UFF bombings, as well as a number of bank robberies and the SMJJU bombings, including the bombing of the Suffolk County courthouse in retaliation for the 1976 Soweto (South Africa) massacre. The trial, which lasted more than 10 months, had more than 200 witnesses and over 1,700 pieces of evidence, making it one of the longest sedition trials in U.S. history. By November 1989, however, all the defendants had been acquitted of the sedition charges.

Laura Lambert

See also Weatherman

Further Readings

James, Joy, ed. *Imprisoned Intellectuals: America's Political Prisoners Write on Life, Liberation, and Rebellion.* Lanham, MD: Rowman & Littlefield, 2004.

Smith, Brent L. *Terrorism in America: Pipe Bombs and Pipe Dreams.* Albany: State University of New York Press, 1994.

UNITED NATIONS

As the premier international lawmaking body, the United Nations (UN) plays a key role in combating international terrorism. However, even as the UN's General Assembly passed one of the most comprehensive resolutions against terrorism in the wake of the September 11, 2001, attacks on the World Trade Center in New York City and the Pentagon just outside Washington, D.C., the international community continued its 30-year struggle to agree on a working definition of terrorism.

The United Nations Charter, which laid out basic principles of international relations, established the UN on October 24, 1945. At its founding, the UN had 51 member countries; it now has almost 200 members. Each member has a seat and a vote in the General Assembly. The UN has five other permanent bodies, including the 15-member Security Council, which is responsible for peacekeeping and international security, and is thus intimately involved in issues of terrorism. (China, France, the United Kingdom, the United States, and Russia are permanent members of the Security Council; representatives of 10 other countries are elected by the General Assembly).

International terrorism became an issue for the UN during the spate of hijackings in the 1960s. In response to the first hijacking, in May 1961, the UN held the Convention on Offences and Certain Other Acts Committed On Board Aircraft—its first high-level meeting on terrorism; from this meeting came a resolution empowering an aircraft commander to act to subdue anyone trying to hijack or jeopardize the flight, and requiring countries to take custody of the offenders. In 1970 another UN convention issued a resolution that required hijackers to be prosecuted or extradited. This piecemeal approach to the problem of terrorism—focusing on terrorist tools, such as hijacking, instead of on terrorism as a whole—would continue for decades.

The UN's inability to define international terrorism gave rise to this kind of legislation. In 1972, the year of the attack on the Israeli athletes during the Olympics in Munich, UN Secretary-General Kurt Waldheim put terrorism on the General Assembly's agenda, under the heading, "Measures to prevent terrorism and other forms of violence which endanger or take innocent lives or jeopardize fundamental freedoms." Several countries, including Australia, Canada, Great Britain, Italy, and Japan, also sponsored a proposal in the UN's legal committee to establish guidelines to punish and prevent terrorism. Concurrently, a second group of predominantly African and Middle Eastern countries proposed that the UN focus on the causes of terrorism. When the second proposal was adopted, Waldheim's already lengthy agenda title was amended to include "and study of the underlying causes of those forms of terrorism and acts of violence which lie in misery, frustration, grievance and despair and which cause some people to sacrifice human lives, including their own, in an attempt to effect radical changes." U.S. President Richard Nixon's proposal for an international treaty against the spread of terrorism beyond areas of conflict foundered in the midst of that debate.

Escalating Terrorism

The subsequent rise in international terrorism, including the Entebbe (Uganda) hostage crisis in 1976 and the Iran hostage crisis in 1979–1981, forced the UN back to the table again and again, resulting in meetings like the 1979 Convention Against the Taking of Hostages, held in New York City. The 1980s saw extensive terrorist activity in war-torn Lebanon, including the bombing of the U.S. embassy and military barracks in Beirut and the kidnapping of American, British, and French nationals by militant Islamic groups. In 1985 alone, four Soviet diplomats were kidnapped in Lebanon, terrorists in Colombia killed 90 people during a siege of the Palace of Justice in Bogotá, and bombs exploded in Paris department stores. In June, Hezbollah terrorists hijacked TWA Flight 847; four months later, Palestinian Liberation Front terrorists hijacked the *Achille Lauro* cruise ship; and an Egypt Air flight was hijacked in

November 1985. More than 75 countries had experienced terrorist attacks by the end of that year.

In December 1985, the UN, through its legal committee, passed the most comprehensive resolution on terrorism in its 40-year history; this resolution declared all acts of international terrorism to be criminal. While the landmark resolution reflected the UN's commitment to condemn terrorism, it did not clearly define terrorism; instead it referred to "acts of international terrorism in all its forms which endanger or take innocent lives, jeopardize fundamental freedoms and seriously impair the dignity of human beings."

The vagueness of the phrase left several members expressing reservations similar to those of Cuba, which criticized the resolution's hesitation to condemn "state terrorism," such as Israeli raids on Arab territories, U.S. support of the Nicaraguan Contras, or South African incursions into neighboring black African states. (Cuba cast a dissenting vote before agreeing to the resolution; Israel abstained.) Although the UN later condemned specific actions, including the U.S. raids on Libya in 1986 and Israel's attacks on civilians in southern Lebanon in the 1990s, no resolution has directly dealt with the overall issue of terrorism.

In 1987, Syria proposed a resolution that would define the difference between international terrorism and the rights of freedom fighters. Critics of this proposal, the fiercest of which was Israel, saw it as an attempt to legitimate acts of terrorism carried out by groups in the Middle East. When Syria lost the support of the Soviet Union and many of the Arab states, a compromise resolution was passed. In May 1995, Syria and several other Arab states reiterated the need to differentiate between terrorism and national liberation when the issue again arose in the General Assembly. In 2011, the distinction remained unclear.

Sanctions

In the 1990s, the UN began to use sanctions as part of its counterterrorism strategy. (The 1990s are sometimes referred to as the "Sanctions Decade.") In 1992 the UN imposed sanctions on Libya to force its government to hand over two suspects in the bombing of Pan Am Flight 103, which had exploded over Lockerbie, Scotland, in

1988. The sanctions were lifted in 1995, when the suspects were handed over for trial in the Netherlands. Similar (largely symbolic) sanctions were levied against Sudan in 1996 to force the Sudanese government to deliver suspects wanted in an assassination attempt on Egyptian president Hosni Mubarak. The UN imposed sanctions on the Taliban government of Afghanistan in an unsuccessful attempt to have Osama bin Laden, wanted for the August 1998 U.S. embassy bombings in Kenya and Tanzania, given over for trial.

In 1994 the UN General Assembly passed the Declaration on Measures to Eliminate International Terrorism, which reiterated the existing conventions on hijackings, prevention and prosecution of attacks on diplomats, hostage takings, attacks on airports and ships, and guidelines for storing nuclear materials. It also established a series of reports, to be produced by the Secretary-General, to aid international cooperation against terrorism.

The embassy bombings, as well as the 1996 attack on the Khobar Towers in Dhahran, Saudi Arabia, prompted further resolutions. In 1997, the International Convention for the Suppression of Terrorist Bombings declared that terrorist bombers would not receive "safe haven" from member states, and that they would be brought to justice through cooperation of member states. In October 1999, the UN Security Council adopted Resolution 1269, which called for all countries to refrain from harboring terrorists and to cooperate in bringing them to justice. At the same time, the Security Council urged the General Assembly to consider two additional resolutions—one, sponsored by Russia, against nuclear terrorism, another, sponsored by France, that would make financing terrorism a crime.

In 1999, in an effort to aid in the growing counterterrorism effort, the UN developed the Terrorism Prevention Branch (TPB), which operates under the UN Office on Drugs and Crime and works with the UN Centre for International Crime Prevention. The TPB researches terrorism and provides information and assistance, while promoting international cooperation with respect to terrorism.

Defining Terrorism

By September 12, 2001, the UN had denounced the terrorist attacks in New York, Pennsylvania, and Washington D.C., and within weeks, the Security Council passed a U.S.-sponsored resolution that greatly increased the UN's role in the U.S.-led "war on terror." Resolution 1373 called for all members to cease supporting, financing, and providing sanctuary to terrorists, and it urged increased cooperation and information sharing between nations. The resolution also established a Counter-Terrorism Committee (CTC) to monitor state compliance.

However, 1373 does not explicitly define terrorism, much less list which states, governments, and organizations should be considered terrorists. Instead, individual states were left to make their own judgments. The result was a confusing mix of overlapping lists and confusing omissions. Russia's list of terrorist organizations, for example, released in July 2006, excludes several groups on the U.S. list, such as Hamas and Hezbollah. Meanwhile, the Arab League and the Organization of the Islamic Conference, among others, have argued that acts related to the struggle against "foreign occupation, aggression, colonialism and hegemony aimed at liberation and self-determination" should be excluded from any definition of terrorism. Indeed, such an exclusion would correspond to UN Resolution 1514, which legitimizes actions taken to achieve national self-determination.

One key weapon in combating terrorism involves cutting off funding sources, a strategy outlined in three UN documents. Resolution 1267 (1999) requires member states to freeze assets, ban travel, and embargo weapons sales or transfers to al Qaeda, the Taliban, and associated individuals and entities. Resolution 1267 has been renewed annually and is monitored by the Al-Qaida and Taliban Sanctions Committee. As mentioned, Resolution 1373 (2001) requires member states to adopt a range of laws and regulations to suppress and prevent terrorist acts. The resolution calls for an imposition of binding regulations against terrorism, but it fails to define what constitutes a "terrorist act." Resolution 1540 (2004) requires member states to adopt domestic controls to prevent terrorist groups from acquiring weapons of mass destruction. All three resolutions included the creation of a dedicated compliance committee. However, none of the resolutions defined the term "terrorism."

In 2004 UN Secretary-General Kofi Annan assembled a committee to establish a definition of terrorism. The panel's resulting statement was clear: terrorism was any act that is "intended to cause death or serious bodily harm to civilians or non-combatants with the purpose of intimidating a population or compelling a government or an international organization to do or abstain from doing any act." The statement was not formally embraced by any country. But two years later, the UN's Global Counter-Terrorism Strategy was adopted by member states. The resolution and an accompanying "plan of action" marked the first time that member states had agreed upon a common counterterrorism strategy. Among other things, the plan calls for increased interstate cooperation in catching and prosecuting terrorists. That said, the majority of the strategy tells states to "encourage," "invite," or "consider" taking particular actions, rather than instructing or forcing them to do so.

The UN also established a Consolidated List of individuals and groups or entities subject to antiterrorism regulations. Instead of imposing sanctions against a country, Resolution 1267 (1999) offered a method to punish al Qaeda terrorists individually and directly. This need arose when the Taliban refused to hand over Osama bin Laden and other al Qaeda leaders to face trial for the bombing of the U.S. embassies in Kenya and Tanzania in 1998. Without a comprehensive definition of terrorism, placement on the list has become an alternate way to identify al Qaeda terrorists and their supporters.

The listing process requires countries to submit names and supporting materials to a screening committee. The nomination file is circulated among the 15 members of the UN Security Council. If no objects are raised after five days (initially just 48 hours), the person is placed on the list. An individual placed on the Consolidated List has no opportunity to present contrary evidence, nor are those listed even notified of their new status. Critics insist that the listing process violates the human rights provisions that that the UN system is designed to protect because it lacks transparency, procedural protections, and judicial oversight. Many countries have been reluctant to submit names, because the evidence needed to list an individual might reveal sensitive intelligence-gathering methods. Initially, there was no provision for regularly reviewing the list and removing individuals who were mistakenly included or who had died.

The UN established a delisting protocol in 2006 with Resolution 1730, but action is only taken if all 15 committee members agree to remove an individual.

Listed persons have filed more than 30 challenges to their designation in national and international courts. In one case before the European Court of Justice, Yassin Abdullah Kadi argued that an order from the European Union to freeze his assets violated his right to property and his right to a fair hearing. The court refused to evaluate the UN Security Council sanctions regime, but it did rule the internal review process "lacked guarantees of judicial protection." Similar cases have been filed in seven other countries, including the United States.

In December 2009 the Security Council unanimously approved a resolution to create an ombudsman to hear appeals to be removed from the list. Sponsored by the United States and Austria, the final version does not allow the ombudsman to rule on removing a person, but provides more of a procedural channel than before. The council established a monitoring team that immediately began to review all 396 individuals and 107 entities on the list. In January 2010, five former senior members of the Taliban were removed from the list, with others to follow.

The United Nations has debated and passed many resolutions regarding specific actions taken by terrorists, such as hijacking airplanes, taking hostages, and detonating bombs. The UN has passed 13 conventions outlawing terrorist acts and formulated a list of counterterrorism measures that member state governments should enact. What it has not accomplished, however, is a universally accepted definition of terrorism, and until there is such a framework in place, any legal provision will have limited use.

Ann E. Robertson and Laura Lambert

See also Counterterrorism; Criminal Prosecution of Terrorists; Financing Terrorism; Hijacking; Hostage Taking; International Relations and Terrorism

Further Readings

Comras, Victor D. "UN Terrorist Designation System Needs Reform." *Perspectives on Terrorism* 2, no. 10 (2008).

Dashti-Gibson, Jaleh, and George A. Lopez. "Taming Terrorism: Sanctions against Libya, Sudan, and Afghanistan." In *The Sanctions Decade: Assessing UN Strategies in the 1990s*, edited by David Cortright and George A. Lopez. Boulder, CO: Lynne Rienner, 2000.

Nesi, Giuseppe, ed. *International Cooperation in Counter-terrorism: The United Nations and Regional Organizations in the Fight against Terrorism.* Aldershot, UK: Ashgate, 2006.

Picco, Giandomenico. *Man without A Gun: One Diplomat's Secret Struggle to Free the Hostages, Fight Terrorism, and End a War.* New York: Times Books, 1999.

Terlingen, Yvonne. "The United States and the UN's Targeted Sanctions of Suspected Terrorists: What Role for Human Rights?" *Ethics and International Affairs* 24, no. 2 (Summer 2010).

United Nations. "United Nations Treaties against International Terrorism." http://www.un.org/News/dh/latest/intreaterror.htm.

UNITED SELF-DEFENSE FORCES OF COLOMBIA

Led by Carlo Castaño, the United Self-Defense Forces of Colombia (Autodefensas Unidas de Colombia, or AUC) is a right-wing paramilitary group formed in 1984 to combat guerrilla militias in Colombia. Its use of terror to destroy the guerrilla's support base has made it a feared and powerful force in that country.

Since the mid-1960s, the Colombian government has been fighting several leftist terror groups, with the two largest being the Revolutionary Armed Forces of Colombia (FARC) and the National Liberation Army–Colombia (ELN). The activities of these groups, combined with the cocaine industry (in which the FARC is heavily involved), have made Colombia a very dangerous country. In addition to bombing, extortion, and attacks on military bases and oil pipelines, both the ELN and the FARC have used kidnapping for ransom as a major source of revenue. Initiated in the late 1970s, kidnappings had become endemic in Colombia by the 1980s.

In the early 1980s, confronted by violence that the government seemed unable to master, right-wing businessmen, ranchers, and members of the military began to train and arm vigilante militias to combat guerrilla forces in their areas. One of the largest such groups was called Muerte a Secuestradores (MAS), which means "Death to Kidnappers." MAS was led by Carlo Castaño, whose father, a rancher, had been kidnapped by guerrillas and murdered when the Castaño family could not meet the full ransom demand. These groups, seen as a way for ordinary people to strike back at the guerrillas, were and continue to be popular with much of the public. Their methods, however, are brutal; for the most part, those killed in the 1980s by the MAS and other vigilante groups were not armed guerrillas but unarmed peasants accused of sympathizing with the guerrilla cause. By 1983, Amnesty International accused MAS of more than 800 extrajudicial killings.

In 1984 the Colombian government initiated a short-lived truce with the guerrilla groups, but many hard-line elements in the military and business communities completely opposed the truce. Support for the vigilantes increased, and they soon formed a coalition, the AUC. Castaño quickly became the leader.

As the AUC grew larger, it began to move beyond the control of the right-wingers who had originally funded it, becoming more like a private army for Castaño. Members attacked villages with roving columns of up to several hundred fighters. AUC's forces lived in jungle camps but also maintained a presence in captured towns. As the AUC took over more villages, it gained control of coca-producing areas. The group then took on the protection of traffickers and growers—just as the guerrillas had—and like the guerrillas, the AUC charged the drug lords handsomely for the service. That drug money enabled the group to equip its fighters with modern weapons and communications equipment, and to pay them a wage much better that that of the average Colombian. Perhaps more important, it also allowed them to pay hefty sums to guerrilla informers, enabling conquered villages to be purged of sympathizers.

Support and Collusion

Many in Colombia's official armed forces are in sympathy with AUC's aims. Poor equipment and training, corruption, and tactical disadvantages have long stymied the army's efforts to combat the guerrillas, and the international community has until very recently been reluctant to provide military aid to Colombia because of the army's human rights' record. Many within the army seem willing to offer the AUC clandestine support, feeling that its brutal tactics are the only effective response to the guerrilla threat. Several major instances suggesting intelligence sharing and tactical support between the AUC and the army have come to light, and significant disparities are apparent in the number of guerrillas and AUC members arrested by the army.

An example of such apparent collusion is an AUC attack on a remote mountain village that occurred in April 2001. The military declined to come to the villagers' aid, claiming that it had been unaware of the attack until too late and, in any case, could not redirect its overstretched forces. In contrast, a FARC attack nearby brought a response within hours. As many people believe the army to be in league with the AUC, they are reluctant to report abuses to civil authorities. The government's attempts at action against the group, however limited, have been largely ineffective. Dozens of villagers were killed by the AUC between April 11 and 13, 2001, and many of them were tortured, their bodies mutilated and beheaded by chain saws. Most of the inhabitants fled the area. Human rights groups estimate that the AUC killed more than 1,000 unarmed civilians in 2001.

On September 10, 2001, the AUC was added to the U.S. State Department's list of terrorist organizations. In 2007, the fruit company Chiquita Brands International admitted that from 1997 to 2004, it had paid the AUC $1.7 million to protect its employees from attacks. Significantly, about half of that money was paid after the AUC was designated as a terrorist organization by the Bush administration. Chiquita eventually paid a fine of $25 million in a plea-bargaining agreement with the U.S. Department of Justice.

In 1998, President Andrés Pastrana withdrew government forces from southern Colombia, allowing the FARC to control over 40 percent of the country as a precondition to peace negotiations. For the next two years, FARC attacks continued while the negotiations went nowhere, and the Colombian people lost faith in the peace process. Those who had always been opposed to the negotiations, the AUC among them, became

convinced that the time was ripe to act. When Pastrana attempted to grant the ELN a similar demilitarized zone in late 2000, AUC forces flooded the area, scoring a series of rapid victories against the ELN. By April the ELN was scrambling to regain its territory. These victories helped further derail the peace process, and by early 2002 it had completely broken down.

Around this period, Castaño became increasingly isolated from the other members of AUC, including his older brother, Vicente Castaño. Observers believe that Carlos Castaño objected to the group's increasing involvement in drug trafficking (though Castaño himself was indicted in absentia by the U.S. Justice Department for cocaine trafficking in 2002). Furthermore, it has been suggested that Castaño the younger was more open to negotiating with the Colombian government that the rest of the AUC. Carlos Castaño was killed in a gunfight at his ranch in 2004, although his charred remains were not identified until 2006.

In the face of increasing pressure from the Colombian government, including large-scale arrests of its members, the AUC appeared to move somewhat closer to reconciliation, even claiming to have demobilized in 2006. However, remaining members of the AUC have rejected proposed terms for negotiation because the terms leave open the possibility that group members may be extradited to the United States for trials on drug-trafficking charges. The AUC reemerged in 2008 with a string of violent attacks in Colombia and Ecuador. In January 2011, six men in Florida were charged with conspiring to provide weapons to men who they believed to be AUC members but were in fact undercover agents.

Colleen Sullivan

See also FARC; Narcoterrorism; National Liberation
   Army–Colombia

Further Readings

Bruce, Victoria, and Karin Hayes. *Hostage Nation:*
   Colombia's Guerilla Army and the Failed War on
   Drugs. New York: Alfred A. Knopf, 2010.
"Castaño, Carlos." *The Independent.* September 6, 2006.
   http://www.independent.co.uk/news/obituaries/
   carlos-castantildeo-414777.html.

Hristov, Jasmin. *Blood & Capital: The Paramilitarization of Colombia.* Athens: Ohio University Press, 2009.

Kline, Harvey F. *State Building and Conflict Resolution in Colombia, 1986–94.* Tuscaloosa: University of Alabama Press, 1999.

Pearce, Jenny. *Colombia: Inside the Labyrinth.* New York: Monthly Review Press, 1990.

Rabasa, Angel, et al. *Ungoverned Territories: Understanding and Reducing Terrorism Risks.* Santa Monica, CA: RAND Corporation, 2007.

Robinson, Linda. "Where Angels Fear to Tread: Colombia and Latin America's Tier of Turmoil." *World Policy Journal* 16, no. 4 (Winter 1999/ 2000): 63.

Safford, Frank, and Marco Palacios. *Colombia: Fragmented Land, Divided Society.* New York: Oxford University Press, 2002.

United States v. Usama Bin Laden, et al.

The criminal case against the Saudi exile Osama bin Laden began in the United States District Court in Lower Manhattan, where federal prosecutors filed the first charges against the alleged terrorist mastermind. A series of superseding indictments obtained by the United States Attorney for the Southern District of New York, *United States v. Usama bin Laden, et al.*, became the most complete set of American accusations against bin Laden prior to the September 11, 2001, terrorist attacks on New York and Washington, D.C.

The first indictment of bin Laden handed down by a grand jury came in June 1998. It contained only one charge: conspiracy to attack national defense utilities of the United States. This indictment, initially sealed from public view, contained what would become the core of the government's case against bin Laden for several years. The indictment accused him of forming an international terrorist group called al Qaeda, meaning "the Base," and labeled bin Laden the *emir,* or leader, to whom members swore a loyalty oath, or *bayat.*

The indictment described al Qaeda as an Islamic extremist group formed in Afghanistan around 1989, and later aligned with anti-American governments in Iran, Iraq, and Sudan, where al Qaeda established its headquarters in the early-to-mid-1990s. The indictment alleged that al Qaeda opposed non-Islamic governments, including the United States, Israel, and Egypt. In particular, the indictment alleged that bin Laden was angered by U.S military and economic support of Israel and U.S. troops being stationed in Saudi Arabia, home of the holiest Muslim shrines, in Mecca and Medina.

From the beginning, the bin Laden indictments alleged that in the early 1990s, al Qaeda sought to attack U.S. military facilities and U.S. troops in Saudi Arabia, sent originally to fight the Gulf War, as well as U.S. troops in the predominant Muslim countries of Yemen and Somalia. The charges claimed that bin Laden's men even trained Somali tribes opposed to U.S. intervention and participated in the infamous October 1993 battle in Mogadishu that left 18 U.S. soldiers dead.

As part of the conspiracy, the indictment stated that bin Laden had established militant training camps in Afghanistan and Sudan, attempted to obtain components of nuclear weapons, attempted to produce chemical weapons, and recruited Americans especially to travel and deliver money. al Qaeda allegedly made fake passports for its operatives and used nongovernmental organizations, such as charities, to transmit funds. The group was governed by a "consultation council," or *majlis al shura,* that supervised military, finance, and media committees.

Evidence of bin Laden's lethal intent were his pair of *fatwas,* or religious decrees, exhorting violence against Americans. In August 1996, bin Laden issued his declaration of *jihad,* or holy war, against the U.S., calling on followers to kill American soldiers. In February 1998, he issued another fatwa, along with other extremist groups, such as Egyptian Islamic Jihad, under the banner of the "International Islamic Front for Jihad against Jews and Crusaders," which advocated the killing of Americans, even civilians, anywhere they could be found.

Two months after the sealed indictment against bin Laden, al Qaeda's East African cell bombed the U.S. embassies in Nairobi, Kenya, and Dar es Salaam, Tanzania. The twin truck bombings of August 7, 1998 killed 224 people, including 12 Americans who worked in the Kenya embassy, and wounded more than 4,500 other people. Claims for the bombings sent to select media outlets were signed by the "Islamic Army for the Liberation of the Holy Places."

The ensuing investigation, the largest at that point in FBI history, led to the quick arrest of two suspected Kenya bombers, Mohamed al Owhali and Mohammed Saddiq Odeh. In the fall of 1998, they were indicted, along with a suspected operational leader of the Kenya bombers, Fazul Abdullah Mohammed, a fugitive, and an accused facilitator of the East Africa cell, Wadih el Hage, a Lebanese-American who lived in Texas after working for years overseas for bin Laden.

United States v. Usama bin Laden, et al. took on a new shape in early November 1998, when U.S. Attorney Mary Jo White announced that bin Laden himself had been indicted for the embassy bombings. In the first of what would become 10 superseding indictments over the next two years, bin Laden was now charged with the murder of those 224 people and a broader terrorism conspiracy to kill Americans worldwide and destroy U.S. property. His alleged military chief, Muhammad Atef, was also publicly charged with the same offenses, bringing the total number of men charged to six.

The indictment alleged that al Qaeda spread its web by allying with jihadi groups in other countries or by establishing its own cells. Besides Kenya and Tanzania, the indictment said there were operatives in Afghanistan, Pakistan, Sudan, Yemen, Saudi Arabia, Somalia, Azerbaijan, the Philippines, England, and the United States, where the Alkifah Refugee Center in Brooklyn had once been a gathering point for anti-Soviet mujahideen, and later for conspirators in the 1993 World Trade Center bombing. The imprisonment of those bombers, followers of the blind Egyptian cleric Sheikh Omar Abdel Rahman, became another stated grievance of al Qaeda.

In characterizing bin Laden's goal as being to drive American troops from Muslim countries, such as Somalia and Saudi Arabia, by violent means, the indictment detailed how the group pursued its goal: by providing military and intelligence training; establishing camps and guesthouses in Afghanistan, Pakistan, Somalia, and Kenya; buying warehouses to store explosives; buying communications gear; and transporting currency. The indictment said al Qaeda would conceal it activities by establishing front companies, creating false identity and travel documents, lying to authorities, and killing informants—methods that would come to light in testimony during the embassy bombings trial in New York in 2001.

At trial, the indictment included 302 counts— 224 of them murder charges for each victim of the embassy bombings—and six terrorism conspiracy counts, the top count being conspiracy to kill U.S. nationals. The indictment also alleged a conspiracy to use weapons of mass destruction and a conspiracy to destroy U.S. property. *United States v. Usama bin Laden, et al.* had ballooned up to 150 pages, and it now contained an encapsulated history of al Qaeda and every accusation against each of nearly two-dozen men accused in the conspiracy. Much of the final indictment was an elaborately detailed account of the Kenya and Tanzania attacks. Most of the counts charged multiple defendants, many of whom were fugitives. Defendant Wadih el Hage faced 19 counts of perjury alone for his two appearances before a federal grand jury investigating al Qaeda. On May 29, 2001, the trial jury found the only four men in court—Hage, Odeh, Owhali, and K.K. Mohamed— guilty of all 302 counts collectively brought against them.

Phil Hirschkorn

See also al Qaeda; bin Laden, Osama; East Africa Embassy Bombings; Mohamed, Khalfan Khamis; Nosair, El Sayyid; Odeh, Mohammed Saddiq; Owhali, Mohamed Rashed al; World Trade Center Bombing (1993)

Further Readings

Bergen, Peter. *Holy War, Inc.: Inside the Secret World of Osama bin Laden.* New York: Free Press, 2001.

Bergen, Peter. *The Longest War: Inside the Enduring Conflict between America and al-Qaeda.* New York: Free Press, 2011.

Bergen, Peter. *The Osama bin Laden I Know: An Oral History of al Qaeda's Leader.* New York: Free Press, 2006.

Gunaratna, Rohan. *Inside al Qaeda: Global Network of Terror.* New York: Columbia University Press, 2002.

Rabasa, Angel, et al. *Beyond al Qaeda.* Part 1, *The Global Jihadist Movement.* Santa Monica, CA: RAND Corporation, 2006.

Reeve, Simon. *The New Jackals: Ramzi Yousef, Osama bin Laden and the Future of Terrorism.* Boston: Northeastern Press, 1999.

Richardson, Louise. *What Terrorists Want: Understanding the Enemy, Containing the Threat.* New York: Random House: 2006.

U.S. District Court for the Southern District of New York. *United States v. Usama bin Laden, et al.* Indictment S(2) 98 Cr. 1023 (LBS), November 4, 1998. http://www.fas.org/irp/news/1998/11/98110602_nlt.html.

U.S. EMBASSY BOMBING, BEIRUT

The April 18, 1983, suicide bombing attack on the U.S. embassy in Beirut, Lebanon, killed 63 people in a blast so powerful it shook the USS *Guadalcanal,* anchored five miles away. The attack was followed by the bombing of U.S. Marine and French military barracks in October of that year. The double horror of these disasters led to a drop in public support of the U.S. military presence in Lebanon and hastened the withdrawal of U.S. and western European troops from the country. The U.S. forces had initially entered war-torn Lebanon in August 1982 as part of a multinational peacekeeping force, which included French, Italian, and British personnel. The peacekeepers intended to negotiate a cease-fire between Lebanon and Israel, who had invaded the country two months prior.

On the afternoon of April 18, a Chevrolet pickup truck, packed with about 2,000 pounds of explosives, sped through the gate of the U.S. embassy in West Beirut and struck the building. The resulting blast killed 46 Lebanese and 17 Americans, including one American journalist and every CIA station chief in the Middle East; 120 others were injured. Islamic Jihad, a group linked to the Iranian-backed Shiite Muslim group Hezbollah, or "Party of God," claimed responsibility for the act.

Six months later, the tragedy was repeated when another suicide bomb attack, this time on the Beirut U.S. Marine Base and French military headquarters, killed 241 U.S. Marines and 58 French paratroopers. This incident was also linked to Islamic Jihad. Five months following the second attack, the Lebanese government authority in West Beirut collapsed. In February 1984, U.S. officials announced the withdrawal of the U.S.

U.S. Embassy in Beirut. (USMC photo)

troops, followed shortly thereafter by the pullout of Italian, British, and French troops.

Erica Pearson

See also Hezbollah; U.S. Marine Barracks Bombing, Beirut

Further Readings

Fisk, Robert. *Pity the Nation: Lebanon at War.* London: Deutsch, 1990.

Freidman, Thomas J. *From Beirut to Jerusalem.* Updated ed. New York: Anchor Books, 1995.

Jaber, Hala. *Hezbollah.* New York: Columbia University Press, 1997.

Norton, Augustus Richard. *Hezbollah: A Short History.* Princeton Studies in Muslim Politics. Princeton, NJ: Princeton University Press, 2007.

Richardson, Louise. *What Terrorists Want: Understanding the Enemy, Containing the Threat.* New York: Random House: 2006.

"U.S. Opens Lebanon Consulate Nearly 20 Years after Attack." *The New York Times,* May 31, 2003. http://www.nytimes.com/2003/05/31/world/us-opens-lebanon-consulate-nearly-20-years-after-attack.html.

U.S. Embassy Bombing, Dar es Salaam

See East Africa Embassy Bombings

U.S. Embassy Bombing, Nairobi

See East Africa Embassy Bombings

U.S. Marine Barracks Bombing, Beirut

On October 23, 1983, 241 American and 58 French service personnel were killed, and many more wounded, in two suicide bombings that destroyed the U.S. Marine barracks and a French paratroop barracks in Beirut, Lebanon. The attack is widely thought to have hastened the end of American military involvement in Lebanon.

American Marines landed in Beirut during summer 1982 as part of a multinational peacekeeping force. They, along with British, French, and Italian military personnel, were sent during U.S.-brokered negotiations among Lebanon, Syria, and Israel. When the multinational troops arrived, both Israeli and Syrian forces occupied Lebanon, fighting on opposite sides of the civil war that pitted Lebanese militia groups against the Lebanese National Movement and the Palestine Liberation Organization.

On the Sunday morning of the attack, an explosive-laden vehicle drove into each military headquarters. The two explosions went off seconds apart, completely destroying their targets. For the U.S. military, the death toll was the largest single-day loss since the Vietnam War.

U.S. officials initially said that the bombing was planned by Iranian and Syrian intelligence services, but both countries denied the charges. Shortly thereafter, Islamic Jihad, an Iranian-backed Shiite Muslim group linked to Hezbollah, or "Party of God," took responsibility for the massacre. This group also claimed responsibility for the April 1983 bombing of the U.S. embassy in West Beirut.

The 1983 Beirut bombings are said to have brought the American military presence in Lebanon to an end. After the collapse of Lebanese government authority in West Beirut in February 1984, the last U.S. troops left Lebanon, followed shortly by the remaining French, British, and Italian troops.

Erica Pearson

See also Bombings and Bomb Scares; Hezbollah; Palestine Liberation Organization; U.S. Embassy Bombing, Beirut

Further Readings

Fisk, Robert. *Pity the Nation: Lebanon at War.* London: Deutsch, 1990.

Freidman, Thomas J. *From Beirut to Jerusalem.* Updated ed. New York: Anchor Books, 1995.

Jaber, Hala. *Hezbollah.* New York: Columbia University Press, 1997.

North, Gretchen. "Lebanon." In *The Middle East*, edited by Robin Surratt. 9th ed. Washington, DC: CQ Press, 2000.

Norton, Augustus Richard. *Hezbollah: A Short History.* Princeton Studies in Muslim Politics. Princeton, NJ: Princeton University Press, 2007.

Pfarrer, Chuck. "One Deadly Morning in Beirut." *The New York Times,* October 23, 2003. http://www.nytimes.com/2003/10/23/opinion/one-deadly-morning-in-beirut.html.

USA PATRIOT ACT

See Patriot Act

USO CLUB BOMBING

On April 14, 1988, a USO club in Naples, Italy, was rocked by a car bomb that killed five people and injured more than a dozen, including several Americans. Further investigations revealed that the attack was in retaliation for the April 1986 bombings of military sites in Tripoli and Benghazi, Libya.

The USO club in Naples was located on a busy, narrow street, just a block from the docks where two American warships were moored. When the car bomb exploded, at about 8 P.M., most American officers were in the entertainment rooms in the basement of club, and they therefore escaped injury. However, four Italians and one U.S. servicewoman walking in the crowded street were killed instantly, and at least 15 others suffered serious injuries from the flying debris and pieces of the car in which the bomb had been hidden.

Initially, Middle Eastern groups with anti-American sentiments were suspected. Responsibility for the attack was claimed by the Brigades of the Holy War, a fundamentalist Muslim group that told a news agency in Rome, "The imperialist American should die today, two years after their barbarous attacks against the Arab-Libyan state." A similar call, also expressing anti-American, anti-imperialist sentiments, was placed to an Italian news agency in Beirut, this time by representatives of the Organization of the Islamic Holy War for the Support of the World's Oppressed.

By the following day, however, Italian officials had linked the rental car and a nearby hotel room to a known international terrorist, Junzo Okudaira. Okudaira was part of the ultra-left-wing Japanese terrorist group known as the Japanese Red Army (JRA), which had been active in the 1970s and had links to the Popular Front for the Liberation of Palestine (PFLP) and the German Baader-Meinhof Gang. After nearly a decade of inactivity, the JRA had resurfaced in mid-1980s. Okudaira and the JRA were thought to have allied with fundamentalist Shiite Muslim groups in Lebanon. Now the JRA was also apparently supported by the Libyan government.

As Italian officials ordered a nationwide manhunt for Okudaira, American officials were questioning another JRA member, Yu Kikumura, who had been arrested by a New Jersey state trooper two days prior to the USO bombing. Kikumura's suspicious behavior at a rest area had drawn the trooper's attention; he had three 18-inch pipe bombs and a map of New York City in the car when he was arrested. The map showed three targets: a navy recruiting office, Manhattan's Garment District, and the United Nations. Apparently, the bombs were to be placed two days later, set to explode at the same time as the USO bomb. Experts claimed that such tactics—striking different sites simultaneously—was typical of the JRA.

In 1989 Kikumura was sentenced to 30 years in prison for his role in the bomb plot. He was released from a Colorado prison in 2007 and returned to Japan, where he was immediately arrested for questioning regarding his relationship with the Japanese Red Army. Kikumura, however, was given a suspended sentence and released. A week before the statute of limitations expired, on April 10, 1993, a U.S. grand jury indicted Okudaira for the bombing, though he remained at large. Okudaira had already been sentenced in absentia to a life term in Italy.

Laura Lambert

See also Baader-Meinhof Gang; Japanese Red Army; Kikumura, Yu; Popular Front for the Liberation of Palestine; Qaddafi, Muammar el; Shigenobu, Fusako; Tripoli and Benghazi Bombing

Further Readings

Farrell, William. *Blood and Rage: The Story of the Japanese Red Army.* Lexington, MA: D.C. Heath, 1990.

Gallagher, Aileen. *The Japanese Red Army.* New York: Rosen Group, 2003.

Smith, Brent L. *Terrorism in America: Pipe Bombs and Pipe Dreams.* Albany: State University of New York Press, 1994.

Steinhoff, Patricia G., and Yoshinori Ito. *Rengo Sekigun to Oumu Shinrikyo.* Tokyo, Japan: Sairyusha, 1996.

Suro, Roberto. "5 Die in Blast outside U.S.O. in Naples" *The New York Times,* April 15, 1988. p. 3. http://www.nytimes.com/1988/04/15/world/5-die-in-blast-outside-uso-in-naples.html.

Suro, Roberto. "A Japanese with Lebanese Links Blamed in Naples U.S.O. Bombing." *The New York Times,* April 16, 1988.

Tumulty, Karen. "Japanese Terrorist Planned 'Mass Murder,' U.S. Says." *The New York Times,* February 4, 1989.

USS *Cole* Bombing

On October 12, 2000, two suicide bombers piloted a rubber boat next to the USS *Cole*, in port in Aden, Yemen, and blew a 40-by-60-foot hole in the side of the 505-foot American naval destroyer. The blast killed 17 U.S. sailors and wounded 39 others on board. Most experts agree that the attack was orchestrated by Osama bin Laden's al Qaeda terror network.

The *Cole* had entered the harbor of Aden to refuel. The crew moored the ship to a buoy and began the refueling process. Within 45 minutes, a small explosive-laden rubber craft positioned itself at the *Cole*'s side. The two men on the boat waved to the men on deck, then detonated the many pounds of explosives.

Within a few hours U.S. agents were en route to Yemen to begin what would become a very strained and lengthy search for clues and suspects. On October 29, the *Cole* was eased out of Aden harbor by tugboat; in the deeper water the ship was loaded onto a massive Norwegian heavy transport ship for return to the United States. After an 18-month, $250 million repair and upgrade project, the USS *Cole* was deemed seaworthy three days after the September 11, 2001, terrorist attacks on the United States; she returned to home port in Norfolk, Virginia, in April 2002, but has since been redeployed on successful missions.

The Search

The attack on the *Cole* is widely accepted to have been a terrorist attack, and although technically unsolved, most of the evidence indicates the involvement of the al Qaeda network. A lesser-known attempt on a U.S. ship had failed in a larger radical Islamic effort to ring in the new millennium with terror attacks. Around that time, a U.S.

Flanked by the USS *Dwight D. Eisenhower*, left, and the USS *Ross*, President Clinton and other military leaders address the families and friends of the sailors killed or missing as a result of the attack on the USS *Cole*. (Photograph by PH3 Larry I. Hess)

warship, the USS *The Sullivans,* was in Yemen, and some terrorists loaded a dinghy with explosives and sailed out to meet the ship. The dingy sank from the weight, and the would-be martyrs swam to shore and disappeared.

Throughout the investigation, a portrait of the *Cole* bombers and their methods emerged. Two men rented an expensive hilltop apartment with a sweeping rooftop view of the Aden harbor. They apparently spent considerable time observing harbor activities, including the comings and goings of large ships. They did not talk much with their neighbors, yet they spoke to local fishermen often, asking various questions, including how far one could sail in a dinghy. Shortly before the attack, the two men told neighbors they were going on a long trip and would be back around late December, the end of Ramadan. They have never been seen or heard from again.

Unearthing hard evidence, though, was next to impossible for investigators, as the American investigation team in Yemen was blocked at nearly every turn. When FBI officials first arrived, less than a day after the attack, Yemeni officials expressed suspicion about their investigation protocols, and FBI requests to interview high-level Yemeni officers were routinely denied. By the summer of 2001, the investigation had stalled and a wave of terror threats against the investigators caused new tensions. The FBI was forced to pull its team from Yemen. After the pullout of FBI agents, a video showing bin Laden praising the *Cole* bombing circulated in the Arab world.

In 2002, the CIA captured Abd al Rahim al Nashiri, a high-ranking member of al Qaeda who was believed to have helped plan the *Cole* attack. Nashri was held at sites in Poland, Thailand, and Morocco before being transferred to the Guantánamo Bay detention facility in 2003, and he was waterboarded as part of his interrogation. A court in Yemen sentenced him to death in absentia in 2004, and a U.S. military tribunal filed charges against him in 2008. The charges were dropped in 2009 pending a review of Guantánamo detentions, but the U.S. Defense Department issued a statement in 2010 that the charges would be refiled at some point in the future.

Yemeni officials eventually tried and sentenced five men, including the ringleader, Jamal al Badawi, for conspiring to blow up the *Cole,* but by 2006 all the defendants had escaped from prison. Badawi turned himself in to authorities but was released in 2007 after telling authorities that he had renounced terrorism. Also in 2007, a U.S. federal court ruled that the country of Sudan was liable for the attack; the suit had been brought by the families of the bombing victims, who argued that al Qaeda members would not have been able to attack the ship without support from the Sudanese government. U.S. District Judge Robert Doumar agreed with the families and declared that Sudan was liable for $13 million in compensatory damages, which are calculated based on potential earnings of the victims had they lived. A second suit was brought by *Cole* families in 2010, this time seeking more than $200 million in damages for pain and suffering caused by the bombing.

Richard McHugh

See also al Qaeda; bin Laden, Osama; Guantánamo Bay

Further Readings

Beaumont, Peter. "Bombshell Report on CIA Interrogations Is Leaked." *The Guardian,* August 22, 2009. http://www.guardian.co.uk/world/2009/aug/22/cia-interrogation-report-leaked.

Bergen, Peter. *Holy War, Inc.: Inside the Secret World of Osama bin Laden.* New York: Free Press, 2001.

Isikoff, Michael. "A Terrorist Walks Free." *Newsweek,* October 27, 2007. http://www.newsweek.com/2007/10/27/a-terrorist-walks-free.html.

Rabasa, Angel, et al. *Beyond al Qaeda.* Part 1, *The Global Jihadist Movement.* Santa Monica, CA: RAND Corporation, 2006.

Sadler, Brent, and David Ensor. "Suspect in USS *Cole* Bombing Kills Self in Yemen." CNN World, February 14, 2002. http://articles.cnn.com/2002-02-13/world/yemen.alqaeda_1_yemeni-security-al-qaeda-yemeni-officials?_s=PM:WORLD.

Sageman, Marc. *Understanding Terror Networks.* Philadelphia: University of Pennsylvania, 2004.

Savage, Charlie. "Trial of Accused Mastermind in *Cole* Attack Tests Tribunal System." *The New York Times,* November 30, 2009. http://www.nytimes.com/2009/12/01/us/01cole.html.

U.S. Navy. "USS *Cole.*" http://www.cole.navy.mil.

Weiss, Murray. *The Man Who Warned America: The Life and Death of John O'Neill.* New York: HarperCollins, 2003.

Whitlock, Craig. "Probe of USS *Cole* Bombing Unravels." *The Washington Post,* May 4, 2008. http://www.washingtonpost.com/wp-dyn/content/article/2008/05/03/AR2008050302047.html.

VIGOROUS BURMESE STUDENT WARRIORS

The Vigorous Burmese Student Warriors (VBSW) is a Burmese terrorist organization opposed to the military junta that rules Myanmar (formerly Burma); the group is best known for a 1999 attack on Myanmar's consulate in Bangkok, Thailand.

In August 1988, student protests helped bring about the downfall of the Burmese dictator Ne Win; the following year, however, a coalition of Burmese military forces calling themselves the State Law and Order Restoration Council (SLORC, now the State Peace and Development Council, or SPDC) took control of the country in a bloody coup, renaming it Myanmar. The SPDC reluctantly allowed elections in 1990. When the elections resulted in a landslide victory for the National League for Democracy (NLD), a student-backed group led by the Nobel Peace Prize winner Aung San Suu Kyi, the junta ignored the results, and Suu Kyi was held under house arrest until 2002.

Since 1990, many of the former student radicals have fled Myanmar for neighboring Thailand. From exile, they have continued their political opposition to the regime, but they have done so peacefully as the All Burma Students' Democratic Front (ABSDF). In late August 1999, as small group of Burmese student activists, frustrated with peaceful protest, formed the Vigorous Burmese Student Warriors. The group released a manifesto that suggested a core of 18 members, including San Naing (aka Ye Thiha), who had hijacked a Myanmar domestic flight and diverted it to Thailand in 1989. Some observers believe Naing to be the group's leader.

On the morning of October 1, 1999, five VBSW members raided the consulate of Myanmar in Bangkok, Thailand, taking 89 hostages, including 14 Westerners. The group then made a number of sweeping demands that, most observers believe, it knew had little chance of being met. In particular, they demanded the release of all Burmese political prisoners, the opening of negotiations between the NLD and the SPDC, and the convening of a parliament based on the results of the 1990 elections. The group later admitted that its true goal had been to focus international attention on Burma. After a few hours, the hostage takers backed down from their initial demands, and the hostages were freed unharmed within two days. VBSW members were allowed to flee by helicopter to the remote jungle along the Thailand-Myanmar border. Following the crisis, some of the hostages and two Thai government officials expressed sympathy for the terrorists, though characterizing their actions as misguided. These comments severely strained Myanmar-Thai relations for the next several months.

After the VBSW members escaped, they linked up with members of God's Army, a small band of ethnic Karen guerrillas led by Johnny and Luther Htoo, twin adolescent boys who had been fighting the Myanmar army since 1997. In late 1999, the

Myanmar military began a series of assaults on the groups' camp, pushing them further into Thai territory. Reluctant to become further involved in Myanmar's conflicts, and angered over the death of four of its soldiers in a landmine incident, the Thai army began shelling the guerrillas from the rear. The guerrillas responded by seizing a hospital in Ratchaburi, Thailand, on January 24, 2000, taking several hundred hostages. The mixed force of God's Army and VBSW members demanded that their soldiers be allowed to retreat into Thailand and receive medical care there. On January 25, Thai security forces launched a commando raid on the hospital compound, freeing all the hostages and killing all 10 terrorists. Some witnesses, including former hostages, claimed that the terrorists were executed after they had surrendered.

Following the hospital debacle, God's Army and the VBSW retreated further into the jungle. God's Army members fled to Thailand in 2001, where they surrendered to authorities. In 2006, Johnny Htoo, then 18 years old, returned to Myanmar and surrendered with eight of his followers; the other twin remains at large. In 2004, after a four-year hiatus, the VBSW claimed responsibility for a bus explosion in Myanmar that killed one person and injured three. Burmese police also blamed the VBSW for an April 2010 bombing at a festival that left 10 dead and 168 injured, though the VBSW did not claim responsibility for the attack.

Colleen Sullivan

Further Readings

"Leader of 'God's Army' Surrenders." *International Herald Tribune,* July 26, 2006.

Lertcharoenchok, Yindee. "Hijacker Not among Embassy Raiders." *Thailand Nation,* October 6, 1999.

Maung Maung Than, Tin. *Myanmar: The Dilemma of Stalled Reforms.* Singapore: Institute of Southeast Asian Studies, 2000.

McDowell, Patrick. "Witnesses: Rebels in Thailand Were Killed after Surrendering." Associated Press, January 26, 2000.

Sanford, Victoria, and Asale Angel-Ajani. *Engaged Observer: Anthropology, Advocacy, and Activism.* Piscataway, NJ: Rutgers University Press, 2006.

Suu Kyi, Aung San. *Freedom from Fear: And Other Writings.* Rev. ed. London and New York: Penguin Books, 1995.

"Thailand Vows to Tighten Security on Myanmar Dissidents." *Thailand Nation,* October 6, 1999.

VOLUNTEERS OF IRELAND

See Real Irish Republican Army

WACO

See Branch Davidian Compound Siege

WAITE, TERRY (1939–)

While serving as secretary for Anglican Communion affairs for the archbishop of Canterbury, Terry Waite negotiated the release of several British hostages in Tehran, Iran, and Libya before being taken hostage himself during the Lebanon hostage crisis.

The archbishop of Canterbury, Dr. Robert Runcie, recruited Waite to be his advisor in 1980. The Anglican Church had no history of intervening in international political affairs, and Waite's role as a hostage negotiator in the Middle East was not part of the job description. Within a year of Waite's appointment, however, three British missionaries had been taken hostage in Tehran. The archbishop appealed to Ayatollah Ruhollah Khomeini as a fellow religious man, and sent Waite as his envoy to negotiate the release of the hostages. Waite's success transformed him from a relatively unknown religious representative to a British personality. On Christmas Day 1984, Waite was received by Colonel Muammar el Qaddafi to negotiate for the release of four more British hostages held in Libya. The hostages were freed the following January.

Nearly a year later, on November 4, 1985, Waite made his first trip to Beirut on behalf of American captives, who had written an open letter to the archbishop asking for assistance. In Waite's first meeting with a representative of Islamic Jihad, Waite brought a Polaroid camera and a copy of the London *Times,* with his signature across the front page, and asked that each of the captives be photographed holding the newspaper. The hostages posed for the photographs and interpreted the newspaper with Waite's signature as a sign that they might soon be released. When the intermediary returned with the photos less than an hour later, Waite was whisked off to the first-ever meeting between a Western emissary and representatives of Islamic Jihad.

On November 26, Waite met with Vice President George Bush of the United States to discuss his progress with Islamic Jihad. The meeting was largely symbolic, as the United States already knew that the price for the American hostages was the release of 17 Muslim prisoners held in Kuwait for their role in the bombing of two U.S. embassies in East Africa. However, the meeting, and the following interview on the White House lawn, established Waite as the public cover for the Reagan administration's covert arms-for-hostages deal with Iran.

Over the next year, Waite continued his efforts to free the American hostages, even after news of the arms-for-hostages deal leaked into the press. He traveled to Lebanon in January 1987, though he had previously been threatened with death if he returned. On January 27, Waite went to the apartment of Dr. Mroueh, an intermediary in the hostage negotiations. Waite believed he was being taken to see Terry Anderson and Thomas Sutherland, who were, according to their captors, depressed and ill. Waite was taken, instead, to a 7-by-10-foot tiled cell. He was held hostage for the next 1,763 days, most of which he spent alone.

In 1990 Waite was moved to an apartment filled with cells that held many of Islamic Jihad's hostages. That fall, Anderson established contact with Waite by tapping out the numerical equivalent of letters of the alphabet on the wall between their two cells. A week later, Waite was allowed to meet other hostages for 15 minutes. He was subsequently moved into their quarters permanently, marking the end of four years of solitary confinement. His condition improved considerably in their company, especially after his fellow hostages lobbied for an inhaler to treat Waite's asthma.

Waite was released on November 18, 1991, along with Thomas Sutherland. The remaining American hostages were freed in December 1991.

Laura Lambert

See also Anderson, Terry A.; East Africa Embassy Bombings; Hezbollah; Sutherland, Thomas

Further Readings

Hewitt, Gavin. *Terry Waite and Ollie North: The Untold Story of the Kidnapping and the Release.* Boston: Little, Brown, 1991.
Martin, David C., and John Walcott. *Best Laid Plans: The Inside Story of America's War against Terrorism.* New York: Harper & Row, 1988.
Ranstorp, Magnus. *Hizb'allah in Lebanon: The Politics of the Western Hostage Crisis.* New York: St. Martin's, 1997.
Waite, Terry. *Taken on Trust.* New York: Harcourt Brace, 1993.

WALL STREET BOMBING

At noon on September 16, 1920, when clerks, receptionists, and brokers were heading for lunch, a horse-drawn cart exploded in front of the offices of J.P. Morgan & Co. at the corner of Wall and Broad streets in downtown New York City. Thirty people were killed instantly, more than 300 were injured, and several later died from their injuries. The noise was heard throughout lower Manhattan and across the East River in Brooklyn. The smoke-filled streets were covered with a layer of shattered glass, debris from the damaged buildings, and bodies; the chief clerk of J.P. Morgan, William Joyce, who had been seated near the front window, was decapitated. Junius Morgan, son of J. P. Morgan Jr., was wounded. The Stock Exchange across Broad Street was closed immediately.

The police and soldiers called in from Governors Island helped the injured, guarded the scene, and searched for evidence. The only evidence found, however, was two charred horse hooves and fragments of sash weights. The investigation ultimately confirmed that a bomb made with TNT and reinforced with sash weights caused the carnage.

Because nobody claimed responsibility for the bombing, the New York Police Department considered a number of possible motives. The assassination of J.P. Morgan Jr. was dismissed as a motive because he was in Europe. Another possibility was an attempt to rob the adjacent Subtreasury Building, where $900 million in gold bars was being moved that day. The bombing was ultimately decided to be an act of terrorism performed by "Reds"—anarchists and communist sympathizers—who wanted to shatter the symbols of American capitalism. A stack of anarchist flyers found in a mailbox a block away from Wall Street supported this theory. Suspicion fell on political radicals, communists, and anarchists of foreign origin—particularly Italians, Russians, and Jews. Although detectives visited every sash-weight manufacturer and dealer in America, as well as 500 stables in every town along the Atlantic coast, they had no success in finding the perpetrators.

Edwin P. Fischer, a lawyer, champion tennis player, and frequent inpatient in mental hospitals, was a suspect. He had predicted an explosion on Wall Street in mid-September in correspondence with friends and in conversations with strangers. On September 16, however, he was in Canada, and his premonition was interpreted by the authorities as the work of a lunatic's mind. Another strong suspect was an Italian, Pietro Angelo, who was connected to the Gimbel Brothers bomb plot of April 1919. Pietro produced an alibi, but he was deported to Italy nonetheless. The Secret Service and the FBI interrogated thousands of people and even arrested many radicals, but no one was charged with the crime, and the investigation was dropped in 1940. No memorial exists to commemorate the event, and Morgan has never repaired the damaged building's facade.

Maria Kiriakova

See also Anarchism; Bombings and Bomb Scares

Further Readings

Barron, James. "After 1920 Blast, the Opposite of 'Never Forget'—No Memorials on Wall Street for Attack That Killed 30." *The New York Times*, September 17, 2003. http://www.nytimes.com/2003/09/17/nyregion/after-1920-blast-opposite-never-forget-no-memorials-wall-st-for-attack-that.html.

Brooks, John. *Once in Golconda: A True Drama of Wall Street, 1920–1938*. New York: Harper & Row, 1969.

Gage, Beverly. *The Day Wall Street Exploded: A Story of America in Its First Age of Terror*. Oxford: Oxford University Press, 2009.

Isaacs, Ana B. "Seventy Years before the Twin Towers." *American Heritage* 45, no. 2 (April 1994): 40–41.

McCann, Joseph. *Terrorism on American Soil: A Concise History of Plots from the Famous to the Forgotten*. Boulder, CO: Sentient Publications, 2006.

Preston, William. *Aliens and Dissenters: Federal Suppression of Radicals, 1903–1933*. Cambridge, MA: Harvard University Press, 1963.

Ward, Nathan. "The Fire Last Time." *American Heritage* 52, no. 8 (December 2001): 46–48.

WEAPONS OF MASS DESTRUCTION

The term *weapons of mass destruction* (or "WMD") refers to those weapons whose destructive capacity far exceeds that of conventional weaponry. Nuclear, chemical, and biological weapons, whether used by organized military units or by terrorist and paramilitary groups, could inflict large numbers of casualties. The suggestion that terrorists might use weapons of mass destruction to achieve their purposes instills great concern and fear.

There is little doubt that terrorists would use such weapons if they had them. Computer files captured from the al Qaeda group in Afghanistan in 2001 revealed that it was seeking to obtain chemical and biological weapons, although none were ever found. The Aum Shinrikyo cult in Japan prepared and used chemical and biological weapons in attacks on the Japanese subway system and other targets in the mid-1980s. Although relatively ineffective, the attacks in Japan demonstrated that a well-funded group could prepare and carry out such attacks.

Nuclear Terrorism

Nuclear weapons pose the largest threat because of their immense power of destruction. The technical difficulty and high cost of mounting a nuclear weapons program is a substantial deterrent to a terrorist group unable to obtain, from an existing stockpile, the uranium or plutonium needed to manufacture a nuclear weapon, or unable to obtain an intact weapon from a nuclear weapons state such as Russia or the United States. Stockpiles of plutonium and uranium, not to mention nuclear weapons themselves, are heavily protected by the nations that possess them, but the very size of these stockpiles and their worldwide distribution are sources of concern.

A deteriorating Russian economy in the 1990s posed a special threat. Had Russian facilities not been adequately protected, and had scientists and security personnel not been adequately paid, it would only have been a matter of time before a subversive group succeeded in obtaining uranium or plutonium. The international community, led by the United States, provided substantial assistance to Russia to strengthen its protective systems for nuclear materials. The heightened sensitivity of the world's nuclear establishments following the September 11, 2001, attacks on the World Trade Center in New York City and the Pentagon outside of Washington, D.C., has led to further improvements in materials and weapon security.

A second form of nuclear terrorism involves the use of radioactive materials combined with an explosive package to make radiological weapons, or "dirty bombs." This capability is surely within the grasp of a well-organized group, but the effects of such a weapon would be far less extensive than those of a nuclear explosion. While the extent of damage caused by a dirty bomb depends upon the amount of radioactive substances dispersed and the time it takes the material to decay into a relatively harmless state, such a weapon would probably result in evacuation and clean-up efforts rather than mass casualties.

An attack on a nuclear power reactor is another version of a radiological weapon. Crashing a heavy aircraft or vehicle into a reactor or its spent-fuel storage area would release harmful radioactive material. Nations possessing nuclear reactors are now attempting to enhance their security to reduce the probability of successful attacks on these complex systems.

Chemical Terrorism

Chemical weapons are sometimes touted as the "poor man's atomic bomb." They have not been used often since World War II because military units are usually well protected with masks and special clothing. However, they would be effective against unprotected civilians if employed by organized military units with the ability to disperse them widely. That capability involves the development of chemical agents as well as the necessary dispersal vehicles, such as aircraft bombs, artillery shells, missiles containing small containers of the chemicals called "bomblets," or spray tanks fitted on aircraft. Such delivery capabilities are likely to be difficult for a terrorist group to obtain. Nerve gases, the most powerful chemical agents, are not easy to manufacture. To produce them in significant quantity requires access to well-trained chemists and sophisticated equipment.

Terrorists do not need to inflict mass casualties to frighten a large population. Aum Shinrikyo dispersed the nerve gas known as sarin in the Tokyo subway system by placing plastic bags of the toxic substance on subway platforms and perforating them with umbrellas. Fortunately, that method was not very effective as a weapon of mass destruction, though it resulted in 12 deaths and a few thousand sickened people. Nevertheless, the attacks were successful in that they caused a massive disruption of the subway system and frightened millions of riders. Other possible (and potentially more destructive) forms of chemical terrorism involve attacks on chemical plants located near large population centers, or attacks on rail cars or trucks carrying toxic materials. Such an attack would release large quantities of toxic materials and force an evacuation.

Biological Weapons

Terrorists considering the use of biological weapons face many of the same difficulties of production and dispersion associated with chemical weapons. The effectiveness of a biological weapon would be similarly linked to its ability to frighten a population rather than kill or sicken large numbers of people. The letter-borne anthrax attacks in the United States in October 2001 demonstrated how a small amount of material was sufficient to paralyze parts of the mail system and shut down important government facilities.

While anthrax cannot be spread by contact with sickened individuals, more deadly viral diseases such as smallpox can spread rapidly. An uncontained outbreak of smallpox has the capability of killing tens of thousands, and perhaps millions, of people if not stopped quickly. It is difficult for terrorists to obtain large quantities of infectious diseases, and these substances are extremely dangerous to handle, but governments recognize the existence of such a threat and are increasing the production and stockpiling of vaccines to protect vulnerable populations if necessary. Agricultural systems are more likely to be vulnerable than human populations to bioterror attacks. Infectious diseases such as foot-and-mouth disease can devastate herds of animals and disrupt whole economies. Governments are hastening to take protective measures against this type of threat as well.

Governments possess the resources needed to deal with terrorist threats involving weapons of mass destruction. Improved physical security at sensitive facilities, strengthened public health and information systems, a prepared medical community, and a knowledgeable public are all important in the containment of and response to terrorist attacks.

Les Paldy

See also Agricultural Terrorism; al Qaeda; Anthrax; Aum Shinrikyo; Biological Terrorism; Chemical Terrorism; Nuclear Terrorism

Further Readings

Alexander, Yonah, and Milton M. Hoenig, eds. *Super Terrorism: Biological, Chemical, and Nuclear*. New York: Transnational Publishers, 2001.

Borrelli, J. V. *Bioterrorism: Prevention, Preparedness, and Protection.* New York: Nova Science Publishers, 2007.

Prasad, S. K. *Chemical Weapons.* New Delhi: Discovery Publishing House, 2009.

Ranstorp, Magnus, and Magnus Normark, eds. *Unconventional Weapons and International Terrorism: Challenges and a New Approach.* New York: Routledge, 2009.

Tucker, Jonathan B. *Toxic Terror: Assessing Terrorist Use of Chemical and Biological Weapons.* Cambridge: MIT Press, 2000.

WEATHERMAN

Weatherman (aka Weather Underground; Weather Underground Organization [WUO]; Weathermen), a militant group of young white Americans that grew out of the anti–Vietnam War movement, engaged in bombing campaigns across the United States for more than five years. Led by Bernardine Dohrn, Weatherman sought to advance communism through violent revolution, and the group called on America's youth to create a rearguard action against the U.S. government that would bring about its downfall.

Weatherman evolved from the Third World Marxists, a faction within Students for a Democratic Society (SDS), the major national organization representing the burgeoning New Left in the late 1960s. Led by Dohrn, James Mellen, and Mark Rudd, this "action faction" of the (by this point skeletal) SDS advocated street fighting as a method for weakening U.S. imperialism. At the SDS national convention in June 1969, the Third World Marxists presented a position paper titled "You Don't Need a Weatherman to Know Which Way the Wind Blows" in the SDS newspaper, *New Left Notes*. The article, the title of which was taken from a Bob Dylan song, asserted, among other things, that black liberation was key to the movement's anti-imperialist struggle, and it emphasized the need for a white revolutionary movement to support liberation movements internationally. This article became the founding statement of Weatherman.

Weatherman launched an offensive that summer. In one action in the Northeast, it tried to recruit members at community colleges and high schools by marching into classrooms, tying up and gagging teachers, and presenting revolutionary speeches. At the Harvard Institute for International Affairs, they smashed windows, tore out phones, and beat up professors.

From October 8 to October 11, 1969, Weatherman worked to organize thousands of young people in a direct assault on the police, or the "pigs." The group called this a "National Action," but newspapers called it "Days of Rage." The protests were to begin on the second anniversary of Che Guevara's death and coincide with the trial of the Chicago 8—eight men charged with conspiracy for their actions during the Democratic Convention in Chicago one year earlier. On October 6, 1969, Weatherman members blew up a statue in Chicago's Haymarket Square that commemorated a policeman who died in a riot in 1886. That message of confrontation and violence was echoed in Weatherman's signs and slogans, which read, "Bring the war home" and "The time has come for fighting in the streets." However, "Days of Rage" proved to be only minimally successful. The demonstrations had a low turnout—as low as 100 by some counts—as well as several incidents of random, pointless rioting. By the end of the weekend, 284 people, including local youth and SDS members, had been arrested; total bail amounted to over $1.5 million.

Frustrated with the inefficacy of traditional forms of political protest after "Days of Rage" and other antiwar demonstrations throughout November, Weatherman called for a national "war council" meeting of the SDS that December. Members of the group discussed the need to instruct themselves in the use of firearms and bombs in order to target and attack sites of power in the United States, as well as the need to kill police. Much of this discussion was fueled by the recent killings of two members of the Black Panthers, Mark Clark and Fred Hampton, by Chicago police. In that meeting, held in Flint, Michigan, Weatherman decided to go underground and become a small-scale paramilitary operation carrying out urban guerrilla warfare.

The Organization Goes Underground

By early 1970, Weatherman had split into several underground cells throughout the country. These cells, usually with three to five men and women living together in a house, were connected to the Weatherman leadership, called the Weather Bureau, by active members who provided aboveground support. The FBI, which began investigating the group in June 1969, estimated Weatherman's total strength at this time at 400 members. The cells were located predominantly in Berkeley, Chicago, Detroit, and New York City.

Within months, Weatherman made its way into headlines and the public imagination. On March 6, 1970, three founding members of Weatherman—Diana Oughton, Ted Gold, and Terry Robbins—died in an explosion while making bombs in a Greenwich Village townhouse. Two other members, Kathy Boudin and Cathy Wilkerson, escaped. Investigators found 57 sticks of dynamite, 30 blasting caps, and timing devices in the rubble. The FBI stepped up its investigation. By April, federal indictments for the "Days of Rage" action came down against 12 Weatherman members, and Weatherman, collectively, was charged with conspiracy.

Weatherman members also began bombing targets across the country in 1970, using tactics from the handbook *Firearms and Self-Defense: A Handbook for Radicals, Revolutionaries and Easy Riders,* and from Carlos Marighella's *Minimanual of the Urban Guerilla.* The more significant targets included the New York City Police Department headquarters, the Presidio army base in San Francisco, a Long Island City courthouse, and several banks in Boston and New York. Most of the bombings were preceded by a warning, to prevent casualties, and followed by a communiqué, dubbed "Weather Reports." Weatherman used these "Weather Reports" to justify attacks, citing recent police and government actions, such as the killing of four students by the National Guard at Kent State or the unlawful incarceration of other revolutionaries. The reports also often commemorated revolutionary efforts throughout the world. By year's end, several Weatherman members had made it to the FBI's Ten Most Wanted list, which had been expanded to 16 to accommodate them.

The bombings continued throughout 1971. Weatherman placed two bombs at the Capitol in Washington, D.C., both of which exploded on March 1. In August, the group attacked three offices of the California prison system after the mysterious murder of the prison revolutionary George Jackson in the San Quentin prison yard. Two weeks later, after 30 inmates were killed at in a revolt at New York's Attica Penitentiary, Weatherman bombed the state commissioner of corrections' office in Albany.

Postwar Attacks

The Pentagon bombing on May 19, 1972, Ho Chi Minh's birthday, marked the end of Weatherman's major actions for almost a year-and-a-half. After the signing of the peace treaty between the United States and Vietnam in January 1973, the group grappled with its postwar identity, and soon it was virtually alone in the struggle for armed resistance, joined only by the Black Liberation Army, an offshoot of the New York Black Panthers, the George Jackson Brigade, and the Symbionese Liberation Army. By the spring of 1974, the FBI believed Weatherman (now called Weather Underground) to be one of the last radical groups of the antiwar movement that still endorsed all forms of violence.

The Weather Underground continued to bomb targets for political reasons, but its efforts, though pointed, were sporadic. In 1974, the group issued "Prairie Fire: The Politics of Revolutionary Anti-Imperialism," the first statement of Weather Underground's politics since 1969. Soon, Prairie Fire Organizing Committees sprang up throughout the country as the aboveground arm of the Weather Underground. Dissension struck in 1976, and the West Coast faction split off to form the Weather Underground Organization (WUO), which was infiltrated by the FBI in 1977.

Starting in 1978, members began to resurface, and they either turned themselves in to authorities or were tracked down by authorities. In 1994, one of the last Weatherman members indicted for the "Days of Rage" actions was tried in court, ending nearly 25 years of pursuit by the government agencies and two decades of life underground. This seemed to bring to an end the Weatherman era.

Laura Lambert

See also Black Panther Party; Boudin, Katherine; Dohrn, Bernardine; Marighella, Carlos; May 19 Communist Organization; Symbionese Liberation Army

Further Readings

Chepesiuk, Ron. *Sixties Radicals, Then and Now: Candid Conversations with Those Who Shaped the Era.* Jefferson, NC: McFarland, 2007.

Dohrn, Bernardine, Bill Ayers, and Jeff Jones, eds. *Sing a Battle Song: The Revolutionary Poetry, Statements, and Communiques of the Weather Underground, 1970–74.* New York: Seven Stories Press, 2006.

Gitlin, Todd. *The Sixties: Years of Hope, Days of Rage.* New York: Bantam, 1987.

Jacobs, Ron. *The Way the Wind Blew: A History of the Weather Underground.* New York: Verson, 1997.

Sale, Kirkpatrick. *SDS.* New York: Random House, 1973.

U.S. Senate. Congress. Committee on the Judiciary. Subcommittee to Investigate the Administration of the Internal Security Act and Other Internal Security Laws. *Weather Underground: Report of the Subcommittee to Investigate the Administration of the Internal Security Act and Other Internal Security Laws of the Committee on the Judiciary.* Washington, DC: U.S. Government Printing Office, 1975.

Wilkerson, Cathy. *Flying Close to the Sun: My Life and Times as a Weatherman.* New York: Seven Stories Press, 2007.

WHITE PATRIOT PARTY

The prosecution of members of the White Patriot Party (WPP), a paramilitary white supremacist group, helped bring to light links between white supremacist groups and the U.S. military, most notably the 82nd Airborne Division at Fort Bragg, North Carolina.

In 1985, Frazier Glenn Miller, a former Green Beret at Fort Bragg and leader of the Carolina Knights of the Ku Klux Klan (CKKKK), signed a consent agreement to settle a civil rights suit brought by the Southern Poverty Law Center. Among other things, Miller agreed to disband the CKKKK's paramilitary army and training camps, which he had used to train Klansmen in armed combat. Miller then changed the name of the CKKKK to the White Patriot Party and continued to run training camps in rural North Carolina, in violation of both state law and the 1985 court order.

The WPP, like other Klan offshoots of the time, firmly embraced the tenets of Christian Identity, a fiercely anti-Semitic, racist, and homophobic Christian fundamentalist sect. WPP planned to take over several North Carolina counties, thus creating a southern homeland for white Christians by the early 1990s.

At its height, Miller claimed the WPP had over 2,500 members, though organizations such as the Klanwatch Project in Montgomery, Alabama, estimated membership at 700 to 800. Many of these members were active-duty Marines from Camp Lejeune, North Carolina, and active-duty soldiers from Fort Bragg. Several of these military personnel assisted at the WPP paramilitary camps, training local civilians, many of them former Klan members, in combat and the use of weapons. The WPP also staged marches in cities throughout North Carolina, in which WPP members wore combat fatigues and berets, carried large Confederate flags, and displayed Nazi paraphernalia.

While several members of the WPP were convicted for conspiring to assault blacks in Florida in 1985, the most significant cases brought against the group involved the military. In 1986, Klanwatch identified 10 Marines as WPP members and demanded an investigation by the Department of Defense. Three Marines, including the former WPP member Richard L. Pounder, were eventually discharged for refusing to dissociate from the group.

On January 8, 1987, Miller, his second-in-command, Stephen S. Miller (no relation to Frazier Glenn Miller), Robert Jackson, Tony Wydra, and two others were indicted on charges of conspiring to obtain weapons stolen from a military installation to equip and sustain the WPP's paramilitary force. Robert Norton Jones, a former Fort Bragg marine who was serving a four-year sentence for attempting to purchase stolen military weapons, told the court that he was paid $50,000 to supply the WPP with arms stolen from Fort Bragg and other military institutions. The stolen goods, which Miller supplied to the WPP and other Klan groups in the area, included 13 LAW anti-tank missiles, rifles, CS anti-riot gas, TNT, C-4 plastic explosives, and 10 Claymore mines. The army eventually recovered over 20 blocks of the C-4 explosives and nearly 14,000 rounds of ammunition from the Klan. Miller served three years in a federal prison for the crime. Since his release, he has made several attempts to run for Congress in Missouri.

The WPP case led to a yearlong investigation by the Senate Armed Services Committee Task Force, focusing on upgrading military inventory systems to prevent further weapons theft.

Laura Lambert

See also Ku Klux Klan; Miller, Frazier Glenn; *Turner Diaries, The*; White Supremacy Movement

Further Readings

Berlet, Chip, and Matthew N. Lyons. *Right-wing Populism in America: Too Close for Comfort*. New York: Guilford Press, 2000.

Cunningham, David. *There's Something Happening Here: The New Left, the Klan, and FBI Counterintelligence*. Berkeley: University of California Press, 2005.

Durham, Martin. *White Rage: The Extreme Right and American Politics*. New York: Routledge, 2007.

George, John, and Laird Wilcox. *American Extremists: Militias, Supremacists, Klansmen, Communists and Others*. Amherst, NY: Prometheus Books, 1996.

Smith, Brent L. *Terrorism in America: Pipe Bombs and Pipe Dreams*. Albany: State University of New York Press, 1994.

Walters, Jerome. *One Aryan Nation under God: Exposing the New Racial Extremists*. Cleveland, OH: Pilgrim Press, 2000.

WHITE SUPREMACY MOVEMENT

White supremacy constitutes a belief system that the white race (sometimes described as "Aryan" or "Northern European") is somehow superior to other races. As practiced by far-right militia and terrorist groups in the United States, the belief system of white supremacy ceases to be simply a bigoted ideology and becomes an action plan to create a religious state based on the destruction of perceived infidels and evil forces.

The ideology of white supremacy goes as far back as the colonial slave trade. Historically, slavery was considered to be a normal outcome of war; the victor won the right to enslave the vanquished (as the Spanish enslaved the Moors, for example). However, due to the expanding agrarian economic markets of the Americas, by the seventeenth century the need for slaves began to outweigh the supply. A conundrum arose for the Catholics and Protestants of Europe: How could a religious people, whose faith is rooted in the exodus of the slaves from Egypt, enslave other people?

The answer was to reclassify those other people (in this case, Africans) as less than human, thus clearing the moral way for the massive enslavement of African "savages." The white supremacist ethic of the slave trade allowed African natives to be "rescued" by God-fearing whites. They were saved from the untamed jungle and dressed in the white man's clothes and religion. The slaves were treated like children, with grown men called "boy," as long as they accepted their subordinate role.

The link between white supremacy and terrorism began when African slaves rejected their subordination. White supremacist groups, such as the Ku Klux Klan, rose to power during the Reconstruction Era (1865–1877), in reaction to attempts to empower newly freed slaves. Similarly, twentieth-century racist terrorism (lynchings and the bombing of black churches in the 1960s, for example) took place during periods of black empowerment.

After the African American Jesse Owens defeated Nazi "supermen" in the 1936 Berlin Olympics, presided over by Adolf Hitler, white supremacist rhetoric was forced to change from talk of "physical superiority" to "intellectual superiority." The great gains of African Americans in leadership positions in the 1970s and 1980s refuted this notion, and the language changed again, moving from "intellectual superiority" to "spiritual superiority." Twenty-first-century white supremacists believe that God is white and his people are the beleaguered white people of Earth—a much more difficult theory to disprove. Racists now use conflicting religious arguments to make the case for white supremacy, including Christian Identity, Odinism, and creationism.

White supremacism has manifested as a terrorist dogma throughout the decades. According to the FBI, the most common types of hate crimes are property crimes committed against racial minorities. Cross burnings or vandalism can target an entire community, making them fearful of future attacks. This is why hate crimes are treated as a unique type of transgression—it is just not the immediate victim that is harmed, but a large group of people being terrorized.

The strongest link between white supremacy and terrorism is the desire for a racial civil war, sometimes referred to as "Rahowa" (racial holy war). As outlined in William Pierce's 1978 novel *The Turner Diaries*, it is believed that a racial civil war is required to rid white America of its enemies

(Jews, minorities, homosexuals, and so on). Through acts of terrorism committed by small cells of committed white racists (often referring to themselves as "separatists" rather than "supremacists"), the racist movement will provoke the federal government to crack down on individual liberties. Radicalized white Americans, concerned with the loss of constitutional rights, will then flock to racist organizations to lead them. These groups will wage war on the federal government, which many racists believe is a Zionist agent, bent on destroying ethnic whites.

The desire for racial civil war has led to numerous terrorist acts in the United States. Robert Mathews united a cross-section of white supremacists in the early 1980s with his group, The Order. Members of this group attacked homosexuals in the Northwest, bombed a synagogue in Boise, Idaho, and robbed two armored trucks, netting more than $4 million. It is believed by authorities that much of that money was funneled to the radical right, including a portion to Pierce.

Timothy McVeigh, the man condemned to death for the 1995 bombing of the Alfred P. Murrah Federal Building in Oklahoma City, was also a follower of *The Turner Diaries*. He had spent time in the Michigan Militia and had protested the federal governments siege of David Koresh's Branch Davidian compound in Waco, Texas. Before his execution, McVeigh was clear that the Oklahoma City bombing was part of a plan to create widespread racial unrest in America, as prophesied in Pierce's book. In 2001 the criminologist Mark Hamm established a strong link between McVeigh's attack and a racist terrorist group, the Aryan Republican Army.

When coupled with religion, the racist desire for civil war becomes an even more powerful motivating force. Skinhead bands like Rahowa and Final War sing of the glory of a righteous battle with Jews and subhumans to their skinhead audiences. Benjamin Smith, a member of the World Church of the Creator, went on a four-city shooting spree in 1999, killing four people, based on his belief in white supremacy. Also in 1999, Aryan Nations member Buford Furrow opened fire in a Granada Hills, California, Jewish school and then killed a Filipino letter carrier. Since that incident, Aryan Nations has been relatively inactive. However, when the United States elected its first black president in 2008, analysts expected an upsurge in white supremacist activity.

Randy Blazak

See also Aryan Nations; Aryan Republican Army; Ku Klux Klan; Lynching; Mathews, Robert Jay; McVeigh, Timothy James; Oklahoma City Bombing; Order, The; Sixteenth Street Baptist Church Bombing; Skinheads; *Turner Diaries, The*

Further Readings

Ezekiel, Raphael S. *The Racist Mind: Portraits of American Neo-Nazis and Klansmen*. New York: Penguin Books, 1996.

Hamm, Mark. *Terrorism as Crime: From Oklahoma City to al Qaeda and beyond*. New York: New York University Press, 2007.

Ridgeway, James. *Blood in the Face: The Ku Klux Klan, Aryan Nations, Nazi Skinheads, and the Rise of a New White Culture*. 2nd ed. New York: Thunder's Mouth Press, 1995.

Zeskind, Leonard. *Blood and Politics: The History of the White Nationalist Movement from the Margins to the Mainstream*. New York: Farrar, Straus and Giroux, 2009.

WOMEN TERRORISTS

Women have been involved in organizations engaged in political violence for a very long time, but the significance of their contribution to the history of terrorism is often overlooked. Especially since the 1960s, women have been increasingly important in nationalist and radical left-wing organizations. Nationalist organizations that have had significant female membership include the Irish Republican Army (IRA), Basque Fatherland and Liberty (ETA), Fatah, the Popular Front for the Liberation of Palestine (PFLP), and the Liberation Tigers of Tamil Ealam (LTTE). Left-wing organizations with significant female membership include the Red Army Faction (RAF), the Red Brigades, FARC, the Japanese Red Army (JRA), and the Communist Party of Nepal (Maoist). The Peruvian group Shining Path (Sendero Luminoso) was thought to be as much as 60 percent female, but this level of participation is rare, and in most terrorist organizations it is likely that women are a minority. Organizations with strong religious identities have not generally had significant female membership, but there has been a notable expansion of female members in some of these organizations since 2000. Women are now members of the al Aqsa Martyrs Brigades, Palestine Islamic Jihad (PIJ) and Hamas, and there are indications that al Qaeda is reconsidering their long-standing opposition to women's membership.

Women terrorists can have strategic and tactical advantages over men. Because women are usually not suspected of involvement in terrorism, they can more easily evade security checks and surveillance. There are also powerful cultural taboos against women being searched in public or being searched by men (who make up the majority of security personnel). Indeed, the ability of women to circumvent heightened security may be an explanation for the increasing occurrence of women terrorists. Organizations are finding it necessary to deploy women because men cannot penetrate heightened security around potential targets. It is possible that organizations are also capitalizing on the political importance of women terrorists, for their use may be seen as a statement that the situation has become so dire that even women are turning to violence to assert their rights. Extensive media coverage is also usually guaranteed for an attack by a woman terrorist, which may appeal to an organization's desire for publicity.

Female terrorists have used common perceptions of women's social roles as caregivers in order to carry out attacks. For example, women have hidden bombs in baby carriages, strapped bombs to their abdomens to resemble pregnancy, and transported weaponry under religiously modest clothing.

The roles women perform vary depending on the organization and the sociopolitical context in which the conflict occurs. Women have important roles that provide support and continuity to terrorist organizations, such as maintaining safe houses; smuggling or transporting arms, equipment, or personnel; holding, administering, or raising funds; recruitment; and providing political and emotional support. In many organizations women can hold combatant roles, and women have taken part in various forms of direct violence, including shootings, bombings, and hostage taking. An early example of a woman combatant is Leila Khaled, who was part of the PFLP unit that hijacked a plane in 1969 and participated in a failed second hijacking in 1970.

A particularly controversial area is women's role in suicide bombing. The first documented case of a female suicide bomber occurred in 1985 in Lebanon, when a female member of the Syrian Social Nationalist Party (SSNP) attacked an Israeli convoy in Lebanon. The LTTE was particularly notable in its deployment of women suicide bombers, and 30 to 40 percent of the group's suicide attacks between 1985 and 2010 were conducted by women (over 220 attacks). In 2007, 17 organizations worldwide were found to use suicide bombings as a tactic, and women participated as bombers in 50 percent of these groups.

There has been a significant expansion of female suicide attacks by Islamist groups since 2002. Many of these groups were originally reluctant to permit women to participate as suicide bombers for religious reasons. However, women have now conducted suicide attacks for Chechen Islamist militant separatists, al Aqsa Martyrs Brigades, Palestine Islamic Jihad, and Hamas. This trend toward more organizations using women as suicide bombers is unlikely to change while women continue to have tactical advantages in penetrating security.

The level of leadership that is permitted to women varies across organizations. Some organizations, such as the IRA, FARC, and LTTE, have had women in important midlevel and commando leadership positions. However, women are rarely in the higher echelons of decision making, even if they make up a large proportion of the membership. Organizations with women in leadership positions have tended to be secular with a nationalist or left-wing political ideology. For example, women have headed the Japanese Red Army, the Red Army Faction, and the Red Brigades. In 2009, Spanish and French authorities announced they believed two leaders of Basque Fatherland and Liberty were women. Meanwhile, it has been alleged that the co-leader of the Irish dissident republican group the Real IRA is (or was) Bernadette Sands-McKevitt, the sister of Bobby Sands, an IRA leader who died on hunger strike in the 1980s.

Women's motivation for participating in terrorism has been the subject of debate. Proposed explanations include women's exploitation by the organizations, which have used nationalism, political conviction, financial inducements, and the perceived inability of particular women to meet various social expectations (e.g., virginity, marriage, and motherhood) as motivational tools. Familial and social relationships to current and former members can also be important in women's recruitment, as it seems to have been with Sands-McKevitt, for example.

It is rarely possible to ascribe a women's participation to any single cause. Just as with men, there can be a variety of motivations combining a mix of personal and political factors. Women's liberation as a factor in terrorism is controversial. Some research indicates that female membership occurs if an organization has incorporated some commitment to gender equality, such as the left-leaning organizations the RAF and the IRA. Other research has found that involvement in terrorism is a consciousness-raising experience for women who then demand equality within the organization. The effect of women's involvement in terrorism on the wider social environment is also uncertain: Whether it helps or hinders women's emancipation in the long term appears to change with each conflict.

The cases of Colleen LaRose, known in the media as "Jihad Jane," and Jamie Paulin-Ramirez highlight some of the complexities in understanding women involved in terrorism. These women, who are both U.S. citizens and recent converts to Islam, were charged with conspiracy to provide material support to terrorists and with conspiracy to murder. Prosecutors contend that the women traveled from the United States to Europe in the fall of 2009 with the intention of meeting with others to plan the murder of Lars Vilks, a Swedish cartoonist who has been under threat of death since publishing a cartoon of the Prophet Mohammed with the body of a dog.

Some aspects of these women's alleged involvement in terrorism are similar to the global trends discussed above. First, both women seem to have recognized that their Caucasian appearance, U.S. citizenship, and previous noninvolvement in extremist causes would make them unlikely suspects in the eyes of law enforcement. Second, both women did appear to have social attachments to men in the group. LaRose had agreed to marry a man from South Asia to facilitate his application for a visa into Europe, though the marriage never took place. Paulin-Ramirez married a co-conspirator after she

had made the commitment to the group by traveling to Europe. Usually, when women have familial or social contacts with terrorist organizations, these relationships are established before the women join. In this case, it is not known how extensive these Internet-based relationships were prior to the women committing to terrorist actions.

There are some important differences between global trends and the cases of LaRose and Paulin-Ramirez. Notably, the U.S. Justice Department has stated that after LaRose's arrest in October 2009, she cooperated willingly with the authorities. This is very unusual, particularly among women terrorists operating in Western organizations such as the IRA or ETA. Indeed, such women are generally described by the security services as being more committed and intractable than men.

In addition, the alleged intended victim is an unusual target for women terrorists. Women's targets are normally specifically designed to further the military and political aspirations of the organization, and they tend to be tied to a specific conflict. A conspiracy to murder a Swedish cartoonist, even if he has deeply offended Muslims, diverges from this global trend. These differences have led some commentators to speculate on how realistic the conspirators' plans really were, the objective level of threat they actually posed, and, in the case of LaRose, her mental stability.

Finally, in most other cases around the globe, it is women's direct experience of violence and conflict that is believed to be crucial in their decision to become terrorists. However, in this case, these women were living ordinary suburban American lives, and it is the contacts they made through cyberspace that appear to have triggered their decision to engage in terrorism. It is this aspect of the case that may be the most important lesson for the security services: the possibility of men and women previously unconnected with international conflicts being drawn into violence because they have become politicized through online contacts and relationships.

Rhiannon Talbot-English

See also Baader-Meinhof Gang; Basque Fatherland and Liberty; Communist Party of Nepal (Maoists); FARC; Fatah; Irish Republican Army; Japanese Red Army; Khaled, Leila; Liberation Tigers of Tamil Eelam; Meinhof, Ulrike; Real Irish Republican Army; Red Brigades; Shining Path

Further Readings

Bloom, Mia. *Dying to Kill: The Allure of Suicide Terror.* New York: Columbia University Press, 2007.

Bloom, Mia. "Women as Victims and Victimizers." America.gov, May 11, 2007. http://www.america.gov/st/peacesec-english/2007/May/20080522172353Sre noD0.6383936.html.

Craigin, Kim R., and Sara A. Daly. *Women as Terrorists: Mothers, Recruiters, and Martyrs.* Santa Barbara, CA: Praeger Security International, 2009.

Cunningham, Karla. "Cross-regional Trends in Female Terrorism." *Studies in Conflict and Terrorism* 26 (2003): 171–195.

Eager, Paige Whaley. *From Freedom Fighters to Terrorists: Women and Political Violence.* Burlington, VT: Ashgate, 2008.

Garrison, Carole. "Sirens of Death: Role of Women in Terrorism Past, Present and Future." *Journal of Criminal Justice and Security* 8, no. 3 (2006): 332–339.

Gonzalez-Perez, Margaret. *Women and Terrorism: Female Activity in Domestic and International Terror Groups.* New York: Routledge, 2009.

Sjoberg, Laura, and Caron E. Gentry. *Mothers, Monsters, Whores: Women's Violence in Global Politics.* London: Zed Books, 2007.

Talbot, Rhiannon. "Myths in the Representation of Women Terrorists." *Eire-Ireland* 35, no. 3/4 (2001): 165–186.

WORLD ISLAMIC FRONT FOR JIHAD AGAINST JEWS AND CRUSADERS

See al Qaeda

WORLD TAMIL ASSOCIATION

See Liberation Tigers of Tamil Eelam

WORLD TRADE CENTER BOMBING (1993)

On February 26, 1993, during a typical Friday lunch hour, a truck bomb exploded in a basement-level parking garage under the World Trade Center in New York City, killing six people and injuring more than a thousand. At the time, the bombing was considered the worst act of terrorism to have been perpetrated on U.S. soil. However, that bombing was overshadowed in 1995 by the Oklahoma City bombing, and then by the attacks of September 11, 2001.

The first World Trade Center bombing conspiracy began in the months before September 1, 1992, when two of the main conspirators, Ahmad Ajaj and Ramzi Yousef, arrived in the United States from Pakistan. The Immigration and Naturalization Service (INS) detained Ajaj and confiscated his suitcase, which contained bombing manuals and anti-American propaganda. Yousef, traveling on an Iraqi passport bearing the name Abdel Basit Mahmoud, requested political asylum and was allowed into the country.

While Ajaj waited in jail, Yousef began to implement the bombing plot aimed at toppling the World Trade Center. On October 1, he moved into a rented room in the Little Egypt section of Jersey City, New Jersey, with another conspirator, Mohammad Salameh. Two weeks later, Salameh and another conspirator, Nidal Ayyad, opened a bank account at the National Westminster Bank.

They used money from this account to purchase the chemicals (urea and nitric acid) to make the bomb; these chemicals were stored in a locker rented by Salameh. On January 1, 1993, Salameh also rented a garage apartment in Jersey City, for use as a bomb factory. Over the next several weeks, the group assembled a 1,500-pound bomb, Salameh went on scouting missions to the World Trade Center, and Yousef called an associate in Dallas, Texas, Eyad Ismoil, who arrived in New York just days before the bombing.

On February 23, 1993, Salameh rented a van from a Ryder agency in Jersey City; he reported the van stolen two days later in order to establish an alibi. The men purchased several tanks of hydrogen gas and loaded them onto the van to magnify the power of the explosion. In the early morning hours of February 26, Mahmud Abouhalima, another conspirator, filled the gas tanks of his car and the rented van. Yousef, Abouhalima, Salameh, and Ismoil then drove to lower Manhattan.

The van was left on the B-2 level of the parking garage, under the Vista Hotel. At 12:18 P.M., the explosives detonated, and within two seconds the blast open a crater six stories deep and 200 feet wide. Abouhalima waited and watched from the classical music section of a nearby record store. Within hours, Salameh went to the Ryder agency to claim his $400 deposit for the "stolen" van; he was told to return later. Ismoil fled to Jordan. Yousef, the mastermind of the operation, was on an 11 P.M. flight to Karachi, Pakistan.

By the time Yousef left the country, authorities had already received more than 50 phone calls claiming responsibility for the bombing, and a handful of fake bomb threats at targets throughout New York City. With few leads, the initial suspects included the Serbian Liberation Forces, Libya's leader Muammar el Qaddafi, or Iraq's Saddam Hussein. Hussein seemed the most likely candidate, as the bombing took place on the second anniversary of his defeat by U.S. forces in Kuwait.

Within two days of the bombing, the FBI got its first major break—a charred and mangled piece of the van's chassis that bore a vehicle identification number (VIN) was discovered in the debris. The VIN led authorities to the Ryder agency in Jersey City. On March 4, when Salameh returned to claim the refund on his deposit, the FBI arrested him. The rental agreement in Salameh's pocket bore traces of bomb residue, as well as the address of the Jersey City apartment. At the apartment, authorities found another roommate, Abdul Rahman Yasin, who led them to the bomb factory. Yasin left the country the next day, headed for Iraq. Abouhalima had also fled New York for Saudi Arabia. He was arrested in Egypt on March 10, the same day Ayyad was arrested in New York.

With Yasin in Iraq and Yousef still at large, a federal grand jury in Manhattan handed down an 11-count indictment against Salameh, Abouhalima, Ayyad, and a man named Bilal Alkaisi, who turned himself in to police in late March. Ajaj, Yousef's traveling companion in 1992, was indicted in May 1993.

The trial began on September 16, 1993. The cases against Salameh and Ayyad were the strongest. Salameh was linked to each stage of the plot through phone, bank, and rental records. Ayyad was considered the spokesman for the plot. Authorities recovered a draft of a communiqué sent to *The New York Times* from his computer; this document claimed the bombing for the 5th

Battalion of the Liberation Army and demanded that the United State cease giving aid to Israel. Abouhalima was placed at the garage apartment on many occasions, and at the gas station the morning of the bombing. Ajaj, who had spent the duration of the plot in jail, was implicated as Yousef's associate and charged with carrying the bombing manuals from Pakistan. Various defense attorneys repeated the argument that Yousef, the apparent architect of the bombing, had duped the defendants, who were portrayed as unwitting participants. On March 4, 1994, after four months, 1,000 exhibits, and over 200 witnesses, Salameh, Ayyad, Abouhalima, and Ajaj were all convicted and each sentenced to 240 years in prison.

After a two-year manhunt, Yousef was captured in Pakistan in February 1995. He and Ismoil, who was charged in connection to the plot in August 1995, were tried and convicted in the fall of 1997. They are both serving their sentences in Colorado's "supermax" prison. Yasin is the only remaining conspirator in the World Trade Center bombing case still at large; it is suspected he is, or was, living in Iraq.

Laura Lambert

See also Abdel Rahman, Omar; Hussein, Saddam; Yousef, Ramzi Ahmed

Further Readings

Dwyer, Jim, David Kocieniewski, Deidre Murphy, and Peg Tyre. *Two Seconds under the World: Terror Comes to America—The Conspiracy behind the World Trade Center Bombing.* New York: Crown, 1994.

Federal Bureau of Investigation. "Most Wanted Terrorists: Abdul Rahman Yasin." http://www.fbi.gov/wanted/terrorists/teryasin.htm.

Mylroie, Laurie. *Study of Revenge: Saddam Hussein's Unfinished War against America.* Washington, DC: AEI Press, 2000.

Reeve, Simon. *The New Jackals: Ramzi Yousef, Osama bin Laden and the Future of Terrorism.* Boston: Northeastern University Press, 2002.

Richardson, Louise. *What Terrorists Want: Understanding the Enemy, Containing the Threat.* New York: Random House, 2006.

U.S. Congress. House Committee on the Judiciary. Subcommittee on Crime and Criminal Justice. *World*

Trade Center Bombing: Terror Hits Home: Hearing before the Subcommittee on Crime and Criminal Justice of the Committee on the Judiciary, House of Representatives, One Hundred Third Congress, First Session, March 9, 1993. Washington, DC: U.S. Government Printing Office, 1994.

WRATH OF GOD

Wrath of God (aka Mivtzah [or Mivtza] Elohim) was a covert Israeli assassination campaign carried out to avenge the 1972 kidnapping and murder of 11 Israeli athletes by Palestinian militants at the Munich Olympics.

A secret Israeli committee chaired by Prime Minister Golda Meir and Defense Minister Moshe Dayan is said to have authorized the assassination of everyone directly or indirectly involved in the Munich killings. The Wrath of God hit squad, made up of members of the Mossad, Israel's secret foreign intelligence service, spent six years tracking down and killing the suspects.

The hit squad first killed Wael Zwaiter, a Palestine Liberation Organization (PLO) organizer and cousin of Yasir Arafat, shooting him in the lobby of his Rome apartment building in October 1972. Mahmoud Hamshari was targeted next. After a Wrath of God member, posing as an Italian journalist, scheduled a telephone interview with Hamshari for December 8, 1972, members of the Wrath of God broke into his home and planted a bomb in his telephone. Hamshari was then called at the time arranged for the interview; when he identified himself, the Wrath of God activated the telephone bomb remotely. He died in the explosion.

Four other suspects, Dr. Basil al Kubaisi, Hussein Abad al Chir, Zaid Muchassi, and Mohammed Boudia, were all killed during the next few months. Boudia was killed by a car bomb in Paris, while Abad al Chir died when a bomb placed under the mattress in his Nicosia hotel room exploded. In 1973, the squad missed one of their targets and mistakenly killed an Arab waiter in Norway. The final Wrath of God killing took place in 1979, when the squad assassinated Ali Hassan Salameh with a car bomb placed along a route he frequented.

Erica Pearson

See also Counterterrorism; Mossad; Munich Olympics Massacre

Further Readings

Bar-Zohar, Michael, and Eitan Haber. *Massacre in Munich: The Manhunt for the Killers behind the 1972 Olympics Massacre.* Guilford, CT: Globe Pequot, 2005.

Calahan, Alexander. "Countering Terrorism: The Israeli Response to the 1972 Munich Olympic Massacre and the Development of Independent Covert Action Teams." MMS dissertation, Marine Corps Command and General Staff College, April 1995. http://www.fas.org/irp/eprint/calahan.htm.

Hunter, Thomas B. "Wrath of God: The Israeli Response to the 1972 Munich Olympic Massacre." *Journal of Counterterrorism & Security International* 7, no. 4 (2001).

Jonas, George. *Vengeance: The True Story of an Israeli Counter-terrorist Team.* New York: Simon & Schuster, 2005.

Klein, Aaron J. *Striking Back: The 1972 Munich Olympics Massacre and Israel's Deadly Response.* New York: Random House, 2007.

Xinjiang

Xinjiang is an autonomous region in China and is home to an estimated 9 million Turkic-speaking Uighurs. Beijing's policy of settling Han Chinese in Xinjiang has been a source of tension, because Uighurs fear that they will soon be marginalized in their native territory. Politicized Uighurs claim that Hans have moved into Xinjiang to exploit its oil, natural gas, and agricultural resources. Despite government economic support that has turned Xinjiang into one of the most productive regions in the country, some Uighurs resent Beijing's assimilation and integration policies. Support for the separatist movement in Xinjiang amongst natives grew significantly in the early twenty-first century.

In July 2009, ethnic clashes between local Uighur Muslims and Han Chinese settlers resulted in the deaths of nearly 200 people, with more than 1,700 injured. The riot was China's worst since 1949, and, such ethnic and religious violence may be the biggest national challenge China faces in the near future. Wu Shimin, vice minister of China's State Ethnic Affairs Commission, says the riot was perpetrated by the "three forces of evil": extremism, terrorism, and separatism. Meanwhile, the local Turkestan Islamic Party (TIP) and its militant wing, the East Turkestan Islamic Movement (ETIM), have accused China of genocide.

While outside observers say that "genocide" is an extreme description of the situation in Xinjiang, it is true that the Chinese government restricts Islamic practices and bans practicing Muslims from most government jobs. Further, most Han employers in Xinjiang prefer not to employ Uighurs because they are perceived as untrustworthy, aggressive, and inclined toward crime. Although none of these stereotypes are fair, the perceptions themselves have intensified the gulf between the two ethnic groups. Propaganda by both nonviolent Uighur separatists as well as the violent ETIM, which is associated with al Qaeda, has served to intensify the hatred. Some al Qaeda ideologues have declared that once they defeat the United States, the Muslims' next enemy will be China.

The ETIM was responsible for a series of bombings, both in Xinjiang and elsewhere in China, in the lead-up to the 2008 Beijing Olympics. The ETIM leadership, which is located in Waziristan, receives training, weapons, finance, and ideology from al Qaeda. Their attacks are not limited to China; the ETIM has also struck in Pakistan and Afghanistan. ETIM suicide bombers trained by al Qaeda present a growing threat both to coalition forces in Afghanistan and to China's security. In addition to the ETIM, Uighur separatist groups in the United States, Canada, and Europe are working to radicalize the Uighur communities in China.

Despite its close relationship with al Qaeda, TIP/ETIM has been careful not to attack the United States. This is largely because of the U.S. position on the Uighur detainees in Guantánamo Bay, Cuba. More than 20 Uighurs have been captured

Han Chinese armed with sticks break through a paramilitary police line as they attempt to attack Uighur areas in Urumqi, western China's Xinjiang province on July 7, 2009. Scattered mobs of Muslim Uighurs and Han Chinese roamed the streets and beat passers-by as the capital of China's Xinjiang region degenerated into communal violence. (AP Photo/Ng Han Guan. © 2011 The Associated Press. All Rights Reserved)

by U.S. forces in Afghanistan and held at Guantánamo since the "war on terror" began in 2001. After several years of detention, which included long episodes of solitary confinement, in 2008 the majority of the Uighurs were determined to no longer be "enemy combatants" and were eligible for release. Knowing that they would be executed in China, the United States found other countries—such as Bermuda, Albania, and Palau—to take the Uighurs. The Uighur separatists consider their lobbying campaign in Washington, D.C., where they have built multiple platforms, a success.

Nonetheless, the TIP expressed displeasure in April 2009 after a TIP leader, Abdul Haq, was labeled a Specially Designated Global Terrorist by the U.S. government. Although the TIP/ETIM has not directly targeted U.S. interests thus far, it seems likely that it may move in that direction in the future. After China, its tier one target, the TIP/ETIM views Pakistan and the United States as its enemies.

The ethnic conflict in Xinjiang presents a greater challenge to the Chinese government even that of Tibet. Bordering Afghanistan, Pakistan, India, Russia, Kazakhstan, and Kyrgyzstan, Xinjiang is important to China in both geopolitical and geo-strategic terms. As terrorist threats are increasingly transnational, Beijing will have to take extra care to secure Xinjiang and build counterterrorism partnerships with its neighbors. Episodic violence between the Uighur and Han communities seems likely to spread beyond Xinjiang.

Meanwhile, the Chinese hard-line approach toward Uighur separatists fails to distinguish between terrorists, supporters, and sympathizers. By the standards of most analysts, this policy stance has failed, and a long-term policy to manage and mitigate the emerging and existing drivers of separatism will be needed.

Rohan Gunaratna

See also al Qaeda; East Turkestan Islamic Movement

Further Readings

Ho, Stephanie. "China Blames Separatists for Deadly Xinjiang Riots." VOANews.com, July 21, 2009. http://www.voanews.com/english/news/a-13-2009-07-21-voa13-68828702.html.

Jacobs, Andrew. "Countering Riots, China Rounds Up Hundreds." *The New York Times,* July 19, 2009. http://www.nytimes.com/2009/07/20/world/asia/20xinjiang.html.

Kaltman, Blaine. *Under the Heel of the Dragon: Islam, Racism, Crime, and the Uighur in China.* Athens: Center for International Studies, Ohio State University, 2007.

Leow, Jason, and Gordon Fairclough. "Clash at Factory Employing Uighurs Triggered Riot." *The Wall Street Journal,* July 8, 2009.

Reed, J. Todd, and Diana Raschke. *The ETIM: China's Islamic Militants and the Global Terrorist Threat.* Santa Barbara, CA: Praeger, 2010.

Tyler, Christian. *Wild West China: The Taming of Xinjiang.* New Brunswick, NJ: Rutgers University Press, 2004.

Yacoub, Ibrahim Salih Mohammed al (1966–)

In October 2001, Ibrahim Salih Mohammed al Yacoub was placed on the FBI's Most Wanted Terrorists list for his alleged involvement in the 1996 bombing of the Khobar Towers air force barracks near Dhahran, Saudi Arabia. The attack, attributed to the Saudi Hezbollah organization, killed 19 U.S. military service members and wounded approximately 500.

On June 21, 2001, the United States indicted Yacoub and 13 others for this bombing. The indictment claimed that Yacoub, who was born in Tarut, Saudi Arabia, was a prominent member of Saudi Hezbollah during the 1990s, and that he was involved in recruiting new members and in planning and executing terror attacks. Yacoub is also said to have worked as a liaison between his organization and the Lebanese and Iranian branches of Hezbollah. Members of Saudi Hezbollah, also called Hezbollah al Hijaz, are mostly Shiite Muslim young men whose loyalty is to Iran, not to Saudi Arabia.

The indictment states that, about three years before the bombing, Ahmad Ibrahim al Mughassil, the head of Saudi Hezbollah's military wing, instructed Yacoub and several others to begin gathering information on U.S. nationals and interests in Saudi Arabia. Yacoub directed other members to survey possible locations for an attack that would drive the United States from the country. Mughassil eventually selected the Khobar Towers, which housed approximately 2,000 U.S. military personnel, as a bombing target. According to the indictment, on the evening of June 25, 1996, Mughassil drove a tanker truck filled with over 5,000 pounds of explosives and parked it near the Khobar Towers. He and a cohort then jumped into a waiting getaway car and drove off. The truck bomb exploded within minutes, killing 19 members of the U.S. Air Force and wounding about 500.

Fellow Saudi Hezbollah members Mughassil, Ali Saed bin Ali el Hoorie, and Abdelkarim Hussein Mohamed al Nasser, were indicted with Yacoub and are also on the FBI's Most Wanted list. Eleven of the men charged are in Saudi custody; three remain fugitives. The Saudi government has disputed U.S. jurisdiction in the Khobar case and has refused to extradite the men on the grounds that the attack was made on Saudi soil and was committed, for the most part, by Saudi citizens. A reward of up to $5 million for information leading directly to the arrest or indictment of Yacoub is being offered by the U.S. State Department.

Erica Pearson

See also Hezbollah; Hoorie, Ali Saed bin Ali el; Khobar Towers Bombing; Mughassil, Ahmad Ibrahim al; Nasser, Abdelkarim Hussein Mohamed al

Further Readings

Federal Bureau of Investigation. "Most Wanted Terrorists." http://www.fbi.gov/wanted/terrorists/fugitives.htm.

Jamieson, Perry D. *Khobar Towers: Tragedy and Response*. Washington, DC: Air Force History and Museums Program, 2008.

"A Nation Challenged: The Hunted; The 22 Most Wanted Suspects, in a Five-act Drama of Global Terror." *The New York Times*, October 14, 2001, p. 1B.

Strobl, Staci, and Jon R. Lindsay. "Lost in Transition: Khobar Towers and the Ambiguities of Terrorism in the 1990s." In *A New Understanding of Terrorism: Case Studies, Trajectories and Lessons Learned*, edited by M.R. Haberfeld and Agostino von Hassell. New York: Springer, 2009.

U.S. District Court for the Eastern District of Virginia, Alexandria Division. *United States v. Ahmed al-Mughassil, et al.* Indictment, June 21, 2001 (Khobar Indictment). http://fl1.findlaw.com/news.findlaw.com/cnn/docs/khobar/khobarindict61901.pdf.

Walsh, Elsa. "Louis Freeh's Last Case." *The New Yorker*, May 14, 2001.

YASIN, ABDUL RAHMAN (1960–)

U.S.-born Abdul Rahman Yasin (aka Aboud Yasin, Abdul Rahman S. Taha, Abdul Rahman S. Taher) is the only suspect in the 1993 bombing of the World Trade Center who has thus far eluded U.S. officials.

Witnesses at the bombing trial of the other defendants said that they saw Yasin meet many times with fellow conspirators. Days before the attack, convicted bomber Mohammad Salameh rented a Ryder van in Jersey City. The conspirators then filled the vehicle with 1,200 pounds of explosives and drove the van to the World Trade Center, parking it in an underground garage. The bomb exploded at 12:18 P.M. on February 26, 1993, killing six people and injuring about 1,000.

Federal agents found Yasin in Salameh's apartment less than a week after the attack and questioned him. He took authorities to the garage apartment in Jersey City, New Jersey, that had been rented by Salameh. Prosecutors in the attack trial often referred to the apartment as a makeshift bomb laboratory. It was there that the conspirators had mixed the chemicals for the bomb, made telephone calls, and received mail. After Yasin cooperated as an informant, U.S. authorities released him. On March 5, Yasin fled to Jordan. According to press reports, he was thought to be hiding somewhere north of Baghdad in the later 1990s, and he may still be in Iraq.

In 1994, a New York court convicted four men, all followers of Sheikh Omar Abdel Rahman, an Egyptian-born cleric living in New Jersey, of various roles in the bombing. Abdel Rahman himself was later charged in a larger conspiracy and is now serving a life sentence. In 1995, officials captured Ramzi Ahmed Yousef, the alleged mastermind behind the 1993 attack on the World Trade Center; he was convicted by a New York court in 1997.

Erica Pearson

See also Abdel Rahman, Omar; World Trade Center Bombing (1993); Yousef, Ramzi Ahmed

Further Readings

Cohen, Patricia. "Bomb Puzzle 1,000 Pieces; Prosecution's Evidence Snowballs." *Newsday*, February 9, 1994.

Federal Bureau of Investigation. "Most Wanted Terrorists." http://www.fbi.gov/wanted/wanted_terrorists.

"A Nation Challenged: The Hunted; The 22 Most Wanted Suspects, in a Five-act Drama of Global Terror." *The New York Times*, October 14, 2001, p. 1B.

Reeve, Simon. *The New Jackals: Ramzi Yousef, Osama bin Laden and the Future of Terrorism*. Boston: Northeastern University Press, 2002.

Richardson, Louise. *What Terrorists Want: Understanding the Enemy, Containing the Threat*. New York: Random House: 2006.

Risen, James. "Iraq Said to Have Tried to Reach Last-Minute Deal to Avert War." *The New York Times*, November 6, 2003. http://www.nytimes.com/2003/11/06/world/struggle-for-iraq-diplomacy-iraq-said-have-tried-reach-last-minute-deal-avert.html.

YOUNIS, FAWAZ (1959–)

The Lebanese hijacker Fawaz Younis (aka Fawaz Yunis) was captured in an elaborate FBI operation and brought to trial in the United States under anti-terrorism laws passed in the 1980s. During his trial, members of the gallery gave Younis the nickname "teddy bear terrorist," because of his affable demeanor and because no hostages were harmed during the 1985 hijacking of Royal Jordanian Airlines Flight 402.

Younis was born in Baalbeck, Lebanon, but his family moved to the Shiite slums of Beirut when he was very young. He was just 15 when the Lebanese civil war began in 1974. In 1979, Younis joined the Shiite militant party Amal. During the early 1980s, he worked as a used car salesman, but when Amal took control of West Beirut in 1984, Younis became a full-time officer in the Amal militia.

On June 11, 1985, under orders from Amal, Younis and four hijackers, armed with hand grenades and other weapons, took control of Flight 402 from Beirut to Amman, Jordan. The group planned to reroute the flight to Tunisia, where the Arab League was meeting, and demand that all Palestinians be expelled from Lebanon.

The hijacked plane flew to Cyprus, to Tunisia, to Italy, back to Tunisia, and finally to Beirut. Two Americans were among the 10 passengers and crew aboard the flight. On the plane, the heavily armed Younis was videotaped reading a statement calling for all Palestinians to be forced out of Lebanon. After the plane landed in Beirut and all of the passengers were allowed to leave the plane, Younis and the other hijackers blew it up. The next day, a Palestinian hijacked a Middle East Airlines flight in protest of Amal's demands. The two Americans on board the first hijacked airplane were also aboard the second hijacked flight.

In September 1987, a Lebanese informant working for the United States lured Younis onto a luxury yacht in international waters off Cyprus by promising him access to a big drug deal. Once aboard, Younis was caught in a trap engineered by the Pentagon, the CIA, the FBI, the Drug Enforcement Agency, and the State Department. U.S. officials arrested him and brought him to the United States to stand trial.

Nabih Berri, Lebanon's justice minister and the leader of the Amal Party, denounced the capture, calling it close to piracy and an attack on Lebanon's honor. In October 1989, an U.S. court sentenced Younis to 30 years in prison. The judge said that Younis was not given a life sentence because he showed sensitivity during the hijacking, ushering those with medical conditions off the plane. During the trial, press accounts revealed that Jamal Hamadan, the informant that U.S. officials used to lure Younis to the yacht, had been convicted of

murder in Lebanon. In exchange for facilitating Younis's capture, Hamadan, who did not testify at the trial, was brought to the United States and placed in the witness protection program. Younis was released in March 2005 after serving approximately half his sentence.

Erica Pearson

Further Readings

Lardner, George, Jr. "Terrorism Suspect Set Up by Friend; Drug Deal Said to Lure Alleged Hijacker." *The Washington Post*, September 19, 1987.

Maogoto, Jackson Nyamura. *Battling Terrorism: Legal Perspectives on the Use of Force and the War on Terror*. Burlington, VT: Ashgate, 2005.

Noble, Kenneth B. "Lebanese Suspect in '85 Hijacking Arrested by the F.B.I. while at Sea." *The New York Times*, September 17, 1987.

Smith, Brent L. *Terrorism in America: Pipe Bombs and Pipe Dreams*. Albany: State University of New York Press, 1994.

Wright, Robin, and Ronald J. Ostrow. "Arab Hijacker's Trial to Pose Test of U.S. Terrorism Policy." *Los Angeles Times*, February 20, 1989.

YOUSEF, RAMZI AHMED (1968–)

Ramzi Ahmed Yousef (aka Adbul Basit Mahmoud Abdul Karima), the convicted mastermind of the 1993 World Trade Center bombing, was part of one of the most ambitious terrorist conspiracies discovered to date, including a thwarted plot to blow up a dozen U.S. airliners over the Pacific Ocean.

While New York City struggled to piece together what happened on February 26, 1993, when a truck bomb exploded in an underground garage in the World Trade Center, Yousef, the man who had orchestrated the plot, was bound for Pakistan. He left behind the small gang of men he had recruited for the bombing—Mohammad Salameh, Mahmud Abouhalima, Nidal Ayyad, and Ahmad Ajaj—who were quickly tried and convicted for their roles in the bombing. The defense attorneys in the trial would later suggest that these men were less Yousef's fellow conspirators than his "dupes." Yousef, some suggest, had taken an existing small-scale bombing conspiracy and elevated it to a plan to topple the twin towers.

Yousef's activities following the bombing are basically unknown, though he is believed to have stayed in a safe house in Quetta, Pakistan, for some time. Authorities believe that by July 1993, militant Islamic forces had approached Yousef to coordinate and carry out an assassination plot against Benazir Bhutto, former prime minister of Pakistan who was again a candidate for that post, before the October 1993 elections.

Yousef used two long-time associates, Abdul Hakim Murad and Abdul Shakur, for this plot. In late July, the three men allegedly went to Bhutto's residence to plant a bomb near her driveway. While setting the bomb, part of the detonator exploded in Yousef's face, injuring one eye. The bomb itself did not explode, but the men abandoned the bomb and rushed Yousef to a hospital. Allegedly, Yousef again failed to assassinate Bhutto when a gun to be used by a sniper was not delivered in time for one of her public addresses.

By spring 1994, Yousef had headed to Thailand, where he coordinated a plot to bomb the Israeli embassy in Bangkok. On March 11, 1994, a stolen van loaded with a bomb drove toward the embassy. Within blocks, however, the van was in an accident and the driver fled. Authorities discovered the bomb, still undetonated, days after the van was impounded.

Three months later, Yousef arranged the bombing of a Shiite shrine in Masshad, Iran, in which 26 people died. He then left for the Philippines, where he trained members of Abu Sayyaf, a militant Islamic group, in the use of explosives. Because of his expertise, they reportedly called him "the chemist." At the time, bin Laden was financing Abu Sayyaf. Through the group, it is believed that bin Laden requested that Yousef assassinate U.S. President Bill Clinton during his trip to the Philippines on November 12, 1994. The attempt was a logistical nightmare and proved too difficult for Yousef. Yousef turned his attention to a plot he had been working on since arriving in Manila, called Project Bojinka (Serbo-Croatian for "loud explosion").

Oklahoma City Connections

Project Bojinka was Yousef's most elaborate and ambitious scheme to date. He planned to blow up 11 U.S. airliners, almost simultaneously, over the Pacific Ocean, using small but strategically placed bombs made of liquid nitroglycerin, which could pass through airport detectors unnoticed and be assembled in an airplane bathroom using little more than two batteries and a watch.

While planning Project Bojinka, Yousef also hatched a plan to assassinate Pope John Paul II. During this time, he may also have taken part in yet another ambitious conspiracy. Sources, most notably Timothy McVeigh's trial lawyer, Stephen Jones, believe Yousef consulted with Terry Lynn Nichols, one of the men convicted in the Oklahoma City bombing. In November 1994, Nichols flew to the Philippines for an extended stay. A former member of Abu Sayyaf turned informant claimed that a man called "the farmer," who may or may not have been Nichols, met with Yousef and two of his Project Bojinka associates, Murad and Wali Khan Amin Shah, to discuss bomb-making and other terrorist activities.

On December 8, 1994, Yousef rented a street-facing room along the route the pope would travel on his visit to Manila. Three days later, Yousef boarded Philippines Airlines Flight 434 in Manila; once on board, he assembled a bomb in the bathroom and placed it under his seat. Yousef disembarked in Cebu, and the plane continued on to Tokyo. At approximately 11:45 AM, the bomb exploded, killing one Japanese passenger and injuring several others. Abu Sayyaf claimed responsibility for the bombing, while Yousef continued to fine-tune his plot to assassinate the pope.

On January 6, 1995, while mixing chemicals intended for bombs, Yousef and Murad started a small fire in their room; when police arrived, both men had already fled, leaving bomb-making materials and, more important, Yousef's laptop. The laptop provided authorities with information related to the planned assassination of the pope, as well as a file named "Bojinka," which detailed how five men were to plant bombs on 11 American planes in the Far East. The date for bombing the first plane was January 21, 1995, just weeks away.

After fleeing, Yousef returned to Pakistan, where he tried to enlist the help of a man who later alerted authorities to his presence in Islamabad. On February 7, 1995, Pakistani authorities captured Yousef in his hotel room. Yousef was flown back to United States quickly after his arrest to await trial for the World Trade Center bombing in 1993 and the Bojinka plot. On September 5, 1996, Yousef, Murad, and Shah were all convicted for the bombing and assassination conspiracy. Yousef was also found guilty of the bombing of Flight 434 and the death of Haruki Ikegami, the passenger who died in the bombing. In November 1997, he was also found guilty of the World Trade Center bombing.

At his sentencing, in January 1998, Yousef stated, "Yes, I am a terrorist," before he was sentenced to 240 years in prison, plus a life sentence, to be served in near solitary confinement at the "supermax" high-security prison in Florence, Colorado. Some of the biggest questions about Yousef, including his true identity, however, remain unanswered.

Laura Lambert

See also Abdel Rahman, Omar; Abu Sayyaf Group; al Qaeda; bin Laden, Osama; Hussein, Saddam; World Trade Center Bombing (1993)

Further Readings

Dwyer, Jim, David Kocieniewski, Deidre Murphy, and Peg Tyre. *Two Seconds under the World: Terror Comes to America—The Conspiracy behind the World Trade Center Bombing.* New York: Crown, 1994.

Mylroie, Laurie. *Study of Revenge: Saddam Hussein's Unfinished War against America.* Washington, DC: AEI Press, 2000.

Pearlstein, Richard Merrill. *Fatal Future? Transnational Terrorism and the New Global Disorder.* Austin: University of Texas Press, 2005.

Reeve, Simon. *The New Jackals: Ramzi Yousef, Osama bin Laden and the Future of Terrorism.* Boston: Northeastern University Press, 1999.

Richardson, Louise. *What Terrorists Want: Understanding the Enemy, Containing the Threat.* New York: Random House, 2006.

U.S. Congress. House Committee on the Judiciary. Subcommittee on Crime and Criminal Justice. *World Trade Center Bombing: Terror Hits Home: Hearing before the Subcommittee on Crime and Criminal Justice of the Committee on the Judiciary, House of Representatives, One Hundred Third Congress, First Session, March 9, 1993.* Washington, DC: U.S. Government Printing Office, 1994.

Weiser, Benjamin. "Judges Uphold Convictions in '93 Bombing." *The New York Times*, April 5, 2003. http://www.nytimes.com/2003/04/05/nyregion/judges-uphold-convictions-in-93-bombing.html.

Y2K Plot

On December 14, 1999, Ahmed Ressam, an Algerian traveling on a fake Canadian passport, was arrested in Port Angeles, Washington, with nearly 200 pounds of explosives in the trunk of his rental car. The ensuing investigation revealed that Ressam, with the help of several others, was planning to blow up a terminal at Los Angeles International Airport (LAX) on New Year's Eve. This plan became known as the Y2K plot or the millennium bomb plot.

The plot was formed in 1998 at one of Osama bin Laden's terrorist training camps in Afghanistan. Ressam, together with at least four other militant Islamic Algerians, planned to travel to Canada. Once there, the plot called for them to rob banks to fund a terrorist attack on a significant site within the United States. When Ressam returned to Canada, where he had been living since 1994, he decided the target should be a terminal at LAX. The group hoped to carry out the bombing on New Year's Eve 1999.

Ressam was the only member of the European-based cell to gain entry to Canada. When he decided to proceed with the plan, he enlisted the help of several associates. Mokhtar Haouari, Ressam's associate from Montreal, knew Ressam was planning some sort of mission, gave him false identification documents and $3,000, and promised more aid. In Vancouver, Ressam relied on Abdelmajid Dahoumane for assistance. Dahoumane housed Ressam when he first returned from Afghanistan, and he was in the rental car with Ressam on the ferry from Victoria, Canada, to Port Angeles. Dahoumane escaped unnoticed.

When Ressam was captured, authorities found the Brooklyn, New York, phone number of Abdelghani Meskini in his pocket. Unbeknownst to authorities, Meskini, traveling under the alias Eduardo Rocha, was actually in Seattle, waiting to connect with Ressam at a Best Western Inn in that city. (Ressam, using the alias Benni Antoine

Norris, had booked the hotel room, as well as an escape flight from Washington to London.) On December 17, after hearing of Ressam's arrest, Meskini returned to New York, where his home was already under surveillance by federal authorities. Within days, he called Haouari in Montreal. Meskini was arrested on Christmas Eve 1999; Haouari's arrest followed soon after.

On April 6, 2000, Ressam was found guilty on nine counts. Both Ressam and Meskini, who pled guilty, turned government witness in order to shorten their sentences, and they eventually testified against Haouari, who was convicted of supporting the Y2K plot and sentenced, in January 2002, to 24 years in prison. Dahoumane was apprehended by Algerian authorities in March 2001. He faces trial in Algeria for terrorist activities before he can be extradited to the United States. Another man, Samir Ait Mohamed, was later indicted for helping Ressam commit credit card fraud. (Lucy Garofalo, a woman caught at the U.S.–Canada border in Vermont shortly after Ressam's arrest was initially charged in relation to the Y2K plot. She was ultimately found guilty of other charges, including transporting Algerian aliens across the U.S. border, for which she served a short sentence.)

Since Haouari's trial, Meskini has provided vital information about the activities of the Armed Islamic Group (GIA), an Algerian terrorist organization with active cells in New York, Boston, and Montreal. Ressam has been instrumental in the U.S. investigations against several terrorists related to bin Laden and the September 11, 2001, attacks on New York City's World Trade Center and the Pentagon, just outside Washington, D.C. Meskini was released in 2005 after serving a year of his 72-month sentence, but he was rearrested in 2007 for allegedly violating the terms of his release and committing new offenses. In 2005 Ressam was sentenced to 22 years in federal prison, but in February 2010 the U.S. Court of Appeals ruled the sentence was too lenient and threw out the decision, reinstating the 65-year minimum term. The case is currently being appealed.

Laura Lambert

See also Armed Islamic Group; bin Laden, Osama; Ressam, Ahmed

Further Readings

Feuer, Alan. "Man Pleads Guilty to Role in Millennial Terrorism Plot." *The New York Times,* March 10, 2001, p. B2.

Mansnerus, Laura. "Prosecutors Promise Chilling Glimpse of Millennium Bomb Plot." *The New York Times,* June 28, 2001, p. B5.

PBS/Frontline. "Trail of a Terrorist." *Frontline,* October 25, 2001. http://www.pbs.org/wgbh/pages/frontline/shows/trail.

Pearlstein, Steven. "Algerian Charged in Bombing Plot Aids FBI Probe." *The Washington Post.* January 21, 2000, p. A21.

Richardson, Louise. *What Terrorists Want: Understanding the Enemy, Containing the Threat.* New York: Random House, 2006.

Sageman, Marc. *Leaderless Jihad: Terror Networks in the Twenty-first Century.* Philadelphia: University of Pennsylvania, 2008.

"Times Topics: Ahmed Ressam." *The New York Times Online.* http://topics.nytimes.com/top/reference/timestopics/people/r/ahmed_ressam/index.html.

Weiser, Benjamin. "New Trouble for Terrorist Who Aided Prosecutors." *The New York Times,* July 30, 2010.

ZARQAWI, ABU MUSAB AL (1966–2006)

Abu Musab al Zarqawi was the *nom de guerre* of Ahmad Fadil Nazal al Khalayleh, the leader of al Qaeda in Iraq (AQI), an extremist Sunni insurgent group with links to the transnational al Qaeda terrorist network. He is responsible for introducing beheadings and massive suicide bombings to the Iraqi insurgency. Prior to his demise on June 7, 2006, in a U.S. airstrike on one of his hideouts north of Baquba, Iraq, Zarqawi was one of the most hunted international terrorists. Zarqawi's notoriety secured him a place in the pantheon of fallen jihadist leaders to take on the United States and its allies in direct military confrontation. He is revered by global jihadists for his defiance of a superpower and reviled by Iraqis for bringing their country to the brink of sectarian civil war.

Zarqawi was born on October 30, 1966, to members of the Bani Hassan tribe in Zarqa, Jordan (hence the Arabic appellation *al Zarqawi*, meaning "of Zarqa"). Located northeast of

U.S. Army soldiers of Charlie Company, 14th Engineer Battalion, assigned to Forward Operating Base Warhorse, and Iraqi army soldiers work to clear rubble left from the attack that killed Abu Musab al Zarqawi, the leader of al Qaeda in Iraq, in the Diyala Province on June 11, 2006. (U.S. Air Force photo by Tech. Sgt. Ken Bergmann/Released)

Amman, the capital, Zarqa is the third largest city in Jordan. It is an impoverished and dilapidated industrial region crammed with concrete housing blocks connected together by narrow, poorly paved streets. It residents live modestly, making do with few of the amenities of modern life.

Zarqawi's formative years are shrouded in mystery, but those who knew him well say that he was street tough before turning to religious zealotry in the late 1980s. In 1989, he and some of his childhood friends volunteered to go to Afghanistan at the tail end of the Soviet occupation of that country. He was among the few Arab Afghans to have engaged in some battles against the remaining Afghani Communist regime before its collapse in 1992.

Zarqawi returned to Jordan in 1993 with plans of spreading the Salafist ideology associated with his mentor, Isam Muhammad Tahir al Barqawi, better known as Abu Muhammad al Maqdisi. Salafism is a puritanical form of Sunni Islamism that rejects the separation of religion from politics and insists on a strict, almost literal, application of Islamic law in the modern world. Zarqawi, however, was an impetuous activist and had little patience for the gradual propagation of Salafism. Instead, he wanted to jump headlong into a violent jihad against the ruling regime in Jordan. Inspired by the historic examples of Nur al Din Zangi and Salah al Din al Ayubi (Saladin), both of whom led campaigns against the Crusaders in the 12th century, Zarqawi aspired to be the modern-day liberator of Jerusalem and the leader to revive the Islamic caliphate in the contemporary world.

His haste ultimately proved counterproductive, as he was quickly implicated in a plot to use small arms against the monarchical system in Jordan. This came to be known as the *Bay'at al-Imam* case (literally, declaring allegiance to the prayer leader). In 1994, Zarqawi and his cohorts were sentenced to several years in prison, but King Abdullah II, who succeeded his father, the late King Hussein, released them in March 1999 under a general amnesty.

After his release, Zarqawi opted to go to Pakistan and, later, to Afghanistan to resurrect his militant career. Initially, he was interested in fighting in Chechnya, where a nationalist insurgency against the Russian federal government was being aided by foreign fighters from the Middle East and North Africa. Saif al Adl, an Egyptian al Qaeda operative, convinced Zarqawi to stay in Afghanistan

in the hope of recruiting him to al Qaeda's cause. Although Zarqawi did not pledge loyalty to Osama bin Laden and the al Qaeda leadership due to their disagreements over strategy, he accepted their help in setting up a guerrilla training camp in the city of Herat in western Afghanistan near the border with Iran. The purpose of the camp, named Monotheism and Jihad, was to train recruits from Jordan, Palestine, Syria, Lebanon, Iraq, and Turkey—areas in which al Qaeda wanted a presence. During this time, Zarqawi was able to establish funding networks through Syrians located in Turkey and Germany. He also made links with the Kurdish Ansar al Islam group, based in northern Iraq, which proved fateful for his future role in the Iraqi insurgency.

The September 11, 2001, terrorist attacks and the subsequent U.S. invasion of Afghanistan forced Zarqawi to seek a new haven. He seems to have been unaware of the 9/11 plot, but he eventually joined fleeing al Qaeda members in eastern Afghanistan as they were contemplating what to do next. He was injured, reportedly with broken ribs, as a result of an American aerial bombardment on al Qaeda positions. Fleeing through Pakistan was increasingly difficult, and there was talk of using Iran as an escape route. Anticipating a U.S. invasion of Iraq, Zarqawi and some of his men eventually escaped to northern Iraq through Iran with the help of Ansar al Islam.

In the lead up to its invasion of Iraq, the United States presented Zarqawi's connection to Ansar al Islam as evidence that the regime of Saddam Hussein harbored international terrorists linked to al Qaeda. The post-invasion intelligence consensus, however, challenges this evidence because Ansar al Islam operated in an autonomous region that was outside of the *de facto* control of the Iraqi government; it had a special protection status extended to the Kurds by the United States and Britain following the 1991 Gulf War.

In 2003, Zarqawi emerged as an insurgent leader of the Monotheism and Jihad group in Iraq, adopting the same name as his training camp in Afghanistan. Zarqawi immediately captured the spotlight through massive suicide attacks on leading Shiite religious figures, including the influential Mohammed Baqir al Hakim. He is also responsible for the bombing of the United Nations headquarters building in Baghdad that killed Sérgio Vieira de Mello, the top UN envoy to Iraq. Zarqawi is most notorious, however, for the televised beheading of Nicholas Berg, an American businessman taken into captivity while seeking contracts in Iraq.

In October 2004, Zarqawi changed the name of his organization to al Qaeda in Iraq (AQI), pledging fealty to bin Laden's al Qaeda movement for the first time. This move was intended to give AQI global recognition and material support from al Qaeda's transnational network. This merger, however, did not end disagreements over strategy between Zarqawi and the al Qaeda leadership. The latter wanted Zarqawi to focus his attacks on coalition forces, while Zarqawi himself was bent on unleashing a civil war between Sunnis and Shiites.

Zarqawi's ambitions were not limited to fighting in Iraq; he also launched attacks in his home country, Jordan, in an effort to destabilize the ruling monarchy. On November 9, 2005, Zarqawi sent suicide bombers to attack three hotels in Amman—the Grand Hyatt Hotel, the Radisson SAS Hotel, and the Days Inn—killing and injuring over 160 people, mainly fellow Jordanians. These attacks against his birthplace were not the first orchestrated by Zarqawi. In September 2001, the Jordanian regime sentenced Zarqawi to 15 years in prison in absentia for planning attacks on major tourist sites on the occasion of the new millennium. In April 2004, Zarqawi was sentenced to death in absentia by the Jordanian authorities for his presumed role in the October 28, 2002, assassination of Laurence Foley, an American diplomat working as the head of USAID in Amman. That same month the Jordanian government announced that it foiled a plot by Zarqawi's network to use chemical-laden truck bombs against the Jordanian intelligence headquarters, the U.S. embassy, and the prime minister's office, all located in Amman.

Zarqawi's biggest impact, however, was in Iraq. As the leader of AQI, his cadres were few, alien, and overmatched by coalition forces. He devised a diabolical strategy to win over the Sunni population: attacking the Shiites and sparking sectarian warfare became the centerpiece of his grand plan. Zarqawi was explicit about the need to attack Shiites to galvanize Sunni support for the insurgency. In January 2004, coalition forces intercepted a courier for Zarqawi with a 17-page document

sent to al Qaeda leaders in Afghanistan or Pakistan. It was an internal report in which he outlined his strategy for fighting in Iraq. Zarqawi viewed Shiites as the key to getting the neutral Sunnis to join the insurgency, embrace suicide bombings, and create a base of support for the foreign jihadists. He calculated that a sustained campaign of violence against Iraq's Shiite communities, their political leaders, and symbols of identity would provoke them to undertake indiscriminate retaliatory violence against Sunnis. Sectarian polarization would create fertile soil for recruitment, enabling outsiders with an extreme worldview to survive, grow, and set up a safe haven for their transnational jihad on the ashes of a failed Iraqi state.

The demise of Zarqawi, like his early life, is mysterious. There are reports that a member of his organization betrayed him while under interrogation; others credit the Jordanian intelligence service for providing the critical tips on how to track him down. What is known for certain is that at 6:12 PM on June 7, 2006, U.S. fighter jets dropped two 500-pound bombs on a safe house used by Zarqawi, killing him and five others in the building.

Mohammed Hafez

See also Afghan Arabs; al Qaeda; al Qaeda in Iraq; Ansar al Islam; Iraq War

Further Readings

Bennet, James. "The Mystery of the Insurgency." *The New York Times,* May 15, 2005. http://www.nytimes.com/2005/05/15/weekinreview/15bennet.html?pagewanted=print.

Gambill, Gary. "Abu Mos'ab al Zarqawi: A Biographical Sketch." Special issue, *Terrorism Monitor* 2, no. 24 (December 16, 2004).

Hafez, Mohammed M. *Suicide Bombers in Iraq: The Strategy and Ideology of Martyrdom.* Washington, DC: United States Institute of Peace, 2007.

Hashim, Ahmed S. "Iraq's Chaos: Why the Insurgency Won't Go Away." *Boston Review* (October–November 2004).

Levitt, Matt, and Julie Sawyer. "Zarqawi's Jordanian Agenda." Special issue, *Terrorism Monitor* 2, no. 24 (December 2004). an Egyptian physician, is alleged to

Napoleoni, Loretta. *Insurgent Iraq: al-Zarqawi and the New Generation.* New York: Seven Stories Press, 2005.

ZAWAHIRI, AYMAN AL (1951–)

Ayman al Zawahiri (aka Abu Abdallah; Abu al Mu'iz; Abu Fatima; Abu Muhammad; Muhammad Ibrahim; The Doctor; Abu Mohammed Nur al Deen; Abdel Muaz), an Egyptian physician, is alleged to have been both Osama bin Laden's closest advisor and his doctor. Viewed by many as the mastermind who led bin Laden and al Qaeda into creating instruments of mass murder, Zawahiri is one of the FBI's "most wanted terrorists." He is said to be the most likely successor to bin Laden and is suspected of playing a key role in the September 11, 2001, attacks on the World Trade Center and the Pentagon. The Council on Foreign Relations has stated that Zawahiri probably had a more direct role in the planning of 9/11 than bin Laden did.

Zawahiri's family is prominent in both Egypt's politics and religion. His father taught at the University of Cairo, his grandfather was a well-known and moderate imam, and his uncle was the first secretary general of the Arab League. Zawahiri took a different path; he was arrested at age 15 for involvement in Muslim Brotherhood, a militant group banned in Egypt.

According to his autobiography, Zawahiri was transformed in 1980 after leaving work at a Cairo Muslim Brotherhood clinic to go to Pakistan and give medical aid to Afghan refugees. A founding member of Egyptian Islamic Jihad, Zawahiri built up the organization during the 1970s and became its leader. The group, said to be a major influence on bin Laden's al Qaeda, opposes the secular Egyptian government and advocates its overthrow through violence. Zawahiri admitted planning the 1981 assassination of Egyptian president Anwar Sadat, in which Islamic Jihad members disguised themselves as soldiers to reach and assassinate Sadat in full view of Egyptian television. Zawahiri was arrested for illegal possession of firearms and spent three years in jail following Sadat's death, but he was never charged in the killing.

In the aftermath of Sadat's death, Egyptian security officials held suspects without trial and tortured many of them. Members of Islamic Jihad began to flee Egypt in large numbers. Zawahiri left Egypt in 1986 and went to Saudi Arabia, then traveled to Pakistan, caring for Afghan soldiers wounded in the guerrilla war against the Soviet Union. During this time Al-Zawahiri met bin Laden and merged his Islamic Jihad group with al Qaeda in the mid-1990s, giving al Qaeda a more radical anti-American stance. Using disguises and false documents, Zawahiri traveled through many western countries, even visiting the United States in the 1990s on a fund-raising mission.

Zawahiri worked very closely with bin Laden in al Qaeda's *majlis al shura*, or consultation council. al Qaeda, an Arabic word meaning "the Base," is an international network that uses force and violence in an effort to drive the United States from Saudi Arabia and other Islamic countries. The al Qaeda network, which serves as an umbrella group for other militant organizations, establishes cells in areas it plans to attack.

The United States indicted Zawahiri for his involvement in the planning of the 1998 bombings of U.S. embassies in East Africa, in which 224 people were killed and thousands wounded. Coordinated truck bombs went off within minutes of each other at the U.S. embassies in Nairobi, Kenya, and Dar es Salaam, Tanzania, cities 400 miles apart.

Shortly after the embassy bombings, the U.S. government announced that bin Laden and al Qaeda operatives were responsible. In retaliation, President Clinton ordered air attacks on al Qaeda training grounds in Afghanistan and a pharmaceutical plant in Khartoum, Sudan. International criticism of the air raids was vociferous, as many debated whether the factory in Sudan had any relation to bin Laden or chemical weapons. In 2001, four men tied to al Qaeda were convicted in the United States of various roles in the bombings.

Zawahiri appeared with bin Laden and Muhammad Atef, another high-ranking al Qaeda member, in a video released to coincide with the first U.S. attacks on Afghanistan following the September 11 attacks. Speaking first, the doctor's remarks on al Qaeda's "holy war" made many experts—including Hamid Mir, bin Laden's "official" biographer—speculate about who truly leads al Qaeda, Zawahiri or bin Laden.

As the U.S. and Afghan rebel assault on the Taliban intensified in the winter of 2001, Zawahiri sent his autobiography, *Knights under the Banner of the Prophet*, to the London-based newspaper *Asharq al Awsat* by way of an unidentified courier. Lengthy excerpts appeared in December 2001.

There have been numerous near misses in the quest to capture Zawahiri; rumors circulated that he was injured during the assault on Tora Bora, Afghanistan, in 2002, and he narrowly avoided being hit by a predator drone attack in 2006. In the spring of 2009, the U.S. government publicly acknowledged that Zawahiri was, for all intents and purposes, the leader of al Qaeda. Soon after, an audiotape was circulated that seemed to feature Zawahiri criticizing a speech that President Barack Obama had recently delivered in Cairo. In September 2010, Zawahiri released another tape, this one on the occasion of the ninth anniversary of the September 11 attacks, in which he continued to urge jihad and also criticized the government of Pakistan for doing too little for its people during severe flooding that summer.

After bin Laden was killed by U.S. Navy SEALs in May 2011, experts speculated that Zawahiri might replace bin Laden—not only as the titular head of al Qaeda but also as the new "world's most wanted man."

Erica Pearson

See also al Qaeda; Atef, Muhammad; bin Laden, Osama; East Africa Embassy Bombings; September 11 Attacks

Further Readings

Baldauf, Scott. "The 'Cave Man' and al Qaeda." *Christian Science Monitor*, October 31, 2001. http://www.csmonitor.com/2001/1031/p6s1-wosc.html.

Bergen, Peter. *The Longest War: Inside the Enduring Conflict between America and al-Qaeda*. New York: Free Press, 2011.

Bergen, Peter. *The Osama bin Laden I Know: An Oral History of al Qaeda's Leader*. New York: Free Press, 2007.

Levy, Glen. "Ayman al-Zawahiri: The Man Most Likely to Succeed bin Laden." *Time*, May 2, 2011. http://newsfeed.time.com/2011/05/02/ayman-al-zawahri-the-man-most-likely-to-succeed-bin-laden.

MacFarquhar, Neil. "Word for Word/Jihad Lit; Beware of Hidden Enemies and Their Wolves and Foxes." *The New York Times*, December 9, 2001. http://www.nytimes.com/2001/12/09/weekinreview/word-for-word-jihad-lit-beware-of-hidden-enemies-and-their-wolves-and-foxes.html.

Riedel, Bruce. *The Search for al Qaeda: Its Leadership, Ideology, and Future*. Washington, DC: Brookings Institution Press, 2008.

Smith, Martin, and Lowell Bergman. "Hunting bin Laden." *Frontline*, PBS, September 13, 2001. http://www.pbs.org/wgbh/pages/frontline/shows/binladen.

Ungoed-Thomas, Jon. "Egypt Used Torture to Crack Network." *Sunday Times* (London), November 25, 2001.

U.S. District Court for the Southern District of New York. *United States v. Usama bin Laden, et al.* Indictment S(2) 98 Cr. 1023 (LBS), November 4, 1998. http://www.fas.org/irp/news/1998/11/98110602_nlt.html.

Wright, Lawrence. "The Man behind bin Laden." *The New Yorker*, September 16, 2002. http://www.newyorker.com/archive/2002/09/16/020916fa_fact2.

Zayyat, Montasser al. *The Road to al Qaeda: The Story of bin Laden's Right-hand Man*. Translated by Ahmed Fekry. New York: Pluto Press, 2004.

ZETAS, LOS

Los Zetas was formed in 1997 as the enforcement arm of the Gulf drug-trafficking organization based in Tamaulipas state in northeast Mexico. Osiel Cárdenas Guillén, who was competing for leadership of the organization, recruited about 30 members and former members of Mexico's Special Forces (GAFE), led by Lieutenant Arturo Guzmán Decenas. It is often claimed that some of these defectors had been trained by the United States. After Decenas was killed and his deputy captured, Heriberto Lazcano (also known as El Lazco or Z3) took over the leadership of the group.

After Cárdenas was arrested in 2003, Los Zetas became more directly involved in the drug business. In 2005 and 2006, the paramilitary force also played a major role in beating back the attempt by the Sinaloa organization to wrest control from Gulf in Nuevo Laredo, a key city for warehousing cocaine and moving it into the United States. In the process, Los Zetas developed a reputation for violence and brutality.

Indeed, Los Zetas broadened its role beyond protection and enforcement, extending its activities to people smuggling, kidnapping, extortion, and arms trafficking. In 2009, human rights and church groups claimed that the Zetas dominated both human trafficking and migrant kidnapping from Tabasco in the south to the border city of Reynosa in Tamaulipas. The same year reports surfaced that the Zetas had corrupted officials at Pemex, Mexico's national oil company, and had stolen between $70 million and $90 million worth of oil and fuel.

The paramilitary group also distanced itself from its employer, emerging as an independent entity that Samuel Logan termed the Zetas Organization. This transformation was linked in part to the death or arrest of most of the original members: in response, the group began to recruit more widely and, among others, brought in former Guatemalan Special Forces known as the Kaibiles. In 2005, reports suggested that the Kaibiles were assisting the Zetas with training new members. The Zetas also encouraged the emergence of a new trafficking organization, La Familia Michoacan, although this organization subsequently tried to expel Los Zetas from the state.

The size of Los Zetas remains uncertain, with estimates ranging from several dozen to several thousand. The uncertainty stems partly from the overlap between the Zetas and the Gulf trafficking organization, partly from the fact that the Zetas typically operate in small cells, and partly from the very fact of the Zetas brand name, which has become a byword for intimidation and encouraged a rash of imitators. Nevertheless, there is some evidence that the organization is larger and more extensive than often suspected. Since 2006, for example, the Zeta presence in the states of San Luis Potosi and Zacatecas has become very blatant, with members intimidating police and politicians and extorting a wide range of businesses. A clue to the size and scope of Los Zetas was found in the arrest in Monterrey in October 2009 of a high-ranking Zeta member in possession of envelopes containing bank deposit receipts for more than 4,000 people from all parts of Mexico. The operational capacity of Los Zetas is also impressive. In March 2010, when Army units clashed with about 40 Zetas in Nueva Leon, other Zetas blocked 31 roads in the Monterrey area. The Zetas organization also has a significant presence in Guatemala, where it has used corrupt policemen as informants.

All this suggests that Los Zetas remains powerful and has an extensive reach. It appears to do a good job in recruitment—in Veracruz state the group has recruited teenagers and trained them in

Federal police officers stand guard as seized weapons are shown to the media in Mexico City, October 22, 2010. Two people were arrested after the arsenal allegedly seized from Los Zetas drug cartel of high-power rifles, grenades and ammunition were found hidden in a horse trailer, according to police. (AP Photo/Miguel Tovar. © 2011 The Associated Press. All Rights Reserved)

weapons and tactics. The Zetas organization has also recruited women, who are known as Las Panteras. Other personnel branches have specialized tasks, such as warning, acquisition of weapons, and communications. The group even uses prostitutes, who can obtain valuable intelligence.

The emergence and evolution of Los Zetas can be understood as both a symptom and a cause of the militarization of the Mexican drug wars. In recent years competition among major trafficking organizations has intensified, while clashes between traffickers and the police and military have become more frequent. The Zetas have been at the heart of much of this violence. Yet, in an ultimate irony, in the early months of 2010 they found themselves facing an alliance of the Gulf and Sinaloa organizations and La Familia—one their former employer, the second their traditional enemy, and the third their protégé—all of whom claimed that the Zetas had undermined and discredited "true drug traffickers."

Philip Williams

See also Narcoterrorism

Further Readings

Campbell, Howard. *Drug War Zone: Frontline Dispatches from the Streets of El Paso and Juárez.* Austin: University of Texas Press, 2009.

Grayson, George W. "Los Zetas: the Ruthless Army Spawned by a Mexican Drug Cartel." Philadelphia: Foreign Policy Research Institute, May 2009. http://www.fpri.org/enotes/200805.grayson.loszetas.html.

Logan, Samuel. "Los Zetas: Evolution of a Criminal Organization." Zurich: International Relations and Security Network, March 11, 2009. http://www.isn.ethz.ch/isn/Current-Affairs/Security-Watch/Detail/?id=97554&lng=en.

Thompson, Barnard. "The Drug War in Mexico: By Any Other Name It's Terrorism." Mexidata.Info, August 9, 2010. http://www.mexidata.info/id2755.html.

ZUBAYDAH, ABU (1971–)

In March 2002, Abu Zubaydah (aka Zayn al-Abidin Muhammad Husayn), believed to be a top-level member of al Qaeda, was captured in eastern Pakistan. Since being taken into custody, Zubaydah has undergone intense interrogations by U.S. officials and has revealed information about possible terrorist attacks in the future. However, the nature and intensity of those interrogations have left the veracity of his statements open to question.

Zubaydah, a Saudi-born Palestinian, is believed to have been the chief of operations for Osama bin Laden's terrorist network. According to the testimony of the Ahmed Ressam, the Algerian terrorist convicted in the bin Laden–supported Y2K bombing plot, Zubaydah vetted recruits for the various terrorist training camps in Afghanistan, working out of the "House of Martyrs," an al Qaeda compound in Peshawar, Pakistan. Zubaydah also briefed newly trained terrorists and coordinated travel and other activities for the vast international network of terrorist cells.

Zubaydah's relationship with bin Laden can be traced to the mid-1990s, when Islamic Jihad, Ayman al Zawahiri's Egypt-based terrorist group, merged with al Qaeda. Zubaydah, then a member of Islamic Jihad, rose quickly to become a top al Qaeda lieutenant. By age 25, he was running bin Laden's camps.

Zubaydah has also been linked to numerous recent terrorist plots, including Ressam's Y2K plot and another millennium plot in Jordan (for which he was sentenced to death, in absentia, in Jordan). He allegedly recruited individuals to carry out bombing plots against U.S. embassies in Paris and Sarajevo. Authorities suspect Zubaydah was a "field commander" for the attack on the USS *Cole* in Yemen in October 2000. He is also believed to have briefed Richard Reid, the alleged "shoe bomber." Zubaydah is assumed to have had a significant role in coordinating the September 11, 2001, attacks on New York City's World Trade Center and the Pentagon, just outside Washington, D.C. Reports suggest that he hand-picked at least three of the hijackers.

Zubaydah apparently took over as chief of military operations for al Qaeda after Muhammad Atef was killed in a November 2001 bombing raid in Afghanistan. With Atef dead, and bin Laden and Zawahiri in hiding, the responsibility for reviving the terrorist network, including activating "sleeper cells" in various countries, fell to Zubaydah.

On March 28, 2002, U.S. and Pakistani forces raided a safe house in Faisalabad, Pakistan, capturing two-dozen Arabs. Zubaydah was shot in the stomach, groin, and thigh. During his recovery, he was interrogated, first in a secret CIA prison, and subsequently at the Guantánamo Bay facility, where he was moved in 2004. In the course of these interrogations, Zubaydah was waterboarded as many as 80 times. Officials suspected that Zubaydah knew the identities and locations of sleeper cells throughout the world, and may also have information regarding the whereabouts of bin Laden and other top al Qaeda figures, including Khaled Sheik Mohammed. Official opinions about the veracity of Zubaydah's statements have varied, although some have proved to be accurate.

Laura Lambert

See also al Qaeda; bin Laden, Osama; Reid, Richard; Ressam, Ahmed; September 11 Attacks; Y2K Plot

Further Readings

Burke, Jason. "How the Perfect Terrorist Plotted the Ultimate Crime." *The Observer*, April 7, 2002.

Burns, John F. "A Nation Challenged: The Fugitives; In Pakistan's Interior, a Troubling Victory in Hunt for al Qaeda." *The New York Times*, April 14, 2002. p. 20.

Gunaratna, Rohan. *Inside al Qaeda: Global Network of Terror*. New York: Columbia University Press, 2002.

Reeve, Simon. *The New Jackals: Ramzi Yousef, Osama bin Laden and the Future of Terrorism*. Boston: Northeastern University Press, 1999.

Shenon, Philip, and James Risen. "A Nation Challenged: Bin Laden's Network; al Qaeda Leader Is Reported to Plan New Raids on US." *The New York Times*, February 13, 2002. p. A1.

Bibliography

Note: Books may be listed under more than one category.

General

Anderson, Sean, and Stephen Sloan. *Historical Dictionary of Terrorism.* 2nd ed. Lanham, MD: Scarecrow, 2002.

Bell, J. Bower. *Transnational Terror.* Washington, DC: American Enterprise Institute, 1975.

Carr, Caleb. *The Lessons of Terrorism: A History of Warfare against Civilians: Why It Has Always Failed and Why It Will Fail Again.* New York: Random House, 2002.

Chaliand, Gerald. *Terrorism: From Popular Struggle to Media Spectacle.* Atlantic Highlands, NJ: Saqi, 1987.

Clutterbuck, Richard. *Terrorism in an Unstable World.* New York: Routledge, 1994.

Cragin, Kim, et al. *Sharing the Dragon's Teeth: Terrorist Groups and the Exchange of New Technologies.* Santa Monica, CA: RAND Corporation, 2007.

Crelinsten, Ronald D., and Denis Szabo. *Hostage-taking.* Lexington, MA: Lexington Books, 1979.

Eager, Paige Whaley. *From Freedom Fighters to Terrorists: Women and Political Violence.* Burlington, VT: Ashgate, 2008.

Freedman, Lawrence Zelic, and Yonah Alexander, eds. *Perspectives on Terrorism.* Wilmington, DE: Scholarly Resources, 1983.

Gardner, Hall. *American Global Strategy and the "War on Terrorism."* Aldershot, UK: Ashgate, 2005.

Gay, Kathleen. *Encyclopedia of Political Anarchy.* Santa Barbara, CA: ABC-CLIO, 1999.

Haberfeld, M. R., and Agostino von Hassell, eds. *A New Understanding of Terrorism: Case Studies, Trajectories, and Lessons Learned.* New York: Springer, 2009.

Hacker, Frederick J. *Criminals, Crusaders, Crazies: Terror and Terrorism in Our Time.* New York: W.W. Norton, 1976.

Heiberg, Marianne, Brendan O'Leary, and John Tirman, eds. *Terror, Insurgency, and the State: Ending Protracted Conflicts.* Philadelphia: University of Pennsylvania Press, 2007.

Hewitt, Christopher. *Understanding Terrorism in America: From the Klan to al Qaeda.* London and New York: Routledge, 2003.

Hoffman, Bruce. *Inside Terrorism.* New York: Columbia University Press, 1998.

Holmes, Jennifer S. *Terrorism and Democratic Stability Revisited.* Manchester, UK: Manchester University Press, 2008.

Huntington, Samuel P. *The Clash of Civilizations and the Remaking of World Order.* New York: Simon & Schuster, 1996.

Jenkins, Brian. *International Terrorism: The Other World War.* Santa Monica, CA: RAND Corporation, 1985.

Köcher, Hans, ed. *Terrorism and National Liberation: Proceedings of the International Conference on the Question of Terrorism.* Frankfurt: Peter Lang, 1988.

Kushner, Harvey W., ed. *The Future of Terrorism: Violence in the New Millennium.* Thousand Oaks, CA: Sage, 1998.

Laqueur, Walter. *The New Terrorism: Fanaticism and the Arms of Mass Destruction.* New York: Oxford University Press, 1999.

Laqueur, Walter. *History of Terrorism.* New York: Transaction Publishers, 2001.

Lutz, James M., and Brenda J. Lutz. *Global Terrorism.* 2nd ed. New York: Routledge, 2008.

Martin, Gus. *Essentials of Terrorism: Concepts and Controversies.* 2nd ed. Thousand Oaks, CA: Sage, 2011.

McKnight, Gerald. *The Terrorist Mind: Why They Hijack, Kidnap, Bomb and Kill.* New York: Bobbs-Merrill, 1974.

Mitchell, Thomas G. *When Peace Fails: Lessons from Belfast for the Middle East.* Jefferson, NC: McFarland, 2010.

Mueller, Robert. *Atomic Obsession: Nuclear Alarmism from Hiroshima to Al Qaeda.* New York: Routledge, 2009.

Netanyahu, Benjamin. *The Terrorism Reader*. New York: Meridian, 1986.

Ochberg, Frank M., and David A. Soskis, eds. *Victims of Terrorism*. Boulder, CO: Westview, 1982.

Reich, Walter, ed. *Origins of Terrorism: Psychologies, Ideologies, Theologies, States of Mind*. Washington, DC: Woodrow Wilson Center Press, 1998.

Richardson, Louise. *What Terrorists Want: Understanding the Enemy, Containing the Threat*. New York: Random House, 2006.

Rose, Gideon, and James F. Hoge. *How Did This Happen? Terrorism and the New War*. New York: Public Affairs, 2001.

Segaller, Stephen. *Invisible Armies: Terrorism in the 1990s*. San Diego, CA: Harcourt Brace Jovanovich, 1987.

Smith, Brent L. *Terrorism in America: Pipe Bombs and Pipe Dreams*. Albany: State University of New York Press, 1994.

Stern, Jessica. *Terror in the Name of God: Why Religious Militants Kill*. New York: Ecco, 2008.

Surrat, Robin, ed. *The Middle East*. 9th ed. Washington, DC: CQ Press, 2000.

Tuman, Joseph S. *Communicating Terror: The Rhetorical Dimensions of Terrorism*. London: Sage, 2003.

U.S. Department of State. *Patterns of Global Terrorism*. Washington, DC [Annual].

White, Jonathan R. *Terrorism and Homeland Security*. Belmont, CA: Wadsworth, 2009.

Whittaker, David J., ed. *The Terrorism Reader*. London and New York: Routledge, 2001.

Wiktorowicz, Quintan. *Islamic Activism: A Social Movement Theory Approach*. Bloomington: Indiana University Press, 2004.

Wiktorowicz, Quintan. *Radical Islam Rising*. Lanham, MD: Rowman, & Littlefield, 2005.

Zeskind, Leonard. *Blood and Politics: The History of the White Nationalist Movement from the Margins to the Mainstream*. New York: Farrar, Straus and Giroux, 2009.

Counterterrorism

Aid, Matthew. *The Secret Sentry: The Untold History of the National Security Agency*. New York: Bloomsbury, 2010.

Alexander, Matthew, with John R. Bruning. *How to Break a Terrorist: The U.S. Investigators Who Used Brains, Not Brutality, to Take Down the Deadliest Man in Iraq*. New York: Free Press, 2008.

Batvinis, Raymond J. *The Origins of FBI Counterintelligence*. Lawrence: University Press of Kansas, 2009.

Berntsen, Gary. *Human Intelligence, Counterterrorism, and National Leadership: A Practical Guide*. Dulles, VA: Potomac Books, 2008.

Beyer, Cornelia, and Michael Bauer, eds. *Effectively Countering Terrorism: The Challenges of Prevention, Preparedness and Response*. Eastbourne, East Sussex, UK: Sussex Academic Press, 2009.

Bolz, Frank, Jr., Kenneth J. Dudonis, and David P. Schulz. *The Counter-terrorism Handbook: Tactics, Procedures, and Techniques*. 3rd ed. Boca Raton, FL: Taylor & Francis, 2005.

Borrelli, J. V. *Bioterrorism: Prevention, Preparedness, and Protection*. New York: Nova Science Publishers, 2007.

Bullock, Jane, George Haddow, Damon P. Coppola, and Sarp Yeletaysi. *Introduction to Homeland Security, Third Edition: Principles of All-hazards Response*. Burlington, MA: Butterworth-Heinemann, 2009.

Burton, Fred. *Ghost: Confessions of a Counterterrorism Agent*. New York: Random House, 2008.

Coen, Bob, and Eric Nadler. *Dead Silence: Fear and Terror on the Anthrax Trail*. Berkeley, CA: Counterpoint, 2009.

Cole, Leonard. *The Anthrax Letters: A Medical Detective Story*. Washington, DC: Joseph Henry Press, 2003.

Coll, Steve. *Ghost Wars: The Secret History of the CIA, Afghanistan, and bin Laden, from the Soviet Invasion to September 10, 2001*. New York: Penguin, 2004.

Cortright, David, and George A. Lopez, with Richard W. Conroy, Jaleh Dashti-Gibson, and Julia Wagler. *The Sanctions Decade: Assessing UN Strategies in the 1990s*. Boulder, CO: Lynne Rienner, 2000.

Das, Dilip K., and Peter C. Kratcoski. *Meeting the Challenges of Global Terrorism: Prevention, Control, and Recovery*. Lanham, MD: Lexington Books, 2003.

Davis, Paul K., ed. *New Challenges for Defense Planning: Rethinking How Much Is Enough*. Santa Monica, CA: RAND Corporation, 1994.

Dickey, Christopher. *Securing the City: Inside America's Best Counterterror Force—the NYPD*. New York: Simon & Schuster, 2009.

Dolnik, Adam, and Keith M. Fitzgerald. *Negotiating Hostage Crises with the New Terrorists*. Westport, CT: Praeger, 2007.

Donohue, Laura K. *The Cost of Counterterrorism: Power, Politics, and Liberty*. Cambridge, UK: Cambridge University Press, 2008.

Dorn, Nicholas, Karim Murji, and Nigel South. *Traffickers: Drug Markets and Law Enforcement*. London and New York: Routledge, 1992.

Esposito, Richard, and Ted Gerstein. *Bomb Squad: A Year Inside the Nation's Most Exclusive Police Unit*. New York: Hyperion, 2007.

Ganor, Boaz. *The Counter-terrorism Puzzle: A Guide for Decision Makers.* New Brunswick, NJ: Transaction Publishers, 2005.

Ginbar, V. *Why Not Torture Terrorists?* Oxford: Oxford University Press, 2008.

Graff, Garrett M. *The Threat Matrix: The FBI at War in the Age of Global Terror.* New York: Little, Brown, 2011.

Gregg, Judd, ed. *Counterterrorism and Infrastructure Protection: Hearing before the Committee on Appropriations.* Collingdale, PA: Diane Publishing, 1999.

Harclerode, Peter. *Secret Soldiers: Special Forces in the War against Terrorism.* London: Cassell, 2000.

Harris, Daniel C. *Combating Terrorism: FBI's Use of Federal Funds for Counterterrorism and Related Activities, 1995–98.* Collingdale, PA: Diane Publishing, 1998.

Hashim, Ahmed S. *Insurgency and Counterinsurgency in Iraq.* Ithaca, NY: Cornell University Press, 2006.

Howard, Russell, James Forest, and Joanne C. Moore. *Homeland Security and Terrorism: Readings and Interpretations.* New York: McGraw-Hill, 2006.

Hulnick, Arthur S. *Keeping Us Safe: Secret Intelligence and Homeland Security.* Santa Barbara, CA: Praeger, 2004.

International Policy Institute for Counter Terrorism. *Countering Suicide Terrorism.* 2nd ed. New York: Anti-Defamation League of B'nai B'rith, 2002.

Jacobson, Michael. *The West at War: U.S. and European Counterterrorism Efforts, Post 9/11.* Washington, DC: Washington Institute for Near East Policy, 2006.

Jenkins, Brian Michael. *No Path to Glory: Deterring Homegrown Terrorism—Testimony Presented before the House Homeland Security Committee, Subcommittee on Intelligence, Information Sharing and Terrorism Risk Assessment on May 26, 2010.* RAND Corporation Report CT-348 (May 2010). Santa Clara, CA: RAND Corporation. http://www.rand.org/pubs/testimonies/2010/RAND_CT348.pdf.

Jones, George. *Vengeance: The True Story of an Israeli Counter-terrorist Team.* New York: Simon & Schuster, 2005.

Katona, Peter, Michael D. Intriligator, and John P. Sullivan, eds. *Countering Terrorism and WMD: Creating a Global Counter-terrorism Network.* London: Routledge, 2006.

Kushner, Harvey W. *Terrorism in America: A Structured Approach to Understanding the Terrorist Threat.* Springfield, IL: Charles C Thomas, 1998.

Lesser, Ian O., et al. *Countering the New Terrorism.* Santa Monica, CA: RAND Corporation, 1999.

Levitt, Geoffrey M. *Democracies against Terror: The Western Response to State-sponsored Terrorism.* New York: Praeger, 1988.

Livingston, Neil C., and Terrell E. Arnold, eds. *Fighting Back: Winning the War against Terrorism.* Lexington, MA: Lexington Books, 1986.

MacWillson, Alastair C. *Hostage-taking Terrorism: Incident-response Strategy.* New York: St. Martin's, 1992.

McCoy, Alfred W., Cathleen B. Read, and Leonard Palmer Adams. *The Politics of Heroin: CIA Complicity in the Global Drug Trade.* Rev. and exp. ed. New York: Lawrence Hill, 1991.

Miller, Abraham H. *Terrorism and Hostage Negotiations.* Boulder, CO: Westview, 1980.

Mockaitis, Thomas R., and Paul B. Rich. *Grand Strategy in the War against Terrorism.* London: Frank Cass, 2003.

Monje, Scott C. *The Central Intelligence Agency: A Documentary History.* Westport, CT: Greenwood, 2008.

Naftali, Timothy. *Blind Sport: The Secret History of American Counterterrorism.* New York: Basic Books, 2005.

Netanyahu, Benjamin. *Fighting Terrorism: How Democracies Can Defeat Domestic and International Terrorism.* New York: Farrar, Straus and Giroux, 1995.

Pedahzur, Ami. *The Israeli Secret Services and the Struggle against Terrorism.* New York: Columbia University Press, 2010.

Perkins, Samuel. *Homegrown Terror and American Jihadists: Assessing the Threat.* Hauppauge, NY: Nova Publishers, 2011.

Pushies, Fred J. *Deadly Blue: Battle Stories of the U.S. Air Force Special Operations Command.* New York: American Management Association, 2009.

Rothkopf, David J. *Running the World: The Inside Story of the National Security Council and the Architects of American Power.* New York: Public Affairs, 2005.

Rubin, Barry, ed. *The Politics of Counterterrorism: The Ordeal of Democratic States.* Washington, DC: Johns Hopkins University Foreign Policy Institute, 1990.

Schawb, Stephen Irving Max. *Guantánamo, USA: The Untold History of America's Cuban Outpost.* Lawrence: University Press of Kansas, 2009.

Scheuer, Michael. *Imperial Hubris: Why the West Is Losing the War on Terror.* Dulles, VA: Potomac Books, 2005.

Schwartau, Winn. *CyberShock: Surviving Hackers, Phreakers, Identity Thieves, Internet Terrorists, and Weapons of Mass Disruption.* New York: Thunder's Mouth, 2000.

Shulsky, Abram N. *Silent Warfare: Understanding the World of Intelligence.* 2nd ed. Revised by Gary J. Schmitt. Washington, DC: Brassey's, 1993.

Siljander, Raymond P. *Terrorist Attacks: A Protective Service Guide for Executives, Bodyguards and Policemen.* Springfield, IL: Charles C Thomas, 1980.

Sloan, Stephen. *Simulating Terrorism.* Norman: University of Oklahoma Press, 1981.

Smith, Michael. *Killer Elite: The Inside Story of America's Most Secret Special Operations Team.* New York: St. Martin's, 2006.

Snyder, Rodney A. *Negotiating with Terrorists: TWA Flight 847.* Pew Case Studies in International Affairs Case 333. Pittsburgh, PA: Pew Charitable Trusts, 1994.

St. John, Peter. *Air Piracy, Airport Security, and International Terrorism: Winning the War against Hijackers.* New York: Quorum, 1991.

Thomas, Gordon. *Gideon's Spies: The Secret History of the Mossad.* 5th ed. New York: St. Martin's, 2009.

Tophoven, Rolf. *GSG 9: German Response to Terrorism.* Koblenz, Germany: Bernard and Graefe, 1984.

U.S. Department of the Army. *U.S. Army Intelligence and Interrogation Handbook.* Guildford, CT: The Lyons Press, 2005.

Wardlaw, Grant. *Political Terrorism: Theory, Tactics, and Counter-measures.* New York: Cambridge University Press, 1989.

Whitcomb, Christopher. *COLD ZERO: Inside the FBI Hostage Rescue Team.* New York: Little, Brown, 2001.

White, Jonathan R. *Terrorism and Homeland Security.* Belmont, CA: Wadsworth, 2009.

Wolf, John B. *Fear of Fear: A Survey of Terrorist Operations and Controls in Open Societies.* New York: Plenum, 1981.

Worthington, Andy. *The Guantánamo Files.* Ann Arbor: Pluto Press, 2007.

Yallop, H. J. *Protection against Terrorism.* Chichester, UK: Barry Rose, 1980.

Culture and Ideology of Terrorism

Alali, A. Odasuo, and Kenoye Kelvin Eke, eds. *Media Coverage of Terrorism: Methods of Diffusion.* Newbury Park, CA: Sage, 1991.

Alexander, Yonah, and Richard Latter, eds. *Terrorism & the Media: Dilemmas for Government, Journalists & the Public.* Washington, DC: Brassey's, 1990.

Bar, Shmuel. *Warrant for Terror: Fatwas of Radical Islam and the Duty of Jihad.* Lanham, MD: Rowman & Littlefield, 2006.

Berko, Anat. *The Path to Paradise: The Inner World of Suicide Bombers.* Westport, CT: Praeger Security International, 2009.

Best, Steven, and Anthony J. Nocella II, eds. *Igniting a Revolution: Voices in Defense of the Earth.* Oakland, CA: AK Press, 2006.

Brabazon, T. *Thinking Popular Culture: War, Terrorism, and Writing.* Burlington, VT: Ashgate, 2008.

Clutterbuck, Richard. *The Media and Political Violence.* London: Macmillan, 1981.

Cook, David. *Understanding Jihad.* Berkeley: University of California Press, 2005.

Dolnik, Adam. *Understanding Terrorist Innovation: Technology, Tactics and Global Trends.* London: Routledge, 2007.

Forest, James J.F., ed. *The Making of a Terrorist: Recruitment, Training, and Root Causes.* Vol. 2, *Training.* Westport, CT: Praeger Security International, 2006.

Gerges, Fawaz A. *The Far Enemy: Why Jihad Went Global.* Cambridge, UK: Cambridge University Press, 2009.

Glucklich, Ariel. *Dying for Heaven: Holy Pleasure and Suicide Bombers.* New York: HarperOne, 2009.

Gonzalez-Perez, Margaret. *Women and Terrorism: Female Activity in Domestic and International Terror Groups.* New York: Routledge, 2009.

Hafez, Mohammed M. *Suicide Bombers in Iraq: The Strategy and Ideology of Martyrdom.* Washington, DC: United States Institute of Peace, 2007.

Han, Henry H., ed. *Terrorism and Political Violence: Limits and Possibilities of Legal Control.* New York: Oceana Publications, 1993.

Johnson, James Turner. *The Holy War Idea in Western and Islamic Traditions.* University Park: Pennsylvania State University Press, 2002.

Juergensmeyer, Mark. *Terror in the Mind of God: The Global Rise of Religious Violence.* Updated ed. Berkeley: University of California Press, 2001.

Kavoori, Anandam P., and Todd Fraley, eds. *Media, Terrorism, and Theory: A Reader.* Lanham, MD: Rowman & Littlefield, 2006.

Keane, Michael. *Dictionary of Modern Strategy and Tactics.* Annapolis, MD: Naval Institute Press, 2005.

Kelsay, John, and James Turner Johnson, eds. *Just War and Jihad: Historical and Theoretical Perspectives on War and Peace in Western and Islamic Tradition.* New York: Greenwood, 1991.

Kressel, Neil J. *Bad Faith: The Danger of Religious Extremism.* Amherst, NY: Prometheus Books, 2007.

Kropotkin, Peter. *The Black Flag: Peter Kropotkin on Anarchism.* St. Petersburg, FL: Red and Black Publishers, 2010.

Kurst-Swanger, Karl. *Worship and Sin: An Exploration of Religion-related Crime in the United States.* New York: Peter Lang, 2008.

Marshall, Peter. *Demanding the Impossible: A History of Anarchism.* Oakland, CA: PM Press, 2010.

Martin, A., and P. Petro, eds. *Rethinking Global Security. Media, Popular Culture, and the "War on Terror."* New Brunswick, NJ: Rutgers University Press, 2006.

Mohaddessin, Mohammad. *Islamic Fundamentalism: The New Global Threat.* Washington, DC: Seven Locks, 1993.

Morgan, Robin. *The Demon Lover: On the Sexuality of Terrorism.* New York: W.W. Norton, 1989.

Nacos, Brigitte L. *Mass-mediated Terrorism: The Central Role of the Media in Terrorism and Counterterrorism.* 2nd ed. Lanham, MD: Rowman & Littlefield, 2007.

Ness, Cindy D. *Female Terrorism and Militancy: Agency, Utility, and Organization.* New York: Routledge, 2008.

Oliverio, Annamarie. *The State of Terror: SUNY Series in Deviance and Social Control.* Albany: State University of New York Press, 1998.

Palmer, Nancy, ed. *Terrorism, War, and the Press.* Cambridge, MA: The Joan Shorenstein Center on the Press, Politics and Public Policy, 2003.

Pape, Robert Anthony. *Dying to Win: The Strategic Logic of Suicide Terrorism.* New York: Random House, 2005.

Perkins, Samuel. *Homegrown Terror and American Jihadists: Assessing the Threat.* Hauppauge, NY: Nova Publishers, 2011.

Peters, Rudolph. *Jihad in Classical and Modern Islam.* Princeton, NJ: Markus Wiener, 1996.

Picard, Robert G. *Media Portrayal of Terrorism: Functions and Meaning of News Coverage.* Ames: Iowa State University Press, 1993.

Purkis, Jon, and James Bowen, eds. *Twenty-first Century Anarchism: Unorthodox Ideas for a New Millennium.* London: Cassell, 1997.

Quarles, Chester L. *Christian Identity: The Aryan American Bloodline Religion.* Jefferson, NC: McFarland, 2004.

Rashid, Ahmed. *Jihad: The Rise of Militant Islam in Central Asia.* New Haven, CT: Yale University Press, 2002.

Reich, Walter, ed. *Origins of Terrorism: Psychologies, Ideologies, Theologies, States of Mind.* Washington, DC: Woodrow Wilson Center Press, 1998.

Rubenstein, Richard E. *Alchemists of Revolution: Terrorism in the Modern World.* New York: Basic Books, 1987.

Schmid, Alex P., and Janny de Graaf. *Violence as Communication: Insurgent Terrorism and the Western News Media.* London: Sage, 1982.

Schopp, A., and M. B. Hill, eds. *The War on Terror and American Popular Culture.* Teaneck, NJ: Fairleigh Dickinson University Press, 2009.

Sjoberg, Laura, and Caron E. Gentry. *Mothers, Monsters, Whores: Women's Violence in Global Politics.* London: Zed Books, 2007.

Sonn, Richard D. *Anarchism.* New York: Twayne, 1992.

Spaaij, Ramon. *Lone-wolf Terrorism.* The Hague, Netherlands: COT Institute for Safety, Security and Crisis Management, 2007.

Stern, Jessica. *Terror in the Name of God: Why Religious Militants Kill.* New York: Ecco, 2008.

Thiel, M., ed. *The "Militant Democracy" Principle in Modern Democracies.* Aldershot, UK: Ashgate, 2009.

Tuman, Joseph S. *Communicating Terror: The Rhetorical Dimensions of Terrorism.* 2nd ed. London: Sage, 2010.

Weber, Eugen. *Apocalypses: Prophesies, Cults, and Millennial Beliefs through the Ages.* Cambridge, MA: Harvard University Press, 1999.

Zeskind, Leonard. *Blood and Politics: The History of the White Nationalist Movement from the Margins to the Mainstream.* New York: Farrar, Straus and Giroux, 2009.

Economics, Politics, and the Law

Adams, James. *The Financing of Terrorism: How the Groups That Are Terrorizing the World Get the Money to Do It.* New York: Simon & Schuster, 1986.

Antokol, Norman, and Mayer Nudell. *No One a Neutral: Political Hostage-taking in the Modern World.* Medina, OH: Alpha, 1990.

Ashcroft, John. *Never Again: Securing America and Restoring Justice.* New York: Center Street, 2006.

Baker, Stewart A. *Patriot Debates: Experts Debate the USA Patriot Act.* Chicago: American Bar Association, 2005.

Bazan, Elizabeth B., ed. *The Foreign Intelligence Surveillance Act: Overview and Modifications.* Hauppauge, NY: Nova Science Publishers, 2008.

Becker, Tal. *Terrorism and the State: Rethinking the Rules of State Responsibility.* Portland, OR: Hart Publishing, 2006.

Beckman, James. *Comparative Legal Approaches to Homeland Security and Anti-terrorism.* Aldershot, UK: Ashgate, 2007.

Bianchi, Andrea, ed. *Enforcing International Law Norms against Terrorism.* Oxford, UK: Hart Publishing, 2004.

Biersteker, Thomas J., and Sue E. Eckert, eds. *Countering the Financing of Terrorism.* London: Routledge, 2008.

Bonner, D. *Executive Measures, Terrorism and National Security*. Aldershot, UK: Ashgate, 2007.

Byman, Daniel. *Deadly Connections: States that Sponsor Terrorism*. Cambridge, UK: Cambridge University Press, 2007.

Clarke, Richard A. *Against All Enemies*. New York: Free Press, 2004.

Crenshaw, Martha. *Terrorism, Legitimacy, and Power*. Middletown, CT: Wesleyan University Press, 1983.

Donohue, Laura K. *The Cost of Counterterrorism: Power, Politics, and Liberty*. Cambridge, UK: Cambridge University Press, 2008.

Drake, Laura. *Hegemony and Its Discontents: United States Policy toward Iraq, Iran, Hamas, the Hezbollah and Their Responses*. Annandale, VA: United Association for Studies and Research, 1997.

Duffy, H. *The "War on Terror" and the Framework of International Law*. Cambridge, UK: Cambridge University Press, 2005.

Durham, Martin. *White Rage: The Extreme Right and American Politics*. New York: Routledge, 2007.

Elias, Bartholomew. *Airport and Aviation Security: U.S. Policy and Strategy in the Age of Global Terrorism*. Boca Raton, FL: Auerbach Publications/Taylor & Francis, 2010.

Enders, Walter, and Todd Sandler. *The Political Economy of Terrorism*. New York: Cambridge University Press, 2006.

Fisher, Barry A.J., William Tilstone, and Catherine Woytowicz. *Introduction to Criminalistics: The Foundation of Forensic Science*. Burlington, MA: Elsevier Academic Press, 2009.

Gardner, Hall. *American Global Strategy and the "War on Terrorism."* Aldershot, UK: Ashgate, 2005.

Goldstein, Joshua S. *The Real Price of War: How You Pay for the War on Terror*. New York: New York University Press, 2004.

Gross, O., and F. Ní Aoláin. *Law in Times of Crisis*. Cambridge, UK: Cambridge University Press, 2006.

Gurr, Ted Robert. *Handbook of Political Conflict: Theory and Research*. New York: Free Press, 1980.

Haimes Yacov Y. *Risk Modeling, Assessment, and Management*. Hoboken, NJ: Wiley-Interscience, 2004.

Han, Henry H., ed. *Terrorism & Political Violence: Limits & Possibilities of Legal Control*. New York: Oceana, 1993.

Herman, Edward S. *The Real Terror Network: Terrorism in Fact and Propaganda*. Boston: South End, 1982.

Honigsberg, Peter Jan. *Our Nation Unhinged: The Human Consequences of the War on Terror*. Berkeley: University of California Press, 2009.

Inderfurth, Karl F., and Loch K. Johnson, eds. *Fateful Decisions: Inside the National Security Council*. New York: Oxford University Press, 2004.

Kushner, Harvey W., ed. *Essential Readings on Political Terrorism: Analyses of Problems and Prospects for the 21st Century*. New York: Gordian Knot, 2002.

Lakdawalla, Darius, and George Zanjani. *Insurance, Self-protection, and the Economics of Terrorism*. Santa Monica, CA: RAND Corporation, 2004.

Lewis, Bernard. *The Political Language of Islam*. Chicago: University of Chicago Press, 1988.

Lipset, Seymour Martin, and Earl Raab. *The Politics of Unreason: Right-wing Extremism in America, 1790–1977*. 2nd ed. Chicago: University of Chicago Press, 1978.

Marguiles, Joseph. *Guantanamo and the Abuse of Presidential Power*. New York: Simon & Schuster, 2006.

McEvoy, Joanne. *The Politics of Northern Ireland*. Edinburgh: University of Edinburgh Press, 2008.

Merkl, Peter H., ed. *Political Violence and Terror: Motifs and Motivations*. Berkeley: University of California Press, 1986.

Michel-Kerjan, E., and P. Raschky. *The Effects of Government Intervention in the Market for Corporate Terrorism Insurance*. Working paper. Philadelphia: The Wharton School, University of Pennsylvania, 2010.

Napoleoni, Loretta. *Terror Incorporated: Tracing the Dollars behind the Terror Networks*. New York: Seven Stories Press, 2005.

Nesi, Giuseppe, ed. *International Cooperation in Counter-terrorism: The United Nations and Regional Organizations in the Fight against Terrorism*. Aldershot, UK: Ashgate, 2006.

Orttung, Robert, and Andrey Makarychev, eds. *National Counter-terrorism Strategies: Legal, Institutional, and Public Policy Dimensions in the US, UK, France, Turkey, and Russia*. NATO Security through Science Series E: Human and Societal Dynamics, Vol. 14. Amsterdam: IOS Press, 2006.

Pillar, Paul R., and Michael H. Armacost. *Terrorism and U.S. Foreign Policy*. Washington, DC: Brookings Institution Press, 2001.

Poland, James M., and Michael J. McCrystle. *Practical, Tactical, and Legal Perspectives of Terrorism and Hostage-taking*. Lewiston, NY: E. Mellon, 1999.

Roth, John, et al. *Monograph on Terrorist Financing*. Washington, DC: National Commission on Terrorist Attacks upon the United States (9/11 Commission), 2010. http://govinfo.library.unt.edu/911/staff_statements/index.htm.

Schamis, Gerardo Jorge. *War and Terrorism in International Affairs*. New Brunswick, NJ: Transaction Publishers, 1980.

Schott, Paul Allen. *Reference Guide to Anti-money Laundering and Combating the Financing of Terrorism*. 2nd ed. Washington, DC: International Bank for Reconstruction and Development/The World Bank, 2006.

Shah, Niaz A. *Self-Defense in Islamic and International Law*. New York: Palgrave Macmillan, 2008.

Singular, Steven. *The Wichita Divide: The Murder of Dr. George Tiller, the Battle over Abortion, and the New Civil War*. New York: St. Martin's, 2011.

Smith, Cary Stacy. *The Patriot Act: Issues and Controversies*. Springfield, IL: Charles C Thomas, 2010.

Staun, Jørgen, Kasper Ege, and Ann-Sophie Hemmingsen. *The Evolving Threat of Terrorism in Policymaking and Media Discourse*. The Hague, Netherlands: COT Institute for Safety, Security and Crisis Management, 2008.

Tanter, Raymond. *Rogue Regimes: Terrorism & Proliferation*. New York: St. Martin's, 1998.

Walker, Clive. *The Law and Terrorism*. Oxford: Oxford University Press, 2011.

Walter, Ingo. *Secret Money: The World of International Financial Secrecy*. London: Allen and Unwin, 1985.

Wardlaw, Grant. *Political Terrorism: Theory, Tactics, and Counter-measures*. New York: Cambridge University Press, 1989.

Weiss, Thomas George, David P. Forsythe, and Roger A. Coate. *The United Nations and Changing World Politics*. 3rd ed. Boulder, CO: Westview, 2001.

Wills, Henry H., et al. *Estimating Terrorism Risk*. Santa Monica, CA: RAND Corporation, 2005.

Woo, Gordon. *Quantifying Insurance Terrorism Risk*. Newark, CA: Risk Management Solutions, 2002.

Zabel, Richard B. *In Pursuit of Justice: Prosecuting Terrorism Cases in the Federal Courts*. New York: Human Rights First, 2008.

Zinn, Howard. *Terrorism and War*. New York: Seven Stories, 2002.

Ziring, Lawrence, Robert E. Riggs, and Jack C. Plano. *The United Nations: International Organization and World Politics*. 3rd ed. Fort Worth, TX: Harcourt College, 2000.

Individuals, Groups, and Events

Aburish, Said K. *Arafat: From Defender to Dictator*. New York: Bloomsbury, 1998.

Akhahenda, Elijah F. *When Blood and Tears United a Country: The Bombing of the American Embassy in Kenya*. Lanham, MD: University Press of America/Rowman & Littlefield, 2002.

Alegría, Claribel, and Darwin Flakoll. *Tunnel to Canto Grande: The Story of the Most Daring Prison Escape in Latin American History*. Translated by Darwin Flakoll. Willimantic, CT: Curbstone, 1996.

Anderson, Jon Lee. *Che Guevara: A Revolutionary Life*. New York: Grove, 1997.

Anderson, Terry A. *Den of Lions: Memoirs of Seven Years*. New York: Crown, 1993.

Atwan, Abdel Bari. *The Secret History of al Qaeda*. Berkeley: University of California Press, 2006.

Ayers, Bill. *Fugitive Days: A Memoir*. Boston: Beacon Press, 2001.

Baer, Robert. *See No Evil: The True Story of a Ground Soldier in the CIA's War on Terrorism*. New York: Crown, 2002.

Bar-Zohar, Michael, and Eitan Haber. *The Quest for the Red Prince*. New York: William Morrow, 1983.

Bauer, Karin, ed. *Everybody Talks about the Weather . . . We Don't: The Writings of Ulrike Meinhof*. New York: Seven Stories Press, 2008.

Becker, Jillian. *Hitler's Children: The Story of the Baader-Meinhof Terrorist Gang*. Philadelphia: J. B. Lippincott, 1977.

Bergen, Peter I. *A Very Long War: The History of the War on Terror and the Battles with al Qaeda Since 9/11*. New York: Free Press, 2011.

Betancourt, Ingrid. *Even Silence Has an End: My Six Years of Captivity in the Colombian Jungle*. New York: Penguin, 2010.

Blundy, David, and Andrew Lycett. *Qaddafi and the Libyan Revolution*. Boston: Little, Brown, 1987.

Bodansky, Yossef. *Bin Laden: The Man Who Declared War on America*. Rocklin, CA: Forum, 1999.

Braudy, Susan. *Family Circle: The Boudins and the Aristocracy of the Left*. New York: Alfred A. Knopf, 2003.

Busic, Julienne Eden. *Lovers and Madmen: A True Story of Passion, Politics, and Air Piracy*. San Jose, CA: Writers Club Press, 2000.

Busic, Julienne Eden. *Your Blood and Mine*. Raleigh, NC: Lulu Enterprises, 2010.

Cambanis, Thanassis. *A Privilege to Die: Inside Hezbollah's Legions and Their Endless War against Israel*. New York: Free Press, 2010.

Carlson, Kurt. *One American Must Die: A Hostage's Personal Account of the Hijacking of Flight 847*. New York: Congdon and Weed, 1986.

Castellucci, John. *Big Dance: The Untold Story of Weather-man Kathy Boudin and the Terrorist Family*

That Committed the Brinks Robbery Murders. New York: Dodd Mead, 1986.

Collins, Aukai. *My Jihad: The True Story of an American Mujahid's Amazing Journey from Usama bin Laden's Training Camps to Counterterrorism with the FBI and CIA.* New York: Lyons, 2002.

Coughlin, Con. *Saddam Hussein: His Rise and Fall.* New York: Ecco/HarperCollins, 2005.

Dekker, Ted, and Carl Medearis. *Tea with Hezbollah: Sitting at the Enemies' Table.* New York: Doubleday, 2010.

Dwyer, Jim, David Kocieniewski, Deidre Murphy, and Peg Tyre. *Two Seconds under the World: Terror Comes to America—The Conspiracy Behind the World Trade Center Bombing.* New York: Crown, 1994.

Emerson, Steven, and Christina Del Sesto. *Terrorist: The Inside Story of the Highest Ranking Iraqi Terrorist Ever to Defect to the West.* New York: Villard, 1991.

Follian, John. *Jackal: The Complete Story of the Legendary Terrorist, Carlos the Jackal.* New York: Arcade Publishing, 2011.

Foner, Philip S., ed. *The Black Panthers Speak.* New York: Da Capo, 1995.

Gage, Beverly. *The Day Wall Street Exploded: A Story of America in Its First Age of Terror.* Oxford: Oxford University Press, 2009.

Gordon, Michael R., and Bernard Trainor. *Cobra II: The Inside Story of the Invasion and Occupation of Iraq.* New York: Vintage, 2007.

Gowers, Andrew, and Tony Walker. *Behind the Myth: Yasser Arafat and the Palestinian Revolution.* New York: Olive Branch, 1991.

Graebmer, William. *Patty's Got a Gun: Patricia Hearst in 1970s America.* Chicago: University of Chicago Press, 2008.

Guevara, Ernesto Che. *Guerrilla Warfare.* Translated by J. P. Morray. New York: Monthly Review, 1961.

Hart, Alan. *Arafat: A Political Biography.* Rev. ed. Bloomington: Indiana University Press, 1989.

Hart, Joseph, ed. *Che: The Life, Death, and Afterlife of a Revolutionary.* New York: Thunder's Mouth Press, 2003.

Hearst, Patricia Campbell. *Patty Hearst: Her Own Story.* New York: Avon, 1988.

Hoffman, David. *The Oklahoma City Bombing and the Politics of Terror.* Venice, CA: Feral House, 1998.

Jamal, Arif. *Shadow War: The Untold Story of Jihad in Kashmir.* Hoboken, NJ: Melville, 2010.

Jamieson, Perry D. *Khobar Towers: Tragedy and Response.* Washington, DC: Air Force History and Museums Program, 2008.

Kaczynski, Theodore. *Technological Slavery: The Collected Writings of Theodore J. Kaczynski, a.k.a. "The Unabomber."* Port Townsend, WA: Feral House, 2010.

Kakar, M. Hassan. *Afghanistan: The Soviet Invasion and the Afghan Response, 1979–1982.* Berkeley: University of California Press, 1997.

Katz, Robert. *Days of Wrath: The Ordeal of Aldo Moro—The Kidnapping, the Execution, the Aftermath.* Garden City, NY: Doubleday, 1980.

Katz, Samuel M. *Israel Versus Jibril: The Thirty-year War against a Master Terrorist.* New York: Paragon, 1993.

Kee, Robert. *Trial and Error: The Maguires, the Guildford Pub Bombings, and British Justice.* London: Hamish Hamilton, 1986.

Khaled, Leila. *My People Shall Live: The Autobiography of a Revolutionary,* edited by George Hajjar. London: Hodder and Stoughton, 1973.

Klein, Aaron J. *Striking Back: The 1972 Munich Olympics Massacre and Israel's Deadly Response.* New York: Random House, 2007.

Kukis, Mark. *My Heart Became Attached: The Strange Journey of John Walker Lindh.* Washington, DC: Brassey's, 2003.

Laqueur, Walter, ed. *Voices of Terror: Manifestos, Writings, and Manuals of Al Qaeda, Hamas, and Other Terrorists from around the World and Throughout the Ages.* New York: Reed Press, 2004.

Levitt, Matthew. *Hamas: Politics, Charity, and Terrorism in the Service of Jihad.* New Haven, CT: Yale University Press, 2006.

Maddox, Eric. *Capturing Saddam: The Hunt for Saddam Hussein.* New York: HarperCollins, 2008.

Maley, William. *The Afghanistan War.* 2nd ed. New York: Palgrave MacMillan, 2009.

Mansoor, Peter R. *Baghdad at Sunrise: A Brigade Commander's War in Iraq.* New Haven, CT: Yale University Press, 2008.

Margolis, Eric S. *War at the Top of the World: The Struggle for Afghanistan, Kashmir, and Tibet.* New York: Routledge, 2002.

Martinez, Thomas, and John Guinther. *Brotherhood of Murder.* New York: McGraw-Hill, 1988.

Melman, Yossi. *The Master Terrorist: The True Story Behind Abu Nidal.* New York: Adama, 1986.

Miniter, Richard. *Mastermind: The Many Faces of the 9/11 Architect, Khalid Shaikh Mohammed.* New York: Sentinel HC, 2011.

Mishel, Shaul. *The PLO under Arafat: Between Gun and Olive Branch.* New Haven, CT: Yale University Press, 1986.

Newkirk, Ingrid. *Free the Animals! The Untold Story of the U.S. Animal Liberation Front & Its Founder, "Valerie."* Chicago: Noble, 1992.

Newton, Huey P. *To Die for the People: The Writings of Huey P. Newton,* edited by Toni Morrison. New York: Writers and Readers, 1999.

Newton, Michael A., and Michael P. Sharf. *Enemy of the State: The Trial and Execution of Saddam Hussein.* New York: St. Martin's, 2008.

Norton, Augustus Richard. *Hezbollah: A Short History.* Princeton, NJ: Princeton University Press, 2007.

Ocalan, Abdullah. *Prison Writings: The Roots of Civilisation,* translated by Klaus Happel. London: Pluto Press, 2007.

Pearl, Mariane. *A Mighty Heart: The Brave Life and Death of My Husband, Danny Pearl.* New York: Scribner, 2003.

Proll, Astrid. *Baader Meinhof: Pictures on the Run 67–77.* Berlin and New York: Scalo, 1998.

Raab, David. *Terror in Black September: The First Eyewitness Account of the Infamous 1970 Hijacking.* New York: Palgrave Macmillan, 2007.

Rashid, Ahmed. *Descent into Chaos: The United States and the Failure of Nation Building in Pakistan, Afghanistan, and Central Asia.* New York: Viking, 2008.

Reeve, Simon. *The New Jackals: Ramzi Yousef, Osama bin Laden, and the Future of Terrorism.* Boston: Northeastern University Press, 1999.

Reeve, Simon. *One Day in September: The Full Story of the 1972 Munich Olympics Massacre and the Israeli Revenge Operation "Wrath of God."* New York: Arcade, 2000.

Robinson, Adam. *Bin Laden: Behind the Mask of Terrorism.* New York: Arcade, 2002.

Schiller, Margit. *Remembering the Armed Struggle: Life in Baader Meinhof.* Darlington, NSW, Australia: Zidane Press, 2009.

Schofield, Victoria. *Kashmir in Conflict: India, Pakistan, and the Unending War.* New York: I.B. Tauris, 2010.

Seale, Patrick. *Abu Nidal: A Gun for Hire.* New York: Random House, 1992.

Sharif, Bassam Abu. *Arafat and the Dream of Palestine: An Insider's Account.* New York: Palgrave Macmillan, 2009.

Sutherland, Tom, and Jean Sutherland. *At Your Own Risk: An American Chronicle of Crisis and Captivity in the Middle East.* Golden, CO: Fulcrum, 1996.

Tamimi, Azzam. *Hamas: A History from within.* Northampton, MA: Olive Branch, 2007.

Tanner, Stephen. *Afghanistan: A Military History from Alexander the Great to the War against the Taliban.* Updated edition. New York: Da Capo, 2009.

Tarrants, Tomas A. *The Conversion of a Klansman: The Story of a Former Ku Klux Klan Terrorist.* Garden City, NY: Doubleday, 1979.

Timmerman, Kenneth R. *In Their Own Words: Interviews with Leaders of Hamas, Islamic Jihad, and the Muslim Brotherhood: Damascus, Amman, and Gaza.* Los Angeles: Simon Wiesenthal Center, 1994.

Varon, Jeremy. *Bringing the War Home: The Weather Underground, the Red Army Faction, and Revolutionary Violence in the Sixties and Seventies.* Berkeley: University of California Press, 2004.

Verbitsky, Horacio. *The Flight: Confessions of an Argentine Dirty Warrior,* translated by Esther Allen. New York: New Press, 1996.

Vollers, Maryanne. *Lone Wolf: Eric Rudolph: Murder, Myth, and the Pursuit of an American Outlaw.* New York: HarperCollins, 2006.

Waite, Terry. *Taken on Trust.* New York: Harcourt Brace, 1993.

Wakhlu, Khem Lata. *Kidnapped: 45 Days with Militants in Kashmir.* Delhi: Konark, 1993.

Walker, Tony, and Andrew Bowers. *Arafat: The Biography.* London: Virgin Books, 2003.

Weir, Ben, and Carol Weir. *Hostage Bound, Hostage Free.* Philadelphia: Westminster, 1987.

Wells, Tim. *444 Days: The Hostages Remember.* New York: Harcourt Brace Jovanovich, 1986.

Wilkerson, Cathy. *Flying Close to the Sun: My Life and Times as a Weatherman.* New York: Seven Stories Press, 2007.

September 11 and Aftermath

AbuKhalil, As'ad. *Bin Laden, Islam, and America's New "War on Terrorism."* New York: Seven Stories, 2002.

Atwan, Abdel Bari. *The Secret History of al Qaeda.* Berkeley: University of California Press, 2006.

Barreveld, Dirk J. *Can America Win the War on Terrorism: A Look into the Root Causes of World Terrorism.* New York: Writer's Club, 2002.

Bennett, William J. *Why We Fight: Moral Clarity and the War on Terrorism.* New York: Doubleday, 2002.

Bergen, Peter. *Holy War, Inc.: Inside the Secret World of Osama bin Laden.* New York: Free Press, 2001.

Bergen, Peter. *The Longest War: Inside the Enduring Conflict between America and al-Qaeda.* New York: Free Press, 2011.

Bergen, Peter. *The Osama bin Laden I Know: An Oral History of al Qaeda's Leader.* New York: Free Press, 2006.

Bonney, Richard. *Jihad: From Qur'an to Bin Laden.* New York: Palgrave Macmillan, 2004.

Chomsky, Noam. *9/11*. New York: Seven Stories, 2001.

Clarke, Richard. *Against All Enemies: Inside America's War on Terror*. New York, Free Press, 2004.

Coll, Steve. *The Bin Ladens: An Arabian Family in the American Century*. New York, Penguin, 2008.

Crews, Robert D., and Amin Tarzi, eds. *The Taliban and the Crisis of Afghanistan*. Cambridge, MA: Harvard University Press, 2009.

Dixon, W.W. *Film and Television after 9/11*. Carbondale: Southern Illinois University Press, 2004.

El-Nawawy, Mohammed et al. *Al Jazeera: How the Free Arab News Network Scooped the World and Changed the Middle East*. Boulder, CO: Westview, 2002.

Emerson, Steven. *Jihad Incorporated: A Guide to Militant Islam in the U.S.* Amherst, NY: Prometheus Books, 2006.

Fishman, Brian. *Dysfunction and Decline: Lessons Learned from Inside al Qaeda in Iraq*. West Point, NY: Harmony Project, The Combating Terrorism Center, 2009.

Griffin, David Ray. *Osama Bin Laden: Dead or Alive?* Northampton, MA: Olive Branch, 2009.

Gunaratna, Rohan. *Inside al Qaeda: Global Network of Terror*. New York: Columbia University Press, 2002.

Jacobson, Michael. *The West at War: U.S. and European Counterterrorism Efforts, Post 9/11*. Washington, DC: Washington Institute for Near East Policy, 2006.

Jenkins, Brian Michael. *Countering Al Qaeda*. Santa Monica, CA: RAND Corporation, 2002.

Kepel, Gilles, Jean-Pierre Milelli, and Pascale Ghazaleh. *Al Qaeda in Its Own Words*. Cambridge, MA: Belknap of Harvard University Press, 2008.

Lebovic, James H. *Deterring International Terrorism and Rogue States: US National Security after 9/11*. New York: Routledge, 2006.

Mahajan, Rahul. *The New Crusade: America's War on Terrorism*. New York: Monthly Review, 2002.

McDermott, Terry. *Perfect Soldiers: The Hijackers: Who They Were, Why They Did It*. New York: HarperCollins, 2005.

Murphy, John F. *Sword of Islam: Muslim Extremism from the Arab Conquests to the Attack on America*. Amherst, NY: Prometheus, 2002.

National Commission on Terrorist Attacks upon the United States. *The 9/11 Commission Report: Final Report of the National Commission on Terrorist Attacks upon the United States*. New York: W.W. Norton, 2004. http://www.9-11commission.gov.

Parenti, Michael. *The Terrorist Trap: September 11 and beyond*. San Francisco: City Lights Books, 2002.

Rabasa, Angel, et al. *Beyond al Qaeda*. Part 1, *The Global Jihadist Movement*. Santa Monica, CA: RAND Corporation, 2006.

Rashid, Ahmed. *Taliban: Militant Islam, Oil and Fundamentalism in Central Asia*. 2nd ed. New Haven, CT: Yale University Press, 2010.

Reeve, Simon. *The New Jackals: Ramzi Yousef, Osama bin Laden, and the Future of Terrorism*. Boston: Northeastern Press, 1999.

Riedel, Bruce. *The Search for al Qaeda: Its Leadership, Ideology and Future*. Washington, DC: Brookings Institution Press, 2010.

Satloff, Robert B. *War on Terror: The Middle East Dimension*. Washington, DC: Washington Institute for Near East Policy, 2002.

Siniver, Asaf, ed. *International Terrorism Post-9/11: Comparative Dynamics and Responses*. London: Routledge, 2010.

Snow, Donald. *September 11, 2001: The New Face of War?* New York: Pearson Higher Education, 2001.

Talbott, Strobe, and Nayan Chandra, eds. *The Age of Terror: America and the World after September 11*. New York: Basic Books, 2002.

Vidino, Lorenzo. *Al Qaeda in Europe: The New Battleground of International Jihad*. Amherst, NY: Prometheus Books, 2006.

Wright, Lawrence. *The Looming Tower: Al-Qaida and the Road to 9/11*. New York: Knopf, 2006.

Yourdon, Edward. *Byte Wars: The Impact of September 11 on Information Technology*. Upper Saddle River, NJ: Prentice Hall, 2002.

Types and Methods of Terrorism

Alexander, Yonah, and Michael S. Swetnam, eds. *Cyber Terrorism and Information Warfare: Threats and Responses*. Ardsley, NY: Transnational, 2001.

Antokol, Norman, and Mayer Nudell. *No One a Neutral: Political Hostage-taking in the Modern World*. Medina, OH: Alpha Publications, 1990.

Arquilla, J., and D. Ronfeldt, eds. *Networks and Netwars: The Future of Terror, Crime and Militancy*. Santa Monica, CA: RAND Corporation, 2001.

Best, Steven, and Anthony J. Nocella II, eds. *Terrorists or Freedom Fighters? Reflections on the Liberation of Animals*. New York: Lantern, 2004.

Burton, Anthony. *Urban Terrorism: Theory, Practice, Response*. London: Cooper, 1975.

Dajami-Shakeel, Hadia, and Ronald A. Messier, eds. *The Jihad and Its Times*. Ann Arbor: University of Michigan Center for Near Eastern and North African Studies, 1991.

Devji, Faisal. *Landscapes of the Jihad: Militancy, Morality, Modernity.* Ithaca, NY: Cornell University Press, 2005.

Dolnike, Adam, and Keith M. Fitzgerald. *Negotiating Hostage Crises with the New Terrorists.* Westport, CT: Praeger Security International, 2008.

Gartenstein-Ross, Daveed, and Laura Grossman. *Homegrown Terrorists in the U.S. and U.K.* Washington, DC: FDD Press, 2009.

George, Alexander, ed. *Western State Terrorism.* New York: Routledge, 1991.

Glucklich, Ariel. *Dying for Heaven: Holy Pleasure and Suicide Bombers.* New York: HarperOne, 2009.

Grayson, George W. *Narco-violence and a Failed State?* Piscataway, NJ: Transaction Publishers, 2010.

Hero, Eneli. *The Stockholm Syndrome: Towards an Integrated Approach.* Copenhagen: University of Copenhagen, Institute of Psychology, 2006.

Kellner, Douglas. *Guys and Guns Amok: Domestic Terrorism and School Shootings from the Oklahoma City Bombing to the Virginia Tech Massacre.* Boulder, CO: Paradigm Publishers, 2008.

Levi, Michael. *On Nuclear Terrorism.* Cambridge, MA: Harvard University Press, 2009.

Liddick, Donald R. *Eco-terrorism: Radical Environmental and Animal Liberation Movements.* Westport, CT: Praeger, 2006.

Lutherer, Lorenz Otto, and Margaret Sheffield Simon. *Targeted: The Anatomy of an Animal Rights Attack.* Norman: University of Oklahoma Press, 1992.

Mann, Michael. *The Dark Side of Democracy: Explaining Ethnic Cleansing.* New York: Cambridge University Press, 2005.

Marighella, Carlos. *Minimanual of the Urban Guerrilla.* Chapel Hill, NC: Documentary Publications, 1985.

Moss, Robert. *Urban Guerrilla Warfare.* London: International Institute for Strategic Studies, 1971.

O'Neill, Bard E. *Insurgency and Terrorism: Inside Modern Revolutionary Warfare.* Washington, DC: Brassey's, 1990.

Pape, Robert Anthony. *Dying to Win: The Strategic Logic of Suicide Terrorism.* New York: Random House, 2005.

Perkins, Samuel. *Homegrown Terror and American Jihadists: Assessing the Threat.* Hauppauge, NY: Nova Publishers, 2011.

Ranstorp, Magnus, and Magnus Normark, eds. *Unconventional Weapons and International Terrorism: Challenges and a New Approach.* New York: Routledge, 2009.

Sageman, Marc. *Leaderless Jihad: Terror Networks in the Twenty-first Century.* Philadelphia: University of Pennsylvania Press, 2008.

Scarce, Rik. *Eco-warriors: Understanding the Radical Environmental Movement.* 2nd ed. Walnut Creek, CA: Left Coast Press, 2006.

Schweitzer, Glenn E., with Carole C. Dorsch. *Superterrorism: Assassins, Mobsters, and Weapons of Mass Destruction.* New York: Plenum Trade, 1998.

Sofaer, Abraham D., and Seymour E. Goodman. *The Transnational Dimension of Cyber Crime and Terrorism.* Stanford, CA: Hoover Institution, 2001.

Spaaij, Ramon. *Lone-wolf Terrorism.* The Hague, Netherlands: COT Institute for Safety, Security and Crisis Management, 2007.

Stern, Jessica. *The Ultimate Terrorists.* Cambridge, MA: Harvard University Press, 1999.

Thornton, Rod. *Asymmetric Warfare: Threat and Response in the Twenty-first Century.* Cambridge, UK: Polity Press, 2007.

Tucker, Jonathan B. *Toxic Terror: Assessing Terrorist Use of Chemical and Biological Weapons.* Cambridge: MIT Press, 2000.

Tucker, Jonathan B. *War of Nerves: Chemical Warfare from World War I to al-Qaeda.* New York: Pantheon Books, 2006.

Verton, Dan. *Black Ice: The Invisible Threat of Cyber-terrorism.* New York: McGraw-Hill, 2003.

Index

Entry titles and their page numbers are in **bold**. Page numbers for photos, figures, and tables are in *italics*.

decommissioning, 154–156
international relations and terrorism, 286–297
law and terrorism, 345, 347
Loyalist Volunteer Force, 366–367
media and terrorism, 385
Omagh bombing, 444–446, *445*
Orange Volunteers, 448–449
popular culture, terrorism in, 481
Real IRA, 498–499
Red Hand Defenders, 502–503
Ulster Defense Association, 597–598
Ulster Freedom Fighters, *599*, 599–600
Ulster Volunteer Force, 600–601
See also Britain
Northern Ireland Civil Rights Association, 304
Nosair, El Sayyid, 2, 315, 321, **433.** *See also* **Kahane, Meir;
World Trade Center bombing (1993)**
November 17. *See* **Revolutionary Organization 17 November**
Nuclear terrorism, 284, **434–437,** 623–624. *See also*
Counterterrorism
Nuremberg Files, 54

Oakland Police Department, 105
Obama, Barack:
Afghanistan war, 15, 16
CIA and, 125
Department of Justice, U.S., and, 160–161
Ghailani, Ahmed Khalfan, and, 231
Guantánamo Bay, 238, 240
international relations and terrorism, 284, 286
Iraq War, 301
Israel-Palestine negotiations, 199
law and terrorism, 346
National Security Council and, 425–426, *426*
Patriot movement and, 472
rendition, extraordinary, 513, 581
September 11 attacks, 538
Ocalan, Abdullah, *336*, 336–337, **439–440**
Odeh, Abdul Aziz, 457
Odeh, Alex, 315
Odeh, Mohammed Saddiq, 440–441
Abdullah, Abdullah Ahmed, and, 4
al Qaeda, 30, 440–441
East Africa embassy bombings, 168, 170, 440–441
United States v. Usama bin Laden, et al., 612
See also **East Africa embassy bombings**
Official Irish Republican Army, 303, 304–305. *See also* **Irish
Republican Army**
Ohio Seven. *See* **United Freedom Front**
Ojeda Rios, Filiberto, 372
Okello, Tito, 364
Oklahoma City bombing, 441–444, *442*
April 19, 57, 443
Branch Davidian Compound siege and, 115
Bureau of Alcohol, Tobacco, Firearms and Explosives, 118
insurance and terrorism, 276
lone-wolf terrorism, 361
McVeigh, Timothy James, 381–382, 441, 442, 443–444
Nichols, Terry Lynn, 429–430, 441, 442–443, 444
Patriot movement and, 472
Snell, Richard Wayne, 549
See also **McVeigh, Timothy James; Nichols, Terry Lynn**

Okot, Innocent, *365*
Okudaira, Junzo, 615
Olivetto, Washington, 374–375
Olympics. *See* **Centennial Park bombing;
Munich Olympics massacre**
Omagh bombing, 113, **444–446,** *445*, 498–499. *See also* **Real
Irish Republican Army**
Omar, Mohammed, 571, 572, 573–574, 576
Omar, Yassin, 360
Omega 7, 65–66, **446–447,** 558. *See also* **Arocena, Eduardo**
"On the Origin of Domestic and International Terrorism"
(Kis-Katos, Liebert, and Schulze), 176
Operation Bite Back, 44, 46–47, 140
Operation Bite Back II, 44, 47
Operation Bluestar, 544
Operation Defensive Shield, 293
Operation Desert Shield, 478
Operation Desert Storm, 478. *See also* **Persian Gulf War**
Operation Eagle Claw, 294, **447–448.** *See also* **Iranian hostage
crisis**
Operation Enduring Freedom, 12–13, 31, 99. *See also*
Afghanistan war
Operation Kibya, 317
Operation Orange Justice, *49*
Operation Rescue, 53, 237
Opportunity-cost argument, 175
Opsahl, Myrna Lee, 569, 570
Orange Volunteers, 448–449
Order, The, 449–451
Aryan Nations and, 66
Covenant, the Sword and the Arm of the Lord, The, and, 146
financing, 207
Fort Smith, Arkansas, trial, 219–220
Mathews, Robert Jay, 378, 379, 450–451
Scutari, Richard, 450–451, 531–532
Turner Diaries, The (Pierce), 592
white supremacy movement, 449–451, 629
See also **White supremacy movement**
Ordine Nuovo, 451–452
Oregon v. Mathiason, 290
Organization of Petroleum Exporting Countries, 528–529
Organized crime, 154, 343–344
Orphanides, Athanasios, 177
Ortiz Montengro, Patricio
Oslo Accords, 292–293
Osman, Hussain, 360
Our Palestine: The Call to Life (magazine), 58, 198
Owhali, Mohamed Rashed al, 168, 170, **452–453,** 612.
See also **East Africa embassy bombings**

Padilla, José, 455–456. *See also* **al Qaeda**
Padilla, Lana, 443
Pakistan:
Harakat ul-Mujahideen, 250–252
international relations and terrorism, 286
Jaish-e-Mohammed, 311–312
Lashkar-e-Taiba, 341, 342
nuclear weapons, 435, 437
Sikh terrorism, 544–545
state-sponsored terrorism, 556
Taliban, 573–574, 575, 576
Tehrik-i-Taliban Pakistan, 576–579, *578*